When should I travel to get the best airfare?
Where do I go for answers to my travel questions?
What's the best and easiest way to plan and book my trip?

frommers.travelocity.com

Frommer's, the travel guide leader, has teamed up with **Travelocity.com**, the leader in online travel, to bring you an in-depth, easy-to-use resource designed to help you plan and book your trip online.

At **frommers.travelocity.com**, you'll find free online updates about your destination from the experts at Frommer's plus the outstanding travel planning and purchasing features of Travelocity.com. Travelocity.com provides reservations capabilities for 95 percent of all airline seats sold, more than 47,000 hotels, and over 50 car rental companies. In addition, Travelocity.com offers more than 2,000 exciting vacation and cruise packages. Travelocity.com puts you in complete control of your travel planning with these and other great features:

Expert travel guidance from Frommer's - over 150 writers reporting from around the world!

Best Fare Finder - an interactive calendar tells you when to travel to get the best airfare

Fare Watcher - we'll track airfare changes to your favorite destinations

Dream Maps - a mapping feature that suggests travel opportunities based on your budget

Shop Safe Guarantee - 24 hours a day / 7 days a week live customer service, and more!

Whether traveling on a tight budget, looking for a quick weekend getaway, or planning the trip of a lifetime, Frommer's guides and Travelocity.com will make your travel dreams a reality. You've bought the book, now book the trip!

Travelocity.com
A Sabre Company

Frommer's®

A New Star-Rating System & Other Exciting News from Frommer's!

In our continuing effort to publish the savviest, most up-to-date, and most appealing travel guides available, we've added some great new features.

Frommer's guides now include a new **star-rating system.** Every hotel, restaurant, and attraction is rated from 0 to 3 stars to help you set priorities and organize your time.

We've also added **seven brand-new features** that point you to the great deals, in-the-know advice, and unique experiences that separate travelers from tourists. Throughout the guide look for:

Finds	Special finds—those places only insiders know about
Fun Fact	Fun facts—details that make travelers more informed and their trips more fun
Kids	Best bets for kids—advice for the whole family
Moments	Special moments—those experiences that memories are made of
Overrated	Places or experiences not worth your time or money
Tips	Insider tips—some great ways to save time and money
Value	Great values—where to get the best deals

We've also added a **"What's New"** section in every guide—a timely crash course in what's hot and what's not in every destination we cover.

Other Great Guides for Your Trip:

Frommer's Caribbean

Frommer's Caribbean Cruises & Ports of Call

Frommer's Caribbean Ports of Call

Frommer's Portable Aruba

Frommer's Puerto Rico

Frommer's Jamaica

Frommer's Virgin Islands

*Frommer's®

Caribbean
from $70 a day

4th Edition

by Darwin Porter & Danforth Prince

Here's what the critics say about Frommer's:

"Amazingly easy to use. Very portable, very complete."

—*Booklist*

"The only mainstream guide to list specific prices. The Walter Cronkite of guidebooks—with all that implies."

—*Travel & Leisure*

"Complete, concise, and filled with useful information."

—*New York Daily News*

"Hotel information is close to encyclopedic."

—*Des Moines Sunday Register*

"The best series for travelers who want one easy-to-use guidebook."

—*US Air Magazine*

Hungry Minds™

Best-Selling Books • Digital Downloads • e-Books • Answer Networks
e-Newsletters • Branded Web Sites • e-Learning
New York, NY • Cleveland, OH • Indianapolis, IN

About the Authors

A native of North Carolina, **Darwin Porter** was a bureau chief for the *Miami Herald* when he was 21 and later worked in TV advertising. This veteran travel writer is the author of numerous bestselling Frommer's guides, including *Frommer's Caribbean,* the most candid and up-to-date guide to island vacations on the market. He is assisted by **Danforth Prince,** formerly of the Paris bureau of the *New York Times.* Both writers have traveled widely in the Caribbean for years and happily share their secrets and discoveries with you.

Published by:

Hungry Minds, Inc.

909 Third Ave.
New York, NY 10022

ISBN 0-7645-6466-8
ISSN 1082-5053

Editor: Kitty Wilson Jarrett
Production Editor: Heather Gregory
Cartographer: Elizabeth Puhl
Photo Editor: Richard Fox
Production by Hungry Minds Indianapolis Production Services

Special Sales

For general information on Hungry Minds' products and services please contact our Customer Care department; within the U.S. at 800-762-2974, outside the U.S. at 317-572-3993 or fax 317-572-4002. For sales inquiries and reseller information, including discounts, bulk sales, customized editions, and premium sales, please contact our Customer Care department at 800-434-3422.

Manufactured in the United States of America

5 4 3 2

Contents

List of Maps   xii

What's New in the Caribbean   1

1   Choosing the Perfect Island: The Best of the Caribbean from $70 a Day   4

1 The Best Destinations for Low-Cost Vacations 4

2 The Best Beaches 5

3 The Best Snorkeling 8

4 The Best Dive Sites 9

5 The Best Adventures That Deliver Bang for Your Buck 10

6 The Friendliest Islands 11

7 The Best Experiences You Can Have for Free (or Almost) 12

8 The Best Destinations for Serious Shoppers Who Insist on Bargains 13

9 The Best Reasonably Priced Honeymoon Resorts 14

10 The Best Family Resorts for Parents Who Don't Want to Blow the Kids' College Fund ...15

11 The Best Camping 15

12 The Best Places to Get Away From It All Without Spending a Fortune 16

13 The Best Authentic Dining 16

14 The Best Places for Sunset Cocktails 18

15 The Best Nightspots Without Sky-High Cover Charges 18

2   Planning an Affordable Trip to the Caribbean   20

1 The Islands in Brief 20

2 Visitor Information 27

3 Entry Requirements & Customs 27

What Things Cost in the Caribbean 29

4 Money 30

The U.S. Dollar, the British Pound, the Canadian Dollar, the French Franc, and the Euro 31

5 When to Go 32

6 Health & Insurance 33

7 Tips for Travelers with Special Needs 35

8 40 Money-Saving Tips 38

9 Package Deals 40

10 Finding the Best Airfare 42

11 Cruises That Don't Cost a Fortune 44

12 Getting the Best Value in Accommodations 50

13 Saving Money on Car Rentals 53

14 Getting Married in the Caribbean 54

15 Planning Your Trip Online 56

Frommers.com: The Complete Travel Resource 57

3 Antigua 60

1 Essentials 61
Fast Facts: Antigua 63
2 Accommodations You Can
Afford .64
3 Great Deals on Dining 66
4 Hitting the Beaches 68
5 Sports & Other Outdoor
Pursuits 70

6 Seeing the Sights 71
Into the Volcano 72
7 Shopping 73
*Cheap Thrills: What to See &
Do for Free (Well, Almost) on
Antigua* 74
8 Antigua After Dark 77

4 Aruba 78

1 Essentials 78
Fast Facts: Aruba 82
2 Accommodations You
Can Afford 83
3 Great Deals on Dining 86
4 Hitting the Beaches 87
5 Sports & Other Outdoor
Pursuits 88

6 Seeing the Sights 89
An Underwater Journey 90
7 Shopping 91
*Cheap Thrills: What to See &
Do for Free (Well, Almost)
on Aruba* 92
8 Aruba After Dark 94

5 Barbados 96

1 Essentials 96
Special Events 99
Fast Facts: Barbados 100
2 Accommodations You
Can Afford 102
3 Great Deals on Dining 107
4 Hitting the Beaches 111

5 Sports & Other Outdoor
Pursuits 112
6 Seeing the Sights 114
7 Shopping 119
*Cheap Thrills: What to See &
Do for Free (Well, Almost)
on Barbados* 120
8 Barbados After Dark 122

6 Bonaire 125

1 Essentials 125
Fast Facts: Bonaire 128
2 Accommodations You
Can Afford 129
3 Great Deals on Dining 131
4 Hitting the Beaches 133
5 Sports & Other Outdoor
Pursuits 133

A Trip to Klein Bonaire 134
6 Seeing the Sights 136
*Cheap Thrills: What to See &
Do for Free (Well, Almost)
on Bonaire* 137
7 Shopping 139
8 Bonaire After Dark 140

7 The British Virgin Islands   141

1 Essentials 141

Fast Facts: The British Virgin Islands 142

2 Tortola 144

The Wreck of the Rhone & Other Top Dive Sites 154

Cheap Thrills: What to See & Do for Free (Well, Almost) in the British Virgins 156

3 Virgin Gorda 160

4 Anegada 166

5 Jost Van Dyke 167

8 The Cayman Islands   170

1 Essentials 170

Fast Facts: The Cayman Islands 172

2 Grand Cayman 173

Swimming with the Stingrays 179

Into the Deep: Submarine Dives 180

Cheap Thrills: What to See & Do for Free (Well, Almost) in the Cayman Islands 182

3 Cayman Brac 185

4 Little Cayman 187

9 Curaçao   190

1 Essentials 190

Fast Facts: Curaçao 192

2 Accommodations You Can Afford 193

3 Great Deals on Dining 195

4 Hitting the Beaches 198

5 Sports & Other Outdoor Pursuits 199

6 Seeing the Sights 201

Cheap Thrills: What to See & Do for Free (Well, Almost) on Curaçao 204

7 Shopping 206

8 Curaçao After Dark 208

10 Dominica   209

1 Essentials 209

Fast Facts: Dominica 212

2 Accommodations You Can Afford 213

3 Great Deals on Dining 215

4 Hitting the Beaches 217

5 Sports & Other Outdoor Pursuits 217

6 Seeing the Sights 219

Cheap Thrills: What to See & Do for Free (Well, Almost) on Dominica 220

7 Shopping 221

8 Dominica After Dark 222

11 The Dominican Republic   224

1 Essentials 224

Fast Facts: The Dominican Republic 227

2 Santo Domingo 228

Un, Dos, Tres Strikes, You're Out 235

3 Barahona Peninsula 241

4 La Romana & Altos
de Chavón 242

5 Puerto Plata 245

*Cheap Thrills: What to See &
Do for Free (Well, Almost) in
the Dominican Republic* 246

6 Sosúa 252

7 Cabarete 256

8 Samaná 259

*Exploring a Rain Forest &
Watching Whales* 260

12 Grenada 262

1 Essentials 262

Fast Facts: Grenada 265

2 Accommodations You
Can Afford 266

3 Great Deals on Dining 268

4 Hitting the Beaches 270

5 Sports & Other Outdoor
Pursuits 271

6 Seeing the Sights 272

*Cheap Thrills: What to See &
Do for Free (Well, Almost)
on Grenada* 274

7 Shopping 276

8 Grenada After Dark 278

9 A Side Trip to Carriacou 278

13 Guadeloupe 282

1 Essentials 282

Fast Facts: Guadeloupe 284

2 Pointe-à-Pitre 286

3 Gosier 288

4 Ste-Anne 291

5 St-François 292

6 An Excursion to the Eastern
End of Guadeloupe 293

7 Driving Around the Northern
Coast of Grande-Terre 294

8 Driving Around Basse-Terre ...295

*Cheap Thrills: What to See &
Do for Free (Well, Almost)
on Guadeloupe* 298

Up the Volcano 304

9 Hitting the Beaches 306

10 Sports & Other Outdoor
Pursuits 307

11 Guadeloupe After Dark 309

12 Side Trips from Guadeloupe ...310

14 Jamaica 317

1 Essentials 318

*Catch a Fire: Jamaica's
Reggae Festivals* 321

Fast Facts: Jamaica 322

2 Montego Bay 324

3 Negril 336

Ann Bonney & Her Dirty Dog ...339

*Cheap Thrills: What You Can See
& Do for Free (Well, Almost)
on Jamaica* 344

4 Falmouth 346

5 Runaway Bay 348

6 Ocho Rios 350

7 Port Antonio 359

Exploring Blue Mountain 364

8 Kingston 365

9 Mandeville 371

10 The South Coast 373

15 Martinique 376

1 Essentials 378
Fast Facts: Martinique 380
2 Fort-de-France 382
Begin the Beguine 387
3 Pointe du Bout &
Les Trois-Ilets 388

Cheap Thrills: What to See &
Do for Free (Well, Almost)
on Martinique 390
4 The South Loop 393
5 The North Loop 398

16 Nevis 404

1 Essentials 405
Fast Facts: Nevis 406
2 Accommodations You Can
Afford 407
3 Great Deals on Dining 408
4 Hitting the Beaches 410
5 Sports & Other Outdoor
Pursuits 411

Eco-Tours: Finding the
Beauty of Nevis 412
6 Seeing the Sights 413
Cheap Thrills: What to See &
Do for Free (Well, Almost)
on Nevis 414
7 Shopping 415
8 Nevis After Dark 416

17 Puerto Rico 417

1 Essentials 417
Fast Facts: Puerto Rico 422
2 San Juan 423
Touring El Yunque Tropical
Rain Forest 438
3 Dorado 449
Cheap Thrills: What to See &
Do for Free (Well, Almost) on
Puerto Rico 450
4 Northwestern Puerto Rico 451
5 Rincón 452
6 Mayagüez 454

A Side Trip to Mona Island ...456
7 Boquerón & Cabo Rojo 457
8 Ponce 459
9 Northeastern Puerto Rico 465
10 Two Island Drives 467
Driving Tour 1: The Rain Forests
& Beaches of the East 468
Driving Tour 2: Western Puerto
Rico & the Southwest
Coast 471
11 Vieques 476
12 Culebra 480

18 Saba 483

1 Essentials 483
Fast Facts: Saba 484
2 Accommodations You Can
Afford 486
3 Great Deals on Dining 487
4 Sports & Outdoor Pursuits ...489

Cheap Thrills: What to See &
Do for Free (Well, Almost)
on Saba 490
5 Seeing the Sights 491
6 Shopping 492
7 Saba After Dark 493

19 St. Eustatius 494

1 Essentials 495

Fast Facts: St. Eustatius 496

2 Accommodations You
Can Afford 497

3 Great Deals on Dining 498

*Cheap Thrills: What to See &
Do for Free (Well, Almost)
on St. Eustatius* 499

4 Hitting the Beaches 500

5 Sports & Other Outdoor
Pursuits 500

6 Seeing the Sights 501

7 Shopping 502

8 St. Eustatius After Dark 502

20 St. Kitts 503

1 Essentials 503

Fast Facts: St. Kitts 505

2 Accommodations You
Can Afford 506

3 Great Deals on Dining 508

*Cheap Thrills: What to See &
Do for Free (Well, Almost)
on St. Kitts* 509

4 Hitting the Beaches 510

5 Sports & Other Outdoor
Pursuits 511

6 Seeing the Sights 512

Into the Volcano 513

7 Shopping 513

8 St. Kitts After Dark 514

21 St. Lucia 516

1 Essentials 516

Fast Facts: St. Lucia 518

2 Accommodations You
Can Afford 519

3 Great Deals on Dining 522

4 Hitting the Beaches 524

5 Sports & Other Outdoor
Pursuits 524

6 Seeing the Sights 526

*Cheap Thrills: What to See &
Do for Free (Well, Almost)
on St. Lucia* 528

7 Nature Reserves 530

8 Shopping 531

9 St. Lucia After Dark 533

22 St. Maarten & St. Martin 535

1 Essentials 538

*Fast Facts: St. Maarten &
St. Martin* 540

2 Accommodations You Can
Afford 542

3 Great Deals on Dining 545

4 Hitting the Beaches 550

5 Sports & Other Outdoor
Pursuits 552

*Cheap Thrills: What to See &
Do for Free (Well, Almost)
on St. Maarten & St. Martin* ...553

6 Cruises & Sightseeing Tours ...555

7 Shopping 556

8 St. Maarten & St. Martin
After Dark 559

23 St. Vincent & the Grenadines   562

1 Essentials 563

*Fast Facts: St. Vincent &
the Grenadines* 564

2 Accommodations You Can
Afford 565

3 Great Deals on Dining 567

4 Hitting the Beaches 569

5 Sports & Other Outdoor
Pursuits 569

6 Seeing the Sights 570

*Cheap Thrills: What to See &
Do for Free (Well, Almost)
on St. Vincent &
the Grenadines* 572

7 Shopping 573

8 St. Vincent After Dark 574

9 The Grenadines: Bequia,
Union Island & Mayreau 575

24 Trinidad & Tobago   582

1 Essentials 582

*Fast Facts: Trinidad &
Tobago* 583

2 Trinidad 584

The Carnival of Trinidad 586

*Cheap Thrills: What to See &
Do for Free (Well, Almost) on
Trinidad & Tobago* 596

3 Tobago 598

25 The U.S. Virgin Islands   607

1 Essentials 607

*Fast Facts: The U.S. Virgin
Islands* 609

2 St. Thomas 610

*Cheap Thrills: What to See &
Do for Free (Well, Almost) on
the U.S. Virgin Islands* 632

3 St. John 635

4 St. Croix 648

*Buck Island: Unspoiled Nature
& World-Class Snorkeling* 658

The Heritage Trail 668

Index   673

List of Maps

The Caribbean Islands   6
Antigua   61
Aruba   79
Barbados   97
Bonaire   127
The British Virgin Islands   143
Tortola   145
Virgin Gorda   161
The Cayman Islands   171
Curaçao   191
Dominica   211
The Dominican Republic   225
Santo Domingo   229
Grenada   263
Guadeloupe   283
Jamaica   318
Montego Bay   326
Negril   337

Ocho Rios   351
Martinique   377
Nevis   405
Puerto Rico   419
San Juan   424
Old San Juan   439
Saba   485
St. Eustatius   495
St. Kitts   505
St. Lucia   517
St. Maarten & St. Martin   536
St. Vincent   563
The Grenadines   577
Trinidad   585
Tobago   599
St. Thomas   611
St. John   637
St. Croix   649

An Invitation to the Reader

In researching this book, we discovered many wonderful places—hotels, restaurants, shops, and more. We're sure you'll find others. Please tell us about them, so we can share the information with your fellow travelers in upcoming editions. If you were disappointed with a recommendation, we'd love to know that, too. Please write to:

Frommer's Caribbean from $70 a Day, 4th Edition
Hungry Minds, Inc. • 909 Third Avenue • New York, NY 10022

An Additional Note

Please be advised that travel information is subject to change at any time—and this is especially true of prices. We therefore suggest that you write or call ahead for confirmation when making your travel plans. The authors, editors, and publisher cannot be held responsible for the experiences of readers while traveling. Your safety is important to us, however, so we encourage you to stay alert and be aware of your surroundings. Keep a close eye on cameras, purses, and wallets, all favorite targets of thieves and pickpockets.

New! Frommer's Star Ratings & Icons

Every hotel, restaurant, and attraction listing in this guide has been ranked for quality, value, service, amenities, and special features, using a star-rating scale. In country, state, and regional guides, we also rate towns and regions, to help you narrow down your choices and budget your time accordingly. Hotels and restaurants are rated on a scale of zero (recommended) to two stars (very highly recommended); exceptional "worth a splurge" options may get three stars. Attractions, towns, and regions are rated according to the following scale: zero stars (recommended), one star (highly recommended), two stars (very highly recommended), and three stars (must-see).

In addition to the rating system, we also use seven icons to highlight insider information, useful tips, special bargains, hidden gems, memorable experiences, kid-friendly venues, places to avoid, and other useful information:

(Finds   (Fun Fact   (Kids   (Moments   (Overrated   (Tips   (Value

The following abbreviations are used for credit cards:

AE American Express	DISC Discover	V Visa
DC Diners Club	MC MasterCard	

FROMMERS.COM

Now that you have the guidebook to a great trip, visit our website, **www.frommers.com,** for travel information on nearly 2,000 destinations. With features updated regularly, we give you instant access to the most current trip-planning information available. At Frommers.com, you'll also find the best prices on airfares, accommodations, and car rentals—and you can even book travel online through our travel booking partners. At Frommers.com you'll also find the following:

- Daily Newsletter highlighting the best travel deals
- Hot Spot of the Month/Vacation Sweepstakes & Travel Photo Contest
- More than 200 Travel Message Boards
- Outspoken Newsletters and Feature Articles on travel bargains, vacation ideas, tips & resources, and more!

THE DISAPPEARANCE OF CLAUDIA KIRSCHHOCH

Claudia Kirschhoch, an assistant editor for Frommer's Travel Guides, went on a Sandals Resort press trip with a group of journalists on May 24, 2000. The itinerary was originally New York City to Cuba by way of Montego Bay, Jamaica. The American journalists were unexpectedly denied entry into Cuba. Because all return flights to New York were full, Claudia decided to stay on in Jamaica, at Sandals' Beaches Resort in Negril, until her return flight to New York on June 1, 2000.

The last confirmed sighting of Claudia was on the resort's beach on Saturday, May 27. Her clothes, purse, passport, cash, credit cards, and camera were found in her room. Although the American Embassy, the FBI, and the Jamaican police worked diligently to find her throughout the summer of 2000, investigative activity on the case has slowed substantially. Claudia's parents, Fred and Mary Ann Kirschhoch, have held press conferences and blanketed the island with posters bearing Claudia's picture; they are now focusing their efforts on keeping Claudia's story in the media and lobbying government representatives to investigate Claudia's disappearance as a possible crime. The Kirschhochs believe that their best hope for a break in the case may come from information offered anonymously. A substantial reward is being offered for information about Claudia's disappearance.

Claudia Kirschhoch is 30 years old. She is 5'2" and 105 lbs. She has long dark brown hair, brown eyes, and fair skin. If you have any information, please contact the police department in Jamaica (✆ 888/991-4000) or the information hot line in the U.S. (✆ 888/967-9300).

Frommer's is fully supportive of the ongoing investigation. As Claudia's colleagues and friends, we are distressed about the lack of new information, but we remain optimistic that Claudia will be found. Because we do not know the full story of Claudia's disappearance, Frommer's is not currently advising travelers against visiting Jamaica. According to the Bureau of Consular Affairs, however, crime is a serious problem in Jamaica. Thus, we encourage you to consult the bureau's website (http://travel.state.gov) for Consular Information Sheets, travel advisories, and safety tips on travel in the Caribbean. Frommer's stands by its general safety advice: Always stay alert, be aware of your surroundings, and avoid walking alone at night, particularly on beaches. Our readers' safety is important to us, and we will continue to provide you with pertinent information to assist your safe and happy travel experiences.

For more information about Claudia and the latest media coverage of her disappearance, please visit the "Find Claudia" website, which is dedicated to her safe return, at http://findclaudia.homestead.com.

What's New in the Caribbean

The volatile archipelago of mostly independent island nations explodes with change year after year. Today's popular resort might be swept away in a hurricane, or last winter's hot restaurant dining choice might be a sea of empty tables this season. Even the beaches come and go. Here are some new developments.

ARUBA The opening of **Sunset Boulevard Studios,** Palm Beach (© 297/8-63940), in high-priced Aruba comes as a welcome relief. The complex rents a series of comfortably furnished accommodations, some of which attract families. See chapter 4 for more details.

BARBADOS BWIA (© 800/538-2942) has introduced nonstop air service from Boston to Barbados, with a continuation to Trinidad and Tobago. **Cayman Airways** and **Air Jamaica** have joined forces to provide an air link from Grand Cayman to Barbados and Trinidad going via Kingston in Jamaica. Flights wing out of Grand Cayman on Monday, Wednesday, and Friday, linking up in Kingston with continuing flights to Barbados and Port-of-Spain, with return flights scheduled for Thursday, Friday, and Sunday. For reservations and information, call © 800/523-5585. See chapter 5 for more details.

BONAIRE The frugal traveler who can settle for a rather rawbone hostelry is checking into the ocean-front **Hotel Rochaline,** Kaya Grandi 7, Kralendijk (© 599/717-8286), in the tiny island's capital. The small rooms, simply furnished and well maintained, overlook harbor views. Its City Café is a local hot spot at night. See chapter 6 for more details.

DOMINICAN REPUBLIC In Santo Domingo, Bettye Marshall, an ex-pat from Tennessee, runs **Galeria Toledo,** Calle Isabel La Catolica 163 (© 809/688-7649), a three-in-one offering—art gallery, guesthouse, and outdoor restaurant—opening onto Plaza Maria de Toledo. Compact rooms are comfortable and inviting, and the price is a steal. See chapter 11 for more details.

GRENADA Sudden fame has come to a little Grenadian eatery, **Deyna's Tasty Food** (© 473/440-6795), which is reached by heading up Melville Street to a modest three-story building overlooking the sea. You might even get invited back into the kitchen to see what's cookin'. The duenna of the stove, Deyna Hercules, looks like she lives up to her namesake and eats her own food. Where else can you get someone to fry you up a tasty batch of *tee-tee-ree,* those minnow-sized fish just plucked from the Caribbean and washed down with "bush tea" steeped from black sage leaves? See chapter 12.

GUADELOUPE At long last the remote offshore island Marie-Galante, a dependency of the French-held island off Guadeloupe, has a new three-star hotel. **La Cohoba Hotel,** Folle Anse (© 800/322-2223), offers an array of 100 tasteful and well-furnished bedrooms, opening onto a white sandy beach. Amenities include items the island's modest hostelries have never seen before—hair dryers, air-conditioning, and even kitchenettes in some 30 accommodations. The resort also offers two French-inspired restaurants. See chapter 13.

JAMAICA   The island's most expensive attraction, the $20 million **Aguasol Theme Park** (② 876/940-1344), has opened at Montego Bay. Themed around the sea and sun, it boasts a giant waterslide, a go-kart track, a large sandy beach, tennis courts, a nightclub, and an international restaurant and sports bar with 42 big TV screens. A ferry service is provided for cruise-line passengers, hauling them over for an afternoon of fun. An upper deck is open for sunbathing, and a picnic area has been marked off. Activities fill the daily calendar with such live events as games, reggae shows, contests, dances, and fashion shows.

A $16-million attraction, **Entertainment Village,** a massive complex of sights and amusements, is scheduled to open on 4 acres of land at the western end of Ocho Rios between Turtle Beach and Reynolds Pier. The site will be a re-created Jamaican village with gardens, a lagoon, and a number of entertainment options. Shops and restaurants along with craft outlets, a theater, an amphitheater, a children's play area, and even a Cyber Center will complete the offerings. Naturally, there will be Jamaican reggae music, both in the form of a museum and also live. See chapter 14 for more details.

PUERTO RICO   The capital, San Juan, continues to announce the opening of various little inexpensive guesthouses. Some of the latest discoveries—all at dirt-cheap prices—are **Villa Verde Inn,** Urbanización Villamar (② 787/727-9457), in Isla Verde, about a 5-minute walk from the beach. It's plain but affordable. For those who want to stay in the historic old walled city of San Juan (that is, not on the beach), there is a newly opened **Hotel Milano,** Calle Fortaleza 307 (② 787/729-9050), a five-story colonial-style hotel within walking distance of the best shops and all the major sights.

The hippest dining joint in San Juan is now the **Carli Café Concierto,** in Old San Juan (② 787/725-4927). It's run by Carli Muñoz, who was once one of the singing group The Beach Boys (there's a gold record on the wall to prove it). A long-time presence who sang at fine dining rooms in San Juan, Carli decided to open his own place. As his chef prepares delightful dishes, Carli entertains at his Steinway grand each evening, often accompanied by visiting local singers and musicians. Diners can eat inside or under the stars, enjoying a first-class menu.

After hurricane damage, **El Morro Trail** in Old San Juan, a jogger's paradise, has been reconstructed. The trail provides Old Town's most scenic views across the harbor. The first part of the trail extends to the San Juan Gate. The walk then goes by El Morro, a 16th-century fort, and eventually reaches a scenic area known as Bastion de Santa Barbara. The walk passes El Morro's well-preserved walls until the trail ends at the entrance to the fortress. The walkway is designed to follow the undulating movement of the ocean, and sea grapes and tropical vegetation surround benches for your rest. It's more romantic at night when the walls of the fortress are illuminated. See chapter 17.

U.S. VIRGIN ISLANDS   A place of "barefoot elegance," the newly opened **Divi Casino,** in the Divi Carina Bay Resort, 25 Estate Turner Hole (② 340/773-9700), has introduced gambling for the first time to the U.S.

Virgin Islands. The 10,000-square-foot casino boasts 12 gaming tables and 275 slot machines, plus two bars.

The island has recently launched the **St. Croix Heritage Trail** to help visitors relive its Danish colonial past. Specially designed maps and road signs lead visitors along the trail, which is one of the 50 nationwide millennium Legacy Trails inaugurated in 2000. The 72-mile road is teeming with historical and cultural sights, and a free brochure and easy-to-follow maps guide travelers along. The route, among other of the trail's historic sites, connects the two major towns of Christiansted and Frederiksted and goes past once-prosperous sugar plantations.

A funky native bar, **Fungi's on the Beach** (© 340/775-4145), has opened on Pineapple Beach in St. Thomas, serving regional dishes and brews. Come here for some of the juiciest burgers on island and the most delectable tasting pizza. You can also order Caribbean specialties such as conch in butter sauce.

The port of Charlotte Amalie, capital of St. Thomas, remains the shopping mecca of the Caribbean. Among stores that have vastly upgraded their stock is **Modern Music,** Nisky Center (© 340/777-7877), which features nearly every genre of music from rock to jazz, concentrating, of course, on the music of the islands. **Mr. Tablecloth** (© 340/774-4343) has received new shipments of top-quality linen from the Republic of China (also Hong Kong). Now he has the best selection of tablecloths and accessories, plus doilies, place mats, aprons, and runners in Charlotte Amalie.

It had to happen. **The Virgin Islands Brewing Company,** across from the Havensight Mall (© 340/777-8888), was originally founded on St. Croix but has invaded St. Thomas with two local beers, Blackbeard Ale and Foxy's Lager. At the company store, you're given free samples and can purchase six-packs of the home-brewed suds along with T-shirts, caps, and polo shirts.

The major venue for nightlife in St. Thomas has recently become **The Old Mill,** 193 Contant (© 340/776-3004), the largest and newest entertainment complex to open on the island, with three separate venues. The courtyard sports bar offers a variety of games, including four pool tables. The more elegant wine and champagne bar is in a restored 18th-century historic sugar mill, where guests can relax to the sound of jazz and blues. More than 100 different types of wines and champagnes from all over the world are served here. There's also a dance club, the largest of its kind in the U.S. Virgins. See chapter 25.

1

Choosing the Perfect Island: The Best of the Caribbean from $70 a Day

You can hike through national parks and scuba dive along underwater mountains. But perhaps your idea of the perfect Caribbean vacation is to plunk yourself down on a beach and do nothing at all. This guide will show you the best of the islands and prove to you that memorable vacations don't have to cost a fortune. In this chapter, we'll share an opinionated list of our favorite finds and bargains to help you start planning. For a thumbnail portrait of each island, see "The Islands in Brief" in chapter 2.

1 The Best Destinations for Low-Cost Vacations

Some islands, such as pricey St. Barts or Anguilla, are best left to the rich and famous—and so they are not covered in this book. If you're not a movie star who commands $18 to $25 million per picture, this book is for you. The following are some of the best lovely, yet inexpensive, options.

- **Dominica:** This island nation with a British/French-Creole flavor has rugged mountains and lush forests. But it lacks great beaches, which has hindered its development as a resort island. That lack of a tourist boom is good news for bargain hunters. If you enjoy lush settings and landscapes, Dominica is for you. The locals are among the friendliest hosts in the West Indies. See chapter 10.

- **The Dominican Republic:** Canadians, whose dollar is weaker in the Caribbean than the Yankee buck, have long flocked to this island nation for its sun, sand, and bargains. It's one of the cheapest destinations in the West Indies.

And new resort areas are under development, including the peninsula at Samaná and the Barahona Peninsula, each charging resort prices we haven't seen in 25 years. See chapter 11.

- **Jamaica:** Sure, there's a long list of posh resorts and pricey all-inclusives in Jamaica. But beyond these guarded compounds is another Jamaica, where the prices are as appealing as a frosty Red Stripe beer. Jamaica is riddled with small inns, and new resort areas are being developed, including along the south coast around Treasure Beach, east of Negril on the long road to Kingston. Even such normally tony areas as Montego Bay are filled with affordable B&Bs and small inns. See chapter 14.

- **Puerto Rico:** You can go for broke in Puerto Rico, but you can also find incredible bargains. Ignore those ritzy resorts: Puerto Rico is filled with B&Bs, small inns, and even government-run *paradors* out in the countryside, where you can stay for just a fraction of the price you'd pay along the Condado in San Juan. You can find terrific dining at inexpensive roadside kiosks, small cafes, and little family-run dining rooms frequented by locals. See chapter 17.

- **Saba:** This is a Dutch-held island, but it's like none other in the Caribbean. Only 5 square miles, it's not everyone's cup of tea. But if you can do without great beaches, try this volcanic island, which is ringed with steep cliffs and offers some of the finest diving in the Caribbean—the hiking is terrific, too. On this beautiful island, the hotels are some of the most affordable in the Caribbean. See chapter 18.

- **St. Eustatius:** Called "Statia" for short, this Dutch-held island is for escapists on a lean budget. It's sleepy, it's undiscovered—and that means great bargains for you. You'll just have to forgo white-sand beaches for some gray- or black-sand ones. It's filled with terrific hiking trails and panoramic dive sites that line the coast, the islanders are friendly, and you can find mom-and-pop hotels that charge prices "the way they were." See chapter 19.

2 The Best Beaches

Good beaches can be found on virtually every island of the Caribbean, with the possible exceptions of Saba (which has rocky shores) and Dominica. The following are some of our favorites.

- **Cane Garden Bay** (Tortola, British Virgin Islands): One of the most spectacular stretches of beach, it extends for 1½ miles of white sand and is a favorite with joggers. Its beach with sheltering palms is a living cliché of Caribbean charm. See chapter 7.

- **Seven Mile Beach** (Grand Cayman, Cayman Islands): It's really about 5½ miles long, but the 7-mile label has stuck. And who cares? Lined with condos and plush resorts, this beach is known for its array of watersports and its translucent aquamarine waters. Australian pines dot the background, and the average winter temperature of the water is a perfect 80°F. See chapter 8.

- **Playa Grande** (Dominican Republic): One of the Caribbean's least crowded beaches and one of the best, Playa Grande lies along the island's north shore. The long stretch of sand is powdery and beautiful. See chapter 11.

- **Grand Anse Beach** (Grenada): Although the island has some 45 beaches, most with white sand, this 2-mile stretch of sand is reason enough to go to Grenada. There's enough space and so few visitors that you'll likely find a spot just for yourself. The sugar-white sands of Grand Anse extend into deep waters far offshore. See chapter 12.

- **Seven Mile Beach** (Jamaica): In the northwestern section of the island, this beach stretches for 7 miles. Not for the conservative, the beach also contains some nudist patches along with bare-all Booby Island offshore. See chapter 14.

- **Diamond Beach** (Martinique): This bright white-sand beach stretches for about 6½ miles, much of it undeveloped. It faces a rocky offshore island, Diamond Rock, which has uninhabited shores. See chapter 15.

- **Pinney's Beach** (Nevis): With its golden sands and clean waters, this strip of beach front is not only the best beach on the little island of

The Caribbean Islands

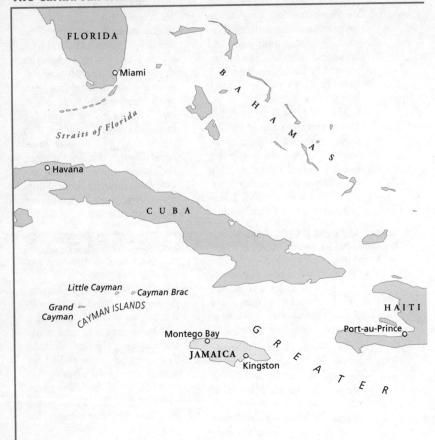

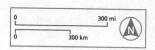

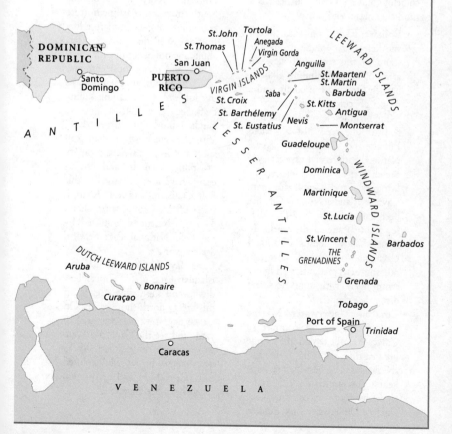

ATLANTIC OCEAN

TURKS AND
CAICOS ISLANDS

DOMINICAN
REPUBLIC

St. John   Tortola
St. Thomas   Anegada
San Juan   Virgin Gorda
PUERTO   Anguilla
Santo   RICO   VIRGIN ISLANDS   St. Maartenl
Domingo   St. Martin
St. Croix   Saba   Barbuda
St. Kitts
St. Barthélemy   St. Kitts
Nevis   Antigua
St. Eustatius   Montserrat

LEEWARD ISLANDS

A N T I L L E S

L E S S E R   A N T I L L E S

Guadeloupe

Dominica

Martinique   WINDWARD ISLANDS

St. Lucia

St. Vincent   Barbados
THE
GRENADINES

Grenada

DUTCH LEEWARD ISLANDS
Aruba
Bonaire
Curaçao

Tobago
Port of Spain
Trinidad

Caracas

V E N E Z U E L A

Nevis, but it's one of the finest in the Caribbean. Three miles of golden sands mean you won't be crowded in these waters, which are ideal for swimming. Shallow waters near the coast make this beach popular with families who have young children. See chapter 16.

- **Luquillo Beach** (Puerto Rico): This crescent-shaped public beach, with white sands and towering palms, lies 30 miles east of San Juan and is the local favorite. Coral reefs protect the crystal-clear lagoon, and tent sites and picnic facilities are available. See chapter 17.

- **Trunk Bay** (St. John, U.S. Virgin Islands): Protected by the U.S. National Park Service, this is one of the Caribbean's most popular beaches. A favorite with cruise ship passengers, it's known for its underwater trail, where markers guide snorkelers along the reef that lies just off the white sandy beach. See chapter 25.

3 The Best Snorkeling

While diving in the islands is excellent (see below), you won't need tanks and a regulator to enjoy the abundant sea life swimming among the Caribbean's colorful coral reefs. All you need is a snorkel, a mask, and fins.

- **Bonaire:** Right from their hotels, snorkelers can wade from the shore to the reefs and view an array of coral, including elkhorn barrier, fire, and leaf corals, and a range of colorful fish, such as redlip blennies, jewelfish, and parrotfish. The reefs just off Klein Bonaire and Washington-Slagbaai National Park receive rave reviews. See chapter 6.

- **Stingray City** (Grand Cayman, Cayman Islands): Stingray City has been called the best 12-foot dive (or snorkel) site in the world. In these shallow depths in Grand Cayman's North Sound, more than 30 southern Atlantic stingrays swim freely with snorkelers and divers. See chapter 8.

- **Curaçao Underwater Marine Park** (Curaçao): In contrast to Curaçao's sterile terrain, the marine life that rings the island is rich and spectacular. The best-known snorkeling sites stretch for 12½ miles along its southern coastline—the Curaçao Underwater Park. Sunken shipwrecks, gardens of coral, and millions of fish are your reward. See chapter 9.

- **Buccoo Reef** (Tobago): The shallow, sun-flooded waters off the South American coastline nurture enormous colonies of marine life. Buccoo Reef on Tobago offers abundant opportunities for snorkeling, and many local entrepreneurs take snorkeling enthusiasts out for junkets on various sailing craft. See chapter 24.

- **Buck Island** (St. Croix, U.S. Virgin Islands): More than 250 species of fish, as well as a variety of sponges, corals, and crustaceans, have been recorded at this 850-acre island and reef system, 2 miles off St. Croix's north shore. The reef is strictly protected by the U.S. National Park Service. See chapter 25.

- **Cane Bay** (St. Croix, U.S. Virgin Islands): One of St. Croix's best diving and snorkeling sites is off this breezy north-shore beach. On a clear day, you can swim out 150 yards and see the Cane Bay Wall, which drops off dramatically to deep waters below. Multicolored fish and elkhorn and brain coral thrive here. See chapter 25.

- **Trunk Bay** (St. John, U.S. Virgin Islands): This self-guided 225-yard-long trail has large underwater signs that identify species of coral and other items of interest. There are freshwater showers, changing rooms, equipment rentals, and a lifeguard on duty. See chapter 25.
- **Leinster Bay** (St. John, U.S. Virgin Islands): With easy access from land or sea, Leinster Bay offers calm, clear, and uncrowded waters, with an abundance of sea life. See chapter 25.
- **Haulover Bay** (St. John, U.S. Virgin Islands): A favorite with locals, this small bay is rougher than Leinster and is often deserted. The snorkeling is dramatic, with ledges, walls, nooks, and sandy areas set close together. At this spot, only about 200 yards separate the Atlantic Ocean from the Caribbean Sea. See chapter 25.
- **Magens Bay** (St. Thomas, U.S. Virgin Islands): On the north shore of St. Thomas, Coki Point offers year-round snorkeling, especially around the ledges near Coral World's underwater tower, a favorite with cruise ship passengers. See chapter 25.

4 The Best Dive Sites

Scuba diving, as everyone knows, is hardly cheap. But if it's your primary reason for visiting the Caribbean, look for a diver's package to get the best deal. Many resorts, including those on Bonaire and the Cayman Islands (the best spots for divers), offer packages that include room, meals, and limited scuba diving.

If diving is only a sometimes passion, you can stay at a budget hotel and visit a local dive operator. Prices can vary, of course, but most one-tank dives cost $45 to $55; two-tank dives, $65 to $75. Full certification courses start at $350.

- **Bonaire:** Here, local license plates read A DIVER'S PARADISE. The highly accessible reefs that surround Bonaire have never suffered from exploitation, poaching, or pollution, and the island's environmentally conscious dive industry will ensure that they never do. For the first-timer or the certified diver, the island is one of the world's top underwater environments—it's an underwater mountain created from volcanic eruptions. Diving is possible 24 hours a day. **Captain Don's Habitat Dive Shop** (© 599/717-8290) offers some of the most all-around reasonable packages that combine accommodations, meals, and diving. See chapter 6.
- **Virgin Gorda** (British Virgin Islands): Many divers plan their entire vacations around exploring the famed wreck of the HMS *Rhone*, off Salt Island. This royal mail steamer, which went down in 1867, is the most celebrated dive site in the Caribbean. See chapter 7.
- **The Cayman Islands:** Grand Cayman is consistently called "the best known dive destination in the Caribbean—if not the world," by *Skin Diver* magazine. There are 34 dive operations on Grand Cayman (plus 5 more on Little Cayman, and 3 on Cayman Brac). A full range of professional dive services is available, including equipment sales, rentals, and repairs; instruction at all levels; and underwater photography, video schools, and processing services. Stingray City has become Grand Cayman's most famous dive (and snorkel) site. On Little Cayman, **Sam McCoy's Diving**

& **Fishing Lodge** (© 800/ 626-0496) offers reasonable dive packages, most of which include all meals. This resort attracts divers who pursue the sport with a passion. See chapter 8.

- **Saba:** Islanders can't brag about Saba's beaches, but the waters around the island are blessed with some of the Caribbean's richest marine life. It's one of the premier diving locations in the Caribbean, with 38 official dive sites. The unusual setting includes underwater lava flows, black-sand bottoms, very large strands of black coral, millions of fish, and underwater mountaintops. The **Saba Deep Dive Center** (© 599/416-63347), one of the best-organized dive outfitters anywhere, offers an assortment of lodgings, many of them affordable choices with charm and a sense of Saban history as part of the package. See chapter 18.

- **Mona Island** (Mayagüez, Puerto Rico): Surrounded by some of the most beautiful coral reefs in the Caribbean, Mona Island has the most pristine, extensive, and well-developed reefs in Puerto Rican waters. The tropical marine ecosystem around Mona includes patch reefs, black coral, spore and groove systems, underwater caverns, deep-water sponges, fringing reefs, and algae reefs. The lush environment attracts octopuses, lobster, queen conch, rays, barracuda, snapper, jack, grunt, angelfish, trunkfish, filefish, butterfly fish, dolphin, parrotfish, tuna, flying fish, and more. The crystal waters afford exceptional horizontal vision for 150 to 200 feet as well as good views down to the shipwrecks that mark the site—including some Hispanic galleons. Five species of whales visit the island's offshore waters. Instead of booking an expensive tour, negotiate with a local fisherman to take you over for a look. See chapter 17.

- **St. Croix** (U.S. Virgin Islands): Increasingly known as a top diving destination, St. Croix hasn't overtaken Grand Cayman yet, but it has a lot going for it. Beach dives, reef dives, wreck dives, nighttime dives, wall dives—it's all here. But none can compete with the underwater trails of the national park at Buck Island, lying off St. Croix's "mainland." Other sites include the drop-offs and coral canyons at Cane Bay and Salt River. Davis Bay is the location of the 12,000-foot-deep Puerto Rico Trench, the fifth-deepest body of water on earth. See chapter 25.

5 The Best Adventures That Deliver Bang for Your Buck

- **Going Deep into Harrison's Cave** (Barbados): If you can explore only one cave in the Caribbean, make it Harrison's, one of the finest cave systems in the world. Open to the public since 1981, these limestone caverns are a fairytale world of stalagmites, subterranean streams, and stalactites—everything reaching its crescendo with a 40-foot waterfall. See chapter 5.

- **Trekking to a Boiling Lake** (Dominica): The highlight of Dominica National Park, this sulfurous lake is like a large cauldron of steaming gray-blue water—a flooded fumarole. It's the world's second-largest boiling lake. Getting here is part of the fun: It's a really arduous climb. The trail (which you should follow only with a guide) takes you through Titou Gorge and along forested mountains until you reach the aptly named Valley of Desolation. After that, it's a rough valley crossing, until you ascend to the mysterious lake on the far side. The trick is to not fall through the thin crust that blankets the steaming lava below! See chapter 10.

- **Exploring Luxuriant Guadeloupe:** The mountainous terrain of Basse-Terre is extraordinarily beautiful. Whereas the island's coastline is lined with beach resorts and fishing villages, the mountainous interior is a sparsely inhabited region devoted almost completely to a French national forest, Le Parc Naturel de Guadeloupe. Near the park's southernmost boundary stands the 4,812-foot volcanic peak, La Soufrière. The park contains more than 200 miles of hiking trails, allowing physically fit hikers to visit a wealth of gorges, ravines, rivers, and (at points north of La Soufrière) some of the highest waterfalls in the Caribbean. See chapter 13.

- **Discovering the Greatest Sight in the Avian World** (Trinidad): The Caroni Bird Sanctuary (© **868/645-1305**), spread across 40 square miles in Trinidad, is without equal in the Caribbean. Home of the national bird of Trinidad and Tobago, the scarlet ibis, this is the world's premier site for birders. Even *Audubon* magazine agrees. Beginning in the late afternoon, fire-engine-red birds arrive by the thousands, settling into roost for the night. As if this weren't enough, snowy egrets and herons fly in to join them in their slumber. The birds arrive in such vast numbers that they look like flaming scarlet and white Christmas tree decorations. See chapter 24.

- **Spending a Day on Buck Island** (off St. Croix, U.S. Virgin Islands): Legendary throughout the Caribbean for its underwater life, Buck Island is riddled with a network of hiking trails. On this 300-acre island surrounded by 550 acres of underwater coral gardens, the snorkeling possibilities are stunning. A circular underwater trail on the island's easternmost side has arrow markers to guide viewers along the inner reef. The elkhorn coral here is among the most massive in the world. See chapter 25.

6 The Friendliest Islands

A few islands are plagued with racial tensions and violent crime, and visitors might not feel welcome. In particular, Jamaica's portside cities (especially Ocho Rios, Kingston, and Montego Bay) are known for crowds of hawkers and peddlers who aggressively pressure tourists to buy unwanted souvenirs. St. Thomas and St. Croix are not very welcoming either and also have crime problems. And both Puerto Rico and the Dominican Republic are populous enough to have an urban atmosphere where some visitors might feel anonymous, but many locals there are pretty jaded about the hordes of tourists who arrive each year. So, with these caveats expressed, let's proceed to friendlier oases.

- **Bonaire:** With a tiny population of about 11,000 souls, Bonaire has a small-town atmosphere with a pace slow enough for the most diehard escapist. Residents are usually curious about off-islanders. See chapter 6.

- **Virgin Gorda** (British Virgin Islands): Many locals leave their houses and cars unlocked (although we don't recommend that you become that casual). But it's the lazy, peaceful life here. Visitors are welcomed into most places with a smile. See chapter 7.

- **Grenada and St. Vincent and the Grenadines:** The islands of the southern Caribbean are English-speaking, music-loving outposts. Locals can be warm and welcoming to outsiders. See chapters 12 and 23.
- **Nevis:** Nevis has a small, intimate feeling. Most accommodations are charming and historic inns, with a British tradition of good manners. See chapter 16.
- **Saba:** The residents here refer to their island as the "Unspoiled Caribbean Queen" because there are no beaches, casinos, or large

hotels, and only a handful of bars. The 1,200 shy but cautiously friendly residents follow traditions that were established by the Dutch settlers who first arrived in the 1600s. You'll be very safe here, but you'll be expected to behave with dignity and respect for island traditions. See chapter 18.

- **St. John** (U.S. Virgin Islands): St. John remains an unspoiled and relatively safe destination. The locals aren't as jaded about tourism here as they are on St. Thomas, and in most places you'll receive a genuine welcome. Many places appreciate your business and want you to return, so they make you feel welcome. See chapter 25.

7 The Best Experiences You Can Have for Free (or Almost)

- **Floating Over to "Treasure Island"** (British Virgin Islands): South of Tortola, east of St. John, and accessible only by boat, Norman Island has serviced the needs of smugglers and ruffians since the 1600s, when pirates used its hillocks to spot Spanish galleons to plunder. Legend has it that this was the island that inspired Robert Louis Stevenson's *Treasure Island*, first published in 1883. In a dinghy, you can row into the southernmost cave on the island—with bats overhead and phosphorescent patches floating on the water. This is where Stevenson's Mr. Fleming, according to legend, took his precious treasure. It was reported that in 1750 treasure from the sunken *Nuestra Señora* was recovered here. The island has a series of other caves, whose bottoms are filled with seawater teeming with marine life. Intrepid hikers climb through scrubland to the island's central ridge, Spy Glass Hill, to appreciate the panoramic view of the land and sea, although hiking

trails are either nonexistent or poorly maintained. See chapter 7.
- **Calling on the Once-Hostile Caribs** (Dominica): The Carib Indian Reservation, along the eastern coast of Dominica, is home to the once-hostile tribe for which the Caribbean is named. Reviled by the Spanish invaders because of their cannibalism, the Caribs now live peacefully in half a dozen villages, the largest of which are Bataka, Sineku, and Salybia. See chapter 10.
- **Exploring Two Unspoiled Islands Near Guadeloupe:** Marie-Galante and the Iles des Saintes are rarely visited islands near the coast of Guadeloupe. They preserve a raffish, seafaring atmosphere you might have found in Marseille during the 1930s. Come to sunbathe, explore by bike, and savor the seclusion. See chapter 13.
- **Rafting on the Río Grande** (Port Antonio, Jamaica; © 876/993-5778): Until the late actor Errol Flynn discovered what fun it was, rafting on this river was simply a

means of transporting bananas. Now it's the most amusing sport in Jamaica. Propelled by stout bamboo poles, you're guided down the river for 8 miles, during which you see a lush backdrop of coconut palms and banana plantations. You're even taken through the Tunnel of Love. See chapter 14.

8 The Best Destinations for Serious Shoppers Who Insist on Bargains

Since the U.S. government allows its citizens to take (or send) home more duty-free goods from the U.S. Virgin Islands than from other ports of call, the U.S. Virgin Islands remain the shopping bazaar of the Caribbean. U.S. citizens are allowed to carry home $1,200 worth of goods untaxed, as opposed to only $400 to $600 worth of goods from most islands in the Caribbean. (The only exception to this rule is Puerto Rico, where any purchase, regardless of the amount, can be carried tax-free back to the U.S. mainland.)

- **Aruba:** The wisest shoppers on Aruba are the cost-conscious souls who have carefully checked the prices of comparable goods before leaving home. Duty here is relatively low (only 3.3%). Much of the European china, jewelry, perfumes, wristwatches, and crystal has a habit of reappearing everywhere, so after you determine exactly which brand of watch or china you want, you can comparison-shop. See chapter 4.
- **Barbados:** Bajan shops seem to specialize in all things English. Merchandise includes bone china from British and Irish manufacturers, china, wristwatches, jewelry, and perfumes. Bridgetown's Broad Street is the shopping headquarters of the island, although there are malls along the congested southwestern coast. Duty-free status is extended to anyone who shows a passport or an ID and an airline ticket with a date of departure from Barbados. And except for cigarettes and tobacco,

any buyer can haul off duty-free items as soon as they're paid for. See chapter 5.
- **Curaçao:** Curaçao has been a mercantile center since the 1700s. In the island's capital, tidy and prosperous Willemstad, hundreds of merchants will be only too happy to cater to your needs. A handful of malls lie on Willemstad's outskirts, but most shops are clustered within a few blocks of the center of town. During seasonal sales, goods might be up to 50% less than comparable prices in the U.S.; most of the year, you'll find luxury goods (porcelain, crystal, watches, and gemstones) priced at about 25% less than in the States. Technically, you'll pay import duties on virtually everything you buy, but rates are so low that you might not even notice. See chapter 9.
- **Dominican Republic:** The island's best buys include handcrafts, amber from Dominican mines, and the distinctive pale-blue semiprecious gemstone larimar. However, the amber you buy from a streetside vendor might be nothing more than orange-colored transparent plastic, so buy only from well-established shops. Other charming souvenirs might include a Dominican rocking chair (remember the one JFK used to sit in?), which is sold boxed, in pieces. Shopping malls and souvenir stands abound in Santo Domingo, in Puerto Plata, and along the country's northern coast. See chapter 11.

- **Jamaica:** The shopping was better in Jamaica during the good old days, before new taxes added a 10% surcharge. Nevertheless, Jamaica offers a wealth of desirable goods, including flavored rums, Jamaican coffees, handcrafts (such as woodcarvings, woven baskets, and sandals), original paintings and sculptures, and cameras and wristwatches. Unless you're a glutton for handmade souvenirs—available on every beach and street corner—you'd be wise to limit most of your purchases to bona fide merchants and stores. See chapter 14.

- **Puerto Rico:** U.S. citizens don't have to pay any duty on anything—yes, anything—bought in Puerto Rico. Jewelry and watches abound, often at competitive prices, especially in the island's best-stocked area, Old San Juan. Also of great interest are such Puerto Rican handcrafts as charming papier-mâché Carnival masks. See chapter 17.

- **St. Thomas** (U.S. Virgin Islands): Charlotte Amalie, the capital of the U.S. Virgin Islands, attracts hordes of cruise ship passengers on a sometimes frantic hunt for bargains, real or imagined. Many of the busiest shops occupy restored warehouses built in the 1700s, and they're stocked with more merchandise than can be found anywhere else in the entire Caribbean. Despite all the fanfare, however, real bargains are hard to come by here. Look for two local publications, *This Week* and *Best Buys;* either might steer you to the type of low-cost merchandise you're seeking. If at all possible, try to avoid shopping when more than one cruise ship is in port—the shopping district is a madhouse on those days. See chapter 25.

- **St. Croix** (U.S. Virgin Islands): This island is the poor stepchild of St. Thomas. You'll see many of the same shops and chains here that you will on St. Thomas. Prices are about the same, but the crowds aren't nearly as bad here. But still, there's much to interest the born-to-shop visitor here, and merchandise has never been more wide-ranging than it is today. Even though most cruise ships call at Frederiksted, a colorful but isolated town near the island's western tip, most shops are in Christiansted, the island's capital. See chapter 25.

9 The Best Reasonably Priced Honeymoon Resorts

More and more couples are exchanging vows in the Caribbean. Many resorts will arrange everything from the preacher to the flowers, so we've included in the following list some resorts that provide wedding services. For more information about weddings on some of the most popular Caribbean islands, see "Getting Married in the Caribbean" in chapter 2.

- **The Catamaran Hotel & Marina** (Antigua; ℂ **268/460-1036**): For honeymooners, this beachside complex offers self-sufficient accommodations at Falmouth Harbour. With its own sandy beach, it is an informal, laid-back choice for a honeymoon, with comfortably furnished apartments where you can impress your new partner with your culinary skills. See chapter 3 for details.

- **Jake's** (Calabash Bay, Jamaica; ℂ **800/OUTPOST** or 876/965-0635): If you're looking for the perfect honeymoon hideaway, make it Jake's, a 3-hour drive east of Montego Bay's airport. On a cliff by the sea, it's a compound of flamboyant cottages that offer a lot of pizzazz for little money. It's off-beat, and it's just plain fun, mon. What to do in this sleepy backwater? Swim, eat, sleep, snorkel, and do whatever else honeymooners do. If you get bored, you can walk up to a cafe called Trans Love and catch up on the latest gossip between the Rasta men and their girlfriends. See chapter 14.

- **Villa Blanca** (St. Thomas, U.S. Virgin Islands; © **800/231-0034** or 340/776-0749): In Charlotte Amalie, Villa Blanca was the former home of the heiress to the Dodge fortune. Now it's the honeymoon bargain of the island, with 12 guest rooms, each with a private balcony and a kitchenette. The "Honeymoon Hideaway" package, for 8 days and 7 nights, costs $875 per couple in winter and only $575 per couple from May 1 to mid-December, and it includes welcome drinks, a bottle of champagne, and flowers. See chapter 25.

10 The Best Family Resorts for Parents Who Don't Want to Blow the Kids' College Fund

- **Mango Bay Resort** (Virgin Gorda, British Virgin Islands; © **800/223-6510** or 284/495-5652): On the western shore, little villas open right onto the beach, and each has its own fully equipped kitchen (including a dishwasher), plus maid service. Shaded by palm trees and surrounded by wide terraces, the villas can be configured to accommodate large and small families. This is an ideal family hideaway. See chapter 7.

- **Calypso Cove** (Grand Cayman, Cayman Islands; © **345/949-3730**): Just off Seven Mile Beach, one of the Caribbean's greatest beaches, this is a bargain on a rather high-priced island. Both one-bedroom and two-bedroom accommodations are available, with the latter housing as many as six. All accommodations have full kitchens, and such extras as washers and dryers help keep the expenses down. The place is relatively bare-bones as to facilities, but restaurants, grocery stores, and other services are just a short walk away. See chapter 8.

- **Trinidad Guest House** (Puerto Rico; © **787/889-2710**): This modest but comfortable inn stands right at Luquillo, the finest and most famous beach in Puerto Rico. For the family who likes to spend the day on the beach, this is a fine and modestly priced choice. To break the routine, the attractions and shops of San Juan are within an easy commute. See chapter 17.

11 The Best Camping

- **Brewers Bay Campground** (Tortola, British Virgin Islands; © **284/494-3463**): At one of the prime snorkeling sites in the BVI, this campground offers you a choice—either a bare site or a pre-pared one. It's fairly basic here, but it's a safe, clean location. See chapter 7.

- **White Bay Campground** (Jost Van Dyke, British Virgin Islands; © **284/495-9312**): At Little Harbour, on this practically deserted island (a former pirate's stamping ground), you get both tent and bare-site options. Running water and flush toilets are available, as are cookout areas. You can wander endlessly without encountering another soul at times. See chapter 7.

- **Cinnamon Bay Campground** (St. John, U.S. Virgin Islands; © 340/776-6330): Directly on the beach, this U.S. National Park Service campground is the most complete in the Caribbean. Sleeping in tents, cottages, or bare sites, you're surrounded by thousands of acres of tropical foliage. You can get up in the morning and take a running leap into the warm waters

off Cinnamon Bay Beach before breakfast. Bare-siters can make use of a picnic table and grill. There are ample facilities, including a cafeteria, watersports, and bathhouses. See chapter 25.

- **Maho Bay Camps** (St. John, U.S. Virgin Islands; © 800/392-9004 or 340/776-6226): At Maho Bay you can camp close to nature—in style and comfort. Boardwalks and ramps link its three-room tent cottages and lead to the beach. Electric lamps, propane stoves, bathhouses, barbecue areas, watersports, a commissary, even a restaurant—it's all here. See chapter 25.

12 The Best Places to Get Away From It All Without Spending a Fortune

- **Papillote Wilderness Retreat** (Dominica; © 767/448-2287): This retreat is situated in the heart of the Papillote Forest, one of the wildest and least-explored rain forests in the Caribbean. If frequent rain showers don't bother you (and it rains a lot in this incessantly lush region of Dominica), Papillote might provide a suitable escape at a surprisingly reasonable price. See chapter 10.

- **La Sagesse Nature Center** (Grenada; © 473/444-6458): Even though you're near the airport here, the opportunities for exploring the glories of nature are almost unlimited. Trails wind through the neighboring landscape, and ample opportunities for bird-watching are within an easy walk. See chapter 12.

- **La Casa del Francés** (Vieques, off the coast of Puerto Rico; © 787/741-3751): This house was built in 1905 as the headquarters of a sugar plantation. Since the 1950s it's been an eccentric but very appealing hideaway, although it's not for everyone. The house includes a collection of primitive art objects scattered amid dozens of potted plants and climbing vines. See chapter 17.

- **Laguna Mar Beach Resort** (Trinidad; © 868/628-3731): This place lies in the heart of 28 acres of rain forest. You can swim in freshwater springs or in the lagoons of swift-flowing rivers, watch (from afar) the beaches where leatherback turtles lay their eggs, and eat grilled fish caught by local fishers. See chapter 24.

13 The Best Authentic Dining

- **Atlantis Hotels Restaurant** (Barbados; © 246/433-9445). For a look at Barbados as it was in the 1950s, head for this battered old hotel beloved by Bajans. Here the

aging Enid I. Maxwell presides over some of the best and most authentic cookery on the island, including the island's best stew, a Bajan pepperpot. For details, see chapter 5.

- **North Shore Shell Museum Bar & Restaurant** (Tortola, British Virgin Islands; ✆ **284/495-4714**): The showcase for the culinary talents of Egberth and Mona Donovan, this restaurant succeeds admirably in serving the most authentic island cuisine. Mona is the daughter of the locally famous Mrs. Scatliffe, for decades considered the island's most "authentic" chef. The chefs take the produce of the island when available and shape the foodstuff into all sorts of delectable island fare, ranging from soupsop daiquiris to spicy conch fritters. See chapter 7.

- **New Golden Star** (Curaçao; ✆ **599/9-4654795**): It's nothing but a down-home roadside diner, but it's got authentic Antillean grub—all that good stuff like *tia chiki* (goat stew), well-seasoned grilled conch, shrimp Creole, and *keshi yena* (baked Gouda cheese stuffed with spicy meat filling). See chapter 9.

- **Mamma's** (Grenada; ✆ **473/440-1459**): Mamma used to welcome visitors with one of her rum punches and tasty regional cuisine. And we're really talking regional here. When Mamma could get them, she served armadillo or manicou (possum), or even monkey. Regrettably, Mamma isn't with us any more, but daughter Cleo learned all of Mamma's culinary secrets. Try her fresh seafood, such as octopus or crayfish, her *callaloo* soup, or one of her curries. See chapter 12.

- **Cosmo's Seafood Restaurant & Bar** (Negril, Jamaica; ✆ **876/957-4784**): At a laid-back *bohio* bordering the beach, Cosmo Brown makes Jamaica's best conch soup. His eatery may be rustic, but it's the place to find authentic Jamaican flavor and escape the bland international fare of the hotel restaurants. Fresh fish is your best bet here, and on some nights you can get lobster, curried or grilled. See chapter 14.

- **Chez Mally Edjam** (Martinique; ✆ **0596/78-51-18**): It's said that Martinique chefs serve the Caribbean's zestiest cuisine. If you'd like to find out for yourself, head to this little dive, where you'll encounter a virtuosa cook. On the island's northernmost tip, the home is modest—but the meals are not. The Creole dishes here are delicacies, with everything from stuffed land crab with hot seasoning to the best pork curry on the island. Save room for one of the cook's original confitures, tiny portions of fresh island fruit such as guava preserved in vanilla syrup. See chapter 15.

- **Jemma's Seaview Kitchen** (Tobago; ✆ **868/660-4467**): Mrs. Jemma Sealey will feed you well after squeezing some fresh orange or pineapple juice to settle your stomach. She doesn't put on airs—she just serves up the most authentic Tobagonian cuisine on the island. Tucked away on the beach, her place is cheap, good, and may be permanently etched in your memory, especially after you try her kingfish steak dipped in batter and accompanied with a spicy sweet sauce. On some nights, she might serve you a lobster if she has them, or perhaps crab and dumplings. See chapter 24.

- **Nolan's Tavern** (St. Croix, U.S. Virgin Islands; ✆ **340/773-6660**): The tastiest and most authentic West Indian cuisine on St. Croix is served in this cozy tavern by a Trinidad-born chef, Nolan Joseph. Called "King Conch" on the island, he prepares delectable versions of that mollusk, as well as some of the island's best curries. See chapter 25 for details.

14 The Best Places for Sunset Cocktails

- **Admiral's Inn** (Antigua; ✆ 268/ 460-1027): At one of the most atmospheric inns in the Caribbean, you can enjoy a cocktail and watch the sun go down over the loveliest harbor in the West Indies. After the sun sets, you can play a game of English darts with whatever crew has arrived at the dockyard. See chapter 3.
- **John Moore Bar** (Barbados; ✆ 246/422-2258): On the waterfront, this is the most famous little bar on Barbados. It's the social center of the island, so you can catch up on the latest gossip while enjoying a rum punch. See chapter 5.
- **Karel's Beach Bar** (Bonaire; ✆ 599/717-8434): Join the diving set at this Tahitian-styled alfresco bar perched above the sea on stilts. The convivial crowd starts gathering around 5pm, and on weekends, a local band entertains, making it a great place to linger. See chapter 6.
- **Cruise Bar** (Jamaica; ✆ 876/ 993-8751): At Dragon Bay, in the seaside town of Port Antonio on the north coast of Jamaica, the resort's most popular bar honors the actor Tom Cruise, who came here to film the movie *Cocktail*, in which he played a bartender. We can't guarantee that Cruise himself will be here to prepare your sundowner, but we can tell you that it's the best place on the north coast to watch the sun go down. See chapter 14 for more details.
- **Frangipani Hotel** (Bequia, the Grenadines; ✆ 784/458-3255): Any of the watering holes along Admiralty Bay would be lovely for a sundowner, although we give this hotel the edge, since it's where the locals go. A lot of yachties gather here, some of whom fly the skull-and-crossbones flag. Often you can hear steel bands playing along the shore, and the whole place becomes festive, making you want to linger long after the sun has disappeared. See chapter 23.
- **The Bar at Paradise Point** (St. Thomas, U.S. Virgin Islands; ✆ 340/777-4540): Head here for your sundowner, and get the bartender to serve you his specialty: a Bushwacker. Sometimes a one-man steel band is on hand to serenade the sunset-watchers, who after a few drinks don't know whether the sun has set. See chapter 25.

15 The Best Nightspots Without Sky-High Cover Charges

- **Bomba's Surfside Shack** (Tortola, British Virgin Islands); ✆ 284/ 495-4148): For uninhibited nightlife, this joint, covered with Day-Glo graffiti, rocks until the early hours. Built from the flotsam of a junkyard, it's fun, funky, and wild. The all-you-can-eat barbecue (on some nights) and the live reggae music keep the joint jumping until the early hours. See chapter 7.
- **Palm Court** (in El San Juan Hotel & Casino, Isla Verde, Puerto Rico; ✆ 787/791-1000): This is the most beautiful bar in the Caribbean (but not for sunset watching, as it's enclosed). And when you walk through the elegant lobby, you'll feel quite posh. But drink prices are reasonable, and many nights you can hear live music emanating from the adjoining El Chico Bar. There's no finer place for drinking in San Juan. See chapter 17.

- **Cheri's Café** (St. Maarten; ℂ **599/ 54-53361**): This is the local hot spot on this popular island divided between the Netherlands and France. Cheri's is on the Dutch side. *Caribbean Travel and Life* magazine announced it as their readers' pick for the best bar in the West Indies, where the competition is rough. Go here for an inexpensive night of uninhibited fun and revelry. After a few Straw Hats (the bartender's specialty), the night is yours. See chapter 22.

- **The Green House** (Charlotte Amalie, St. Thomas, U.S. Virgin Islands; ℂ **340/774-7998**): If you must be in Charlotte Amalie at night (there are safer places to be), head here for drinking, dining, and perhaps listening to some of the best music on the island, either live or recorded. What's even better are the two-for-one happy hours, which include a generous free buffet Monday through Saturday. There's only a modest cover charge when live bands play. See chapter 25.

- **Blue Moon** (St. Croix, U.S. Virgin Islands; ℂ **340/772-2222**): This is the hottest dive on the island, located in the capital, Frederiksted. Thursday and Friday are the best nights to show up. It's hip, and it's fun—and it also offers good bistro-type food. Live entertainment is often featured, and a convivial crowd of locals and visitors shows up nightly. See chapter 25.

2

Planning an Affordable Trip to the Caribbean

This chapter is designed to provide most of the nuts-and-bolts information you'll need before setting off on your island escape. We'll show you how to save money when booking your trip and how to scout out the best airfare and cruise bargains.

1 The Islands in Brief

The first decision you'll have to make is where to go in the Caribbean. Here is a brief rundown of the region to help get you started. See the following chapters for details.

ANTIGUA Antigua claims to have a different lovely beach for each day of the year. Some British traditions (including a passion for cricket) linger on, although this nation became independent in 1981; its British legacy means that you can see some of the most interesting historic naval sites in the world here. The island has a population of 80,000, mostly descended from the African slaves of plantation owners. Although there are many conservative but very glamorous resorts, we've found some affordable accommodations with charming island atmosphere. Antigua is politically linked to the sparsely inhabited and largely undeveloped island of Barbuda, about 30 miles north. See chapter 3.

ARUBA Until its beaches were "discovered" in the late 1970s, Aruba was an almost-forgotten outpost of Holland, mostly valued for its oil refineries and salt factories. Today it's favored for its unique terrain—an almost lunar landscape of desert, plus spectacular beaches where you can bask under

constant sunshine. There's an almost total lack of racial tensions, although its population of 70,000 is culturally diverse, with roots in Holland, Portugal, Spain, Venezuela, India, Pakistan, and Africa. A building boom in the 1980s has transformed this island into a pale version of Las Vegas (it's one of the islands most noted for casinos). Unfortunately, it's next to impossible to find real budget accommodations, though we've scouted out a few for you. See chapter 4.

BARBADOS Cosmopolitan Barbados has the densest population of any island in the Caribbean, and its people have an avid interest in cricket. Here you'll find many stylish, medium-size hotels. Its topography varies from rolling hills and savage waves on the eastern (Atlantic) coast to densely populated flatlands and sheltered beaches in the southwest. Barbados is generally an expensive destination. See chapter 5.

BONAIRE Bonaire is the place to be for serious divers and bird-watchers. The landscape is as dry and inhospitable as anything you'll find in the Caribbean. The beaches aren't the best, but there's a wealth of rich marine life along the island's miles of offshore reefs. There's little nightlife or shopping here; most visitors come for diving or nature. Bonaire is a terrific destination for cost-conscious travelers. See chapter 6.

THE BRITISH VIRGIN ISLANDS

Still a British Crown Colony, this lushly forested archipelago consists of about 50 mountainous islands (depending on how many rocks, cays, and uninhabited islets you want to include). A superb destination for sailing, the BVI is less densely populated, less developed, and has fewer social problems than its neighbors, the U.S. Virgin Islands. Tortola is the main island, followed in importance by Virgin Gorda. See chapter 7.

THE CAYMAN ISLANDS

Flat and prosperous, this tiny nation of three islands south of Cuba is dependent on Britain for its economic survival. It attracts millionaire expatriates from all over because of its lenient tax and banking laws. The landscapes aren't as lush and lovely as others in the Caribbean—these islands are covered with scrubland and swamp—but they do have great beaches and world-class diving. Many of these beaches are lined with upscale (and horrendously expensive) private homes and condominiums, but we've found some affordable places to stay. See chapter 8.

CURAÇAO

Because much of the island's surface is an arid desert that grows only cactus, its canny Dutch settlers ruled out farming and developed Curaçao into one of the Dutch Empire's busiest trading posts. Until the post–World War II collapse of the oil refineries, Curaçao was a thriving mercantile society with a capital (Willemstad) that somewhat resembled Amsterdam. Tourism began to develop here during the 1980s, and many new hotels—usually in the Dutch colonial style—have been built. Overall, Curaçao is more than just a tourist mecca: It's a well-defined society in its own right. See chapter 9.

DOMINICA

An English-speaking island set midway between Guadeloupe and Martinique, Dominica is the largest and most mountainous island of the Windwards. A mysterious, rarely visited land of waterfalls, rushing streams, and rain forests, it has only a few beaches, which are mainly lined with black volcanic sand. Some 82,000 people live here, including 2,000 remaining descendants of the Carib Indians. Dominica is one of the poorest islands in the Caribbean, with the misfortune of lying directly in the hurricane belt. But if you like the offbeat and unusual, you might find this the most fascinating island in the Caribbean, with beautiful, lush landscapes to explore—and it's one of the best bargain destinations. See chapter 10.

THE DOMINICAN REPUBLIC

Occupying the eastern two-thirds of Hispaniola (it shares the island with Haiti), this mountainous country is the second largest in the Caribbean and boasts gorgeous beaches. An endless series of military dictatorships once wreaked havoc on its social fabric, but today there's a more favorable political climate. The "D.R." offers some of the least expensive vacation options in the entire Caribbean, although there are some drawbacks: The contrast between the wealth of foreign tourists and the poverty of locals is especially obvious here, and it's not the safest of the islands. The crowded capital, Santo Domingo, has a population of two million. The island offers lots of Hispanic color, wonderful *merengue* music, and many opportunities to dance, drink, and otherwise party. Unfortunately, Hurricane Georges hit the Dominican Republic hard in 1998. See chapter 11.

GRENADA

The southernmost nation of the Windward Islands, Grenada is one of the lushest in the Caribbean. Extravagantly fertile, it's one of the largest producers of spices in the Western Hemisphere, the result of a gentle climate, rich volcanic soil, and a corps of good-natured islanders. There's a lot of very appealing local color on Grenada, particularly since the political troubles of the 1980s have ended. The beaches are white and sandy, and the populace (a mixture of English expatriates and islanders of African descent) is friendly. Once a British Crown Colony but now independent, the island nation includes Carriacou and Petit Martinique, two smaller islands that have few tourist facilities. Grenada's capital, St. George's, is one of the most raffishly charming towns in the Caribbean. See chapter 12.

GUADELOUPE It isn't as sophisticated or cosmopolitan as the two outlying islands (St. Barthélemy and the French sector of St. Martin) over which it holds administrative authority, but there's a lot of natural beauty in this *département* of France. With a relatively low population density (only 340,000 people live here, mostly along the coast), butterfly-shaped Guadeloupe is actually two distinctly different volcanic islands separated by a narrow saltwater strait, the rivière Salée. It's ideal for scenic drives and Creole color, offering an unusual insight into the French colonial world. See chapter 13.

JAMAICA A favorite of North American honeymooners, mountainous Jamaica rises abruptly from the sea 90 miles south of Cuba and about 100 miles west of Haiti. One of the most densely populated nations in the Caribbean, with a vivid sense of its own identity, Jamaica has a tragic history rooted in slavery, and today a legacy of poverty and political turbulence remains. Yet despite that poverty and a regrettable increase in crime and harassment of tourists by vendors in such resort areas as Ocho Rios, Jamaica is one of the most successful predominately black democracies in the world. The island is large enough to allow the more-or-less peaceful coexistence of all kinds of people, from expatriate English aristocrats to dyed-in-the-wool Rastafarians. Overall, Jamaica is a fascinating island, with a vibrant culture, a rich musical heritage, and an astounding diversity of landscapes. Many super-expensive resorts line its lovely beaches, fenced off and isolated from the life of the island, but there are countless bargains to be had, too—we'll round them up for you in chapter 14.

MARTINIQUE One of the most exotic French-speaking destinations in the Caribbean, Martinique was once the site of a settlement that was demolished by the volcanic activity of St. Pierre, which is now only a pale shadow of a once-thriving city. Like Guadeloupe, Martinique is legally and culturally French (certainly many islanders drive with a Gallic panache—read: very badly), although many Creole customs and traditions continue to flourish. The beaches are beautiful, the Creole cuisine is full of flavor and flair, and the island has lots of tropical charm. See chapter 15.

NEVIS Now forging its own road to independence from St. Kitts, from which it is separated by 2 miles of water, Nevis was spotted by Columbus in 1493 on his second voyage to the New World. He called it *Nieves*—Spanish for "snows"—when he saw the cloud-crowned volcanic isle that evoked for him the snow-capped peaks of the Pyrenees. Known for its long beaches of both black and white sand, Nevis, more than any other island in the Caribbean, has turned its former great houses, built during the plantation era, into some of the most charming inns in the West Indies. The capital city, Charlestown, looks like a real Caribbean backwater, but it is home to hundreds of worldwide businesses that

Value Websites for Divers

For useful information on scuba diving in the Caribbean, check out the website of the **Professional Association of Diving Instructors (PADI): www.padi.com**. This site provides descriptions of dive destinations throughout the Caribbean and a directory of PADI-certified dive operators. *Rodale's Scuba Diving Magazine* also has a helpful website at **www. scubadiving.com**. Both sites list dive package specials and display gorgeous color photos of some of the most beautiful dive spots in the world.

are drawn to Nevis for its tax laws and bank secrecy. See chapter 16.

PUERTO RICO   Home to 3.3 million Spanish-speaking people, the Commonwealth of Puerto Rico is under the jurisdiction of the United States. It's one of the Caribbean's most urban islands, with glittering casinos, lots of traffic, a relatively high crime rate, and a more-or-less comfortable mixture of Latin and U.S. cultures. The island's interior is filled with ancient volcanic mountains and lush rain forest; the coastline is ringed with sandy beaches. San Juan, the island's 16th-century capital, contains beautifully preserved Spanish colonial neighborhoods and the Condado, its beach strip of high-rise hotels, which evokes Miami Beach. Outside the glitzy resorts are many charming and reasonably priced places to stay, lots of wonderful down-home restaurants, and a host of affordable adventures. See chapter 17.

SABA   Saba is a cone-shaped extinct volcano that rises abruptly and steeply from the watery depths of the Caribbean. It has no beaches to speak of, but the local Dutch- and English-speaking populace has traditionally made a living from fishing, trade, and needlework rather than tourism. Visitors usually come to Saba to dive (which is expensive, but worth it), to visit the rain forest (which is free), and to totally get away from it all. Hotel choices are limited, often designed in the traditional Saban style of stone

foundations terraced into sloping hillsides with white walls and red roofs. See chapter 18.

ST. EUSTATIUS   Known as "Statia," St. Eustatius is among the poorest islands in the Caribbean, with 8 square miles of arid landscape, beaches that have strong and sometimes dangerous undertows, a population of around 1,700 people, and a sleepy capital, Oranjestad. The island is very committed to maintaining its political and fiscal links to the Netherlands. See chapter 19.

ST. KITTS   The first English settlement in the Leeward Islands, St. Kitts has a rich sense of British maritime history. With 68 square miles of land, St. Kitts (also known as St. Christopher) enjoyed one of the richest sugarcane economies of the plantation age. This island lies somewhat off the beaten tourist track and has a very appealing, intimate charm. A lush, fertile mountain island with a rain forest and waterfalls, it is crowned by the 3,792-foot Mount Liamuiga—a crater that thankfully has remained dormant (unlike the one at Montserrat). Come here for the beaches and the history, for lush natural scenery, and to stay at a restored plantation home that's been turned into a charming inn. See chapter 20.

ST. LUCIA   St. Lucia (*Loo*-sha) is the second largest of the Windward Islands. A volcanic island with lots of rainfall and great natural beauty, it has

Which Island Is for You?	Vacation Costs	All-Inclusive Resorts	Beaches	Above-Average Food	Campgrounds	Casinos	Condo/Villa Rentals	Family-Friendly	Cruise-Ship Port	Deluxe Resorts
Antigua	$$$	✔	✔	✔		✔		✔	✔	✔
Aruba	$$	✔	✔	✔		✔	✔	✔	✔	✔
Barbados	$$$	✔	✔	✔			✔	✔	✔	✔
Bonaire	$$		✔							
Cayman Islands	$$$	✔	✔	✔			✔	✔	✔	✔
Curaçao	$$		✔			✔			✔	✔
Dominica	$									
Dominican Republic	$	✔	✔			✔		✔	✔	✔
Grenada	$$		✔					✔	✔	✔
Guadeloupe	$$	✔	✔	✔	✔	✔			✔	
Jamaica	$$	✔	✔	✔	✔		✔	✔	✔	✔
Martinique	$$$	✔	✔	✔	✔	✔			✔	✔
Nevis	$$$		✔	✔						✔
Puerto Rico	$		✔	✔	✔	✔	✔	✔	✔	✔
Saba	$									
St. Croix	$$		✔	✔			✔	✔	✔	✔
St. Eustatius	$		✔							
St. John	$$$		✔	✔	✔		✔	✔		✔
St. Kitts	$$	✔	✔			✔		✔		✔
St. Lucia	$$$	✔	✔					✔	✔	✔
St. Martin/St. Maarten	$$$	✔	✔	✔		✔	✔	✔	✔	✔
St. Thomas	$$	✔	✔	✔			✔	✔	✔	✔
St. Vincent	$		✔							
Tobago	$$		✔							✔
Tortola	$$		✔		✔		✔	✔	✔	✔
Trinidad	$		✔							
Virgin Gorda	$$$	✔	✔	✔	✔			✔		✔

Golf	Hiking	Historic Sites	Mountainous Terrain	Music/Entertainment Nightlife	Nonstop Flights from U.S.	Public Transport	Rain Forest	Romantic Getaways	Sailing	Scenic Beauty	Scuba Diving/Snorkeling	Secret Hideaways	Shopping	Verdant & Lush Terrain	Very Dry Climate
✓	✓	✓			✓			✓	✓	✓	✓	✓			
✓	✓	✓	✓					✓		✓		✓			
✓	✓	✓		✓	✓	✓			✓	✓		✓			
	✓			✓						✓				✓	
✓	✓	✓	✓			✓		✓		✓					
	✓	✓	✓	✓	✓					✓		✓		✓	
	✓	✓	✓			✓	✓			✓		✓		✓	
✓	✓	✓	✓	✓	✓	✓				✓			✓	✓	
✓	✓	✓	✓		✓	✓	✓	✓	✓	✓	✓	✓		✓	
✓	✓	✓	✓		✓	✓		✓	✓	✓			✓		
✓	✓	✓	✓	✓	✓	✓	✓	✓		✓	✓	✓	✓	✓	
✓	✓	✓	✓	✓		✓	✓			✓	✓			✓	
✓	✓	✓	✓					✓		✓		✓		✓	
✓	✓	✓	✓	✓	✓	✓	✓	✓	✓	✓	✓	✓	✓	✓	
	✓		✓							✓	✓	✓		✓	
✓	✓	✓		✓		✓	✓			✓	✓		✓	✓	
	✓														
	✓	✓	✓					✓	✓	✓	✓	✓		✓	
✓	✓	✓						✓		✓		✓			
✓	✓		✓		✓		✓	✓		✓		✓		✓	
✓	✓	✓	✓			✓				✓		✓			
✓	✓	✓	✓	✓	✓			✓				✓			
	✓		✓						✓					✓	
✓	✓			✓	✓		✓								
	✓		✓			✓			✓	✓	✓	✓		✓	
	✓			✓	✓	✓	✓			✓				✓	
	✓		✓			✓		✓	✓	✓	✓	✓		✓	

both white and black sandy beaches, bubbling sulfur springs, and panoramic mountain scenery. Most tourism is concentrated on the island's northwestern tip, near the capital (Castries), but the arrival of up to 200,000 visitors per year has inevitably altered St. Lucia's old agrarian lifestyle throughout the island. Nevertheless, it remains a beautiful and welcoming place. See chapter 21.

ST. MAARTEN & ST. MARTIN This "twin nation" of 37 square miles has been divided between the Dutch (St. Maarten) and the French (St. Martin) since 1648. Regardless of how you spell it, it's the same island, although the two sides of the unguarded border are quite different from one another. The Dutch side contains the island's major airport, as well as many shops and tourist facilities. St. Martin, whose capital is Marigot, has some of the poshest hotels and the best food on the island. Both sides of the island are modern, urban, and proudly international. Each suffers from traffic jams, a lack of parking space in the capitals, tourist-industry burnout (especially on the Dutch side), and a disturbing increase in crime. See chapter 22.

ST. VINCENT & THE GRENADINES Despite its natural beauty, this mini-archipelago has only recently emerged from obscurity. It has always been known to divers and yachties, who find its north-to-south string of cays and coral islets some of the most panoramic sailing regions in the world. St. Vincent is by far the largest and most fertile island in the country. Its capital is the sleepy, somewhat dilapidated town of Kingstown. Stretching like a pearl necklace to the south of St. Vincent are some 32 neighbor islands called the Grenadines. These include the boat-building community of Bequia and chic Mustique. Less densely populated islands in the chain include the tiny outposts of Mayreau, Canouan, Palm Island, and Petit St. Vincent, whose sun-blasted surfaces were for the most part covered with scrub until around the late 1960s, when hotel owners planted groves of palms and hardwood trees. See chapter 23.

TRINIDAD & TOBAGO The southernmost of the West Indies, this two-island nation lies just 7 miles off the coast of Venezuela. Trinidad is the most industrial island in the Caribbean, with oil deposits and a polyglot population derived from India, Pakistan, Venezuela, Africa, and Europe. Known for its calypso music and carnivals, Trinidad is one of the most culturally distinct nations in the Caribbean. It has a rich artistic tradition, a bustling capital (Port-of-Spain), and exotic flora and fauna.

About 20 miles northeast of Trinidad, tiny Tobago is calmer and less heavily forested, with a rather dull capital (Scarborough) and a spectacular array of white-sand beaches. Whereas Trinidad seems to consider tourism as only one of many viable industries, Tobago is absolutely dependent on it. For details on both islands, see chapter 24.

THE U.S. VIRGIN ISLANDS Formerly Dutch possessions, these islands became part of the United States in 1917. St. Croix is the largest and flattest of the U.S. Virgins; the more mountainous St. Thomas and St. John are also popular destinations. St. Thomas and, to a lesser degree, St. Croix, offer all the diversions, facilities, and amusements you'd find on the U.S. mainland, including bars, restaurants, and lots of modern resort hotels. St. Thomas is sometimes referred to as the "shopping mall of the Caribbean," and crowds of cruise ship visitors frequently pass through. Much of the surface of St. John is devoted to a national park, a gift from Laurence Rockefeller. All three islands offer sailing, snorkeling, and unspoiled vistas. Crime is on the increase, however—an unfortunate fly in the ointment of what would otherwise be a corner of paradise. See chapter 25.

2 Visitor Information

All the major islands have tourist representatives who will supply information before you go; we list them in the "Visitor Information" sections of the individual island chapters. The **Caribbean Tourism Organization,** 80 Broad St., 32nd floor, New York, NY 10004 (© **212/635-9530**), can also provide general information.

INFO ON THE WEB

The Internet is a great source of travel information. **Yahoo!** (www.yahoo. com), **Excite** (www.excite.com), **Lycos** (www.lycos.com), **Infoseek** (www. infoseek.com), and the other major Internet indexing sites all have subcategories for travel, country/regional information, and culture.

Other good clearinghouse sites for information are **Microsoft Expedia** (www.expedia.msn.com), **Travelocity** (www.travelocity.com), the **Internet Travel Network** (www.itn.com), and **TravelWeb** (www.travelweb.com). Another good site is **Excite Travel** (http://travel.excite.com), which can point you toward a wealth of Caribbean travel information on the Web.

Of the many, many online travel magazines, two of the best are **Arthur Frommer's Budget Travel Online** (www.frommers.com), written and updated by the guru of budget travel himself, and **Condé Nast's Epicurious** (www.epicurious.com), based on articles from the company's glossy magazines *Traveler* and *Bon Appétit*.

In addition to these general websites, as often as possible throughout this chapter, we've included specific websites along with phone numbers and addresses. We've also provided each hotel and resort's website, if it has one, so you can see pictures of a property before you make reservations.

TRAVEL AGENTS

A good travel agent can also provide information and save you plenty of time and money by hunting down the best airfare for your route and arranging for cruises and rental cars. For the time being, most travel agents still charge you nothing for their services—they're paid through commissions from the airlines and other agencies they book for you. However, a number of airlines have begun cutting commissions, and increasingly agents are finding that they have to charge you a fee to hold the bottom line—or else unscrupulous agents will offer you only the travel options that bag them the juiciest commissions. Shop around and ask hard questions; use this book to become an informed consumer. If you decide to use a travel agent, make sure the agent is a member of the **American Society of Travel Agents (ASTA)**, 1101 King St., Alexandria, VA 22314 (© **703/739-8739;** www. astanet.com). If you send ASTA a self-addressed stamped envelope, it will mail you its free booklet *Avoiding Travel Problems*.

3 Entry Requirements & Customs

ENTRY REQUIREMENTS

Even though the Caribbean islands are, for the most part, independent nations and thereby classified as international destinations, passports are not generally required, unless you're coming from outside North America. You'll certainly need identification, and, since a passport is the best form for speeding you through Customs and Immigration, we recommend carrying one anyway. Other acceptable documents include an ongoing or return ticket plus a birth certificate (the original or a copy that has been certified by your local registrar of deeds and birth certificates). You will also need some photo ID, such as a driver's license or an expired passport; however, a driver's license is not acceptable as a sole form of ID.

Visas are usually not required, but some countries may require you to fill out a tourist card (see the individual island chapters for details).

Before leaving home, make two copies of your documents—including your passport, your driver's license, your airline ticket, and any hotel vouchers—and leave them home with someone. If you're on medication, you should also make copies of prescriptions.

CUSTOMS

Each island has specific requirements that are detailed in the destination chapters that follow. Generally, you're permitted to bring in items intended for your personal use, including tobacco, cameras, film, and a limited supply of liquor—usually 40 ounces. Here's what you can bring home from the islands:

U.S. CUSTOMS The U.S. government generously allows $1,200 worth of duty-free imports every 30 days from the U.S. Virgin Islands; if you go over this amount, you're taxed at 5% rather than the usual 10%. The duty-free limit is $400 for such international destinations as the French islands of Guadeloupe and Martinique, and $600 for many other islands. If you visit only Puerto Rico, you don't have to go through Customs at all, since the island is a U.S. commonwealth.

Joint Customs declarations are possible for members of a family traveling together. For instance, if you are a husband and wife with two children, your purchases in the U.S. Virgin Islands become duty-free up to $4,800! Unsolicited gifts can be sent to friends and relatives at the rate of $100 per day from the U.S. Virgin Islands and $50 a day from the other islands. U.S. citizens, or returning residents at least 21 years of age, traveling directly or indirectly from the U.S. Virgin Islands to the United States, are allowed to bring in free of duty 1,000 cigarettes, 5 liters of alcohol, and 100 cigars (but not Cuban cigars). Duty-free limitations on articles from other countries are generally 1 liter of alcohol, 200 cigarettes, and 200 cigars.

Be sure to collect receipts for all purchases made abroad. You must also declare on your Customs form the nature and value of all gifts received during your stay abroad. It's prudent to carry proof that you purchased expensive cameras or jewelry on the U.S. mainland. If you purchased such an item during an earlier trip abroad, you should carry proof that you have previously paid Customs duty on the item.

Sometimes merchants suggest a false receipt to undervalue your purchase. *Warning:* You could be involved in a sting operation—the merchant might be an informant for U.S. Customs.

If you use any medication that contains controlled substances or requires injection, carry an original prescription or note from your doctor.

For more specifics, write to the **U.S. Customs Service,** 1301 Constitution Ave., P.O. Box 7407, Washington,

What Things Cost in the Caribbean

Country	Local Phone Call	Average Budget Double Room	Average Budget Lunch	Average Budget Dinner	Coffee	Film
Antigua	15¢	$100	$15	$25	$2	$12
Aruba	25¢	$125	$15	$28	$2	$10
Barbados	25¢	$135	$14	$25	$1.25	$12
Bonaire	16¢	$95	$15	$36	$1.50	$6
BVIs	30¢	$85	$15	$25	$1	$8.50
Cayman Islands	70¢	$125	$15	$32	$1.80	$8
Curaçao	25¢	$100	$20	$30	$1.50	$10
Dominica	10¢	$80	$10	$18	$1.40	$10
Dominican Republic	10¢	$90	$8	$20	$1	$7.50
Grenada	10¢	$90	$15	$22	$1.50	$6.50
Guadeloupe	65¢	$110	$15	$35	$2	$7
Jamaica	15¢	$110	$20	$25	$2	$7
Martinique	65¢	$120	$20	$35	$2	$8
Nevis/St. Kitts	12¢	$110	$15	$30	$1.50	$9
Puerto Rico	30¢	$90	$15	$30	$1.50	$6
Saba	15¢	$90	$15	$30	$1.50	$7
St. Eustatius	25¢	$85	$15	$20	$1.50	$8
St. Lucia	20¢	$110	$15	$20	$1.50	$7
St. Maarten	30¢	$130	$15	$28	$2	$7
St. Martin	65¢	$110	$15	$30	$1.75	$7
St. Vincent	15¢	$75	$10	$20	$1.50	$6
Trinidad/Tobago	25¢	$100	$10	$20	$1.50	$6
USVIs	30¢	$90	$15	$20	$1	$7

DC 20044 (© 202/927-6724; www.customs.ustreas.gov), and request the free pamphlet *Know Before You Go.*

U.K. CUSTOMS U.K. citizens returning from a non-EU country such as one of the Caribbean nations have a customs allowance of 200 cigarettes; 50 cigars; 250 grams of smoking tobacco; 2 liters of still table wine; 1 liter of spirits or strong liqueurs (over 22% volume); 2 liters of fortified wine, sparkling wine, or other liqueurs; 60cc (ml) perfume; 250cc (ml) of toilet water; and £145 worth of all other goods, including gifts and souvenirs. People under age 17 cannot have the tobacco or alcohol allowance. For more information, contact **HM Customs & Excise,** Passenger Enquiry Point, 2nd Floor Wayfarer House, Great South West Road, Feltham, Middlesex, TW14 8NP (© 020/8910-3744; www.hmce.gov.uk).

CANADIAN CUSTOMS For a clear summary of Canadian rules, write for the booklet *I Declare,* issued by **Revenue Canada,** 2265 St. Laurent Blvd., Ottawa K1G 4KE (© **506/ 636-5064;** www.ccra-adrc.gc.ca). Canada allows its citizens a $750 exemption, and you're allowed to bring back duty-free 200 cigarettes, 200 grams of tobacco, 1.5 liters of liquor, and 50 cigars. In addition, you're allowed to mail gifts to Canada from abroad at the rate of Can$60 a day, provided they're unsolicited and don't contain alcohol or tobacco (write on the package "Unsolicited gift, under $60 value"). All valuables should be declared on the Y-38 form before departure from Canada, including serial numbers of valuables you already own, such as expensive foreign cameras. *Note:* The $750 exemption can be used only once a year and only after an absence of 7 days.

4 Money

CURRENCY

Widely accepted on many of the islands, the **U.S. dollar** is the legal currency of the U.S. Virgin Islands, the British Virgin Islands, and Puerto Rico. Many islands use the **Eastern Caribbean dollar,** even though your hotel bill will most likely be presented in U.S. dollars. French islands use the **French franc,** although many hotels often quote their prices in U.S. dollars. From January of 2002 the French franc will be phased out and replaced by the **euro,** the single European currency of 11 countries. For details, see "Fast Facts" in the individual island chapters.

TRAVELER'S CHECKS

Traveler's checks are something of an anachronism from the days before the ATM made cash accessible at any time. These days, traveler's checks seem less necessary, as most islands have 24-hour ATMs that allow you to withdraw small amounts of cash as needed. However, if you want to avoid ATM service charges, or if you want the security of knowing you can get a refund in the event that your wallet is stolen, you might want to purchase traveler's checks, which you can do at almost any bank. **American Express** offers denominations of $10, $20, $50, $100, $500, and $1,000. You'll pay a service charge ranging from 1% to 4%. You can also get American Express traveler's checks over the phone by calling © **800/221-7282** (www.americanexpress.com); by using this number, Amex gold and platinum cardholders are exempt from the 1% fee. AAA members can obtain checks without a fee at most AAA offices.

Visa (© **800/227-6811**) offers traveler's checks at **Citibank** locations nationwide and several other participating banks. The service charge ranges from 1½% to 2%; checks come in denominations of $20, $50, $100, $500, and $1,000. **MasterCard** also offers traveler's checks. Call © **800/ 223-7373** for a location near you.

If you opt to carry traveler's checks, be sure to record their serial numbers, and keep the list separate from the checks so you're ensured a refund in case of loss or theft.

ATMS

ATMs are linked to an international network that most likely includes your bank at home. **Cirrus** (© **800/ 424-7787;** www.mastercard.com/ cardholderservices/atm/) and **Plus** (© **800/843-7587;** www.visa.com) are the two most popular networks; check the back of your ATM card to see which network your bank belongs to. Use the toll-free numbers or websites to locate ATMs in your destination.

The U.S. Dollar, the British Pound, the Canadian Dollar, the French Franc, and the Euro

During the lifetime of this edition, each of the currencies listed in the chart below will be accepted somewhere within the Caribbean. Because exchange rates fluctuate, it should be used only as a general guide, with the understanding that changes in economic policies can and will certainly affect the values of international currencies. Be sure to confirm the exchange rates before you make any serious transactions.

At this writing, US$1 = about UK£0.65, Can$1.50, 6.90 French francs, and 1.10 euros.

US$	UK£	Can$	French Franc	Euro
0.25	0.15	0.40	1.70	0.30
0.50	0.35	0.75	3.45	0.55
0.75	0.50	1.15	5.20	0.85
1.00	0.65	1.50	6.90	1.10
2.00	1.35	3.00	13.80	2.20
3.00	2.00	4.50	20.65	3.30
4.00	2.65	6.00	27.55	4.40
5.00	3.35	7.50	34.45	5.50
6.00	4.00	9.00	41.35	6.60
7.00	4.65	10.50	48.25	7.70
8.00	5.35	12.00	55.10	8.80
9.00	6.00	13.50	62.00	9.90
10.00	6.65	15.00	68.90	11.00
15.00	10.00	22.50	103.35	16.50
20.00	13.30	30.00	137.80	22.00
25.00	16.65	37.50	172.25	27.50
30.00	20.00	45.00	206.70	33.00
35.00	23.30	52.50	241.15	38.50
40.00	26.65	60.00	275.60	44.00
45.00	29.95	67.50	310.05	49.50
50.00	33.30	75.00	344.50	55.00
60.00	39.95	90.00	413.40	66.00
70.00	46.60	105.00	482.30	77.00
80.00	53.30	120.00	551.20	88.00
90.00	59.95	135.00	620.10	99.00
100.00	66.60	150.00	689.00	110.00
125.00	83.25	187.50	861.25	137.50
150.00	99.90	225.00	1,033.50	165.00
175.00	116.55	262.50	1,205.75	192.50
200.00	133.20	300.00	1,378.00	220.00
250.00	166.50	375.00	1,722.50	275.00
500.00	333.00	750.00	3,445.00	550.00

If you're traveling abroad, ask your bank for a list of overseas ATMs. Be sure to check the daily withdrawal limit before you depart, and ask whether you need a new PIN to make transactions from abroad.

CREDIT CARDS

Credit cards are invaluable when traveling. They're a safe way to carry money and provide a convenient record of all your expenses. You can also withdraw cash advances from your credit cards at any bank (but you'll start paying hefty interest on the advance the moment you receive the cash, and you won't get frequent-flyer miles on an airline credit card). At most banks, you don't even need to go to a teller; you can get a cash advance at the ATM if you know your PIN.

Almost every credit card company has an emergency toll-free number that you can call if your wallet or purse is stolen. They may be able to wire you a cash advance off your credit card immediately, and in many places, they can deliver an emergency credit card in a day or two. The issuing bank's toll-free number is usually on the back of the credit card—though of course that doesn't help you much if the card was stolen. In that case, call the toll-free information directory at ℂ **800/555-1212. Citicorp Visa**'s U.S. emergency number is ℂ **800/ 336-8472. American Express** cardholders and traveler's check holders should call ℂ **800/221-7282** for all money emergencies. **MasterCard** holders should call ℂ **800/307-7309. Diners Club** users should call ℂ **800/ 234-6377,** and **Discover Card** users should call ℂ **800/347-2683.**

Odds are that if your wallet is gone, the police won't be able to recover it for you. However, after you realize that it's gone and you cancel your credit cards, it is still worth informing them. Your credit card company or insurer might require a police report number.

CASH It's always a good idea to carry around some cash for small expenses, like cab rides, or for that rare occasion when a restaurant or small shop doesn't take plastic, which can happen if you're dining at a neighborhood joint or buying from a small vendor. U.S. dollars are accepted nearly everywhere, and in some countries, such as Jamaica, most locals prefer their tips to be in U.S. dollars. Perhaps $100 in small bills will see you through.

5 When to Go

WEATHER

The temperature variations in the Caribbean are surprisingly slight, averaging between 75° and 85° Fahrenheit (24°C–29°C) in both winter and summer, although it can get really chilly, especially in the early morning and at night. The Caribbean winter is usually like a perpetual northern-U.S. May. Overall, daytime high temperatures in the mid-80s prevail throughout most of the region, and trade winds make for comfortable days and nights, even without air-conditioning. If you go in summer to get the best bargains, you must be prepared for fierce sun.

The humidity and insects can be a problem here year-round. However, more mosquitoes come out during the rainy season, which is traditionally from September to December.

The curse of Caribbean weather, the **hurricane season** lasts—officially, at least—from June 1 to November 30. But there's no cause for panic. Satellite forecasts give adequate warnings so that precautions can be taken.

To get a weather report before you go, call the nearest branch of the National Weather Service, listed in phone directories under "U.S. Department of Commerce." You can also call

Weather Trak; for the telephone number for your particular area, call ℂ **900/WEATHER** (a taped message gives you the three-digit access code for the place you're interested in; the call costs 95¢ per inquiry). Or you can log onto the **Weather Channel** web-site: **www.weather.com**.

THE "SEASON" & THE "OFF-SEASON"

The Caribbean has become a year-round destination. The "season" runs roughly from mid-December to mid-April. Hotels charge their highest prices during this peak winter period, which is generally the driest time of year. It can be rainy in mountainous areas, however, and you can expect showers especially in December and January on Martinique, Guadeloupe, Dominica, St. Lucia, on the north coast of the Dominican Republic, and in northeast Jamaica.

For a winter vacation, make reservations 2 to 3 months in advance—or earlier for trips at Christmas time and in February.

The "off-season" in the Caribbean runs roughly from mid-April to mid-December—it varies from hotel to hotel—and amounts to a summer sale. In most cases, hotels, inns, and condos slash rates by 20% to 60%.

Dollar for dollar, you'll spend less money by renting a summer house or self-sufficient unit in the Caribbean than you would on Cape Cod, Fire Island, Laguna Beach, or the coast of Maine. Sailing and watersports are better, too, because the West Indies are protected from the Atlantic on their western shores, which border the calm Caribbean Sea. However, you have to be able to take strong sun and heat.

Because there's such a drastic difference in high-season and low-season rates at most hotels, we've included both on every property we review. You'll see the incredible savings you can enjoy if your schedule is flexible enough to wait a couple of months for your fun in the sun!

6 Health & Insurance

STAYING HEALTHY

Vaccinations are not required to enter the Caribbean if you're coming from the United States, Great Britain, or Canada.

If you're staying in a regular Caribbean hotel, few preventive measures are generally needed. Take along an adequate supply of any prescription drugs that you need and a written prescription that uses the generic name of the drug, not the brand name. You might want to pack first-aid cream, insect repellent, aspirin, bandages, and other basic remedies for minor injuries or illnesses.

The Caribbean sun can be brutal. Limit your exposure, especially during the first few days of your trip. Use sunscreen with a high protection factor, and apply it liberally. Wear sunglasses and a hat. And remember that children need more protection than adults do.

Finding a doctor in the Caribbean is not a problem, except perhaps on the smallest islands. Most Caribbean doctors—virtually 100% of them—speak English. See the "Fast Facts" section in each chapter for specific names or listings of medical help or assistance.

One of the biggest menaces is the "no-see-ums," which appear mainly in the early evening. You can't see these tiny flies, but you sure can "feel-um." Screens can't keep these critters out, so carry your favorite bug repellent.

Mosquitoes are a nuisance, too, but malaria-carrying mosquitoes are confined largely to Haiti and the Dominican Republic. If you're visiting either, consult your doctor for preventive medicine at least 8 weeks before you leave home.

Dengue fever is prevalent in the islands, most prominently on Antigua, St. Kitts, Dominica, and the Dominican Republic. Once thought to have been nearly eliminated, it has made a comeback. To date, no satisfactory treatment has been developed; visitors are advised to avoid mosquito bites— as if that were possible.

Infectious hepatitis has been reported on such islands as Dominica and Haiti. Unless you have been immunized for both hepatitis A and B, consult your doctor about the advisability of getting a gamma-globulin shot before you leave.

The **U.S. Centers for Disease Control and Prevention** (CDC; ℂ **800/311-3435** or 404/639-3534; www.cdc.gov) provides up-to-date information on necessary vaccines and health hazards by region or country. The CDC provides an informational booklet ($25 by mail; free on the Internet).

SOME PRECAUTIONS If you suffer from a chronic illness, consult your doctor before your departure. For conditions such as epilepsy, diabetes, and heart problems, wear a **Medic Alert Identification Tag** (ℂ **800/825-3785;** www.medic alert.org), which will immediately alert doctors to your condition and give them access to your records through Medic Alert's 24-hour hotline. Membership is $35, plus a $15 annual fee.

Pack prescription medications in your carry-on luggage. Carry written prescriptions in generic, not brand-name form, and dispense all prescription medications from their original labeled vials. Also, bring along copies of your prescriptions in case you lose your pills or run out.

INSURANCE

There are three kinds of travel insurance: trip-cancellation, medical, and lost-luggage coverage.

Trip-cancellation insurance is a good idea if you have paid a large portion of your vacation expenses up front, say, by purchasing a package or a cruise. Trip-cancellation insurance should cost approximately 6% to 8% of the total value of your vacation. (Don't buy it from the same company from which you've purchased your vacation—talk about putting all your eggs in one basket!)

The other two types of insurance, however, don't make sense for most travelers. Check your existing policies before you buy any additional coverage.

Your existing health insurance should cover you if you get sick on vacation (although if you belong to an HMO, you should check to see whether you are fully covered while you're away from home). If you need hospital treatment, most health insurance plans and HMOs will cover out-of-country hospital visits and procedures, at least to some extent. Most make you pay the bills up front at the time of care, however, and you'll get a refund only after you've returned and filed all the paperwork. Members of **Blue Cross/Blue Shield** can now use their membership cards at select hospitals in most major cities worldwide. Call ℂ **800/810-BLUE** or visit www.bluecares.com for a list of hospitals.

Note that **Medicare** covers U.S. citizens traveling only in Mexico and Canada.

Your homeowner's insurance should cover stolen luggage. The airlines are responsible for providing you with some compensation if they lose your luggage; if you plan to carry anything valuable, keep it in your carry-on bag.

If you do require additional insurance, try one of the following companies: **Access America,** 6600 W. Broad St., Richmond, VA 23230 (© **800/ 284-8300;** www.accessamerica.com); **Travel Guard International,** 1145 Clark St., Stevens Point, WI 54481 (© **800/826-1300**); **Travel Insured International, Inc.,** P.O. Box 280568, East Hartford, CT 06128 (© **800/ 243-3174;** www.travel insured.com); Columbus Direct, 279 High St., Croydon CR0 1QH (© **020/7375-0011** in London; www.columbusdirect.net).

For medical coverage, try **MEDEX International,** P.O. Box 5375, Timonium, MD 21094-5375 (© **888/ MEDEX-00** or 410/453-6300; fax 410/453-6301;www.medexassist.com); or **Travel Assistance International** (Worldwide Assistance Services, Inc.), 1133 15th St. NW, Suite 400, Washington, DC 20005 (© **800/821- 2828** or 317/575-2652; www.travel assistance.com). The **Divers Alert Network** (DAN; © **800/446-2671** or 919/684-8111; www.diversalert network.org) insures scuba divers.

7 Tips for Travelers with Special Needs

FOR TRAVELERS WITH DISABILITIES

At times, getting around the Caribbean seems only for Olympic athletes, as you traverse rough, steep roads, ascend hills to reach accommodations, wade through sand to the door of your beachfront cottage, get on and off boats in turbulent waters, board small planes with cramped seating, and walk potholed streets even in the larger cities. Wheelchair ramps, TTY phone systems, and the like are in short supply. However, persons with disabilities are visiting the islands in greater numbers every year, and the travel industry, especially the airlines, is beginning to pay attention to their needs. However, such a trip involves careful planning, plus a detailed talk with the hotel of your choice about whether it has facilities equipped for disabled guests.

There are more resources out there than ever before. *A World of Options,* a 658-page book of resources for disabled travelers, covers everything from biking trips to scuba outfitters. It is available from **Mobility International USA,** P.O. Box 10767, Eugene, OR 97440 (© **541/343-1284,** voice and TDD; www.miusa.org). Annual membership for Mobility International is

$35, which includes the quarterly newsletter, *Over the Rainbow.* In addition, **Twin Peaks Press,** P.O. Box 129, Vancouver, WA 98666 (© **360/ 694-2462**), publishes travel-related books for people with disabilities.

The **Moss Rehab Hospital** (© **215/ 456-9600**) has been providing friendly and helpful phone advice and referrals to disabled travelers for years through its **Moss Rehab Resource.Net** (© **215/456-9603;** www.mossresource net.org).

You can join the **Society for Accessible Travel & Hospitality** (**SATH**), 347 Fifth Ave. Suite 610, New York, NY 10016 (© **212/447-7284;** fax 212-725-8253; www.sath.org) for $45 annually, $30 for seniors and students, to gain access to SATH's vast network of connections in the travel industry. SATH provides information sheets on travel destinations and referrals to tour operators that specialize in traveling with disabilities. Its quarterly magazine, *Open World for Disability and Mature Travel,* is full of good information and resources. A year's subscription is $13 ($21 outside the U.S.).

Travelers with disabilities might also want to consider joining a tour that caters specifically to them. One of the best operators is **Flying Wheels**

Travel, 143 West Bridge (P.O. Box 382), Owatonna, MN 55060 (© **800/ 535-6790** or 507/451-5005; www. flyingwheelstravel.com). It offers various escorted tours and cruises, with an emphasis on sports, as well as private tours in minivans with lifts. Other reputable specialized tour operators include **Access Adventures** (© **716/ 889-9096**), which offers sports-related vacations; **Accessible Journeys** (© **800/TINGLES** or 610/521-0339), for slow walkers and wheelchair travelers; **The Guided Tour, Inc.** (© 215/782-1370); **Wilderness Inquiry** (© **800/728-0719** or 612/ 379-3858); and **Directions Unlimited** (© **800/533-5343**).

Vision-impaired travelers should contact the **American Foundation for the Blind,** 11 Penn Plaza, Suite 300, New York, NY 10001 (© **800/ 232-5463**), for information on traveling with Seeing Eye dogs.

FOR GAY & LESBIAN TRAVELERS

Some Caribbean islands are more gay-friendly than others. The most gay-friendly islands are the U.S. possessions—most notably Puerto Rico, which is hailed as the "gay capital of the Caribbean" and offers gay guesthouses, nightclubs, bars, and discos. To a lesser extent, much of St. Thomas, St. John, and St. Croix are welcoming, but they have nowhere near the number of gay-oriented establishments that Puerto Rico has.

The French islands—St. Barts, St. Martin, Guadeloupe, and Martinique—are technically an extension of mainland France, and the French have always regarded homosexuality with a certain blasé tolerance. On the other hand, the Dutch islands of Aruba, Bonaire, and Curaçao are quite conservative, so discretion is suggested.

Gay life is fairly secretive in many of the sleepy islands of the Caribbean. It's actively discouraged in places like the homophobic Cayman Islands. Homosexuality is illegal in Barbados, and there is often a lack of tolerance there in spite of the large number of gay residents and visitors. Jamaica is the most homophobic island in the Caribbean, with harsh antigay laws, even though there is a large local gay population. One local advised that it's not smart for a white gay man to wander the streets of Jamaica at night. Gay travelers might also note that the Cayman Islands once refused to allow an all-gay cruise ship to dock on Grand Cayman, and several gay advocacy groups have even called for a boycott on travel to the Caymans in response.

The **International Gay & Lesbian Travel Association (IGLTA;** © **800/ 448-8550** or 954/776-2626; fax 954/ 776-3303; www.iglta.org) links travelers with the appropriate gay-friendly service organization or tour specialist. With around 1,200 members, it offers quarterly newsletters, marketing mailings, and a membership directory that's updated quarterly. Membership often includes gay or lesbian businesses but is open to individuals for $150 yearly, plus a $100 administration fee for new members. Members are kept informed of gay and gay-friendly hoteliers, tour operators, and airline and cruise-line representatives. Contact IGLTA for a list of its member agencies, who will be tied into IGLTA's information resources.

General gay and lesbian travel agencies include **Above and Beyond Tours** (© **800/397-2681;** mainly gay men) and **Kennedy Travel** (© **800/ 988-1181** or 516/352-4888). There are many others, all over the United States; you'll find a list of gay-friendly travel agencies across the United States on the RSVP Vacations website mentioned below.

Several companies now assemble gay travel packages. **RSVP Vacations** (© **800/328-RSVP** or 619/379-4697; www.rsvp.net) offers gay cruises on ships both large and small in the Caribbean. **Atlantis Events** (© **800/ 628-5268** or 310/281-5450; www. atlantisevents.com) books Club Med resorts for all-gay, all-inclusive vacations; they also do all-gay cruises, often in the Caribbean.

There are also two good, biannual English-language gay guidebooks, both focused on gay men but including information for lesbians as well. You can get *Spartacus International Gay Guide* or *Odysseus* from most gay and lesbian bookstores, or order them from **Giovanni's Room** (© **215/ 923-2960**). Both lesbians and gays might want to pick up a copy of *Gay Travel A to Z* ($16). **The Ferrari Guides** (www.ferrariguides.com) is yet another very good series of gay and lesbian guidebooks.

The magazine **Our World,** 1104 N. Nova Rd., Suite 251, Daytona Beach, FL 32117 (© **904/441-5367;** www. ourworldmag.com), covers options and bargains for gay and lesbian travel worldwide. It costs $35 for 10 issues. ***Out and About,*** 657 Harrison St., San Francisco, CA 94107 (© **800/929- 2268** or 415/229-1793; www.outand about.com), has been hailed for its "straight" reporting about gay travel. It profiles the best gay or gay-friendly hotels, gyms, clubs, and other places at destinations throughout the world. It costs $49 for 10 information-packed issues.

FOR SENIORS

In general, seniors are treated like all other visitors to the Caribbean, in that there are no special facilities or discounts for them at theaters, museums, and other attractions. It might be possible, however, to negotiate a lower rate off-season at a Caribbean hotel (usually a major hotel as opposed to a small inn). In the high season, everybody is charged virtually the same price unless you book on a package tour deal.

In planning your trip, keep in mind that members of the **American Association of Retired Persons (AARP),** 601 E St. NW, Washington, DC 20049 (© **800/424-3410** or 202/ 434-aarp; www.aarp.org), get discounts on airfares and car rentals. AARP offers members a wide range of special benefits, including *Modern Maturity* magazine and a monthly newsletter.

Sears Mature Outlook, P.O. Box 9390, Des Moines, IA 50306 (© **800/336-6330** or 847/286- 5024), began as a travel organization for people over 50, but it now caters to people of all ages. Members get discounts on hotels and receive a bimonthly magazine. Annual membership is $39.95, which entitles members to discounts and, often, free coupons for discounted merchandise from Sears.

The ***Mature Traveler,*** a monthly 12-page newsletter on senior citizen travel is a valuable resource. It is available by subscription ($30 a yr.) from GEM Publishing Group, Box 50400, Reno, NV 89513-0400. GEM also publishes ***The Book of Deals,*** a collection of more than 1,000 senior discounts on airlines, lodging, tours, and attractions; it's available for $9.95 by calling © **800/460-6676.** Another helpful publication is ***101 Tips for the Mature Traveler,*** available from **Grand Circle Travel,** 347 Congress St., Suite 3A, Boston, MA 02210 (© **800/221-2610** or 617/350-7500; fax 617/346-6700).

Grand Circle Travel is also one of hundreds of travel agencies that specialize in vacations for seniors. Many of these packages, however, are of the tour-bus variety, with free trips thrown in for those who organize groups of 10 or more. Seniors seeking more independent travel should probably consult a regular travel agent. **SAGA International Holidays,** 222 Berkeley St., Boston, MA

02116 (© **800/343-0273;** www.saga holidays.com), offers inclusive tours and cruises for those 50 and older. SAGA also sponsors the more substantial **"Road Scholar Tours"** (© **800/ 621-2151**), which are fun-loving but with an educational bent.

FOR SINGLES

Unfortunately for the 85 million or so single Americans, the travel industry is geared toward couples, so singles often wind up paying the penalty. One company that resolves the problem is **Travel Companion Exchange,** which matches single travelers with like-minded companions. It's headed by Jens Jurgen, who charges $159 for an annual listing in his well-publicized records. People seeking travel companions fill out forms stating their preferences and needs and receive a listing of potential travel partners. Companions of the same or opposite sex can be requested. For $48 you can get a bimonthly newsletter, averaging 70 large pages, that also gives numerous money-saving tips of special interest to solo travelers. A sample copy is available for $6. For an application and more information, contact Jens Jurgen at **Travel Companion Exchange,** P.O. Box 833, Amityville, NY 11701 (© **800/392-1256** or 631/454-0880; fax 631/454-0170; www.whytravelalone.com).

8 40 Money-Saving Tips

AIRFARES

1. Start out by shopping around for air/land packages. Particularly in the Caribbean, a week's stay at even a top-of-the-line resort is often much cheaper if it's arranged as part of a package booked with airfare. The savings might make a stay at an expensive hotel completely affordable.
2. Try booking through a consolidator, or "bucket shop." See "Finding the Best Airfare," later in this chapter, for recommendations of reputable companies to try.
3. Make sure you're flying into the right airport. On some islands, such as St. Lucia, you can rack up substantial transfer costs by flying into the wrong airport. Whenever an island has more than one international airport, be sure to figure out its position in relation to your hotel and plan your incoming flight accordingly. Taxi costs across the length of a mountainous island can total more than $60.
4. Fly off-season. Airfares plummet from April to late June and from mid-September until about 10 days before Christmas.

5. Shop for the best deal on the Web. See "Finding the Best Airfare," later in this chapter, for tips on how to do this.

ACCOMMODATIONS

6. Find out what "extras" are included in the hotel price. A moderately priced hotel that tacks on charges for everything from beach chairs to snorkeling equipment could wind up costing you more than a luxury hotel that includes these extras in its price. And be sure to ask what taxes and surcharges might be added to your final bill.
7. If you're traveling off-season, don't always assume that a large hotel costs more than an inn with a limited number of amenities. Especially during off-season promotions, a mega-resort might be more generous with discounts, add-ons, and packages.
8. An oceanfront room will cost more than a room without a view, so you can save if you can live without seeing the water from your window.

9. If you're traveling with kids, consider housing up to two of your children in your room with you on foldaway beds. Many places offer free accommodations to anyone under 12, under 16, or (in some cases) under 18. We've noted these policies on every hotel we review.

10. Especially if you're traveling in a group of four or more, rent an apartment or villa that has kitchen facilities so you can cook for yourself.

11. Many hotels slash their rates during the slow month of January, right after New Year's, when postholiday business is slow. Sometimes the discounts you get at this time even match off-season rates!

12. If a hotel is not on the beach, find out if there's a charge to get there. The hotel rates might be lower, but will you wind up spending a lot of time and money to get to the sands every day?

13. In small B&Bs and guesthouses, rooms without private bathrooms, although they often have a sink with hot and cold running water, sometimes save you an average of 40% off the regular rate.

14. Ask if a hotel charges extra for paying with a credit or charge card. Although this is against the bylaws of such lenders as American Express, hoteliers often do it anyway. If you're penalized for plastic, consider bringing enough cash or traveler's checks.

15. If you're an avid golfer, tennis player, or scuba diver, shop around for the best packages without all the frilly stuff.

16. Consider camping. It's not always available on all islands, but on those where it is (St. John's, for example), it may be the way to go.

17. Check the surcharge for either local or long-distance calls, which can be an astonishing 40%. Make your calls outside at a pay phone or the post office.

18. Determine whether breakfast is included in the rates. An extra daily breakfast charge can make a big difference in your final bill.

19. If you're going to spend at least a week at a resort, ask about a discount. If they're not full, some hotels might give you the seventh night free.

20. Book the MAP (Modified American Plan), including breakfast and dinner, if it looks good. It'll save a lot over the a la carte menu.

DINING

21. Scan advertisements in local tourist guides and newspapers that publicize specialty buffets and special discounts on meals.

22. Opt for local foods, like fresh fish, chicken, fruit, and vegetables. Most other food is imported at a high cost, and it arrives frozen to boot.

23. Stick to rum-based drinks—the island favorite—and watch out for those high price tags on imported booze such as scotch.

24. In most cases, the fixed-price menu or daily specials might be one-third cheaper than ordering a la carte.

OUTDOOR ACTIVITIES

25. Enjoy free or cheap activities like hiking through a nature preserve or snorkeling. And, of course, the beach provides you with free amusement all day long!

NIGHTLIFE

26. Scan the local press for reggae concerts, community groups sponsoring "bashes" (all reasonable in price), charity bazaars, whatever. There's always something going on in the Caribbean, and at these events, you can learn about island life, too.

27. Hit a bar at happy hour, usually from 5 to 6:30 or even 7pm, when drinks are traditionally discounted 20% to 50%, and hors d'oeuvres are often discounted as well.

SHOPPING

28. Before you leave home, stop by your local discount shops to check the latest prices. Only then can you comparison shop to determine whether you're getting a bargain in a Caribbean discount outlet.

29. Don't be afraid to haggle over a price. Savvy shoppers pride themselves on almost never paying retail for anything. If you think the price is too high, make a lower offer. Sometimes you'll get yes for an answer.

30. If you're traveling as a family, submit a joint declaration to Customs—that is, combine the duty allowance of all members of your group into one bulk package. Even a child gets a duty-free allowance ranging from $400 to $1,200, depending on the island.

31. Buy handcrafted arts and crafts, which in most cases are duty-free regardless of the amount you paid.

32. Remember that Puerto Rico has the same tariff barriers as the U.S. mainland. You can take home as many bargains as you find here without paying duty.

33. U.S. Customs allows you to take back home duty-free $600 worth of merchandise (per family member) from such islands as Jamaica and Barbados, but only $400 from such islands as St. Barts and Martinique (because these islands are technically part of France).

34. The best shopping deal of all is the U.S. Virgin Islands (St. Thomas, St. Croix, and St. John), where you can bring back $1,200 per person in duty-free purchases. If you go over the limit, you're charged at a flat rate of 5% up to $1,000 rather than the usual 10% imposed on goods from other countries.

35. Save your big purchases for so-called duty-free islands as opposed to those that have a heavy sales tax.

TRANSPORTATION

36. Think about whether you can skip a rental car altogether. You might not be as mobile without one, but your hotel might offer minivan transport that will get you to shops, a local beach, and snorkeling facilities. It's worth asking when you make your reservation.

37. Renting a local taxi for a day's outing might work out to be less expensive than an entire week's rental of a car. See all the sights over a 1- or 2-day period, and plan to relax close to your hotel on other days.

38. If you do rent a car, weekly rentals are more cost-efficient (on a day-to-day basis) than a single day's rental.

39. Rent bikes to get around. Although bicycles are definitely not recommended for nighttime use (Caribbean roads are notoriously dark at night), they can be an invigorating and efficient mode of transportation.

40. Stay at a hotel in one of the beach towns, such as Charlotte Amalie, Christiansted, Montego Bay, or Puerto Rico's Condado or Isla Verde. With dozens of restaurants, bars, and nightclubs nearby, you'll almost never need a car.

9 Package Deals

For popular destinations like the Caribbean, packages can save you a ton of money. Especially in the Caribbean, package tours are *not* the same thing as escorted tours. You'll be on your own, but in most cases, a package to the Caribbean includes airfare, hotel, and transportation to and from the airport—and it costs you less than just the hotel alone if you booked it yourself. This is really the way to save hundreds and hundreds of dollars! It might not be for you if you want to stay in a more intimate inn or guesthouse, but if you like resorts, read on.

You'll find an amazing array of packages to popular Caribbean destinations. Some packages offer a better class of hotels than others. Some offer the same hotels for lower prices. Some offer flights on scheduled airlines, and others book charters. In some packages, your choices of accommodations and travel days might be limited. Remember to comparison shop among at least three different operators, and always compare apples to apples.

The best place to start your search is the travel section of your local Sunday newspaper. Also check the ads in the back of national travel magazines like *Travel & Leisure, National Geographic Traveler,* and *Condé Nast Traveler.* **Liberty Travel** (© 888/271-1584 to be connected with the agent closest to you; www.libertytravel.com) is one of the biggest packagers in the Northeast, and it usually boasts a full-page ad in Sunday papers. You won't get much in the way of service, but you will get a good deal. **Certified Vacations** (© 800/241-1700; www.clik vacations.com) is another option. Check out its **Last Minute Travel Bargains** site (www.lastminute.com), offered in conjunction with Continental Airlines, with deeply discounted vacation packages and reduced airline fares that differ from the E-savers bargains that Continental e-mails weekly to subscribers. **Northwest Airlines** (www.nwa.com) offers a similar service. Posted on Northwest's website every Wednesday, its **Cyber Saver Bargain Alerts** offer special hotel rates, package deals, and discounted airline fares.

Another good resource is the airlines themselves, which often package their flights together with accommodations. Fly-by-night packagers are uncommon, but they do exist; when you buy your package through an airline, however, you can be pretty sure the company will still be in business when your departure date arrives. Among the airline packagers, your options include **American Airlines Vacations** (© 800/321-2121; www.aavacations. com), **Delta Vacations** (© 800/872-7786; www.deltavacations.com), and **USAirways Vacations** (© 800/455-0123; www.usairwaysvacations. com).

The biggest hotel chains, casinos, and resorts also offer package deals. If you already know where you want to stay, call the resort itself and ask if it offers land/air packages.

To save time comparing the prices and value of all the package tours out there, consider calling **TourScan, Inc.,** P.O. Box 2367, Darien, CT 06820 (© 800/962-2080 or 203/655-8091; www.tourscan.com). Every season, the company computerizes the contents of travel brochures that contain about 10,000 different vacations at 1,600 hotels in the Caribbean, the Bahamas, and Bermuda. TourScan selects the best-value vacation at each hotel and condo. Two catalogs are printed each year, which list a choice of hotels on most of the Caribbean islands in all price ranges. Write to TourScan for catalogs, the price of which ($4) is credited toward any TourScan vacation.

Other tour operators include the following:

- **Caribbean Concepts Corp.,** 99 Jericho Turnpike, Jericho, NY 11793 (© 800/423-4433 or 516/417-9917), offers low-cost air-and-land packages to the islands, including apartments, hotels, villas, and condo rentals, plus local sightseeing (which can be arranged separately).

- **Horizon Tours,** 1010 Vermont Ave. NW, Suite 202, Washington, DC 20005 (✆ **202/393-8390;** www.horizontours.com), specializes in good deals for all-inclusive resorts in the Bahamas, Jamaica, Aruba, Puerto Rico, Antigua, and St. Lucia.
- **Club Med,** Club Med Sales, P.O. Box 4460, Scottsdale, AZ 85261-4460 (✆ **800/258-2633;** www.clubmed.com), has various all-inclusive options throughout the Caribbean and the Bahamas.
- **Globus & Cosmos,** 5301 S. Federal Circle, Littleton, CO 80123 (✆ **800/851-0728,** ext. 7518; www.globusandcosmos.com), gives escorted island-hopping expeditions to three or four islands, focusing on the history and culture of the West Indies.

10 Finding the Best Airfare

You shouldn't have to pay a regular fare to the Caribbean. Why? There are so many deals out there—in both summer and winter—that you can certainly find a discount fare. That's especially true if you're willing to plan on the spur of the moment: If a flight is not fully booked, an airline will discount tickets to try to fill it up.

Before you do anything else, read the section "Package Deals," above. But if a package isn't for you, and you need to book your airfare on your own, keep in mind these money-saving tips:

- **If you fly in spring, summer, and fall, you're guaranteed substantial reductions on airfares to the Caribbean.** You can also ask if it's cheaper to fly Monday through Thursday. And don't forget to consider air-and-land packages, which offer considerably reduced rates. Most airlines charge different fares according to the season. *Peak season,* which is winter in the Caribbean, is most expensive; *basic season,* in the summer, offers the lowest fares. *Shoulder season* refers to the spring and fall months in between.
- **Keep an eye out for sales.** Check your newspaper for advertised discounts or call the airlines directly and ask if any promotional rates or special fares are available. You'll almost never see a sale during the peak winter vacation months of February and March or during the Thanksgiving or Christmas seasons, but in periods of low-volume travel, you should find a discounted fare. If your schedule is flexible, ask if you can get a cheaper fare by staying an extra day or by flying midweek. (Many airlines won't volunteer this information.) If you already hold a ticket when a sale breaks, it might even pay to exchange your ticket, which usually incurs a $50 to $75 charge. Note, however, that the lowest-priced fares are often nonrefundable, require advance purchase of 1 to 3 weeks and a certain length of stay, and carry penalties for changing dates of travel.
- **Consolidators, also known as "bucket shops," are a good place to find low fares.** Consolidators buy seats in bulk from the airlines and then sell them back to the public at prices below even the airlines' discounted rates. Their small-boxed ads usually run in the Sunday travel section of newspapers at the bottom of the page. Before you pay a consolidator, however, ask for a record locator number and confirm your seat

with the airline itself. Be prepared to book your ticket with a different consolidator—there are many to choose from—if the airline can't confirm your reservation. Also, be aware that bucket-shop tickets are usually nonrefundable or rigged with stiff cancellation penalties, often as high as 50% to 75% of the ticket price.

Council Travel (© 888/ COUNCIL; www.counciltravel. com) and **STA Travel** (© 800/ 781-4040; www.statravel.com) cater especially to young travelers, but their bargain-basement prices are available to people of all ages. **1-800/AIR-FARE** (© 800/ AIR-FARE; www.1800airfare. com) was formerly owned by TWA and now offers the deepest discounts on many other airlines, with a 4-day advance purchase. Other reliable consolidators are **1-800-FLY-CHEAP** (www.1800 flycheap.com); **TFI Tours International** (© 800-745-8000 or 212/736-1140), which serves as a clearinghouse for unused seats; or "rebators" such as **Travel Avenue** (© 800/333-3335 or 312/876-1116), which rebate part of their commissions to you.

• **Consider a charter flight.** Discounted fares have pared the number of charters available, but they can still be found. Most charter operators advertise and sell their seats through travel agents, thus making these local professionals your best source of information for available flights. Before deciding to take a charter flight, however, check the restrictions on the ticket: You might be asked to purchase a tour package, to pay in advance, to be flexible if the day of departure is changed, to pay a service charge, to fly on an airline you're not familiar with (this usually is not the case), and to pay harsh penalties if you

cancel—but be understanding if the charter doesn't fill up and is canceled up to 10 days before departure. Summer charters fill up more quickly than others and are almost sure to fly, but if you decide on a charter flight, seriously consider getting cancellation and baggage insurance.

• **Join a travel club.** Clubs such as **Moment's Notice** (© 718/234-6295; www.moments-notice. com) or **Sears Discount Travel Club** (© 800/433-9383, or 800/255-1487 to join) supply unsold tickets at discounted prices. You pay an annual membership fee to get the club's hotline number. Of course, you're limited to what's available, so you have to be flexible.

• **Search for the best deal on the Web.** The websites highlighted below are worth checking out, especially since all services are free. Always check the lowest published fare, however, before you shop for flights online.

Arthur Frommer's Budget Travel (www.frommers.com) offers detailed information on destinations around the world and up-to-the-minute ways to save dramatically on flights, hotels, car rentals, and cruises. Book an entire vacation online and research your destination before you leave. Consult the message board to set up "hospitality exchanges" in other countries, to talk with other travelers who have visited a hotel you're considering, or to direct travel questions to Arthur Frommer himself. The newsletter is updated daily to keep you abreast of the latest breaking ways to save, to publicize new hot spots and best buys, and to present veteran readers with fresh, ever-changing approaches to travel.

Microsoft Expedia (www. expedia.com) offers a Fare Tracker feature that e-mails you weekly with the best airfare deals from your hometown on up to three destinations. The site's Travel Agent will steer you to bargains on hotels and car rentals, and with the help of hotel and airline seat pinpointers, you can book everything right online. Before you depart, log on for maps and up-to-date travel information, including weather reports and foreign exchange rates.

Travelocity (www.travelocity. com) is one of the best travel sites out there, especially for finding cheap airfares. In addition to its Personal Fare Watcher, which notifies you via e-mail of the lowest airfares for up to five different destinations, Travelocity will track the three lowest fares for any routes on any dates in minutes. You can book a flight, then find the best hotel or car-rental deals via the SABRE computer reservations system. Click on "Last Minute Deals" for the latest travel bargains.

The Trip (www.thetrip.com) is really geared toward the business traveler, but vacationers-to-be can also use its exceptionally powerful fare-finding engine, which will e-mail you weekly with the best city-to-city airfare deals for as many as 10 routes. The Trip uses the Internet Travel Network, another reputable travel-agent database, to book hotels and restaurants.

Here's a partial list of airlines and their websites, where you can not only get on the e-mailing lists but also book flights directly: **Air Jamaica** (www.airjamaica.com); **American Airlines** (www.im.aa. com); **British Airways** (www. britishairways.com); **BWIA** (www. bwee.com); **Air Canada** (www. aircanada.ca); **Continental Airlines** (www.continental.com); **Delta** (www.delta.com); and **US Airways** (www.usairways.com).

11 Cruises That Don't Cost a Fortune

Except for peak-season cruises between Christmas and New Year's, forget the prices listed in the cruise-line brochures. Overcapacity and fierce competition have ushered in the age of the discounted fare. There are great bargains out there, enough at times to baffle even the most experienced cruise-line travel specialists. These low prices make cruising the Caribbean a viable money-saving option.

Don't succumb to sticker shock when you look in a cruise line's brochure, because these rates are the maritime equivalent of new car prices: a fiction. The price you'll actually pay will be far less, sometimes from 20% to 50% less. And remember that your cruise fare doesn't just pay for transportation—you also get accommodations, as many as eight (!) meals a day, a packed roster of activities, free use of fitness and entertainment facilities, as well as cabaret, jazz performances, dance bands, and discos.

Cruises typically cost less than comparable land-based vacations. The key word, of course, is *comparable*. If you stay at a Motel 6 and eat only at the local burger joint, you'll generally do better on land, but there are a few cruise lines out there that would even give that arrangement a run for its money.

Almost everything is included in the cruise price. But know before you go that even the sweetest cruise-related deal contains its share of hidden extras, and if you're not careful, you might get some unpleasant surprises when you eventually pay your piper. You'll have to pay extra for your bar and wine tabs, some shore excursions, gambling, tips, the exorbitant cost of any ship-to-shore phone calls or faxes, any special pampering (hairdressers, manicurists/pedicurists, massages, and/or skin treatments), purchases in the shipboard boutiques and at the ports of call, and medical treatments in the ship's infirmary. There may also be the question of port charges, although most lines now include them in their fares (be sure to ask when you book, just to be on the safe side).

BOOKING A CRUISE FOR THE BEST PRICE

How should you book your cruise and get to the port of embarkation before the good times roll? It's best to use a travel agent, particularly one who specializes in cruises. He or she will be able to steer you toward any of the special promotions that come and go as frequently as Caribbean rainstorms, and may also be able to give specific advice on individual ships. To get to the port on time, many cruise lines offer deals that include airfare from your local airport to the cruise-departure point. It's possible to purchase your air ticket on your own and book your cruise ticket separately, but in most cases you'll save money by combining the fares into a package deal.

Here are some travel agencies to consider: **Cruises, Inc.,** 5000 Campuswood Dr. E., Syracuse, NY 13057 (© **800/854-0500** or 315/463-9695); **Cruise Masters,** Century Plaza Towers, 2029 Century Park E., Suite 950, Los Angeles, CA 90067 (© **800/456-4FUN** or 310/556-2925); **The Cruise Company,** 10760 Q St, Omaha, NE 68127 (© **800/289-5505** or 402/339-6800); **Kelly Cruises,** 1315 W. 22nd St., Suite 105, Oak Brook, IL 60523 (© **800/837-7447** or 630/990-1111); **Hartford Holidays Travel,** 129 Hillside Ave., Williston Park, NY 11596 (© **800/828-4813** or 516/746-6670); and **Mann Travel** and **Cruises,** 6010 Fairview Rd., Suite 104, Charlotte, NC 28210 (© **800/849-2301** or 704-556-8311). These companies stay tuned to last-minute price wars; cruise lines don't profit if these megaships don't fill up near peak capacity, so sales pop up all the time.

You're likely to sail from Miami, which has become the cruise capital of the world. Other departure ports include San Juan, Port Everglades, New Orleans, Tampa, and (via the Panama Canal) Los Angeles.

For much more detailed information, including specific information about saving money and reviews of each individual ship, pick up a copy of *Frommer's Caribbean Cruises & Ports of Call 2002.*

DISCOUNT CRUISE LINES

The lines listed in this section offer consistently low prices. You won't be sailing on those space-age-looking megaships that the major lines are bringing out in packs these days, but some of these ships have the kind of character you don't see in the new ships. Examples? Windjammer's fleet, which consists almost entirely of old sailing ships, or Commodore's *Enchanted Capri,* which was purchased from the former Soviet Union.

- **American Canadian Caribbean** (© **800/556-7450** or 401/247-0955; www.accl-smallships.com). These tiny, 80- to 100-passenger coastal cruisers make 10- to 11-day excursions through the Caribbean, visiting smaller, more out-of-the-way ports than the big cruise ships and offering an experience that's quiet and completely unpretentious. The line operates three almost identical ships, at least one of which spends part of the winter cruising around the Bahamas, Puerto Rico, the Virgin

Islands, the Panama Canal, and the coasts of Central America.

- **Windjammer Barefoot Cruises** (© 800/327-2601 or 305/672-6453; www.windjammer.com). Windjammer operates five sailing ships, most of which are faithful renovations of antique schooners or sail-driven private yachts. The company offers a real "yo ho ho and a bottle of rum" kind of cruise, and true to its name, few passengers ever bring more than shorts and T-shirts for their time aboard. From bases as divergent as San Juan, St. Martin, Tortola, Antigua, and Grenada, the ships travel to rarely visited outposts, with special emphasis on the scattered reefs and cays of the Virgin Islands and the Grenadines. Port calls often mean just anchoring off a small beach and shuttling passengers ashore, and the ships often stay in port late into the evening, giving passengers an opportunity to enjoy nightlife ashore.

  Some of the best deals (and some of the most amazing itineraries) are to be had aboard the company's durable but not very exciting supply ship, *Amazing Grace*, a freighter-style vessel that carries provisions and supplies for the company's sailing ships (and carries passengers between ports while it's at it). *Amazing Grace* makes continuous 13-day trips between Freeport, the Bahamas, and Trinidad, stopping frequently en route to supply other ships in the company's fleet. You can sometimes snag a cruise fare aboard this ship for less than $60 per day (plus airfare to and from the port). Cruises aboard the line's sailing ships generally stay in the $800 to $1,100 dollar range for week-long cruises, but if you're able to travel on short notice, check the line's website, which offers e-mail updates of last-minute bargains, with weeklong cruises often going for under $500.

MAINSTREAM LINES

If you catch them during off-season and book a relatively small, simple cabin, you can often get steeply discounted rates from these lines, which are the main players in the Caribbean cruise industry (and thus are engaged in some fierce competition—meaning good prices for you). In fact, you might be able to get a cruise aboard one of these lines for the same price you'd pay aboard a budget line, but you have to catch a sale. Again, talk to your travel agent, who will be up on the latest deals.

- **Carnival Cruise Lines** (© 800/327-9502 or 305/599-2200; www.carnival.com). Offering affordable vacations on some of the biggest and most brightly decorated ships afloat, Carnival is the boldest, brashest, and most successful mass-market cruise line in the world. Twelve of its vessels depart for the Caribbean from Miami, Tampa, New Orleans, Port Canaveral, and San Juan, and eight of them specialize in 7-day or longer tours that feature stopovers at selected ports throughout the eastern, western, and southern Caribbean, including St. Lucia, San Juan, Guadeloupe, Grenada, Grand Cayman, and Jamaica; four others offer 3- to 5-day itineraries visiting such ports as Nassau, Key West, Grand Cayman, and Playa del Carmen/Cozumel. Its fleet has many ships, including the megaship *Paradise*. Launched in 1998 and weighing in at 70,367 tons, it's noteworthy as the only completely smoke-free cruise ship in the Caribbean. Most of the company's Caribbean cruises offer good value and feature nonstop activities. Food and party-colored drinks are plentiful, and the overall atmosphere is comparable to a floating theme park. Lots of single passengers opt for this line, as do families attracted by the line's well-run children's program. The average onboard age is a relatively youthful 42, although ages range from 3 to 95.

- **Celebrity Cruises** (✆ **800/ 327-6700** or 305/539-6000; www. celebritycruises.com). Celebrity maintains six newly built, stylish, medium to large ships with cruises that last between 7 and 11 nights to ports such as Key West, San Juan, Grand Cayman, St. Thomas, Ocho Rios, Antigua, and Cozumel, Mexico, to name a few. It's classy but not stuffy, several notches above mass-market, and provides an experience that's both elegant and fun— and all for a price that's competitive with lines offering much less. Accommodations are roomy and well-equipped, cuisine is the most refined of any of its competitors, and its service is impeccable.

- **Costa Cruise Lines** (✆ **800/ 462-6782** or 305/358-7325; www. costacruises.com). Costa, the U.S.-based branch of a cruise line that has thrived in Italy for about a century, maintains hefty to mega-size vessels, three of which offer virtually identical jaunts through the western and eastern Caribbean on alternate weeks, each of them departing from Fort Lauderdale. Ports of call during the eastern Caribbean itineraries of both vessels include stopovers in San Juan, St. Thomas, Serena Cay (a private island off the coast of the Dominican Republic known for its beaches), and Nassau. Itineraries through the western Caribbean include stopovers at Grand Cayman; either Ocho Rios or Montego Bay, Jamaica; Key West; and Cozumel. There's an Italian flavor and lots of Italian design on board

here, and an atmosphere of relaxed indulgence.

- **Holland America Line–Westours** (✆ **800/426-0327** or 206/ 281-3535; www.hollandamerica. com). Holland America is the most high-toned of the mass-market cruise lines, with nine respectably hefty and good-looking ships, seven of which spend substantial time cruising the Caribbean. They offer solid value, with very few jolts or surprises, and attract a solid, well-grounded clientele of primarily older travelers (so late-night revelers and serious partiers might want to book cruises on other lines, such as Carnival). Cruises stop at deep-water mainstream ports throughout the Caribbean and last for an average of 7 days, but in some cases for 10 days, visiting such ports as Key West, Grand Cayman, St. Maarten, St. Lucia, Curaçao, Barbados, and St. Thomas.

- **Norwegian Cruise Line** (✆ **800/ 327-7030** or 305/436-4000; www. ncl.com). Norwegian operates a diverse fleet ranging from the classic though now massively renovated *Norway* (formerly the *France*) to the medium-sized *Norwegian Majesty, Norwegian Wind, Norwegian Dream,* and *Norwegian Sea,* to the megaship *Norwegian Sky.* The first three are based throughout the winter in Miami and embark on 7-day jaunts through the eastern and/or western Caribbean. Ships on either itinerary usually spend a day allowing passengers to sun, swim, and surf at the company's private island, Great Stirrup Cay. *Norwegian Dream* follows a year-round 7-day itinerary departing from San Juan, Puerto Rico, to such ports as Aruba, Curaçao, Tortola, Virgin Gorda, St. Thomas, St. Lucia, Antigua, St. Kitts, and St. Croix. The *Norwegian Sea* sails year-round from Houston, making continuous circuits across the Gulf of Mexico to such Yucatán ports as Cancún and Cozumel, and Honduras's Roatan Bay. On board the ships, NCL administers a snappy, high-energy array of activities and, in many cases, a revolving array of international sports figures for game tips and lectures.

- **Princess Cruises** (© **800/ 421-0522** or 310/553-1770; www. princesscruises.com). Currently operating 10 mega-vessels, four of which cruise through Caribbean and Bahamian waters, Princess offers a cruise experience that's part Carnival- or Royal Caribbean–style party-time fun and part Celebrity-style classy enjoyment. The *Ocean Princess, Dawn Princess,* and *Sea Princess,* almost identical vessels all built in the late 1990s, offer the bulk of Princess's Caribbean itineraries, with the *Dawn* and *Ocean* running two alternating 7-night southern Caribbean itineraries round-trip from San Juan, while the *Sea* sails 7-night western Caribbean runs round-trip from Fort Lauderdale. Depending on the exact itinerary, ports on the southern Caribbean runs include Curaçao, Isla Margarita (Venezuela), La Guaira/Caracas (Venezuela), Grenada, Dominica, St. Vincent, St. Kitts, St. Thomas, Trinidad, Barbados, Antigua, Martinique, St. Lucia, and St. Maarten. Western Caribbean itineraries visit Ocho Rios (Jamaica), Grand Cayman, Cozumel, and Princess Cays, the line's private island. The *Grand Princess* sails 7-night eastern Caribbean itineraries round-trip from Fort Lauderdale, visiting St. Thomas, St. Maarten, and Princess Cays. All of the line's ships are stylish and comfortable, but the *Grand* ups it a notch in the style department, offering amazing open deck areas and some really beautiful indoor public areas.

- **Royal Caribbean International (RCI;** © **800/327-6700** or 305/ 539-6000; www.royalcaribbean. com). RCI leads the industry in the development of megaships. Most of this company's dozen or so vessels weigh in at around 73,000 tons. In November 1999 RCI launched what was to that point the biggest cruise ship, the 142,000-ton, 3,114-passenger *Voyager of the Seas,* with a year-round itinerary taking in such Caribbean ports as Jamaica's Ocho Rios and Mexico's Cozumel. In October 2000, RCI launched yet another megaship, the 142,000-ton, 3,838-passenger *Explorer of the Sea.* This vessel has a year-round Caribbean itinerary; it leaves from Miami and makes stops at ports such as Nassau, St. Thomas, and San Juan. Fall 2001 saw the debut of the 142,000-ton, 3,114-passenger *Adventure of the Seas,* sailing 7-night South Caribbean cruises out of Miami, with stops at such ports as San Juan, Aruba, Curaçao, St. Maarten, and St. Thomas. The announcement of two more *Voyager*-class ships for 2002 and 2003 means RCI will have a new 3,114-passenger, 142,000-ton ship every year for 5 years.

RCI's ships offer such cruise ship firsts as an ice-skating rink and a rock-climbing wall. A mass-market company that has everything down to a science, RCI encourages a house-party theme that's just a little less frenetic than the mood aboard Carnival.

There are enough onboard activities to suit virtually any taste and age level. Although accommodations on RCI ships are more than adequate, they are not upscale, and they tend to be a bit more cramped than the industry norm. Using either Miami, Fort Lauderdale, or San Juan as their home port, RCI ships call regularly at St. Thomas, San Juan, Ocho Rios, St. Maarten, Grand Cayman, St. Croix, Curaçao, and one or the other of the line's private beaches—one in the Bahamas, the other along an isolated peninsula in northern Haiti. Most of the company's cruises last 7 days, although some weekend jaunts from San Juan to St. Thomas are available for 3 nights, and some Panama Canal crossings last for 11 and 12 nights.

MORE WAYS TO CUT CRUISE COSTS

BE FLEXIBLE WITH DATES & ITINERARIES Cruise discounters can often get you some amazing fares, but you'll have to take what they've got. (They usually negotiate those fares by reserving cabins in bulk from the cruise lines.)

DON'T CRUISE ALONE When booking a cabin, you'll pay a premium for traveling alone. Most ships impose a supplement of between 125% and 200% of the per-person price for single occupancy of a double cabin. To avoid this penalty, you could let the cruise line match you with a (same-sex) stranger in a shared cabin. Some devoted party lines like Carnival will put up to four single cruisers in a quad cabin at bargain-basement prices. You'll lose your privacy, but you'll love the price.

You can also tap into the "singles" and "senior singles" phone network run by **The Cruise Line, Inc.,** 150 NW 168th St., North Miami Beach, FL 33169 (© **800/777-0707**). When you call this number, you'll hear information geared to general passenger needs before you get to information pertinent to the solo traveler.

SHARE A CABIN WITH FAMILY OR FRIENDS Many lines offer cabins that can house a total of three and four passengers (sometimes even five)—two in regular beds and two in bunk-style berths that pull down from the ceiling or upper part of the wall. So for families of four or groups of very good friends, if you're willing to be a bit (or a lot) crowded, you can save money by sharing your cabin. The rates for the third and fourth passengers in a cabin, adults or children, are typically half the normal adult fare, and are sometimes less than half. Also, look into sharing a suite; most ships have some.

BOOK YOUR CRUISE WITH A GROUP Many cruise lines offer reduced rates to groups occupying at least eight cabins (some as few as five cabins), with two adults in each cabin (for a total of 16 passengers). Based on two people per cabin, typically the 16th person in the group gets a free cruise, and the entire group can split the savings. In general, discounts for this type of group travel can be significant, but they are wholly determined by the cruise line and seasonal demand at the time you're booking. Some high-volume cruise agencies might be able to team you up with a "group" of their own devising that they're booking aboard a certain ship; ask about the possibility when you talk to the agency.

READ THE FINE PRINT You never know what obscure special deals might apply to you. Carnival, for instance, offers really low rates on the *Carnival Destiny* if you book one of the cabins that is one deck directly above the disco (and all the noise it generates at night). The brochure calls them "Night Owl Staterooms," and if you're planning on being in the disco yourself till the wee hours of the night, you might want to consider these cabins, which are discounted at 50%

or more than other, quieter cabins in the same category!

TAKE ADVANTAGE OF SAIL-AND-STAY PROMOTIONS If you want to add a few more days to your vacation, cruise lines often offer good prices for hotels in the cities of embarkation. These days, cruises are departing from ports that are tourist attractions in their own right. You might want to explore Miami before you sail, drive to Disney World from Port Canaveral, or spend a few days in San Juan. Many cruise lines negotiate group hotel discounts for passengers interested in prolonging their vacation. These packages usually include transportation from the hotel to the ship (before the cruise) or from the docks to the hotel (after a cruise).

TAKE ADVANTAGE OF TWO-FERS Promotions called "two-fers"—two-for-one deals that let you bring a companion for free—come and go like hurricane winds, but if you see one, it's worth considering. A cruise specialist should know if some cut-rate discount for two is being offered at the time you plan to sail. (These deals don't happen during the peak winter season in the Caribbean.) You'll have to negotiate these two-fers carefully, and compare them with various air/sea packages to see if you're indeed getting a discounted deal. If airfare is included for both of you, then go for it. But if airfare has to be booked separately, compare the cost of a two-fer without airfare to an air/sea package for two to see which one is the better deal.

TAKE ADVANTAGE OF SENIOR DISCOUNTS Don't keep your age a secret. Membership in any of dozens of clubs, such as AAA or AARP, can afford discounts of anywhere from 5% to 50%. Always ask when you're booking.

12 Getting the Best Value in Accommodations

WATCH OUT FOR EXTRAS!

Nearly all islands charge a government tax on hotel rooms, usually 7½%, but that rate varies from island to island. This tax mounts quickly, so ask if the rate you're quoted includes this room tax. Sometimes the room tax depends on the quality of the hotel; it might be relatively low for a guesthouse but steeper for a first-class resort. Determine the tax before you accept the rate.

In addition, most hotels routinely add 10% to 12% for "service," even if you didn't like the service or didn't see much evidence of it. That means that with tax and service, some bills are 17% or even 25% higher than originally quoted to you! Naturally, you need to determine just how much the hotel, guesthouse, or inn plans to add to your bill at the end of your stay.

That's not all. Some hotels slip in little hidden extras that mount quickly. For example, it's common for many establishments to quote rates that include a continental breakfast. Should you prefer ham and eggs added to the order, that will mean extra charges. Sometimes if you request special privileges, such as extra towels for the beach or laundry done in a hurry, surcharges mount. It pays to watch those extras.

HOTELS & RESORTS

Many budget travelers assume that they can't afford the big hotels and resorts. But there are so many packages out there (see the section "Package Deals," earlier in this chapter) and so many frequent sales, even in winter, that you might be pleasantly surprised.

The rates given in this book are "rack rates"—that is, the officially posted rate that you'd be given if you just walked in off the street. Almost no one actually pays them! Always ask about packages and discounts. Think of the rates in this book as guidelines to help you comparison shop.

WHAT THE ABBREVIATIONS MEAN

Rate "sheets"—that is, statements of a hotel's room rates—often have these classifications, which we've also used in this guide:

> **MAP (Modified American Plan)** usually means room, breakfast, and dinner, unless the room rate has been quoted separately, and then it means only breakfast and dinner.
> **CP (Continental Plan)** includes room and a light breakfast.
> **EP (European Plan)** means room only.
> **AP (American Plan)** includes room plus three meals a day.

A savvy travel agent can help save you serious money. Some hotels can be flexible about their rates, and many offer discounts and upgrades whenever they have a big block of rooms to fill and few reservations. The smaller hotels and inns are not as likely to be generous with discounts, much less upgrades. Even if you book into one of these bigger hotels, ask for the cheaper rooms—that is, those that don't open directly onto the ocean. Caribbean hoteliers charge dearly for the view alone.

ALL-INCLUSIVE RESORTS

The promises are persuasive: "Forget your cash, put your plastic away." Presumably, everything's all paid for in advance at an "all-inclusive" resort. But is it?

The all-inclusives have a reputation for being expensive, and many of them are, especially the giant Super-Clubs of Jamaica or even the Sandals properties (unless you book in a slow period or off-season).

In the 1990s, so many competitors entered the all-inclusive game that the term now means different things to the various resorts using that form of marketing. The ideal all-inclusive is just that—a place where everything, even drinks and watersports, is included. But in the narrowest sense it means a room and three meals a day, with drinks, sports, whatever, appearing as extra charges. Of course, when booking, it's important to ask and to understand exactly what's included in your so-called all-inclusive. Watersports programs and offerings vary greatly at the various resorts. Extras might include options for horseback riding or sightseeing on the island.

The all-inclusive market is geared to the active traveler who likes to participate in organized entertainment, a lot of sports, workouts at fitness centers, and who also likes a lot of food and drink.

If you're single or gay, avoid Sandals. If you have young children, stay away from Hedonism II in Negril, Jamaica, which lives up to its name. Even some Club Meds are targeted more for singles and couples, although many now aggressively pursue the family market. Some Club Meds have Mini Clubs, Baby Clubs, and Teen Clubs at some of their properties, at least during holiday and summer seasons.

This guide doesn't review the high-priced all-inclusives, but it does review the resorts that are within the range of the traveler on a budget—for example, only one Sandals in Jamaica (see "Montego Bay," in chapter 14) falls in our price range. Forget Jamaica's SuperClubs—consider one of the Jack Tar Villages, including those in Jamaica (Montego Bay), the Dominican Republic (north coast), and St. Kitts instead. The Pineapple resort on Antigua is at least moderate in price, a good splurge choice, and most Club Meds fall within the moderate (if not budget) range.

The trick is to look for that special deal and to travel in off-peak periods, which doesn't always mean just from mid-April to mid-December. Discounts are often granted during certain slow periods for hotels, most often after the New Year's holiday. If you want a winter vacation at an all-inclusive, choose the month of January—not February or the Christmas holidays, when prices are at their all-year highs.

One good deal might be **Club Med's "Wild Card,"** geared to singles and couples. You must be 18 or over. Reservations must be made 2 or more weeks prior to departure. One week prior to departure, Club Med advises passengers which "village" on which island they're going to. If this uncertainty doesn't bother you, you can save $150 to $300 per weekly package. The complete per-person Wild Card cost for a week's package is a flat $999 per person. Each package includes round-trip air transportation from New York, double-occupancy accommodations, all meals with complimentary wine and beer (other alcoholic drinks extra), use of all sports facilities except scuba (extra charges), nightly entertainment, and other recreational activities, such as boat rides, snorkeling expeditions, and picnics. For more information, call ℂ **800/CLUB-MED.**

Consult a good travel agent for other good deals that might be available.

GUESTHOUSES

An entirely different type of accommodation is the guesthouse, where most of the Antilleans themselves stay when they travel. In the Caribbean, the term *guesthouse* can mean anything. Sometimes so-called guesthouses are really like simple motels built around swimming pools. Others are small individual cottages, with their own kitchenettes, constructed around a main building in which you'll often find a bar and a restaurant serving local food. Some are surprisingly comfortable, often with private bathrooms and swimming pools. You may or may not have air-conditioning.

For value, the guesthouse can't be topped. You can always journey over to a big beach resort and use its seaside facilities for only a small charge, perhaps no more than $5. Although bereft of frills, the guesthouses we've recommended are clean and safe for families or single women. The cheapest ones are not places where you'd want to spend time, because of their simple, modest furnishings.

COOKING FOR YOURSELF

Particularly if you're a family or a group of friends, a "housekeeping holiday" can be one of the least expensive ways to vacation in the Caribbean. Accommodations with kitchens are now available on nearly all the islands. Some are individual cottages you can rent, some are housed in one building, and some are private homes rented when the owners are away. Many self-catering places have maid service included in the rental, and you're given fresh linen as well.

In the simpler rentals, doing your own cooking and laundry or even your own maid service might not be your idea of a good time in the sun, but it saves money—a lot of money.

The disadvantage to many of these self-catering cottages is that they're in inaccessible places, which may mean you'll need a car. Public transportation on any island in the Caribbean is simply inadequate, if it exists at all.

You have to approach these rental properties with a certain sense of adventure and a do-it-yourself independence. These rentals are not for everybody, but they can make a Caribbean vacation possible for families or other groups on a tight budget.

For a list of agencies to arrange rentals, refer to the accommodations sections of the individual island chapters.

PRIVATE APARTMENTS, EFFICIENCIES & COTTAGES

There are lots of private apartments for rent, either with or without maid service. This is more of a no-frills option than a villa or condo would be. The apartments may not be in buildings with swimming pools, and they may not have front desks to help you.

Cottages are the most freewheeling way to stay. Most are fairly simple; many open onto a beach, whereas others may be clustered around a communal swimming pool. Many contain no more than a simple bedroom with a small kitchen and bathroom. For the peak winter season, reservations should be made at least 5 or 6 months in advance.

Dozens of agents throughout the United States and Canada offer these types of rentals; we've noted some in the island chapters that follow. You can also write to local tourist offices for good suggestions.

Travel experts agree that savings are great, especially for a family of three to six people, or two or three couples; you're likely to pay 50% to 60% of what a hotel would cost. If there are only two in your party, these savings don't apply.

If you intend to prepare your own meals, be aware that groceries are often priced 35% to 60% higher than the average on the U.S. mainland because nearly all foodstuffs have to be imported. Even so, preparing your own food will cost a lot less than dining at restaurants (whose foods, obviously, are also imported).

13 Saving Money on Car Rentals

Refer to the individual chapter listings for special driving rules (sometimes a local license is required) and for major car-rental companies serving a particular island. In many Caribbean islands, including the U.S. Virgin Islands, driving is on the left.

Car-rental rates vary even more than airline fares. The price you pay depends on the size of the car, where and when you pick it up and drop it off, the length of the rental period, where and how far you drive the car, whether you purchase insurance, and a host of other factors. A few key questions could save you hundreds of dollars.

If you decide to rent a car, shop around and ask a lot of questions. The rental firms aren't going to volunteer to save you money, but competition in their industry is fierce. Their reservations clerks are used to being asked for the lowest rate available, and most will find it to get your business. You might have to try different dates, different pickup and drop-off points, and different discount offers yourself to find the best deal because the deals change constantly. Also, if you're a member of an organization such as AARP or AAA, be sure to ask whether you're entitled to discounts.

Check the rental firms' websites. Most automatically bring up the lowest available rate, and there are boxes to click if you are an association member or have a discount coupon. **Microsoft Expedia** (www.expedia.com) and **Travelocity** (www.travelocity.com) help you compare prices and locate car rental bargains from various companies nationwide. They will even make your reservation for you once you've found the best deal. See the "Finding the Best Airfare" section earlier in this chapter for more tips about using the Internet.

Most of the companies pad their profits by selling loss/damage waiver (LDW) insurance. Your insurance carrier or a credit card company might already cover you, so check with them before succumbing to a hard sell.

Also, some rental companies will offer to refill your gas tank at "competitive" prices when you return. Some of their come-ons for this service quote the "average" price of a gallon of gasoline in town. Regular gas usually is less expensive in town than the rental company's rate.

Most also require a minimum age, ranging from 19 to 25, and some also set maximum ages. Others deny cars to anyone who has a bad driving record. Ask about rental requirements and restrictions when you book to avoid problems later. You must have a valid credit card to rent a vehicle.

Some travel packages include airfare, accommodations, and a rental car with unlimited mileage. Compare these prices with the cost of booking airline tickets and renting a car separately to see if these offers are good deals.

14 Getting Married in the Caribbean

If you yearn to take the plunge on a sun-dappled island, check out these wedding basics for the islands where weddings are most commonly held:

ANTIGUA   There is a 24-hour waiting period for marriages on Antigua. A couple appears at the Ministry of Justice in the capital, St. John, to complete and sign a declaration before a marriage coordinator and pay a $190 license fee. The coordinator will arrange for a marriage officer to perform a civil ceremony at any of Antigua's hotels or another place the couple selects. The fee for the marriage officer is $50. Several hotels and resorts offer wedding/honeymoon packages. For more information on civil or religious wedding ceremonies, contact the **Antigua Department of Tourism,** 610 Fifth Ave., Suite 311, New York, NY 10020 (© **212/ 541-4117**).

ARUBA   Civil weddings are possible on Aruba only if one of the partners is an Aruban resident. Because of this restriction, the average couple marries elsewhere, then visits Aruba for a honeymoon. For more information about planning a wedding on Aruba, contact the **Aruba Tourism Authority,** 1000 Harbor Blvd., Weehawken, NJ 08707 (© **800/TO-ARUBA** or 201/ 330-0800).

BARBADOS   Couples can now marry the same day they arrive on Barbados, but they must first get a marriage license from the **Ministry of Home Affairs** (© **246/228-8950**). Bring either a passport or a birth certificate and photo ID, $150 (U.S.) in fees, and $25 for the revenue stamp that can be obtained at the local post office, a letter from the authorized officiant who will perform the service, plus proof, if applicable, of pertinent deaths or divorces of any former spouse(s). A Roman Catholic wedding on Barbados carries additional requirements. For more information, contact the **Barbados Tourism Authority,** 800 Second Ave., New York, NY 10017 (© **800/221-9831** or 212/986-6516).

BONAIRE   Either the bride or groom must have a temporary residency permit, obtained by writing a letter to the governor of the Island Territory of Bonaire, Wilhelminaplein 1, Kralendijk, Bonaire, N.A. (© **599/ 717-5350**). The letter, submitted within 2 months of departure for Bonaire, should request permission to marry on Bonaire, apply for temporary residency, as well as inform the governor of your arrival and departure dates and the date on which you want to marry. The partner who applies for residency must be on the island for 7 days prior to the wedding. The governor must issue a special dispensation if there is less than a 10-day time period between the announcement of the marriage and actually getting married. In addition, send three passport photos, copies of the bride's and groom's passports, birth certificates, and proof of divorce or, in the case of widows and widowers, the death certificate of the deceased spouse.

You can arrange your wedding on Bonaire through **Multro Travel and Tours,** Attn: Mrs. Marvel Tromp, Lighthouse Beach Resort #22 (P.O. Box 237), Bonaire, N.A. (© **599/7-8334;** fax 599/717-8834), or check with the hotel where you're planning to stay. Some hotels arrange weddings on special request. For further information, contact the **Bonaire Tourist Office** (© **800/BONAIRE** or 212/956-5911).

THE BRITISH VIRGIN ISLANDS In the British Virgin Islands, there is no requirement of island residency, but a couple must apply for a license at the attorney general's office, and must stay in the B.V.I. for 3 days while the application is processed. You must present a passport or an original birth certificate and photo identification, plus certified proof of your marital status, as well as any divorce or death certificates that apply to any former spouse(s). Two witnesses must accompany the couple. The fee is $110. Marriages can be performed by the local registrar or by the officiant of your choice. Contact the **Registrar's Office,** P.O. Box 418, Road Town, Tortola, B.V.I. (© **284/494-3134** or 284/468-3701, ext. 5001).

THE CAYMAN ISLANDS Visitors must arrange for a marriage officer before arriving in the Cayman Islands in order to name the individual who will be officiating on the application. The application for a marriage license, which costs $200, can be obtained from the **Deputy Secretary's Office,** Third Floor, Government Administration Building, George Town (© **345/949-7900**). There is no waiting period. You must present a birth

certificate plus the embarkation/disembarkation cards issued by the island's immigration authorities, along with divorce decrees or proof of a former spouse's death (if applicable). Complete wedding services and packages are offered by **Cayman Weddings of Grand Cayman,** owned and operated by Cayman marriage officers Vernon and Francine Jackson. For more information, contact them at P.O. Box 678, Grand Cayman (© **345/949-8677;** fax 345/949-8237). A brochure, *Getting Married in the Cayman Islands,* is available from **Government Information Services,** Broadcasting House, Grand Cayman (© **345/949-8092;** fax 345/949-5936).

CURAÇAO Couples must be on the island 2 days before applying for a marriage license, for which there is a 14-day waiting period. Passport, birth certificate, return ticket, and divorce papers (if applicable) are required. The fee is subject to change, so check in advance. For further information, call the **Curaçao Tourist Board,** 475 Park Ave. S., Suite 2000, New York, NY 10016 (© **212/683-7660;** fax 212/683-9337).

JAMAICA In high season, some Jamaican resorts witness several weddings a day. Many of the larger Jamaican resorts can arrange for an officiant, a photographer, and even the wedding cake and champagne. Some resorts will even throw in your wedding with the cost of your honeymoon at the hotel. Both the Jamaican Tourist Board and your hotel will assist you with the paperwork. Participants must reside on Jamaica for 24 hours before the ceremony. Bring birth certificates and affidavits saying you've never been married before, or, if you've been divorced, bring copies of your divorce papers; widows and widowers must bring a copy of the deceased spouses' death certificate. The cost of the marriage license and stamp duty is $200.

The cost of the ceremony can range from $50 to $200, depending on how much legwork you want to do yourself. You can apply in person at the **Ministry of National Security and Justice,** 12 Ocean Blvd., Kingston, Jamaica (© **876/922-9500**).

PUERTO RICO There are no residency requirements. You'll need parental consent if either party is under 18. Blood tests are required, although a test conducted within 10 days of the ceremony on the U.S. mainland will suffice. A doctor in Puerto Rico must sign the license after conducting an examination of the bride and groom. For complete details, contact the **Commonwealth of Puerto Rico Health Department,** Demographic Register, 171 Quisaueya St., Hato Rey, PR 00917 (© **787/ 767-9120**).

ST. LUCIA For a wedding on St. Lucia, both parties must have remained on the island for 48 hours prior to the ceremony. Present your passport or birth certificate, plus (if either participant has been widowed or divorced) proof of death or divorce from the former spouse(s). Before the ceremony, it usually takes about 2 days to process all the paperwork. Fees run around $150 for a lawyer (which you usually need for the application to the governor-general), $25 for the registrar to perform the ceremony, and $37.75 for the stamp duty and the license. Some resorts and vacation properties also offer wedding packages that include all the necessary arrangements for a single fee. For more information, contact the **St. Lucia Tourist Board,** 800 Second Ave., 9th Floor, New York, NY 10017 (© **212/ 867-2950;** fax 212/867-2795).

THE U.S. VIRGIN ISLANDS If you plan to wed in the U.S. Virgin Islands, no blood tests or physical examinations are necessary, but there is a $25 license fee, a $25 notarized application fee, and an 8-day waiting period, which is sometimes waived, depending on circumstances. Civil ceremonies before a judge of the territorial court cost $200 each; religious ceremonies performed by clergy are equally valid. Fees and schedules for church weddings must be negotiated directly with the officiant. More information is available from the **U.S. Virgin Islands Division of Tourism,** 1270 Ave. of the Americas, New York, NY 10020 (© **212/332-2222**).

The guide *Getting Married in the U.S. Virgin Islands* is distributed by U.S.V.I. tourism offices; it provides information on all three islands, including wedding planners, places of worship, florists, and limousine services. The guide also provides a listing of island accommodations that offer in-house wedding services.

Couples can apply for a marriage license for St. Thomas or St. John by contacting the **Territorial Court of the Virgin Islands,** P.O. Box 70, St. Thomas, U.S.V.I. 00804 (© **340/ 774-6680**). For weddings on St. Croix, applications are available by contacting the **Territorial Court of the Virgin Islands,** Family Division, P.O. Box 929, Christiansted, St. Croix, U.S.V.I. 00821 (© **340/ 778-9750**).

15 Planning Your Trip Online

With a mouse, a modem, and a little do-it-yourself determination, Internet users can tap into the same travel-planning databases that were once accessible only to travel agents. Sites such as **Travelocity, Expedia,** and **Orbitz** allow consumers to comparison shop for airfares, book flights, learn of last-minute bargains, and reserve rooms and rental cars.

But don't fire your travel agent just yet. Although online booking sites

Frommers.com: The Complete Travel Resource

For an excellent travel-planning resource, we highly recommend **Arthur Frommer's Budget Travel Online** (www.frommers.com). We're a little biased, of course, but we guarantee you'll find the travel tips, reviews, monthly vacation giveaways, and online-booking capabilities thoroughly indispensable. Among the special features are **"Ask the Expert"** bulletin boards, where Frommer's authors answer your questions via online postings; **Arthur Frommer's Daily Newsletter,** for the latest travel bargains and inside travel secrets; and Frommer's **Destinations archive,** where you'll get expert travel tips, hotel and dining recommendations, and advice on the sights to see for more than 200 destinations around the globe. Once your research is done, the **Online Reservation System** (www.frommers.com/booktravelnow) takes you to Frommer's favorite sites for booking your vacation at affordable prices.

offer tips and data to help you bargain shop, they cannot endow you with the hard-earned experience that makes a seasoned, reliable travel agent an invaluable resource, even in the Internet age. And for consumers with a complex itinerary, a trusty travel agent is still the best way to arrange the most direct flights to and from the best airports.

Still, there's no denying the Internet's emergence as a powerful tool in researching and plotting travel time. The benefits of researching your trip online can be well worth the effort:

- **Last-minute specials,** known as **E-Savers,** such as weekend deals or Internet-only fares, are offered by airlines to fill empty seats. Most of them are announced on Tuesday or Wednesday and must be purchased online. They are valid only for travel that weekend, but some can be booked weeks or months in advance. Sign up for weekly e-mail alerts at airline websites or check megasites that compile comprehensive lists of E-savers, such as Smarter Living (www.smarter living.com) or WebFlyer (www. webflyer.com).

- Some sites will send you **e-mail notification** when a cheap fare to your favorite destination becomes available. Some will also tell you when fares to a particular destination are lowest.
- The best of the travel planning sites are now **highly personalized;** they track your frequent-flier miles, and store your seating and meal preferences, tentative itineraries, and credit card information, letting you plan trips or check agendas quickly.
- All major airlines offer **incentives**— bonus frequent-flier miles, Internet-only discounts, sometimes even free cellphone rentals—when you purchase online or buy an e-ticket.
- Advances in mobile technology provide business travelers and other frequent travelers with **the ability to check flight status, change plans, or get specific directions** from hand-held computing devices, mobile phones, and pagers. Some sites will e-mail or page a passenger if a flight is delayed.

TRAVEL PLANNING & BOOKING SITES

The best travel planning and booking sites cast a wide net, offering domestic and international flights, hotel and rental-car bookings, plus news, destination information, and deals on cruises and vacation packages. Keep in mind that free (one-time) registration is often required for booking. Because several airlines are no longer willing to pay commissions on tickets sold by online travel agencies, be aware that these online agencies will either charge a $10 surcharge if you book a ticket on that carrier—or neglect to offer those air carriers' offerings.

The sites in this section are not intended to be a comprehensive list, but rather a discriminating selection to get you started. Recognition is given to sites based on their content, value, and ease of use and is not paid for—unlike some website rankings, which are based on payment. Remember: This is a press-time snapshot of leading websites—some undoubtedly will have evolved or moved by the time you read this.

- **Travelocity** (www.travelocity.com or www.frommers.travelocity.com) and **Expedia** (www.expedia.com) are the most longstanding and reputable sites, each offering excellent selections and searches for complete vacation packages. Travelers search by destination and dates coupled with how much they are willing to spend.
- The latest buzz in the online travel world is about **Orbitz** (www.orbitz.com), a site launched by United, Delta, Northwest, American, and Continental airlines. It shows all possible fares for your desired trip, offering fares lower than those available through travel agents. (Stay tuned: At press time, travel-agency associations were waging an antitrust battle against this site.)

- **Qixo** (www.qixo.com) is another powerful search engine that allows you to search for flights and hotel rooms on 20 other travel-planning sites (such as Travelocity) at once. Qixo sorts results by price, after which you can book your travel directly through the site.

SMART E-SHOPPING

The savvy traveler is one who is armed with good information. Here are a few tips to help you navigate the Internet successfully and safely:

- **Know when sales start.** Last-minute deals might vanish in minutes. If you have a favorite booking site or airline, find out when last-minute deals are released to the public. (For example, Southwest's specials are posted every Tues at 12:01am central time.)
- **Shop around.** Compare results from different sites and airlines—and against a travel agent's best fare, if you can. If possible, try a range of times and alternative airports before you make a purchase.
- **Follow the rules of the trade.** Book in advance, and choose an off-peak time and date if possible. Some sites will tell you when fares to a particular destination tend to be cheapest.
- **Stay secure.** Book only through secure sites (some airline sites are not secure). Look for a padlock icon at the bottom of your Web browser before you enter credit card information or other personal data.
- **Avoid online auctions.** Sites that auction airline tickets and frequent-flier miles are the number-one perpetrators of Internet fraud, according to the National Consumers League.
- **Maintain a paper trail.** If you book an e-ticket, print out a confirmation, or write down your

confirmation number, and keep it safe and accessible—or your trip could be a virtual one!

ONLINE TRAVELER'S TOOLBOX

Veteran travelers usually carry some essential items to make their trips easier. Following is a selection of online tools to bookmark and use:

- **Visa ATM Locator** (www.visa.com/pd/atm) or **MasterCard ATM Locator** (http://www.mastercard.com/cardholder services/atm/). Find ATMs in hundreds of cities in the U.S. and around the world.
- **Foreign Languages for Travelers** (www.travlang.com). Here you can learn basic terms in more than 70 languages and click on any underlined phrase to hear what it sounds like. *Note:* To use this site, you must have speakers and downloadable free audio software.
- **Intellicast** (www.intellicast.com). Get weather forecasts for all 50 states and cities around the world. *Note:* Temperatures are in Celsius for many international destinations.
- **Mapquest** (www.mapquest.com). This best of the mapping sites lets you choose a specific address or destination, and in seconds, it returns a map and detailed directions.
- **Cybercafes.com** (www.cybercafes.com) or **Net Café Guide** (www.netcafeguide.com/mapindex.htm). Locate Internet cafes at hundreds of locations around the globe. Catch up on your e-mail and log onto the Web for a few dollars per hour.
- **Universal Currency Converter** (www.xe.net/currency). See what your dollar or pound is worth in more than 100 other countries.
- **U.S. State Department Travel Warnings** (www.travel.state.gov/travel_warnings.html). Reports on places where health concerns or unrest might threaten U.S. travelers. It also lists the locations of U.S. embassies around the world.

Antigua

Antiguans boast that they have a different beach for every day of the year (which is a bit of an exaggeration). Most of them protected by coral reefs, and with sand often sugar-white, these beaches are reason enough for most visitors to come here. But Antigua is also known for its sailing facilities, centered at historic English Harbour, where Lord Nelson built a base for his English fleet in the late 18th century. The principal "tourist zone" lies north of the capital of St. John's in the northwest. Here you'll find some of the best hotels (but not *the* best) and an array of restaurants, beach bars, and watersports facilities.

Old-timers claim that their island is trying to imitate Miami Beach with its sprawling resorts. To some extent, that's true. Some of the Caribbean's largest resort hotels have opened in Antigua, which also means that the island boasts some of the most expensive places to stay in all the West Indies. The island's guesthouses, small inns, and B&Bs just haven't kept pace with all the gigantic mega-resorts that sometimes discount their packages dramatically to fill cavernous floors. There's a dearth of really good budget accommodations, but you'll find a number of small, less expensive restaurants, especially in St. John's.

The islands of Antigua, Barbuda, and Redonda form the independent nation of Antigua and Barbuda, within the Commonwealth of Nations. Redonda is an uninhabited rocky islet of less than a square mile,

located 20 miles southwest of Antigua. Sparsely populated Barbuda, which lies 26 miles to the north of Antigua, is expensive to get to and super-expensive once you're there. If your fortune approaches that of Bill Gates, the hoteliers will be only too glad to welcome you. Independence has come, but Antigua is still British in many of its traditions.

Rolling, rustic Antigua has as its highest point Boggy Peak, 1,360 feet above sea level. Antigua has a population of about 67,000 and an area of 108 square miles. Stone towers, once sugar mills, dot the landscape, although its inland scenery isn't as dramatic as on St. Kitts. But, oh, those beaches!

The capital is **St. John's,** a large, neatly laid-out town, 6 miles from the airport and less than a mile from Deep Water Harbour Terminal, where cruise ships dock. The town is the focal point of commerce and industry, as well as the seat of government and visitor shopping. Trade winds keep the streets fairly cool, as they were built wide just for that purpose. Protected in the throat of a narrow bay, St. John's consists of cobblestone sidewalks, weather-beaten wooden houses, corrugated iron roofs, and louvered Caribbean verandas.

Most locals will treat you with respect if you show them respect, but Antigua is hardly the friendliest of islands in the Caribbean—too much unemployment, too great a gap between rich and poor.

The Admiral's Inn **1**
Catamaran Hotel
& Marina **2**
Island Inn **4**
Lashings Beach Café
& Inn at Sandhaven **3**

1 Essentials

VISITOR INFORMATION

Before you leave, you can contact the **Antigua and Barbuda Department of Tourism,** 610 Fifth Ave., Suite 311, New York, NY 10020 (© **212/541-4117**), or 25 SE Second Ave., Suite 300, Miami, FL 33131 (© **305/381-6762**). A new toll-free number also provides information: © **888/268-4227.** Live operators are available Monday to Friday 9am to 5pm eastern standard time. You can also look up the department's website, at **www.antigua-barbuda.org**.

In Canada, contact the **Antigua and Barbuda Department of Tourism & Trade,** 60 St. Clair Ave. E., Suite 304, Toronto, ON M4T 1N5 (© **416/ 961-3085**).

In the United Kingdom, information is available at **Antigua House,** 15 Thayer St., London, England W1M 5LD (© **020/7486-7073**).

On the island, the **Antigua and Barbuda Department of Tourism,** at Thames and Long streets in St. John's (© **268/462-0480**), is open Monday to Thursday 8am to 4:30pm and on Friday 8am to 3pm.

GETTING THERE

Be sure to read the section "Package Deals" in chapter 2 before you book your airline ticket—it can save you a ton of money!

The major airline that flies to Antigua's V. C. Bird Airport is **American Airlines** (© **800/433-7300** in the U.S.; www.im.aa.com), which offers four daily

---

Fun Fact **Special Events**

The week before the first Tuesday in August, summer **Carnival** envelops the streets in exotic costumes that recall Antiguans' African heritage. Festivities include a beauty competition and calypso and steel band competitions. The big event in spring is Antigua's annual **Sailing Week** in late April or early May.

---

nonstop flights to Antigua from its hub in San Juan, Puerto Rico; flights take about 1½ hours. Each of them departs late enough in the day to allow easy transfers from other flights.

Continental (© **800/231-0856** or 268/462-5355; www.continental.com) has daily flights out of Newark, New Jersey.

British Airways (© **800/247-9297** in the U.S.; www.british-airways.com) offers flights four times a week from London's Gatwick Airport.

Air Canada (© **888/247-2262;** www.aircanada.ca) has regularly scheduled flights from Toronto to Antigua on Saturday only.

BWIA (© **800/538-2942** in the U.S.; www.bwee.com) is increasingly popular. Each week, three flights depart for Antigua from Miami; one from Toronto; five from Kingston, Jamaica; and five from London.

GETTING AROUND

BY TAXI   Taxis meet every airplane, and drivers wait outside the major hotels. In fact, if you're going to be on Antigua for a few days, you may find that a particular driver has "adopted" you, although budget travelers will want to avoid this expensive luxury. The typical one-way fare from the airport to St. John's is $12; to English Harbour, it's $25 and up. The government of Antigua fixes the rates, and the taxis have no meters.

While it's costly, the best way to see Antigua is by private taxi whose drivers also act as guides. Most taxi tours are from the St. John's area to English Harbour. Drivers generally charge $40 for three or four passengers and usually wait at least 30 minutes or maybe more while you sightsee around English Harbour. If you split the cost with another couple, it falls within the range of most budgets.

To call a taxi in St. John's, dial © **268/462-0711;** after 6pm, call © **268/462-5190.**

BY RENTAL CAR   Newly arrived drivers quickly (and ruefully) learn that the island's roads are among the worst, most potholed, and most badly signposted in the Caribbean. Considering that you have to *drive on the left* and are often tempted to have one piña colada too many, renting a car on Antigua is usually not a great idea.

If you insist on driving, you must get an Antiguan **driver's license,** which costs an overpriced $20. To obtain one, you must produce a valid driver's license from home. Most car-rental firms are authorized to issue you an Antiguan license, which they usually do without a surcharge.

Several different car-rental agencies operate on Antigua, although they're sometimes precariously financed local operations with cars best described as "battered." The best of them are affiliated with major car-rental companies in the United States. **Avis** (© **800/331-1212** in the U.S. or 268/462-2840 in Antigua; www.avis.com) and **Hertz** (© **800/654-3131** in the U.S. or 268/462-6450 in Antigua; www.hertz.com) are both represented on Antigua, each offering pickup service at the airport. Another agency to try is **Dollar** on Nevis Street, St. John's (© 800/800-4000 in the U.S., or 268/462-0362 in Antigua; www.dollarcar.com). **Budget** is also represented on Antigua with a kiosk at the airport (© 800/472-3325 in the U.S., or 268/462-3009 in Antigua; www.budgetrentacar.com). Although not as reliable as the big companies, you can always call a local company and see if they'll make a cheaper deal. The cars might not be as well maintained, but it could be easier on your pocketbook. Try **Anjam Rent-a-car,** Sunset Cove, Dickenson Bay (© 268/462-0959). The average rental is about $50 a day. But if you're arriving off-season, be firm about wanting a "summer discount"—it's often granted. Of course, the longer you book the car, especially for use over several days, the cheaper the daily rate is likely to be.

BY MOTORCYCLE & SCOOTER   For the cheapest wheels on the island, rent a motorcycle or scooter from **Shipwreck,** English Harbour (© 268/464-7771). Yamaha or Honda motorcycles rent for about $35 per day or $150 per week; scooters cost $25 per day or $85 per week. You'll save so much that you might not even mind the bumpy ride.

BY BUS   Buses are not recommended for the average visitor, although they do exist and are cheap. Service is erratic and undependable along impossibly bumpy roads. Officially, buses operate between St. John's and the villages daily 5:30am to 6pm, but don't count on it. In St. John's, buses leave from two different "stations"—near the Central Market and near the Botanical Gardens. Most fares are $1.

 FAST FACTS: **Antigua**

Banking Hours Banks are usually open Monday to Thursday 8am to 1pm and Friday 8am to 1pm and 3 to 5pm.

Currency The **Eastern Caribbean dollar (EC$)** is used on these islands. However, nearly all hotels bill you in U.S. dollars, and only certain tiny restaurants present their prices in EC dollars. Make sure you know which dollars are referred to when you inquire about a price. The EC dollar is worth about 37¢ in U.S. currency (EC$2.70 = U.S.$1). Unless otherwise specified, *rates quoted in this chapter are given in U.S. dollars.*

Customs Arriving visitors are allowed to bring in 200 cigarettes and 1 quart of liquor, plus 6 ounces of perfume.

Documents A valid passport is preferred when U.S., British, and Canadian nationals are visiting the island. An original birth certificate accompanied by a photo ID is also acceptable, but we recommend that you bring your passport anyway. All arriving visitors must have a departing ticket.

Electricity Most of the island's electricity is 220 volts AC (60 cycles), meaning that U.S. appliances need transformers. However, the Hodges Bay area and some hotels are supplied with 110 volt AC (60 cycles).

Emergencies In an emergency, contact the police (© 268/462-0125), the fire department (© 268/462-0044), or an ambulance (© 268/462-0251). In addition, you can also call © 911 or 999 for any type of emergency.

Hospital The principal medical facility on Antigua is **Holberton Hospital,** on Hospital Road, St. John's (© 268/462-0251).

Language The official language is English.

Liquor Laws Beer and liquor are sold in many stores, 7 days a week. It's legal to have an open container on the beach.

Safety Antigua is generally safe, but that doesn't mean you should go wandering alone at night on the practically deserted streets of St. John's. Don't leave valuables unguarded on the beach.

Taxes & Service Charges A departure tax of U.S.$20 is imposed, and an 8.5% government tax is added to all hotel bills. Most hotels also add a 10% service charge.

Telecommunications Telephone calls can be made from hotels or from the office of **Cable & Wireless,** 42–44 St. Mary's St., in St. John's (© **268/462-0840**). Faxes and telegrams can also be sent from here.

Time Antigua is on Atlantic standard time year-round, so it's 1 hour ahead of U.S. eastern standard time. When daylight saving time takes over in the States, then Antigua's time is the same as in the eastern United States.

Tipping Most hotels and restaurants add a 10% charge to your bill to cover service. Even so, it is still customary to add another 5% to restaurant checks. Tip most cabbies 10%, with porters and bellmen getting $1 per piece of luggage. If you're staying at an all inclusive, tips have been figured into your overall bill; otherwise, tip maids about $2 a night at other hotels.

Water Tap water is generally safe to drink here, but many visitors prefer to drink only bottled water.

Weather The average year-round temperature ranges from 75° to 85°F (24°C–29°C).

2 Accommodations You Can Afford

Antigua's hotels are among the best and most plentiful in the eastern Caribbean, but you have to hunt for bargains. Watch out for summer closings, which often depend on the caprice of the owners, who might decide to shut down if business isn't good. Incidentally, air-conditioning, except in first-class hotels, isn't as common as some visitors think it should be. Chances are, your hotel will be on a beach. You can also rent an apartment or cottage if you want to cook for yourself.

Remember that an 8.5% government tax and 10% service charge are added to your hotel bill, which makes quite a difference in your final tab.

The Admiral's Inn ★★ This is one of the most atmospheric inns in the Caribbean, a great place for a sunset cocktail. Designed in 1785, the year Nelson sailed into the harbor as captain of the HMS *Boreas,* and completed in 1788, the building once here used to house dockyard services. In the heart of Nelson's Dockyard and loaded with West Indian charm, the hostelry is constructed of weathered brick brought from England as ships' ballast. It has a terrace opening onto a centuries-old garden. The ground floor, with brick walls, giant ship beams, and island-made furniture, has a tavern atmosphere, with decorative copper, boat lanterns, old oil paintings, and wrought-iron chandeliers.

There are three types of character-filled accommodations. The lowest rate is for smaller rooms on the top floor, which may get warm during the day in summer but are quiet, with dormer-window views over the yacht-filled harbor.

The most expensive are some ground-floor rooms in a tiny brick building—on the site of a provisions warehouse for Nelson's troops—across the courtyard from the main structure. Each of these spacious rooms has a little patio and a garden entry as well as optional air-conditioning. The same superior rate applies to front rooms on the first floor of the main building, with views of the lawn and harbor. A medium rate applies to the back rooms on this floor, all of which have air-conditioning. All rooms have ceiling fans and twin beds with good mattresses. The Inn's bathrooms are small and well maintained, with some shelf space, plus compact shower stalls. The Joiner's Loft is an upstairs suite adjacent to the annex rooms of the inn, with a large living room looking out over the water; there are two bedrooms, two bathrooms, and a full kitchen. The inn has a restaurant that serves lobster, seafood, and steaks in a 17th-century setting. On Saturday night, a steel band plays.

English Harbour (P.O. Box 713), St. John's, Antigua, W.I. ℂ **800/223-5695** in the U.S. or 268/460-1027. Fax 268/460-1534. 15 units. Winter $108–$115 single; $145–$160 double; $350 triple; $400 suite. Off-season $82–$86 single; $100–$110 double; $210 triple; $250 suite. AE, MC, V. Closed Sept to mid-Oct. Take the road southeast from St. John's, following the signs to English Harbour. **Amenities:** Restaurant, bar, snorkeling, free transport to beaches, room service, babysitting, laundry. *In room:* A/C (some units), hair dryer (upon request at desk), ceiling fans.

The Catamaran Hotel & Marina ✵✵ This is a longtime favorite on Antigua. At Falmouth Harbour, a 2-mile drive from English Harbour, the Catamaran opens onto a palm-lined beach. When we first discovered the property years ago, a film crew had taken it over while making a movie about pirates of the West Indies. The management had to post a sign: TODAY'S "PIRATES" MUST WEAR BATHING SUITS ON THE BEACH. It's not as wild around here anymore, and peace and tranquility prevail. It is an informal, laid-back choice for a honeymoon, with comfortably furnished apartments where you can impress your new partner with your culinary skills.

On the second floor are eight self-contained rooms, each with a four-poster bed, a good queen-size mattress, and a balcony opening onto the water. The most luxurious and spacious rental is called the Captain's Cabin. The standard rooms are quite small but well maintained and comfortable enough, and the efficiencies at water's edge can be rented by one person or two. Each efficiency has a balcony and a kitchen, plus a small bathroom with shower. Boaters will like the hotel's location at the 30-slip Catamaran Marina. You can purchase supplies at a nearby grocery store, or enjoy the hotel's own reasonably priced meals at the hotel restaurant and bar. Sportfishing and diving can be arranged, and the hotel offers Sunfish, dinghies, and rowboats.

Falmouth Harbour (P.O. Box 958), St. John's, Antigua, W.I. ℂ **268/460-1036.** Fax 268/460-1339. www. catamaran-antigua.com. 16 units. Winter $70 single; $120 double. Off-season $55 single; $70–$115 double. Extra person $25 over age 10; children $15 under age 10. AE, MC, V. Closed Sept–Oct. **Amenities:** Restaurant, bar, sportfishing, diving, boat rentals. *In room:* Kitchen (some units), coffeemaker, safe, ceiling fans, no phone.

Island Inn This white concrete building trimmed in green enjoys a well-kept garden setting only a 10-minute walk from the beach at Dickenson Bay. It features self-contained, one-bedroom studios with king-size or double beds with good mattresses. The studios all have ceiling fans, individual balconies, or patios, plus fully equipped kitchenettes. Bathrooms are tiny and absolutely standard, each with a tiled shower, but the plumbing is up-to-date. Locals often use the inn for wedding receptions. There's a swimming pool and a simple and modestly priced restaurant that serves low-cost breakfasts and dinners. The food is only standard, but portions are generous and filling.

Anchorage Rd. (P.O. Box 1218), St. John's, Antigua, W.I. © **268/462-4065.** Fax 268/462-4066. 10 units. Winter $80 studio for 1; $90 studio for 2. Off-season $75 studio for 1; $80 studio for 2. Extra person $10; children 11 and under stay free in parents' room. AE, DISC, MC, V. **Amenities:** Restaurant, pool, room service, babysitting. *In room:* A/C, TV, kitchenette, no phone.

Lashings Beach Café & Inn at Sandhaven This is a small hotel on a good beach 3 miles north of St. John's. Richie Richardson, the island's cricketing legend, has teamed up with close friend, David Folb, an Englishman, to take over this small inn. Located at Dry Hill, this hotel is a friend of the budget traveler. It's the lazy life here in this secluded spot, and you can see hotel guests finding their favorite spot underneath the palms or ordering a cool rum punch at the beach bar. The interior of this two-story cinder-block structure is a bit spartan, with small guest rooms with concrete floors and ceiling fans. Beds are twins or doubles, but the mattresses were recently upgraded. Bathrooms offer shower stalls, and patios or balconies contain plastic furnishings. Traditionally, Antigua's cheapest hotel has been known as the "barracks on the beach," but management has made improvements. This might be a good bet for high-priced Antigua if you're not the fussy type and you plan to spend most of your time at the beach.

The on-site bar is an island hot spot and can get noisy at night. It's beachside, as is the restaurant, which serves everything from fresh lobster to a mug of chili, all at a reasonable price.

Sandhaven, Runaway Beach, St. John's, Antigua, W.I. © **268/462-4438.** Fax 268/462-4491. www. lashings.com. 16 units. Winter $65 single; $95 double; $110 triple; $145 family room. Off-season $50 single; $70 double; $90 triple; $100 family room. MC, V. **Amenities:** Beach restaurant/bar. *In room:* No phone.

3 Great Deals on Dining

Many independently operated restaurants serve West Indian food, which is not readily available in hotel dining rooms. Some dishes, especially the curries, show an East Indian influence, and Caribbean lobster is a specialty. Although you'll find expensive items on some menus, most dishes at the restaurants listed here are at the lower end of the price scale. You get such big helpings that one plate of food will fortify most appetites for the day or night.

Some restaurants present their prices in the local currency, the Eastern Caribbean dollar (EC$). When you inquire about a price, make sure you know which type of dollar is being quoted. Rates quoted in this section are given in U.S. dollars.

Big Banana Holding Company ⭐ PIZZA In former slave quarters, this place serves up some of the best pizza in the eastern Caribbean. It stands amid the most stylish shopping and dining emporiums in town, a few steps from the Heritage Quay Jetty. Its ceiling fans and laid-back atmosphere will almost make you expect Sydney Greenstreet to stop in for a drink. The frothy libations, coconut or banana crush, are practically desserts. You can also order overstuffed baked potatoes, fresh-fruit salad, or conch salad. On Thursday a reggae band entertains from 10pm to 1am.

Redcliffe Quay, St. John's. © **268/480-6986.** Main courses $8–$32. AE, DC, MC, V. Mon–Sat 8am–11:30pm.

Hemingway's ⭐ *Value* CREOLE/INTERNATIONAL Set on the second floor of a building in the heart of St. John's and accented with intricate ginger-bread painted in bright tropical colors, this charming cafe attracts a crowd of shoppers and sightseers. It's very busy when cruise ships dock. From its upper verandas, you can see the landing dock and enjoy the sight of pedestrian traffic

> ### (Finds) Antigua's Best Beach Bar
>
> As you whiz along the winding road, you spot the initials **O.J.**, Crab Hill
> (**© 268/460-0184**). O.J. stands for Oliver Joseph, who has returned to his
> childhood home after a stint as what he calls a "Toronto suit." His bar
> overlooks the sea, on a half-acre between the deluxe Curtain Bluff and
> Jolly Harbour, both south of St. John's along the coastal road. This is the
> classic cliché of a Caribbean beach bar, with seashells, tablecloths in flam-
> boyant prints, plus sea fans and coral from the reefs. Here in a laid-back
> atmosphere, you can sample Wadadli beer (the local brew) or one of the
> dark Cavalier rums so beloved by Antiguans. The piña coladas, made
> from homegrown plantains, guava, coconuts, and mangos, are the
> island's best. O.J. grows his own herbs, which are used in his chicken,
> fresh fish, and lobster dishes. If you want to stay for a big lunch, it'll cost
> around $12 and rarely more than $20 for dinner. The big resort hotels
> don't have this kind of atmosphere.

in the street below. Menu items include salads, sandwiches, burgers, sautéed
filets of fish, pastries, ice creams, and an array of brightly colored tropical drinks.
This is a place for a convenient, casual meal and great value rather than for serious gourmet fare.

Jardine Court, St. Mary's St., St. John's. © 268/462-2763. Dinner main courses $11–$26; lunch main courses
$5.50–$29; breakfast $5.50–$9. AE, MC, V. Mon–Sat 8:30am–11pm.

Joe Mike's Restaurant WEST INDIAN Popular with the locals, this
restaurant is on the ground floor of Joe Mike's Hotel (see "Accommodations You
Can Afford," above). Hang out here if you'd like to connect with the bustling
life of St. John's, at least during the day. People show up for the good food,
affordable prices, and happy times. Daily specials feature local foods, including
fresh fish. Try one of the homemade soups such as pepper pot, which seems to
taste different every day, depending on what went into it. Cream of pumpkin is
a soothing delight, too. A specialty of the chef is *ducana* and saltfish. (*Ducana* is
a dumpling made with sweet potatoes, pumpkin, and coconut.) Tuesday to
Friday a one-man band entertains at lunchtime.

In Joe Mike's Hotel, Nevis St., St. John's. © 268/462-1142. Main courses $8–$10. AE, DISC, MC, V. Tues
7:30am–10pm; Wed–Sat 7:30am–11pm.

Pizzas in Paradise PIZZA/CARIBBEAN Young islanders and cruise ship
passengers alike gravitate to this spot, which offers excellent pizzas and a satisfying assortment of seafood salads, fruit platters, pastas, and grilled flying-fish sandwiches. All types of subs are also on the menu. The most expensive item is a
delectable mammoth seafood pizza. Situated in a historic building, this restaurant
offers both indoor and outdoor dining. The deck has picnic tables with umbrellas and overlooks the town's shops. A large selection of CDs is available for background music, except on Thursday night, when there's live entertainment.

Redcliffe St., Redcliffe Quay, St. John's. © 268/462-2621. Pizzas, pastas, and main courses $8–$34. AE, DC,
MC, V. Mon–Sat 7am–midnight.

Redcliffe Tavern CARIBBEAN/INTERNATIONAL If you don't want
pizza (see above), this is one of your best bets along the water at Redcliffe Quay,
especially at lunch. This waterside restaurant was originally a warehouse

constructed by the British in the 18th century. The place displays plantation-era water pumps and other Antiguan artifacts from that time. Don't expect a quiet and romantic evening here, however; the place is usually crowded. The menu features zesty items such as plantain-stuffed chicken breasts in tomato or basil sauce, brie wrapped in phyllo with tomato-raspberry vinaigrette, and steaks with mushrooms or peppercorn sauce. The Normandy-style apple tart is superb.

Redcliffe Quay, St. John's. ⓒ 268/461-4557. Reservations recommended. Main courses $15–$25; lunch from $9. AE, DISC, MC, V. Mon–Sat 8am–11pm.

Russell's INTERNATIONAL   Set in a dark-stained wooden house, on a hill-side about 20 feet above sea level directly north of St. John's, this restaurant is best known for its bar (which sometimes features live music) and the potent drinks that sometimes turn Russell's into a raucous party. The most appealing time to visit is during the cocktail hour, especially when live music is playing. That's usually every Wednesday to Saturday between 7 and 10pm, although hours and days vary widely according to the availability of local artists. Rum-based drinks, especially those that are pink and flavored with guava, pawpaw, and perhaps a touch of cinnamon, are especially popular. Menu items range from the simple and unpretentious (burgers, salads, and hot dogs) to more ambitious platters such as grilled wahoo or grouper with hollandaise or butter sauce, Creole-style snapper, Caribbean lobster, and shrimp.

Fort James, St. John's. ⓒ 268/462-5479. Reservations recommended. Lunch main courses $6–$22; dinner main courses $12–$22. MC, V. Daily noon–3pm and 6–11pm. Hours vary according to the owner's whims during low season.

PIZZA, BARBECUE & LUNCH ON THE RUN

At Jolly Harbour, you can visit **Al Porto** (ⓒ 268/462-7695) for a selection of some of the best pizzas on the island. If you're frequenting one of the beaches in the area, this makes an ideal stopover for a fast lunch. It also serves freshly caught seafood when available, as well as some tasty pasta dishes. Everything is offered in a laid-back alfresco setting.

At the Jolly Harbour Beach Resort, **The Dog Watch Tavern Bar & Grill** (ⓒ 268/462-6550) is one of the most popular pub-style bars on the island, offering great barbecue, drinks, and some mighty fine music most of the time. It's good for a quick bite or ideal as a rendezvous point to meet a friend over a drink.

Facing Nelson's Dockyard, you can call at **Catherine's Café,** Antigua Slipway (ⓒ 268/460-5050), for lunch on the run. It's cheap and good; light fare, even breakfast, is served on a lovely waterfront terrace facing the historical dockyard.

4 Hitting the Beaches

ON THE CARIBBEAN SIDE

There's a lovely white-sand beach on **Pigeon Point** at Falmouth Harbour, about a 4-minute drive from The Admiral's Inn (see "Accommodations You Can Afford," earlier in this chapter). With calm waters and pristine sands, this is the best beach near English Harbour, but it's likely to be crowded, especially when a cruise ship is in port. It's ideal for snorkelers and swimmers of most ages and abilities.

Dickenson Bay in the northwest, directly north of St. John's, is one of the island's finest beaches, with its wide strip of powder-soft sand and blissfully calm turquoise waters. This safe beach often attracts families with small children in tow. The center point here is the **Halcyon Cove Hotel** (ⓒ 268/462-3483), where you can rent watersports equipment. You can visit the hotel for refreshments, or mosey over to the casual bars and restaurants nearby.

On the north side of Dickenson Bay, you'll find more secluded beaches and some ideal snorkeling areas along this fan-shaped northern crown of Antigua. For a fee, locals will sometimes take beachcombers to one of the uninhabited offshore islets, such as **Prickly Pear Island,** enveloped by beautiful coral gardens. Glass-bottomed boat excursions often visit one of the island's best snorkeling spots—**Paradise Reef,** a mile-long coral garden of stunning beauty north of Dickenson Bay (see "Scuba Diving, Snorkeling & Other Watersports," below).

If you want to escape from everybody, flee to **Johnson's Point.** Between the hamlets of Johnson's Point and Urlings, at Antigua's southwestern tip below Jolly Harbour, it opens onto the tranquil Caribbean Sea. There are no facilities, but the sand is a dazzling white, and the waters, usually clear and calm, are populated with schools of rainbow-hued tropical fish.

Near Johnson's Point on the southwest coast, **Turner's Beach** is idyllic. This is one of the best places to lie out in the tropical sun, cooled by trade winds. The beach has fine white sand and gin-clear waters. If the day is clear (as it usually is), you can see the volcanic island of Montserrat.

If you head east of Urlings, toward the hamlet of Old Road, you'll reach **Carlisle Bay,** site of one of the island's most celebrated shores. Against a backdrop of coconut groves, two long beaches extend from the spot where Curtain Bluff, the island's most deluxe hotel, sits atop a bluff. The waters are impossibly blue here, where the calm Caribbean Sea meets the more turbulent Atlantic.

South of Jolly Harbour, **Driftwood Beach** is directly north of Johnson's Point, in the southwest. The white sands and calm, clear waters are delightful. It is close to all the villas at Jolly Harbour Beach Resort Marina, however, and might be overcrowded.

In the same vicinity is **Darkwood Beach,** a 5-minute drive south of Jolly Harbour Marina and the Jolly Harbour Golf Club. Here the shimmering waters are almost crystal blue. The snorkeling is great, and you can bet that gentle trade winds will keep you cool. Located in a tourist zone, it is likely to be crowded—almost impossibly so when cruise ships are in port.

If you continue north toward St. John's and cut west at the turnoff for Five Islands, you'll reach the four secluded **Hawksbill Beaches** on the Five Islands peninsula. The beaches here have white sands, dazzling blue and green waters, and coral reefs ideal for snorkeling. On one of them, you can sunbathe and swim in the buff. The Five Islands peninsula is the site of major hotel developments. Although it's secluded, the beaches might be crowded.

ON THE ATLANTIC SIDE

So far we've been on the Caribbean or western side of Antigua, but if you'd like to escape to the eastern side, fronting the Atlantic, you can head for what is perhaps Antigua's most beautiful beach, **Half Moon Bay,** which stretches for nearly a mile of white sand. It is perhaps the most beautiful beach on Antigua. Since it is on the Atlantic side, the surf is likely to be rough at times, although it draws a never-ending stream of snorkelers and windsurfers. Half Moon is now a public park and is an ideal choice for a family outing, as it is completely protected by its reef. The location is a 5-minute drive from Freetown village on the southeast coast. Because of its fine pink sand, evocative of Bermuda, this has long been a favorite of ours with its trade winds and active surf. The Half Moon Bay lies to the east of English Harbour in the vicinity of Mill Reef.

On the far eastern coast of Antigua, directly north of Half Moon Bay and to the east of the little town of Willikies, is **Long Bay,** site of Long Bay Hotel and the Pineapple Beach Club. Patrons of either property are likely to be the major beach bums on this sandy strip. Unlike the beaches previewed above, the stunning coral here are in water so shallow that you can actually walk to the reefs, although you're not supposed to harm them in any way.

In the same vicinity, **Pineapple Beach** lies a 5-minute drive from the village of Willikies heading east. It opens onto Long Bay and the east coast (Atlantic side) of Antigua. This is a fine white-sand beach, with crystal-blue waters that make it ideal for snorkeling. Most beach buffs come here just to relax in the sun on near-perfect sands.

5 Sports & Other Outdoor Pursuits

Sports such as scuba diving and fishing are very expensive in the Caribbean, often priced outside the realm of the average budget traveler's wallet. Proceed cautiously when booking a program with an outfitter, and always agree upon the cost in advance.

DAY CRUISES   All the major hotel desks can book a day cruise on the 108-foot "pirate ship," the *Jolly Roger,* Redcliffe Quay (© **268/462-2064**), the largest sailing ship in Antiguan waters. For $60 for adults and $30 for children under 12, you get a fun-filled day of sightseeing, with drinks and barbecued steak, chicken, or lobster. Lunch is combined with a snorkeling trip. On the poop deck, members of the crew teach passengers how to dance calypso. Cruises last 4 hours and sail on Tuesday and Friday. A Saturday-night dinner cruise is $50, leaving Heritage Quay in St. John's at 7pm and returning at 11pm. In spite of the high price, many budget travelers book this cruise.

GOLF   Antigua's facilities are not on par with some of the other islands', but its premier course is good. The 18-hole, par-69 **Cedar Valley Golf Club,** Friar's Hill Road (© **268/462-0161**), is 3 miles east of St. John's, near the airport. With panoramic views of Antigua's northern coast, the island's largest course was designed by the late Richard Aldridge to fit the contours of the area. Daily greens fees are $35 for 18 holes. Cart fees are $30 for 18 holes, and club rentals are $15.

HIKING   The best hiking tours in Antigua are offered by **Tropikelly Trails** (© **268/461-0383**). The trail leads through a tropical rain forest and climbs to the top of the hills in the south. Tours cost $35 per person.

PARASAILING   This sport is gaining popularity on Antigua. Facilities are available during the day, Monday to Saturday, on the beach at Dickenson Bay.

SCUBA DIVING, SNORKELING & OTHER WATERSPORTS   The reefs that fringe Antigua are home to beautiful, brilliantly colored fish. Many of the island's beaches (see "Hitting the Beaches," above) have clear, pure, calm waters that make for great snorkeling, and the most popular beaches, like Dickenson Bay, have concessions where you can rent snorkel gear and other equipment if it isn't available from your hotel.

Scuba diving is best arranged through **Dive Antigua,** at the Rex Halcyon Cove, Dickenson Bay (© **268/462-3483**), Antigua's most experienced dive operation. A resort course is $88, and a two-tank dive costs $73. A five-dive package goes for $305, and open-water certification costs $492. Prices do not include equipment; add $20.

On the northeastern coast of the island, **Long Bay Hotel** (© 268/463-2005) is a good location for swimming, sailing, water-skiing, and windsurfing. The hotel also has complete scuba facilities. Beginning snorkelers and divers alike are welcome. A boat will take groups of four or more to Green Island and Great Bird Island. The shallow side of the double reef across Long Bay is ideal for the novice, and the northeastern tip has many reefs of varying depths. A one-afternoon resort course costs $85.

An outfitter known as **Splish Splash** (© 268/462-3483) regularly offers 2-hour snorkeling jaunts over to Paradise Reef.

TENNIS   Tennis buffs will find courts at most of the major hotels, and some are lit for night games. If your hotel doesn't have a court, you can find them at the **Royal Antiguan Resort,** Deep Bay (© 268/462-3733), which has eight courts each. If you're not a guest, you'll have to book a court and pay charges that vary from hotel to hotel. Guests of a hotel usually play for free. You might also try the **Temo Sports Complex** at Falmouth Bay (© 268/463-1781), which offers two floodlit tennis courts.

WINDSURFING   Located at the Lord Nelson Beach Hotel, on Dutchman's Bay, **Windsurfing Antigua** (© 268/462-9463) offers windsurfing for the absolute beginner, the intermediate sailor, and the hard-core windsurfer. The outlet guarantees to get beginners to enjoy the sport after a 2-hour introductory lesson for $60. A 1-hour rental costs $20, a half-day $50.

6 Seeing the Sights

IN ST. JOHN'S

St. John's Cathedral, the Anglican church between Long Street and Newgate Street at Church Lane (© 268/461-0082), has resurrected itself time and again—it's been destroyed by earthquakes and rebuilt on the same site at least three times since the original structure was constructed in 1683. The present structure dates from 1845.

Exhibits at the **Museum of Antigua & Barbuda,** at Market and Church streets (© 268/462-1469), cover the island-nation's prehistoric days up to its independence from Britain in 1981. The full-size replica of a house built by Arawaks, the earliest settlers, is most intriguing. You can also see models of sugar plantations, paintings, and historical prints. It's open Monday through Friday 8:30am to 4pm and on Saturday 10am to 2pm; admission is by donation.

AROUND THE ISLAND

Eleven miles southeast of St. John's is **Nelson's Dockyard National Park** ✹✹✹ (© 268/460-1379), one of the eastern Caribbean's biggest attractions. English ships took refuge from the hurricanes in this harbor as early as 1671. The park's centerpiece is the restored Georgian naval dockyard, which was used by Admirals Nelson, Rodney, and Hood, and was the home of the British fleet during the Napoleonic Wars. From 1784 to 1787, Nelson commanded the British navy in the Leeward Islands and made his headquarters at English Harbour. The dockyard museum recaptures the 18th-century era of privateers, pirates, and battles at sea. A sort of Caribbean Williamsburg, its colonial naval buildings stand as they did when Nelson was here. Although Nelson never lived at **Admiral House** (© 268/460-8181)—it was built in 1855—his telescope and tea caddy are displayed here, along with other nautical memorabilia. Hours are daily 8am to 6pm; admission is $2.

Finds **Into the Volcano**

Ever so slowly, adventurous visitors are returning to the partially destroyed island of Montserrat, where two-thirds of the population of 12,000 had to be evacuated in 1995 after the island's volcano, Chance's Peak, blew its top. On our most recent visit, we found some 4,000 residents—both locals and ex-pats—going about their daily lives and living in the sequestered northern half of the 12-mile-long island. The volcano last stirred again in November 1999, and the path of future pyroclastic flows can more or less be predicted. That has allowed tourism to return, in ever so small a volume, to the island. In fact, the volcano has led to the promotion of Montserrat as one of the most haunting natural spectacles in the Caribbean.

The island's new commercial center is Little Bay, since the capital, Plymouth, lies under volcanic ash. The island is reached from Antigua, but its airport was destroyed by the volcano. However, twice-daily helicopter service, costing $60 one-way, wings in from Antigua, landing at Little Bay. There is also twice-daily ferry service from Antigua, costing $56 round-trip. For transportation on either, call **New World Travel** at © **800/308SURF.**

Accommodations are extremely limited, but if you want to spend the night, book into **Tropical Mansions** (© **664/491-8273**), in Sweeneys, a hotel with a pool and restaurant. When Emmanuel Galloway, the owner, built the hotel, his wife thought he was crazy. But this contractor and hardware store owner pressed on and opened this $2 million, 18-room inn, located near the heliport, just a short drive from the ferry landing.

The park itself has sandy beaches and tropical vegetation, with various species of cactus and mangroves. A migrating colony of African cattle egrets shelters in the mangroves. Archaeological sites here predate Christ. Nature trails, with coastal views, lead you through the flora. Tours of the dockyard last 15 to 20 minutes; nature walks along the trails can last anywhere from 30 minutes to 5 hours. The entrance fee is $5. Children 12 and under are admitted free. The dockyard is open daily 9am to 6pm.

The best **nature trail** on Antigua, a well-tended footpath, goes up the hill from English Harbour to **Shirley Heights** ⋆, beginning at the Galleon Beach Hotel. Follow the sign that points TO THE LOOKOUT. The trail is marked with tape on the branches of trees. Eventually you reach a summit of nearly 500 feet where you're rewarded with a panoramic view. If you'd like to get more information about the walk, you can pick up a free brochure at the dockyard at the office of the **National Parks Authority** (© **268/460-1379**). This walk is easy; it takes less than an hour to reach the peak.

Another major attraction is the **Dow's Hill Interpretation Center** (© **268/460-2777**), just 2½ miles south of the dockyard. The only one of its kind in the Caribbean, it offers multimedia presentations that cover six periods of the island's history, including the era of Amerindian hunters, the era of the British military, and the struggles connected with slavery. A belvedere opens onto a panoramic view of the park. Admission to the center, including the multimedia show, is $5. Hours are daily 9am to 5pm.

On a low hill overlooking Nelson's Dockyard, English stonemasons built **Clarence House** (✆ **268/463-1026**) to accommodate Prince William Henry, later known as the Duke of Clarence—and even later known as William IV. The future king stayed here when he was in command of the *Pegasus* in 1787. At present it's the country home of the governor of Antigua and Barbuda and is open to visitors when His Excellency is not in residence. A caretaker will show you through (it's customary to tip), and you'll see many pieces of furniture on loan from the National Trust. Princess Margaret and Lord Snowdon stayed here on their honeymoon.

On the way back, take **Fig Tree Drive** ✿, a 20-some-mile circular drive across the main mountain range. It passes through lush tropical hills and fishing villages along the southern coast. You can pick up the road just outside Liberta, north of Falmouth. Winding through a rain forest, it passes thatched villages, every one with a church and lots of goats and children running about. But don't expect fig trees (*fig* is an Antiguan name for "bananas").

Betty's Hope (✆ **268/462-1469**), just outside the village of Pares on the eastbound route to Long Bay, is Antigua's first sugar plantation (from 1650). You can tour it for $2 for adults, free for children, Tuesday to Saturday, 10am to 4pm. Exhibits in the visitor center trace the sugar era, and you can also see two windmills. Plans are underway to excavate the adjacent slave village—the first dig of a slave village in the Caribbean.

Indian Town is one of Antigua's national parks, on the island's northeastern point. Over the centuries, Atlantic breakers have lashed the rocks and carved a natural bridge known as Devil's Bridge. It's surrounded by numerous blowholes spouting surf, a dramatic sight. An environmentally protected area, Indian Town Point lies at the tip of a deep cove, Indian Town Creek. The park fronts the Atlantic at Long Bay, just west of Indian Town Creek at the eastern side of Antigua. Birders flock here to see some 36 different species. The park is blanketed mainly by the acacia tree, a dry shrub locally known as "cassie." A large, meadowy headland around Devil's Bridge makes a great spot for a picnic. Arm yourself with directions and a good map before you start out. The main highway ends at Long Bay, but several hiking trails lead to the coastline. Our favorite hike is to Indian Town Point, at a distance of 1½ miles. This is the most scenic walk in the park, passing through a protected area of great natural beauty. Long Bay is also great for snorkeling, but you need to bring your own gear.

Megaliths, at Greencastle Hill, reached by a long climb, are said to have been set up by human hands for the worship of a sun god and a moon goddess. Some experts believe, however, that the arrangement is an unusual geological formation, a volcanic rockfall.

Antigua Rum Distillery, at Rat Island (✆ **268/462-1072**), turns out fine Cavalier rum. Check at the tourist office about arranging a visit. Established in 1932, the plant is next to Deep Water Harbour.

7 Shopping

Most of the shops are clustered on St. Mary's Street or High Street in St. John's. Some shops are open Monday to Saturday 8:30am to noon and 1 to 4pm, but this varies greatly from store to store—Antiguan shopkeepers are an independent lot. Many of them close at noon on Thursday.

Value Cheap Thrills: What to See & Do for Free (Well, Almost) on Antigua

- **Enjoy Beaches, Beaches & More Beaches.** All of Antigua's beaches are open to the public, and they're free. The only time you'll pay is when you want to buy something—perhaps some handcrafts being hawked right on the beach, even a cold beer, and most definitely watersports rentals, which can be expensive (so be duly warned). If a cruise ship docks, beaches tend to be crowded on the western or Caribbean side, so head for the Atlantic or eastern side. The waters aren't as tranquil here, but you'll escape the hordes.

- **Explore Indian Town National Park.** An environmentally protected area, Indian Town Point lies at the tip of a deep cove, Indian Town Creek. This area of natural beauty is found at Long Bay, just west of Indian Town Creek, on the eastern side of Antigua, fronting the Atlantic. Birders flock here to see some 36 different species. Along the shore a cove called Devil's Bridge has been created by the ocean pounding against the cliffs. It took eons of time to hollow out this natural bridge across the crashing surf. The water throws up a neat display of foam from time to time. Around Devil's Bridge there is a large, meadowy headland that would make an ideal spot for a picnic. At several blowholes, sprays of water surge violently through vents in the rocky coast. It's a dramatic sight—and it's free. Arm yourself with directions and a good map before starting out. The main highway ends at Long Bay, but several trails lead to the coastline, and they're ideal for hikes. Long Bay is also a great place for snorkeling.

- **Drive Along Fig Tree Drive.** There's no better drive on Antigua, even though the road is bumpy and potholed, than Fig Tree Drive. The road has no fig trees; in Antigua, *fig* is the name for "banana." The road is unmarked—in fact, there are almost no road signs on Antigua. But the drive begins at the little coral-built Catholic church just outside the hamlet of Liberta, north of Falmouth. Once you're here, it's easy to spot. Head southwest, going through the island's only rain forest and its hilliest section. The road rises and falls steeply. Of course, you'll see plenty of bananas along with coconut groves and mango trees—a lush tropical setting. The drive descends to the village of Old Road and the Curtain Bluff area.

- **Take in View from Shirley Heights.** The view from Shirley Heights, on the southern rim of Antigua, is arguably the most famous in the

You'll find many duty-free items for sale, including English woolens and linens, and you can also purchase several specialized items made on Antigua, such as original pottery, local straw work, Antiguan rum, and silk-screened, hand-printed local designs on fabrics, as well as mammy bags, floppy foldable hats, and shell curios.

If you want an island-made bead necklace, don't bother to go shopping; just lie on the beach, anywhere, and some "bead lady" will find you.

Caribbean. The road here lies to the east side of English Harbour, all named for General Thomas Shirley, the governor of the British Leeward Islands from 1781 to 1791. While you take in the view, you are likely to be entertained by a Rastafarian steel band (which would like a tip, of course). On the way here, you'll pass signs of former British colonialism—barracks, fortifications, powder magazines, all in picturesque ruins now, remains of a bygone era. A restaurant on the bluff provides light refreshments after you take in that stunning view.

- **Forage in a Fortress.** In the 1700s, the coastline of the island was ringed with British forts, all in ruins today. Fort and archaeology buffs can enjoy rummaging through the ruins. Even if there isn't much left to see, the views from these former military strongholds are among the most panoramic in the Caribbean—and you can visit them for free. You can begin at St. John's harbor, which was once guarded by Fort Barrington on the south and Fort James on the north. Later you can head down to Fort James Bay, where you'll find a couple of bars right on the sand, including Russell's Beach Bar, an ideal place to unwind with a beer on Sunday afternoon, when it's most active.

- **Take a Bus to the Market.** If you're staying outside St. John's, take a local bus into the city on market day on Saturday morning. It's best between 8am and noon. Hop on the bus and be prepared for anything. Many of the locals with stuff to sell get right on the bus with what they'll be peddling in town at the market. Often their wares are live—chickens, birds, whatever. Sometimes it's luscious fruit or the island's most beautiful flowers, and certainly plenty of handcrafts. Locals will immediately sense you're a foreigner and start bargaining with you before you even get to the market.

- **Shop the Quays.** Even if you don't buy anything, the thrill is in the adventure of shopping two of the Caribbean's most colorful quays, Heritage Quay and Redcliffe Quay, both in St. John's. Sometimes live musicians entertain you as you browse. Heritage Quay sells a little bit of everything—sexy lingerie, T-shirts, designer luggage, you name it. At Redcliffe, which was transformed from old dockside warehouses, you can wander and browse among Antiguan handcrafts and clothing, see the latest French fashions, purchase jewelry and pottery, and have a pizza.

If you're in St. John's on a Saturday morning, you can attend the **fruit and vegetable market** at the lower end of Market Street. Locally made handcrafts are also offered for sale. And the incredibly sweet and juicy Antiguan black pineapple is worth the trip into town alone.

Begin your bargain-shopping jaunt at St. John's at **Redcliffe Quay** on the waterfront at the southern edge of town. Set around landscaped courtyards, all tree-shaded, you'll find nearly three dozen boutiques, many offering specialty items sold nowhere else. Redcliffe Quay was a slave-trading quarter, but after the abolition of slavery the quay was filled with grog shops and merchants selling various wares. Now it has been redeveloped and contains interesting shops in former warehouses, all open Monday to Saturday. Our favorite is **A Thousand Flowers** (✆ **268/462-4264**), which sells Indonesian batiks crafted on Antigua into sundresses, knock-'em-dead shirts, sarongs, and rompers.

At the **Gazebo** (✆ **268/460-2776**), expect a little bit of everything, a mass of south-of-the-border pottery to Indonesian wood items and stunning blue-glaze plates. **West Indies Oil Co.** (✆ **268/462-0141**) is a big hit with kids, offering British toys, beach games, island crafts, and more. Additional Redcliffe Quay shops include **Isis** (✆ **268/462-4602**) for unique Egyptian jewelry, leather, finely woven cotton, and handcrafts, and **The Goldsmitty** (✆ **268/462-4601**), where precious stones are set in unique, exquisite creations of 14- and 18-karat gold.

Noreen Phillips, Redcliffe Quay (✆ **268/462-3127**), is one of the island's major fashion outlets. Cruise ship passengers beeline here for both casual wear and beaded glitzy dress clothes. **Island Hopper,** Jardine Court, St. Mary's Street (✆ **268/462-2972**), specializes in Caribbean-made gifts and clothing, including T-shirts and casual wear, spices, coffees, and handcrafts.

The Scent Shop, Lower High Street (✆ **268/462-0303**), is the oldest and best perfume shop on the island, and also stocks an array of crystal. **Shoul's Chief Store,** St. Mary's Street at Market Street (✆ **268/462-1140**), is an all-purpose department store selling fabric, appliances, souvenirs (more than 300 kinds), and general merchandise.

Heritage Quay, Antigua's first shopping-and-entertainment complex, features some 40 duty-free shops and an arcade for local artists and craftspeople. Its restaurants and food court offer a range of cuisines and views of St. John's Harbour. Many shops are open all day, Monday through Saturday.

At the foot of St. Mary's Street, stop in at **Benjies Photo Centre** (✆ **268/462-3619**), a Kodak distributor and photofinisher, selling film and brand-name cameras. **Fashiondock** (✆ **268/462-9672**) is known for its duty-free Versace jeans and accessories, plus other Italian styles. **Sunseakers** (✆ **268/462-4523**) carries the largest collection of duty-free swimwear in the Caribbean. **Colombian Emeralds** (✆ **268/462-3462**) is the world's largest retailer of these gemstones. **Albert's Jewelry** (✆ **268/462-3108**) sells the best selection of watches on Antigua, as well as china and crystal. Nick Maley, a makeup artist who worked on *Star Wars* and *The Empire Strikes Back,* founded **Island Arts,** upstairs at Heritage Quay (✆ **268/462-2787**). You can purchase his own fine-art reproductions or browse through everything from low-cost prints to works by artists exhibited at the Museum of Modern Art in New York. You can also visit Nick's home and studio at Aiton Place, on Sandy Lane directly behind the Hodges Bay Club, 4 miles from St. John's. The residence is open Monday to Wednesday and on Friday, but call first (✆ **268/461-6324**).

Other worthwhile specialty stores include **Caribelle Batik,** St. Mary's Street (✆ **268/462-2972**), a reasonably priced outlet for the Romney Manor workshop on St. Kitts. The Caribelle label consists of batik and tie-dye beach wraps, scarves, and casual wear for women and men.

Rain Boutique, Lower St. Mary's (✆ **268/462-0118**), offers casual clothes, formal wear, hats, scarves, shoes, jewelry, and handbags.

At Falmouth Harbour, **Seahorse Studios, Art Gallery & Gift Shop** (✆ **268/460-1457**) specializes in original art and limited-edition prints, with lots of seascapes, plus batiks, T-shirts, and the pottery of Nancy Nicholson, considered the island's best craftsperson.

The best for last: Head for **Harmony Hall,** in Brown's Bay Mill, near Free-town (*(C) 268/460-4120*), following the signs along the road to Freetown and Half Moon Bay. This restored 1843 plantation house and sugar mill overlooking Nonsuch Bay is ideal for a lunch stopover or a shopping expedition. It displays an excellent selection of Caribbean arts and crafts. Lunch is served daily from noon to 4pm, featuring Green Island lobster, flying fish, and other specialties. Sunday is barbecue day.

8 Antigua After Dark

Antigua has some of the best steel bands in the Caribbean. Most nightlife revolves around the hotels, unless you want to roam Antigua at night, looking for a hot local club. If you're going out for the night, make arrangements to have a taxi pick you up; otherwise, you could end up stranded in the wild somewhere. Regrettably, taxis can be expensive, so make sure you ask your hotel what taxi fare is likely to cost before you set out.

The **Royal Casino,** in the Royal Antiguan Hotel, Deep Bay (*(C) 268/462-3733*), has blackjack, baccarat, roulette, craps, and slot machines. It's open daily from 2pm until around 1am, and there's no cover. Far better and the most glamorous place to go if you have time for only one casino is the **St. James's Club** at Mamora Bay (*(C) 268/463-1113*), which has the island's most flamboyant gambling palace. Other action is found at **King's Casino** on Heritage Quay (*(C) 268/462-1727*), the only casino in St. John's proper.

Steel bands, limbo dancers, calypso singers, folkloric groups—there's always something happening by night on Antigua. Your hotel can probably tell you where to go on any given night. The following clubs are reliable hot spots:

Ribbit Night Club, in Donovans, Green Bay (*(C) 268/462-7996*), is the liveliest club on Antigua and attracts mostly locals, ranging from the prime minister to young couples. Overlooking Deep Water Harbour and St. John's, it's known for hot music and dancing that lasts until all hours. You can hear reggae, some of the best Caribbean steel bands, and international music. There's a cover charge on weekends.

Stop in at the **Bay House,** Tradewinds Hotel, Marble Hill (*(C) 268/462-1223*), for the island's best mix of singles (both straight and gay). Live reggae is often performed on Monday and Wednesday night at **Colombo's** at the Galleon Beach Club in English Harbour (*(C) 268/460-1452*).

Live nightly entertainment takes place right on the beach at **Millers by the Sea,** at Runaway Beach (*(C) 268/462-9414*). Spilling over onto the sands, its happy hour is the best in town.

At English Harbour, action centers on **The Admiral's Inn** (*(C) 268/460-1027*), a barefoot-friendly kind of place where you can always find a game of darts. Thursday and Saturday nights feature live music, most often a local 14-piece steel band. Try one of Norman's daiquiris (the island's best) and ask the bartender about the famous guests he's served, from Richard Burton to Prince Charles.

4

Aruba

Honeymooners, sun worshipers, snorkelers, sailors, and weekend gamblers find that the Dutch island of Aruba suits their needs just fine. Forget lush vegetation here—that's impossible with only 17 inches of rainfall annually. Aruba is dry and sunny almost year-round, with clean, exhilarating air like that found in the desert of Palm Springs, California. Along with the very low humidity, trade winds keep the island from becoming uncomfortably hot.

The smallest of the ABC Islands (Aruba, Bonaire, and Curaçao), Aruba is 20 miles long and 6 miles wide, with a landmass of 115 square miles. Its coastline on the leeward side is smooth and serene, with white-sand beaches; but on the eastern coast, the windward Atlantic side, it looks rugged and wild.

Aruba's Palm Beach, one of the best beaches in the world, draws visitors in droves, as do its glittering casinos. As you lie back along the 7-mile stretch of white-sand beach, enjoying an 82°F

(28°C) daytime temperature, you're not harassed by the locals peddling wares you don't want. There's almost no racial tension and, chances are, you won't get mugged.

Aruba is not the best island for vacationers on a budget. In winter, the large resort hotels and timeshare units are expensive; rates begin at around $150 a night. And Aruba does not have the number of inexpensive guesthouses and small inns that many other islands do. However, there are numerous package deals, which a good travel agent can help you find (see "Package Deals" in chapter 2). Restaurant tabs can also be high, since all food has to be imported onto desert-dry Aruba, but we've found a few affordable choices for you.

Aruba stands outside the hurricane path. Its coastline on the leeward side is smooth and serene, with sandy beaches; but on the eastern coast, the windward side, the look is rugged and wild, typical of the windswept Atlantic.

1 Essentials

VISITOR INFORMATION

Before you leave home, contact the **Aruba Tourism Authority** at the following locations: 1000 Harbor Blvd., Weehawken, NJ (© **201/330-0800;** fax 201/330-8757; newjersey@toaruba.com); One Financial Plaza, Suite 136, Fort Lauderdale, FL 33394 (© **954/767-6477;** fax 954/767-0432; ata.florida@toaruba.com); 199 14th St., NE, Suite 2008, Atlanta, GA 39309 (© **404/892-7822;** fax 404/873-2193; ata.atlanta@toaruba.com); 12707 North Freeway, Suite 138, Houston, TX 77060 (© **713/872-7822;** fax 713/872-7872; ata.houston@toaruba.com); Suite 201, Business Centre 5875, Highway 7, Vaughan, Ontario L4L 8Z7 (© **905/264-3434**). There is no information office in the U.K.

Information is on the Web at **www.aruba.com.**

Aruba

Andicuri Inn **4**
Aruba Blue Village Suites **7**
Cactus Apartments **10**
Caribbean Town Beach Resort **2**
Coconut Inn **5**
Mi Cielo Apartments **3**
The Mill Resort **6**
Sunset Boulevard Studios **8**
Turibana Plaza **9**
Vistalmar Apartments **1**

California Lighthouse
California Point
Malmok Beach
Hadicurari (Fishermen's Hut)
Palm Beach
Alto Vista Chapel
Eagle Beach
Noord
Manchebo Beach
Druif Beach
Oranjestad
Casibari
Caribbean Sea
Bushiribana
Natural Bridge
Ayo Rock Formations
Queen Beatrix Airport
Hooiberg
Santa Cruz
Caves of Canashito
ARIKOK
NATIONAL
PARK
Boca Prins Sand Dunes
Fontein Cave
Quadirikiri Cave
Huliba Cave
Spanish Lagoon
Jamanota
Caribbean Sea
Savaneta
San Nicolas
Boca Grandi
Rodger's Beach
Seroe Colorado
Baby Beach
Colorado Point

✈ Airport
🏖 Beach
⚲ Lighthouse

0   3 mi
0   3 km

N

Once you're on the island, for information go to the **Aruba Tourism Authority** at L. G. Smith Blvd. 172, Oranjestad (© 297/8-23777).

GETTING THERE

Before you book your airline tickets, read the section on "Package Deals" in chapter 2—it could save you a bundle. Even if you don't book a package, see that chapter's tips on finding the best airfare.

On **American Airlines** (© 800/433-7300; www.im.aa.com), Aruba-bound passengers can catch a daily nonstop 4½-hour flight from New York's JFK airport. American also offers daily nonstop flights from Boston, Miami, and San Juan, Puerto Rico. American offers lots of great-value packages to Aruba, including a selection of several resorts. Ask for their tour department, or talk to your travel agent.

ALM (© 800/327-7230; www.alm-airlines.com) has good connections into Aruba from certain parts of the United States, but no direct flights. All flights stop first in Curaçao.

US Airways (© 800/428-4322; www.usairways.com) offers daily nonstop flights from Charlotte, NC, Philadelphia, and Pittsburgh.

Delta (© 800/241-4141; www.delta.com) operates nonstop service from Atlanta, and it also flies in from Kennedy Airport in New York.

Continental Airlines (© 800/231-0856; www.continental.com) also flies to Aruba from Houston. There are also nonstop flights from Newark on Monday, Wednesday, and Friday.

United Airlines (© 800/241-6522; www.ual.com) has weekend service from Chicago, but only in winter.

Air Canada (© 800/776-3000 in the U.S., or 888/247-2262 in Canada; www.aircanada.ca) has good connections from Toronto and Quebec to Miami. Once in Miami, Canadians and other passengers can fly Air Aruba to the island.

GETTING AROUND

BY TAXI   In Aruba, the taxis are unmetered but rates are fixed, so tell the driver your destination and ask the fare before getting in. The main office is on Sands Street between the bowling center and Taco Bell. A **dispatch office** is located at the Bosabao (©) **297/8-22116**). A ride from the airport to most of the hotels, including those at Palm Beach, costs about $16 to $18 per car, with a maximum of four passengers allowed. Some locals don't tip, although we suggest tipping, especially if the driver has helped you with luggage. Additionally, since it's next to impossible to locate a taxi on some parts of the island, it's a good idea to ask the taxi driver to return to pick you up at a certain time if you're going to a remote destination.

You'll also usually find the English-speaking drivers willing tour guides. Most seem well informed about their island and eager to share it with you. A 1-hour tour (and you don't need much more than that) costs from $30 for a maximum of four passengers.

BY RENTAL CAR   Unlike most Caribbean islands, Aruba makes it easy to rent a car. The roads connecting the major tourist attractions are excellent, and a valid U.S. or Canadian driver's license is accepted by each of the major car-rental companies. The three major U.S. car-rental companies maintain offices on Aruba, and also have airport branches and kiosks at the major hotels. No taxes are imposed on car rentals on Aruba, but insurance can be tricky. Even

---

Fun Fact Festival Time

Many visitors come here for the annual pre-Lenten **Carnival,** a month-long festival held in February or March with events day and night. With music, dancing, parades, costumes, and "jump-ups" (Caribbean hoe-downs), Carnival is the highlight of Aruba's winter season.

---

with the purchase of a collision-damage waiver, a driver is still responsible for the first $300 to $500 worth of damage. (Avis doesn't even offer this waiver, so in the event of an accident—unless you have private insurance—you'll be liable for up to the full value of damage to your car.) Rental rates range between $50 and $70 per day.

Try **Budget Rent-a-Car,** at Divi Aruba Beach Resort, L. G. Smith Blvd. 93 (© **800/472-3325** in the U.S., or 297/8-24185); **Hertz,** L. G. Smith Blvd. 142 (© **800/654-3001** in the U.S., or 297/8-24545), and **Avis,** Kolibristraat 14 (© **800/331-1084** in the U.S., or 297/8-25496). Budget requires that renters be at least 25; Avis, 23; and Hertz, 21.

Car rentals are also available at **Dollar Rent-a-Car** (© **800/800-4000** in the U.S.; www.dollarcar.com), whose two branches are at Grendeaweg 15 (© 297/8-22783), and at the Queen Beatrix Airport (© **297/8-25651**). **National** (© **800/CAR-RENT** in the U.S.; www.nationalcar.com) has branches at Tanki Leendert 170 (© **297/8-71967**), and at the Queen Beatrix Airport (© **297/8-25451**).

For a better deal, consider **Hedwina Car Rental,** Bubali 93A (© **297/8-76442,** or 297/8-30880 at the airport). If you take a car for a week, you sometimes pay for only 5 days. Another agency to consider is **Thrifty Car Rental,** Balashi 65 (© **297/8-55300,** or 297/8-35335 at the airport), which offers good deals, with many rentals beginning at $42 to $52 per day. You can also rent Jeeps from $65 per day.

BY MOTORCYCLE & MOPED   Since Aruba's roads are good, and the terrain is flat, many visitors like to rent mopeds and motorcycles. They're available at **George's Scooter Rental,** L. G. Smith Blvd. 136 D (© **297/8-25975**), and **Nelson Motorcycle Rental,** Gasparito 10A, Noord (© **297/8-66801**). Scooters rent for $30 per day and motorcycles for $45 to $100.

Melcor Cycle Rental, Bubali 106B (© **297/8-75203**), in front of the Adventure Golf Club, rents scooters for $32 per day. You can also rent dirt bikes and street bikes, beginning at $45 per day. These are cash prices; a 4% handling charge is assessed if you use a credit card. You can also find rentals at **Semver Cycle Rental,** Noord 22 (© **297/8-66851**), where bikes begin at $25 per day.

BY BUS   Aruba has excellent bus service, with a round-trip fare between the beach hotels and Oranjestad of $2. Bus schedules are available at the Arubus Office at the central bus station on Zoutmanstraat. Your hotel reception desk will also know the approximate times the buses pass by where you're staying. There's regular daily service from 6am to midnight. Try to have the exact change. For **bus schedules and information,** call the **Arubus Co.** (© 297/8-27089).

 **FAST FACTS: Aruba**

Banks   Banks are open Monday to Friday 8am to noon and 1:30 to 3:45pm. The most central bank is **Aruba Bank** at Caya Betico Croes 41 (© **297/ 8-21550**). It's not hard to find an ATM (including one at the airport).

Currency   The currency is the **Aruba florin (AFl)**, which is divided into 100 cents. Silver coins are in denominations of 5, 10, 25, and 50 cents and 1 and 2½ florins. The 50¢ piece, the square "yotin," is Aruba's best-known coin. The current exchange rate is 1.77AFl to U.S.$1 (1AFl is worth about 56¢). U.S. dollars, traveler's checks, and major credit and charge cards are widely accepted throughout the island. *Note:* Unless otherwise stated, *prices quoted in this chapter are in U.S. dollars.*

Documents   To enter Aruba, U.S. and Canadian citizens and British subjects may submit a valid passport or a birth certificate. We recommend that you bring a passport whenever you're visiting a foreign country.

Electricity   The electricity is 110 volts AC, 60 cycles, the same as in the United States.

Emergencies   For the **police,** dial © **11100.** For a **medical emergency,** dial © **74300.** For the **fire** department, call © **115.**

Language   The official language is Dutch, but nearly everybody speaks English. Spanish is also widely spoken.

Medical Care   To receive medical care, go to the **Horacio Oduber Hospital** on L. G. Smith Boulevard (© **297/8-74300;** also the number to call in case of a medical emergency). It's a modern building near Eagle Beach, with excellent medical facilities. Hotels also have medical doctors on call, and there are good dental facilities as well (appointments can be made through your hotel).

Safety   Aruba is one of the Caribbean's safest destinations, in spite of its numerous hotels and gambling casinos. Of course, some pickpockets and purse-snatchers are around, so guard your valuables. Never leave them unattended on the beach or even in a locked car.

Taxes & Service   The government of Aruba imposes a 6% room tax, as well as a $34.25 airport departure tax. At your hotel, you'll have a 15% to 20% service charge added to charges for room, food, and beverages.

Telecommunications   To call Aruba from the United States, dial **011** (the international access code), then **297** (the country code for Aruba), and then **8** (the area code) and the five-digit local number. Once on Aruba, only the five-digit local number is necessary to call another number on the island.

Time   Aruba is on Atlantic standard time year-round, so most of the year Aruba is 1 hour ahead of Eastern standard time (when it's 10am on Aruba, it's 9am in New York). When daylight saving time is in effect in the United States, clocks in New York and Aruba show the same time.

Tipping   A service charge of 11% is added to most hotel bills, and restaurants in general add a 10% to 15% service charge to the final tab. If you're not sure whether this charge has been added, you can ask. If it's not added, Arubans traditionally add 10% to the check. Taxi drivers get 10%

to 15%, and porters and bellmen get about $1 per bag, with hotel maids in budget and moderate hotels getting $1.50 a day.

Water   The water, which comes from the world's second-largest desalination plant, is pure.

2 Accommodations You Can Afford

Most of Aruba's hotels are bustling and self-contained resorts. Unfortunately for the budget traveler, there's a dearth of family or budget hotels. The few guesthouses tend to be booked up early in winter by faithful returning visitors. In season, you must make reservations well in advance; don't ever arrive expecting to find a room on the spot—you must have an address to give Immigration when you arrive on Aruba. Don't forget to ask if the 6% room tax and any service charge are included in the rates quoted when you make your reservation.

Andicuri Inn   If you'd like to stay in the capital, Oranjestad, just 5 minutes from the center and only 10 minutes from the nearest good beach, consider this affordable little choice. It offers fully furnished and comfortable apartments, each with a king-size bed with a good mattress, cable TV, and walk-in closet, plus a kitchen with a built-in stove and a small but tidy bathroom with shower stalls. There's little style here, but you get reasonable comfort at a good price. The place is for independent types who don't expect resort-style amenities. For your other diversions, you have to go outside the property.

De La Sallestraat 13, Oranjestad, Aruba. ⒸⓉ **297/8-21539.** Fax 297/8-29922. 18 apts. Winter $55 apt for 1 or 2. Off-season $50 apt for 1 or 2. Two children 11 and under stay free in parents' room. MC, V. *In room:* A/C, TV.

Aruba Blue Village Suites ⭐ *Value*   If you can forgo a beachfront location, you'll find one of Aruba's best deals at this complex. Off-season, it's a sweet bargain if four people share a junior suite or six people share a two-bedroom suite. The accommodations are in the typical resort style, plain but comfortable, yet features include cable TV, a separate bathroom with shower, and a fully equipped kitchenette. More than half of the suites come with pull-out sofas. The mattresses are firm, and the bathrooms are motel standard but adequate. The complex of single-story apartments lies in a residential area removed from the hotel strip. A free bus service will haul you to the beach, 5 minutes away, and you're close to casinos and nightlife.

Cunucu Abao 37, Aruba. ⒸⓉ **297/8-78618.** Fax 297/8-70081. www.arubabluevillage.com. 56 units. Winter $111–$140 single or double. Off-season $88–$105 single or double. AE, MC, V. **Amenities:** Poolside bar, 2 pools, 2 sun terraces, table tennis, children's playground. *In room:* A/C, TV.

Cactus Apartments   This is a small, inexpensive apartment complex whose mustard-colored exterior blends into the surrounding arid, cactus-dotted landscape. Its oldest section was built in the early 1980s. The nearest beach is 2 miles away, so a car is recommended for anyone who wants to stay here—although owner Jacinto Tromp is happy to tell you how to get around on the island's network of buses and other public transport. There's neither a bar nor restaurant on the premises, but each basic and rather small guest room contains its own kitchenette. Each room also has a rather thin mattresses and a tiny, shower-only bathroom. Nevertheless, the place is reasonably comfortable.

Matadera 5, Aruba. © **297/8-22903.** Fax 297/8-20433. cactus.apts@setarnet.aw. 13 apts. Winter $55 apt for 1 or 2; $65 apt for 3. Off-season $45 apt for 1 or 2; $55 apt for 3. AE, MC, V. **Amenities:** Laundry. *In room:* A/C, TV, kitchenette, no phone.

Coconut Inn   Within a 7-minute walk from the landlocked village of Noord, this affordable hotel is built in five sections. Considering what beachfront hotels a 10-minute drive away charge, the Coconut's rates are a steal. The location is convenient to supermarkets, and a public bus stops a short walk away. Units come in an array of styles that include relatively cramped studios as well as conventional rooms and one-bedroom suites, which both contain almost the same amount of floor space. All accommodations are furnished in a somewhat unimaginative motel style, each with a balcony or patio and a kitchenette or at least a microwave and refrigerator. The beds are good, with fairly new mattresses, but the shower bathrooms are typically small, with not enough room to spread out your stuff. There's no maid service on Sunday.

Noord 31, Aruba. © **297/8-66288.** Fax 297/8-65433. www.coconutinn.com. 40 units. Winter $75 studio for 1 or 2; $90 double or 1-bedroom suite for 2. Off-season $60 studio for 1 or 2; $70 double or 1-bedroom suite for 2. Extra person $20 in winter; $15 in off-season. Rates include breakfast. MC, V. **Amenities:** Restaurant, bar, pool. *In room:* A/C, TV, kitchenette (some units).

Mi Cielo Apartments   Although these incredible rates—at least for Aruba—might not hold indefinitely, Mi Cielo offers one of the island's lowest-priced places to stay. A local lawyer runs the property, and there's little on-site management, so this choice is really for self-sufficient types. You're in a good location, however, between beach and town, about a 10-minute walk each way. In this one-story property, the units are absolutely standard, with no frills or style, but each is reasonably comfortable and pleasantly furnished, with firm mattresses, a patio, and a tiny bathroom with a shower stall.

Italiesstraat 12, Aruba. © **297/8-20021.** Fax 297/8-30076. 7 apts. Winter $75 1-bedroom apt. Off-season $65 1-bedroom apt. V. *In room:* A/C, TV, kitchenette, no phone.

Sunset Boulevard Studios *Value*   In high-priced Aruba, this complex comes as a welcome relief to the purse. Facing a garden, the studios are comfortably furnished, each with a small but adequately equipped kitchenette and a compact bathroom with shower. The most desirable accommodations face the ocean, so you can enjoy a sunset drink on your terrace. One of the units is large enough for a family.

Palm Beach, Aruba. © **297/8-63940.** www.arubasunsetstudios.com. 9 units. Winter $85–$100 double. Off-season $65–$80 double. MC, V. **Amenities:** Pool, room service, babysitting, laundry/dry cleaning. *In room:* A/C, TV, kitchenette, minibar, coffeemaker, safe.

Turibana Plaza ★ *Value*   This modern complex of rather standard apartments is only minutes from the best white, sandy beaches of Aruba as well as some terrific restaurants near Oranjestad. And its prices are among the island's most affordable. For those cooking in, a supermarket is less than a mile away. Because of their low rates, the apartments are booked early in winter, so reserve as far in advance as possible. The medium-size bedrooms have wall-to-wall carpeting and plain, simple furnishings, with a full kitchenette. The mattresses, although not new, are still rather firm, and the bathrooms are well maintained and rather efficient, with adequate shelf space and a shower. Some guests like the place so much that they check in for a month. On the ground level is an excellent restaurant. Although the Turibana Plaza isn't a full-service hotel, it does offer daily maid service and laundry facilities.

Noord 124, Aruba. © **297/8-67292.** Fax 297/8-62658. 19 apts. Winter $75 apt for 2; $152.50 apt for 4. Off-season $50 apt for 2; $95 apt for 4. Extra person $15 in winter; $10 in off-season. AE, MC, V. **Amenities:** Restaurant, maid service, laundry. In room: A/C, TV, kitchenette.

Vistalmar Apartments (Value An affordable and intimate place to stay on Aruba, this property doesn't have access to the celebrated beaches, but it lies across from the water in a residential section near the airport. It's quite a bargain, however, for not only will you have complimentary use of boats, bikes, picnic coolers, snorkeling equipment, beach towels, and an outdoor grill, you also get a car! The complex of apartments is in two similar buildings, each with a balcony or courtyard offering water views. A little more stylish than some of the more barebones apartment units rented on the island, the accommodations here are spacious and furnished for comfort. Your hosts, among the island's more personable, are Aby and Karty Yarzagaray, who have a wealth of island information. They even stock your refrigerator with food for your first night here.

Each apartment has a king-size bed with a good mattress, a well-maintained bathroom with a tub and shower, a separate dressing area, a fully equipped kitchen, and a living room with a sleeper sofa. There's also a second sleeping room and a sun porch.

Bicutiweb 28, Aruba. © **297/8-28579.** Fax 297/8-22200. 8 units. Winter $100 apt with car. Off-season $75 apt with car. No credit cards. **Amenities:** Boats, snorkeling equipment, car, bikes. In room: A/C, kitchenette, fridge and complimentary food upon arrival, no phone.

WORTH A SPLURGE

Caribbean Town Beach Resort   It's seen the wear and tear of the years, but this longtime favorite has long been known as one of the best moderately priced choices on Aruba. On the south side of Oranjestad, it's really like a motel and is frequented by business travelers. An upgraded and enlarged beach is 200 yards (182m) across the street. The bedrooms are a bit dark, and both standard and superior rooms have ceiling fans, balconies, refrigerators, and microwaves, whereas the studios and apartments offer fuller kitchenettes. New owners have spruced up the bedrooms with furniture and mattresses and rejuvenated the plumbing with new shower units.

A daily happy hour with free snacks and live music is a draw for the budget traveler, and you can eat all the prime rib you want at Friday night's carvery, one of Aruba's best food values. The hotel's beach club has reopened as Havana Beach Club and is now one of the island hot spots.

L. G. Smith Blvd. 2, Aruba. © **297/8-23380.** Fax 297/8-33208. info@aruba-caribtownresort.com. 62 units. Winter $135 single; $145 double; $165–$175 1-bedroom studio; $205–$215 2-bedroom apt. Off-season $100–$110 single or double; $135 1-bedroom studio; $140–$150 2-bedroom apt. Extra person $10; children 11 and under stay free in parents' room. MAP (breakfast and dinner) $35 per person extra. AE, MC, V. **Amenities:** 2 restaurants, bar, beach club. In room: A/C, TV, no phone.

The Mill Resort ★★   Opened in 1990 and enlarged in 1994, this complex of two-story concrete buildings with red roofs is set in an arid, rather dusty location inland from the beach but within a 7-minute trek of Eagle Beach (which is used by such mega-hotels as the Hilton). It's adjacent to a large, modern re-creation of a Dutch windmill, which has become a kitschy Aruban landmark. Units ring a large swimming pool. The room decor is tropical, with white rattan, carpeting or white floor tiles, and pastel-colored curtains and draperies. The rooms and furnishings are standard motel. Mattresses are renewed every 2 years. The bathrooms, although small, are adequate, with well-maintained plumbing, including shower stalls.

This hotel is best for independent types who don't mind exploring Aruba for dining, drinking, and diversions. Since most units have kitchenettes (or at least a refrigerator), many guests cook in. In many rooms you'll find king-size beds and Jacuzzi-style bathtubs.

L. G. Smith Blvd. 330, Palm Beach, Aruba. ✆ **297/8-67700.** Fax 297/8-67271. www.themillresort.com. 200 units. Winter $170–$205 single or double with refrigerator; $290–$385 minisuite with kitchenette for 1 or 2. Off-season $70–$105 single or double with refrigerator; $175–$200 studio or minisuite with kitchenette for 1 or 2. AE, DC, MC, V. **Amenities:** Pool, fitness center, sauna, salon, massage, laundry. *In room:* A/C, TV.

3 Great Deals on Dining

Regrettably, nearly all food on the island has to be imported, making Aruba one of the higher-priced dining destinations in the Caribbean. But there are some bargains here. The trick is, you have to order from the lower end of the menu and avoid the high-priced fish dishes, which often cost from $25 or more.

Brisas del Mar ✶ *Finds* SEAFOOD   A 15-minute drive east of Oranjestad, near the police station, Brisas del Mar, in very simple surroundings right at the water's edge, is a little hut with an air-conditioned bar where locals gather to drink the day away. The place is often jammed on weekends with many of the same locals who come here to drink and dance. In back, the tables are open to sea breezes, and nearby you can see the catch of the day, perhaps wahoo, being sliced and sold to local buyers. Specialties include a mixed seafood platter, baby shark, and broiled lobster; you can order meat and poultry dishes as well, including tenderloin steak and broiled chicken. It's all solid, traditional fare—nothing too subtle or fancy.

Savaneta 222A. ✆ **297/8-47718.** Reservations required. Main courses $12–$32. AE, MC, V. Tues–Sun noon–2:30pm; daily 6–9:30pm.

Charlie's Bar and Restaurant SEAFOOD/INTERNATIONAL   Charlie's is the best reason to visit San Nicolas. The bar dates from 1941 and is the most overly decorated joint in the West Indies, sporting an array of memorabilia and local souvenirs. Where roustabouts and roughnecks once brawled, you'll now find tables filled with contented visitors admiring thousands of pennants, banners, and trophies dangling from the high ceiling. Two-fisted drinks are still served, but the menu has improved since the good old days, when San Nicolas was one of the toughest towns in the Caribbean. You can now enjoy freshly made soup, grilled scampi, Creole-style squid, and *churrasco* (grilled meat). Sirloin steak and red snapper are usually featured. Come here for the good times and the brew, not necessarily for the food, although it isn't bad.

Main St., San Nicolas (a 25-min. drive east of Oranjestad). ✆ **297/8-45086.** Daily soup $6; main courses $10–$20. AE, DISC, MC, V. Mon–Sat noon–9:30pm (bar open till 10pm).

Hadicurari ✶ *Finds* ARUBAN/SEAFOOD   Increasingly, visitors to Aruba are escaping restaurants in the high-rise hotels along Palm Beach to discover local dives that serve seafood. Hadicurari lies on a beach just to the north of the Marriott Hotel on Palm Beach. This dive is run by a local fisherman, so naturally the catch of the day—always perfectly grilled—is the specialty of the kitchen. You can also order shrimp Creole or sautéed conch. Live music from local bands is a feature on Saturday and Sunday.

L. G. Smith Blvd. 97. ✆ **297/8-60820.** Main courses $7–$15. No credit cards. Daily 8am–10pm.

Le Petit Café CONTINENTAL   This local hangout's specialty is called Romance on the Stone—meals cooked on hot stones, including steak, chicken, jumbo shrimp, fish, and lobster. Dinner is not for the price-conscious, but lunch offers a wide selection of dishes at reasonable prices. The menu spotlights chicken kebabs with peanut sauce and whatever happens to be the catch of the day. For a quick bite, try one of the salads (chicken, tuna, fruit, and chef) or a sandwich, such as a BLT, club, or steak. Le Petit Café offers indoor-outdoor dining with seating on two floors and also on the terrace.

Emmastraat 1, Strada Complex II. ℭ 297/8-26577. Reservations recommended. Main courses $16.50–$32.50; lunch $5.50–$13. AE, DC, MC, V. Mon–Sat 11am–4:30pm; daily 6–11pm.

Mama's & Papa's ℟ ARUBAN/SPANISH   Located north of Oranjestad, this small place serves Aruban and Spanish specialties and some West Indian dishes. The cooks here serve the island's best paella. Local favorites include *keshi yena,* a casserole of chicken and cheese, and *kreeft di cay reef,* broiled lobster. Fish selections are served in a variety of sauces, including Creole and garlic butter. If you're in the mood for West Indian, try the curried chicken, stewed goat, or conch stew. Most nights a guitar player entertains with music from the 1960s. Desserts include carrot cake and sweet-potato pie.

Noord 41C. ℭ 297/8-67913. Main courses $11–$25. AE, DC, MC, V. Mon–Sat 6–11pm.

The Paddock INTERNATIONAL   In the heart of Oranjestad, this cafe and bistro overlooks the harbor, a short walk from virtually every shop in town. Much of the staff is hip and European. No one will seem to mind whether you opt for a drink, a cup of tea or coffee, a snack of sliced sausage and Gouda cheese, or a full-fledged meal. The menu offers crab, salmon, shrimp, and tuna sandwiches; salads; pita-bread sandwiches stuffed with sliced beef and an herb sauce with plenty of tang; fresh poached or sautéed fish; and a glazed tenderloin of pork. Happy hours change frequently, but whenever they're offered, this place becomes packed with a festive crowd.

L. G. Smith Blvd. 13, Oranjestad. ℭ 297/8-32334. Sandwiches, snacks, and salads $3.70–$5.50; main courses $9.50–$14.50. AE, MC, V. Mon–Thurs 10:30am–2am; Fri–Sun 10:30am–3am.

4 Hitting the Beaches

The major resort hotels are built on the southwestern and more tranquil strip of Aruba, called the Turquoise Coast. These beaches open onto calm waters, ideal for swimming. The beaches on the northern side of Aruba, although quite beautiful, face choppy waters with stronger waves. Along this stretch, Palm Beach and Eagle Beach (the latter closer to Oranjestad) are the best. No hotel along the strip owns these beaches; all beaches are open to the public (if you use any of the hotel's facilities, however, you'll be charged).

Palm Beach is a superb stretch of wide white sand that fronts hotels such as the Allegro Resort. It's great for swimming, sunbathing, sailing, fishing, and snorkeling. Unfortunately, it's crowded in the winter. The waters off this beach are incredibly blue and teeming with neon-yellow fish and flame-bright coral reefs. Billowing rainbow-colored sails complete the picture. Along Palm Beach, all the resorts are set in flowering gardens. Of course, a river of water keeps these gardens blooming in this otherwise arid landscape, but the gardens take on a special beauty precisely because the island is so dry.

Also worth seeking out is **Hadikurari** (Fisherman's Huts), where swimming conditions, in very shallow water, are excellent. The only drawback to this white powder-sand beach is some pebbles and stones at water's edge. This beach is known for some of the finest windsurfing on island. It is, in fact, the site of the annual **Hi-Winds Pro-Am Windsurfing Competition.** Facilities include picnic tables.

Quite similar to Palm Beach, **Eagle Beach** is next door on the west coast, fronting a number of timeshare units. With gentle surf along miles of white-powder sand, swimming conditions here are excellent. Hotels along the strip organize watersports and beach activities.

The white-powder sands of **Punta Brabo,** also called **Manchebo Beach,** are a favorite among topless sunbathers. Actually, Manchebo is part of the greater Eagle Beach (see above), and the Manchebo Beach Resort is a good place to stop, as it offers a dive shop and will rent snorkeling gear. It's also set amid 100 acres of gardens, filled with everything from cacti to bougainvillea.

Practically every visitor winds up on Eagle Beach and Palm Beach. If you'd like something more private, head for **Baby Beach** on the southeastern end of Aruba. The beach has white-powder sand and tranquil, shallow waters, making it an ideal place for swimming and snorkeling. There are no facilities other than a refreshment stand and shaded areas. (Our local friends love this beach and may be furious at us for telling you about it!) You'll spot the Arubans themselves here on weekends. Baby Beach opens onto a vast lagoon shielded by coral rocks that rise from the water. Bring your own towels and snorkeling gear.

Next to Baby Beach on the eastern tip of the island, **Rodger's Beach** also has white-powder sand and excellent swimming conditions. The backdrop, however, is an oil refinery at the far side of the bay. But the waters remain unpolluted, and you can admire large and small multicolored fish here and strange coral formations. The trade winds will keep you cool.

5 Sports & Other Outdoor Pursuits

DAY CRUISES   Visitors interested in combining a boat ride with a few hours of snorkeling should contact **De Palm Tours,** which has offices in eight of the island's hotels, and its main office at L. G. Smith Blvd. 142, in Oranjestad (© **800/766-6016** or 297/8-24400). De Palm Tours offers a 1½-hour glass-bottomed boat cruise that visits two coral reefs and the German shipwreck *Antilla* on Thursday and Friday. The cost is $19.50 per person.

DEEP-SEA FISHING   In the deep waters off the coast of Aruba you can test your skill and wits against the big ones—wahoo, marlin, tuna, bonito, and sail-fish. **De Palm Tours,** L. G. Smith Blvd. 142, in Oranjestad (© **800/766-6016** or 297/8-24400), takes out a maximum of six people (four of whom can fish at the same time) on one of its four boats, which range in length from 27 to 41 feet. Half-day tours, with all equipment included, begin at $250 for up to four people and $30 per person for five or six. The prices are doubled for full-day trips. Boats leave from the docks in Oranjestad. De Palm maintains 8 branches, most of which are in Aruba's major hotels.

GOLF   Visitors can play at the **Aruba Golf Club,** Golfweg 82 (© **297/ 8-42006**), near San Nicolas on the southeastern end of the island. Although it has only 10 greens, they are played from different tees to simulate 18-hole play. Twenty-five different sand traps add an extra challenge. Greens fees are $25 for 18 holes and $15 for 9 holes. The course is open daily 7:30am to 5pm, although anyone wishing to play 18 holes must begin the rounds before 1pm. Golf carts and clubs can be rented in the pro shop. There's an air-conditioned restaurant and changing rooms with showers on the premises.

HORSEBACK RIDING   De Palm Tours, L. G. Smith Blvd. 142 (© 297/
8-24400), will make arrangements for you to ride at **Rancho Del Campo**
(© 297/8-50290). Two rides a day are offered, lasting 3 hours and cutting
through a park to a natural pool where you can dismount and cool off with a
swim. The price is $50 per person, and the minimum age is 10 years.

SCUBA DIVING & OTHER WATERSPORTS   You can snorkel in rather
shallow waters, and scuba divers find stunning marine life with endless varieties
of coral as well as tropical fish in infinite hues; at some points visibility is up to
90 feet. The goal of most divers is the German freighter *Antilla*, which was
scuttled in the early years of World War II off the northwestern tip of Aruba, not
too far from Palm Beach.

   Red Sails Sports, Palm Beach (© 297/8-61603), is the best watersports
center on the island. It has an extensive variety of activities, including sailing,
water-skiing, and scuba diving. Red Sail dive packages include shipwreck dives
as well as exploration of marine reefs all in one day. Guests are first given a poolside resort course in which Red Sail's certified instructors teach procedures that
ensure safety during dives. For those who want to become certified, full PADI
certification can be achieved in as little as 4 days for $350. One-tank dives cost
$40; two-tank dives cost $65.

   Divi Winds Center, J. E. Irausquin Blvd. 41 (© 297/8-37841), near the
Tamarind Aruba Beach Resort, is the windsurfing headquarters of the island.
Equipment is made by Fanatic and is rented for $15 per hour, $35 per half day,
or $45 all day. The resort is on the tranquil (Caribbean) side of the island and
doesn't face the fierce Atlantic waves. Sunfish lessons can also be arranged for
$50 (private) or $30 (if in a group). Snorkeling gear can also be rented.

TENNIS   If your hotel doesn't have a tennis court, head to the **Aruba Racket
Club** (© 297/8-60215), the island's first world-class tennis facility, with eight
courts, an exhibition center court, a pool, a bar, a small restaurant, an aerobics
center, and a fitness center. The club is open Monday through Saturday 8am to
11pm and on Sunday 3 to 8pm. Rates are $10 per hour per court. The location
is part of the Tierra del Sol complex on Aruba's northwest coast, near the
California Lighthouse.

6 Seeing the Sights

IN ORANJESTAD 👁

Aruba's capital, Oranjestad, attracts more shoppers than sightseers. The bustling
city has a very Caribbean flavor, with part-Spanish, part-Dutch architecture.
The main thoroughfare, Lloyd G. Smith Boulevard, cuts in from the airport
along the waterfront and on to Palm Beach, changing its name along the way to
J. E. Irausquin Boulevard. Most visitors cross it to head for **Caya G. F. Betico
Croes** and the best duty-free shopping.

   After a shopping trip, you might return to the harbor where fishing boats and
schooners, many from Venezuela, are moored. Nearly all newcomers to Aruba
like to photograph the **Schooner Harbor.** Colorful boats dock along the quay,
and boat people display their wares in open stalls. The local patois predominates.
A little farther along, at the **fish market,** fresh fish is sold directly from the
boats. **Wilhelmina Park,** named after Queen Wilhelmina of the Netherlands, is
also on the sea side of Oranjestad. The park features a tropical garden along the
water and a sculpture of the Queen Mother.

Finds **An Underwater Journey**

One of the island's most fun activities is an underwater journey on one of the world's few passenger submarines, operated by **Atlantis Submarines** ⭐, Seaport Village Marina (opposite the Sonesta), Oranjestad (© **800/253-0493** or 297/8-36090). Even nondivers can witness a coral reef firsthand without risking the obstacles and dangers of a scuba expedition. Carrying 46 passengers to a depth of up to 150 feet, the ride provides all the thrills of an underwater dive—but keeps you dry. In 1995 an old Danish fishing vessel was sunk to create a fascinating view for divers and submariners.

There are four departures from the Oranjestad harbor front every hour on the hour, Monday to Sunday 10am to 12:30pm. Each tour includes a 30-minute catamaran ride to Barcadera Reef, 2 miles southeast of Aruba—a site chosen for the huge variety of its underwater flora and fauna. At the reef, participants are transferred to the submarine for a 1-hour underwater lecture and tour.

Allow 2 hours for the complete experience. The cost is $74 for adults and $35 for children 4 to 16 (children under 4 are not admitted). Advance reservations are essential. A staff member will ask for a credit-card number (and give you a confirmation number) to hold the booking for you.

IN THE COUNTRYSIDE

If you can lift yourself from the sands for an afternoon, you might like to drive into the *cunucu*, which in Papiamento means "the countryside." Here Arubans live in modest, colorful, pastel-washed houses, decorated with tropical plants that require expensive desalinated water. Visitors who venture into the center of Aruba will want to see the strange **divi-divi tree** ⭐, with its trade-wind-blown coiffure.

From Oranjestad, take Caya G. F. Betico Croes (7A) toward Santa Cruz. Soon you'll reach **Hooiberg,** affectionately known as "The Haystack," Aruba's most outstanding landmark. Anybody with the stamina can climb steps to the top of this 541-foot-high hill. On a clear day, you can see Venezuela from here.

Aruba is studded with massive boulders. You'll find the most impressive ones at **Ayo** and **Casibari,** northeast of Hooiberg. Diorite boulders stack up as high as urban buildings. The rocks weigh several thousand tons and puzzle geologists. Ancient Amerindian drawings appear on the rocks at Ayo. At Casibari, you can climb to the top for a panoramic view of the island or a close look at rocks that nature has carved into seats or prehistoric birds and animals. Pay special attention to the island's unusual species of lizards and cacti. Casibari is open daily from 9am to 5pm, with no admission charge. There's a lodge at Casibari where you can buy souvenirs, snacks, soft drinks, and beer.

Guides can also point out drawings on the walls and ceiling of the **Caves of Canashito** (© 297/8-23777), south of Hooiberg. You might get to see some giant green parakeets here as well. The caves are open daily from 8am to 6pm.

On the jagged, windswept northern coast, the unrelenting surf carved the **Natural Bridge** out of coral rock. You can order snacks in a little cafe overlooking the coast. You'll also find a souvenir shop with trinkets, T-shirts, and wall hangings for reasonable prices.

NEAR SAN NICOLAS

As you drive along the highway toward the island's southernmost section, you may want to stop at the **Spaans Lagoen** (Spanish Lagoon), where pirates hid and waited to plunder rich cargo ships in the Caribbean. Today it's an ideal place for snorkeling, and you can picnic at tables under the mangrove trees.

To the east, you'll pass an area called **Savaneta,** where some of the most ancient traces of human habitation have been unearthed. You'll see here the first oil tanks that marked the position of the **Lago Oil & Transport Company,** the Exxon subsidiary around which the town of San Nicolas developed. San Nicolas was a company town until 1985, when the refinery curtailed operations. Twelve miles from Oranjestad, it is now called the Aruba Sunrise Side, and tourism has become its main economic engine.

Boca Grandi, on the windward side of the island, is a favorite windsurfing location; if you prefer quieter waters, you'll find them at Baby Beach and Rodgers Beach, on Aruba's leeward side. Baby Beach offers the island's best beach-based snorkeling. **Seroe Colorado** (Colorado Point) overlooks the two beaches. From here, you can see the Venezuelan coastline and the pounding surf on the windward side. If you climb down the cliffs, you're likely to spot an iguana; protected by law, the once-endangered saurians now proliferate in peace.

You can see cave wall drawings at the **Guadarikiri Cave** and **Fontein Cave.** At the **Huliba** and **Tunnel of Love** caves, guides and refreshment stands await visitors. In spite of its name, the Tunnel of Love cave requires some physical stamina to explore. It is filled with steep climbs, and its steps are illuminated only by hand-held lamps. Wear sturdy shoes and watch your step. Call © 297/ 8-23777 for information.

7 Shopping ⋆⋆

Aruba manages to compress the offerings of six continents into the half-mile-long **Caya G. F. Betico Croes,** the main shopping street of Oranjestad. While it is not technically a duty-free port, the duty is so low (3.3%) that articles are attractively priced—and Aruba has no sales tax. You'll find the usual array of Swiss watches; German and Japanese cameras; jewelry; liquor; English bone china and porcelain; Dutch, Swedish, and Danish silver and pewter; French perfume; British woolens; Indonesian specialties; and Madeira embroidery. Delft blue pottery is an especially good buy. Other good buys include Dutch cheese (Edam and Gouda), as well as Dutch chocolate and English cigarettes in the airport departure area.

Philatelists interested in the wealth of colorful and artistic stamps issued in honor of the changed governmental status of Aruba can purchase a complete assortment, as well as other special issues, at the post office in Oranjestad.

The budget shopper might want to stick to one of the major shopping centers instead of the more expensive specialty stores. Aruba has some of the best-stocked shopping malls in the Caribbean.

If you have time for only one center, check out the **Seaport Mall/Seaport Market Place,** L. G. Smith Blvd. 82 (© 297/8-24622), a pair of two-story malls with a lot of the stuff U.S. visitors may want to buy. Overlooking the harbor, each mall contains its own casino. There's also a **movie theater** (© 297/ 8-30318) with six screens and recently released films from Europe and the U.S.

Cheap Thrills: What to See & Do for Free (Well, Almost) on Aruba

- **Wander the Beach Gardens.** Along Palm Beach, all the seaside hotels are set in flowering gardens. This is unusual for Aruba, which is an otherwise barren landscape. Of course, a river of water is needed to keep these gardens blooming, but they take on a special beauty on such a dry island. As you walk along the beach you can wander through garden after garden, watching the tropical mockingbirds feeding on juicy local fruits. You'll also see the black-faced grass quit or the green-throated carib hovering around these flowers and flowering shrubs. If you stop to have a drink at one of the hotel open-air bars, chances are you'll be joined soon by a banana quit hoping to steal some sugar from you.
- **Enjoy Sunset at Bubali Pond.** This bird sanctuary lies on the north side of Eagle Beach (see above) at Post Chikito. It is south of De Olde Molen, a 19th-century windmill, now turned into a restaurant and the most famous landmark on Aruba. Flocks of birds cluster at the pond, particularly at sunset, making for one of the most memorable sights on Aruba. Mostly they are pelicans, but you can see many other species, too, including black olivaceous cormorants and the black-crowned night herons. Great egrets with long, black legs and yellow bills will also delight you, as will spotted sandpipers. You'll even see visitors flying in from Venezuela, especially the large wood stork and the glossy scarlet ibis.
- **Stroll Through Oranjestad.** The old Dutch capital city is incongruous in the Caribbean. You expect to find something like this in the Netherlands, not off the coast of South America. Wander past the tall multicolored houses of Wilhelminastraat, combining carved wooden doors and traditional Dutch tiles with air-open galleries and sloping Aruban-style roofs. At Fort Zoutman, the oldest building on the

mainland, a convention center, several bars and cafes, and at least 200 stores. **Agatha at Les Accessories,** in the Seaport Mall (© **297/8-37965**), features the exclusive designs of Agatha Brown, an award-winning American designer, including stunning knitwear handbags. **Jewelers Warehouse,** in the Seaport Mall (© **297/8-36045**), carries a complete line of rings, earrings, and bracelets, most of them inexpensively priced. Most shops within the complex are open Monday to Saturday 9am to 6pm, and the bars and cafes usually operate on Sunday as well.

Try **Alhambra Moonlight Shopping Center,** adjacent to the Alhambra Casino, L. G. Smith Boulevard (© **297/8-35000**), with international shops, outdoor marketplaces, cafes, and restaurants. It's good for casual late-night shopping.

Its major competitor is **Royal Plaza Mall,** L. G. Smith Blvd. 94, a bustling shopping center across from the cruise-ship terminal. It has a little bit of everything, including big-name Caribbean chains such as Gandelman Jewelers and Little Switzerland (see below). You'll also find outlets for American chains,

island, a weekly Bonbini Festival offers up local food, crafts, folkloric dancing, and free shows. Oranjestad is also the place to do some duty-free shopping as you browse in the market place for Aruban art and local handcrafts.

- **Spelunk in Former Private Hideouts.** In the San Nicolas area, you'll come across underground caves, unusual on a tropical island. At the Guadirikiri Cave, sunlight filters through two inner chambers, providing the perfect photo opportunity for cave explorers. The cave's 100-foot long tunnel is home to hundreds of harmless bats. Nearby, the Fontein Cave is testimony to the island's native population. Still visible drawings by the Arawak Indians decorate the cave's ceilings and are a powerful reminder of the island's indigenous history. Another cave in the area is called the Tunnel of Love, because of its heart-shaped entrance. A 300-foot-long tunnel winds through eerie rock formations and narrow passages. Helmets and flashlights can be rented for $6 from Arubans who are positioned at the entrances to the Guadirikiri and Tunnel of Love Caves.

- **Explore a Desert in the Caribbean.** On the northeastern coast, Arikok National Park is a desert-like ecological preserve. The island's rich crust makes it one of the rare places in the world where you can trace its geological origins with a naked eye. Hiking trails make it easy for visitors to explore the unusual terrain and diverse flora and fauna of the preserve. Iguanas and many species of migratory birds nest in the park, and goats and donkeys graze on nearby brush trees. Some of the island's best examples of early Indian art and artifacts are preserved within its boundaries. Visitors feeling particularly active can try dune sliding with the locals at the nearby Boca Prins dunes. At dusk, parakeets and other birds bid a cacophonous farewell in Jaburibari.

including Tommy Hilfiger and Nautica. At the **Internet Café** (© 297/ 8-24500), you can send e-mail and order coffee.

SPECIALTY SHOPS

Notable specialty shops include the **Artistic Boutique,** Caya G. F. Betico Croes 25 (© **297/8-23142**), which carries 14- and 18-karat fine gold jewelry set with precious or semiprecious stones. It also sells porcelain figurines, Oriental antiques, handmade dhurries and rugs, fine linens, and organdy tablecloths. Its collections of Indonesian imports is the best on the island.

The **Aruba Trading Company,** Caya G. F. Betico Croes 12 (© **297/8-22602**), has the island's best and most moderately priced selection of perfume, plus cosmetics, shoes, clothing for men and women, liquor, and cigarettes.

Because of the low duty imposed on Aruba, even the budget traveler can sometimes find a good deal on jewelry. **Gandelman Jewelers,** Royal Plaza (© **297/8-34433**), offers an extensive collection of fine gold jewelry and famous-name timepieces at duty-free prices. Go here if you're in the market for a deluxe watch or some piece of jewelry you'll have for a lifetime. Prices are reasonable. There are branch stores in the Americana Aruba Hotel, Airport Departure Hall, Wyndham Hotel, Royal Plaza, and Hyatt Regency Aruba. **Little Switzerland Jewelers,** Caya G. F. Betico Croes 14 (© **297/8-21192**), is famous for its duty-free 14- and 18-karat gold jewelry and watches.

New Amsterdam Store, Caya G. F. Betico Croes 50 (© **297/8-21152**), is the leading department store for linens, with napkins, place mats, and embroidered tablecloths from as far away as China.

Penha, Caya G. F. Betico Croes 11–13 (© **297/8-24161**), has offered large selections of top-name perfumes and cosmetics since 1865. A household name on Aruba, it's one of the most dependable stores around. A Tommy Hilfiger boutique has been added to the store, and the men's department on the second floor is Aruba's finest. Prices are usually lower than in the States.

8 Aruba After Dark

CASINOS: LET THE GOOD TIMES ROLL

The casinos of the big hotels along Palm Beach are the liveliest nighttime destinations. They stay open as long as business demands, often into the wee hours. In plush gaming parlors, guests try their luck at roulette, craps, blackjack, and, of course, the one-armed bandits. Limits and odds are about the same as in the United States.

Excelsior Casino, J. E. Irausquin Blvd. 230 (© **297/8-67777**), wins the prize for all-around action. Its casino doors are open 8am to 4am. The **Aruba Grand,** J. E. Irausquin Blvd. 79 (© **297/8-63900**), opens its games at 10am; it stays open until 1:30am. **Casino Masquerade,** at the Radisson Aruba Caribbean Resort & Casino, J. E. Irausquin Blvd. 81, Palm Beach (© **297/8-66555**), is one of the newest casinos on Aruba. On the lower-level lobby of the hotel, it's open from 10am to 4am daily. It offers blackjack, single deck, roulette, Caribbean stud, craps, and Let It Ride.

One of the island's best is the **Crystal Casino** at the Aruba Sonesta Resort & Casino at Seaport Village (© **297/8-36000**), open daily 24 hours. The 14,000-square-foot casino offers 11 blackjack tables, 270 slot machines, four roulette tables, three Caribbean stud-poker tables, two craps tables, one minibaccarat table, and three baccarat tables. This place has luxurious furnishings, ornate moldings, marble, and crystal chandeliers.

Visitors have a tendency to flock to the newest casinos on the island, like the one at the **Wyndham Hotel and Resort,** J. E. Irausquin Blvd. 77 (© **297/8-64466**), or the **Hyatt Regency Aruba,** J. E. Irausquin Blvd. 85 (© **297/8-61234**). The **Royal Cabana Casino,** at the **La Cabana All Suite Beach Resort & Casino,** J. E. Irausquin Blvd. 250 (© **297/8-79000**), outdraws them all. It's known for its multitheme three-in-one restaurant and its showcase cabaret theater and nightclub, with Las Vegas–style revues, female impersonators, and comedy series on the weekend. The largest casino on Aruba, it offers 33 tables and games, plus 320 slot machines.

Alhambra, J. E. Irausquin Blvd. 47 (© **297/8-35000**), is a complex of buildings and courtyards designed like an 18th-century Dutch village. About a dozen shops here sell souvenirs, leather goods, jewelry, and beachwear. From the outside, the complex looks Moorish, with serpentine mahogany columns, arches, and domes. A busy casino operates on the premises (open from 10am till very early in the morning, usually 3am).

THE CLUB & BAR SCENE

Nongamblers can usually drink in hotel cocktail lounges and any of the restaurants previously recommended. You don't have to be a guest to see shows, but you should make a reservation. Tables at the big shows, especially in season, are likely to book up early in the day.

Mumbo Jumbo, in the Royal Plaza Mall, L. G. Smith Boulevard (© 297/8-33632), is sultry and relaxing. Expect a cosmopolitan blend of Dutch and Latino visitors, and lots of Latin rhythms. The volume is kept at a tolerable level for wallflowers and anyone who wants to have a conversation. There's an array of specialty drinks; imagine coconut shells, very colorful straws, and large fruit. Hours are from sunset until between 2 and 3am, depending on the night of the week.

Havana Beach Club, L. G. Smith Blvd. 4 (© 297/8-23380), rents chairs and umbrellas during the day and has a swimming pool. After 8pm, it transforms into one of the island's busiest nightclubs, with recorded or live salsa music and lots of high-energy exhibitionism on the dance floor. It's open every night until 5am. The cover ranges from $6 to $10.

Other hot spots worth checking out include **E-Zone,** Bayside Mall, Westraat 5 in Oranjestad (© 279/9-36784), with a large dance floor. It's a fun kind of place—the bartenders wear hard hats, for example—and the walls are decorated with whatever could be retrieved from the junkyard. Far classier is **La Fiesta,** Aventura Mall, Plaza Daniel Leo (© 297/8-35896), where you can drink indoors or out in the moonlight. Yachties often frequent this place. Another favorite is **Café Bahia,** Westraat 7 in Oranjestad (© 297/8-89982), both a bar and a dance club. Some of the best island bands show up here.

5

Barbados

Bajans like to think of their island as "England in the tropics," but endless pink- and white-sand beaches are what really put Barbados on the map. Rich in tradition, Barbados has a grand array of hotels (many of them super-expensive). Although it doesn't offer casinos, it has more than beach life. It offers much to travelers interested in learning about the local culture, and it has more sightseeing attractions than most islands of the West Indies.

Afternoon tea remains a tradition at many places on Barbados, cricket is still the national sport, and many Bajans speak with a British accent. Crime has been on the rise in recent years, although Barbados is a relatively safe destination. The difference between the haves and the have-nots doesn't cause the sometimes-violent clash here that it does on some other islands, such as Jamaica.

Don't rule out Barbados if you're seeking a peaceful island getaway. Although the south coast is known for its nightlife and the west-coast beach strip is completely built up, some of the island remains undeveloped. The east coast is fairly tranquil, and you can often be alone here (but because it faces the Atlantic, the waters aren't as tranquil as they are on the Caribbean side). Many escapists, especially Canadians seeking a low-cost place to stay in the winter, don't seem to mind the Atlantic waters at all.

Because it's so built up with hotels and condos, Barbados offers more package deals than most islands. You can often get a steal in the off-season, which lasts from April until mid-December. You don't necessarily have to pay the rack rate (the published or highest rate for individual bookings) at hotels if you'll take the time to shop around. Barbados is filled with bargains, especially along its southern coast, directly below Bridgetown. This strip of beachfront isn't the most glamorous, but it's the most reasonable in price. Read the section "Package Deals" in chapter 2 before you try to book on your own.

1 Essentials

VISITOR INFORMATION

In the United States, you can contact the following offices of the **Barbados Tourism Authority:** 800 Second Ave., New York, NY 10017 (© **800/ 221-9831**); 3440 Wilshire Blvd., Suite 1215, Los Angeles, CA 90010 (© **213/380-2198**); or 158 Alhambra Circle, Suite 1270, Miami, FL 33134 (© **305/442-7471**).

In Canada, contact the **Barbados Tourism Authority** at 105 Adelaide St. W., Suite 1010, Toronto, ON M5H 1P9 (© **416/214-9880**). In the United Kingdom, contact the **Barbados Tourism Authority** at 263 Tottenham Court Rd., London W1P 0LA (© **020/7636-9448**).

Barbados

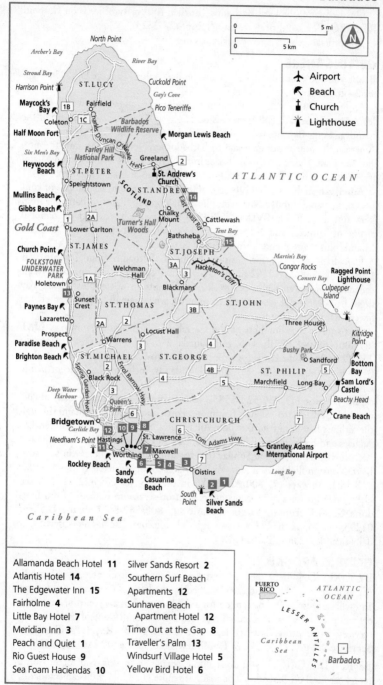

0	5 mi
0	5 km

N

✈ Airport
🏄 Beach
⛪ Church
🔦 Lighthouse

North Point
Archer's Bay
Stroud Bay
River Bay
Harrison Point
Cuckold Point
ST. LUCY
Gay's Cove
Maycock's Bay 1B
Fairfield
Pico Teneriffe
Coleton 1C
Half Moon Fort
Barbados Wildlife Reserve
Morgan Lewis Beach
Six Men's Bay
Farley Hill National Park
Heywoods Beach
Greenland 2
ST. PETER
St. Andrew's Church
Speightstown
ST. ANDREW
ATLANTIC OCEAN
Mullins Beach
14
Gibbs Beach
Chalky Mount
Cattlewash
1
2A
Gold Coast
Lower Carlton
Turner's Hall Woods
Bathsheba
Tent Bay
15
ST. JAMES
ST. JOSEPH
Church Point
Martin's Bay
FOLKSTONE UNDERWATER PARK
Welchman Hall
3A
Congor Rocks
Consett Bay
Ragged Point Lighthouse
Holetown
1A
3
Hackleton's Cliff
Culpepper Island
13
Sunset Crest
Blackmans
ST. JOHN
Paynes Bay
ST. THOMAS
Lazaretto
2
3B
Three Houses
Kitridge Point
Prospect
2A
Locust Hall
Paradise Beach
Warrens
3
Bushy Park
Brighton Beach
ST. MICHAEL
ST. GEORGE
Sandford
Bottom Bay
2
4
5
Black Rock
4B
ST. PHILIP
Sam Lord's Castle
3
Marchfield
Long Bay
Deep Water Harbour
5
Beachy Head
Queen's Park
4
Crane Beach
Bridgetown
6
CHRISTCHURCH
7
Carlisle Bay
12 10 9 8
6
Needham's Point
Hastings
St. Lawrence
Tom Adams Hwy
Grantley Adams International Airport
11
7
Worthing
Maxwell
Rockley Beach
6 5 4 3
7
Sandy Beach
Oistins
Long Bay
Casuarina Beach
2 1
Caribbean Sea
South Point
Silver Sands Beach

Allamanda Beach Hotel **11**	Silver Sands Resort **2**
Atlantis Hotel **14**	Southern Surf Beach
The Edgewater Inn **15**	Apartments **12**
Fairholme **4**	Sunhaven Beach
Little Bay Hotel **7**	Apartment Hotel **12**
Meridian Inn **3**	Time Out at the Gap **8**
Peach and Quiet **1**	Traveller's Palm **13**
Rio Guest House **9**	Windsurf Village Hotel **5**
Sea Foam Haciendas **10**	Yellow Bird Hotel **6**

PUERTO RICO
ATLANTIC OCEAN
LESSER ANTILLES
Caribbean Sea
Barbados

On the island, the local **Barbados Tourism Authority** office is on Harbour Road (P.O. Box 242), Bridgetown (© **246/427-2623**). The official website is **www.barbados.org**.

GETTING THERE

Before you book your flight, be sure to read the section "Package Deals" in chapter 2—it can save you a bundle!

More than 20 daily flights arrive on Barbados from all over the world. **Grantley Adams International Airport** is on Highway 7, on the southern tip of the island at Long Bay, between Oistins and the village The Crane. From North America, the four major gateways to Barbados are New York, Miami, Toronto, and San Juan. Flying time to Barbados from New York is 4½ hours, from Miami it's 3½ hours, from Toronto it's 5 hours, and from San Juan, 1½ hours.

American Airlines (© 800/433-7300; www.im.aa.com) has dozens of connections passing through San Juan, plus daily nonstop flights to Barbados from New York and Miami. **BWIA** (© 800/538-2942; www.bwee.com), the national airline of Trinidad and Tobago, also offers daily flights from New York and Miami, plus many flights from Trinidad.

Canadians may opt for nonstop flights to Barbados from Toronto. **Air Canada** (© 888/247-2262 in the U.S., or 800/268-7240 in Canada; www.aircanada.ca) has seven flights per week from Toronto in winter plus one Sunday flight from Montreal year-round. In summer, when demand slackens, there are fewer flights from Toronto.

Barbados is a major hub of the Caribbean-based airline known as **LIAT** (© 800/468-0482 in the U.S. and Canada, 246/434-5428 for reservations, or 246/428-0986 at the Barbados airport), which provides generally poor service to Barbados from a handful of neighboring islands, including St. Vincent in the Grenadines, Antigua, and Dominica.

Air Jamaica (© 800/523-5585; www.airjamaica.com) offers daily flights that link Barbados to Atlanta, Baltimore, Fort Lauderdale, and Miami through the airline's new Montego Bay hub. Air Jamaica has added service between Los Angeles and Barbados on Friday and Sunday, and service between Orlando and Barbados on Thursday and Sunday (but requiring an overnight stay in Montego Bay). Nonstop flights from New York to Barbados are available 6 days a week.

British Airways (© 800/AIRWAYS in the U.S., or 0345/222-111 in the U.K.; www.british-airways.com) offers nonstop service to Barbados from London's Gatwick Airport. **Virgin Atlantic** (© 800/862-8621 in the U.S., or 01293/747-747 in the U.K.; www.virgin-atlantic.com) also has one direct flight daily from London to Barbados.

GETTING AROUND

BY TAXI   Taxis aren't metered, but the government fixes rates (at about $20 per hr.). Taxis on the island are identified by the letter Z on their license plates and will carry up to five passengers for a single fare. Taxis are plentiful, and drivers will produce a list of standard rates. To call a taxi, dial one of the following services: **Paramount Taxi Service** (© 246/429-3718), **Royal Pavilion Taxi Service** (© 246/422-5555), or **Lyndhurst Taxi Service** (© 246/436-2639).

BY RENTAL CAR   If you don't mind *driving on the left*, you might find a rental car ideal on Barbados. The roads are quite good by Caribbean standards, although they're poorly signposted (newcomers invariably get lost, at least once). None of the major U.S.-based car-rental companies maintains an affiliate on

Fun Fact Special Events

One of the hottest "cool" jazz festivals in the Caribbean takes place at the Barbados jazz festival, called **Paint It Jazz**, and scheduled for mid-January in 2002. International artists appear, along with the best in local jazz talent. For tickets and further details, contact the festival organizers at bdosjazz@caribsurf.com.

In mid-February, the **Holetown Festival** takes place in St. James. It is a weeklong event that commemorates the landing of the first European settlers at Holetown in 1627. Highlights include street fairs, police band concerts, a music festival in the parish church, and a road race.

In the second week of April, the **Oistins Fish Festival** commemorates the signing of the charter of Barbados. You'll find fishing, boat racing, fish-boning competitions, a Coast Guard exhibition, food stalls, arts and crafts, dancing, singing, and road races.

Beginning in late June and lasting until the first week of August, the **Crop Over Festival** is the island's major national festival, celebrating the completion of the sugarcane harvest and recognizing the hardworking men and women in the sugar industry. Communities all over the island participate in fairs, concerts, calypso competitions, car parades, and other cultural events. The climax of the festival occurs at Kadooment Day, a national holiday on the first Monday in August, which becomes the biggest party of the year in Barbados.

For information on these festivals, contact the Barbados Tourism Authority.

Barbados, however, and many vehicles rented by local companies are in bad shape. Many local car-rental companies continue to draw serious complaints from readers, both for overcharging and the condition of the rental vehicles. Proceed very cautiously with rentals here, and be sure to check out the insurance and liability issues carefully when you rent.

Except in the peak midwinter season, cars are usually readily available without a prior reservation. Most renters pay for a taxi from the airport to their hotel and then call for the delivery of a rental car. This is especially advisable because of frequent delays at airport counters.

The island's most frequently recommended car-rental firm is **National Car Rentals,** Bush Hall, Main Road, St. Michael (© 246/426-0603), which offers a wide selection of Japanese cars (note that it's not affiliated with the U.S. chain National Car Rental). Located near the island's national stadium (the only one on the island), it lies 3 miles northeast of Bridgetown. Cars will be delivered to almost any location on the island upon request, and the driver who delivers it will carry the necessary forms for the Bajan driver's license, which can be purchased for $5.

Other companies, which charge approximately the same prices and offer approximately the same services, include **Sunny Isle Motors,** Dayton, Worthing Main Road, Christ Church (© 246/435-7979), and **P&S Car Rentals,** Pleasant View, Cave Hill, St. Michael (© 246/424-2052). One company that's conveniently close to hotels on the remote southeastern end of Barbados is

Stoutes Car Rentals, Kirtons, St. Philip (© **246/435-4456**). Closer to the airport than its competitors, it can theoretically deliver a car to the airport within 10 minutes of when you place a call after arrival.

A temporary driving permit is needed if you don't have an International Driver's License. All the rental agencies listed above can issue you a visitor's permit, or you can go to the police desk upon your arrival at the airport. You're charged a registration fee of BD$10 ($5), and you must have your own license. The speed limit is 20 mph inside city limits, 45 mph elsewhere on the island. No taxes apply to car rentals on Barbados.

BY BUS   Unlike most of the British Windwards, Barbados has a reliable bus system, which fans out from Bridgetown to almost every part of the island. On most major routes, there are buses running every 20 minutes or so. Bus fares are BD$1.50 (75¢) wherever you go, exact Bajan change required.

The nationally owned **buses** of Barbados are blue with yellow stripes. They're not numbered, but their destinations are marked on the front. Departures are from Bridgetown, leaving from Fairchild Street for the south and east, and from Lower Green and the Princess Alice Highway for the north going along the west coast. Call the **Barbados Tourist Board** (© **246/427-2623**) for bus schedules and information.

Privately operated **minibuses** run shorter distances and travel more frequently. They are bright yellow, with their destinations displayed on the bottom-left corner of the windshield. Minibuses in Bridgetown are boarded at River Road, Temple Yard, and Probyn Street. They, too, cost BD$1.50 (75¢).

 FAST FACTS: Barbados

American Express   The island's American Express affiliate is **Barbados International Travel Services,** Horizon House, McGregor Street (© **246/ 431-2423**), in the heart of Bridgetown.

Business Hours   Most banks on Barbados are open Monday to Thursday 9am to 3pm and Friday 9am to 1pm and 3 to 5pm. Stores are open Monday to Friday 8am to 4pm and Saturday 8am to noon. Most government offices are open Monday to Friday 8:30am to 4:30pm.

Consulates & High Commissions   The U.S. Consulate is located in the ALICO Building, Cheapside, Bridgetown (© **246/431-0225**); the Canadian High Commission at Bishop Court Hill, Pine Road (© **246/429-3550**); and the British High Commission at Lower Collymore Rock, St. Michael (© **246/436-6694**).

Currency   The **Barbados dollar (BD$)** is the official currency, available in $5, $10, $20, and $100 notes, as well as 10¢, 25¢, and $1 silver coins, plus 1¢ and 5¢ copper coins. The Bajan dollar is worth 50¢ in U.S. currency. Unless otherwise specified, *currency quotations in this chapter are in U.S. dollars.* Most stores take traveler's checks or U.S. dollars. However, it's best to convert your money at banks and pay in Bajan dollars.

Customs   Most items for personal use (within reason, of course) are allowed into Barbados, except agricultural products and firearms. You can bring in perfume for your use if it's not for sale. You're also allowed a carton of cigarettes and a liter of liquor.

Documents A U.S. or Canadian citizen coming directly from North America to Barbados for a visit not exceeding 3 months must have proof of identity and national status, such as a passport. A birth certificate (either an original or a certified copy) is also acceptable, provided that it's backed up with photo ID, but we recommend that you carry a passport. For stays longer than 3 months, a passport is required. An ongoing or return ticket is also necessary. British subjects need a valid passport.

Electricity The electricity is 110-volt AC (50 cycles), so in most places you can use U.S.-made appliances.

Emergencies In an **emergency**, call © **119**. Other important numbers include the **police** at © **112**, the **fire** department at © **113**, and an **ambulance** at © **115**.

Language The Barbadians, or Bajans, as they're called, speak English, but with a unique island lilt.

Medical Care The **Queen Elizabeth Hospital** is on Martinsdale Road in St. Michael (© **246/436-6450**). There are several private clinics as well; one of the most expensive and best recommended is the **Bayview Hospital,** St. Paul's Avenue, Bayville, St. Michael (© **246/436-5446**). Your hotel might have a list of doctors on call, although some of the best recommended are **Dr. J. D. Gibling** (© **246/432-1772**) and **Dr. Adrian Lorde** or his colleague **Dr. Ahmed Mohamad** (© **246/424-8236**), any of whom will pay house calls to patients unable to leave their hotel rooms. **Dr. Derek Golding,** with two other colleagues, maintains one of the busiest practices on Barbados. Located at the Beckwith Shopping Mall in Bridgetown (© **246/426-3001**), he accepts most emergency dental problems; otherwise, hours are Monday to Saturday 8am to 2:30pm.

Safety Crimes against tourists used to be rare, but the U.S. State Department reports rising crime, such as purse snatching, pickpocketing, armed robbery, and even sexual assault on women. The department advises that you not leave cash or valuables in your hotel room; beware of purse snatchers when walking; exercise caution when walking on the beach or visiting tourist attractions; and be wary of driving in isolated areas of Barbados.

Taxes When you leave, you'll have to pay a BD$25 ($12.50) departure tax. A 7½% government sales tax is added to hotel bills, and a 15% VAT (value-added tax) is added to all restaurant meals. For example, if your hotel costs $200 per night, and you are charged $50 per person for MAP, you are levied a 7½% government tax plus the 10% additional service charge for the $200 room rate, then an additional 15% VAT on the MAP rate. Comprende? Some visitors have viewed these additional charges as "larcenous." They certainly won't make you happy when you go to pay your final bill.

Telecommunications To call Barbados from the United States, dial **1**, then **246** (the area code for Barbados) and the local number. Once on Barbados, to call another number on the island, only the local number is necessary. To charge an overseas call on a major credit card, call © **800/744-2000**.

Time Barbados is on Atlantic standard time year-round, placing it 1 hour ahead of New York. However, when the United States is on daylight saving time, Barbados matches the clocks of the U.S. east coast.

Tipping Most hotels and restaurants add at least a 10% service charge to your bill. If service is extremely good, you might want to supplement that. If it has not been included, you might want to tip your waiter 10% to 15%. Taxi drivers expect a 10% tip.

Water Barbados has a pure water supply. It's pumped from underground sources in the coral rock that covers six-sevenths of the island, and it's safe to drink.

Weather Daytime temperatures are in the 75°F to 85°F (24°C–29°C) range throughout the year.

2 Accommodations You Can Afford

There are bargains to be found, but to find them you'll have to avoid the resorts on fashionable St. James Beach and instead head south from Bridgetown to such places as Hastings and Worthing. The best buys are often self-contained efficiencies or studio apartments where you can do your own cooking. You can usually find good package deals to Barbados, too; see the section "Package Deals" in chapter 2.

Prices in this section, unless otherwise indicated, are in U.S. dollars. Remember that the government hotel tax of 7½% and a 10% service charge will be added to your final bill.

Some of the best and least expensive rental deals can be made through **Homar Rentals,** Europa, Sunset Crest, St. James (© **246/432-6750;** fax 246/432-7229), which controls 109 apartments. These accommodations are two-apartment bungalows, some on one floor, others in two-story buildings, all constructed from concrete. Furnishings for the most part are basic, in a West Indian motif, with rattan pieces or leatherette. There are phones, and some bedrooms have ceiling fans, but TVs must be rented. Daily maid service is provided. Air-conditioning is token-operated at $5 for 10 hours. In winter a single or double begins at $95 daily, with off-season prices lowered to $70. An extra person is charged $10, and one child under 12 can stay for free in his or her parents' room. Homar is one of several companies that manage the Sunset Crest Resort, privately owned condos where apartments are rented when the owners are off-island. Sunset Crest has two pools, plus a restaurant that serves three standard meals a day. The nearby Beach Club also has a pool, a bar, and water-sports equipment for rent.

Allamanda Beach Hotel *Kids* *Value* These apartments, last renovated in 1995, represent one of the best bargains on Barbados and are ideal for families. Directly on a rocky shoreline 2½ miles southeast of Bridgetown, the hotel is in the heart of the village of Hastings. The U-shaped apartment complex is built around a pool terrace overlooking the sea. Functional and minimalist in decor, it's clean and comfortable. All units have balconies or decks, and some have air-conditioning. Bedrooms are small, as are the shower bathrooms, but the beds are good and the plumbing is well maintained. Supermarkets, stores, and banks are within easy walking distance. Although some athletic guests attempt to swim off the nearby rocks, most walk 5 minutes to the white sands of nearby Rockley (Accra) Beach. A small restaurant on the property serves American and Bajan fare.

Hastings, Christ Church, Barbados, W.I. © **246/435-6694**. Fax 246/435-9211. www.allamandabeach.com. 48 units. Winter $125–$130 studio apt for 1 or 2; $165 1-bedroom apt for 1 or 2; $215 2-bedroom apt for up to 4. Off-season $90–$95 studio apt for 1 or 2; $110 1-bedroom apt for 1 or 2; $135 2-bedroom apt for up to 4. Extra person $12. AE, MC, V. **Amenities:** Restaurant, pool, bike rental, babysitting, laundry. *In room:* A/C in some units, kitchenette, fridge, hair dryer.

Atlantis Hotels This boxy, concrete-sided hotel offers virtues (and drawbacks) not associated with more modern resorts in better-developed regions of Barbados. It's one of the most durable establishments on the island, with a long history of feeding large numbers of lunchtime visitors (see "Great Deals on Dining," below). It's in an isolated position on Barbados's rocky and turbulent Atlantic coast, where strong currents, winds, and undertows usually make swimming a bad idea. If that doesn't deter you, here are the pluses: The scenery is among the most beautiful on Barbados; the welcome is warm and the ambience authentically Bajan. The Atlantis is respectable, well known by virtually everyone on the island. The accommodations are clean but simple affairs, with white walls, carpeted floors, wooden furniture, and (in many cases) views and balconies overlooking the surging Atlantic. Mattresses are rather old and lumpy, but the diehard devotees of this place rarely complain. Bathrooms are really too tiny, but each has a shower. You stay here more for old Bajan atmosphere than for any grand comfort. Mrs. Enid Maxwell and members of her family are the longtime owners.

Bathsheba, St. Joseph, Barbados, W.I. © **246/433-9445**. www.atlantisbarbados.com. 15 units. Winter $45 single; $75 double. Off-season $45 single; $70 double. Extra adult $35 each in winter, $30 each in off-season; extra child 11 and under $20 each in winter, $15 each in off-season. Rates include half-board. AE. **Amenities:** Restaurant, bar. *In room:* No phone.

The Edgewater Inn ★★ Built as a dramatically isolated private home and converted into a hotel in 1947, this inn is directly on the Atlantic coast, a short drive southeast of the island's Scotland district. The beach closest to the hotel can be treacherous, but the staff will direct you to a 9-mile coral sand beach to the north. You will also be directed to Joe's River, the only free-flowing river in Barbados. Located in an 85-acre tropical rain forest atop a low cliff, the property opens onto ocean views, and a nearby wildlife sanctuary invites exploration. Cozy and intimate, the small inn is decorated with beveled leaded-glass windows from Asia; furnishings reflect an island motif, with mahogany pieces handcrafted by local artisans. If they're available, request rooms 215 or 216 for their upgraded furnishing and panoramic views. The shower-only bathrooms are small.

The freshwater pool, shaped like the island of Barbados, is the focal point of the resort. Surfers and nonguests often drop by for a drink or a meal. The restaurant serves excellent West Indian and continental cuisine.

Bathsheba (13 miles northeast of Bridgetown on Hwy. 3), St. Joseph, Barbados, W.I. © **246/433-9900**. Fax 246/433-9902. www.edgewaterinn.com. 20 units. Winter $105–$199 single or double. Off-season $85–$145 single or double. Breakfast and dinner $35 per person. AE, DISC, MC, V. **Amenities:** Restaurant, bar, pool. *In room:* A/C in some units, TV.

Fairholme ★ Fairholme is a converted plantation house that has been enlarged during the past 20 years with a handful of connected annexes. The main house and its original gardens are just off a major road 6 miles southeast of Bridgetown. The hotel is a 5-minute walk to the beach and across from its neighbor, the Sea Breeze, which has a waterfront cafe and bar that Fairholme guests may use. The older part of Fairholme has 11 double rooms, each with a living-room area and a patio overlooking an orchard and a pool. Fairly recently added are 20 Spanish-style studio apartments, each with a balcony or patio, built in the old plantation style, with cathedral ceilings, dark beams, and traditional furnishings. Bedrooms range from small to medium; the mattresses are firm and the bathrooms tend to be tiny but tidy, with shower stalls. The restaurant has a reputation for home-cooking—wholesome, nothing fancy, but the ingredients are fresh. Air-conditioning is available only in the studios. (At the reception desk you buy a brass token for $3 that you insert into your air conditioner for around 8 hr. of cooling-off time.)

Maxwell, Christ Church, Barbados, W.I. ✆ 246/428-9425. Fax 246/420-2389. 31 units. Winter $35 single or double; $65 studio apt. Off-season $32 single or double; $35 studio apt. No credit cards. **Amenities:** Pool. *In room:* A/C in some units, no phone.

Little Bay Hotel   This small apartment complex consists of an older core, which has been upgraded and renovated by its owners, the Patterson family. It's a pastel-colored building with a tiled roof and pleasant, unfrilly accommodations with brick-tile floors, utilitarian furniture, and views over Barbados's well-developed southwestern coastline. Accommodations are a bit small but adequate for one or two guests, although very crowded when four share a unit. Mattresses are firm and comfortable, and the shower-only bathrooms are tiny but clean. Each unit has a small bathroom with a shower, and three units have tub/shower combinations. There are ample opportunities for affordable drinking, nightclubbing, and dining within a brisk walk of your room. You can cook your meals in-house, as you'll have a private kitchenette and access to several grocery stores and mini-marts nearby. No breakfast is served on site, but Italian dinners are available at Bellini's restaurant, which is vaguely associated with this hotel.

St. Lawrence Gap, Christ Church, Barbados, W.I. ✆ 246/435-7246. Fax 246/435-8574. www.barbados.org/apt/a72.htm. 10 units. Winter $95–$110 studio for 1 or 2; $145 1-bedroom apt for up to 4. Off-season $65–$75 studio for 1 or 2; $90 1-bedroom apt for up to 4. AE, MC, V. **Amenities:** Room service, massage, babysitting. *In room:* A/C, TV, kitchenette, fridge, coffeemaker.

Meridian Inn *(Kids*   Close to shopping, restaurants, and nightclubs, this four-story, white-painted building right on the street is about a minute's walk to a good beach. It offers some of the least-expensive rooms on the island. The units are clean and comfortable, but some of them evoke Miami motels of the 1960s, although a recent refurbishment included installation of new mattresses. Units have small shower-only bathrooms and private balconies, along with daily maid service. TVs can be rented, and phones are available in the corridors. A simple restaurant features fresh seafood at both lunch and dinner.

Dover, Christ Church, Barbados, W.I. ✆ 246/428-4051. Fax 246/420-6495. www.meridianinn.com. 16 studio apts. Winter $79 studio apt for 1 or 2. Off-season $48 studio apt for 1 or 2. Children under 12 stay free in parents' studio. AE, MC, V. **Amenities:** Restaurant, maid service, babysitting. *In room:* A/C, kitchenette, fridge, no phone.

Peach and Quiet   This budget hotel complex is set on 4 acres of tropical gardens. It boasts the only sea rock pool on island. Clean and comfortable, its accommodations are inviting, although they have no great style. Each unit has a small bathroom, equipped with shower. This is not a place for families with children as the Peach and Quiet prefers only grown-ups.

Inch Marlow, Barbados, W.I. ✆ 246/428-5682. Fax 246/428-24567. www.barbados.org/hotels/h48.htm. 22 units. Winter $99 double. Off-season $69 double. DISC, MC, V. Closed Sept. **Amenities:** Restaurant, pool, laundry. *In room:* Hair dryer, safe, no phone.

Rio Guest House   Built as a private home in the 1940s, this simple black-and-white-painted guesthouse is maintained by the resident owner, Mrs. Denise

Harding. It features low rates and clean, no-frills bedrooms. None of the single rooms has a private bathroom; there are no private kitchens, except in the studio. Accommodations are small, and the mattresses have been used many, many times before, but they are still comfortable. Accommodations that have private bathrooms are a bit cramped for shelf space; the communal bathrooms are kept neat and tidy. The mini-marts, bars, nightclubs, and hamburger joints of St. Lawrence Gap are within walking distance; Dover Beach is within a 2-minute walk. Guests share a communal kitchen, in which a large refrigerator is divided into compartments, each reserved more or less exclusively for one of the units.

Paradise Village, St. Lawrence Gap, Christ Church, Barbados, W.I. ℭ **246/428-1546.** Fax 246/428-1546. 8 units, 5 with bathroom; 1 studio. Winter $26 single without bathroom, $37 single or double with bathroom; $55 studio. Off-season $21 single without bathroom, $27 single or double with bathroom; $45 studio. MC, V. **Amenities:** Communal kitchen. *In room:* Ceiling fans, no phone.

Southern Surf Beach Apartment *Kids*   Close to the famous Accra Beach at Rockley, this is a good, serviceable choice in a centrally located complex. It's convenient for nearby dining, shopping, and entertainment. Four rooms are in the Great House, and the studio apartments are in a four-story concrete-block building. There are three apartments per floor, each simply but comfortably furnished, with a balcony and beach view. The rooms don't have phones, but there is one for public use in the apartment block, and the only TV is in the office reception area. Rooms in the main house, although not as large, have an old-time Bajan feeling. The apartment complex renews mattresses as needed and keeps the plumbing in a good state in its small but well-maintained shower-only bathrooms. Children are housed free in a studio apartment if an extra cot is not needed; otherwise a $15-per-day surcharge applies. Southern Surf owns the land between it and the ocean, so there's an unobstructed view of the beach.

Rockley Beach, Christ Church, Barbados, W.I. ℭ **246/435-6672.** Fax 246/435-6649. www.barbados. org/apt/a61.htm. 16 units, including 12 studio apts. Winter $50–$60 single or double; $80 studio apt for 2. Off-season $40 single or double; $50–$60 studio apt for 2. Extra person in apt $15. MC, V. **Amenities:** Pool, garden, babysitting. *In room:* Ceiling fans, no phone.

Sunhaven Beach Apartment Hotel   This small, rather innocuous-looking complex offers both conventional bedrooms and one-bedroom apartments with kitchenettes. It's close to the sands of Rockley Beach, near many fast-food and inexpensive pub-style restaurants. The accommodations are small and a bit dowdy, with functional furniture and dour, floral-patterned carpeting, but if you're traveling with friends or children in tow, it's hard to beat the savings. Each unit has a sea view and a balcony. The mattresses are good and are replaced as needed, and the shower-only bathrooms are neatly arranged, with some shelf space for your stuff. At one edge of the pool, overlooking the beach, is an open-air restaurant.

Rockley Beach, Christ Church, Barbados, W.I. ℭ **246/435-8905.** Fax 246/435-6621. 35 units, including 26 apts. Winter $60 single; $70 double; $75 1-bedroom apt for 1; $90 1-bedroom apt for 2; $105 1-bedroom apt for 3. Off-season $45 single; $50 double; $50 1-bedroom apt for 1; $60 1-bedroom apt for 2; $70 1-bedroom apt for 3. Children 4 and under stay free in parents' unit; children 5–12 $10 per child extra. MAP (breakfast and dinner) $30 per person extra. AE, DC, MC, V. **Amenities:** Restaurant, pool. *In room:* A/C, kitchenette (apartments), no phone.

Time Out at the Gap   In 1998, new management took over the premises of a faded four-story relic from the 1970s and radically upgraded the old furniture and amenities. Almost all the accommodations here have tiled floors and walls, plus vibrant color schemes. Nearly all the mattresses are new; shower-only bathrooms are a bit small, but adequate. On the premises is a whimsical sports bar

and restaurant, the Whistling Frog, which is recommended in "Great Deals on Dining," below.

St. Lawrence Gap, Christ Church, Barbados, W.I. ✆ **246/420-5021.** Fax 246/420-5021. www.gemsbarbados. com/timeout. 76 units. Winter $140–$150 single or double. Off-season $115–$125 single or double. Extra person $15. AE, MC, V. **Amenities:** Restaurant, sports bar. *In room:* TV, fridge.

Traveller's Palm   Within a 10-minute walk of a good beach, this is for self-sufficient types who are not too demanding and who like to save money. There's a choice of simply furnished, one-bedroom apartments with fully equipped kitchens. They're simple, slightly worn apartments, with bright but fading colors, but they're quite a deal in this high-rent district. The apartments have living and dining areas, as well as patios where you can have breakfast or a candlelit dinner you've prepared yourself (no meals are served here).

265 Palm Ave., Sunset Crest, St. James, Barbados, W.I. ✆ **246/432-7722.** homar@caribsurf.com. 16 units. Winter $95 apt for 2. Off-season $70 apt for 2. MC, V. **Amenities:** Pool. *In room:* A/C.

Windsurf Village Hotel   Although this hotel assumes that windsurfers appreciate proximity to other windsurfers, many guests who don't have very much interest in the sport have been happy here, too. Designed in a two-story, white-walled format with balconies, with at least two patios for outdoor mingling of guests, it attracts a youngish crowd of sports enthusiasts, as well as older non-participants who appreciate the lighthearted setting. The small bedrooms have white-painted walls, wooden furnishings, ceiling fans, and tile-covered floors. Mattresses are a bit thin, and the bathrooms contain only showers, but this is a grade above college dorm living. Budget travelers like the location, amid Barbados's densest concentration of nightclubs, supermarkets, and cheap restaurants, all of which are in the same parish (Christ Church), within an easy walk or drive. The Windsurf maintains a snack-style restaurant on the beach.

Despite the establishment's name, it doesn't own or rent any windsurfers. Instead, windsurfing enthusiasts are directed to the watersports facilities at the nearby Club Mistral.

Maxwell Main Rd., Christ Church, Barbados, W.I. ✆ **246/428-9095.** Fax 246/435-6621. www.windsurfbeach. com. 15 units. Winter $60 single or double; $90–$115 studio with kitchenette for 2; $170 2-bedroom apt for 4. Off-season $45 single or double; $65–$75 studio with kitchenette for 2; $125 2-bedroom apt for 4. AE, MC, V. **Amenities:** Beach snack bar. *In room:* Ceiling fans, no phone.

Yellow Bird Hotel   At the much-frequented St. Lawrence Gap, this property comes as an affordable relief, easing the plight of pricey Barbados. It's been spruced up and now offers tidy and well-furnished apartments, each with a kitchenette and a small tiled bathroom with tub. Each accommodation also has a balcony that opens onto views of the Caribbean.

St. Lawrence Gap, Barbados, W.I. ✆ **246/435-8444.** Fax 246/435-8522. www.barbados.org/hotels/h67.htm. 20 units. Winter $100 double. Off-season $70 double. AE, MC, V. **Amenities:** Restaurant, bar, pool, room service, laundry. *In room:* A/C, kitchenette, hair dryer.

WORTH A SPLURGE

Sea Foam Haciendas ⭐ (Value)   Centrally located on Worthing Beach, this Spanish-style property lies between the airport and Bridgetown. It's also convenient to supermarkets, banks, a post office, and a small shopping plaza. All the drinking and dining facilities of the St. Lawrence area are close at hand, so you don't need to rent a car. Each good-size unit is fully furnished, with two air-conditioned bedrooms with fine mattresses, a modern kitchen with electric stove, and a large refrigerator with a microwave. Each unit also has its own private phone and radio, and there's a wall safe in the master bedroom. Bathrooms are fairly standard and routine; each has a shower and enough space to spread out your toilet articles. The living and dining room area opens onto a large private balcony overlooking the ocean. Because of this place's good value, it enjoys a high repeat clientele.

Worthing, Christ Church, Barbados, W.I. ✆ **800/8-BARBADOS** in the U.S. and Canada, or 246/435-7380. Fax 246/435-7384. www.seafoamhaciendas.com. 12 units. Winter $135 single or double; $185 quad. Off-season $95 single or double; $130 quad. Extra person $15. MC, V. *In room:* A/C, TV, kitchen, safe.

Silver Sands Resort ✿ *Value*   This is a beachfront resort of six mushroom-colored buildings on 6 acres of handsomely landscaped grounds. Each is well furnished, and, although not particularly stylish, all come with balconies and a number of conveniences, including pay-per-view TV. All the studios have kitchenettes, and the suites have full kitchens. The least desirable rooms are classified as standards; they are small and evoke dormitory living. Studios are suitable for one or two. The one-bedroom suites are the most desirable as they are rather spacious and decently furnished. Closets are tiny, as are the shower bathrooms. Mattresses, however, are fairly new throughout. The best views of the ocean are on the third floor of the main building. You can dine here or patronize several restaurants nearby. The Sands is a true resort. The place might not be for the hopelessly romantic—it's too sterile for that. It's a good, all-around, reliable resort, one of the best in the area, and it charges only a fraction of the price of the mega-resorts.

Silver Sands, Christ Church, Barbados, W.I. ✆ **800/GO-BAJAN** in the U.S., 800/822-2077 in Canada, or 246/428-6001. Fax 246/428-3758. http://barbados.org/hotels/silvsnd. 106 units. Winter $130 single or double; $145 studio for 2; $175 suite for 2; $190 triple; $205 quad. Off-season $70 single or double; $80 studio for 2; $95 suite for 2; $110 triple; $125 quad. Extra person $15; children 12 and under stay free in parents' room. AE, DC, DISC, MC, V. **Amenities:** Restaurant, bar, room service, babysitting. *In room:* A/C, TV, kitchenette (some units), no phone.

3 Great Deals on Dining

Angry Annie's Restaurant & Bar ✿ *Value* INTERNATIONAL   Don't ask Annie why she's angry—she might tell you! Annie and Paul Matthews, both from the United Kingdom, run this friendly, cozy, 34-seat joint. It's decorated in tropical colors with a circular bar, and rock-and-roll classics play on the excellent sound system. The dishes are tasty, with lots of local flavor. The place is known for its ribs, the most savory on the island. We like the garlic-cream potatoes and the use of local vegetables whenever possible. Annie also turns out fresh fish and excellent pasta dishes. Try the takeout service if you'd like to dine back in your room.

First St., Holetown, St. James. ✆ **246/432-2119.** Main courses $12.50–$27.50. MC, V. Daily 6–10pm (sometimes until midnight).

Atlantis Hotels ✿✿ *Finds* BAJAN   Harking back to the Barbados of many years ago, the slightly run-down Atlantis is often filled with both Bajans and visitors. It's located between Cattlewash-on-Sea and Tent Bay on the east (Atlantic) coast. From the sunny, breeze-filled restaurant, with a sweeping view of the turbulent ocean, Enid Maxwell has been welcoming visitors from all over the world ever since she opened the place in 1945. Her copious buffets are one of the best values on the island. From loaded tables, you can sample such Bajan foods as pumpkin fritters, peas and rice, macaroni and cheese, chow mein, souse (pigs' feet marinated in lime juice), and Bajan pepper pot. No one ever leaves here hungry.

⌒Finds The Island's Freshest Fish

Savvy locals will guide you to the **Oistins Fish Market,** a historic fish market southeast of Bridgetown and past the settlements of Hastings and Worthing. This is where Bajan fishermen unload their catch of the day, selling it directly to the customer. This is ideal if you have an accommodation with a kitchen. If not, you'll find nearly a dozen run-down shacks that sell fried fish you know is fresh. Flying fish is in the fryer and fish steaks such as wahoo are on the grill. Buy a beer or a soft drink, and the day is yours.

In the Atlantis Hotels, Bathsheba, St. Joseph. ℂ **246/433-9445.** Reservations required for Sun buffet and 7pm dinner, recommended at all other times. 2-course fixed-price lunch $13.50; fixed-price dinner $17; Sun buffet $20. AE. Daily 11:30am–3pm; dinner Mon–Sat at 7pm (don't be late).

Barbecue Barn BAJAN   This basic restaurant serves simple fare, often to families staying in south-coast hotels. There's a fully stocked self-service salad bar. Try the barbecued chicken as a main course or in a sandwich. The menu also includes roast chicken, burgers, steak, and fried chicken nuggets. Most main courses are served with a choice of potato or spiced rice and garlic bread. A small selection of wines complements your meal.

Rockley, Christ Church. ℂ **246/430-3402.** Main courses $10.50–$12.50. MC, V. Daily 11am–11pm.

Bombas INTERNATIONAL   Simple and unpretentious though it is, this place is worth a detour. Right on the water at Paynes Bay, it's so inviting that you might adopt it as your local hangout. The avocados on Barbados are said to be ethereal, and you can find out why here. You can sample an array of other Bajan specialties, including dishes designed to appeal to the vegetarian market. The drinks here are made with fresh juices and not overly loaded with sugar. The owners Gaye and Wayne, a Scottish/Bajan couple, are hospitable hosts, chalking up their latest offerings on a blackboard menu. You can visit just for a snack, perhaps to enjoy rôti or seasoned flying fish. The main dishes are certainly worth trying, including the catch of the day, which can be blackened Cajun style or deep-fried in crispy batter, served with chips in the English style. They also make a wicked Bomba curry or, for a taste of the Highlands of Scotland, will serve you sautéed chicken breast on a bed of saffron rice with a Drambuie-cream sauce.

Paynes Bay, St. James. ℂ **246/432-0569.** Main courses $10–$16.50; lunch from $8. MC, V. Daily 11am–11pm.

Café Calabash ⭐ ⌒Finds BAJAN/AFTERNOON TEA   On the site of a Jacobean plantation great house, this is the most romantic place on Barbados to have afternoon tea or to stop in for a Bajan lunch of Creole fare. Nick Hudson, a restaurateur who became famous islandwide when he operated the restaurant La Cage aux Folles, opened this cafe in 1997. Now you can eat or drink at one of the premier tourist attractions of Barbados. The cafe looks out onto one of the few remaining virgin rain forests in the Caribbean. A typical meal might include one of the local homemade soups, such as pumpkin or fish. Sandwiches and burgers are always available, or you can order one of the fresh fish dishes of the day. Barracuda is often featured, as are swordfish and mahimahi. The cooks also make a mean chicken pot and some of the island's best banana bread.

St. Nicholas Abbey, on the St. Peter/St. Lucy border. ✆ 246/422-8725. Creole lunch $5–$18; snacks, traditional English tea from $4. No credit cards. Mon–Fri 10am–4pm.

Café Sol TEX-MEX   Even though this cafe has a gringo section on the menu, designed for diehard meat-and-potatoes Yankees, most people come for some of the best Tex-Mex food on the island. The burritos and tacos don't get much bigger than here. If you're looking for flavorful and zesty meals, good prices, oversized portions, and enthusiastic service, eat here. Feast on the tostados, fajitas, nachos, and all the good-tasting beef, shrimp, and chicken dishes, each served with rice and beans or fries. For non-Mexican foods, such as burgers, barbecued chicken, hot dogs, and steaks, you can fare better elsewhere.

St. Lawrence Gap, Christ Church. ✆ 246/435-9531. Main courses $12–$17. AE, MC, V. Daily 6–11pm.

Rôti Hut RÔTIS   The island's best rôtis are served here at this little Worthing hut, an off-white concrete structure with an enclosed patio for dining. Count on these zesty pastries to be filled with good-tasting and spicy meats, or whatever. The crowd pleaser is the mammoth chicken or beef potato rôti. The locals like their rôtis with bone, but you can order yours without if you wish. You can also order other food items, including beef burgers, fried chicken, and beef or chicken curry with rice. This is also a good place to pick up a picnic box.

Worthing, Christ Church. ✆ 246/435-7362. Snacks and plates $2–$4.50; picnic box $5. No credit cards. Mon–Thurs 11am–10pm; Fri–Sat 11am–11pm.

T.G.I. Boomers *Value* AMERICAN/BAJAN   South of Bridgetown near Rockley Beach along Highway 7, T.G.I. Boomers offers some of the best bargain meals on the island. It has an active bar and a row of tables for diners, who usually order frothy pastel-colored drinks as well. The cook prepares a special catch of the day, which is served with soup or salad, rice or baked potato, and a vegetable. You can always count on seafood, steaks, and hamburgers. For lunch, there's the daily Bajan special and jumbo sandwiches. Be sure to try one of the 16-ounce daiquiris.

St. Lawrence Gap, Christ Church. ✆ 246/428-8439. American breakfast $6.50; lunch specials $3.50–$7; dinner main courses $9–$25. AE, MC, V. Daily noon–10pm.

39 Steps ✦ INTERNATIONAL   This south-coast choice, one of the area's most popular, is the best wine bar in Hastings. Diners walk the 39 steps (or however many) to reach this convivial place where performers sometimes entertain on the sax and guitar. It's laid-back and casual, and the food and wine are not only good but affordable. Look to the chalkboard for the tasty favorites of the day. Whenever possible the cooks use fresh, local produce to concoct dishes that appeal to a wide cross-section, including English pub grub–style pies such as steak and kidney or chicken and mushroom. They also turn out lasagna and other pastas, along with seafood crêpes, shrimp and chicken curry, and blackened fish. The most famous dish of Barbados, flying fish, appears only on the lunch menu. They're not big on vegetables, however, serving only a mixed green salad. This pleasant restaurant and bar has lots of windows and a balcony for outdoor dining.

Chattel Plaza, Hastings, Christ Church. ✆ 246/427-0715. Main courses $14–$17. MC, V. Mon–Fri noon–midnight; Sat 6:30pm–midnight. Closed Sept.

Waterfront Café INTERNATIONAL/BAJAN   This is your best bet if you're in Bridgetown shopping or sightseeing. In a turn-of-the-century warehouse originally built to store bananas and freeze fish, this cafe serves international fare with a strong emphasis on Bajan specialties. Try the fresh catch of the day prepared Creole style, peppered steak, or the fish burger, made with kingfish or dolphin. For vegetarians, the menu features such dishes as pasta primavera, vegetable soup, and usually a special of the day. Both diners and drinkers are welcome here for Creole food, beer, and pastel-colored drinks. Tuesday nights bring live steel-band music and a Bajan buffet. To see the Thursday night Dixieland bands, reserve about a week in advance. There's jazz on Friday and Saturday.

The Careenage, Bridgetown. ℂ 246/427-0093. Reservations required. Main courses $14–$23. AE, DC, MC, V. Mon–Sat 10am–10pm.

Whistling Frog INTERNATIONAL　The decor of this restaurant is one of the most themed, but also one of the most charming, of the many that line the edges of St. Lawrence Gap. The decor includes lots and lots of images of every kind of frog. (Most of them are adorable, a fact that may or may not jibe with your particular point of view about amphibians.) Menu items manage to elevate bar food to slightly more respectable levels, thanks to stuffed peppers and platters of fresh fish that augment the traditional roster of nachos and burgers that form the basis of sports bar menus throughout the known world. Look for salads, platters of fried fish, and rum-based drinks such as the Time Bomb or Smoothie.

In the Time Out at the Gap hotel, St. Lawrence Gap, Christ Church. ℂ 246/420-5021. Main courses $10–$25. AE, MC, V. Daily 7am–10:45pm.

ALL-YOU-CAN-EAT BARGAINS

The Coach House ⓥalue BAJAN　The Coach House is a green-and-white house said to be 200 years old. The atmosphere is a Bajan version of an English pub, with an outdoor garden bar. Businesspeople and sun worshippers from nearby beaches come here for buffet lunches, where Bajan food is served Sunday to Friday noon to 3pm. The price is $14 for an all-you-can-eat lunch that includes local vegetables and salads prepared fresh daily. The bar menu, which ranges from burgers and fries to fried shrimp and flying fish, is a great deal as well. Dinner is from an a la carte menu with steak, chicken, fish, curried dishes, fresh salads, and a wide range of desserts, from cheesecake to banana flambé. Live music is available every night of the week.

Paynes Bay, St. James (on the main Bridgetown–Holetown Rd., just south of Sandy Lane, about 6 miles north of Bridgetown). ℂ 246/432-1163. Reservations recommended. Dinner main courses $7–$24; lunch buffet $14.50. AE, MC, V. Daily noon–2am.

The Ship Inn ENGLISH PUB/BAJAN　South of Bridgetown between Rockley Beach and Worthing, The Ship Inn is a traditional English-style pub with an attractive, rustic nautical decor. You can also enjoy a drink in the garden bar's tropical atmosphere. Many guests come to play darts, to meet friends, and especially to listen to top local bands (see "Barbados After Dark," later in this chapter). The Ship Inn serves substantial bar food, such as homemade steak-and-kidney pie, shepherd's pie, and chicken, shrimp, and fish dishes. For more formal dining, visit the Captain's Carvery, where you can have your fill of succulent cuts from prime roasts from the buffet, plus an array of traditional Bajan food, like filets of flying fish.

St. Lawrence Gap, Christ Church. ℂ 246/435-6961. Reservations recommended for the Captain's Carvery only. Main courses $8–$15; all-you-can-eat carvery meal $14 at lunch, $21 (plus $7.50 for appetizer and dessert) at dinner. DC, MC, V. Daily noon–3pm and 6–10:30pm (last order).

4 Hitting the Beaches

Bajans will tell you that their island has a beach for every day of the year. If you're visiting for only a short time, however, you'll probably be happy with the ones that are easy to find. They're all open to the public—even those in front of the big resort hotels and private homes—and the government requires that there be access to all beaches, via roads along the property line or through the hotel entrance. The beaches on the west, the so-called **Gold Coast** 🏖🏖, are the most popular. Swimming and sunbathing are best on the western coast, in the clear, buoyant waters of the Caribbean, although you might also want to visit the surf-pounded Atlantic coast in the east, which is better for the views than for swimming.

ON THE WEST COAST The waters are calm here. Major beaches include **Paynes Bay,** which is accessed from the Coach House, south of Holetown, and has a parking area. This is a good choice for watersports, especially snorkeling. The beach can get rather crowded, but the beautiful bay is worth the effort. Directly south of Payne's Bay, at Fresh Water Bay, are three of the best west-coast beaches: **Brighton Beach, Brandon's Beach,** and **Paradise Beach.**

We also recommend **Mullins Beach,** where the glassy blue waters attract snorkelers. There's parking on the main road and some shady areas. At the Mullins Beach Bar, you can order that rum drink you've been craving.

ON THE SOUTH COAST **Casuarina Beach** is accessed from Maxwell Coast Road, going across the property of the Casuarina Beach Hotel. This is one of the wider beaches of Barbados, and we've noticed that it's swept by trade winds even on the hottest days of August. Windsurfers are especially fond of this one. Food and drinks can be ordered at the hotel.

Silver Sands Beach, to the east of Oistins, is near the southernmost point of Barbados, directly east of South Point Lighthouse and near the Silver Rock Hotel. This white-sand beach is a favorite with many Bajans (who probably want to keep it a secret from tourists). Drinks are sold at the Silver Rock Bar.

Sandy Beach, reached from the parking lot on the Worthing main road, has tranquil waters opening onto a lagoon, the epitome of Caribbean charm. This is a family favorite, especially boisterous on weekends. Food and drinks are sold here.

ON THE SOUTHEAST COAST The southeast coast is the site of the big waves, especially at **Crane Beach,** the white-sand strip set against a backdrop of palms that you've probably seen in all the travel magazines. The beach is spectacular, as Prince Andrew, who has a house overlooking it, might agree. It offers excellent bodysurfing, but at times the waters might be too rough for all but the strongest swimmers. The beach is set against cliffs, with the Crane Beach Hotel towering above it. This is the ocean, not the calm Caribbean, so take precautions.

Bottom Bay, north of Sam Lord's Castle Resort, is one of our all-time Bajan favorites. Park on the top of a cliff, then walk down the steps to this much-photographed tropical beach with its grove of coconut palms; there's even a cave. The sand is brilliantly white against the aquamarine sea, a picture-postcard perfect beach paradise.

ON THE EAST (ATLANTIC) COAST There are miles and miles of uncrowded beaches along the east coast, but this is the Atlantic side, thus swimming here is potentially dangerous. Many travelers like to visit the beaches here, especially those in the **Bathsheba/Cattlewash** areas, for their rugged grandeur. Waves are extremely high on these beaches, and the bottom tends to be rocky. The currents are also unpredictable. But the beaches are ideal for strolling, if not for going into the water.

5 Sports & Other Outdoor Pursuits

DEEP-SEA FISHING   The fishing is first-rate in the waters around Barbados, which are rich with dolphin (mahimahi), marlin, wahoo, barracuda, sailfish, and cobia, to name only the most popular catches.

The Dive Shop, Pebbles Beach, Aquatic Gap, St. Michael (© **800/693-3483** or 246/426-9947) can arrange half-day charters for one to six people (all equipment and drinks included), costing $350 per boat. Under the same arrangement, the whole-day jaunt goes for $700.

HIKING   The **Barbados National Trust** (© **246/426-2421**) offers Sunday morning hikes throughout the year, often attracting more than 300 participants. Led by young Bajans and members of the National Trust, the hikes cover a different area of the island each week, giving you an opportunity to learn about the natural beauty of Barbados. The guides give brief talks on subjects such as geography, history, geology, and agriculture. The hikes, free and open to participants of all ages, are divided into fast, medium, and slow categories, with groups of no more than 10. All hikes leave promptly at 6am, are about 5 miles long, and take about 3 hours to complete. There are also hikes at 3:30 and 5:30pm, the latter conducted only on moonlit nights. For more information, contact the Barbados National Trust.

In 1998, Barbados created a nature trail that explores the natural history and heritage of Speightstown, once a major sugar port and even today a fishing town with old houses and a bustling waterfront. The **Arbib Nature & Heritage Trail** takes you through town, the mysterious gully known as "the Whim," and the surrounding districts. The first marked trail is a 4.7-mile trek that begins outside St. Peter's Church in Speightstown, traverses the Whim, crosses one of the last working plantations in Barbados (Warleight), and leads to the historic 18th-century Dover Fort, following along white-sand beaches at Heywoods before ending up back in town. Guided hikes are offered on Wednesday, Thursday, and Saturday. For information and reservations, call the Barbados National Trust, and ask for a trail map at the tourist office.

The rugged, dramatic **east coast** stretches about 16 miles from the lighthouse at Ragged Point, the easternmost point of Barbados, north along the Atlantic coast to Bathsheba and Pico Teneriffe. This is the island's most panoramic hiking area. Some hardy souls do the entire coast; if your time is limited, hike our favorite walk, the 4-mile stretch from Ragged Point to Consett Bay, along a rough, stony trail that requires only moderate endurance. Allow at least 2½ hours. A small picnic facility just north of Bathsheba is a popular spot for Bajan families, especially on Sundays. As for information, you're pretty much on your own, although if you stick to the coastline, you won't get lost.

HORSEBACK RIDING   The **Caribbean International Riding Centre,** St. Andrew, Sarely Hill (© **246/422-7433**), offers a different view of Barbados. With nearly 40 horses, Mrs. Roachford and her daughters offer a variety of trail rides for all levels of experience, ranging from a 1½-hour jaunt for $60 to a 2½-hour trek for $90. You'll ride through some of the most panoramic parts of Barbados, including the hilly terrain of the Scotland district. Along the way, you can see wild ducks and water lilies, with the rhythm of the Atlantic as background music.

SCUBA DIVING & SNORKELING   The clear waters off Barbados have a visibility of more than 100 feet most of the year. More than 50 varieties of fish inhabit the shallow inside reefs, and there's an unusually high concentration of hawksbill turtles. On night dives, you can spot sleeping fish, night anemones, lobsters, moray eels, and octopuses. Diving is concentrated on the leeward west and south coasts, where hard corals grow thick along the crest of the reef, and orange elephant ear, barrel sponge, and rope sponge cascade down the drop-off of the outer reef.

On a mile-long coral reef 2 minutes by boat from **Sandy Beach,** sea fans, corals, gorgonias, and reef fish are plentiful. *J.R.,* a dredge barge sunk as an artificial reef in 1983, is popular with beginners for its coral, fish life, and 20-foot depth. The *Berwyn,* a coral-encrusted tugboat that sank in Carlisle Bay in 1916, attracts photographers for its variety of reef fish, shallow depth, good light, and visibility.

Asta Reef, with a drop of 80 feet, has coral, sea fans, and reef fish in abundance. It's the site of a Barbados wreck that was sunk in 1986 as an artificial reef. **Dottins,** the most beautiful reef on the west coast, stretches 5 miles from Holetown to Bridgetown and has numerous dive sites at an average depth of 40 feet and drop-offs of 100 feet. The SS *Stavronikita,* a Greek freighter, is a popular site for advanced divers. Crippled by fire in 1976, the 360-foot freighter was sunk a quarter of a mile off the west coast to become an artificial reef in **Folkestone Underwater Park,** north of Holetown. The mast is at 40 feet, the deck at 80 feet, and the keel at 140 feet. While you explore the site, you might spot barracuda, moray eels, and a vibrant coat of bright yellow tube sponge, delicate pink rope sponge, and crimson encrusting sponge. The park has an underwater snorkel trail, plus glass-bottomed boat rides, making it a family favorite.

The **Dive Shop,** Pebbles Beach, Aquatic Gap, St. Michael (© 800/693-3483 or 246/426-9947), offers some of the best scuba diving on Barbados, charging $55 for a one-tank dive and $80 for a two-tank dive. Every day, three dive trips go out to the nearby reefs and wrecks; snorkeling trips and equipment rentals are also available. Visitors with reasonable swimming skills who have never dived before can sign up for a resort course. Priced at $70, it includes pool training, safety instructions, and a one-tank open-water dive. The establishment is NAUI- and PADI-certified and open daily 9am to 5pm. Some other dive shops in Barbados that rent or sell snorkeling equipment include the following: **Carib Ocean Divers,** St. James (© 246/422-4414); **Hazel's Water World,** Bridgetown, St. Michael (© 246/426-4043); and **Explore Sub,** Christ Church, near Bridgetown (© 246/435-6542).

Several companies also operate snorkeling cruises that take you to particularly picturesque areas; see "Submerged Sightseeing" under "Seeing the Sights," below.

TENNIS   The big hotels have tennis courts that you can reserve even if you're not a guest. In Barbados, most tennis players still wear traditional whites. **Folkestone Park,** Holetown (© 246/422-2314), is a public tennis court available for free. The **National Tennis Centre,** Sir Garfield Sobers Sports Complex, Wildey Street, St. Michael (© 246/437-6010), charges $12 per hour; you must reserve in advance. Courts at the **Barbados Squash Club,** Marine House, Christ Church (© 246/427-7913), can be reserved for $12.50 for 45 minutes.

WINDSURFING   Experts say the windsurfing off Barbados is as good as any this side of Hawaii. Judging from the crowds that flock here, they're right. Windsurfing on Barbados has turned into a very big business between November and April, attracting thousands of windsurfers from as far away as Finland, Argentina, and Japan. The shifting of the trade winds between November and May and the shallow offshore reef of **Silver Sands** create unique conditions of wind and wave swells. This allows windsurfers to reach speeds of up to 50 knots and do complete loops off the waves. Silver Sands is rated the best spot in the Caribbean for advanced windsurfing (skill rating of 5–6), so you've gotta be good.

The **Barbados Windsurfing Club,** with two branches on the island, can get you started. Beginners and intermediates usually opt for the branch in Oistins (© **246/428-7277**), where winds are constant but the sea is generally flat and calm. Advanced intermediates and experts usually go to the branch adjacent to the Silver Sands Hotel, in Christ Church (© **246/428-6001**), where stronger winds and higher waves allow surfers to combine aspects of windsurfing and conventional Hawaii-style surfing. Both branches use boards and equipment provided by the Germany-based Club Mistral. Lessons at either branch cost between $40 and $65 per hour, depending on how many people are in your class. Equipment rents for $25 per hour, or $55 to $65 per half day, depending on where and what you rent; rates are less expensive at the Oistins branch.

6 Seeing the Sights

TOURS & CRUISES

Barbados is worth exploring, either in a rental car or with a taxi-driver guide. Unlike on so many islands of the Caribbean, the roads are fair and quite passable. They are, however, poorly signposted, and newcomers invariably get lost, not only once, but several times. If you get lost, the people in the countryside are generally helpful.

ORGANIZED TOURS   Bajan Tours, Eric Court, Bishops Court Hill, St. Michael (© **246/437-9389**), is a locally owned and operated company. The best bet for the first-timer is the Exclusive Island Tour, which departs daily between 8:30 and 9am and returning between 3:30 and 4pm. It covers all the highlights of the island, including the Barbados Wildlife Reserve, the Chalky Mount Potteries, and the rugged east coast. On Friday, the Heritage Tour takes in mainly the island's major plantations and museums. Monday through Friday, the Eco Tour explores the natural beauty of the island. All tours cost $56 per person and include a full buffet lunch.

CRUISES   **Most popular and fun are the **Jolly Roger "Pirate" Cruises run by Jolly Roger Cruises (© **246/436-6424**), operating out of Bridgetown Harbour. Passengers can rope swing, swim, snorkel, and suntan on the top deck. Even mock weddings are staged. A buffet lunch with rum punch is presented Tuesday, Thursday, and Saturday 10am to 2pm. Lunch cruises cost $61.50 per person. You can also sail on a catamaran lunch cruise, a 4-hour cruise offered daily 10am to 3pm, costing $65 per person. Children 12 and under sail for half-price.

Part cruise ship, part nightclub, the **M/V _Harbour Master_** (© **246/ 430-0900**) is a 100-foot, four-story vessel with theme decks, a modern gallery, and three bars. It boasts a dance floor and a sit-down restaurant, also offering formal buffets on its Calypso Deck. On the Harbour Master Deck, there's a bank of TVs for sports buffs. The showpiece of the vessel is an onboard semi-submersible, which is lowered hydraulically to 6 feet beneath the ship. This is, in effect, a "boat in a boat," with 30 seats. Lunch and dinner cruises cost $61.50 per person; the semi-submersible experience costs another $10.

**SUBMERGED SIGHTSEEING   **You no longer have to be an experienced diver to see what lives 150 feet below the surface of the sea. Now anybody can view the sea's wonders on sightseeing submarines. The air-conditioned submersibles seat 28 to 48 passengers and make several dives daily 9am to 4pm. Passengers are transported aboard a ferryboat from the Careenage in downtown Bridgetown to the submarine site, about a mile from the west coast of Barbados. The ride offers a view of the west coast of the island.

The submarines *Atlantic I* and *III* have viewing ports that allow you to see a rainbow of colors, tropical fish, plants, and even a shipwreck that lies upright and intact below the surface. The cost is $80 for adults, $40 for children. For reservations, contact **Atlantis Submarines** (**Barbados**), Shallow Draught, Bridgetown (*©* **246/436-8929**).

It's also possible to go cruising over one of the shore reefs to observe marine life. You sit in air-conditioned comfort aboard the *Atlantis Seatrec*, a semi-submersible boat, which gives you a chance to get a snorkeler's view of the reef through large viewing windows. You can also relax on deck as you take in the scenic coastline. A second *Seatrec* tour explores wreckage sites. Divers go down with video cameras to three different wrecks on Carlisle Bay, and the video is transmitted to TV monitors aboard the vessel. Both tours cost $35 for adults, half-price for children 4 to 12 (not suitable for kids 3 and under). For reservations, call the number above.

EXPLORING BRIDGETOWN

Often hot and clogged with traffic, the capital, **Bridgetown,** merits a morning's shopping jaunt (see "Shopping," later in this chapter), plus a visit to some of its major sights.

Because some half a million visitors arrive on Barbados by cruise ship each year, the government has opened a $6 million **cruise-ship terminal** with 20 duty-free shops, 13 local retail stores, and scads of vendors. Cruise passengers can choose from a range of products, including the arts and crafts of Barbados, jewelry, liquor, china, crystal, electronics, perfume, and leather goods. The interior was designed to re-create an island street scene; some storefronts appear as traditional chattel houses in brilliant island colors, complete with streetlights, tropical landscaping, benches, and pushcarts.

Begin your tour at the waterfront, called **the Careenage** (French for "turning vessels on their side for cleaning"). This was a haven for clipper ships, and even though today it doesn't have the color of yesteryear, it's still worth exploring.

At **Trafalgar Square,** the long tradition of British colonization is immortalized. The monument here, honoring Lord Nelson, was executed by Sir Richard Westmacott and erected in 1813. The great gray Victorian/Gothic **Public Buildings** on the square look like those you might expect to find in London. The east wing contains the meeting halls of the Senate and the House of Assembly, with some stained-glass windows representing the sovereigns of England. Look for the "Great Protector" himself, Oliver Cromwell.

Behind the Financial Building, **St. Michael's Cathedral,** east of Trafalgar Square, is the symbol of the Church of England. This Anglican church was built in 1655 but was completely destroyed in a 1780 hurricane. Reconstructed in 1789, it was again damaged by a hurricane in 1831. George Washington supposedly worshiped here on his visit to Barbados.

The **Synagogue,** Synagogue Lane (no phone), is one of the oldest in the western hemisphere and is surrounded by a burial ground of early Jewish settlers. The present building dates from 1833. It was constructed on the site of an even older synagogue, erected by Jews from Brazil in 1654. It's now part of the National Trust of Barbados—and a synagogue once again. It's open Monday to Friday 9am to 4pm; a donation is requested for admission.

First made popular in 1870, **cricket** is the national pastime on Barbados. Matches can last from 1 to 5 days. If you'd like to see a local match, watch for announcements in the newspapers or ask at the **Tourist Board,** on Harbour Road (✆ **246/427-2623**). From Bridgetown, you can take a taxi to **Garrison Savannah,** just south of the capital, a venue for frequent cricket matches and horse races.

Barbados Gallery of Art, Bush Hill (✆ **246/228-0149**), in a restored old building in the historic Garrison district, displays the very best Bajan and Caribbean visual art. The gallery also pays tribute to the memory of the late actress Claudette Colbert, longtime resident of Barbados. She is memorialized in a beautiful garden here, and the gallery even owns one of her own paintings. Hours are Tuesday through Saturday 10am to 5pm. Admission is $2.50 for adults, free for children.

Barbados Museum, St. Ann's Garrison, St. Michael (✆ **246/427-0201**), is housed in a former military prison. Extensive collections show the island's development from prehistoric to modern times, as well as fascinating glimpses into the natural environment and fine examples of West Indian maps and decorative arts. The museum sells a variety of quality publications, reproductions, and handcrafts. Its cafe is a good place for a snack or light lunch. Hours are Monday to Saturday 9am to 5pm, Sunday 2 to 6pm. Admission is $6 for adults, $3 for children.

Nearby, the russet-red **St. Ann's Fort,** on the fringe of the savanna, garrisoned British soldiers in 1694. The fort wasn't completed until 1703. The Clock House survived the hurricane of 1831.

A GREAT HOUSE OUTSIDE BRIDGETOWN

Tyrol Cot Heritage Village ✪   If you arrived at the airport, you'll recognize the name of Sir Grantley Adams, the leader of the Bajan movement for independence from Britain. Tyrol Cot Heritage Village was once his home, and his wife, Lady Adams, lived in the house until her death in 1990. Once you had to wrangle a highly prized invitation to visit, but it's now open to all. It was built sometime in the mid-1850s from coral stone, in a Palladian style. The grounds have been turned into a museum of Bajan life, including small chattel houses where potters and artists work. The museum attracts mainly those with a genuine interest in Bajan culture; it might not be for the average visitor intent on getting to the beach on time. The Old Stables Restaurant is located in the former stables and serves meals until 4pm. Reservations are recommended for the Friday buffet, by calling ✆ **246/425-7777.**

Codrington Hill, St. Michael. ✆ **246/424-2074.** Admission $6 adults, $3 children. Mon–Fri 9am–5pm.

INLAND SIGHTS ✪✪

Many visitors stay on the fabulous west-coast beaches, but the island's true beauty is its lush interior. If you have the time, we highly recommend a hike, drive, or tour through such rarely visited parishes as St. Thomas and St. George (both of which are landlocked) and the wild Atlantic coast parishes of St. Andrews and St. John.

Flower Forest ✪   This old sugar plantation stands 850 feet above sea level near the western edge of the Scotland district, a mile from Harrison's Cave. Set in one of the most scenic parts of Barbados, it's more than just a botanical garden; it's where people and nature came together to create something beautiful. After viewing the grounds, visitors can purchase handcrafts at Best of Barbados (see "Shopping," below).

Richmond Plantation, St. Joseph. ☏ **246/433-8152**. Admission $7 adults, $3.50 children 5–16, free for children 4 and under. Daily 9am–5pm.

Francia Plantation ☄

A fine family home, the Francia Plantation stands on a wooded hillside overlooking the St. George Valley and is still owned and occupied by descendants of the original owner. Built in 1913, the house blends both West Indian and European architectural influences. You can explore several rooms, including the dining room with its family silver and an 18th-century James McCabe bracket clock. On the walls are antique maps and prints, including a map of the West Indies printed in 1522.

St. George, Barbados. ☏ **246/429-0474**. Admission $5. Mon–Fri 10am–4pm. On the ABC Hwy., turn east onto Hwy. 4 at the Norman Niles Roundabout (follow the signs to Gun Hill); after going ½ mile, turn left at the Francia sign (follow the signs to Gun Hill); after another mile, turn right at the Shell gas station and follow the road past St. George's Parish Church and up the hill for a mile, turning left at the sign to Francia.

Gun Hill Signal Station

One of two such stations owned and operated by the Barbados National Trust, the Gun Hill Signal Station is strategically placed on the highland of St. George and commands a panoramic view from the east to the west. Built in 1818, it was the finest of a chain of signal stations and was also used as an outpost for the British army. The restored military cookhouse houses a snack bar and gift shop.

Hwy. 4. ☏ **246/429-1358**. Admission $5 adults, $2.30 children 13 and under. Mon–Sat 9am–5pm. Take Hwy. 3 from Bridgetown, then go inland from Hwy. 4 toward St. George Church.

Harrison's Cave ☄☄

The underground world here, the number-one tourist attraction of Barbados, is viewed from aboard an electric tram and trailer. On the tour, you'll see bubbling streams, tumbling cascades, and subtly lit deep pools, while all around stalactites hang overhead like icicles, and stalagmites rise from the floor. Visitors can disembark and get a closer look at this natural phenomenon at the Rotunda Room and the Cascade Pool. Although it's interesting, it might not impress Americans who have been to the far more spectacular Carlsbad or Luray Caverns.

Welchman Hall, St. Thomas. ☏ **246/438-6640**. Tour reservations recommended. Admission $13 adults, $6 children. Daily 9am–4pm. Closed Good Friday, Easter Sun, and Christmas Day.

Morgan Lewis Sugar Mill

Created in 1727 when Barbados was one of Britain's major sugar colonies, this mill is now restored, one of the only two intact sugar mills in the Caribbean (the other is in Antigua). The Barbados National Trust maintains it. The mill includes an exhibit of the equipment once used to make sugar. The on-site plantation house has seen better days, but makes a picturesque ruin with its rubble walls. The mill lies on a scenic mount in the northeast of the island, offering panoramic views of the east coast. Before its restoration, this mill appeared on a list of the 100 most endangered historical sites in the world.

Signposted near the Barbados Wildlife Reserve, St. Andrew. ☏ **246/422-7429**. Admission $5 adults, $2.50 children. Mon–Fri 9am–5pm.

Welchman Hall Gully ☄

The Barbados National Trust owns this lush, tropical garden. You'll see some specimens of plants that were here when the English settlers landed in 1627. Many of the plants are labeled—clove, nutmeg, tree fern, and cocoa, among others—and occasionally you'll spot a wild monkey. You can also see breadfruit trees that are supposedly descendants of the seedlings brought ashore by Captain Bligh, of *Bounty* fame.

Welchman Hall, St. Thomas. ☏ **246/438-6671**. Admission $5.75 adults, $3 children 6–12, free for children 5 and under. Daily 9am–5pm. Take Hwy. 2 from Bridgetown.

EXPLORING THE SOUTHEAST (ST. PHILIP)

While you're driving around this part of the island, you might like to stop off at the **Crane Beach Hotel,** on Crane Bay, St. Philip (© **246/423-6220**). We don't recommend staying here, but nonguests can buy a day pass for $10. Take a dip in the pool (a Roman-style affair, complete with columns), have a drink at the bar, and enjoy the fabulous views over the Atlantic.

Heritage Park & Rum Factory   After driving through cane fields, you'll arrive at the first rum distillery to be launched on the island since the 19th century. Inaugurated in 1996, this factory is located on a former molasses and sugar plantation dating back some 350 years. Produced on site is ESA Field, a white rum praised by connoisseurs. Adjacent is an admission-free park where Bajan handcrafts are displayed in the Art Foundry (see "Shopping," below). You'll also find an array of shops and carts selling global foods, handcrafts, and products.

Foursquare Plantation, St. Philip. © **246/420-1977.** Admission $15. Daily 9am–5pm.

Sunbury Plantation House 🐾   If you have time to visit only one plantation or great house in Barbados, make it this one. It's the only great house on Barbados where all the rooms are open for viewing. The 300-year-old plantation house is steeped in history, featuring mahogany antiques, old prints, and a unique collection of horse-drawn carriages. Take the informative tour, then stop in the Courtyard Restaurant and Bar for a meal or drinks; there's also a gift shop. A candlelight dinner is offered at least once a week; this five-course meal, served at a 200-year-old mahogany table, costs $75 per person.

6 Cross Rd., St. Philip. © **246/423-6270.** Admission $7 adults, $3.50 children. Daily 9:30am–4:30pm.

EXPLORING THE NORTHEAST

Andromeda Botanic Gardens 🐾   On a cliff overlooking the town of Bathsheba on the rugged east coast, limestone boulders make for a natural 8-acre rock-garden setting. Thousands of orchids, hundreds of hibiscus and heliconia, and many varieties of ferns, begonias, palms, and other species grow here in splendid profusion. You'll occasionally see frogs, herons, lizards, hummingbirds, and sometimes a mongoose or a monkey.

Bathsheba, St. Joseph. © **246/433-9384.** Admission $6 adults, $3 children, free for kids 5 and under. Daily 9am–5pm.

Barbados Wildlife Reserve   Across the road from Farley Hill National Park, in northern St. Peter Parish, the reserve is set in a mahogany forest that's maintained by the Barbados Primate Research Center. Visitors can stroll through what is primarily a monkey sanctuary and an arboretum. Aside from the uncaged monkeys, you can see wild hares, deer, tortoises, otters, wallabies (which were brought into Barbados), and a variety of tropical birds.

⌒*Tips* The Great Tour

From mid-January through the first week of April, you can tour a different **great house** every Wednesday afternoon. Houses include those rarely seen by the public, as well as major attractions such as Francia Plantation. You'll see a great array of plantation antiques and get a feeling for the elegant colonial lifestyle once commonplace on Barbados. For more information, call © **246/426-2421.**

(*Moments* A Beautiful Picnic Spot

Farley Hill National Park surrounds what used to be one of the greatest houses of Barbados, **Farley Hill,** a mansion in ruins. The park lies in the north of the parish of St. Peter, directly across the road leading into the Barbados Wildlife Reserve. You can wander in the park overlooking the turbulent waters of the Atlantic, and pack along a picnic. You can enter the park for free if you're walking, but it costs $1.50 to bring a car in. Hours are daily 8:30am to 6pm.

Farley Hill, St. Peter. ℂ **246/422-8826.** Admission $10 adults, $5 for children 12 and under. Daily 10am–5pm.

St. Nicholas Abbey Surrounded by sugarcane fields, this Jacobean plantation great house has been around since about 1650. It was never actually an abbey—around 1820 an ambitious owner simply christened it as such. More than 200 acres are still cultivated each year. The house, characterized by its curved gables, is believed to be one of three Jacobean houses in the western hemisphere. At least the ground floor of the structure is open to the public. You can have lunch or afternoon tea at the cafe and perhaps catch an intriguing home movie from the 1930s.

On Cherry Tree Hill, Hwy. 1. ℂ **246/422-8725.** Admission $5 adults, free for children 12 and under. Mon–Fri 10am–3:30pm.

7 Shopping ⋆⋆

You might find duty-free merchandise here at prices 20% to 40% lower than in the United States and Canada—but you need to be a smart shopper to spot bargains and you should be familiar with prices back in your hometown. Duty-free shops have two prices listed on items of merchandise: the local retail price, and the local retail price less the government-imposed tax.

Some of the best duty-free buys include cameras, watches, crystal, gold jewelry, bone china, cosmetics and perfumes, and liquor (including locally produced Barbados rum and liqueurs), along with tobacco products and cashmere sweaters, tweeds, and sportswear from Britain. If you purchase items made on Barbados, you don't have to pay duty.

The outstanding item in Barbados handcrafts is black-coral jewelry. Another Bajan craft, clay pottery, originated at **Chalky Mount Potteries,** which is worth a visit. Potters turn out different products, some based on designs that are centuries old. The potteries (which are signposted) are north of Bathsheba on the east coast, in St. Joseph Parish near Barclay's Park. In shops across the island, you'll also find a selection of locally made vases, pots, pottery mugs, glazed plates, and ornaments.

Wall hangings are woven from local grasses and dried flowers, and island craftspeople also turn out straw mats, baskets, and bags with raffia embroidery. Still in its infant stage, leatherwork is also found on Barbados, particularly handbags, belts, and sandals.

IN BRIDGETOWN Cruise passengers generally head for the **cruise-ship terminal** at Bridgetown Harbour, which has some 20 duty-free shops, 13 local shops, and many vendors (see "Exploring Bridgetown" under "Seeing the Sights," earlier in this chapter).

> **Value** **Cheap Thrills: What to See & Do for Free (Well, Almost) on Barbados**
>
> - **Go Native at the Market.** The major markets are found in the center of the main towns of Bridgetown (the capital), Oistins, and Speightstown. To get you in the mood for a taste treat, order a glass of mauby from one of the vendors. This is a refreshing but slightly bitter iced tea made from a tree bark. On our recent rounds we discovered a delightful new way of doing gazpacho: From the mango trees. It's addictive. Every hawker in these markets has something good to eat: One woman was cooking some pumpkin fritters, formed into a ball and fried in butter, and another was luring you to taste her bowl of pepperpot, a meat stew preserved by cassava juice and kept for several days (it dates from the time of the Arawaks). For dessert, seek out a Rastaman pushing an oversized cart filled with coconut. On command he'll take his machete to a green coconut and whack it off to offer you a cool drink, followed by "the jelly," that soft essence that slithers sweetly down your throat.
> - **Journey into Yesteryear.** Bridgetown, the capital of this island known as "Little England," retains its British influence even though independent. Stroll around the city center for a nostalgic look at a time gone by. A relatively small city, its heart lies on the north bank of the Careenage in the heart of the old port. Broad Street leads into Trafalgar Square, the city's main drag. Here is a monument to Lord Horatio Nelson, predating the column in London's Trafalgar Square by 27 years. As a 19-year-old lieutenant, Nelson was based in Barbados in 1777. A short walk from Trafalgar, St. Michael's Cathedral was completed in 1789 and makes for a peaceful oasis in the heart of the bustling city. The classier stores are along Broad Street, including Cave Shepherd, the largest department store.

At **Articrafts,** Broad Street (© **246/427-5767**), John and Rosyln Watson have assembled an impressive display of Bajan arts and crafts. Roslyn's distinctive wall hangings are decorated with objects from the island, including sea fans and coral. The unique **Colours of De Caribbean,** the Waterfront Marina, next to the Waterfront Café, on the Careenage (© **246/436-8522**), carries original hand-painted and batik clothing, all made in the West Indies, plus jewelry and decorative objects.

Cave Shepherd, Broad Street (© **246/431-2121**), is the largest department store on the island and the best place for duty-free merchandise. There are branches at Sunset Crest in Holetown, Da Costas Mall, Grantley Adams Airport, and the Bridgetown cruise-ship terminal, but if your time is limited, try this outlet, as it has the widest selection. The store sells perfumes, cosmetics, fine crystal and bone china, cameras, jewelry, swimwear, leather goods, men's designer clothing, handcrafts, liquor, and souvenirs. You can take a break in the cool comfort of the Balcony, overlooking Broad Street, which serves vegetarian dishes and has a salad bar and beer garden.

Want something esoteric to look up? Head for George Washington House atop Bush Hill in the historic Garrison area south of Bridgetown. Although it's now filled with the offices of Barbados Light & Power Co., this is where in 1751 Washington stayed with his brother Lawrence, to recover from tuberculosis.

- **Visit a Pirate's Castle.** The finest mansion in Barbados has had a notorious history. Today the property is the site of **Sam Lord's Castle Resorts,** Long Bay at St. Philip (© 246/423-7350), but in 1820 it was the great house built by one of the island's most notorious scoundrels. According to the legend, Samuel Hall Lord—called "the Regency Rascal"—constructed the estate with money acquired by luring ships to wreck on the jagged but hard-to-detect rocks of Cobbler's Cove Reef. The great house, still standing today, features double verandas on all sides and magnificent plaster ceilings created by Charles Rutter, who crafted the ceilings of Windsor Castle in England. A lot of the original mahogany furniture and gilt mirrors remain intact today. The castle is open to the public daily and charges admission of only $1.25.

- **Hike a Self-Guided Nature Trail.** In October 1998 Barbados launched two nature trails that explore the natural history and heritage of Speightstown, once a major sugar port and today a fishing town with old houses and a bustling waterfront. The **Arbib Nature & Heritage Trail** offers insights into this old Caribbean town (see "Sports & Other Outdoor Pursuits," earlier in this chapter). Equally enchanting is the 3.4-mile trail designed for those looking for a more relaxing hike. There are two guided hikes, at 9am and 2:30pm, on Wednesday, Thursday, and Saturday. The trail begins outside St. Peter's Church in Speightstown. To prebook a hike and learn more information, call the **Barbados National Trust** at © 246/426-2421.

Harrison's, 1 Broad St. (© 246/431-5500), has 14 branch stores, all selling a wide variety of duty-free merchandise, including china, crystal, jewelry, leather goods, and perfumes—all at fair prices. Also for sale are some fine leather products handcrafted in Colombia. Harrison's is the major competitor to Cave Shepherd on the island, but we'd give the edge to Cave Shepherd.

Little Switzerland, in the Da Costas Mall, Broad Street (© 246/431-0030), offers a wide selection of fragrances and cosmetics, watches, fine jewelry, Mont Blanc pens, and an array of goodies from Waterford, Lalique, Swarovski, Baccarat, and others. Also on Broad Street, at Mall 34, is a branch of **Best of Barbados** (© 246/436-1416); see "Elsewhere Around the Island," below.

Just a 10-minute drive south of Bridgetown, **Luna Jewelers,** Bay Street at Bedford Avenue, about four buildings over from Barbados's Parliament (© 246/430-0355), sells diamonds and precious stones, watches and gift items. What makes Luna unusual is its emphasis on Art Nouveau and Art Deco designs set into gold and silver, crafted on Barbados in alluring designs. Fossilized Bajan coral is carefully polished and set into gold or silver settings and, in some cases, intricate mosaic-style inlays.

Pelican Village, Harbour Road (© 246/426-4391), offers bargains from Bajan artisans. In Bridgetown, go down Princess Alice Highway to the city's Deep Water Harbour, where you'll find this tiny colony of thatch-roofed shops. Some of the shops here are gimmicky, but interesting items can be found. Sometimes you can see craftspeople at work.

ELSEWHERE AROUND THE ISLAND   The best shop on the island for local products is **Best of Barbados,** in the Southern Palms, St. Lawrence Gap, Christ Church, on the south coast (© 246/420-8040). Part of an islandwide chain of 12 stores, this tasteful shop sells only products designed and/or made on Barbados, such as prints, coasters, T-shirts, pottery, dolls, games, and cookbooks. Also in the town of St. Lawrence Gap is **Walker's Caribbean World** (© 246/428-1183), near the Southern Palms, which offers many locally made items for sale, as well as handcrafts from the Caribbean Basin and the famous Jill Walker prints.

The **Art Foundry,** Rum Factory & Heritage Park, Foursquare Plantation, St. James (© 246/418-0714), is operated by R. L. Seale, the rum distiller. It displays some of the finest works of art on Barbados in its ground-floor gallery, with changing exhibitions upstairs.

Earthworks Pottery/The Potter's House Gallery, Edgehill Heights 2, St. Thomas (© 246/425-0223), is one of the artistic highlights of Barbados. Deep in the island's central highlands, Canadian-born Goldie Spieler and her son, David, create whimsical ceramics in the colors of the sea and sky; many objects are decorated with Antillean-inspired swirls and zigzags. On the premises are a studio and a showroom that sells the output of at least half a dozen other island potters. Purchases can be shipped. The **Great House Gallery,** at the Bagatelle Restaurant, Highway 2A, St. Thomas (© 246/421-6767), in one of the most historic great houses on Barbados, displays oils and watercolors by Caribbean, Latin American, and British artists.

The **Shell Gallery,** Carlton House, St. James (© 246/422-2593), has the best collection of shells in the West Indies and features the art of Maureen Edghill, the finest artist in this field and the founder of this unique gallery. Also offered are hand-painted china, shell jewelry, local pottery and ceramics, and batik and papier-mâché artwork. **Greenwich House Antiques,** Greenwich Village, Trents Hill, St. James (© 246/432-1169), a 25-minute drive from Bridgetown, feels like a genteel private home where the objects for sale seem to have come from the attic of your favorite slightly dotty great-aunt. Dozens of objects fill every available inch of tabletop or display space.

8 Barbados After Dark

ON THE WEST COAST   A lot of the evening entertainment around here revolves around the big resorts, all of which have lovely bars and many of which host bands and beach parties in the evening. See "Accommodations You Can Afford," earlier in this chapter.

Attracting mostly visitors, **Coach House,** Paynes Bay, St. James (© 246/432-1163), is a Bajan version of an English pub, with an outdoor garden bar. From 6 to 10:30pm, you can order bar meals, including flying-fish burgers, priced at $8 and up. Most nights, there's live music—everything from steel bands to jazz, pop, and rock, attracting an attentive crowd from 9pm on. The lunchtime buffet, offered Monday through Friday ($14), is popular.

John Moore Bar ✦✦, on the waterfront, Weston, St. James (📞 **246/422-2258**), is the most atmospheric and least pretentious bar on Barbados. It's the nerve center of this waterfront town, filled throughout the day and night with a congenial group of neighborhood residents, with a scattering of foreigners. Most visitors opt for a rum punch or beer, but you can order up a platter of local fish as long as you don't mind waiting.

Head for **Upstairs at Olives,** Holetown, St. James (📞 **246/432-2112**), where you can order excellent drinks while seated in an atmosphere of potted palms and old-fashioned ceiling fans that's straight out of *Casablanca.*

IN BRIDGETOWN   For the most authentic Bajan evening possible, head for **Baxters Road** in Bridgetown, where there's always something cooking on Friday and Saturday after 11pm. In fact, if you stick around until dawn, the party's still going strong. Some old-time visitors have compared Baxters Road to the back-streets of New Orleans in the 1930s. If you fall in love with the place, you can "caf crawl" up and down the street, where nearly every bar is run by a Bajan mama.

The most popular cafe on Baxters Road is **Enid's** (she has a phone, "but it doesn't work"), a little ramshackle establishment where Bajans come to devour fried chicken at 3 in the morning. Enid's is open daily 8:30pm to 8:30am, when the last satisfied customer departs into the blazing morning sun and Enid heads home to get some sleep before the new night begins. Stop in for a Banks beer.

The Rusty Pelican, the Careenage (📞 **246/436-7778**), is an atmospheric choice if you're in Bridgetown at night. It's right on the waterfront, and in addition to the good drinks, the club often has a musician (or musicians) to entertain. **The Boatyard,** Bay Street, Bridgetown (📞 **246/436-2622**), has a pubby atmosphere, with a DJ and occasional live bands.

Harbour Lights, Marine's Villa, Lower Bay Street, about a mile southeast of Bridgetown (📞 **246/436-7225**), is the most popular weekend spot for dancing, drinking, and flirting on all of Barbados. In a modern seafront building with an oceanfront patio (which gives dancers a chance to cool off), the place plays reggae, soca, and whatever else is popular until the wee hours every night. The barbecue pit/kiosk serves up grilled meats and hamburgers. Monday is beach party night; the $44 charge includes transportation to and from your hotel, a barbecue buffet, drinks, and a live band. On Wednesday and Friday, there's a cover of $12 to $17.50. The place attracts a large following among locals, with a few foreign visitors showing up.

ON THE SOUTH COAST   **Cafe Sol,** St. Lawrence Gap, Christ Church (📞 **246/435-9531**), has an encircling veranda opening onto a view of the water. A very convivial crowd gathers here to enjoy the bustling activity. As a specialty of the house, the bartender rubs the margarita glasses with Bajan sugar instead of the usual salts.

Plantation Restaurant and Garden Theatre, Main Road (Hwy. 7), St. Lawrence, Christ Church (📞 **246/428-5048**), is the island's main showcase for evening dinner theater and Caribbean cabaret. It's completely touristy, but despite that, most people enjoy it. Every Wednesday and Friday, dinner is served at 6:30pm, followed by a show, *Plantation Tropical Spectacular II,* at 8pm. Expect elaborate costumes and lots of reggae, calypso, and limbo. For $75, you get dinner, the show, and transport to and from your hotel; the show alone costs $37.50. Reserve in advance.

Another tourist show, **1627 and All That,** Barbados Museum, Highway 7, Garrison, St. Michael (📞 **246/428-1627**), effectively combines music with entertainment and dancing. It's the most interesting place on Barbados on a Thursday night. A night out here involves a cocktail hour, a large buffet of Bajan food, and a historic and cultural presentation. The $57.50 charge includes transportation to and from your hotel. Dinner is served at 7pm; the show lasts from 6:30 to 10pm.

The Ship Inn, St. Lawrence Gap, Christ Church (© **246/435-6961**), recommended earlier, in "Great Deals on Dining," is now among the leading entertainment centers on the south coast. The pub is the hot spot: Top local bands perform nightly, offering reggae, calypso, and Top 40 music. The entrance fee, which changes daily, is redeemable for food or drink at any of the other bars or restaurants in the Ship Inn complex, so you're actually paying only a small fee for the live entertainment. The place draws an equal mixture of visitors and locals.

Bert's Bar, at the Abbeville Hotel in Worthing, on the Main Road in Christ Church (© **246/435-7924**), is known for making the best daiquiris on the island. Sports fans head for **Bubba's Sports Bar,** Rockley Main Road, Christ Church (© **246/435-6217**), which offers a couple of satellite dishes, a 10-foot video screen, and a dozen TVs. The longest bar on the island is at **After Dark,** St. Lawrence Gap, Christ Church (© **246/435-6547**), where you can often hear live reggae, soca, Bajan calypso, and jazz.

Bonaire

Untrampled by hordes of tourists, Bonaire is one of the world's premier destinations for diving and snorkeling. Unlike some islands, Bonaire isn't just surrounded by coral reefs—it *is* the reef, sitting on the top of a dry, sunny underwater mountain. Its shores are thick with rainbow-hued fish. Powdery white sands and turquoise waters beckon. Spearfishing isn't allowed in its waters, nor is the taking or destruction of any coral or other living animal from the sea.

Bonaire is also a bird-watcher's haven, home to some 135 species. You'll spot flamingos (which nearly outnumber the sparse human population), as well as big-billed pelican, bright green parrots, snipes, terns, parakeets, herons, and hummingbirds. Bring binoculars.

This sleepy island doesn't have the glitz of Aruba, its sibling in the Netherlands Antilles (an autonomous part of the Netherlands). In fact, Bonaireans treasure their precious environment and go to great lengths to protect it. Although they eagerly seek tourism, they don't want to create "another Aruba," with its high-rise hotels.

If you're a serious diver, be sure to book a package deal. Bonaire has a number of moderately priced inns and hotels and a handful of small guesthouses. Budget travelers can also rent an apartment with a kitchen to keep dining costs low. Even so, you'll be shocked at grocery-store prices, since everything has to be imported.

Bonaire has a population of about 10,000. Its capital is **Kralendijk** (*Krall*-en-dike). It's most often reached from its neighbor island of Curaçao, 30 miles to the west. Like Curaçao, it's desertlike, with a dry and brilliant atmosphere. Only 5 miles wide and 24 miles long, Bonaire is poised in the Caribbean close to the coast of South America and comprises about 112 square miles. Its northern sector is hilly, tapering up to Mount Brandaris, all of 788 feet. However, the southern half, flat as a flapjack, is given over to bays, reefs, beaches, and a salt lake that attracts flamingos.

1 Essentials

VISITOR INFORMATION

Before you go, you can contact the **Bonaire Government Tourist Office** at Adams Unlimited, 10 Rockefeller Plaza, Suite 900, New York, NY 10020 (© **800/BONAIRE** or 212/956-5911).

For tourist information on Bonaire, go to the **Bonaire Government Tourist Bureau,** Kaya Libertad Simón Bolivar 12, Kralendijk (© **599/717-8322**). It's open Monday to Friday 7:30am to noon and 1:30 to 5pm.

Bonaire's official website is **www.bonaire.org**.

GETTING THERE

Before you book your flight, be sure to read the section "Package Deals" in chapter 2; it can save you a bundle. Even if you don't book a package, see that chapter's tips on finding the best airfare.

> **Fun Fact A Special Event**
>
> The big annual event is the **October Sailing Regatta,** a 5-day festival of racing sponsored by the local tourist bureau. Now an international affair, the event attracts sailors and spectators from around the world, as a flotilla of sailboats and yachts anchor in Kralendijk Bay. If you're planning to visit during regatta days, make sure you have an ironclad hotel reservation.

ALM (© 800/327-7230) is one of your best bets for flying to Bonaire. The airline flies from Miami and Atlanta daily. **Air Aruba** (© 800/882-7822) flies from Newark to Bonaire on Thursday, Saturday, and Sunday. These are direct flights. On Monday, Tuesday, Wednesday, and Friday, it has air links to Bonaire via Aruba.

American Airlines (© 800/433-7300) offers one daily nonstop flight to Curaçao from its hub in Miami. These flights depart late enough in the day (11am) to allow easy connections from cities all over the Northeast. They reach Curaçao early enough to allow immediate transfers on to Bonaire. American will book (but not ticket) your connecting flight to Bonaire on Bonaire Airways.

Other routings to Bonaire are possible on any of American's daily nonstop flights to Aruba through American's hubs in New York, Miami, and San Juan, Puerto Rico. Once on Aruba, ALM will transfer passengers on to Bonaire, usually after a brief touchdown (or change of equipment) on Curaçao. Although these transfers are somewhat complicated, American will set up any of them, and will also offer reduced rates at some Bonairean hotels if you book your reservation simultaneously with your air passage.

GETTING AROUND

Even though the island is flat, renting mopeds or motor scooters is not always a good idea. The roads are often unpaved, pitted, and peppered with rocks. Touring through Washington National Park is best done by van, Jeep, or car.

BY TAXI Taxis are unmetered, but the government has established rates. All taxicabs carry a license plate with the letters *TX*. Each driver should have a price list available to be produced on request. As many as four passengers can go along for the ride unless they have too much luggage. A trip from the airport to your hotel should cost about $10 to $12. From 8pm to midnight, fares are increased by 25%, and from midnight to 6am they go up by 50%.

Most taxi drivers can take you on a tour of the island, but you'll have to negotiate a price according to how long a trip you want and what you want to see. For more information, call **Taxi Central Dispatch** (© 599/717-8100).

BY RENTAL CAR You might want to rent a four-wheel-drive vehicle, especially from October to January, which can be a muddy season.

It pays to shop around: Sometimes—but not always—you can make a better deal with a local agency. Among local agencies, **Island Rentals,** Kaya Industria 31 (© 599/717-2100), offers soft-top Jeeps for $45 a day.

Avis (© 800/331-1212 in the U.S.; www.avis.com) is also at Flamingo Airport. Weekly arrangements are cheaper, but daily rates range from $43 to $68, with unlimited mileage. At the airport, **Budget Rent-a-Car** (© 599/717-7424)

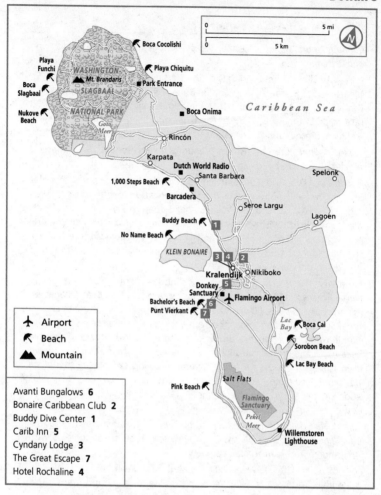

Avanti Bungalows **6**
Bonaire Caribbean Club **2**
Buddy Dive Center **1**
Carib Inn **5**
Cyndany Lodge **3**
The Great Escape **7**
Hotel Rochaline **4**

rents such vehicles as four-wheel drives and Suzuki minivans. Some automatic, air-conditioned four-door sedans are available.

Your valid U.S., British, or Canadian driver's license is acceptable for driving on Bonaire, and you must be 25 or older to rent a car. *Driving on Bonaire is on the right.*

BY BICYCLE You might consider renting a bike, although you'll have to contend with the hot sun and powerful trade winds. Nevertheless, much of the island is flat, and if you follow the main road you'll go along the water's edge. The best deals are at **Cycle Bonaire,** Kaya L. D. Gerjharts (© **599/717-7558**), where you can rent a 21-speed or an 830 Trek for $15 to $20 per day. Rental includes a water bottle, lock, helmet, repair kit, and pump. A map is provided free for a 6-day rental; otherwise, you're charged $5.

FAST FACTS: Bonaire

Banking Hours Banks are usually open Monday to Friday 8:30am to noon and 2 to 4pm.

Currency Like the other islands of the Netherlands Antilles (Curaçao, St. Maarten, St. Eustatius, and Saba), Bonaire's coin of the realm is the **Netherlands Antillean florin (NAf)**, sometimes called a guilder. The official rate at press time is Naf1.77 to the U.S. dollar. However, U.S. dollars are widely accepted, and the rates in this chapter are quoted in U.S. dollars.

Customs There are no Customs requirements for Bonaire. See chapter 2 for details on what you can bring home.

Documents U.S. and Canadian citizens don't need passports to enter Bonaire, but without one, a birth or naturalization certificate or an alien registration card is required. You also need a return ticket. British subjects may carry a British Visitor's Passport, obtainable at post offices on Bonaire, although a valid passport issued in the United Kingdom is preferred. We strongly suggest that you bring your passport whenever you travel to a foreign country anyway.

Electricity The electricity on Bonaire is slightly different from that used in North America (110–130 volts, 50 cycles, as opposed to U.S. and Canadian voltages of 110 volts, 60 cycles). Adapters and transformers are necessary for U.S. and Canadian appliances, but you should still proceed with caution in using any appliance on Bonaire and try to avoid usage if possible because of the erratic current. Be warned, further, that electrical current used to feed or recharge finely calibrated diving equipment should be stabilized with a specially engineered electrical stabilizer. Every dive operation on the island has one of these stabilizers as part of its standard equipment for visiting divers to use.

Language English is widely spoken, but you'll also hear Dutch, Spanish, and Papiamento, a patois that combines the three major tongues with Amerindian and African dialects.

Medical Care The **St. Franciscus Hospital** is at Kayasoeur Bartola 2 in Kralendijk (© 599/717-8900). A plane on standby at the airport takes seriously ill patients to Curaçao for treatment.

Safety Bonaire is a remarkably safe destination. But remember, any place that attracts tourists also attracts people who prey on them. Safeguard your valuables.

Taxes & Service Charges The government requires a $5.50-per-person daily room tax on all hotel rooms. Most hotels and guesthouses add a 10% service charge in lieu of tipping. Restaurants generally add a service charge of 15% to the bill. Upon leaving Bonaire, you'll be charged an airport departure tax of $10, so don't spend every penny. There's also an interisland departure tax of $5.75.

Telecommunications Service for telephone, Telex, telegraph, radio, and TV is available in English. To call Bonaire from the United States, dial **011** (the international access code), then **599** (the country code for Bonaire), and then **717** (the area code) and the four-digit local number. Once you're on Bonaire, to call another number on the island, only the four-digit local number is necessary.

Time Bonaire is on Atlantic standard time year-round, 1 hour ahead of Eastern standard time (when it's noon on Bonaire, it's 11am in Miami). When daylight saving time is in effect in the United States, clocks in Miami and Bonaire show the same time.

Tipping Most hotels and guesthouses add a 10% service charge in lieu of tipping. Taxi drivers expect a 10% tip.

Water Drinking water is pure and safe. It comes from distilled seawater.

Weather Bonaire is known for its fine climate, with midday temperatures hovering at 82°F (28°C). The water temperature averages 80°F (27°C). It's warmest in August and September, coolest in January and February. The average rainfall is 22 inches, and December to March are the rainiest months.

2 Accommodations You Can Afford

Hotels, most of which face the sea, are low-key, hassle-free, and personally run operations where everybody gets to know everybody else rather quickly.

Taxes and service charges are seldom included in the prices you're quoted, so ask about them when making your reservations.

Avanti Bungalows   A block in from Bachelor's Beach, south of the airport, this complex of bungalows is managed by a family business, Happy Holiday Homes. The basic units are comfortable, with an on-site washer and a living/dining-room area. There aren't a lot of graceful notes around here; it's pretty much a do-it-yourself affair. The bungalows are in rows of two or three units each, and all have front terraces and gardens. The area is heavily planted with foliage for more privacy. Each unit is furnished differently with a sofa, Venetian blinds, just-adequate tables and chairs, and color-coordinated curtains and bed linens, plus good mattresses. The bedrooms are air-conditioned and the living/dining areas are cooled by ceiling fans. Bathrooms are small but well maintained, with tiled shower stalls. The kitchens are fully furnished, with refrigerators and microwaves. There's no pool.

Punt Vierkant, Belnem, Bonaire, N.A. ℭ **599/717-8405.** Fax 599/717-8605. www.bonaire.org/happy-holiday. 13 bungalows. Winter $75 1-bedroom bungalow; $100 2-bedroom bungalow; $130 3-bedroom bungalow. Off-season $65 1-bedroom bungalow; $90 2-bedroom bungalow; $120 3-bedroom bungalow. Extra person $15. MC, V. **Amenities:** Laundry. *In room:* A/C, cable TV, kitchens, ceiling fans.

Bonaire Caribbean Club   A mile north of the hotel strip, this Dutch-owned complex rents bungalow apartments, some with their own porches. Some good dive sites lie about a block away, although the property fronts a coral beach. The nearest good sandy beach, however, is about 1½ miles away. The apartments are two to a unit, in a parklike setting, with gardens and flowering vines around the porches. The furnishings are simple, with colorful seat cushions and curtains in a vague tropical motif. All have kitchens and air-conditioning, and some offer ceiling fans as well, although there are no phones or TVs. Mattresses are replaced as needed. The shower-only bathrooms are cramped, with not enough room for your stuff. A pool with a mural of underwater life is the big on-site attraction, and there's a simple restaurant serving breakfast and dinner. Daily maid service is provided except on Sunday, and babysitting can be arranged, with advance notice.

Tourist Rd., Kralendijk, Bonaire, N.A. © 800/748-8733 or 599/717-7901. Fax 599/717-7900. 20 units. Year-round $65–$95 1-bedroom apt; $125 2-bedroom apt. Apr–July 1 and Nov–Dec 15, guests receive 7th night free. Extra person $9; children 4 and under stay free in parents' apt. MC, V (5% extra fee for use of charge card). **Amenities:** Restaurant, pool, babysitting, maid service. *In room:* A/C, kitchen, no phone.

Buddy Dive Center On the island's western edge amid a strip of other hotels, many of which are more expensive, this hotel consists of three buildings. The oldest contains bedrooms but not apartments. The pair of newer buildings (ca. 1992–93) has white concrete walls, red roofs, and apartments with kitchens. As you'd guess from the hotel's name, most visitors check in here for the diving opportunities, which are abundant off the nearby coast. PADI and NAUI dive options are available on site. The accommodations are ultra-simple and not particularly large. Each unit is outfitted with rattan furniture and white walls, and each has a balcony. Mattresses are firm, but bathrooms are barely adequate; they are rather cramped and have shower units. There's a pool, although most visitors swim at Buddy Beach, a few steps away. Each apartment has its own kitchen, and there's also an in-house restaurant, Buddy's Reef.

Kaya Gobernador N. E. Debrot (P.O. Box 231), Kralendijk, Bonaire, N.A. © 800/786-3483 or 599/717-5080. Fax 599/717-8647. www.buddydive.com. 34 units, including 30 apts with kitchen. Winter $119 single or double; $179 1-bedroom apt for 2; $254 2-bedroom apt for up to 4; $312 3-bedroom apt for up to 6. Off-season $116 single or double; $164 1-bedroom apt for 2; $231 2-bedroom apt for up to 4; $286 3-bedroom apt for up to 6. Ask about dive packages. AE, MC, V. **Amenities:** Restaurant, pool, car rental, limited maid service. *In room:* A/C, TV, kitchen.

Carib Inn ★★ *Value* On a sliver of a beach, this inn, owned and managed by the American diver Bruce Bowker, is occupied by dedicated scuba divers who are drawn to the hotel's five-star PADI dive facility. This is the most intimate little dive resort on Bonaire, and it remains one of the island's best values. Eight rooms have kitchens, all units are equipped with fridges, and maid service is provided daily. The accommodations are furnished with tropical rattan pieces, and the bathrooms have been enlarged and refurbished, each with a shower stall. Repeat guests are likely to book this place far in advance for winter visits.

J. A. Abraham Blvd. (P.O. Box 68), Kralendijk, Bonaire, N.A. © 599/717-8819. Fax 599/717-5295. www.caribinn.com. 10 apts. Year-round $109 studio efficiency apt; $129 1-bedroom apt; $149 2-bedroom apt; $159 3-bedroom house. Extra person $10. DISC, MC, V. **Amenities:** Maid service. *In room:* A/C, kitchenette, fridge, no phone.

Cyndany Lodge In a tranquil residential area of Kralendijk, within a short walk of a good beach, this is a small inn known for its good value. The units are only in the basic motel style, but guests who check in here are more interested in saving money than in fancy resort amenities. Opened in summer 1995, this hotel offers bedrooms with either two double beds or one queen size, each with a good mattress. All the units have tiled floors and feature large bathrooms with showers. The location is behind the landmark Divi Flamingo Beach Resort and near several dive and snorkeling outfitters. It is peaceful, private, and welcoming, somewhat like a Bonaire-style country inn. There is a bar and a restaurant, the latter serving breakfast only.

J. A. Abraham Blvd. 51, Kralendijk, Bonaire, N.A. © 599/717-7075. Fax 599/717-4047. http://bestofbonaire.com/hotel. 12 units. Year-round $75–$78 single or double. MC, V. **Amenities:** Restaurant (breakfast only), bar, laundry service, maid service. *In room:* A/C, TV, wet bar, fridge.

The Great Escape About half a mile south of the airport, near Bachelor's Beach, this is one of the newest B&Bs on the island, a welcoming and homey two-story white stone building. The lobby is large and open, and guests gather to watch TV in a lounge on the wide upstairs balcony. Although not noted for any particular style, except for the flowery courtyard with a freshwater swimming pool, the medium-size accommodations range from standard through deluxe to the most expensive of all, a suite. Special budget honeymoon arrangements can be made. The rooms are pleasantly furnished and well maintained and offer a double bed or two twins, each with a good mattress. The suites have two double beds and a pullout sofa. Shower-only bathrooms are small. This place is family friendly, with a small playground with a tiny zoo and babysitting services. A simple restaurant serves three meals a day.

Blvd. Europese Economische Gemeenschap 97, Belnem, Bonaire, N.A. ℭ/fax **599/717-7488.** 12 units. Winter $110 single or double; $140 suite. Off-season $100 single or double; $130 suite. Extra person $20; children stay free in parents' room. Rates include breakfast. AE, MC, V. **Amenities:** Restaurant, bar, TV lounge, pool, babysitting. In room: A/C, ceiling fans.

Hotel Rochaline *(Value)*   An oceanfront hotel in the heart of Kralendijk, this small hotel lies above a bustling cafe. It's a rather rawboned stopover for the frugal traveler who wants to be in the bull's-eye center of town sans beach location. The best aspect of this little inn is the rooms with balconies opening onto harbor views. All the small rooms are well maintained but simply furnished, although the beds are comfortable. The compact tiled bathrooms come with shower. A special feature is the cozy outdoor terrace at the waterfront, where you can order specialties from the grill. For nighttime diversions, the City Café itself is one of the local hot spots, especially during happy hour, 5:30 to 7:30pm.

Kaya Grandi 7, Kralendijk, Bonaire, NA. ℭ **599/717-8286.** Fax 599/717-8258. hotelrochaline@ bonairenet.com. 25 units. $50 single; $65 double; $80 triple. AE, MC, V. **Amenities:** 2 restaurants, bar. In room: A/C, TV.

3 Great Deals on Dining

At the restaurants below, fish dishes are expensive, but most other selections are at the lower end of the price scale.

If you're striking out for Washington-Slagbaai National Park or one of the island's remote beaches, you can stop at the **Sand Dollar Grocery** at Kaya Gobernador N. E. Debrot (ℭ **599/717-5490**) and rent a cooler for $4.60 to $8.60, plus a $10.60 deposit.

Blue Moon *ⓡ* INTERNATIONAL   This seafront bistro near the Divi Flamingo Beach Resort is in one of the island's oldest houses. Intimate tables and candlelight create a romantic ambience in the main restaurant, and you can dine less formally outside on the terrace overlooking the harbor. The menu always features the catch of the day as well as steak dishes. Sample a delectable stuffed chicken breast with mango, or jumbo shrimp hollandaise, followed by one of the homemade desserts. Finish off with one of the rich, Cuban-style coffees. Flavors are precisely defined, although nearly all ingredients have to be imported. Specials change daily.

Kaya C.E.B. Hellmund 5. ℭ **599/717-8617.** Reservations recommended. Main courses $11–$25. AE, MC, V. Tues–Sun 6–10pm.

Green Parrot Restaurant CONTINENTAL   On a breezy pier, this place is part of a resort complex that's a 15-minute drive from the airport. It serves burgers, pasta, sandwiches, and seafood dishes. You can gaze at the waves, enjoy a frozen tropical-fruit drink, and watch the sunset. The food consistently ranks as some of the island's best, especially the charcoal-grilled fish (based on the catch of the day). You might also try the barbecued chicken and ribs, various U.S. beef cuts (from T-bone to filet mignon), garlic shrimp, or the highly flavored onion strings (like an onion loaf). Saturday nights bring a barbecue buffet with entertainment. Come here for fun and good times.

In the Sand Dollar Condominium Resort, Kaya Gobernador N. E. Debrot 79. ℂ 599/717-5454. Reservations recommended. Main courses $12.50–$30; lunch $7–$10. AE, MC, V. Daily 7:30am–10pm.

Mi Poron ⚔ BONAIRIAN   This place serves the island's most authentic Antillean cuisine. The *konfó* (hibachi) and *karbón* (charcoal) are still used as the original cooking methods to prepare such mouthwatering dishes as *stobá* (stew). You can sample all those dishes you've dreamed about here, ranging from tripe soup to okra soup. The conch dishes are delectable, and you can also sample goat specialties. Start your repast with a crab salad of locally smoked marlin. After dinner you can browse through the antique house, with its original artifacts. On the first Sunday of the month there is live mariachi music and a barbecue.

Kaya Caracas 1. ℂ 599/717-5199. Reservations recommended. Main courses $6–$10. MC, V. Tues–Sat noon–2pm and 5–10pm; Sun 5–10pm.

Old Inn INDONESIAN/INTERNATIONAL   Few other restaurants on Bonaire present so strong a Dutch colonial theme. Low-slung and unpretentious, the setting includes plaster walls lined with murals of Indonesian landscapes, with a menu whose unerring specialty is *rijsttafel,* the Indonesian rice dish whose curried flavors are enhanced with at least a dozen condiments and spices served on the side. Also look for *satay* (skewered Indonesian beef), and *nasi goreng,* an Indonesian fried-rice special. Service is attentive by a mostly Dutch-born staff, and prices are reasonable.

J. A. Abraham Blvd. ℂ 599/717-6666. Reservations recommended. Main courses $12–$24. MC, V. Thurs–Tues 5–10pm.

t'ankertje INTERNATIONAL   A winning little choice, this inviting restaurant (pronounced "tan-ker-jay") is across the street from the water in Kralendijk. Open-air tables are set near the ocean. For inspiration, the cooks roam the world—everything from Italian-style pizza to Mexican tacos. Our favorite dish is their Indonesian satay with marinated chicken and a delectable peanut sauce. The "Arabian sandwich," similar to a gyro, appears on pita bread stuffed with pork. Your best bet? Look for the daily specials chalked up on a blackboard menu. If it's fresh fish, go for it; otherwise, you can sample what's frozen from the larder—perhaps a blackened sirloin steak or a Wiener schnitzel.

Kaya C.E.B. Hellmund. ℂ 599/717-5216. Main courses $11–$18. MC, V. Mon–Fri 5–10pm.

WORTH A SPLURGE

Rendez-Vous Restaurant & Espresso Bar ⚔ INTERNATIONAL   This restaurant is known for its renowned chef, Martin Bouwmeester, who prepares some of the island's finest fare. Opt for a table on the terrace of this cafe where you can watch the people of Bonaire parade before you. You can do all this while enjoying an array of both cold or hot appetizers, ranging from locally smoked marlin to escargots in herb butter. Everyone tries to get the recipe for the shrimp bisque. A number of main courses, each well prepared, will tempt you nightly—perhaps the catch of the day baked in puff pastry and served with a creamy white wine sauce or the pork tenderloin medallions stuffed with a nut filling. A touch of the islands appears in the ensemble of fresh salmon and shrimp with a passion fruit sauce. For dessert, save room for the island's most delectable apple strudel.

Kaya L. D. Gerharts 3. ℂ 599/717-8454. Reservations recommended. Main courses $16–$22. MC, V. Fri–Wed 5:30–10pm.

4 Hitting the Beaches

You should come to Bonaire for the diving (see "Sports & Other Outdoor Pursuits," below), not the beaches. For the most part, the beaches are full of coral and feel gritty to bare feet. The beaches on the leeward side (the more tranquil side of the island) are often narrow strips. To compensate, some hotels have shipped in extra sand for their guests.

Pink Beach, south of Kralendijk, out past Salt Pier, is the best, despite its narrow strip of sand, shallow water, and lack of shade. It's aptly named: The beach really is a deep pink color, from the corals that have been pulverized into sand by the waves. Bring your own cooler and towels, as there are no refreshment stands or equipment rentals to mar the panoramic setting. It's also wise to bring along some sun protection, as the few palm trees bordering the dunes offer little shade. Enter the water at the southern end of this beach, as the northern tier has some exposed rock. Many Bonaireans flock here on weekends, but during the week you'll have the beach to yourself.

Playa Funchi, within Washington-Slagbaai National Park, is good for snorkeling. Regrettably, it has almost no sand, there are no facilities, and the area surrounding the beach is a bit smelly. On one side of the beach, there's a lagoon where flamingos nest; snorkelers find the water most desirable on the other side. Also within the park, the more desirable **Boca Slagbaai** draws snorkelers and picnickers. You can spot flamingos nearby. A 19th-century building houses decent toilets and showers; drinks and snacks are also available. Don't venture into the waters barefoot, as the coral beach can be quite rough. A final beach at the national park is **Boca Cocolishi,** a black-sand strip on the northern coast. This is the windiest beach on Bonaire; you'll certainly stay cool as the trade winds whip up the surf. The waters are too rough for swimming, but this is a good picnic spot.

Many of Bonaire's beaches are situated along the east coast. The best spot for windsurfers is **Lac Bay Beach,** on the southern shore of Lac Bay. There are mangroves at the north end of the bay. A couple of windsurfing concessions usually operate here, and food and drink are available. One of the more unusual is **Nukove Beach,** a minicave in a limestone cliff with a small white-sand channel, which cuts through the dense wall of elkhorn coral near the shore, giving divers and snorkelers easy access to the water. Farther north is **1,000 Steps Beach,** where 67 steps (although it can feel like 1,000 on the way back up) carved out of the limestone cliff lead to the white-sand beach. This beach offers good snorkeling and diving, a unique location and view, and nearly perfect solitude.

5 Sports & Other Outdoor Pursuits

The true beauty on Bonaire is under the sea, where visibility is 100 feet 365 days of the year, and the water temperatures range from 78°F to 82°F (25.5°C–27.7°C). Many dive sites can be reached directly from the beach, and sailing is another favored pastime. The bird-watching is among the best in the Caribbean, and for beachcombers there are acres and acres of driftwood, found along the shore from the salt flats to Lac.

BIRD-WATCHING   Bonaire is home to 190 species of birds, 80 of which are indigenous to the island. But most famous are its flamingos, which can number 15,000 during the mating season. For great places to bring your binoculars, see "Seeing the Sights," below.

Moments A Trip to Klein Bonaire

Bonaire's offshore island, **Klein Bonaire,** which lies just three-fourths of a mile offshore, offers some of the island's most pristine beaches. This 1,500-acre island is flat and rocky. Its vegetation will make you think you're in Arizona. The little island is known for its almost deserted white sandy beaches, of which **No Name Beach** is deservedly the most popular, ideal for both a picnic lunch or a snorkeling adventure. As you enter the waters off the coast here, expect to encounter such friends as the yellowtail snapper, the tiger grouper, the parrotfish or the trumpetfish, and certainly the white mullet. The spotted moray eel might also be seen, but these are rather elusive creatures and will not harm you if you don't touch them. The island is known for its spectacular reefs, 16 sites of which are world class. They're filled with stunning elkhorn coral as well as large star corals and brain corals. Great varieties of sponges and gorgonians can also be spotted. Check with the tourist office ((C) **599/717-8322**) for information on hiring a boat to visit Klein Bonaire.

DIVING   One of the richest reef communities in the entire West Indies, Bonaire has plunging walls that descend to a sand bottom at 130 or so feet. The reefs are home to various coral formations that grow at different depths, ranging from the knobby brain coral at 3 feet, to staghorn and elkhorn up to about 10 feet deeper, and gorgonians, giant brain, and others all the way to 40 to 83 feet. Swarms of rainbow-hued tropical fish inhabit the reefs, and the deep reef slope is home to a range of basket sponges, groupers, and moray eels. Most of the diving is done on the leeward side where the ocean usually is lake flat. There are more than 40 dive sites on sharply sloping reefs.

The **Bonaire Marine Park** ⋆⋆ ((C) **599/717-8322**) was created to protect the coral-reef ecosystem off Bonaire. The park incorporates the entire coastline of Bonaire and neighboring **Klein Bonaire.** Scuba diving and snorkeling are all popular here. The park is policed, and services and facilities include a visitor information center at the **Karpata Ecological Center,** lectures, slide presentations, films, and permanent dive-site moorings.

Visitors are asked to respect the marine environment and to refrain from activities that could damage it, including sitting or walking on the coral. All marine life is completely protected. This means there's no fishing or collecting fish, shells, or corals—dead or alive. Spearfishing is forbidden, as is anchoring; all craft must use permanent moorings, except for emergency stops (boats shorter than 12 ft. may use a stone anchor). Most recreational activity in the marine park takes place on the island's leeward side and among the reefs surrounding Klein Bonaire.

Bonaire has a unique program for divers; the major hotels offer personalized, close-up encounters with the island's fish and other marine life under the expertise of Bonaire's dive guides.

Dive I and *Dive II,* at opposite ends of the beachfront of the Divi Flamingo Beach Resort & Casino, J. A. Abraham Boulevard ((C) **599/717-8285**), north of Kralendijk, are among the island's most complete scuba facilities. They're open daily 8am to 12:30pm and 1:30 to 5pm. Both operate out of well-stocked beachfront buildings, rent diving equipment, charge the same prices, and offer the same type of expeditions. A resort course for first-time divers costs $88; for experienced divers, a one-tank dive goes for $38.50, a two-tank dive for $55.

Captain Don's Habitat Dive Shop ★★, Kaya Gobernador N. E. Debrot 103 (© 599/717-8290), is a PADI five-star training facility. The open-air, full-service dive shop includes a classroom, photo/video lab, camera-rental facility, equipment repair, and compressor rooms. Habitat's slogan is "Diving Freedom," and divers can take their tanks and dive anywhere, any time of day or night, most often along "The Pike," a half-mile of protected reef right in front of the property. The highly qualified staff is here to assist and advise, not to police or dictate dive plans. Diving packages include boat dives, unlimited offshore diving (24 hr. a day), unlimited air, tanks, weights, and belt. Some dive packages also include accommodations and meals. If you're not staying at the hotel as part of a dive package, you can visit for a beach dive, costing $21. If you want to rent snorkeling equipment, the charge is $7.45 a day. A half-day of diving, with all equipment included, goes for $37.

Sand Dollar Dive and Photo, at the Sand Dollar Condominium & Beach Club, Kaya Gobernador N. E. Debrot (© 599/717-5252), offers dive packages, PADI and NAUI instruction, and equipment rental and repairs; boat and shore trips with an instructor are available by appointment. The photo shop offers underwater photo and video shoots, PADI specialty courses by appointment, E-6 processing, print developing, and equipment rental and repair. It's open daily 8:30am to 5:30pm.

FISHING   The island's offshore fishing grounds offer some of the best fishing in the Caribbean. A good day's catch might include mackerel, tuna, wahoo, dolphin (mahimahi), blue marlin, Amber Jack, grouper, sailfish, or snapper. Bonaire is also one of the best-kept secrets of bonefishing enthusiasts.

Your best bet is Chris Morkos of **Piscatur Fishing Supplies,** Kaya Herman 4, Playa Pabao (© 599/717-8774). A native Bonairean, he has been fishing almost since he was born. His company takes a maximum of six people on a 42-foot boat with a guide and captain, at a cost of $350 for a half day or $500 for a whole day, including all tackle and bait. Reef fishing is another popular sport, in boats averaging 15 and 19 feet. A maximum of two people can go out for a half-day at $225 or a whole day at $400. For the same price, a maximum of two people can fish for bonefish and tarpon on the island's large salt flats.

MOUNTAIN BIKING   Biking on Bonaire can be a rewarding experience; you can explore more than 186 miles of trails and dirt roads where you can venture off the beaten path to enjoy the scenery and contrasting geography. Check

---

⸨Fun Fact⸩ The *Hooker*

The waters off the coast of Bonaire received an additional attraction in 1984. A rust-bottomed general cargo ship, 80 feet long, was confiscated by the police, along with its contraband cargo, about 25,000 pounds of marijuana. Known as the *Hilma Hooker* (familiarly dubbed "The Hooker" by everyone on the island), it sank unclaimed (obviously) and without fanfare one calm day, in 90 feet of water. Lying just off the southern shore near the capital, its wreck is now a popular dive site.

with your hotel about arranging a trip, or call **Cycle Bonaire,** Kaya L. D. Gerharts 11D (© **599/717-7558**), which rents 21-speed mountain bikes and arranges half- or full-day excursions costing from $40 to $65, respectively, in addition to the bike rental charges.

SEA KAYAKING   You can paddle the protected waters of Lac Bay, or head for the miles of flats and mangroves in the south (the island's nursery) where baby fish and wildlife can be viewed. Kayak rentals are available at **Jibe City,** Lac Bay (© **599/717-5233**), for $10 per hour, $25 per half day, or $35 for a full day.

SNORKELING   Bonaire's **snorkeling** ⭐⭐⭐ is amazing, and it can be accessed easily from many spots. Some of the highlights include **Boca Slagbaai** and **Playa Funchi,** both in Washington-Slagbaai National Park; **1,000 Steps Beach;** and **Klein Bonaire,** the offshore island.

Snorkeling gear can be rented at **Carib Inn,** J. A. Abraham Blvd. (© **599/ 717-8819**); **Sand Dollar Dive and Photo,** Kaya Gobernador N. E. Debrot (© **599/717-5252**), and **Captain Don's Habitat Dive Shop,** Kaya Governador N. E. Debrot (© **599/717-8290**).

TENNIS   There are two tennis courts at the **Sand Dollar Condominium & Beach Club** at Kaya Governador N. E. Debrot 79 (© **800/288-4773**), and there are also courts at the **Divi Flamingo Beach Resort,** J. A. Abraham Boulevard (© **800/367-3484**). All the courts are lit for night play.

WINDSURFING   Consistent conditions, enjoyed by windsurfers with a wide range of skill levels, make the shallow, calm waters of Lac Bay the island's home to the sport. Call **Bonaire Windsurfing** (© **599/717-2288**) for details. A halfday costs $40.

6 Seeing the Sights

THE CAPITAL

The capital's name, **Kralendijk,** means "coral dike" and is pronounced *Krall-en-dike*, although most denizens refer to it as *Playa*, Spanish for "beach." A dollhouse town of some 2,500 residents, it's small, neat, pretty, Dutch-clean, and just a bit dull. Its stucco buildings are painted pink and orange, with an occasional lime green. The capital's jetty is lined with island sloops and fishing boats.

Kralendijk is nestled in a bay on the west coast, opposite **Klein Bonaire** ("Little Bonaire"), the uninhabited, low-lying islet a 10-minute boat ride away (see "Hitting the Beaches," earlier in this chapter).

The main street of town leads along the beachfront on the harbor. A Protestant church was built in 1834, and **St. Bernard's Roman Catholic Church** has some interesting stained-glass windows.

At **Fort Oranje** you'll see a lone cannon dating from the days of Napoléon. If possible, try to get up early to see the **Fish Market** on the waterfront, where you'll see a variety of strange and brilliantly colored fish.

EXPLORING THE BEAUTIFUL NORTH

The road that heads north on Bonaire is one of the most beautiful stretches in the Antilles, with turquoise waters on the left and coral cliffs on the right. You can stop at several points along this road, where you'll find paved paths for strolling or bicycling.

After leaving Kralendijk and passing the Sunset Beach Hotel and the desalination plant, you'll come to **Radio Nederland Wereld Omroep (Dutch World**

(*Value* **Cheap Thrills: What to See & Do for Free (Well, Almost) on Bonaire**

- **Investigate Washington-Slagbaai National Park.** One of the first national parks in the Caribbean, this land mass is home to some 190 species of birds, thousands of towering candle cacti, herds of goats, stray donkeys, and lizards and more lizards. The park terrain is varied, and those ambitious enough to climb some of its steep hills are rewarded with panoramic views. You can take your Jeep or car through the park on one of two driving trails, and, of course, the hiking possibilities are seemingly endless. Small hidden beaches with crashing waters by the cliffs provide an ideal place for a picnic.
- **Watch Flamingos at the Salt Flats.** Bonaire's flamingo population during the breeding season swells to almost 10,000, nearly outnumbering the island's human population. The best place to watch flamingos is at the island's salt ponds in the National Park, at Goto Meer, or at the southern end of the island at the solar salt works. While the solar sanctuary within the salt works requires a special permit for entry, the pink flamingos can be seen from the road. Every day at sunset, the entire flock flies the short 50-mile trip to Venezuela for feeding.
- **Explore Bonaire's Reefs.** Nature has blessed Bonaire with gorgeous coral reefs that start in just inches of water and have dense coral formations in very shallow surf. To a snorkeler, this is an underwater paradise. Most snorkeling on the island is conducted in 15 feet of water or less, and there's plenty to see, even at this depth.
- **Mountain Bike Around the Island.** Biking is an ideal way to see Bonaire's hidden beauty off the beaten track. There are more than 300 kilometers of trails on the island, ranging from goat paths to unpaved roads. Other than hiking, this is the only way to explore the wonders of Bonaire's terrestrial natural resources. You can take along a picnic to enjoy at some scenic vista. Along these paths you'll encounter panoramic views of Caribbean flora and wildlife. Ask at the tourist office for a trail map, which outlines the most scenic routes. You can find a little cafe for a quick lunch in the town of Rincón or else have a picnic on the windward side of the island, as you're cooled by the trade winds.

Radio). It's a 13-tower, 300,000-watt transmitting station. Opposite the transmitting station is a lovers' promenade, built by nature and an ideal spot for a picnic.

Continuing, you'll pass the storage tanks of the Bonaire Petroleum Corporation, the road heading to **Gotomeer,** the island's inland sector, with a saltwater lake. Several flamingos prefer this spot to the salt flats in the south.

Down the hill the road leads to a section called **Dos Pos,** or "two wells," which has palm trees and vegetation in contrast to the rest of the island, where only the drought-resistant *kibraacha* and divi-divi trees, tilted before the constant wind, can grow, along with forests of cacti.

Bonaire's oldest village is **Rincón.** Slaves who used to work in the salt flats in the south once lived here. There are a couple of bars, and the Rincón Ice Cream Parlour makes homemade ice cream in a variety of interesting flavors. Above the bright roofs of the village is the crest of a hill called Para Mira, or "stop and look."

A side path outside Rincón takes you to some Arawak inscriptions that are supposedly 500 years old. The petroglyph designs are in pink-red dye. At nearby **Boca Onima,** you'll find grotesque grottoes of coral.

Before going back to the capital, you might take a short bypass to **Seroe Largu,** which has a good view of Kralendijk and the sea. Lovers frequent the spot at night.

WASHINGTON-SLAGBAAI NATIONAL PARK ★★

Occupying 15,000 acres of Bonaire's northwestern end, **Washington-Slagbaai National Park (© 599/717-8444)** conserves the island's fauna, flora, and landscape, and is a changing vista highlighted by desertlike terrain, secluded beaches, caverns, and a bird sanctuary. The park was once plantation land, producing divi-divi, aloe, and charcoal. It was purchased by the Netherlands Antilles government, and since 1967 part of the land, formerly the Washington plantation, has been a wildlife sanctuary. The southern part of the park, the Slagbaai plantation, was added in 1978.

You can see the park in a few hours, although it takes days to appreciate it fully. Touring the park is easy, with two self-guided routes: a 15-mile "short" route, marked by green arrows, and a 22-mile "long" route, marked by yellow arrows. The trails are well-marked and easy to follow although somewhat rugged (they're gradually being improved). Admission to the park is $5 for adults and $1 for children 11 and under. The park is open daily except holidays 8am to 5pm. No one is allowed to enter after 3pm because there isn't enough time left to explore before closing. Also, be aware when arranging for car rental that only four-wheel-drive vehicles are allowed into the park because of the poor quality of the mostly unpaved roads, and that the park is sometimes closed to visitors during the rainy season because the roads become impassable.

Whichever route you take, there are a few important stops you should make. Just past the gate is **Salina Mathijs,** a salt flat that's home to flamingos during the rainy season. Beyond the salt flat on the road to the right is **Boca Chikitu,** a white-sand beach and bay. A few miles up the beach lies **Boca Cocolishi,** a two-part black-sand beach. Many a couple has raved about the romantic memories of this beach, perfect for picnics, privacy, and seclusion. Its deep, rough seaward side and calm, shallow basin are separated by a ridge of calcareous algae. The basin and the beach were formed by small pieces of coral, mollusks, and their shells (*cocolishi* means "shells"), thus the "black sand." The basin itself has no current, so it's perfect for snorkeling close to shore, where hermit crabs scuttle through the shallow water and black sands.

The main road leads to **Boca Bartol,** a bay full of living and dead elkhorn coral, seafans, and reef fish. A popular watering hole good for bird-watching is **Poosdi Mangel. Wajaca** is a remote reef, perfect for divers and home to the island's most exciting sea creatures, including turtles, octopuses, and triggerfish. Immediately inland towers 788-foot **Mount Brandaris,** Bonaire's highest peak, at whose foot is **Bronswinkel Well,** a watering spot for pigeons and parakeets. Some 130 species of birds live in the park, many with such exotic names as banana quit and black-faced grass quit. Bonaire has few mammals, but you'll see goats and donkeys, and perhaps a wild bull.

TOURING THE SOUTH

Leaving the capital again, you pass another radio transmitter, the **Trans World Radio antennas.** Towering 500 feet in the air, they blast their signals at 810,000 watts, making it one of the hemisphere's most powerful medium-wave radio stations and the most powerful nongovernmental broadcast station in the world. It sends out interdenominational gospel messages and hymns in 20 languages to places as far away as Eastern Europe and the Middle East.

Later, you arrive at the **salt flats** (★), where the island's brilliantly colored pink flamingos live. Bonaire shelters the largest accessible nesting and breeding grounds in the world. The flamingos build high mud mounds to hold their eggs. The best time to see the birds is in spring when they're usually nesting and tending their young. The salt flats were once worked by slaves, and the government has rebuilt some primitive stone huts, bare shelters little more than waist high. The slaves slept in these huts and returned to their homes in Rincón in the north on weekends. The centuries-old salt pans have been reactivated by the International Salt Company. Near the salt pans you'll see some 30-foot obelisks in white, blue, and orange, built in 1838 to help mariners locate their proper anchorages.

Farther down the coast is the island's oldest lighthouse, **Willemstoren,** built in 1837. Still farther along, **Sorobon Beach** and **Boca Cai** come into view. They're at highly protected Lac Bay, which is ideal for swimming and snorkeling. Conch shells are stacked up on the beach. The water here is so vivid and clear you can see coral 65 to 120 feet down in the reef-protected waters.

ORGANIZED TOURS

Bonaire Sightseeing Tours (℗ 599/717-8778) can transport you on tours of the island, both north and south, to take in the flamingos, slave huts, conch shells, Goto Lake, the Amerindian inscriptions, and other sights. Each of these tours lasts 2 hours and costs $18 per person. You can also take a half-day "City and Country Tour," which lasts 3 hours and costs from $24 per person; this tour allows you to see the entire northern section and the southern part, as far as the slave huts.

7 Shopping

Kralendijk features an assortment of goods, including gemstone jewelry, wood, leather, sterling, ceramics, liquors, and tobacco, priced 25% to 50% less than in the United States and Canada. Prices are often quoted in U.S. dollars. Walk along Kaya Grandi in Kralendijk to sample the merchandise.

Benetton, Kaya Grandi 49 (℗ **599/717-5107**), has invaded the island and offers its brightly colored merchandise at prices about one-quarter less than most stateside outlets, or so it is said.

Littman Jewelers, Kaya Grandi 33 (℗ **599/717-8160**), sells Tag Heuer dive watches and also carries Daum French crystal and Lladró Spanish porcelain. Next door is **Littman's Gifts,** which sells standard and hand-painted T-shirts, plus sandals, hats, Gottex swimsuits, gift items, costume jewelry, and toys.

Although hardly great, there are some other stores you might want to visit, including **Best Buddies,** Kaya Grandi 32 (℗ **599/717-7570**), which is known for its *pareos,* or beach wraps, and its batiks from Indonesia. Nearby at **Island Fashions,** Kaya Grandi 5 (℗ **599/71-7565**), you can pick up the latest swim wear. Acquiring island art? Check the local gallery display at **BonTki,** Kaya C.E.B. Hellmund 3 (℗ **599/717-6877**). A more upgraded display is offered at

Harmony Art Gallery, Kaya L. D. Gerharts 10 (© **599/717-8539**), which has work by not only local artists, but by Dutch and U.S. artists as well.

8 Bonaire After Dark

Underwater **slide shows** provide entertainment for both divers and nondivers. The best shows are at **Captain Don's Habitat** (© **599/717-8290**). Shows are presented in the hotel bar, Rum-Runner, Thursday night from 7 to 8:30pm.

Karel's Beach Bar 𝖗𝖗, on the waterfront (© **599/717-8434**), is almost Tahitian in its high-ceilinged, open-walled design. This popular bar is perched above the sea on stilts. You can sit at the long rectangular bar with many of the island's dive and boating professionals or select a table near the balustrades over-looking the illuminated surf. On weekends local bands entertain. If you show up for happy hour from 5:30 to 7pm, drink prices are reduced.

Call **Klein Bonaire,** Kaya C.E.B. Hellmund 5 (© **599/717-8617**), to check to see if they are offering live jazz on the weekends, as they so often do.

We'd nominate the **City Café,** Kaya Isla Riba 3 (no phone) as the island's funkiest bar. Painted in vibrant Caribbean colors of electric blue, scarlet, magenta, and banana, this bar is a popular local hangout, but "only for the crazy ones," in the words of one regular. You can also order snack food here.

The **Plaza Resort Casino,** J. A. Abraham Blvd. 80 (© **599/717-2500**), is the larger of Bonaire's two casinos, and it's also usually the noisier and more ani-mated. It glitters, vibrates, and jangles with the sound of slot machines that cover entire walls, and gaming tables offer several games of chance. It's open daily 6pm to 4am. Jackets and ties aren't required, but shorts after dark are frowned upon.

The island's other casino, the **Divi Flamingo Beach Resort & Casino,** in a former residence on J. A. Abraham Boulevard (© **599/717-8285**), promotes itself as "The World's First Barefoot Casino." It offers blackjack, roulette, poker, wheel of fortune, video games, and slot machines. Entrance is free, and it's open Monday to Saturday from 8pm to 2am.

A local dive, **Paradiso,** Kaya Grandi 38A (no phone), swings Thursday to Sunday often until the wee hours. Saturday nights are wild and woolly, but this is hardly a first-class club.

At the marina tapas bar, **Admiral's Tavern,** part of the Harbour Village Beach Resort, Kaya Gobernador N. E. Debrot (© **599/717-7500**), you can sit out with a plate of tapas on the moonlit terrace while enjoying a beer: heavenly. Closed Tuesday.

The British Virgin Islands

With their small bays and hidden coves, the British Virgin Islands are among the world's loveliest cruising grounds. Strung over the northeastern corner of the Caribbean, about 60 miles east of Puerto Rico, are some 40 islands, including some small uninhabited cays or spits of land. Only three of the British Virgins are of any significant size: Virgin Gorda (the "Fat Virgin"), Tortola ("Dove of Peace"), and Jost Van Dyke. Other islands have such names as Fallen Jerusalem and Ginger. Norman Island is said to have been the inspiration for Robert Louis Stevenson's *Treasure Island.* On Dead Chest Island on Deadman's Bay, Blackbeard marooned 15 pirates and a

bottle of rum, which gave rise to the ditty.

There are predictions that mass tourism is on the way, but so far the British Virgins are still a place to escape the world. The good news for budget travelers is that you can find a number of moderately priced or inexpensive hotels and restaurants here. Many of these places have recently opened, so in the pages that follow, we'll introduce you to some hotels, inns, guesthouses, restaurants, and taverns that haven't yet appeared in any other guidebook. You'll also find some of the best campgrounds in the Caribbean here, although those on St. John in the U.S. Virgin Islands are even better (see chapter 25).

1 Essentials

VISITOR INFORMATION

Before you go, you can obtain information from the **British Virgin Islands Tourist Board,** 370 Lexington Ave., Suite 313, New York, NY 10017 (© **212/ 696-0400**). Other sources are the **British Virgin Islands Information Offices,** 1804 Union St., San Francisco, CA 94123 (© **415/775-0344**); 3450 Wilshire Blvd., Suite 108-17, Los Angeles, CA 90010 (© **310/287-2200**); and 3390 Peachtree Rd. NE, Suite 1000, Lenox Towers, Atlanta, GA 30326 (© **404/ 240-8018**).

In the United Kingdom, contact the **B.V.I. Information Office,** 110 St. Martin's Lane, London WC2N 4DY (© **020/7240-4259**).

The official website is **www.bviwelcome.com**.

Once on the islands, you'll find the **B.V.I. Tourist Board** is in the center of Road Town (Tortola), close to the ferry dock, south of Wickhams Cay (© **284/494-3134**).

GETTING THERE

BY PLANE There are no direct flights from North America or Europe to the British Virgin Islands, but you can make connections from San Juan and St. Thomas to Tortola's airport on Beef Island. (See chapters 17 and 25 for information on flying to these islands.) The one-lane Queen Elizabeth Bridge connects Beef Island to Tortola.

Your best bet to reach Tortola is to take **American Eagle** (© 800/433-7300 in the U.S.), the most reliable airline in the Caribbean, with at least four daily trips from San Juan to Beef Island/Tortola.

Another choice, if you're on one of Tortola's neighboring islands, is the much less reliable **LIAT** (© 800/468-0482 in the U.S. and Canada, 284/495-2577 or 284/495-1187 locally). This Caribbean carrier makes the short hops to Tortola from St. Kitts, Antigua, St. Maarten, St. Thomas, and San Juan in small planes not known for their frequency or careful scheduling. Reservations are made through travel agents or through the larger U.S.-based airlines that connect with LIAT hubs.

BY FERRY   You can travel from Charlotte Amalie on St. Thomas in the U.S. Virgin Islands by public ferry to West End and Road Town on Tortola, a 45-minute voyage on Drake's Channel, which runs through the islands. Boats making this run include **Native Son** (© 284/495-4617), **Smith's Ferry Service** (© 284/495-4495), and **Inter-Island Boat Services** (© 284/495-4166). The latter specializes in a somewhat obscure routing—that is, from St. John to the West End on Tortola.

 FAST FACTS: The British Virgin Islands

Banks   Banks are generally open Monday to Thursday 9am to 3pm and Friday 9am to 5pm.

Currency   The U.S. dollar is the legal currency, much to the surprise of many travelers.

Customs   You can bring items intended for your personal use into the British Virgin Islands. For U.S. residents, the duty-free allowance is only $400, providing you have been out of the country for 48 hours. You can send unsolicited gifts home if they total less than $50 per day to any single address. You don't pay duty on items classified as handcrafts, art, or antiques.

Documents   To enter the British Virgins, visitors need a valid passport or an original birth certificate with a raised seal, accompanied by a government-issued photo identification. We always recommend traveling to another country with your passport in hand.

Electricity   The electrical current is 110 volts AC (60 cycles), as in the United States.

Embassies & Consulates   There are no embassies or consulates in the British Virgin Islands.

Liquor Laws   The legal minimum age for purchasing liquor or drinking alcohol in bars or restaurants is 21.

Mail   Postal rates in the British Virgin Islands are 30¢ for a postcard (airmail) to the U.S. or Canada, and 45¢ for a first-class airmail letter (½ oz.) to the United States or Canada, or 35¢ for a second-class letter (½ oz.) to the United States or Canada.

Medical Care   In Road Town, you can go to **Peebles Hospital,** Porter Road (© 284/494-3497). A number of doctors practice on the islands. If you need medical help, your hotel can put you in touch with the islands' medical staff.

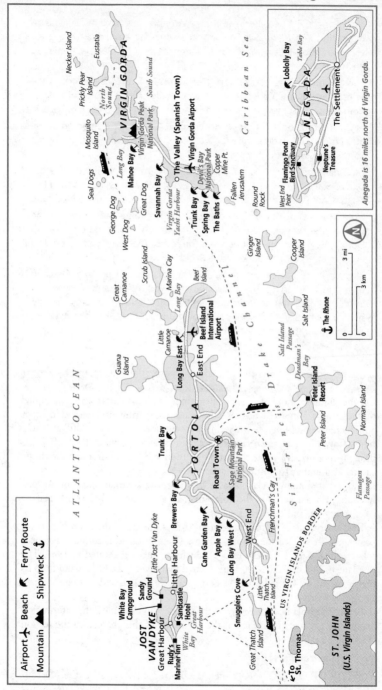

The British Virgin Islands

Legend:
Airport ✈ Beach ⌐ Ferry Route ⌐
Mountain ▲ Shipwreck ⚓

ATLANTIC OCEAN

Caribbean Sea

VIRGIN GORDA
Necker Island
Eustatia
Prickly Pear Island
Mosquito Island
North Sound
South Sound
Seal Dogs
Long Bay
Mahoe Bay
Virgin Gorda Peak National Park
George Dog
Great Dog
West Dog
Savannah Bay
The Valley (Spanish Town)
Virgin Gorda Airport
Virgin Gorda Yacht Harbour
Trunk Bay
Devil's Bay National Park
Copper Mine Pt.
Spring Bay
The Baths
Fallen Jerusalem
Round Rock
Scrub Island
Great Camanoe
Marina Cay
Long Bay
Ginger Island
Cooper Island
Little Camanoe
Beef Island
Beef Island International Airport
Salt Island
Guana Island
Long Bay East
East End
Drake Channel
Salt Island Passage
Deadman's Bay
Trunk Bay
TORTOLA
Road Town
Sage Mountain National Park
Peter Island Resort
Sir Francis
Brewers Bay
Cane Garden Bay
Apple Bay
Long Bay West
West End
Frenchman's Cay
Peter Island
Norman Island
Smugglers Cove
Little Thatch Island
Flanagan Passage
US VIRGIN ISLANDS BORDER
Little Jost Van Dyke
White Bay Campground
Sandy Ground
Little Harbour
JOST VAN DYKE
Great Harbour
Rudy's Mariner Inn
Sandcastle Hotel
White Bay
Great Harbour
Great Thatch Island
To St. Thomas
ST. JOHN (U.S. Virgin Islands)

ANEGADA
Loblolly Bay
Table Bay
The Settlement
West End Point
Flamingo Pond Bird Sanctuary
Neptune's Treasure

Anegada is 16 miles north of Virgin Gorda.

⚓ The Rhone

3 mi
3 km
0

143

Newspapers & Magazines The British Virgin Islands have no daily newspaper, but *The Island Sun,* published Wednesday and Friday, is a good source of information on local entertainment, as is *The Beacon,* published on Thursday.

Safety Crime is rare here; in fact, the British Virgin Islands are among the safest places in the Caribbean. Still, you should take all the usual precautions you would anywhere, and don't leave items unattended on the beach.

Taxes There is no sales tax. A government tax of 7% is imposed on all hotel rooms. A $10 departure tax is collected from everyone leaving by air, $5 for those departing by sea.

Telecommunications You can call the British Virgins from the continental United States by dialing **1**, the area code **284**, followed by **49**, and then five digits. Once you're there, omit both the 284 and the 49 to make local calls.

Time The islands operate on Atlantic standard time year-round. In the peak winter season, when it's 6am in the British Virgins, it's only 5am in Florida. However, when Florida and the rest of the East Coast go on daylight saving time, the clocks in the British Virgins do not change.

Tipping Porters at airports or bellmen at hotels get $1 per bag. Check to see if the 10% service charge is included on your restaurant tab. Even if it is, it's a local custom to leave another 5%. Most taxi drivers aren't tipped since most cabs are owned by their own drivers. Maids get about $2 per day in moderate or budget-priced hotels.

2 Tortola ★★

On the southern shore of this 24-square-mile island, **Road Town** is the capital of the British Virgin Islands. It's the seat of Government House and other administrative buildings, but it seems more like a village. The landfill at **Wickhams Cay,** a 70-acre town center development and marina in the harbor, has brought in a massive yacht-chartering business and has transformed the sleepy capital into more of a bustling center.

Rugged mountain peaks characterize the entire southern coast of Tortola, including Road Town. On the northern coast are white sandy beaches, banana trees, mangoes, and clusters of palms.

Beef Island, close to Tortola's eastern end, is the site of the main airport for passengers arriving in the British Virgins. The tiny island is connected to Tortola by the Queen Elizabeth Bridge, which the queen dedicated in 1966. The one-lane bridge spans the 300-foot channel that divides the little island from its bigger neighbor, Tortola. On the north shore of Beef Island is a good beach, Long Bay East.

Because Tortola is the gateway to the British Virgin Islands, the information on how to get there is covered at the beginning of this chapter, in the section "Getting There."

TORTOLA ESSENTIALS

VISITOR INFORMATION   There is a **B.V.I. Tourist Board Office** (✆ **284/ 494-3134**) at the center of Road Town near the ferry dock. You'll find information about hotels, restaurants, tours, and more. Pick up a copy of *The Welcome Tourist Guide,* which has a useful map of the island.

Tortola

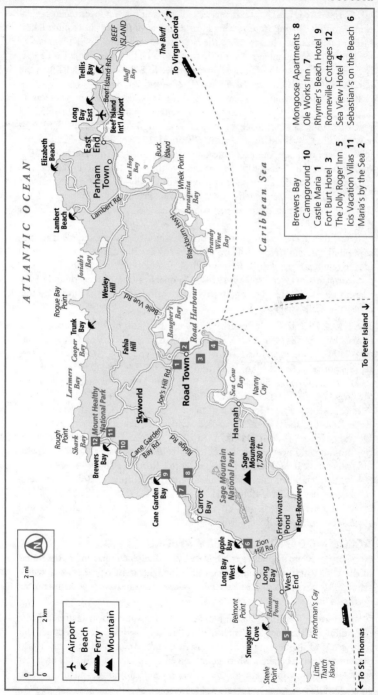

ATLANTIC OCEAN

BEEF ISLAND

The Bluff

To Virgin Gorda

Trellis Bay

Bluff Bay

Beef Island Rd.

Long Bay East

Beef Island Int'l Airport

Elizabeth Beach

East End

Parham Town

Buck Island

Whelk Point

Fat Hogs Bay

Lambert Beach

Paraquita Bay

Lambert Rd.

Josiah's Bay

Blackburn HWY

Brandy Wine Bay

Rogue Bay Point

Wesley Hill

Belle Vue Rd.

Road Harbour

Caribbean Sea

Cooper Bay

Trunk Bay

Larimers Bay

Baugher's Bay

Fahia Hill

Joe's Hill Rd.

1

2

3

4

Road Town

To Peter Island

Rough Point

Shark Bay

Brewers Bay

12

11

10

Skyworld

Mount Healthy National Park

Cane Garden Bay Rd.

Ridge Rd.

Sea Cow Bay

Hannah

Nanny Cay

Cane Garden Bay

9

7

8

Carrot Bay

Sage Mountain National Park

Sage Mountain 1,780 ft.

Freshwater Pond

Fort Recovery

Apple Bay

6

Zion Hill Rd.

Long Bay West

Long Bay

West End

Belmont Point

Belmont Pond

Frenchman's Cay

Smugglers Cove

5

Steele Point

Little Thatch Island

To St. Thomas

Brewers Bay Campground 10
Castle Maria 1
Fort Burt Hotel 3
The Jolly Roger Inn 5
Icis Vacation Villas 11
Maria's by the Sea 2

Mongoose Apartments 8
Ole Works Inn 7
Rhymer's Beach Hotel 9
Ronneville Cottages 12
Sea View Hotel 4
Sebastian's on the Beach 6

Airport
Beach
Ferry
Mountain

0 ____ 2 mi
0 ____ 2 km

N

GETTING AROUND   **Taxis** meet every arriving flight. Government regulations prohibit anyone from renting a car at the airport, so visitors must take a taxi to their hotels. The fare from the Beef Island airport to Road Town is $15 for one to three passengers. Your hotel can call a taxi for you. A **taxi tour** lasting 2½ hours costs $45 for one to three people. To call a taxi in Road Town, call ℂ **284/494-2322**; on Beef Island dial ℂ **284/495-2378**.

Because of the volume of tourism to Tortola, you should reserve a **car** in advance, especially if you want to rent in winter. A handful of local companies rent cars, plus U.S.-based chains. On Tortola, **Itgo** (ℂ **284/494-2639**) is at 1 Wickhams Cay, Road Town. **Avis** (ℂ **800/331-1212** or 284/494-3322) maintains offices opposite the police headquarters in Road Town. **Hertz** (ℂ **800/654-3001** or 284/495-4405) has offices on the island's West End, near the ferryboat landing dock. Rental companies will usually deliver your car to your hotel. All three companies require a valid driver's license and a temporary B.V.I. driver's license, which the car-rental company can sell you for $10; it's valid for 3 months.

Remember to *drive on the left* in the British fashion. Because island roads are narrow, poorly lit, and have few, if any, lines, driving at night can be risky. It's a good idea to rent a taxi to take you to that difficult-to-find beach, restaurant, or bar.

Scato's Bus Service (ℂ **284/494-2365**) operates from the north end of the island to the west end, picking up passengers who hail it down. Fares for a trek across the island are $1 to $3.

FAST FACTS   To cash traveler's checks, try the **Bank of Nova Scotia,** Wickhams Cay (ℂ **284/494-2526**), or **Barclays Bank,** Wickhams Cay (ℂ **284/494-2171**), both near Road Town on Tortola. The local **American Express** representative is **Travel Plan,** Waterfront Drive (ℂ **284/494-2347**).

The main **police** headquarters is on Waterfront Drive near the ferry docks on Sir Olva Georges Plaza (ℂ **284/494-3822**).

If you need a **drugstore,** the best place to go is **J. R. O'Neal,** Main Street, Road Town (ℂ **284/494-2292**); closed Sunday. For dental emergencies, contact **Dental Surgery** (ℂ **284/494-3274**), which is in Road Town, behind the Skeleton Building and next to the *BVI Beacon,* the local newspaper. Road Town also offers medical care at **Peebles Hospital,** Porter Road (ℂ **284/494-3497**).

The best place for film and camera repair on Tortola is **Bolo's Brothers,** Wickhams Cay (ℂ **284/494-3641**).

The best **map** of the British Virgin Islands is published by Vigilate and is sold at most bookstores in Road Town.

ACCOMMODATIONS YOU CAN AFFORD

None of the island's hotels is as big, splashy, and all-encompassing as the hotels in the U.S. Virgin Islands, and that's just fine with most of the islands' repeat visitors. All rates are subject to a 10% service charge and a 7% government tax on the room.

Castle Maria   This inn sits on a hill overlooking Road Town Harbour, just a few minutes' walk from the center of Road Town. The lush, tropical garden out front is one of the best in the British Virgin Islands. An orchard produces avocados, mangoes, and bananas, which guests can enjoy. Rooms are basic, but offer reasonable comfort, with balconies, patios, shower-only bathrooms, and kitchenettes.

P.O. Box 206, Road Town, Tortola, B.V.I. ℂ 284/494-2553. Fax 284/494-2111. www.islandsonline.com/hotel castlemaria. 31 units. Winter $90–$95 double; $105–$110 triple; $130–$140 quad. Off-season $80–$85 double; $99–$105 triple; $120–$130 quad. MC, V. **Amenities:** Restaurant, bar, pool, room service. *In room:* A/C, TV, some kitchenettes, fridge, coffeemaker.

Fort Burt Hotel   This inn, which is covered with flowering vines, rents rooms but devotes much of its energy to its popular pub and restaurant (Fort Burt Restaurant & Pub; see "Great Deals on Dining," later in this chapter). Built in 1960 on the ruins of a 17th-century Dutch fort, the rooms are set at a higher elevation than any others in Road Town, offering views from their private terraces to the waterfront below. Simple, sun-flooded, and cozy, they have a colonial charm and freewheeling conviviality. The suite rentals are a bit expensive, but the regular doubles are spacious enough and have recently been refurbished. There's a pool on the grounds, or guests can walk to Garden Bay Beach or Smuggler's Cove Beach in just 3 minutes. Its major competitor is Fort Recovery, which is also built around the ruins of a sugar mill, but Fort Recovery has a beach.

P.O. Box 3380, Fort Burt, Road Town, Tortola, B.V.I. ℭ 284/494-2587. Fax 284/494-2002. www. pussers.com/ftburt. 18 units. Year-round $99–$135 double; $155–$205 suite with kitchen, $225–$295 suite with private pool, but no kitchen. AE, MC, V. **Amenities:** Restaurant, pub, pool. *In room:* A/C, TV, no phone.

The Jolly Roger Inn ★ *Value*   This small harbor-front hotel is located at Soper's Hole, only 100 yards from the dock for the ferry to St. Thomas and St. John. The accommodations are clean and very simple. The small rooms have recently been refurbished with new draperies, bedspreads, and fresh paint, but only two have a private bathroom. There's no air-conditioning, but the rooms are breezy. The atmosphere is fun, casual, and definitely laid-back. The beach at Smuggler's Cove is a 20- to 30-minute walk over the hill.

West End, Tortola, B.V.I. ℭ 284/495-4559. Fax 284/495-4184. www.jollyrogerbvi.com. 5 units, 2 with bathroom. Winter $66 double without bathroom, $76 double with bathroom; $88 triple without bathroom, $99 triple with bathroom. Off-season $59 double without bathroom, $70 double with bathroom; $65 triple without bathroom, $83 triple with bathroom. AE, MC, V. Closed Aug 10–Oct 1. **Amenities:** Dinghy dock, fax service, sports-fishing, sailing, diving trips. *In room:* Ceiling fans, no phone.

Maria's by the Sea   This enterprise is centrally located in Road Town, with a panoramic view of the harbor. It's a 10- to 15-minute drive to the nearest beach. The rooms are decorated with rattan furniture and locally created murals. Each unit has a balcony and a small, shower-only bathroom.

P.O. Box 206, Road Town, Tortola, B.V.I. ℭ 284/494-2595. Fax 284/494-2420. www.islandsonline.com/ mariasbythesea. 41 units. Winter $110–$125 double. Off-season $95–$125 double. AE, DC, MC, V. **Amenities:** Restaurant, bar, pool, watersports. *In room:* A/C, TV, kitchenette.

Rhymer's Beach Hotel *Finds*   This comfortable, unpretentious mini-resort is housed in a low-slung pink building that sits next to a white-sand beach on the island's north shore. The hotel's social center is a wide ground-floor veranda where beach life and bar orders merge. The simple accommodations have small, shower-only bathrooms. Music lovers can head for the bar of the nearby Ole Works Inn (see "Worth a Splurge," below), where island star Quito Rhymer presents live music.

P.O. Box 570, Cane Garden Bay, Tortola, B.V.I. ℭ 284/495-4639. Fax 284/495-4820. 21 units. Winter $90 double. Off-season $55 double. Extra person $10. AE, MC, V. **Amenities:** Restaurant, commissary, salon. *In room:* A/C, TV, kitchenette, ceiling fans.

Sea View Hotel   Set at the western perimeter of Road Town, this concrete-sided modern guesthouse occupies a sloping site that affords a view over the boats bobbing at anchor in Road Town Harbour, but it's a 10-mile ride to the nearest beach. It's about as simple (and inexpensive) a hotel as you're likely to find, with few frills, although all rooms were recently renovated. Each efficiency apartment has a sitting room, a concrete-sided porch, ceiling fans, two bedrooms, and a modest kitchen. Each smallish suite has a radio and a mini-fridge. Mattresses are a bit used but still comfortable, and the bathrooms are very tiny, with shower stalls. Only breakfast is served, but the bars, sandwich shops, and grocery stores of Road Town are a 5-minute walk away.

P.O. Box 59, Road Town, Tortola, B.V.I. (C) **284/494-2483.** Fax 284/494-4952. Jumukhal@caribsurf.com. 34 units. Year-round $55 single or double; $76 suite for 2; $135 efficiency apt with kitchenette for 4. MC, V. **Amenities:** Breakfast room, pool, maid service. *In room:* A/C (in suites), mini-fridge, ceiling fans.

WORTH A SPLURGE

Ole Works Inn ✦ *Finds*   This hotel occupies the historic premises of a 300-year-old sugar refinery. It is also a far less expensive alternative to the island's other Sugar Mill, although it doesn't have the cuisine or the facilities of the more famed and expensive property. Still, it puts you right on the beach. It's set inland from Cane Garden Bay, across the road from a beautiful white-sand beach, and has the best musical venue on Tortola—the rustic indoor-outdoor bar, Quito's Gazebo. The rooms are cozy, outfitted with angular furniture and pastel colors; many have water views. Each contains a small refrigerator and ceiling fan. Some are built as hillside units with ceiling fans (plus air-conditioning), refrigerators, and clock radios. Others are older and smaller. Regardless, the shower-only bathrooms are all a bit cramped. The most romantic unit is the honeymoon suite in the venerable tower; it's larger than you'd expect. On the premises is a boutique-style art gallery showing watercolors by local artists and souvenirs. There are seven different restaurants on the beach.

The in-house bar is a magnet for fans of modern calypso music, largely because it's supervised by the hotel owner Quito (Enriquito) Rhymer, who's the most famous recording star ever produced on Tortola. Quito himself performs several times a week.

P.O. Box 560, Cane Garden Bay, Tortola, B.V.I. (C) **284/495-4837.** Fax 284/495-9618. oleworks@ candwbvi.net. 18 units. Winter $80–$200 double; from $165 suite. Off-season, $60–$175 double; from $140 suite. Extra person $25; children age 11 and under stay free in parents' room. Rates include continental breakfast. MC, V. Closed Sept. **Amenities:** Bar. *In room:* Fridge, ceiling fan.

Sebastian's on the Beach ✦   The hotel is located at Little Apple Bay, about a 15-minute drive from Road Town, on a long beach that offers a view of Jost Van Dyke and some of the best surfing in the B.V.I. The rooms are housed in three buildings, with only one on the beach. All the floral-accented rooms are furnished with rattan furniture; six units have air-conditioning, balconies, and porches. You should be careful here about room selection, as accommodations vary considerably, so ask lots of questions. Most sought after are the beachfront rooms, only steps from the surf; they have an airy tropical feeling with tile floors, balconies, patios, and screened jalousies. The rear accommodations on the beach side are less desirable. Not only do they lack views but they are subject to traffic noise. Also, avoid if possible the two bedrooms above the commissary, as they are likely to be noisy. If you're economizing, you can opt for one of the dozen rather spartan rooms in the back of the main building, as they are much less expensive; they don't have any view, but they're only a short walk from the beach.

The restaurant overlooks the bay and offers an international menu. On Saturday and Sunday guests can enjoy live entertainment in the bar. The hotel features dive packages along with packages that include a MAP plan, a welcome cocktail, a dozen assorted postcards, a pictorial guide to the B.V.I., and a bottle of rum.

Little Apple Bay (P.O. Box 441), West End, Tortola, B.V.I. (C) **800/336-4870** in the U.S., or 284/495-4212. Fax 284/ 495-4466. www.sebastiansbvi.com. 26 units. Winter $135–$230 double. Off-season $85–$140 double. Extra person $15; MAP $40 per person extra. AE, DISC, MC, V. **Amenities:** Restaurant, bar. *In room:* Fridge, ceiling fans, no phone.

APARTMENT & VILLA RENTALS

Icis Vacation Villas   These apartment units, though rather basic, are spotlessly maintained, and they're just yards from Brewers Bay, which has good swimming. Doors open onto a patio or porch in three white-and-pink concrete buildings. There's lots of foliage. The rooms have both air-conditioning and ceiling fans, plus small, shower-only bathrooms. There are no room phones, but an on-site coin phone is available. This place is in a tranquil part of the island.

P.O. Box 383, Road Town, Tortola, B.V.I. *(C)* **284/494-6979.** Fax 284/494-6980. www.icisvillas.com. 11 units. Winter $99–$115 efficiency; $159 1-bedroom apt; $260 3-bedroom apt. Off-season $69–$79 efficiency; $89–$99 1-bedroom apt; $179 3-bedroom apt. Children age 11 and under stay free in parents' unit. DC, DISC, MC, V. **Amenities:** Pool, car rental, secretarial services, babysitting, laundry. *In room:* A/C, TV, kitchenette, coffeemaker, ceiling fans, no phone.

Mongoose Apartments *(Value)*   Just minutes from the beach, in the Cane Garden Bay area, lies one of the most reasonably priced apartment units on the island. Each of the apartments, although simply furnished, has a living room, balcony, shower-only bathroom, and twin sleeper couch in the living room. Two units have TV, but you'll have to rely on the office phone. The apartments are in a U-shaped two-story building. Some have ocean views. A number of restaurants are close at hand. The owner, Sandra Henley, grows herbs for medicinal teas, which guests are invited to try.

P.O. Box 581, Cane Garden Bay, Tortola, B.V.I. *(C)* **284/495-4421.** Fax 284/495-9721. www.mongooseapartments. com. 6 1-bedroom apts. Winter $135 apt for 2. Off-season $95 apt for 2. Extra person $20; children age 12 and under $10. AE, MC, V. **Amenities:** Babysitting. *In room:* Kitchen, coffeemaker, ceiling fans, no phone.

Ronneville Cottages   If you'd like an inexpensive, weeklong vacation in the Brewers Bay area, this is a good choice. The cottages might not be romantic, but they're well designed for basic beach living. They're set in concrete structures on ground level and feature lots of tropical foliage and flowers. The units are clean and basic, with ceiling fans in the living rooms and standing fans in the bedrooms. Each has a porch or patio and TV, plus a small, shower-only bathroom. There's no pool, however, and no restaurant. But if you'd like some local cookery, the owner will prepare a dinner (given sufficient notice), and a beach bar that serves burgers and the like is only a 5-minute walk away.

P.O. Box 2652, Brewers Bay, Tortola, B.V.I. *(C)* **284/494-3337.** 2 2-bedroom cottages, 1 3-bedroom/2-bathroom house. Winter $675 cottage per week. Off-season $475 cottage per week. Extra person $25 year-round; children age 2 and under stay free with parents. No credit cards. **Amenities:** Meals prepared. *In room:* TV, fans, no phone.

CAMPING

Brewers Bay Campground *★★*   Most camping buffs appreciate this place, located 3 miles from Road Town, for its low costs and its easy access to some of the best snorkeling off the coast of Tortola. Both tent and bare-site options are available, and both include access to cookout areas, showers, and flush toilets. There's also a simple beachfront bar that sells sandwiches, hot dogs, and beer. With advance notice, dinner can be provided. On Friday night there's a communal fish fry and on Sunday night a barbecue—both meals cost $10 per person. There's no on-site commissary, but shops in Road Town sell groceries and camping paraphernalia.

Brewers Bay (P.O. Box 185), Road Town, Tortola, B.V.I. *(C)* **284/494-3463.** 20 tents, 20 bare sites. Year-round, $35 tent for 2; $10 bare site for 2. No credit cards. A camp shuttle is sometimes available. **Amenities:** Beachfront bar. *In room:* No phone.

GREAT DEALS ON DINING

Cafesito INTERNATIONAL   No one will object if you stop into this hip and popular place just for one of its Bahama Mamas, a seductive, mildly psychedelic drink that's deceptively pink and laced with rum. But if you want a meal, there's a full menu of culinary temptations that range from simple rôtis and BLTs to more complicated fare such as coconut-flavored shrimp, pasta with shrimp and lobster-flavored cream sauce, blackened red snapper, and barbecued baby-back ribs. Most dishes are on the low end of the price scale. There's some kind of live entertainment, usually either a steel band or a calypso band, that performs every Friday, Saturday, and Sunday from 7:30pm till around 11pm (no cover). There's no sea view from this place's terrace, but whenever the drinks are flowing and the music is playing, no one ever really seems to care.

Romasco Place, Wickhams Cay, Road Town. ⒸⒷ **284/494-7412.** Lunch main courses $3.50–$13.50; dinner main courses $11–$35. AE, DISC, MC, V. Daily 10:30am–11pm.

Capriccio di Mare ⸙ ITALIAN   This place is small, casual, laid-back, and a local favorite. It's the most authentic-looking Italian *caffe* in the Virgin Islands. At breakfast time, many locals stop in for a refreshing Italian pastry, along with a cup of cappuccino, or a full breakfast. You can come back for lunch and dinner. If it's evening, you might also order the mango Bellini, a variation of the famous cocktail served at Harry's Bar in Venice (which is made with fresh peaches). Begin with such appetizers as *piedini* (flour tortillas with various toppings), then move on to fresh pastas with succulent sauces, the best pizza on the island, or even well-stuffed sandwiches. We prefer the pizza topped with grilled eggplant. If you arrive on the right night, you might even be treated to lobster ravioli in a rose sauce. Also try one of the freshly made salads: We like the *insalata mista,* with large, leafy greens and slices of fresh Parmesan.

Waterfront Dr., Road Town. ⒸⒷ **284/494-5369.** Reservations not accepted. Main courses $6–$13. MC, V. Mon–Sat 8am–9pm.

Flying Iguana *Value* CARIBBEAN/CONTINENTAL   Don't make a special trip here, but if you're in the vicinity, this is a good lunch spot. It also serves tasty dinners as well. Don't be scared off by the $45 price for surf and turf. Most dishes are under $7, and the portions are large. This open-air restaurant is painted in vivid Caribbean colors. At lunch order one of the iguana burgers (actually, made with beef), the conch chowder, or one of the spicy conch fritters, along with a selection of sandwiches and pasta. The kitchen shines brighter at dinner, with an array of steak and seafood dishes, filet mignon, and roast duck. Puck, the chef and co-owner, will also prepare pretty much what you want to eat that night—within reason, of course. Just tell him your culinary desires, and he'll try to whip something up for you.

At the airport. ⒸⒷ **284/495-5277.** Main courses $3–$45; lunch $3–$16. MC, V. Daily 7am–10pm.

The Jolly Roger ⸙ SEAFOOD/INTERNATIONAL   This open-air bar and restaurant is a local favorite. People come for the stewed and cracked conch, unique pizzas, and great burgers—but the best thing about the Jolly Roger is the people. Just stick your head into the kitchen and ask Wanda for one of her great omelets for breakfast (she's here for lunch, too). The house specialty is homemade Key lime pie—don't miss it. The bar is very popular with locals and sailors. Check the schedule or call to ask about the weekend Caribbean barbecue and live entertainment several nights a week.

West End (just past the ferry dock). ⒸⒷ **284/495-4559.** Main courses $12–$22; pizzas from $10.25; breakfast $1.75–$6. AE, MC, V. Daily 8am–10pm. Closed mid-Aug to Oct 1.

Marlene's WEST INDIAN   This centrally located restaurant provides takeout as well as casual dining indoors. Try the Caribbean patés—conch, swordfish, chicken, or beef wrapped in pastry dough, then baked or fried. Other examples of local fare include rôtis and curries. You can also order baked chicken, steak, or seafood such as lobster and other shellfish. The desserts are made from scratch.

Wickhams Cay. ⓒ 284/494-4634. Patés $1.50–$2.50; main courses $6.50–$12; breakfast $2.50–$5. No credit cards. Mon–Sat 7:30am–6pm.

Midtown Restaurant CARIBBEAN   Set in the heart of Road Town, this hangout offers typical local fare such as curried chicken and mutton. The menu also includes soups, such as conch, pea, and even boiled cow-foot soup. Other choices are stewed beef ribs, baked chicken, and a wide selection of fresh seafood, depending on the day's catch. Most dishes come with your choice of *fungi*, plantains, or Caribbean carrots. There's also a good breakfast here.

Main St., Road Town. ⓒ 284/494-2764. Main courses $6–$15. No credit cards. Mon–Sat 7am–10pm; Sun 7am–5pm.

North Shore Shell Museum Bar & Restaurant 🌟🌟 *Finds* WEST INDIAN   When Egberth and Mona Donovan, both chefs, got married, they naturally decided to open a restaurant to showcase their culinary talents. They have succeeded admirably. Mona learned from her mother, Mrs. Scatliffe, who is the most celebrated local chef in the British Virgin Islands. The cuisine here is local and authentic. If you're in the area for breakfast, by all means drop in to sample the pancakes, made with coconut, guava, and mango—they're delectable. At lunch you can sample typical island fare along with some spicy conch fritters. For dinner you can try what was good at the market that day—the best soursop daiquiri on the island will get you in the mood. Tuesday and Saturday are barbecue nights, with chicken, lobster, and ribs. After dining, patrons hang out for a hoedown, a music fest, featuring such instruments as a ukulele, a washtub, or a gourd maraca.

Main Rd., Carrot Bay. ⓒ 284/495-4714. Dinner $28; breakfast from $5; lunch $5–$10. No credit cards. Daily 7am–10pm.

Paradise Pub INTERNATIONAL   This establishment is housed in a low-slung timbered building on a narrow strip of land between the coastal road and the southern edge of Road Town's harbor. It has a grangelike interior and a rambling veranda built on piers over the water. The pub attracts many of the island's yachties, as well as the local sports teams, who celebrate here after their games. More than 25 different kinds of beer are available. If you're here for a meal, you can order Bahamian fritters, Caesar or Greek salad, pasta, four kinds of steaks, and burgers. The chef also prepares a catch of the day. Different nights of the week are devoted to all-you-can-eat theme dinners, including pasta on Tuesday, prime rib on Thursday, mussels on Wednesday, and barbecue on Saturday. Happy hour brings discounted drinks 5 to 7pm Monday to Thursday and 11am to 7pm on Friday, when hot wings and raw vegetable platters are offered.

Fort Burt Marina, Harbour Rd. ⓒ 284/494-2608. Reservations recommended. Main courses $8.50–$22. AE, MC, V. Mon–Sat 6am–10pm.

Pusser's Landing 🌟🌟 CARIBBEAN/ENGLISH PUB/MEXICAN   This second Pusser's (see below for the first) is even more desirably located in the West End, opening onto the water. Within this nautical setting you can enjoy fresh grilled fish, or perhaps an English-inspired dish like shepherd's pie. Begin with a hearty bowl of homemade soup and follow it with filet mignon, West Indian roast chicken, or a filet of mahimahi. Mud pie is the classic dessert here, or you can try Key lime pie or, even better, the mango soufflé. Some dishes occasionally miss the mark, but on the whole this is a delightful choice. Happy hour is daily 4 to 6pm.

Frenchman's Cay, West End. ✆ 284/495-4554. Reservations recommended. Main courses $13–$22. AE, DISC, MC, V. Daily 11am–10pm.

Pusser's Road Town Pub ✦ CARIBBEAN/ENGLISH PUB/MEXICAN
Standing on the waterfront across from the ferry dock, the original Pusser's serves Caribbean fare, English pub grub, and good pizzas. This is not as fancy or as good as the Pusser's in the West End, but it's a lot more convenient and has faster service. The complete lunch and dinner menu includes English shepherd's pies and deli-style sandwiches. *Gourmet* magazine asked for the recipe for its chicken-and-asparagus pie. John Courage ale is on draft, but the drink to order here is the famous Pusser's Rum, the same blend of five West Indian rums that the Royal Navy has served to its men for more than 300 years. Thursday is nickel beer night.

Waterfront Dr. and Main St., Road Town. ✆ 284/494-3897. Reservations recommended. Main courses $7–$19. AE, DISC, MC, V. Daily 10am–midnight.

Quito's Gazebo ✦ *Finds* WEST INDIAN   This restaurant, owned by Quito Rhymer, the island's most acclaimed musician, is the most popular of the restaurants located along the shore of Cane Garden Bay. Quito himself performs after dinner several nights a week. The place, which is designed like an enlarged gazebo, is set directly on the sands of the beach. It serves frothy rum-based drinks (ask for the piña colada or a Bushwacker, made with four different kinds of rum). Lunch includes sandwiches, salads, and platters. Evening meals are more elaborate, and might feature conch or pumpkin fritters, mahimahi with a wine-butter sauce, a conch dinner with (Callwood) rum sauce, chicken rôti, and steamed local mutton served with a sauce of island tomatoes and pepper. On Friday night for only $16 you can enjoy an all-you-can-eat buffet of barbecue ribs, chicken, rôti, corn on the cob, and johnnycakes. The food has a true island flavor and a lot of zest.

Cane Garden Bay. ✆ 284/495-4837. Main courses $12–$18; lunch platters, sandwiches, and salads $5–$10. AE, MC, V. Mon–Fri 7am–6pm; Fri–Sat 7am–4pm. Bar, Tues–Sun 11am–midnight.

Rita's Restaurant *Value* CARIBBEAN/AMERICAN   If you're looking for an inexpensive eatery with a touch of the island, then stop at Rita's for some local fare. The surroundings are simple, but the atmosphere is lively. Breakfast ranges from the standard American fare to local favorites such as fried fish or saltfish, which is chopped up with a variety of spices and sautéed in butter. Both are served with johnnycakes. The lunch menu includes pea soup, curried chicken, and stewed mutton. For those who want a taste of the mainland, try the barbecued chicken and ribs, sandwiches, or that old standby, spaghetti and meatballs.

Round-A-Bout, Road Town. ✆ 284/494-6165. Breakfast $3–$8; lunch or dinner $10–$16. No credit cards. Daily 8am–10pm.

Rôti Palace *Value* INDIAN   The best rôtis in the British Virgin Islands are served here, right on the old main street of the island's capital—they're just as good as those in Port-of-Spain, Trinidad. This is primarily a lunch stop, although it's also a good choice for an affordable dinner or a standard breakfast. Choices include a wide selection of vegetables and local conch, along with lobster, beef, and chicken dishes, often spicy and tasty. Sea snails are a specialty; they're mixed with onions, garlic, and celery, and spiced with curries, served in a butter sauce. Ginger beer, along with juices and wines, might accompany your meal.

Abbot Hill, Road Town. ✆. 284/494-4196. Main courses $6–$18. No credit cards. Mon–Sat 7am–9:30pm.

Scuttlebutt Bar & Grill INTERNATIONAL/CARIBBEAN This cafe's greatest asset is its location—it's 1 mile west of the center of Road Town, beside a small, charming marina. You can order your meal at the counter, and then carry it to one of the picnic tables, which are sheltered from the sun, but not from the breezes off the water. The simple setting here keeps prices down, and the food—especially breakfast—is plentiful and good. Specialties include beef crêpes, crabmeat salads, sandwiches, burgers, and a house drink that combines several kinds of rum into a lethal combination known as a Painkiller. The place is especially popular at breakfast, when eight different kinds of "rooster omelets" draw the yachters. Upstairs is a more expensive restaurant, Callaloo.

In the Prospect Reef Resort, Slaney Hill, Drake's Hwy. ℭ 284/494-3311. Sandwiches, platters, and salads $5.50–$14. AE, MC, V. Daily 7am–1am.

Virgin Queen WEST INDIAN/ENGLISH This restaurant offers casual dining in a modest cinder-block building with nautical pictures scattered throughout. The menu includes a wide spectrum of dishes ranging from local fare, such as curried chicken, to a more international offering of pastas, such as the fettuccine served with a tomato-basil sauce, and barbecued chicken and baby-back ribs. Included among the British specialties are shepherd's pie, bangers and mash, and steak-and-ale pie. The portions are substantial.

Cane Garden Bay. ℭ 284/495-4837. Main courses $12–$18; lunch platters, sandwiches, and salads $5–$10. AE, MC, V. Mon–Thurs 7am–6pm; Fri–Sat 7am–4pm. Bar, Tues–Sun 11am–midnight.

WORTH A SPLURGE

Fort Burt Restaurant & Pub INTERNATIONAL The food here is quite good, although hardly the best on the island. It's more of a local favorite. This restaurant was built on rocks mortared together with lime and molasses in the 17th century by the Dutch and French. Lunches consist of soups, salads, grilled fish, and sandwiches. Dinners are by candlelight and are more elaborate, with such choices as fresh asparagus with aïoli sauce, conch fritters, shepherd's pie, baby-back ribs, and roast duck with orange-and-tarragon sauce.

Fort Burt, Road Town. ℭ 284/494-2587. Reservations recommended for dinner. English breakfast $8.75; dinner platters $15–$25; lunch sandwiches and platters $5–$8.50. AE, MC, V. Daily 8–10am, noon–3pm, and 6–11pm. Bar open daily 10am–midnight.

Mrs. Scatliffe's Restaurant ✦ *Finds* WEST INDIAN This Tortola Mama offers home-cooked meals on the deck of her island home, and some of the vegetables come right from her garden, although others might be from a can. You'll be served excellent authentic West Indian dishes, perhaps spicy conch soup, followed by curried goat, "old wife" fish, or possibly chicken in a coconut shell. After dinner, your hostess and her family will entertain you with a *fungi*-band performance (except on Sun) or gospel singing. *Be duly warned:* This entertainment isn't for everyone, including one reader who compared the hymns to a "screeching caterwaul." Service, usually from an inexperienced teenager, is not exactly efficient.

You might also be exposed to Mrs. Scatliffe's gentle and often humorous form of Christian fundamentalism. A Bible reading and a heartfelt rendition of a gospel song might be served up with a soft custard dessert. She often serves lunch in winter, but call ahead just to be sure.

Carrot Bay. ℭ 284/495-4556. Reservations required by 5:30pm. Fixed-price meal $25–$30. No credit cards. One seating daily begins 7–8pm.

Finds   The Wreck of the Rhone & Other Top Dive Sites

The wreck of the HMS *Rhone* ★★★ is perhaps the premier dive spot in the Caribbean. *Skin Diver* magazine called this "the world's most fantastic shipwreck dive." The *Rhone* sank in 1867 near the western point of Salt Island, and its wreck teems with marine life and coral formations.

Although it's no *Rhone, Chikuzen* is another intriguing dive site off Tortola. This 270-foot steel-hulled refrigerator ship sank off the island's east end in 1981. The hull, still intact under about 80 feet of water, is now home to a vast array of tropical fish, including yellowtail, barracuda, black-tip sharks, octopus, and drum fish.

Another top dive site is a brilliant coral wall with the evocative name of **Alice in Wonderland.** It lies off Ginger Island. The wall slopes from 40 feet to a sandy bottom at 100 feet. This dreamlike site earned its name because of its monstrous overhangs, large mushroom-shaped corals, rainbow-hued colors, and wide variety of sea animals, including everything from the longnose butterfly fish to garden eels.

The best way for novice and expert divers to see these and other great dive sites is with one of the following outfitters:

- **Baskin in the Sun** (✆ **800/233-7938** in the U.S., or 284/494-2858), a PADI five-star facility on Tortola, is a good outfitter, with locations at the Prospect Reef Resort, near Road Town, and at Soper's Hole, on Tortola's West End. Baskin's most popular trip is the supervised "Half-Day Scuba Diving" experience for $95, catered to beginners, but there are trips for all levels of experience. Daily excursions are scheduled to the HMS *Rhone,* as well as "Painted Walls" (an underwater canyon, the walls of which are formed of brightly colored coral and sponges) and the "Indians" (four pinnacle rocks sticking out of the water, which divers follow 40 ft. below the surface).

- **Underwater Safaris** (✆ **284/494-3235**) takes you to all the best sites, including the HMS *Rhone,* "Spyglass Wall," and "Alice in Wonderland." It has two offices: Safari Base in Road Town and Safari Cay on Cooper Island. Get complete directions and information when you call. The center offers a complete PADI and NAUI training facility. An introductory resort course and three dives costs $168, while an open-water certification, with 4 days of instruction and four open-water dives, goes for $385, plus $40 for the instruction manual.

HITTING THE BEACHES

Beaches are rarely crowded on Tortola unless a cruise ship is in port. You can rent a car or a Jeep to reach them, or take a taxi (but be sure to arrange for a time to be picked up).

Tortola's finest beach is **Cane Garden Bay** ★★★, on Cane Garden Bay Road directly west of Road Town. You'll have to navigate some roller-coaster hills to get there, but these fine white sands, with sheltering palm trees, are among the most popular in the B.V.I., and the lovely bay is beloved by yachties. There are outfitters that rent Hobie Cats, kayaks, and sailboards. Windsurfing is possible as well. Beware of crowds in high season. There are some seven places here to eat, along with a handful of bars. **Rhymer's** (© 284/495-4639) is our favorite, offering cold beer and refreshing rum drinks. If you're hungry, try the conch or lobster, black-bean gazpacho, or barbecued spareribs. The beach bar and restaurant is open daily 8am to 9pm, with steel-drum bands entertaining on some evenings. Ice and freshwater showers are available (and you can rent towels). Ask about renting Sunfish and windsurfers next door.

Surfers like **Apple Bay,** west of Cane Garden Bay, along North Shore Road. The beach isn't very big, but that doesn't diminish activity when the surf's up. Conditions are best in January and February. After enjoying the white sands here, you can have a drink at Bomba's Surfside Shack, a classic dive of a beach bar at the water's edge (see "Tortola After Dark," below).

Smugglers Cove, known for its tranquility and the beauty of its sands, lies at the extreme western end of Tortola, opposite the offshore island of Great Thatch and just north of St. John. It's a lovely crescent of white sand, with calm turquoise waters. A favorite local beach, it's at the end of bumpy Belmont Road. Once you get here, a little worse for wear, you'll think the crystal-clear water and the beautiful palm trees are worth the effort. Snorkelers like this beach, which is sometimes called "Lower Belmont Bay." It's especially good for beginning snorkelers, since the reef is close to shore and easily reached. You'll see sea fans, sponges, parrotfish, and elkhorn and brain corals.

East of Cane Garden Bay and site of a campground, **Brewers Bay,** reached along the long, steep Brewers Bay Road, is ideal for snorkelers and surfers. This clean, white-sand beach is a great place to enjoy walks in the early morning or at sunset. Sip a rum punch from the beach bar, and watch the world go by.

The mile-long, white-sand beach at **Long Bay West,** reached along Long Bay Road, is one of the most beautiful in the B.V.I. Joggers run along the water's edge, and it's also a lovers' walk at dusk, with spectacular sunsets. The Long Bay Beach Resort stands on the northeast side of the beach; many visitors like to book a table at the resort's restaurant overlooking the water.

At the very east end of the island, **Long Bay East,** reached along Beef Island Road, is a great spot for swimming. Cross Queen Elizabeth Bridge to reach this mile-long beach with great views and white sands.

EXPLORING AN ANCIENT RAIN FOREST

No visit to Tortola is complete without a trip to **Sage Mountain National Park** ⊛, a national park whose Mount Sage rises to 1,780 feet. Here you'll find traces of a primeval rain forest, and you can enjoy a picnic while overlooking neighboring islets and cays. Go west from Road Town to reach the mountain. Before you head out, stop by the tourist office and pick up a brochure called *Sage Mountain National Park.* It has a location map, directions to the forest (where there's a parking lot), and an outline of the main trails through the park.

Covering 92 acres, the park was established in 1964 to protect the remnants of Tortola's original forests not burned or cleared during the island's plantation era. From the parking lot, a trail leads to the main entrance to the park. The two main trails are the Rain Forest Trail and the Mahogany Forest Trail.

Moments **Gourmet Picnic, Anyone?**

Fort Wines Gourmet, Main Street, Road Town (© **284/494-2211**), offers fabulous fixings, including Hediard paté terrines and fine chocolates.

> ## (Value Cheap Thrills: What to See & Do for Free (Well, Almost) in the British Virgins
>
> - **Sample Mango Pancakes.** Head for a place called **North Shore Shell Museum/Home Made Banana Bread,** on Main Road at Carrot Bay on in Tortola (© **284/495-4714**). There's no more down-home spot than this. Come for breakfast and look for the special on the chalk-board: mango pancakes (or coconut, guava, or banana), along with the homemade bread of the day—guava, mango, or banana, each pan-toasted for extra flavor. Ask owner Egbert Donovan to wrap an extra three or four slices for treats later on the beach. Come back at night to hear an ad hoc *fungi* band with such instruments as a grooved gourd or a metal scratching stick. Enjoy cracked conch or barbecued chicken, and certainly one of those to-die-for guava daiquiris.
> - **Visit a Remarkable Tropical Forest.** If you like to explore mountain-ous landscape that looks no doubt as it did when Columbus first landed, you'll find the B.V.I. filled with wonder. At the Sage Mountain National Park on Tortola, you'll see the results of reforestation and the reintroduction of vegetation that's quite remarkable. Although it gets only 100 inches of rain a year, the park nevertheless has the makings of a rain forest.
> - **Discover Dead Chest.** For a small fee (to be negotiated), a local boatman will also take you over to Dead Chest Island, part of the Rhone National Marine Park, a half-mile south of Peter Island. Dead Chest also has historic appeal, being the reputed island where Blackbeard marooned 15 crew members with only their sea chests and a bottle of rum—hence the ditty "Yo, ho, ho . . ."
> - **Check Out Treacherous Anegada.** In the overcrowded Caribbean, tiny Anegada is a remote limestone and coral atoll. The population is only 250, so you can often walk for miles without seeing anyone. You'll feel like a modern-day Robinson Crusoe here. More than 300 ships have been sent to the bottom of the sea because of the dangerous coral shelf extending out from it, and that's more wrecks than anywhere else in the Caribbean. Here's the good news: The

Shadow's Ranch, Todman's Estate (© **284/494-2262**), offers horseback rides through the national park or down to the shores of Cane Garden Bay. Call for details, Monday to Saturday 9am to 4pm. The cost is from $30 per hour.

ORGANIZED TOURS

Travel Plan Tours, Romasco Place, Wickhams Cay 1, Road Town (© **284/ 494-2872**), will organize 3½-hour tours that touch on the panoramic highlights of Tortola (a minimum of four participants is required) for $28 per person, with a supplement of $5 per person if you want to extend the tour with a bout of hill-climbing in the rain forest. The company also offers 2½-hour snorkeling tours for $35 per person, or full-day (with lunch included) snorkeling tours for $42 per person. A half-day sailing tour aboard a catamaran that moves from Tortola

entire island is surrounded by white sandy beaches, making it a paradise for divers and snorkelers.

- **Find Hidden Pools in The Baths.** The most celebrated site on Virgin Gorda is The Baths, where giant boulders were brought to the surface eons ago by a vast volcanic eruption. The huge rocks strewn along the beach on the island's southwest shore are granite; it's been suggested they were placed here by some race of giants, but scientists think they were spewed up by volcanic activity. The important thing is not to solve this mystery, but to explore the cave-like passages between them and find hidden pools just right for a quick dip.

- **Snorkel Off "Treasure Island"** 🐬🐬. Across Drake Channel from Tortola lies Norman Isle. Although it used to be a pirate den with treasure ships at anchor, it is now deserted by all except some seabirds and small wild animals. Legend has it that this tiny isle was the inspiration for Robert Louis Stevenson's *Treasure Island,* first published in 1883. You can row a dinghy into the southernmost cave of the island—with bats overhead and phosphorescent patches—where Stevenson's Mr. Fleming supposedly stowed his precious treasure. Norman Isle has a series of other caves whose waters are teeming with marine life. The caves are one of the most well-known snorkeling spots in the B.V.I. Intrepid hikers climb through scrubland to the island's central ridge, Spy Glass Hill. To cut costs, ask three or four other people to go in with you and rent a sailboat to go over for a cheap adventure.

- **Check Out the Botanic Gardens. J.R. O'Neal Botanic Gardens,** Botanic Station (☎ **284/494-4997**), is free and it's a gem. This 3-acre park in Road Town was created by the B.V.I. National Parks Trust and is run by local volunteers eager to show you around. The orchid house and a small rain forest are reached by crossing a charming lily pond, and other paths lead to a cactus garden and a palm grove. The aptly named flamboyant tree, with its brilliant scarlet flowers, is just one of the highlights here.

to Peter Island or Norman Island costs $80.85 per person; a full-day tour that goes farther afield to as far away as the Baths at Virgin Gorda and includes lunch costs $80 per person. And if deep-sea fishing appeals to you, a half-day excursion, with equipment, for four fishers and up to two "non-fishing observers" will cost $600 to $700.

A **taxi tour** that lasts 2½ hours costs $45 for two passengers or $55 for 3 hours. To call a taxi in Road Town, dial ☎ **284/494-2322;** on Beef Island, ☎ **284/495-2378.**

SHOPPING

Most of the shops are on Main Street in Road Town.

Caribbean Corner Spice House Co., Soper's Hole (☎ **284/495-9567**), offers the island's finest selection of spices and herbs, along with local handcrafts and botanical skin-care products, most of which you'll find useful in the fierce sun. There's also a selection of Cuban cigars, but Americans will have to smoke them on-island, as U.S. Customs does not allow their importation. **Caribbean Fine Arts Ltd.,** Main Street, Road Town (© **284/494-4240**), has one of the most unusual collections of art from the West Indies. It sells original watercolors and oils, limited-edition serigraphs and sepia photographs, and pottery and primitives. **Caribbean Handprints,** Main Street, Road Town (© **284/ 494-3717**), features island handprints, all hand-done by local craftspeople. **Flamboyance,** Soper's Hole (© **284/495-4099**), is the best place to shop for perfume. There is also an upscale assortment of quality cosmetics. None of these products is particularly cheap, but since they are hawked without duty, you'll save money.

Fort Wines Gourmet, Main Street, Road Town, (© **284/494-2211**), is a store-cum-cafe and a good place to stock up on a truly gourmet picnic. A decorative and home accessories store, **J. R. O'Neal,** Upper Main Street, Road Town (© **284/ 494-2292**), across from the Methodist church, has an extensive collection of terra-cotta pottery, wicker and rattan home furnishings, Mexican glassware, dhurrie rugs, baskets, ceramics, fine crystal, china, and more, all at good prices.

Bargain hunters also gravitate to **Sea Urchin,** Columbus Centre, Road Town (© **284/494-3129**), where you'll find print shirts and shorts, along with stuff for the beach, including T-shirts, cover-ups, bathing suits, and sandals. Good prices in swimwear are also available at **Turtle Dove Boutique,** Fleming Street, Road Town (© **284/494-3611**), which has a wide international selection. Women can also purchase linen and silk dresses here at reasonable prices.

Pusser's Company Store, Main Street and Waterfront Drive, Road Town (© **284/494-2467**), is for nautical memorabilia. There's a long, mahogany-trimmed bar accented with many fine nautical artifacts. The store sells a proprietary line of Pusser's sports and travel clothing and gift items. Pusser's Rum is one of the best-selling items here, or perhaps you'd prefer a Pusser's ceramic flask as a memento.

Sunny Caribbee Herb and Spice Company, Main Street, Road Town (© **284/494-2178**), in an old West Indian building, was the first hotel on Tortola. Today it's a shop that specializes in Caribbean spices, seasonings, teas, condiments, and handcrafts. You can buy two world-famous specialties here: the West Indian hangover cure and the Arawak love potion. A Caribbean cosmetics collection, Sunsations, is also available and includes herbal bath gels, island perfume, and sunshine lotions. With its aroma of spices permeating the air, this factory is an attraction in itself. There's a daily sampling of island products, something different every day—perhaps tea, coffee, sauces, or dips. Right next door is the Sunny Caribbee Gallery, featuring original paintings, prints, wood-carvings, and hand-painted furniture, plus crafts from throughout the Caribbean. In the Sunny Caribbee Art Gallery, adjacent to the spice shop, you'll find an extensive collection of original art, prints, metal sculpture, and many other Caribbean crafts.

TORTOLA AFTER DARK

Ask around to find out which hotel has entertainment on any given evening. Steel bands and *fungi* or scratch bands (African-Caribbean musicians who improvise on locally available instruments) appear regularly, and nonguests are usually welcome. Pick up a copy of *Limin' Times,* an entertainment magazine listing what's happening locally; it's usually available at your hotel.

Bomba's Surfside Shack ✰✰, Cappoon's Bay (℗ **284/495-4148**), is the oldest, most memorable, and most uninhibited nightspot on the island. It sits on a 20-foot-wide strip of unpromising coastline near the West End. It's covered with Day-Glo graffiti and laced into a semblance of coherence with wire and rejected odds and ends of plywood, driftwood, and abandoned rubber tires. Despite its makeshift appearance, the shack has the electronic amplification system to create a really great party. Every month (dates vary), Bomba's stages a full-moon party when free house tea is spiked with hallucinogenic mushrooms. "We don't make it really strong any more," says Bomba Smith, the owner. "But it still gets you plenty high." The tea is free because it's illegal to sell it. The place is also wild on Wednesday and Sunday nights, when there's live music and a $8 all-you-can-eat barbecue. Open daily 10am to midnight (or later, depending on business).

The Moorings/Mariner Inn, Wickhams Cay (℗ **284/494-2332**), is the preferred watering hole of some upscale yacht owners, maybe because the drink prices are low. Open to a view of its own marina and bathed in a dim and flattering light, the place is nautical and relaxed. The two drink specials are Moorings Delight, made with vodka, rum, cointreau, and cream of coconut, or a Tortola Sunset, made with tequila, orange juice, and cranberry juice. A *fungi* band sometimes provides a backdrop to the socializing.

Another popular watering hole is **Spyglass Bar,** in the Treasure Isle Hotel, at the eastern end of Road Town (℗ **284/494-2501**). This popular bar is in a little house designed with Haitian gingerbread. The sunken bar on the terrace overlooks the swimming pool and faraway marina facilities of this popular hotel. Bar specialties include Treasure Island rum punch with dark rum, orange juice, strawberry syrup, and apricot brandy, and Windstorm, made with Galliano, rum, fruit punch, and 7-Up.

The Bat Cave, Waterfront Drive at Road Town (℗ **284/494-4880**), on the ground floor of the restaurant Spaghetti Junction, is one of the newest hot spots. It's a full bar where you can eat spaghetti at tables if the restaurant upstairs is too packed. On Friday night they play "pre-released" music or songs just being released on radio stations. The latest recorded music on the charts is presented to the convivial crowd nightly. On the last Friday of each month the staff throws a big costume party—it's an island hit.

De Loose Mongoose, Beef Island (℗ **284/495-2302**), should be near the top of the list of funky beach bars in the Caribbean. Sailors on sailboats or the yachting crowd on their yachts like to drop anchor at this laid-back haven overlooking Trellis Bay near the airport. The bar is set right on the water. You're welcomed into the domain of Michele Gill, who runs the bar with her husband, Ken, who is often heard strumming the guitar. Their house specialty is called No-See-Um, named after the pesky biting gnat of the Caribbean, the plague of every sunset watch. Michele says if you drink enough of her potent rum concoction, "these biting insects won't bother you—nothing will!"

Other little island hot spots, worth at least a drop-in on a barhopping jaunt include **Bing's Drop in Bar,** Fat Hog's Bay in the East End (℗ **284/495-2627**), where the locals gather at night. In winter there's a DJ playing the latest music. At **Jolly Roger,** West End (℗ **284/495-4559**), you can hear local bands or perhaps some from America, playing everything from reggae to blues. On Friday and Saturday nights, starting at 8pm, the joint rocks and rolls. You can count on a jumping dance crowd at **Myett's,** Cane Garden Bay (℗ **284/495-9543**), on Friday and Saturday evenings and also after 3pm on Sunday afternoon when the B.V.I. usually gets pretty dull. Also in Cane Garden Bay, visit **Stanley's**

Welcome Bar (© 284/495-9424), where a rowdy fraternity-type crowd gathers on the beach to drink, talk, and drink some more. Finally, check out **Sebastian's,** Apple Bay (© 284/495-4212), especially on Saturday and Sunday when you can dance to live music under the stars—at least in the winter season.

The joint is jumping at the **Tower Night Club,** West End (© 284/494-1776), on Friday to Sunday nights. The place is packed with locals and a scattering of visitors who come to listen to a DJ but often live salsa and reggae.

3 Virgin Gorda ★★★

In 1493, on his second voyage to the New World, Columbus named this island Virgin Gorda, or "fat virgin" (from a distance, the island looks like a reclining woman with a protruding stomach). The second largest of the British Virgin Islands, Virgin Gorda is 10 miles long and 2 miles wide, with a population of some 1,400. It's 12 miles east of Road Town and 26 miles from St. Thomas.

The island was a fairly desolate agricultural community until Laurence S. Rockefeller established the Little Dix Bay Hotel in the early 1960s, following his success with Caneel Bay on St. John in the 1950s (see chapter 25). He envisioned a "wilderness beach," where privacy and solitude reign, and he literally put Virgin Gorda on the map. Other major hotels followed in the wake of Little Dix, but you can still find that privacy and solitude.

In 1971 the Virgin Gorda Yacht Harbour opened. Operated by the Little Dix Bay Hotel, it accommodates 120 yachts.

VIRGIN GORDA ESSENTIALS

GETTING THERE **Air St. Thomas** (© 340/776-2722) flies to Virgin Gorda daily from St. Thomas. The 40-minute flight costs $71 one-way, $140 round-trip.

Speedy's Fantasy (© 284/495-5240) operates a ferry service between Road Town and Virgin Gorda. Five ferries a day leave from Road Town Monday to Saturday, reduced to two on Sunday. The trip costs $10 one-way or $19 round-trip. From St. Thomas to Virgin Gorda there's service three times a week (on Tues, Thurs, and Sat), costing $31 one-way or $50 round-trip.

GETTING AROUND Independently operated open-sided **safari buses** run along the main road. Holding up to 14 passengers, these buses charge upward of $3 per person to transport a passenger from, say, The Valley to The Baths.

If you'd like to rent a car, try one of the local firms, including **Mahogany Rentals,** The Valley, Spanish Town (© 284/495-5469), across from the yacht harbor. A representative will meet you at the airport or ferry dock and do the paperwork there. This company is the least expensive on the island, beginning at around $50 daily for a Suzuki Samurai. An alternative is **Andy's Taxi and Jeep Rental** (© 284/495-5252), 7 minutes from the marina in Spanish Town. A representative here will also meet you at the airport of ferry dock for the paperwork. Rates begin at $50 daily.

FAST FACTS The local **American Express** representative is **Travel Plan Ltd.,** Virgin Gorda Yacht Harbour (© 284/495-5586). You can call the local police station at © 284/495-5222.

ACCOMMODATIONS YOU CAN AFFORD

Sometimes, particularly in the off-season, you can get a good deal on a villa rental. The best agency for that is **Virgin Gorda Villa Rentals Ltd.,** P.O. Box 63, The Valley, Virgin Gorda, B.V.I. (© 284/495-7421; fax 284/495-7367).

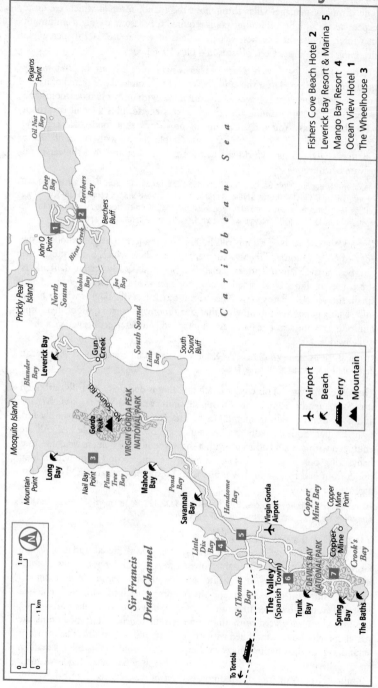

Virgin Gorda

Fishers Cove Beach Hotel **2**
Leverick Bay Resort & Marina **5**
Mango Bay Resort **4**
Ocean View Hotel **1**
The Wheelhouse **3**

Parjaros Point

Oil Nut Bay

Deep Bay

Berchers Bay

Berchers Bluff

John O Point

Birra Creek

Caribbean Sea

Prickly Pear Island

North Sound

Robin Bay

Joe Bay

South Sound

Mosquito Island

Blunder Bay

Leverick Bay

Gun Creek

Little Bay

South Sound Bluff

ON Sound Rd.

Gorda Peak

VIRGIN GORDA PEAK NATIONAL PARK

Mountain Point

Long Bay

Nail Bay Point

Plum Tree Bay

Mahoe Bay

Savannah Bay

Pond Bay

Handsome Bay

Virgin Gorda Airport

Copper Mine Bay

Copper Mine Point

Sir Francis Drake Channel

Little Dix Bay

Copper Mine

Crook's Bay

St Thomas Bay

The Valley (Spanish Town)

DEVIL'S BAY NATIONAL PARK

Trunk Bay

Spring Bay

The Baths

To Tortola

✈ Airport
↖ Beach
┄ Ferry
▲ Mountain

N

1 mi
0

1 km
0

161

The company manages villas throughout the island, most of which are quite expensive. A 5-night minimum stay is required off-season, a 7-night minimum in winter. About the cheapest weekly rentals in winter are $1,150 per week, dropping to $800 per week off-season—plus 19% tax.

Fischers Cove Beach Hotel 🏖️🏖️   There's swimming at your doorstep in this group of units nestled near the sandy beach of St. Thomas Bay. Erected of native stone, each of the eight cottages is self-contained, with one or two bedrooms and a combination living/dining room with a kitchenette, plus a small bathroom with shower stall. You can stock up on provisions at a food store near the grounds. There are also 12 pleasant but simple rooms with views of Drake Channel. Each has its own private bathroom (with hot and cold showers) and private balcony.

The Valley (P.O. Box 60), Virgin Gorda, B.V.I. ☎ **284/495-5252.** Fax 284/495-5820. fischers@candwbvi.net. 20 units. Winter $145–$150 double; $170–$285 studio cottage. Off-season $100 double; $125–$205 studio cottage. MAP (breakfast and dinner) $40 per person extra. AE, MC, V. **Amenities:** Occasional live entertainment, Jeeps available, children's playground. *In room:* A/C, kitchenette in cottages, no phone.

Ocean View Hotel   This no-frills hotel is in a residential neighborhood at the edge of Virgin Gorda's largest settlement, The Valley, which is the site of the ferryboat arrivals from Tortola. Small, simple, and family operated, it offers sheetrock- or cinder block-sided rooms with a sense of Caribbean aesthetics and small, shower-only bathrooms. The nearest beach (Devil's Bay) is within half a mile. Many guests abandon their rather small rooms to spend most of their time outdoors near the sea. The bars, restaurants, and launderettes of town are a short walk away.

P.O. Box 66, Virgin Gorda, B.V.I. ☎ **284/495-5230.** 12 units. Year-round $85 double. AE, MC, V. **Amenities:** Restaurant, bar. *In room:* A/C, TV, ceiling fans.

The Wheelhouse   This cinder-block building is definitely no-frills, although it is conveniently located near a shopping center and the Virgin Gorda Marina and a 15-minute walk from the beach. The rooms are clean and simply furnished, often done in pastels, with two single beds or a double bed. All are equipped with a small bathroom with a shower stall. Children are welcome, and babysitting can be arranged. The rooms are on the second floor with a long porch front and back, and downstairs is an inexpensive restaurant. There's also a garden in back.

P.O. Box 66, Spanish Town, Virgin Gorda, B.V.I. ☎ **284/495-5230.** 12 units. Year-round $85 double. AE, MC, V. **Amenities:** Restaurant, bar. *In room:* A/C, TV, ceiling fan.

VILLA & CONDO RENTALS

Leverick Bay Resort & Marina 🏖️🏖️   Set on the sheltered waters of Virgin Gorda's North Sound, this establishment offers a well-designed row of town house–style hotel rooms on a white sand beach. The facade of each unit is painted a different pastel color, and the building is capped with an orange-red roof and fronted by three tiers of ocean-facing balconies. The units are stylish, comfortable, and graced with fine architectural touches. The bedrooms are pastel-colored, breezy, and filled with original art, and have seafront balconies or verandas, plus tiled bathrooms with showers. The site contains a food market, an art gallery and two small beaches (a larger beach at Savannah Bay is within a 10-min. drive). A quartet of condo units is set in modern, red-roofed hexagons flanked on four sides by wraparound porches.

North Sound (P.O. Box 63), Virgin Gorda, B.V.I. ☎ **800/848-7081** in the U.S., 800/463-9396 in Canada, or 284/495-7421. Fax 284/495-7367. www.virgingordabvi.com. 16 units, 4 condos. Winter $149 double.

Off-season $119 double. Extra person $36 in winter; $24 off-season. Condos (by the week only) winter $1,470 for 2; $1,800 for 6. Condos off-season $1,200 for 2; $1,350 for 6. AE, MC, V. **Amenities:** Restaurant, bar, pool, dive shop. *In room:* A/C, TV.

Mango Bay Resort *Value Kids*   This well-designed compound of eight white-sided villas is set on lushly landscaped grounds overlooking the scattered islets of Drake's Channel on the island's western shore. The accommodations are the most adaptable on the island—doors can be locked or unlocked to divide each villa into as many as four independent units, which is especially handy for families of various sizes. Costs vary with the proximity of the unit to the nearby beach. Interiors are stylish yet simple, often dominated by the same turquoise as that of the seascape in front of you. Each unit has a compact, tiled bathroom with a shower stall. Daily maid service is included. You can cook in or dine on site at Georgio's Table, which is quite good and serves three meals a day.

Mahoe Bay (P.O. 1062), Virgin Gorda, B.V.I. © 800/223-6510 in the U.S., 800/424-5500 in Canada, or 284/495-5672. Fax 284/495-5674. www.bvi-resort.com. 12 units. Winter $220 efficiency studio for 2; $450 2-bedroom villa for 4; $645–$900 3-bedroom villa for 6. Off-season $99–$130 efficiency studio for 2; $235–$465 2-bedroom villa for 4; $365–$515 3-bedroom villa for 6. Extra person on foldaway couch $25–$45. AE, MC, V. **Amenities:** Restaurant, bar, maid service. *In room:* A/C, kitchen, ceiling fans, no phone.

GREAT DEALS ON DINING

Bath & Turtle Pub INTERNATIONAL   At the end of the waterfront shopping plaza in Spanish Town sits the most popular pub on Virgin Gorda, packed with locals during happy hour 4 to 6pm. Even if you don't care about food, you might join the regulars over midmorning guava coladas or peach daiquiris. There's live music every Wednesday and Sunday night, in summer only (no cover). From its handful of indoor and courtyard tables, you can order fried fish fingers, nachos, very spicy chili, pizzas, fresh pasta, barbecue chicken, steak, lobster, and daily seafood specials such as conch fritters.

Virgin Gorda Yacht Harbour, Spanish Town. © 284/495-5239. Reservations recommended. Breakfast $4.50–$8.95; main courses $6.75–$9 lunch, $9–$20 dinner. AE, MC, V. Daily 7am–11pm.

The Crab Hole WEST INDIAN   This is a clean and decent West Indian restaurant, far removed from the expense and glitter of such resorts as Little Dix Bay and Biras Creek Estate. It's located in the private home of Kenroy and Janet Millington (look for a concrete house surrounded by fields and other simple private dwellings). You order food from the chalkboard posted above the bar. They have their good days and their bad days here, depending on what the market turned up. You might get stewed whelk with Creole sauce made from local spices or tomatoes, perhaps stewed chicken, and most definitely fried fish. Stewed oxtail is sometimes on the menu, and guests, often hotel workers in the area, drop in for a noonday hamburger.

South Valley. © 284/495-5307. Main courses $10–$15. No credit cards. Mon–Sat 9am–9pm. Head south along the road to The Baths, and turn left at the sign to The Crab Hole.

The Lighthouse Restaurant CONTINENTAL   Glass cases containing ship models lend a nautical feel to this restaurant, and dark wooden beams and an antique English bar add a touch of quiet elegance. Although there are a few tables inside, the main dining area is on the deck overlooking North Sound. The menu selections range from the very simple to the more elaborate, such as sesame seed–encrusted tuna. The real bargains here are the meals served until 6pm, when dinner begins. The breakfasts are hearty, lunches are filling, and to beat the higher prices at night, opt for an early dinner of pizza, which is served 11am to 6pm every day.

Leverick Bay, North Sound. ⓒ **284/495-7154.** Reservations recommended. Main courses $13–$25; lunch $6–$14; pizzas from $5. AE, MC, V. Daily 8:30am–10pm.

Mad Dog ⚹ *Finds* PIÑA COLADAS/SANDWICHES This is the most skillful and charming reconstruction of a West Indian cottage on Virgin Gorda. The wide veranda and the brightly painted 19th-century wooden timbers and clapboards create a cozy and convivial drink and sandwich bar. The piña coladas are absolutely divine. The owner and supervisor of this laid-back place is London-born Colin McCullough, a self-described "mad dog" who sailed the British Virgin Islands for almost 30 years before establishing his domain here.
The Baths, The Country. ⓒ **284/495-5830.** Sandwiches $5; piña coladas $4. No credit cards. Daily 9am–7pm.

Thelma's Hideout ⚹ *Finds* WEST INDIAN Mrs. Thelma King, one of the most outspoken *grandes dames* of Virgin Gorda (who worked in Manhattan for many years before returning to her native B.V.I.), runs this convivial gathering place for the island's local community. It's located in a concrete house with angles softened by ascending tiers of verandas. Food choices include grilled steaks, fish filets, and West Indian stews containing pork, mutton, or chicken. Limeade and mauby are available, but many stick to rum or beer. Live music is presented on Saturday night in winter and every other Saturday off-season.
The Valley. ⓒ **284/495-5646.** Reservations required by 3pm for dinner. Dinner $15–$18; lunch $9–$10. No credit cards. Daily 7–10am, 11:30am–2:30pm, and 6–10pm. Bar, daily 11am–midnight.

Top of the Baths WEST INDIAN This aptly named green-and-white restaurant offers a patio with a pool. Locals gather here to enjoy the food they grew up on. At lunch, you can order an array of appetizers, sandwiches, and salad plates. You're invited to swim in the pool either before or after dining. At night, the kitchen turns out good home-style cookery, including fresh fish, lobster, chicken, and steaks. Look for one of the daily specials, and save room for a piece of that rum cake! On Wednesday and Thursday live steel bands perform.
The Valley. ⓒ **284/495-5497.** Dinner $16–$26; sandwiches and salad plates $6.50–$10. AE, MC, V. Daily 8am–10pm.

SWIMMING AT THE BATHS & OTHER OUTDOOR PURSUITS

On everyone's to-do list is a visit to **The Baths** ⚹⚹, where house-size boulders form a series of tranquil pools and grottoes flooded with seawater. As these boulders toppled over one another, they formed saltwater grottoes, suitable for exploring. The pools around The Baths are excellent for swimming and snorkeling (equipment can be rented on the beach).

Neighboring The Baths is **Spring Bay,** one of the best of the island's beaches, with white sand, clear water, and good snorkeling. **Trunk Bay** is a wide sandy beach that's reachable by boat or along a rough path from Spring Bay. **Savannah Bay** is a sandy beach north of the yacht harbor, and **Mahoe Bay,** at the Mango Bay Resort, has a gently curving beach with neon-blue water.

Devil's Bay National Park can be reached by a trail from the roundabout for The Baths. The walk to the secluded coral-sand beach takes about 15 minutes through boulders and dry coastal vegetation.

The Baths and surrounding areas are part of a proposed system of parks and protected areas in the B.V.I. The protected area encompasses 682 acres of land, including sites at Little Fort, Spring Bay, and Devil's Bay on the east coast.

DIVING Kilbrides Sunchaser Scuba, at the Bitter End Resort at North Sound (ⓒ **800/932-4286** in the U.S., or **284/495-9638**), offers the best diving in the British Virgin Islands, visiting 15 to 20 dive sites, including the wreck of the ill-fated HMS *Rhone* 🐠🐠🐠 (see the box earlier in this chapter). Prices range from $80 to $90 for a two-tank dive on one of the coral reefs. A one-tank dive in the afternoon costs $60. Equipment, except wet suits, is supplied at no charge, and videos of your dives are available.

HIKING   Consider a trek up the stairs and hiking paths that crisscross **Virgin Gorda Peak National Park,** the island's largest stretch of undeveloped land. To reach the best departure point for your uphill trek, drive for about 15 minutes north of The Valley on the only road leading to North Sound (it's very hilly, so a four-wheel-drive vehicle is a very good idea). Stop at the base of the stairway leading steeply uphill. There's a sign pointing to the park.

Depending on your speed, you'll embark on a trek of between 25 and 40 minutes to reach the summit of Gorda Peak, the highest point on the island, where views out over many scattered islets of the Virgin archipelago await you. There's a tower at the summit, which you can climb for enhanced views. Admire the flora and the fauna (birds, lizards, nonvenomous snakes) that you're likely to run across en route. Because the vegetation you'll encounter is not particularly lush, wear protection against the intense noonday sun, and consider bringing a picnic as tables are scattered along the hiking trails.

EXPLORING THE ISLAND

The northern side of Virgin Gorda is mountainous, with Gorda Peak reaching 1,370 feet, the highest spot on the island. However, the southern half is flat, with large boulders appearing at every turn.

Coppermine Point, the site of an abandoned copper mine and smelter at the island's southeastern tip, is an interesting place to visit. Legend has it that the Spanish worked these mines in the 1600s; however, the only authenticated document reveals that the English sank the shafts in 1838 to mine copper.

The best way to see the island if you're over for a day trip is to call **Andy Flax** at the Fischers Cove Beach Hotel. He runs the **Virgin Gorda Tours Association** (✆ **284/495-5252**), which will give you a tour of the island for $20 per person. The tour leaves twice daily, or more often based on demand. You can be picked up at the ferry dock if you give them 24 hours notice.

SHOPPING

There isn't much to buy here. Your best bet is the **Virgin Gorda Craft Shop** at Yacht Harbour (✆ **284/495-5137**), which has some good arts and crafts, especially straw items. Some of the more upscale hotels have boutiques, notably the **Bitter End Yacht Club's Reeftique** (✆ **284/494-2745**), with its selection of sports clothing, including sundresses and logo wear. You can also purchase a hat here to protect you from the sun. You might also check **Island Silhouette in Flax Plaza,** near Fischers Cove Beach Hotel (no phone), which has a good selection of resortwear hand-painted by local artists. **Pusser's Company Store,** Leverick Bay (✆ **284/495-7369**), sells rum products, sportswear, and gift and souvenir items—a good selection. **Tropical Gift Collections,** The Baths (✆ **284/495-5380**), is the best place for local crafts. Here you'll find island spices, bags, and pottery on sale, all at good prices.

VIRGIN GORDA AFTER DARK

There isn't a lot of action at night, unless you want to make some of your own. The **Bath & Turtle Pub,** at Yacht Harbour (✆ **284/495-5239**), brings in local bands for dancing on Wednesday and Sunday at 8pm. Most evenings in winter the **Bitter End Yacht Club** (© 284/494-2746) has live music. Reachable only by boat, this is the best bar on the island. With its dark wood, it evokes an English pub and even serves British brews. Sailors from all over the world (usually rich ones) keep the place lively deep into the night with talk of Lasers and Boston whalers. Call to see what's happening at the time of your visit.

Andy's Chateau de Pirate, at the Fischers Cove Beach Hotel, The Valley (© 284/495-5252), is a sprawling, sparsely furnished local hangout. It has a simple stage, a very long bar, and huge oceanfront windows that almost never close. The complex also houses the Lobster Pot Restaurant, the Buccaneer Bar, and the nightclub EFX. The Lobster Pot is open 7am to 10pm. The place is a famous showcase for the island's musical groups, which perform Wednesday to Sunday 8pm to midnight; lots of people congregate to listen and kibitz. There's a $5 cover charge Friday to Sunday nights.

4 Anegada ⊀

The most northerly and isolated of the British Virgins, 30 miles east of Tortola, Anegada has a population of about 250, none of whom has found the legendary treasure from the more than 500 wrecks lying off its notorious Horseshoe Reef. It's different from the other British Virgins in that it's a flat coral-and-limestone atoll. Its highest point reaches 28 feet, and it hardly appears on the horizon if you're sailing to it.

At the northern and western ends of the island are some good beaches, which might be your only reason for coming here. This is a remote little corner of the Caribbean: Be prepared to put up with some inconveniences, such as mosquitoes.

Most of the island has been declared off-limits to settlement and reserved for birds and other wildlife. The B.V.I. National Parks Trust has established a flamingo colony in a bird sanctuary, which is also the protected home of several different varieties of heron as well as ospreys and terns. It has also designated much of the interior of the island as a preserved habitat for Anegada's animal population of some 2,000 wild goats, donkeys, and cattle. Among the endangered species being given a new lease on life is the rock iguana, a fierce-looking but quite harmless reptile that can grow to a length of 5 feet and a weight of up to 20 pounds. Although rarely seen, these creatures have called Anegada home for thousands of years. The environment they share with other wildlife has hardly changed in all those years.

ANEGADA ESSENTIALS

GETTING THERE   The only carrier with regular service from Tortola to Anegada, **Clair Aero Service** (© 284/495-2271), uses six- to eight-passenger prop planes. It operates four times a week, on Monday, Wednesday, Friday, and Sunday, charging $59 per person round-trip. In addition, **Fly BVI** (© 284/495-1747) operates a charter/sightseeing service between Anegada and Beef Island off Tortola. The one-way cost is $125 for two to three passengers.

GETTING AROUND   Limited taxi service is available on the island—not that you'll have many places to go. **Tony's Taxis** (© 284/495-8027), which you'll spot when you arrive, will take you around the island. It's also possible to rent **bicycles**—ask around.

> (*Finds* **Loblolly Bay**
>
> Any trip to Anegada has to include a visit to the fantastic beach and reef at **Loblolly Bay.** If you're taking a day trip from Tortola, make sure you call **Tony's Taxis** (📞 **284/495-8027**) ahead of time; Tony will take you across the island to the bay, with one quick stop to see the legendary pink flamingos on the way. Once you pull up at Loblolly Bay, stake out a place on the beach and enjoy some of the most spectacular snorkeling in the B.V.I. Break for lunch at Big Bamboo, and have a drink at the small thatched-roof bar where scrawled signatures on the bar and roof supports are from Cindy Crawford, Brooke Shields, and Andre Agassi (the bartender swears they're real).

ACCOMMODATIONS YOU CAN AFFORD & GREAT DEALS ON DINING

Neptune's Treasure 🌴 *Finds* INTERNATIONAL   Set near its own 24-slip marina, near the southern tip of the island in the same cluster of buildings that includes the more high-priced Anegada Reef Hotel, this funky bar and restaurant usually hosts a mix of yacht owners and local residents. Dining is in a spacious indoor area whose focal point is a bar and lots of nautical memorabilia. The Soares family and their staff serve platters of swordfish, lobster, fish fingers, chicken, steaks, and ribs; dispense information about local snorkeling sites; and generally maintain order and something approaching a (low-key) party atmosphere.

They also offer four simple bedrooms and about four tents for anyone looking for super-low-cost lodgings. Depending on the season, rooms with private bathroom rent for $70 to $95 double. Tents share the plumbing facilities of the restaurant and go for $25 a night for two. Continental breakfast is included in the rates, and discounts are offered for stays of a week or more.

Between Pomato and Saltheap points, Anegada, B.V.I. 📞 284/495-9438, or VHF Channel 16 or 68. www.islandsonline.com/neptunes. Breakfast $9; fixed-price meals $26–$40. AE, MC, V. Daily 8am–10pm.

5 Jost Van Dyke

About 130 people live on the 4 square miles of mountainous Jost Van Dyke. On the south shore, White Bay and Great Harbour are good beaches. Although there are only a handful of places to stay, there are several dining choices, as Jost Van Dyke is a popular stopping-over point not only for the yachting set, but also for many cruise ships, including Club Med, Cunard, and often all-gay cruises. So you'll only experience the peace and tranquility of yesteryear when the cruise ships aren't here.

JOST VAN DYKE ESSENTIALS

GETTING THERE   Take the ferry from either St. Thomas or Tortola. Be warned that departure times can vary widely throughout the year, and they often don't adhere very closely to the printed timetables. Ferries from St. Thomas depart from Red Hook Friday, Saturday, and Sunday, about twice a day. More convenient (and more frequent) are the daily ferryboat shuttles from Tortola's isolated West End. The latter departs three times a day on the 25-minute trip, and costs $8 each way, $15 round-trip. Call the **Jost Van Dyke Ferryboat**

service (② 284/494-2997) for information about departures from any of the abovementioned points. If all else fails, carefully negotiate a transportation fee with one of the handful of privately operated water taxis.

FAST FACTS You can reach the local **police station** at ② 284/495-9828.

ACCOMMODATIONS YOU CAN AFFORD

The **White Bay Campground** ★★ (② 284/495-9312) rents bare sites that cost $15 for three people or equipped tent sites for $35 for two. Facilities include showers and toilets.

Don't try to write to these accommodations (or anywhere else) on Jost Van Dyke, as it can take months for mail to arrive.

Rudy's Mariner Inn This simple place is modesty itself, but it's got a lot of yachties who like the hospitality of Rudy George, the owner. It's also one of the best places to eat on the island (see below), with simply prepared food. This place is the social gathering point for much of the island. It's also a bar and nightclub of sorts and a ship's commissary. Expect a bare-bones room with a bed and shower, and that's about it.

Great Harbour (next to the boat dock at the west end of the harbor), Jost Van Dyke, B.V.I. ② 284/495-9282, or 284/775-3558 in the U.S.V.I. 5 units. Winter $125–$240 double. Off-season $90–$160 double. DISC, MC, V. **Amenities:** Restaurant, bar, snorkeling, fishing, windsurfing. *In room:* Ceiling fan, no phone.

GREAT DEALS ON DINING

Abe's by the Sea WEST INDIAN In this local bar and restaurant, sailors are satisfied with a menu of fish, lobster, conch, and chicken. Prices are low, too, and it's money well spent, especially when a *fungi* band plays for dancing. For the price of the main course, you get peas and rice, coleslaw, and dessert. Some nights, Abe's hosts festive pig roasts.

Little Harbour. ② 284/495-9329. Reservations recommended for groups of 5 or more. Dinner $12–$35; nightly barbecue $20. MC, V. Daily 8–11am, noon–3pm, and 7–10pm. Take the private motor launch or boat from Tortola; as you approach the east side of the harbor, you'll see Abe's on the right.

Foxy's Tamarind Bar ★ *(Finds* WEST INDIAN Arguably the most famous bar in the B.V.I., this mecca of yachties and other boat people spins entirely around a sixth-generation Jost Van Dyke native, Philicianno ("Foxy") Callwood. He opened the place some 3 decades ago, and sailors and the world have been coming back ever since. A songwriter and entertainer, Foxy is part of the draw. He creates impromptu calypso—almost in the Jamaican tradition—around his guests. If you're singled out, he'll embarrass you, but it's all in good fun. He also plays the guitar and takes a profound interest in preserving the environment of his native island.

Thursday through Saturday nights, a live band entertains. On other evenings, it's rock-and-roll, perhaps reggae or soca. The food and drink aren't neglected, either—try Foxy's Painkiller Punch. During the day, flying-fish sandwiches, rôtis, and the usual burgers are served, but evenings might bring freshly caught lobster, spicy steamed shrimp, or even grilled fish, depending on the catch of the day. No lunch is served on Saturday and Sunday.

Great Harbour ② 284/495-9258. Reservations recommended. Dinner $12–$26; lunch $7–$12. AE, MC, V. Daily 9am "until."

Rudy's Mariner's Rendezvous WEST INDIAN Rudy's, at the western end of Great Harbour, serves good but basic West Indian food—and plenty of it.

The place looks and feels like a private home with a waterfront terrace for visiting diners. A welcoming drink awaits sailors and landlubbers alike, and the food that follows is simply prepared and inexpensive. Conch always seems to be available, and a catch of the day is featured. Most dinners are inexpensive, unless you order lobster, of course.

Great Harbour. ✆ **284/495-9282.** Reservations required by 6:30pm. Dinner $18–$35. MC, V. Daily 7pm–midnight.

The Cayman Islands

Don't go to the Cayman Islands expecting fast-paced excitement. Island life focuses on the sea. Snorkelers will find a paradise, beach lovers will relish the powdery sands of Seven Mile Beach—but party-hungry travelers in search of urban thrills might be disappointed. Come here to relax and get away from it all.

The Caymans, 480 miles due south of Miami, consist of three islands: Grand Cayman, Cayman Brac, and Little Cayman. Despite its name, Grand Cayman is only 22 miles long and 8 miles across at its widest point. The other islands are considerably smaller, of course, and contain very limited tourist facilities, in contrast to well-developed Grand Cayman. George Town on Grand Cayman is the capital and is therefore the hub of government, banking, and shopping.

English is the official language of the islands, although it's often spoken with an English slur mixed with an American southern drawl and a lilting Welsh accent.

Winter vacations in the Caymans can be pricey affairs. The cost of living here is about 20% higher than in the United States. Because so much food has to be imported from the U.S. mainland, restaurant tabs are second only to the high-priced French islands such as St. Barts and Martinique (we've included tips on how to save on dining costs below). But you can make a trip here affordable. The key is advance planning and visiting the islands between mid-April and mid-December, when room rates are 20% to 40% lower than in winter. And in recent years several low-cost or moderately priced lodgings have opened, many of them with provisions for cooking simple meals.

Gay and lesbian travelers, take note: In 1998, the Cayman Islands government turned away Norwegian Cruise Line's *Leeward,* which was carrying 900 gay passengers. The tourism directors of the Caymans claimed that "we cannot count on this group to uphold the standards of appropriate behavior expected of visitors to the Cayman Islands." This decision drew massive protest, but the government arrogantly refused to change its stand.

1 Essentials

VISITOR INFORMATION

The **Cayman Islands Department of Tourism** has the following offices in the United States: 6100 Blue Lagoon Dr., 6100 Waterford Bldg., Suite 150, Miami, FL 33126 (© **305/266-2300**); 9525 W. Bryn Mawr, Suite 160, Rosemont, IL 60018 (© **847/678-6446**); Two Memorial City Plaza, 820 Gessner, Suite 170, Houston, TX 77024 (© **713/461-1317**); 3440 Wilshire Blvd., Suite 1202, Los Angeles, CA 90010 (© **213/738-1968**); 6100 Blue Lagoon Dr., Suite 150, Miami, FL 33126 (© **305/266-2300**); and 420 Lexington Ave., Suite 2733, New York, NY 10170 (© **212/682-5582**).

The Cayman Islands

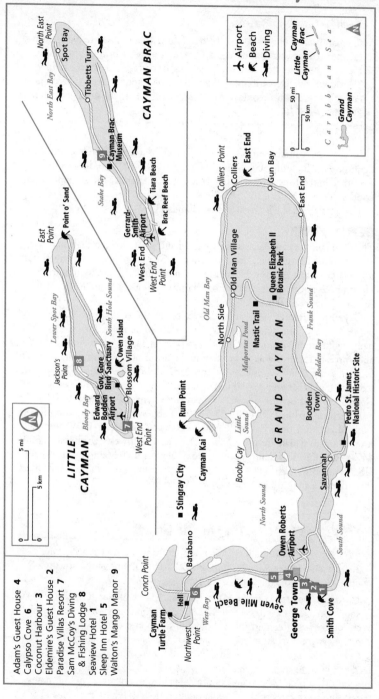

Adam's Guest House 4
Calypso Cove 6
Coconut Harbour 3
Eldemire's Guest House 2
Paradise Villas Resort 7
Sam McCoy's Diving & Fishing Lodge 8
Seaview Hotel 1
Sleep Inn Hotel 5
Walton's Mango Manor 9

✈ Airport
🏖 Beach
🤿 Diving

Caribbean Sea

Little Cayman
Cayman Brac

Grand Cayman

50 mi
50 km

CAYMAN BRAC

North East Point
Spot Bay
Tibbetts Turn
North East Bay
Cayman Brac Museum
Stake Bay
Point o' Sand
East Point
Tiara Beach
Gerrard-Smith Airport
Brac Reef Beach
West End
West End Point

LITTLE CAYMAN

Jackson's Point
Lower Spot Bay
Bloody Bay
Edward Bodden Airport
Gov. Gore Bird Sanctuary
Owen Island
Blossom Village
South Hole Sound
West End Point

East End
Gun Bay
Colliers Point
Colliers
East End
Old Man Village
Old Man Bay
Queen Elizabeth II Botanic Park
North Side
Mastic Trail
Malportas Pond
Frank Sound
Bodden Bay

GRAND CAYMAN

Rum Point
Cayman Kai
Stingray City
Little Sound
Booby Cay
North Sound
Batabano
Conch Point
Bodden Town
Pedro St. James National Historic Site
Savannah
Owen Roberts Airport
Seven Mile Beach
George Town
Smith Cove
South Sound
Cayman Turtle Farm
Hell
West Bay
Northwest Point

171

> **Fun Fact Ahoy, Matey!**
>
> **Cayman Islands Pirates' Week,** held in late October, is a national festival in which cutlass-bearing pirates and sassy wenches storm George Town, capture the governor, throng the streets, and stage a costume parade. The celebration pays tribute to the nation's past and its cultural heritage. For the exact dates, contact the **Pirates Week Festival Administration** (© **345/949-5078**).

In Canada, contact Earl B. Smith, **Travel Marketing Consultants,** 234 Eglinton Ave. E., Suite 306, Toronto, ON M4P 1K5 (© **416/485-1550**).

In the United Kingdom, the contact is **Cayman Islands,** 100 Brompton Rd., London SW3 1EX (© **020/7581-9960**).

The official website is **www.caymanislands.ky.**

GETTING THERE

The Caymans are easily accessible. Only a handful of nonstop flights are available from the heartland of North America to Grand Cayman, so many visitors use Miami as their gateway. Flying time from Miami is 1 hour 20 minutes; from Houston, 2 hours 45 minutes; from Tampa, 1 hour 40 minutes; and from Atlanta, 3 hours 35 minutes.

Cayman Airways (© **800/422-9626** in the U.S. and Canada, or 345/949-2311), offers the most frequent service to Grand Cayman, with three daily flights from Miami, four flights a week from Tampa, three from Orlando, and three nonstop flights a week from Houston and Atlanta. Once in the Caymans, the airline's subsidiary, **Island Air Ltd.** (© **345/949-5152**), operates frequent flights between Grand Cayman and Little Cayman and Cayman Brac. Round-trip fares between Grand Cayman and Cayman Brac begin at $154.

American Airlines (© **800/433-7300**) operates three daily nonstop flights from Miami and from Raleigh/Durham. **Delta** (© **800/221-1212**) flies daily into Grand Cayman from its hub in Atlanta. **Northwest Airlines** (© **800/447-4747**) flies to Grand Cayman from Detroit and Memphis via Miami. **US Airways** (© **800/428-4322**) flies daily nonstop from Tampa, and offers three flights a week from Pittsburgh and Charlotte.

  ***FAST FACTS:* The Cayman Islands**

Business Hours Normally, banks are open Monday to Thursday 9am to 2:30pm and Friday 9am to 1pm and 2:30 to 4:30pm. Shops are usually open Monday to Saturday 9am to 5pm.

Currency The legal tender is the **Cayman Islands dollar (CI$)**, currently valued at U.S.$1.25 (U.S.$1 equals 80¢ CI$). Canadian, U.S., and British currencies are accepted throughout the Cayman Islands, but you'll save money if you exchange your U.S. dollars for Cayman Islands dollars. The Cayman dollar breaks down into 100 cents. Coins come in 1¢, 5¢, 10¢, and 25¢. Bills come in denominations of $1, $5, $10, $25, $50, and $100 (there is no CI$20 bill). Most hotels quote rates in U.S. dollars, although many restaurants quote prices in Cayman Islands dollars, which might lead you to think that food is much cheaper than it is. Unless otherwise noted, *prices in this chapter are in U.S. dollars, rounded off.*

Documents No passports are required for U.S. or Canadian citizens, but entering visitors must have proof of citizenship (such as a birth certificate) and a return ticket. We suggest that you carry a passport anyway whenever you visit a foreign country.

Electricity It's 110 volts AC (60 cycles), so U.S. and Canadian appliances do not need adapters or transformers.

Emergencies For medical or police emergencies, dial ℂ **911** or 555.

Taxes A government tourist tax of 10% is added to your hotel bill. Also, a departure tax of CI$10 ($12.50) is collected when you leave the Caymans.

Telecommunications You can dial the Cayman Islands direct from the United States. The area code is ℂ **345.**

Time U.S. eastern standard time is in effect all year; however, daylight saving time is not observed.

Tipping Most restaurants add a 10% to 15% charge in lieu of tipping. Hotels also add a 10% service charge to your bill. Taxi drivers expect a 10% to 15% tip, and porters and bellmen get $1 per bag.

2 Grand Cayman ★★

The largest of the three islands and a real diving mecca, Grand Cayman is one of the hottest destinations in the Caribbean. With more than 500 banks, its capital, George Town, is the offshore banking center of the Caribbean. Retirees are drawn to the peace and tranquility of this British Crown Colony, site of a major condominium development. Almost the entire 32,000-person population of the Cayman Islands lives on Grand Cayman. The civil manners of the locals reflect their British heritage.

GRAND CAYMAN ESSENTIALS

VISITOR INFORMATION   The **Department of Tourism** is in the Pavilion Building, Cricket Square (P.O. Box 67), George Town, Grand Cayman, B.W.I. (ℂ **345/949-0623**).

GETTING AROUND   All arriving flights are met by taxis. The rates are fixed by the **director of civil aviation** (ℂ **345/949-7811**); typical one-way fares from the airport to Seven Mile Beach range from $10 to $12. Taxis (which can hold five people) will also take visitors on around-the-island tours. **Cayman Cab Team** (ℂ **345/947-1173**) offers 24-hour service. You can also call **A.A. Transportation** at ℂ **345/949-7222.**

Several car-rental companies operate on the island, including **Cico Avis** (ℂ **800/331-1212** in the U.S., or 345/949-2468), **Budget** (ℂ **800/527-0700** in the U.S., or 345/949-5605), and **Ace Hertz** (ℂ **800/654-3131** in the U.S., or 345/949-2280). Each will issue the mandatory Cayman Islands driving permit for an additional $7.50. All three require that reservations be made between 6 and 36 hours before pickup. At Avis drivers must be at least 21, and at Hertz, 25. Budget requires that drivers be between 25 and 70 years old. It pays to call around for the lowest rate. Cars generally range in price from $266 to $315 and up per week, including unlimited mileage. An optional collision-damage waiver

(CDW) costs from $12 a day. All three rental companies maintain kiosks within walking distance of the airport, although most visitors find it easier to take a taxi to their hotels and then arrange for the cars to be brought to them.

Remember to drive on the left and to reserve your car as far in advance as possible, especially in midwinter.

FAST FACTS   Island Pharmacy, West Shore Centre, Seven Mile Beach (© **345/ 949-8987**), is open Monday to Saturday 8:30am to 5:30pm. The only hospital is **George Town Hospital,** Hospital Road (© **345/949-8600**).

In George Town, the **post office** and Philatelic Bureau is on Edward Street (© **345/949-2474**), open Monday to Friday 8:30am to 5pm and Saturday 8:30am to noon. There's also a counter at the Seven Mile Beach Post Office, open the same hours.

The **Cable and Wireless,** Anderson Square, George Town, on Grand Cayman (© **345/949-7800**), is open Monday to Friday 8:15am to 5pm, Saturday 9am to 1pm, and Sunday 9am to noon.

ACCOMMODATIONS YOU CAN AFFORD

True budget travelers will rent an apartment or condo (shared with friends or families), so they can cut costs by cooking their own meals. Divers will want to find hotels or small resorts that include a half-day's dive in their tariffs. Hotels, unlike many Caymanian restaurants, generally quote prices in U.S. dollars.

Adam's Guest House ☆ *Value*   Tom and Olga Adam advertise their guesthouse as "the best at the lowest." While it may not be the fanciest place to stay, it's among the best values on the island. This 1950s-style West Indian ranch bungalow is located in a residential area a mile south of George Town, which is a long 4-mile haul from Seven Mile Beach. However, there's excellent snorkeling at Smith Cove Bay, only about a 10-minute walk away, and scuba-diving facilities—five different outfits—lie within a 5-minute stroll. For a restaurant and bar, you can stroll over to the Seaview Hotel, about 5 minutes away. A supermarket and a drugstore are also nearby, as are some breakfast places.

Each no-frills room has a private entrance, twin beds with good mattresses, and a small private bathroom with a shower stall. The two-bedroom apartment, which can hold up to six, is ideal for families.

Melmac Ave., George Town, Grand Cayman, B.W.I. © **345/949-2512.** Fax 345/949-0919. www. adamsguesthouse.com.ky. 3 units, 1 apt. Winter $95 single or double. Off-season $185 single or double. MC, V (accepted only for room deposit; pay with cash or traveler's checks). **Amenities:** Laundry. *In room:* A/C, TV, microwave, fridge, ceiling fans.

Eldemire's Guest House ☆ *Kids*   This casual and friendly place is owned by Erma Eldemire, an old-time Caymanian, now in her 80s, who established the first guesthouse on the island. No one knows the island better than dear Mrs. Eldemire, who will not only regale you with tall tales of Caymanian life but might also share her recipe for coconut jelly. About a mile from the center of George Town and ½ mile from great snorkeling at Smith Cove Beach, this rambling West Indian ranch-style house offers small bedrooms and studio apartments. The place is simple yet comfortable and suitable for families. Each unit has a tiny private bathroom with shower, air-conditioning, and a ceiling fan. Beds are quite comfortable, the mattresses having been recently replaced. Guests also have access to a fridge, toaster oven, hotplate, and coffeemaker. The apartments have their own kitchenettes, with maid service Monday to Saturday.

Within walking distance are dive sites, a snorkeling area, the "Cove" (a white sandy beach with crystal-clear water), and a number of restaurants. Seven Mile

Beach lies 2 miles away, and the house is 3 miles from the airport. Families or groups might want to use the barbecue pit and the picnic table in the garden. A launderette is nearby. Across the street is a restaurant where you can order breakfast for $6.

S. Church St. (P.O. Box 482), George Town, Grand Cayman, B.W.I. © 345/949-5387. Fax 345/949-6987. www.eldemire.com. 6 units, 3 apts. Winter $94 single or double; $105 apt. Off-season $67 single or double; $110 apt. Extra person $10. No credit cards. **Amenities:** Maid service. *In room:* A/C, TV, ceiling fans.

Seaview Hotel   This seafront property lies on the south side of George Town, about a 10-minute walk from the downtown area or a 10-minute walk to the beach at Smith Cove. It's about a 2- to 3-minute drive to Seven Mile Beach. One of the island's oldest properties, the hotel still retains its '50s-style look. It's being improved and upgraded, but is still a tin-roofed wooden hotel. Bright Caribbean fabrics have enlivened some rooms, and 10 accommodations face the ocean in a central veranda style. Rooms range in size from small to medium, but each has a good bed with a firm mattress, plus a tiny but well-maintained private bathroom (with showers instead of tubs). The on-site pool is large and inviting, and there's also an inside restaurant and bar, offering three meals a day, with rather excellent seafood. Boat dives can be arranged.

S. Church St., George Town, Grand Cayman, B.W.I. © 345/945-0558. Fax 345/945-0559. 15 units. Winter $100 single; $110 double. Off-season $80 single; $90 double. Extra person $10; children 11 and under stay free in parents' room. AE, MC, V. **Amenities:** Restaurant, bar, pool, dive facility, laundry. *In room:* A/C, TV.

GREAT CHOICES FOR DIVERS

Coconut Harbour *Value*   This resort property just south of George Town, with a friendly staff and a convivial crowd, offers one of the best values for divers. There's excellent diving right offshore, and on site is a full-service dive shop operated by Parrots Landing (which you might check out even if you don't stay here). The clean and comfortable rooms, with kitchenettes, are furnished in a plain Florida-motel style. Upper rooms have balconies overlooking the sea, and lower accommodations open onto patios. Rooms range from small to medium but there is reasonable comfort here, although the mattresses are a bit thin. Your bathroom will be like a cubicle, with a shower (no tub), plus meager shelf space. The hotel operates an open-air bar, a good place for a drink, and a rather standard restaurant that's open until 10pm.

S. Church St., George Town, Grand Cayman, B.W.I. © 800/552-6281 in the U.S., or 345/949-7468. Fax 345/949-7117. coccayman@aol.com. 35 units. Winter $182 double. Off-season $174 double. Rates include continental breakfast. AE, MC, V. **Amenities:** Restaurant, bar, pool, dive shop, maid service. *In room:* A/C, TV, kitchenette.

Sleep Inn Hotel *Value*   Opened in 1992, the Sleep Inn is on Seven Mile Beach and near the center of George Town. On rather bleak grounds, it lies 250 feet from the sands and about a 5-minute drive from the international airport. It's one of the more reasonably priced hotels on the island, offering value for your money, and a good choice for families. A franchise of Choice Hotels International, it offers both smoking and nonsmoking rooms and units that are accessible for persons with disabilities. Furnishings are rather nondescript but perfectly comfortable. The rooms have modern tropical furnishings and a small safe for valuables; the suites contain kitchenettes. Each unit contains a small bathroom with shower stalls.

West Bay Rd. (P.O. Box 30111), George Town, Grand Cayman, B.W.I. © 345/949-9111. Fax 345/949-6699. www.choicecaribbean.com. 121 units. Winter $150–$165 double; $195 suite. Off-season $109–$120 double; $179 suite. Rates include buffet breakfast. Children 12 and under stay free in parents' room. AE, DC, DISC, MC, V. **Amenities:** 2 fast-food restaurants, pool bar and grill, pool, Jacuzzi, dive shop, laundry/dry cleaning. *In room:* A/C, TV, kitchenette (in suites), safe.

VILLA & CONDO RENTALS

Grand Cayman offers a wide choice of condos and villas; renting one can cut your accommodation costs considerably. Most are owned as second or third homes (or purely as untaxed investments) by absentee owners, and are available for short-term rentals by qualified vacationers.

Most places have some kind of kitchen or kitchenette as well as a washing machine and dryer (or access to coin-operated laundry facilities on site). Some even have barbecue grills in the garden area, so you can stock up at a grocery store for a cookout. You may be able to arrange maid service. Or you can go for a bare-bones rental, even bringing from home your own sheets and towels.

For more deals, you can contact the following condo and villa rentals yourself. Try the **Grape Tree Cocoplum** (© **345/949-5640**), **The Retreat at Rum Point** (© **345/947-9135**), or the **Victoria House Apartments** (© **345/945-4233**).

Calypso Cove ★★ *Kids*   Just a dozen or so steps from the northernmost fringe of Seven Mile Beach, this guesthouse—renovated in 1998—is run by Sonia and Leif Barkinge. It is often booked by airline employees stopping over on Grand Cayman. They know what a good bargain it is on this high-priced island. It's a condo facility, in two pink concrete-block buildings in West Bay, with three studios for two, two one-bedroom units for up to four, and two two-bedroom/two-bathroom units housing as many as six (great for families!). The two-bedroom units are each equipped with a washer and dryer. All accommodations have front and back patios and are furnished in standard style with various combinations of twin, queen-size, and king-size beds and sofa sleepers, all with firm mattresses. Bathrooms are a bit cramped but tidily maintained, each with shower. There is no pool, restaurant, or bar on the premises, but a number of places are within walking distance.

West Bay, Grand Cayman, B.W.I. ©/fax **345/949-3730**. 7 units. Winter $100–$145 studio; $145 1-bedroom unit; $220 2-bedroom unit. Off-season $75–$105 studio; $105 1-bedroom unit; $160 2-bedroom unit. Children 11 and under stay free in parents' room. MC, V. *In room:* A/C, TV, kitchen, ceiling fans.

GREAT DEALS ON DINING

Make sure you understand which currency the menu is printed in. If it's not written on the menu, ask the waiter if the prices are in U.S. dollars or Cayman Island dollars (CI$), as this will make a big difference when you get your final bill.

Billy's Place JAMAICAN/CARIBBEAN/INDIAN   Don't come here if you feel like dressing up and hitting the town. But if you like to stay in your T-shirt and shorts and enjoy the laid-back island style, this is the local favorite. A pink-and-blue house in the Kirk Shopping Center with flowers on both sides and a garden and fountain in front, it's the creation of Jamaican-born Billy MacLaren, a real raconteur. He wanders through the restaurant making sure everything is running smoothly, but he sits only with people he knows. While calypso and reggae rock play in the background, you can check out the menu.

The Indian curries are the best on the island, as are the Jamaican-inspired jerk dishes, such as chicken and pork. He even serves the island's only "jerk" pizza. Try one of the Indian *pakoras* (vegetable fritters) or tandoori chicken or shrimp. There's very little difference between the lunch and dinner menus except the prices.

N. Church St., George Town. © **345/949-0470**. Main courses CI$12–CI$34 ($15–$42.50); lunch CI$8–CI$24 ($10–$30). AE, MC, V. Mon–Sat 11am–10pm; Sun 6–10pm.

Champion House WEST INDIAN   The Champion House has two grades of restaurants; this particular location is the less expensive. Here you'll get down-home West Indian food such as curried goat and chicken, stewed beef, peppered steak, and barbecued beef and ribs. There's also a variety of fresh seafood, but the West Bay location has a greater selection. The casual and friendly atmosphere has a certain quaint charm about it.

Eastern Ave., West Bay. © **345/949-2190.** Reservations recommended. Soups CI$3–CI$4 ($3.75–$5); main courses CI$5–CI$7 ($6.25–$8.75). No credit cards. Sun–Thurs 11:30am–midnight; Fri–Sat 10am–3am.

Chicken! Chicken! CHICKEN   The chicken here is marinated in a sauce of lemon, lime, rosemary, parsley, garlic, and thyme, and served with fresh vegetables. A dinner includes your choice of two side dishes, including garlic-and-herb potatoes, wild-mushroom pilaf, sweet tarragon carrots, potato salad, spinach pesto pasta, and coleslaw. For a slightly different taste, this restaurant serves two kinds of chicken salad (one with ginger, oranges, soy sauce, and water chestnuts). For a finish, they'll bring you the congo square, a chocolate brownie smothered in chocolate, coffee, and rum. This enterprise also offers fixed-price feasts for four or more people.

In the West Shore Centre, West Bay Rd., along Seven Mile Beach. © **345/945-2290.** Main courses CI$8–CI$11.50 ($10–$14.40); lunch specials CI$5.25–CI$7.50 ($6.55–$9.40); fixed-price meal CI$23.50–CI$46 ($29.40–$57.50). AE, MC, V. Daily 11am–10pm.

Corita's Copper Kettle ★ *Finds* CARIBBEAN/AMERICAN   This place is generally packed in the mornings, when diners can enjoy a full American breakfast or West Indian breakfast specialties. Included are green bananas served with fried dumplings, fried flying fish, and Corita's Special (ham, melted cheese, egg, and jelly all presented on a fried fritter). For lunch, the menu varies from salads to chicken and beef, along with conch, turtle, or lobster prepared as burgers or served up in a hearty stew.

In Dolphin Center, George Town. © **345/949-7078.** Reservations required. Lunch CI$6.75–CI$12 ($8.45–$15); breakfast CI$6.50–CI$8.50 ($8.15–$10.65). No credit cards. Mon–Sat 7am–5pm; Sun 7am–3pm.

Eats Crocodile Rock Café AMERICAN/INTERNATIONAL   Also called Eats Café, this restaurant offers a Hard Rock Cafe atmosphere, with a bright interior with leopard spots and tiger stripes. It serves hearty fare at reasonable prices. Lunch features salads, sandwiches, and burgers. Dinner spotlights stir-fries, including Szechuan teriyaki and mix-and-match pastas (a selection of five pastas with a choice of seafood, tomato, pesto, alfredo, or meat sauce). Other dishes include black-bean soup, coconut shrimp, and rum-garlic shrimp. Breakfast can also be ordered.

In Falls Centre, West Bay Rd. (just north of the Holiday Inn Grand Cayman). © **345/945-5288.** Main courses CI$6–CI$14 ($7.50–$17.50); lunch CI$4.50–CI$7 ($5.65–$8.75); breakfast CI$5–CI$7 ($6.25–$8.75). AE, DC, MC, V. Daily 6:30am–11pm.

Golden Pagoda CHINESE   Craving Chinese? This friendly restaurant is located in front of the Radisson Resort Grand Cayman on West Bay Road. When you see the sign TAKEE OUTEE, you've found it! In front is a fountain with a modest garden and a small red bridge that leads to the front door. One house specialty is the mango chicken, a stir-fry dish with mango chutney, water chestnuts, and green peppers. The Hakka-style cooking features such fare as Mongolian beef, butterfly shrimp, kung pao chicken, and (the dish that the locals love) sweet-and-sour chicken.

West Bay Rd., along Seven Mile Beach. © **345/949-5475.** Reservations recommended in winter. Main courses CI$8–CI$18 ($10–$22.50); buffet lunches CI$8 ($10). AE, MC, V. Mon–Fri 11:30am–2:30pm and 6–10pm; Sat–Sun 6–10pm.

Liberty's West Bay (Value) CAYMANIAN   Visitors rarely find this local dive in the center of the West Bay shopping area, but it offers some of the best values on the island, especially at its all-you-can-eat dinner buffets on Wednesday, Friday, and Sunday nights. The place is a real dollar-stretcher, and a local patron told us that the food was "real he-man." Presumably by that he meant such regional fare as codfish and ackee (the national dish of Jamaica), curried goat, and zesty oxtail, the latter a mite greasy but good. On many nights a "seafood feast" is offered up, with lobster, shrimp, and the local catch. At lunch you might opt for burgers and sandwiches.

Reverend Blackman Rd., West Bay. (C) **345/949-3226.** Main courses CI$8–CI$24 ($10–$30); lunch CI$6.50–CI$18.50 ($8.15–$23.15); dinner buffet CI$16 ($20). MC, V. Daily 11am–4pm and 6–10pm.

WORTH A SPLURGE
Captain Brian's (★) CARIBBEAN/ENGLISH   On a plot of seafront land near the beginning of West Bay Road, this restaurant enjoys a loyal following. In a low-slung cottage, whose verandas are vivid shades of pink, blue, and yellow, the place has both an amusingly decorated pub and a Caribbean-inspired dining room open to a view of the harbor. In the pub, you can order such British staples as fish-and-chips or cottage pie, and such drinks as a Snake Bite (equal parts of hard English cider and English lager) or a frothy tropical concoction. The food is competently prepared and satisfying, but not a lot more. Don't overlook this as a possible site for breakfast, where you can devour *huevos rancheros*.

N. Church St., George Town. (C) **345/949-6163.** Reservations recommended in winter for dinner. Main courses CI$9–CI$20 ($11.25–$25); breakfast CI$6–CI$8 ($7.50–$11). AE, MC, V. Daily 8am–10pm (last order); bar open till 1am.

HITTING THE BEACHES
One of the finest beaches in the Caribbean, Grand Cayman's **Seven Mile Beach** (★★★), which lies north of George Town, has sparkling white sands rimmed with Australian pines and palms. Although it's not actually 7 miles long, it is still a honey, with 5½ miles of white, white sands stretching all the way to George Town, the capital. There are lots of sunbathers near the big resorts, but the beach is so big you can always find some room to spread out your towel.

The waters are clear and warm here, with no great tide. Because the beach is on the more tranquil side of Grand Cayman, the water is generally placid and inviting, ideal for families, even those with small children. A sandy bottom slopes gently to deep water. The water's so clear you can generally see what's swimming in it; it's great for snorkelers and swimmers of most ages and abilities.

From one end of the beach to the other, there are hotels and condos, many with beachside bars you can visit. All sorts of watersports concessions can be found along this beach, including rental of snorkel and diving equipment. You can parasail, take a tour of the waters off the beach, go water-skiing, and rent windsurfing equipment, wave runners, paddlecats, and aqua trikes. Unlike the beaches of Jamaica, this beach is without peddlers. It is also beautifully maintained, so you shouldn't encounter litter.

Although they pale in comparison to Seven Mile Beach, Grand Cayman also has a number of minor beaches. Visit them if you want to escape the crowds. Those on the east and north coasts are also good, filled with white sand. They are protected by an offshore barrier reef, so waters are generally tranquil.

One of our favorites is on the north coast, bordering the **Cayman Kai Beach Resort.** This beach is a Caribbean cliché of charm, with palm trees and beautiful sands. You can snorkel along the reef to Rum Point. The beach is also ideal as a Sunday afternoon picnic spot. There are changing facilities, and **Red Sail Sports** (© 345/947-9203) at Rum Point offers windsurfers, wave runners, sailboats, water-skiing, and even glass-bottomed boat tours to see the stingrays offshore. It also offers scuba diving.

Locals often go to **Smith's Cove,** which is off South Church Street. It is especially popular on Saturday and Sunday. The best windsurfing is just off the beaches of the East End, at Colliers, bordered by Morritt's Tortuga Club.

SPORTS & OTHER OUTDOOR PURSUITS

DIVING   Grand Cayman is one of the top **diving** ✶✶✶ destinations in the world. Coral reefs and coral formations encircle the islands and are filled with lots of marine life—which scuba divers are forbidden to disturb, by the way.

It's easy to dive close to shore here, so boats aren't necessary, but there are plenty of boat diving operations. On certain excursions, we recommend a trip with a qualified divemaster. There are many dive shops for rentals, but they won't rent you scuba gear or supply air unless you have a NAUI or PADI certification card. Hotels also rent diving equipment to their guests, as well as arrange snorkeling and scuba-diving trips.

Universally regarded as the most up-to-date and best-equipped watersports facility in the Cayman Islands, **Red Sail Sports** maintains its headquarters at the Hyatt Regency Grand Cayman, West Bay Road (© **800/255-6425** or 345/949-8745). Other locations are at the Westin Casuarina (© **345/949-8732)**

Moments Swimming with the Stingrays

The offshore waters of Grand Cayman are home to one of the most unusual (and ephemeral) underwater attractions in the world, **Stingray City** ✶✶. Set in the sun-flooded 12-foot-deep waters of North Sound, about 2 miles east of the island's northwestern tip, the site originated in the mid-1980s when local fishers cleaned their catch and dumped the offal overboard. They quickly noticed scores of stingrays (which usually eat marine crabs) feeding on the debris, a phenomenon that quickly attracted local divers and marine zoologists. Today, between 30 and 50 relatively tame stingrays hover in the waters around the site for daily handouts of squid and ballyhoo from increasing hordes of amateur snorkelers and scuba enthusiasts.

Most of the stingrays that feed here are females; the males prefer to remain in deeper waters offshore. To capitalize on the phenomenon, about half a dozen entrepreneurs lead expeditions from points along Seven Mile Beach, traveling around the landmass of Conch Point to the feeding grounds. One well-known outfit is **Treasure Island Divers** (© 345/949-4456), which charges divers $50 and snorkelers $30. Trips are made on Sunday, Wednesday, and Friday at 1:30pm.

Be warned that stingrays possess deeply penetrating and viciously barbed stingers capable of inflicting painful damage to anyone who mistreats them. (Above all, the divers say, never try to grab one by the tail.) Despite the dangers, divers and snorkelers seem amazingly adept at feeding, petting, and stroking the velvet surfaces of these bat-like creatures without unpleasant incidents.

Tips Into the Deep: Submarine Dives

So scuba diving's not enough for you? You want to see the real undiscovered depths of the ocean? On Grand Cayman, you can take the *Atlantis* reef dive. It's expensive, but it's a unique way to go underwater—and it might be the highlight of your trip.

One of the island's most popular attractions is the **Atlantis XI** ☆, Goring Avenue (© **345/949-7700**), a submersible that's 65 feet long, weighs 80 tons, and was built at a cost of $3 million to carry 48 passengers. You can view the reefs and colorful tropical fish through the 26 large viewpoints 2 feet in diameter, as it cruises at a depth of 100 feet through the maze of coral gardens at a speed of 1½ knots; a guide keeps you informed.

There are two types of dives. The premier dive, *Atlantis* Odyssey, features such high-tech extras as divers communicating with submarine passengers by wireless underwater phone and moving about on underwater scooters. This dive, operated both day and night, costs $82. On the *Atlantis* Expedition dive, you'll experience the reef and see the famous Cayman Wall; this dive lasts 55 minutes and costs $72. Children 4 to 12 are charged half-price (no children under 4 allowed). *Atlantis XI* dives Monday to Saturday, and reservations are recommended 3 days in advance.

and at Rum Point (© **345/947-9203**). A two-tank morning dive includes exploration of two different dive sites at depths ranging from 50 to 100 feet, and costs $75. Beginners can take a daily course that costs $120 per person. They have a wide range of offerings, from deep-sea fishing to sailing, diving, and more. Red Sail can also arrange water-skiing for $75 per half-hour (the cost can be divided among several people).

Established in 1957, the best dive operation in the Caymans is **Bob Soto's Diving Ltd.** (© **800/262-7686** or 345/949-2022). Owned by Ron Kipp, the operation includes full-service dive shops at Treasure Island, the SCUBA Centre on North Church Street, and Soto's Coconut in the Coconut Place Shopping Centre. A full-day resort course, designed to teach the fundamentals of scuba to beginners who know how to swim, costs $99: The morning is spent in the pool and the afternoon is a one-tank dive from a boat. All necessary equipment is included. Certified divers can choose from a wide range of one-tank ($50) and two-tank ($85) boat dives daily on the west, north, and south walls, plus shore diving from the SCUBA Centre. A one-tank night dive costs $55. Nondivers can take advantage of daily snorkel trips ($25–$30), including Stingray City. The staff is helpful and highly professional.

SNORKEL CRUISES   Red Sail Sports (see "Diving," above) offers a number of inexpensive ways you can go sailing in Cayman waters, including a glass-bottomed boat ride costing $30 without snorkeling equipment or $35 with snorkeling equipment. It also offers sunset cruises that cost $27.50 (half-price for children under 12). A 10am to 2pm sail to Stingray City, with snorkeling equipment and lunch included in the price of $65 per person, leaves once daily. Children under 12 go for half-price.

EXPLORING THE ISLAND

The capital, **George Town,** can easily be explored in an afternoon; stop by for its restaurants and shops (and banks!)—not sights. The town does offer a clock monument to King George V and the oldest government building in use in the Caymans today, the post office on Edward Street. Collectors avidly seek stamps sold here.

The island's premier museum, the **Cayman Islands National Museum,** Harbor Drive, in George Town (© 345/949-8368), is in a much-restored old building directly on the water. Today the museum incorporates a gift shop, theater, cafe, and more than 2,000 items portraying the natural, social, and cultural history of the Caymans. Admission is CI$4 ($5) for adults, CI$2 ($2.50) for children 7 to 12 and senior citizens, and free for children 6 and under. It's open Monday to Friday 9am to 5pm and Saturday 10am to 2pm (last admission is half an hour prior to closing).

Elsewhere on the island, you might go to **Hell!** That's at the north end of West Bay Beach, a jagged piece of rock named Hell by a former commissioner. There the postmistress will stamp "Hell, Grand Cayman" on your postcard to send back home.

The **Cayman Turtle Farm** ✭, Northwest Point (© 345/949-3893), is the only green-sea-turtle farm of its kind in the world, and it's the most popular land-based tourist attraction in the Caymans. Once the islands had a multitude of turtles in the surrounding waters (which is why Columbus called the islands "Las Tortugas"), but today these creatures are sadly few in number (and they're practically extinct elsewhere in the Caribbean), and the green sea turtle has been designated an endangered species. (You cannot bring turtle products into the United States.) The turtle farm has a twofold purpose: to provide the local market with edible turtle meat and to replenish the waters with hatchling and yearling turtles. Visitors today can look at 100 circular concrete tanks in which these sea creatures can be observed in every stage of development; the hope is that one day their population in the sea will regain its former status. Turtles here range in size from 6 ounces to 600 pounds. At a snack bar and restaurant, you can sample turtle dishes (we couldn't bring ourselves to, though). The turtle farm is open daily 8:30am to 5pm. Admission is $6 for adults, $3 for children 6 to 12, free for children 5 and under.

At **Botabano,** on the North Sound, fishers tie up with their catch, much to the delight of photographers. You can buy lobster (in season), fresh fish, and even conch. A large barrier reef protects the sound, which is surrounded on three sides by the island and is a mecca for diving and sports fishing.

If you're driving, you might want to go along **South Sound Road,** which is lined with pines and, in places, old wooden Caymanian houses. After leaving the houses behind, you'll find good spots for a picnic.

Pedro St. James National Historic Site, Savannah (© 345/947-3329), is a restored great house dating from 1780, when only 400 people lived on the island. It outlasted all the hurricanes until 1970, but it was destroyed by fire that year. Now it's been rebuilt and is the centerpiece of a new heritage park with a visitor center and an audiovisual theater with a laser light show. Because of its size, the great house was called "the Castle" by generations of Caymanians. Its primary historic importance dates from December 5, 1831, when residents met here to elect Grand Cayman's first legislative assembly. Therefore, Pedro St. James is the cradle of the island's democracy. The great house sits atop a limestone bluff with a panoramic view of the sea. Guests enter via a $1.5 million

---

Value **Cheap Thrills: What to See & Do for Free (Well, Almost) in the Cayman Islands**

- **Stroll Through Historic George Town.** Arm yourself with a map (the tourist office will help you plot a route) and start at the Old Courts Building, now the Cayman Islands National Museum, on Harbour Drive. It has exhibits of the natural and cultural history of the island. To your left as you leave is Panton Square, with three old Cayman houses distinguished by pitched gables and ornate fretwork. On Harbour Drive, past the cruisedock, is Elmslie Memorial Church, built by Captain Rayal Bodden, a well-known shipwright. To the right, by the car park, are old grave markers shaped like houses, with small ones for children. In the churchyard is a War Memorial, and across the street, the Seamen's Memorial, with names of 153 Caymanians lost at sea. Next to it are the remains of Fort George, built in 1790 for defense against the Spaniards who raided the islands, carrying inhabitants captive to Cuba.

- **View an Underwater Ecosystem.** Snorkeling in the Caymans is one of the reasons to come here, and it doesn't cost much to rent equipment. Many sites are close to shore, in calm, shallow waters. Virtually any shoreline in Grand Cayman, and the lesser islands, too, offer great opportunities for the snorkeler, often with no boat required. Among the more popular sites are Parrot's Reef and Smith's Cove south of George Town. Lush reefs abound with parrotfish, coral, sea fans, and sponges. Also great for snorkelers is Turtle Farm Reef, a short swim from shore, offering a mini-wall rising from a sandy bottom.

- **Spend a Day on Seven Mile Beach.** Soaking up the sun on these brilliant white sands must rank among the great beach experiences

---

visitor center with a landscaped courtyard, a gift shop, and a cafe. Self-guided tours are possible. You can explore the house's wide verandas, rough-hewn timber beams, gabled framework, mahogany floors and staircases, and wide-beam wooden ceilings. Guides in 18th-century costumes are on hand to answer questions. Admission is $8 for adults and $4 for children (free for those 5 and under). Hours are daily from 9am to 5pm.

On the road again, you reach **Bodden Town,** once the largest settlement on the island. At Gun Square, two cannons commanded the channel through the reef. They are now stuck muzzle-first into the ground.

On the way to the **East End,** just before Old Isaac Village, you'll see the onshore sprays of water shooting up like geysers. These are called "blowholes," and they sound like the roar of a lion.

Old Man Bay is reached by a road that opened in 1983. From here you can travel along the north shore of the island to **Rum Point,** which has a good beach and is a fine place to end the tour. After visiting Rum Point, you can head back toward Old Man Village, where you can go south along a cross-island road through savannah country that eventually leads west to George Town.

On 60 acres of rugged wooded land off Frank Sound Road, North Side, the **Queen Elizabeth II Botanic Park** ⚜ (© 345/947-9462) offers visitors a short

of a lifetime. Even Tom Cruise succumbed to its charm in the movie *The Firm.* Lie back on the powdery white sand, without the annoyance of peddlers, and enjoy one of the few hassle-free experiences left in a troubled world.

- **Go to Hell!** Back in the 1930s, the island commissioner, Alan Cardinall, was enthralled with the bleak, forbidding-looking landscape in the West Bay area, and he christened it Hell. Word spread, and a tourist stop was born. In 1962 the destination became so popular that the Cayman Islands government established a district post office here, and it's open daily, including Sunday, from 8:30am to 1pm and 2 to 3:30pm. Literally thousands of visitors want to send postcards back home from Hell. The messages go somewhat like this: "We went to Hell and back today." "Greetings from a Hell of a place." Hell is set in an unusual geological formation of weathered and blackened local rock called ironshore. It's a rather bleak place, but then you wouldn't expect Hell to be a Garden of Eden.

- **Sip a Rum Punch at Rum Point.** Rum Point got its name from barrels of rum that once washed ashore here after a shipwreck. Today, it is dreamy and quaint, surrounded by towering causarina trees blowing in the trade winds. Most of these trees have hammocks hanging from their trunks, inviting you to enjoy the leisurely life. With its cays, reefs, mangroves, and shallows, Rum Point is a refuge that extends west and south for 7 miles. The sound's many spits of land and its plentiful lagoons are ideal for snorkeling, swimming, wading, and birding. It you get hungry, drop in to the Wreck Bar for a juicy hamburger.

walk through wetland, swamp, dry thicket, mahogany trees, orchids, and bromeliads. You'll likely see chickatees, the freshwater turtles found only on the Caymans and in Cuba. Occasionally you'll spot the rare Grand Cayman parrot, or if not that, perhaps the anole lizard, with its cobalt-blue throat pouch. Even rarer is the endangered blue iguana. There are six rest stations with visitor information along the trail. The park is open daily 9am to 5:30pm. Admission is CI$6 ($7.50) for adults, CI$4 ($5) for children, free for children 5 and under. There's a visitor center with changing exhibitions, plus a canteen for food and refreshments. It's set in a botanic park adjacent to the woodland trail and includes a heritage garden with a re-creation of a traditional Cayman home, garden, and farm; a floral garden with 1½ acres of flowering plants, and a 2-acre lake with three islands, home to many native birds.

Mastic Trail is a restored 200-year-old footpath through a 2-million-year-old woodland area in the heart of the island. The trail lies west of Frank Sound Road, about a 45-minute drive from the heart of George Town. Named for the majestic mastic tree, the trail showcases the reserve's natural attractions, including a native mangrove swamp, traditional agriculture, and an ancient woodland area—home to the largest variety of native plant and animal life found in the Cayman Islands. Guided tours, lasting 2½ to 3 hours and limited to eight

---

Finds **Yo Ho Ho & a Bottle of Rum**

Blackbeard's Liquors has several locations, the most convenient of which is at the Strand, opposite Foster's Food Fair (© **345/949-8763**). Their liquors are bottled in the Cayman Islands; try various rum flavors, such as banana, coconut, and mango, all based on original recipes. The **Tortuga Rum Company,** Selkirk Plaza (© **345/945-7655**), not only sells rum but is also famous locally for its chocolate rum cake. Of course, most people come here for a bottle of its premium gold, 151-proof superb light rum, at the duty-free price of $8.50 per liter.

---

participants, are offered Monday to Friday at 8:30am and 3pm, and again on Saturday at 8:30am. Reservations are required, and the cost is $50 per person (expensive, but if you're really into plants you might want to splurge on it). The hike is not recommended for children under 6, the elderly, or persons with physical disabilities. Wear comfortable, sturdy shoes, and carry water and insect repellent. For reservations, call © **345/945-6588** Monday to Friday 7 to 9am.

SHOPPING ★★
Although duty-free shopping in George Town encompasses silver, china, crystal, Irish linen, French perfumes, British woolen goods, and such local crafts as black-coral jewelry and thatch-woven baskets, there aren't any real bargains. Americans shouldn't purchase turtle products—they cannot be brought into the United States.

Ayurvedic Concepts, Elizabethan Square (© **345/949-1769**), is one of the most unusual stores in the Cayman Islands. It's been known for its natural herbal remedies since 1930. Some of their products include MindCare, said to calm a "racing mind" and help enhance memory.

For reasonably priced resort wear for men, women, and children, head for **Island Casuals,** Galleria Plaza, West Bay Road (© **345/949-8094**).

Kayman Kids, Galleria Plaza on West Bay Road (© **345/945-2356**), sells a vast array of items, mainly children's clothing, plus a large selection of bathing suits for boys and girls. They also sell dollhouses designed to look like a typical Caymanian cottage. A lot of specialty gifts are also hawked.

Kirk Freeport Plaza, Cardinal Avenue and Panton Street, George Town (© **345/949-7477**), is the largest store of its kind on the Caymans, with a treasure trove of gold jewelry, watches, china, crystal, perfumes, and cosmetics. The store holds a Cartier franchise, with items priced 15% to 35% below suggested retail prices stateside. Also stocked are crystal and porcelain from Wedgwood, Waterford, Lladró, and Baccarat, priced 30% to 50% less than recommended retail prices stateside.

Pure Art, South Church Street, George Town (© **345/949-9133**), is good for some local souvenirs and is your best bet for arts and crafts. One room is devoted to original art, including locally produced Christmas ornaments. Another room stocks art prints and note cards. The shop also carries carvings, ceramics, thatch work, and baskets, plus pottery made by the youngsters at the Bodden Town primary school.

Tropical Trader Market & Bazaar, Edward St. (© **345/949-6538**), is a good bet on an island of overpriced art galleries. You can pick up some typical Caymanian scenes here—not only paintings, but drawings and prints as well—for $15 and up. Local artists painted many of the island scenes in water-colors. The outlet is a true bazaar, selling gold, silver, and black-coral jewelry (the latter among the most inexpensive on the island). You can also purchase watches by Anne Klein, Casio, and Swiss Army, plus Tommy Bahama men's sports clothing. Bags and luggage by Kipling and Tumi are also sold.

An offbeat shopping adventure can be found at **Caribbean Charlie's,** Hut Village, 4 miles from Rum Point (© **345/947-9452**), on the north side of the island in a typical Caymanian settlement. This is the workshop and home of the remarkable Charlie Ebanks, who is known on the island for his brightly painted wooden *waurie* boards. This game was believed to have been imported to the island by slaves. It is said that everybody from Blackbeard to Ernest Hemingway has enjoyed playing this game. Charlie also makes birdhouses in the shape of the traditional Cayman cottages. One of the few native artisans still on the island, Charlie is aided by his American-born wife, Elaine, who adds bright colors and fanciful designs to his creations.

GRAND CAYMAN AFTER DARK

Lone Star Bar & Grill, West Bay Road (© 345/945-5175), is a transplanted corner of the Texas Panhandle. You can enjoy juicy burgers in the dining room or head immediately for the bar in back. Here, beneath murals of Lone Star beauties, you can watch several sports events simultaneously on 15 different TV screens and sip lime and strawberry margaritas. Monday and Thursday are fajita nights, all-you-can-eat affairs at CI$13 ($16.25), and Tuesday is all-you-can-eat lobster night at CI$36 ($45). There's a new volleyball court, too.

The Planet, about a block inland from West Bay Road (© 345/949-7169), adjacent to the island's only cinema, offers the island's largest dance floor, plus the biggest indoor stage and four bars dispensing reasonably priced drinks along with bar food. The mix of locals and tourists form a wide age range—from 18 to 50. Expect a $5 cover.

3 Cayman Brac ⟨⋆⟩

The "middle" island of the group, Cayman Brac is a piece of limestone and coral-based land 12 miles long and a mile wide, about 89 miles east-northeast of Grand Cayman. It was given the name Brac (Gaelic for "bluff") by 17th-century Scottish fishers who settled here. The bluff for which the island was named is a towering limestone plateau rising to 140 feet above the sea, covering the eastern half of Cayman Brac. Caymanians refer to the island simply as Brac, and its 1,400 inhabitants, a hospitable bunch of people, are called *Brackers*.

The big attraction of the bluff is the more than 170 caves honeycombing its limestone height. In the early 18th century, pirates occupied the Caymans, and Edward Teach, the infamous Blackbeard, is supposed to have spent quite a bit of time around Cayman Brac. Some of the caves are at the bluff's foot; others can be reached only by climbing over jagged limestone rock. One of the biggest caves is Great Cave, with a number of chambers. Harmless fruit bats cling to the roofs of the caverns.

On the south side of the bluff, you won't see many people, and the only sounds are of the sea crashing against the lavalike shore. The island's herons and wild green parrots are seen here. Most of the Brackers live on the north side, many in traditional wooden seaside cottages, some built by the island's pioneers. The islanders must all have green thumbs, as attested to by the variety of flowers, shrubs, and fruit trees in many of the yards. On Cayman Brac, you'll see poinciana trees, bougainvillea, Cayman orchids, croton, hibiscus, aloe, sea grapes, cactus, and coconut and cabbage palms. The gardeners grow cassava, pumpkins, breadfruit, yams, and sweet potatoes.

There are no actual towns on the island, only settlements, such as Stake Bay (the "capital"), Spot Bay, the Creek, Tibbitt's Turn, the Bight, and West End, where the airport is located.

CAYMAN BRAC ESSENTIALS

Flights from Grand Cayman to Cayman Brac are operated on **Cayman Airways** (© **800/422-9626** in the U.S., or 345/949-2311). The airline uses relatively large 737 jets carrying 122 passengers each. There is an evening flight here, plus a morning return. The round-trip cost is $107 to $135 per person.

The only hospital is the 18-bed **Faith Hospital** (© **345/948-2243**).

ACCOMMODATIONS YOU CAN AFFORD

The two major resorts on the island, Brac Reef Beach Resort and Divi Tiara Beach Resort, are pretty high-priced, and the other accommodations here aren't exactly inexpensive.

Walton's Mango Manor ★★ *Finds* Unique on Cayman Brac, this is a personalized, small-scale B&B that's more richly decorated, elegant, and appealing than you might have thought was possible in such a remote place. Originally the home of a sea captain, it was moved to a less exposed location and rebuilt from salvaged materials shortly after the disastrous hurricane of 1932. Set on 3 acres of land on the island's north shore, within a lush garden, it contains such intriguing touches as a banister salvaged from the mast of a 19th-century schooner. The most desirable accommodations are on the upper floor, partly because of their narrow balconies that offer views of the sea. Each room has a small bathroom equipped with a shower stall. Your hosts are Brooklyn-born Lynne Walton and her husband, George, a former USAF major who retired to his native Cayman Brac.

Stake Bay (P.O. Box 56), Cayman Brac, B.W.I. ©/fax 345/948-0518. www.waltonsmangomanor.com. 5 units. Winter $90–$100 double. Off-season $80–$90 double. Rates include full breakfast. AE, MC, V. *In room:* A/C, no phone.

GREAT DEALS ON DINING

Captain's Table AMERICAN The decor is vaguely nautical, with oars over and around the bar and pieces of boats forming the restaurant's entryway. In the same building as a scuba shop and the hotel's reception desk, the restaurant offers both indoor and air-conditioned seating, along with outside dining by the pool. Begin with shrimp and lobster cocktail or perhaps a conch fritter, then follow with one of the soups such as black bean. Main dishes include everything from the catch of the day, often served pan-fried, to barbecue ribs. At lunch, you can order burgers and sandwiches.

In Brac Caribbean Beach Village, Stake Bay. © 345/948-1418. Reservations recommended. Main courses $17–$28.15; lunch from $6. AE, MC, V. Mon–Sat 11am–3pm and 6–10pm; Sun noon–3pm.

FUN ON & OFF THE BEACH

The biggest attraction on Cayman Brac is the variety of **watersports**— swimming, fishing, snorkeling, and some of the world's best diving and exploration of coral reefs. There are undersea walls on both the north and south sides of the island, with stunning specimens lining their sides. The big attraction for divers is the **M.V. *Tibbetts,*** a 330-foot-long Russian frigate that rests under 100 feet of water, a relic of the Cold War sunk in September of 1996. It is complete with guns both fore and aft. Hatches into the ship have been barred off to ensure diver safety. Marine life is becoming more pronounced on this relic, which now rests in a watery grave far, far from its home. The best dive center is **Peter Hughes Dive Tiara** at the Divi Tiara Beach Resort (℗ **800/367-3484** or 345/945-1553).

History buffs might check out the **Cayman Brac Museum,** in the former Government Administration Building, Stake Bay (℗ **345/948-2622**), which has an interesting collection of Caymanian antiques, including pieces rescued from shipwrecks and items from the 18th century. Open Monday to Friday 9am to noon and 1 to 4pm, Saturday 9am to noon, and Sunday 1 to 4pm. Admission is free.

4 Little Cayman ⚹

The smallest of the Cayman Islands is cigar-shaped Little Cayman, 10 miles long and about a mile across at its widest point. It lies about 75 miles northeast of Grand Cayman and some 5 miles from Cayman Brac. The entire island is coral and sand.

The islands of the Caymans are mountaintops of the long-submerged Sierra Maestra Range, which runs north and into Cuba. Coral formed layers over the underwater peaks, eventually forming the islands. Beneath Little Cayman's Bloody Bay is one of the mountain's walls—a stunning sight for snorkelers and scuba divers.

The island seems to have come into its own now that fishing and diving have taken center stage; this is a near-perfect place for such pursuits. The waters around the little island were hailed by the late Jacques Cousteau as one of the three finest diving spots in the world. Fine bonefishing is available just offshore, and a brackish inland pool can be fished for tarpon. Even if you don't dive or fish, you can row 200 yards off Little Cayman to isolated and uninhabited Owen Island, where you can swim from the sandy beach and picnic by a blue lagoon.

There may still be pirate treasure buried on the island, but it's in the dense interior of what is now the largest bird sanctuary in the Caribbean. Little Cayman is also home to a unique species of lizard that predates the iguana.

Blossom Village, the island's "capital," is on the southwest coast.

LITTLE CAYMAN ESSENTIALS
Most visitors fly from Grand Cayman to Little Cayman. **Cayman Airways** (℗ **345/949-5252** on Grand Cayman) is the reservations agent for Island Air, a charter company that charges $159 round-trip.

ACCOMMODATIONS YOU CAN AFFORD
Paradise Villas Resort ⚹ *(Kids)*   On this high-priced little island, this resort on the beach is your best deal, and it's also the best choice if you're traveling with family (baby-sitting can be arranged). The style is typically Caymanian, with gingerbread decoration, metal roofs, and porches front and back. Guests prepare their own meals. Bordering the sea are six duplex cottages, each divided into two one-bedroom units. Pullout couches in the living room easily accommodate extra guests. Rooms are small and mattresses are well used, but there is basic comfort here. The compact bathrooms contain shower stalls. The resort is on the island's south side, near the little airport from which pickup is provided free. A

grocery store, boutique, two auto rentals, and a liquor store are all within walking distance, and Paradise Resort offers free bikes. On the premises is the best affordable restaurant on the island, The Hungry Iguana (see "Great Deals on Dining," below). Diving is arranged through Paradise Divers. Its two-tank dive, at $75, is the island's best value.

P.O. Box 30, Little Cayman, Cayman Islands, B.W.I. ℂ 877-3CAYMAN or 345/948-0001. Fax 345/948-0002. www.paradisevillas.com. 12 units. Winter $175 single; $200 double; $225 triple. Off-season $156 single; $169 double; $200 triple. Children 11 and under stay free in parent's room. AE, MC, V. **Amenities:** Restaurant, free bikes, airport shuttle. *In room:* A/C, TV, ceiling fans.

Sam McCoy's Diving & Fishing Lodge ★★ Set on the island's northwestern shore, this hotel reflects the personalities of Sam McCoy and his family, who include their guests in many aspects of their day-to-day lives. There's not really a bar or restaurant in the traditional sense; rather, you'll pour your own drinks (usually from your own bottle) or drink at a beach bar that rises from the sands of Bloody Bay a short walk from the hotel. Light snacks and simple platters are offered at outdoor tables near the main lodge with Sam and his gang, many of whom are associated in one way or another with diving operations on the reefs offshore. The bedrooms are ultra-simple, with few adornments other than beds with a firm mattress, a table and chair, and a ceiling fan. Bathrooms are small with dated plumbing and a shower stall. Maid service is included in the price. There's a pool on the premises, but most visitors opt for dips in the wide blue sea instead, usually taking part in any of the wide choice of scuba explorations offered by Sam and his staff. (Jackson Beach lies nearby.) Picnics can be arranged to the offshore sands of Owens Cay. This is a place built by divers, and intended for divers, even those with children in tow.

P.O. Box 12, Little Cayman, Cayman Islands, B.W.I. ℂ 800/626-0496 in the U.S. and Canada, or 345/948-0026. Fax 345/949-0057. www.mccoyslodge.com.ky. 8 units. $80 per person double; $65 per person triple. Dive packages $536.50 for 3 nights/2 days, and $1,354.50 for 7 nights/6 days, per person, double occupancy. Rates include all meals and all dives. AE, MC, V. **Amenities:** Pool, watersports, maid service. *In room:* A/C, ceiling fans.

GREAT DEALS ON DINING

Birds of Paradise AMERICAN/CONTINENTAL This spot caters primarily to hotel guests but welcomes anyone. The specialty is buffet-style dinners—the kind your parents might have enjoyed back in the 1950s or 1960s. Tuesday night features the island's most generous barbecue spread—all the ribs, fish, and Jamaican-style jerk chicken you'd want. On other nights, try the prime rib, fresh fish Caribbean style (your best bet), or chicken either Russian style (Kiev) or French style (cordon bleu). There's a freshly made salad bar, and homemade desserts are yummy, especially the key lime pie. At night, opt for an outdoor table under the stars.

At Little Cayman Resort. ℂ 345/948-1033. Reservations recommended for dinner. Dinner CI$31.75 ($39.70); lunch CI$18.75 ($23.45); breakfast CI$15 ($18.75). AE, MC, V. Daily 7–8:30am, 12:30–1:30pm, and 6:30–8pm.

The Hungry Iguana AMERICAN/CARIBBEAN At the beach, you'll spot this place immediately, with its mammoth iguana mural. The island's tastiest dishes are served here, a winning combination of standard American fare along with some zesty flavors from the islands south of here. It's the most macho place on the island, especially the sports bar with its satellite TV in the corner, with a sort of TGI Friday's atmosphere. Lunch is the usual burgers and fries along with some well-stuffed sandwiches. We always prefer the grilled chicken salad.

Dinner gets a little more elaborate—there's usually a special meat dish of the day, depending on the market (supplies are shipped in once a week by barge). Try one of the seafood platters. The chef always seems willing to prepare you a steak as you like it. Marinated shrimp with rémoulade is a tasty choice as well. Most dishes are at the lower end of the price scale.

Paradise Resort. ✆ **345/948-0007.** Reservations recommended. Dinner CI$15–CI$34 ($18.75–$42.50); lunch CI$7.25–CI$10. ($9.05–$12.50). AE, MC, V. Daily noon–9:30pm. Bar Mon–Fri noon–1am; Sat–Sun noon–midnight.

SPORTS & OTHER OUTDOOR PURSUITS

Established in 1994, the **Governor Gore Bird Sanctuary** (✆ **345/949-1021**) is home to some 5,000 pairs of red-footed boobies. As far as it is known, this is the largest colony of such birds in the western hemisphere. The sanctuary, lying near the small airport, is also home to dramatic colonies of snowy egrets and black frigates. Many bird-watchers from the United States fly into Little Cayman just to see these bird colonies.

The best fishing is at Bloody Bay, lying off the island's north coast. It is especially noted for its bonefishing and tarpon catches. For fishing, contact Sam McCoy's Diving and Fishing Lodge (see "Accommodations You Can Afford," above).

The Bloody Bay Wall is also the best dive site on island, lying just 20 minutes offshore and reached by boat. The drop here begins at only 20 feet but plunges to more than 1,200 feet. This is one of the great dive spots in the Caymans. For more information about how to enjoy it, call **Paradise Divers** at ✆ **800/ 450-2084** or 345/948-0004. You can also make arrangements at Sam McCoy's as well (see "Accommodations You Can Afford," above).

9

Curaçao

Just 35 miles north of the coast of Venezuela, Curaçao, the "C" of the Dutch ABC islands of the Caribbean, is the most populous in the Netherlands Antilles. It attracts visitors because of its distinctive culture, warm people, duty-free shopping, lively casinos, and watersports. Heading out from its harbor, fleets of tankers carry refined oil to all parts of the world.

Curaçao, together with Bonaire, St. Maarten, St. Eustatius, and Saba, is in the Kingdom of the Netherlands as part of the Netherlands Antilles. Curaçao has its own governmental authority, relying on the Netherlands only for defense and foreign affairs. Its population of 171,000 represents more than 50 nationalities.

The largest of the Netherlands Antilles, Curaçao is 37 miles long and 7 miles across at its widest point. Because of all the early Dutch building, Curaçao is the most important island architecturally in the entire West Indies, with more European flavor than anywhere else in the Caribbean. After leaving the capital, **Willemstad,** you plunge into a strange, desertlike countryside that evokes the American Southwest. The landscape is an amalgam of browns and russets, studded with three-pronged cactus, spiny-leafed aloes, and the divi-divi trees, with their coiffures bent by centuries of trade winds. Classic Dutch-style windmills are in and around Willemstad and in some parts of the countryside. These standard farm models pump water from wells to irrigate vegetation.

Only in the 1990s did tourism become the biggest money earner for this island. As a result, you can find a number of inexpensive or moderately priced hotels, inns, and apartment complexes here.

1 Essentials

VISITOR INFORMATION

In the United States, contact the **Curaçao Tourist Board** at 475 Park Ave. S., Suite 2000, New York, NY 10016 (© 800/270-3350 or 212/683-7660), or at 330 Biscayne Blvd., Suite 330, Miami, FL 33132 (© 305/374-5811).

The official website is **www.curacao-tourism.com.**

On the island, go to the **Curaçao Tourist Board,** Pietermaai (© 599/9-4616000).

GETTING THERE

The air routes to **Curaçao International Airport,** Plaza Margareth Abraham (© 599/9-682288), are still firmly linked to those leading to nearby Aruba. In recent years, however, developments at such airlines as American have initiated direct or nonstop routings into Curaçao from such international hubs as Miami.

ALM (© 800/327-7230) is Curaçao's national carrier. It flies 14 times a week from Miami to Curaçao. Although 10 of these flights stop in either Aruba,

Legend

✈ Airport
🏖 Beach
🔺 Mountain

Hotel Holland **2**
Hotel Seru Coral **4**
Landhuis Daniel Inn **1**
Otrabanda Hotel & Casino **3**

Playa Kenepa
Noordpunt
Westpunt
Westpunt
Boca Tabla
Playa Abao
Knip Bay
CHRISTOFFEL NATIONAL PARK
Playa Lagun
St. Christoffelberg
St. Christoffelberg
Santa Cruz
Santa Marta Bay
Soto
Barber
San Juan Bay
Country House Museum
Caribbean Sea
Port Marie Beach
St. Willibrordus
Daaibooi
Habitat Curaçao Beach
Boca St. Marie
Curaçao International Airport
Boca Hato
Hato Caves
St. Michiel
Julianadorp
Brievengat
Blauwbaai
Piscadera Bay
Emmastad
Santa Catarina
St. Anna Bay
Santa Rosa
St. Joris Bay
Willemstad
Montagne
Caribbean Sea
Seaquarium
Jan Thiel Bay
Spanish Water
Santa Barbara Beach
Curaçao Underwater Marine Park
Ostpunt

0   5 mi
0   5 km

Bonaire, or Haiti, the others are nonstop. ALM also flies two times a week to Curaçao from Atlanta, usually with a stop in Bonaire en route.

American Airlines (📞 800/433-7300) offers a daily nonstop flight to Curaçao from its hub in Miami, which departs late enough in the day to permit easy connections from cities all over the northeast. Fortunately, it arrives early enough in the day (around 3pm) to allow guests to unpack and enjoy a leisurely dinner the same evening. American also offers flights to Curaçao's neighbor, Aruba, from New York, Miami, and San Juan, Puerto Rico. Once on Aruba, many clients transfer on to Curaçao on any of ALM's many shuttle flights. An American Airlines sales representative can also sell discounted hotel packages if you book your airfare and overnight accommodations simultaneously.

Air Aruba (📞 800/88ARUBA) flies daily from Newark, New Jersey, to Aruba, with two flights on Saturday and Sunday (one of the Sun flights stops in Baltimore to pick up passengers). The same airline also offers daily nonstop flights to Aruba from Miami and Tampa and direct service from Baltimore. On Aruba, regardless of their points of origin, Curaçao-bound passengers either remain on the same plane for its continuation on to Curaçao or transfer to another aircraft after a brief delay.

GETTING AROUND

BY TAXI Because taxis don't have meters, ask your driver to quote you the rate before getting in. Drivers are supposed to carry an official tariff sheet, which they'll produce upon request. Charges go up by 25% after 11pm. Generally there's no need to tip, unless a driver helped you with your luggage. The charge from the airport to Willemstad is about $15, and the cost can be split among four passengers. If a piece of luggage is so big that the trunk lid won't close, you'll be assessed a surcharge of $1.

In town, the best place to get a taxi is on the Otrabanda side of the floating bridge. To summon a **taxi,** call *©* **599/9-8690752.** Cabbies will usually give you a tour of the island for around $20 per hour for up to four passengers.

BY RENTAL CAR Because all points of interest on Curaçao are easily accessible by paved roads, you might want to rent a car. U.S., British, and Canadian visitors can use their own licenses, if valid, and *traffic moves on the right.* International road signs are observed.

Avis (*©* **800/331-2112** or 599/9-8681163) and **Budget** (*©* **800/472-3325** or 599/9-8683420) offer some of the lowest rates. **Hertz** (*©* **800/654-3001** in the U.S., or 599/9-8681182) may also offer good deals. Rentals are often cheaper if you reserve from North America at least a week before your departure, and rates vary depending on the time of year.

Local car-rental firms include **Rent a Yellow,** Santa Rosa 9 (*©* **599/9-7673777**), whose cars are painted like a yellow cab. The lowest rates are for vehicles without air-conditioning, costing from $47.75 daily, rising to $58 with air-conditioning. Rates include tax and insurance.

BY BUS Some hotels operate a free bus shuttle that will take you from the suburbs to the shopping district of Willemstad. A fleet of DAF yellow buses operates from Wilhelmina Plein, near the shopping center, to most parts of Curaçao. Some limousines function as "C" buses. When you see one listing the destination you're heading for, you can hail it at any of the designated bus stops.

 FAST FACTS: Curaçao

Banks Banking hours are Monday to Friday 8:30am to noon and 1:30 to 4:30pm. However, the Banco Popular and the Bank of America remain open during the lunch hour, doing business Monday to Friday 9am to 3pm.

Currency Whereas Canadian and U.S. dollars are accepted for purchases on the island, the official currency is the **Netherlands Antillean florin (NAf),** also called a guilder, which is divided into 100 NA (Netherlands Antillean) cents. The exchange rate is U.S.$1 to 1.80NAf (1NAf = 56¢ U.S.). Shops, hotels, and restaurants usually accept most major U.S. and Canadian credit and charge cards. *Rates in this chapter are quoted in U.S. dollars unless otherwise specified.*

Documents To enter Curaçao, U.S. or Canadian citizens need proof of citizenship, such as a birth certificate or a passport, along with a return or continuing airline ticket out of the country. We always recommend carrying your passport when visiting a foreign country. British subjects need a valid passport.

Electricity The electricity is 110–130 volts AC, 50 cycles, the same as in North America, although many hotels will have transformers if your appliances happen to be European.

Language Dutch, Spanish, and English are spoken on Curaçao, along with Papiamento, a patois that combines the three major tongues with Amerindian and African dialects.

Medical Care Medical facilities are well equipped, and the 534-bed **St. Elisabeth Hospital,** Breedestraat 193 (© **599/9-4624900**), near Otrabanda in Willemstad, is one of the most up-to-date facilities in the Caribbean.

Police The police emergency number is © **114.**

Safety Although Curaçao is not plagued with crime, it is wise to safeguard your valuables.

Taxes & Service Curaçao levies a room tax of 7% on accommodations, and most hotels add 12% for room service. There's a departure tax of $12.50 for international flights, $5.65 for flights to other islands in the Netherlands Antilles.

Telecommunications To call Curaçao from the United States, dial **011** (the international access code), then **599** (the country code for Curaçao), and then **9** (the area code) and the local number (the number of digits in the local number varies).

Once on Curaçao, to call another number on the island, only the local number is necessary; to make calls to an off-island destination, dial **021** and then the area code and number.

Time Curaçao is on Atlantic standard time year-round, 1 hour ahead of eastern standard time and the same as eastern daylight saving time.

Tipping Most restaurants and hotels include a service charge—usually 10%. If service has been very good in a restaurant, locals often add another 5% to the tab. Cabbies get a 10% tip, and bellmen and porters get $1 per bag. Maids are given about $2 a day on the average.

Water The water comes from a modern desalination plant and is safe to drink.

Weather Curaçao has an average temperature of 81°F (22.7°C). Trade winds keep the island fairly cool, and it is flat and arid, with an average rainfall of only 22 inches per year—hardly your idea of a lush, palm-studded tropical island.

2 Accommodations You Can Afford

Your hotel will be in Willemstad or one of the suburbs, which are 10 to 15 minutes from the shopping center. The bigger hotels often have free shuttle buses running into town, and most of them have their own beaches and pools.

Remember that Curaçao is a bustling commercial center, and the downtown hotels often fill up fast with business travelers and visitors from neighboring countries on shopping holidays. Therefore, reservations are always important.

When making reservations, ask if the 7% room tax and 12% service charge are included in the price you're quoted.

Hotel Holland ★   A 2-minute drive from the airport, Hotel Holland contains the Flying Dutchman Bar, a popular gathering place, plus a casino. For a few brief minutes of every day, you can see airplanes landing from your perch at the edge of the poolside terrace, where well-prepared breakfasts, lunches, and dinners from The Cockpit restaurant are served in good weather (see "Great Deals on Dining," below, for a review). And you probably will hang around the pool because it's a 30-minute drive to the nearest good beach. You definitely need a rental car if you stay here. This property is the domain of former Navy frogman Hans Vrolijk and his family. Hans still retains his interest in scuba and arranges dive packages for his guests. The comfortably furnished accommodations have shower-only bathrooms and balconies.

F. D. Rooseveltweg 524, Curaçao, N.A. ℭ 599/9-8688044. Fax 599/9-688114. 45 units. Year-round $85 double; from $125 suite. AE, DC, MC, V. **Amenities:** Restaurant, bar, casino, pool, room service, babysitting. *In room:* A/C, TV/VCR, fridge.

Hotel Seru Coral *Kids*   Built in the early 1990s, this is a landscaped hotel complex whose white-walled buildings are clustered around the edges of a very large circular pool terrace. It lies on Curaçao's eastern edge, about 4 miles from the nearest beach (Santa Barbara Beach), but the inconvenience of reaching the beach is offset by the fact that this hotel is home to the largest freshwater pool on Curaçao. At least five room configurations are available, allowing groups of travelers to cut their costs to very reasonable levels by sharing. Each has white walls with pastel trim, white tile floors, and a mixture of rattan and wooden furniture, including good beds with firm mattresses and standard bathrooms with stall showers only. Watersports, boat trips, and tennis can be arranged nearby. Families are welcome.

Koraal Partier 10, Curaçao, N.A. ℭ 599/9-7678499. Fax 599/9-7678256. 86 units. July–Aug and Dec $101 studio; $130 apt; $196 bungalow for 4; $257 villa for 6. Off-season $73 studio; $90 apt; $140 bungalow for 4; $257 villa for 6. Extra bed for 1 additional occupant $9 per day; children 12 and under stay free in parents' room. AE, DC, MC, V. **Amenities:** Restaurant, bar, pool, children's wading pool, minimart, babysitting, laundry. *In room:* A/C, TV.

Landhuis Daniel Inn ★ *Value*   South of Westpunt, near the island's westernmost point, this mustard-colored plantation house is most often visited by locals for its on-site restaurant. If you don't mind a location away from the beach, it offers the best value on the island. The nearest worthwhile beaches are Porto Marie or Habitat Curaçao, which are a 7- to 10-minute drive away.

Very simple but comfortable bedrooms, located a floor above the restaurant, are tidily maintained and have small private bathrooms with shower units. Only two rooms are air-conditioned, but all units have ceiling fans—or you can rely on the trade winds to keep cool. Ask for a room in the main house: The converted slave quarters are small, but charming. This place's basic rooms and communal TV room give it something of the aura of a youth hostel; guests also play billiards and darts.

Wegnaar, Westpunt, Curaçao, N.A. ℭ/fax 599/9-8648400. www.danieldivers.com. 10 units. Year-round $60 double. AE, DC, MC, V. **Amenities:** Restaurant, bar, pool, dive shop. *In room:* TV, ceiling fans.

Otrabanda Hotel & Casino   This six-story, somewhat anonymous hotel serves both tourists and business travelers in the heart of Willemstad. Although the nearest beach is a 15-minute drive away, there's a pool and lots of diversions, shopping, bars, and inexpensive restaurants within an easy stroll. The bedrooms are simple, spartan, and clean, with white walls, carpets, and wooden furniture. Maintenance is good, and the units are medium in size with carpeted floors, floor-to-ceiling windows, and excellent mattresses. Bathrooms are spacious, with combination shower and tub bathrooms and adequate shelf space. On the premises are the Bay Sight Terrace restaurant and the Pontoon Bar. The ground-floor casino, although not particularly memorable, seems relatively busy.

Breedestraat, Otrabanda, Curaçao, N.A. ✆ **599/9-4627400.** Fax 599/9-627299. www.otrobandahotel.com. 48 units. Winter $105 single; $115 double; $150 suite. Off-season $95 single; $105 double; $140 suite. Rates include breakfast. AE, DISC, MC, V. **Amenities:** Restaurant, bar, casino, pool. *In room:* A/C, TV.

3 Great Deals on Dining

Although the restaurants reviewed below offer some high-priced dishes—mostly fresh fish—most items are at the lower end of the price scale.

The Cockpit *(Value)* DUTCH/INTERNATIONAL   The restaurant's dining room has the nose of an airplane cockpit as its focal point; there's also seating outside, around the pool. Located on the scrub-bordered road leading to the airport, a few minutes from the landing strips, The Cockpit serves international cuisine with an emphasis on Dutch and Antillean specialties. Guests enjoy fresh fish in season (served Curaçao style: with red peppers, onions, and tomatoes), Dutch-style steak, Caribbean curried chicken, split-pea soup, and various pasta dishes, such as shrimp linguine *della mama* in a lobster sauce. All dishes are accompanied by fresh vegetables and Dutch-style potatoes. No one pretends the food is gourmet fare—it's robust, hearty, filled with good country flavor, and a terrific value to boot.

In the Hotel Holland, F. D. Rooseveltweg 524. ✆ **599/9-8688044.** Reservations required. Main courses $12–$25. AE, DC, MC, V. Daily 7am–11pm.

The Grill King GRILLED MEATS/FISH   This casual place draws locals and visitors to an open-air site near the harbor with a panoramic view of the passing ships. It's a lively, bustling place, specializing in grilled meats and fish, although there are other choices as well. The grilled steaks are succulent, as is the fresh catch of the day. You can also order pepper steak, a platter full of seafood (shrimp, calamari, conch, and lobster). Savvy foodies often gravitate to the mixed grill with pork, beef, conch, and chicken, all served with fresh vegetables. Burgers are also available, and there's not only a soup of the day but a daily special, often regional. The bar often stays open until 1am, and it attracts a convivial crowd.

Water Foort 2–3. ✆ **599/9-4616870.** Main courses $7–$26. AE, DC, DISC, MC, V. Mon–Thurs noon–midnight; Fri–Sat noon–12:30am; Sun 5:30pm–midnight.

Il Barile ITALIAN   Many Italian meals in Curaçao are very expensive, but this winning little two-story trattoria-style place not only offers affordable prices, but serves a very good cuisine. It's really only an informal cafe with an outdoor terrace on the ground floor. Many locals, including some Italians, cite it for its good food. You can drop in for breakfast, stick around for such lunch offerings as burgers and sandwiches, and definitely stay for dinner. In the evening the kitchen really shines, turning out a number of pasta dishes, such as linguine al pesto. The fresh basil in the pesto sauce is grown at the owner's home. You can also order excellent grilled red snapper or shrimp in garlic butter.

Hanhi Sna 12, Punda. ℂ **599/9-4613025.** Main courses $6–$15. AE, DISC, MC, V. Mon–Sat 8am–8pm.

Jaanchi's SEAFOOD   In the village of Westpunt, on the island's northern tip, this local dive continues to make a name for itself because of its fried fresh fish. Many locals drive out here for a feast that ranges from shrimp to conch and octopus—each dish prepared according to time-tested traditional recipes. For those with exotic palates, the menu offers a number of very rare regional dishes, even iguana soup! If the spicy local goat doesn't interest you, you can always opt for a good steak instead. Platters are served with rice, french fries, fried bananas, salad, and *fungi* polenta. The restaurant is built ranch style, offering open-air dining. Birds looking for handouts (bread crumbs) will often join you at your table. On Sunday and holidays there's live music, and Jaanchi's becomes rather festive.

Westpunt 15. ℂ **599/9-8640126.** Main courses $12–$18; lunch from $12. AE, DC, MC, V. Daily noon–8:30pm.

Mambo Beach INTERNATIONAL   Set 2 miles south of Willemstad, on an isolated stretch of sandy beachfront near the Prince's Beach Hotel, this bar and restaurant consists of little more than a wooden deck that's raised above the sand, less than 60 feet from the water's edge. Don't expect a ceiling or a roof to shelter you from a view of the stars, but parasols will shade you at noontime. Although most of the energy at this place is devoted to its restaurant and bar trade, it does an active business every Saturday and Sunday night between 11pm and 3am on the nightlife circuit. Then you'll see up to six Dutch or Caribbean bands at a time, or at least a DJ spinning the kind of tunes that encourage you to shake, rattle, and roll. If there's a cover charge at all, it won't exceed $5.60 per person and will apply only during the rare super-concert that occurs only a few times a year. If you arrive during mealtimes, menu items at lunch include pastas, pancakes and crêpes, salads, and grilled fish or chicken. Evening meals are more substantial, and often include grilled shark with lobster sauce, tuna with teriyaki sauce, salmon with mayonnaise sauce, shrimp with garlic sauce, and tournedos with sun-dried tomatoes. The food is surprisingly good and excellently prepared with first-rate ingredients.

Seaquarium Beach. ℂ **599/9-4618999.** Lunch main courses $3.65–$14; dinner main courses $7–$17.10. MC, V. Mon–Fri 10am–1pm; Sat–Sun 10am–3am.

New Golden Star ★★ *Finds* CREOLE   The best place to go on the island for *criollo* (local) food is inland from the coast road leading southeast from St. Anna Bay, at the corner of Dr. Hugenholtzweg and Dr. Maalweg, southeast of Willemstad. Evoking a roadside diner, the air-conditioned restaurant is very simple, but it has a large menu of very tasty Antillean dishes, such as *carco stoba* (conch stew), *bestia chiki* (goatmeat stew), *bakijauw* (salted cod), and *concomber stoba* (stewed meat and marble-size spiny cucumbers). Other specialties include *criollo* shrimp (*kiwa*) and *sopi carni* (meat stew). Everything is served with a side order of *fungi*, the cornmeal staple. The place has a large local following with an occasional tourist dropping in.

Socratesstraat 2. ℂ **599/9-4654795.** Main courses $7.50–$25.70. AE, DC, MC, V. Daily 9am–1am.

WORTH THE SPLURGE

Froets Garden of Eaten ★ *Finds* SEAFOOD/INTERNATIONAL   Across from the Princess Beach, this is a winning and inviting little eatery for an alfresco dinner. Attracting a fun-loving crowd, it serves tasty dishes that are never sublime but always satisfying. We often begin with the seafood soup or one of the fish dishes. For one price you get a starter, main course, and dessert (tiramisu or banana cake on our last visit). Succulent pastas and fresh salads are a regular feature as well; many guests finish off with a cappuccino, sometimes enjoyed with a regional plum cake flavored with cinnamon sauce.

Koraal Swpechtweg 11. C 599/9-4657565. Fixed-price menus $17–$25. AE, MC, V. Daily 6–10:30pm.

Pisces Seafood ☆ CREOLE/SEAFOOD
This West Indian restaurant might be difficult to find, as it's on a flat, industrial coastline near a marina and an oil refinery, about 20 minutes from Willemstad on the island's southernmost tip. There's been a restaurant here since the 1930s, when sailors and workers from the oil refinery came for home-cooked meals. This place offers food the way the locals used to eat long before the cruise ships started arriving and the sprawling resorts opened. The simple frame building offers seating near the rough-hewn bar or in a breeze-swept inner room. The menu depends on the catch of the day. Main courses, served with rice, vegetables, and plantains or potatoes, might include *sopi*, "seacat" (squid), mula (similar to kingfish), or red snapper; if you wish, the Pisces platter combines any of these in copious quantities for two or more people. Shrimp and conch are each prepared three different ways: with garlic, with curry, or Creole style. It's simple, straightforward, affordable, and often quite good.

Caracasbaaiweg 476. C 599/9-7672181. Reservations recommended. Main courses $16–$33. MC, V. Tues–Sun 5–10:30pm.

Rijsttafel Restaurant Indonesia and Holland Club Bar (Value) INDONESIAN
This is the best place on the island to sample the Indonesian *rijsttafel,* the traditional rice table with all the zesty side dishes. At lunchtime, the selection of dishes is more modest, but for dinner, Javanese cooks prepare the specialty of the house—a *rijsttafel* consisting of 16, 20, or 25 dishes. There's even an all-vegetarian *rijsttafel.* Warming trays are placed on your table; the service is buffet style. You're allowed to season your plate with peppers rated hot, very hot, and palate melting. It's best to go with a party so that all of you can share in the feast. The spicy food is a good change of pace when you tire of seafood and steak.

Mercuriusstraat 13, Salinja. C 599/9-4612606. Reservations recommended. Main courses $14–$43; *rijsttafel* $22 for 16 dishes, $27 for 20 dishes, $42.85 for 25 dishes; all-vegetarian *rijsttafel* $22.85 for 16 dishes. AE, DC, MC, V. Mon–Sat noon–2pm and 6–9:30pm. Take a taxi to this villa in the suburbs near Salinja, near the Princess Beach Resort & Casino southeast of Willemstad.

Small World International Cuisine ☆ (Finds) INTERNATIONAL
There is no more eclectic dining on the island than you'll find here. The owner, Darryll Circkens, set out to open a restaurant that roamed the world for its culinary inspiration. He has succeeded admirably in this place, which opened in 1998. The specialties are mainly Creole, Spanish, French, and Chinese. Dinner can be outside on the terrace overlooking the sea or inside where the ideal table is a glass-top over an aquarium. Some West Indian specialties will put hair on your chest, including *lengua,* or tongue in a savory sauce. We prefer the Spanish food, especially the paella and grilled seafood. Many French dishes lean heavily on beef as evoked by the chateaubriand or the filet mignon. On our last visit we enjoyed a well-flavored Chinese chicken served with a medley of mushrooms. For us, nothing quite tops the shrimp in garlic sauce offered with rice and fresh

vegetables. There's a bar if you want to drop in early for a drink. Most dishes are at the lower end of the price scale.

Waterfort Boogies 18–19. (C) 599/9-4645575. Reservations recommended. Main courses $6–$25. AE, DC, MC, V. Mon–Sat 11am–11pm; Sun 5–11pm.

4 Hitting the Beaches

Its beaches aren't the best in the Dutch Leewards, but Curaçao does have nearly 40 of them, ranging from hotel sands to secluded coves. Beaches are called *playas* or *bocas*. *Playas* are the larger, classic sandy beaches, while *bocas* are small inlets placed between two large rock formations. The northwest coast is generally rugged and difficult for swimming, but the more tranquil waters of the west coast are filled with sheltered bays, offering excellent swimming and snorkeling.

The human-made **Seaquarium Beach,** just east of the center of Willemstad, charges a fee of $2.50 for access to its complete facilities, including two bars, two restaurants, a watersports shop, beach-chair rentals, changing facilities, and showers. The calm waters make this beach ideal for swimming.

Just northwest of Willemstad, **Blauwbaai** (Blue Bay) is the largest and most popular beach on Curaçao, with enough white sand for everybody. Along with showers and changing facilities, there are plenty of shady places to retreat from the noonday sun. To get here, follow the road that goes past the Holiday Beach Hotel, heading in the direction of Juliandorp. Follow the sign that tells you to bear left for Blauwbaai and the fishing village of San Michiel.

Farther up the west coast, about 30 minutes from Willemstad in the Willibrordus area on the west side of Curaçao, **Daaibooi** is a good beach, although there are no showers or changing rooms. Wooden umbrellas provide shade. Snorkelers are attracted to the sides of the bay, as the cliffs rise out of the surf. Small rainbow-hued fish are commonplace, and many varying corals cover the rocks. This beach gets very crowded on Sunday with locals.

A beach popular with families and a base for fishing boats, **Playa Lagun** lies well concealed in the corner of the village of Lagun as you approach from Santa Cruz. The narrow cove is excellent for swimming because of the tranquil, shallow water. Rainbow-hued fish appear everywhere, so the beach is also a favorite with snorkelers. Some concrete huts provide shelter from the scorching sun; a snack bar is open on weekends.

Knip Bay, just north of Playa Lagun, has white sands, rocky sides, and beautiful turquoise waters, making it suitable for snorkeling, swimming, and sunbathing. The beach tends to be crowded on weekends, often with locals. Manzanilla trees (also called machineel trees) provide some shade, but their fruit is poisonous; never seek shelter under the trees when it rains, as drops falling off the leaves will cause major skin irritation. Changing facilities and refreshments are available.

Playa Abao, with crystal turquoise waters, is at the northern tip of the island. One of Curaçao's most popular strands, this is often called Playa Grandi ("Big Beach"). It can get very, very hot at midday, but *pergolas* (thatched shade umbrellas) provide some protection. A stairway and ramp lead down to the excellent white sands. There's a snack bar in the parking lot. Near the large cove at Playa Abao is **Playa Kenepa,** which is much smaller but gets our nod as one of the island's most beautiful strips. Partially shaded by trees, it's a good place for sunbathing, swimming, and shore diving. A 10-minute swim from the beach leads to a reef where visibility is often 100 feet. Baby sea turtles are often spotted here. A snack bar is open on weekends.

Tips **A Word of Caution to Swimmers**

Beware of stepping on the spines of the sea urchins that sometimes abound in these waters. To give temporary first aid for an embedded urchin's spine, try the local remedies of vinegar or lime juice. If you're tough, you can try a burning match, as the locals advise. While the urchin spines are not dangerous, they can cause several days of real discomfort.

Westpunt, a public beach on the northwestern tip of the island, is known for the Sunday divers who jump from its gigantic cliffs into the ocean below. You can spot rainbow-hued little boats and fishermen's nets hanging out to dry here. There are no facilities at this beach, which tends to be exceptionally hot and has no shade trees (bring lots of sunscreen). The calm waters offer excellent swimming, but they're not good for snorkeling.

South of Willemstad is **Santa Barbara Beach.** It's between the open sea and the island's primary watersports and recreational area known as Spanish Water. A mining company owns this land, which also contains Table Mountain, a remarkable landmark, and an old phosphate mine. The natural beach has pure-white sand and calm water. A buoy line protects swimmers from boats. Facilities include rest rooms, changing rooms, a snack bar, and a terrace; water bicycles and small motorboats are available for rent. The beach, open daily 8am to 6pm, has access to the Curaçao Underwater Marine Park.

5 Sports & Other Outdoor Pursuits

DAY CRUISES **Taber Tours,** Dokweg (© 599/9-7376637), offers a handful of seagoing tours, such as a 5-hour sunset/snorkel trip to Santa Barbara Beach, which includes round-trip transportation to excellent reef sites, use of snorkeling equipment, and snacks for a cost of $43 per person. Children 9 and under pay half-price. A 2-hour sunset cruise leaves Friday at dusk and includes wine and cheese. This trip costs $30 for adults, $15 for children.

Travelers looking for an experience similar to the sailing days of yore should book a trip on the *Insulinde,* Handelskade (© 599/9-5601340 [note that this is a cellular phone and the connection may be poor]; www.insulinde.com). The 120-foot traditionally rigged sail clipper is available for day trips and chartering. On Saturday, you can enjoy a full-day excursion to Klein Curaçao. The boat departs at 7am and returns at 6pm. Included in the $63 cost is breakfast, lunch, and all snorkeling gear. For a shorter trip, try the sunset cruise to Santa Barbara Beach, which departs every Thursday afternoon and makes several stops before returning by sail into the sunset. This excursion costs $43 and includes snacks and all snorkeling gear. Advance reservations are required for both trips.

Like a ghost ship from ancient times, a dual-masted, five-sailed wooden schooner cruises silently through the waters of Curaçao. It carries a name steeped in history—the *Bounty* (© 599/9-5601887), although it's not a replica of its famous namesake. On Friday, the 90-foot, gaff-rigged schooner heads to the secluded white-sand beach of Porttomarie Bay. On Sunday, the ship sets out for Klein Curaçao, a desert island that's a favorite of snorkelers. Each Monday, the *Bounty* visits Spanish Bay, a coastal community surrounded by terraced hills. The Friday, Sunday, and Tuesday trips cost $55 and include a buffet lunch.

DIVING & SNORKELING   Most hotels offer their own watersports programs. However, if your hotel isn't equipped, we suggest that you head for one of the most complete watersports facilities on Curaçao, **Seascape Dive and Watersports,** at the Four Points Resort Curaçao (© **599/9-4625000**). Specializing in snorkeling and scuba diving to reefs and underwater wrecks, it operates from a hexagonal kiosk set on stilts above the water, just offshore from the hotel's beach. Open 8am to 5pm daily, it offers snorkeling excursions for $25 per person in an underwater park offshore from the hotel, water-skiing for $40 per half hour, and rental of jet skis for $50 per half hour. A Sunfish can be rented for $20, and an introductory scuba lesson, conducted by a competent dive instructor with PADI certification, goes for $40; four-dive packages cost $110. Seascape can also arrange deep-sea fishing for $336 for a half-day tour, carrying a maximum of six people; the cost is $560 for a full-day tour. Drinks and equipment are included, but you'll have to get your hotel to pack your lunch.

Underwater Curaçao, in Bapor Kibrá (© **599/9-4618131**), has a complete PADI-accredited underwater-sports program. A fully stocked modern dive shop has retail and rental equipment. Individual dives and dive packages are offered, costing $33 per dive for experienced divers. An introductory dive for novices is priced at $65, and a snorkel trip costs only $20, including equipment.

Scuba divers and snorkelers can expect spectacular scenery in waters with visibility often exceeding 100 feet at the **Curaçao Underwater Marine Park** 🐠🐠, which stretches along 12½ miles of Curaçao's southern coastline. Although the park technically begins at Princess Beach and extends all the way to East Point, the island's most southeasterly tip, some scuba aficionados and island dive operators are aware of other, excellent dive sites outside the official boundaries of this park. Lying beneath the surface of the water are steep walls, at least two shallow wrecks, gardens of soft corals, and more than 30 species of hard corals. Although access from shore is possible at Jan Thiel Bay and Santa Barbara Beach, most people visit the park by boat. For easy and safe mooring, the park has 16 mooring buoys, placed at the best dive and snorkel sites. A snorkel trail with underwater interpretive markers is laid out just east of the Princess Beach Resort & Casino and is accessible from shore. Spearfishing, anchoring in the coral, and taking anything from the reefs, except photographs, are strictly prohibited.

GOLF   The **Curaçao Golf and Squash Club,** Wilhelminalaan, in Emmastad (© **599/9-7373590**), is your best (well, only) bet if you want to hit the links. Greens fees are $30, and both clubs and carts can be rented. The nine-hole course is open to nonmembers only in the morning, Friday to Wednesday 8am to noon. Afternoon tee times are reserved for members and for tournaments. Thursday hours for nonmembers are 10am until sundown.

HORSEBACK RIDING   At Christoffel National Park, **Rancho Christof** (© **599/9-8640535**) specializes in outdoor horseback riding, private rides along unspoiled trails, and riding smooth-gaited "paseo" horses suitable even for non-riders. You can call for reservations daily between 8am and 4pm. Most trail rides cost $45, with departures daily at 9am.

TENNIS   Most of the deluxe hotels have tennis courts, but we frugal travelers won't be staying there. So if you want to play tennis, head for the **Santa Catherine Sports Complex** at Club Seru Coral, Koraal Partier 10 (© **599/9-7677028**), where courts cost $20 per hour.

6 Seeing the Sights

Most cruise ship passengers see only Willemstad—or, more accurately, the capital's shops—but you might want to get out into the *cunucu*, or countryside, and explore the towering cacti and rolling hills topped by *landhuizen* (plantation houses) built more than 3 centuries ago.

SIGHTSEEING IN WILLEMSTAD ★★

The Spanish founded Willemstad as Santa Ana in the 1500s. Dutch traders found a vast natural harbor, a perfect hideaway along the Spanish Main, and they renamed it Willemstad in the 17th century. Not only is Willemstad the capital of Curaçao, it's also the seat of government for the Netherlands Antilles. Today it boasts rows of pastel-colored, red-roofed town houses in the downtown area. After more than a decade of restoration, the historic center of Willemstad and the island's natural harbor, Schottegat, have been inscribed on UNESCO's World Heritage List.

The city grew up on both sides of a canal. It's divided into **Punda** (Old World Dutch ambience and the best shopping) and **Otrabanda** (the contemporary "other side"). The **Queen Emma Pontoon Bridge,** a pedestrian walkway, connects both sections. Powered by a diesel engine, it swings open many times every day to let ships from all over the globe pass in and out of the harbor.

The view from the bridge is of the old **gabled houses** ★ in harmonized pastel shades. The bright colors, according to legend, are a holdover from the time when one of the island's early governors is said to have had eye trouble and flat white gave him headaches. The colonial-style architecture, reflecting the Dutch influence, gives the town a storybook look. The houses, built three or four stories high, are crowned by "step" gables and roofed with orange Spanish tiles. Hemmed in by the sea, a tiny canal, and an inlet, the streets are narrow, and they're crosshatched by still narrower alleyways.

Except for the pastel colors, Willemstad might remind you of old Amsterdam. It has one of the most intriguing townscapes in the Caribbean. But the city can be rather dirty, despite its fairy-tale appearance.

A **statue of Pedro Luis Brion** dominates the square known as Brionplein right at the Otrabanda end of the pontoon bridge. Born in Curaçao in 1782, he became the island's favorite son and best-known war hero. Under Simón Bolívar, he was an admiral of the fleet and fought for the independence of Venezuela and Colombia.

In addition to the pontoon bridge, the **Queen Juliana Bridge** opened to vehicular traffic in 1973. Spanning the harbor, it rises 195 feet, which makes it the highest bridge in the Caribbean and one of the tallest in the world.

The waterfront originally guarded the mouth of the canal on the eastern or Punda side, but now it has been incorporated into the Plaza Hotel. The task of standing guard has been taken over by **Fort Amsterdam,** site of the Governor's Palace and the 1769 Dutch Reformed church. The church still has a British cannonball embedded in it. The arches leading to the fort were tunneled under the official residence of the governor.

A corner of the fort stands at the intersection of Breedestraat and Handelskade, the starting point for a plunge into the island's major shopping district.

At some point save time to visit the **Waterfort Arches,** stretching for a quarter mile. They rise 30 feet high and are built of barrel-vaulted 17th-century stone set against the sea. Waterfort offers a chance to explore boutiques, have

---

Moments The Floating Market

A few minutes' walk from the pontoon bridge, at the north end of Handelskade, is the **Floating Market** ⊛, where scores of schooners tie up alongside the canal, a few yards from the main shopping area. Boats arrive from Venezuela and Colombia, as well as other West Indian islands, to dock here and sell tropical fruits and vegetables—a little bit of every-thing, in fact, including handcrafts. The modern market under its vast concrete cap has not replaced this unique shopping expedition, which is fun to watch; arrive early or stay late.

---

film developed quickly, cash a traveler's check, or purchase fruit-flavored ice cream. You can walk through to a breezy terrace on the sea for a local Amstel beer or a choice of restaurants. At night the grand buildings and cobbled walk-ways are illuminated.

Between the I. H. (Sha) Capriles Kade and Fort Amsterdam, at the corner of Columbusstraat and Hanchi di Snoa, stands the **Mikve Israel-Emanuel Synagogue** (© 599/9-4611067), the oldest synagogue building in the western hemisphere. Consecrated on the eve of Passover in 1732, it houses the oldest Jewish congregation in the New World, dating from 1651. A fine example of Dutch colonial architecture, covering about a square block in the heart of Willemstad, it was built in a Spanish-style walled courtyard, with four large por-tals. Sand covers the sanctuary floor following a Portuguese Sephardic custom, representing the desert where Israelites camped when the Jews passed from slavery to freedom. The highlight of the east wall is the Holy Ark, rising 17 feet, and a raised *banca,* canopied in mahogany, is on the north wall. Joaño d'Illan led the first Jewish settlers (13 families) to the island in 1651, almost half a century after their expulsion from Portugal by the Inquisition. The settlers came via Amsterdam to Curaçao.

Adjacent to the synagogue courtyard is the **Jewish Cultural Historical Museum,** Kuiperstraat 26–28 (© 599/9-4611633), housed in two buildings dating back to 1728. They were originally the rabbi's residence and the bath-house. The 2½-centuries-old *mikvah,* or bath for religious purification purposes, was in constant use until around 1850 when this practice was discontinued and the buildings sold. They have been reacquired and turned into the present museum. On display are a great many ritual, ceremonial, and cultural objects, many of which date back to the 17th and 18th centuries and are still in use by the congregation for holidays and events.

The synagogue and museum are open to visitors Monday to Friday 9 to 11:45am and 2:30 to 4:45pm; if there's a cruise ship in port, they are also open Sunday 9am to noon. Services are Friday at 6:30pm and Saturday at 10am. Visitors are welcome, with appropriate dress required. There's a $2.50 entrance fee to the museum.

WEST OF WILLEMSTAD

You can walk to the **Curaçao Museum,** Van Leeuwenhoekstraat (© 599/9-4626051), from the Queen Emma Pontoon Bridge. The tiny museum was built in 1853 by the Royal Dutch Army Corps of Engineers as a military quarantine hospital for yellow fever victims and was carefully restored in 1946–48 as a fine example of 19th-century Dutch architecture. Equipped with paintings, objets d'art, and antique furniture made in the 19th century by local cabinetmakers, it re-creates the atmosphere of an era gone by. The museum contains a large collection from the Caiquetio tribes, the early inhabitants described by Amerigo Vespucci as 7-foot-tall giants. There's also a reconstruction of a traditional music pavilion in the garden where Curaçao musicians give regular performances. It's open Monday to Saturday 9am to noon and 2 to 5pm and Sunday 10am to 4pm. Admission is $2.50 for adults, $1.25 for children 13 and under.

Opened in 1998, the **Maritime Museum,** Van De Brandhof Straat 7 (© 599/9-4652327), traces the story of Curaçao in various exhibits, beginning with the arrival of the island's original inhabitants in 600 B.C. In the historic Scharloo neighborhood of Willemstad, the museum stands just off the old harbor of St. Ana Bay. Video presentations include the development of Curaçao's harbor and the sad role of the island as one of the largest slave depots in the Caribbean. Five oral histories are also presented, one from a 97-year-old Curaçaoan who served on the cargo vessel *Normandie.* Other exhibits include antique miniatures, 17th-century ship models, and a collection of maps, some dating from the 16th century. Admission is $6 adults and $4 children, and hours are Monday to Saturday 10am to 5pm. Guided tours are available by arrangement only.

Curaçao Underwater Marine Park (© 599/9-4624242) stretches from the Princess Beach Resort & Casino to the east point of the island, a strip of about 12½ miles of untouched coral reefs. For information on snorkeling, scuba diving, and trips in a glass-bottomed boat to view the park, see "Sports & Other Outdoor Pursuits," above.

The **Country House Museum,** Doktorstuin 27 (© 599/9-8642742), 12 miles west of Willemstad, is a small-scale restoration of a 19th-century manor house that boasts thick stone walls, a thatched roof, and artifacts that represent the old-fashioned methods of agriculture and fishing. It's open Tuesday to Friday 9am to 4pm, and Saturday and Sunday 9am to 5pm. Admission is $2.

En route to Westpunt, you'll come across a seaside cavern known as **Boca Tabla,** one of many such grottoes on this rugged, uninhabited northwest coast.

In the Westpunt area, a 45-minute ride from Punda in Willemstad, **Playa Forti** is a stark region characterized by soaring hills and towering cacti, along with 200-year-old Dutch land houses, the former mansions that housed slave owners.

Out toward the western tip of Curaçao in Savonet, a high-wire fence surrounds the entrance to the 4,500-acre **Christoffel National Park** ★★ (© 599/9-8640363), about a 45-minute drive from the capital. A macadam road gives way to dirt, surrounded on all sides by abundant cactus and bromeliads. In the higher regions you can spot rare orchids. Rising from flat, arid countryside, 1,230-foot-high St. Christoffelberg is the highest point in the Dutch Leewards. Donkeys, wild goats, iguanas, the Curaçao deer, and many species of birds thrive in this preserve, and there are some Arawak paintings on a coral cliff near the two caves.

The park has 20 miles of one-way trail-like roads, with lots of flora and fauna along the way. The shortest trail is about 5 miles long and, because of the rough terrain, takes about 40 minutes to drive through. Various walking trails are available also. One of them will take you to the top of **St. Christoffelberg** in about 1½ hours. (Come early in the morning, when it isn't so hot.) The park is open Monday to Saturday 8am to 4pm and Sunday 6am to 3pm. The admission fee is $10 for both adults and children, and it includes admission to the museum.

The park also has a museum with varying exhibitions year-round set in an old storehouse leftover from plantation days. Phone to arrange a guided tour. Next

> ⌒ *Value* **Cheap Thrills: What to See & Do for Free (Well, Almost) on Curaçao**
>
> - **Stroll Across Curaçao's Golden Gate.** Walking from Punda to Otrabanda (Papiamento for "other side") takes you across the Queen Emma Pontoon Bridge (circa 1888), which locals hold in the same high regard as citizens of San Francisco do their Golden Gate bridge. This pontoon bridge is affectionately known as the "Swinging Old Lady." It floats open and closed to let maritime traffic enter the harbor. Guarding the harborside entrance is a restaurant, Bistro Le Clochard, where you can dine in a former jail or a former rain cistern. From the galleys on top, you can sip a drink at the Harbour Side Terrace, enjoying a panoramic view of Punda across the harbor entrance.
>
> - **Taste the Original and Authentic Curaçao.** When Spaniards landed on the island in the early 16th century, they planted hundreds of Naranja orange trees. But the island's arid climate and sparse rainfall didn't provide good growing conditions for their citrus crop. An inedible, bitter fruit, known locally as the *lahara* orange, was produced. By accident it was discovered that the peel of this orange, when dried in the sun, provided an aromatic oil that families used to make liqueur. Exotic spices were added, and the unique Curaçao liqueur was the result. Today the Curaçao Liqueur Factory still distills and distributes this popular beverage, created from the original and very secret recipe. You can take a free tour of the factory at Landhuis Chobolobo and sample the real thing.
>
> - **Sample Authentic Curaçaoan Food.** At the Old Marshé (The Old Market), which lies behind the post office at De Ruyterkade, you can sample all the famous Antillean dishes of the island at a fraction of the price you'd pay in a restaurant. This is the most boisterous, authentic, and popular local lunch spot on the island. Stop by this

door, the park has opened the **National Park Shete Boka** (Seven Bays). It's a turtle sanctuary and contains a cave with pounding waves off the choppy north coast. Admission to this park is $2.50 per person.

NORTH & EAST OF WILLEMSTAD

Just northeast of the capital, **Fort Nassau** was completed in 1797 and christened by the Dutch as Fort Republic. Built high on a hill overlooking the harbor entrance to the south and St. Anna Bay to the north, it was fortified as a second line of defense in case the waterfront gave way. (Today, it is a restaurant).

In addition, the **Curaçao Liqueur Distillery,** Landhuis Chobolobo, Saliña Arriba (© 599/9-4613526), offers a chance to visit and taste at Chobolobo, the 17th-century *landhuis* where the famous Curaçao liqueur is made. It's made by a secret formula handed down through generations. One of the rewards of a visit here (Mon–Fri 8am–noon and 1–5pm) is a free snifter of the liqueur.

On Schottegatweg West, northwest of Willemstad, past the oil refineries, lies the **Beth Haim Cemetery,** the oldest Caucasian burial site still in use in the western hemisphere. Meaning "House of Life," the cemetery was consecrated

famous old market around noon. Family seating is on a first-come, first-served basis. The portions are generous. You can feast on *fungi,* their version of the cornmeal-made polenta, goat stew, fried fish, peas and rice, *keshi yena,* and fried plantains.

- **Watch the Crashing Waves.** At Shete Boka, which means "Seven Inlets" in the local dialect, the islanders have created a new national park, along Westpunt Highway, just past the village of Soto. Here you can hike along the rugged, crag-strewn cliffs where the sea has carved out dramatic caverns. You can also join park rangers for some turtle-monitoring every morning. The showcase of the park is Boka Tabla, one of Curaçao's most spectacular sites. Millions of years of pounding surf have carved out a wide cavern underneath a limestone terrace where you can watch and listen to the surf roll in. A path along the bluff takes you to the edge where you can see waves crashing against the north coast for miles in each direction. Flocks of parakeets emerge in formation, birds of prey such as hawks soar and dip, and seagulls dive-bomb for luckless fish.

- **Hike Through a National Park.** At the western end of the island, Christoffel National Park is centered on Mount Christoffel, the island's highest point at 1,237 feet. A protected wildlife preserve and garden covers 4,500 acres of land. The park consists of three former plantations and offers 20 miles of one-way driving trails through abundant flora and fauna, including divi-divi trees, exotic flowers, and prickly pear cactus. Protected wildlife includes iguanas, rabbits, donkeys, several species of birds, and some 200 white-tail Curaçao deer. Visitors can explore the park on foot, by horseback, by mountain bike, by car, or by Jeep.

before 1659. On about 3 acres are some 2,500 graves. The carving on some of the 17th- and 18th-century tombstones is exceptional.

Landhuis Brievengat ✦, Brienvengat (☏ 599/9-7378344), gives visitors a chance to visit a Dutch version of an 18th-century West Indian plantation house. This stately building, in a scrub-dotted landscape on the eastern side of the island, contains a few antiques, high ceilings, and a gallery facing two entrance towers, said to have been used to imprison slaves. It's open daily 9:15am to 12:15pm and 3 to 6pm; admission is $1.

Hato Caves, F. D. Rooseveltweg (☏ 599/9-8680379), have been called "mystical." Every hour, professional local guides take visitors through this Curaçao world of stalagmites and stalactites, found in the highest limestone terrace of the island. Actually, they were once old coral reefs, which were formed when the ocean water fell and the landmass was lifted up over the years. Over thousands of years, limestone formations were created, some mirrored in an underground lake. After crossing the lake, you enter the "Cathedral," an underground cavern. The caves are open daily 10am to 4pm. Admission is $6.25 for adults and $4.75 for children 4 to 11 (free for kids 3 and under).

The **Curaçao Seaquarium,** off Dr. Martin Luther King Boulevard at a site called Bapor Kibrá (© **599/9-4616666**), has more than 400 species of fish, crabs, anemones, sponges, and coral displayed and growing in a natural environment. Located a few minutes' walk along the rocky coast from the Princess Beach Resort & Casino, the Seaquarium is open daily 8:30am to 6pm. Admission is $12.50 for adults, $7 for children 14 and under.

A special feature of the aquarium is a "shark and animal encounter," which costs $57.75 for divers or $28.85 for snorkelers. Divers, snorkelers, and experienced swimmers are able to feed, film, and photograph sharks, which are separated from them by a large window with feeding holes. In the Animal-Encounters section, swimmers are able to swim among stingrays, lobsters, tarpons, parrotfish, and other marine life, feeding and photographing these creatures in a controlled environment where safety is always a consideration. The Seaquarium is also home to Curaçao's only full-facility, palm-shaded, white-sand beach.

Seaworld Explorer 𝄇 is a semi-submersible submarine that departs daily at 4:30pm on hour-long journeys into the deep. You're taken on a tour of submerged wrecks off the shores of Curaçao and are treated to close encounters of coral reefs with their rainbow-hued tropical fish. The *Explorer* has a barge top that submerges only 5 or so feet under the water, but the submerged section has wide glass windows allowing passengers underwater views, which can extend for 110 feet or so. Reservations must be made a day in advance by calling © **599/ 9-4610011.** Adults pay $33; children 11 and under are charged $19.

SIGHTSEEING TOURS

Taber Tours, Dokweg (© **599/9-7376637**), offers several tours to points of interest on Curaçao. The tour through Willemstad, to the Curaçao Liqueur distillery, through the residential area and the Bloempot shopping center, and to the Curaçao Museum (admission fee included in the tour price) costs $12.50 for adults, $6.25 for children 11 and under.

The easiest way to go exploring is to take a 1¼-hour **trolley tour,** visiting the highlights of Willemstad. The open-sided cars, pulled by a silent "locomotive," make two tours each week—Monday at 11am and Wednesday at 4pm. The tour begins at Fort Amsterdam near the Queen Emma Pontoon Bridge. The cost is $10 for adults or $5 for children 2 to 12 (free for children 1 and under). Call © **599/9-4610011** for more information.

7 Shopping 𝄇𝄇

Curaçao is a shopper's paradise. Some 200 shops line the major shopping malls of such streets as Heerenstraat and Breedestraat. Right in the heart of Willemstad, the **Punda** shopping area is a 5-block district. Most stores are open Monday to Saturday 8am to noon and 2 to 6pm (some 8am–6pm). When cruise ships are in port, stores are also open for a few hours on Sunday and holidays. To avoid the cruise ship crowds, do your shopping in the morning.

Look for good buys in French perfumes, Dutch Delft blue souvenirs, finely woven Italian silks, Japanese and German cameras, jewelry, silver, Swiss watches, linens, leather goods, liquor, and island-made rum and liqueurs, especially Curaçao liqueur, some of which has a distinctive blue color. The island is famous for its 5-pound "wheels" of Gouda or Edam cheese. It also sells wooden shoes, although we're not sure what you'd do with them. Some of its stores also stock some good buys in intricate lacework imported from Portugal, China, and everywhere between. If you're a street shopper and want something colorful, consider one of the woodcarvings or flamboyant paintings from Haiti or the Dominican Republic. Street vendors hawk both at any of the main plazas.

Incidentally, Curaçao is not technically a free port, but import levies are low, so its prices are often inexpensive.

Kas di Arte Kursou, Breedestraat 126, Otrabanda (© **599/9-46238888**), in a 19th-century mansion in Otrabanda near the cruise ship terminal, sells unique souvenirs such as one-of-a-kind T-shirts, all handmade by local artists. The gallery also has changing exhibits of paintings, plus a sculpture gallery.

Every garment sold in **Bamali,** Breedestraat 2 (© **599/9-4612258**), is designed and, in many cases, crafted by the storeowners. Influenced largely by Indonesian patterns, the airy attire includes V-neck cotton pullovers perfect for a casual, hot-weather climate, as well as linen shifts, often in batik prints, appropriate for a glamorous cocktail party. Most pieces here are for women; all are made from all-natural materials, such as cotton, silk, and linen, and there's also a limited array of sandals and leather bags. **Benetton,** Madurostraat 4 (© **599/9-4614619**), has invaded Curaçao with all its many colors. Some items are marked down by about 20% off stateside prices (this is done to get rid of surplus stock from the previous season); in-season clothing is available as well.

Bert Knubben Black Koral Art Studio, in the Princess Beach Resort & Casino, Dr. Martin Luther King Blvd. (© **599/9-4652122**), is a name synonymous with craftsmanship and quality. Although it's illegal to collect black coral here, an exception was made for Bert, a diver who has been harvesting corals and fashioning them into fine jewelry and objets d'art for more than 35 years. Collectors avidly seek out this type of coral, not only for the quality of its craftsmanship, but also because it's becoming increasingly rare and might one day not be offered for sale at all.

Gandelman Jewelers, Breedestraat 35, Punda (© **599/9-4611854**), is the island's best and most reliable source for jewelry, often exquisitely designed and set with diamonds, rubies, emeralds, sapphires, and other gemstones. You'll also find watches and the unique line of Prima Classe leather goods embossed with the world map.

Little Holland, Braedestraat 37, Punda (© **599/9-4611768**), specializes in silk neckties, Nautica shorts and shirts, and, most important, a sophisticated array of cigars. Crafted in Cuba, the Dominican Republic, and Brazil, they include some of the most prestigious names in smoke, including Montecristos, Cohiba, and Churchills. (Remember, it's still illegal to bring Cuban cigars into the United States; smoke them here.)

Electronics are a good buy on Curaçao, as they can be sold duty-free; we recommend the very reliable **Boolchand's,** Heerenstraat 4B, Punda (© **599/9-4612262**), in business since 1930. If you can't find what you're looking for, try **Palais Hindu,** Heerenstraat 17 (© **599/9-4616897**), which sells a wide range of video and cassette recorders, photographic equipment, and watches.

Penha & Sons, Heerenstraat 1 (© **599/9-4612266**), in the oldest building in town (1708), has a history dating from 1865. It has long been known for its fine selection of perfumes, cosmetics, and designer clothing (for both men and women). It distributes such names as Calvin Klein, Yves Saint Laurent, Elizabeth Arden, Clarins, and Estée Lauder, among others.

La Casa Amarilla (The Yellow House), Breedestraat 46 (© **599/9-4613222**), in a yellow-and-white 19th-century building and operating since 1887, sells an intriguing collection of perfume and cosmetics from all over the world and is an agent of Christian Dior, Guerlain, Cartier, and Van Cleef & Arpels.

At **Landhuis Groot Santa Martha,** Santa Martha (© **599/9-8641559**), crafts-people with disabilities fashion unusual handcrafts, some evoking those found in South America. **Yoqui,** De Rouvilleweg 9A (© **599/9-4627533**), sells an unusual collection of artifacts from the Incas and the Mayan Indians, most made of clay and onyx. There's also contemporary tribal paintings done on leather and bark.

Should you, like many visitors from Venezuela, develop a shopping craze, there are a lot more stores to check out, including **Perfume Place,** Braastraat 23 (© **599/9-4617462**), offering all the big names in perfume and cosmetics, and **New Amsterdam,** Gomerzpein 14 (© **599/9-4612437**), a long-established store known for its Hummel figurines and hand-embroidered tablecloths, among other items. Handcrafts from the region and items from South America are displayed at the **Arawak Craft Factory,** Cruise Terminal, Otrabanda (© **599/9-4627249**). For novelties and souvenirs, head for **Warenhaus Van Der Ree,** Breedestraat 5, Punda (© **599/9-4611645**).

8 Curaçao After Dark

Most of the nightlife spins around the island's **casinos:** the **Marriott Beach Resort,** Piscadera Bay (© **599/9-7368800**); **Holiday Beach Hotel & Casino,** Pater Euwensweg 31, Otrabanda (© **599/9-4625400**); **Plaza Hotel & Casino,** Plaza Piar, in Willemstad (© **599/9-4612500**); **Porto Paseo Hotel & Casino,** De Rouvilleweg 47 in Willemstad (© **599/9-4627878**); and **Princess Beach Resort & Casino,** Martin Luther King Blvd. 8 (© **599/9-7367888**).

Emerald Casino at the Marriott is especially popular, designed to resemble an open-air courtyard. It features 143 slot machines, 6 blackjack tables, 2 roulette wheels, 2 Caribbean stud poker tables, a craps table, a baccarat table, and a mini-baccarat table. The casino at the **Princess Beach Hotel** is the liveliest on the island. These hotel gaming houses usually start their action at 2pm, and some of them remain open until 4am. The Princess Beach serves complimentary drinks.

The historic **Landhuis Brievengat** (see "Seeing the Sights," above), in addition to being a museum with island artifacts, is also the site of Wednesday, Friday, and Sunday *rijsttafel* parties. They begin at 7:30pm, require an admission fee of $8 (which includes the first drink), and feature heaping portions of *rijsttafel* that start at $16.50 each. A platform is set up amid the flamboyant trees nearby, and two bands alternate with each other to provide a pleasant ambience. Call before you go, as this event is very popular, especially on Friday night.

The landlocked, flat, and somewhat dusty neighborhood of **Salinja** is now the nightlife capital of Curaçao. Among the best of them is **Blues,** in the Avila Beach Hotel, Penstraat 130 (© **599/9-4614377**), a restaurant with a hopping bar that's packed every night except Mondays. Live jazz is offered Thursday 7pm to midnight and Saturday 9pm to 1:30am. No cover.

Façade, Lindbergh 32 (© **599/9-4614640**), in the Salinja district, is one of the most popular discos on the island. Spread over several different levels of a modern building, it has a huge bar, three dance floors, and live music nightly. It's open Wednesday to Sunday 8pm to 3am. The cover is $5 to $10.

For other nighttime diversions, begin the evening with wine and tapas served at **Rum Runners,** Otrabanda Waterfront, De Rouvilleweg 9 (© **599/9-4623038**), which gets rowdy at times. On Friday and Saturday nights the place to be is **Ole! Ole!,** Salina (© **599/9-4617707**), offering live music. If you like to party on the beach, head for **Hook's Hut,** Piscadera Bay (© **599/9-4626575**), where jazz is a regular feature, and you can find some of the best Cuban salsa.

10

Dominica

Dominica's meager beaches aren't worth the effort to get here, but its landscape is. Untamed, unspoiled Dominica (pronounced "Dom-in-*ee-ka*") is known for clear rivers and waterfalls, hot springs, and boiling lakes. According to myth, it has 365 "rivers"—one for each day of the year. This is the most rugged of the Caribbean islands, too. Nature lovers will experience a wild Caribbean setting, as well as the rural life that has largely disappeared on the more developed islands. This is, after all, one of the poorest and least developed islands in the Caribbean. Many of Dominica's citizens make a subsistence living from fishing or living off the land. Come here for lush tropical beauty, not fancy beach resorts.

The cost of living here is the lowest of all the West Indies islands. Imported items, of course, carry high price tags, but if you stick to local produce, you can eat well and inexpensively. Hotel rates are very low, but the rooms will be quite basic—spartan but clean.

Dominica, with a population of 71,000, lies in the eastern Caribbean, between Guadeloupe to the north and Martinique to the south. English is the official language, but a French patois is widely spoken. The Caribs, the indigenous people of the Caribbean, live as a community on the northeast of the island. The art and craft of traditional basketry is still practiced and is unique to today's Carib community, whose numbers have dwindled to 3,000.

The mountainous island is 29 miles long and 16 miles wide, with a total land area of 290 square miles, many of which have never been seen by explorers.

Because of the pristine coral reefs, dramatic drop-offs, and shipwrecks found in the crystal-clear waters with visibility of 100 feet plus, scuba diving is becoming increasingly popular, particularly off the west coast, site of Dominica's two dive operations.

Yearly rainfall varies from 50 inches (1.3m) along the dry west coast to as much as 350 inches (8.9m) in the tropical rain forests of the mountainous interior, where downpours are not uncommon.

Clothing is casual, including light summer wear for most of the year. However, take along walking shoes for those trips into the mountains and a sweater for cooler evenings. Bikinis and swimwear should not be worn on the streets of the capital city, Roseau, or in the villages.

1 Essentials

VISITOR INFORMATION

Before you go, you can contact the **Dominica Tourist Office** at 10 E. 21st St., Suite 600, New York, NY 10010 (✆ **212/475-7542**). In England, contact the **Office of the Dominica High Commission London,** 1 Collingham Gardens, London SW5 0HW (✆ **020/7370-5194**). The official website is **www. dominica.dm.**

On the island, the **Dominica Tourist Information Office** is on the Old Market Plaza, Roseau, with administrative offices at the National Development Corporation offices, Valley Road (© **767/448-2186**). It's open Monday 8am to 5pm and Tuesday to Friday 8am to 4pm. Also, there are **information bureaus** at Melville Hall Airport (© **767/445-7051**) and Canefield Airport (© **767/449-1242**).

GETTING THERE

BY PLANE   There are two airports on Dominica, neither of which is large enough to handle a jet; therefore, there are no direct flights from North America. The **Melville Hall Airport** (© **767/445-7100**) is on the northeastern coast, almost diagonally across the island from the capital, Roseau, which is on the southwestern coast. Should you land at Melville Hall, there's a 1½-hour taxi ride into Roseau, a tour across the island through the forest and coastal villages. The fare from Melville Hall to Roseau is $18 per person, and drivers have the right to gather up at least four passengers in their cabs. Private use of a taxi could cost $50.

The newer **Canefield Airport** (© **767/449-1199**) is about a 15-minute taxi ride to the north of Roseau. The 2,000-foot airstrip accommodates smaller planes than those that can land at Melville Hall. From here, the typical taxi fare into town is $15. There's also a public bus (with an *H* that precedes the number on the license plate), which charges $2 per person. The buses come every 20 minutes and hold between 15 and 18 passengers.

For many Americans, the easiest way to reach Dominica is to take the daily **American Eagle** (© **800/433-7300**) flight from San Juan. From Thursday to Sunday there is also a second flight. From Antigua, you can board one of the two daily **LIAT** (© **800/468-0482** in the U.S. and Canada, or 767/448-2422) flights to Dominica.

It's also possible to fly to Guadeloupe (see "Getting There" in chapter 13) and make a connection to Dominica on **Air Caraíbe** (© **767/448-2181**). This airline has two flights a day to Dominica except on Sunday, when there is no morning flight (flying time is 30 min.).

Two minor airlines also serve Dominica: **Helen Air** (© **767/448-2181**) flies in from Barbados and St. Lucia, arriving two times a day at both the Canefield and Melville Hall airports, and **Cardinal Airlines** (© **767/449-0600**) wings in from the islands of Antigua, Barbados, and Dutch St. Maarten, arriving at Canefield daily.

BY BOAT   The *Caribbean Express* (© **596/63-12-11,** or 767/448-2181 on Dominica), sailing from the French West Indies, runs between Guadeloupe in the north to Martinique in the south, and Dominica is a port of call along the way. Call for exact schedules. Departures are Friday to Wednesday.

In addition, car ferries sail from Pointe-à-Pitre on Martinique to Roseau five to seven times a week, depending on demand. For information about schedules, contact **White Church Travel,** 5 Great Marlborough St. in Roseau (© **767/448-2181**). A round-trip fare costs EC$224.50 ($83.15), and a one-way fare is EC$113 ($41.85).

GETTING AROUND

Many of the places to stay are found in or very close to Roseau, the capital.

BY TAXI   At either the Melville Hall or Canefield airports, you can rent a taxi. The government regulates prices (airport fares are covered under "Getting There," above). If you want to see the island by taxi, rates are about $18 per car for each hour of touring, and as many as four passengers can go along at the same time.

Airport
Beach
Mountain

Anchorage Hotel **6**
Castle Comfort Lodge **5**
Floral Gardens **2**
Hummingbird Inn **4**
Papillote Wilderness Retreat **3**
Picard Beach Cottage Resort **1**
Zandoli Inn **7**

BY RENTAL CAR If you rent a car, a fee of EC$30 ($11.10) is charged to obtain a driver's license, which is available at the airports. There are 310 miles of newly paved roads on Dominica, and only in a few areas is a four-wheel-drive necessary. *Driving is on the left.*

Most U.S. vacationers reserve their car in advance from the local representative of **Avis,** 4 High St. in Roseau (© **800/331-1212** or 767/448-2481), although we've found the service here poor.

There are also a handful of small, usually family-owned car-rental companies, the condition and price of whose vehicles vary widely. Their ranks include **Valley Rent-a-Car,** Goodwill Road in Roseau (© **767/448-3233**); **Wide Range,** 79 Bath Rd., Roseau (© **767/448-2198**); and **Best Deal Car Rental,** 15 Hanover St. in Roseau (© **767/449-9204**).

BY MINIBUS The public transportation system consists of private minibus service between Roseau and the rest of Dominica. These minibuses, each of which is painted and sometimes garishly decorated according to the tastes of their individual owners, are filled mainly with schoolchildren, workers, and country people who need to come into Roseau. They're identified by the letter *H* preceding their license number. Taxis may be a more reliable means of transport for visitors, but there are hotels at which buses call during the course of the day. Fares range from $1.25 to $3.35.

 Fun Fact SPECIAL EVENTS

National Day celebrations on November 3 commemorate Columbus's discovery of Dominica in 1493 and its independence in 1978. Cultural celebrations of the island's traditional dance, music, song, and storytelling begin in mid-October and continue to Community Day, November 4, when people undertake community-based projects.

FAST FACTS: Dominica

Banking Hours Banks are open Monday to Thursday 8am to 3pm and Friday 8am to 5pm.

Currency Dominica uses the **Eastern Caribbean dollar (EC$)**, worth about EC$2.70 to U.S.$1. *Prices in this chapter are given in U.S. dollars unless otherwise indicated.*

Customs Dominica is lenient, allowing you to bring in personal and household effects, plus 200 cigarettes, 50 cigars, and 40 ounces of liquor or wine per person.

Documents To enter, U.S. and Canadian citizens must have a passport). In addition, an ongoing or return ticket must be shown. British visitors should have a valid passport.

Drugstores The island's best-stocked drugstore is **Jolly's Pharmacy,** with two branches in Roseau at 37 Great George St. and at 12 King George V St. Both branches share the same phone number and hours (© **767/ 448-3388**). It's open Monday to Thursday 8am to 4:30pm, Friday 8am to 5pm, and Saturday 8am to 1:30pm. They also have a 24-hour prescription service available at the same number for after-hours needs.

Electricity The electricity is 220–240 volts AC (50 cycles), so both adapters and transformers are necessary for North American appliances. It's advisable to take a flashlight with you to Dominica, in case of power outages.

Emergencies Dial © **999** to reach the police, report a fire, or summon an ambulance.

Hospitals The island hospital is **Princess Margaret Hospital,** Federation Drive, Goodwill (© **767/448-2231**). However, those with serious medical complications might want to forgo a visit to Dominica, as island medical facilities are often inadequate.

Language English is the official language. Locals often speak a Creole-French patois.

Safety Although crime is rare here, you should still safeguard your valuables. Never leave them unattended on the beach or left alone in a locked car.

Taxes A 10% government room tax is added to every hotel accommodation bill, and a 3% tax is tacked onto the price of alcoholic drinks and food items. Anyone who remains on Dominica for more than 24 hours must pay a $12 (U.S.) departure tax.

Telecommunications Dominica maintains phone, telegraph, teletype, Telex, and fax connections with the rest of the world. International direct dialing (IDD) is available, as well as U.S. direct service through AT&T. To call Dominica from another island within the Caribbean, just dial **767**, plus the seven-digit local number.

Time Dominica is on Atlantic standard time, 1 hour ahead of eastern standard time in the United States. Dominica does not observe daylight saving time, so when the United States changes to daylight saving time, clocks in Dominica and the U.S. east coast tell the same time.

Tipping Most hotels and restaurants add a 10% service charge to all bills. When this charge has not been included, tipping is up to you.

Water The water is drinkable from the taps and in the high mountain country. Pollution is hardly a problem here.

Weather Daytime temperatures average between 70°F and 85°F (21°C and 29.4°C). Nights are much cooler, especially in the mountains. The rainy season is June to October, when there can be warnings of hurricane activity. Regrettably, Dominica lies in the "hurricane path," and fierce storms have taken their toll on the island over the years.

2 Accommodations You Can Afford

Anchorage Hotel   Recently renovated, the Anchorage is at Castle Comfort, a half-mile south of Roseau. For the active traveler, there is no finer choice, as scuba diving, whale-watching, hiking, fishing, and bird-sighting are given great emphasis here. The Armour family provides small rooms with two double beds and a shower or bathtub, plus a balcony overlooking a pool. The best rooms open onto views of the Caribbean Sea and each contain two double beds with firm mattresses. The other rooms are more standard, with comfortable twin beds or one double. Recent renovations have much improved this property, and bathrooms are adequate, with showers and decent shelf space.

Despite being located at the shore, there's little or no sandy beach available here, so guests spend their days around the pool. However, the hotel has its own jetty, you can swim off a pebble beach, and there's a squash court. The hotel's French and Caribbean cuisine is simple, with an emphasis on fresh fish and vegetables. Nonresidents must ask permission to use the pool, and they can also visit for meals. A West Indian band plays music twice a week for dancing. On Thursday night, there's a buffet accompanied by a live band.

Castle Comfort (P.O. Box 34), Roseau, Dominica, W.I. ℂ **767/448-2638.** Fax 767/448-5680. anchorage@ mail.tod.dm. 32 units. Year-round $60–$80 single; $80–$100 double. Children 11 and under granted 50% reductions. MAP (breakfast and dinner) $35 per person extra. AE, DC, DISC, MC, V. **Amenities:** Restaurant; pool, room service, babysitting, laundry. *In room:* A/C, TV.

Floral Gardens   Everything about this place pays homage to the surrounding scenic jungles. Situated near the edge of the Carib Indian Reservation, adjacent to the Layou River, it appeals to hikers, naturalists, birders, and students of Indian culture. The Floral Gardens is quietly proud of its allure as a funky, nonstandard hotel, quite different from its larger and more anonymous competitors. The older part is designed vaguely like a tropical version of a Swiss chalet, with latticed windows and flowerboxes. The bedrooms in the newer section are preferable to those in the original house because they're larger, not as noisy, and get more sunlight. Furnishings, including beds with well-worn mattresses, are utterly basic, with small showers that may or may not have hot water. An on-site restaurant (Floral Gardens Restaurant; see "Great Deals on Dining," below) serves simple West Indian cuisine to residents and group tours, which sometimes stop in as part of guided jaunts through Dominica. Your host is O. J. Seraphin, a former prime minister. His wife, Lily, ably assists him, and as a team they are the most welcoming and dynamic hosts on the island.

Concord Village (P.O. Box 192), Roseau, Dominica, W.I. ☎ 767/445-7636. Fax 767/445-7333. 15 units. Year-round $45 single; $60 double; $70 apt for 2 with kitchenette. AE, MC, V. **Amenities:** Restaurant.

Hummingbird Inn ☆ *Value*   A short drive from Roseau and the Canefield Airport and a 2-minute walk to the beach, this hilltop retreat is a great little bargain. Opening onto panoramic views, the rooms are in two bungalows and have louvered windows and doors to capture the breezes in lieu of air-conditioning. Ceiling fans hum day and night, and you can also retreat to terraces with hammocks. Each accommodation has bedside tables and reading lamps (not always a guarantee on Dominica). The handmade quilts on the beds, which have excellent mattresses, add a homey touch. One four-poster bed, a mammoth wooden affair, is 250 years old. Bathrooms are small but well maintained, and each has a shower. This is a friendly, family-style place, and there are lovely gardens with exotic plants that attract both hummingbirds and iguanas. The local cook is one of the best on the island, and she'll pack a picnic lunch for you. The restaurant is open to nonguests without a reservation. Many diners come here to sample "mountain chicken" (frogs' legs).

Morne Daniel (P.O. Box 1901), Roseau, Dominica, W.I. ☎/fax 767/449-1042. www.thehummingbirdinn.com. 10 units. Winter $65 single or double; $110 suite. Off-season $55 single or double; $80–$92 suite. Extra person $20; children 11 and under stay free in parents' room. MAP $20 per person extra. AE, DC, DISC, MC, V. **Amenities:** Restaurant. *In room:* Ceiling fans.

Papillote Wilderness Retreat ☆☆ *Finds*   This property is run by the Jean-Baptistes: Cuthbert, who handles the restaurant, and his wife, Anne Grey, who was a marine scientist. Their unique resort, 4 miles east of Roseau, stands right in the middle of Papillote Forest, at the foothills of Morne Macaque. In this remote setting, you're surrounded by exotic fruits, flowers, and herb gardens. The rooms have a rustic, log-cabin atmosphere, but modern comforts, such as up-to-date bathrooms with plenty of hot water, await you.

Don't expect constantly sunny weather, since this part of the jungle is known for its downpours, but that's what keeps the orchids, begonias, and brilliantly colored bromeliads lush. The 12 acres of sloping and forested land have a labyrinth of stone walls and trails, beside which flow freshwater streams, a few of which come from hot mineral springs. Natural hot mineral baths are available, and you'll be directed to a secluded waterfall where you can swim in the river. The Jean-Baptistes also run a boutique that sells Dominican products, including appliquéd quilts made by local artisans. Even if you don't stay here, it's an experience to dine on the thatch-roofed terrace.

Trafalgar Falls Rd. (P.O. Box 2287), Roseau, Dominica, W.I. ☎ 767/448-2287. Fax 767/448-2285. www.papillote.dm. 7 units. Year-round $90 single; $95 double; $105 suite. MAP (breakfast and dinner) $35 per person extra. AE, MC, V. Closed Aug 15–Oct 15. **Amenities:** Restaurant, bar, room service, laundry. *In room:* Ceiling fans, no phone.

WORTH A SPLURGE

Picard Beach Cottage Resort ☆   This is the best deal on the island if you want to stay in a cozy West Indian cottage. Here you'll find eight Dominican-style, stained-wood cottages, built in the 18th century, set on landscaped grounds opening on the beach. There's space in the living and dining area for two single beds. The decor is plain motel style, with flowery bed linens and good mattresses. The shower-only bathrooms are small but well kept. A dive shop is about a 5-minute walk away.

Picard Beach, Portsmouth, Dominica, W.I. (C) **767/445-5142.** Fax 767/445-5599. www.delphis.dm/ picard.htm. 8 cottages. Winter $100–$120 cottage for 1; $160–$180 cottage for 2. Off-season 50% reductions. Children 12 and under stay free in parents' room. MAP (breakfast and dinner) $30 per person extra. AE, MC, V. **Amenities:** Restaurant, pool. *In room:* Kitchenette, ceiling fan.

Zandoli Inn   On the most southerly coast of the island, a 25-minute drive from Roseau, this country inn attracts discerning guests who want maximum comfort but don't want to pay a lot of money for it. The hamlet of Stowe itself offers the rugged geography and abundant flora for which Dominica is known. The inn is nestled 80 feet above the sea in a secluded 6-acre forest garden. From the balconies and dining terrace, there are panoramas in all directions. Footpaths riddle the property, inviting hikes. The accommodations are spacious, with good beds and balconies that open onto views of either the coastline or the mountains. Each room has a small private bathroom with solar-generated hot water showers. There are mosquito nets and fans in each room. Other features include a shaded plunge pool area with a sea view. There's even a stargazing terrace. As there are a fair number of stairs, it is not wheelchair accessible, nor is it suitable for children under 12. The food is excellent, relying on local ingredients whenever possible.

Roche Cassee, Stowe (P.O. Box 2099), Dominica, W.I. (C) **767/446-3161.** Fax 767/446-3344. www.zandoli. com. 5 units. Winter $145 single; $160 double. Off-season $125 single; $135 double. Extra person $40. AE, DISC, MC, V. **Amenities:** Restaurant, pool, hiking paths. *In room:* Ceiling fans, mosquito nets, no phone.

3 Great Deals on Dining

It's customary to eat at your hotel, although Dominica has a string of independent restaurants. Dress is casual. If you're going out in the evening, always call to make sure your dining choice is actually open and that you have proper transportation there and back.

Callaloo Restaurant WEST INDIAN   When you enter this restaurant, you're greeted by a collection of local art on the walls, including straw mats, paintings, and maps of the route Christopher Columbus used when he sailed the Caribbean. Touted as one of the few remaining original Caribbean restaurants in the region, it offers patrons a taste of the island. The dinner prices include three courses, but lunch is the best time to find a real bargain. The Callaloo's forte is the mountain chicken (frogs' legs) served in a variety of ways, including fried, Creole style, and in a garlic-butter sauce. The menu also features *callaloo* soup (puréed *dasheen* leaves seasoned with herbs, spices, coconut cream, and bits of crayfish); curried conch; and chicken, baked or fried. For a finale, try one of the homemade desserts. Rooms above the restaurant are available for rent and cost $40 to $65 per night.

66 King George V St. (C) **767/448-3386.** Reservations recommended. Main courses EC$20–EC$45 ($7.40–$16.65); lunch EC$30–EC$55 ($11.10–$20.35). AE, DISC, MC, V. Mon–Sat 8am–10pm; Sun 8am–9pm.

Floral Gardens Restaurant WEST INDIAN   Located at the Floral Gardens Hotel about 10 miles from the Melville Hall Airport, this simple eatery specializes in Creole cuisine. For starters, try the pumpkin *accras* (grated pumpkin mixed with herbs and spices, then deep-fried and served with a pepper sauce) or the *callaloo* soup. The main courses include chicken, mountain goat, mutton, rabbit, and seafood such as lobster, codfish, and crab. Save room for dessert, such as the banana flambé lit up in Dominica's local rum.

In the Floral Gardens Hotel, Concord Rd. © **767/445-7636.** Reservations recommended. Main courses EC$20–EC$45 ($7.40–$16.65). AE, MC, V. Daily 7am–11pm.

Forest Bistro CARIBBEAN   On the southwestern coast, the Forest Bistro is set in a lush tropical section of the island, cozy, and secluded, with cliffs as a backdrop and a panoramic vista of the Caribbean from the tables. Cows roam among the acres of lime trees, and the whole place has such a bucolic setting, you'd want to come here even if the food weren't good. But the cuisine is excellent, well prepared, and made whenever possible with the freshest of ingredients, often grown by your hosts, Andre and Joyce Charles. The restaurant on this 5-acre dairy farm is actually the top floors of the Charles home. Joyce is a topnotch chef, having worked at some of the island's finest restaurants. Her talent is particularly obvious in her fresh fish dishes. The farm also provides an endless source of refreshing drinks, including lime squash, passion fruit, grapefruit, and fresh coconut water. At lunch you can order some of the island's most delightful soups, made with peas, pumpkin, *callaloo*, or papaya. Stick to the fish unless you're a total vegetarian; then you might opt for one of the delicious Creole-style vegetarian dishes, such as savory eggplant.

Soufrière. © **767/448-7104.** Reservations essential. Main courses EC$25–EC$35 ($9.25–$12.95). Daily 11am–9pm.

Papillote Wilderness Retreat ⋆ *Finds* CREOLE/CARIBBEAN   Even if you're not staying here, come by taxi for lunch; it's only 4 miles east of Roseau. For dinner, you'll need to make arrangements. Amid exotic flowers, century-old trees, and filtered sunlight, you'll dine overlooking a gorgeous vista of rivers and mountains. The array of healthful food includes flying fish and truly delectable freshwater prawns known as *bookh.* Mountain chicken (frogs' legs) appears in season, as does kingfish. Breadfruit or *dasheen* puffs merit a taste if you've never tried them, and tropical salads are filled with flavor. Our favorite dishes include "the seafood symphony" and chicken rain forest (sautéed with orange, papaya, and banana, and wrapped in a banana leaf).

Trafalgar Falls Rd. © **767/448-2287.** Reservations recommended for lunch, required for dinner. Main courses EC$25–EC$60 ($9.25–$22.20). AE, DISC, MC, V. Daily 7:30am–10pm; dinner served at 7:30pm.

Pearl's Cuisine ⋆ *Finds* CARIBBEAN   In this restored Creole house with a veranda, Chef Pearl is the hearty empress and enjoys a certain celebrity in town for her island delicacies. Come here for a true taste of Dominica. Begin with one of her tropical fruit juices, then go on to sample mountain chicken (frogs' legs) or perhaps freshly caught crayfish. Whenever lobster is available, it's served at dinner any way you want it. She also makes some mean pork chops, and her curried goat will make a man of you, even if you're a woman. Try the rice and spareribs or the codfish and plantains if you want to really go local.

50 King George V St., Rouseau. © **767/448-8707.** EC$5–EC$30 ($1.85–$11.10) lunch, EC$20–EC$60 ($7.40–$22.20) dinner. AE, DC, MC, V. Daily 9am–9pm.

World of Food Restaurant and Bar ⋆⋆ CREOLE   This is one of the most charming Creole restaurants in town. In the 1930s, the garden containing this restaurant belonged to the novelist Jean Rhys, author of *Wide Sargasso Sea.* Some say that its owner, Vena McDougal, is the best Creole cook in town, and we more or less agree, although the competition is stiff. You can have a drink at the stone-walled building at the far end of the garden, but many guests select one of the tables in the shadow of a large mango tree. Specialties include steamed fish or fish steak, curried goat, chicken-filled rôti, black pudding, breadfruit puffs, conch, and *tee-tee-ree* (fried fish cakes). Vena also makes the best rum punches on the island.

In Vena's Hotel, 48 Cork St. (with another entrance on Field's Lane). ☎ **767/448-3286.** Main courses EC$28–EC$58 ($10.35–$21.50). MC, V. Daily 7:30am–11pm.

4 Hitting the Beaches

If you demand great beaches as part of your Caribbean vacation, don't come here, for Dominica has some of the worst beaches in the Caribbean. Most of the island's beaches are rocky with gray-black volcanic sand. Some beaches, even though they don't have great sand or shade, nevertheless are still good for diving or snorkeling in the turquoise waters surrounding the island.

The best beach on the island, **Picard Beach,** lies on the northwest coast. It stretches for about 2 miles, a strip of grayish sand with palm trees as a backdrop. It is ideal for snorkeling or windsurfing, but not much else. Guests can drop in for food and drink at the Picard Beach Cottage Resort (see "Accommodations You Can Afford," earlier in this chapter) or the Coconut Beach Hotel, both of which lie along this beach.

On the northeast coast, a quartet of beaches is among the island's most beautiful, although none is ideal for swimming. They are **L'Anse Noire, Hodges Beach, Woodford Hill Bay,** and **Hampstead Beach.** Divers and snorkelers seek them out, although at times their turbulent waters make the pursuit of either of those sports less than ideal. The waters off the coasts of all these beaches have strong currents, so be duly warned. That island you can see in the distance is Marie Galante, which is an offshore island of Guadeloupe.

The southwest coast also has some beaches, but the sand here is black and studded with rocks. Nonetheless, snorkelers and scuba divers flock to **Soufrière Bay Beach** and **Scotts Head Beach.** The snorkeling and diving here are excellent because of the gin-clear waters, the sudden drop-offs, and the underwater walls, which are stunning. At one point along the coast, volcanic vents puff steam into the sea. Divers claim it's like swimming in champagne, and locals have dubbed the spot "Champagne."

Near the hamlet of La Plaine, on the southeast coast, is one final beach, **Bout Sable Bay.** Again, it's not suitable for swimming, but it is a dramatic beach nonetheless, set against towering chalky red cliffs overlooking the turbulent Atlantic. Waters are too churned up for safe swimming.

5 Sports & Other Outdoor Pursuits

HIKING   Wild and untamed Dominica offers very experienced and physically fit hikers some of the most bizarre geological oddities in the Caribbean. Sights include scalding lava covered with a hot, thin, and not-very-stable crust; a boiling lake where mountain streams turn to vapor as they come into contact with super-heated volcanic fissures; and a barren wasteland known as the Valley of Desolation.

All these attractions are in the 17,000 heavily forested acres of the **Morne Trois Pitons National Park,** in the island's south-central region (see "Seeing the Sights," below). You should go with a guide—they're in plentiful supply, waiting for your business in the village of Laudat. Or go to the office of the **Dominica National Park,** in the Botanical Gardens in Roseau (☎ **767/448-2401**), or to the Dominica Tourist Board (see "Essentials," earlier in this chapter).

Few markers appear en route, but the trek, which includes a real assortment of geological oddities, stretches 6 miles in both directions from Laudat to the Boiling Lake. Hikers bring their lunch and walk cautiously, particularly in districts peppered with bubbling hot springs. Regardless of where you turn, you'll run into streams and waterfalls, the inevitable result of an island whose mountaintops receive up to 400 inches of rainfall a year. Winds on the summits are strong enough to have pushed one recreational climber to her death several years ago, so be careful. Ferns, orchids, trees, and epiphytes create a tangle of underbrush; insect, bird, and reptilian life is profuse.

During your trek, pay a visit to the **Titou Gorge,** a deep and very narrow ravine whose depths were created as lava floes cooled and contracted. On the way, there might be views of rare Sisserou and Jacquot parrots, monkeys, and vines whose growth seems to increase visibly on an hourly basis. The hill treks of Dominica have been described as "sometimes easy, sometimes hellish," and if it should happen to rain during your climb (and it rains very frequently on Dominica), your path is likely to become very slippery. But botanists and geologists agree with the assessment of experienced hikers, that climbs through the jungles of Dominica are the most rewarding in the Caribbean.

Locals warn that to proceed alone or in pairs on the island's badly marked trails into areas that can be physically treacherous is not a good idea. Forestry officials recommend **Ken's Hinterland Adventure Tours & Taxi Service,** 10A Old St., in Roseau (② 767/448-4850). Depending on their destination and the attractions they feature, treks cost $25 to $50 per person for up to four participants and require 4 to 8 hours round-trip. Transportation from Roseau in a minivan to the starting point of your hill climb is usually included in the price.

KAYAKING   Dominica is probably the best place in all the Caribbean for kayaking. You can rent a kayak for $26 for a half-day, then go on a unique adventure around the rivers and coastline of the lushest island in the West Indies. **Nature Island Dive,** in Roseau (② 767/449-8181), offers rentals and gives the best advice. You can combine bird-watching, swimming, and snorkeling as you glide along. Consider Soufrière Bay, a marine reserve in southwest Dominica. Off the west coast, you can discover tranquil Caribbean waters with rainbow-hued fish along the beaches in Mero, Salisbury, and the region of the Layou and Macoucherie Rivers.

SCUBA DIVING   Diving holidays in Dominica are becoming more and more popular. The underwater terrain is spectacular. Most of the diving is on the southwestern end of the island, with its dramatic drop-offs, walls, and pinnacles. These volcanic formations are interwoven with cuts, arches, ledges, and overhangs. A myriad of sponges, gorgonians, and corals cloak these ledges. An abundance of invertebrates, reef school fish, and unusual sea creatures such as sea horses, frogfish, batfish, and flying gunards attract the underwater photographer.

You can discover diving on the island with **Dive Dominica,** in the Castle Comfort Diving Lodge (P.O. Box 2253, Roseau Castle Comfort, Dominica, W.I.; ② 767/448-2188). Open-water certification (both NAUI and PADI) instruction is given. Two diving catamarans (45- and 33-ft. long, respectively), plus a handful of other, smaller boats used for groups of divers, get you to the dive sites in relative comfort. The dive outfit is closely linked to its on-site hotel, a 15-room lodge where at least 90% of the clientele check in as part of the outfit's dive packages. A 7-night dive package, double occupancy, where breakfasts and dinners are included as part of the price, along with five two-tank dives and one night dive, begins at $995 per person. A single tank dive goes for $45, a two-tank dive for $75, with a night dive costing $50. All rooms in the lodge are air-conditioned, and about half have TV and a telephone. On the premises is a bar (for residents and their guests only) and a Jacuzzi.

Divers from all over the world patronize the **Dive Centre,** at the Anchorage Hotel in Castle Comfort (© **767/448-2638**). A fully qualified PADI and NAUI staff awaits divers there. A single-tank dive costs $50; a double-tank dive, $65; and a one-tank night dive, $55. A unique whale and dolphin watch from 2pm to sunset is a popular feature, where all participants are actively engaged in trying to sight the faraway plumes of pods of whales, herds of dolphins, and even schools of flying fish. The price for a 3½-hour experience of communal straining to catch sight of the animals is $45 per person. On the way home (and not before), rum punches are served. Celebrity participants of this experience in the past have included author Peter Benchley. With a pool, classrooms, a private dock, a mini-flotilla of dive boats, and a well-trained and alert staff, this is the most complete dive resort on Dominica.

SWIMMING　The beaches might be lousy, but Dominica has some of the best river swimming in the Caribbean. It is said the little island has 365 rivers, one for every day of the year. The best bets for such activity are on the west coast at the **Picard** or the **Machoucherie rivers.** On the east coast the finest swimming is at **White River.** All the rivers are unpolluted, and you can do a little sunbathing or perhaps bring along a picnic lunch to enjoy along their banks. Consider also the **Layou River** and its gorges. Layou is the island's largest river, ranging from tranquil beach-lined pools ideal for swimming to deep gorges and turbulent rapids.

6 Seeing the Sights

Those making day trips to Dominica from other Caribbean islands will want to see the **Carib Indian Reservation** ★★ (© **767/448-2186**), in the northeast. In 1903 Britain got the Caribs to agree to live on 3,700 acres of land. Hence, this is the last remaining turf of the once-hostile tribe for whom the Caribbean was named. Their look is Mongolian, and they are no longer "pure-blooded," as they have married outside their tribe. Today they survive by fishing, growing food, and weaving baskets and vertiver grass mats, which they sell to the outside world. They still make dugout canoes, too.

It's like going back in time when you explore **Morne Trois Pitons National Park** ★★, a primordial rain forest. Mists rise gently over lush, dark-green growth, drifting up to blue-green peaks that have earned Dominica the title "Switzerland of the Caribbean." Framed by banks of giant ferns, rivers rush and tumble. Trees sprout orchids, and everything seems blanketed with some type of growth. Green sunlight filters down through trees, and roaring waterfalls create a blue mist.

One of the best starting points for a visit to the park is the village of **Laudat,** 7 miles from Roseau. Exploring the heart of Dominica is for serious botanists and only the most skilled hikers, who should never penetrate unmarked trails without a very experienced guide (see "Sports & Other Outdoor Pursuits," above).

Deep in the park is the **Emerald Pool Trail,** a half-mile nature trail that forms a circuit loop on a footpath passing through the forest to a pool with a beautiful waterfall. Downpours are frequent in the rain forest, and at high elevations cold winds blow. It lies 3½ miles northeast of Pont Casse.

(Value) **Cheap Thrills: What to See & Do for Free (Well, Almost) on Dominica**

- **Explore Jungle Jim Country.** In the Morne Trois Pitons National Park, you can explore one of the last island-based rain forests in the world. This lush, majestic blanket supports thousands of plants and animals. Precious and endangered wildlife are found in the area, which is the last refuge of the Sisserou or Imperial parrot. More than 160 other bird species live in the rain forest as well, particularly in the forested region of Syndicate in the foothills of Morne Diabolotin. The trail to the summit of the mountain also starts in Syndicate. The tour to the top takes 4 to 6 hours. If you'd like a close encounter with the rain forest, consider making the Floral Gardens hotel your choice of accommodations (see "Accommodations You Can Afford," earlier in this chapter).

- **Take a River Dip.** Almost everywhere you go on the island, you come across a river. The best places for swimming are under a waterfall, and there are dozens of them on the island. Almost all waterfalls have a refreshing pond at the base of them, ideal for a dip. The best places for a swim on the west coast are the Picard and Machoucherie rivers. The finest spot on the east coast is White River, near the village of La Plaine. The source for this river is a boiling lake. For a lazy day on the river, float and clamber down the Layou River, which starts in the settlement of Belles in the rain forest and works its way down through the Layou flats to the west coast.

- **Snorkel over Flamboyant Colors.** The western side of the Island, where nearly all the snorkeling takes place, is the leeside, meaning the waters are tranquil. In all, there are some 30 separate and

Five miles up from the **Roseau River Valley,** in the south-central sector of Dominica, **Trafalgar Falls** can be reached after you drive through the village of Trafalgar. You have to approach on foot, as the slopes are too steep for vehicles. After a 20-minute walk past growths of ginger plants and vanilla orchids, you arrive at the base, where a trio of falls converge into a rock-strewn pool.

The **Sulphur Springs** and the Boiling Lake east of Roseau are evidence of the island's volcanic past. Jeeps or Land Rovers can get quite close. This seemingly bubbling pool of gray mud sometimes belches smelly sulfurous fumes—the odor is like rotten eggs. Only the very fit should attempt the 6-hour round-trip to **Boiling Lake** ★★, the world's second-largest boiling lake. Go only with an experienced guide, as according to reports, some tourists lost their lives in the **Valley of Desolation;** they stumbled and fell into the boiling waters.

Finally, **Titou Gorge** is a deep and narrow gorge where it's possible to swim under a waterfall. Later you can get warm again in a hot sulfur spring close by. Again, a visit here is best attempted only with an experienced guide (arranged at the tourist office). The guide will transport you to the gorge and will know if swimming is dangerous, which it can be after heavy rainfall.

first-rate snorkeling areas immediately off the coast. Snorkelers can, for example, explore the underwater hot springs at Champagne and Toucari, or else the Coral Gardens off Salisbury, and they can meander along the southern shoreline of Scotts Head Beach and marvel at the outrageously flamboyant colors of more than 190 species of fish that call Dominica home. You'll see abundant marine life, prolific corals, and orange and yellow sponges, along with densely packed schools of rainbow-colored fish. The closeness of the reefs to shore makes snorkeling here among the best in the Caribbean, although it isn't a highly organized operation.

- **Bus Your Way Around the Island.** On most Caribbean islands we don't recommend buses; they're hot, inconvenient, and undependable. But Dominican buses—really minivans—afford great insights into local life. They're also a cheap way to get around. A trip between most towns costs only $3 one-way. These are privately owned vehicles, and everybody comes aboard, often loaded with parcels. Some are taking their wares, including fresh vegetables, to market. One driver told us, "We don't consider visitors who ride buses strangers—we consider them friends." Packed into the tight confines of these minivans, you can set out for adventures in all directions, going to the Carib Indian reservation or stopping off to wander around the old port city of Portsmouth. These vans cruise the island like taxis. Just hail one when you see one and tell the driver where you want to go. They travel daily from about 6am to 8pm. On some vans you'll get to meet the most interesting chickens—live ones, that is. What a way to go!

On the northwestern coast, **Portsmouth** is Dominica's second largest settlement. You can row up the Indian River in native canoes, visit the ruins of Fort Shirley in Cabrits National Park, and bathe at Sandy Beach on Douglas Bay and Prince Rupert Bay.

Cabrits National Park 🕸🕸, on the northwestern coast, 2 miles south of Douglas Bay (© **767/448-2732**), is a 1,313-acre protected site containing mountain scenery, tropical forests, swampland, volcanic sand beaches, coral reefs, and the ruins of a fortified, 18th-century garrison of British, then French construction. The park's land area is a panoramic promontory formed by twin peaks of extinct volcanoes, overlooking beaches, with Douglas Bay on one side and Prince Rupert Bay across the headland. Entrance is EC$5.30 ($1.95).

7 Shopping

Store hours are usually Monday to Friday 8am to 5pm and Saturday 9am to 1pm.

In Roseau, the **Old Market Plaza,** of historical significance as a former slave-trading market and more recently the site of a Wednesday-, Friday-, and Saturday-morning vegetable market, now houses three craft shops, each specializing in coconut, straw, and Carib craft products.

Tips **Searching for Moby Dick**

You'll see more sperm whales, pilot whales, killer whales, and dolphins during **whale- and dolphin-watching trips** off Dominica than off any other island in the Caribbean. The **Anchorage Hotel,** at Castle Comfort (© **767/448-2638**), offers the best tours; a 4-hour trip costs $40 (children under 12 pay half-price). The vessels leave the dock every Wednesday and Sunday at 2pm.

Tropicrafts Island Mats, 41 Queen Mary St. and Turkey Lane (© **767/448-2747**), offers the well-known grass rugs handmade and woven in several intricate patterns at the Tropicrafts factory. They also sell handmade dolls, shopping bags, and place mats, all appliquéd by hand. The Dominican vetiver-grass mats are known throughout the world, and you can watch the weaving process during store hours. There's another outlet on Bay Street opposite Burroughs Square in Portsmouth (© **767/445-5956**).

Caribana, 31 Cork St. (© **767/448-7340**), displays Dominica's arts and crafts, especially straw-weaving. The staff is usually pleased to explain the dyeing processes that turn the straw into one of three different earth tones.

Other outlets for crafts include **Dominica Pottery,** Bayfront Street at Kennedy Avenue, Roseau (no phone), run by a local priest. An array of pottery made from local clays is on sale, as well as other handcrafts. **Balisier's,** 35 Great George St., Roseau (no phone), is run by a young and talented artist, Hilroy Fingol, an expert in airbrush painting. The shop also has some of the most original T-shirts on the island as well as an assortment of Carnival dolls and handmade jewelry.

Goods from all over the Caribbean are featured at the **Rainforest Shop,** 17 Old St., Roseau (© **767/448-8834**), including flamboyantly painted gifts and souvenirs. The shop contributes $1 from every purchase to protecting the rain forest.

8 Dominica After Dark

It's not very lively, but there is some evening activity. A couple of the major hotels, such as the **Castaways Beach Hotel,** at Mero (© **767/449-6244**), and **Reigate Hall Hotel** on Mountain Road (© **767/448-4031**), have entertainment on weekends, usually a combo or "jing ping" (traditional local music). In the winter season, the Castaways sponsors a weekend barbecue on the beach with live music. The **Anchorage Hotel** at Castle Comfort (© **767/448-2638**) also has live entertainment and a good buffet on Thursday. Call for details.

The clubs and bars in these hotels attract mainly foreign visitors. But if you'd like to go where the locals go, head for one of the following recommendations.

The Warehouse, Checkhall Estate (© **767/449-1303**), a 5-minute drive north of Roseau, adjacent to Canefield Airport, is the island's major dance club, packed every Saturday. Recorded disco, reggae, and other music is played from 11pm to 5am in this 200-year-old stone building, once used to store rum. The cover is EC$10 ($3.70).

If you're seeking more action, such as it is, head for **Wykie's Tropical Bar,** 51 Old St. (© **767/448-8015**), in Roseau. This is little more than a cramped hole-in-the-wall, yet curiously enough it draws the power brokers of the island. Happy hour on Friday is the time to show up. You might be offered some black pudding or stewed chicken to go with your local tropical drink. A homegrown calypso band is likely to entertain. You'll definitely hear some "jing ping." The **Dominica Club,** 49 High St. (© 767/448-2995), in Roseau, is another choice. It has two tennis courts, a lively bar, and live music on Friday night.

Other hot spots include **QClub,** corner of Bath Road and High Street, Roseau (© 767/448-2995), the place to be on a Friday night. Records, both local and American, are played till dawn breaks. If you get bored here, head for **Symes Zee's,** 34 King George V St., Roseau (© 767/448-2494), the domain of Symes Zee, the island's best blues man. A local band entertains with blues, jazz, and reggae. Here's your chance to smoke a reasonably priced Cuban cigar.

11

The Dominican Republic

Sometimes called "the fairest land under heaven" because of its sugar-white beaches and mountainous terrain, the Dominican Republic has long attracted visitors not only for its natural beauty but also for its rich colonial heritage. Its Latin flavor sharply contrasts with the character of many nearby islands, especially the British- and French-influenced ones. Often mistakenly thought of as "a poorer Puerto Rico," the Dominican Republic has its own distinctive cuisine and heritage. Five centuries of culture and tradition converge here.

There's also grinding poverty, which you can't help but see during your visit. Many Dominicans risk their lives to cross the 54-mile-wide Mona Passage and slip into Puerto Rico, and from there to the U.S. mainland. Crime, especially muggings and robbery of tourists, is on the rise.

The greatest threat to the Dominican these days comes from hurricanes, which periodically flatten entire cities. The major resorts have become adept at getting back on their feet quickly after a hurricane, as evidenced by the quick rebound from the devastation of Hurricane Georges (1998). Still, if a hurricane hits the country before your trip, you might want to call ahead and make sure your room is still standing.

In the heart of the Caribbean archipelago, the country has 870 miles of coral-edged coastline, about a third of it given to magnificent beaches. The republic occupies the eastern third of Hispaniola (Haiti has the rest). Columbus sighted this lush landmass in 1492 during his first voyage to the New World, and ruins of the first permanent European settlement in the Americas, founded in 1493, remain near Montecristi in the northeastern part of the island. The country has had a bloody history almost from the beginning, and it climaxed with the infamous reign of dictator Rafael Trujillo (1930–61) and the civil wars that followed. Today the Dominican Republic is being rebuilt and restored, and it offers visitors a chance to enjoy the sun and sea, as well as to learn about the history and politics of a developing society.

The Dominican Republic is one of the least expensive places in the West Indies to vacation. Too many hotels, too few guests, and underpaid workers keep costs down. Package deals are often available; refer to chapter 2 for hints on how to find them. American and Canadian dollars are traded extremely favorably against the Dominican peso.

1 Essentials

VISITOR INFORMATION

Before your trip, go to **www.dominicana.com.do** on the Web or contact any of the following **Dominican Republic Tourist Information Centers:** 136 E. 57th St., Suite 803, New York, NY 10022 (© **888/374/6361** or 212/588-1012); 2355 Salzedo St., Suite 307, Coral Gables, FL 33134 (© **888/358-9594** or

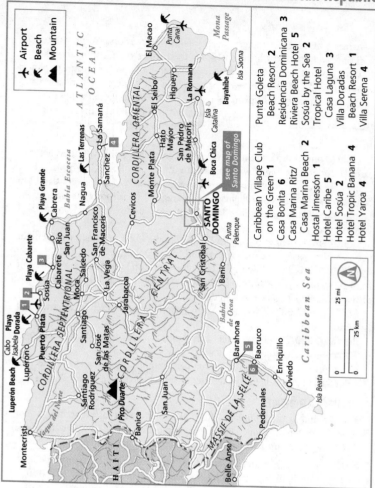

The Dominican Republic

Legend:
- ✈ Airport
- ✗ Beach
- ▲ Mountain

Caribbean Village Club on the Green **1**
Casa Bonita **6**
Casa Marina Ritz/ Casa Marina Beach **2**
Hostal Jimessón **1**
Hotel Caribe **5**
Hotel Sosúa **2**
Hotel Tropic Banana **4**
Hotel Yaroa **4**

Punta Goleta Beach Resort **2**
Residencia Dominicana **3**
Riviera Beach Hotel **5**
Sosúa by the Sea **2**
Tropical Hotel
Casa Laguna **3**
Villa Doradas
Beach Resort **1**
Villa Serena **4**

305/444-4592; fax 305/444-4845); 2080 Crescent St., Montréal, PQ H3G 2B8, Canada (© **800/563-1611** or 514/499-1918; fax 514/499-1393); or 35 Church St., Unit 53, Toronto, ON M5E 1TE, Canada (© **888/494-5050;** fax 416/361-2130). Don't expect too many specifics.

The major tourist information office in the Dominican Republic is at Av. Mexico, Esquina 30 de Marzo, Oficinas Gobernamentales, Edificio D (© **809/ 221-4660**).

GETTING THERE

American Airlines (© **800/433-7300;** www.im.aa.com) offers the most frequent service, with at least a dozen flights daily from cities throughout North America to Santo Domingo or Puerto Plata. Flights from hubs like New York's JFK, Miami International, or San Juan's Luís Muñoz Marin airports are usually nonstop. You can also make connections to the Dominican Republic from other cities through Miami. American also offers some good package deals. If you're

---

Tips A Traveler's Advisory

Arriving at Santo Domingo's Las Américas International Airport is confusing and chaotic. Customs officials tend to be rude and overworked
and give you a very thorough check! Stolen luggage is not uncommon
here; beware of "porters" who offer to help with your bags. Arrival at La
Unión International Airport, 23 miles east of Puerto Plata on the north
coast, is generally smoother and safer, but you should still be cautious.

---

heading to one of the Dominican Republic's smaller airports, your best bet is to
catch a connecting flight with **American Eagle** (© 800/433-7300), whose
small-scale (up to a maximum of 64 passengers) planes depart every day from
San Juan (with connecting flights from Mayagüez) for airports throughout the
Dominican Republic, including Santo Domingo, Puerto Plata, La Romana, and
Punta Cana.

Continental Airlines (© 800/525-0280 in the U.S.) maintains a daily flight
between New Jersey's Newark airport and Santo Domingo.

TWA (© 800/221-2000 in the U.S.) flies nonstop every morning at 9:40am
from New York's JFK to Santo Domingo, arriving there at 2:19pm local time,
early enough to let you enjoy a midafternoon sunbath.

ALM (© 809/687-4569) links Santo Domingo with Dutch St. Maarten and
Curaçao.

Iberia (© 800/772-4642) offers daily flights from Madrid to Santo Domingo,
each making a brief stop in San Juan.

For information on flights into Casa de Campo/La Romana, see the section
"La Romana & Altos de Chavón," later in this chapter.

GETTING AROUND

Getting around in the Dominican Republic is not always easy, especially if your
hotel is in a remote location. The most convenient modes of transport are shuttle
flights, taxis, rental cars, *públicos* (multipassenger taxis), and *guaguas* (public buses).

BY AIR   The quickest and easiest way to get across a difficult landscape is on
one of the shuttle flights offered by **Air Santo Domingo** (© 809/683-8006),
flying from Santo Domingo to Puerto Plata, Punta Cana, La Romana, Samaná,
and Santiago, among other towns. In general, each one-way flight costs about
$70 a ticket.

BY TAXI   Taxis aren't metered, and determining the fare in advance (which
you should do) might be difficult if you and your driver don't speak the same
language. Taxis can be hailed in the streets, and you'll definitely find them at the
major hotels and at the airport. The minimum fare within Santo Domingo is
$6, but most drivers try to get more. In Santo Domingo, the most reliable taxi
company is **Tecni-Taxi** (© 809/567-2010). In Puerto Plata, call **Tecni-Taxi**
(© 809/320-7621). Don't get into an unmarked street taxi. Many visitors,
particularly in Santo Domingo, have been assaulted and robbed by doing that.

BY RENTAL CAR   The best way to see the Dominican Republic is to drive;
island buses tend to be erratic, hot, and overcrowded. If you want seat belts, you
have to ask.

To rent a car, a Canadian or American driver's license is suitable documentation, along with a valid credit card or a substantial cash deposit. Unlike many

Caribbean islands, you *drive on the right* here. Although major highways are relatively smooth, the country's secondary roads, especially those in the east, are covered with potholes and ruts. Roads also tend to be badly lit and badly marked in both the city and the countryside. Drive carefully and give yourself plenty of time when traveling between island destinations. Watch out for policemen who flag you down and accuse you (often wrongly) of some infraction. Many locals give these low-paid policemen a $5 *regalo,* or gift "for your children," and are then free to go.

The high accident and theft rate in recent years has helped to raise car-rental rates here. Prices vary, so call around for last-minute quotes. Make sure you understand your insurance coverage (or lack thereof) before you leave home. Your credit-card issuer may already provide you with this type of insurance; contact the issuer to find out.

For reservations and more information, call the rental companies at least a week before your departure: **Avis** (© **800/331-1212** or 809/535-7191), **Budget** (© **800/527-0700** or 809/562-6812), and **Hertz** (© **800/654-3001** or 809/221-5333) all operate in the Dominican Republic. Although the cars might be not as well maintained as the big three, you can often get a cheaper deal at a local firm, notably **McBeal,** Av. George Washington, Santo Domingo (© **809/ 688-6518**).

BY PUBLIC TRANSPORTATION   Unmetered multi-passenger taxis known as *públicos* travel along main thoroughfares, stopping often to pick up people waving from the side of the street. A *público* is marked by a white seal on the front door. You must tell the driver your destination when you're picked up to make sure the *público* is going there. A ride is usually RD$4 (25¢).

Public buses, often in the form of minivans or panel trucks, are called *guaguas.* They provide the same service as *públicos* and cost about the same, but they're generally more crowded. Larger buses provide service outside the towns. Beware of pickpockets on board.

 FAST FACTS: **The Dominican Republic**

Currency   The Dominican monetary unit is the **peso (RD$)**, made up of 100 centavos. Coin denominations are 1, 5, 10, 25, and 50 centavos, and 1 peso. Bill denominations are RD$5, RD$10, RD$20, RD$50, RD$100, RD$500, and RD$1,000. Price quotations in this chapter appear in U.S. dollars or Dominican currency, depending on the policy of the establishment. The use of any currency other than Dominican pesos is technically illegal, but few seem to bother with this mandate. At press time, we got about RD$16 to U.S.$1. Bank booths at the international airports and major hotels will change your currency at the prevailing free-market rate. You'll be given a receipt for the amount of foreign currency you've exchanged. If you have pesos left at the end of your trip, present this receipt at the Banco de Reservas booth at the airport, and you can trade in your pesos for American dollars.

Documents   To enter the Dominican Republic, citizens of the United States and Canada need only proof of citizenship, such as a passport or an original birth certificate. However, citizens might have trouble returning home without a passport—a reproduced birth certificate is not acceptable. Save yourself the hassle and just bring a passport. Upon your arrival at the airport in the Dominican Republic, you must purchase a tourist card for $10. You can avoid waiting in line by purchasing this card when checking in for your flight to the island.

Electricity The country generally uses 110-volt AC (60 cycles), so adapters and transformers are usually not necessary for U.S.-made appliances.

Embassies All embassies are in Santo Domingo, the capital. The Embassy of the **United States** is on Calle Cesar Nicholas Penson at the corner of Leopold Navarro (✆ **809/221-2171**); the Embassy of the **United Kingdom** is at Febrero 27 (✆ **809/472-7111**); and the Embassy of **Canada** is at Av. Máximo Gómez 39 (✆ **809/685-1136**).

Language The official language is Spanish; many people also speak some English.

Safety The Dominican Republic has more than its fair share of crime (see "Getting There," above, for a warning about crime at airports). Avoid unmarked street taxis, especially in Santo Domingo; you could be assaulted and robbed. While strolling around the city, beware of hustlers selling various wares. Pickpockets and muggers are common here, and visitors are easy targets. Don't walk in Santo Domingo at night. Locals like to offer their services as guides, and it is often difficult to decline. Hiring an official guide from the tourist office is your best bet.

Taxes A departure tax of $10 is assessed and must be paid in U.S. currency. The government imposes a 13% tax on hotel rooms, which usually is configured in conjunction with a 10% service charge that's automatically added to your hotel bill, which adds up to a staggering surcharge that helps support the country.

Telecommunications The area code for the Dominican Republic is **809**. You place calls to or from the Dominican Republic just as you would from any other area code in North America.

Time Atlantic standard time is observed year-round. When New York and Miami are on eastern standard time and it's 6am, it's 7am in Santo Domingo. However, during daylight saving time, when it's noon on the U.S. east coast, it's noon in Santo Domingo, too.

Tipping In most restaurants and hotels, a 10% service charge is added to your check. Most people usually add 5% to 10% more, especially if the service has been good.

Weather The average temperature is 77°F (25°C). August is the warmest month and January the coolest month, although even then it's warm enough to swim.

2 Santo Domingo ✦✦✦

Bartholomeo Columbus, brother of Christopher, founded the city of New Isabella, later renamed Santo Domingo, on the southeastern Caribbean coast on August 4, 1496. It's the oldest city in the New World and the capital of the Dominican Republic. It has had a long, sometimes glorious, more often sad, history. At the peak of its power, Diego de Velásquez sailed out to settle Cuba, Ponce de León went forth to conquer and settle Puerto Rico and Florida, and

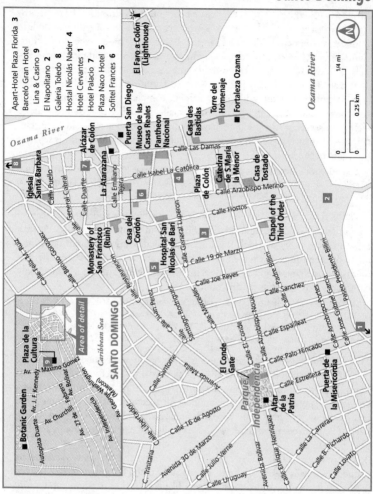

Santo Domingo map key:

Apart-Hotel Plaza Florida **3**
Barceló Gran Hotel
Lina & Casino **9**
El Napolitano **2**
Galeria Toledo **8**
Hostal Nicolás Nader **4**
Hotel Cervantes **1**
Hotel Palacio **7**
Plaza Naco Hotel **5**
Sofitel Frances **6**

El Faro a Colón (Lighthouse)

Torre del Homenaje
Fortaleza Ozama
Casa des Bastidas
Puerta San Diego
Museo de las Casas Reales
Pantheon Nacional
Alcázar de Colón
Iglesia Santa Barbara
La Atarazana
Calle Las Damas
Calle Isabel La Católica
Catedral de S.María la Menor
Casa de Tostado
Plaza de Colón
Calle Arzobispo Merino
Calle Emiliano Tejera
Calle Hostos
Casa del Cordón
Hospital San Nicolas de Bari
Chapel of the Third Order
Monastery of San Francisco (Ruin)
Calle 19 de Marzo
Calle Joe Reyes
Calle Sanchez
Calle Padre Billini
Botanic Garden
Plaza de la Cultura
Area of detail
SANTO DOMINGO
Caribbean Sea
El Conde Gate
Parque Independencia
Altar de la Patria
Puerta de la Misericordia
Ozama River

Cortés set out for Mexico. The city still reflects its long history today—French, Haitian, and especially Spanish.

SANTO DOMINGO ESSENTIALS

In Santo Domingo, **24-hour drugstore** service is provided by San Judas Tadeo, Av. Independencia 57 (© **809/685-8165**). An emergency room operates at the **Centro Médico Universidad,** Av. Máximo Gómez 68, on the corner of Pedro Enrique Urena (© **809/221-0171**). For the **police,** call © **911**.

ACCOMMODATIONS YOU CAN AFFORD

Even the highest-priced hotels in Santo Domingo might be classified as medium-priced in most of the Caribbean. However, remember that taxes and service will be added to your bill, which will make the rates around 20% higher. When making reservations, ask if these charges are included in the rates quoted—usually they aren't. And remember, all prices quoted are in U.S. dollars; if local prices are listed, the U.S. equivalent follows in parentheses.

Apart-Hotel Plaza Florida   Favored by business travelers from nearby Caribbean nations, this three-story hotel dates from 1978, when it was built in a modern commercial district near the larger (and more expensive) Hotel Commodoro. The small accommodations are simple, airy, and clean, with few frills, although the beds are comfortable and have decent mattresses. Bathrooms don't have much room to spread out your stuff, but each has a tiled shower. The hotel resembles something like an apartment complex, where residents tend to stay longer than conventional tourists, usually preparing at least breakfast in their rooms. About half the units have small balconies. There's a simple restaurant on site, which serves Dominican specialties, but its management is separate from that of the hotel.

Av. Bolívar 203 (Calle Armando Rodriguez), Santo Domingo, Dominican Republic. © **809/541-3957.** Fax 809/540-5582. 32 units. Year-round RD$650 ($40.65) single; RD$700 ($43.75) double. Extra person RD$100 ($6.25). AE, MC, V. **Amenities:** Restaurant. *In room:* A/C, TV, kitchenette.

Barceló Gran Hotel Lina & Casino 🍀🍀   Rising nine floors in the heart of the capital in a sterile design, the Lina offers a wide range of amenities. At least a third of the units overlook the Caribbean. Bedrooms are comfortable, and many of them quite spacious, but the decor is standard motel style. The best rooms, on the eighth and ninth floors, have balconies. The tiled, shower-only bathrooms have spacious marble vanities.

Avs. Máximo Gómez and 27 de Febrero, Santo Domingo, Dominican Republic. © **800/942-2461** in the U.S., or 809/563-5000. Fax 809/686-5521. www.barcelo.com. 217 units. Year-round $120 single or double; from $149 suite. Extra person $28. Rates include breakfast. AE, DC, MC, V. **Amenities:** Restaurant, bar, snack bar, piano bar, casino, pool, health club, Jacuzzi, sauna, 24-hour room service, laundry. *In room:* A/C, TV, minibar, fridge.

El Napolitano *Value*   El Napolitano is a safe haven and a good bargain along the Malecón, which is usually lively—and potentially dangerous—until the wee hours. Popular with Dominicans, the hotel rents comfortably furnished but simple units, many large enough for families. All accommodations open onto the sea. Mattresses are frequently renewed, and you'll probably get a good night's sleep. The bathrooms, which have shower stalls, are barely adequate in size but well maintained.

The restaurant, Da Luz, is open 24 hours a day, and the chefs specialize in seafood (especially lobster). There's a disco and a piano bar, plus a terrace casino, with both live and recorded music. If you like crowds, lots of action, and informality, El Napolitano may be for you.

Av. George Washington 51 (between Calle Cambrunal and Calle del Número), Santo Domingo, Dominican Republic. © **809/687-1131.** Fax 809/687-6814. www.hotelnapolitano.com. 72 units. Year-round RD$1,248–RD$1,398 ($78–$87.40) single or double. AE, DC, MC, V. **Amenities:** Restaurant, disco, bar, casino, pool, room service. *In room:* A/C, TV.

Galeria Toledo *Finds*   An exile from the state of Tennessee, Bettye Marshall runs this establishment, which is a three-in-one offering: an art gallery, a guesthouse, and an unpretentious though highly popular outdoor restaurant on Plaza de Toledo. In keeping with the artistic focus of the place, the decor is tasteful and inviting. The rooms are compact but quite comfortable and neatly maintained, each with a small, tiled bathroom with shower. The restaurant serves light, simple, yet tasty food consisting mainly of excellent salads and various takes on pasta.

Calle Isabel La Catolica 163, Plaza Maria de Toledo, Santo Domingo, Dominican Republic. © **809/688-7649.** Fax 809/221-4167. 8 units. Year-round $70 double. Breakfast and dinner $10 per person extra. MC, V. **Amenities:** Restaurant. *In room:* A/C, TV.

Hostal Nicolás Nader   The family owners of this spacious hotel will proudly tell you that two former residents of this building were eventually elected president of the Dominican Republic. Originally a private home in the 1930s, it provides clean and inviting lodgings, with battered colonial furniture, some of them antiques. The guest rooms overlook either the street or a small Andalusian courtyard with cast-iron furniture. Most rooms have excellent twin beds with firm mattresses, although there are some with double beds. The walk-in closets are ideal for storing your clothing, and the tub-and-shower bathrooms are a bit small but well maintained, with compact vanities. Breakfast is the only meal served.

Calle Admiral Luperón 251 (at Calle Duarte, 4 blocks west of calle Las Damas), Santo Domingo, Dominican Republic. ✆ **809/687-6674.** Fax 809/565-6204. 9 units. Year-round RD$750 ($46.90) single; RD$850 ($53.15) double. AE, V. **Amenities:** Breakfast room. *In room:* A/C, TV.

Hotel Cervantes ⓥₐₗᵤₑ   Long a favorite among budget travelers, the family-oriented Cervantes, with a security guard on staff, offers nicely furnished but small bedrooms. Most bedrooms are reasonably comfortable, although some mattresses need to be replaced. Bathrooms are also a bit cramped, and each has a tiled shower. It might not have the most tasteful decor in Santo Domingo, but the Hotel Cervantes is nevertheless clean and efficient, and the staff is pleasant. The hotel is known for its Bronco Steak House.

Av. Cervantes 202, Santo Domingo, Dominican Republic. ✆ **809/688-2261.** Fax 809/686-5754. 170 units. Year-round RD$720 ($45) single; RD$900 ($56.25) double. AE, MC, V. Free parking. **Amenities:** Restaurant, pool. *In room:* A/C, TV, fridge.

Hotel Palacio ✦   History buffs often opt to stay here, since the hotel is within walking distance of the city's major historical sights. It's in the heart of the historic zone, only 2 blocks from the cathedral. The Palacio is also popular with business travelers. Built in the 1600s, it was the family home of a former president of the Dominican Republic, Buenaventura Báez, and it still retains its original iron balconies and high ceilings. Kitchenettes were added to all rooms in the early 1990s. Not all rooms are the same size; if you want a more spacious unit, just ask. The shower-only bathrooms tend to be small.

Calle Duarte 106 (at Calle Solomé Urena), Santo Domingo, Dominican Republic. ✆ **809/682-4730.** Fax 809/687-5535. h.palacio@codetel.net.do. 17 units. Year-round $65–$90 single or double. Children 12 and under stay free in parents' room. AE, MC, V. **Amenities:** Small gym, rooftop Jacuzzi. *In room:* A/C, TV, kitchenette.

Plaza Naco Hotel   An ideal accommodation for business travelers or for visitors seeking a lot of space and facilities, the Plaza Naco offers handsomely decorated accommodations equipped with computer safe-lock doors, good beds, dining rooms, and tiled showers in the bathrooms. Each unit was renovated in 1998. There's a good restaurant and a cafeteria, plus a gift shop, a deli, and a mini-market.

In the Plaza Naco Mall, Av. Presidente Gonzalez at Av. Tiradentes (Apdo. Postal 30228), Santo Domingo, Dominican Republic. ✆ **809/541-6226.** Fax 809/549-7743. www.naco.com.do/plaza.html. 220 units. Year-round $129 junior suite for 1 or 2; $172–$184 1-bedroom suite for up to 4. Extra person RD$300 ($18.75). Rates include breakfast. AE, MC, V. **Amenities:** Restaurant, bar, cafeteria, disco, health club, sauna, rental car desk, business services, room service, laundry/dry cleaning. *In room:* A/C, TV, kitchenette, hair dryer, safe.

Sofitel Frances ✦✦   Our favorite small hotel in the old city, this intimate inn lies within a stone-fronted town house dating from the 16th century. Sofitel has upgraded the accommodations, while retaining many of its original architectural features. Arches surround an Iberian-style fountain, and columns reach up to the second-floor patios, with palms and tropical plants surrounding the rooms. You'll think you've been delivered to Seville. A gracefully winding stone staircase leads to the high-ceilinged and thick-walled bedrooms outfitted in a somber, rather dark colonial style. Accommodations are simple but tasteful, with rugs resting on the tile floors; each has a somewhat cramped but tidily kept bathroom with a shower stall.

Calle las Mercedes (corner Arzobispo Merion), Santo Domingo, Dominican Republic. © **809/685-9331.** Fax 809/685-1289. www.sofitel.com. 19 units. Year-round $100–$126 single or double. AE, MC,V. **Amenities:** Restaurant, bar. In room: A/C, TV, minibar.

GREAT DEALS ON DINING

El Conuco ⭐ DOMINICAN   Come to "the countryside" (its English name) for the best-tasting and most authentic Dominican dishes in the capital. La Bahía (see below) might have better seafood, but otherwise this place is superb even if a bit corny. The waiters in costume will even dance a wicked merengue with you. Few restaurants have been as successful at commercializing the charms of rural Dominican life, and as such, it has attracted many of the country's sports and pop-music stars. You'll find it within an upscale residential neighborhood near the Malécon, close to the Jaragua Resort. Inside, you'll find everything you might need to cope with country living in the Spanish-speaking tropics: hammocks, domino tables, colorful weavings, and thatch-covered *bohios*. Familiar menu items here include six kinds of steak, and chicken "merengue," prepared with red wine, onions, and mushrooms. Only the venturesome dare try cow's foot stew. A specialty here is the "Dominican flag," a traditional platter whose various colors derive from artfully arranged portions of white rice, beans, meat, fried bananas, and salad.

Calle Casimiro de Moya 152. © **809/686-0129.** Reservations recommended. Main courses RD$75–RD$240 ($4.75–$15); buffet RD$219 ($13.75). AE, DC, MC, V. Daily noon–2am.

Fonda La Atarazana CREOLE/INTERNATIONAL   This patio restaurant offers regional food in a colonial atmosphere, with either live or recorded music for dancing. Just across from the Alcázar, it's a convenient stop if you're shopping and sightseeing in the old city. A cheap, good dish is *chicharrones de pollo*, tasty fried bits of Dominican chicken. Or you might try curried baby goat in a sherry sauce. Sometimes the chef cooks lobster Thermidor and Galician-style octopus. If you don't mind waiting half an hour, you can order the *sopa de ajo* (garlic soup). Many fans come here especially for the fricasseed pork chops.

Calle Atarazana 5. © **809/689-2900.** Main courses RD$110–RD$280 ($6.90–$17.50). AE, DC, MC, V. Daily noon–midnight.

La Bahía ⭐ *(Finds* SEAFOOD   You'd never know that this unassuming place right on the Malecón serves some of the best and freshest seafood in the Dominican Republic. One predawn morning as we passed by, fishermen were waiting outside to sell the chef their latest catch. Rarely in the Caribbean will you find a restaurant with such a wide range of seafood dishes. To start, you might try *ceviche* (sea bass marinated in lime juice) or lobster cocktail. Soups usually contain big chunks of lobster as well as shrimp. Our favorite specialties include kingfish in coconut sauce, sea bass Ukrainian style, baked red snapper, and a savory kettle of seafood in the pot. The chef also works his magic with conch. Desserts are superfluous. The restaurant stays open until the last customer departs.

Av. George Washington 1. © **809/682-4022.** Main courses RD$95–RD$270 ($6–$17). AE, MC, V. Daily 9am–2am.

La Baquette SANDWICHES   Don't expect fancy service and culinary chi-chi at this French bakery wannabe. You stand up and place your order at the counter, then either carry your goodies away or sit at the limited number of tables in the corner. Menu items lean toward the snack food and tasty morsel category and include the town's largest selection of pastries plus brochettes of pork, chicken, and beef, among other selections. Our favorite dessert is the mango mousse, but you can also order flan, tarts, cookies, slices of cake, and other goodies.

Calle Gustavo Meija Ricart 126. ℂ 809/565-6432. Snacks and pastries RD$10–RD$95 (65¢–$6). MC, V. Mon–Sat 8:30am–8pm.

La Canasta DOMINICAN/INTERNATIONAL   The best late-night dining spot in the capital is set back from the Malecón, between the El Diamante Casino and the Azucar Disco. It's not only economical but serves popular Dominican dishes culled from favorite recipes throughout the country, including *sancocho* (a typical stew with a variety of meats and yucca) and *mondongo* (tripe cooked with tomatoes and peppers). Other unusual dishes are goat meat braised in rum sauce, and pigs' feet vinaigrette Creole style. La Canasta is locally known for its *pollo a la plancha,* grilled chicken flavored with fresh Dominican herbs. The late-night dining hours are perfectly suited to the young Dominican clientele the restaurant serves, many of whom frequent the discos in the wee hours.

In the Melia Santo Domingo Hotel & Casino, Av. George Washington 365. ℂ 809/221-6666. Main courses RD$85–RD$350 ($5.25–$22). AE, DC, MC, V. Daily 8pm–6am.

Mesón de la Cava ✿✿ DOMINICAN/INTERNATIONAL   At first we thought this was a mere gimmicky club—you descend a perilous iron stairway into an actual cave with stalactites and stalagmites—but the cuisine is among the finest in the capital. The quality ingredients are well prepared and generously served, with accurate timing and full flavors. Recorded merengue, Latin jazz, blues, and salsa give the place a festive ambience. Launch your repast with the small shrimp sautéed in a delicate sauce of garlic and white wine, perhaps a "sexy" conch gratinée. The gazpacho is also an excellent beginning, as is the bubbling *sopa de pescado* (red snapper chowder). Follow it up with the grilled Caribbean rock lobster or the double French lamb chops, which are done to tender perfection.

Av. Mirador del Sur 1. ℂ 809/533-2818. Reservations required. Main courses at lunch RD$160–RD$320 ($10–$20), at dinner RD$195–RD$348 ($12.25–$21.75). AE, DC, MC, V. Daily noon–4pm and 5:30pm–1am.

Pat 'e Palo ✿ INTERNATIONAL   Part of Pat 'e Palo's charm derives from its location, overlooking Plaza Colón, the graceful arcades of the Alcazar de Colón, and the amiable clusters of Dominican families who promenade with their children every night at dusk. During the 1500s, the building was a bistro under the supervision of a mysterious Dutch buccaneer known as Peg-Leg (Pat 'e Palo), who's credited with establishing the first tavern in the New World.

In the late 1990s, another Dutchman and his four partners transformed the place into a gregarious and engaging bistro that on weekends is one of the most crowded and popular singles bars in the country. Tables are thick-topped wooden affairs, set either on the plaza outside or within the antique walls of the dark and shadowy interior. The food is some of the best in the capital, and is usually accompanied by live guitar music every Thursday to Sunday 6 to 10pm. Having dined here many times, we feel at home with the menu and can most recommend the sautéed shrimp in coconut curry sauce. On festive occasions, ask for the brochette of mixed meats; the meat has been marinated in fresh spices and herbs and is artfully flambéed at your table. The sea bass with white wine sauce is perfectly prepared, although the fancy continental dishes such as char-broiled steak with onion sauce and a grilled rack of lamb might be more suited for the cold Alps.

La Atarazana 25, Zona Colonial. ℂ **809/687-8089**. Burgers and salads RD$95–RD$115 ($6–$7.25); main courses RD$195–RD$320 ($12.25–$20). AE, MC, V. Daily 11am–1:30pm.

Scherezade MEDITERRANEAN   Its name (heroine of the Arabic legend of *A Thousand and One Nights*) and decor (a simulation of a Moorish palace) evoke the Middle East better than anything else in town. The main dining room is divided into two sections. The bustling kitchen makes a roster of international dishes that are ambitious and for the most part successful. Menu items include pastas, *osso buco*, fresh fish, Turkish-style shish kebabs, and well-flavored versions of Lebanese dishes such as tabouleh, tahini, and roast lamb with Mediterranean herbs. The service is much better than we've typically found in Santo Domingo.

Calle Roberto Pastoriza 226 (at Calle Lope de Vega). ℂ **809/227-2323**. Reservations recommended. Main courses RD$170–RD$390 ($10.75–$24.50). AE, MC, V. Daily noon–midnight.

Spaghettissimo ITALIAN   Convivial and unpretentious, this restaurant manages to convey the sense that a chef somewhere in a steamy kitchen will be genuinely disappointed if you don't manage to actually finish your pasta. You might begin your meal with a drink in the bar near the entrance, then segue into a simple but dignified dining room where part of the visual distraction derives from a generously appointed antipasti buffet (most of the selections are fish or grilled vegetables that have marinated succulently in olive oil and herbs). Starters might include shellfish, fish soup, foie gras, and the inevitable pastas such as penne with artichokes, which can be configured as main courses if you prefer. Meats and fish are often grilled, well seasoned, and redolent of the traditions of faraway Italy.

13 Paseo de Los Locubres. ℂ **809/565-3708**. Main courses RD$155–RD$365 ($9.75–$22.75). AE, MC, V. Daily noon–3pm and 7:30pm–midnight.

Tu Casona DOMINICAN/ARGENTINEAN   Set within an antique build-ing in the colonial zone, just around the corner from the Plaza Colón, this restaurant is graced with tiles and rough-hewn ceiling beams. Within a pair of dining rooms, you'll find simple wooden chairs, starched linens, and a cheerful Dominican staff. Menu items stress grilled beefsteak prepared in the way you might expect on the pampas of Argentina. The cuisine isn't spectacular, but it is well crafted, even heartfelt, and full of brawny flavors. You might begin with a portion of Manchego cheese or Serrano ham, followed by grilled chicken or ten-der grilled filets of beef or pork (served in 12-oz. or huge 16-oz. portions).

Calle Emilano Tejera 101. ℂ **809/687-8970**. RD$160–RD$290 ($10–$18.15). AE, DISC, MC, V. Daily noon–midnight.

HITTING THE BEACHES

The Dominican Republic has some great beaches, but they aren't in Santo Domingo. The principal beach near the capital is **Boca Chica,** less than 2 miles east of the international airport and about 19 miles from the center of Santo Domingo. Here you'll find clear, shallow blue water, a white-sand beach, and a natural coral reef. The east side of the beach, known as "St. Tropez," is popular with Europeans. In recent years the backdrop of the beach has become rather

---

Moments Un, Dos, Tres Strikes, You're Out

Dominicans were crazy about baseball long before their countryman Sammy Sosa set the United States on fire with his annual home run race against Mark McGwire. Almost every major-league baseball team has at least one player from the Dominican Republic on its roster these days. Pedro Martinez, Manny Ramirez, and Armando Benitez are just a few of the veritable all-star team of players who hail from the Dominican Republic.

If you're here between October and January, you might want to catch a game in the Dominican's Professional Winter League. The **Liga de Beisbol stadium** (© **809/567-6371**) is in Santo Domingo; check local newspapers for game times, or ask at your hotel. There are also games at the Tetelo Vargas Stadium in San Pedro de Marcoris, known to die-hard sports fans as the "land of shortstops" for the multitude of infielders who call this tiny town home.

---

tacky, with an array of pizza and fast-food stands, beach cottages, chaise longues, watersports concessions, and plastic beach tables.

Slightly better maintained is the narrow white-sand beach of **Playa Juan Dolio** or **Playa Esmeralda,** a 20-minute drive east of Boca Chica. Several resorts have recently located here. The beach used to be fairly uncrowded, but with all the resort hotels now lining it, it's likely to be as crowded as Boca Chica any day of the week.

SPECTATOR SPORTS

HORSE RACING   Santo Domingo's racetrack, **Hipódromo V Centenario,** on Avenida Las Américas (© **809/687-6060**), schedules races Tuesday, Thursday, and Saturday. You can spend the day here and have lunch at the track's restaurant. Admission is free.

EXPLORING HISTORIC SANTO DOMINGO

Santo Domingo, a treasure trove of historic, sometimes crumbling buildings, is undergoing a major government-sponsored restoration. The old town is still partially enclosed by remnants of its original city wall. The narrow streets, old stone buildings, and forts are like nothing else in the Caribbean, except Old San Juan. The only thing missing is the clank of the conquistadors' armor.

Old and modern Santo Domingo meet at the **Parque Independencia,** a big city square whose most prominent feature is its Altar de la Patria, a shrine dedicated to Duarte, Sanchez, and Mella, who are all buried here. These men led the country's fight for freedom from Haiti in 1844. As in provincial Spanish cities, the square is a popular family gathering point on Sunday afternoon. At the entrance to the plaza is **El Conde Gate,** named for the count (El Conde) de Penalva, the governor who resisted the forces of Admiral Penn, the leader of a British invasion. It was also the site of the March for Independence in 1844, and holds a special place in the hearts of Dominicans.

In the shadow of the Alcázar, **La Atarazana** is a fully restored section that centered on one of the New World's finest arsenals. It extends for a city block, a catacomb of shops, art galleries (both Haitian and Dominican paintings), boutiques, and some good regional and international restaurants.

Just behind river moorings is the oldest street in the New World, **Calle Las Damas** (Street of the Ladies). Some visitors assume that this was a bordello district, but actually it wasn't. Rather, the elegant ladies of the viceregal court used to promenade here in the evening. It's lined with colonial buildings.

Alcázar de Colón ✵ The most outstanding structure in the old city is the Alcázar, a palace built for Columbus's son, Diego, and his wife, who was also the niece of Ferdinand, king of Spain. Diego became the colony's governor in 1509, and Santo Domingo rose as the hub of Spanish commerce and culture in America. For more than 60 years, this coral limestone structure on the bluffs of the Ozama River was the center of the Spanish court, entertaining such distinguished visitors as Cortés, Ponce de León, and Balboa. The nearly two dozen rooms and open-air loggias are decorated with paintings and period tapestries, as well as 16th-century antiques.

Calle Emiliano Tejada (at the foot of Calle Las Damas). ℂ **809/687-5653.** Admission RD$20 ($1.25). Mon and Wed–Fri 9am–5pm; Sat 9am–4pm; Sun 9am–2pm.

Casa del Cordón Near the Alcázar de Colón, the Cord House was named for the cord of the Franciscan order, which is carved above the door. Francisco de Garay, who came to Hispaniola with Columbus, built the casa in 1503–04, which makes it the oldest stone house in the western hemisphere. It once housed the first royal audience of the New World, which acted as the Supreme Court of Justice for the entire West Indies. On another occasion, in January 1586, the noble ladies of Santo Domingo gathered here to donate their jewelry as ransom demanded by Sir Francis Drake in return for his promise to leave the city.

At Calle Emiliano Tejera and Calle Isabel la Católica. No phone. Free admission. Tues–Sun 8:30am–4:30pm.

Catedral de Santa María la Menor ✵ This, the oldest cathedral in the Americas, was begun in 1514 and completed in 1540. With a gold coral limestone facade, the church combines elements of both Gothic and baroque, with some lavish Plateresque styles, as exemplified by the high altar chiseled out of silver. The cathedral was the center for a celebration of the 500th anniversary of the European Discovery of America in 1992. The treasury boasts an excellent art collection of ancient woodcarvings, furnishings, funerary monuments, and silver and jewelry.

Calle Arzobispo Meriño (on the south side of Columbus Sq.). ℂ **809/689-1920.** Free admission. Cathedral Mon–Sat 9am–4pm, Sun masses begin at 6am; treasury Mon–Sat 9am–4pm.

El Faro a Colón (Columbus Lighthouse) Built in the shape of a cross, the towering 688-foot-tall El Faro a Colón monument is both a sightseeing attraction and a cultural center. In the heart of the structure is a chapel containing the Columbus tomb, and, some say, his mortal remains. The "bones" of Columbus were moved here from the Cathedral of Santa María la Menor (see above). (Other locations, including the Cathedral of Seville, also claim to possess the explorer's remains.) The most outstanding and unique feature is the lighting system composed of 149 searchlights and a 70-kilowatt beam that circles out for nearly 44 miles. When illuminated, the lights project a gigantic cross in the sky that can be seen as far away as Puerto Rico.

Although the concept of the memorial is 140 years old, the first stones were not laid until 1986, following the design submitted in 1929 by J. L. Gleave, the winner of the worldwide contest held to choose the architect. The monumental lighthouse was inaugurated on October 6, 1992, the day Columbus's "remains" were transferred from the cathedral.

Av. España (on the water side of Los Tres Ojos, near the airport in the Sans Souci district). ℭ **809/591-1492.** Admission RD$20 ($1.25) adults, RD$5 (30¢) children 11 and under. Tues–Sun 9am–5:30pm.

Museo de las Casas Reales (Museum of the Royal Houses) Through artifacts, tapestries, maps, and re-created halls, including a courtroom, this museum traces Santo Domingo's history from 1492 to 1821. Gilded furniture, arms and armor, and other colonial artifacts make it the most interesting museum of Old Santo Domingo. It contains replicas of the *Niña,* the *Pinta,* and the *Santa Maria,* and one exhibit is said to hold part of the ashes of the famed explorer. You can see, in addition to pre-Columbian art, the main artifacts of two galleons sunk in 1724 on their way from Spain to Mexico, along with remnants of another 18th-century Spanish ship, the *Concepción.*

Calle Las Damas (at Calle Las Mercedes). ℭ **809/682-4202.** Admission RD$20 ($1.25). Daily 9am–5pm.

OTHER SIGHTS

In total contrast to the colonial city, modern Santo Domingo dates from the Trujillo era. A city of broad, palm-shaded avenues, its seaside drive is called **Avenida George Washington,** more popularly known as the **Malecón.** This boulevard is filled with restaurants, as well as hotels and nightclubs. Use caution at night—there are pickpockets galore.

We also suggest a visit to the **Paseo de los Indios,** a sprawling 5-mile park with a restaurant, fountain displays, and a lake.

About a 20-minute drive from the heart of the city, off the Autopista de las Américas on the way to the airport and the beach at Boca Chica, is **Los Tres Ojos** or "The Three Eyes," which stare at you across the Ozama River from Old Santo Domingo. There's a trio of lagoons set in scenic caverns, with lots of stalactites and stalagmites. One lagoon is 40 feet deep, another 20 feet, and yet a third—known as the "Ladies Bath"—only 5 feet deep. A Dominican Tarzan will sometimes dive off the walls of the cavern into the deepest lagoon. The area is equipped with walkways.

Jardín Botánico Sprawled over 445 acres in the northern sector of the Arroyo Hondo, these are among the largest gardens of their kind in Latin America. They emphasize the flowers and lush vegetation native to the Dominican Republic, and require at least 2 hours to even begin to explore. A small, touristy-looking train makes a circuit through the park's major features, which include a Japanese park, the Great Ravine, and a floral clock.

Av. República de Colombia (at the corner of de los Proceres). ℭ **809/567-6211.** Admission RD$20 ($1.25) adults, RD$5 (30¢) children. Tour by train RD$25 ($1.55) adults, RD$7 (45¢) children. Tues–Sun 9am–5pm.

Museo de Arte Moderno The former site of the Trujillo mansion, plaza de la Cultura has been turned into a park and contains the Museum of Modern Art, which displays national and international works (the emphasis, of course, is on native-born talent).

Plaza de la Cultura, Calle Pedro Henríquez Ureña. ℭ **809/685-2153.** Admission RD$20 ($1.25). Tues–Sat 9am–5pm.

Also in the center are the **National Library** (ℭ **809/688-4086**) and the **National Theater** (ℭ **809/687-3191**), which sponsor, among other events, folkloric dances, opera, outdoor jazz concerts, traveling art exhibits, classical ballet, and music concerts.

SHOPPING ✿✿

The best buys are handcrafted native items, especially amber jewelry. **Amber** deposits, petrified tree resin that has fossilized over millions of years, is the national gem. Look for pieces of amber with objects, such as insects and spiders, trapped inside. Colors range from a bright yellow to black, but most of the gems are golden in tone. Fine-quality amber jewelry, along with lots of plastic fakes, is sold throughout the country.

A semiprecious stone of light blue (sometimes a dark-blue color), larimar is the Dominican turquoise. It often makes striking jewelry, and is sometimes mounted with wild boars' teeth.

Ever since the Dominicans presented John F. Kennedy with what became his favorite rocker, visitors have wanted to take home a rocking chair. To simplify transport, these rockers are often sold unassembled.

Other good buys include Dominican rum, handknit articles, macramé, ceramics, and crafts in native mahogany. The best shopping streets are El Conde, the oldest and most traditional shop-flanked avenue, and Avenida Mella.

In the colonial section, **La Atarazana** is filled with galleries and gift and jewelry stores, all charging inflated prices. Duty-free shops are found at the airport, in the capital at the **Centro de los Héroes,** and at both the Hotel Santo Domingo and the Hotel Embajador. Shopping hours are generally 9am to 12:30pm and 2 to 5pm Monday to Saturday.

Head first for the National Market, **El Mercado Modelo,** Avenida Mella, filled with stall after stall of crafts and spices, fruits, and vegetables. The merchants will be most eager to sell, and you can easily get lost in the crush. You'll see a lot of tortoiseshell work here, but exercise caution, since many species, especially the hawksbill, are on the endangered-species list and could be impounded by U.S. Customs if discovered in your luggage. Rockers are for sale here, as are mahogany-ware, sandals, baskets, hats, clay braziers for grilling fish, and so on.

Ambar Marie, Caonabo 9, Gazcue (© **809/682-7539**), is a reliable source for amber. In case you're worried that the piece of amber you like might be plastic, you can be assured of the real thing at Ambar Marie, where you can even design your own setting for your chosen gem. Look especially for the beautiful amber necklaces, as well as the earrings and pins. Another reliable source is **Ambar Nacionale,** Calle Restauración 110 (© **809/686-5700**), around the corner from the Amber World Museum. This outlet hawks items for sale that include many stunning pieces of amber as well as coral and larimar. In general prices here are a bit less expensive than those at the more prestigious Amber World Museum. Look for some stunning jewelry fashioned from larimar or ancient amber and placed in silver settings.

In the colonial section of the old city, **Ambar Tres,** La Atarazana 3 (© **809/688-0474**), sells jewelry made from amber and black coral, as well as mahogany carvings, watercolors, oil paintings, and other Dominican products. **Amber World Museum,** 452 Arzobispo Meriño (© **809/682-3309**), lives up to its name. In the wake of the film *Jurassic Park,* more and more visitors are flocking to this display to see plants, butterflies, insects, and even scorpions fossilized in resin millions of years ago during the age of the dinosaurs. Although some of the display is not for sale, in an adjoining salon you can watch craftspeople at work, polishing and shaping raw bits of ancient amber for sale. Admission is RD$15 (95¢) adults.

In the center of the most historical section of town is a well-known gallery, **Galería de Arte Nader,** Rafael Augusto Sanchez 22 (© **809/687-6674**), that sells so many Latin paintings that they're sometimes stacked in rows against the walls. Many of these paintings appear quite worthy, and works by some leading artists are displayed here. But others, especially those shipped in by the truck-load from Haiti, seem to be mere tourist junk. In recent years, the focus has shifted away from Haiti. Today you get a more diversified collection of art, including some from such other countries as Colombia, Peru, Venezuela, and even Cuba.

Although the name implies that it's new, **Novo Atarazana,** La Atarazana 21 (© **809/689-0582**), is actually one of the longest-established shops in town. If you don't have time to survey a lot of shops looking for local art and crafts, you'll find a wide cross-section here. You can purchase pieces of amber, black coral, leather goods, woodcarvings, and Haitian paintings.

Plaza Criolla, at the corner of Avenidas 27 de Febrero and Anacaona, is a modern shopping complex. Its shops are set amid gardens with tropical shrubbery and flowers, facing the Olympic Center. The architecture makes generous use of natural woods, and a covered wooden walkway links the stalls together.

Columbus Plaza (Decla, S.A.), Calle Arzobispo Merino 204 (© **809/689-0565**), is one of the largest supermarket-style gift and artifacts store in the country. Well-organized and imaginative, with a helpful English-speaking staff, it sprawls over three floors of a modern building divided into boutiques specializing in amber, larimar, gold and silver jewelry, cigars, paintings and sculpture, plus crafts items.

SANTO DOMINGO AFTER DARK

La Guácara Taína, Calle Mirador, in Parque Mirador del Sur (© **809/533-1051**), is the best *discoteca* in the Dominican Republic. As you dance to the music within this underground cave, you might be worried that the reverberations of the state-of-the-art dance music might loosen one of the overhead rocks and send it crashing to the dance floor. Fortunately, that hasn't happened (or if it has, we haven't heard about it.) The site lies underground, within a verdant park surrounded by a middle-class neighborhood. The specialty is merengue, salsa, and other international sounds. Inside you'll find three bars, two dance floors, and banquettes and chairs nestled into irregularities within the rocky walls. Entrance is RD$150 ($9.50) per person.

Azucar Disco/Diamante Bar, in the Melia Santo Domingo Hotel & Casino, Av. George Washington 361 (© **809/221-6666**), is a hot spot along the Malecón. Anyone could while away an intriguing evening by dividing his or her time between these two watering holes, both of which lie on the premises of this hotel. The Azucar Disco is one of the most artfully decorated discos in town, with mirrors and gray, green, and blue decor that functions as background for the throbbing, pulsating recorded music. If you consider yourself older and a bit more sedate (at least by D.R. standards), avoid the place on Tuesday nights, when it's college night. After a while many visitors move on to the Diamante Bar, the showcase bar in the Sheraton's casino, in an annex building adjacent to the hotel itself. Here, live bands perform merengue, salsa, and more. Both bars are open daily 8pm to 4am. The disco charges a cover of RD$60 ($3.75).

Fantasy Disco, Avenida Heroes de Luperón (© **809/535-5581**), is one of the capital's most popular discos, about a block inland from the Malecón. Once you get past the vigilant security staff, you'll find lots of intimate nooks and crannies, a small dance floor, and one of the country's best-chosen medleys of nonstop merengue music. Entrance is free, and beer costs RD\$45 (\$2.80) a bottle. The place is open daily 4pm till 6am.

Jet Set, Centro Comercial El Portal, Avenida Independencia (© **809/ 533-9707**), is one of the capital's most formal and elaborate nightclubs, admitting couples only, and nobody who is too rowdy. Most of the tables and chairs slope down toward an amphitheater-style dance floor, giving the place the feel of a bullfighting arena. The collection of live orchestras that play here are better than anywhere else in town. Entrance costs between RD\$65 to RD\$300 (\$4–\$18.75), depending on the artist. Open 9pm until the early morning.

In the colonial zone stands **Bachata Rosa,** La Atarazana 9 (© **809/ 688-0969**), which takes its name from a popular song on the island. In fact, Juan Luís Guerra, the Dominican merengue megastar who made the song a hit, is part owner. Currently, this is the island's best dance club, with action taking place on two floors. This club draws a heavier concentration of locals than of visitors. There's also a restaurant here, which serves local specialties. Open daily 5pm to 2am.

Disco Free, Avenida Ortega y Gaset (© **809/565-8100**), which is open Thursday to Sunday only, is the country's leading gay dance club, and also has some of the best music in town. The club is known for its salsa and merengue.

Many other chic stops are in the big hotels. **Las Palmas,** in the Hotel Santo Domingo, Av. Independencia (© **809/221-7111**), occupies premises originally decorated by Oscar de la Renta. Today it's best compared to a cross between a conventional bar and a disco, where the emphasis is on the bar trade between 5:30 and 9:30pm, and live music, such as salsa and merengue, from 9:30pm till closing time (4am). When someone isn't performing, large-screen TVs broadcast music videos beamed by satellite in from the U.S. mainland. Drink prices are reduced from 5:30 to 8pm.

Merengue Bar, in the Jaragua Renaissance Resort & Casino, Av. George Washington 367 (© **809/221-2222**), has a party atmosphere that often spills out into the sophisticated Jaragua Casino. High-ceilinged and painted in dark, subtly provocative colors, it includes a sprawling bar area, a sometimes overcrowded dance floor, and rows of banquettes and tables that face a brightly lit stage. Here, animated bands from as far away as the Philippines crank out high-energy sounds daily beginning at 4pm and going strong until the wee hours of the morning. The joint really gets jumping around 10pm, when this bar/ nightclub seems to forget that it operates in a jangling casino.

Santo Domingo has several major casinos, all of which are open nightly till 4 or 5am. The most spectacular is the **Renaissance Jaragua Resort & Casino,** Av. George Washington 367 (© **809/221-2222**), whose brightly flashing sign is the most dazzling light along the Malecón at night. The most glamorous casino in the country is fittingly housed in the capital's poshest hotel, and offers blackjack, baccarat, roulette, and slot machines. You can gamble in either Dominican pesos or U.S. dollars. Another casino is at the **Hispaniola Hotel,** Avenida Independencia (© **809/221-7111**). One of the most stylish casinos is the **Casino Diamante,** in the Melia Santo Domingo Hotel & Casino, Av. George Washington 361 (© **809/221-6666**). Its bilingual staff will help you play blackjack, craps, baccarat, and keno, among other games. There's also a piano bar.

3 Barahona Peninsula ★

True bargain hunters are deserting the high-priced resorts such as Casa de Campo at La Romana and those sprawling megahotels at Punta Cana. Instead, they're heading for more remote parts of the island nation, where tourist structures are just developing. There is no more remote corner than the Barahona Peninsula, often called "a closely guarded secret" in the travel industry.

You're certainly off the beaten track here. This seldom-visited southwestern region is still unspoiled, unlike the overly developed north coast around Puerto Plata. It's a 3-hour drive west of Santo Domingo. The peninsula's chief city is Barahona, whose locals are called *Barahoneros*. Even more remote is the tiny fishing village of Baoruco, some 15 miles of coastal scenery southwest of Barahona.

GETTING THERE & GETTING AROUND

If you don't have a car, call **Caribe Tours** (© **809/221-4422**) in Santo Domingo. This agency runs a minibus to the peninsula daily, charging RD$70 ($4.40) per person round-trip.

Once here, you can rent a car in Barahona from **Challenger Taxi** (© **809/524-2457**), which offers cars with their own drivers only on a daily or weekly basis.

ACCOMMODATIONS & MEALS YOU CAN AFFORD

Casa Bonita   Built around 1990 in the village of Baoruco, a 15-minute drive south of Barahona, this low-key, slow-paced cottage colony offers accommodations that consist of a dozen earth-toned *casitas* whose architecture emulates the natural, simple outdoor life favored in this obscure corner of the D.R. The furnishings are simple, but the beds are good, and room space is generous. Six accommodations contain air-conditioning, and most of them open onto a view of the water or the rain forest of the Sierra de Bahoruco. Shower-only bathrooms are small but adequate for the job. There's a swimming pool, a bar, a staff that speaks virtually no English, and both a river (the Baoruco) and a beach a short walk away. The food is a good reason to stay here. The chefs have their own secret recipes and will feed you well.

Carretera de la Costa, km 16, Baoruco (near Barahona), Dominican Republic. © **809/685-5184.** Fax 809/472-2163. casa_bonita@hotmail.com. 12 bungalows. Winter RD$935–RD$1,025 ($58.50–$64) double. Off-season RD$840–RD$925 ($52.50–$57.80) double. Rates include breakfast and dinner. AE, MC, V. **Amenities:** Restaurant, bar, pool. *In room:* A/C in 6 rooms, TV, ceiling fans.

Hotel Caribe   Painted pale blue both inside and out, this three-story hotel lies a few steps from the larger Riviera Beach Hotel (see below). Unpretentious and carefully maintained by the Tesanos family, it occupies a strip of land near the sea, although anyone who wants to go swimming usually walks for 5 minutes to a more hospitable stretch of sand nearby. There's no pool, no tennis courts, and few other facilities. But the price represents extremely good value, the greeting is friendly, and the bedrooms offer comfortable retreats from the sun and sand. Furnishings are simple and basic, but mattresses are firm; the bathrooms, though small, are well maintained, each with a shower.

Av. Enriquillo, Barahona, Dominican Republic. © **809/524-4111.** Fax 809/524-4115. 31 units. Year-round RD$409.50–RD$514.80 ($25.50–$32.25) single or double. Rates Mon–Fri include breakfast. AE, MC, V. **Amenities:** Restaurant, bar. *In room:* A/C, TV.

THE BEST ALL-INCLUSIVE DEAL IN BARAHONA

Riviera Beach Hotel ★ *Value*   This is the largest and most upscale hotel in Barahona. It encourages guests to check in as part of all-inclusive plans.

Accented with touches of marble, it rises five stories above one of the best beaches in town. There's a generously proportioned swimming pool on the premises, a tennis court, and two restaurants, one (El Curro) specializing in a la carte dishes, the other (El Manglar) featuring an almost endless roster of buffets. The bedrooms are simple but comfortable, white-walled, and airy, each with a balcony but few other architectural pretensions. Most of the rooms are a bit small, but beds are firm and comfortable, and the tiny bathrooms have decent plumbing and tiled showers.

Av. Enriquillo 6, Barahona, Dominican Republic. © 809/524-5111. Fax 809/524-5798. 108 units. Winter RD$895 ($56) per person double. Off-season RD$1,200 ($75) double. Rates include all meals and drinks. AE, DC, MC, V. **Amenities:** 2 restaurants, bar, pool, tennis courts, room service. *In room:* A/C, TV.

PRISTINE BEACHES & UNTAMED NATURE

"The southwest," as it's known, is filled in part with small coffee plantations and weekend homes of the upper class of Santo Domingo. The beaches here are white sand, set against a terrain that looks like rain forest in parts. The beaches are all but deserted, although we did spot Oscar de la Renta here one time, surveying the land for a fashion layout for *Vogue.*

There's also a series of three government parks, among the most untamed in the Caribbean. **Parque Nacional Isla Cabritos** is one of three islands in the **Lago Enriquillo,** bordering Haiti. This is the largest lake in the Caribbean, 21 miles in length. At 144 feet below sea level, it's also the lowest point in the Caribbean. Because of the lack of rain, it's a rather barren place with a few cacti and gnarled plants. However, people visit in hopes of getting a look at the American crocodile, which was imported to the lake in the early 1930s from Florida.

To visit, contact the **Dirección Nacional de Parques** (© 809/221-4660), which escorts visitors to the island twice a day. Nearly a dozen passengers are taken on a small launch for the 20-minute ride across a passage. The island is also home to wild goats, poisonous scorpions, and iguanas. If you want to spot a croc, it's best to take the first boat leaving at 7am.

Another national park, **Parque Nacional Bahoruco,** doesn't have adequate facilities for visitors. However, the most intrepid might want to explore **Parque Nacional Jaragua,** named for a Taíno Indian chief. This very arid land covers some 520 square miles, the largest in the Dominican Republic. It's covered with desertlike vegetation, including many species of birds. Pink flamingos also live here. The park embraces Lago Oviedo, a saltwater lake east of the town of Oviedo. Pink flamingos frequent this lake. You'll really need to take a guided tour to reach this park on the Haitian border. Only trucks and Jeeps can get through, and there are no tourist facilities.

4 La Romana ✦ & Altos de Chavón ✦✦✦

On the southeast coast, **La Romana** was once a sleepy sugarcane town that also specialized in cattle raising, and unless one had business here with either industry, no tourist bothered with it. But then **Casa de Campo** (© 809/523-3333) was built on its outskirts, a tropical resort of refinement and luxury, and La Romana soon became known among the jet-set travelers. Casa de Campo today remains one of the most expensive resorts in the Caribbean, attracting the well-heeled who demand top service and amenities. There is no other place to stay in this area. (But don't give up—ask your travel agent about package deals. Casa de Campo can often be booked at surprising bargain rates.)

LA ROMANA & ALTOS DE CHAVÓN   243

Just east of La Romana is **Altos de Chavón,** a village built specially for artists. For the frugal traveler, Altos de Chavón remains the reason to visit. You can visit in a day, but leave Santo Domingo early in the morning to get back to the city by early evening.

GETTING THERE

The easiest air routing to Casa de Campo from almost anywhere in North America is through San Juan, Puerto Rico, on **American Eagle** (© **800/ 433-7300** in the U.S.). See "Getting There" in chapter 17 for details.

From Santo Domingo, you can drive here in about an hour and 20 minutes from the international airport, along Las Américas Highway. (Allow another hour if you're in the center of the city.) Of course, everything depends on traffic conditions. (Watch for speed traps—low-paid police officers openly solicit bribes, whether you were speeding or not.)

LA ROMANA
GREAT DEALS ON DINING

Even if you can't afford to stay at Casa de Campo, you might want to enjoy a meal here, as some of its restaurants are moderate in price.

El Patio *Value* CARIBBEAN/AMERICAN   Originally designed as a disco, El Patio now contains a shield of lattices, banks of plants, and checkerboard tablecloths. Technically it's a glamorized bistro, offering good value, considering the quality of both the cookery and the first-class ingredients that go into meal preparations. You can feast on selections from the constantly changing menu. Try such pleasing dishes as grilled snapper in a savory lime sauce or filet of salmon with a perfectly prepared vinaigrette. The fettuccine in seafood sauce also wins a thumbs-up. If you like your dishes plainer, opt for half a roast chicken or the classic beef tips in mushroom and onion sauce.

In Casa de Campo. © **809/523-3333**. Main courses RD$155–RD$330 ($9.75–$20.75). AE, DC, MC, V. Daily 7am–2pm and 3–10pm.

Lago Grill CARIBBEAN/AMERICAN   Lago Grill is ideal for breakfast; in fact, it has one of the best-stocked morning buffets in the country. Your view is of a lake, a sloping meadow, and the resort's private airport, with the sea in the distance. At the fresh-juice bar, an employee in colonial costume will extract juices in any combination you prefer from 25 different tropical fruits. Then you can select your ingredients for an omelet, and an employee will whip it up while you wait. The lunchtime buffet includes sandwiches, burgers, *sancocho* (the famous Dominican stew), and fresh conch chowder. There's also a well-stocked salad bar.

In Casa de Campo. © **809/523-3333**. Buffet RD$300 ($18.75). AE, DC, MC, V. Daily 7–11am and noon–4pm.

BEACHES & SPORTS GALORE AT CASA DE CAMPO

Casa de Campo has one of the most complete watersports facilities in the Dominican Republic. If you can stay at the resort, which is fabulous, on a bargain package rate, great; if not, you can still take advantage of some of the resort's facilities. Reservations and information on any seaside activity can be arranged through the resort's concierge; call © **809/523-3333**.

A large, palm-fringed sandy crescent, **Bayahibe** is a 20-minute launch trip or a 30-minute drive from La Romana. In addition, **La Minitas** is a tiny, but nice, immaculate beach and lagoon. Transportation is provided on the bus, or you can rent a horse-drawn buckboard. Finally, **Catalina** is a turquoise beach on a deserted island just 45 minutes away by motorboat. You can charter a boat for snorkeling. The resort maintains eight charter vessels, with a minimum of eight people required per outing. Wednesday to Monday, full-day snorkeling trips to Isla Catalina cost $28 per snorkeler.

Trail rides at Casa de Campo cost $30 for 1 hour, $52 for 2.

For **tennis** buffs, 13 clay courts at Casa de Campo are lit for night play. The courts are available daily 7am to 9pm. Charges are RD$330 ($20.75) during the day and RD$289 ($18) at night.

ALTOS DE CHAVÓN: AN ARTISTS' COLONY

In 1976 a plateau 100 miles east of Santo Domingo was selected by Charles G. Bluhdorn, then chairman of Gulf + Western Industries, as the site for a remarkable project. Dominican stonecutters, woodworkers, and ironsmiths began the task that would produce Altos de Chavón, today a flourishing Caribbean art center set above the canyon of the Río Chavón and the Caribbean Sea.

A walk down one of the cobblestoned paths of Altos de Chavón reveals at every turn architecture reminiscent of another era. Coral block and terra-cotta brick buildings house artists' studios, craft workshops, galleries, stores, and restaurants. Mosaics of black river pebbles, sun-bleached coral, and red sandstone spread out to the plazas. The **Church of St. Stanislaus** is centered on the main plaza, with its fountain of the four lions, colonnade of obelisks, and panoramic views.

School of Design at Altos de Chavón has offered a 2-year Associate in Applied Science degree, in the areas of communications, fashion, environmental studies, product design, and fine arts/illustration, since its inauguration in 1982. The school is affiliated with the Parsons School of Design in New York and Paris, providing local and international graduates with the opportunity to acquire the advanced skills needed for placement in design careers.

From around the world come artists-in-residence, the established and the aspiring. Altos de Chavón provides them with lodging, studio space, and a group exhibition at the culmination of their 3-month stay.

The **galleries** at Altos de Chavón offer a varied and engaging mix of exhibits. In three distinct spaces—the Principal Gallery, the Rincón Gallery, and the Loggia—the work of well-known and emerging Dominican and international artists is showcased. The gallery has a consignment space where finely crafted silk-screen and other multiple works are available for sale.

Altos de Chavón's *talleres* are craft ateliers, where local artisans have been trained to produce ceramic, silk-screen, and woven-fiber products. From the clay apothecary jars with Carnival devil lids to the colored tapestries of Dominican houses, the richness of island myth and legend, folklore, and handcraft tradition is much in evidence. The posters, notecards, and printed T-shirts that come from the silk-screen workshops are among the most sophisticated in the Caribbean. All the products of Altos de Chavón's *talleres* are sold at **La Tienda,** the foundation village store.

Thousands of visitors annually view the Altos de Chavón **Regional Museum of Archaeology** (© **809/523-8554**), which houses the objects of Samuel Pion, an amateur archaeologist and collector of treasures from the vanished Taíno tribes, the island's first settlers. The timeless quality of some of the museum's objects makes them seem strangely contemporary in design—some of the sculptural forms recall the work of Brancusi or Arp. The museum is open daily 9am to 8pm.

At the heart of the village's performing-arts complex is the 5,000-seat open-air **amphitheater.** Since its inauguration over a decade ago by the late Frank Sinatra and Carlos Santana, the amphitheater has hosted renowned concerts, symphonies, theater, and festivals, including concerts by Julio Iglesias and Gloria Estefan. The annual Heineken Jazz Festival has brought together such diverse talents as Dizzy Gillespie, Toots Thielemans, Tania Maria, and Randy Brecker.

GREAT DEALS ON DINING

Café del Sol ITALIAN   The pizzas at this stone-floored indoor/outdoor cafe, which is positioned one flight above the medieval-looking piazza outside, are the best on the south coast. The favorite seems to be *quattro stagioni,* topped with mushrooms, artichoke hearts, ham, and olives. The chef makes a soothing minestrone in the true Italian style, served with freshly made bread. To reach the cafe, climb a flight of stone steps to the rooftop of a building whose ground floor houses a jewelry shop.

Altos de Chavón. © **809/523-3333,** ext. 2346. Pizzas RD$153–RD$220 ($9.50–$13.75); salads RD$90–RD$250 ($5.75–$15.75). AE, MC, V. Daily 11am–11pm.

El Sombrero MEXICAN   In this thick-walled, colonial-style building, the jutting timbers and roughly textured plaster evoke a corner of Old Mexico. There's a scattering of rattan furniture and an occasional example of Mexican weaving, but the main draw is the spicy cuisine. Red snapper in garlic sauce is usually very successful. Most guests dine outside on the covered patio, within earshot of a group of wandering minstrels wearing sombreros. Chances are you've had better versions of the standard nachos, enchiladas, black-bean soup, and grilled steaks served here, but a margarita or two will make it a fun night out anyway.

Altos de Chavón. © **809/523-3333.** Reservations recommended. Main courses RD$185–RD$350 ($11.50–$22). AE, MC, V. Daily 6–11pm.

La Piazzetta ITALIAN   La Piazzetta snuggles in the 16th-century-style "village" set high above the Chavón River. Well-prepared Italian dinners might begin with an antipasto *misto,* followed with filet of sea bass with artichokes–and–black olive sauce, chicken *saltimbocca* (with ham), or beef brochette with a walnut-and-arugula sauce. Your fellow diners are likely to be guests of the deluxe Casa de Campo nearby.

Altos de Chavón. © **809/523-3333.** Reservations required. Main courses RD$180–RD$450 ($11.25–$28). AE, MC, V. Daily 6–11pm.

SHOPPING

At **Everett Designs,** Altos de Chavón (© **809/523-3333,** ext. 8331), the designs here are so original that many visitors mistake this place for a museum. Each piece of jewelry is handcrafted in a mini-factory at the rear of the shop. Minnesota-born Bill Everett is the inspirational force for many of these pieces, which include Dominican larimar and amber, 17th-century Spanish pieces-of-eight from sunken galleons, and polished silver and gold.

5 Puerto Plata ⌖

Columbus intended to found a city at Puerto Plata and name it La Isabela. But a tempest detained him, and it wasn't until 1502 that Nicolás de Ovando founded Puerto Plata ("Port of Silver"), 130 miles northwest of Santo Domingo.

Value   Cheap Thrills: What to See & Do for Free (Well, Almost) in the Dominican Republic

---

- **Explore the National Parks.** This island nation has 16 national parks and 7 nature reserves—unequalled in the Caribbean. Here you can climb mountains—Pico Durate in J. Armando Bermúdez National Park is the highest mountain in the West Indies at 10,700 feet—and cascade, an ecosport involving climbing to the top of a waterfall, then rappelling down the middle of the cascade. In the southwestern tip of the country, Parque Nacional Jaragua is one of the largest in the Caribbean, with everything from offshore islands to inland deserts. Home to turtles and reptiles, it also has more than half of all the bird species found on the island. Dominican tourist offices will provide complete details about how to tour these parks on your own.

- **Call on the Crocs.** In the southwest part of the country, a rare collection of endangered American crocodiles still live around Lake Enriquillo, a vast body of saltwater that is the biggest lake in the West Indies. In the center of the lake is Parque Nacional Isla Cabritos ("Goat Island"), home to the native American crocodile, as well as flocks of pink flamingos, roseate spoonbills, terns, herons, and other birdlife. Like the crocodile, the similarly endangerd rhinoceros iguana and the variegated shell turtle call the lake home. The drive down from Santo Domingo to the lake goes through the ocean-bordering town of Barahona and takes more than 3 hours. *Be duly warned:* This area is one of the hottest in the Caribbean, even in winter. But to see nature in the wild like this, it's worth a little heat and inconvenience.

- **Spend a Day in a "Medieval Village."** Altos de Chavón, on the southern coast near the chic resort of Casa de Campo, is without equal in the Caribbean. You can spend a delightful day here—it's free to enter—wandering around this re-creation of a 16th-century village created by an Italian set designer. It's a combination of a living museum and an artisans' colony. Some of the Caribbean's

---

The port became the last stop for ships going back to Europe, their holds laden with treasures taken from the New World.

Puerto Plata appeals to vacationers who might shun more expensive resorts, and some hotels boast a nearly full occupancy rate almost year-round. It's already casting a shadow on business at longer-established resorts throughout the Caribbean, especially in Puerto Rico.

Most of the hotels are not actually in Puerto Plata itself but are in a special tourist zone called **Playa Dorada.** The backers of this usually sun-drenched spot have poured vast amounts of money into a flat area between a pond and the curved and verdant shoreline. (It rains a lot in Puerto Plata during the winter, whereas the south is drier.) There are major hotels, a coterie of condominiums and villas, a famed golf course, and a riding stable with horses for each of the major properties.

finest artisans can be seen at work here. There's a little bit of everything, ranging from an ornate stone church to a Grecian-style amphitheater; there's even a museum with artifacts from the extinct Taíno Indians. Workshops, galleries, and studios can be visited, and the local shops hold equal fascination. There are also a lot of inexpensive dining places if you're staying over for lunch.

• **Explore Santo Domingo's Colonial Past.** Except for the historic core of Old San Juan, no other place in the Caribbean has as much history as the restored colonial zone of Santo Domingo, the heart of this ancient city. It's filled with attractions at every turn, including Calle Las Damas, one of the oldest and most beautiful streets in the New World, named for the ladies of the viceregal court who once lived here and used to promenade up and down.

• **Hang Out at Samaná.** The Samaná peninsula, along the east coast, was settled in the 1820s by thousands of escaped U.S. slaves who established a new life here in little fishing villages. Samaná is just awakening to tourism, and a journey here will show you how the Caribbean used to be before the big developers moved in. The location, reached across rugged terrain, is 168 miles east of the airport at Puerto Plata. Las Terrenas on the north coast of the peninsula alone boasts 17 miles of virgin beach. You can meet and talk to many of the descendants of the runaway slaves, who still speak English.

• **Journey to the Dominican Alps.** Most visitors come to enjoy white sandy beaches, but for an offbeat adventure you can go inland to the resort towns of Jarabacoa and Constanza, the heartland of the "Dominican Alps." These resorts are unexpected on a tropical island. The evenings are cool up here. Evoking Switzerland, chalets instead of beachside homes dominate the landscape. Lying along 90 miles north of Santo Domingo, and easily reached by car, the beauty of the forests, the towering "Alps," and the rushing waterfalls await you.

PUERTO PLATA ESSENTIALS

GETTING THERE The international airport is actually not in Puerto Plata but east of Playa Dorado on the road to Sosúa. For information about flights from North America, see "Getting There" at the beginning of this chapter.

From Santo Domingo, the 3½-hour drive directly north on Autopista Duarte passes through the lush Cibao Valley, home of the tobacco industry and Bermudez rum, and through Santiago de los Caballeros, the second-largest city in the country, 90 miles north of Santo Domingo.

GETTING AROUND **Taxi service** is available; just be sure to agree with the driver on the fare before your trip starts, as the vehicles are not metered. You'll find taxis on Central Park at Puerto Plata. At night it's wise to rent your cab for a round-trip. If you go in the daytime by taxi to any of the other beach resorts or villages, check on reserving a vehicle for your return trip. Note that a taxi from Puerto Plata to Sosúa will cost around RD$320 to RD$360 ($20–$22.50) each way, and it will hold up to four occupants.

The cheapest way of getting around is on a *motoconcho,* found at the major corners of Puerto Plata and Sosúa. This motorcycle *concho* (taxi) offers a ride to practically anywhere in town. You can also go from Puerto Plata to Playa Dorada (site of most of the hotels). Fares range from RD$25 to RD$35 ($1.55–$2.20).

For information on renting a car, see "Getting Around" at the beginning of this chapter. You might find that a **motor scooter** will be suitable for transportation in Puerto Plata or Sosúa, although the roads are potholed.

Minivans are another means of transport, especially if you're traveling outside town. They leave from Puerto Plata's Central Park and will take you all the way to Sosúa. Determine the fare before getting in. Usually a shared ride between Puerto Plata and Sosúa costs RD$15 (95¢) per person. Service is daily 6am to 9pm.

FAST FACTS Round-the-clock drugstore service is offered by **Farmacia Deleyte,** Calle John F. Kennedy 89 (✆ 809/586-2583). Emergency medical service is provided by **Clínica Dr. Brugal,** Calle José del Carmen Ariza 15 (✆ 809/586-2519). To summon the **police** in Puerto Plata, call ✆ 809/586-2331. Tourist information is available in Puerto Plata at the **Office of Tourism,** Playa Long Beach (✆ 809/586-3676).

ACCOMMODATIONS YOU CAN AFFORD

Hostal Jimessón This is about as simple a hotel as we will recommend. It lies in the commercial heart of downtown Puerto Plata, in what was originally a rather grand wood-sided house whose vestiges of gingerbread trim still remain. The public rooms have high ceilings, remnants of a faded grandeur, and some unusual antiques. The bedrooms, however, lack the charm of the front rooms. In a cinder-block addition in back, they're small, anonymous, and somewhat cramped. Mattresses are well used, and shower-only bathrooms are tiny. There are almost no resort-style amenities to speak off, but the staff is polite and the price really can't be beat. No more than two occupants are ever allowed in any bedroom. Only coffee is served in the morning, but there are several cafes in the neighborhood, as well as the many inexpensive restaurants in town.

Calle John F. Kennedy 41, Puerto Plata, Dominican Republic. ✆ 809/586-5131. Fax 809/586-7313. 22 units. Year-round RD$300 ($18.75) single or double. Rates include morning coffee. AE, MC, V. **Amenities:** Guest lounge. *In room:* A/C.

THE BEST ALL-INCLUSIVE DEALS IN PUERTO PLATA

Caribbean Village Club on the Green ⋆ 𝒱𝑎𝑙𝑢𝑒 Upgraded in 1996 by a hotel chain, this modern low-rise property is near a cluster of competitors east of the airport, a 10-minute walk to the nearest good beach. The hotel offers comfortable but simple bedrooms, and the all-inclusive rates include three meals a day, all beverages, and some watersports. Accommodations are decorated in tropical Caribbean colors, with private safes, two queen-size beds with firm mattresses (some rooms have king-size beds), and medium-size bathrooms with good showers and excellent maintenance.

Playa Dorada, Puerto Plata, Dominican Republic. ✆ 809/320-1111, or 305/269-5909 in Miami. Fax 809/320-5386. www.allegroresorts.com/cv_s/cotg. 336 units. Winter $147 single; $95 per person double. Off-season $131 single; $77 per person double. Rates include meals, beverages, and some watersports. AE, MC, V. **Amenities:** 3 restaurants, bar, pool; 7 tennis courts, health club, sauna; watersports. *In room:* A/C, TV, safe.

Villas Doradas Beach Resort ⋆ 𝐾𝑖𝑑𝑠 This collection of town houses east of the airport is arranged in landscaped clusters, usually around a courtyard. There's no beachfront here. Each unit is pleasantly furnished with louvered doors and windows. The units have sleek tropical styling with tile floors, rattan and bamboo furnishings, and wooden ceilings. Most of the bedrooms have either queen-size or twin beds, each with firm, frequently renewed mattresses. Many also have tiny kitchenettes and balconies or patios. Shower-only bathrooms are small but tidily arranged. We didn't get the impression that you'd get any personal service here.

A focal point of the resort is the restaurant Las Garzas, where shows entertain guests every evening. The management also features barbecues around the pool area, where a net is sometimes set up for volleyball games. Of course, it would be tempting never to leave the shade of the cone-shaped thatch-roofed pool bar, which is one of the most popular parts of the whole resort.

Playa Dorada (Apdo. Postal 1370), Puerto Plata, Dominican Republic. (℃ **809/320-3000.** Fax 809/320-4790. 244 units. Year-round $66–$90 per person single or double. Rates are all-inclusive. AE, MC, V. **Amenities:** Restaurant, bar, pool, kiddie pool, tennis court, horseback riding. *In room:* A/C, TV, kitchenette.

GREAT DEALS ON DINING

Hemingway's Café INTERNATIONAL   The rough-hewn character of this place stands in stark contrast to the manicured exterior of the shopping center that contains it. Inside, you'll find a dark and shadowy plank-sheathed bar and grill, dotted with accessories you might have found on a pier in Key West. We can just imagine Papa himself digging into the succulent pastas, fajitas, meal-sized salads, burgers, and huge New York steaks, while downing one of the "Floridita" cocktails. After around 9pm, a karaoke machine cranks out romantic or rock-and-roll favorites.

Playa Dorada Plaza. (℃ **809/320-2230.** Sandwiches, salads, and pastas RD$55–RD$105 ($3.50–$6.50); main course platters RD$105–RD$310 ($6.50–$19.50). AE, MC, V. Daily 11am–1am.

Jardín de Jade CHINESE   A high-ceilinged, airy, modern restaurant, Jardín de Jade offers the finest Chinese food in the area. Typical menu items include barbecued Peking duck, sautéed diced chicken in chile sauce, and fried crab claws. The chefs specialize in Cantonese and Szechwan cuisine. You've probably eaten better-prepared versions of these dishes before, but at least this restaurant provides a change of pace. Because it's located in a heavily booked resort, it has a captive audience, yet it remains solid and reliable. We haven't had good service here, though.

In the Villas Doradas Beach Resort, Playa Dorada. (℃ **809/586-3000.** Reservations recommended. Main courses RD$170–RD$350 ($10.75–$22). AE, MC, V. Daily 7–10pm.

Porto Fino ★ ITALIAN/DOMINICAN   This popular restaurant, just across from the entrance of the Hotel Montemar in Puerto Plata, serves generous helpings of Parmesan breast of chicken, eggplant Parmesan, ravioli, and pizzas, and such regional dishes as *arroz con pollo* (chicken with rice). You'll get off cheap if you order only pizza. Locals and visitors mingle freely here. This is a place to go for a casual meal in casual clothes.

Av. Las Hermanas Mirabal. (℃ **809/586-2858.** Main courses RD$85–RD$250 ($5.30–$15.65). AE, MC, V. Daily 8am–midnight.

Roma II INTERNATIONAL   This air-conditioned restaurant is staffed by an engaging crew of well-mannered young employees who work hard to converse in English. The menu includes 13 varieties of pizza, such as cheese, shrimp, and garlic. Seafood dishes include paella and several preparations of lobster and sea bass. The menu is unfussy, as is the preparation. Don't look for any new taste sensations (except for octopus vinaigrette, one of the chef's specialties). The meat dishes, such as filet steak, are less successful than the fish offerings.

Calle Emilio Prud'homme 45 at the corner of Calle Beller. ℂ 809/586-3904. Main courses RD$90–RD$305 ($5.75–$19); pizza RD$70–RD$210 ($4.50–$13). AE, MC, V. Daily 10am–11pm.

BEACHES, WATERSPORTS & OTHER OUTDOOR PURSUITS

The north coast is a watersports scene, although the sea here tends to be rough. Snorkeling is popular, and the windsurfing is among the best in the Caribbean.

Although they face the sometimes turbulent waters of the Atlantic, and it rains a lot in winter, beaches put the north coast of the Dominican Republic on the tourist map. The beaches at **Playa Dorada** are known collectively as the "Amber Coast" for all the deposits of amber that have been discovered here. Playa Dorada has one of the highest concentrations of hotels on the north coast, so the beaches here, although good, are likely to be crowded at any time of the year, both with tourists and locals. The beaches have lovely white or powdery beige sand. The Atlantic waters here are very popular for water-skiing and windsurfing. Many concession stands along the beach rent equipment.

Another good choice in the area, **Luperón Beach** lies about a 60-minute drive to the west of Puerto Plata. This is a wide beach of powdery white sand, set amid palm trees that provide wonderful shade when the noonday sun grows too fierce. It's more ideal for windsurfing, scuba diving, and snorkeling than for general swimming. Various watersports concessions can be found here, along with several snack bars.

The watersports options in Puerto Plata are numerous. Most of the kiosks on the beach here are ultimately run by the same company, and prices don't vary among them. If there isn't one close to your hotel, try **Playa NACO Centro de Deportes Acuaticos** (ℂ **809/320-2567**), a rustic clapboard-sided hut on the beachfront of the Dorado NACO Hotel. Prices are as follows: banana boat rides RD$80 ($5) for a 10- to 12-minute ride; water-skiing RD$240 ($15) for a 10- to 15-minute ride; sea kayak and Sunfish sailboat rental RD$160 ($10) per hour; sailboards RD$290 ($18.25) per day; and paragliding at RD$350 ($22) for a 10-minute ride.

There are watersports kiosks about every 100 yards along the beach, any of which will rent you snorkeling gear and tell you the best spots for seeing fish. Puerto Plata isn't great for snorkeling, but you can take a boat trip to some decent sites.

GOLF   Robert Trent Jones, Jr., designed the par-72, 18-hole **Playa Dorada** ★★ championship golf course (ℂ **809/320-3344**), which surrounds the resorts and runs along the coast. Even nongolfers can stop at the clubhouse for a drink or a snack to enjoy the views. It's best to make arrangements at the activities desk of your hotel. Greens fees are RD$950 ($59.50) for 18 holes, including the cart. Another Jones design, **Playa Grande Golf Course** at Playa Grande, Carretera Rio San Juan–Cabrera, km 9 (ℂ **800/858-2258** or 809/582-0860), is generating a lot of excitement. Some pros have already hailed it as one of the best of the Caribbean's golf courses. Ten of its holes border the Atlantic, and many of these are also set atop dramatic cliffs overlooking the turbulent waters. When you're not concentrating on your game of golf, you can take in the panoramic views of the ocean and of Playa Grande Beach. The course is 4,888 yards, par-72, and greens fees are $90 year-round, with carts.

SEEING THE SIGHTS

Fort San Felipe, the oldest fort in the New World, is a popular attraction. Philip II of Spain ordered its construction in 1564, a task that took 33 years to complete. Built with 8-foot-thick walls, the fort was virtually impenetrable, and the moat surrounding it was treacherous—the Spaniards sharpened swords and embedded them in coral below the surface of the water to discourage enemies from fording the moat. The doors of the fort are only 4 feet high, another deterrent to swift passage. During Trujillo's rule, Fort San Felipe was used as a prison. Standing at the end of the Malecón, the fort was restored in the early 1970s. Admission is RD$20 ($1.25). Open daily 8am to 5pm.

Isabel de Torres, a tower with a fort built when Trujillo was in power, affords a panoramic view of the Amber Coast from a point near the top, 2,595 feet above sea level. You reach the observation point by cable car (*teleférico*), a 7-minute ascent. Once here, you're also treated to 7 acres of botanical gardens. The round-trip costs RD$100 ($6.25) for adults, RD$30 ($1.90) for children 12 and under. The aerial ride is operated Thursday to Tuesday 9am to 5pm. There's often a long wait in line for the cable car, and at certain times it's closed for repairs, so check at your hotel before you head out.

You can see a collection of rare amber specimens at the **Museum of Dominican Amber,** Calle Duarte 61 (© 809/586-2848). The museum, open Monday to Friday 8am to 5pm and Saturday 9am to 5pm, is near Puerto Plata's Central Park. Guided tours in English are offered. Admission is RD$40 ($2.50) for adults, RD$7 (45¢) for children. The neoclassical house sheltering the Amber Museum also contains the densest collection of **boutiques** in Puerto Plata. Merchandise is literally packed into seven competing establishments. A generous percentage of the paintings are from neighboring Haiti, but the amber, larimar, and mahogany woodcarvings are from the Dominican Republic. On the premises is also a patio bar.

SHOPPING

Plaza Turisol Complex, the largest shopping center on the north coast, has about 80 different outlets. Each week, or so it seems, a new store opens. You might want to head here to get a sampling of the merchandise available in Puerto Plata before going to any specific recommendation. The plaza lies about 5 minutes from the centers of Puerto Plata and Playa Dorada, on the main road heading east. Nearby is a smaller shopping center, **Playa Dorada Plaza,** with about 20 shops, selling handcrafts, clothing, souvenirs, and gifts. Both centers are open daily 9am to 9pm.

Plaza Isabela, in Playa Dorada about 500 yards from the entrance to the Playa Dorada Hotel complex, is a collection of small specialty shops constructed in the Victorian gingerbread style, although much of its inventory has a Spanish inspiration and flair. Here you'll find the main branch of the Dominican Republic's premier jeweler, **Harrison's,** Plaza Isabela, Playa Dorada (© 809/586-3933), which specializes in platinum. Although there are almost two dozen branches of Harrison's in the Dominican Republic, the chain—at least as yet—has no outlets anywhere else in the world. Celebrities wearing the jewelry have included Madonna, Michael Jackson, Keith Richards of the Rolling Stones, and Patrick Swayze. It's possible to take a tour of this outlet. Any merchandise that sits for a year in a store is automatically marked down and placed in a special sale section. There's another branch of this store in the Playa Dorada Shopping Plaza (© 809/320-2219) in the Playa Dorada Hotel complex.

ROLLING THE DICE & OTHER AFTER-DARK DIVERSIONS

AMHSA Paradise Beach Casino (© 809/586-3663) has the most appealing design of Puerto Plata's three casinos. It is decorated in shades of hot pink, with a soaring ceiling and lots of mahogany trim and louvers. **Allegro's Jack Tar Village,** Playa Dorada (© 809/320-3800), has a casino as well as a disco, a European-style restaurant, and five bars. It's built in Spanish Mediterranean colonial style with a terra-cotta roof. **Playa Dorada Casino,** in the Playa Dorada Hotel (© 809/586-3988), has mahogany gaming tables reflected in the silver ceiling. If you have time to visit only one casino, make it this one. No shorts are permitted inside the premises after 7pm, and beach attire is usually discouraged.

The Playa Dorada Hotel complex contains about 20 hotels, five of which have **discos** that welcome anyone, guest or not, into their confines. These after-dark diversions tend to be filled mainly with foreign visitors, although they occasionally attract locals looking to hook up with tourists. None charges a cover, and the almost-universal drink of choice, Presidente Beer, costs RD$50 ($3.15) a bottle. **Andromeda,** in the Hotel Heaven (© 809/586-5250), is a high-voltage club off the lobby that opens nightly at 11pm. **Crazy Moon,** adjacent to the lobby of the AMHSA Paradise Hotel (© 809/320-3663), is the hottest, hippest, and most sought-after nightclub in Puerto Plata. Fronted by an artful re-creation of a clapboard-sided Creole cottage, and outfitted in party colors of pink, green, and yellow, it's open Monday to Saturday 10pm to 4am. Admission charges range from RD$20 to RD$80 ($1.25–$5).

La Barrica, Av. Manolo Tavares Justo 106 (© 809/586-6660), lies behind an ochre-colored Spanish colonial facade on the dusty highway leading from Puerto Plata to Santiago, about a mile south of the town center. It's mobbed with locals every night after 11pm. They talk, smoke, drink, flirt, and often neck with each other on any of the thousands of folding chairs, many of which you're likely to trip over. If you enjoy active, sometimes aggressive merengue bars where a man will positively never need to be alone, you might find it fascinating. Entrance is free, but know in advance that you might be frisked for weapons before you enter. Open daily noon to 6am.

6 Sosúa (*

About 15 miles east of Puerto Plata is one of the finest beaches in the Dominican Republic, Sosúa Beach, a strip of soft white sand more than half a mile wide in a cove sheltered by coral cliffs. The beach connects two communities, which together make up the town known as Sosúa. But, regrettably, you might not be able to enjoy a day on the beach in peace, as vendors and often beggars pursue visitors aggressively. To the east is our favorite beach, **Playa Grande** (**, a long stretch of white sand that has the consistency of powder. The swimming is safe in shallows close to shore. In summer, the waters are calmer and more hospitable, and that's true anywhere along the north coast. Playa Grande beach is great for picnics, sunset watching, walking, and hanging out. It's rapidly being developed, and the Playa Grande Hotel is just one of many projects planned. Beachcombers delight in walking along this beach, picking up driftwood and anything else that might have washed ashore.

At one end of the beach is **El Batey,** an area with residential streets, gardens, restaurants, shops, and hotels that can be visited by those who can tear themselves away from the beach. Real-estate transactions have been booming in El Batey and its environs, where many streets have been paved and villas constructed. At the other end of Sosúa Beach lies **Los Charamicos,** a sharp contrast to El Batey. Here you'll find tin-roofed shacks, vegetable stands, chickens scrabbling in the rubbish, and warm, friendly people. This community is a typical Latin American village, recognizable through the smells, sights, and sounds in the narrow, rambling streets.

Sosúa was founded in 1940 by European Jews seeking refuge from Hitler, when Trujillo invited 100,000 of them to settle in his country on a banana plantation. Actually, only 600 or so Jews were allowed to immigrate, and of those, only about a dozen or so remained. However, there are some 20 Jewish families living in Sosúa today, and, for the most part, they are engaged in the dairy and smoked-meat industry the refugees began during the war. Many of the Jews intermarried with Dominicans, and the town has taken on an increasingly Spanish flavor; women of the town are often seen wearing both the Star of David and the Virgin de Altagracia. Nowadays, many German expatriates are also found in the town.

GETTING THERE

Taxis, charter buses, and *públicos* from Puerto Plata and Playa Dorada let passengers off at the stairs leading down from the highway to Sosúa beach. Take the *autopista* east for about 30 minutes from Puerto Playa. If you venture off the main highway, anticipate potholes that fall all the way to China.

ACCOMMODATIONS YOU CAN AFFORD

Hotel Sosúa ⭐ *Value*   This place is one of the best choices for affordable accommodations in Sosúa. It's in a suburban community about a 2-minute drive from the center of town. Its simple and attractive layout includes a reception area designed to conceal a flagstone-rimmed pool from the street outside. The medium-size bedrooms are strung along a wing extending beside the pool and contain simple furniture that was, for the most part, crafted locally. The bedrooms contain ceiling fans, a mini-fridge, and an occasional pinewood balcony. Light furnishings, including good beds with firm mattresses, add a graceful note, but the shower-only bathrooms are only routine and a bit cramped. On the premises are a restaurant (Caballo Blanco; see "Great Deals on Dining," below), a mini-gym, a bar, and a boutique that sells the day-to-day necessities that tourists might need.

Calle Dr. Alejo Martínez, El Batey, Sosúa, Dominican Republic. ✆ 809/571-2683. Fax 809/571-2180. hotel. sosua@net.do. 40 units. Winter $40 single; $50 double. Off-season $30 single; $40 double. Rates include continental breakfast. AE, MC, V. **Amenities:** Restaurant, bar, pool, small fitness center. In room: A/C, TV, mini-fridge, ceiling fan.

Hotel Yaroa   Clean, decent, and well managed, this hotel, a short walk from the beach, gets its name from a long-ago native village. Inside, you'll find a two-story atrium illuminated by a skylight that's shaped like a Star of David, lots of exposed wood and stone, and a well-designed garden that rings a sheltered pool. Each bedroom has more space than you might expect, with a decor that's based on varnished mahogany louvers and trim; terra-cotta tile floors; white walls, and a ceiling fan. Shower-only bathrooms are cramped but serviceable, and the overall ambience is pleasant and reasonably priced.

Calle Dr. Rosens, El Batey, Sosúa, Dominican Republic. ✆ 809/571-2651. Fax 809/571-3814. www.hotelyaroa. com. 24 units. Year-round $56–$68 double or single. Rates include breakfast. MC, V. **Amenities:** Restaurant, bar. In room: A/C, ceiling fan.

THE BEST ALL-INCLUSIVE DEALS

Casa Marina Ritz/Casa Marina Beach ⭐   These twin hotels were built in 1987, as part of the building boom that swept over Sosúa. Originally conceived as different entities, they were enlarged and combined in 1996. What's the difference between the two? Residents of the Casa Marina's 32 bedrooms have to walk about 3 minutes to reach the resort's main cluster of dining, drinking, entertainment, and watersports facilities at Playita Beach, a short drive from the center of Sosúa. By far the larger hotel is the Casa Marina Ritz, with units scattered among eight separate annexes. (Except for their views, over a pool or a garden, the units at the Casa Marina Branch are equivalent in virtually every way, but cost less because of their relative isolation from the heart of the resort's action.)

Throughout the complex, color schemes are brightly tropical, with locally made furniture and touches of rattan. Guest rooms are fairly compact, with either twin beds or double beds, each with firm mattresses. The floors are tile, and the mirrored closets have safes inside. Bathrooms, which have tubs and showers, are small, but maintenance and plumbing are good. If possible, try for one of the rooms on the 10th or 11th floors, where the views of the sea are panoramic. The big drawback here is massive group bookings.

Residents of both properties share access to three pools, a medley of bars, and four restaurants (meals are included in the price).

La Playita, Sosúa, Dominican Republic. ℂ **809/571-3690.** Fax 809/571-3110. 332 units. Year-round, Casa Marina Ritz $105 single; $157 double. Casa Marina Beach $75 single; $105 double. Rates are all-inclusive. AE, MC, V. **Amenities:** 4 restaurants, several bars, 3 pools, watersports. *In room:* A/C, TV, safe.

Punta Goleta Beach Resort   Built in 1986, and set on about 100 acres of sandy, palm-dotted soil, this all-inclusive resort makes it a point to include enough distractions to keep a guest busy. The resort has a neo-Victorian theme, with gingerbread trim and pastel colors. The location is private, without being isolated. Bedrooms are a bit cramped, but each one has a tropical motif, with decent beds (firm mattresses) and a tiled bathroom with a shower that is tiny but well kept. Windsurfing is excellent in the waters offshore.

Cabarete Rd., Cabarete, Sosúa, Dominican Republic. ℂ **809/571-0700.** Fax 809/571-0707. www.puntagoleta. com. 254 units. Winter RD$1,575 ($98.50) single; RD$2,250 ($140.75) double. Off-season RD$700 ($43.75) single; RD$1,300 ($81.25) double. Rates include all meals. AE, MC, V. **Amenities:** 2 restaurants, 3 bars, disco, pool, 2 tennis courts; watersports. *In room:* A/C, TV.

Sosúa by the Sea   The blue-and-white main building here is softened with inviting wooden lattices. The pool area opens onto Sosúa Bay, and the resort stands on a coral cliff above the beach. From the open-air rooftop lounge you have a view of Mount Isabel de Torres. The accommodations lie along meandering paths through tropical gardens. Reached by elevator, the airy but rather basic bedrooms come with private safes. They are generous in size with light tropical furnishings, often cane, and quilted bedspreads over firm mattresses. The oceanfront units open onto views but lack balconies, but the French windows allow the trade winds to drift in if you don't prefer air-conditioning. Bathrooms with shower are very routine and a bit cramped.

A formal restaurant, Sunset Place, serves both Dominican specialties and international cuisine, with live entertainment, and you can have lunch at the poolside bar and grill.

Sosúa Beach, Sosúa (Apdo. Postal 361), Puerto Plata, Dominican Republic. ℂ **809/571-3222.** Fax 809/ 571-3020. 81 units. Year-round $65–$72 single or double; $92–$115 suite. Rates include half-board. AE, MC, V. **Amenities:** Restaurant, bar, rooftop lounge, pool, massage, salon. *In room:* A/C, TV, kitchenette, minibar, safe.

GREAT DEALS ON DINING

Caballo Blanco DOMINICAN/ITALIAN   This dining room overlooks a pool and a small but pleasant garden. It serves a medley of inexpensive Italian wines, which go well with such dishes as melon slices with Italian ham, shellfish salads, tortellini, spaghetti (with either meat or shellfish sauce), paella (for two diners only), and veal parmigiana. If you want to divide your meal into pasta for an appetizer and a meat dish for a main course, the staff will acquiesce. Main courses include four different preparations of chicken, and your choice of beef filet prepared with cognac, with peppers, with mushrooms, or with ham and cheese, Cordon Bleu–style. These dishes are perfectly acceptable, even well prepared, if not imaginative.

In the Hotel Sosúa, Calle Dr. Alejo Martínez, El Batey. ① 809/571-2683. Main courses $8–$18. AE, MC, V. Daily 7am–6pm.

Caribae INTERNATIONAL   Set within a few steps of Sosúa's police station, a short walk from the center of Sosúa, this restaurant occupies the open-sided premises of a high-ceilinged thatch-covered building that's set in the midst of a verdant garden that's studded with dozens of exotic shrubs and flowering trees. Part of its charm derives from the eco-sensitive efforts of owner Antonio Isa, a biological engineer who appreciates the good life he's created within an environment that stresses harmony of humans with nature. The decor consists of stone-topped tables supported by segments of thick natural logs, and views out over the garden. Ingredients include several kinds of herbs that the owners grow themselves, as well as copious amounts of shrimp they produce in their own shrimp farms. These farms, incidentally, can be toured as part of the owners' eco-tourism endeavors. One of the tastiest dishes served here is a grilled combination platter of seafood, filet of mahimahi or snapper, shrimp, and lobster. Salads here are meal-sized main courses, usually studded with shrimp or seafood. Wines are imported from Europe, California, or Chile. The perfect appetizer? Check out such tapas as smoked pork ribs served with tamarind sauce. Looking for something ethnic, simple, and satisfying? Consider a wholesome, time-tested version of *arroz con pollo* that's served with a generous helping of herb-flavored beans.

Camino Libre 70. ① 809/571-3138. Main courses RD$120–RD$310 ($7.50–$19.50). AE, DC, MC, V. Daily 4–midnight.

La Puntilla de Piergiorgio ⊛ ITALIAN   A 10-minute walk west of Sosúa's center, this place serves the best Italian food in town, attracting an animated clientele of Europeans looking for a change from Creole and Dominican cuisine. The setting, located in the hotel of the same name, is a series of outdoor terraces, some of them covered, most of them open-air, that cascade down to the edge of a seacliff. There's enough space to allow conversational privacy for virtually any intimate dinner, and a pair of gazebo-style bars that provide an ongoing supply of mimosas and rum-based drinks. We've had better versions of every dish served here, but for the area, it is outstanding, especially the different preparations of fresh fish caught off local waters. You can even order the fish barbecued. Sometimes the chef gets fancy, as when he flames the prawns with cognac, or goes Continental with his filet steak in green peppercorn sauce. The cannelloni Rossini (chopped meat and spinach) isn't bad at all.

Calle La Puntilla. ① 809/571-2215. Main courses RD$195–RD$320 ($12.25–$20). AE, MC, V. Daily noon–4pm and 6pm–midnight.

Morua Mai ⊛ INTERNATIONAL   This is the most visible, and most deeply entrenched, restaurant in downtown Sosúa. Established by German entrepreneurs in the 1970s, it is set at the town's busiest intersection. The patio in front is the closest thing in town to a European cafe. The restaurant was designed of timbers and palm thatch, like an enormous Taíno teepee, under which ceiling fans slowly spin, and wicker and wooden furniture help create an ambience conducive to the consumption of leisurely tropical drinks and well-prepared food. Steaks and seafood are ongoing staples here. Depending on the arrival of fresh supplies that day, the menu might also include four different preparations of lobster; several kinds of shrimp, including a version with spicy tomato sauce and fresh vegetables; four different preparations of sea bass, including a version flavored with Chablis; orange-flavored chicken spiced with ginger; steak Diana, flavored with bacon; and pork in mustard-flavored cream sauce. An excellent version of paella contains chunks of lobster and fresh shrimp.

Pedro Clisante 5, El Batey. ℭ 809/571-2966. Pizzas and pastas RD$90–RD$270 ($5.75–$17); main courses RD$130–RD$380 ($8.25–$23.75). AE, MC, V. Daily 8am–midnight.

ECO-TOURING THE SOSÚA AREA

Caribae Tours, at the Caribae restaurant, Camino Libre 70, Sosúa (ℭ **809/ 571-3138**), is owned by biological engineer Antonio Isa, whose education and values emphatically stress the need for harmony between humans and the natural environment of the Dominican Republic's north shore. The most appealing of the trips involves a Jeep and kayak tour of the upper reaches of the Yasica River valley, the north shore's most fertile. This full-day experience costs RD$1,050 ($65.65) per person, and it includes tours of the organization's shrimp farms and the 20 riverside ponds they comprise. There are also options for kayak riding, horseback riding, and guided commentary on an appropriate application of fertilizers and organic farming, particularly as it applies to the production of coffee and guava.

7 Cabarete ⟨★

In some ways Cabarete evokes Malibu, California, before it was overdeveloped. The winds that blow constantly southward off the Atlantic swept in a hip young crowd in the 1990s, as Cabarete emerged as the premier windsurfing site in the Caribbean. But only a small portion of the visitors who come here are actually interested in the waves. Hundreds of the young, the beautiful, and the restless who throng here, mostly from Europe, never even think about jumping on a board. Instead, they come to bask in the reflected glitter, or the bare-chested sex appeal, of a hard-core cadre of young men who spend lots of time riding the waves by day and strutting their stuff in the hyperhip town bars by night.

To service the needs of the growing number of visitors, the town has attracted some of the most aggressive prostitutes in the Dominican Republic, all ages, all skin tones, all degrees of blatancy. If you're a heterosexual male in Cabarete, you'll absolutely never, ever, lack for female companionship, paid or unpaid.

News of Cabarete's allure has spread, some might say like a contagious virus, among the 20-something populations of Europe. Especially prevalent are visitors from northern Europe, including Germany, Benelux, Switzerland, Scandinavia; France (some chic boutiques cater to the sense of French aesthetics); Spain; and Italy. (There are fewer U.S. and Canadian young people here than you'd think.) The big attraction remains **Cabarete Beach,** with its white sands and ideal wind and surf conditions

Cabarete isn't particularly distinguished architecturally, consisting of a series of relatively small-scale hotels, restaurants, and gift shops lining either side of the highway that parallels the north coast. Virtually everything in town lies along

> **Tips** **Serious Windsurfing**
>
> Cabarete hosts an annual weeklong windsurfing tournament every June. Only amateurs are allowed to participate. For more information, contact the Happy Surf School, Calle Principal (© **809/571-0784**), or any staff member at the AHMSA Hotel Estrella del Mar (© **809/571-0808**).

this street (Calle Principal), with the exception of small shops that are found on narrow alleyways that bisect the main street. But as word of the resort has spread, there have been increasing numbers of large all-inclusive hotels built on the outskirts of town.

GETTING THERE

To reach Cabarete from Sosúa, continue east along the *autopista* for about 8 miles. Taxis and *públicos* from Sosúa can also take you there.

ACCOMMODATIONS YOU CAN AFFORD

Residencia Dominicana   Well located just a short walk from the beach, this three-story, no-frills *residencia* is a favorite with frugal holidaymakers. Be warned: It's rather bare-bones, but it's clean and decent. Some of the 11 main rooms were recently renovated, and each has a small, compact shower-only bathroom. On the ground floor are some air-conditioned apartments, each of which has a kitchenette and fridge. The staff is helpful and friendly, and will invite you to dine on Dominican and international cuisine at the affordable second-floor restaurant.

Proyecto Procab, Cabarete, Dominican Republic. © **809/571-0890**. www.hispaniola.com/res-dom. 20 units, 2 apts. Year-round $30 single or double; $35 apartment. MC, V. **Amenities:** Restaurant, bar. *In room:* A/C in apts, ceiling fans, no phone.

Tropical Hotel Casa Laguna   One of the better lodging values in Cabarete is this circa-1980s hotel, just across the street from the beach, within a pleasant walled-in garden. Each of the rooms has mahogany louvers and lattices, plus functional furniture. Most have sparsely equipped kitchenettes, and each has a tiled, shower-only bathroom.

Calle Principal, Cabarete, Dominican Republic. © **809/571-0956**. Fax 809/571-0709. www.tropicalclubs.com. 81 units. Winter $54 per person single or double. Off-season $49 per person single or double. Rate includes all meals. AE, DC, MC, V. **Amenities:** Restaurant, bar, pool, laundry. *In room:* A/C, fridge.

GREAT DEALS ON DINING

Casa del Pescador SEAFOOD   Since 1988, Casa del Pescador has served sophisticated seafood in an engagingly hip environment. It's right on the beach, in the heart of town. To begin, sample the chef's flavor-filled fish consommé. He does very well with shrimp, too, either with a pastis sauce or, more zestily, with curry and fresh garlic. On a hot day, the seafood salads are a welcome relief and tasty, too, as are the grilled octopus in spicy Creole sauce and fresh lobster in garlic sauce (the latter spice, however, overpowers a good thing when a butter sauce might have sufficed). Although there's a full wine list, Presidente beer seems the best accompaniment to the fish, especially on hot, sultry nights.

Calle Principal. © **809/571-0760**. Reservations recommended for dinner. Main courses RD$140–RD$280 ($8.75–$17.50). AE, DC, MC, V. Daily 11am–11pm.

La Casita de Don Alfredo (Chez Papy) ★ DOMINICAN/FRENCH   This quirky and durable bistro is one of our favorite restaurants in Cabarete. It's located on a battered pavilion directly on the sands of Cabarete's beachfront, and it's accessible from the town's Calle Principal. Don Alfredo himself, a French expatriate from Strasbourg, keeps a firm grip on things. Menu items sure to entice include spiny Caribbean lobster with garlic and saffron sauce or with pastis; filet mignon with peppercorn sauce; and an array of whatever local fishermen bring in that day. We nearly always go for the fresh fish, which can be prepared almost any way you like it. As you'd expect from an articulate Frenchman, the wines are well chosen and urbane.

Playa de Cabarete. No phone. Reservations not accepted. Main courses RD$160–RD$250 ($10–$15.75). No credit cards. Bar and cafe daily 8:30am–midnight. Meals 8:30–10:30am, noon–2:30pm, and 6–10:30pm.

SPORTS & OTHER OUTDOOR PURSUITS

Cabarete, the best **windsurfing** ★★ resort destination in the Caribbean, is also home to the best windsurfing school. **Club Nathalie Simon,** Calle Principal (© 809/571-0848; www.hispaniola.com/nathalie-simon), is one of the most prominent branches of an international windsurfing organization. It's devoted to teaching proper windsurfing techniques and to renting state-of-the-art equipment. Group lessons are included free with any rental. Rentals cost $25 for 1 hour, $48 for 3 hours, between $55 and $68 for a full day, and between $210 and $240 for a full week. Individual lessons cost $30 per hour if you bring your own board, or $50 per hour if you use one of theirs. On the premises is an alfresco snack bar.

Iguana Mama at Cabarete (© 809/571-0908), offers the best **mountain biking** and **hiking.** Going strong since 1993, it features a trek to Mount Isabel de Torres with experienced guides, lasting a full day and costing $45 to $55 per person. If enough people book, this tour is offered daily. Another trek involves a 3,000-foot downhill cruise with time for cycling down rolling hills, costing $35 per person and held only Monday, Wednesday, and Friday.

The finest and safest **dive center** is **Hippocampo Dive Center** at Cabarete, which is PADI certified. It features one dive for $28 or three dives for $75. The outfitter will lead you to 20 different dive sites on walls and coral heads, all reachable by boat.

The best **adventure tours** are offered by **Cabarete Tours** (© 809/571-0505), which will take you on a daylong Jeep safari for $26 per person, exploring river banks, small caves, and a tropical rain forest. It can also take you **deep-sea fishing,** for $65 per angler. Finally, **Gipsy Ranch** (© 809/571-1373) is the most complete riding stable in the Dominican Republic; they'll take you **horseback riding** at a cost of $30 per person.

SHOPPING

Atlantis, Calle Principal (© 809/571-2286), has the largest and most intriguing repository of Haitian sculptures along the north coast of the Dominican Republic. Most of them are bas-relief cutouts fashioned from sheet metal (sometimes the tops of oil drums). Many reflect mystical and, in some cases, voodoo-related themes that are invariably intriguing and usually very dramatic. There's also elaborate jewelry from both the Dominican Republic and Haiti, and large-scale Haitian banners, many inspired by voodoo rituals, fashioned from intricate layerings of beads and sequins.

Island Clothes, Calle Principal (© 809/571-0921), is run by a local family with strong ties to the United States. This shop is loaded with Dominican handcrafts, Haitian paintings, souvenirs, costume jewelry, beach accessories, and tropical-weight clothing.

CABARETE AFTER DARK

New Wave Café, Calle Principal (© **809/571-0826**), attracts raucous, hip young windsurfers from as far away as Stockholm and Los Angeles. Set between the resort's main street and the beachfront, and designed without walls beneath a simple shanty-style roof, it rocks and rolls every day of the week 9am to 4am, but gets especially sexy and especially cool after 9pm. There's live music every Monday, Friday, and Saturday, and recently released recorded music every other night of the week. There's no cover charge; drinks cost RD$40 to RD$50 ($2.50–$3.15).

Las Brisas, Calle Principal (© **809/571-0614**), is the second most important and the most popular nightlife venue in Cabarete, but arrive after 10:30pm. The dance floor is illuminated with strobe lights and lasers, and the bar is always busy. Many patrons here arrive with dates of their own, but if you're a single man flying solo, never fear, as a bevy of attractive working women are invariably on hand to provide companionship.

8 Samaná ⊛

Another offbeat destination, where prices are still affordable, Samaná is an undeveloped 30-mile-long peninsula located in the northeastern corner of the country. It's about as Casablanca as the Caribbean gets. Hiding out here is an international expatriate enclave of rampant individualists. It also has some of the finest white sandy beaches in the Dominican Republic. The best beach, **Las Terrenas,** lies on the north coast of the peninsula. At any minute you expect to encounter Robinson Crusoe here. Although the strand strip is narrow, it is filled with white sand set against a backdrop of palms. The beach is never crowded. About the only visitors you'll encounter are at sea: the several thousand humpback whales who swim in from Antarctica to birth their calves from January through March. The main town, **La Samaná,** lies on the southern side of the peninsula, overlooking a bay. The north coast of the peninsula is more accessible by boat. The roads are a bit of a joke, better suited for donkeys than cars.

In 1824 the *Turtle Dove,* a sailing vessel, was blown ashore at Samaná. Dozens of American slaves from the Freeman Sisters' underground railroad escaped to these shores. They settled in Samaná, and today their offspring are waiting to greet you. Although Spanish is the major language, you can still hear some form of 19th-century English, and you'll see villages with names such as Philadelphia or Bethesda.

GETTING THERE

To reach Samaná from Sosúa, head east through Cabarete. East of here lies Playa Grande, a long stretch of beach strip, among the best in the West Indies. After leaving Playa Grande, you still have 120 miles to go east before reaching remote Samaná. Allow about 3 hours, unless you're tempted by one of the beaches along the way.

It's also possible to fly here from Santo Domingo. A small carrier in Santo Domingo, **Air Santo Domingo** (© **809/683-8006**), has regularly scheduled flights to Samaná.

ACCOMMODATIONS YOU CAN AFFORD

Hotel Tropic Banana On a pancake-flat 7-acre parcel of beachfront midway between the ocean and a range of rolling hills and mountains, this is one of the most escapist and otherworldly hotels in northeastern Hispaniola. Composed of an administrative headquarters and at least four white-and-yellow annexes, this

Moments Exploring a Rain Forest & Watching Whales

You can ask your hotel staff about arrangements for day trips to **Los Haitisses,** a national park in nearby Sánchez. Ancient Taíno inscriptions still adorn the cave walls here. This remote, unspoiled rain forest has crystal lakes, mangrove swamps, and limestone knolls. This karst region comprises some 100 miles of mangrove estuaries and land. You can also visit **Las Terrenas,** a remote stretch of coastline with nearly deserted beaches that are only now being discovered, although some German tourists have found them.

Nature lovers also flock here to see some 3,000 **humpback whales** off the coast in winter. Many whale-watching expeditions come here in January and February.

Sport-fishing off the coast is among the finest in the entire western hemisphere. The staff or owner of your hotel can put you in touch with local fishermen who will take you out

place has a Swiss, French, and Dominican staff that will help you get away from it all and relax. The accommodations have just enough furniture and amenities to be livable, but not enough to be plush. The rooms open to private porches and are cooled by ceiling fans and trade winds rather than air-conditioning. Bedrooms have firm mattresses and bathrooms that, although small, are tidily maintained and have tiled showers.

The restaurant features Gallic/Caribbean and Italian food that's more stylish than you might imagine. It offers live music and merengue dancing at least one night a week.

The hotel lies in the town of **Las Terrenas,** with a population of around 8,000 people, set about 9 miles north of the larger town of Sánchez. From Sánchez, the drive is mountainous, requiring 30 minutes negotiating winding mountain roads. Las Terrenas lies 155 miles north of Santo Domingo. Despite that relatively short-sounding distance, the roads are awful and require 5 hours of driving.

Las Terrenas, Provincia de Samaná, Dominican Republic. (℃) **809/240-6110.** Fax 809/240-6112. 27 units. Winter $50 single; $75 double. Off-season $45 single; $60 double. AE, MC, V. **Amenities:** Restaurant, bar, pool, tennis court, horseback riding, car rental. *In room:* TV, ceiling fans.

WORTH A SPLURGE

Villa Serena ✦ Some 26 miles east of the town of Samaná, beside the only road that runs along the edge of the peninsula, this hotel was built in the early 1990s along the lines of a rambling, two-story Victorian house with a wrap-around balcony. Painted white with a blue-green roof and a large front garden, it sits above a rocky coastline, a 3-minute walk from a relatively uncrowded beach. Each accommodation has a private balcony and a decor that's different from its neighbors—yours might be Chinese, neoclassical gold-and-white, or Laura Ashley romantic. The more expensive rooms are air-conditioned; others have ceiling fans. The beds are most comfortable here, and the bathrooms, which have tub-and-shower combos, are tidily kept. Conceived for honeymooners and anyone else who's looking for a place to escape urban life, the site is quiet, isolated, and low-key, with little to do other than swim in the oval-shaped pool, visit the beach, read, and chat with other guests. Many guests order lunch from operators of small charcoal grills set up on the beach (simple platters of pork or fish). The in-house restaurant, however, is the best of the three or four mainstream restaurants in Las Galeras, opening every day for breakfast, lunch, and dinner.

Apdo. Postal 51-1, Las Galeras, Samaná, Dominican Republic. © 809/538-0000. Fax 809/538-0009. www. villaserena.com. 11 units. Winter $125–$135 single or double. Off-season $110–$120 single or double. MC, V. **Amenities:** Restaurant, pool. *In room:* A/C in some rooms, ceiling fans.

12

Grenada

Grenada is famous for being invaded by the U.S. Marines in 1983, but the political troubles are long over on this sleepy island. Today it's a good place to relax in the midst of fairly friendly people and the lovely and popular white sands of Grand Anse Beach. Exploring the lush interior, especially Grand Etang National Park, also is worthwhile. Crisscrossed by nature trails and filled with dozens of secluded coves and sandy beaches, Grenada has moved beyond the 1980s and is now safe and secure. It's not necessarily for the serious party person—and definitely not for those seeking action at a casino. Instead, it attracts visitors who like snorkeling, sailing, fishing, and doing nothing more invigorating than lolling on a beach under the sun.

Because it shelters so many elegant inns and hotels, Grenada has long been known as an upmarket target for well-heeled visitors, some of whom arrive on yachts. However, in recent years it has developed a number of at least moderately priced inns and small hotels, even guesthouses, which makes traveling here much more possible than ever before for the budget traveler. Even cheaper is the offshore island of Carriacou, which is—until it's discovered—one of the major bargains of the Caribbean.

Grenada has a number of inexpensive places to eat, existing alongside the more expensive restaurants. Unlike many islands of the Caribbean, Grenada has abundant produce, so all the foodstuff doesn't have to be imported—hence, the lower costs in restaurants that rely on locally produced items.

The "Spice Island," Grenada (pronounced Gre-*nay*-dah) is part of an independent three-island nation that also includes Carriacou, the largest of the Grenadines, and Petit Martinique. The southernmost of the Windward Islands, it lies 60 miles southwest of St. Vincent and about 90 miles north of Trinidad. An oval island, it's 21 miles long and about 12 miles wide, and it is volcanic in origin.

The air on Grenada is full of the fragrance of spice and exotic fruits; the island has more spices per square mile than any other place in the world—cloves, cinnamon, mace, cocoa, tonka beans, ginger, and one-third of the world's supply of nutmeg. "Drop a few seeds anywhere," the locals will tell you, "and you have an instant garden." The central area is like a jungle of palms, oleander, bougainvillea, purple and red hibiscus, crimson anthurium, bananas, breadfruit, birdsong, and ferns.

1 Essentials

VISITOR INFORMATION
In the United States, the **Grenada Board of Tourism** has an information office at 800 Second Ave., Suite 400K, New York, NY 10017 (© **800/927-9554** or 212/687-9554).

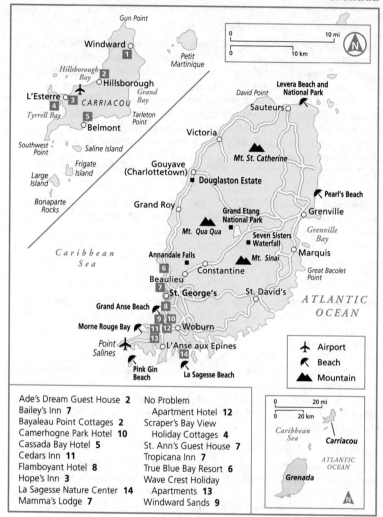

Grenada

Ade's Dream Guest House 2
Bailey's Inn 7
Bayaleau Point Cottages 2
Camerhogne Park Hotel 10
Cassada Bay Hotel 5
Cedars Inn 11
Flamboyant Hotel 8
Hope's Inn 3
La Sagesse Nature Center 14
Mamma's Lodge 7

No Problem
  Apartment Hotel 12
Scraper's Bay View
  Holiday Cottages 4
St. Ann's Guest House 7
Tropicana Inn 7
True Blue Bay Resort 6
Wave Crest Holiday
  Apartments 13
Windward Sands 9

In Canada, contact the **Grenada Board of Tourism,** 439 University Ave., Suite 820, Toronto, ON M5G 1Y8 (© **416/595-1339**). In London, contact the **Grenada Board of Tourism,** 1 Collingham Gardens, Earl's Court, London, SW5 0HW (© **020/7370-5164**).

On the island, go to the **Grenada Board of Tourism,** The Carenage, in St. George's (© **473/440-2279**), open Monday to Friday 8am to 4pm. Maps, guides, and general information are available.

The official website of Grenada is **www.grenada.org**.

GETTING THERE

The **Point Salines International Airport** lies at the southwestern toe of Grenada. The airport is about 5 to 15 minutes by taxi from the major hotels.

Moments   Carnival on Grenada

The second weekend of August brings colorful Carnival parades, music, and dancing. The festivities begin on Friday and continue practically non-stop to Tuesday. Steel bands and calypso groups perform at Queen's Park. Jouvert, one of the highlights of the festival, begins at 5am Monday, with a parade of Djab Djab/Djab Molassi, devil-costumed figures daubed with a black substance. (*Be warned:* Don't wear nice clothes to attend this event—you might get sticky from close body contact.) The Carnival finale, a gigantic "jump-up" (like a hoedown), ends with a parade of bands from Tanteen through The Carenage into town.

American Airlines (© 800/433-7300) offers a daily morning flight from Kennedy Airport in New York to Grenada. If you live in many cities of the southeast, such as Atlanta, the better connection is via Miami.

BWIA (© 800/292-1183) has direct service from New York's Kennedy Airport on Thursday and Sunday. The rest of the week they fly from Kennedy to Grenada with stopovers in Antigua, St. Lucia, or Barbados.

LIAT (© 800/468-0482 in the U.S. and Canada, or 268/462-0700) also has scheduled service between Barbados and Grenada (at least four flights daily, although they are sometimes canceled with little notice—we've often spent hours and hours waiting in the Barbados airport for a plane). Through LIAT or BWIA, you can connect on Barbados with several international airlines, including British Airways, Air Canada, American Airlines, and Air France.

Air Jamaica (© 473/444-4121) offers nonstop flights from New York to Grenada two times a week.

British Airways (© 0345/222-111 in England) flies to Grenada every Wednesday and Friday from London's Gatwick Airport, making a single stop at Antigua en route.

GETTING AROUND

BY TAXI   Taxi fares are set by the government. Most arriving visitors take a cab from the Point Salines International Airport to one of the hotels near St. George's, at a cost of $15. The fare increases to $20 from 6pm to 6am. You can also use most taxi drivers as a guide for a day's sightseeing, and the cost can be divided among three or four passengers. The price can be negotiated, depending on what you want to do.

BY RENTAL CAR   First, remember to *drive on the left.* A U.S., British, or Canadian driver's license is valid on Grenada; however, you must obtain a local permit, costing EC$30 ($11.10), before getting onto the roads. These permits can be obtained from the car-rental companies or the traffic department at The Carenage in St. George's.

Among the major U.S.-based car-rental firms, **Avis** (© 800/331-1212 or 473/440-3936) operates out of a Shell gasoline station on Lagoon Road, on the southern outskirts of Saint George's. Avis will agree to meet you at the airport but requires at least 24-hour notice before its toll-free reservations service will guarantee availability. To get the best deal, it pays to shop around. Try **Dollar Rent-a-Car** at the Point Salines Airport (© 473/444-4786). You might also try some local concerns, such as **McIntyre Brothers Ltd.,** in the True Blue area (© 473/444-3944).

A word of warning about local drivers: There's such a thing as Grenadian driving machismo; the drivers take blind corners with abandon. An extraordinary number of accidents are reported in the lively local paper. Gird yourself with nerves of steel, and be extra alert for children and roadside pedestrians while driving at night. Many foreign visitors, in fact, find any night-driving hazardous.

BY BUS   Minivans, charging EC$1 to EC$6 (35¢–$2.20), are the cheapest way to get around. The most popular run is between St. George's and Grand Anse Beach. Most minivans depart from Market Square or from the Esplanade area of St. George's.

 FAST FACTS: **Grenada**

Banks In St. George's, the capital, **Barclays** is at Church and Halifax streets (✆ **473/440-3232**); **Scotiabank,** on Halifax Street (✆ **473/440-3274**); the **National Commercial Bank (NCB),** at the corner of Halifax and Hillsborough streets (✆ **473/440-3566**); the **Grenada Bank of Commerce,** at the corner of Halifax and Cross streets (✆ **473/440-3521**); and the **Grenada Cooperative Bank,** on Church Street (✆ **473/440-2111**).

Currency The official currency is the **Eastern Caribbean dollar (EC$),** worth about 17¢ at press time, or EC$2.70 = U.S.$1. Always determine which dollars—EC or U.S.—you're talking about when someone on Grenada quotes you a price. *Rates in this chapter are quoted in U.S. dollars, unless otherwise noted.*

Documents A valid passport is required of U.S., British, and Canadian citizens entering Grenada, as is a return or an ongoing ticket.

Electricity Electricity is 220- to 240-volt AC (50 cycles), so transformers and adapters will be needed for U.S.-made appliances.

Embassies & High Commissions Grenada, unlike many of its neighbors, has a **U.S. Embassy** at Point Salines in St. George's (✆ **473/444-1173**). It also has a **British High Commission,** on Church Street, St. George's (✆ **473/440-3536**).

Emergencies Dial ✆ **911** to summon the police, report a fire, or call an ambulance.

Language English is commonly spoken on this island of some 100,000 people because of the long years of British influence. Creole English—a mixture of several African dialects, English, and French—is spoken informally by the majority.

Medical Care There is a general hospital, **St. George's Hospital** (✆ **473/440-2051**), with an x-ray department and operating room. Private doctors and nurses are available on call.

Pharmacies Try **Gittens Pharmacy,** Halifax Street, St. George's (✆ **473/440-2165**), open Monday, Tuesday, Wednesday, and Friday 8am to 6pm, Thursday 8am to 5pm, and Saturday 8am to 3pm.

Post Office The **General Post Office** is at The Pier, St. George's, open Monday to Friday 8am to 3:30pm.

Safety Street crime occurs here. Tourists have been victims of armed robbery in isolated areas, and thieves frequently steal U.S. passports and alien registration cards in addition to money. Muggings, purse-snatchings, and other robberies occur in areas near hotels, beaches, and restaurants, particularly after dark. Visitors should exercise appropriate caution when walking after dark, or they should rely on taxis. Visitors might want to consult with local authorities, their hotels, and/or the U.S. Embassy for current information. Valuables left unattended on beaches are subject to theft. The loss or theft of a U.S. passport overseas should be reported to the local police and the nearest U.S. embassy or consulate. A lost or stolen birth certificate and/or driver's license generally cannot be replaced outside the United States.

Taxes A 10% value-added tax is imposed on food and beverages, and there's an 8% room tax. Upon leaving Grenada, you must fill out an immigration card and pay a departure tax of $20.

Telecommunications International telephone service is available 24 hours a day from pay phones. Public telegraph, telex, and fax services are also provided from The Carenage offices of **Grenada Telecommunications (Grentel)** in St. George's (© **473/440-1000** for all Grentel offices), open Monday to Friday 7:30am to 6pm, Saturday 7:30am to 1pm, and Sunday and holidays 10am to noon. To call another number on Grenada, dial all seven digits, as the island is divided among four telephone exchanges: 440, 442, 443, and 444. The most commonly used is 440.

Tipping A 10% service charge is added to most restaurant and hotel bills.

Weather Grenada has two distinct seasons: dry and rainy. The dry season is from January to May; the rest of the year is the rainy season, although the rainfall doesn't last long. The average temperature is 80°F (26.7°C). Because of constant trade winds, the humidity is seldom oppressive.

2 Accommodations You Can Afford

Don't forget that your hotel or inn will probably add a service charge to your bill—ask in advance about this. Also, there's an 8% government room tax, as well as a 10% tax on food and beverage tabs.

Camerhogne Park Hotel   About a 5-minute stroll over to the fabled sands of Grand Anse Beach, this family-owned and -operated hotel is about a 10-minute drive to the international airport at Point Salines. The small rooms are simply but comfortably furnished and have more amenities than many comparably priced hotels, including bathrooms with showers. Most rooms have verandas as well. You'll get a 10% discount for stays of 6 or more nights. The on-premises restaurant, Cathy's Tavern, makes use of Grenadian produce when available. The staff will help you arrange tours of the island and a car rental.

Grand Anse (P.O. Box 378), St. George's, Grenada, W.I. © **473/444-4587.** Fax 473/444-3111. camhotel@ caribsurf.com. 25 units. Winter $55–$65 single or double; $75–$150 apt. Off-season $45–$65 single or double; $65–$125 apt. AE, DISC, DC, MC, V. **Amenities:** Restaurant, bar. *In room:* A/C, TV, ceiling fans.

Cedars Inn   Conveniently located only minutes from both the international airport and Grenada's main attraction, Grand Anse Beach, this is a two-floor block of rooms and apartments. Each accommodation opens onto a private patio and has a small private bathroom with shower. The standard rooms are a bit cramped but with good beds, and the apartments are generous in size. The setting is in a tropical landscape, although the rooms themselves are in a very simple motel-type style. West Indian meals are served in the hotel restaurant, and guests can also enjoy the pool bar. A free shuttle takes guests to the airport.

True Blue (P.O. Box 73), St. George's, Grenada, W.I. © 800/223-6510 in the U.S., or 473/444-4641. Fax 473/444-4652. 20 units. Winter $95–$110 single or double; $130–$140 apt. Off-season $75–$85 single or double; $90–$120 apt. Extra person $20; children 11 and under stay free in parents' room. MAP $30 per person extra. AE, MC, V. Amenities: Restaurant, bar, pool, airport shuttle. In room: A/C, TV, private patio.

La Sagesse Nature Center ★★ (Finds)

On a sandy, tree-lined beach 10 miles from the airport, La Sagesse consists of a seaside guesthouse and art gallery. Nearby are trails for hiking and exploring, a haven for wading and shore birds, hummingbirds, hawks, and ducks. Rivers, mangroves, and a salt pond sanctuary enhance the natural beauty of the place. The original great house of what was once La Sagesse plantation contains two apartments, one with a fully equipped kitchen, and each with high ceilings and comfortable beds, plus shower-only bathrooms. Guests can also rent a two-bedroom beach cottage, with comfortable furnishings and a wraparound porch. The least desirable accommodations are two small, economy-priced bedrooms in back of the inn's patio restaurant.

St. David's (P.O. Box 44, St. George's), Grenada, W.I. © 473/444-6458. Fax 473/444-6458. lsnature@caribsurf.com. 6 units. Winter $95–$125 single or double. Off-season $50–$80 single or double. AE, MC, V. Amenities: Restaurant, bar, snorkeling, laundry. In room: Ceiling fans, no phone.

Mamma's Lodge ★★ (Value)

This is the best bargain on Grenada. Mamma's is named after the island's most celebrated cook (now deceased), who became famous in the press during the U.S. invasion of Grenada. Her restaurant, Mamma's (it's a 5-min. walk from here; see "Great Deals on Dining," below), became a hangout for U.S. service personnel. The lodge is about 5 minutes from Grand Anse Beach and about 3 minutes from St. George's. Built in the typical two-floor motel style, it's locally owned and managed. Ceiling fans cool the somewhat cramped rooms, and furnishings are rather sparse. Bathrooms, which have shower units, are barely adequate for the job, but the place is clean and decent.

Lagoon Rd. (P.O. Box 248), St. George's, Grenada, W.I. © 473/440-1623. Fax 473/440-4181. dovetail@caribsurf.com. 10 units. Year-round $30 single; $42 double. Extra person $20. Rates include breakfast. No credit cards. Amenities: Restaurant. In room: TV, ceiling fans.

No Problem Apartment Hotel ★ (Value)

The small one-bedroom apartments at this all-suites hotel are one of the best deals on the island. The motel-style lodging is just 5 minutes from the airport and Grand Anse Beach. The simply furnished units open onto a pool and bar area; each has a good bed, plus a small, shower-only bathroom.

True Blue (P.O. Box 280, St. George's), Grenada, W.I. © 800/74-CHARMS in the U.S., or 473/444-4634. Fax 473/444-2803. noprob@mail.idt.net. 20 units. Winter $75–$85 single or double. Off-season $55–$65 single or double. Extra person $20. Breakfast and dinner $30 per person extra. AE, DISC, MC, V. Amenities: Coffeebar, pool, free bikes, beach shuttle, reading room, laundry. In room: A/C, TV, kitchenette.

Tropicana Inn

A 5-minute walk from The Carenage in St. George's, this relatively new hotel is ideal for those who want to be within walking distance of one of the Caribbean's most charming port cities rather than at the beach. There is no pool, but the prices are extremely reasonable. Accommodations in the front overlook the lagoon and one of the island's yacht services—and regrettably, a lot of traffic. Rooms in the back are more spacious but don't have any view at all. Amenities include air-conditioning, but the furnishings are rather basic and the shower-only bathrooms are quite small, although the beds are good. The place can get quite lively at times, with buffets, barbecues, and entertainment.

Lagoon Rd., St. George's. © 473/440-1586. Fax 473/440-9797. www.tropicanainn.com. 20 units. Year-round $65 single; $77 double. AE, MC, V. Amenities: Bar, babysitting, laundry. In room: A/C, TV.

Windward Sands *Value*   This place is for those seeking a typical West Indian guesthouse that's short on luxury but high on friendliness. You're welcome by a Grenadian family, the Phillipses. Some of the better rooms contain old-fashioned four-poster beds, and each unit has a small bathroom with a shower. Don't expect hot water, however, although after a day on the beach the cool water is refreshing. The location is only 1 block from Grand Anse Beach. Yes, the place could do with a coat of paint, but it's cozy and comfortable, except for one or two rooms, which are mere cubicles. Guests meet fellow guests over the excellent homemade breakfast served here each morning. Some of the rooms are air-conditioned, some have TV, and some have kitchenettes.

Grande Anse Beach (P.O. Box 1299, St. George's), Grenada, W.I. ℂ/fax **473/444-4238**. 8 units. Winter $40 single, $55 double; off-season $35 single, $50 double. Rates include breakfast. No credit cards. **Amenities:** Restaurant, bar. *In room:* No phone.

WORTH A SPLURGE

True Blue Bay Resort ✦   This resort takes its name from an old indigo plantation that once stood on this spot. It's still appropriately named because of the panoramic views of the blue waters of Prickly Bay. You can select one-bedroom apartments with verandas overlooking the bay or two-bedroom cottages nestled in tropical gardens. Children are allowed in the cottages (but not in the one-bedroom apartments). The accommodations are tastefully furnished in pastels, with tropical rattan pieces and excellent beds, either king-size or twin. Each unit has a tiled, shower-only bathroom.

Old Mill Ave., True Blue (P.O. Box 1414, St. George's), Grenada, W.I. ℂ **473/443-8783**. Fax 473/444-5929. www.truebluebay.com. 15 units. Winter $155 1-bedroom apt; $220 2-bedroom cottage. Off-season $120 1-bedroom apt; $177 2-bedroom cottage. Extra person $25. AE, MC, V. **Amenities:** 2 restaurants, bar, pool, dock, boating, laundry. *In room:* A/C, TV, kitchen.

3 Great Deals on Dining

The Boatyard ✦ INTERNATIONAL   This medical student hangout overlooks the marina where the yachts are moored. It attracts visiting yachties, most of whom seem to prefer the liquid lunch. Lunch consists of a Caribbean daily special and might include stewed pork or Creole chicken served in tomato sauce with rice. Some of the best featured dishes are stewed and barbecued chicken, baked conch Parmesan, and grilled steak; most are served with rice, salad, and fresh vegetables. Mexican specialties and Italian pastas also appear on the menu, but they are not reason enough to come here. On Friday nights a steel-drum band plays; when the band is done, the sound system is cranked up for indoor-outdoor dancing until the wee hours.

L'Anse aux Epines, Prickly Bay. ℂ **473/444-4662**. Main courses EC$29.50–EC$75 ($10.95–$27.80). AE, MC, V. Daily 8:30am–midnight.

Deyna's Tasty Food ✦ *Finds* GRENADIAN   This little eatery is a closely guarded secret among locals. It's reached by heading up Melville Street to a modest three-story building overlooking the sea. You might even get invited back into the kitchen to see what's cookin'. The duenna of the stove, Deyna Hercules, looks like she lives up to her namesake and eats her own food. Where else can you get someone to fry you up a tasty batch of *tee-tee-ree,* minnow-sized fish just plucked from the Caribbean and washed down with "bush tea" steeped from black sage leaves? Her savory stuffed crabs are the island's best, and you can check out her specials, scribbled on a countertop chalkboard. Her specialty is a "fix-up"—a sampling of the best food of the day, perhaps "stew fish," green plantains, and curried goat. She also serves the national dish of Grenada, an "oil down," made with salted meat and breadfruit cooked in coconut milk. Diners with hair in their chest can opt for two of her gamey specialties—*manicou* (a cross between an opossum and a large rat) and *tatou,* akin to armadillo. Stewed turtle and fried sea eggs round out this offbeat menu.

Melville St. ✆ 473/440-6795. Reservations recommended. Main courses $8–$9. MC, V. Mon–Sat 8am–8pm; Sun 10am–4pm.

La Boulangerie FRENCH Don't be deterred by the shopping center location. This French coffee shop and bakery is an ideal spot for a good breakfast or light lunch (served throughout the afternoon). And prices at dinner are very reasonable. In the early morning visitors throng here for the freshly brewed coffee, downed with pastries or croissants. The afternoon crowd devours well-stuffed baguettes, sandwiches, and pizzas. More substantial dishes, including roast chicken and fresh fish, are offered in the evening.

Le Marquis Shopping Complex, Grand Anse Beach. ✆ 473/444-1131. Sandwiches and pizzas EC$8–EC$30 ($2.95–$11.10); dinner main courses EC$18–EC$30 ($6.65–$11.10). AE, MC, V. Daily 8am–9pm.

Mamma's ★★ CREOLE Every trip to the Caribbean should include a visit to an establishment like this. Serving copious meals, this mamma became particularly famous during the intervention in Grenada, as U.S. soldiers adopted her as their own island mama. Mamma (Insley Wardally) is now deceased, but her daughter, Cleo, carries on.

Meals include such dishes as *callaloo* soup with coconut cream, shredded cold crab with lime juice, freshwater crayfish, fried conch, rôtis made of curry and yellow chickpeas, and a casserole of cooked bananas, yams, and *dasheen,* along with ripe baked plantain, and followed by sugar-apple ice cream for dessert. The more venturesome might want to try crab backs or octopus in a hot-and-spicy sauce. Mamma is also known for her "wild meats," which might include (depending on availability) armadillo, opossum, game birds, and even monkey (yes, that's right, monkey). The specialty drink of the house is rum punch whose ingredients are a secret.

Lagoon Rd., St. George's. ✆ 473/440-1459. Reservations required a day in advance. Fixed-price meal EC$45 ($16.65). MC, V. Daily 9am–10pm. Take the road that leads to Grenada Yacht Services.

Morne Fendue ★ *Finds* CREOLE This plantation house is the ancestral home of the late owner, Betty Mascoll. It was built in 1912, the year Miss Mascoll was born, of carefully chiseled river rocks held together with a mixture of lime and molasses. Miss Mascoll died in 1998, but her loyal staff carries on her tradition. Of course, they need time to prepare food for your arrival, so it's imperative to give them a call to let them know you're coming by. Lunch is likely to include yam and sweet-potato casserole, curried chicken with lots of hot spices, and a hot pot of pork and oxtail. Because this is very much a private home, tipping should be done with the greatest tact. Nonetheless, the hardworking cook and maid seem genuinely appreciative of a gratuity.

St. Patrick's, 25 miles north of St. George's. ✆ 473/442-9330. Reservations required. Fixed-price lunch EC$45 ($16.65). No credit cards. Mon–Sat 12:30–2pm. Follow the coastal road north out of St. George's. After you pass through Nonpareil, turn inland (east) and continue through Buguesng and follow the signs to Morne Fendue.

The Nutmeg ★ SEAFOOD/CREOLE Right on the harbor, The Nutmeg is a rendezvous point for the yachting set. It's suitable for a snack or a full-fledged dinner in an informal atmosphere. The drinks are very good; try one of the Grenadian rum punches, made with Angostura bitters, grated nutmeg, rum, lime juice, and syrup. There's always fresh fish, and usually *callaloo* or pumpkin soup, plus potato croquettes. *Lambi* (that ubiquitous conch) is done very well here. A small wine list has some California, German, and Italian selections, and you can drop in just for a glass of beer to enjoy the sea view. Sometimes you'll be asked to share a table.

The Carenage, St. Georges's. ⓒ 473/440-2539. Main courses EC$16–EC$70 ($5.95–$25.95) lunch, EC$35–EC$70 ($12.95–$25.95) dinner. AE, MC, V. Mon–Sat 8am–11pm; Sun 4–11pm.

Papa Hall's ⭐ *Finds* CREOLE   If you're looking for a casual atmosphere with lots of local color, then stop here for a drink and a bite to eat. If you order carefully, you can enjoy a meal at a sensible price, especially when the chef decides to run specials. The breakfast choices range from $5.50 to $7 and include not only the standard fare of eggs and bacon, but also West Indian favorites such as smoked herring, codfish, and other local fish served with tomatoes, onions, and fresh local vegetables. The lunch and dinner menus include favored choices like Creole fish, calypso chicken, and various curried dishes, including beef, lamb, and lobster. The selection of rôtis includes beef, fish, chicken, shrimp, vegetable, and lamb. Beverages include specialty juices made from seamoss or the bark of the mauby tree, and punches made from fresh local fruits, even one made with peanut butter.

At the Cot Bam Resort, Grand Anse. ⓒ 473/444-2050. Reservations recommended. Main courses EC$30–EC$50 ($11.10–$18.50); lunch EC$6–EC$30 ($2.20–$11.10); breakfast EC$15–EC$19 ($5.55–$7.05). AE, MC, V. Daily 9am–11pm.

Rick's Café AMERICAN   The main dining area here is bordered on one side by an open kitchen, containing a stone oven and barbecue, and a 30-foot counter with stools on the other. The diner-style atmosphere (there's no table service) offers relatively inexpensive meals. They're not preset; you mix and match items to suit your own taste. For example, if you order barbecued chicken or ribs, you could pair it with a side order of fries or a potato served with your choice of toppings. If you're famished, consider a burger. The pizzas are served with a choice of the typical toppings; the most expensive option, a large with six toppings, costs EC$42 ($15.55). At the counter you can dine on banana splits, milkshakes, and 35 to 40 flavors of ice cream, including local favorites like passion fruit, coconut, rum raisin, and soursop.

Grand Anse Shopping Center. ⓒ 473/444-4597. Main courses EC$11–EC$25 ($4.05–$9.25). No credit cards. Tues–Thurs 11am–9:30pm; Fri–Sat 11am–10pm; Sun 4–9:30pm.

4 Hitting the Beaches

The best of the 45 beaches on Grenada are in the southwestern part of the island. The granddaddy of them all is **Grand Anse Beach** ⭐⭐⭐, which is 2 miles of sugar-white sand fronting a sheltered bay. This beach is really the stuff of dreams—it's no surprise why so many of the major resort hotels are here. Many visitors never leave this part of the island. Protected from strong winds and currents, the waters here are relatively safe, making Grand Anse a family favorite. The clear, gentle waters are populated with schools of rainbow-hued fish. Palms and sea-grape trees offer shade. Watersports concessions here offer water-skiing, parasailing, windsurfing, and scuba diving; vendors peddle coral jewelry, local crafts, and the inevitable T-shirts.

The beach at **Morne Rouge Bay** is less frequented than Grande Anse but just as desirable, with its white sands bordering clear waters. Morne Rouge is noted for its calm waters and some of the best **snorkeling** in Grenada. It's about a mile south of Grand Anse Beach.

Pink Gin Beach lies near the airport at Point Salinas, bordering two large resorts. This is also a beach of white sand and clear waters, ideal for swimming and snorkeling. You'll find a restaurant and kayak rentals here.

Also on Grenada's southern coast, **La Sagesse Beach** is part of La Sagesse Nature Center (see "Accommodations You Can Afford," earlier in this chapter). This especially powdery strip of white sand is a lovely, tranquil area; in between time spent on the beach, you can go for nature walks in most directions. A small restaurant opens onto the beach.

If you like your waters more turbulent, visit the dramatic **Pearl's Beach,** north of Grenville on the Atlantic coast. The light gray sand stretches for miles and is lined with palm trees. You'll practically have the beach to yourself.

Part of Levera National Park, **Levera Beach,** at the northeastern tip of the island, is one of the most beautiful on Grenada. Its sand fronts the Atlantic, which most often means rough waters. Many locals come here for Sunday picnics.

5 Sports & Other Outdoor Pursuits

GOLF   At the **Grenada Golf Course and Country Club,** Woodlands (© 473/444-4128), you'll find a 9-hole course, with greens fees of $16 for 9 holes, or $23 if you want to play 18 holes on the 9-hole course. The course is open Monday to Saturday 8am to 7pm and on Sunday 8am to 1:30pm. The course offers a view of both the Caribbean Sea and the Atlantic.

HIKING   Because of its lushness and beauty, Grenada is one of the Caribbean's best islands for hiking. The best trails wind through **Grand Etang National Park and Forest Preserve** (© 473/440-6160 for information). You can take a self-guided nature trail around Crater Lake or go on a more elaborate jaunt, perhaps to the peak of Mount Qua Qua, at 2,373 feet. The latter should be done with a guide, which costs $25 per person for a 4-hour hike. You can also hike to Mount St. Catherine, at 2,757 feet, but this should also be done with a guide, which costs $35. For information about hikes, call **Telfor Bedeau Hiking Tours** at © 473/442-6201 or **Arnold's Tours** at © 473/440-0531.

SCUBA DIVING & SNORKELING   Along with many other watersports, Grenada offers the diver an underwater world rich in submarine gardens, exotic fish, and coral formations, sometimes with underwater visibility stretching to 120 feet. Off the coast is the wreck of the ocean liner *Bianca C,* which is nearly 600 feet long. Novice divers might want to stick to the west coast of Grenada, whereas more experienced divers might search out the sights along the rougher Atlantic side.

Daddy Vic's Watersports, in the Grenada Renaissance, Grand Anse Beach (© 473/444-4371, ext. 638), is directly on the sands. The island's premier dive outfit, it offers night dives or two-tank dives for $65, and PADI instructors offer an open-water certification program for $350 per person. In addition, this is the best center for other watersports, offering snorkeling trips for $18 (1½–2 hr.) or windsurfing with board rentals for $16 per hour. Sunfish rentals are $16 per hour, parasailing is $30 per 10 minutes, jet-skiing runs $44 per half hour, and water-skiing is $15 per run. Even deep-sea-fishing arrangements can be made.

Giving Daddy Vic's serious competition is **Grand Anse Aquatics,** at the Coyaba Beach Resort on Grand Anse Beach (© 473/444-7777). Canadian-run, it's welcoming and inviting to divers, and there's a PADI instructor on site. The dive boat is well equipped with well-maintained gear. Both scuba diving and snorkeling jaunts to panoramic reefs and shipwrecks teaming with marine life are offered. A single dive costs $35, a resort course $75, and a night dive $55. A snorkeling trip can be arranged for $20 in winter or $15 in off-season. Diving instruction, including a resort course, is available.

If you'd rather strike out on your own, take a drive to Woburn and negotiate with a fisherman for a ride to **Glovers Island,** an old whaling station, and snorkel away. Glovers Island is an uninhabited rock spit a few hundred yards offshore from the hamlet of Woburn.

Warning: Divers should know that Grenada doesn't have a decompression chamber. If you should get the bends, you'll have to take an excruciatingly painful air trip to Trinidad.

SAILING   Two large "party boats," designed for 120 and 250 passengers, operate out of St. George's harbor. The *Rhum Runner* and *Rhum Runner II,* c/o Best of Grenada, P.O. Box 188, St. George's, Grenada, W.I. (© **473/ 440-4FUN**), make shuttle-style trips, three times a day, with lots of emphasis on strong liquor, steel-band music, and good times. Four-hour daytime tours, conducted every morning and afternoon, coincide with the arrival of cruise ships, but will carry independent travelers if space is available. Rides cost $20 per person and include snorkeling stops at reefs and beaches along the way. Evening tours are much more frequently attended by island locals, and are more bare-boned, louder, and usually less restrained. They cost $7.50 per person. Regardless of when you take it, your cruise will include rum, reggae music, and lots of hoopla.

TENNIS   The big resorts for the most part have tennis courts for their guests. But if you're staying at a small inn, you won't find such facilities. There are public courts, however, both at Grand Anse (adjacent to the Grande Anse Beach resort) and in Tanteen in St. George's (adjacent to T.A. Marryshow Community College).

6 Seeing the Sights

There's much to see here, both in the capital city of St. George's and around this lush island.

ST. GEORGE'S

The capital city of Grenada, **St. George's** ✺✺, is one of the most attractive ports in the West Indies. Its nearly landlocked inner harbor is said to be the deep crater of a long-dead volcano.

In the town you'll see some of the most charming Georgian colonial buildings to be found in the Caribbean, still standing in spite of a devastating hurricane in 1955. The streets are mostly steep and narrow, which enhances the attractiveness of the ballast bricks, wrought-iron balconies, and red tiles of the sloping roofs. Many of the pastel warehouses date back to the 18th century. Frangipani and flamboyant trees add to the palette of color.

The port, which some have compared to Portofino, Italy, is flanked by old forts and bold headlands. Among the town's attractions is an 18th-century pink Anglican **church,** on Church Street, and the **Market Square** where colorfully attired farm women offer even more colorful produce for sale.

Fort George, on Church Street, built by the French, stands at the entrance to the bay, with subterranean passageways and old guardrooms and cells.

Everyone strolls along the waterfront of **The Carenage** or relaxes on its Pedestrian Plaza, with seats and hanging planters providing shade from the sun.

On this side of town, the **Grenada National Museum,** at the corner of Young and Monckton streets (© **473/440-3725**), is set in the foundations of an old French army barrack and prison built in 1704. Small but interesting, it houses finds from archaeological digs, including petroglyphs, native fauna, the first telegraph installed on the island, a rum still, and memorabilia depicting Grenada's history. The most comprehensive exhibit traces the native culture of Grenada. One of the exhibits shows two bathtubs—the wooden barrel used by the fort's prisoners and the carved marble tub used by Joséphine Bonaparte during her adolescence on Martinique. The museum is open Monday to Friday 9am to 4:30pm and Saturday 10am to 1pm. Admission is $2.

The Outer Harbour is also called the **Esplanade.** It's connected to The Carenage by the Sendall Tunnel, which is cut through the promontory known as St. George's Point, dividing the two bodies of water.

You can take a drive up to Richmond Hill, where **Fort Frederick** stands. The French began construction on the fort in 1779; however, after Grenada was returned to Britain, following the Treaty of Versailles in 1783, the English carried on the work until its completion in 1791. From its battlements you'll have a superb view of the harbor and of the yacht marina.

An afternoon tour of St. George's and its environs takes you into the mountains northeast of the capital. About a 15-minute drive delivers you to **Annandale Falls** ✪, a tropical wonderland, where a cascade about 50-feet high falls into a basin. The overall beauty is almost Tahitian, and you can have a picnic surrounded by liana vines, elephant ears, and other tropical flora and spices. The **Annandale Falls Centre** (© **473/440-2452**) houses gift items, handcrafts, and samples of the indigenous spices of Grenada. Nearby, an improved trail leads to the falls, where you can enjoy a refreshing swim. Swimmers can use the changing cubicles at the falls free. The center is open daily 8am to 4pm.

A SPECTACULAR RAIN FOREST & MORE AROUND THE ISLAND

If you head north out of St. George's along the western coast, you can take in the beaches, spice plantations, and fishing villages that are so typical of Grenada.

You pass through **Gouyave,** a spice town, which is the center of the nutmeg and mace industry. Both spices are produced from a single fruit. Before reaching the village, you can stop at the Dougaldston Estate, where you'll witness the processing of nutmeg and mace. At the **Grenada Cooperative Nutmeg Association** (© **473/444-8337**), near the entrance to Gouyave, huge quantities of the spice are aged, graded, and processed. Most of the work is done within the ocher walls of the factory, which sport such slogans as "Bring God's peace inside and leave the Devil's noise outside." Workers sit on stools in the natural light from the open windows of the aging factory and laboriously sort the raw nutmeg and its byproduct, mace, into different baskets for grinding, peeling, and aging. It's open Monday to Friday 10am to 1pm and 2 to 4pm, and a visit costs $1.

Proceeding along the coast, you reach **Sauteurs,** at the northern tip of Grenada. This is the third-largest town on the island. It was from this great cliff that the Caribs leaped to their deaths instead of facing enslavement by the French.

To the east of Sauteurs is the palm-lined **Levera Beach,** an idyll of sand where the Atlantic meets the Caribbean. This is a great spot for a picnic lunch, but swimming can sometimes be dangerous. On the distant horizon you'll see some of the Grenadines.

Value Cheap Thrills: What to See & Do for Free (Well, Almost) on Grenada

- **Journey to Forgotten Petite Martinique.** In a 20-minute ride aboard the mailboat from Hillsborough on the island of Carriacou, you can be on an island that time forgot. The fare is only $5 one-way. This 486-acre dependency of Grenada is home to some 900 people. The island is really one large hill whose slopes run down to the coast. The eastern shore is rocky, but there are some fine beaches on the western (leeward) side, which is more tranquil. It was first settled by the French, and many islanders still have names of French origin. The islanders have long supported themselves through boatbuilding, fishing, and a little smuggling. A visit to this remote outpost is like a time capsule. Right on the beach, you'll spot the **Palm Beach Restaurant** (© 473/443-9103) as you arrive on a boat. It offers simple but good Creole lunches, featuring fish dishes on the beach at picnic tables. The cost for a meal is around $8.

- **Visit the Caribbean's Kayak Capital.** A major attraction of visiting Carriacou, Grenada's sibling island, is to watch tiny, lightweight kayaks being made. Up at the hamlet of Windward, on the northern part of Carriacou, the island's formidable reputation for boatbuilding comes into sharp perspective. Here you'll see sturdy 70- and 80-foot schooners and sloops in the making, a tradition that goes back to Scottish settlers who came here in the 1800s. You can watch as builders work on their new craft without blueprints along the shoreline. Completion time for the average wooden boat: about 5 months, with six good men.

- **Cool Off Under Concord Falls.** Just off the Coast Road, about 8 miles north of St. George's, are the Concord Falls, set in a lush landscape of bamboo, palms, mango, and breadfruit trees. Here you can take wooden steps to the base of the 65-foot Concord Falls for photos and, perhaps, a refreshing swim. These are actually a trio of waterfalls with a viewing platform and a small visitor's center. There's even a changing room where you can put on a bathing suit. In the dry months, usually January to May, you can stand under the waterfall, because the flow isn't too powerful then. To approach the two other waterfalls, you have to take an hour's hike through the rain forest. It's worth it. The third and final fall is the most panoramic of all, as water thunders down some 70 feet over massive boulders. Although this creates a pool at the base, no swimming is permitted here.

Opened in 1994, the 450-acre **Levera National Park** has several white sandy beaches for swimming and snorkeling, although the surf is rough here, where the Atlantic meets the Caribbean. It's also a hiker's paradise, and offshore are coral reefs and seagrass beds. The park contains a mangrove swamp, a lake, and a bird sanctuary. Perhaps you'll see a rare tropical parrot. Its interpretative center (© 473/442-1018) is open Monday to Friday 8am to 4pm, Saturday 9am to 4pm, and Sunday 9am to 5pm.

- **Visit Birds and Monkeys in Grand Etang National Park.** In the deep heart of mountainous Grenada is the Grand Etang National Park, encompassing a spine of mountains that dominate the interior of the island nation. The highest peaks are Mount Sinai at 2,309 feet and Mount Qua Qua at 2,373 feet. With miles of hiking trails, fishing streams, and panoramic lookout posts, this is one grand adventure for the hiker and Jungle Jim–type explorer. Our favorite trail (the visitor center here will assist you) is the Seven Sisters Trail in the central mountains. It begins southwest of Grand Etang Lake and leads to a beautiful spot with seven waterfalls and reflecting pools. You're also surrounded by wild birds and other animals, including monkeys. Allow about 3 hours for hiking this trail, Grenada's most intriguing.

- **Buy Some Essence of Grenada.** No small wonder that Grenada is called the "Spice Island." It is the second largest producer of nutmeg in the world. At the Gouyave Nutmeg Processing Cooperative, in the little town of Gouyave (© **473/444-8337**), for only $1 you can take a tour, climbing the narrow wooden stairs to the "drying floor" of the biggest processing factory on the island's western coast. Guides will show you the whole process of how nutmeg is produced, from the time it is first received at the station until it is carefully graded by hand and bagged for shipment. Visitors can also take along some essence of Grenada with them, in the form of jams, jellies, syrup, or plain ground nutmeg, all for sale here.

- **Stroll Around St. George's.** There is little dispute that St. George's, the capital of Grenada, is the prettiest harbor town in the West Indies. It is stacked on an amphitheatrical hillside and filled with houses with red tin roofs, a picture postcard waiting to be photographed. Named after King George III of England, it is split into two main halves: The Carenage on the inner harbor and the Esplanade itself fronting the Caribbean. You can spend an entire day wandering around and taking in its beauty, including old warehouses that overlook the sea. There's a fish market that amuses when the catch is brought in at the end of the day, and the harbor itself is always filled with ferries, tour boats, and schooners. Cruise ships even dock here, and the whole place takes on a festive, fun atmosphere. When a windjammer appears in harbor, as happens frequently on weekends, the place takes on the aura of the 1800s.

Heading down the east coast of Grenada, you reach **Grenville,** the island's second city. If possible, pass through here on a Saturday morning, when you'll enjoy the hubbub of the native fruit-and-vegetable market. There's also a fish market along the waterfront. A nutmeg factory here welcomes visitors. From Grenville, you can cut inland into the heart of Grenada. Here you're in a world of luxuriant foliage, passing along nutmeg, banana, and cocoa plantations.

In the center of the island, reached along the major interior road between Grenville and St. George's, is **Grand Etang National Park** ⚶, containing the island's spectacular rain forest, which has been made more accessible by hiking trails. Beginning at the park's forest center, the Morne LeBaye Trail affords a short hike along which you can see the 2,309-foot Mount Sinai and the east coast. Down the **Grand Etang Road,** trails lead to the 2,373-foot summit of Mount Qua Qua and the Ridge, and the Lake Circle Trail, which takes hikers on a 30-minute trek along Grand Etang Lake, the crater of an extinct volcano lying in the midst of a forest preserve and bird sanctuary. Among the birds you're likely to see are the yellow-billed cuckoo and the emerald-throated hummingbird. The park is also a playground for Mona monkeys. All three trails offer the opportunity to see a wide variety of Grenada's flora and fauna. Guides for the park trails are available, but they must be arranged for in advance. After a rainfall the trails can be very slippery (much of the rain falls on Grenada between June and Nov); hikers should wear sneakers or jogging shoes, and carry drinking water as well. The park's **Grand Etang Interpretation (Nature) Centre,** on the shores of Grand Etang Lake (✆ **473/440-6160**), is open Monday to Friday 8am to 4pm, featuring a video show about the park. An admission of $1 is charged.

As you begin your descent from the mountains, you'll pass hanging carpets of mountain ferns. Going through the tiny hamlets of Snug Corner and Beaulieu, you eventually come back to the capital.

Another good trip is to drive south from St. George's to the beaches and resorts spread along Grand Anse, which is one of the most beautiful beaches in the West Indies. Water taxis can also take you from The Carenage in St. George's to **Grand Anse.**

Point Salines, where the airport is located, is at the southwestern tip of the island, where a lighthouse stood for 56 years. A sculpture of the lighthouse has been constructed on the grounds, just outside the airport terminal building. A panoramic view ranging from the northwest side of Grenada to the green hills in the east to the undulating plains in the south can be seen from a nearby hill.

Along the way you'll pass through the village of **Woburn,** which was featured in the film *Island in the Sun,* and go through the sugar belt of **Woodlands,** with its tiny sugarcane factory.

7 Shopping

Everybody who visits Grenada goes home with a basket of spices, better than any you're likely to find in your local supermarket. Wherever you go, you'll be besieged by spice vendors selling handwoven panniers of palm leaf or straw, filled with items grown on the island, including the inevitable nutmeg, as well as mace, cloves, cinnamon, bay leaf, vanilla, and ginger. The local stores also sell a lot of luxury imports, mainly from England, at prices that are almost duty-free. Grenada is no grand merchandise mart of the Caribbean like St. Thomas and St. Maarten, but you might locate some local handcrafts, gifts, and even art.

If you like to attend Caribbean markets as much as we do, head for **Market Square** at the foot of Young Street in St. George's. The market is at its liveliest on Saturday morning but is also open Monday to Friday. It's best to go between 8am and noon. An array of handcrafts is for sale, but fresh spices to bring home are more plentiful.

At **Arawak Islands,** Upper Belmont Road, St. George's (✆ **473/444-3577**), look for at least nine different fragrances distilled from frangipani, wild lilies, cinnamon, nutmeg, and cloves; an all-natural insect repellent that some insist is the most effective (and safest) they've ever used; caffeine-free teas distilled from local plants; bitters that will perk up any rum-based drink; and soaps made in small batches and scented with nutmeg. Especially interesting is the root of the khus-khus plant, which, when pulverized and stuffed into potpourri bags, will sweeten the scents emanating from musty closets in hot climes.

Spice Island Perfumes, The Carenage (© 473/440-2006), is a little gem, a virtual treasure trove of perfumes made from the natural extracts of all those herbs and spices grown on Grenada. If you're a collector of exotic scents, this is your store. The workshop produces and sells perfumes, potpourri, and teas made from the locally grown flowers and spices. If you like, they'll spray you with a number of desired scents, including island flower, spice, frangipani, jasmine, patchouli, and wild orchid. The shop stands near the harbor entrance, close to the Ministry of Tourism and the public library.

Few other shops on Grenada convey as vivid an impression of the labor and detail that go into the manufacture of a yard of the boldly patterned batik cloth as **Art Fabrik,** Young Street, St. George's (© 473/440-0568). Your visit can combine a look at the showroom, where shirts, shifts, shorts, skirts, T-shirts, and virtually every other warm-weather garment you can think of, are sold. A quick visit to the studio is also worthwhile, partly as a means of seeing the hot wax applications and multiple dyeing rituals that go into the psychedelic patterns of the merchandise. If you fancy yourself a seamstress or couturier, or if you're just looking for upholstery fabric, you can buy it here, by the bulky bolt.

Gift Remembered, Cross Street, St. George's (© 473/440-2482), in the center of town a block from the water, sells handcrafts, straw articles, jewelry, batiks, film, beach wear, postcards, high-quality T-shirts, books, and wood carvings. It's mainly for a sort of aimless shopping, but could come in handy if you promised to bring some remembrance back from the islands for a relative or friend.

In the Grand Anse Beach area, you can break up your time in the sun with some handcraft purchases at **Imagine,** Grand Anse Shopping Centre (© 473/444-4028). The resort wear isn't the most fashionable we've ever seen, but it's ideal if you're seeking some minor gift item. This shop also offers excellent value in Caribbean handcrafts, all made of natural materials—dolls, ceramics, and straw items.

Sea Change Bookstore, The Carenage (© 473/440-3402), is cramped, crowded, and the staff here might remind you of the dissatisfied teachers who used to punish you during elementary school. But despite these drawbacks, it's the largest repository of pretty recent British and American newspapers on Grenada, piled untidily on overflowing shelves. There's also a collection of paperback books, island souvenirs, postcards, and film.

Tikal, Young Street, St. George's (© 473/440-2310), is located in an early 18th-century brick building off The Carenage, next to the museum. You'll find an array of tastefully chosen handcrafts from around the world, as well as the finest selection of crafts made on Grenada, including batiks, ceramics, woodcarvings, paintings, straw work, and clothing. The owner, Jeanne Fisher, is the designer of the local crafts.

Yellow Poui Art Gallery, Cross Street, St. George's (© 473/440-3001), is a 2-minute walk from Market Square and the most interesting shop for souvenirs and artistic items. Here you can see oil paintings and watercolors, sculpture, prints, photography, rare antique maps, engravings, and woodcuts, with prices beginning at $10 and going up. There's also a comprehensive display of newly acquired works from Grenada, the Caribbean area, and other sources, shown in three rooms.

8 Grenada After Dark

Regular evening entertainment is provided by the resort hotels and includes steel bands, calypso, reggae, folk dancing, and limbo—even crab racing. Ask at your hotel desk to find out what's happening at the time of your visit.

The island's most popular nightspot is **Fantazia 2001,** Morne Rouge Beach (© **473/444-2288**). It's air-conditioned, with state-of-the-art equipment, good acoustics, and fantastic disco lights, and plays the best in regional and international sounds. Live shows are presented on Friday and Saturday. The cover is EC$10 to EC$15 ($3.70–$5.55), depending on the entertainment.

Catbam, Grand Anse Beach, next to the Coyaba Beach Resort (© **473/ 444-2050**), offers dancing to calypso and reggae, and dining on rôtis and Carib beer on its open terrace. It stays open late. You can also try **Boatyard,** Prickly Bay, L'Anse aux Epines (© **473/444-4662**), down by the marina. Friday night after 11pm, a local DJ spins dance music until dawn.

La Sucrier, Sugar Mill, Grand Anse (© **473/444-1068**), has comedy acts, oldies, and a disco scene. A young local crowd, both visitors and residents, shows up any time after 9pm, Wednesday through Saturday nights.

Casablanca, Grand Anse (© **473/444-1631**), is the island's major sports bar. It's also a piano bar. The **Beachside Terrace** at the Flamboyant Hotel, Grande Anse (© **473/444-4247**), is a laid-back spot featuring **crab races** on Monday, a steel band on Wednesday and Saturday, and, our favorite, a beach barbecue with live calypso music on Friday.

One of our favorite bars is **The Aquarium** at Point Salines (© **473/ 444-1410**), which also serves delectable food. From the sprawl of decks open to the trade winds, you can enjoy the lights of St. George's Harbour here at night.

For those seeking culture, the 200-seat **Marryshow Folk Theatre,** Herbert Blaize Street near Bain Alley, St. George's (© **473/440-2451**), offers performances of Grenadian, American, and European folk music, drama, and West Indian interpretative folk dance. Check with the theater or the tourist office to see what's on. Tickets cost EC$15 to EC$20 ($5.55–$7.40).

9 A Side Trip to Carriacou ⊛

Largest of the Grenadines, Carriacou, "land of many reefs," is populated by about 8,000 inhabitants, mainly of African descent, who are scattered over its 13 square miles of mountains, plains, and white-sand beaches. There's also a Scottish colony, and you'll see such names as MacFarland on the island. In the hamlet of Windward, on the east coast, villagers of mixed Scottish and African descent carry on the tradition of building wooden schooners. Large skeletons of boats in various stages of readiness line the beach where workers labor with the most rudimentary of tools, building the West Indian trade schooner fleet. If you stop for a visit, a master boatbuilder will let you climb the ladder and peer inside the shell, and will explain which wood came from which island and why the boat was designed in its particular way. Much of the population, according to reputation, is involved in smuggling; otherwise, they're sailors, fisherfolk, shipwrights, and farmers.

ESSENTIALS
VISITOR INFORMATION For information about the island, go to the **Carriacou Board of Tourism** in Hillsborough (© **473/443-7948**). Open Monday to Friday 8am to noon and 1 to 4pm.

GETTING THERE   From Grenada's Point Salines International Airport you can fly to Carriacou in just 25 minutes. It's also possible to fly **Airlines of Carriacou** (© 473/444-3549), which has daily scheduled service not only to Carriacou but to St. Vincent and the Grenadines as well. There are two flights per day on Monday and Friday. For reservations, contact a travel agent, LIAT, or Airlines of Carriacou itself at the Point Salines airport. **SVG Air** (© 473/444-0328) also operates a nine-seat propeller plan between Grenada and Carriacou.

Ferries also run to Carriacou, including the *Osprey Express* (© 473/443-7984), a hovercraft departing Thursday to Tuesday, taking 90 minutes and costing $15 per person one-way or $28 round-trip. From the harbor at St. George's, the schooners *Alexia II, Alexia III,* and *Adelaide B* head for Carriacou daily except Monday and Thursday. These schooners carry both cargo and people, taking 4 hours and costing $7.50 one-way or $12 round-trip.

ACCOMMODATIONS YOU CAN AFFORD

Carriacou is a beautiful but remote island that hasn't yet experienced the onslaughts of hotel developments that have, in many cases, disfigured the landscapes of some other islands.

Bayaleau Point Cottages ★ *Finds*   Locals call it "Dave and Ulla's Place." A real discovery, this is the happy domain of Dave Goldhill, who escaped from New York to this place, evoking the Harrison Ford movie *The Mosquito Coast.* Here he met Ulla, a Dane, and they joined forces and established this homestead, where they receive guests, and fish and farm. In addition, Ulla creates batiks and David builds boats. They offer four pastel wooden cabins with porches, each cottage different and charmingly rustic. They're not screened, so mosquitoes can be a problem, but the beds are covered in netting. Our favorite cottages include The Little Blue Cottage, arranged in a small one-room house, and The Little Yellow Cottage, which is newer and perched higher than the others. With its large writer's desk, it might be the place where you'll at long last tackle that novel you were planning to write.

Windward, Carriacou, Grenada, WI. ©/fax **473/443-7984.** www.grenadines.net/carriacou/bayaleau/bayaleau.htm. 4 units. Winter $345–$545 weekly. Off-season $245–$445 weekly. MC, V. *In room:* Kitchenette, fridge, no phone.

Hope's Inn   This is one of the cheapest yet acceptable inns you're likely to find in all of Carriacou or Grenada. Although none of the bedrooms has a private bathroom, the raffishly informal place seems to suit its position on an island that's rarely visited by outsiders. It was built in 1992, with white walls, a red roof, and ultra-simple amenities such as curtained showers in the hall. The accommodations come with the use of a fan (set on a stand, not hung from the ceiling). Only the apartment has its own private kitchen; residents of the simple bedrooms share two communal cooking areas. (Guests usually prepare their own meals, but some hire cooks.) There's a modest grocery store nearby for purchases of liquor, supplies, soft drinks, cigarettes, and groceries. L'Esterre Beach begins about 50 feet from the hotel's foundations.

L'Esterre, Carriacou, Grenada, W.I. © **473/443-7457.** 6 units, none with bathroom; 1 apt. Year-round $25 single; $29 double; $40 1-bedroom apt for 2; $50 1-bedroom apt for 3. No credit cards. *In room:* Fan.

Scraper's Bay View Holiday Cottages   The administration of this 1970s hotel contributes a lot to its sense of somewhat disorganized fun. It consists of a main building and three white-sided outbuildings, flower gardens with picket fences and lots of hibiscus and oleander, and a restaurant that in its way is the best known on the island. Bedrooms have shower-only bathrooms that are small and utterly basic, but decently maintained.

You'll enjoy the bar (where rum punch is a specialty) and the rapid-fire dialogue of the owner, Scraper, whose real name is Stephen Gay. Scraper sometimes performs at his bar or restaurant (see "Great Deals on Dining," below). Don't expect the formality or services of a full-fledged resort here. If you appreciate nonstandard, aggressively informal hotels with a funky, strongly emphasized ethnic wit, this might be the place for you. The nearest beach is Tyrrel Bay, and the resort lies near the island's southern tip, in the village of Harvey Vale.

Tyrrel Bay, Carriacou, Grenada, W.I. ⓒ 473/443-7403. 6 units. Year-round $45 single; $55 double. DISC, MC, V. **Amenities:** Restaurant, bar. *In room:* A/C, TV, ceiling fans.

VILLA RENTALS

Some of the island's most alluring accommodations are in privately owned houses, whose off-island owners surrender the keys to a local management company whenever they don't need access. **Down Island Villa Rentals,** Hillsborough, Carriacou, Grenada, W.I. (ⓒ 473/443-8182; www.islandvillas.com), manages about 15 privately owned villas and apartments located in quiet residential spots. You need to book well ahead for stays in December to March. All the rentals are fully equipped homes with full kitchens and are built to take advantage of the trade winds. In winter, units range from $65 to $220 daily depending on their size, dropping in off-season to $50 to $185, plus $20 per extra person. Children 2 to 12 are housed for $12. Homes can accommodate from two to six guests. Villas are either on, over, or within walking distance of coves and beaches.

GREAT DEALS ON DINING

Scraper's SEAFOOD   At this restaurant in Scraper's Bay View Holiday Cottages, you can order some of the island's finest cuisine in relaxed, friendly surroundings, where everybody gets to know everybody else. The decor is hardly elegant, but no one comes here for that. They visit for the good food and the low prices. Stephen Gay himself (a.k.a. Scraper) makes the best conch on the island, and it's served Creole style or with curry. Lobster is occasionally featured on the menu. All these seafood delectables are freshly caught that day. Local seasonings add the right touch to bring out the fresh flavor in the food. Begin with Scraper's *callaloo* soup. The restaurant is right on the beach, and guests can dine inside or on the beach. Three times a week there's a steel band for entertainment.

At Scraper's Bay View Holiday Cottages, Tyrrel Bay. ⓒ 473/443-7403. Main courses EC$16–EC$60 ($5.95–$22.20); lunch from EC$15 ($5.55). DISC, MC, V. Daily 7am–midnight.

Finds When You're Tired of Restaurants

If you want a real home-cooked meal, West Indian style, you can call **Bayaleau Point Cottages** at Windward (ⓒ 473/443-7984), where Ulla Goldhill, a Dane, is the island's finest chef. She blends local herbs, spices, and produce with her Continental-sharpened skills, and the result is marvelous. The bread is freshly baked, and you can usually count on some fish specialty for the night, depending on the catch of the day. A meal is likely to cost around $15.

Guadeloupe

adeloupe consists of two islands ...rated by a narrow seawater chan-... known as the Rivière Salée. ...rande-Terre, the eastern island, is ...pical of the charm of the Antilles, ...ith its rolling hills and sugar planta-tions. **Basse-Terre,** to the west, is a rugged mountainous island, domi-nated by the 4,800-foot still-alive vol-cano La Soufrière. Guadeloupe's mountains are covered with tropical forests, impenetrable in many places. Bananas grown on plantations are the main crop, and the island is ringed by beautiful beaches, which have attracted much tourism.

Guadeloupe isn't the least expensive island in the West Indies. As in all French islands, the cost of dining in restaurants is usually high, but we've found some suitable budget selections. The island has big expensive resorts, but it also offers a number of Relais Creoles, really like West Indian B&Bs, that charge reasonable rates. Some vis-itors prefer renting a villa, a cottage, or an apartment with a kitchenette.

1 Essentials

VISITOR INFORMATION

For information before you go, call the **French Government Tourist Office** (© **800/391-4909** or 202/659-7779; www.francetourism.com).

The major tourist information office on Guadeloupe is the **Office Départe-mental du Tourisme,** Square de la Banque 5, in Pointe-à-Pitre (© **590/82-09-30**).

GETTING THERE

Most flights into Guadeloupe are tied in with air connections to Martinique. See "Getting There," in chapter 15.

Air Canada (© **800/268-7240** in Canada or 800/776-3000 in the U.S.) flies between Montréal and Guadeloupe (but not Martinique) every Saturday throughout the year. Air Canada can also route passengers on one of its daily non-stop flights from Toronto to Barbados, where clients connect to other carriers (usually LIAT) to Guadeloupe.

GETTING AROUND

BY TAXI You'll find **taxis** when you arrive at the airport, but no limousines or buses. From 9pm to 7am, cabbies are legally entitled to charge you 40% more than the regular rates. In practice, either day or night, they charge you whatever they think the market will bear, although technically fares are regulated by the government. Always agree on the price before getting in a taxi. Approximate fares are 130F to 140F (€19.75–€21.30, $18.75–$20.25) from the airport to Gosier hotels or 80F (€12.15, $11.50) from the airport to Pointe-à-Pitre. **Radio taxis** can be called at © **590/82-99-88** (on Basse-Terre, © **590/81-79-70**).

If you're traveling with more than two people, it's possible to do your sight-seeing by taxi. Usually the concierge at your hotel will help you make this

13

Moments The Gems of the Gr

Although most visitors come to Carriacou
even escape paradise on a boat built by D
Bayaleau Point Cottages (see "Accommo
above). He takes sightseers out in his 28-foot ↑
no more than a dozen at one time. The cost o
lunch and drinks. One favorite jaunt in the Grena
Cays, where you can swim in the half-moon-shapeo
The small collection of uninhabited islets called Toba
preserve. The area offers some of the best snorkeling in
typical fare that would include both a visit to the Toba
island of Mayreau costs $60 per person, everything include

EXPLORING THE ISLAND

The best time to visit Carriacou is in August, in time for its **regatta,**
begun by J. Linton Rigg in 1965 with the work boats and schooners fo
the Grenadines are famous. Now work boats, three-masted schooner
miniature "sailboats" propelled by hand join the festivities. Banana boats o
ing at the pier are filled with people rather than bananas, and sailors fro
Bequia and Union Island camp on tiny Jack-a-Dan and Sandy Isle, only 20 min
utes away by outboard motor from Hillsborough. The people of the Grenadines
try their luck at the greased pole, footraces, and of course the sailing races. Music
fills the air day and night, and impromptu parties are held. At the 3-day celebration, Big Drum dancers perform in the Market Square.

The **Big Drum dance** is part of the heritage of Carriacou brought from Africa
and nurtured here more purely than perhaps on any other Caribbean island. The
"Go Tambo," or Big Drum, is an integral part of such traditional events as stone
feasts (marking the setting of a tombstone) and the accompanying rites. The
feast, called *saraca,* and setting of the tombstone might be as long as 20 years
after a death. Another event involving the Big Drum and *saracas* is the *maroon.*
This can involve a dream interpretation, but it seems actually to be just a regular
festivity, held in various places during the dry season, with dancing and feasting.
A boat launching might also be accompanied by the Big Drum and the *saraca*
and usually draws crowds of participants.

The **Carriacou Parang Festival** is usually held on the weekend closest to
December 25. The festival serves to maintain the indigenous culture of the people of Carriacou. Bands are formed out of guitar, cuatro, bass drum, and violin.

Hillsborough is the chief port and administrative center of Carriacou, handling the commerce of the little island, which is based mainly on growing limes
and cotton. The capital bustles on Monday when the produce arrives, then
settles down again until "mail day" on Saturday. The capital is nestled in a mile-
long crescent of white sand.

Carriacou Museum, on Paterson Street in Hillsborough (© **473/443-8288**),
opposite Grentel, has a display of Amerindian artifacts, European china, glass
shards, and exhibits of African culture. In two small rooms, it preserves the history of Carriacou, which parallels that of its neighbor island, Grenada. It's open
Monday to Friday 9:30am to 3:45pm. Admission is EC$5 ($1.85) per person.

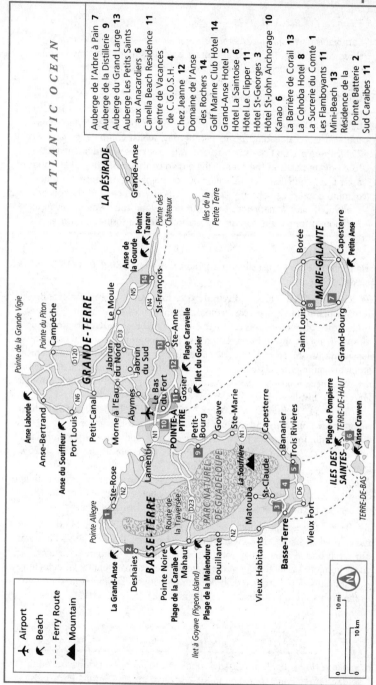

ATLANTIC OCEAN

Auberge de l'Arbre à Pain **7**
Auberge de la Distillerie **9**
Auberge du Grand Large **13**
Auberge Les Petits Saints
  aux Anacardiers **6**
Canella Beach Residence **11**
Centre de Vacances
  de C.G.O.S.H. **4**
Chez Jeanne **12**
Domaine de l'Anse
  des Rochers **14**
Golf Marine Club Hôtel **14**
Grand-Anse Hotel **5**
Hôtel La Saintoise **6**
Hôtel Le Clipper **11**
Hôtel St-Georges **3**
Hôtel St-John Anchorage **10**
Kanao **6**
La Barrière de Corail **13**
La Cohoba Hotel **8**
La Sucrerie du Comté **1**
Les Flamboyants **11**
Mini-Beach **13**
Résidence de la
  Pointe Batterie **2**
Sud Caraïbes **11**

GRANDE-TERRE

LA DÉSIRADE

Grande-Anse

Pointe de la Grande Vigie
Pointe du Piton
Campêche
Port Louis
Anse-Bertrand
Anse Laborde
Anse du Souffleur

Petit-Canal
Le Moule
Jabrun du Nord
Jabrun du Sud
Morne à l'Eau
Abymes

Anse de
la Gourde
Pointe
Tarare
Pointe des
Châteaux

Iles de la
Petite Terre

St-François
Ste-Anne
Plage Caravelle

Le Bas
du Fort
Gosier
Ilet du Gosier

POINTE-A-
PITRE

Petit-
Bourg
Goyave
Ste-Marie
Capesterre
Bananier
Trois Rivières

Lamentin

Ste-Rose

BASSE-TERRE

La Grand-Anse
Deshaies

Pointe Noire
Plage de la Caraïbe
Mahaut

Route de
la Traversée

PARC NATUREL
DE GUADELOUPE

La Soufrière
St-Claude
Matouba

Plage de la Malendure
Bouillante

Ilet à Goyave (Pigeon Island)

Vieux Habitants

Basse-Terre
Vieux Fort

Pointe Allègre

MARIE-GALANTE

Borée
Capesterre
Petite Anse

Saint Louis
Grand-Bourg

ILES DES
SAINTES

TERRE-DE-HAUT
Plage de Pompierre
Anse Crawen

TERRE-DE-BAS

Airport
Beach
Ferry Route
Mountain

N

10 mi
10 km
0

Fun Fact   Carnival

Carnival is particularly exuberant in Guadeloupe—the parades rival even those of Trinidad. The celebrations are a wild blend of old-time Catholicism, African music, and a French propensity toward exhibitionism. The best marching bands in the French West Indies parade through the streets of Pointe-à-Pitre in outrageous costumes, all trying to offer the most contagious blend of danceable music. It all happens on the Sunday before Fat Tuesday and Ash Wednesday. Lots of low-key partying marks the entire week leading up to parade day, which will be February 25, 2002. There are no tickets to buy, and you won't even need an invitation to a private party, as the roar of the crowd continues in the streets long after the parade itself ends. Bring your own libations, a sense of humor, general good cheer, and if you want, a wacky costume, and chances are that you'll have a marvelous time. But book your hotel well in advance. For more information, contact the island's tourist information office.

---

arrangement. Fares are usually negotiated but are around 800F (€121.60, $116) per day.

BY RENTAL CAR   Having a **rental car** enables you to circumnavigate Basse-Terre, which is one of the most panoramic drives in the Caribbean. Car-rental kiosks at the airport are open to meet international flights. Rental rates at local companies might appear lower than rates of the major international companies, depending on the agency, but several readers have complained of mechanical problems, billing irregularities, and difficulties in resolving insurance disputes in the event of accidents. So we recommend reserving a car in advance through **Hertz** (© **800/654-3001** or 590/21-09-35), **Avis** (© **800/331-1212** or 590/21-13-54), or **Budget** (© **800/527-0700** or 590/21-13-48), each of which is represented on the island and has its headquarters at the airport.

In addition to the rental rates, you'll have to pay a one-time airport surcharge of 100F (€15.20, $14.50) and VAT of 9.5%. Prices are usually 20% to 25% lower between March and early December.

Driving is on the right-hand side of the road. There are several gas stations along the island's main routes. Because of the distance between gas stations away from the capital, try not to let your gas gauge fall below the halfway mark.

BY BUS   **Buses** link almost every village with Pointe-à-Pitre. However, you might need to know some French to use the system. From Pointe-à-Pitre you can catch one of these jitney vans, either at the Gare Routière de Bergevin if you're going to Basse-Terre or at the Gare Routière de Mortenol if Grande-Terre is your destination. Service is daily 5:30am to 7:30pm. The fare from the airport to the Pointe-à-Pitre terminal on rue Peynier is 8F (€1.20, $1.15).

   FAST FACTS: Guadeloupe

Banking Hours   Banks on Guadeloupe are usually open Monday through Friday 9am to 3pm. There are about a dozen banks in Pointe-à-Pitre, most with ATMs (they're called *distributeurs des billets*).

Currency The official monetary unit is the **French franc (F)**, which is divided into 100 centimes. Occasionally, a shop will accept U.S. dollars, converting them into francs at a rate somewhat less favorable than you'd have gotten if you had changed them at a bank or *bureau de change*.

The exchange rate used to calculate the dollar values given in this chapter is 6.9F to U.S.$1 (1F = U.S.14½¢). As this is sure to fluctuate a bit, use this rate for general guidance only. Be aware that beginning February of 2002, during the lifetime of this edition, the **euro (€)** will be accepted for general use throughout France, even though authorities expect both the French franc and the euro to coexist, even if not altogether comfortably, for an indeterminate time after the euro's introduction. At press time, the euro converted into French francs at a rate of €1 = 6.58F, and the U.S. dollar converted into euros at a rate of U.S.$1 = €.92.

Customs Items for personal use "in limited quantities" can be brought in tax free.

Documents For stays of less than 21 days, U.S., British, or Canadian residents need a passport, plus a return or ongoing plane ticket.

Electricity The local electricity is 220-volt AC (50 cycles), meaning that those using U.S.-made appliances will need to bring a transformer and an adapter.

Emergencies Call the **police** at ✆ **17**; report a **fire** or summon an **ambulance** at ✆ **18**. If the situation involving the police is less urgent than an emergency, call ✆ **590/93-00-66**.

Language The official language is French, and Creole is the unofficial second language. English is spoken only in the major tourist centers, rarely in the countryside.

Medical Care There are five modern hospitals on Guadeloupe, plus 23 clinics. Hotels and the Guadeloupe tourist office can assist in locating English-speaking doctors. A 24-hour emergency room operates at the **Centre Hôpitalier de Pointe-à-Pitre,** Abymes (✆ **590/89-10-10**).

Pharmacies The pharmacies carry French medicines, and most over-the-counter U.S. drugs have French equivalents. Prescribed medicines can be bought if you have a prescription. At least one drugstore is always open, but the schedule is always changing. The tourist office can tell you what pharmacies are open at what time.

Safety Guadeloupe is relatively free of serious crime. But don't go wandering alone at night on the streets of Pointe-à-Pitre; by nightfall they're relatively deserted and might be dangerous. Purse-snatching by fast-riding motorcyclists have been reported, so exercise caution.

Taxes A departure tax, required on scheduled flights, is included in all airfares. Hotel taxes are included in all room rates.

Telephone To call Guadeloupe from the United States, dial **011** (the international access code), then **590** (the area code for Guadeloupe), plus the rest of the local number, which will be six digits.

St. Barts, French St. Martin, and offshore dependencies of Guadeloupe (such as Ile des Saints and La Desirade) are all directly linked to the phone network of Guadeloupe, so no telephone prefix is required when calling from Guadeloupe; simply dial the six-digit phone number of whomever you want to reach. If you call Martinique, however, you'll have to punch in the prefix for Martinique (0596), followed by a six-digit phone local number.

Time Guadeloupe is on Atlantic standard time year-round, 1 hour ahead of eastern standard time (when it's 6am in New York, it's 7am on Guadeloupe). When daylight saving time is in effect in the United States, clocks in New York and Guadeloupe show the same time.

Tipping Hotels and restaurants usually add a 10% to 15% service charge. Most taxi drivers who own their own cars do not expect a tip.

2 Pointe-à-Pitre

The port and chief city of Guadeloupe, **Pointe-à-Pitre** lies on Grande-Terre. Having been burned and rebuilt many times, the port has emerged as a town lacking in character, with modern apartments and condominiums forming a high-rise backdrop over jerry-built shacks and industrial suburbs. The rather narrow streets are jammed during the day with a colorful crowd, creating a permanent traffic tie-up. However, at sunset, the town becomes quiet again and almost deserted.

The real point of interest in Pointe-à-Pitre is shopping. It's best to visit the town in the morning—you can easily cover it in half a day—taking in the waterfront and outdoor market (the latter is livelier in the early hours). Be careful about walking alone on the nearly deserted streets of Pointe-à-Pitre at night.

The town center is **place de la Victoire,** a park shaded by palm trees and poincianas. Here you'll see some old sandbox trees said to have been planted by Victor Hugues, the mulatto who organized a revolutionary army of both whites and blacks to establish a dictatorship. In this square he kept a guillotine busy, and the death-dealing instrument still stood here (but not in use) until modern times.

With the recent completion of the **Centre St-Jean-Perse,** a $20-million project that had been on the drawing boards for many years, the waterfront of Pointe-à-Pitre has been transformed from a bastion of old warehouses and cruise-terminal buildings into an architectural complex comprising a hotel, 3 restaurants, 80 shops and boutiques, a bank, and the expanded headquarters of Guadeloupe's Port Authority.

Named for Saint-John Perse, the 20th-century poet and Nobel laureate who was born just a few blocks away, the center is tastefully designed in contemporary French Caribbean style, which blends with the traditional architecture of Pointe-à-Pitre. It offers an array of French Caribbean attractions: duty-free shops selling Guadeloupean rum and French perfume; small tropical gardens planted around the complex; and a location right near the open-air markets and small shops of this bustling port of call. For brochures, maps, and data on sightseeing, the Guadeloupe tourist office is just minutes away.

ACCOMMODATIONS YOU CAN AFFORD

Hôtel St-John Anchorage   This hotel rises four stories above the harbor front, near the quays. We'd recommend that you stay here only if you have business in town or need to be here for an early morning flight. The small rooms are clean, simple, and furnished with locally crafted mahogany pieces. Very few units have views over the sea. Shower-only bathrooms are small, with no frills. Once you check in, the laissez-faire staff might leave you alone until the end of your stay.

There's a simple coffee shop/cafe on street level. To reach a beach, you have to travel 2 miles to the east, to Le Bas du Fort and the Gosier area (see "Gosier," below).

Centre St-John-Perse, quai de Croisières (at the harborfront), 97110 Pointe-à-Pitre, Guadeloupe, F.W.I. ② 590/82-51-57. Fax 590/82-52-61. 44 units. Year-round 535F (€81.30, $77.55) single or double. Rates include continental breakfast. MC, V. **Amenities:** Coffee shop. *In room:* A/C, TV.

GREAT DEALS ON DINING

Restaurant Sucré-Salé TRADITIONAL FRENCH   In the heart of Pointe-à-Pitre, adjacent to an Air France office and near several banks, this restaurant is always filled at lunchtime with dealmakers and office workers. The decorative theme revolves around jazz, with portraits of Louis Armstrong, Billie Holliday, and Miles Davis. A covered terrace overlooking the busy boulevard serves as an animated singles bar every evening after work. The charming Marius Pheron, the Guadeloupe-born owner who did an 18-year stint in Paris, offers filets of snapper served with *pommes soufflés* and black pepper, meal-sized salads, entrecôte steaks, and an impressive medley of grilled fish. The restaurant hosts a jazz concert one evening a month; posters announcing the event appear all over town.

Bd. Légitimus. ② 590/21-22-55. Reservations recommended. Main courses 60F–120F (€9.10–€18.25, $8.75–$17.50). DC, MC, V. Mon–Sat noon–3pm; Tues–Sat 7–9:30pm.

SHOPPING

Your best buys on Guadeloupe are French luxury imports, such as perfumes, fashions, Vuitton luggage, Lalique crystal, and Limoges dinnerware. Sometimes (but don't count on it) prices are as much as 30% to 40% below those in the United States.

If you pay in U.S. dollars, store owners supposedly will give you a 20% discount; however, the exchange rates vary considerably from store to store, and almost invariably they are far less favorable than the rate offered at the local banks. You're usually better off shopping in the smaller stores, where prices are 8% to 12% lower on comparable items, and paying in francs that you have exchanged at a local bank.

Purchases are duty-free if brought directly from the store to the airplane. In addition to the places below, there are also duty-free shops at **Raizet Airport** (② **590/21-14-66**) selling liquor, rums, perfumes, crystal, and cigarettes.

Most shops open at 9am, close at 1pm, then reopen between 3 and 6pm. They're closed on Saturday afternoon, Sunday, and holidays. When the cruise ships are in port, many eager shopkeepers stay open longer.

One of the best places to buy French perfumes, at prices often lower than those charged in Paris, is **Phoenicia,** 8 rue Frébault (② **590/83-50-36**). The shop also has a good selection of imported cosmetics. U.S. traveler's checks will get you further discounts. Other leading perfume shops are **Au Bonheur des Dames,** 49 rue Frébault (② **590/82-00-30**), which is also known for its skincare products. **L'Artisan Parfumeur,** Centre St-John-Perse (② **590/83-80-25**), carries not only top French perfumes, but also leading American brands at discounted prices.

Rosébleu, 5 rue Frébault (② **590/82-93-44**), sells fine crystal, fine porcelain, and tableware from all the grand chic names of Europe's leading porcelain manufacturers, including Christofle, Kosta Buda, and Villeroy & Boch, always at prices 20% less than on the French mainland. **Vendôme,** 8–10 rue Frébault (ⓒ **590/83-42-84**), has imported fashions for both men and women, as well as a large selection of gifts and perfumes, including the big names. Usually you can find someone who speaks English to sell you a Cardin watch.

If you're interested in foodstuffs imported from France, including everything from cheese to chocolate, head for **Délice Shop,** 45 rue Achille René-Boisneuf (ⓒ **590/82-98-24**). The **Distillerie Bellevue,** rue Bellevue-Damoiseau, 97160 Le Moule (ⓒ **590/23-55-55**), produces "the essence of the island"—*rhum agricole,* a pure rum fermented from sugarcane juice. Once this rum was available in great abundance, but now only two distilleries process it. On the island, savvy locals say that the rum there (whose brand name is Rhum Damoiseau) is the only rum you can drink without suffering the devastation of a rum hangover (comparable to a gin hangover) the next morning. You're allowed to taste the product.

If you're adventurous, you might want to seek out some native goods in little shops along the back streets of Pointe-à-Pitre. Collector's items are the **straw hats** (*salakos*) made in Iles des Saintes. They look distinctly related to Chinese coolie hats and are usually well designed, often made of split bamboo. Native **doudou dolls** are also popular gift items.

Open-air stalls surround the **covered market** (*marché couvert*) at the corner of rue Frébault and rue Thiers. Here you can discover the many fruits, spices, and vegetables that are enjoyable just to view, if not to taste. In madras turbans, Creole women make deals over their strings of fire-red pimientos. The bright fabrics they wear compete with the rich tones of oranges, papayas, bananas, mangos, and pineapples, and the sounds of an African-accented French fill the air.

THE "SOUTH RIVIERA"

Saint-John Perse once wrote about the fine times sailors had in Pointe-à-Pitre, as a stopover on the famous Route du Rhum. But because that day is long gone, you might want to move on to the "South Riviera," along Grand-Terre's south coast from Pointe-à-Pitre to Pointe des Châteaux. This area has long stretches of white sands, although the beaches here aren't spectacular, and are often narrow and artificially created.

The first tourist complex you come to, just 2 miles east of Pointe-à-Pitre, is **Le Bas du Fort,** near Gosier. Here you can visit the **Aquarium de la Guadeloupe,** place Créole, Marina Bas-du-Fort (ⓒ **590/90-92-38**), rated as one of the three most important of France and the largest and most modern in the Caribbean. Just off the highway near Bas-du-Fort Marina, the aquarium is home to tropical fish, coral, underwater plants, huge sharks, and other sea creatures. It's open daily 9am to 7pm. Admission is 36F (€5.45, $5.25) for adults and 20F (€3.05, $3) for children 6 to 12; free for kids 5 and under.

3 Gosier

Some of the biggest and most important hotels of Guadeloupe are at this holiday center, with its nearly 5 miles of beach, stretching east from Pointe-à-Pitre.

For an excursion, you can climb to **Fort Fleur-d'Epée,** dating from the 18th century. Its dungeons and battlements are testaments to the ferocious fighting between the French and British armies seeking to control the island in 1794. The well-preserved ruins command the crown of a hill. From here you'll have good views over the bay of Pointe-à-Pitre, and on a clear day you can see the neighboring offshore islands of Marie-Galante and the Iles des Saintes.

ACCOMMODATIONS YOU CAN AFFORD

Canella Beach Residence 🜚 Near the tip of the Gosier peninsula, this resort evokes an apartment or condominium complex more than a hotel, as virtually everyone opts to prepare at least some of their own meals. Each of the summery-looking units, which are scattered amid a trio of three-story pink buildings, has a kitchenette. Interiors are monochromatically outfitted in wicker and varnished hardwoods, and many open onto views of the beach. Suites come in one-level or duplex form. Accommodations are medium in size, with sturdy beds and tidily maintained (though small) bathrooms, most of which have both a tub and a shower. Look for lots of families—most from France—who arrive for stays of at least a week. There are lots of pleasant corners and hideaways here. The in-house restaurant, La Véranda, is appealing enough to be visited by residents of nearby hotels (see "Great Deals on Dining," below).

Pointe de la Verdure (B.P. 73), Gosier, Guadeloupe, F.W.I. ✆ **590/90-44-00.** Fax 590/90-44-44. www. canellabeach.com. 145 units. Winter 1,020F (€155, $148) single or double; 1,770F (€269, $256.50) suite. Off-season 710F (€107.90, $103) single or double; 1,300F (€197.55, $188.50) suite. AE, DC, MC, V. **Amenities:** Restaurant, bar, pool, babysitting, laundry. *In room:* A/C, TV, kitchenette, minibar, safe.

Hotel le Clipper
Opened in 1997, this is Gosier's most theme-based hotel, designed to look like a five-story ocean liner rising from the sands. Each unit has its own balcony, angled along the building's curved sides for a view over the sea, and contains durable and practical wooden furniture. Each bathroom has a tub and shower and a round-sided window evocative of a porthole; the bedrooms have oversized bay windows. Guests have access to tennis courts at a neighboring hotel. A good percentage of the guests check in as part of tour groups from France, often arriving with their children in tow.

Pointe de la Verdure, Gosier, Guadeloupe, F.W.I. ✆ **590/840-175.** Fax 590/843-815. 88 units. Winter 900F (€136.80, $130.50) single; 980F (€148.95, $142) double. Off-season 515F (€78.25, $74.75) single; 600F (€91.20, $87) double. AE, MC, V. **Amenities:** Restaurant, bar, pool, access to tennis nearby, babysitting, laundry. *In room:* A/C, TV, fridge, hair dryer, safe.

Les Flamboyants
On a clifftop overlooking the sea and panoramic views of the coast, this complex lies within a 15-minute walk of a small strip of golden sand. Small scale and—at least in theory—more personalized than the massive hotels in the same neighborhood, this was developed around the core of a pink-sided Creole house in a pleasant garden. The main house was built just before World War II, and the various bungalows were constructed without much style in the mid-1970s, many with views over the seacoast and the offshore island, Islet du Gosier. The nine rooms with kitchenettes are the most expensive. Bathrooms are cramped but generally adequate, each with a tiled shower stall. The hotel offers discounts of around 15% for stays of a week or more.

Périnet, chemin des Phares et Balises, 97190 Gosier, Guadeloupe, F.W.I. ✆ **590/84-14-11.** Fax 590/84-53-56. 18 units. Winter 320F–360F (€48.65–€54.70, $46.40–$52.15) single; 360F–420F (€54.70–€63.85, $52.15–$60.85) double. Summer 260F–320F (€39.50–€48.65, $37.70–$46.40) single; 300F–360F (€45.60–€54.70, $43.50–$52.15) double. Rates include breakfast. AE, DC, MC, V. **Amenities:** Small pool. *In room:* A/C, kitchenette (some units), no phone.

Sud Caraibes *Finds*
Part of this place's appeal (and the reason for its relatively low costs) is its location on the perimeter of the fishing village of Petit Havre, far removed from the shops, casinos, and bustle of Gosier. Opened in the mid-1980s, the resort has gradually developed a roster of guests who don't care much about its lack of resort amenities and appreciate the individual attention they get from the owners. Each room has rattan furniture, but, except for a small refrigerator, none has any cooking facilities. There's no restaurant on site, but a

mom-and-pop grocery store is within a 10-minute walk. Each unit has a small but efficiently organized tiled shower-only bathroom. There's a large rectangular pool and a poolside replica of a Creole cottage outfitted with a blue-and-white decor inspired by the traditions of Tunisia, with North African artifacts and ceramics. Many visitors opt for dips in the nearby sea and serious sunbathing beside the pool. Other than breakfast, meals are not served on a regular basis, except by special arrangement.

Chemin de la Plage, Petit Havre, 97190 Gosier, Guadeloupe, F.W.I. © 590/85-96-02. Fax 590/85-80-39. 12 units. Winter 590F (€89.65, $85.55) single; 790F (€120.05, $114.50) double. Off-season 490F (€74.45, $71) single; 590F (€89.65, $85.50) double. Rates include breakfast. MC, V. **Amenities:** Bar; pool; health club; laundry. *In room:* A/C, fridge, no phone.

GREAT DEALS ON DINING

La Véranda FRENCH/CARIBBEAN   In an indoor/outdoor beachfront building on the grounds of the Canella Beach Residence, this well-managed restaurant offers food that's better than you might imagine. It manages to import a certain Gallic savoir-faire. Accompanied by the sound of the waves, you can enjoy dishes like steamed lobster with shallot butter, fricassee of chicken with freshwater crayfish, and snapper filet with creamy onion sauce.

In the Canella Beach Residence, Pointe de la Verdure, Gosier. © 590/90-44-00. Reservations recommended. Lunch main courses 50F–90F (€7.60–€13.70, $7.25–$13.05); dinner main courses 70F–90F (€10.65–€13.70, $10.15–$13.05). AE, DC, MC, V. Daily noon–2pm and 7–10pm.

Le Bananier ⊕ *Finds* CREOLE   Well-established Guadeloupe-born entrepreneurs Élixe Virolan (maître-d'hôtel) and chef Yves Clarus joined forces years ago to create a restaurant where some of the most imaginative dishes in the Creole repertoire are handled with finesse and charm. Within an air-conditioned, 50-year-old clapboard-sided cottage, you'll enjoy old-fashioned staples, such as stuffed crab backs and *accras* (beignets) of codfish. Much more appealing, however, are dishes like filet mignon served with pulverized blood sausage, port wine, and a reduction of crayfish bisque; a *clafoutis* (gratinated medley) of shellfish; and a *tourtière d'oeufs aux crabes* (an omelet with breaded and baked crabmeat, fresh tomatoes, and reduction of *callaloo* leaves). The menu's most appealing dessert is banana flambéed in *Schrubb*, an obscure island liqueur made from fermented orange peels and prized by the owners' grandparents.

Rue Principale de Gosier, Montauban. © 590/84-34-85. Reservations recommended. Main courses 75F–175F (€11.40–€26.60, $11–$25.50). AE, DC, MC, V. Tues–Sun noon–2:30pm and 7–10:30pm.

SHOPPING

Gosier is a good place to shop for souvenirs and some Haitian paintings. Try **Boutique de la Plage,** blvd. Général de Gaulle (© **590/84-52-51**), which has all sorts of handcrafts. Many are quite junky, but some are amusing. The island's best selection of Haitian art is found at **Centre d'Art Haitien,** Montauban 65 (© **590/84-32-60**).

ACCOMMODATIONS & DINING NEARBY

Chez Jeanne ⊕ *Finds* CREOLE   This hotel is a 10-minute drive from Gosier on the coastal road to Ste-Anne and adjacent to a small apartment house that's under the same ownership. Madame Jeanne rents 16 simple rooms in the cement-sided apartment house next door, each with TV and phone and furnished in the simplest possible way. The beach at Gosier is about 2 miles away.

The on-site restaurant, La Nouvelle Table Créole, serves richly authentic Creole cuisine supervised, and in many cases personally prepared, by Mme

Jeanne Carmelite, matriarch extraordinaire. Her versions of recipes handed down by her forebears are well seasoned, with a strong emphasis on grilled fish, steamed or stewed conch or octopus, goat meat or pork stew, and court bouillons of fish. These are in addition to what's de rigueur as a part of any proper Creole meal, *accras de morue* and perhaps a *blaff* of chicken or seafood. The restaurant is open daily noon to 3pm and Monday through Saturday 7 to 9pm. Main courses are 50F to 100 F (€7.60–€15.20, $7.25–$14.50).

In the Village Caraibes Carmelita, St-Félix. (℡ **590/84-28-28.** Winter 620F (€94.20, $90) double with kitchen, 470F (€71.45, $68) double without kitchen. Off-season 420F (€63.85, $61) double with kitchen, 300F (€45.60, $43.50) double without kitchen. DC, MC, V. **Amenities:** Restaurant, bar, pool. *In room:* TV.

4 Ste-Anne

About 9 miles east of Gosier, little Ste-Anne is a sugar town and resort area, offering many fine sandy beaches and lodgings. It's the most charming of the villages of Guadeloupe, with its town hall in pastel colors, its church, and its principal square, **Place de la Victoire,** where a statue of Schoelcher commemorates the abolition of slavery in 1848.

All the rainbow colors of the Caribbean are for sale at **La Case à Soie** in Ste-Anne (℡ **590/88-11-31**), known for its flamboyantly colored scarves and its flowing silk dresses.

ACCOMMODATIONS YOU CAN AFFORD

Auberge du Grand Large   This cottage colony is near the beachfront of Ste-Anne, close to the hamlet's center. Among the more unusual aspects of this hotel is that each kitchenette is under the sheltering eaves of outdoor verandas guarded by shrubs and flowering vines and with views of the beach or a garden. Bedrooms and shower-only bathrooms are small and routine, but the overall comfort is reasonable for the price. There's no pool and only a moderate number of amenities, but the independent travelers these bungalows attract don't seem to mind. You can rent a bungalow for a full week, and forgo the usual maid service, for 3,200F (€486.30, $464) in high season or 2,100F (€319.15, $304.50) in the off-season.

Route de la Plage, 97180 Ste-Anne, Guadeloupe, F.W.I. (℡ **590/85-48-28.** Fax 590/88-16-69. 10 units. Winter 600F (€91.20, $87) bungalow for 1 or 2. Off-season 350F (€53.20, $50.75) bungalow for 1 or 2. Extra person 100F (€15.20, $14.50). MC, V. **Amenities:** Laundry. *In room:* A/C, TV, kitchenette.

La Barrière de Corail   About ¾ mile from the center of Ste-Anne, adjacent to the Club Med Caravelle and close to clusters of equivalent (but more expensive) competitors, this is a complex of white cottages with corrugated (usually red) roofs and brown trim. The nearest beach is the one shared by the permissive and somewhat topless crowd at Club Med. Expect no frills here, but if you're looking for a woodsy back-to-the-earth kind of ambience and don't need amenities or maid service, one of these bungalows might be for you. The bedrooms, containing beds with well-used mattresses, are cramped, with tiny shower-only bathrooms and bare-bones kitchenettes, but few guests spend much time inside anyway. A handful of restaurants are within a brisk walk. No breakfast of any kind is served, and once you arrange for your accommodations, you might not see any staff members for days at a time.

Durivage, 97180 Ste-Anne, Guadeloupe, F.W.I. (For information and reservations, write Mme Giroux, rue Bébian 4, 97110 Pointe-à-Pitre, Guadeloupe, F.W.I.) (℡ **590/88-20-03.** 27 units. Winter 300F (€45.60, $43.50) single or double. Off-season 200F (€30.40, $29) single or double. Extra 60F (€9.10, $8.75) for 3rd or 4th person. Air-conditioning 20F (€3.05, $3) per night. MC, V. *In room:* Kitchenette, no phone.

Mini-Beach   Beneath a canopy of trees near the isolated northern edge of Ste-Anne's beach, this small hotel is personally managed by the resident-owner Nicole Poinard. Opened in the early 1980s, it consists of a main building containing half a dozen tiny rooms, a restaurant, and three one-room bungalows close to the water's edge. Surprisingly, the rooms, not the bungalows, sell out fastest. Each accommodation features a different decor, with tropical accents and mosquito nets on the beds, plus small bathrooms with shower stalls. There's no pool, no tennis courts, and no other resort-type amenities, but many guests enjoy the blasé, vaguely permissive ambience of this very French hotel. The restaurant has an open kitchen where diners can watch the chef (Philippe) at work, preparing lobsters from a holding tank.

B.P. 77, 97180 Plage Ste-Anne, Guadeloupe, F.W.I. ✆ 590/88-21-13. Fax 590/88-19-29. 9 units, including 3 bungalows with kitchenettes. Winter 500F (€76, $72.50) single, double, or bungalow for 1 or 2. Off-season 300F (€45.60, $43.50) single, double, or bungalow for 1 or 2. Rates include breakfast. MC, V. **Amenities:** Restaurant, bar. *In room:* A/C, minibar, safe.

5 St-François ⍟

Continuing east from Ste-Anne, you'll notice many old round towers named for Father Labat, the Dominican founder of the sugarcane industry. These towers were once used as cane-grinding mills. St-François, 25 miles east of Pointe-à-Pitre, used to be a sleepy fishing village, known for its native Creole restaurants. Then Air France discovered it and opened a Méridien hotel with a casino. That was followed by the promotional activities of J. F. Rozan, a native, who invested heavily to make St-François a jet-set resort. Now the once-sleepy village has first-class accommodations (and even some budget choices), as well as an airport that's available to private jets, a golf course, and a marina.

ACCOMMODATIONS YOU CAN AFFORD

Domaine de l'Anse des Rochers   With no neighbors except a nearby hotel, this low-slung resort sits amid carefully landscaped grounds adjacent to the sea. Built in 1990, its somewhat cramped accommodations are in a network of detached bungalows or in a series of gingerbread-laced two-story annexes. Beds are good and have firm mattresses, and shower-only bathrooms don't really have enough room to spread out your stuff, though the plumbing is decent and maintenance is high. Each building is painted a different Creole-inspired color (green, pink, red, or yellow), and paths leading from each of them end up at the resort's pool. The overall effect is that of a small laid-back village that rocks to disco music after dark.

Every unit has a kitchenette, so most guests prepare their own breakfast and lunch from ingredients they buy at an on-site superette, then opt for a dinner in any of three on-site restaurants: Le Blanc-Mangé, focusing almost exclusively on buffets and open only for breakfast and dinner; La Villa Romaine, a French and Mediterranean bistro open daily for lunch and dinner; and Le Tilolo, an informal place for grilled fish and Creole food.

L'Anse des Rochers, 97118 St-François, Guadeloupe, F.W.I. ✆ 590/93-90-00. Fax 590/93-91-00. www.hotels-anchorage.com. 356 units. Winter 650F–845F (€98.80–€128.45, $94.25–$122.50) single; 745F–1,335F (€113.25–€202.90, $108–$193.50) double. Off-season 515F–660F (€78.30–€100.30, $74.75–$95.75) single; 595F–755F (€90.45–€114.75, $86.25–$109.50) double. AE, MC, V. **Amenities:** 3 restaurants, 2 bars, pool, laundry. *In room:* A/C, kitchenette, safe.

Golf Marine Club Hôtel   Critics of this hotel claim its name is deliberately misleading: The golf club it promises is a municipal course across the street; the marine facilities are within walking distance but not associated with the hotel in any way; and the nearest beach is a 5-minute walk away. Despite these caveats, the hotel is a good bet for simple bedrooms with good mattresses and tiny but tidy shower-only bathrooms. Some have balconies, but those facing the rear garden are quieter than those opening onto the busy main street of St-François. The staff isn't the most organized on the island, but once you've checked in, you might appreciate the low-key attitude.

Ave. de l'Europe (B.P. 204), 97118 St-François, Guadeloupe, F.W.I. ℭ 590/88-60-60. Fax 590/85-51-43. 61 units. Winter 600F (€91.20, $87) single; 640F (€97.25, $92.75) double. Off-season 450F (€68.40, $65.25) single; 480F (€72.95, $69.50) double. AE, V. **Amenities:** Pool, laundry. *In room:* A/C, TV, minibar, safe.

GREAT DEALS ON DINING

Oiseau de Paradis ✦ *Value* FRENCH/CREOLE   Cool, confident, and well-managed, this restaurant attracts diners from throughout the island, thanks to well-prepared cuisine and the kind of decor that invites you to linger over drinks or after-dinner coffee. There's a bar attached to this place, in case you're more interested in drinking than dining. Within rooms that are painted in tones of—among others—celery green, you can order dishes that include grilled freshwater crayfish, grilled conch, tagliatelle with lobster, court bouillon of fish, curried, slow-cooked goat meat, and shellfish stew. The menu also lists *métropolitain* (mainland France staples) that include magret of duckling with honey and lime sauce; rack of lamb, and the kind of shellfish sauce that has everybody asking for the secret ingredients.

Rue de la République, St-François. ℭ 590/88-77-97. Reservations recommended. Main courses 100F–140F (€15.20–€21.30, $14.50–$20.25); fixed-price menus 120F–180F (€18.25–€27.35, $17.50–$26). AE, MC, V. Thurs–Tues noon–2:30pm and 6–10:30pm.

6 An Excursion to the Eastern End of Guadeloupe

POINTE DES CHÂTEAUX

The Atlantic meets the Caribbean 7 miles east of St-François at **Pointe des Châteaux,** the easternmost tip of Grand-Terre. Here, where crashing waves sound around you, you'll see a cliff sculpted by the sea into castle-like formations, the erosion typical of France's Brittany coast. The view from here is splendid. At the top is a cross put there in the 19th century.

You might want to walk to **Pointe des Colibris,** the extreme end of Guadeloupe. From here you'll have a view of the northeastern sector of the island, and to the east a look at La Désirade, another island, which has the appearance of a huge vessel anchored far away. Among the **beaches** found in coves around here, Tarare Point is *au naturel.*

GREAT DEALS ON DINING

Restaurant Les Châteaux CREOLE   Many visitors make this gazebo-style restaurant the final destination of drives to the extreme eastern tip of Grande-Terre. Although some fixed-price meals are prohibitively expensive, many others cost only 80F (€12.15, $11.50). Lunches are informal affairs where at least some guests may dine in bathing suits. Dinner, served only Saturday, is a bit more formal, but still has a barefoot kind of charm heightened by the isolation you might feel on flat, sandy, and scrub-covered Pointe des Châteaux. For savory local fare, try squid in Creole sauce, a court bouillon of fish (it's been simmering on the stove all day), several preparations of lobster, and an unusual *salade* *de coffre* from the tenderized and grilled flesh of a local fish (*le coffre*), whose armor is so tough that local fishers compare it to a crustacean.

Pointe des Châteaux. © **590/88-43-53**. Fixed-price menus 80F–150F (€12.15–€22.80, $11.50–$21.75). V. Tues–Sun noon–2pm; Sat 7:30–10pm.

LE MOULE

To go back to Pointe-à-Pitre from Pointe des Châteaux, you can use an alternative route, N5 from St-François. After a 9-mile drive you reach the village of Le Moule, which was founded at the end of the 17th century and known long before Pointe-à-Pitre. It used to be a major shipping port for sugar. Now a tiny coastal fishing village, it never regained its importance after it and many other villages of Grand-Terre were devastated in the great hurricane of 1928. Because of its more than 10-mile-long crescent-shaped beach, it's developing as a holiday center. Modern hotels built along the beaches have opened to accommodate visitors.

Specialties of this Guadeloupean village are *palourdes*, the clams that thrive in the semi-salty mouths of freshwater rivers. Known for being more tender and less rubbery than saltwater clams, they often, even when fresh, have a distinct sulfur taste not unlike that of overpoached eggs. Local gastronomes prepare them with saffron and aged rum or cognac.

Nearby, the sea unearthed some skulls, grim reminders of the fierce battles fought among the Caribs, French, and English. It's called the **Beach of Skulls and Bones.**

Three miles from Le Moule heading toward Campêche, the **Edgar Clerc Archaeological Museum La Rosette,** Parc de la Rosette (© **590/23-57-57**), shows a collection of both Carib and Arawak artifacts gathered from various islands of the Lesser Antilles. The museum is open Tuesday to Sunday 9am to noon and 2 to 5pm. Admission is 10F (€1.50, $1.50) adults, 5F (€.75, 70¢) students.

To return to Pointe-à-Pitre, we suggest you use route D3 toward Abymes. The road winds around as you plunge deeply into Grand-Terre. As a curiosity, about halfway along the way a road will bring you to **Jabrun du Nord** and **Jabrun du Sud.** These two villages are inhabited by Caucasians with blond hair, said to be survivors of aristocrats slaughtered during the French Revolution. Those members of their families who escaped found safety by hiding out in Les Grands Fonds. The most important family is named Matignon, which gave its name to the colony known as Les Blancs Matignon. These citizens are said to be related to Prince Rainier of Monaco.

7 Driving Around the Northern Coast of Grande-Terre

To explore the northern coast of Grande-Terre, from Pointe-à-Pitre, head northeast toward Abymes, passing next through Morne à l'Eau. After 13 miles you'll reach **Petit Canal.** This is Guadeloupe's sugarcane country, where a sweet smell fills the air.

PORT LOUIS

Continuing northwest along the coast from Petit Canal, you come to Port Louis, well known for its beautiful beach, **Anse du Souffleur,** which we find best in spring, when the brilliant white sand is effectively shown off against a contrast of the flaming red poinciana. During the week the beach is an especially quiet spot. The little port town is asleep under a heavy sun and has some good restaurants.

GREAT DEALS ON DINING

Le Poisson d'Or ★ *Finds* CREOLE   You enter this white-sided Antillean house by walking down a narrow corridor and emerging into a rustic dining room lined with varnished pine. Despite the simple setting, the food is well prepared and satisfying. Don't even think of coming here at night without an advance reservation—you might find the place locked up and empty. Lunch is the real time to come, when there will be a mix of locals and tourists from France. Try the stuffed crabs or the beef bouillon, topped off by coconut ice cream, which is homemade and tastes it. The place is a fine choice for an experience with Creole cuisine, complemented by a bottle of good wine.

2 rue Sadi-Carnot, Port Louis. © 590/22-88-63. Reservations required for dinner. Main courses 70F–85F (€10.65–€12.90, $10.25–$12.25); fixed-price menu 90F–120F (€13.70–€18.25, $13–$17.50). AE, MC, V. Daily 9am–5pm. Drive northwest from Petit Canal along the coastal road.

ANSE-BERTRAND

About 5 miles from Port Louis lies Anse-Bertrand, the northernmost village of Guadeloupe. What's now a fishing village was the last refuge of the Carib tribes, and a reserve was once created here. Everything now, however, is sleepy.

GREAT DEALS ON DINING

Chez Prudence (Folie Plage) ★ CREOLE   About a mile north of Anse-Bertrand at Anse Laborde, this place is owned by Prudence Marcelin, who enjoys local acclaim for her Creole cooking. She draws people from all over the island, especially on Sunday. Island children frolic in the saltwater pool, while, in between courses, diners shop for crafts, clothes, and souvenirs sold by a handful of nearby vendors. Her court bouillon is excellent, as is the goat or chicken *colombo* (curried). The *palourdes* (clams) are superb, and she makes a zesty sauce to serve with fish. The place is relaxed and casual.

Chez Prudence also rents half a dozen very basic motel-style bungalows priced at 300F (€45.60, $43.50), double occupancy.

Anse Laborde, Anse-Bertrand. © 590/22-11-17. Reservations recommended for dinner. Main courses 70F–150F (€10.65–€22.80, $10.15–$21.75). AE. Daily noon–3pm and 7–10pm.

CONTINUING AROUND THE NORTHERN TIP

From Anse-Bertrand, you can drive along a graveled road heading for **Pointe de la Grande Vigie,** the northernmost tip of the island, which you reach after 4 miles of what we hope will be cautious driving. Park your car and walk carefully along a narrow lane that'll bring you to the northernmost rock of Guadeloupe. The view of the sweeping Atlantic from the top of rocky cliffs is remarkable— you stand at a distance of about 280 feet above the sea.

A 4-mile drive south on quite a good road will bring you to **Porte d'Enfer** ("Gateway to Hell"). Here you'll find the sea rushing violently against two narrow cliffs. After this kind of awesome experience in the remote part of the island, you can head back, going to either Morne à l'Eau or Le Moule before connecting to the road taking you back to Pointe-à-Pitre.

8 Driving Around Basse-Terre ★★★

Leaving Pointe-à-Pitre on route N1, you can explore the lesser windward coast. After 1½ miles you cross the Rivière Salée at Pont de la Gabarre. This narrow strait separates Guadeloupe's two islands. For the next 4 miles the road runs straight through sugarcane fields.

At the sign, on a main crossing, turn right on N2 toward **Baie Mahault.** Leaving that town on the right, head for **Lamentin.** This village was settled by corsairs at the beginning of the 18th century, and scattered about are some colonial mansions.

STE-ROSE

From Lamentin, you can drive 6½ miles to Ste-Rose, where you'll find several good beaches. On your left, a small road leads to **Sofaia,** from which you'll have a panoramic view over the coast and forest preserve. The locals claim that a sulfur spring here has curative powers.

ACCOMMODATIONS YOU CAN AFFORD

La Sucrerie du Comté ⭐ You'll see the ruins of a 19th-century sugar factory (including a rusting locomotive) on the 8 acres of forested land overlooking the sea, but most of the resort is modern (it opened in 1991). The medium-size accommodations are in 26 pink-toned bungalows. Each cozy bungalow has chunky and rustic handmade furniture and a bay window overlooking either the sea or a garden. (Each bungalow contains two units, both with ceiling fans; none have TVs or phones.) The firm mattresses will put you to sleep; shower-only bathrooms are tiny but tidy. The nearest major beach is La Grand-Anse, a 10- to 15-minute drive from the hotel; a small, unnamed beach is within a 10-minute walk, although the swimming there isn't very good.

Comté de Loheac, 97115 Ste-Rose, Guadeloupe, F.W.I. ℂ **590/28-60-17.** Fax 590/28-65-63. 52 units. Winter 560F (€85.10, $81.25) single or double. Off-season 350F (€53.20, $50.75) single or double. Rates include breakfast. 3-night minimum bookings. AE, MC, V. **Amenities:** Restaurant, bar, pool, scuba diving, snorkeling, fishing. *In room:* A/C, no phone.

GREAT DEALS ON DINING

Restaurant Clara ⭐⭐ CREOLE On the waterfront near the center of town is the culinary statement of Clara Lesueur. Clara lived for 12 years in Paris as a member of an experimental jazz dance troupe, but years ago she returned to Guadeloupe, her home, to set up this breezy restaurant. Try for a table on the open patio, where palm trees complement the color scheme.

Clara artfully melds the classic French style of fine dining with authentic Creole flavors. Specialties include *ouassous* (freshwater crayfish), brochette of swordfish, *palourdes* (small clams), several different preparations of conch, sea-urchin omelets, and *crabes farcis* (red-orange crabs with a spicy filling). The "sauce chien" that's served with many of the dishes is a blend of hot peppers, garlic, lime juice, and "secret things." The house drink is made with six local fruits and ample quantities of rum.

Ste-Rose. ℂ **590/28-72-99.** Reservations recommended. Main courses 45F–120F (€6.85–€18.25, $6.50–$17.50). MC, V. Mon–Tues and Thurs–Sat noon–3pm and 7–11pm; Sun noon–2:30pm.

DESHAIES & LA GRAND-ANSE

A few miles farther along, you'll reach Pointe Allegre, the northernmost point of Basse-Terre. At **Clugny Beach,** you'll be at the site where the first settler landed on Guadeloupe. A couple miles farther will bring you to **La Grand-Anse,** which has black volcanic sand and is one of the best beaches on Guadeloupe. It's very large and still secluded, sheltered by many tropical trees.

At **Deshaies,** snorkeling and fishing are popular pastimes. The narrow road winds up and down and has a corniche look to it, with the blue sea underneath, and the view of green mountains studded with colorful hamlets.

Some 9 miles from Deshaies, **Pointe Noire** comes into view. Its name comes from black volcanic rocks. Look for the odd polychrome cenotaph in town.

ACCOMMODATIONS YOU CAN AFFORD

Grand-Anse Hotel   Built in the 1970s and renovated in 1996, this secluded hotel is removed from the tourist hordes but near the ferry piers of the hamlet of Trois-Rivières. Its beige interconnected bungalows are set in a garden with a view of the mountains and (in some cases) the sea. The small accommodations are mostly modern, with sliding glass doors, hints of French colonial styling, and mahogany furniture, including good beds. All units contain small but efficient bathrooms with shower stalls. The bar and Creole restaurant here are well recommended. The closest beach, La Grand-Anse, is ¾ mile away, but the hotel has a rectangular pool. The staff is unpretentious and polite.

La Grand-Anse, 97114 Trois-Rivières, Guadeloupe, F.W.I. ℂ 590/92-92-21. Fax 590/92-93-69. 16 bungalows. Winter 400F (€60.80, $58) single or double. Off-season 300F (€45.60, $43.50) single or double. Rates include breakfast. MC, V. **Amenities:** Restaurant, bar, pool. *In room:* TV, minibar.

Résidence de la Pointe Batterie (Value)   Built in 1996 on steeply sloping land near the edge of both the rain forest and the sea, these all-wood villas each contain a veranda, an American-built kitchen, good beds with firm mattresses, a small, shower-only bathroom, and summery furniture made from rattan, local hardwoods, and wicker. The nearest beach, La Grand-Anse, is a 3-minute drive or a long uphill walk away.

97126 Pointe Batterie Deshaies, Guadeloupe, F.W.I. ℂ 800/322-2223 in the U.S., or 590/28-57-03. Fax 590/28-57-28. 20 units. Winter 1,200F (€182.40, $173.90) 1-bedroom villa without pool (for up to 4), 1,600F (€243.20, $232) 1-bedroom villa with pool (for up to 4); 2,000F (€304, $290) 2-bedroom villa with pool (for up to 6). Off-season 550F (€83.60, $79.75) 1-bedroom villa without pool, 750F (€114, $108.75) 1-bedroom villa with pool; 950F (€144.40, $137.75) 2-bedroom villa with pool. MC, V. **Amenities:** Restaurant, bar. *In room:* A/C, TV, ceiling fans.

GREAT DEALS ON DINING

Chez Jacky ⭐ (Finds) CREOLE/AFRICAN   Named after its owner, Creole matriarch Jacqueline Cabrion, this place enjoys a loyal following. In a French-colonial house about 30 feet from the sea, it features lots of exposed wood, verdant plants, tropical furniture, and a bar that sometimes does a respectable business in its own right. Some of the dishes and spices were inspired by Africa, and others are in the classic Creole repertoire. Our favorites are the *colombo* of conch and the fricassee of conch. If it's available, go for the freshwater crayfish or several preparations of grilled catch of the day. The ragout of lamb is a winner, as is the fresh grilled lobster. After all that, the bananas flambé are a bit much. Lighter fare includes a limited choice of sandwiches and salads, which tend to be offered only during daylight hours. The cuisine here seems to have more zest than Les Gommiers (see below). But it's a close tie, so try Chez Jacky first, and if there's no room, head for Les Gommiers instead. Both kitchens will feed you well, on rather similar cuisine.

Anse Guyonneau, Pointe Noire. ℂ 590/98-06-98. Reservations recommended at dinner. Main courses 70F–150F (€10.65–€22.80, $10.25–$21.75); fixed-price menu 90F–120F (€13.730–€18.25, $13–$17.50). MC, V. Tues–Sat 9am–10pm; Sun–Mon 9am–3pm.

La Cafeière Beausejour ⭐ (Finds) CREOLE   In the green Pointe-Noire Valley, you come upon one of the dining secrets of Guadeloupe: La Cafeière Beausejour. This is the domain of the hearty empress of the mountain, Bernadette Hayot-Beauzelin, who grows her own produce and herbs, used in many of her

Value   Cheap Thrills: What to See & Do for Free (Well, Almost) on Guadeloupe

- **Explore the Parc Naturel de Guadeloupe.** Basse-Terre has one of the largest and most spectacular parks in the Caribbean, the Parc Naturel de Guadeloupe. The 74,100-acre park has much to offer. A highlight is Chutes du Carbet, one of the tallest waterfalls in the Caribbean, with a drop of 800 feet. The park boasts 180 miles of marked trails through forests to lowlands, taking in rain forests and the wooded slopes of the 4,813-foot-high Soufrière volcano. You can hike for only 15 minutes or all day, encountering hot springs, rugged gorges, and rushing streams. Many locals bring a picnic lunch and a bottle of wine.

- **Spend a Day at Pointe des Châteaux.** At the eastern tip of Guadeloupe, Pointe des Châteaux is a rocky headland extending for almost a mile into the sea. It's one of the most dramatic coastlines in Guadeloupe, bordered by miles of white-sand beaches. Most of them are safe for swimming, except at the point where the waves of the turbulent Atlantic churn up the waters of the otherwise tranquil Caribbean Sea. There's a nudist enclave at Tarare, but most visitors run around in skimpy bikinis. You can also visit Grand Saline, a salt pond. If you're a bird-watcher, you will be enthralled at the hundreds of shorebirds that congregate here. The point also has varied vegetation, ranging from the Indian almond to cinnamon. You might be able to get a local boatman to take you to Iles de la Petit Terre, two deserted islets offshore. You'll share the island with a colony of iguanas. The sandy beaches here are almost deserted.

nouvelle Creole dishes. On the site of a coffee plantation more than 2 centuries old, Ms. Hayot-Beauzelin welcomes you into her home. Since early morning she has been gathering up the bounty of the day—everything from tomatoes and bananas to passion fruit and avocados. The house was constructed in 1764, years after Louis XIV sent the first coffee plant to Guadeloupe in 1721. Ms. Hayot-Beauzelin is called a *bèkè*—that is, a white Creole whose family came here from France some 3 centuries ago to colonize the French West Indies.

Don't expect a menu. You'll be told what the kitchen prepared that day. Chances are it'll be your most memorable meal in the French West Indies. We still remember the quiche made with fresh onions and papaya. She also makes papaya tarts. Your main course might be a delectable smoked duck served with some pan-Asian sauce that tastes of ginger, with side dishes of fries (cut like french fries) from the breadfruit tree and pumpkin purée. Ms. Hayot-Beauzelin's coffee is the island's best. Always call for a reservation before heading up into the mountains, and get good directions.

Pointe Noire. ✆ **590/98-10-09.** Reservations required. Fixed-price menu 185F–250F (€28.10–€38, $27–$36.25). No credit cards. Tues–Sun 12:15–2:30pm. Dinner available for groups.

- **Wander Around a Nostalgic, Almost Forgotten Town.** Most visitors assume that Pointe-à-Pitre is the capital of Guadeloupe. But the capital is Basse-Terre, a sleepy town of some 14,000 inhabitants, lying 20 miles from Pointe-à-Pitre. Founded in 1643, the town was constructed on a hill and is much lovelier than the larger city of Pointe-à-Pitre. Much of the antique flavor of the town is still in evidence, as evoked by its upper floors of shingle-wood tiles and clapboard buildings along narrow streets. Wrought-iron balconies still grace many buildings. For the most interesting views, seek out place du Champ d'Arbaud and the Jardin Pichon. At the harbor on the southern tier of town you can see Fort Delgrès, which once protected the island from the English. There are acres of ramparts with panoramic vistas to be walked.

- **See Where Columbus Was Peppered.** The sleepy little town of Ste-Marie, south of Petit-Bourg on the east coast of Basse-Terre, enjoyed its moment in history, for it was here Columbus first set foot on Guadeloupe in 1493. The people today are a lot friendlier than the cannibalistic Indians who greeted the great explorer by peppering him with poison arrows. Columbus just had time to name the island for Spain's Virgin of Guadalupe before fleeing to friendlier places. A statue of Columbus in the town square honors him. The people are mainly descended from freed East Indian slaves who had been imported to work on plantations. Take time to visit the south of town and the Allée Dumanoir, a ½-mile stretch of road lined with towering palms that were planted in the 1800s by Pinel Dumanoir. His claim to fame was that he dramatized the French version of *Uncle Tom's Cabin*.

Le Karacoli CREOLE   At least three large signs point you to this place, at the edge of the region's most famous beach. The setting is airy and tropical, with streaming sunlight, tables set outdoors in a garden, and a bar area that's sheltered from storms. No one will mind if you drop in just for a drink, but if you want lunch, consider ordering any of such dishes as a *boudin Creole* (blood pudding), stuffed crab backs, scallops prepared "in the style of the chef," court bouillon of fish, fricassee of octopus, or fried chicken. The choice of the ingredients and the quality of the craftsmanship in the kitchen is topnotch. Sunday is usually more popular than other days.

La Grand-Anse (1¼ miles north of Deshaies). ℂ **590/28-41-17.** Reservations recommended. Main courses 80F–110F (€12.15–€16.70, $11.50–$16). MC, V. Daily noon–2pm; Fri–Sat 5–9:30pm.

Les Gommiers CREOLE   Named after the large rubber trees (*les gommiers*) that grow nearby, this popular Creole restaurant serves well-flavored dishes in a dining room lined with plants. You can order such Creole staples as *accras de morue* (codfish), *boudin Creole* (blood pudding), fricassee of freshwater crayfish, seafood paella, and a custardlike dessert known as *flan coucou*. Dishes inspired by France include filet of beef with Roquefort sauce and veal scallops. We consistently return year after year, and we have never detected any slip-off in the quality. As one chef told us, "We are not technically perfect, but we cook from the heart."

Rue Baudot, Pointe Noire. © **590/98-01-79.** Main courses 70F–150F (€10.65–€22.80, $10.25–$21.75); fixed-price menus 90F–150F (€13.70–€22.80, $13–$21.75). MC, V. Daily 11:30am–3pm; Tues–Sat 7–10pm.

ROUTE DE LA TRAVERSÉE
PARC NATUREL DE GUADELOUPE: A TROPICAL FOREST
Four miles from Pointe Noire, you reach **Mahaut.** On your left begins the **Route de la Traversée** 🎯🎯, the Transcoastal Highway. This is the best way to explore the scenic wonders of **Parc Naturel de Guadeloupe,** passing through a tropical forest as you travel between the capital, Basse-Terre, and Pointe-à-Pitre.

Guadeloupe has set aside 74,100 acres, about one-fifth of its entire terrain, in the Parc Naturel. Reached by modern roads, this is a huge tract of mountains, tropical forests, and magnificent scenery. It's home to a variety of tame animals, including Titi (a raccoon adopted as the park's official mascot), and birds like the wood pigeon, turtledove, and thrush. Small exhibition huts, devoted to the volcano, the forest, or coffee, sugarcane, and rum, are scattered throughout the park. The park has no gates, no opening or closing hours, and no admission fee.

From Mahaut you climb slowly in a setting of giant ferns and luxuriant vegetation. Four miles after the fork, you reach **Les Deux Mamelles** ("The Two Breasts"), where you can park your car and go for a hike. Some of the trails are for experts only; others, such as the Pigeon Trail, will bring you to a summit of about 2,600 feet, with a panoramic view. Expect to spend at least 3 hours going each way. Halfway along the trail you can stop at Forest House. From that point, many lanes, all signposted, branch off on trails that can be completed in anywhere from 20 minutes to 2 hours. Try to find the **Chute de l'Ecrevisse** ("Crayfish Waterfall"), a little pond of very cold water you'll discover after a quarter mile.

From the park, the main road descends toward pretentiously named **Versailles,** a hamlet about 5 miles from Pointe-à-Pitre.

GREAT DEALS ON DINING
Chez Vaneau CREOLE Set in an isolated pocket of forest about 18 miles north of Pointe Noire, far from any of its neighbors, Chez Vaneau offers a wide, breezy veranda overlooking a gully. Neighbors often gather here to play cards, while steaming Creole specialties emerge from the kitchen. This is the domain of Vaneau Desbonnes, who is assisted by his wife, Marie-Gracieuse, and their children. Their best specialties include oysters with piquant sauce, crayfish bisque, ragout of goat, fricassee of conch, different preparations of octopus, and roast pork. All these dishes bespeak admirable talents in the kitchen, and authenticity and personality go into everything that's served. Lobsters are featured heavily on the menu.

Mahaut/Pointe Noire. © **590/98-01-71.** Main courses 50F–150F (€7.60–€22.80, $7.25–$21.75); fixed-price menu 70F–150F (€10.65–€22.80, $10.15–$21.75). AE, MC, V. Daily noon–4pm and 7–10:30pm.

BOUILLANTE
If you don't take the Route de la Traversée at this time but want to continue exploring the west coast, you can head south from Mahaut until you reach **Bouillante.** This village is exciting for only one reason: You might encounter former French film star and part-time resident Brigitte Bardot.

Try not to miss seeing the small island called **Ilet à Goyave** or Ilet du Pigeon. Jacques Cousteau often explored the silent depths around it.

After a meal, you can explore around the village of Bouillante, known for its thermal springs. In some places if you scratch the ground for only a few inches you'll feel the heat.

GREAT DEALS ON DINING

Chez Loulouse ✪ CREOLE   A good choice for lunch, this place offers plenty of offhanded charm, and it stands on the well-known beach opposite Pigeon Island. Many guests prefer their rum punches on the lovely veranda, overlooking a scene of loaded boats preparing to depart and merchants hawking their wares. The equally colorful dining room inside has a ceiling of palm fronds, wraparound Creole murals, and reggae music emanating from the bar. The charming Mme Loulouse Paisley-Carbon holds court here, assisted by her children. She offers house-style Caribbean lobster, spicy versions of conch, octopus, *accras* (codfish), gratin of *christophine* (squash), and savory *colombos* (curries) of chicken or pork. She's perfected these dishes that she must have learned from her grandmother.

Malendure Plage. ✆ **590/98-70-34.** Reservations required for dinner. Main courses 50F–200F (€7.60–€30.40, $7.25–$29); fixed-price menu 80F–200F (€12.15–€30.40, $11.50–$29). AE, MC, V. Daily noon–3:30pm and 7–10pm.

Le Rocher de Malendure FRENCH/CREOLE   On a rocky peninsula 30 feet above the rich offshore reefs near Pigeon Island, this restaurant offers gorgeous views. Each table is sheltered from direct sunlight (and rain) by a shed-style roof, which also affords a sense of privacy. Much of the cuisine served here is seafood caught in offshore waters: grilled red snapper, fondues of fish, marinated marlin steaks, and different preparations of lobster and conch. Meat dishes include veal in raspberry vinaigrette and filet of beef with any of three different sauces.

The restaurant also rents 11 bungalows, which cost 350F (€53.20, $50.70) per night, single or double occupancy. Each small unit has a sea view, a tiny bathroom, and a simple kitchenette, where many visitors cook most of their meals.

Malendure Plage, Pointe Batterie, Bouillante. ✆ **590/98-70-84.** Reservations recommended. Main courses 78F–150F (€11.85–€22.80, $11.25–$21.75); fixed-price menus 85F–250F (€12.90–€38, $12.25–$36.25). MC, V. Daily 11am–2pm; Mon–Sat 7–10pm.

BASSE-TERRE ✪

Another 10 miles of winding roads brings you to Basse-Terre, Guadeloupe's seat of government. The town lies between the water and La Soufrière, the volcano. Founded in 1634, it's the oldest town on the island, and it still has a lot of charm; its market squares are shaded by tamarind and palm trees.

The town suffered heavy destruction at the hands of British troops in 1691 and again in 1702. It was also the center of fierce fighting during the French Revolution, when the political changes that swept across Europe caused explosive tensions on Guadeloupe. As it did in the mainland of France, the guillotine claimed many lives on Guadeloupe during the infamous Reign of Terror.

In spite of the town's history, there isn't much to see in Basse-Terre except for a 17th-century **cathedral** and **Fort St-Charles,** which has guarded the city—not always well—since it was established.

ACCOMMODATIONS YOU CAN AFFORD

Centre de Vacances de C.G.O.S.H.   For rock-bottom rates, consider staying here, the closest thing to a youth hostel on Guadeloupe, within a 15-minute walk from the sleepy town of Basse-Terre and 5 minutes from Plage de Rivières Sens, a beach noted for its black sands. You don't have to be a member of a youth-hostel organization to stay here. There are 19 clapboard-covered bungalows built in the mid-1980s, and although they're far from luxurious, they're somewhat better than you might expect. Each bungalow has between four and six beds in an air-conditioned bedroom, two more beds in a living area, a terrace, and a private bathroom.

Rivières-Sens, 97113 Gourbeyre, Guadeloupe, F.W.I. ℂ 590/81-36-12. 19 bungalows. Year-round 452F (€68.70, $65.50) bungalow for up to 6. AE, DC, MC, V. **Amenities:** Bar; pool; nearby marina. *In room:* A/C, TV, kitchenette, safe.

Hôtel St-Georges   Built in 1996, this tastefully modern inn is set on a hill and has sweeping views over the town and the sea. A series of three-story buildings is centered around a large pool. The medium-size bedrooms are outfitted, Creole style, with dark-grained and rattan furniture, tiled floors, and small, shower-only bathrooms trimmed with touches of marble. Overall, this place has the feel of a business hotel. Expect lots of amiable goodwill from the 20 or 30 students registered at the hotel training school that's associated with the St-Georges.

Rue Gratien, Parize, 97120 St-Claude, Guadeloupe, F.W.I. ℂ 590/80-10-10. Fax 590/80-30-50. http:// pro.wanadoo.fr/hotel.st.georges. 40 units. Year-round 660F–740F (€100.30–€112.50, $95.75–$107.25) single or double; 890F (€135.30, $129) suite. MAP (breakfast and dinner) 120F (€18.25, $17.50) per person extra. AE, DC, MC, V. **Amenities:** Restaurant; bar; pool; fitness center. *In room:* A/C, TV.

GREAT DEALS ON DINING

Le Bison Bleu ⓕ FRENCH/INTERNATIONAL   This is one of Basse-Terre's most appealing restaurants, always filled with representatives of the city's many legal offices, government agencies, hospitals, and cultural organizations. It occupies what was built in 1823 as the home of a slave-owning French aristocrat, the comte de Desmarets. Tables fill both the Creole-inspired interior and the verandas, and are supervised by director Christophe Roubenne. The food represents a sophisticated adaptation of local ingredients, and includes brochettes of sharkmeat served with your choice of four different sauces including versions with shallots and green peppercorns. There's also grilled fish, such as red snapper with lemon sauce, lobster-stuffed veal filet with tagliatelle and a confit of gingerinfused vegetables, served with pepper sauce. Views from most of the tables encompass a sprawling French-Caribbean garden loaded with tropical fruit trees.

Lieu-dit Desmarais, ¾ mile north of Basse-Terre, on border of Basse-Terre and Saint-Claude. ℂ 590/ 81-01-01. Reservations recommended. Main courses 90F–120F (€13.70–€18.25, $13–$17.50); fixed-price lunches 99F–250F (€15.05–€38, $14.25–$36.25). Daily noon–2:30pm and 7:30–10pm.

LA SOUFRIÈRE ⓕⓕ

The big attraction of Basse-Terre is the famous sulfur-puffing La Soufrière volcano, which is still alive but dormant—for the moment at least. Rising to a height of some 4,800 feet, it's flanked by banana plantations and lush foliage.

From the capital at Basse-Terre, you can drive to **St-Claude,** a suburb, 4 miles up the mountainside, at a height of 1,900 feet. It has an elegant reputation for its perfect climate and tropical gardens.

From St-Claude, you can begin the climb up the narrow, winding road the Guadeloupeans say leads to hell—that is, **La Soufrière.** The road ends at a parking area at La Savane-à-Mulets, at an altitude of 3,300 feet. That is the ultimate

---

Moments **Off the Beaten Path**

From St-Claude, if you have time, you can follow a small signposted road for 2 miles to the settlement of **Matouba**, in a countryside of clear mountain spring water. The only sounds you're likely to hear are birds and the running water of dozens of springs. This is really an idyllic spot to commune with nature. The village, which rarely gets visitors, was settled long ago by Hindus. You'll see a small office of the Maison Forestière ("Forestry House") at an altitude of 2,235 feet. If it's open, you might be able to arrange for a guided hike of the surrounding area.

---

point to be reached by car. Hikers are able to climb right to the mouth of the volcano. However, the appearance of ashes, mud, billowing smoke, and earthquake-like tremors in 1975 proved that the old beast was still alive. No deaths were reported, but 75,000 inhabitants were relocated to Grande-Terre. The inhabitants of Basse-Terre still keep a watchful eye on the smoking giant.

Even in the parking lot, you can feel the heat of the volcano merely by touching the ground. Steam emerges from fumaroles and sulfurous fumes from the volcano's "burps." Of course, fumes come from its pit and mud cauldrons as well.

GREAT DEALS ON DINING

Chez Paul de Matouba CREOLE/INTERNATIONAL   You'll find good food in this family-run restaurant, which sits beside the banks of the small Rivière Rouge ("Red River"). The dining room on the second floor is enclosed by windows, allowing you to drink in the surrounding dark-green foliage of the mountains. The cooking is Creole, and the specialty is crayfish dishes, although well-prepared East Indian meals are also available. By all means, drink the mineral or spring water of Matouba. Hearty meals include perfectly executed stuffed crab, *colombo* (curried) of chicken, and an array of French, Creole, and Hindu specialties. You're likely to find the place overcrowded in winter with the tour-bus crowd.

Rivière Rouge. © **590/80-01-77.** Main courses 55F–150F (€8.35–€22.80, $7.95–$21.75); fixed-price menu 110F (€16.70, $16). No credit cards. Daily noon–3pm. Follow the clearly marked signs; it's beside a gully close to the center of the village.

THE WINDWARD COAST ☆☆

From Basse-Terre to Pointe-à-Pitre, the road follows the east coast, called the Windward Coast. The country here is richer and greener than elsewhere on the island.

To reach **Trois-Rivières** you have a choice of two routes. One goes along the coastline, coming eventually to Vieux Fort, from which you can see Les Saintes archipelago. The other heads across the hills, Monts Caraïbes.

Near the pier in Trois-Rivières you'll see the pre-Columbian petroglyphs carved by the original inhabitants, the Arawaks. They're called merely **Roches Gravées,** or "carved rocks." In this **Parc Archéologique** at Bord de la Mer (© **590/92-91-88**), the rock engravings are of animal and human figures, dating most likely from A.D. 300 or 400. You'll also see specimens of plants, including cocoa, pimento, and banana, that the Arawaks cultivated long before the Europeans set foot on Guadeloupe. Hours are daily 9am to 5pm; admission is 4F (€.60, 60¢).

Up the Volcano

The mountainous terrain of Guadeloupe's Basse-Terre is some of the most beautiful in the entire Caribbean. Although the coastline of Basse-Terre is lined with beach resorts and fishing villages, the mountainous interior (about 20% of the landmass) is devoted almost completely to the protected terrain of a French national forest, the **Parc Naturel de Guadeloupe.** Near the park's southernmost tip rise the misty heights of one of the island's most distinctive natural features, the 4,812-foot volcanic peak of **La Soufrière.** Since recorded history on Guadeloupe began, the volcano has erupted in 1560, 1797, 1975, and 1976–77. Dozens of lava flows along its slopes attest to the potential violence that reigns in the volcano's core. Today its many pits and craters offer the rare ability for geologists and hikers to gaze down into the rumbling and smoking primeval forces that shaped the planet.

The park contains an intricate network of more than 200 miles of hiking trails, allowing physically fit hikers to visit a wealth of gorges, ravines, rain forests, rivers, and (at points north of La Soufrière) some of the highest waterfalls in the Caribbean. The watershed from the peak of La Soufrière pours rainwater down a ring of black sandy beaches along Basse-Terre's southern coastline.

Surprisingly, the trek up the mountainside isn't particularly strenuous, although you should wear a hat or some other form of sun protection. Most of your walk is through scrubland and, at higher elevations, rocky plateaux covered with moss and lichens. Total time expended round-trip, without accounting for admiration of the views, is about 3 hours.

After leaving Trois-Rivières, continue on route N1. Passing through the village of Bananier, you turn left at Anse St-Sauveur to reach the famous **Chutes du Carbet** ✦, a trio of waterfalls. The road to two of them is narrow, winds over many steep hills, and passes through banana plantations as you move deeper into a tropical forest.

After 3 miles, a lane, suitable only for hikers, brings you to **Zombie Pool.** Half a mile farther along, a fork to the left takes you to **Grand Etang,** or large pool. At a point 6 miles from the main road, a parking area is available, and you have to walk the rest of the way on a less than easy trail toward the second fall, Le Carbet. Expect to spend around 20 to 30 minutes, depending on how slippery the lane is. Then you'll be at the foot of this second fall, where the water drops from 230 feet. The waters here average 70°F (21°C), which is warm for a mountain spring.

The first fall is the most impressive, but it takes 2 hours of rough hiking to get here. The third fall is reached from Capesterre on the main road by climbing to Routhiers. This fall is less impressive in height, only 70 feet. When the Carbet water runs out of La Soufrière, it's almost boiling.

Begin your walking tour to the volcano's summit from one of the highest-altitude parking lots on Guadeloupe, **Savane-à-Mulets**. Savane-à-Mulets has no amenities of any kind. Set on the volcano's western slope at about 3,400 feet above sea level, 3 miles west of the village of St-Claude, it marks the farthest point a conventional vehicle can proceed along route de la Soufrière. (The road between St-Claude and Savane-à-Mulets is very steep—put your transmission in low gear en route.) Park your car in the parking lot, then hike along a network of carefully marked trails toward the summit. If a wind is blowing, it'll probably clear away much of the mist that sometimes envelops the peak. Along the way you'll pass a string of small craters and crevasses, many of them bubbling up mud and fumes. As you pass each pit, the scent of sulfur and the radiant heat become very powerful. Of special note is the **South Crater** (Crader Sud), which spews lots of noise, steam, and sulfurous odors.

On the way back down near the parking lot you can visit **La Maison du Volcan** (© **590-78-15-16**), a little museum devoted to volcanoes in general and La Soufrière in particular. Charging 15F (€2.30, $2.25) admission, it is open daily 9am to 5pm.

A handful of hikers have had their valuables stolen during scattered incidents in this park. Lock anything extremely valuable in a safe back at your hotel, and carry minimal amounts of cash with you as you proceed on this itinerary. For more information about this and other hikes in the national park, contact the employees of the national park at © **590/80-24-25.**

If you'd like to stop over along the Windward Coast before returning to Grande-Terre, the area of Petit-Bourg, north of Ste-Marie and Goyave and directly southwest of Pointe-à-Pitre, makes the best stopover. To reach Vernou from Petit-Bourg, cut inland (west) along D23.

ACCOMMODATIONS YOU CAN AFFORD

Auberge de la Distillerie   This inn attracts more of a hiking crowd than a beach-going one. Outfitted in a tropical-woodsy motif, it lies close to the entrance of the Parc Naturel, near the hamlet of Vernou, in a luxuriantly verdant setting. You'll have to drive about 15 minutes to reach the black sands of the nearest beach (Plage de Viard), but hiking trails through the volcanic oddities of Basse-Terre are nearby. Each small accommodation contains a writing table, a good bed, a balcony with a hammock, and a radio, plus a tiny but tidy bathroom with shower or shower-and-tub combo. Boating excursions can be arranged on the Lezard River, where a waterfall (Cascade aux Ecrevisses) is one of the primary attractions.

Tabanon, C.D. 23, 97170 Petit-Bourg, Guadeloupe, F.W.I. © **590/94-25-91.** Fax 590/94-11-91. Winter 450F (€68.40, $65.25) single; 650F (€98.80, $94.25) double. Off-season 350F (€53.20, $50.75) single; 450F (€68.40, $65.25) double. AE, MC, V. **Amenities:** Restaurant, bar, pool, babysitting, laundry. *In room:* A/C, TV, minibar.

9 Hitting the Beaches

Chances are, your hotel will be right on a beach, or no more than 20 minutes from a good one. Plenty of natural beaches dot the island, from the surf-brushed dark strands of western Basse-Terre to the long stretches of white sand encircling Grande-Terre. Public beaches are generally free, but some charge for parking. Unlike hotel beaches, public beaches have few facilities. Hotels welcome nonguests but charge for changing facilities, beach chairs, and towels.

Sunday is family day at the beach. Topless sunbathing is common at hotels, less so on village beaches.

Most of the best beaches lie between Gosier and St-François on Grande-Terre. Visitors usually head for the hotel beaches at **Gosier.** Stone jetties were constructed here to protect the beaches from erosion. Since this area has the largest concentration of tourists, it's likely to be crowded.

The beaches near Gosier are not peas-in-a-pod; each one is different. There's no shade at the **Creole Beach** fronting Creole Beach Hotel, although you can retreat to the bar there for a drink. A stone retaining wall blocks access to the water. Nearby, the **Salako Beach** has more sand and is set against a backdrop of palms that offer some shade. Part of this beach also leads up to a jetty. This is a fine sandy beach, although a little too crowded at times, and it also contains a snack bar.

Also nearby, **Arawak Beach** is a gorgeous spot, with plenty of swaying palm trees providing a bit of shade on the beige sands. It, too, is protected by jetties. Close at hand, **Callinago Beach** is smaller than Arawak, but still has a pleasant crescent of beige sand and palms.

Le Bas du Fort, 2 miles east of Pointe-à-Pitre and close to Gosier, is another popular area. Its beaches, also protected by jetties, are shared by guests at the Hotels Fleu d'Epée and Marissol. This is a picture-postcard tropical beach with tranquil waters, plenty of sand, and palms for shade. There are hotel bars as well as snack bars, and vendors, too (some of whom are rather aggressive).

Some of Grande-Terre's best beaches are in the **Ste-Anne** area, site of a Club Med. **Plage Caravelle** is heaped with white sand, attracting crowds of sunbathers; snorkelers, too, are drawn to the beach's reef-protected waters.

The French visitors here often like to go nude, and there is no finer nude beach than **Tarare Point,** a 45-minute drive from Gosier. This beach lies east of St-François at Pointe des Châteaux. It's one of the island's most pristine, tranquil beaches, but there's no shade to protect you from the fierce noonday sun. You can snorkel here if the water's not kicking up. There's a good restaurant by the parking lot. *Warning:* The tourist office doesn't recommend that women come here unaccompanied.

If you're not a nudist, you can enjoy the lovely strip of white sand at **Anse de la Gourde,** lying between St-François and Pointe des Châteaux. It has good sand, but tends to become crowded on weekends.

The eastern coast of Grande-Terre is less desirable for swimming, as it fronts the more turbulent Atlantic. Nonetheless, the sands at **Le Moule** make for an idyllic beach because a reef protects the shoreline. There are also beach bars here—and the inevitable crowds, especially on weekends. You'll find a more secluded strip of sand north of here at **La Porte d'Enfer.**

There are two other excellent beaches on the northwestern coast: one at **Anse Laborde** just outside the village of Anse-Bertrand, the other called **Anse du Souffleur** at Port Louis. We especially like the beach at Souffleur for its brilliant, flamboyant trees that bloom in the summer. There are no facilities here, but you can pick up provisions in the shops in the little village, then enjoy a picnic on the beach.

In Basse-Terre, a highly desirable beach is **La Grande-Anse,** just outside Deshaies, reached by heading west from Ste-Rose along N2. You won't find any facilities here, but we think you'll enjoy the powdery sands, tranquil waters, and palm trees. Another desirable beach is **Plage de la Malendure,** on the west coast (the more tranquil side) of Basse-Terre across from Pigeon Island. This is a major center for scuba diving, but the sand tends to be dark here.

If you want to escape the crowds, seek out the spurs and shoulders produced by the mountains of Basse-Terre. In the northwest is a string of fine sandy beaches. Although small, these are highly desirable enclaves for sunbathing and swimming. Favorites include **La Plage de Cluny** (near Pointe Allegre), **Plage de la Tillette,** and **Plage de la Perle.**

South of Pointe Noire, also on the west coast, is **Plage de La Caraïbe,** with its calm waters and sandy strip. This beach has picnic facilities, a shower, and toilets.

Warning: The beaches on the north coast of Basse-Terre are exceedingly dangerous for swimming. **Plage de Clugny** is especially treacherous, and there have been several deaths by drowning.

Other good beaches are found on the offshore islands, **Iles des Saintes** and **Marie-Galante** (see the section "Side Trips from Guadeloupe," below).

10 Sports & Other Outdoor Pursuits

HIKING   **Parc Naturel de Guadeloupe** contains the best hiking grounds in the Caribbean (see the "Up the Volcano" box, earlier in this chapter). Marked trails cut through the park's deep foliage of rain forests until you come upon a waterfall or a cool mountain pool. The big excursion, of course, is around the volcano, La Soufrière. Hiking brochures are available from the tourist office. Hotel tour desks can arrange this activity. For information about this and other hikes in the national park, contact the **Organisation des Guides de Montagne de la Caraïbe,** Maison Forestière, Matouba (© **590/94-29-11**).

Warning: The annual precipitation on the higher slopes is 250 inches per year, so be prepared for downpours.

SAILING   Sailboats of varying sizes, crewed or bareboat, are plentiful. Information can be secured at any hotel desk. Sunfish sailing can be arranged at almost every beachfront hotel.

SCUBA DIVING   Scuba divers are drawn more to the waters off Guadeloupe than to any other point in the French-speaking islands. The allure is the relatively calm seas and **La Réserve Cousteau,** a kind of French national park with many intriguing dive sites, where the underwater environment is rigidly protected. Jacques Cousteau once described the waters off Guadeloupe's Pigeon Island as one of the world's 10 best diving spots. During a typical dive, sergeant majors become visible at a depth of 30 feet, spiny sea urchins and green parrotfish at 60 feet, and magnificent stands of finger, black, brain, and star coral at 80 feet. Despite the destruction of some branch coral in a 1995 hurricane, the reserve is still one of the most desirable underwater sites in the French-speaking world.

The most popular dive sites are Aquarium, Piscine, Jardin de Corail, Pointe Carrangue, Pointe Barracuda, and Jardin Japonais. Although scattered around the periphery of the island, many are in the bay of Petit Cul-de-Sac Marin, south of Rivière Salée, the channel separating the halves of Guadeloupe. North of the Salée is another bay, Grand Cul-de-Sac Marin, where the small islets of Fajou and Caret also boast fine diving.

Centre International de la Plongée (C.I.P.), B.P. 4, Lieu-Dit Poirier, Malendure Plage, 97125 Pigeon, Bouillante, Guadeloupe, F.W.I. (℃ **590/ 98-81-72**), is the island's most professional dive operation. In a wood-sided house on Malendure Plage, close to a well-known restaurant, Chez Loulouse, it's well-positioned at the edge of the Cousteau Underwater Reserve. Certified divers pay 220F (€33.45, $32) for a one-tank dive. What the Americans usually refer to as a resort course for first-time divers (the French refer to it as a *baptême*) costs 280F (€42.55, $40.50) and is conducted one-on-one with an instructor. Packages of 6 or 12 dives are offered for 1,100F to 2,000F (€167.20–€304, $159.50–$290), respectively.

Nearby, **Les Heures Saines,** Rocher de Malendure, 97132 Pigeon-Malendure (℃ **590/98-86-63**), has a trio of dive boats departing daily at 10am, 12:30pm, and 3pm for explorations of the waters in the reserve. With all equipment included, dives cost 270F (€41.05, $39.25) each. Novices pay 320F (€48.65, $46.50) for a *baptême.* Les Heures Saines maintains its own 11-room hotel, **Le Paradis Creole** (℃ **590/98-71-62**), where motel-style accommodations rent for 450F to 670F (€68.40–€101.85, $65.25–$97.25), breakfast included, depending on the season. Rooms, which are occupied almost exclusively by avid divers on holiday from the French mainland, are air-conditioned but contain few other real amenities.

A miniresort, **Le Jardin Tropical** (℃ **590/98-77-23**), patronized almost exclusively by dive enthusiasts from France, lies adjacent to this school. The 16 rooms—each with air-conditioning and phone—rent for 560F (€85.10, $81.25) per person, with breakfast, dinner, and two dives included, with lots of price breaks for divers who purchase accommodations as part of a hotel-dive package.

TENNIS All the large resort hotels have tennis courts, many of them lit. If your hotel doesn't have courts, you can play at **St-François Plage,** in St-François, a durable but somewhat weathered facility that is often unused despite the fact that it's free. For information, contact **La Mairie** (Town Hall) of St-François, at ℃ **590/88-48-74.**

WINDSURFING & WATER-SKIING Each of the large-scale hotels on Guadeloupe provides facilities and instructions for windsurfing and water-skiing, but if you prefer to strike out on your own or your hotel doesn't provide it, head for the **Surfing Club,** Plage de St-François, St-François (℃ **590/ 88-72-04**). Thirty-minute windsurfing lessons go for around 120F (€18.25, $17.50) per hour, and rentals, depending on the size and make of the board you rent, average 150F (€22.80, $21.75) per hour.

If you're interested in a more in-depth exposure to windsurfing or perhaps a week-long deep immersion in the sport, head for **UCPA** (Union National des Centres Sportifs de Plein-Air), 97118 St-François (℃ **590/98-89-00**), a 60-room resort whose quarters are available only by the week and come with all meals. A week's sojourn, double occupancy, is 2,860F (€434.65, $414.50) per person, including windsurfing, surfing and surfboard-riding, golf, and physical fitness.

Value Begin the Beguine

The folkloric dance troupe **Ballets Guadeloupeans** makes frequent appearances at the big hotels, whirling and moving to the rhythms of island music in colorful costumes and well-choreographed routines. Some resorts, including the Club Med–Caravelle, use their weekly visit to set the theme for the evening, serving up a banquet of traditional island dishes to accompany the dance, music, and costumes.

Ask at your hotel where the Ballets Guadeloupeans will be appearing during your stay, as their schedule tends to vary as they tour the island. You can catch them as they rotate through the hotels Arawak, Salako, L'Auberge de le Vieille Tour, and Fleur d'Epée Novotel, as well as the Club Med–Caravelle. On the night of any of these performances, you can order a drink at the bar and catch the show, or join in the hotel buffet for a flat price. Buffets usually start around 8pm, with the show beginning at 8:30pm. The troupe also performs on some cruise ships.

11 Guadeloupe After Dark

Guadeloupeans claim that the beguine was invented here, not on Martinique, and they dance the beguine as if they truly do own it. Of course, calypso and the merengue move rhythmically, too—the islanders are known for their dancing.

THE BAR & CLUB SCENE

Nighttime diversions in Guadeloupe tend to be seasonal, with winter being the busiest time. **Lele Bar,** at Le Méridien in St-François (© 590/88-51-00), is the most active on the island, attracting Guadeloupeans along with visitors.

Cuban salsa and Latin dancing draw patrons to **Lollapalooza,** 122 Montauban, Gosier (© 590/84-58-58), where pictures of dictator Fidel and the long-dead Che Guevara decorate the walls. If you get tired of this joint, try **Fanzy Bar,** Mathurin Poucette (© 590/84-41-34), where you'll hear everything from Bob Marley reggae to Edith Piaf singing old French songs. These bars are free, but the island's discos charge a uniform fee of about $20, which includes the cost of a first drink. After that, most cocktails are a pricey $10. If you've got money to waste, head for **Caraïbes 2,** Carrefour de Blanchard, Bas-du-Fort (© 590/90-97-16), whose specialty is Brazilian music. **Zenith,** Route de la Riviera (© 590/90-72-04), is currently the island's hottest club.

If you want to escape all the tourist joints and find some real local color, make it **Les Tortues,** off the N2 near Bouillante, signposted near the main road on Basse-Terre's western coast (© 590/98-82-83). This bar is a local hangout, often filled with scuba divers downing Corsaire beer and telling tall tales of the deep. The bartender's rum specialty is *ti punch,* cut with lime and cane syrup. You can also dine here on good food, especially the catch of the day (marlin, kingfish, ray, snapper, or Caribbean lobster). Les Tortues is closed all day Sunday and on Monday night.

ROLLING THE DICE

One of the island's two gambling emporia, **Casino Gosier-les-Bains,** 43 Pointe de la Verdure (© 590/84-79-68), in Gosier, is in the resort community. Although dress tends to be casually elegant, coat and tie for men aren't required.

The bulk of the place is open nightly 7:30pm to 3am (to 4am Fri–Sat), although an area containing only slot machines is open daily 10am to 3 or 4am, depending on the night of the week. There's no cover charge and no ID requested for admission to the area with the slot machines, but entrance to the gaming tables and roulette wheels costs 69F (€10.50, $10) and requires a photo ID.

A smaller casino, with fewer slot machines, is **Casino de la Marina,** avenue de l'Europe (© **590/88-41-31**), near the Hôtel Mèridien in St-François. Slot machines begin whirring every day at noon, continuing to 2am on Sunday to Thursday and to 3am on Friday and Saturday. The more interesting main core of the casino, containing tables devoted to blackjack, roulette, and chemin-de-fer, doesn't open until 8pm. Entrance costs 69F (€10.50, $10). Dress codes are the same as those at the casino at Gosier-les-Bains, and both casinos contain bars.

12 Side Trips from Guadeloupe

ILES DES SAINTES ✿
A cluster of eight islands off the southern coast of Guadeloupe, the Iles des Saintes are certainly off the beaten track. The two main islands and six rocks are Terre-de-Haut, Terre-de-Bas, Ilet-à-Cabrit, La Coche, Les Augustins, Grand Ilet, Le Redonde, and Le Pâté. Only Terre-de-Haut ("Land of High"), and to a lesser extent Terre-de-Bas ("Land Below"), attract visitors.

Some claim that Iles des Saintes have one of the nicest bays in the world, a Lilliputian Rio de Janeiro with a sugarloaf. The isles, just 6 miles from the main island, were discovered by Columbus (who else?) on November 4, 1493, and he named them Los Santos.

The history of Iles des Saintes is very much the history of Guadeloupe itself. In years past, the islands have been heavily fortified, as if they were Guadeloupe's Gibraltar. The climate is very dry, and until the desalination plant opened, water was often rationed.

If you're planning a visit, **Terre-de-Haut** is the most interesting island to call on, and it's the only one with facilities for overnight guests. The population of Terre-de-Haut is mainly Caucasian fisherfolk or sailors, descended from Breton corsairs. The very skilled sailors maneuver large boats called *saintois,* and wear coolie-like headgear called a *salako,* which is shallow and white with a sun shade covered in cloth, built on radiating ribs of thick bamboo—it looks very much like a small parasol. If you want to take a photograph of these sailors, please make a polite request (in French; otherwise they won't know what you're talking about). Visitors often like to buy these hats (if they can find them) for use as beach wear.

Terre-de-Haut is a place for discovery and lovers of nature, many of whom stake out their exhibitionistic space on the nude beach **Anse Crawen.**

Centre Nautique des Saintes, Plage de la Colline, at Bourg in Terre-de-Haut (© **590/99-54-24**), rents scuba diving gear and will direct you to the dozen or so top dive sights around the island.

GETTING THERE
BY PLANE   The fastest way to get to Terre-de-Haut is by plane. The airport is a truncated landing strip accommodating nothing larger than 20-seat Twin Otters. **Air Guadeloupe** (© **590/82-47-00** on Guadeloupe, or 590/99-51-23 on Terre-de-Haut) has two round-trip flights daily from Pointe-à-Pitre, which take 15 minutes and cost around 394F (€59.90, $57.25) per person round-trip.

BY FERRY Most islanders reach Terre-de-Haut via one of the several ferries that travel from Guadeloupe daily. Visitors opt for one of the two boats that depart from Pointe-à-Pitre's Gare Maritime des Iles, on quai Gatine, across the street from the open-air market. The trip requires 60 minutes each way and costs 180F (€27.35, $26) round-trip. The most popular departure time for Terre-de-Haut from Pointe-à-Pitre is 8am Monday to Saturday and 7am Sunday, with returns scheduled every afternoon at 4pm. Be at the ferryboat terminal at least 15 minutes prior to the anticipated departure.

Other ferries (two per day) also depart from Trois Rivières, and one additional ferry leaves daily from the island's capital of Basse-Terre. Transit from either of these last two cities requires 25 minutes each way and costs 90F (€13.70, $13) round-trip.

For more information and last-minute departure schedules, contact **Frères Bru-dey** (© **590/90-04-48**) or **Trans Antilles Express,** Gare Maritime, quai Gatine, Pointe-à-Pitre (© **590/21-05-68**).

GETTING AROUND

On an island that doesn't have a single car-rental agency, you get about by walking or renting a bike or motor scooter from a hotel or in town near the pier. **Localizé,** at Bourg in Terre-de-Haut (© **590/99-51-99**), rents both motorboats and scooters.

There are also minibuses called **Taxis de l'Ile,** which take six to eight passengers.

ACCOMMODATIONS YOU CAN AFFORD

Auberge Les Petits Saints aux Anacardiers Set in a hilltop garden a 5-minute walk from the nearest beach, this cost-conscious guesthouse occupies a 1970s building that was once the home of the island's mayor; it was transformed into a guesthouse in the early 1990s by expats from the French mainland. The small rooms are simple but appealing and comfortable, with new beds and very tiny bathrooms with shower stalls. Some units have TVs and minibars. On the premises is a restaurant, on a terrace surrounded with plants, that serves health-conscious foods with an emphasis on fresh fish.

La Savane, 97137 Terre-de-Haut, Les Saintes, Guadeloupe, F.W.I. © 590/99-50-99. Fax 590/99-54-51. www. petitssaints.com. 12 units. Winter 600F–750F (€91.20–€114, $87–$108.75) single or double; 800F (€121.60, $116) bungalow with kitchenette for up to 6. Off-season 450F–550F (€68.40–€83.60, $65.25–$79.75) single or double; 600F (€91.20, $87) bungalow with kitchenette for up to 6. AE, MC, V. **Amenities:** Restaurant, bar, pool, room service (drinks and snacks only, 7am–10pm). In room: A/C.

Hôtel La Saintoise 🅐 Originally built in the 1960s, La Saintoise is a modern two-story building set near the almond trees and widespread poinciana of the town's main square, near the ferryboat dock, across from the town hall. As in a small French village, the inn places tables and chairs on the sidewalk, where you can sit and observe what action there is. The owner will welcome you and show you through the uncluttered lobby to one of his modest, second-floor bedrooms, each outfitted with a small shower-only bathroom. Housekeeping is good, beds have firm mattresses, and the comfort level is suitable. This is a friendly and unpretentious place.

Place de la Mairie, 97137 Terre-de-Haut, Les Saintes, Guadeloupe, F.W.I. ©/fax 590/99-52-50. 8 units. Year-round 370F (€56.25, $53.75) double. MC, V. In room: A/C.

Kanao Named after the open-sided log canoes used by the Arawaks, this modern concrete-sided structure is on a little beach at Pointe Coquelet, about a

10-minute walk north of the town center. All the small accommodations have private showers in cramped bathrooms and rather spartan furnishings, including narrow beds. Five have views of the sea and Anse Mire cove. Although very limited English is spoken, Kanao may still be ideal for non-French-speaking vacationers wanting to get away from it all.

97137 Terre-de-Haut, Les Saintes, Guadeloupe, F.W.I. ⓒ **590/99-51-36.** Fax 590/99-55-04. 19 units, including 4 bungalows with kitchenettes. Winter 600F (€91.20, $87) single; 700F (€106.40, $101.50) double; 750F–950F (€114–€144.40, $108.75–$137.75) bungalow for 2. Off-season 250F (€38, $36.25) single; 340F (€51.70, $49.30) double; 400F–500F (€60.80–€76, $58–$72.50) bungalow for 2. Rates include breakfast. MC, V. **Amenities:** Restaurant, bar, pool, laundry. *In room:* A/C.

GREAT DEALS ON DINING

Many French-speaking visitors used to come to Terre-de-Haut to eat roast iguana, the large but harmless lizard found on many of these islands. The species is now endangered, so we don't recommend that you order this dish. Instead, try conch (called *lambi*), Caribbean lobster, or fresh fish. For dessert, you can try the sweet island specialty, *tournament d'amour* (agony of love), a coconut pastry available in the restaurants but best sampled from the barefoot children who sell the delicacy near the boat dock.

The island's most popular bar is **Nilce's Bar** at Bourg in Terre-de-Haut (ⓒ **590/99-56-80**), which also serves good food. You're welcomed by Ghislain Laps and his wife, Nilce, who hails from Rio de Janeiro. Her fresh salads are among the island's best, and her fresh fish is truly excellent and never allowed to overcook. This is also the best place for people-watching, as you can see passengers disembarking or boarding the ferries to take them back to the mainland of Guadeloupe. In the late evening music is played until midnight, when local law dictates that Les Saintes quiets down. Nilce, a Brazilian chanteuse, will sometimes sing.

Chez Jeannine (Le Casse-Croûte) ⭐ *Value* CREOLE The creative statement of Mme Jeannine Bairtran, originally from Guadeloupe, this restaurant is a 3-minute walk south of the town center in a simple Creole house decorated with modern Caribbean accessories. The fixed-price meal includes avocado stuffed with crabmeat, *gâteau de poissons* (literally "fish cake"), and several curry-enhanced stews (including one made with goat). Crayfish and grilled catch of the day appear daily on the menu. Local vegetables are used. The ambience is that of a Creole bistro—in other words, a hut with nautical trappings and bright tablecloths.

Fond-de-Curé, Terre-de-Haut. ⓒ **590-99-53-37.** Reservations recommended for large groups only. Fixed-price 3-course meal 75F (€11.40, $10.85). V. Daily 9–10am, noon–3pm, and 7pm–midnight.

Les Amandiers ⭐ CREOLE Across from the town hall on the main square of Bourg is the most traditional Creole bistro on Terre-de-Haut. Monsieur and Madame Charlot Brudey are your hosts in this beige-painted building, with tables and chairs on the upper balconies for open-air dining. A TV set (at loud volumes) might be providing entertainment in the bar when you stop in. Conch (*lambi*) is prepared in a fricassee or a *colombo*, a savory curry stew. Also offered are a court bouillon of fish, a *gâteau* (terrine) of fish, and a seemingly endless supply of grilled crayfish, a staple of the island. The catch of the day is also grilled the way you like it. You'll find an intriguing collection of stews, concocted from fish, bananas, and *christophine* (chayote). Knowledge of French is helpful around here.

Place de la Mairie. ⓒ **590/99-51-77.** Reservations recommended. Fixed-price menu 80F–100F (€12.15–€15.20, $11.50–$14.50). AE, MC, V. Daily 8am–3pm and 6:30–9:30pm.

HITTING THE BEACHES

Most visitors to Terre-de-Haut flock to the beaches. There is none finer than **Plage de Pompierre,** which curves around the bay like a half moon, and is set against a backdrop of palms. The beach lies only a 15- to 20-minute walk from where the ferry docks from Guadeloupe. Unless a cruise ship is in port, the beach is generally uncrowded, filled with mainland French enjoying the powdery white sand wearing next to nothing. If you want to bare all, head for **Plage Anse Crawen** on the western coastline. It is the legal nudist beach, although visitors often go nude on the other beaches, too. The best snorkeling is on the southern coast, at **Plage Figuier,** which, chances are, you'll have almost to yourself.

EXPLORING THE ISLAND

Terre-de-Haut's main settlement is **Bourg,** a single street following the curve of the fishing harbor. A charming hamlet, it has little houses with red or blue doorways, balconies, and Victorian gingerbread gewgaws. Donkeys are the beasts of burden, and everywhere you look are fish nets drying in the sunshine. You can also explore the ruins of **Fort Napoléon,** left over from those 17th-century wars, including the naval encounter known in European history books as the Battle of the Saints. You can see the barracks and prison cells, as well as the drawbridge and art museum. Occasionally you'll spot an iguana scurrying up the ramparts. Directly across the bay, atop Ilet-à-Cabrit, sits the fort named in honor of Empress Joséphine. Open daily 9am to 12:30pm, the admission is 20F (€3.05, $3).

You can hike to **Le Grand Souffleur,** with its beautiful cliffs, and to **Le Chameau,** the highest point on the island, rising to a peak of 1,000 feet. You might also get a sailor to take you on his boat to the other main island, **Terre-de-Bas,** which has no accommodations.

The underwater world off Iles des Saintes has attracted scuba divers as renowned as Jacques Cousteau, but even the less experienced can explore its challenging depths and multicolored reefs. You can also explore the intriguing underwater grottoes found near Fort Napoléon on Terre-de-Haut.

SHOPPING

Few come here to shop, but there's one offbeat choice at **Kaz an Nou Gallery** on Terre-de-Haut (© **590/99-52-29**), where a local artist, Pascal Fay, carves miniature wooden house facades, all candy-colored and trimmed in gingerbread. His most popular reproduction graces the cover of the bestselling picture book *Caribbean Style.* Mr. Fay will point the way to the real house, a few blocks away, which has become a sightseeing attraction all on its own because of the book's popularity. The houses measure about 16 by 13 inches and sell for $100 to $400 each.

If you're looking for an authentic *salako* hat, similar to the hat of a Chinese coolie, head to **José Beaujour** at Terre-de-Bas (© **590/99-80-20**). At **Mahogany Artisanat,** Bourg in Terre-de-Haut (© **590/99-50-12**), you'll find Yves Cohen's batik and hand-painted T-shirts.

MARIE-GALANTE ✥

Full of rustic charm, this offshore dependency of Guadeloupe is an almost-perfect circle of about 60 square miles. Almost exclusively French-speaking, Marie-Galante lies 20 miles south of Guadeloupe's Grand-Terre.

Columbus noticed Marie-Galante before he did Guadeloupe, on November 3, 1493. He named it for his own vessel but didn't land here. In fact, it was 150 years later that the first European came ashore. The first French governor of the island was Constant d'Aubigné, father of the marquise de Maintenon. Several captains from the West Indies Company attempted settlement, but none of them succeeded. In 1674, Marie-Galante was given to the Crown, and from that point on its history was closely linked to that of Guadeloupe.

After 1816, the island settled down to a slumber so quiet you could almost hear the sugarcane growing on its plantations. Many windmills were built to crush the cane, and lots of tropical fruits were grown.

Now some 30,000 inhabitants live here and make their living from sugar and rum, the latter said to be the best in the Caribbean. The island's climate is rather dry, and there are many good beaches. Brilliantly white, one of them covers at least 5 miles. However, swimming can be dangerous in some places. The best beach is at **Petite Anse,** 6½ miles from **Grand-Bourg,** the main town that sports an 1845 baroque church. The 18th-century Grand-Anse rum distillery can be visited, as can the historic fishing hamlet of Vieux Fort.

GETTING THERE & GETTING AROUND
Air Guadeloupe (✆ **590/82-74-00**) flies to Marie-Galante in just 20 minutes from Pointe-à-Pitre, landing at Les Basse Airport, about 2 miles from Grand-Bourg. Round-trip fare is 394F (€59.90, $57.25).

Antilles Trans Express (Exprès des Iles), Gare Maritime, quai Gatine, Pointe-à-Pitre (✆ **590/83-12-45** or 590/91-13-43), operates boat service to the island with three daily round-trips between Point-à-Pitre and Grand-Bourg costing 170F (€25.85, $24.75). Departures from Pointe-à-Pitre are daily at 8am, 12:30pm, and 5pm, with returns from Grand-Bourg at 6am, 9am, and 3:45pm.

A limited number of **taxis** are available at the airport; negotiate a fare before you drive off.

ACCOMMODATIONS YOU CAN AFFORD
On the island are only a few accommodations, which, even if they aren't very up-to-date in amenities, are clean and hearty. The greetings are friendly, but they might be bewildering if you speak no French. You can also find lodgings as well as good meals at **Le Touloulou** (see "Great Deals on Dining," below).

Auberge de l'Arbre à Pain   Set behind a clapboard facade close to the street, about a 5-minute stroll from the harborfront, this place is named after the half-dozen breadfruit trees (*les arbres à pain*) that shelter its courtyard and its simple but pleasant bedrooms from the blazing sun. You'll get a taste of Old France at this respectable *auberge,* which has easy access to nearby beaches. Each room has uncomplicated furnishings and a private shower-only bathroom.

34 rue Jeanne-d'Arc, 97112 Grand-Bourg, Marie-Galante, Guadeloupe, F.W.I. ✆ 590/97-73-69. 7 units. Year-round 300F (€45.60, $43.50) single or double. V. At the harbor, take the 1st street going toward the church. **Amenities:** Restaurant. *In room:* A/C, no phone.

La Cohoba Hotel   On Folle Anse, an uncrowded, white-sand beach that's edged with sea grape and mahogany trees, La Cohaba Hotel is a bargain and a comfortable nest. The hotel takes its name from the cohoba plant, known to the Caribs as a plant whose red pods have hallucinogenic powers. The hotel, the largest ever on Marie-Galante, has small suite-like rooms decorated with white tile and ghost-white walls, along with bright Caribbean colors and tiny but efficient shower-only bathrooms. Thirty of the accommodations have kitchenettes.

Folle Anse, Marie-Galante, Guadeloupe, F.W.I. ✆ 800/322-2223 in the U.S., or 590/97-50-50. Fax 590/97-97-96. www.cohoba.gp. 100 units. Winter $148–$218 double. Off-season $110–$130 double. Rates include continental breakfast. AE, MC, V. **Amenities:** 2 restaurants, pool, 2 tennis courts. *In room:* A/C, TV, hair dryer, safe.

GREAT DEALS ON DINING

Don't expect elaborate restaurants here, but you can often eat well, even if the choice for dining is housed in a shack.

In the center of Grand-Bourg you can dine right on the beach at **Le Neptune** (✆ **590/97-96-90**) or **City Plat** (✆ **590/97-76-25**). Naturally, the grilled fish is the way to go. In town itself, opt for **La Charette** (✆ **590/97-52-34**). The island's best pizzas are made at **Pizzeria Le Moana & Crêperie** (✆ **590/97-85-97**), also in the town center. The specialty is a pizza topped with shellfish. Only a 15-minute drive east from Grand-Bourg, **Tatie Zézette** (✆ **590/97-36-02**) is known for its spicy seafood dishes. Another good bet nearby, **Chez Henri** (✆ **590/97-04-57**) is really a bar but has an alfresco dining area. The grilled lobster and shrimp are special treats. Local vegetables like breadfruit and *dasheen* accompany the main courses.

Crêperie La Pergola CREOLE/FRENCH   Most locals view the crêperie aspect of this place as a Gallic-style fast-food joint, where a sweet or salted crêpe will provide a late-night pick-me-up. The setting combines aspects of both a bar and a cafe, and this noteworthy local hangout perks up with gossip and recorded music, including the island's only karaoke machine, every evening except Tuesday, beginning around 9pm. Crêpes are available in simple (with butter and a dusting of sugar) to complex (the kitchen sink that includes salted versions laden with ham, cheese, and vegetables) versions.

A wider variety of more substantial platters, most of them Creole, is available in the restaurant Le Touloulou, which sits immediately adjacent (see below).

Plage de Petite Anse, Marie-Galante. ✆ 590/97-32-63. Crêpes 20F–45F (€3.05–€6.85, $3–$6.50); main courses 60F–130F (€9.10–€19.75, $8.75–$19). MC, V. MC, V. Daily 7pm–1am.

Le Touloulou ★ (Finds) CREOLE   Set adjacent to the beach, with a hardworking staff and a casual crowd, Le Touloulou specializes in shellfish and crayfish culled from local waters. If sea urchins or lobster are your passion, you'll find them here in abundance, prepared virtually any way you want. Other standbys include a savory, and highly ethnic, version of *bébélé* (cow tripe enhanced with breadfruit, dumplings, and plantains) and conch served as fricassee or in puff pastry. Developed during the days of extreme poverty by slaves, it consists of entrails, offal, green bananas, flour dumplings, and vegetables. Here, it's served as a cleaned-up version of an appetizer, in ways that are considerably more elegant than in the old days.

The inn has also added five very basic units, each with air-conditioning and a small private bathroom. In winter, a double costs 280F (€42.55, $40.60); a double with kitchenette, 300F (€45.60, $43.50). A two-bedroom bungalow with kitchenette, suitable for four, rents for 450F (€68.40, $65.25). In the off-season, a double ranges from 240F to 280F (€36.45 to €42.55, $34.75 to $40.50), with the bungalow going for 400F (€60.80, $58).

Plage de Petite Anse, Marie-Galante. ✆ 590/97-32-63. Fax 590/97-33-59. Main courses 50F–150F (€7.60–€22.80, $7.25–$21.75); fixed-price menu 90F–120F (€13.70–€18.25, $13–$17.50) for lunch, 175F (€26.60, $25.50) for dinner. MC, V. Tues–Sun noon–2:30pm and 7–9:30pm. Closed Sept 15–Oct 15.

LA DÉSIRADE

The ubiquitous Columbus spotted this *terre désirée,* or sought-after land, after his Atlantic crossing in 1493. Named La Désirade, the island, 5 miles off the eastern tip of Guadeloupe, is less than 7 miles long and about 1½ miles wide. A single potholed road runs along its length. This former leper colony is often visited as a day excursion.

The island has fewer than 1,700 inhabitants, including the descendants of Europeans exiled here by royal command. Tourism has hardly touched the place. Most visitors opt to spend only a day on La Désirade, sunning or perhaps touring the island's barren expanses. There are, however, a handful of exceptionally simple guesthouses, which charge from 300F (€45.60, $43.50) for two. Don't expect anything grand.

The main hamlet is **Grand-Anse,** which has a small church with a presbytery and flower garden. **Le Souffleur** is a village where boats are constructed, and at **Baie Mahault** you can see the ruins of the old leper colony (including a barely recognizable chapel) from the early 18th century.

The best **beaches** are Souffleur, a tranquil oasis near the boat-building hamlet, and **Baie Mahault,** a small beach that's a Caribbean cliché of white sand and palm trees.

GETTING THERE & GETTING AROUND
Air Guadeloupe (© 590/82-47-00) offers flights to La Désirade from Guadeloupe's Le Raizet Airport three times a week. The round-trip fare is 394F (€59.90, $57.25) per person, and the trip takes between 15 to 20 minutes each way. Unless a respectable number of passengers shows up for the flight, Air Guadeloupe might cancel it, leaving passengers to fend for themselves and find other means of transport.

Most travelers opt to ride the **ferry** that leaves every day at 8am and 5pm (and sometimes at 3pm as well, depending on the season) from the wharves at St-François, near Guadeloupe's eastern tip. Return voyages include a daily departure at 3pm, allowing convenient access for day-trippers. Trip time is around 50 minutes each way, depending on conditions at sea. Round-trip passage costs 170F (€25.85, $24.75) per person. Call © **590/83-12-45** for schedules.

On La Désirade, three or four **minibuses** run between the airport and the towns. To get around, you might negotiate with a local driver. **Bicycles** are also available at the hotels.

If you'd like to spend the night, call **L'Oasis** (© **590/20-02-12**) or **Le Mirage** (© **590/20-01-08;** fax 590/20-07-45). Both are at Beauséjour, half a mile from the airport. Oasis has six plain rooms and charges 280F (€42.55, $40.50) for a double, including breakfast. Built in 1990 of concrete, it's simple and boxy, lying a short walk from a good beach. A bit closer to the sea, Le Mirage offers seven rather drab rooms at 260F (€39.50, $37.75) for a double, including breakfast. Built of concrete around the same time as Oasis, it offers a simple bar and restaurant.

14

Jamaica

Most visitors have a mental picture of Jamaica before they arrive: a boisterous culture of reggae and Rastafarianism, with white-sand beaches, tropical forests, rivers, mountains, and clear waterfalls. Jamaica's art, music, and cuisine (particularly jerk) are also remarkable.

Jamaica can be tranquil and intriguing, but there's no denying that it's plagued by crime, drugs, and muggings. There's also palpable racial tension. But many visitors are unaffected—they're escorted from the airport to their heavily patrolled hotel grounds and venture out only on expensive organized tours. Those who want to see the real Jamaica, or at least see the island in greater depth, had better be prepared for some hassle. Vendors on the beaches and in the markets can be particularly aggressive.

Most Jamaicans, despite economic hard times, have unrelenting good humor and genuinely welcome visitors to the island, with that famous "no problem, mon" charm. Others harm the tourism business, so many visitors vow never to return. Jamaica's appealing aspects have to be weighed against its poverty and problems, the legacy of traumatic political upheavals that have characterized the island since the 1970s.

Should you go? By all means, yes. Be prudent and cautious, though—just as if you were visiting New York, Miami, or Los Angeles. But Jamaica is worth it! The island has fine hotels and a zesty cuisine, and it is well-geared to couples who come to tie the knot or honeymoon. Jamaica's landscape affords visitors lots of outdoor activities, such as rafting and serious hiking. The island also has some of the finest diving waters in the world, with an average diving depth of 35 to 95 feet. Visibility is usually 60 to 120 feet. Most of the diving is done on coral reefs, protected by underwater parks where fish, shells, coral, and sponges are plentiful. Experienced divers can also see wrecks, hedges, caves, drop-offs, and tunnels.

Jamaica is known for its all-inclusive resorts, most of which are expensive. But you can save money by staying at local B&Bs, small hotels, and guesthouses. And if you steer clear of the pricey restaurants that cater almost exclusively to tourists and eat where many Jamaicans do, you'll cut your meal costs by two-thirds—and maybe more. Every town from Kingston to Montego Bay to Negril has a jerk center, and you almost can't go wrong by patronizing one of these local dives for a true taste of Jamaica. A jerk chicken or pork lunch runs about $6 in most places.

Jamaica lies 90 miles south of Cuba, with which it was chummy in the 1970s (when much of the world feared that Jamaica was going Communist). It's the third largest of the Caribbean islands, with some 4,400 square miles of predominantly green land, a mountain ridge peaking at 7,400 feet above sea level, and many white-sand beaches with clear blue sea on the north coast.

Jamaica

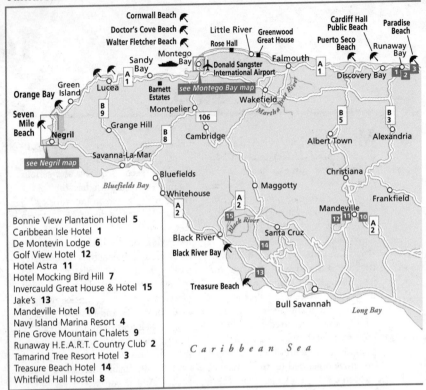

Bonnie View Plantation Hotel **5**
Caribbean Isle Hotel **1**
De Montevin Lodge **6**
Golf View Hotel **12**
Hotel Astra **11**
Hotel Mocking Bird Hill **7**
Invercauld Great House & Hotel **15**
Jake's **13**
Mandeville Hotel **10**
Navy Island Marina Resort **4**
Pine Grove Mountain Chalets **9**
Runaway H.E.A.R.T. Country Club **2**
Tamarind Tree Resort Hotel **3**
Treasure Beach Hotel **14**
Whitfield Hall Hostel **8**

1 Essentials

VISITOR INFORMATION

Before you go, you can obtain information from the **Jamaica Tourist Board** at the following U.S. addresses: 500 N. Michigan Ave., Suite 1030, Chicago, IL 60611 (© 312/527-1296); 1320 S. Dixie Hwy., Suite 1101, Coral Gables, FL 33146 (© 305/665-0557); 3440 Wilshire Blvd., Suite 805, Los Angeles, CA 90010 (© 213/384-1123); and 801 Second Ave., New York, NY 10017 (© 212/856-9727). In Atlanta, information can be obtained only by phone (© 770/452-7799).

In **Canada,** contact 1 Eglinton Ave. E., Suite 616, Toronto, ON M4P 3A1 (© 416/482-7850). Brits can call the **London** office: 1–2 Prince Consort Rd., London SW7 2BZ (© 020/7224-0505).

Once on **Jamaica,** you'll find tourist board offices at 2 St. Lucia Ave., Kingston (© 876/929-9200); Cornwall Beach, St. James, Montego Bay (© 876/952-4425); Shop no. 29, Coral Seas Plaza, Negril, Westmoreland (© 876/957-4243); in the Ocean Village Shopping Centre, Ocho Rios, St. Ann (© 876/974-2582); in City Centre Plaza, Port Antonio (© 876/993-3051); and in the Hendriks Building, 2 High St., Black River (© 876/965-2074).

The Internet address for Jamaica is **www.jamaicatravel.com.**

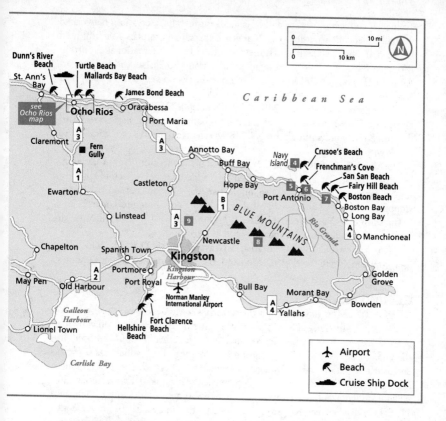

GETTING THERE

Before you book your own airfare, read the section "Package Deals" in chapter 2—it can save you a bundle!

There are two **international airports** on Jamaica: **Donald Sangster** in Montego Bay (© 887/952-3124) and **Norman Manley** in Kingston (© 876/924-8235). The most popular flights to Jamaica are from New York and Miami. Remember to reconfirm all flights, going and returning, no later than 72 hours before departure. Flying time from Miami is 1¼ hours; from Los Angeles, 5½ hours; from Atlanta, 2½ hours; from Dallas, 3 hours; from Chicago and New York, 3½ hours; and from Toronto, 4 hours.

Some of the most convenient and popular routes to Jamaica are provided by **American Airlines** (© 800/433-7300 in the U.S.), via its hubs in New York and Miami. Throughout the year, three daily nonstop flights depart from New York's Kennedy Airport for Montego Bay, continuing on to Kingston. Return flights to New York from Jamaica usually depart from Montego Bay, touch down briefly in Kingston, then continue nonstop back to Kennedy. From Miami, at least two daily flights depart for Kingston and two daily flights for Montego Bay.

Air Jamaica (© 800/523-5585 in the U.S.), the national carrier, operates about 14 flights a week from New York's JFK, most of which stop at both Montego Bay and Kingston. It offers even more frequent flights from Miami. The airline has connecting service within Jamaica through its reservations network to a small independent airline, **Air Jamaica Express,** whose planes usually hold between 10 and 17 passengers. It flies from the island's international airports at Montego Bay and Kingston to small airports around the island, including Port Antonio, Boscobel (near Ocho Rios), Negril, and Tinson Pen (a tiny airport near Kingston).

Air Canada (© **800-268-7240** in Canada or 800/776-3000 in the U.S.) flies to Jamaica from Toronto. In winter, service is daily; off-season flights are Saturday and Sunday only. But all this is subject to change depending on demand, so check with the airline.

US Airways (© **800/428-4322**) has two daily flights from New York, stopping in Charlotte or Philadelphia to take on added passengers before continuing to Jamaica. Likewise, it also offers two daily flights out of Baltimore, stopping in either Charlotte or Philadelphia before continuing to Jamaica.

In addition, **Northwest Airlines** (© **800/225-2525**) flies directly to Montego Bay daily from Minneapolis and Tampa.

British travelers usually take **British Airways** (© **0345/222-111**), which has four nonstop flights weekly to Montego Bay and Kingston from London's Gatwick Airport.

GETTING AROUND

BY PLANE   Most travelers enter the country via Montego Bay. If you want to fly elsewhere, you'll need to use the island's domestic air service, provided by Air Jamaica Express. Reservations are handled by **Air Jamaica** (© **800/523-5585** in the U.S., or 876/923-8680 in Kingston and Montego Bay), which has consolidated its reservation system. You can also reserve flights before you leave home through a travel agent or through Air Jamaica. Air Jamaica Express offers 30 scheduled flights daily, covering all the major resort areas. For example, there are 11 flights a day between Kingston and Montego Bay and 3 a day between Negril and Port Antonio. (Incidentally, Tinson Pen Airport in the heart of downtown Kingston is for domestic flights only.) Car-rental facilities are available only at the international airports at Kingston and Montego Bay.

Air SuperClub (© **876/940-7746**) also provides shuttle service between Montego Bay and Ocho Rios and between Montego Bay and Negril. **Tropical Airlines** (© **876/968-2473** in Kingston or 876/979-3565 in Montego Bay) flies between Montego Bay and Kingston.

BY TAXI & BUS   Kingston has no city taxis with meters, so agree on a price before you get in. In Kingston and on the rest of the island, special taxis and buses for visitors are operated by **JUTA** (Jamaica Union of Travelers Association) and have the union's emblem on the side of the vehicle. All prices are controlled,

---

⌐Fun Fact **Illegal Flights to Cuba**

Many residents of the United States use **Tropical Airlines** (see above) to take illegal flights from Montego Bay to Havana, where Castro's boys don't stamp their passports. After some "Havana heat," the Americans then fly back to Montego Bay, where they take another flight—no doubt, on American Airlines—for their return to the U.S. mainland, where, in theory at least, U.S. immigration authorities are none the wiser.

> ### (Finds Catch a Fire: Jamaica's Reggae Festivals
>
> Jamaica comes alive to the pulsating sounds of reggae during August's **Reggae Sunsplash,** the world's largest annual reggae festival. This week-long music extravaganza features some of the most prominent reggae groups and artists, which in the past have included Ziggy Marley and the Melody Makers. Sunsplash takes place at different venues; check with the Jamaican Tourist Board for the latest details.
>
> Some time during the second week of August a **Reggae Sunfest** is staged in Montego Bay. Usually this is a 4-day musical event, with some of the biggest names in reggae, both from Jamaica and worldwide, performing. Many local hotels are fully booked for the festivals, so advance reservations are necessary. The Jamaican Tourist Board's U.S. and Canadian offices can give you information about packages and group rates for the festivals. Call for information about Sunfest.
>
> Other reggae concerts and festivals featuring top performers are held throughout the year on Jamaica. Ask the tourist board for details.

and any local JUTA office will supply a list of rates. JUTA drivers handle nearly all the ground transportation, and some offer sightseeing tours.

BY RENTAL CAR   Jamaica is big enough, and public transportation unreliable enough, that a rental car is a necessity if you plan to do much independent sightseeing. In lieu of this, you can always take an organized tour to the major sights and spend the rest of the time on the beaches near your hotel.

Depending on road conditions, driving time for the 50 miles from Montego Bay to Negril is 1½ hours; from Montego Bay to Ocho Rios, 1½ hours; from Ocho Rios to Port Antonio, 2½ hours; from Ocho Rios to Kingston, 2 hours.

Unfortunately, prices of car rentals on Jamaica have skyrocketed recently, making it one of the most expensive rental scenes in the Caribbean. There's also a 15% government tax on rentals. Equally unfortunate are the unfavorable insurance policies that apply to virtually every car-rental agency on Jamaica.

It's best to stick to branches of U.S.-based outfits. **Avis** (© **800/331-1212** in the U.S.) maintains offices at the international airports in both Montego Bay (© **876/952-4543**) and Kingston (© **876/924-8013**). The company's least-expensive car requires a 24-hour advance booking. There's also **Budget** (© **800/527-0700** or 876/952-3838 at the Montego Bay Airport, 876/924-8762 in Kingston); with Budget, a mandatory daily collision-damage waiver costs another $15. **Hertz** (© **800/654-3001** in the U.S.) operates branches at the airports at both Montego Bay (© **876/979-0438**) and Kingston (© **876/924-8028**). If you'd like to shop for a better deal with one of the local companies, try **Jamaica Car Rental** in Montego Bay (© **876/952-5586**) or in Ocho Rios (© **876/974-2505**).

In Montego Bay, some local options are **United Car Rentals,** 49 Gloucester Ave. (© **876/952-3077**), which rents Mazdas, Toyota Starlets, Hondas, and Suzuki Jeeps from $48 per day for a two-door car without air-conditioning. You can also try **Jamaica Car Rental,** 23 Gloucester Ave. (© **876/952-5586**), with a branch at the Donald Sangster International Airport at Montego Bay (© **876/952-9496**). Daily rates begin at $70.

In Kingston, try **Island Car Rentals,** 17 Antigua Ave. (© **876/926-5991**), with a branch at Montego Bay's Sangster International Airport (© **876/952-5771**). It rents Hondas and Samurais, beginning at $115 daily in winter and $96 off-season.

Driving is on the left, and you should exercise more than your usual caution because of the unfamiliar terrain. Be especially cautious at night. Speed limits are 30 mph in town and 50 mph outside town. Gas is measured in the Imperial gallon (a British unit of measure that'll give you 25% more than a U.S. gal.), and the charge is payable only in Jamaican dollars; most stations don't accept credit cards. Your valid driver's license from back home is acceptable for driving during short-term visits to Jamaica.

BY BIKE & SCOOTER   If you have a valid driver's license, you can rent bikes and scooters in Montego Bay. **Montego Honda/Bike Rentals,** 21 Gloucester Ave. (© **876/952-4984**), rents Honda scooters for $30 to $35 a day (24 hr.), plus a $300 deposit. Bikes cost $10 a day, plus a $150 deposit. Deposits are refundable if the vehicles are returned in good shape. It's open daily 7:30am to 5pm.

 FAST FACTS: Jamaica

Banking Hours   Banks islandwide are open Monday to Friday 9am to 5pm. You'll find ATMs in all the major resort areas and towns, including Port Antonio, Ocho Rios, and Kingston. There are lots in Montego Bay, of course, and even one or two in sleepy Negril.

Currency   The unit of currency on Jamaica is the **Jamaican dollar,** using the same symbol as the U.S. dollar ($). There's no fixed rate of exchange for the Jamaican dollar. Subject to market fluctuations, it's traded publicly. Visitors to Jamaica can pay for any goods in U.S. dollars. In this guide we've generally followed the price-quotation policy of the establishment, whether in Jamaican dollars or U.S. dollars. The symbol **J$** denotes prices in Jamaican dollars; the conversion into U.S. dollars follows in parentheses. When dollar figures stand alone, they're always U.S. currency.

Jamaican currency is issued in banknotes of J$10, J$20, J$50, J$100, and J$500. Coins are available in denominations of 5¢, 10¢, 25¢, 50¢, J$1, and J$5. Five-dollar banknotes and 1¢ coins are also in circulation but increasingly rare. At press time (but subject to change), the exchange rate of Jamaican currency is J$46 to U.S.$1 (J$1 = about U.S.2.2¢). There are 58 Jamaican dollars in 1 pound sterling. When asking a sale price, always ask if the quotation is in U.S. dollars or Jamaica dollars. The difference can mean whether you get robbed or not!

There are Bank of Jamaica exchange bureaus at both international airports (Montego Bay and Kingston), at cruise ship piers, and in most hotels.

Customs   Do not bring in or take out illegal drugs from Jamaica. Your luggage will be searched. Marijuana-sniffing police dogs are stationed at the airport. Otherwise, you can bring in most items intended for personal use.

Documents   U.S. and Canadian residents don't need passports, but must have proof of citizenship (or permanent residency) and a return or ongoing ticket. In lieu of a passport, an original birth certificate or a certified copy, plus photo ID, will do. Always double-check, however, with the airline you're flying in case document requirements have changed. Other visitors, including British subjects, need passports, good for a maximum stay of 6 months. Immigration cards, needed for bank transactions and currency exchange, are given to visitors at the airport arrivals desks.

Drugstores In Montego Bay, try **Overton Pharmacy,** 49 Union St., Overton Plaza (✆ **876/952-2699**); in Ocho Rios, **Great House Pharmacy,** Brown's Plaza (✆ **876/974-2352**); and in Kingston, **Moodie's Pharmacy,** in the New Kingston Shopping Centre (✆ **876/926-4174**). Prescriptions are accepted by local pharmacies only if issued by a Jamaican doctor. Hotels have doctors on call. If you need any particular medicine or treatment, bring evidence, such as a letter from your own physician.

Electricity Most places have the standard 110-volt AC (60 cycles), as in the United States. However, some operate on 220-volt AC (50 cycles). If your hotel is on a different current from your U.S.-made appliance, ask for a transformer and an adapter.

Embassies Calling embassies or consulates in Jamaica is a challenge. Phones will ring and ring before being picked up, if they're answered at all. Extreme patience is needed to reach a live voice. The Embassy of the **United States** is at the Jamaica Mutual Life Centre, 2 Oxford Rd., Kingston 5 (✆ **876/929-4850**). The High Commission of **Canada** is in the Mutual Security Bank Building, 30–36 Knutsford Blvd., Kingston 5 (✆ **876/926-1500**), and there's a **Canadian** Consulate at 29 Gloucester Ave., Montego Bay (✆ **876/952-6198**). The High Commission of the **United Kingdom** is at 28 Trafalgar Rd., Kingston 10 (✆ **876/926-9050**).

Emergencies For the **police** and **air rescue,** dial ✆ **119**; to report a **fire** or call an **ambulance,** dial ✆ **110**.

Hospitals In Kingston, the **University Hospital** is at Mona (✆ **876/927-1620**); in Montego Bay, the **Cornwall Regional Hospital** is at Mount Salem (✆ **876/952-5100**); and in Port Antonio, the **Port Antonio General Hospital** is at Naylor's Hill (✆ **876/993-2646**).

Safety Major hotels have security guards who protect the grounds, so most vacationers don't have any real problems. It's not wise to accept an invitation to see "the real Jamaica" from some stranger you meet on the beach. Exercise caution when traveling around Jamaica. Safeguard your valuables and never leave them unattended on a beach. Likewise, never leave luggage or other valuables in a car or even the trunk of a car. The U.S. State Department has issued a travel advisory about crime rates in Kingston, so don't go walking around alone at night. Caution is also advisable in many north-coast tourist areas, especially remote houses and isolated villas that can't afford security.

Shopping Hours Hours vary widely, but as a general rule most stores are open Monday to Friday 8:30am to 4:30 or 5pm. Some shops are open Saturday until noon.

Taxes The government imposes a 12% room tax. You'll be charged a J$1,000 ($22) departure tax at the airport, payable in Jamaican or U.S. dollars. There's also a 15% government tax on rental cars and a 15% tax on all overseas phone calls.

Telecommunications From the United States, call Jamaica by dialing **1** and then the area code, **876**. Most hotels provide direct phone services to the U.S.

Time Jamaica is on eastern standard time year-round. However, when the United States is on daylight saving time, at 6am in Miami it's 5am in Kingston.

Tipping Tipping is customary. A general 10% or 15% is expected in hotels and restaurants on occasions when you would normally tip. Some places add a service charge to the bill. Tipping isn't allowed in the all-inclusive hotels.

Water It's usually safe to drink piped-in water, islandwide, as it's filtered and chlorinated. But, as always, it's more prudent to drink bottled water if it's available.

Weather Expect temperatures around 80° to 90°F on the coast. Winter is a little cooler. In the mountains it can get as low as 40°F. There is generally a breeze, which in winter is noticeably cool. The rainy periods in general are October and November (although it can extend into Dec) and May and June. Normally rain comes in short, sharp showers; then the sun shines.

TIPS ON FINDING AFFORDABLE ACCOMMODATIONS

CAMPING   Recent attacks against tourists have put a severe damper on many visitors' willingness to sleep in the Jamaican wild. Although you can, at your own risk, pitch a tent beneath any coconut palm, it's usually wiser (and in some cases, much wiser) to stick to the limited number of bona-fide campsites scattered around the island.

A source of information about camping is the **Jamaica Alternative Tourism Camping and Hiking Association (JATCHA)**, P.O. Box 216, Kingston 7, Jamaica, W.I. (© **876/702-0314**). This organization offers alternatives to traditional luxury resorts, which include lodgings in old plantation houses, run-down but respectable guesthouses, and (in rare cases) outdoor camping under carefully controlled circumstances. For $15 you can get a pamphlet listing around 100 options. The organization also dispenses information to special-interest travelers like bird-watchers and botanists.

VILLA RENTALS   Certain villa rentals in the off-season (mid-Apr to mid-Dec) become quite reasonable, especially for families or groups that want to do their own cooking. **Selective Vacation Services,** 154 Main St. (P.O. Box 335), Ocho Rios, Jamaica, W.I. (© **876/974-5187**), offers some of the best deals in the Ocho Rios area. Available are two- and three-bedroom apartments and villas, and car rentals can also be arranged. In summer, the least expensive villa, a two-bedroom unit, begins at $1,700 to $2,900 per week, although this same villa will rent for $2,300 to $3,900 per week in winter.

2 Montego Bay ★★★

On the northwestern coast of Jamaica, Montego Bay first attracted tourists in the 1940s, when Doctor's Cave Beach was popular with the wealthy who bathed in the warm water fed by mineral springs. Now it's Jamaica's second-largest city. In spite of the large influx of visitors, Montego Bay retains its own identity, with

---

Tips **A Word on Ganja**

Someone selling ganja will almost certainly approach you—in fact, that's why many travelers come here. However, we should warn you that drugs (including marijuana) are illegal, and imprisonment is the penalty for possession. You don't want to experience the Jamaican penal system first-hand. Don't smoke pot openly in public. Of course, hundreds of visitors do and get away with it, but you might be the one who gets caught, and the person selling to you might even be a police informant. Above all, don't even try to bring marijuana back into the United States. There are drug-sniffing dogs stationed at the Jamaican airports, and they will check your luggage. U.S. Customs agents, well aware of the drug situation on Jamaica, have arrested many tourists who have tried to take a chance on bringing some home.

---

a thriving business and commercial center and cruise ship piers, and it functions as the market town for most of western Jamaica. The history of Mo Bay, as the islanders call it, goes back to 1494, when it was discovered as an Arawak settlement.

Because Montego Bay has its own airport, the Donald Sangster International Airport, those who vacation here have little need to visit Kingston, the island's capital, unless they're seeking its cultural pleasures. Otherwise, you have everything in Mo Bay, the most cosmopolitan of Jamaica's resorts.

ACCOMMODATIONS YOU CAN AFFORD

Blue Harbour Hotel On a hillside overlooking the harbor, midway between the airport and town, off A1, this small hotel offers basic service in a friendly atmosphere. The standard rooms are simple, but the suites also contain TVs and kitchenettes. Mattresses are firm, and maintenance is generally quite acceptable. Each unit has a compact, tiled bathroom with a shower stall. For dinner, the hotel offers the option of a dine-around plan that includes 10 Montego Bay restaurants (transportation provided). Tennis is nearby, and arrangements can be made for golf, deep-sea fishing, scuba diving, and island tours. The beach is a 5-minute walk from the hotel, which provides free transportation to and from the shore.

6 Sewell Ave. (P.O. Box 212), Montego Bay, Jamaica, W.I. © 876/952-5445. Fax 876/952-8930. robbyg@ cwjamaica.com. 24 units. Winter $40–$64 single; $56–$72 double; $94 suite. Off-season $29–$48 single; $42–$58 double; $70–$75 suite. Children 11 and under stay free in parents' room. AE, MC, V. **Amenities:** Coffee shop, lounge, pool, beach shuttle. *In room:* A/C, TV.

Ocean View Guest House *Value* Opened in the 1960s when the grandparents of the present owners began to rent extra rooms in their home, this super-bargain is half a mile from the airport and the same distance from the public beach. You'll need a taxi to get here, although the owner sometimes provides transportation to and from the airport. The small rooms are supplemented with a library and satellite TV room; all but two are air-conditioned, all have fans, and most open onto a veranda or the spacious front porch. It's quietest at the back. A few drawbacks: The mattresses are a bit tired, the shower-only bathrooms really are cubicles, cleanliness and service are minimal, and the hotel doesn't take reservations (you'll have to wait until you're on the island before you know if there are rooms available). The owner will arrange island tours, tennis,

Montego Bay

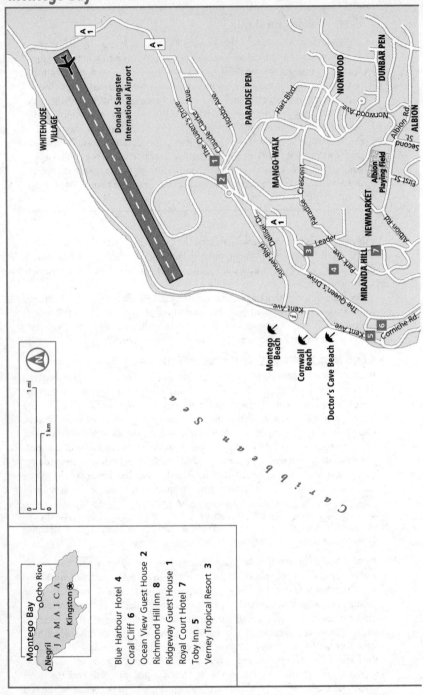

Blue Harbour Hotel **4**
Coral Cliff **6**
Ocean View Guest House **2**
Richmond Hill Inn **8**
Ridgeway Guest House **1**
Royal Court Hotel **7**
Toby Inn **5**
Verney Tropical Resort **3**

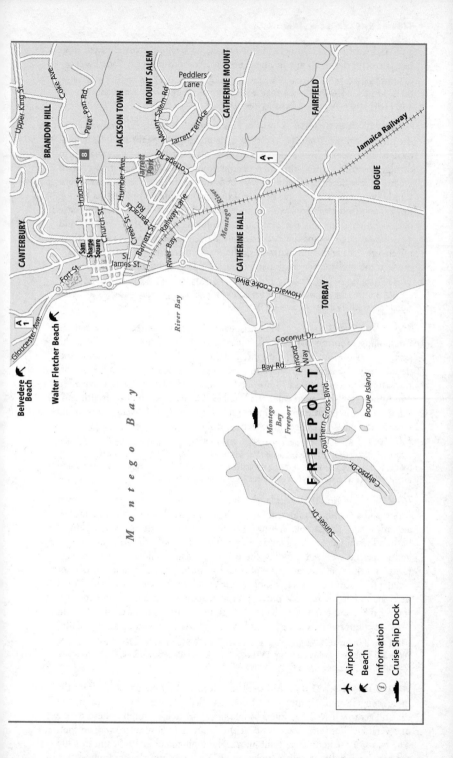

golf, and watersports. Dinners (T-bone steak, pork chops, roast chicken, fresh fish) are offered only to guests, and dinner reservations must be made by 2pm.

26 Sunset Blvd. (P.O. Box 210), Montego Bay, Jamaica, W.I. ℂ **876/952-2662.** 12 units. Winter $35 single; $41–$43 double. Off-season $23–$28 single; $34–$36 double. No credit cards. **Amenities:** Restaurant (guests only). *In room:* A/C in most, TV, ceiling fans.

Ridgeway Guest House ⭐ *Finds* This hospitable B&B, far removed from the impersonal mega-resorts (and their megaprices), is a great find. The helpful owners, Brenda and Bryan (Bryan is actually his last name, as he doesn't like to divulge his first name), offer free pickup from the airport and transport to Doctor's Cave Beach, a 15-minute walk or 5 minutes by car. The Bryans are constantly improving their property, a two-story white-painted building set among flowers and fruit trees from which guests may help themselves. Guests can have before-dinner drinks in the roof garden, enjoying a view of the airport and ocean. The large rooms are decorated in a tropical motif, with two or three queen-size beds with firm mattresses. The medium-size marble bathrooms have modern tub-and-shower combinations, and TV is available in a public area.

34 Queen's Dr., Montego Bay, Jamaica, W.I. ℂ **876/952-2709.** 10 units. Year-round $35–$45 single; $45–$55 double. Children 11 and under stay free in parents' room. DISC, MC, V. **Amenities:** Restaurant, bar, pickup from airport, TV lounge. *In room:* A/C, TV.

Royal Court Hotel ⭐⭐ This reasonable choice is located on the hillside overlooking Montego Bay, above Gloucester Avenue and off Park Avenue. The small rooms are outfitted in bright, tasteful colors, and all have patios and decent beds; the larger ones have fully equipped kitchenettes. Each has a neat, tiled shower-only bathroom. This hotel is clean and attractive, has a charming atmosphere, and is a good value. Its Wellness Center offers holistic health consultation and hypnotherapy sessions. You'll find better-than-average food at its restaurant, which specializes in vegetarian dishes.

Sewell Ave. (P.O. Box 195), Montego Bay, Jamaica, W.I. ℂ **876/952-4531.** Fax 876/952-4532. 20 units. Winter $65–$80 double; $90 suite. Off-season $50–$65 double; $75 suite. AE, MC, V. **Amenities:** Restaurant, bar, health club, Jacuzzi, steam room, massage, shuttle to town, shuttle to beach (a 10-min. ride away), shuttle to tennis club, TV room, Wellness Center. *In room:* A/C, kitchenette (some units).

Toby Inn Its location beside the busy main thoroughfare of downtown Montego Bay (and a 5-min. walk from Doctor's Cave Beach) is an advantage or a disadvantage, depending on how easy you want your access to the inexpensive bars and restaurants to be. Despite the traffic and crowds, the almond, mango, and grapefruit trees surrounding the two-story main building, a series of cottages, and the pool create a sense of rural isolation. You'll also find a restaurant serving Jamaican cuisine, a gift shop, a bandstand for the rare concerts presented here, and a bar where a TV provides at least some of the entertainment. Each room has either a terrace or a balcony. Each unit's king-size, queen-size, or twin beds are comfortable, and each unit has a small bathroom with a shower stall.

1 Kent Ave. (P.O. Box 467), Montego Bay, Jamaica, W.I. ℂ **876/952-4370.** Fax 876/952-6591. 65 units. Winter $55 single; $65 double. Off-season $50 single; $55 double. Extra person $15. AE, MC, V. **Amenities:** Restaurant, bar, pool, small fitness center. *In room:* A/C, TV.

Verney Tropical Resort In a verdant setting just far enough away from the urban congestion of Montego Bay, this hotel offers a feeling of remote calm. You can still get to where the action is by taking a short trek downhill or head to one of several beaches (like Cornwall Beach) that are only 5 minutes away on foot. The two-story structure was built on steeply sloping land in 1945, and in 1995 the pastel-colored rooms were freshened up. Each medium-size accommodation

---

> ### Moments   Going Native on the Street
>
> MoBay has some of the finest and most expensive dining on the island.
> But if you're watching your wallet and have an adventurous streak, you
> can find lots of terrific street food. On **Kent Avenue** you might try
> authentic jerk pork or seasoned spareribs grilled over charcoal fires and
> sold with extra-hot sauce; order a Red Stripe beer to go with it. Cooked
> shrimp are also sold on the streets of MoBay; they don't look it, but
> they're very spicy, so be warned. And if you have an efficiency unit with
> a kitchenette, you can buy fresh lobster or the catch of the day and make
> your own dinner.

---

has white walls, simple furnishings, a small shower-only bathroom, and a good
bed. The Kit-Kat restaurant and bar overlook the pool. The staff is usually
gracious.

3 Leader Ave. (P.O. Box 18), Montego Bay, Jamaica, W.I. (℃ **876/952-8628.** Fax 876/979-2944. 25 units.
Winter $45 single; $55 double; $75 triple; $95 quad. Off-season $40 single; $50 double; $60 triple; $80 quad.
MAP $18 per person. AE, MC, V. **Amenities:** Restaurant, pool. *In room:* A/C, TV.

WORTH A SPLURGE

Coral Cliff ★ *Value*   The Coral Cliff lies only 2 minutes from Doctor's Cave
Beach. The hotel grew from a colonial-style building that was once the private
home of Harry M. Doubleday (of the famous publishing family). It's located
about a mile west of the center of town. Many of the light, airy, and spacious
bedrooms open onto a balcony with a view of the sea. The rooms, as befits a
former private house, come in a wide variety of shapes and sizes, most of them
containing old colonial furniture, wicker, and rattan. Most units also have twin
beds with firm mattresses. The bathrooms are small in the older bedrooms, but
more spacious in the newer wing out back. Each is tidily maintained and has a
combination tub/shower.

165 Gloucester Ave. (P.O. Box 253), Montego Bay, Jamaica, W.I. (℃ **876/952-4130.** Fax 876/952-6532.
www.coralcliffjamaica.com. 30 units. Winter $90–$100 double; $110–$120 triple; from $160 suite. Off-
season $80–$90 double; $92–$105 triple; from $140 suite. MC, V. **Amenities:** Restaurant, bar. *In room:* A/C.

Richmond Hill Inn ★★   High on a forested slope, 500 feet above Montego
Bay's center, this is the much-restored site of what was once the homestead of
the Dewar family (the scions of scotch). Little of that villa remains, but what
you'll find is an aerie ringed by urn-shaped concrete balustrades, a pool terrace
suitable for sundowner cocktails, and comfortable, slightly fussy rooms with
lace-trimmed curtains and homey bric-a-brac. Rooms come in a variety of sizes,
and all are comfortable and have firm mattresses. Bathrooms, which have tub-
and-shower combinations, are small but tidy. If you're an avid beach lover, know
in advance that the nearest beach (Doctor's Cave) is a 15-minute drive away.

Union St. (P.O. Box 362), Montego Bay, Jamaica, W.I. (℃ **876/952-3859.** Fax 876/952-6106. www.
richmond-hill-inn.com. 20 units. Winter $90 single; $115 double; $198 1-bedroom suite; $230 2-bedroom
suite for up to 4; $300 3-bedroom penthouse suite. Off-season $75 single; $90 double; $168 1-bedroom suite;
$220 2-bedroom suite for up to 4; $250–$320 3-bedroom penthouse suite. Extra person $27–$32. MAP
$41–$48 per person. AE, MC, V. **Amenities:** Restaurant, bar, pool, maid service, laundry. *In room:* A/C, TV.

GREAT DEALS ON DINING

The Brewery AMERICAN/JAMAICAN   This restaurant/bar not only serves
good food, but might also be your entertainment choice for the evening. It has

extended its patio and built a roof over it so you can eat out regardless of the weather, with a view of the ocean. Burgers, salads, and sandwiches are available, and there's a nightly Jamaican dinner special, a freshly made soup of the day, and an excellent chicken gumbo. The chef is known for his pasta dishes, and you can also order classics like rib-eye steak and mesquite turkey. One night a week is devoted to shrimp, with a bevy of choices; another night ribs might be featured. Call ahead to find out what the special nights are and to learn if any entertainment is offered. The best time to come for drinks is the daily 4-to-6pm happy hour, when drinks made with local liquor are half-price. If you're daring, you might want to try the bartender's special firewater—he won't disclose the ingredients but promises it lives up to its name.

In Miranda Ridge Plaza, Gloucester Ave. ✆ 876/940-2433. Main courses J$350–J$850 ($7.50–$18.50). AE, MC, V. Daily 11am–2am.

Le Chalet INTERNATIONAL/JAMAICAN   In the densest concentration of stores and souvenir shops on Montego Bay's tourist strip, this high-ceilinged restaurant lies across Gloucester Avenue from the sea and looks somewhat like a Howard Johnson's. The well-prepared food is served in copious portions: The lunch selection might include burgers, sandwiches, barbecued ribs, and salads, and the dinner selection chicken platters, steaks, fresh fish, and lobster, which seems to taste best here if prepared with Jamaican curry. The staff is articulate and helpful.

32 Gloucester Ave. ✆ 876/952-5240. Main courses $6–$24 at dinner, $4–$19 at lunch. AE, MC, V. Mon–Sat 10am–10pm; Sun 4–10pm.

The Native Restaurant ✿✿ JAMAICAN/INTERNATIONAL   Open to the breezes, this casual restaurant with panoramic views serves some of the finest Jamaican dishes in the area. Appetizers include jerk reggae chicken and ackee and saltfish, which you can follow with steamed fish or jerk chicken. The most tropical offering is "goat in a boat" (that is, a pineapple shell). A more recent specialty is Boononoonoos; billed as "A Taste of Jamaica," it's a big platter with a little bit of everything—meats and several kinds of fish and vegetables.

29 Gloucester Ave. ✆ 876/979-2769. Reservations recommended. Main courses $8.50–$32. AE, MC, V. Daily 7:30–10:30pm.

The Pelican (Kids) JAMAICAN   A Montego Bay landmark, the family-friendly Pelican has been serving good food at reasonable prices for more than a quarter of a century. Most of the dishes are at the lower end of the price scale, unless you order shellfish. Many diners come here at lunch for one of the well-stuffed sandwiches, juicy burgers, or barbecued chicken. You can also choose from a wide array of Jamaica dishes, including stewed peas and rice, curried goat, Caribbean fish, fried chicken, and curried lobster. A "meatless menu" includes such dishes as a vegetable plate and vegetable chili. The soda fountain serves old-fashioned sundaes with real whipped cream.

Gloucester Ave. ✆ 876/952-3171. Reservations recommended. Main courses $6–$28. AE, DC, MC, V. Daily 7am–11pm.

Pork Pit ✿ (Finds) JAMAICAN   This joint is the best place to go for the famous Jamaica jerk pork and jerk chicken, and the location is right in the heart of Montego Bay, near Walter Fletcher Beach. Many beachgoers desert their towels at noontime and head over here for a big, reasonably priced lunch. Picnic tables encircle the building, and everything is open-air and informal. A half-pound of

---

Fun Fact The Naked Truth

Nude bathing is allowed at a number of hotels, clubs, and beaches (especially in Negril), but only where there are signs stating SWIMSUITS OPTIONAL. Elsewhere, the law won't allow even topless sunbathing.

---

jerk meat, served with a baked yam or baked potato and a bottle of Red Stripe, is usually sufficient for a meal. The menu also includes steamed roast fish.

27 Gloucester Ave. ✆ 876/952-1046. 1 lb of jerk pork J$400 ($11.50). AE, MC, V. Daily 11am–11pm.

HITTING THE BEACHES

Cornwall Beach (✆ 876/952-3463) is a long stretch of white sand with dressing rooms, a bar, and a cafeteria. The grainy sand and good swimming have made Cornwall a longtime favorite. Unlike some of Jamaica's remote, hard-to-get-to beaches, this one is near all the major hotels, especially the moderately priced ones. Unfortunately, it can be crowded in winter (mostly with tourists, not locals). This is a good beach for kids, with gentle waters and a gently sloping ocean bottom. The beach is open daily 9am to 5pm. Admission is J$80 ($1.75) for adults, J$40 (90¢) for children.

Doctor's Cave Beach, on Gloucester Avenue (✆ 876/952-2566 for the beach club), arguably the loveliest stretch of sand bordering Montego Bay, helped put Montego Bay on the map in the 1940s. Its gentle surf, golden sands, and fresh turquoise water make it one of the most inviting places to swim and there's always a beach-party atmosphere. Placid and popular with families, it's the best all-around beach in Montego Bay. Sometimes schools of tropical fish weave in and out of the waters, but usually the crowds of frolicking people scare them away. Since it's almost always packed, especially in winter, you have to get there early to stake out a beach-blanket–sized spot. Admission is $3 for adults, $1.50 for children 12 and under. The beach club here has well-kept changing rooms, showers, rest rooms, a food court, a bar, a cybercafe, and a sundries shop. Beach chairs and umbrellas can be rented daily.

One of the premier beaches of Jamaica, **Walter Fletcher Beach** (✆ 876/ 979-9447), in the heart of Mo Bay, is noted for its tranquil waters, which makes it a particular favorite for families with children. This is one of the most beautiful beaches along the southern coast of Jamaica. Easy to reach, it's generally crowded in winter and enjoyed by visitors and locals alike. Some people bring picnics, but be careful not to litter, as patrols might fine you. From December to March, there seems to be a long-running beach party here. Somehow, regardless of how many people show up, there always seems to be a place in the sun for them. Visitors show up in almost anything (or lack of anything), although actual nudity is prohibited. There are changing rooms, a restaurant, and lifeguards. Hours are daily 10am to 10pm. Admission is J$100 ($2.20) for adults, J$50 ($1.10) for children.

You might want to skip all these public beaches entirely and head instead for the **Rose Hall Beach Club** (✆ 876/953-2323), on the main road 11 miles east of Montego Bay. The club offers half a mile of secluded white-sand beach with crystal-clear water, plus a restaurant, two bars, a covered pavilion, an open-air dance area, showers, rest rooms, hammocks, changing rooms, beach volleyball courts, beach games, a full watersports program, and live entertainment. Admission is $15 for adults, $10 for children. Hours are daily 9am to 6pm.

⌠*Moments* Rum & Reggae—and an Escape

When you want to escape, head for **Time 'n' Place,** just west of Falmouth (*℡* **876/954-4371**). From Montego Bay, you'll spot the sign by the side of the road before you reach Falmouth, reading IF YOU GOT THE TIME, THEN WE GOT THE PLACE. On an almost deserted 2-mile beach sits this funky beach bar, built of driftwood. Sit back in this relaxed, friendly place and listen to the reggae from the local stations. You can order the island's best daiquiris, made from fresh local fruit, or stick around for peppery jerk chicken or lobster. Time 'n' Place isn't completely undiscovered: The fashion editors of *Vogue* have swooped down on the place, using it as a backdrop for beach fashion shots.

SPORTS & OTHER OUTDOOR PURSUITS

DIVING, SNORKELING & OTHER WATERSPORTS   **Seaworld Resorts,** Rose Hall Main Road (*℡* **876/953-2180**), operates scuba-diving excursions, plus many other watersports, including sailing and windsurfing. Its scuba dives plunge to offshore coral reefs, among the most spectacular in the Caribbean. There are three certified dive guides, one dive boat, and all the necessary equipment for either inexperienced or certified divers. One-tank dives cost $40 and night dives are $65. In Montego Bay, the waters right on the beach are fine for snorkeling. However, it's more rewarding to go across the channel. Here Cayaba Reef, Seaworld Reef, and Royal Reef are full of barjacks, blue and brown chromis, yellow-headed wrasses, and spotlight parrotfish. You must have a guide to go here because the currents are strong and the wind picks up in the afternoon. If you're not staying at a resort that offers snorkeling expeditions, Seaworld is your best bet; the charge of $25 per hour might be a bit steep, but the guides swim along with you, pointing out the various tropical fish.

HORSEBACK RIDING   A good program for equestrians is offered at the **Rocky Point Riding Stables,** at the Half Moon Club, Rose Hall (*℡* **876/953-2286**). Housed in the most beautiful barn and stables in Jamaica, built in the colonial Caribbean style in 1992, it offers around 30 horses and a helpful staff. A 90-minute beach or mountain ride costs $50, and a 2½-hour combination ride (including treks along hillsides, forest trails, and beaches, and ending with a saltwater swim) goes for $70.

RAFTING   **Mountain Valley Rafting,** 31 Gloucester Ave. (*℡* **876/956-4920**), offers rafting excursions on the Great River departing from the Lethe Plantation, about 10 miles south of Montego Bay. Rafts, composed of bamboo trunks with a raised dais to sit on, are available for $36 for up to two people. In some cases, a small child can accompany two adults on the same raft, although due caution should be exercised if you choose to do this. Trips last 45 minutes and operate daily 8am to 5pm. Ask about pickup by taxi at the end of the rafting run to return you to your rented car. For $45 per person, a half-day experience will include transportation to and from your hotel, an hour's rafting, lunch, a garden tour of the Lethe property, and a taste of Jamaican liqueur.

TENNIS   The **Half Moon Golf, Tennis, and Beach Club,** outside Montego Bay (*℡* **876/953-2211**), has the finest tennis courts in the area. Its 13 state-of-the-art courts, 7 of which are lit for night games, attract tennis players from around the world. Lessons cost $25 to $35 per half hour or $50 to $65 per hour.

Residents play free throughout the day or night. The pro shop, which accepts reservations for court times, is open daily 7am to 9pm. If you want to play after those hours, you switch on the lights yourself. If you're not a guest of the hotel, you must buy a day pass ($50 per person) at the front desk. It'll allow you access to the resort's tennis courts, gym, sauna, Jacuzzi, pools, and beach facilities.

The **Wyndham Rose Hall Golf & Beach Resort,** Rose Hall (© 876/ 953-2650), outside Montego Bay, is an outstanding tennis resort, although it's not the equal of Half Moon. Wyndham offers six hard-surface courts, each lit for night play. As a courtesy, nonguests are sometimes invited to play for free, but permission has to be obtained from the manager. You can't play unless you're invited. The resident pro charges $30 per hour for lessons, or $20 for 30 minutes.

WATERSPORTS A "water world" for the family, the $20-million **Aguasol Theme Park** (© 876/940-1344), Walter Fletcher Beach, lures with its array of watersports activities, including a giant water slide, a go-kart track, a large sandy beach, plus planned amusements that cover everything from fashion shows to presentations of reggae. There's also an outdoor restaurant and a sports bar featuring 42 big-screen televisions. An upper deck is ideal for sunbathing, and there's also a picnic area. At night a dance club dominates the action. Open long hours daily 10am to 3am, the attraction charges J$100 ($2.20) adults, J$50 ($1.10) for children 12 and under. Rentals of beach chairs or umbrellas go for J$50 ($1.10) each.

TOURING THE GREAT HOUSES

Occupied by plantation owners, the Great Houses of Jamaica were built on high ground so that they could overlook the plantations and provide a view of the next house in the distance. It was the custom for the owners to offer hospitality to travelers crossing the island by road; travelers were spotted by the lookout, and bed and food were given freely.

Barnett Estates and Bellfield Great House Once a private estate sprawled across 50,000 acres, this Great House has hosted everybody from President Kennedy to Churchill and even Queen Elizabeth II. Now anybody who pays admission can come in and take a look. The domain of the Kerr-Jarret family during 300 years of high society, this was once the seat of a massive sugar plantation. At its center is the 18th-century Bellfield Great House, a grand example of Georgian architecture (restored in 1994, but not as ornate as Rose Hall, below). Costumed guides offer narrated tours of the property. After the tour, drop in to the old Sugar Mill Bar for a tall rum punch.

Granville Main Road, Granville. (The hamlet of Granville lies on the southern border of Montego Bay, away from the sea. Granville Main Road begins in the center of Montego Bay and heads southeast. Near Granville, the attraction is signposted.) © 876/952-2382. Admission $10. Daily 9:30am–5pm.

Greenwood Great House 𝄞 Some people find the 15-room Greenwood even more interesting than Rose Hall because it's been less restored and has more literary associations. Erected on its hillside perch between 1780 and 1800, the Georgian-style building was the residence of Richard Barrett (cousin of poet Elizabeth Barrett Browning). Elizabeth Barrett Browning herself never visited Jamaica, but her family used to be one of the largest landholders here. An absentee planter who lived in England, her father once owned 84,000 acres and some 3,000 slaves. On display is the original library of the Barrett family, with rare books dating from 1697, along with oil paintings of the family, Wedgwood china, rare musical instruments, and a fine collection of antique furniture.

On Rte. A1, 14 miles east of Montego Bay. © 876/953-1077. Admission $12 adults, $6 children under 12. Daily 9am–6pm.

Rose Hall Great House ⚘   The legendary Rose Hall is the most famous Great House on Jamaica. The subject of at least a dozen Gothic novels, it was immortalized in the H. G. deLisser book *White Witch of Rose Hall.* John Palmer, a wealthy British planter, built the house from 1778 to 1790. At its peak, this was a 6,600-acre plantation, with more than 2,000 slaves. However, it was Annie Palmer, wife of the builder's grandnephew, who became the focal point of fiction and fact. Called "Infamous Annie," she was said to have dabbled in witchcraft. She took slaves as lovers and then killed them off when they bored her. Servants called her "the Obeah woman" (*Obeah* is Jamaican for "voodoo"). Annie was said to have murdered several of her husbands while they slept and eventually suffered the same fate herself. Long in ruins, the house has now been restored and can be visited by the public. Annie's Pub is on the ground floor.

Rose Hall Hwy., 9 miles east of Montego Bay. © 876/953-2323. Admission $15 adults, $10 children. Daily 9am–6pm.

ORGANIZED TOURS & CRUISES

The **Croydon Plantation** (© 876/979-8267), is a 25-mile ride from Montego Bay and can be visited on a half-day tour from Montego Bay (or Negril) on Wednesday and Friday. Included in the $45 price are round-trip transportation from your hotel, a tour of the plantation, a taste of tropical fruits in season, and a barbecued-chicken lunch. Most hotel desks can arrange this tour.

For a plantation tour, go on a **Hilton High Day Tour,** through Beach View Plaza (© 876/952-3343). The tour includes round-trip transportation on a scenic drive through historic plantation areas. Your day starts at a plantation house with a continental breakfast. You can roam the plantation's 100 acres and visit the German village of Seaford town or St. Leonards village nearby. Calypso music is played throughout the day, and a Jamaican lunch is served at 1pm. The charge is $55 per person for the plantation tour, breakfast, lunch, and transportation. Tour days are Tuesday, Wednesday, Friday, and Sunday.

Day and evening cruises are offered aboard the *Calico,* a 55-foot gaff-rigged wooden ketch sailing from Margeuritaville on the Montego Bay waterfront. An additional vessel, *Calico B,* also carries another 40 passengers per boat ride. You can be transported to/from your hotel, for either cruise. The day voyage, departing at 10am and returning at 1pm, provides a day of sailing, sunning, and snorkeling (with equipment supplied). The cruise costs $35 per person and is offered daily. On the *Calico's* evening voyage, which goes for $25 per person and is offered Wednesday to Saturday 5 to 7pm, cocktails and wine are served as you sail through sunset. For information and reservations, call Capt. Bryan Langford at **North Coast Cruises** (© 876/952-5860). A 3-day notice is recommended.

SHOPPING ⚘⚘

When you go shopping in Montego Bay, be prepared for aggressive vendors. Since selling a craft item might affect whether or not they put food on the table that night, there's often a feverish attempt to peddle goods to potential customers, all of whom are viewed as rich. Therefore, prepare yourself for being pursued persistently. If you want some item, also be prepared for some serious negotiation, as bargaining on your part will lead to substantial discounts.

The main shopping areas are at **Montego Freeport,** within easy walking distance of the pier; **City Centre,** where most of the duty-free shops are, aside from those at the large hotels; and **Holiday Village Shopping Centre.**

SHOPPING CENTERS   The **Old Fort Craft Park,** a shopping complex with 180 vendors (all licensed by the Jamaica Tourist Board), fronts Howard Cooke

> **Tips Is It a Bargain?**
>
> Some so-called duty-free prices are actually lower than stateside prices, but then the government hits you with a 10% "general consumption tax" on all items purchased. But you can still find good duty-free items here, including Swiss watches, Irish crystal, Italian handbags, Indian silks, and liquors and liqueurs. Appleton's rums are an excellent value. Tia Maria (coffee-flavored) and Ruymona (rum-flavored) are the best liqueurs. Khus Khus is the local perfume. Jamaica arts and crafts are available throughout the resorts and at the Crafts Market.

Boulevard (up from Gloucester Avenue in the heart of Montego Bay, on the site of Fort Montego). A market with a varied assortment of handcrafts, it's grazing country for both souvenirs and more serious purchases. You'll see a selection of wall hangings, handwoven straw items, and wood sculpture. You can even get your hair braided. At the **Crafts Market,** near Harbour Street in downtown Montego Bay, you can find the best selection of handmade souvenirs, including straw hats and bags, wooden platters, straw baskets, musical instruments, beads, carved objects, and toys. That *jipijapa* hat is important if you're going to be out in the island sun.

One of the newest and most intriguing places for shopping is **Half Moon Plaza,** set on the coastal road about 8 miles east of the commercial center of Montego Bay. This upscale mini-mall caters to the shopping and gastronomic needs of residents of one of the region's most elegant hotels, the Half Moon Club. On the premises are a bank and about 25 shops arranged around a central courtyard and selling a wide choice of carefully selected merchandise.

ARTS & CRAFTS   The **Ambiente Art Gallery,** 9 Fort St. (© **876/ 952-7919**), is housed in a 100-year-old clapboard cottage close to the road. The Austrian-born owner, Maria Hitchins, is one of the *doyennes* of the Montego Bay art scene. She has personally encouraged and developed scores of fine artworks and prints by local artists. At **Blue Mountain Gems Workshop,** in the Holiday Village Shopping Centre (© **876/953-2338**), you can take a tour of the workshops to see the process of jewelry creation, from raw stone to the finished product you can buy later. Wooden jewelry, local carvings, and one-of-a-kind ceramic figurines are also sold.

Neville Budhai Paintings, Budhai's Art Gallery, Holiday Village Center, (© **876/979-2568**), is the art center of a distinguished artist, Neville Budhai, the president and cofounder of the Western Jamaica Society of Fine Arts. He has a distinct style and captures the special flavor of the island and its people. The artist can sometimes be seen sketching or painting in Montego Bay or along the highways of rural Jamaica. **Things Jamaican,** at the Donald Sangster Airport (© **876/952-1936**), is a showcase for the artisans of Jamaica. A wealth of products is displayed, even food and drink, including rums and liqueurs, along with jerk seasoning and orange-pepper jelly. Look for Busha Browne's fine Jamaican sauces, especially spicy chutneys or planters' spicy piquant sauce. Other items for sale are wood sculpture, salad bowls, trays, and handwoven baskets. Also look for reproductions of the Port Royal collection. Port Royal was buried by an earthquake and tidal wave in 1692. After resting underwater for 275 years, beautiful pewter items were recovered and are reproduced here. They include rat-tail spoons, a spoon with the heads of the monarchs William and Mary, and splay-footed lion rampant spoons. Many items are reproduced faithfully, right down to the pit marks and scratches.

Golden Nugget, 8 St. James Shopping Centre, Gloucester Ave. (© **876/ 952-7707**), is a duty-free shop with an impressive collection of watches and a fine assortment of jewelry, plus cameras and a wide assortment of French perfumes. **Copasetic,** Half Moon Shopping village (© **876/953-3838**), is a good outlet for Jamaican crafts, including pottery and jewelry. There are also good buys here in straw products. The best selection of native art is found at the **Gallery of West Indian Art,** 1 Orange Lane (© **876/952-4547**), with a wide selection of paintings not only from Haiti and Jamaica, but Cuba as well, along with Jamaican hand-carved wooden animals—even some painted hand-turned pottery.

FASHION Klass Kraft Leather Sandals, 44 Fort St. (© **876/952-5782**), next door to Things Jamaican, offers sandals and leather accessories made on location by a team of Jamaican craftspeople.

JEWELRY Golden Nugget, 8 St. James Shopping Centre, Gloucester Ave. (© **876/952-7707**), is a duty-free shop with an impressive collection of watches for both women and men and a fine assortment of jewelry, especially gold chains. The shop also carries leading brand-name cameras and a wide assortment of French perfumes.

MONTEGO BAY AFTER DARK

Marguerite's Seafood by the Sea and Margeuritaville Sports Bar & Grill, Gloucester Avenue (© **876/952-4777**), is a two-in-one restaurant across from the Coral Cliff Hotel specializing in moderately priced seafood served on a breezy terrace overlooking the sea. The sports bar and grill features a 110-foot hydroslide, live music, satellite TV, a sundeck, a CD jukebox, and a straightforward menu of seafood, sandwiches, pasta, pizza, salads, and snacks—nothing fussy. Naturally, the bartenders specialize in margaritas.

Cricket Club, at Wyndham Rose Hall (© **876/953-2650**), is more than just a sports bar; it's where people go to meet and mingle with an international crowd. Televised sports, karaoke singalongs, tournament darts, and backgammon are all part of the fun. It's open daily 7pm to 1am; there's no cover.

We've enjoyed the atmosphere at **Walter's,** 39 Gloucester Ave. (© **876/ 952-9391**), which has an authentic Jamaican laid-back feel—complete with a constant flow of calypso and reggae music from as early as 10am daily (for the diehards) until 2am. There's never a cover, and they have live bands on the weekends.

The Brewery, Gloucester Avenue (© **876/940-2433**), is one of the city's most popular nightlife hangouts. It's a cross between an English pub and a Jamaican jerk pork pit. There's a woodsy-looking bar where everyone is into Red Stripe and reggae, lots of neo-medieval memorabilia, and a covered veranda in back, overlooking busy Gloucester Avenue.

3 Negril ⟨★⟩⟨★⟩⟨★⟩

On the western tip of the island, this once-sleepy village has turned into a tourist mecca, with visitors drawn to its beaches along three well-protected bays: Long Bay, Bloody Bay (now Negril Harbour), and Orange Bay. It's 50 miles and about a 2-hour drive from Montego Bay's airport, along a winding road and past ruins of sugar estates and Great Houses. Negril became famous in the late 1960s, when it attracted laid-back American and Canadian youths, who liked the idea of a place with no phones and no electricity; they rented modest little houses on

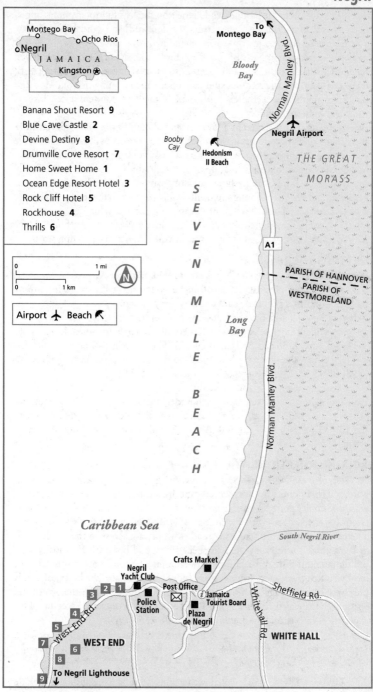

Negril

Banana Shout Resort **9**
Blue Cave Castle **2**
Devine Destiny **8**
Drumville Cove Resort **7**
Home Sweet Home **1**
Ocean Edge Resort Hotel **3**
Rock Cliff Hotel **5**
Rockhouse **4**
Thrills **6**

Montego Bay
Ocho Rios
Negril
J A M A I C A
Kingston

0   1 mi
0   1 km

Airport ✈ Beach ⌐

To Montego Bay

Bloody Bay

Norman Manley Blvd.

Negril Airport ✈

THE GREAT MORASS

Booby Cay

Hedonism II Beach

A1

PARISH OF HANNOVER
PARISH OF WESTMORELAND

S E V E N   M I L E   B E A C H

Long Bay

Norman Manley Blvd.

Caribbean Sea

South Negril River

Crafts Market

Negril Yacht Club

Post Office
✉

Jamaica Tourist Board ℹ

Sheffield Rd.

Police Station ■

Plaza de Negril

Whitehall Rd.

WHITE HALL

West End Rd.

3 2 1
4
5
7
6
8
9 To Negril Lighthouse ↓

WEST END

the West End where the locals extended their hospitality. But today more sophisticated hotels and all-inclusive resorts like Hedonism II and Sandals Negril draw a better-heeled and less rowdy crowd, including Europeans.

There are really two Negrils: The **West End** is the site of many little eateries, such as Chicken Lavish, and cottages that still receive visitors. The other Negril is the **East End,** which you first approach on the road coming in from Montego Bay. Here are the upscale hotels, with some of the most panoramic beachfronts (such as Negril Gardens).

Chances are you'll stake out a favorite spot along Negril's famed **Seven Mile Beach.** You don't need to get up for anything, as somebody will be along to serve you. Perhaps it'll be the banana lady, with a basket of fruit perched on her head. Maybe the ice-cream man will set up a stand right under a coconut palm. Surely the beer lady will find you as she strolls along with a carton of Jamaican beer on her head, and hordes of young men will peddle illegal ganja whether you smoke it or not. At some point you'll want to explore **Booby Cay** (or Key), a tiny islet off the Negril coast. Once, it was featured in the Walt Disney film *20,000 Leagues Under the Sea,* but now it's overrun with nudists from Hedonism II.

GETTING THERE

If you're going to Negril, you'll fly into **Donald Sangster Airport** in Montego Bay. Some hotels, particularly the all-inclusive resorts, will arrange for airport transfers from that point. Be sure to ask when you book.

If your hotel doesn't provide transfers, you can **fly** to Negril's small airport on the independent carrier **Air Jamaica Express,** booking your connection through Air Jamaica (© 800/523-5585 in the U.S.). The airfare is $45 one-way. Or you can take a **bus;** the fare is $20 for the 2-hour trip. We recommend **Tour Wise** (© 876/979-1027 in Montego Bay, or 876/974-2323 in Ocho Rios).

Or you can **rent a car** and make the 76-mile, 2-hour drive east of Montego Bay. Information on car rentals is given under "Getting There," at the beginning of this chapter. Or you can take a **taxi.** A typical one-way fare from Montego Bay to Ocho Rios is $50 to $60. Always negotiate and agree on a fare *before* getting into the taxi.

ACCOMMODATIONS YOU CAN AFFORD

Banana Shout Resort ⋆ *Finds*   On 2½ acres of landscaped grounds with waterfalls, lily ponds, tropical flowers, and fruit trees, you'll find seven cottages with three units poised on a cliff overlooking the sea. In front of the property is a series of tiered decks with concrete steps leading down the rocks to the water. The garden cottages are across the road, with private access to the beach. Each of the secluded units contains a kitchenette, a good bed with firm mattress, a ceiling fan, and a small bathroom with shower. The rooms are furnished with locally crafted pieces and artwork from Indonesia and Bali. The best deal at this hideaway is the cottage with the patio barbecue. Mark Conklin, the owner, has written a book called *Banana Shout,* a humorous and fictionalized account of his experiences in Negril, building his resort in the early 1970s.

West End Rd. (P.O. Box 4), Negril, Jamaica, W.I. ©/fax 876/957-0384. www.negril.com/bananashout. 7 units. Winter $45–$100 cottage for 1 or 2; $85–$120 cottage for 4; $200 cottage for 8. Off-season $35–$60 cottage for 1 or 2; $60–$70 cottage for 4; $160 cottage for 8. MC, V. *In room:* Kitchenette, ceiling fan.

Blue Cave Castle ⋆ *Value*   Filled with whimsy and fun, this little mock castle may be the Caribbean's best bargain. It's been featured by the Jamaica Tourist Board in its TV ads, and the 1997 Dallas Cowboys cheerleaders calendar was

Fun Fact **Ann Bonney & Her Dirty Dog**

At Bloody Bay, off the coast of Negril, one of the most notorious pirates of all time, Calico Jack Rackham, was finally captured in 1720. His is a name that'll live in infamy, along with Blackbeard's. He was captured with his lover Ann (also Anne) Bonney, the most famous female pirate of all time. (The bay isn't called bloody, however, because of these pirates. Whalers used to disembowel their catch here, turning the waters red with blood.)

After tracking her husband, a penniless ne'er-do-well sailor named James Bonney, to a brothel in the Virgin Islands, Ann slit his throat. However, she soon fell for Capt. Jack Rackham, who was known as Calico Jack. Some say he came by his nickname because of the colorful shirts he wore; others claim it was because of his undershorts.

Until he met this lady pirate, Calico Jack hadn't done so well as a pirate, but she inspired him to greatness. In a short time, they became the scourge of the West Indies. No vessel sailing the Caribbean Sea was too large or too small for them to attack and rob. Ann is said to have fought alongside the men, and she was a much tougher customer than Calico Jack himself. With her cutlass and marlinspike, she was usually the first to board a captured vessel.

Late in October, off the Negril coast, Calico Jack and all the pirates were getting drunk on rum when a British Navy sloop attacked. Calico Jack ran and hid, but Ann fought bravely. She flailed away with battle-ax and cutlass. Calico Jack and the other captured pirates were sentenced to be hanged. Ann, however, pleaded with the court that she was pregnant. Since British law didn't allow the killing of unborn children, she got off though her comrades were sentenced to death.

Her final advice to Calico Jack: "If you'd fought like a man, you wouldn't be hanged like the dirty dog you are." So much for a lover's parting words. Ann's father in Ireland bought her release, and she opened a gaming house in St. Thomas and prospered until the end.

shot here. Battlements and turrets re-create medieval days, and the resort, covering an acre, is built over a cave. There are steps down to the cave from the garden, where wedding receptions are held regularly. The small guest rooms are decorated with handmade mahogany furniture and antique Turkish carpets covering the walls; only three are air-conditioned, but all have sea views and tiny bathrooms with showers. There's no pool, but you can swim off the cliffs in lieu of a beach. An on-site restaurant has closed, but guests interested in cooking can still use the kitchen. If a group of guests staying here would like a barbecue outside, it can be arranged.

Lighthouse Rd., Negril, Jamaica, W.I. © 876/957-4845. www.bluecavecastle.com. 10 units. Winter $50 single; $65 double. Off-season $35 single; $45 double. Extra person $10. No credit cards. *In room:* A/C in 3 units, fridge, ceiling fans.

Devine Destiny About 550 yards from the West End cliffs, this funky retreat in a medley of styles is about a 20-minute walk from the beach; there's a shuttle to Seven Mile Beach. The two-story structure with a terra-cotta roof is surrounded by gardens where wedding receptions are often held. The motel-like rooms are furnished in a standard style, and although most are small, all are comfortable and boast patios or balconies; the shower-only bathrooms are tiny. The suites are the best deal, with ceiling fans, kitchens, living rooms with pull-out beds, TVs, and patios. The most expensive rooms are air-conditioned. The restaurant serves simple fare three times a day.

Summerset Rd., West End (P.O. Box 117), Negril, Jamaica, W.I. ✆ **876/957-9184**. Fax 876/957-3846. www.devinedestiny.com. 44 units. Winter $77–$88 single or double; $180 suite. Off-season $58–$69 single or double; $125 suite. Children 11 and under stay free in parents' room. AE, MC, V. **Amenities:** Restaurant, 2 bars, pool, TV room, games room, tour desk, room service, babysitting. *In room:* Fridge, ceiling fans.

Drumville Cove Resort   This resort overlooks the sea near the lighthouse. All the medium-size rooms and cottages have radios, ceiling fans, and tiny shower-only bathrooms, but only seven of the rooms and none of the cottages are air-conditioned; four rooms offer TVs. These basic lodgings are furnished with a mixture of wicker and hardwood and decorated with floral prints. The mattresses could stand to be replaced, but the beds are generally comfortable. Included on the property is a restaurant that serves Jamaican specialties and a few American dishes. The nearest beach is a 5-minute car ride away (the hotel provides transportation).

West End Rd. (P.O. Box 72), Negril, Jamaica, W.I. ✆ **876/957-0198**. Fax 876/929-7291. www.negril.com/dcmain.htm. 25 units. Winter $65–$95 single or double. Off-season $55–$70 single or double. AE, MC, V. **Amenities:** Restaurant. *In room:* Ceiling fans, radio.

Home Sweet Home   On the cliff side, 1½ miles from the town center, this cozy down-home place at times seems to re-create Negril's 1960s hippie heyday. You may find your groove here, as writer Terry McMillan did when she visited many little inns while researching *How Stella Got Her Groove Back*. Home Sweet Home is a single pink concrete building with a garden with lots of greenery and flowering plants. Each cramped accommodation has a routine bed, a shower-only bathroom, and a balcony or veranda. There's a sun deck on the cliffs, and swimming, diving, and snorkeling are possible. A simple restaurant serves three inexpensive Jamaican-style meals a day.

West End Rd., Negril, Jamaica, W.I. ✆ **800/925-7418** in the U.S., or 876/957-4478. Fax 800/925-7418. www.homesweethomeresort.net. 14 units. Winter $100–$120 single or double. Off-season $65–$80 single or double. Extra person $15; children 11 and under stay free in parents' room. AE, DC, MC, V. **Amenities:** Restaurant, bar, pool, Jacuzzi, watersports. *In room:* Ceiling fans, radio/cassette player.

Ocean Edge Resort Hotel   On a cliff on the West End Road across from Kaiser's Café, this hotel offers simple small accommodations in a laid-back atmosphere. They're modestly decorated in a tropical motif, with hardwood furnishings, decent beds, and compact shower-only bathrooms. If you must have air-conditioning, don't stay in one of the villa rooms, which are cooled only by ceiling fans. The suite and villas have kitchenettes. The Seven Seas restaurant specializes in fresh seafood. The hotel provides transportation to and from the beach, a 5-minute drive away.

West End Rd. (P.O. Box 71), Negril, Jamaica, W.I. ✆ **876/957-4362**. Fax 876/957-0086. www.negril.com/oemain.htm. 28 units. Winter $65 single or double; $120 villa; $75 suite. Off-season $55 single or double; $100 villa; $65 suite. Children 11 and under stay free in parents' unit. AE, MC, V. **Amenities:** Restaurant; pool, Jacuzzi, beach shuttle. *In room:* TV, ceiling fans.

Rockhouse ★★   This funky boutique inn stands in stark contrast to the hedonistic all-inclusive resorts such as Sandals, and offers very affordable rates.

It seems like a cross between a South Seas island retreat and an African village, with thatched roofs capping stone-and-pine huts. A team of enterprising young Aussies restored and expanded this place, which was one of Negril's first hotels (the Stones hung out here in the 1970s). The rooms have ceiling fans, four-poster beds draped in mosquito netting, and open-air showers. One cottage is divided into two studios; other units contain queen-size beds. A quarter mile from the beach, Rockhouse has a ladder down to a cove where you can swim and snorkel. After a refreshing dip in the cliff-side pool, you can dine in the open-sided restaurant pavilion that serves spicy and excellent local fare three times a day.

West End Rd. (P.O. Box 24), Negril, Jamaica, W.I. ⓒ/fax 876/957-4373. www.rockhousehotel.com. 28 units. Winter $120 studio; $195 villa. Off-season $85 studio; $120 villa. Children 11 and under stay free in parents' unit. AE, MC, V. **Amenities:** Restaurant, 2 bars, pool, snorkeling. *In room:* Fridge, safe, ceiling fans, no phone.

Thrills   Southwest of Negril's center, on palm-dotted land sloping toward a rocky beach, this is a simple but well-managed resort. Its centerpiece is a hex-agonal tower adjacent to a low-slung motel-like complex. Each rather small room has white walls, island-made mahogany furniture, louvered doors, and tiled floors. Bathrooms are small, with a shower stall. An in-house restaurant serves international cuisine. Beach-lovers take a 10-minute drive (or a 20-min. walk) east to Negril's legendary beach. Snorkelers, however, find ample oppor-tunities for pursuing their favorite sport off the low cliffs and caves along the coast. The resort has its own tennis courts, and a wide choice of dive shops and watersports facilities is nearby.

West End (P.O. Box 99, Negril), Westmoreland, Jamaica, W.I. ⓒ 876/957-4390. Fax 876/957-4153. www. negril.com/thrills. 25 units. Winter $65 single; $75 double; $85 triple. Off-season $45 single or double; $55 triple. MAP $21 per person. MC, V. **Amenities:** Restaurant, tennis courts, access to watersports. *In room:* No phone.

GREAT DEALS ON DINING

Chicken Lavish ⭐⭐ *Finds* JAMAICAN   We've found that Chicken Lavish, whose name we love, is the best of the low-budget eateries. Just show up on the doorstep of this place along the West End beach strip, and see what's cooking. Curried goat is a specialty, as is fresh fried fish. The red snapper is caught in local waters. But the big draw is the restaurant's namesake, the chef's special Jamaican chicken. He'll tell you, and you may agree, that it's the best on the island. Ironically, this utterly unpretentious restaurant has achieved something like cult status among counterculture travelers who have eaten here since the 1970s. It's amazingly consistent, specializing in chicken, chicken, and more chicken that's fried, served with curry, or with sweet and sour sauce. Dine on the roofed-over veranda if you want, or ask for takeout and dine back at your room.

West End Rd. ⓒ 876/957-4410. Main courses $5–$13. MC, V. Daily 10am–10pm.

Choices JAMAICAN   This no-frills open-air restaurant offers a bustling atmosphere and simple local food in hearty portions. You'll pay about $5 to $6 for breakfast, which includes ackee and salt codfish prepared with Jamaican spices, onions, green peppers, and tomatoes. Daily soup specials might include pumpkin or red pea. For a real island experience, try the spicy jerk chicken, fish, or lobster. Other dishes may be stewed beef, curried goat, or a dish of oxtail. Most dishes come with salad and a choice of vegetable.

West End Rd. ⓒ 876/957-4841. Main courses $4.20–$11.20. Daily 7am–11pm.

Cosmo's Seafood Restaurant & Bar ☆☆ SEAFOOD/JAMAICAN One of the best places to go for local seafood is centered on a Polynesian thatched *bohio* (beach hut) that's open to the sea and borders the main beachfront. In this rustic setting, Cosmo Brown entertains locals as well as visitors. You can order his famous conch soup, or conch in a number of other ways, including steamed or curried. He's also known for his savory kettle of curried goat, or you might prefer freshly caught seafood or fish, depending on what the catch turned up. Unless you order expensive shellfish, most dishes are rather cheap, making this place a friend of the budget traveler.

Norman Manley Blvd. ✆ 876/957-4784. Main courses $7–$31. AE, MC, V. Daily 9am–10pm.

Hungry Lion ☆ JAMAICAN/INTERNATIONAL Some of the best seafood and vegetarian dishes are found at this laid-back alfresco hangout on the cliffs. The first floor of this green concrete-and-wood building has an open-air section with booths inside, but on the second floor it's all windows. Menus change daily, depending on what's available in the markets. About seven main courses are offered nightly—not only seafood and vegetarian platters, but many tasty chicken dishes as well, and even shepherd's pie, pasta primavera, grilled kingfish steak, and pan-fried snapper. Lobster is prepared in many ways, and everything is accompanied by rice and peas, along with steamed vegetables. The homemade desserts are luscious, especially the pineapple-carrot cake, our favorite. You can visit the juice bar and sample the tropical punches. The restaurant may be closed for parts of September, October, and November; closings depend on the whim of the staff, so call to see if they're open before heading here.

West End Rd. ✆ 876/957-4486. Main courses $8.50–$18. MC, V. Daily 5–10pm.

Mariners Inn & Restaurant (*Value* JAMAICAN/AMERICAN/CONTINEN-TAL Many people escaping from their all-inclusive dining rooms head here, looking for some authentic Jamaican flavor. The bar is shaped like a boat, and you enter the adjoining restaurant through a tropical garden. As you drink or dine, the sea breezes waft in. The one appetizer is a bacon-wrapped banana, not everybody's favorite way to begin a meal, but the food picks up considerably after that. The chef knows how to use curry effectively in the lobster and chicken dishes, and even the goat. The *coq au vin* has never been to France, so you're better off sticking to dishes like pan-fried snapper or fried chicken.

West End Rd. ✆ 876/957-0392. Pizzas $6.50–$10.25; main courses $8–$20; all-you-can-eat dinner buffet $14. AE, MC, V. Daily 8am–10pm.

Margueritaville ☆ AMERICAN/INTERNATIONAL It's practically Disney-gone-Jamaican at this rowdy bar, restaurant, and entertainment complex. Thanks to the loaded buses that pull in as a field trip from some of Negril's all-inclusive hotels, it's a destination in its own right. People party here all day and night. There's an on-site art gallery, where most of the works are by the very talented American-born artist Geraldine Robbins, and gift shops where you might actually be tempted to buy something. Every evening, beginning around 9pm, there's live music or perhaps karaoke. Permanently moored a few feet offshore is a pair of Jamaica's largest trampolines, whale-sized floaters that feature high-jumping contests. Drinks are deceptively potent. In all this party atmosphere, you don't expect the food to be that good, but it might happily surprise you, even though it consists of such fare as a shrimp and tuna kebab. Try the Southern fried chicken, the "Pacific paella," or a club steak or burger.

Norman Manley Blvd. ✆ 876/957-4467. Burgers and sandwiches $6.50–$8.50; main courses $13–$26. AE, MC, V. Daily 9am–11pm.

The Pickled Parrot MEXICAN/JAMAICAN/AMERICAN You know you'll have a night of fun at a place called The Pickled Parrot. The restaurant stands at the edge of a cliff and is open to the trade winds, and there's a rope swing and a water slide for fun outside. Slot machines inside add to the funky ambience. The cook claims he serves the best lobster fajitas in town (we agree). You can also order the usual burgers, sandwiches, and freshly made salads at lunch. Actually, you can order the full dinner menu at lunch if you like. They prepare a predictable array of burritos and nachos, but you might be tempted by the fresh fish, lobster or shrimp Jamaican-style, and famous jerk chicken.

West End Rd. (*C* 876/957-4864. Main courses $6–$24. AE, MC, V. Daily 10am–10pm.

Rick's Café ✪ SEAFOOD/STEAKS At sundown, everybody in Negril heads toward the lighthouse along the West End strip to Rick's Café, whether they want a meal or not. Of course, the name was inspired by the old watering hole of Bogie's *Casablanca.* There was a real Rick (Richard Hershman), who first opened this bar back in 1974, but he's long gone. This laid-back cafe was made famous in the '70s as a hippie hangout, and ever since it's attracted the bronzed and the beautiful (and some who want to be). The sunset here is said to be the most glorious in Negril, and after a few fresh-fruit daiquiris (pineapple, banana, or papaya), you'll agree. Casual dress is the order of the day, and reggae and rock compose the background music. If you want dinner, you can order imported steaks along with a complete menu of blackened dishes, Cajun style. The fish (red snapper, fresh lobster, or grouper) is always fresh. The food is rather standard fare, and expensive for what you get, but that hardly keeps the touristy crowds away from the sunset party. You can also buy plastic bar tokens at the door, which you can use instead of money, a la Club Med. A bit tacky, we'd say. Bogie would never have tolerated this.

West End Rd. (*C* 876/957-0380. Reservations accepted for parties of 6 or more. Main courses $12–$28. AE, MC, V. Daily noon–10pm.

Sweet Spice ✪ *Finds* JAMAICAN This is everybody's favorite mom-and-pop eatery, a hangout beloved by locals as well as scantily clad visitors. The Whytes welcome guests warmly and serve them good food in an alfresco setting. The portions are large and most satisfying. You get what's on the stove or in the kettle that night, perhaps the fresh catch of the day or conch steak. The grilled chicken is done to perfection, and shrimp is served with garlic butter or cooked in coconut cream. A number of curry dishes tempt, like concoctions made with goat, lobster, and chicken. Meals come with freshly cooked Jamaica-grown vegetables. The fruit juices (in lieu of alcoholic beverages) are truly refreshing.

1 White Hall Rd. (*C* 876/957-4621. Main courses $5.50–$17. MC, V. Daily 8:30am–10:30pm.

Tenby Beach Bar & Restaurant JAMAICAN/INTERNATIONAL The Lawrences, a native family who offer warm hospitality, own this waterfront restaurant decorated in cool tones of blue and white. You can get a variety of dishes, including stewed chicken with brown gravy (similar to chicken fricassee but a little spicier) and curried chicken and goat. The islanders recommend the seafood. You can order lobster in a variety of ways, like curried, grilled with butter sauce, with garlic, or Thermidor. If you don't see what you want on the menu, just ask—any reasonable request will be granted. The portions are huge, and the atmosphere is inviting.

West End Rd. (*C* 876/957-4372. Reservations recommended. Main courses $6–$20. MC, V. Daily 8:30am–8pm.

Value Cheap Thrills: What You Can See & Do for Free (Well, Almost) on Jamaica

- **A Visit to Cockpit Country.** Only 15 miles inland from Montego Bay on the south coast is the Caribbean's most primitive and undeveloped area. Nature created this harsh terrain with pitfalls and potholes carved in limestone, which evoked a cockpit where cock fights were staged. Once it was known as the Land of Look Behind, because English soldiers were always nervous when riding through here and they were constantly looking over their shoulders. The region was settled by the fierce Maroons, fugitive slaves who refused to surrender to invading British troops and were in a state of constant war. The descendants of these historic freedom fighters continue to live in the area, just as ungoverned today as they were back then; no one pays taxes, for example. Head for their main hamlet at Accompong, where you can walk through the village and look at a few historic structures. You'll meet some of the Maroons, known as the island's finest herbalists.

- **Experience Market Day in Falmouth.** Lying 23 miles east of Montego Bay, this town, with its decaying Georgian architecture, is like a place time forgot. The best time to arrive is on Wednesday morning, when it hosts the country's biggest flea market, with hundreds of booths linking the marketplace and overflowing into the streets. Buyers from all over the island flock here to pick up bargains (later sold at inflated prices). Named after the British birthplace in Cornwall of Trelawny's parish's first governor, it still evokes a nostalgic atmosphere of the early 18th century. The most interesting buildings lie along Market Street near Water Square. Take time out to buy a loaf of *bammy* (cassava bread) and pick up the makings of a picnic.

- **Spend an Afternoon on Errol Flynn's Island.** The swashbuckling star who gave the world the expression "in like Flynn" may no longer be around, but his island—reached by a short boat ride—still lies off the coast of Port Antonio. Navy Island was once his hideaway. Of course, he didn't wear his famous green tights from *Robin Hood* here. Actually, according to reports, he didn't wear much at all. You can do the same when you visit the island if you go to its nudie beach, known as Trembly Knee Cove. There's also a non-nudie beach. The restaurant and bar feature plenty of posters of Flynn's movies.

HITTING THE BEACHES

Beloved by the hippies of the 1970s, **Seven Mile Beach** ★★ is still going strong, but it's no longer the idyllic retreat it once was. Resorts now line this beach, attracting an international crow. Nudity, however, is just as prevalent as it's always been, especially along the stretch near Cosmo's. There's a carefree, laid-back vibe in the air. On the western tip of the island, the white powdery sand stretches from Blood Bay in Hanover to Negril Lighthouse in Westmoreland; clean, tranquil aquamarine waters, coral reefs, and a backdrop of palm trees add

- **Swim in the Blue Lagoon.** Remember the young Brooke Shields? She made the film *The Blue Lagoon* in a calm, protected cove 10 miles east of Port Antonio. The water is so deep, nearly 20 feet or so, that it turns a cobalt blue; there's almost no more scenic spot in all of Jamaica. The Blue Lagoon, with its small, intimate beach, is a great place for a picnic (you can pick up plenty of jerk pork, smoked at various shacks along the Boston Bay Beach area).

- **Head for the Hellshire Hills.** Southwest of Kingston, reached along the coastal road, the limestone Hellshire Hills are different from the image of lush Jamaica. This is more like Arizona, a terrain of dry cacti and cassia growing in a semi-desert landscape. Many Kingstonians retreat here for the weekend to enjoy its beaches, where they're rarely disturbed by tourists. The backdrop for the Hellshire Hills is filled with salt ponds, mangroves, and undeveloped caves (some with petroglyphs). This is also snake country, including the endemic Jamaican boa, called the yellow snake. It often grows 6 to 8 feet long and is one of the largest in the Caribbean. However, it isn't poisonous. South of Port Henderson, you can take a marked hiking trail up to Rodney's Looking for the most panoramic overview of Kingston and the eastern coast.

- **Bite into Some Jerk Pork.** Wherever you go in Jamaica, you'll encounter ramshackle stands selling jerk pork or jerk chicken. There's no more authentic Jamaican experience than to stop at one of these stands and order a lunch of jerk pork, preferably washed down with a Red Stripe beer. Jerk is a special way Jamaicans have of barbecuing highly spicy meats over a wood fire set in the ground. The Maroons who lived in the mountains are said to have developed this technique. What goes into the seasoning isn't clear, but the taste is definitely of peppers, pimento (allspice), and ginger. The meat is cooked on slats of pimento wood, giving it a unique flavor. You can also order jerk sausage, fish, and even lobster. As you place your order, the cook will haul out a machete and chop the meat into bite-size pieces for you and throw it into a paper bag.

to the appeal. When you tire of the beach, you'll find all sorts of resorts, clubs, beach bars, open-air restaurants, and the like. Vendors will try to sell you everything from Red Stripe beer to ganja.

Many of the big resorts have nude beaches as well. The hottest and most exotic is found at **Hedonism II,** although **Grand Lido** next door draws its fair share. Nude beaches at each of these resorts are in separate and "private" areas of the resort property. Total nudity is required for strolling the beach, and security guards keep peeping Toms at bay. Photography is not permitted.

SCUBA DIVING & SNORKELING

The **Negril Scuba Centre,** in the Negril Beach Club Hotel, Norman Manley Boulevard (© **800/818-2963** or 876/957-9641), is the most modern, best-equipped facility. A professional staff of internationally certified scuba instructors and dive masters teach and guide divers to Negril's colorful coral reefs. Beginners' dive lessons are offered daily, and certified divers can purchase multiple-dive packages. Full scuba certifications and specialty courses are also available. A resort course, designed for first-timers with basic swimming abilities, includes all instruction, equipment, a lecture on water and diving safety, and one open-water dive. It begins at 10am daily and ends at 2pm, costing $75. A one-tank dive costs $30 per dive, plus $20 for equipment rental (not necessary if divers bring their own). More economical is a two-tank dive that must be completed in 1 day, costing $55, plus the optional $20 rental of equipment. This organization is PADI-registered, although it accepts all recognized certification cards.

The best area of **snorkeling** is off the cliffs in the West End. The coral reef here is extremely lively, with marine life at a depth of about 10 to 15 feet. The waters are so clear and sparkling that just by wading in and looking down, you'll see lots of marine life. The fish are small but extremely colorful.

NEGRIL AFTER DARK

Although smaller than Mo Bay, Negril isn't without spots to have a good time, although you're likely to spend most evenings enjoying the entertainment in your own resort. Fun places are easy to find, as nearly *everything* is on Norman Manley Boulevard, the only major road in Negril.

Alfred's, Norman Manley Boulevard (© 876/957-4735), is a truly Jamaican place where travelers will still feel welcome. There's no cover, and in addition to grabbing a drink, you can order a bite to eat until midnight. Particularly interesting is the beach-party area, with a stage for live reggae and jazz acts. You can also boogie on the dance floor inside, shaking to hits you'd hear at clubs stateside.

De Buss, Norman Manley Boulevard (© 876/957-4405), is probably the most popular and versatile hangout on Negril Beach. It was named after the rusted carcass of a Kingston double-decker bus that was hauled to this site in the 1960s. Nearby is an imposing-looking courtyard area flanked with a stage that was bashed together from two-by-fours and plywood, and brightly painted in Rastafarian colors, where live bands perform every Thursday and Saturday in off-season, and virtually every night in winter. You can order heaping and low-priced platters of jerk chicken with french fries, and naturally, the rum and beer flow freely. It's open daily 9am to at least 11pm, and during show nights until at least 1:30am.

Risky Business, Norman Manley Boulevard (© 876/957-3008), sits a few feet from the waves. It can be sleepy or manic, depending on what music is playing. In season, you can order up burgers and sandwiches, and the Red Stripe is cheap all year round. Basically, it's a hangout kind of place whose traditional party nights are Monday, Thursday, and Saturday, beginning at 9pm. There's no cover, even when the place is rocking and rolling.

4 Falmouth

This port town lies on the north coast of Jamaica, only about 23 miles east of Montego Bay. The Trelawny Beach Hotel originally put it on the tourist map (though we no longer recommend staying there). The Georgian town itself is interesting but ramshackle. There's talk about fixing it up for visitors, but no one has done it yet. If you leave your car at Water Square, you can explore the town in about an hour. The present courthouse was reconstructed from the early 19th-century building, and fisherfolk still congregate on Seaboard Street. You'll pass the Customs Office and a parish church dating from the late 18th century. Later you can go on a shopping expedition to Caribatik, outside town.

There's a dearth of accommodations in the area, so visitors usually seek lodgings in Montego Bay.

GREAT DEALS ON DINING

Glistening Waters Inn and Marina ★ (*Finds* SEAFOOD   Residents of Montego Bay often make the 28-mile drive out here, along A1, just to sample the ambience of Old Jamaica. This well-recommended restaurant, with a veranda overlooking the lagoon, is housed in what was a private clubhouse of the aristocrats of nearby Trelawny. The furniture might remind you of a stage set for Tennessee Williams's *Night of the Iguana*. Menu items usually include local fish dishes, like snapper or kingfish, served with *bammy* (a form of cassava bread). Other specialties are three lobster dishes, three preparations of shrimp, three conch viands, fried rice, and pork chops.

The waters of the lagoon here contain a rare form of phosphorescent microbe that, when the waters are agitated, glows in the dark. Ask at the restaurant about evening booze cruises, which cost $10 per person and include one drink and plenty of phosphorescent microbes. Departures are nightly at about 6:30pm. You don't have to be a customer of the restaurant to take these cruises. Anybody can show up and ask to be included for the regular fee.

Rock Falmouth (between Falmouth and the Trelawny Beach Hotel). © 876/954-3229. Main courses $10–$25. AE, MC, V. Daily 9:30am–9:30pm.

RIVER RAFTING NEAR FALMOUTH

Rafting on the **Martha Brae** is an adventure. To reach the starting point from Falmouth, drive approximately 3 miles inland to **Martha Brae's Rafters Village** (© 876/952-0889). The rafts are similar to those on the Río Grande, near Port Antonio, and cost $40 per raft, with two riders allowed on a raft, plus a small child if accompanied by an adult (but use caution). The trips last 1¼ hours and operate daily 9am to 4pm. You sit on a raised dais on bamboo logs. Along the way you can stop and order cool drinks or beer along the banks of the river. You'll find a bar, a restaurant, and two souvenir shops in the village.

SHOPPING

Two miles east of Falmouth on the north-coast road is **Caribatik Island Fabrics,** at Rock Wharf on the Luminous Lagoon (© 876/954-3314). You'll recognize the place easily, as it has a huge sign painted across the building's side. This is the private living and work domain of Keith Chandler, who opened the place with his late wife, Muriel, in 1970. Today the batiks created by Muriel Chandler before her death in 1990 are viewed as stylish and sensual garments by the chic boutiques in the United States. The shop has a full range of fabrics, scarves, garments, and wall hangings, some patterned after such themes as Jamaica's doctor bird and various endangered animal species. Muriel's gallery continues to sell a selection of her original batik paintings. Either Keith or a member of the staff will be glad to describe the intricate process of batiking during their open hours of 9am to 4pm Tuesday to Saturday. They're closed in September and on national holidays.

5 Runaway Bay

Once Runaway Bay was a mere western satellite of Ocho Rios. However, with the opening of some large resort hotels, plus a colony of smaller hostelries, Runaway Bay is now a destination in its own right.

This part of Jamaica's north coast has several distinctions: It was the first part of the island seen by Columbus, the site of the first Spanish settlement on the island, and the point of departure of the last Spaniards leaving Jamaica following their defeat by the British.

Jamaica's most complete equestrian center is the **Chukka Cove Farm and Resort,** at Richmond Llandovery, St. Ann (© **876/972-2506**), less than 4 miles east of Runaway Bay. A 1-hour trail ride costs $30, and a 2-hour mountain ride goes for $40. The most popular ride is a 3-hour beach jaunt where, after riding over trails to the sea, you unpack your horse and swim in the surf. Refreshments are served as part of the $55 charge. A 6-hour beach ride, complete with picnic lunch, goes for $130. Polo lessons are also available, costing $50 for 30 minutes.

ACCOMMODATIONS YOU CAN AFFORD

Caribbean Isle Hotel   This hotel, which is directly on the beach, offers 8 superior and 15 standard rooms, with personalized service in an informal atmosphere. The small, tattered rooms have ocean views and tiny bathrooms with showers, and the so-called superior units have private balconies. The hotel has a TV in the bar-lounge and a dining room leading onto a sea-view patio. Meals are served 7:30am to 11pm daily, with dinner including lobster, fish, shrimp, pork chops, chicken, and local dishes prepared on request. This place is mainly for beach buffs who like to spend most of their time in the outdoors and not much time in the rooms.

P.O. Box 119, Runaway Bay, St. Ann, Jamaica, W.I. © 876/973-2364. Fax 876/973-4835. 23 units. Year-round $65 single or double. AE, MC, V. **Amenities:** Restaurant, bar, TV lounge. *In room:* A/C.

Runaway H.E.A.R.T. Country Club ★★ *Value*   This place wins hands-down as the bargain of the north coast. One of Jamaica's few training and service institutions, the club and its adjacent academy are operated by the government to provide a high level of training for young Jamaicans interested in the hotel trade. The helpful staff of both professionals and trainees offers the finest service of any hotel in the area.

The good-size rooms are bright and airy. Bathrooms have generous shelf space and shower stalls. The accommodations open onto private balconies with views of well-manicured tropical gardens or vistas of the bay and golf course. Guests enjoy having a drink in the piano bar (ever had a cucumber daiquiri?) before heading for the dining room, the Cardiff Hall Restaurant, which serves a superb Jamaican and continental dishes.

Ricketts Ave. (P.O. Box 98), Runaway Bay, St. Ann, Jamaica, W.I. © 876/973-2671. Fax 876/973-2693. runaway.heart@cwjamaica.com. 20 units. Winter $98 single; $125–$144 double. Off-season $90 single; $106–$124 double. Rates include MAP (breakfast and dinner). AE, MC, V. **Amenities:** Restaurant, bar, laundry. *In room:* A/C, TV, safe.

Tamarind Tree Resort Hotel   This small family-style hotel was named after a lavishly blossoming tamarind tree that once grew near its entrance. Red-roofed stucco buildings with awnings and pastel-trimmed balconies house cream-colored and carpeted rooms. The most appealing rooms are on the second floor, where cooling breezes offer refreshment. All units are medium in size and comfortably furnished; the shower-only bathrooms are a bit small. There's a pool terrace, and the nearest beach is within a 5-minute walk. Although the occupants of the cottages usually cook meals in their lodgings, the simple Bird Wing restaurant serves breakfast and dinner. The Stinger is a disco whose drinks and recorded music relieve some of the evening monotony of this out-of-the-way hotel.

P.O. Box 235, Runaway Bay, St. Ann, Jamaica, W.I. ℂ 876/973-4819. Fax 876/973-5013. www.in-site.com/tamtree. 16 units, 3 three-bedroom cottages with kitchenette. Year-round $45 single or double; $165 cottage for up to 6. MC, V. **Amenities:** Restaurant, piano bar, disco, pool. *In room:* A/C, TV.

HITTING THE BEACHES

The two best beaches at Runaway Bay are **Paradise Beach** and **Cardiff Hall Public Beach.** Both have wide strips of white sand and are clean and well maintained. There's a great natural beauty to this part of Jamaica, and many visitors, especially Canadians, seek it out, preferring its more raffish look to the more publicized tourist meccas of Ocho Rios. You don't get a lot of facilities, however, so if you're going to the beach you'd better bring along whatever you need. Both of these beaches are ideal for a picnic. Even if you're staying in Ocho Rios, you might want to escape the crowds and come here.

The waters are calm almost all year, but somehow the noonday sun is fierce, and many visitors from far northern climes report massive sunburns on their first day. They literally turn their northern white bodies into lobster-red colors. Prevailing on-shore trade winds will often keep you cool, especially in the morning and late afternoon. In Ocho Rios some vendor will try to sell you something every 5 minutes. Here they'll leave you alone.

Since there are no lifeguards, be especially careful if you're beaching it with children.

WATERSPORTS

Runaway Bay offers some of the best areas for snorkeling. The reefs are close to shore and extremely lively with marine life, including enormous schools of tropical fish like blue chromis, trigger fish, small skate rays, and snapper. Since boats and fishing canoes can be a problem close to shore, you can go on a snorkeling excursion with the best diving facility at Runaway Bay. Try **Resort Divers** in Runaway Bay (ℂ **876/974-5338**) along the beach. This five-star PADI facility takes you out to one of several protected reefs where the water currents aren't dangerous and where fishing boats are required to stay at least 200 yards away from snorkelers. Resort Divers also provides sport-fishing jaunts as well as scuba-diving certification and equipment. A resort dive costs $85; a one-tank dive goes for $35 or a two-tank dive costs $65. Parasailing is available, at $45 per half hour.

EXPLORING THE AREA

Columbus Park Museum, on Queens Highway in Discovery Bay (ℂ **876/973-2135**), is a large open area between the main coast road and the sea. You just pull off the road and walk among the fantastic collection of exhibits; admission is free. There's everything from a canoe made of a solid piece of cottonwood (the way Arawaks did it more than 5 centuries ago) to a stone cross that was placed on the Barrett estate at Retreat (9 miles east of Montego Bay) by Edward Barrett, brother of poet Elizabeth Barrett Browning. You'll see a tally, used to count bananas carried on men's heads from plantation to ship, as well as a planter's strongbox with a weighted lead base to prevent its theft. Other items are 18th-century cannons, a Spanish water cooler and calcifier, a fish pot made from bamboo, a corn husker, and a water wheel. Pimento trees, from which allspice is produced, dominate the park, which is open daily 8:30am to 4:30pm.

You can also visit the **Seville Great House,** Heritage Park (© **876/ 972-2191**), open daily 9am to 5pm. Built in 1745 by the English, the house contains a collection of artifacts once used by everybody from the Amerindians to African slaves. You're treated to an exhibit of 5 centuries worth of Jamaican history. Modest for a Great House, it has a wattle-and-daub construction. A small theater presents a 15-minute historical film about the house. Admission is $4.

6 Ocho Rios (★)

The north-coast resort town of Ocho Rios is a 2-hour drive east of Montego Bay or west of Port Antonio. Ocho Rios was once a small banana and fishing port, but tourism became the leading industry long ago. Short on charm, Ocho Rios is now Jamaica's cruise-ship capital. The bay is dominated on one side by a bauxite-loading terminal and on the other by a range of hotels with sandy beaches fringed with palm trees.

Ocho Rios and neighboring Port Antonio have long been associated with celebrities. Its two most famous writers are Sir Noël Coward, who invited the world to his doorstep, and Ian Fleming, creator of James Bond (see "Exploring the Area," below, for details about their homes here).

Unless you're on a cruise ship, you might want to stay away from the major attractions on cruise ship days. Even the duty-free shopping markets are overrun then, and the hustlers become more strident in promoting their crafts, often junk souvenirs. Dunn's River Falls becomes almost impossible to visit at those times. However, Ocho Rios has its own unique flavor and offers the usual range of sports, including a major fishing tournament every fall, in addition to a wide variety of accommodations.

If you're going to Ocho Rios, you'll fly into the **Donald Sangster Airport** in Montego Bay. Some hotels, particularly the larger resorts, will arrange for airport transfers from that point. Be sure to ask when you book.

If your hotel doesn't provide transfers, you can take a **bus** for $25 one-way. We recommend **Tour Wise** (© **876/979-1027** in Montego Bay, or 876/ 974-2323 in Ocho Rios). The bus will drop you off at your hotel. The trip takes 2 hours. You can **rent a car** for the 67-mile drive east along A1 (see "Getting There," at the beginning of this chapter). Or you can take a **taxi;** the typical one-way fare from Montego Bay is $70, but always negotiate and agree on a fare *before* you get into the taxi.

ACCOMMODATIONS YOU CAN AFFORD

Hibiscus Lodge Hotel (★★) This inn offers more value for your money than any other resort at Ocho Rios. The intimate little inn, perched precariously on a cliff along the shore 3 blocks from the Ocho Rios Mall, has character and charm. All medium-size bedrooms, either doubles or triples, have small, shower-only bathrooms and verandas that open to the sea.

After a day spent in a pool suspended over the cliffs, or lounging on the large sundeck, guests can enjoy a drink in the unique swinging bar. The owners provide dining at the Almond Tree Restaurant (see "Great Deals on Dining," below).

83 Main St. (P.O. Box 52), Ocho Rios, St. Ann, Jamaica, W.I. © **876/974-2676.** Fax 876/974-1874. mdoswald@cwjamaica.com. 27 units. Winter $111–$126 single or double; $157 triple. Off-season $99 single or double; $135 triple. Rates include breakfast. AE, DC, MC, V. **Amenities:** Restaurant, bar, tennis court, Jacuzzi. *In room:* A/C, TV, ceiling fans.

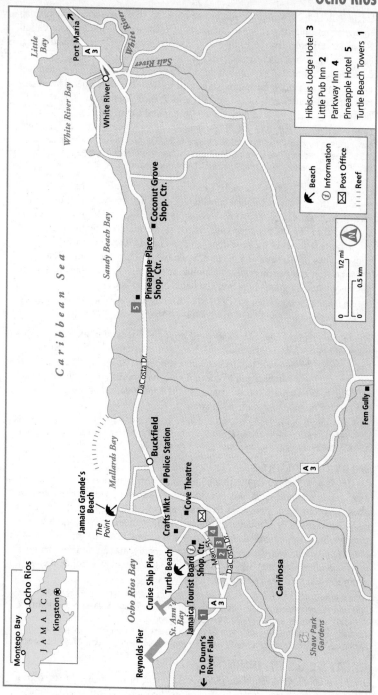

Ocho Rios

Hibiscus Lodge Hotel 3
Little Pub Inn 2
Parkway Inn 4
Pineapple Hotel 5
Turtle Beach Towers 1

↖ Beach
ⓘ Information
☒ Post Office
‖‖‖ Reef

N

0   1/2 mi
0   0.5 km

Little Bay

Port Maria

A 3

White River

White River

Salt River

White River Bay

Coconut Grove Shop. Ctr.

Sandy Beach Bay

Pineapple Place Shop. Ctr.

5

C a r i b b e a n   S e a

DaCosta Dr.

Fern Gully ■

Buckfield

Police Station

Mallards Bay

Jamaica Grande's Beach

The Point

Cove Theatre

Crafts Mkt. ■

☒

A 3

2 3 4

Ocho Rios Bay

Turtle Beach

Cruise Ship Pier

Jamaica Tourist Board ⓘ Shop. Ctr.

Main St.

DaCosta Dr.

Cariñosa

Shaw Park Gardens

St. Ann's Bay

Reynolds Pier

1

A 3

↓ To Dunn's River Falls

Montego Bay

o Ocho Rios

J A M A I C A

Kingston ✪

Little Pub Inn   If you don't mind some noise, try this place, which offers small rooms at sensible prices. It's in the heart of town next to the Jamaica Grand Renaissance Resort, in the Little Pub Complex, which includes a small night-club, slot machines, and a restaurant with indoor and outdoor dining. The air-conditioned rooms have a tropical decor with good beds; some have small bed lofts reached by ladder. Each unit has a small bathroom with shower. The restau-rant serves international cuisine and a few local specialties; guests receive a VIP card for a 15% discount at both the restaurant and the nightclub.

59 Main St. (P.O. Box 256), Ocho Rios, St. Ann, Jamaica, W.I. © 876/974-2324. Fax 876/974-5825. www.caribbean-travel.com/littlepub. 22 units. Year-round $44–$70 single or double. Extra person $20 winter, $15 off-season; children 11 and under stay free in parents' room. Higher rates include full American break-fast. AE, MC, V. **Amenities:** Restaurant, nightclub, slot machines. *In room:* A/C, TV.

Parkway Inn   Built in the early 1990s in the heart of town, this hotel offers rooms in the basic motel tradition, with well-used mattresses, but it's one of the area's best deals. The shower-only bathrooms are cramped. Although no resort-style facilities are on site, guests are invited to use the pool, tennis courts, and watersports facilities at the next-door Jamaica Grand Hotel and any of the Ocho Rios beaches (the nearest is a 10-min. walk away). There's a Chinese/Jamaican restaurant on the premises, serving simple meals, plus a third-floor bar where guests can enjoy a grand view over the lights of Ocho Rios.

Main St., Ocho Rios, St. Ann, Jamaica, W.I. © 876/974-2667. 21 units. Year-round $60–$65 single or double. AE, MC, V. **Amenities:** Restaurant, bar, access to nearby pool, tennis courts, and watersports. *In room:* A/C, TV.

Pineapple Hotel   Next door to the Pineapple Place Shopping Centre, this hotel offers no frills—just tropically decorated quarters with tiny bathrooms, decent beds, shower-only bathrooms, and tile floors. The Pineapple Pizza Pub is on site, serving a combination of cuisines with Italian, American, and Jamaican influences. Watersports can be arranged at the front desk. For a seaside romp, try Turtle Beach, a 20-minute walk away.

Pineapple Place (P.O. Box 263), Ocho Rios, St. Ann, Jamaica, W.I. © 876/974-2727. Fax 876/974-1706. 20 units. Year-round $50 single or double; $62.50 triple. Children 11 and under stay free in parents' room. AE, MC, V. **Amenities:** Restaurant; pool, watersports. *In room:* A/C, TV.

WORTH A SPLURGE

Turtle Beach Towers ★★   In a commercial district opposite the cruise ship pier, these medium-sized accommodations with equipped kitchenettes are housed in four high-rise towers that offer apartment living with the bonus of daily maid service. Mattresses are firm, and maintenance is most acceptable. The compact bathrooms are tiled and have tub-and-shower combinations. The prop-erty has a beach, and the on-site restaurant serves Jamaican and international specialties for breakfast, lunch, and dinner. On Tuesday evening, there's a complimentary manager's rum-punch party.

DaCosta Dr. (P.O. Box 73), Ocho Rios, St. Ann, Jamaica, W.I. © 876/974-2801. Fax 876/974-2806. www. jamaicaresorts.com/turtlebeach. 116 apts. Winter $110–$125 studio apt; $126–$155 1-bedroom apt; $198–$212 2-bedroom apt. Off-season $82–$88 studio apt; $88–$112 1-bedroom apt; $132–$152 2-bedroom apt. Children 11 and under stay free in parents' apt (no children in studio apts). AE, MC, V. **Amenities:** Restaurant; pool, lighted tennis courts, watersports, maid service. *In room:* A/C, TV, kitchenette.

GREAT DEALS ON DINING

BiBiBips   INTERNATIONAL/JAMAICAN   Set in the main tourist strip of Ocho Rios, this restaurant (whose name is the owner's nickname) occupies a sprawling open-air compound of porches and verandas. Lots of single folks come just to hang out at the bar. Drinks and flirtations sometimes segue into dinner at the adjacent restaurant, where well-prepared menu items include Red Stripe shrimp, which is deep-fried in beer-based batter; coconut-curried chicken; vegetarian Rasta Pasta; and a combination Creole-style seafood platter. Lunches are a bit simpler, focusing mostly on sandwiches, salads, and an especially delicious jerk chicken burger. There's live entertainment, usually some kind of rap or reggae band, every Friday, Saturday, and Sunday, beginning at 8pm.

93 Main St. (*) 876/974-8759. Lunch main courses J$230–J$1,092 ($5–$22.50); dinner main courses J$264–J$1,265 ($5.75–$27.75). AE, MC, V. Daily 11am–5:30pm and 6–11:30pm.

Little Pub Restaurant ⭐ JAMAICAN/INTERNATIONAL   Located in a redbrick courtyard with a fishpond and a waterfall in the center of town, this indoor-outdoor pub's centerpiece is a restaurant in the dinner-theater style. Top local and international artists are featured, as are Jamaican musical plays. No one will mind if you just enjoy a drink while seated on one of the pub's barrel chairs. But if you want dinner, proceed to a linen-covered table topped with cut flowers and candles. We are fond of the barbecued chicken and the grilled kingfish, but you might opt for the stewed snapper or the freshly caught lobster.

In the Little Pub Inn, 59 Main St. (*) 876/974-2324. Reservations recommended. Main courses $12–$28. AE, DC, MC, V. Daily 8pm–midnight.

Ocho Rios Village Jerk Centre ⭐ *Finds* JAMAICAN   At this open-air restaurant, you can get the best jerk dishes on this part of the coast. When only a frosty Red Stripe beer can quench your thirst or the fiery taste of Jamaican jerk seasonings ease your stomach growls, head here. Don't dress up and don't expect anything fancy: It's the food that counts, and you'll find fresh daily specials posted on a chalkboard menu on the wall. If a cruise ship is in port, the place is likely to be swamped with passengers, so it's better to go in the evening. The food is hot and spicy, but not overly so; hot spices are presented on the side for those who want to go truly Jamaican. The barbecued ribs are especially good, and the perfectly grilled fresh fish is a delight. Vegetarian dishes are available on request, and if you don't want beer, you can wash it all down with natural fruit juices.

DaCosta Dr. (*) 876/974-2549. Jerk pork $3 for ¼ lb, $11 for 1 lb; whole jerk chicken $14. MC, V. Daily 10am–11pm.

Parkway Restaurant *Value* JAMAICAN   Come here to eat as Jamaicans eat. This popular spot in the commercial center of town couldn't be plainer or more unpretentious, but it's always packed. Locals know they can get some of Ocho Rios's best and most affordable dishes here. It's the local watering hole, and the regulars are a bit disdainful of all those Sandals and Couples resorts, with their contrived international food. Hungry diners dig into straightforward fare such as Jamaican-style chicken, curried goat, sirloin steak, and fillet of red snapper, topping it all off with banana cream pie. The restaurant recently renovated its third floor to offer entertainment and dancing. Tuesday's Reggae Night lets local bands do their best "to let the groove ooze," as they say here.

At the Parkway Inn, 60 DaCosta Dr. (*) 876/974-2667. Lunch main courses $6–$11.25; dinner main courses $6.50–$22.25. AE, MC, V. Daily 8am–11:30pm.

WORTH A SPLURGE

Almond Tree Restaurant ⭐⭐ INTERNATIONAL   The Almond Tree is a two-tiered patio restaurant with a tree growing through the roof. Lobster Thermidor is the most delectable item on the menu, but we also like the bouillabaisse (made with conch and lobster). Other excellent choices are the roast suckling pig, medallions of beef Anne Palmer, and a fondue *bourguignonne.* Jamaican plantation rice is a local specialty. The wine list offers a variety of vintages, including Spanish and Jamaican. Have a cocktail in the unique "swinging bar" (with swinging chairs, that is).

In the Hibiscus Lodge Hotel, 83 Main St. © 876/974-2813. Reservations recommended for dinner. Main courses $16–$37. AE, MC, V. Daily 7:30–10:30am, noon–2:30pm, and 6–9:30pm.

HITTING THE BEACHES

The most idyllic sands are found at the often-overcrowded **Mallards Bay Beach,** shared by hotel guests and cruise ship passengers, but locals may steer you to the white sands of **Turtle Beach** in the south. Turtle Beach lies between the Renaissance Jamaica Grande and Club Jamaica. This is where the islanders themselves go to swim. The most frequented (and to be avoided when cruise ships are in port) is **Dunn's River Beach,** located below the famous falls. Another great spot is **Jamaica Grande's Beach,** which is open to the public. Parasailing is a favorite sport on this beach.

Many exhibitionistic couples check into the famous but pricey **Couples Resort,** known for its private *au naturel* island. A shuttle boat transports visitors offshore to this beautiful little island with a fine sandy beach. A bar, pool, and hot tub on the island are found just a few hundred yards offshore from Couples. Security guards keep the gawkers from bothering guests on this beach.

We always follow the trail of 007 and head for our favorite: **James Bond Beach** (© 876/975-3663), east of Ocho Rios at Oracabessa Beach. Entrepreneur Chris Blackwell reopened writer Ian Fleming's former home, Goldeneye, and the master spy-thriller writer himself often used this beach. For $5, nonguests can enjoy its sand strip any day except Monday. Admission includes a free drink (beer or soda) and use of the changing room. There's also a watersports rental center.

Under a thatched palm roof you can enjoy local specialties: Try the grilled fish and finish off with a local specialty, the *bammy* cake. You can also visit the bar just for drinks, like the Goldfinger (pineapple and orange juices mixed with rum), the Moonraker (a strawberry-flavored rum drink), or the 007 (for this you've got to take a chance, since the bartender refuses to divulge the ingredients).

SPORTS & OTHER OUTDOOR PURSUITS

SNORKELING & SCUBA DIVING The best outfitter is **Resort Divers Shop,** Main Street, Turtle Beach (© 876/974-6632), at the Club Jamaica Resort. The skilled staff can hook you up with dive trips or snorkeling. The best spot for either of these sports is 200 yards offshore (you'll be transported there). A boat leaving daily at 1pm goes to Paradise Reef, where tropical fish are plentiful. Of course, bad weather can lead to a cancellation.

TENNIS **Ciboney Ocho Rios,** Main Street, Ocho Rios (© 876/974-1027), focuses more on tennis than any other area resort. It offers three clay-surface and three hard-surface courts, all lit for nighttime play. Guests play free either day or night, but nonguests must call and make arrangements with the manager. A pro offers lessons for $25 an hour. Ciboney also sponsors twice-a-day clinics for both beginners and advanced players. Frequent guest tournaments are also staged, including handicapped doubles and mixed doubles.

EXPLORING THE AREA

Goldeneye at Oracabessa, St. Mary's (© 876/974-3354), is not open to the public unless you rent one of the 11 units. Yet it's one of the most asked-about sights.

Noël Coward was a frequent guest of Ian Fleming at Goldeneye, made fashionable in the 1950s. It was here in 1952 that the most famous secret agent in the world, 007, was born. Fleming built the house in 1946 and wrote each of the 13 original Bond books in it. Through the large gates with bronze pineapples on the top came a host of international celebs, including Evelyn Waugh, Truman Capote, and Graham Greene. The house was closed and dilapidated for some time after the writer's death, but its present owner, British music publisher Christopher Blackwell, has restored the property. Although Fleming kept the place "just back to the basics," Blackwell sought the help of a designer to revamp the interior. With East Asia, including Timor, as the theme, the place now contains oversized bamboo sofas, totem-like Japanese obisps, and the like. Fleming's original desk, where 007 was born, remains. Look for the Esso (not Exxon) sign and take the narrow lane nearby going to the sea. Since you can't go inside Goldeneye, you might want to settle for a swim at James Bond Beach (see "Hitting the Beaches," above).

A scenic drive south of Ocho Rios along A3 takes you inland through **Fern Gully.** This was originally a riverbed, but now the main road winds up some 700 feet among a profusion of wild ferns, a tall rain forest, hardwood trees, and lianas. There are hundreds of varieties of ferns, and roadside stands offer fruit and vegetables, carved-wood souvenirs, and basketwork. The road runs for about 4 miles, and then at the top of the hill you come to a right turn onto a narrow road leading to **Golden Grove,** a small Jamaican community with a bauxite mine that is of no touristic interest.

Head west when you see the signs pointing to **Lyford,** a small community southwest of Ocho Rios. To approach it, take A3 south until you come to a small intersection directly north of Walkers Wood. Follow the signpost west to Lyford. You'll pass the remains of **Edinburgh Castle,** built in 1763, the lair of one of Jamaica's most infamous murderers, a Scot named Lewis Hutchinson who used to shoot passersby and toss their bodies into a deep pit. The authorities got wind of his activities, and although he tried to escape by canoe, he was captured by the navy under the command of Admiral Rodney and was hanged. Rather proud of his achievements (evidence of at least 43 murders was found), he left £100 and instructions for a memorial to be built. It never was, but the castle ruins remain.

Continue north on A1 to **St. Ann's Bay,** the site of the first Spanish settlement on the island, where you can see the **statue of Christopher Columbus,** cast in his hometown of Genoa, Italy, and erected near St. Ann's Hospital on the west side of town, close to the coast road. In the town are a number of Georgian buildings—the **Court House** near the parish church, built in 1866, is the most interesting.

Brimmer Hall Estate ⟨★★⟩   Some 21 miles east of Ocho Rios, in the hills 2 miles from Port Maria, this 1817 estate is an ideal place to spend a day. You can relax beside the pool and sample a wide variety of brews and concoctions. The Plantation Tour Eating House offers typical Jamaican dishes for lunch, and there's a souvenir shop with a good selection of ceramics, art, straw goods, wood-carvings, rums, liqueurs, and cigars. All this is on a working plantation where you're driven around in a tractor-drawn jitney to see the tropical fruit trees and coffee plants; the knowledgeable guides will explain the various processes necessary to produce the fine fruits of the island. This is a far more interesting and entertaining experience than the trip to Croydon Plantation in Montego Bay. So if you're visiting both Ocho Rios and Montego Bay and have time for only one plantation, make it Brimmer Hall.

Port Maria, St. Mary's. ℂ 876/994-2309. Tours $15. Tours Mon–Fri 8am–4pm.

Coyaba River Garden and Museum A mile from the center of Ocho Rios, at an elevation of 420 feet, this park and museum were built on the grounds of the former Shaw Park plantation. The word *coyaba* comes from the Arawak name for "paradise." Coyaba is a Spanish-style museum with a river and gardens filled with native flora, a cut-stone courtyard, fountains, and a crafts shop and bar. The museum boasts a collection of artifacts from the Arawak, Spanish, and English settlements in the area.

Shaw Park Rd. (C) 876/974-6235. Admission J$190 ($4.25), free for children 12 and under. Daily 8am–5pm. Take the Fern Gully–Kingston road, turn left at St. John's Anglican Church, and follow the signs to Coyaba, just ½ mile farther.

Dunn's River Falls For a fee, you can relax on the beach or climb with a guide to the top of the 600-foot falls. You can splash in the waters at the bottom of the falls or drop into the cool pools higher up between the cascades of water. The beach restaurant provides lackluster snacks and drinks, and dressing rooms are available. If you're planning to climb the falls, wear old tennis shoes or sport sandals to protect your feet from the sharp rocks and to prevent slipping.

Climbing the falls with the crowds is a chance to experience some 610 feet of cold but clear mountain water. In contrast to the heat swirling around you, the splashing water hitting your face and bare legs is cooling on a hot day. The problem here is slipping and falling, especially if you're joined to a chain of hands linking body to body. In spite of the slight danger, there seems to be few accidents. The falls aren't exactly a wilderness experience, with all the tour buses carrying cruise ship passengers here. The place is always overrun.

Rte. A3. (C) 876/974-2857. Admission $6 adults, $3 children 2–11, free for children under 2. Daily 8:30am–5pm (8am–5pm on cruise ship arrival days). From St. Ann's Bay, follow Route A3 east back to Ocho Rios, and you'll pass Dunn's River Falls; there's plenty of parking.

Firefly ⭐ This vacation retreat was the home of Sir Noël Coward and his longtime companion, Graham Payn, who, as executor of Coward's estate, donated it to the Jamaica National Heritage Trust. The recently restored house is more or less as it was on the day Sir Noël died in 1973. His Hawaiian-print shirts still hang in the closet of his austere bedroom, with its mahogany four-poster. The library contains a collection of his books, and the living room is warm and comfortable, with big armchairs and two grand pianos (where he composed several famous tunes). Guests were housed at Blue Harbour, a villa closer to Port Maria; they included Evelyn Waugh, Winston Churchill, Errol Flynn, Laurence Olivier, Vivien Leigh, Claudette Colbert, Katharine Hepburn, Mary Martin, and the Queen Mother. Paintings by the noted playwright/actor/author/composer adorn the walls. An open patio looks out over the pool and the sea. Across the lawn, Sir Noël is buried under a simple white marble gravestone.

Grants Pen, in St. Mary, 20 miles east of Ocho Rios above Port Maria. (C) 876/725-0920. Admission $10. Mon–Sat 8:30am–5:30pm.

Harmony Hall Once, this was the centerpiece of a sugar plantation in the late 19th century. It has been restored and today is the focal point of an art gallery and restaurant that showcases the painting and sculpture of Jamaican artists as well as a tasteful array of arts and crafts. Among the featured gift items are Sharon McConnell's Starfish Oils, which contain natural additives harvested in Jamaica. The gallery shop also carries the Reggae to Wear line of sportswear, designed and made on Jamaica.

Harmony Hall is also the setting for one of the best Italian restaurants along the coast, Toscanini's.

Tower Isles on Rte A3, 4 miles east of Ocho Rios. © 876/975-4222. Free admission. Gallery daily 10am–6pm. Restaurant/cafe Tues–Sun 10am–2:30pm and 6–11pm.

Prospect Plantation   This working plantation adjoins the 18-hole Prospect Mini Golf Course. A visit to this property is an educational, relaxing, and enjoyable experience. On your leisurely ride by covered jitney through the scenic beauty of Prospect, you'll readily see why this section of Jamaica is called "the garden parish of the island." You can view the many trees planted by such visitors as Winston Churchill, Henry Kissinger, Charlie Chaplin, Pierre Trudeau, Noël Coward, and many others. You'll learn about and see pimento (allspice), bananas, cassava, sugarcane, coffee, cocoa, coconut, pineapple, and the famous leucaena ("Tree of Life"). You'll see Jamaica's first hydroelectric plant and sample some of the exotic fruit and drinks.

Horseback riding is available on three scenic trails at Prospect. The rides vary from 1 to 2¼ hours. Advance booking of 1 hour is necessary.

Rte. A3, 3 miles east of Ocho Rios, in St. Ann. © 876/994-1058. Tours $12 adults, free for children 12 and under; 1-hour horseback ride $20. Tours Mon–Sat 10:30am, 2pm, and 3:30pm; Sun 11am, 1:30pm, and 3pm.

SHOPPING

For many, Ocho Rios provides an introduction to shopping Jamaica-style. After surviving the ordeal, some visitors might vow never to go shopping again. Hundreds of Jamaicans pour into town, hoping to peddle something, often something they made, to cruise ship passengers and other visitors. Be prepared for aggressive vendors and some fierce haggling. All vendors ask too much for an item at first, giving them the leeway to negotiate until the price reaches a more realistic level. Is shopping fun in Ocho Rios? A resounding no. Do cruise ship passengers and land visitors indulge in it anyway? A decided yes.

SHOPPING CENTERS   There are seven main shopping plazas. We list them because they're here, not because we heartily recommend them. The **Ocean Village Shopping Centre** (© 876/974-2683) contains numerous boutiques, food stores, a bank, sundries purveyors, a pharmacy, travel agencies, service facilities, and what have you. East of Ocho Rios, the **Pineapple Place Shopping Centre** is a collection of shops in cedar-shingle-roofed cottages set amid tropical flowers.

Ocho Rios Craft Park is a complex of some 150 stalls through which to browse. An eager seller will weave you a hat or a basket while you wait, or you can buy from the mix of ready-made hats, hampers, handbags, place mats, and lampshades. Other stands stock hand-embroidered goods and will make small items while you wait. Woodcarvers work on bowls, ashtrays, wooden-head carvings, and statues chipped from lignum vitae, and make cups from local bamboo. The **Coconut Grove Shopping Plaza** is a collection of low-lying shops linked by walkways and shrubs. The merchandise consists mainly of local craft items. Many of your fellow shoppers may be cruise ship passengers.

Island Plaza is a shopping complex in the heart of Ocho Rios. You can find some of the best Jamaican art here, all paintings by local artists. You can also buy local handmade crafts (be prepared to do some haggling over price and quality), carvings, ceramics, even kitchenware, and most definitely the inevitable T-shirts. **Mutual Security Plaza** contains some 30 shops.

SPECIALTY SHOPS   In general, the shopping is better in Montego Bay. But if you're not going there, wander the Ocho Rios crafts markets, although the selection of merchandise becomes monotonous. Among the places deserving special mention are these:

Swiss Stores, in the Ocean Village Shopping Centre (© **876/974-2519**), sells all the big names in Swiss watches, like Juvenia, Tissot, Omega, Rolex, Patek Philippe, and Piaget. The Rolex watches are real, not those fakes touted by hustlers on the streets of Ocho Rios. The Swiss outlet also sells duty-free handcrafted jewelry.

One of the best bets for shopping is **Soni's Plaza,** 50 Main St., the address of all the shops recommended below. **Casa dé Oro** (© **876/974-5392**) specializes in selling duty-free watches, fine jewelry, and classic perfumes. **Chulani's** (© **876/974-2421**) sells a good assortment of quality watches, brand-name perfumes, and leather bags. Jewelry comes in a wide variety of 14-karat and 18-karat settings with diamonds, emeralds, rubies, and sapphires. **Gem Palace** (© **876/974-2850**) is the place to go for diamond ring solitaires and tennis bracelets, as well as 14-karat gold chains and bracelets. **Taj Gift Centre** (© **876/974-9268**) has a little bit of everything: Blue Mountain coffee, Jamaican cigars, hand-embroidered linen tablecloths, and Jamaican jewelry made from hematite, a mountain stone.

Mohan's (© **876/974-9270**) offers one of the best selections of 14-karat and 18-karat gold chains, rings, bracelets, and earrings, as well as jewelry studded with precious gems like diamonds and rubies. **Soni's** (© **876/974-2303**) dazzles with gold but also sells cameras, French perfumes, watches, china and crystal, linen tablecloths, and even standard Jamaican souvenirs. **Tajmahal** (© **876/ 974-6455**) beats most competition with its name-brand watches, jewelry, and fragrances; it also has Paloma Picasso leatherwear and porcelain by Lladró.

We generally ignore hotel gift shops, but the **Jamaica Inn Gift Shop** in the Jamaica Inn, Main Street (© **876/974-2514**), is better than most, selling everything from Blue Mountain coffee to Walkers Wood products, and even guava jelly and jerk seasoning. If you're lucky, you'll find marmalade from an old family recipe, plus Upton Pimento Dram, a unique liqueur flavored with Jamaican allspice. Local handcrafts include musical instruments for kids, brightly painted tin country cottages, and intricate jigsaw puzzles of local scenes. The constantly replenished collection of antiques ranges from sterling silver collectibles to 18th-century teaspoons and serving pieces. The antique maps of the West Indies are among the finest in Jamaica.

OCHO RIOS AFTER DARK

A $16 million attraction, **Entertainment Village,** a massive complex of sights and amusements, is scheduled to open by the time you read this. On 4 acres of land at the western end of Ocho Rios between Turtle Beach and Reynolds Pier, the site will be a re-created Jamaican village with gardens, a lagoon, and a number of entertainment options. Shops and restaurants, along with craft outlets, a theater, an amphitheater, a children's play area, and even a Cyber Center, will complete the offerings. Naturally, there will be Jamaican reggae music, both in the form of a museum and live.

The **Sports Bar** at the Little Pub Restaurant (see "Great Deals on Dining," above) is open daily 10pm to 3am, and Sunday is disco night. Most evenings are devoted to some form of entertainment, including karaoke.

Hotels often provide live entertainment to which nonguests are invited. Ask at your hotel desk where the action is on any given night. Otherwise, you might want to look in on **Silks Discothèque,** in the Shaw Park Hotel, Cutlass Bay (© 876/974-2552), which has a smallish dance floor and a sometimes-animated crowd of drinkers and dancers. If you're not a hotel guest, you can enter for J$150 ($3.25).

If everything is in a name, then we recommend **Jamaic'N Me Crazy,** at the Jamaican Grande Hotel (© 876/974-2201). An all-inclusive club that will evoke more of a New York–nightclub memory than a Jamaican one, it charges nonguests $30 to cover everything you can shake or drink, daily 10pm to 3am. It has the best lighting and sound system in Ocho Rios (and perhaps Jamaica), and the crowd can include anyone from the passing yachter to the curious tourist.

For more of the same without an overbearing Americanized atmosphere, try the **Acropolis,** 70 Main St. (© 876/974-2633). At least the adventurous traveler can rest assured that this is a lot closer to an authentic Jamaican nightclub than Jamaic'N Me Crazy. Cover is required only on nights they have a live band, and it's rarely any higher than J$200 ($4.25).

7 Port Antonio ⋆

Port Antonio is a verdant and sleepy seaport on the northeast coast of Jamaica, 63 miles northeast of Kingston, where Tom Cruise filmed *Cocktail*. It has been called the Jamaica of 100 years ago. Port Antonio is the mecca of the titled and the wealthy, including European royalty and stars like Bruce Willis, Linda Evans, Raquel Welch, Whoopi Goldberg, Peter O'Toole, and Tommy Tune.

The bustling small town of Port Antonio is like many on the island: clean and tidy, with sidewalks around a market filled with vendors; tin-roofed shacks competing with old Georgian and modern brick-and-concrete buildings; and lots of people shopping, talking, laughing, and some just loafing. The market is a place to browse among local craftwork, spices, and fruits.

In bygone days, visitors arrived by banana boat and stayed at the Tichfield Hotel (which burned down) in a lush, tropical, unspoiled part of the island. Captain Bligh landed here in 1793 with the first breadfruit plants, and Port Antonio claims that the ones grown in this area are the best on the island. Visitors still arrive by water—but now it's in cruise ships that moor close to Navy Island, and the passengers come ashore just for the day.

Navy Island and the long-gone Tichfield Hotel were owned for a short time by film star Errol Flynn. The story is that after suffering damage to his yacht, he put into Kingston for repairs, visited Port Antonio by motorbike, fell in love with the area, and in due course acquired Navy Island (some say he got it in a gambling game). Later he either sold or lost it and bought a nearby plantation, Comfort Castle, still owned by his widow, Patrice Wymore Flynn, who spends most of her time there. He was much loved and admired by the Jamaicans and was totally integrated into the community. They still talk of him in Port Antonio—his reputation for womanizing and drinking lives on.

GETTING THERE

If you're going to Port Antonio, you will fly into the **Donald Sangster Airport** in Montego Bay or the **Norman Manley International Airport** in Kingston. Some hotels, particularly the larger resorts, will arrange for airport transfers from that point. Be sure to ask when you book.

If your hotel doesn't provide transfers, you can **fly** to Port Antonio's small airport aboard the independent carrier **Air Jamaica Express,** booking your connection through Air Jamaica (© 800/523-5585 in the U.S.). The one-way airfare is $50 from Kingston or $60 from Montego Bay. Or you can take a **bus** for $25 one-way. We recommend **Tour Wise** (© **876/979-1027**). The bus will drop you off at your hotel. The trip takes 2 hours, but for safety's sake, we recommend this option only if you fly into Montego Bay. You can **rent a car** for the 133-mile drive east along Route A1 (see "Getting There," at the beginning of this chapter), but we don't advise this 4-hour drive for safety's sake, either from Montego Bay or from Kingston. Or you can take a **taxi;** the typical one-way fare from Montego Bay is $100, but always negotiate and agree on a fare *before* you get into the taxi.

ACCOMMODATIONS YOU CAN AFFORD

Bonnie View Plantation Hotel   The two-story house containing this hotel is the subject of several local legends. Some claim it was built by an expat Englishman as a holiday home around 1900; others maintain it was the center of a large plantation and constructed around 1850. Other stories claim that Errol Flynn owned it briefly and used it as a place to carouse. Regardless of the details, it's obvious that this building once boasted pretensions of grandeur and many of the graceful notes of the Old World. But today it's a battered remnant of its original self, with a much-renovated dining room, 15 rooms in the main house, and 5 in cabaña-style outbuildings in the garden. The somewhat tattered accommodations contain Jamaica-made furniture and often sagging mattresses and virtually no accessories, but a very limited number of units offer sea views. Each unit has a small shower-only bathroom. The nearest beach (Frenchman's Cove) is about a 20-minute drive away.

Richmond Hill (P.O. Box 82), Port Antonio, Jamaica, W.I. © 876/993-2752. Fax 876/993-2862. 20 units. Winter $66 single; $100 double. Off-season $64 single; $95 double. MAP $44 per person. AE, DC, MC, V. **Amenities:** Restaurant, bar, pool. *In room:* TV, ceiling fans.

De Montevin Lodge   This lodge, in the town center on Titchfield Hill, is an ornate yet somewhat shabby version of a Victorian gingerbread house. It stands on a narrow back street whose edges are lined with architectural reminders (some not well-preserved) of the colonial days. Cast-iron accents and elongated red-and-white balconies set a tone for the charm you find inside: cedar doors, Art Deco cupboards, a ceiling embellished with lacy plaster designs, and elaborate cove moldings. Don't expect modern amenities; your room might be a study of another, not-yet-renovated era. The hallway bathrooms are adequate, but the furnishings are a bit spartan and frayed; the mattresses are often lumpy. Try to get an accommodation with a private side porch. The Little Reef Beach is a 5-minute walk away, and Frenchman's Cove and Boston Beach are a 15-minute drive away.

21 Fort George St. (P.O. Box 85), Port Antonio, Jamaica, W.I. © 876/993-2604. 13 units, 3 with bathroom. Year-round $26 single without bathroom; $39 double without bathroom; $52 single or double with bathroom. AE, MC, V. **Amenities:** Restaurant. *In room:* TV, ceiling fans.

WORTH A SPLURGE

Navy Island Marina Resort   Jamaica's only private island getaway, this resort and marina are on that bit of paradise once owned by actor Errol Flynn. Today this cottage colony and yacht club is one of the best-kept secrets in the Caribbean. To reach the resort, you'll have to take a ferry from the dockyards of Port Antonio on West Street for a short ride across one of the most beautiful harbors of Jamaica. Hotel guests travel free.

Each accommodation is designed as a studio cottage or villa branching out from the main club. Ceiling fans and trade winds keep the cottages cool, and mosquito netting over the comfortable beds adds a plantation touch. Bathrooms are fairly small and routine, but at least the plumbing in this remote location works. One of the resort's beaches is a secluded clothing-optional stretch of sand known as Trembly Knee Cove. The grounds are dotted with hybrid hibiscus, bougainvillea, and palms (many of which were originally ordered planted by Flynn himself). At night, after enjoying drinks in the H.M.S. Bounty Bar, guests can dine in the Bounty (see "Great Deals on Dining," below).

Navy Island (P.O. Box 188), Port Antonio, Jamaica, W.I. ✆ **876/993-2667.** 7 units. Year-round $80 double; $105 1-bedroom villa for 2; $130 1-bedroom villa for 3; $225 2-bedroom villa for 3; $250 2-bedroom villa for 4. Children 11 and under stay free in parents' villa. Rates include breakfast. AE, MC, V. **Amenities:** Restaurant, bar, pool, snorkeling. *In room:* Ceiling fans.

ACCOMMODATIONS NEARBY

Hotel Mocking Bird Hill ★★ A 6-mile drive east of Port Antonio, this hotel occupies the much-renovated premises of what was built in 1971 as the holiday home of an American family. In 1993 two imaginative women transformed the place into a blue-and-white enclave of good taste, reasonable prices, and ecological consciousness. About 600 feet above the coastline, on a hillside laden with tropical plants, the accommodations are simple but tasteful, and other than their ceiling fans, are devoid of electronic gadgets. They're tastefully furnished, with excellent beds in the best B&B tradition, and each of them has a neatly kept shower-only bathroom. Much of the interior, including the restaurant (Mille Fleurs; see "Dining Nearby," below), is decorated with artworks by Ms. Walker, the hotel's co-owner and manager; as this hotel grows, the gallery aspect will probably be expanded. The hotel has sweeping views over the Blue Mountains and the Jamaican coastline.

Mocking Bird Hill (P.O. Box 254), Port Antonio, Jamaica, W.I. ✆ **876/993-7267.** Fax 876/993-7133. www. hotelmockingbirdhill.com. 10 units. Winter $190–$230 single or double. Off-season $160–$225 single or double. AE, MC, V. **Amenities:** Restaurant, bar, TV lounge, access to rafting, hiking, and art classes. *In room:* Ceiling fans.

GREAT DEALS ON DINING

Bounty JAMAICAN In Errol Flynn's former retreat (see above), the Bounty, reached by ferry across the Port Antonio harbor, is the perfect place for a romantic tryst at low prices. The kitchen is known for its convivial seafaring ambience, fresh fish, and down-home Jamaican cookery, often appearing on the menu as daily specials. Come early so you can enjoy a drink and take in the view from the bar. (Flynn used to have quite a few, all recorded in *My Wicked, Wicked Ways*, his autobiography.) The lunch and dinner menus are the same. Steak is prepared delectably in a variety of ways, as are lobster, shrimp, chicken, and crayfish.

In the Navy Island Marina Resort, Navy Island. ✆ **876/993-2667.** Reservations recommended for dinner. Lunch or dinner $12–$20. AE, DC, DISC, MC, V. Daily 10am–6pm.

De Montevin Lodge Restaurant *Value* JAMAICAN/AMERICAN At this restaurant at De Montevin Lodge, (see "Accommodations You Can Afford," above), start with pepper pot or pumpkin soup, follow with curried lobster or chicken Jamaican style with local vegetables, and finish with coconut or banana cream pie or bread pudding, washed down with coffee. We suggest an ice-cold Red Stripe beer with the meal. The menu changes according to the availability of fresh supplies, but the standard of cooking and the full Jamaican character of the meal are constant. If you'd like a special dish cooked, you can request it when you make reservations.

In the De Montevin Lodge, 21 Fort George St. ✆ **876/993-2604.** Reservations recommended a day in advance. Fixed-price meal $12–$20. AE, MC, V. Daily 12:30–2:30pm and 7–9:30pm.

Yachtsman's Wharf INTERNATIONAL   This restaurant beneath a thatch-covered roof is at the end of an industrial pier, near the departure point for ferries to Navy Island. The rustic bar and restaurant is a favorite of the expatriate yachting set. Crews from many of the ultra-expensive boats have dined here and have pinned their ensigns on the roughly textured planks and posts. The kitchen opens for breakfast and stays open all day, serving menu items such as burgers, *ceviche,* curried chicken, and ackee with saltfish. Main dishes include vegetables. Come here for the setting, the camaraderie, and the usual array of tropical drinks; the food is only secondary.

16 West St. ✆ 876/993-3053. Main courses $9–$36. No credit cards. Daily 7:30am–10pm.

DINING NEARBY
Mille Fleurs ✦✦ INTERNATIONAL   This restaurant, associated with the Hotel Mocking Bird Hill, is terraced into a verdant hillside about 600 feet above sea level, with sweeping views over the Jamaican coastline and the faraway harbor of Port Antonio. Sheltered from the frequent rains but open on the sides for maximum access to cooling breezes, it features candlelit dinners, well-prepared food, and lots of New Age charm. Menu items at lunch include sandwiches, salads, grilled fish, and soups. Dinners are fixed-price three-course meals that feature wholesome stylish dishes derived from around the world. The restaurant has been acclaimed by *Gourmet* magazine. You might want to try the coconut-and-garlic soup, and the fish with spicy mango-shrimp sauce is a specialty. Breads and most jams are made on the premises. Some of the dishes are designed for vegetarians.

In the Hotel Mocking Bird Hill, Port Antonio. ✆ 876/993-7267. Reservations recommended. Main courses $8–$36. MC, V. Daily 7am–9:30pm.

HITTING THE BEACHES
Port Antonio has several white-sand beaches, some free and some that charge for use of facilities. The most famous is **San San Beach,** which has recently gone private, although guests of certain hotels are admitted with a pass. **Boston Beach** is free and often has light surfing; there are picnic tables as well as a restaurant and snack bar. Before heading here, stop nearby and get the makings for a picnic lunch at the most famous center for peppery jerk pork and chicken on Jamaica. These rustic shacks also sell the much rarer jerk sausage. The dish was said to originate with the Maroons who lived in the hills beyond and occasionally ventured out to harass plantation owners. The location is 11 miles east of Port Antonio and the Blue Lagoon.

Also free is **Fairy Hill Beach** (Winnifred), with no changing rooms or showers. **Frenchman's Cove Beach** attracts a chic crowd to its white-sand beach combined with a freshwater stream. Non-hotel guests are charged a fee. **Navy Island,** once Errol Flynn's hideaway, is a fine choice for swimming (one beach is clothing optional) and snorkeling (at **Crusoe's Beach**). Take the boat from the Navy Island dock on West Street across from the Exxon station. It's a 7-minute ride to the island, and a one-way fare is 30¢. The ferry runs 24 hours a day. The island is the setting for the Navy Island Marina Resort (see "Worth a Splurge," above).

SPORTS & OTHER OUTDOOR PURSUITS
RAFTING   Rafting started on the **Río Grande** ✦✦ as a means of transporting bananas from the plantations to the waiting freighters. In 1871 a Yankee skipper, Lorenzo Dow Baker, decided a seat on one of the rafts was better than walking, but it wasn't until Errol Flynn arrived that the rafts became popular as

a tourist attraction. Flynn used to hire the craft for his friends, and he encouraged the rafters to race down the Río Grande. Bets were placed on the winner. Now bananas are transported by road, and the raft skipper makes one or maybe two trips a day down the waterway. If you want to take a raft trip, contact **Río Grande Attractions Limited,** c/o Rafter's Restaurant, St. Margaret's Bay (© **876/993-5778**).

The rafts, 33-feet long and only 4-feet wide, are propelled by stout bamboo poles. There's a raised double seat about two thirds of the way back for the two passengers. The skipper stands in the front, trousers rolled up to his knees, the water washing his feet, and guides the craft down the lively river, about 8 miles between steep hills covered with coconut palms, banana plantations, and flowers, through limestone cliffs pitted with caves, through the Tunnel of Love, a narrow cleft in the rocks, then on to wider, gentler water.

The day starts at the Rafter's Restaurant, west of Port Antonio, at Burlington on St. Margaret's Bay. Trips last 2 to 2½ hours and are offered 8am to 4pm daily at $45 per raft (suitable for two people). From the Rafter's Restaurant, a fully insured driver will take you in your rented car to the starting point at Grants Level or Berrydale, where you board your raft. The trip ends at the Rafter's Restaurant, where you collect your car, which has been returned by the driver. If you feel like it, take a picnic lunch, but bring enough for the skipper, too.

SNORKELING & SCUBA DIVING   The best outfitter is **Lady Godiva's Dive Shop** in Dragon Bay (© **876/993-8988**), 7 miles from Port Antonio. Full dive equipment is available, and the service is provided daily. Technically, you can snorkel off most of the beaches in Port Antonio, but are likely to see much farther offshore. The very best spot is San San Bay by Monkey Island. The reef is extremely active and full of exciting marine life. Lady Godiva offers two excursions daily to this spot for $12 per person. Snorkeling equipment costs $9 for a full day's rental.

EXPLORING THE AREA

Athenry Gardens and Cave of Nonsuch
Twenty minutes from Port Antonio, it's an easy drive and an easy walk to see the stalagmites, stalactites, fossilized marine life, and evidence of Arawak civilization in Nonsuch. The cave is 1.5 million years old, and you can explore its underground beauty by following railed stairways and concrete walkways on a 30-minute walk. The place is dramatically lit. Although the United States and Europe have far greater cave experiences, this is as good as it gets in Jamaica. From the Athenry Gardens, there are panoramic views over the island and the sea. The gardens are filled with coconut palms, flowers, and trees, and complete guided tours are given.

Portland. © 876/993-3740. Admission (including guide for gardens and cave) $6 adults, $3 children 11 and under. Daily 10am–4pm. From Harbour St. in Port Antonio, turn south in front of the Anglican church onto Red Hassel Rd. and proceed approximately a mile to Breastworks community (fork in road); take the left fork, cross a narrow bridge, go immediately left after the bridge, and proceed approximately 3½ miles to the village of Nonsuch.

Folly Great House
This house was reputedly built in 1905 by Arthur Mitchell, an American millionaire, for his wife, Annie, daughter of Charles Tiffany, founder of the famous New York jewelry store. Seawater was used in the concrete mixtures of its foundations and mortar, and the house began to collapse only 11 years after the family moved in. Because of the beautiful location, it's easy to see what a fine Great House it must have been.

On the outskirts of Port Antonio on the way to Trident Village, going east along the A4. No phone. Free admission.

Exploring Blue Mountain

Jamaica has some of the most varied and unusual topography in the Caribbean, including a mountain range laced with rough rivers, streams, and waterfalls. The 192,000-acre **Blue Mountain–John Crow Mountain National Park** is maintained by the Jamaican government. The mountainsides are covered with coffee fields, producing a blended version that's among the leading exports of Jamaica. But for the nature enthusiast, the mountains reveal an astonishingly complex series of ecosystems that change radically as you climb from sea level into the fog-shrouded peaks.

The most popular climb begins at Whitfield Hall (see "Kingston," below). Reaching the summit of Blue Mountain Peak (3,000 ft. above sea level) requires between 5 and 6 hours each way. En route, hikers pass through acres of coffee plantations and forest, where temperatures are cooler than you might expect and where high humidity encourages thick vegetation. Along the way, watch for an amazing array of bird life, including hummingbirds, warblers, rufous-throated solitaires, yellow-bellied sapsuckers, and Greater Antillean pewees.

The best preparation against the wide ranges of temperature you'll encounter is to dress in layers and bring bottled water. If you opt for a 2am departure to catch the sunrise from atop the peak, carry a flashlight as well. Sneakers are usually adequate, although many climbers bring hiking boots to Jamaica solely in anticipation of their trek up Blue Mountain. Be aware that even during the dry season (Dec–Mar), rainfall is common. During the rainy season (the rest of the year), these peaks can get up to 150 inches of rainfall, and fogs and mists are frequent.

You can always hike alone into the Jamaican wilderness, but considering the dangers of such an undertaking and the crime you might

Somerset Falls Here the waters of the Daniels River pour down a deep gorge through a rain forest, with waterfalls and foaming cascades. You can take a short ride in an electric gondola to the hidden falls. A stop on the daily Grand Jamaica Tour from Ocho Rios, this is one of Jamaica's most historic sites; the falls were used by the Spanish before the English captured the island. At the falls, you can change into a swimsuit and enjoy the deep rock pools and buy sandwiches, light meals, soft drinks, beer, and liquor at the snack bar. The guided tour includes the gondola ride and a visit to both a cave and a freshwater fish farm. On certain days the site is likely to be overrun with camera-toting tourists.

8 miles west of Port Antonio, just past Hope Bay on Rte. A4. (?) 876/913-0108. Tour $4. Daily 9am–5pm.

PORT ANTONIO AFTER DARK

It was bound to happen. Down by the sea, east of Port Antonio, at **Dragon Bay** ((?) 876/993-8751), the cocktail bar has been renamed **"Cruise Bar"** in honor of the movie *Cocktail*, which starred Tom Cruise. Cruise and a Hollywood cast came to Dragon Bay's 55 acres to shoot the movie. Two other films were shot here, including the remake of *Lord of the Flies* and *Club Paradise*. Regrettably, Cruise himself is no longer here serving those rum punches. Come

encounter, we don't advise it. A better bet is engaging one of Kingston's best specialists in eco-sensitive tours, **Sunventure Tours,** 30 Balmoral Ave., Kingston 10, Jamaica, W.I. (✆ **876/960-6685**). The staff can always arrange an individualized tour, but if you're interested in their mainstream offerings, here are two: The Blue Mountain Sunrise Tour is a camp-style overnight in one of Jamaica's most inaccessible areas. For $140 per person, participants are retrieved at their Kingston hotels and driven to an isolated ranger station, Wildflower Lodge, accessible only via four-wheel-drive vehicle. The two-stage hike begins at 4:30pm, and a simple mountaineer's supper is served at 6pm around a campfire at a ranger station near Portland Gap. At 3am, climbers hike by moonlight and flashlight to an aerie selected because of its view of the sunrise. Climbers stay aloft until about noon, then head back down for a return to their hotels by 4pm. There's also an excursion from Kingston Y's Waterfall on the Black River, in southern Jamaica's Elizabeth Parish. Participants congregate in Kingston at 6:30am for a transfer to a raft and boating party near the hamlet of Lacovia and an all-day waterborne excursion to a region of unusual ecological interest. Depending on the number of participants, fees range from $80 to $100 per person, including lunch.

Blue Mountain Bike Tours (✆ 876/974-7075) offers all-downhill bike tours through the Blue Mountains—you pedal only about a half dozen times on this several-mile trip. Visitors are driven to the highest navigable point in the Blue Mountains, where they are provided bikes and protective gear. Lunch, snacks, and lots of information about coffee, local foliage, and history are provided. The cost is about $85 per person.

here for a "sundowner," and you may fall in love with the place—or the bartender—and stick around for dinner. Another recently opened bar drawing a fashionable crowd is the **Tree Bar,** on the grounds of Goblin Hill Villas at San San (✆ **876/993-7443**), high on a hill commanding a panoramic view of 12 acres. The aptly named bar is wrapped around huge ficus trees, whose mammoth aerial roots dangle over the drinking area. Giant-leafed pothos climb down the trunks. It's a sort of "Me Tarzan, You Jane" kind of place and should prove increasingly popular.

8 Kingston ⋆

Kingston, the largest English-speaking city in the Caribbean with a population of more than 650,000, is the capital of Jamaica. It sits on the plain between Blue Mountain and the sea. The buildings are a mix of very modern, graceful, old, and plain ramshackle. It's a busy city, as you might expect, with a natural harbor that's the seventh largest in the world. The University of the West Indies has its campus on the edge of the city. The cultural center of Jamaica is here, along with industry, finance, and government. However, there's a terrible crime problem, and it's best to stay outside the city.

ESSENTIALS

See "Getting There" at the beginning of this chapter for details on the airlines that serve Kingston's international airport.

Since Kingston is a rather confusing place to negotiate, many visitors rely on taxis.

The **University Hospital** is at Mona (© **876/927-1620**). **Moodie's Pharmacy** is in the New Kingston Shopping Centre (© **876/926-4174**).

ACCOMMODATIONS NEARBY

Remember to ask if the 12% room tax is included in the rate quoted when you make your reservation. The rates listed below are year-round unless otherwise noted.

Pine Grove Mountain Chalets   This simple inn occupies what was a coffee plantation in the 1930s, with a view over misty hills and the lights of faraway Kingston, landscaped brick walkways, and topiary trees. The accommodations are in one-story motel-like units, each with basic amenities but good beds and small but tidy bathrooms with showers. Three contain slightly battered kitchenettes, for which there's no extra charge. Owners Ronald and Marcia Thwaites deliberately avoided the installation of air-conditioning in favor of the natural breezes. There's a restaurant, and hiking trips into the nearby mountains can be arranged.

Content Gap P.A., St. Andrew (for information, write Pine Grove Mountain Chalets, 62 Duke St., Kingston, Jamaica, W.I.). © **876/977-8009.** Fax 876/977-8447. 17 units. Year-round $57 single; $73 double. MAP $25 per person. AE, MC, V. **Amenities:** Restaurant. *In room:* Fans.

Whitfield Hall Hostel *(Finds)*   Offbeat Whitfield Hall is a high-altitude hostel about 6 miles from the hamlet of Mavis Bank. It's on a coffee plantation dating from 1776 and is the last inhabited house before you get to the peak of Blue Mountain, at 7,402 feet. The main allure is the opportunity to see Blue Mountain from a hill-climber's viewpoint. The accommodations for 30 guests are in the bleakest dorm mode. Blankets and linen are provided, but personal items (towels, soap, and food) are not. There's a deep freezer and a refrigerator, as well as cooking facilities, crockery, and cutlery. You bring your own food and share the kitchen and the two bathrooms. There's no restaurant. All water comes from a spring, and lighting is by kerosene lamps called Tilleys. A wood fire warms everyone—it gets cold in the mountains at night.

Most visitors come to see the sunrise from the summit of Blue Mountain, which means getting up at around 2 or 3am to walk the final distance along a bridle path through the forest. The route is clearly marked, and you need a good flashlight and warm clothing, along with hiking boots or strong shoes. It's a 3-hour walk each way. It's also possible to hire a mule or a horse to make the jaunt, accompanied by a guide, for $42 round-trip for the 13-mile journey.

To get here, you can drive to Mavis Bank, about 20 miles from Kingston. Head northeast along Old Hope Road to the suburb of Papine, then proceed to Gordon Town. At Gordon Town, turn right over the bridge near the police station and drive into the hills for some 10 miles until you reach Mavis Bank. As alternatives, Whitfield Hall will send a four-wheel-drive for you for $30, or you can walk. You can also get to Mavis Bank by bus from Kingston. Some people request to be picked up in Kingston by a Land Rover for $50 each way for up to six passengers; each extra passenger pays $6.

Halfway up Blue Mountain. Contact John Allgrove, 8 Armon Jones Crescent, Kingston 6, Jamaica, W.I. © **876/ 927-0986** (preferably 7–9pm). 30 beds in 7 units, none with bathroom; 1 cottage with kitchen and bathroom.

Year-round $15 per person in communal room; $60 per night in cottage for up to 4 (extra person, to a maximum of 8, $15). No credit cards. **Amenities:** Communal kitchen. *In room:* No phone.

GREAT DEALS ON DINING

Chelsea Jerk Centre *ಱ* JAMAICAN   Between the New Kingston Shopping Centre and the Wyndham New Kingston Hotel, this is the city's most popular provider of the Jamaican delicacies jerk pork and jerk chicken. You can order food to take out or eat in the comfortably battered dining room. Although no appetizers are served, you can order a side portion of what the scrawled chalkboard refers to as Festival (fried cornmeal dumplings). On Friday nights, steamed fish is the specialty.

7 Chelsea Ave. © 876/926-6322. Reservations recommended. Jerk chicken J$460 ($10); 1 lb jerk pork J$300 ($6.50). AE, MC, V. Mon–Thurs 11am–11pm; Fri–Sat 11am–midnight; Sun 1–10pm.

Devonshire Restaurant/The Grogg Shoppe *ಱಱ* JAMAICAN/SEAFOOD/ STEAK   These two restaurants near New Kingston are in what were the brick-sided servants' quarters of Kingston's most-visited mansion, Devon House. The more formal of the two is the Devonshire, now a steak-and-seafood grill. You can eat on patios under the trees, in sight of the royal palms and the fountain in front of the historic Great House. Appetizers include a tidbit of jerk pork or a bowl of soup (perhaps Jamaican red-pea or pumpkin soup). Main dishes feature Jamaican ackee and saltfish, barbecued chicken, or steamed snapper. Also tasty are the unusual homemade ice creams made of local fruits, such as soursop. Blue Mountain tea or coffee is served. The bars for both restaurants serve 11 rum punches and 10 fruit punches. Especially popular is the Devon Duppy, combining virtually every variety of rum in the bartender's inventory. Many aficionados opt for these drinks on one of the Grogg Shoppe's two terraces.

In Devon House, 26 Hope Rd. © 876/929-7046. Reservations recommended for Devonshire only. Dinner J$350–J$1,200 ($7.75–$26.50); lunch J$270–J$505 ($6–$11). AE, MC, V. Mon–Fri noon–3pm and 6–10pm; Sat 6–10pm.

The Hot Pot JAMAICAN   A short walk from the first-class Pegasus and Wyndham hotels, this uncomplicated Jamaican-run restaurant attracts an animated local crowd and serves simple but straightforward cuisine. In a red-and-white interior, near a view of a modest garden, you can drink Red Stripe beer or rum concoctions. Menu items include red-pea soup, beef stew, roast chicken, steaks, mutton, and fish.

2 Altamont Terrace. © 876/929-3906. Main courses $5–$8. MC, V. Daily 8am–10pm.

HITTING THE BEACHES

You don't really come to Kingston for beaches, but there are some. To the southwest of the sprawling city are black sandy beaches at both **Hellshire Beach** and **Fort Clarence,** popular with locals on weekends. These beaches have changing rooms and heavy security, along with numerous food stands. The reggae concerts at Fort Clarence are legendary on the island. Just past Fort Clarence, the fisherman's beach at **Naggo Head** is an even hipper destination, or so Kingston beach buffs claim. After a swim in the refreshing waters, opt for one of the food stands selling fried fish and *bammy.* The beach closest to the city (though it's not very good) is **Lime Cay,** on the outskirts of Kingston Harbour. The little island can be approached after a short boat ride from Morgan's Harbour at Port Royal.

SEEING THE SIGHTS

Even if you're staying at Ocho Rios or Port Antonio, you might want to visit Kingston for brief sightseeing and for trips to nearby Port Royal and Spanish Town.

IN TOWN   Downtown Kingston, the old part of the town, is centered on **Sir William Grant Park,** formerly Victoria Park, a showpiece of lawns, lights, and fountains. North of the park is the **Ward Theatre,** the oldest theater in the New World, where the traditional Jamaican pantomime is staged from December 26 to early April. To the east is **Coke Methodist Church,** and to the south, the equally historic **Kingston Parish Church.**

One of the major attractions, **Devon House,** 26 Hope Rd. (© **876/929-7029**), was built in 1881 by George Stiebel, a Jamaican who became one of the first black millionaires in the Caribbean. He made his fortune mining in Latin America. A striking classical building, the house has been restored to its original beauty by the Jamaican National Trust. The grounds contain craft shops, boutiques, two restaurants, shops selling the best ice cream in Jamaica (in exotic fruit flavors), and a bakery and pastry shop with Jamaican puddings and desserts. The main house also displays furniture of various periods and styles. Admission to the main house is J$6 (15¢), and it's open Tuesday to Saturday 9:30am to 5pm. Admission to the grounds (including the shops and restaurants) is free. Almost next door to Devon House are the sentried gates of **Jamaica House,** residence of the prime minister, a fine white-columned building set well back from the road.

Continuing along Hope Road, at the crossroads of Lady Musgrave and King's House roads, turn left and you'll see a gate on the left with its own traffic light. This leads to **King's House,** the official residence of the governor-general of Jamaica, the queen's representative on the island. The outside and front lawn of the gracious residence, set in 200 acres of well-tended parkland, is sometimes open to viewing Monday to Friday 10am to 5pm. The secretarial offices are housed next door, in an old wooden building set on brick arches. In front of the house is a gigantic banyan tree in whose roots, legend says, *duppies* (as ghosts are called in Jamaica) take refuge when they're not living in the cotton trees.

Between Old Hope and Mona roads, a short distance from the Botanical Gardens, is the **University of the West Indies** (© **876/927-1660**), built in 1948 on the Mona Sugar Estate. Ruins of old mills, storehouses, and aqueducts are juxtaposed with modern buildings on what must be the world's most beautifully situated campus. The chapel, an old sugar-factory building, was transported stone by stone from Trelawny and rebuilt. The remains of the original sugar factory are well preserved and give a good idea of how sugar was made in slave days.

National Library of Jamaica (formerly the West India Reference Library), Institute of Jamaica, 12 East St. (© **876/922-0620**), a storehouse of the history, culture, and traditions of Jamaica and the Caribbean, is the world's finest working library for West Indian studies. It has the most comprehensive, up-to-date, and balanced collection of materials on the region, including books, newspapers, photographs, maps, and prints. Exhibits highlight different aspects of Jamaica and West Indian life. It's open Monday to Thursday 9am to 5pm and Friday 9am to 4pm.

Bob Marley Museum (formerly Tuff Gong Studio), 56 Hope Rd. (© **876/927-9152**), is the most-visited sight in Kingston, but if you're not a Bob Marley fan, it might not mean much to you. The clapboard house with its garden and high surrounding wall was the famous reggae singer's home and recording studio until his death. You can tour the singer's house and view assorted Marley memorabilia, and you might even catch a glimpse of his various children, who often frequent the grounds. The museum is open Monday to Saturday 9am to 4pm. Admission is J$400 ($8.75) for adults, J$200 ($4.50) for children 4 to 12; free for children 3 and under. It's reached by bus no. 70 or 75 from Halfway

Tree, but take a cab to save yourself the hassle of dealing with Kingston public transportation.

IN PORT ROYAL   From West Beach Dock, Kingston, a ferry ride of 20 to 30 minutes will take you to Port Royal, which conjures up visions of swashbuckling pirates led by Henry Morgan, swilling grog in harbor taverns. This was once one of the New World's largest trading centers, with a reputation for being the wickedest city on earth. Blackbeard stopped here regularly on his Caribbean trips. But the whole thing came to an end at 11:43am on June 7, 1692, when a third of the town disappeared underwater during a devastating earthquake. Nowadays, Port Royal, with its memories of the past, has been designated by the government for redevelopment as a tourist destination.

As you drive along the Palisades, you arrive first at **St. Peter's Church.** It's usually closed, but you may persuade the caretaker, who lives opposite, to open it if you want to see the silver plate, said to be spoils captured by Henry Morgan from the cathedral in Panama. In the ill-kept graveyard is the tomb of Lewis Galdy, a Frenchman swallowed up and subsequently regurgitated by the 1692 earthquake.

Fort Charles (© **876/967-8438**), the only one remaining of Port Royal's six forts, has withstood attack, earthquake, fire, and hurricane. Built in 1656 and later strengthened by Morgan for his own purposes, the fort was expanded and further armed in the 1700s, until its firepower boasted more than 100 cannons, covering both the land and the sea approaches. In 1779, Britain's naval hero, Horatio Lord Nelson, was commander of the fort and trod the wooden walkway inside the western parapet as he kept watch for the French invasion fleet. Scale models of the fort and ships of past eras are displayed. The fort is open daily 9am to 5pm, charging J$100 ($2.20) admission.

Part of the complex, **Giddy House,** once the Royal Artillery storehouse, is another example of what the earth's movements can do. Walking across the tilted floor is an eerie and strangely disorienting experience.

IN SPANISH TOWN   From 1662 to 1872, Spanish Town was the capital of the island. Founded by the Spaniards as Villa de la Vega, it was sacked by Cromwell's men in 1655, and all traces of Roman Catholicism were obliterated. The English cathedral, surprisingly retaining a Spanish name, **St. Jago de la Vega,** was built in 1666 and rebuilt after being destroyed by a 1712 hurricane. As you drive into town from Kingston, the ancient cathedral, rebuilt in 1714, catches your eye with its brick tower and two-tiered wooden steeple, added in 1831. Since the cathedral was built on the foundation and remains of the old Spanish church, it's half-English and half-Spanish and displays two distinct styles: Romanesque and Gothic. Of cruciform design and built mostly of brick, the cathedral is one of the island's most interesting buildings. The black-and-white marble stones of the aisles are interspersed with ancient tombstones, and the walls are heavy with marble memorials that are almost a chronicle of Jamaica's history, dating back as far as 1662.

Beyond the cathedral, turn right, and 2 blocks along you'll reach Constitution Street and the **Town Square.** This little square is surrounded by towering royal palms. On the west side is **King's House,** gutted by fire in 1925, although the facade has been restored. This was the residence of Jamaica's British governors until 1872, when the capital was transferred to Kingston. Many celebrated guests stayed here, among them Lord Nelson, Admiral Rodney, Captain Bligh of HMS *Bounty* fame, and King William IV.

Beyond the house is the **Jamaica People's Museum of Craft & Technology,** Old King's House, Constitution Square (© **876/922-0620**), open Monday to Friday 10am to 4pm. Admission is J$35 (75¢) for adults and J$15 (35¢) for children. The garden contains examples of old farm machinery, an old water mill wheel, a hand-turned sugar mill, a fire engine, and other items. An outbuilding displays a museum of crafts and technology, together with a number of smaller agricultural implements. In the small archaeological museum are old prints, models, and maps of the town's grid layout from the 1700s.

The streets around the old Town Square contain many fine Georgian town houses intermixed with tin-roofed shacks. Nearby is the **market,** so busy in the morning you'll find it difficult, almost dangerous, to drive through. However, it provides a bustling scene of Jamaican life.

SHOPPING

Cool arcades lead off from **King Street,** but everywhere you'll see a teeming mass of people going about their business. There are some beggars and the inevitable salespeople who sidle up and offer "hot stuff, mon," frequently touting highly polished brass lightly dipped in gold and offered at high prices as real gold. The hucksters do accept a polite but firm no, but don't let them keep you talking or you'll end up buying—they're very persuasive!

For many years, the richly evocative paintings of Haiti were viewed as the most valuable contribution to the arts in the Caribbean. However, Jamaica is increasingly perceiving itself as one of the artistic leaders of the developing world. An articulate core of Caribbean critics is focusing the attention of the art world at large on the unusual, eclectic, and sometimes politically motivated paintings being produced on Jamaica.

Frame Centre Gallery, 10 Tangerine Place (© **876/926-4644**), is one of Jamaica's most important galleries, and the founder and guiding force, Guy McIntosh, is widely respected as a patron of the Jamaican arts. Committed to presenting quality Jamaican art, Frame Centre has three viewing areas and carries a varied collection of more than 300 works. The **Mutual Life Gallery,** in the Mutual Life Centre, 2 Oxford Rd. (© **876/926-9025**), is one of the country's most prominent galleries, the corporate headquarters of a major insurance company. After you pass a security check, you can climb to the corporation's mezzanine level for an insight into the changing face of Jamaican art. Exhibits change every 2 weeks.

Kingston Crafts Market, at the west end of Harbour Street downtown, is a large covered area of individually owned stalls; you can reach the market through thoroughfares like Straw Avenue, Drummer's Lane, and Cheapside. All kinds of island crafts are sold: wooden plates and bowls, trays, ashtrays, mats, baskets, and pepperpots made from mahoe, the national wood of the island. Batik shirts and cotton shirts with gaudy designs are sold. Banners for wall decoration are inscribed with the Jamaican coat-of-arms, and wood masks often have elaborately carved faces.

The Shops at Devon House, at Devon House, 26 Hope Rd. (© **876/ 929-7029**), are associated with one of Jamaica's most beautiful and historic mansions. These shops ring the borders of a 200-year-old courtyard once used by slaves and servants. Although about 10 shops operate from these premises, 4 of the largest are operated by Things Jamaican, a nationwide emporium dedicated to the enhancement of the country's handcrafts. Shops include the Cookery, offering island-made sauces and spices, and the Pottery, selling crockery and stoneware. Look for pewter knives and forks, based on designs of pewter items discovered in archaeological digs in the Port Royal area in 1965. Other outlets are a children's shop, a leather shop, and a stained-glass shop, as well as a gallery with paintings, ceramics, and sculpture.

9 Mandeville

The English town Mandeville lies on a plateau more than 2,000 feet above the sea in the tropical highlands. The commercial part of the town is small and surrounded by a sprawling residential area that is popular with the large North American expat population mostly involved with the bauxite-mining industry. Much cooler than the coastal resorts, it's the best center from which to explore the entire island.

Shopping in the town is a pleasure, whether in the old center or in one of the modern complexes, such as **Grove Court.** The **market** in the center of town teems with life, particularly on weekends, when the country folk bus into town. The town has several interesting old buildings. The square-towered **church** built in 1820 has fine stained glass, and the little churchyard tells an interesting story of the past inhabitants of Mandeville. The **Court House,** built in 1816, is a fine old Georgian stone-and-wood building with a pillared portico reached by a sweeping double staircase. There's also **Marshall's Pen,** one of the Great Houses, in Mandeville.

ACCOMMODATIONS YOU CAN AFFORD

Golf View Hotel   This hotel won't win any prizes for architectural finesse—it practically looks like a hospital. But it's one of the best maintained and most efficiently managed hotels in the area. It's the favorite of most of the corporations in town, many of whom advise their clients to sleep here, but to avoid the hotel restaurant in favor of the also-recommended Bloomfield Great House (see "Great Deals on Dining," below). About half of the rooms overlook the verdant fairways of the local golf course (Manchester Golf Club); the others front a pool and a relatively banal-looking courtyard. Rooms are outfitted motel-style with relatively comfortable furnishings based on vaguely colonial models. About a third of them have air-conditioning, and each is equipped with a shower-only bathroom.

5½ Caledonia Rd, Mandeville, Manchester, Jamaica, WI. © 876/962-4477. Fax 876/962-5640. www. thegolfviewhotel.com. 51 units. Year-round $55–$75 double; $60 1-bedroom suite; $80 2-bedroom suite. AE, MC, V. Amenities: Restaurant, bar. In room: A/C (some units), TV.

Hotel Astra   Our top choice for a stay in this area is the family-run Astra, operated by Diana McIntyre-Pike, known to her family and friends as Thunderbird. She's always coming to the rescue of guests, happily picking up people in her own car and taking them around to see the sights, and organizing introductions to island people. The accommodations are mainly in two buildings reached along open walkways. Units are spartan with well-worn beds, but they're well maintained and have basic comforts. You can also spend the afternoon at the Manchester Country Club, where tennis and golf are available. Horses can be provided for cross-country treks.

The Country Fresh Restaurant offers excellent meals. Lunch or dinner includes a choice of a homemade soup like red pea or pumpkin, followed by local fish and chicken specialties. The kitchen is under the personal control of Diana, who's always collecting awards in Jamaican culinary competitions. Someone is on hand to explain the niceties of any Jamaican dish. A complete meal is

$12 to $20, with some more expensive items like lobster and steak. Dinner is served 6 to 9:30pm daily. Thursday is barbecue night, when guests and towns-folk gather around the pool to dine. The Revival Room is the bar, where every-thing including the stools is made from rum-soaked barrels. Try the family's homemade pick-me-up, made of Guinness, rum, egg, condensed milk, and nut-meg. It's open daily 11am to 11pm.

62 Ward Ave., Mandeville, Jamaica, W.I. ℂ 876/962-3725. Fax 876/962-1461. 22 units. Year-round $70 sin-gle or double; $115 suite. Rates include continental breakfast. AE, DISC, MC, V. **Amenities:** Restaurant, bar, pool, access to horseback riding, sauna, massage. *In room:* TV, ceiling fans.

Mandeville Hotel   This ornate hotel dates from the early 1900s, and for a while housed part of the British military garrison. In the 1970s, the venerable hotel was replaced with a modern structure. It lies in the heart of Mandeville, across from the police station. Bedrooms, which range in size from small to spa-cious, are furnished with Jamaican styling, often including a four-poster and other mahogany furniture. Bathrooms are old-fashioned but tidily maintained, each with a shower. There are attractive gardens, and you can play golf or tennis at the nearby Manchester Country Club.

There is no pretension to the restaurant's food at all (see "Great Deals on Dining," below); it's simple homemade fare. From the dining room, you'll have a view of the green hills of central Jamaica.

4 Hotel St. (P.O. Box 78), Mandeville, Jamaica, W.I. ℂ 876/962-2460. Fax 876/962-0700. www.mandevillehotel. com. 56 units. Year-round $65–$125 single or double; from $95 suite. AE, MC, V. **Amenities:** Restaurant, bar. *In room:* TV.

GREAT DEALS ON DINING

Bloomfield Great House ✦ INTERNATIONAL   This is the only restau-rant in town that's viewed as a destination in its own right. Serving excellent food in an intricately restored setting of historic interest, it's a hangout for the town's expatriate Australians, Brits, Americans, and Scandinavians. Surrounded by 5 acres of landscaping, it's perched on a hilltop about a quarter-mile south of the town's commercial core, in a verdant residential neighborhood of upscale private homes. Although its foundations are about 200 years old, it took its present form in 1838, when it was the centerpiece of a coffee plantation.

Today, it feels like England in the tropics, thanks to the devoted labor of Australia-born Ralph Pearce and his Jamaican/American wife, Pamela Grant, who transformed her family's romantic-looking but sleepy real estate investment into the well-orchestrated dining enclave you'll see today. Start off with a drink in the cozy mahogany-trimmed pub before dining on the rambling veranda (with views that sweep out over the town), or a high-ceilinged dining room with colonial-style trim and moldings. Superb menu items include smoked marlin with black caviar and lime-flavored aïoli, char-broiled filet mignon with sherry sauce and crispy onions, plantain-crusted chicken served with a passion-fruit vinaigrette, and a delicious version of jumbo shrimp stuffed with jalapeño pepper, wrapped in bacon, and served with barbecue sauce. Pastas are made fresh on the premises.

8 Perth Rd. ℂ 876/962-7130. Reservations recommended for dinner. Lunch main courses J$250–J$915 ($5.50–$20); dinner main courses J$415–J$995 ($9.25–$22). AE, DISC, MC, V. Mon–Sat noon–9pm.

Mandeville Hotel JAMAICAN   Close to the city center, near the police sta-tion and popular with local businesspeople, the Mandeville Hotel offers a wide selection of sandwiches, plus milkshakes, tea, and coffee. In the restaurant the a la carte menu features Jamaican pepperpot soup, lobster Thermidor, fresh snapper, and kingfish. Potatoes and vegetables are included in the main-dish prices. There's no pretension to the homemade and basic food, almost like that served in the house of a typical Jamaican family. From the restaurant's dining room, you'll have a view of the green hills of central Jamaica.

In the Mandeville Hotel, 4 Hotel St. © 876/962-2460. Reservations recommended. Main courses $8–$25. AE, MC, V. Daily 6:30am–9:30pm.

EXPLORING THE AREA

Mandeville is the sort of place where you can become well acquainted with the people and feel like part of the community. One of the largest and driest **caves** on the island is at Oxford, about 9 miles northwest of Mandeville. Signs direct you to it after you leave Mile Gully, a village dominated by St. George's Church, some 175 years old.

Among the interesting attractions, **Marshall's Pen** is one of the Great Houses. A coffee plantation home some 200 years old, it has been restored and furnished in traditional style. In 1795 it was owned by one of the governors of Jamaica, the earl of Balcarres. It has been in the hands of the Sutton family since 1939; they farm the 300 acres and breed Jamaican Red Poll cattle. This is very much a private home and should be treated as such, although guided tours can be arranged. A contribution of $10 is requested, and a tour can be arranged for one to four people. For information or an appointment to see the house, contact Ann or Robert Sutton, **Marshall's Pen,** Great House (P.O. Box 58), Mandeville, Jamaica, W.I. (© **876/904-5454**). Robert Sutton is coauthor of *Birds of Jamaica,* a photographic field guide published by Cambridge University Press.

10 The South Coast ⊀

Known as "undiscovered Jamaica," the south coast attracts more foreign visitors every year and is a mecca for the budget traveler.

Local adventures are plentiful, too. Among the most popular is South Coast Safaris's boat tour up the Black River—once a major logging conduit (and still home to freshwater crocodiles). Another favorite is the trip to the Y. S. Falls, where seven spectacular cascades tumble over rocks in the foothills of the Santa Cruz Mountains, just north of the town of Middle Quarters (famed for its spicy freshwater shrimp).

The south coast has been called the sunniest on Jamaica, and that's true. It also means the coast is the most arid. The Arawak lived here and were discovered by Columbus when he circumnavigated Jamaica in 1494. Five generations of Spaniards raised cattle on ranches on the broad savannas of St. Elizabeth, when not repelling French pirates.

To reach the south coast, head east from Negril, following the signposts to Savanna-La-Mar. This is Sheffield Road, and the highway isn't particularly good until it broadens into Route A2 at Savanna. After passing through the village of Bluefields, continue southeast to the small town of Black River, opening onto Black River Bay.

ACCOMMODATIONS YOU CAN AFFORD

Invercauld Great House & Hotel   This is an offbeat, slightly funky guesthouse. In 1889, when Black River's port was one of the most important on Jamaica, a Scottish merchant imported most of the materials for the construction of this white-sided manor house. Today, the renovated and much-enlarged house is a hotel. A few rooms are in the original high-ceilinged house; the rest are in a concrete outbuilding added in 1991. The rooms are clean and stripped down, usually with mahogany furniture made by local craftsmen, including the comfortable beds. Each unit has a small bathroom with a shower. All are air-conditioned except for two single rooms that have ceiling fans. On the premises is the conservatively dignified Willow restaurant. It's open daily for lunch and dinner, charging $20 to $25 for three-course meals of lobster, chicken, and fish.

66 High St. (P.O. Box 12), Black River, St. Elizabeth, Jamaica, W.I. ℂ **876/965-2750.** Fax 876/965-2751. 48 units. Winter $85–$95 single or person double; $120 per person suite. Off-season $80–$90 single or double; $110 suite. AE, MC, V. **Amenities:** Restaurant, pool, tennis court. *In room:* A/C, TV, ceiling fans.

Jake's ★★ *(Finds)*   In a setting of cactus-studded hills in the arid southwest (in total contrast to the rest of tropically lush Jamaica), this is a special haven, an ideal place for an off-the-record tryst. Perched on a cliffside overlooking the ocean, this complex of cottages is an explosion of colors, everything from funky purple to toreador red. Each room is individually decorated, everything inspired by Sally Henzell, a Jamaican of British ancestry who's married to Perry Henzell, art director on the classic reggae film *The Harder They Come.* Sally cites contro-versial Catalán architect Antoni Gaudí as her mentor in the creation of Jake's—especially in the generous use of cracked mosaic tile so familiar to Barcelona devotees. The rooms could contain anything Sally might've picked up at the flea market. But be warned: There's no air-conditioning and days are hot in the "desert." Each unit has a neat little bathroom with shower.

The restaurant's fare is simple Jamaican, but it's tasty and good, made with fresh ingredients.

Calabash Bay, Treasure Beach, St. Elizabeth, Jamaica, W.I. ℂ **800/OUTPOST** in the U.S., or 876/965-0635. Fax 876/965-0552. www.islandoutpost.com. 10 units. Year-round $95 single or double; $150 suite. AE, MC, V. **Amenities:** Restaurant, saltwater pool, game room. *In room:* Minibar, ceiling fans, CD player.

Treasure Beach Hotel   This little inn lies midway between Black River and Pedro Cross on a steep but lushly landscaped hillside above Treasure Beach. This white-sided hotel was built in the mid-1970s and renovated about a decade later. Although its staff is young and inexperienced, this is the largest and most elaborate hotel on Jamaica's south coast. Its centerpiece is a long and airy rattan-furnished bar whose windows look down the hillside to the beach and the hotel's 11 acres that flank it. Each unit has a ceiling fan and a veranda or patio. The accommodations are somewhat spartan and have well-used beds and small, shower-only bathrooms. Housekeeping is good, even if the furnishings are a bit tattered.

Treasure Beach (P.O. Box 5), Black River, St. Elizabeth, Jamaica, W.I. ℂ **876/965-0110.** www.treasurebeach jamaica.com. 36 units. Winter $99 single; $110 double; $143 suite. Off-season $88 single; $99 double; $113.30 suite. AE, MC, V. **Amenities:** Restaurant, bar, pool. *In room:* A/C, ceiling fan.

GREAT DEALS ON DINING

Bridge House Inn JAMAICAN   This is an uncomplicated and very Jamaican restaurant in one of the town's few hotels, built in the early 1980s in a concrete beachfront motif in a grove of coconut palms and sea grapes. Guests include a cross-section of the region, as well as tourists. The menu includes complete din-ners (fish, chicken, curried goat, oxtail, stewed beef, or lobster), served politely and efficiently by a staff of hardworking waiters. The chef has a secret recipe for pork chops that's so good people drive for miles around to sample it. A separate bar area dispenses drinks. Main dishes include soup, salad, and your choice of vegetables. Also on the premises are 14 rooms, some air-conditioned, and each with ceiling fan, TV, and simple furniture. Ten rooms are air-conditioned. In winter singles are priced at $33 and doubles $47, the prices lowered off-season to $25 single or $40 double.

14 Crane Rd., Black River, St. Elizabeth, Jamaica, W.I. ℭ 876/965-2361. Reservations recommended. Full meals $7–$18. MC, V. Daily 7am–10pm.

THE ROAD TO ADVENTURE

The **Black River,** the longest stream on Jamaica, has mangrove trees, crocodiles in the wild, and the insectivorous bladderwort, plus hundreds of different species of bird including herons, ospreys, and many of the wading variety. You can indeed go on safari. The best tours are by **South Coast Safaris,** operating out of the town of Black River (ℭ **876/965-2513** for reservations). The cost is $15; children 12 and under go for half price and those 2 and under go for free. Tours last about 1½ hours and cover 12 miles (6 miles upstream, 6 miles back) with a running commentary on the ecology and history of the Black River. Tours are at 9am, 11am, 12:30pm, 2pm, and 3:30pm daily. Specialized tours can be arranged for any number of groups, including bird-watchers, photographers, botanists, and natural-history buffs.

After leaving Black River, where you can find hotels and restaurants, you can continue north along the A2 to Mandeville or go directly southeast to Treasure Beach. A2 north takes you to **Middle Quarters,** a village on the plains of the Great Morass, through which the Black River runs. Day visitors often stop here and order a local delicacy, pepper shrimps.

Just north of the town of Middle Quarters is **Y. S. Falls,** where seven water-falls form crystal pools. Guests take a jitney and go through grazing lands and a horse paddock on the way to the falls, where they cool off in the waters and often enjoy a picnic lunch. After Middle Quarters, the road cuts east toward Mandeville along Bamboo Avenue, a scenic drive along 2 miles of highway covered with bamboo. Here you'll see a working plantation, Holland Estate, growing sugarcane, citrus, papaya, and mango.

If you've decided to take the southern-coast route to **Treasure Beach,** follow the signs to Treasure Beach directly southeast of Black River. The treasures here are seashells in many shapes and sizes. This is the site of the Treasure Beach Hotel (see above). To the east of Treasure Beach in Southfield is **Lovers' Leap,** a cliff plunging hundreds of feet into the sea. Two slave lovers reportedly jumped to their deaths here rather than be sold off to different masters.

15

Martinique

Martinique and Guadeloupe aren't French colonies, as many visitors assume, but the westernmost part of France, meaning that their inhabitants are full-fledged citizens of *la belle France,* a status they've enjoyed since 1946. Martinique has mountains dotted with lush vegetation, rain forests bursting with bamboo and breadfruit trees, and even a patch of desert in the south. But most visitors, including those from mainland France, come just for the white-sand beaches.

In island boutiques you can buy that Hermès scarf you've always wanted, certainly a bottle of Chanel perfume, or even some Baccarat crystal. For breakfast, freshly baked croissants will arrive on your plate. French cheese is shipped in from Marseilles, and the Creole cuisine is among the most distinctive in the West Indies.

Napoléon's empress, Joséphine, was born on Martinique in 1763, the same year France relinquished rights to Canada in exchange for the French West Indies. The mistress of Louis XIV, Mme de Maintenon, also lived here, in the small fishing village of Le Prêcheur. Columbus was the first to chart Martinique. The French took possession of the island, in the name of Louis XIII, in 1635 and then established sugarcane plantations and rum distilleries. In spite of some intrusions by British forces, the French have remained here ever since. In the beginning, the French imported slaves from Africa to work the plantations, but at the time of the French Revolution, the practice began to decline on Martinique. It wasn't until the mid–19th century, however, that Victor Schoelcher, a Paris-born deputy from Alsace, successfully lobbied to abolish slavery.

Almond-shaped Martinique is mountainous, especially in the rain-forested northern part, where Mount Pelée (Montagne Pelée), a volcano, rises to 4,656 feet. In the center of the island, the mountains are smaller, with Carbet Peak reaching a 3,960-foot summit. The high hills rising among the peaks or mountains are called *mornes.* The southern part of Martinique has only big hills, reaching peaks of 1,500 feet at Vauclin and 1,400 feet at Diamant. The irregular coastline provides five bays, dozens of coves, and miles of sandy beaches.

The climate is relatively mild, the average temperature in the 75°F-to-85°F range, but at higher elevations it's considerably cooler. The island is cooled by a wind the French called *alizé,* and rain is frequent but doesn't last very long. Late August to November might be called the rainy season; April to September are the hottest months.

The early Carib peoples, who gave Columbus such a hostile reception, called Martinique the "island of flowers," and indeed it has remained so. The vegetation is lush, and includes hibiscus, poinsettias, bougainvillea, coconut palms, and mango trees. Almost any fruit that can grow in the ground sprouts out of Martinique's soil—pineapples, avocados, bananas, papayas, and custard apples. Bird-watchers are often pleased at the number of hummingbirds, mountain

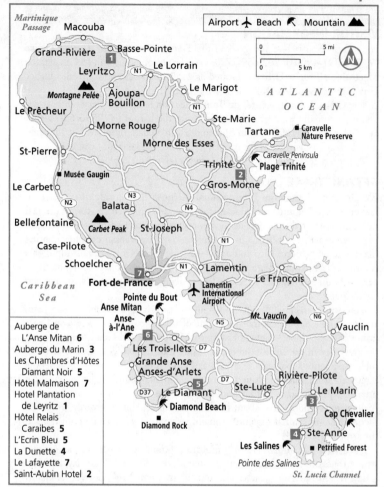

Airport ✈ Beach 🏖 Mountain ▲▲

Martinique Passage

Macouba

Grand-Rivière

Basse-Pointe [1]

Leyritz○

Le Lorrain

N1

Le Marigot

Montagne Pelée ▲▲

Ajoupa-Bouillon

Le Prêcheur

Ste-Marie

N1

ATLANTIC OCEAN

Morne Rouge

Tartane

Caravelle Nature Preserve

Morne des Esses

St-Pierre○

Caravelle Peninsula

Trinité○ [2]

Plage Trinité

■ Musée Gaugin

Gros-Morne

Le Carbet○

N3

N2

Balata○

N4

Bellefontaine

Carbet Peak ▲▲

St-Joseph

N1

Case-Pilote

Schoelcher

N1

Lamentin

Caribbean Sea

Fort-de-France [7]

Le François

Pointe du Bout

Lamentin International Airport

Anse Mitan

Anse-à-l'Ane

N5

Mt. Vauclin ▲▲

N6

Vauclin

[6]

Les Trois-Ilets

D7

Grande Anse Anses-d'Arlets

D7

Rivière-Pilote

[5]

Le Marin

D37

Le Diamant

Ste-Luce

[3]

Diamond Beach

Cap Chevalier

■ Diamond Rock

[4]○ Ste-Anne

Les Salines

■ Petrified Forest

Pointe des Salines

St. Lucia Channel

Auberge de L'Anse Mitan **6**
Auberge du Marin **3**
Les Chambres d'Hôtes Diamant Noir **5**
Hôtel Malmaison **7**
Hotel Plantation de Leyritz **1**
Hôtel Relais Caraïbes **5**
L'Ecrin Bleu **5**
La Dunette **4**
Le Lafayette **7**
Saint-Aubin Hotel **2**

0 — 5 mi
0 — 5 km

whistlers, blackbirds, mongoose, and multicolored butterflies. After sunset there's a permanent concert of grasshoppers, frogs, and crickets.

However, all this lushness, tropical beauty, and French-Creole food come at a price. Martinique has a reputation for being one of the Caribbean's more expensive destinations, especially in the price of its food, a tradition it shares with mainland France. Its hotel and food prices are high. To beat the high cost of dining out, we suggest picnicking during the day and then splurging at dinner. Grocery stores are loaded with choice tidbits from mainland France, and a bottle of French wine will cost you less here than on the non-French islands in the Caribbean.

Taxis and automobile rentals are high, so try to stay at a place on the beach (or near a beach) so you won't have long, expensive commutes every day. True budget hotels are hard to find on Martinique, but we have several suggestions below.

1 Essentials

VISITOR INFORMATION

For information before you go, call the **French Government Tourist Office** (© **800/391-4909** or 202/659-7779; www.francetourism.com). In Canada, the **Martinique Tourist Office** is located at 2159 rue Mackay, Montréal, Quebec H3G 2J2 (© **800/361-9099** or 514/844-8566).

The **Office Départemental du Tourisme** is on boulevard Alfassa in Fort-de-France, across the waterfront boulevard from the harbor (© **0596/63-79-60**), open Monday to Friday 8am to 5pm and Saturday 8am to noon. The information desk at Lamentin Airport is open daily until the last flight comes in.

The Internet site for Martinique is **www.martinique.org**.

GETTING THERE

BY PLANE   Lamentin International Airport lies outside the village of Lamentin, a 15-minute taxi ride east of Fort-de-France and a 40-minute taxi ride northeast of the island's densest concentration of resort hotels (the Trois Islets peninsula). Most flights to Martinique require a transfer on a neighboring island—usually Puerto Rico and occasionally Antigua. Direct or nonstop flights from the U.S. mainland are rare: Air France (see below) offers only one flight per week, on Sunday, which leaves from Miami and stops at Martinique and Guadeloupe.

American Airlines (© **800/433-7300**) flies into its busy hub in San Juan, and from here passengers transfer to one of usually two daily **American Eagle** (same phone number) flights heading to Martinique and Guadeloupe. Taking off every day in the late afternoon, the American Eagle flights usually arrive at their destinations between 1½ and 2 hours later. Off-season, the evening flights are sometimes combined into a single flight. Return flights to San Juan usually depart separately from both islands twice a day. Consult an American Airlines reservations clerk about booking your hotel simultaneously with your flight, since substantial discounts sometimes apply if you handle both tasks at the same time.

Air France (© **800/237-2747**) flies from Miami to Martinique, sometimes with a touchdown in Guadeloupe en route, every Tuesday, Thursday, and Saturday. It also operates separate nonstop flights from Paris's Charles de Gaulle Airport, departing at least once a day or (in some cases, depending on the season and the day of the week) twice a day. The airline also maintains three weekly flights from Port-au-Prince, Haiti, into Martinique, and three flights a week, depending on the season, between Cayenne in French Guyana and Martinique.

Antigua-based **LIAT** (© **800/468-0482** in the U.S. and Canada, 268/462-0700, or through the reservations department of American Airlines) flies from both its home base of Antigua and from Barbados to Martinique and Guadeloupe several times a day. Depending on the season, flights to these islands are either separate or combined into a single flight, with touchdowns en route. Both Antigua and Barbados are important air-terminus links for such larger carriers as American Airlines (see above).

Another option is flying **BWIA** (© **800/538-2942**), the national airline of Trinidad and Tobago, from New York or Miami nonstop to both Barbados and Antigua and from there transferring onto a LIAT flight. **British Airways** (© **800/247-9297** in the U.S., or 0345/222-111 in England) flies separately to Antigua and Barbados three times a week from London's Gatwick Airport. From either of those islands, LIAT connects to Martinique.

Fun Fact **Carnival**

If you like masquerades and dancing in the streets, you should be here in January or February to attend **Carnival**, or *Vaval*, as it's known here. It begins right after the New Year, as each village prepares costumes and floats. Weekend after weekend, frenzied celebrations take place, reaching fever pitch just before Lent. Fort-de-France is the focal point for Carnival, but the spirit permeates the whole island. On Ash Wednesday, the streets of Fort-de-France are filled with *diablesses,* or she-devils (portrayed by members of both sexes). Costumed in black and white, they crowd the streets to form King Carnival's funeral procession. As devils cavort about and the rum flows, a funeral pyre is built at La Savane. When it's set on fire, the dancing of those "she-devils" becomes frantic (many are thoroughly drunk at this point). Long past dusk, the cortège takes the coffin to its burial, ending Carnival until next year.

BY FERRY   You can travel between Guadeloupe and Martinique by boat in a leisurely 3¾ hours, with an intermediate stop in Dominica or Les Saintes. The trip is made on comfortable craft operated by **Exprès des Iles.** The company operates at least one ferryboat a day and, in some cases, two per day, between the two largest islands of the French West Indies. Morning departures from Pointe-à-Pitre for Fort-de-France are usually at 8am, and departures from Fort-de-France for Pointe-à-Pitre are usually at 2pm. One-way fares are 340F to 535F (€51.65–€81.30, $49.30–$77.55) round-trip. For details and reservations, contact **Exprès des Iles,** Gare Maritime, quai Gatine, 97110 Pointe-à-Pitre, Guadeloupe (© 0590-83-12-45), or the office at Terminal Inter-Iles, Bassin de Radoub, 97200 Fort-de-France, Martinique (© 0596/63-12-11).

GETTING AROUND

BY BUS & TAXI COLLECTIF   Two types of buses operate on Martinique. Regular buses, *grands busses,* hold about 40 passengers and cost 5F to 8F (€.75–€1.20, .70¢–$1.15) to go anywhere within the city limits of Fort-de-France. But to travel beyond that, *taxis collectifs* are used. These are privately owned minivans that traverse the island and bear the sign TC. Their routes are flexible and depend on passenger need. A one-way fare is 30F (€4.55, $4.35) from Fort-de-France to Ste-Anne. *Taxis collectifs* depart from the heart of Fort-de-France from the parking lot of Pointe Simon. There's no phone number to call for information about this unpredictable means of transport, and there are no set schedules. Traveling in a *taxi collectif* is for the adventurous visitor—they're crowded and not very comfortable.

BY TAXI   Travel by taxi is popular but expensive. Most of the cabs aren't metered, and you'll have to agree on the price of the ride *before* getting in. Most visitors arriving at Lamentin Airport head for one of the resorts along the peninsula of Pointe du Bout. To do so costs about 180F (€27.35, $26.10) during the day or about 270F (€41.05, $39.25) at night. Night fares are in effect 7pm to 6am, when a 40% surcharge is added. You can call **Radio Taxi** at © 0596/63-63-62.

If you want to rent a taxi for the day, it's best to have a party of at least three or four people to keep costs low. Based on the size of the car, expect to pay from 700F to 850F (€106.40–€129.20, $101.50–$123.25) and up for a 5-hour tour, depending on the itinerary you negotiate with the driver. Generally, four passengers are charged 200F (€30.40, $29) per hour.

BY RENTAL CAR   The scattered nature of Martinique's geography makes renting a car especially tempting. Martinique has several local rental agencies, but clients have complained of mechanical difficulties and billing irregularities. We recommend renting from one of the large U.S. companies. **Budget** has offices at rue Félix-Eboué 12, in Fort-de-France (© **800/527-0700** in the U.S., or 0596/63-69-00); **Avis**, at rue Ernest-Deproge 4, in Fort-de-France (© **800/331-1212** in the U.S., or 0596/70-11-60); and **Hertz**, at Lamentin Airport (© **800/654-3001** or 0596/51-01-01). Prices are usually lower if you reserve a car in North America at least 2 business days before your arrival.

To rent a car, you must be 21 and have a valid driver's license, such as one from the United States or Canada, to rent a car for up to 20 days. After that, an International Driver's License is required. Remember that you'll be hit with a value-added tax (VAT) of 9.5% on top of the final car-rental bill. (VATs for some luxury goods on Martinique, including jewelry, can go as high as 14%.) Collision-damage waivers (CDWs), an excellent idea in a country where the populace drives somewhat recklessly, cost 75F to 190F (€11.40–€28.90, $10.85–$27.55) per day, depending on the value of the car.

BY FERRY   The least expensive way to go between quai d'Esnambuc in Fort-de-France and Pointe du Bout is by ferry (*vedette*); it costs 38F (€5.80, $5.50) round-trip or 19F (€2.90, $2.75) each way. Schedules for the ferries, which usually run daily 6am to midnight, are printed in the free visitor's guide *Choubouloute,* distributed by the tourist office. For information, call © **0596/73-05-53.** If the weather is bad or the seas are rough, all ferry services may be canceled.

A smaller ferry runs between Fort-de-France and the small-scale, unpretentious beach resorts of Anse Mitan and Anse-à-l'Ane, both across the bay and home to many two- and three-star hotels and several modest and unassuming Creole restaurants. A boat departs daily from quai d'Esnambuc in Fort-de-France at 30-minute intervals between 6am and 6:30pm. The trip takes only about 20 minutes. A round-trip goes for 33F (€5, $4.80). For more information, call © **0596/63-06-46.**

BY BICYCLE & MOTORBIKE   You can rent motor scooters from **Funny,** 80 rue Ernest-Deproge in Fort-de-France (© **0596/63-33-05**). The new 18-speed VTT (*velo tout terrain,* or all-terrain bike) is gradually making inroads from mainland France into the rugged countryside of Martinique, but there aren't many places to rent one. **St. Luce Location,** rue Schoelcher 14, St-Luce (© **0596/62-49-66**), about a 30-minute drive from Fort-de-France, rents scooters as well. A deposit of 3,500F (€531.90, $507.25) is required. **Jacques-Henry Vartel,** VT Tilt, Anse Mitan (© **0596/66-01-01**), has moved away from rentals but operates bike tours around Martinique based on demand. Call for more information.

 FAST FACTS: **Martinique**

Banking Hours Banks are open Monday to Friday 7:30am to noon and 2:30 to 4pm.

Consulate The nearest U.S. consulate is on Barbados (see chapter 5).

Currency The official monetary unit is the French franc (F), which is divided into 100 centimes. Occasionally, a shop will accept U.S. dollars, converting them into francs at a rate somewhat less favorable than you'd have gotten if you had changed them at a bank or *bureau de change*. The exchange rate used to calculate the dollar values given in the chapter is 6.9F = U.S.$1 (or 1F = U.S.14½¢). As this is sure to fluctuate a bit, use this rate for general guidance only. Be aware that begining in February 2002, the **euro** (€) will be accepted for general use throughout France and its Caribbean possessions. At press time, the euro converted into French francs at a rate of €1 = 6.58F, and the U.S. dollar converted into euros at a rate of U.S.$1 = €.92.

Customs Items for personal use, such as tobacco, cameras, and film, are admitted without formalities or tax if not in excessive quantity.

Documents U.S. and Canadian citizens need a valid passport. A return or ongoing ticket is also necessary. British subjects, Australians, and New Zealanders also need a valid passport.

Electricity Electricity is 220-volt AC (50 cycles), the same as that used on the French mainland. However, check with your hotel to see if it has converted the electrical voltage and outlets in the bathrooms (some have). If it hasn't, bring your own transformer and adapter for U.S. appliances.

Emergencies Call the **police** at © **17,** report a **fire** at © **18,** and summon an **ambulance** at © **0596/75-15-75.**

Hospitals There are 18 hospitals and clinics on the island, plus a 24-hour emergency room at **Hôpital Pierre Zobda Quikman,** Châteauboeuf, right outside Fort-de-France (© **0596/55-20-00).**

Languages French, the official language, is spoken by almost everyone. The local Creole patois uses words borrowed from France, England, Spain, and Africa. In the wake of increased tourism, English is occasionally spoken in the major hotels, restaurants, and tourist organizations—but don't count on driving around the countryside and asking for directions in English.

Pharmacies Try the **Pharmacie de la Paix,** at the corner of rue Perrinon and rue Victor-Schoelcher in Fort-de-France (© **0596/71-94-83),** open Monday to Friday 7:15am to 6:15pm and Saturday 7:45am to 1pm.

Safety Crime is hardly rampant on Martinique, yet there are still those who prey on unsuspecting tourists. Follow the usual precautions, especially in Fort-de-France and in the tourist-hotel belt of Pointe du Bout. It's wise to protect your valuables and never leave them unguarded on the beach.

Telecommunications To call Martinique from the United States, dial 011 (the international access code), then **596** (the country code for Martinique), and finally the six-digit local number. When making a call from one place on Martinique to another, you'll have to add a **0** (zero) to the country code (**0596** for Martinique) and dial the four-digit country code plus the six-digit local number; in all, 10 digits for calls made on the island.

Time Martinique is on Atlantic standard time year-round, 1 hour earlier than eastern standard time except when daylight saving time is in effect in the United States. Then Martinique time is the same as that on the east coast of the United States.

Tipping Restaurants generally add a 15% service charge to all bills, which you can supplement if you think the service is outstanding. Some hotels also add a 10% service charge to your bill. Tip taxi drivers at least 15% of the fare.

Water Potable water is available throughout the island.

Weather The climate is relatively mild—temperatures are usually in the 75°F-to-85°F range.

TIPS FOR SAVING MONEY ON MARTINIQUE

Often, family-run places are called **Relais Créoles**—a sort of French–West-Indian B&B. Although many are expensive, some are quite reasonable. However, don't expect the management to speak English, and be prepared to find that your fellow guests are French travelers on a budget. Nevertheless, Relais Créoles represent some of the best values on Martinique.

Villa rentals, which can be arranged by the week or the month, are an option for families or groups. The **Villa Rental Service** of the Martinique Tourist Office (② **0596/63-79-60**) can arrange this type of vacation rental for you. You can also contact **Gîtes de France**, B.P. 1122, 97209 Fort-de-France (② **0596/73-67-92**), which offers simple but comfortable studios and apartments in private homes. Also available are independent cottages as well as *chambres d'hôte* (B&B–style lodgings). Rates begin at 1,200F (€182.35, $173.90) per week.

Camping can be done almost everywhere in the mountains, in the forests, and on the beaches, although indiscriminate camping isn't permitted. Only the French authorities can interpret what *indiscriminate* means. Comfortable camps with showers and toilets are located at **Nid Tropical,** at Anse-à-l'Ane near Trois-Ilets (② **0596/68-31-30**); at **Vauclin,** on the southeast Atlantic coast (② **0596/74-40-40**); and one at **Pointe Marin,** near the Ste-Anne public beach (② **0596/76-72-79**). A nominal fee is charged for facilities. Between June and September, camping is allowed in other areas that have no facilities whatsoever. For more details, contact the **Office National des Forêts,** km 3.5, route de Moutte, Fort-de-France (② **0596/71-34-50**).

Recreational vehicles are an ideal way of discovering the natural and cultural riches along Martinique's nearly 500 miles of roadway. A recommended camping car operation is **West Indies Tours,** which offers campers outfitted with beds for four, a refrigerator, a shower, a sink, a 430-gallon water tank, a dining table, a stove, and a radio-cassette player. Weekly rates are $565, $645, and $735, depending on the season. Contact Michel Toula at West Indies Tours, Le François (② **0596/54-50-71**).

2 Fort-de-France

A mélange of New Orleans and Menton (French Riviera), Fort-de-France is the main town of Martinique, at the end of a large bay surrounded by evergreen hills. Iron-grill balconies overflowing with flowers are commonplace.

The proud people of Martinique are even more fascinating than the town, although today the Creole women are likely to be seen in jeans instead of traditional turbans and Empress Joséphine–style gowns, and they rarely wear those massive earrings that used to jounce and sway as they sauntered along. Narrow streets climb up the steep hills on which houses have been built to catch the overflow of the capital's more than 100,000 inhabitants.

ACCOMMODATIONS YOU CAN AFFORD

Rates are sometimes advertised in U.S. dollars, sometimes in French francs, and sometimes in a combination of both. Don't stay in town if you want a hotel near a beach. If you do opt to stay in Fort-de-France, you'll have to take a ferry to reach the beaches at **Pointe du Bout.**

Hôtel Malmaison   This inner-city hotel shows some of the battering it's received since it was built 60 years ago. It welcomes a crowd of business travelers from other parts of the Caribbean and off-island musicians playing at Martinique's resorts. Despite the building's age, the rooms, refurnished in 1997, are outfitted with modern furniture—comfortable beds, wooden tables, chairs, and armoires. Bathrooms are quite small. The staff probably won't pay much attention to you after you've registered, but from here you'll have easy access to the bars and cheap restaurants of Fort-de-France.

Rue de la Liberté 7, 97200 Fort-de-France, Martinique, F.W.I. ✆ **0596/63-90-85.** Fax 0596/60-03-93. 20 units. Year-round 305F–330F (€46.35–€50.15, $44.20–$47.85) single; 335F–415F (€50.90–€63.05, $48.55–$60.15) double. MC, V. **Amenities:** Restaurant, bar. *In room:* A/C, TV, minibar in some.

Le Lafayette   You enter this modest downtown hotel, located right on La Savane, through rue Victor-Hugo; the reception hall is up a few terra-cotta steps. The hotel was renovated in 2000 and its bedrooms are tidy and clean. Most units contain comfortable twin beds, with small pure-white, shower-only bathrooms. The overall impression is neat but simple and unpretentious. The inn is the oldest continuously operating hotel on Martinique, originally built in the 1940s, with quasi–Art Deco hints that are now slightly dowdy. There's no on-site restaurant, but several eateries are within a short walk.

5 rue de la Liberte, 97200 Fort-de-France, Martinique, F.W.I. ✆ **0596/73-80-50.** Fax 0596/60-97-75. 24 units. Winter 350F (€53.20, $50.70) single or double. Off-season 320F (€48.65, $46.40) single or double. AE, MC, V. *In room:* A/C, TV, minibar.

GREAT DEALS ON DINING

The Crew (L'Equipage)   FRENCH-CREOLE   In a wood-sided house built near the port 150 years ago, this restaurant is done in a nautical theme with wood trim. Styled after the kind of workaday brasserie you'd expect to find on the French mainland, it's in the heart of town, does a busy lunch trade with office workers and shopkeepers, and specializes in unfussy but traditional French and grilled cuisine. A choice of appetizers is included in the price of a main course. Menu items feature large platters of such items as escargots, mussels in white-wine sauce, steak tartare, chunky patés, grilled chicken, fish, steak, and even tripe.

Rue Ernest-Deproges 44 ✆ **0596/73-04-14.** Main courses 75F–120F (€11.40–€18.25, $10.85–$17.40); fixed-price menu 92F–150F (€14–€22.80, $13.35–$21.75). MC, V. Mon–Fri noon–3pm and 7–10pm; Sat noon–3pm.

Le Planteur ⚜ FRENCH-CREOLE   A growing number of local fans and members of the island's business community appreciate this restaurant's location on the southern edge of La Savane, in the commercial core of Fort-de-France. Established in 1997, it contains several somewhat idealized painted depictions of colonial Martinique. The hardworking, somewhat distracted staff runs around hysterically trying to be all things to all diners. Menu items are fresh, filled with flavor, and usually received with approval. They feature a hot *velouté*

> ### *Value* The Best Food Bargains Around
>
> For the best food bargains, don't patronize the restaurants but go to **La Savane**, especially the eastern edge of the park along boulevard Chevalier Ste-Marthe. Here dozens of vendors nightly set up little trailers and light the fires to their grills. They serve surprisingly good food—and big portions, too—from their stalls. They'll cook you succulent golden grilled chicken along with fresh conch, brochettes of lamb, and tasty herb-seasoned pork chops. Prices are remarkably low, and your evening can turn into a culinary adventure.

(soup) concocted from shrimp and *giraumons*, a green-skinned tropical fruit with a succulent yellow core; a cassoulet of minced conch; filet of *daurade* with coconut; and a *blanquette* (white, slow-simmered stew) of shellfish that's available only when the local catch makes such a dish possible.

1 rue de la Liberté. ⓒ **0596/63-17-45.** Reservations recommended. Main courses 75F–100F (€11.40–€15.20, $10.85–$14.50); fixed-price menu 100F (€15.20, $14.50), 150F (€22.80, $21.75), and 180F (€27.35, $26.10). AE, MC, V. Mon–Fri noon–2:30pm; daily 7–10:30pm.

Marie-Sainte ⭐ *Finds* CREOLE   You'd expect to find this place out in the countryside, not right in the capital. Your hostess is Agnés Marie-Sainte, a venerable Creole cook whose recipes for *boudin Créole, daube de poisson,* and *colombo* of mutton were derived from her ancestors. In a simple dining room that's likely to be crowded with locals, she offers fixed-price lunches with a strong emphasis on fresh fish (grilled or fried), and perhaps a fricassee of conch, always accompanied by a medley of fresh beans, dasheen, breadfruit, and *christophene*. This is about as authentic as it gets, and also as inexpensive as you're likely to find for meals of such quality and authenticity.

160 rue Victor-Hugo. ⓒ **0596/70-00-30.** Main courses 80F–180F (€12.15–€27.35, $12.75–$26.10); fixed-price lunch 80F (€12.15, $11.60). AE, MC, V. Mon–Sat 8am–4pm.

SPORTS & OTHER OUTDOOR PURSUITS

If it's a beach you're looking for, take the ferry to **Pointe du Bout** (see "Pointe du Bout & Les Trois-Ilets," below, for complete information). The island's only **golf course** is in Les Trois-Ilets (see "Pointe du Bout & Les Trois-Ilets," below).

The personnel of the **Parc Naturel Régional de la Martinique,** Excollège Agricole de Tivoli, B.P. 437, 97200 Fort-de-France (ⓒ **0596/64-42-59**), organize inexpensive guided hiking excursions year-round, and special excursions can be arranged for small groups. If you want to see the waters around Martinique, it's better to go on one of the **sailboat excursions** in the bay of Fort-de-France. Ask at your hotel desk what boats are taking passengers on cruises in Martinique waters. These vessels tend to change from season to season.

EXPLORING FORT-DE-FRANCE

At the center of the town lies a broad garden planted with many palms and mangos, **La Savane,** a handsome savannah with shops and cafes lining its sides. In the middle of this grand square stands a **statue of Joséphine,** Napoléon's little Creole, made of white marble by Vital Debray. With the grace of a Greek goddess, the statue poses in a Regency gown and looks toward Trois-Ilets, where she was born.

At any time of year, your next stop after La Savane should be the **St. Louis Roman Catholic Cathedral,** on rue Victor-Schoelcher, built in 1875. The religious centerpiece of the island, it's an extraordinary iron building, which someone once likened to a sort of Catholic railway station. A number of the island's former governors are buried beneath the choir loft.

A statue in front of the Palais de Justice is of the island's second main historical figure, **Victor Schoelcher** (you'll see his name a lot on Martinique). As mentioned earlier, he worked to free the slaves more than a century ago. The **Bibliothèque Schoelcher,** 21 rue de la Liberté (© **0596/70-26-67**), also honors this popular hero. Functioning today as the island's central government-funded library, the elaborate structure was first displayed at the 1889 Paris Exposition. Back then the Romanesque portal in red and blue, the Egyptian lotus-petal columns, and even the turquoise tiles were imported piece by piece from Paris and reassembled here. Most of the books inside are in French, and it's one of the most stringently protected historic buildings in the French West Indies. It's open Monday 1 to 5:30pm, Tuesday to Thursday 8:30am to 5:30pm, Friday 8:30am to 5pm, and Saturday 8:30am to noon.

Guarding the port is **Fort St-Louis,** built in the Vauban style on a rocky promontory. In addition, **Fort Tartenson** and **Fort Desaix** stand on hills overlooking the port.

The **Musée Départemental de la Martinique,** rue de la Liberté 9 (© **0596/71-57-05**), the one bastion on Martinique that preserves its pre-Columbian past, has relics left from the early settlers, the Arawaks, and the Caribs. The era the museum celebrates is from 3,000 B.C. to A.D. 1635. Everything here stops shortly after the arrival of the first French colonials on the southern tip of Martinique in the early 1600s. It's mostly an ethnological museum that was enlarged and reorganized into a more dynamic and up-to-date place in 1997. The museum faces La Savane and is open Monday to Friday 8am to 5pm and Saturday 9am to noon, charging 25F (€3.80, $3.60) for adults, 15F (€2.30, $2.15) for students, and 10F (€1.50, $1.45) for children.

Sacré-Coeur de Balata Cathedral, at Balata, overlooking Fort-de-France, is a copy of the one looking down from Montmartre on Paris—and this one is just as incongruous, maybe more so. It's reached by going along route de la Trace (N3). Balata is 6 miles northwest of Fort-de-France.

A few minutes away on N3, **Jardin de Balata** (© **0596/64-48-73**) is a tropical botanical park. The park was created by Jean-Philippe Thoze on land that the jungle was rapidly reclaiming around a Creole house that belonged to his grandmother. He has also restored the house, furnishing it with antiques and historic engravings. The garden contains flowers, shrubs, and trees growing in profusion and offering a vision of tropical splendor. Balata is open daily 9am to 5pm. Admission is 40F (€6.10, $5.80) for adults and 15F (€2.30, $2.15) for children 7 to 12; free for children under 6.

SHOPPING

The best buys on Martinique are French luxury imports, such as perfumes, fashions, Vuitton luggage, Lalique crystal, or Limoges dinnerware. Sometimes (but don't count on it) prices are as much as 30% to 40% below those in the United States.

If you pay in U.S. dollars, store owners supposedly will give you a 20% discount; however, when you pay in dollars, the exchange rates vary considerably from store to store, and almost invariably they're far less favorable than the rate offered at one of the local banks. The net result is that you received a 20% discount, but then they take away from 9% to 15% on the dollar exchange, giving you a net savings of only 5% to 11%. You're better off shopping in the smaller stores, where prices are 8% to 12% lower on comparable items and paying in francs you've exchanged at a local bank.

The main shopping street in town is **rue Victor-Hugo.** The other two leading streets are **rue Schoelcher** and **rue St-Louis.** However, the most boutique-filled shopping streets are **rue Antione-Siger, rue Lamartine,** and **rue Moreau de Jones.** Here you'll find the latest French design fashions. Facing the tourist office and alongside **quai d'Esnambuc** is an open market where you can buy local handcrafts and souvenirs. Many of them are pretty tacky, however.

Far more interesting is the display of vegetables and fruit at the **open-air stalls along rue Isambert,** full of local flavor. You can't help but smell the **fish market** alongside the Levassor River. Gourmet chefs will find all sorts of spices in the open-air markets, or such goodies as tinned paté or canned quail in the local *supermarchés.*

For the ubiquitous local fabric, madras, there are shops on every street with bolts and bolts of it, all colorful and inexpensive. So-called haute couture and resort wear are sold in many boutiques dotting downtown Fort-de-France. Try to postpone your shopping trip if a cruise ship is in town, to avoid the stampede.

Cadet-Daniel, rue Antoine-Siger 72 (© **0596/71-41-48**), offers Lalique crystal and Christofle silver flatware, but by far the stars are the gleaming rows of 18-karat gold jewelry, some inset with precious and semiprecious stones. Most of it's manufactured in Martinique, and much of it is fashioned into traditional patterns inspired by the Créles. The **Centre des Métiers d'Art,** rue Ernest-Deproges (© **0596/70-25-01**), is an arts-and-crafts store adjacent to the tourist office. Inside is a mix of valuable and worthless local handmade artifacts, including bamboo, ceramics, painted fabrics, and patchwork quilts suitable for hanging.

Galeries Lafayette, rue Victor-Schoelcher 10, near the cathedral (© **0596/ 71-38-66**), is a small-scale branch of the most famous department store in Paris. Specializing in fashion for men, women, and children, it also offers leather goods, jewelry, watches, and all the predictably famous names in French perfume and fashion. The store offers 20% off for purchases made with U.S. dollar traveler's checks or a credit or charge card.

La Case à Rhum, in the Galerie Marchande, rue de la Liberté 5 (© **0596/ 73-73-20**), is the place to go for the local brew. Aficionados consider Martinique rum to be one of the world's finest. This shop offers all the brands of rum manufactured on Martinique (at least 12), as well as several others famous for their age and taste. Bottles range from 42F to 5,500F (€6.40–€835.85, $6.10–$797.10) for a connoisseur's delight—a bottle of rum distilled by the Bally Company in 1924 in the nearby hamlet of Carbet. They offer samples in small cups to prospective buyers. We suggest you try Clement, a dark mellow Old Mahogany, or a blood-red brown liqueur-like rum bottled by Bally.

La Galleria, route de Lamentin, is midway between Fort-de-France and the Lamentin Airport. This is the most upscale and elegant shopping complex on Martinique. On the premises are more than 60 vendors. You'll find a handful of cafes and simple restaurants to relieve your hunger pangs as you shop, as well as an outlet or two for the local pastries and sweets. **Paradise Island,** 20 rue Ernest-Deproges (© **0596/63-93-63**), features the most upscale collection of

Moments Begin the Beguine

The sexy and rhythmic beguine was *not* an invention of Cole Porter. It's a dance of the islands—although exactly which island depends on whom you ask. Popular wisdom and the encyclopedia give the nod to Martinique. Guadeloupeans claim it for their own, and to watch them dance it you might be convinced.

More famous than the dancers on Guadeloupe is the touring group **Les Grand Ballets Martiniquais.** Everybody who goes to Martinique wants to see the show performed by this bouncy group of about two dozen dancers, along with musicians, singers, and choreographers. This most interesting program of folk dances in the Caribbean was launched in the early 1960s, and their performances of the traditional dances of Martinique have been acclaimed in Europe and the United States. With a swoosh of gaily striped skirts and clever acting, the dancers capture all the exuberance of the island's soul. The group has toured abroad with great success, but they perform best on their home ground, presenting tableaux that tell of jealous brides and faithless husbands, demanding overseers and toiling cane cutters. Dressed in traditional costumes, the island women and men dance the spirited mazurka, which was brought from the ballrooms of Europe, and, of course, the exotic beguine.

Les Grand Ballets Martiniquais usually perform Monday at the Novotel Coralia Diamant, Wednesday at the Novotel Coralia Carayou, Thursday at the Méridien Trois-Ilets, and Friday at the Bakoua Beach, but these schedules can vary, so check locally. In addition, the troupe gives mini-performances aboard visiting cruise ships. The cost of dinner and the show is usually 260F (€39.50, $37.70). Most performances are at 8:30pm, with dinners at the hotels beginning at 7:30pm.

Whoever performs it for you, on whichever island, you'll soon realize the beguine is more than a dance—it's a way of life. See it for yourself, or dance it, if you think you can.

T-shirts on Martinique, each displayed as a kind of couture-conscious art form. Whatever you like will be available in about a dozen colors. The store also sells what it refers to as Les Polos, knit shirts with collars, priced at 229F to 329F (€34.80–€50, $33.20–$47.70), a good value.

Roger Albert, 7–9 rue Victor-Hugo (© **0596/71-71-71**), is by far the largest emporium of luxury goods on Martinique, a department store for locals and cruise ship passengers. It's one of five branches around Martinique, although this, a short walk from the waterfront, is by far the busiest. You'll find wristwatches (both fun and expensive), perfumes, sportswear by Lacoste and Tacchini, Lladró and Limoges porcelain, and crystal by Swarovski and such other manufacturers as Daum and Lalique. For anyone with a non-French passport, there are reductions of 20% off what a local resident would pay, plus discounts of an extra 20%, depending on seasonal discounts and promotions. Even better, the value-added tax isn't added to the price of your purchases.

FORT-DE-FRANCE AFTER DARK

The most exciting after-dark venue is a performance of the folkloric troupe **Les Grand Ballets Martiniquais** (see the box "Begin the Beguine," above).

Jazz sessions are a regular feature at **Westindies,** boulevard Alfassa (© **0596/ 63-63-77**). The popularity of dance clubs rises and falls almost monthly. Most of them charge a cover of 48F (€7.30, $6.95), unless some special entertainment is presented. Current favorites, drawing both locals and visitors, are **L'Alibi,** Morne Tartenson (© **0596/63-45-15**), and **Zenith,** blvd. Allègre 24 (© **0596/60-20-22**). Another local hot spot is **Le Queen,** in the Hotel La Batellière, at Schoelcher, outside Fort-de-France (© **0596/61-49-49**).

For casino action, head for Martinique's new **Casino Batelière Plaza,** at Schoelcher (© **0596/61-73-19**), outside Fort-de-France. You'll need a passport and 70F (€10.65, $10.15) to enter, plus a jacket and tie for men. You can play French baccarat, roulette, and blackjack. However, you can dispense with the formalities and the entrance fee to play the slots on the left as you enter. Slots are open Monday to Saturday noon to 3am. The more formal gambling is daily 8pm to 3am.

As for the gay scene, Martinique remains fairly conservative. However, the attitude of most Martinicans remains laissez-faire regarding your sleeping habits. Although you'll often see same-sex couples dancing together in the local discos, the only gay bar is **Daly's,** Route de Ravine Vilaine (© **0596/79-66-26**), in an affluent suburb of Fort-de-France. It's open only Friday and Saturday, offering two dance floors and both indoor and alfresco bars. Head out of Fort-de-France in the direction of St-Joseph and look for the signs.

3 Pointe du Bout ⭑ & Les Trois-Ilets

Pointe du Bout is a narrow peninsula across the bay from the busy capital of Fort-de-France. It's the most developed resort area of Martinique, with at least four of the island's largest hotels, an impressive marina, about a dozen tennis courts, pools, and facilities for horseback riding and all kinds of watersports. There's also a handful of independent restaurants, a gambling casino, boutiques, and in nearby Les Trois-Ilets, a Robert Trent Jones, Sr.–designed golf course. Except for the hillside that contains the Sofitel Bakoua Caralia, most of the district is flat and verdant, with gardens and rigidly monitored parking zones. All the hotels listed below are near the clean white-sand beaches of Pointe du Bout. Some of the smaller properties are convenient to the white sandy beaches of Anse Mitan. Nearby is also Les Trois-Ilets, the birthplace of Joséphine, the empress of France and wife of Napoléon Bonaparte.

GETTING THERE

If you're **driving** from Fort-de-France, take Route 1, along which you'll cross the plain of Lamentin—the industrial area of Fort-de-France and the site of the international airport. Often the air is filled with the fragrance of caramel because of the large sugarcane factories in the area. After 20 miles, you reach Trois-Ilets. Three miles farther, on the right, take Route D38 to Pointe du Bout. For those who want to reach Pointe du Bout by sea, there's a **ferry service** (more fully described in "Getting Around," earlier in this chapter) running all day long until midnight from the harbor front (quai d'Esnambuc) in downtown Fort-de-France. Round-trip fare is 33F (€5, $4.80).

ACCOMMODATIONS YOU CAN AFFORD

Auberge de L'Anse Mitan   Many guests like this hotel's location at the isolated end of a road whose more commercial side is laden with restaurants and a bustling nighttime parade. The hotel was built in 1930, but the hospitable Athanase family has renovated it several times since then. What you see today is a three-story concrete box–type structure. Six of the units are studios with kitchens and TVs. Rooms are boxy, but the beds are comfortable and have firm mattresses. The shower-only bathrooms are very small and cramped, but tidy. You don't get anything special here, but the price is right.

Anse Mitan, 97229 Trois-Ilets, Martinique, F.W.I. ☎ **0596/66-01-12.** Fax 0596/66-01-05. auberge-ansemitan@wanadoo.fr. 25 units. Winter 450F (€68.40, $65.20) single or double; 420F (€63.85, $60.85) studio. Off-season 330F (€50.15, $47.80) single or double; 300F (€45.60, $43.50) studio. Room (but not studio) rates include breakfast. AE, DC, MC, V. *In room:* A/C.

GREAT DEALS ON DINING

Chez Fanny   CREOLE/FRENCH   On the ground floor of a four-story concrete building facing the sea, this restaurant is the domain of Creole chef Fanny Gallonde, who prepares well-received platters for crowds that at lunchtime fill it to capacity. The decor is unpretentious, and the food includes a traditional roster of tried-and-true staples like *boudin* (blood sausage) Creole, codfish beignets (*accras de morue*), grilled or baked chicken, fricassee of shrimp, and grilled octopus. The menu also contains a short roster of dishes from the French mainland, including *coq au vin* (chicken in wine) and *boeuf bourguignonne.* The chef also makes a wicked couscous, spilling over with chicken, fresh vegetables, and chick peas, but only on Saturdays.

Trois-Ilets, Anse Mitan. ☎ **0596/66-04-34.** Reservations recommended. Main courses 38F–130F (€5.80–€19.75, $5.50–$18.85); fixed-price menus 68F–190F (€10.35–€28.90, $9.85–$27.55). DC, MC, V. Thurs–Tues noon–3pm and 7–10pm.

Pignon sur Mer   CREOLE   Simple and unpretentious, this is an intimate Creole restaurant that has about 15 tables, set within a rustically dilapidated building beside the sea, about a 12-minute drive from Pointe du Bout. Menu items are island-inspired, and might include *delices du Pignon,* a platter of shellfish, or whatever grilled fish or shellfish was hauled in that day. *Lambi* (conch), shrimp, and crayfish are almost always available, and brochettes of chicken are filling and flavorful.

Anse-à-l'Ane. ☎ **0596/68-38-37.** Main courses 70F–180F (€10.65–€27.35, $10.15–$26.10). MC, V. Tues–Sun 12:15–4pm; Tues–Sat 7–9:30pm.

HITTING THE BEACHES

The clean white-sand beaches of **Pointe du Bout,** site of the major hotels of Martinique, were created by developers and tend to be rather small. Most of the tourists head here, so the narrow beaches are among the island's most crowded. It doesn't help that Pointe du Bout is also the site of several marinas lining the shore, as well as the docking point for the ferry from Fort de France. Even if you don't find a lot of space on the beach, with its semiclear waters, you will find toilets, phones, restaurants, and cafes galore. The waters suffer from industrial usage, although apparently the pollution is not severe enough to prevent people from going in. You'll often see the French standing deep in the water, smoking cigarettes—perhaps not your idea of an idyllic beach vacation.

To the south, however, the golden-sand beaches at **Anse Mitan** have always been welcoming visitors, including many snorkelers. The beaches here are far

(Value) **Cheap Thrills: What to See & Do for Free (Well, Almost) on Martinique**

- **Find a Haven for Shutterbugs.** Martinique lends itself to photography, almost more than any other island in the Caribbean. That's why French fashion magazines often come here for shoots. Islanders don't mind being photographed, provided that you ask first. Of course, if they don't consider themselves properly dressed, they might turn down your request. The most picturesque sites are La Savane, in Fort-de-France; St-Pierre, the best place to photograph towering Mount Pelée; La Pagerie, with its decaying ruins of a sugar factory; and from the panoramic overlooks along La Trace, the serpentine road winding through the entire rain forest.

- **Traverse the Route de la Trace.** Cited as one of Martinique's most photographed places, this is one of the grand scenic routes of the French West Indies, going through the island's rain forest. From Fort-de-France, you can pick up the narrow Route de la Trace (or simply La Trace). It heads north through the dense rain forests blanketing the island, part of the Regional Natural Park, going all the way to Deux-Choux, a tunnel on the north side of Pitons du Carbet, the spiked and scarped mountain covering the north and central regions. From every hairpin turn on this corkscrew highway, you'll be rewarded with sweeping views of the capital and its yacht-clogged harbor. The route ultimately leads to Mount Pelée, with its still-active volcano. On the final leg of the trip, the road descends slowly through a beautiful area of pineapple plantations. Once at Morne-Rouge, the route joins with the north cross-island road between the calm Caribbean Sea and the more turbulent Atlantic coast.

- **Have a Bottle of Rum and a Tour.** Martinique still has more than a dozen rhumeries, and you'll find acres still devoted to sugarcane. From January to June, the juice from this cane ends up in one of these rhumeries. It's boiled until it forms a thick syrup and then is distilled into one of the strongest drinks you'll likely ever

less crowded and more inviting, with cleaner waters. However, the steepness of Martinique's shoreline leaves much to be desired by its swimmers and snorkelers. The water declines steeply into depths, no reefs ring the shores, and fish are rarely visible. Nonetheless, beaches here are ideal for sunbathing.

The neighboring beach to Anse-Mitan is **Anse-à-l'Ane,** an ideal place for a picnic on the white sands.

SPORTS & OTHER OUTDOOR PURSUITS

HORSEBACK RIDING   The premier riding facility on Martinique is **Ranch Jack,** Esperanze, Trois-Ilets (© **0596/68-37-69**). It offers morning horseback rides for both experienced and novice riders, at a cost of 350F (€53.20, $50.70) for a 3-hour ride. Jacques and Marlene Guinchard make daily promenades across the beaches and fields of Martinique, with a running explication of the

encounter. It's generally toned down and softened before bottling. Nearly all rhumeries offer free tours and even a free drink. The most fascinating distillery to visit is the Saint James Distillery in Ste-Marie (see "The North Loop," later in this chapter).

- **Explore the Village of Macouba.** At the northern tip of Martinique, between the towns of Grand-Rivière and Basse-Pointe, lies the village of Macouba (named after the Carib word for "fish"), overlooking Martinique Passage. If you're seeking an undiscovered village, head here. In the 17th century it was a thriving tobacco town, but prosperity has long passed it by. From its clifftop location you'll have one of the most panoramic views of the island, with the towering mountains as a backdrop. On a clear day you can see the island of Dominica, between Martinique and Guadeloupe. Here you can also visit the JM Distillery, which produces an excellent vintage rum. Macouba can be your starting point for a panoramic 6-mile drive along the Route du Grand-Rivière, passing groves of giant bamboo and cliffs curtained in vines.

- **Hike Through Martinique.** The northern part of the island is best for hiking, as it's covered by a rain forest guarded by towering volcanic Mount Pelée. The **Parc Naturel Régional de la Martinique** (© 0596/64-42-59) organizes hiking tours. One goes along the east coast to the Caravelle Peninsula, with marked hiking trails along the beach out to the historic ruins of the Château Dubuc. In all, there are 30 hiking trails, each well marked and maintained. Most are designed for hikers to go on their own, as they're relatively safe. However, the most serious hiking tour, a 2-hour climb to Mount Pelée, should be done with a guide, as it's the most difficult, going through thick foliage and along overgrown trails. Fairly easy are hikes at Les Ombrages, a nature trail at Ajoupa-Bouillon, or along the Gorges de la Falaise, a ravine leading to a waterfall where guided canyoning is the local sport.

history, fauna, and botany of the island. Cold drinks are included in the price, and transportation is usually free to and from the hotels of nearby Pointe du Bout. Four to 15 participants are needed to book a tour. This is an ideal way to discover both botanical and geographical Martinique.

SCUBA DIVING & SNORKELING   The beachfront of the Hotel Méridien (at Pointe du Bout) is the headquarters for the island's best-recommended dive outfit, **Espace Plongee Martinique** (© 0596/66-01-00), which welcomes anyone who shows up, regardless of where they happen to be staying. Daily dive trips, depending on demand, leave from Hotel Méridien's pier every day at 9am, returning at noon, and at 2:30pm, returning at 6pm. Popular dive sites within a reasonable boat ride, with enough diversity and variation in depth to appeal to divers of all degrees of proficiency, include *La Baleine* (The Whale) and *Cap*

Solomon. A dive shop stocks everything you'll need to take the plunge, from weight belts and tanks to wet suits and underwater cameras. Divers pay between 220F and 250F (€33.45–€38, $31.90–$36.25) per session. Pool instruction for novice divers, which is conducted in the Méridien's pool every day 11:30am to noon, is free.

Snorkeling equipment is usually available free to hotel guests, who quickly learn that coral, fish, and ferns abound in the waters around the Pointe du Bout hotels.

TENNIS Tennis pros at Bathy's Club at the **Hotel Méridien,** Pointe du Bout (© **0596/66-06-00**), usually allow nonguests to play for free if the courts are otherwise unoccupied, except at night, when the charge is almost always imposed.

You can also play on one of the three courts at **Golf de l'Imperatrice-Joséphine,** at Trois-Ilets (© **0596/68-32-81**). The setting here is one of the most beautiful on Martinique. It costs 80F (€12.15, $11.60) per hour to play. No racquet rentals are available.

WINDSURFING An enduringly popular sport in the French West Indies, windsurfing (*la planche à voile*) is available at most of the large-scale hotels. One of the best equipped is the **Cabane des Sports,** the beachfront facilities at the Hotel Méridien, Pointe du Bout (© **0596/66-00-00**). Lessons cost 150F (€22.80, $21.75) for 1 hour, and boards rent for about 60F (€9.10, $8.70) an hour.

A VISIT TO JOSÉPHINE'S TROIS-ILETS

About 20 miles south of Fort-de-France is Trois-Ilets, a charming little village. Marie Josèphe Rose Tascher de La Pagerie was born here in 1763. At 17, this young woman known as Joséphine married Vicomte Alexandre de Beauharnais and bore two children, but she and her husband were jailed during France's Reign of Terror; he became one of its last victims when he was guillotined. Joséphine then went on to meet the rising Napoléon Bonaparte and become the empress of France from 1804 to 1809. Six years older than her husband, she pretended she'd lost her birth certificate so he wouldn't find out her true age. When she couldn't bear him a child, Napoléon divorced her, and she ended her days at Malmaison. Although many historians call her ruthless and selfish, she's still revered by some on Martinique as an uncommonly gracious lady. Others have less kind words—because Napoléon is said by some historians to have reinvented slavery, and many blame Joséphine's influence.

One mile outside the hamlet, turn left to La Pagerie, where the small **Musée de la Pagerie** (© **0596/68-33-06**), holding mementos relating to Joséphine, has been installed in the former estate kitchen. Along with her childhood bed in the kitchen, you'll see a passionate letter from Napoléon. Dr. Robert Rose-Rosette compiled the collection. Here Joséphine gossiped with her slaves and played the guitar. Still remaining are the partially restored ruins of the Pagerié sugar mill and the church (in the village itself) where she was christened in 1763. The plantation was destroyed in a hurricane. The museum is open Tuesday to Friday 9am to 5:30pm and Saturday and Sunday 9am to 1pm and 2:30 to 5:30pm, charging 20F (€3.05, $2.90) for admission.

A botanical garden, the **Parc des Floralies,** is adjacent to the Golf de l'Imperatrice-Joséphine (see "Sports & Other Outdoor Pursuits," above), as is the Musée de la Pagerie (see above).

Maison de la Canne, Pointe Vatable (℃ **0596/68-32-04**), stands on the road to Trois-Ilets. (From Fort-de-France, you can take a taxi or shuttle bus to La Marina, Pointe du Bout; from here, an unnumbered bus heads for Pointe Vatable.) It was created in 1987 on the premises of an 18th-century distillery to house a permanent exhibit that tells the story of sugarcane and the sweeping role it played in the economic and cultural development of Martinique. Exhibits include models, tools, a miniature slave ship, an ancient cart tethered to life-size models of two oxen, and a restored carriage. Hostesses guide visitors through the exhibit. It's open Tuesday to Sunday 9am to 5:30pm, charging 20F (€3.05, $2.90) for adults and 5F (€.75, 70¢) for children 5 to 12 (free 4 and under).

SHOPPING

The **Marina complex** has a number of interesting boutiques. Several sell hand-crafts and curios from Martinique. They're sometimes of good quality and are expensive, regrettably, particularly if you buy some of the batiks of natural silk and the enameled jewel boxes.

At Christmastime, many of the island's traditional foie gras and pastries are presented in crocks made by the island's largest earthenware factories, the **Poterie de Trois-Ilets,** Quartier Poterie, Trois-Ilets (℃ **0596/68-03-44**). At least 90% of its production is devoted to brick-making. However, one small-scale offshoot of the company devotes itself to producing earth-toned stoneware and pottery whose colors and shapes are a tribute to the folklore of Martinique. In theory, the studios are open Monday to Saturday 7am to 2:30pm, but call before you set out to make sure they'll accept visitors.

POINTE DU BOUT AFTER DARK

Martinique has one of the dullest casinos in the French West Indies, **Casino Trois-Ilets** at Hotel Méridien Trois-Ilets, Pointe du Bout (℃ **0596/66-00-30**), open daily 10pm to 3am, charging 70F (€10.65, $10.15) for entrance to the room where roulette or blackjack is played. A picture ID is required. Entrance to the slot-machine room is free.

A mellow piano bar atmosphere is found at **L'Amphore,** in the rear of Le Bak-oua hotel, at Pointe du Bout (℃ **0596/66-03-09**).

4 The South Loop

South of Pointe du Bout, you can find sun and beaches. Resort centers here include Le Diamant and Ste-Anne. On the way to them from Trois-Ilets, you can follow a small curved road that brings you to **Anse-à-l'Ane, Grande Anse,** and **Anses d'Arlets.** At any of these places are small beaches, quite safe and usu-ally not crowded.

ANSES D'ARLETS

This charming little village features a white-sand beach dotted with brightly painted *gommiers* (fishing boats), a good-size pier from which children swim and adults fish, a pretty steepled church, a bandstand for holiday concerts, and a smattering of modest dining spots. Rue du Président-Kennedy honors the slain American president.

The waters off Anses d'Arlets are a playground for scuba divers, with a wide variety of small tropical fish and colorful coral formations. The area itself has been for many years a choice spot for weekend second homes and is now begin-ning to develop touristically.

From Anses d'Arlets, D37 takes you to Le Diamant. The road offers much scenery.

LE DIAMANT

On the island's southwestern coastline, this village offers a good beach open to the prevailing southern winds. The village is named after one of Martinique's best-known geological oddities, **Le Rocher du Diamant** (**Diamond Rock**), a barren offshore island that juts upward from the sea to a height of 573 feet. Sometimes referred to as the Gibraltar of the Caribbean, it figured prominently in a daring British-led invasion in 1804, when British mariners carried a formidable amount of ammunition and 110 sailors to the top. Despite frequent artillery bombardments from the French-held coast, the garrison held out for 18 months, completely dominating the passage between the rock and the coastline of Martinique. Intrepid foreigners sometimes visit Diamond Rock, but the access across the strong currents of the channel is risky.

Diamond Beach ★★, on the Martinique mainland, offers a sandy bottom, verdant groves of swaying palms, and many surfing and bathing possibilities. The entire district has developed into a resort, scattered with generally small hotels, most of which consist of simple clusters of low-rise buildings with good landscaping and access to the beach.

ACCOMMODATIONS YOU CAN AFFORD

Hôtel Relais Caraibes   Despite its charm (some visitors define it as a tropical inn with an ocean view), the Caraibes looks more expensive than it is. It consists of a main building (with a trio of small rooms above its restaurant) and a dozen medium-size bungalows scattered over carefully clipped lawns. Each bungalow has a porch and a view from the clifftop location over the water to the jagged crags of Diamond Rock. (The rooms don't have oceans views.) Regardless of its classification, each unit is decorated in an eclectic and rather modest style, each with a small salon, plus a sofa bed with a firm mattress and a tiny but tidy bathroom with tub and shower. Some guests prefer the standard rooms, which have a few graceful notes, like hand-painted headboards. Although privacy is ensured by this inn's location about a mile from the main highway, the beach lies within a 5-minute walk, at the bottom of the low cliffs on which the hotel sits.

La Cherry, 97223 Le Diamant, Martinique, F.W.I. Ⓒ **0596/76-44-65.** Fax 0596/76-21-20. relais-caraibes@ wanadoo.fr. 15 units. Nov–July 500F–900F (€76–€136.80, $72.45–$130.45) single; 610F–1,030F (€92.70–€156.55, $88.40–$149.30) double; 610F–1,020F (€92.70–€155, $88.40–$147.80) bungalow for 1; 720F–1,440F (€109.40–€218.85, $104.35–$208.70) bungalow for 2. Rates include breakfast. MC, V. Closed Aug–Oct. **Amenities:** Restaurant, bar, pool, babysitting, laundry. *In room:* A/C, TV, minibar, hair dryer, safe.

L'Ecrin Bleu   In the rocky hills above the hamlet of Le Diamant, this blue-and-white hotel was built in the early 1990s, and it is still well-maintained today by the Tosatos from Marseilles. Isolated on virtually every side and composed of three buildings, it offers carefully decorated rooms with views sweeping out over the sea and the lofty heights of Diamond Rock. Although not large, the rooms are nicely done in a simple French Antillean style, with fine mattresses and renovated shower-only bathrooms that may lack space but not good maintenance. The beach is a 5-minute downhill walk away.

Morne de la Croix, 97223 Le Diamant, Martinique, F.W.I. Ⓒ **0596/76-41-92.** Fax 0596/76-41-90. www. ecrinbleu.com. 19 units. Winter 450F (€68.40, $65.20) single; 550F (€83.60, $79.70) double. Off-season 400F (€60.80, $57.95) single; 450F (€68.40, $65.20) double. Rates include breakfast. AE, MC, V. **Amenities:** Restaurant (dinner only), bar, pool with aquacise classes, exercise room, access to scuba-related activities, babysitting, laundry. *In room:* A/C, no phone.

Les Chambres d'Hôtes Diamant Noir   Much of the allure of this place derives from its charming owners, Dominique and Elléna Bertin. It consists of a 30-year-old main villa, with five units, set in a sprawling well-maintained garden and a 5-year-old, four-unit annex adjacent to the sea. The small rooms have little style and are basic, except for comfortable beds; the shower-only bathrooms are a bit small but well maintained. It's about 1½ miles from Le Diamant, painted white with pink shutters, swathed in trailing strands of bougainvillea and ringed with fruit trees. Breakfast is the only meal served, but at least two restaurants are within an easy walk, and a communal kitchen is available for use by all guests.

Anse Cafard, Dizac, 97233 Le Diamant, Martinique F.W.I. © 0596/76-41-25. Fax 0596/76-28-89. www. sasi.fr/diamnoir. 9 units. Winter 310F–375F (€47.10–€57, $44.95–$54.35) single; 355F–400F (€53.95–€60.80, $51.45–$57.95) double. Off-season 235F (€35.70, $34.05) single; 285F (€43.30, $41.30) double. Rates include breakfast. No credit cards. **Amenities:** Communal kitchen, babysitting, laundry. *In room:* A/C in some rooms, TV.

GREAT DEALS ON DINING

Restaurant Diamant Plage ★ *(Finds)* CREOLE   One of the most gregarious and appealing restaurants in this hamlet is maintained by members of the Octavia family, especially Jules, who has elevated the art of informal dining *à la Creole* to a bemused and beguiling art form. Look for a cement-built, clapboard-sided house, painted green, on the main street of town, with a view over the sea and the faraway offshore rocks of Le Diamant. Menu items include shellfish, lobster, stuffed crabs, *boudin noir,* and grilled fish, any of which can be literally washed down with rum punches, beer, or wine.

Rue Justin-Roc, Bourg-du-Diamant. © 0596/76-40-48. Reservations recommended. Main courses 75F–195F (€11.40–€29.65, $10.85–$28.25). AE, DC, MC, V. Tues–Sun noon–3:30pm and 7–10pm.

LE MARIN

As you follow the road south to Trois-Rivières, you'll come to **Ste-Luce,** one of the island's most charming villages. Beautiful **beaches** surround the town, and it's the site of the **Forêt Montravail.** Continuing, you'll reach Rivière-Pilote, quite a large town, and **Le Marin,** at the bottom of a bay of the same name, 22 miles south of Fort-de-France.

Long a popular stop en route south, Le Marin is the site of one of Martinique's most historic monuments, a **Jesuit-style church** built in 1766. The town has become a sailing center, its marina sheltering the island's single largest yacht charter fleet. Also of interest is Le Marin's biennial **August fête,** a cultural extravaganza. For overnighting, the Auberge du Marin (see below) is a good bet.

After passing Le Marin, you reach **Vauclin,** by going northeast; this is a fishing port and market town that's pre-Columbian. If you have time, stop in at the 18th-century **Chapel of the Holy Virgin.** Visitors like to make an excursion to **Mount Vauclin,** the highest point in southern Martinique, where you'll enjoy one of the most scenic panoramas in the West Indies.

ACCOMMODATIONS YOU CAN AFFORD

Auberge du Marin   This simple inn mimics the tradition of a *restaurant avec chambres,* which is well-established in mainland France but not particularly common in the Antilles. Although most of the management's energies are devoted to running a restaurant (described in "Great Deals on Dining," below), it maintains two no-frills rooms with cramped but serviceable showers on the street level and three larger rooms upstairs that share a bathtub, shower, and toilet. The units without bathrooms are much bigger and more comfortable than the rooms with bathrooms, so the price is the same for both. Don't expect luxury or resort amenities here, as the place is isolated and very simple, and Plage de Ste-Anne is 6 miles away. The advantages of this place are the low rates, the view of the marina from some rooms, the garden setting, and a simple on-site restaurant. The inn has a stunning collection of exotic masks from Haiti, Ecuador, and Venezuela.

Rue Osman-Duquesnay 21, 97290 Le Marin, Martinique, F.W.I. ✆ **0596/74-83-88.** Fax 0596/74-76-47. 5 units, 2 with bathroom. Year-round 200F (€30.40, $29) single with or without bathroom; 250F (€38, $36.25) double with or without bathroom. 100F (€15.20, $14.50) extra bed in any room. Rates include breakfast. MC, V. **Amenities:** Restaurant. *In room:* No phone.

GREAT DEALS ON DINING

Auberge du Marin *Value* FRENCH-CREOLE This restaurant's staff is somewhat blasé, but the place will probably grow more likable as your meal progresses, and the relatively low tab will more than make up for the rustic setting. Decorated with artifacts and carved masks from Venezuela, Haiti, and Brazil, the restaurant is in the heart of Le Marin, overlooking a garden and a marina. The lunch *plat du jour* is a meal in itself, and the fixed-price meal (soup or salad, a main platter of meat or grilled fish, and dessert) is a bargain. The cuisine is French Creole and evocative of southwestern France. The chef makes a delectable *cassoulet* filled with white beans and meat products. His *margret* of duckling is excellent, as is his *confit* of duckling with flap mushrooms. He also prepares an old-fashioned version of sweetbreads.

In the Auberge du Marin hotel, Rue Osman-Duquesnay 21, Le Marin. ✆ **0596/74-83-88.** Reservations recommended. Main courses 64F–145F (€9.75–€22.05, $9.25–$21); lunch *plat du jour* 47F (€7.15, $6.80); fixed-price 3-course lunch or dinner 82F (€12.45, $11.90). AE, MC, V. Mon–Fri noon–1:30pm and daily 7:30–9:30pm. Closed Sept.

STE-ANNE

From Le Marin, a 5-mile drive brings you to Ste-Anne, at the extreme southern tip of Martinique. This sleepy little village is known for **white-sand beaches** (in contrast to those to the north, which are rather gray). In many ways, the beaches at Les Salines are Martinique's finest. The climate is arid like parts of Arizona, and the beaches are almost always sunny, perhaps too much so during the fierce midday sun.

Les Salines tends to be crowded on holidays and weekends, as many islanders and their families flock to this beach during those times. Regrettably, the beach isn't big enough to handle the hordes, and you'd be wise to seek out other beaches at this time. The name of the beach comes from Étang des Salines, a large salt pond that forms a backdrop to the strip of sand. Under no circumstances should you go under the machineel trees here for protection in a rainfall. When it's sunny, you can seek shade here. But when it rains, drops falling from this poisonous tree will be like acid on your tender skin. The trees are found mainly at the southeastern end of the beach.

Salines is the site of Martinique's only real **gay beach.** Drive to the far end of the parking lot, near the sign for Petite Anse des Salines. Here you'll find a trail leading through thick woods to a sun-flooded beach often filled with naked gay men, with an occasional lesbian couple. Technically, there are no legal nudist beaches on Martinique, so it's possible you could be arrested here for going nude, although authorities don't seem to enforce this law. Throughout the island, however, the European custom of topless bathing isn't uncommon on any of the beaches of Martinique or even around hotel pools.

Ste-Anne opens onto views of the Ste-Lucia Canal, and nearby is the Petrified Savanna Forest, which the French call **Savane des Pétrifications.** It's a field of petrified volcanic boulders in the shape of logs. The eerie desertlike site, no-man's-land, is studded with cacti.

ACCOMMODATIONS YOU CAN AFFORD

La Dunette ★★ (Value   A motel-like stucco structure directly beside the sea, this hotel appeals to guests who appreciate its simplicity and its isolation from the more built-up resort areas of other parts of Martinique. A three-story building originally constructed in the late 1960s, it's near the Club Med and the white-sand beaches of Les Salines. Best defined as an unpretentious seaside inn with a simple, summery decor, the hotel is accented with a garden filled with flowers and tropical plants. The furnishings are casual and modern, although some rooms are quite small. The private shower-only bathrooms, although cramped, are well maintained. The in-house restaurant is better than you might expect, thanks to the culinary finesse of the Tanzania-born owner, Gerard Kambona.

97227 Ste-Anne, Martinique, F.W.I. ℂ **0596/76-73-90.** Fax 0596/76-76-05. 18 units. Winter 600F (€91.20, $86.95) single or double. Off-season 500F (€76, $72.45) single or double. Rates include continental breakfast. MC, V. **Amenities:** Restaurant. *In room:* A/C, TV.

GREAT DEALS ON DINING

Aux Filets Bleus ★ CREOLE/FRENCH   This family-run blue-and-white restaurant is a 30-minute drive south of the airport. The seaside exposure of the alfresco dining room and its terrace makes you feel as if you're in an isolated tropical retreat, where the only sound is the splash of waves and the tinkling of ice in glasses. What appears to be a glass-covered reflecting pool set into the floor is actually a lobster tank, supposedly one of only a few on Martinique. The restaurant offers one of the island's cheapest fixed-price menus, unless you opt for the more expensive shellfish menu. Specialties include *bouillabaisse de la mer,* three types of fish covered with a tomato and onion sauce; crabmeat salad with a coulis of tomato, basil, and olive oil; and *pave de daurade aux senteurs des Iles,* white fish with a coriander-and-fennel sauce.

Pointe Marin, Ste-Anne. ℂ **0596/76-73-42.** Reservations required. Fixed-price menu 70F–275F (€10.65–€41.80, $10.15–$39.85). MC, V. Daily noon–3:30pm and 7–10:30pm.

Poï et Virginie ★★ CREOLE   From the outside, this restaurant looks like a ramshackle bungalow beside the beach. Inside, the decor is much more substantial, with terra-cotta floor tiles, primitive Haitian paintings, slowly spinning ceiling fans, and lots of roughly textured wood. If it isn't too hot or rainy, you might sit on a wooden deck whose foundations are sunk into the seabed and hear the waves splashing beneath your table. Menu choices include fresh local lobster, marinated raw conch, stuffed crab back, raw marinated fish, local fresh oysters, and grilled local fish. One fish dish is exceptional: grilled fresh fish with sauce Martiniquaise (vinaigrette with Martinique spices). Most dishes, except for the expensive shellfish platters, are at the lower end of the price scale. The restaurant's name was inspired by a 19th-century romantic novel, *Paul et Virginie,* whose star-crossed protagonists were doomed to everlasting unrequited love.

Place de l'Eglise, rue du Bord-de-Mer, Ste-Anne. ℂ **0596/76-76-86.** Reservations recommended. Main courses 60F–250F (€9.10–€38, $8.70–$36.25). AE, MC, V. Tues 7–9pm; Wed–Sun noon–2:30pm and 7–9:30pm.

5 The North Loop

North of Fort-de-France, our main targets are **Le Carbet, St-Pierre, Mount Pelée,** and **Leyritz.** However, we'll sandwich in many stops along the way. From Fort-de-France there are three ways to head north to Mount Pelée. The first way is to follow the N4 up to St-Joseph. Here you take the left fork for 3 miles after St-Joseph and turn onto D15 toward Marigot.

Another way to Mount Pelée is to take the N3 through the vegetation-rich mornes until you reach Le Morne Rouge. This road is known as the Route de la Trace and is now the center of the Parc Naturel de la Martinique. Yet a third route to reach Mount Pelée is to follow N2 along the coast. Near Fort-de-France, the first town you reach is Schoelcher.

Farther along N2 you come to Case-Pilote, then Bellefontaine. This portion, along the most frequented tourist route on Martinique—that is, Fort-de-France to St-Pierre—will remind many a traveler of the French Riviera. Bellefontaine is a small fishing village with boats stretched along the beach. Note the many houses also built in the shape of boats.

LE CARBET

Leaving Bellefontaine, a 5-mile drive north will deliver you to Le Carbet. Columbus landed here in 1502, and the first French settlers arrived in 1635. In 1887, Gauguin lived here for 4 months before going on to Tahiti. You can stop for a swim at an Olympic-size pool set into the hills or watch the locals scrubbing clothes in a stream. The town lies on the bus route from Fort-de-France to St-Pierre.

Centre d'Art Musée Paul-Gauguin, Anse Turin, Le Carbet (© **0596/78-22-66**), is near the beach represented in the artist's *Bord de Mer.* The landscape hasn't changed in 100 years. The museum, in a five-room building, commemorates the French artist's 1887 stay on Martinique, with books, prints, letters, and other memorabilia. There are also paintings by René Corail, sculpture by Hector Charpentier, and examples of the artwork of Zaffanella. Of special interest are faïence mosaics made of once-white pieces that turned pink, maroon, blue, and black in 1902 when the fires of Mount Pelée devastated St-Pierre. There are also changing exhibits of works by local artists. The museum is open daily 9am to 5:30pm, with an admission of 20F (€3.05, $2.90) for adults and 5F (€.75, 70¢) for children under 8.

ST-PIERRE 🅰

In the early 1900s, St-Pierre was known as the Little Paris of the West Indies. Home to 30,000 inhabitants, it was the cultural and economic capital of Martinique. On May 7, 1902, the citizens read in their daily newspaper that Mount Pelée didn't present any more risk to the population than Vesuvius did to the Neapolitans. However, on May 8, 1902, at 8am, the southwest side of Mount Pelée exploded into fire and lava. At 8:02am all 30,000 inhabitants were dead—that is, all except 1. A convict in his underground cell was saved by the thickness of the walls. When islanders reached the site, the convict was paroled and left Martinique to tour in Barnum & Bailey's Circus. St-Pierre never recovered its past splendor. Now it could be called the Pompeii of the West Indies. Ruins of the church, the theater, and some other buildings can be seen along the coast.

One of the best ways to get an overview of St-Pierre is riding a rubber-wheeled train, the *CV Paris Express* (© **0596/78-31-41**), which departs on tours from the base of the Musée Volcanologique. Tours cost 50F (€7.60, $7.25) for adults and 25F (€3.80, $3.60) for children and run Monday to Friday 10:30am to 1pm and 2:30 to 7pm. In theory, tours depart about once an hour, but they leave only when there are enough people to justify a trip.

Musée Volcanologique, rue Victor-Hugo, St-Pierre (℘ **0596/78-10-32**), was created by American volcanologist Franck Alvard Perret, who turned the museum over to the city in 1933. Here, in pictures and relics dug from the debris, you can trace the story of what happened to St-Pierre. Dug from the lava is a clock that stopped at the exact moment the volcano erupted. The museum is open daily 9am to 5pm, with an admission of 10F (€1.50, $1.45); free for children 7 and under.

GREAT DEALS ON DINING

La Factorerie CREOLE This budget place is between St-Pierre and Le Prêcheur, near the ruins of a 19th-century church, the Eglise du Fort. It's a ramshackle-looking cottage in a grove of mango trees and coconut palms. At least some of the staff have been trained at Martinique's nearby agricultural training school. The restaurant is a bit battered and serves only lunch, but if you're in the neighborhood around noon, it makes a good stop. You'll enjoy dishes like chicken with coconut, conch fricassee, chicken with prawns, fresh-water crayfish served with piquant tomato sauce, *colombo* with chicken, and a dessert flan made with fresh coconuts and sweet potatoes.

Quartier Fort, St-Pierre. ℘ **0596/78-12-53.** Reservations recommended. Main courses 75F–160F (€11.40–€24.30, $10.85–$23.20). AE, MC, V. Daily noon–2pm.

LE PRÊCHEUR

From St-Pierre you can continue along the coast north to Le Prêcheur. Once the home of Mme de Maintenon, the mistress of Louis XIV, it's the last village along the northern coast of Martinique. Here you can see hot springs of volcanic origin and the **Tombeau des Caraïbes (Tomb of the Caribs),** where, according to legend, the collective suicide of many West Indian natives took place after they returned from a fishing expedition and found their homes pillaged by the French.

MOUNT PELÉE

A panoramic and winding road (N2) takes you through a **tropical rain forest.** The curves are of the hairpin variety, and the road is twisty and not always kept in good shape. However, you're rewarded with tropical flowers, baby ferns, plumed bamboo, and valleys so deeply green you'll think you're wearing cheap sunglasses.

The village of **Morne Rouge,** at the foot of Mount Pelée, is a popular vacation spot for Martinicans. From here a narrow and unreliable road brings you to a level of 2,500 feet above sea level, 1,600 feet under the round summit of the volcano that destroyed St-Pierre. Mount Pelée itself rises 4,575 feet above sea level.

If you're a trained mountain climber and would like to do 4 or 5 hours of hiking, you can scale the peak to Grand' Rivière. Realize that this is a mountain, that rain is frequent, and that temperatures drop very low. Tropical growth often hides deep crevices in the earth, and there are other dangers. So if you're really serious about this climb, you should hire an experienced guide. As for the volcano, its death-dealing reign in 1902 apparently satisfied it—at least for the time being.

On your descent from Mount Pelée, drive down to **Ajoupa-Bouillon,** which some describe, justifiably, as the most beautiful town on Martinique. Abounding in flowers and shrubbery with bright yellow and red leaves, this little village is the site of the remarkable **Gorges de la Falaise,** mini-canyons on the Falaise River up which you can travel to reach a waterfall.

GREAT DEALS ON DINING

Le Fromager ★ *Finds* CREOLE-FRENCH   Set about a half mile uphill (east) of the center of St-Pierre, this indoor–outdoor villa, owned by the Rene family, welcomes luncheon guests with a humor and charm that's half French, half Martiniquais. The restaurant, which resembles a covered open-air pavilion, has a sweeping view of the town. Good-tasting menu items include marinated octopus, grilled conch or lobster, curried goat or chicken, and whatever grilled fish is available that day. This is a good lunch stopover during your tour of the island.

Route de Fonds-St-Denis, St-Pierre. ✆ 0596/78-19-07. Reservations recommended. Fixed-price menu 100F–190F (€15.20–€28.90, $14.50–$27.55); main courses 80F–130F (€12.15–€19.75, $11.60–$18.85). AE, DC, MC, V. Daily noon–3pm.

LEYRITZ

If you continue east toward the coast, near the town of Basse-Pointe in northeastern Martinique, turn left a mile before Basse-Pointe and follow a road that goes deep into sugarcane country to Leyritz, where you'll find one of the best-restored plantations on Martinique.

ACCOMMODATIONS YOU CAN AFFORD

Hôtel Plantation de Leyritz ★★   This hotel, which offers spa facilities, dates from 1700, when a plantation owner, Bordeaux-born Michel de Leyritz, built it. It's still a working banana plantation that's been restored to its original character and often hosts a stampede of cruise ship passengers. There are 16 acres of tropical gardens, with views that sweep across the Atlantic and take in fearsome Mount Pelée. At the core of the grounds is an 18th-century great house, with rugged stone walls (20 in. thick), beamed ceilings, and tile and flagstone floors. The interior is cozy, with mahogany tables, overstuffed sofas, and gilt mirrors. About half the accommodations are in a series of small outbuildings scattered around the property; others are in a newer annex adjacent to the spa. The guest rooms come in a variety of different sizes; some have sundecks. The shower-only bathrooms, although tiny, are tidy. Don't expect well-polished luxury—that's not the style here.

The dining room is in a former rum distillery, and provides elaborate dinners, featuring both French and Creole dishes.

97218 Basse-Pointe, Martinique, F.W.I. ✆ 0596/78-53-92. Fax 0596/78-92-44. hleyritz@cgit.com. 67 units. Winter 750F (€114, $108.70) single or double. Off-season 550F (€83.60, $79.70) single or double. Rates include continental breakfast. AE, MC, V. **Amenities:** Restaurant, bar, spa. *In room:* A/C, TV.

GREAT DEALS ON DINING

La Plantation ★ FRENCH-CREOLE   This remains one of the finest restaurants in Martinique, following its move into Leyritz Plantation, the island's showcase manor house at Basse-Pointe.

La Plantation is run by a hardworking staff and a chef who aims to serve an imaginative cuisine. The foie gras comes from France, but the herbs flavoring it are Antillean. We found a traditional version of rack of lamb perfectly cooked and herby. Everything we've sampled here has been noteworthy, especially a soup of gargantuan crayfish. A salad served here was worth getting *Gourmet* magazine on the phone. It was filled with crab, hearts of palm, conch, and baby octopus—all bathed in a champagne vinaigrette with a confetti of pecans, carrots, red bell peppers, diced sweet prunes, and parsley.

In Hotel Plantation de Leyritz, 97218 Basse-Pointe. © 0596/78-53-92. Reservations required. Main courses 120F–250F (€18.25–€38, $17.40–$36.25); fixed-price lunch 200F (€30.40, $29). AE, MC, V, Mon–Fri noon–2pm; Mon–Sat 7:30–9:30pm.

BASSE-POINTE

At the northernmost point on the island, Basse-Pointe is a land of pineapple and banana plantation fields, covering the Atlantic-side slopes of Mount Pelée.

GREAT DEALS ON DINING

Chez Mally Edjam ✶✶ FRENCH-CREOLE This local legend operates from a modest house beside the main road in the town center, 36 miles from Fort-de-France. Appreciating its exotic but genteel charm, many visitors prefer to drive all the way from Pointe du Bout to dine here instead of at the La Plantation. You sit at one of a handful of tables on the side porch, unless you prefer a seat in the somewhat more formal dining room.

Grandmotherly Mally Edjam (ably assisted by France-born Martine Hugé) is busy in the kitchen, turning out her Creole delicacies. They know how to prepare all the dishes for which the island is known: stuffed land crab with hot seasoning, small pieces of conch in a tart shell, and a classic *colombo de porc* (the Creole version of pork curry). Equally acclaimed are the lobster vinaigrette, the papaya soufflé (which must be ordered in advance), and the highly original *confitures* (tiny portions of fresh island fruits, such as pineapple and guava, that have been preserved in a vanilla syrup).

Route de la Côte Atlantique. © 0596/78-51-18. Reservations required. Main courses 75F–180F (€11.40–€27.35, $10.85–$26.10); fixed-price menu 75F (€11.40, $10.85). MC, V. Daily noon–3pm; dinner by special arrangement only. Closed mid-July to mid-Aug.

GRAND' RIVIÈRE

After Basse-Pointe, the town you reach on your northward trek is Grand' Rivière. From here you must turn back, but before doing so, you might want to stop at a good restaurant right at the entrance to the town.

Yva Chez Vava ✶ *Finds* FRENCH-CREOLE Directly west of Basse-Pointe, in a low-slung building painted the peachy-orange of a pawpaw fruit, Yva Chez Vava is a combination private home and restaurant. It represents the hard labor of three generations of Creole women. Infused with a simple country-inn style, it was established in 1979 by a well-remembered, long-departed matron, Vava, whose daughter, Yva, is now assisted by her own daughter, Rosy. Family recipes are the mainstay of this modest bistro. A la carte items include Creole soup, a blaff of sea urchins, lobster, and various *colombos* or curries. Local delicacies used in the kitchen include *z'habitants* (crayfish), *vivaneau* (red snapper), *tazard* (kingfish), and *accras de morue* (cod fritters).

Blvd. Charles-de-Gaulle. © 596/55-72-72. Reservations recommended. Main courses 65F–180F (€9.90–€27.35, $9.40–$26.10); fixed-price menu 100F–150F (€15.20–€22.80, $14.50–$21.75). AE, DC, MC, V. Daily noon–6pm.

STE-MARIE

Heading south along the coastal road, you'll pass Le Marigot to reach a sight-seeing stop in the little town of Ste-Marie. The **Musée du Rhum St-James,** route de l'Union at the Saint James Distillery (© 0596/69-30-02), displays engravings, antique tools and machines, and other exhibits tracing the history of sugarcane and rum from 1765 to the present. When inventories of rum are low and the distillery is functioning (Feb–July), guided tours of both the museum and its distillery are offered. Tours depart at 10am, 11:30am, 1pm, and 2:30pm, costing 20F (€3.05, $2.90) per person, including a rum-tasting. Admission to the museum (open daily 9am–7pm, regardless of whether the distillery is functioning) is free. Samples of rum are available for purchase on site.

From here you can head out the north end of town and loop inland a bit for a stop at Morne des Esses, or continue heading south straight to Trinité.

GREAT DEALS ON DINING

Restaurant la Decouverte/Chez Tatie Simone ★ *Finds* CREOLE   Set near Martinique's northeastern tip, 2½ miles north of Ste-Marie, this restaurant prepares superb versions of traditional Creole cuisine. The cement-sided house, built in the early 1980s, is the showcase for the cuisine of "Auntie" (*Tatie*) Simone Adelise. In a dining room accented with white wainscoting and folkloric paintings, you'll enjoy her *boudin rouge* (blood sausages, in this case accented with habanero chiles and cinnamon), *boudin blanc* (sausages made from pulverized conch and spices), couscous with *fruits de mer* (garnished with shrimp, crayfish, sea urchins, clams, and octopus), and a succulent array of grilled fish.

A member of the staff might propose a short stroll after your meal, along a well-marked trail dotted with signs that give the names of specific trees and plants. At its end, you'll be rewarded with sweeping panoramas over sea and coastline. Estimated round-trip time for the hike, not counting stops to admire the view, is 40 minutes.

Forêt la Philippe, Route du Marigot, Ste-Marie. ✆ 0596/69-44-04. Reservations recommended. Main courses 80F–160F (€12.15–€24.30, $11.60–$23.20); fixed-price menu 120F–200F (€18.25–€30.40, $17.40–$29). AE, DC, MC, V. Daily 11am–10:30pm.

MORNE DES ESSES

This is the *vannerie* (basket-making) capital of Martinique, and you can pick up a sturdy straw food basket in any of the small village shops.

GREAT DEALS ON DINING

Le Colibri (The Hummingbird) ★ CREOLE   This is one of Martinique's oldest restaurants. Well-respected matriarch Mme Clotide Paladino opened this rustic-looking spot. To an increasing degree she is assisted by her daughters, Marie-José and Marie-Joseph, and her son, Joël. (Marie-José and Marie-Joseph are fraternal twins who bear a striking resemblance to each other, and the similarity of their names adds a charming but sometimes confusing spice to a meal here.) The site, which was enlarged and embellished in the mid-1990s with a series of paintings by local artists, is in the heart of town, near the post office. Two terraces, one of which overlooks a view of the busy kitchen, supplement the dining space. The cuisine is deeply rooted in Creole traditions and usually includes steaming bowls of *callaloo* soup garnished with crabmeat, Creole-style *boudin* (blood sausage), *accras* of codfish, and less conventional fare like *buisson d'érevisses* (stew of freshwater crayfish), chicken with coconut, conch tarts, avocado stuffed with crabmeat, and roast suckling pig. Especially appealing is a *salade de Colibri* loaded with seafood that some diners select as a main course and (when they're available) a *tourte des oursins* (sea urchin pie).

Allée de Colibri. ✆ 0596/69-91-95. Reservations recommended. Main courses 100F–250F (€15.20–€38, $14.50–$36.25). AE, DC, MC, V. Daily noon–3pm and 7–10pm.

TRINITÉ

If you're in Mornes des Esses, continue south and then turn east, or from Ste-Marie head south along the coastal route (N1) to reach the small village of Trinité. The town is the gateway to the Carvalle peninsula, where the **Presqui'ile de la Carabelle Nature Preserve** offers excellent hiking and one of the only safe beaches for swimming on the Atlantic coast, **Plage Trinité.** This town would hardly merit a stopover were it not for the Saint-Aubin Hotel.

ACCOMMODATIONS YOU CAN AFFORD

Saint-Aubin Hotel ⭐⭐ A former restaurant owner, Normandy-born Guy Forêt, has sunk his fortune into restoring this three-story Victorian house and turning it into one of the loveliest inns in the Caribbean. Painted a vivid pink with fancy gingerbread, the hotel was originally built in 1920 of brick and poured concrete as a replacement for a much older wood-sided house, which served as the seat of a large plantation. It sits on a hillside above sugarcane fields and the bay, 2 miles from the village of Trinité. It was named after the uninhabited islet of St-Aubin, which lies offshore and is visible from the hotel. There are 800 yards of public beach, plus a pool on the grounds. All the good-size bedrooms sport wall-to-wall carpeting and modern (not antique) furniture; views are of the garden or the sea. There are some family rooms as well. Each unit has a neatly tiled shower-only bathroom.

97220 Trinité, Martinique, F.W.I. ℂ **0596/69-34-77.** Fax 0596/69-41-14. 15 units. Winter 480F–580F (€72.95–€88.15, $69.55–$84.05) single or double. Off-season 380F–480F (€57.75–€72.95, $55.05–$69.55) single or double. Rates include continental breakfast. AE, DC, MC, V. **Amenities:** Restaurant, bar, pool. *In room:* A/C.

LE FRANÇOIS

Continuing your exploration of the east coast of Martinique, you can stop over in Le François to visit the **Musée Rhum Clement** at the Domaine de l'Acajou (ℂ **0596/54-62-07**), about 1½ miles south of the village center. The distillery is in the cellar of an 18th-century mansion with period furnishings. A Christopher Columbus exhibit is set up in caves, and other exhibits trace the institution of slavery in the islands. The museum is located in a botanic park; you could easily spend 2 or 3 hours exploring the exhibits and grounds. It's open daily 9am to 6pm. Admission is 40F (€6.10, $5.80) adults, 20F (€3.05, $2.90) children.

16

Nevis

A local once said the best reason to go to Nevis is to practice the fine art of *limin'*—doing nothing. Limin' might still be the best reason to come to this small volcanic island. You can find lodging in the old plantation houses, now converted to inns, or in the small Antillean guesthouses, and experience all the calm you want. And during the day you can head for reef-protected Pinney's Beach, a 3-mile strip of dark-gold sand set against a backdrop of palms, with panoramic views of St. Kitts.

Columbus sighted Nevis (*Nee*-vis), which lies 2 miles south of St. Kitts, in 1493. He called it Las Nieves, Spanish for "snows," because its mountains reminded him of the snow-capped range in the Pyrenees. When viewed from St. Kitts (see chapter 20), the island appears like a perfect cone, rising gradually to 3,232 feet. A saddle joins the tallest mountain to two smaller peaks, Saddle Hill (1,250 ft.) in the south and Hurricane Hill (only 250 ft.) in the north. Coral reefs rim the shore, and there's mile after mile of palm-shaded white-sand beaches.

Settled by the British in 1628, the island is famous as the birthplace of Alexander Hamilton, the U.S. statesman who wrote many of the articles contained in the *Federalist Papers* and was Washington's secretary of the treasury. (He was killed by Aaron Burr in a duel.) Nevis is also the island on which Adm. Horatio Lord Nelson married a local woman, Frances Nisbet, in 1787. The historical facts are romanticized, but this episode is described in the late James Michener's bestseller *Caribbean*.

In the 18th century, this Queen of the Caribees was the leading spa of the West Indies, made so by its hot mineral springs. It was also once peppered with prosperous sugarcane estates, but they're gone now—many have been converted into some of the most intriguing hotels in the Caribbean.

Although there has been sentiment for Nevis breaking away to form its own island nation, it's still part of a federation with neighboring St. Kitts. Nevis has great sibling rivalry with that island, both competing for upper-market tourists and doing very little to attract budget travelers—hence, prices on both islands tend to be high. Nevis also vies with St. Kitts as a banking island and is noted for its banking secrecy. Already some 10,000 offshore businesses are registered here, which is more than one business for each inhabitant. In some cases, the operators of these businesses have never set foot on Nevis. More than half of these businesses, operating under strict secrecy laws, have opened since the mid-1990s.

As you drive around the island, through tiny villages like Gingerland (named for the spice it used to export), you'll reach the heavily wooded slopes of Nevis Peak, which offer views of the neighboring islands. On the Caribbean side, Charlestown, the capital, was fashionable in the 18th century, when sugar planters were carried around in carriages and sedan chairs. Houses are of locally

Nevis

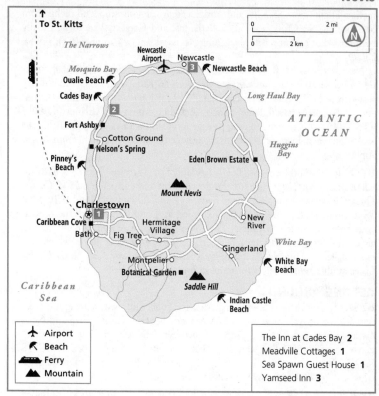

The Inn at Cades Bay 2
Meadville Cottages 1
Sea Spawn Guest House 1
Yamseed Inn 3

✈ Airport
⤴ Beach
🚂 Ferry
▲ Mountain

quarried volcanic stone, encircled by West Indian fretted verandas. A town of wide, quiet streets, this port gets busy only when its major link to the world, the ferry from St. Kitts, docks at the harbor.

1 Essentials

VISITOR INFORMATION

Tourist information is available from the St. Kitts and Nevis tourist boards' **stateside offices** at 414 E. 75th St., New York, NY 10021 (© **800/582-6208** or 212/535-1234), and 1464 Whippoorwill Way, Mountainside, NJ 07092 (© **208/233-6701**).

In **Canada,** an office is at 365 Bay St., Suite 806, Toronto, ON M5H 2V1 (© **416/376-6707**), and in the **United Kingdom** at 10 Kensington Court, London, W8 5DL (© **020/7376-0881**).

The best source for information on the island is the **Tourist Bureau** on Main Street in Charlestown (© **809/469-5521**).

GETTING THERE

BY PLANE The **Newcastle Airport** lies half a mile from Newcastle in the northern part of the island. You can fly to Nevis on **LIAT** (© **800/468-0482** in the U.S. and Canada, or 869/469-9333), which offers regularly scheduled service. Flights from St. Kitts and Antigua are usually nonstop, and flights from St. Thomas, St. Croix, San Juan, Barbados, and Caracas, Venezuela, usually require at least one stop before reaching Nevis. It's only a 7-minute hop from St. Kitts.

Nevis Express (© 869/469-9755) operates a 12-passenger flight daily shuttle service of 10 departures each way between St. Kitts and Nevis. A round-trip ticket from St. Kitts to Nevis costs $40. Call for reservations and information. Any of North America's large carriers, including **American Airlines** (© 800/433-7300), can arrange ongoing passage to Nevis on LIAT through such hubs as Antigua, San Juan, or St. Maarten, connecting with your flight from North America.

BY FERRY You can use the interisland ferry service from St. Kitts to Charlestown on Nevis, aboard the government passenger ferry *M.V. Caribe Queen.* It departs from each island between 7 and 7:30am on Monday, Tuesday, Wednesday, Friday, and Saturday, returning at 4 and 6pm (check the time at your hotel or the tourist office). The cost is $4 each way. You can also take an air-conditioned 110-passenger ferry, *M.V. Spirit of Mount Nevis,* which sails twice daily on Thursday and Sunday, costing $6 one-way. Call **Nevis Cruise Lines** at © 869/469-9373 for more information.

GETTING AROUND

BY TAXI Taxi drivers double as guides, and you'll find them waiting at the airport for the arrival of every plane. A taxi ride between Charlestown and Newcastle Airport costs EC$37 ($13.70); between Charlestown and Old Manor Estate, EC$32 ($11.85); and from Charlestown to Pinney's Beach, EC$18 ($6.65). Between 10pm and 6am, 50% is added to the prices for Charlestown trips. Call © 869/469-5621 for more information.

BY RENTAL CAR If you're prepared to face the winding, rocky, potholed roads of Nevis, you can arrange for a rental car from a local firm through your hotel. Or you can check with **Skeete's Car Rental,** Newcastle Village, near the airport (© 869/469-9458).

To drive on Nevis you must obtain a permit from the traffic department, which costs EC$50 ($18.50) and is valid for a year. Car-rental companies will handle this for you. Remember, *drive on the left side of the road.*

 FAST FACTS: Nevis

Banking Hours Banks are open Monday to Saturday 8am to noon, and most are also open Friday 3:30 to 5:30pm.

Currency The local currency is the **Eastern Caribbean dollar (EC$)**, valued at about $2.70 to the U.S. dollar. Many prices, however, including those of hotels, are quoted in U.S. dollars. Always determine which "dollar" locals are talking about.

Customs You're allowed in duty-free with your personal belongings. Sometimes luggage is subjected to a drug check.

Drugstores Try **Evelyn's Drugstore,** Charlestown (© 869/469-5278), open Monday to Friday 8am to 5:30pm (closes at 5pm Thurs), Saturday 8am to 7pm, and Sunday 7 to 8pm only, to serve emergency needs.

Electricity As on St. Kitts, an electrical transformer and adapter will be needed for most U.S. and Canadian appliances, as the electricity is 230-volt AC (60 cycles). However, check with your hotel to see if it has converted its voltage and outlets.

Emergencies For the **police,** call ✆ **911.**

Entry Requirements U.S. and Canadian citizens can enter with proof of citizenship, such as a birth certificate with a raised seal. British subjects need a passport, but not a visa. A return or ongoing ticket is also mandatory. If you clear Customs in St. Kitts, you don't need to clear Customs again in Nevis.

Hospitals A 24-hour emergency room operates at **Alexandra Hospital,** Government Road, in Charlestown (✆ **869/469-5473).**

Language English is the language of the island and is spoken with a West Indian patois.

Post Office The post office, on Main Street in Charlestown, is open Monday to Wednesday and Friday 8am to 3pm, Thursday 8 to 11am, and Saturday 8am to noon.

Safety Although crime is rare here, protect your valuables and never leave them unguarded on the beach.

Taxes The government imposes a 7% tax on hotel bills, plus a departure tax of EC$27 ($10) per person. You don't have to pay the departure tax on Nevis if you're returning to St. Kitts.

Telecommunications Telegrams and telexes can be sent from the **Cable & Wireless office,** Main Street, Charlestown (✆ **869/469-5000).** International telephone calls, including collect calls, can also be made from the cable office. It's open Monday to Friday 8am to 5pm and Saturday 8am to noon. The area code for Nevis is **869.** You can make calls to or from the United States as you would for any other area code in North America.

Time Like St. Kitts, Nevis is on Atlantic standard time year-round, which means it's usually 1 hour ahead of the U.S. east coast, except when the mainland goes on daylight saving time; then clocks are the same.

Tipping A 10% service charge is added to your hotel bill. In restaurants it's customary to tip 10% to 15% of the tab.

Water In the 1700s, Lord Nelson regularly brought his fleet to Nevis just to collect water, and Nevis still boasts of having Nelson spring water.

2 Accommodations You Can Afford

Meadville Cottages These white concrete buildings lie on the outskirts of Charlestown, in a commercial district. The amenities are few, but the prices are reasonable. The small rooms are simple, with wall-to-wall carpeting, mahogany furniture, decent beds, and tiny shower-only bathrooms. Some have L-shaped verandas, and all have fans (at this elevation, you can usually count on refreshing trade winds). The cottages are near restaurants, shops, and Pinney's Beach.

Craddock Rd. (P.O. Box 66), Charlestown, Nevis, W.I. ✆ 869/469-5235. 11 units. Winter $70 single; $90 double; $170 cottage for 2. Off-season $50 single; $60 double; $150 cottage for 2. Extra person $20. MC, V. *In room:* Kitchenette (some units), ceiling fans.

Sea Spawn Guest House A 2-minute walk from Pinney's Beach, this is just about the island's most no-frills entry, but, hey, you didn't come here to hang out in your hotel room. You're assured of cleanliness and reasonable comfort in this simple white two-story concrete building with verandas all around the upper and ground floors. The tiny rooms are a little bit grander than bunk style. Standing fans attempt to keep you cool. The shower-only bathrooms are barely adequate, and the plumbing isn't state of the art, but hearty types like it here. Guests share a communal kitchen for $5 a day, and the restaurant offers inexpensive local fare for three meals a day. Some of the rooms are air-conditioned.

Old Hospital Rd., Charlestown, Nevis, W.I. © **869/469-5239.** Fax 869/469-5706. 18 units. Year-round $35–$37 single; $44–$59 double; $82.50 triple. Children 11 and under stay free in parents' room. DISC, MC, V. **Amenities:** Restaurant. *In room:* TV, fans.

Yamseed Inn ⚡ *(Finds)* Built as a home in 1964, this charming yellow B&B is in the northernmost part of the island, on a secluded beach that offers panoramic views of St. Kitts. The spacious airy rooms are well appointed with antiques, Oriental rugs (including some from Nepal), and locally crafted headboards crowning comfortable beds with firm mattresses. Each has its own small but tidy bathroom with shower and private entrance. Sybil Siegfried, who owns and operates the Yamseed, serves full breakfasts that include freshly baked multigrain and banana breads, homemade granola cereal, waffles, and fresh fruit. The Yamseed offers hammocks to laze away the days and beautiful surf to enjoy.

Newcastle, Nevis, W.I. © **869/469-9361.** 4 units. Year-round $100 single or double. 3-night minimum stay. Rates include full breakfast. No credit cards. **Amenities:** Breakfast room. *In room:* Ceiling fans.

BEST OFF-SEASON BET

The Inn at Cades Bay ⚡⚡ This hotel is small, charming, and locally owned. On the island's southern coast, occupying a quintet of salmon-colored one-story buildings, it's the creative statement of Eddy and Sheila Williams, who have already proved their skill, thanks to the success of Eddy's restaurant in downtown Charlestown. Each medium-size accommodation contains a tray-shaped ceiling fashioned from pickled pine, a floor layered with terra-cotta Mexican tiles, off-white walls, and summery furniture. Bathrooms are small but tidily arranged and kept, each with a shower stall. There's a long rectangular pool, shuttle bus service from the hotel to Eddy's restaurant, and a knowledgeable staff. The hotel's bar and restaurant, Tequila Sheila's, is described in "Great Deals on Dining," below.

Cades Bay, Nevis, W.I. © **869/469-8139.** Fax 869/469-8129. www.cadesbayinn.com. 16 units. Mid-Dec to mid-Apr $195 single or double. Mid-Apr to mid-Dec $150 single or double. AE, MC, V. **Amenities:** Restaurant, bar, pool, shuttle service. *In room:* TV (some rooms), coffeemaker, hair dryer, ceiling fans.

3 Great Deals on Dining

The local food on Nevis is good. Suckling pig is roasted with many spices, and eggplant and avocado are used in a number of tasty ways. You might see turtle on some menus, but remember that it is an endangered species.

Beachcomber Restaurant & Bar INTERNATIONAL This open-air restaurant on the beach is ideal for dining, especially lunch at any time during the afternoon. Take a table on the veranda, and let the trade winds cool you off. Watch for the changing specials. At lunch you might want to opt for the Nevis burger, made with chopped mahimahi or tuna and served on a sesame bun with cole slaw and fries. We also like to come here for a bowl of one of the soups, made fresh daily—especially tasty are the conch chowder and cream of pumpkin. For a main course, the Creole chicken is always spicy and filled with flavor, as is flying fish sautéed in curried beer batter. Locals are fond of the salt fish with johnnycakes.

Pinney's Beach. ℭ **869/469-1192**. Reservations recommended. Burgers $8–$9; platters $15–$35. AE, MC, V. Daily 10:30am–10pm.

The Courtyard CARIBBEAN/INTERNATIONAL   Near the main docks and the Customs House, this is a simple restaurant whose charms aren't fully realized until you explore the seating options. There's a West Indian bar on the ground floor and a dining room upstairs (used only when it threatens to rain). Most visitors head for the rear garden, where palms, almonds, and sea grape push up through holes in the crumbling concrete deck. Lunch platters include sandwiches, burgers, and fish-and-chips. Dinner is more elaborate; it's very tasty and well-prepared fare ranging from barbecued lobster to Creole-style shrimp. Fresh fish is invariably on the menu, and you can order it fried, stewed, or cooked Creole style, with tomatoes, onions, and peppers. The coffee here is the best on the island.

Main St., Charlestown. ℭ **869/469-1854**. Main courses EC$15–EC$35 ($5.55–$12.95). No credit cards. Daily 6am–11pm.

Eddy's ☆ 𝘝𝘢𝘭𝘶𝘦 INTERNATIONAL   On the upper floor of a plank-sided Nevisian house in the center of Charlestown, this restaurant is open on three sides to the prevailing winds, and its balcony juts out over the pedestrian traffic below. The airy interior contains a tucked-away bar, lattices and gingerbread, and lots of tropical color. The menu items, posted on one of several signs, are among the best prepared in town—perhaps try Eddy's fish cioppino with roasted garlic–mayonnaise croutons or juicy tandoori-sauced chicken. For a new twist on a traditional favorite, try the lime-glazed seafood kebabs with black-bean salsa. No one will mind if you arrive only for a drink at the corner bar, but you'll be missing out on a tasty meal.

Main St., Charlestown. ℭ **869/469-5958**. Main courses EC$28–EC$50 ($10.35–$18.50). AE, MC, V. Mon–Wed and Fri–Sat 11:45am–3pm and 7–9:30pm.

Muriel's Cuisine ☆ 𝘝𝘢𝘭𝘶𝘦 WEST INDIAN   This restaurant is in the back of a concrete building whose front is devoted to a store, Limetree. It's a 6-minute walk from Charlestown's waterfront and set in an outlying neighborhood of low-rise commercial buildings. Head here for a slice of real island life and for real authentic West Indian cuisine. Muriel's curries are the best in town, ranging from the simple goat or chicken to the more elaborate lobster. She also turns out some fabulous chicken or seafood rôtis, and even a lobster Creole for those who want to get fancy. Her jerk pork or chicken would win the approval of a Jamaican, and her preparations of conch, stewed or curried, are worth the trip. If you want to go native all the way, ask for saltfish or goatwater stew.

Upper Happyhill Dr., Charlestown. ℭ **869/469-5920**. Reservations recommended. Lunch EC$18–EC$35 ($6.65–$12.95); dinner EC$35–EC$65 ($12.95–$24.05). AE, MC, V. Daily 8–10am and 11:30am–7pm.

Newcastle Bay Marina Restaurant INTERNATIONAL   This open-air restaurant on the water, housed in a concrete-block building with cathedral ceilings, is part of the Mount Nevis Beach Club. From the deck, you can take in a panoramic sea view. The informal cuisine is usually prepared with flair by the hardworking chef. Examples are a roster of meal-sized pizzas big enough for two (try the version with seafood) as well as chicken parmigiana with pasta, shrimp with salsa verde, and Mexican platters piled high with quesadillas, tacos, flautas, and spicy beef. The best way to begin a meal is with one of the colorful margaritas.

Newcastle Marina, Charlestown. ☎ **869/469-9373**. Reservations recommended. Main courses EC$25–EC$35 ($9.25–$12.95); pizzas for 2 EC$35–EC$55 ($12.95–$20.35). AE, MC, V. Thurs–Tues 6–10pm.

Prinderella's INTERNATIONAL   With a name like Prinderella's (an old joke based on spoonerisms), this place offers some fun and whimsy. As many as 60 diners can enjoy this popular local spot at once, with lattice walls 15 feet from the water on the wharf. The menu ranges from burgers to lobster, and you can count on freshly made salads, homemade soups, and pasta dishes. Even some English pub food, like shepherd's pie and steak-and-kidney pie, appear on the menu, as does a homemade paté. The best bet? The fresh catch of the day, which somehow tastes best grilled—everything from flying fish to wahoo, mahimahi, or yellowfin tuna.

Tamarind Bay. ☎ **869/469-1291**. Main courses $7–$25. MC, V. Daily 10am–midnight.

Tequila Sheila's ⊛ WEST INDIAN/INTERNATIONAL   This restaurant is on the premises of The Inn at Cades Bay, set on a wooden platform less than 60 feet from the seafront, with a covered parapet but without walls. It offers panoramic views as far away as St. Kitts and a menu that incorporates West Indian, Mexican, and international cuisine. Lunchtime brings dishes such as rôti, enchiladas, grilled or jerk chicken, and lobster quesadillas. Dinner platters include vegetable-stuffed chicken, lobster, New York strip steak with horseradish sauce or béarnaise sauce, and fish. Flying fish, wahoo, and mahimahi are very fresh here, and prepared as simply as possible—usually grilled with nothing more than lemon juice and herbs. The bar, fashioned from an overturned fishing boat, offers margaritas, various brands of tequila, and all the usual party-colored drinks you'd expect.

At The Inn at Cades Bay, Cades Bay. ☎ **869/469-8139**. Reservations recommended. Main courses EC$20–EC$35 ($7.40–$12.95) lunch, EC$32–EC$60 ($11.85–$22.20) dinner. AE, MC, V. Mon–Sat noon–3pm and 7–9:30pm; Sun brunch 11:30am–4pm.

4 Hitting the Beaches

Nevis's best beach—in fact, one of the best beaches in the Caribbean—is the reef-protected **Pinney's Beach** ⊛⊛, which has gin-clear water, golden sands, and a gradual slope; it's just north of Charlestown on the west coast. You'll have 3 miles of sand (often virtually to yourself) that culminates in a sleepy lagoon against a backdrop of coconut palms. It's almost never crowded, and its calm, shallow waters are perfect for swimming. It's also ideal for wading, making it a family favorite. The Four Seasons Beach Resort lies in the middle of this beach. It's best to bring your own sports equipment; the hotels are stocked with limited gear that may be in use by its guests. You can go snorkeling or scuba diving here among damselfish, tangs, grunts, blue-headed wrasses, and parrotfish, among other species. The beach is especially beautiful in the late afternoon, when flocks of cattle egrets fly into its north end to roost at the freshwater pond at Nelson's Spring.

If your time on Nevis is limited, go to Pinney's Beach. But if you're going to be around for a few more days, you might want to search out the other beaches, notably beige-sand **Oualie Beach,** known especially for its diving and snorkeling. The location is north of Pinney's and just south of Mosquito Bay. The beach is well maintained and rarely crowded; you can purchase food and drink, as well as rent watersports equipment, at the Oualie Beach Hotel.

Indian Castle Beach, at the southern end of Nevis, is rarely sought out. It has an active surf and a swath of fine gray sand. Indian Castle is definitely for escapists—chances are you'll have the beach all to yourself except for an indigenous goat or two, who might be very social and interested in sharing your picnic lunch.

Newcastle Beach is by the Nisbet Plantation, at the northernmost tip of the island on the channel that separates St. Kitts and Nevis. Snorkelers flock to this strip of soft, ecru sand set against a backdrop of coconut palms.

The beaches along the east coast aren't desirable. They front Long Haul Bay in the north and White Bay in the south. These bays spill into the Atlantic ocean and are rocky and too rough for swimming, although they're rather dramatic to visit if you're sightseeing. Of them all, **White Bay Beach** (sometimes called Windward Beach), in the southeastern section, east of Gingerland, is the most desirable. If you want some chillier Atlantic swimming, head here—but be careful, as the waters can suddenly turn turbulent.

5 Sports & Other Outdoor Pursuits

BOAT CHARTERS   **Scuba Safaris,** an outfit that operates independently on the premises of the Oualie Beach Club (© **869/469-9518**), offers boat charters to Banana Bay and Cockleshell Bay, which can make for a great day's outing, costing only $50 round-trip.

GOLF   The **Four Seasons Golf Course,** Pinney's Beach (© **869/469-1111**), has one of the world's most challenging and visually dramatic golf courses. Designed by Robert Trent Jones, Jr. (who called it "the most scenic golf course I've ever designed"), this 18-hole championship golf course wraps around the resort and offers panoramic ocean and mountain views at every turn. The course is, in the words of one avid golfer, "reason enough to go to Nevis." But there's a high price tag. Guests of the hotel pay $125 for 18 holes, and nonguests are charged $150. Rental clubs are available, costing $40 for 18 holes.

HIKING & MOUNTAIN CLIMBING   Hikers can climb **Mount Nevis,** 3,232 feet up to the extinct volcanic crater, and enjoy a trek to the rain forest to watch for wild monkeys. This is strenuous and recommended only for the stout of heart. Ask your hotel to pack a picnic lunch and arrange a guide (charging about $35 per person). The hike takes about 5 hours, and once at the summit, you'll be rewarded with views of Antigua, Saba, Statia, St. Kitts, Guadeloupe, and Montserrat. Of course, you've got to reach that summit, which means scrambling up near-vertical sections of the trail requiring handholds on not-always-reliable vines and roots. It's definitely not for acrophobes! Guides can be arranged at the **Nevis Historical and Conservation Society,** based at the Museum of Nevis History on Main Street in Charlestown (© **869/469-5786**).

HORSEBACK RIDING   Horseback riding is available at the **Nisbet Plantation Beach Club,** Newcastle (© **869/469-9325**). You can ride English saddle at $55 per person for 45 minutes. A guide takes you along mountain trails to visit sites of long-forgotten plantations.

SNORKELING & SCUBA DIVING   For **snorkeling,** head for Pinney's Beach. You might also try the waters of Fort Ashby, where the settlement of Jamestown is said to have slid into the sea; legend has it that the church bells can still be heard, and the undersea town can still be seen when conditions are just right. So far, to our knowledge, no diver has found the conditions "just right."

For scuba divers, the best site on Nevis is the **Monkey Shoals,** 2 miles west of the Four Seasons. This is a beautiful reef starting at 40 feet, with dives up to 100 feet in depth. Angelfish, turtles, nurse sharks, and extensive soft coral can be found here. **The Caves** are on the south tip of Nevis, a 20-minute boat ride

Moments Eco-Tours: Finding the Beauty of Nevis

Eco-Tours Nevis (© 869/469-2091 for reservations) offers three unique walking tours of the 36-mile island. Tours offer a wealth of fascinating and cultural history, reflecting the tropical climate and some 1,000 years of human activity. The expeditions explore the shore, tropical forests, and historic ruins. Each offers something for the experienced traveler or the first-time visitor and are taken at a leisurely pace, requiring only an average level of fitness.

The Eco-Ramble (2½ hr.) takes place on the windswept east coast of Nevis, where sea, ruins, and mountains combine to provide a panorama. This tour covers the 18th-century New River and Coconut Walk Estates, where you'll experience the diverse ecology of Nevis, discover archaeological evidence of pre-Columbian Amerindian settlers, and explore the remains of the last working sugar factory. It costs $25 per person. The Mountraverse Hike (2½ hr.) takes a close look at Montraverse House, one of Nevis's hidden secrets. These spectacular ruins are the focus of an easy hike into the tropical forest–covered slopes of Nevis Peak. This tour costs $25 per person. The Historic Charlestown tour (1½ hr.) takes you through the capital, with Gallows Bay and Jews Walk two of the reminders of Charlestown's rich and turbulent past. Called at various times "a sink of debauchery" and "a sleepy town with many of its buildings locked from day to day," Charlestown has survived 300 years of fire, earthquake, hurricanes, and warfare to become a charming Victorian-era West Indian town. The cost is $15 per person.

Shorts, socks, and closed shoes are suitable for all three tours. A hat is a welcome addition, and suitable casual attire is appreciated in Charlestown (no swimsuits). The Eco-Ramble is recommended for children over 12 years old. The other tours are not suitable for children. All walking tours are offered on a reservation-only basis.

from the Four Seasons. A series of coral grottos with numerous squirrelfish, turtles, and needlefish make it an ideal dive for both certified and resort divers. **Champagne Garden,** a 5-minute boat ride from the Four Seasons, gets its name from bubbles created from an underwater sulfur vent. Because of the warm water temperature, large numbers of tropical fish are found here. Finally, **Coral Garden,** 2 miles west of the Four Seasons, is another beautiful coral reef with schools of Atlantic spadefish and large seafans. The reef is at a maximum depth of 70 feet and suitable for both certified and resort divers.

Scuba Safaris, Oualie Beach (© 869/469-9518), on the island's north end, offers PADI scuba diving and snorkeling in an area rich in dive sites. It also offers resort and certification courses, dive packages, and equipment rental. A one-tank scuba dive costs $45; a two-tank dive, $80. Full certification courses cost $450 per person. Snorkeling trips cost $35 per person. Boat charters to Banana Bay, Cockleshell Bay, and other beaches are offered.

TENNIS Some of the big hotels have tennis courts, but you must call in advance and see if nonguests are allowed to play (you might have to pay a fee). Outside the posh Four Seasons, the best courts are at **Pinney's Beach Hotel,**

Pinney's Beach, just outside Charlestown (© **869/469-5207**); **Golden Rock,** Gingerland (© **869/469-9325**); and **Nisbet,** Newcastle Beach (© **869/ 469-9325**).

WINDSURFING The waters of Nevis are often ideal for windsurfing, especially for beginners and intermediates. **Windsurfing Nevis** at the Oualie Beach Hotel (© **869/469-9682**) offers the best equipment, costing $25 for 30 minutes.

6 Seeing the Sights

You can negotiate with a taxi driver to take you around Nevis. The distance is only 20 miles, but you might find yourself taking a long time if you stop to see specific sights and talk to all the people who'll want to chat. A 3-hour sightseeing tour around the island will cost $60; the average taxi holds up to four people, so when the cost is sliced per passenger, it's a reasonable investment. No sightseeing bus companies operate on Nevis, but a number of individuals own buses they use for taxi service. Call **All Seasons Streamline Tours** at © **869/ 469-5705** or 869/469-1138.

The major attraction is the **Museum of Nevis History,** in the house where Alexander Hamilton was born, on Main Street in Charlestown (© **869/ 469-5786**). Hamilton was the illegitimate son of a Scotsman and Rachel Fawcett, a Nevisian of Huguenot ancestry. The family immigrated to St. Croix and from there Hamilton made his way to the U.S. colonies, where he became the first secretary of the U.S. Treasury. His picture appears on the U.S. $10 bill. The lava-stone house by the shore has been restored, and the museum, dedicated to the history and culture of Nevis, houses the island's archives. The museum is open Monday to Friday 9am to 4pm and Saturday 9am to noon. Admission is $2 for adults and $1 for children.

Eden Brown Estate, about 1½ miles from New River, is said to be haunted. Once it was the home of a wealthy planter, whose daughter was to be married, but her husband-to-be was killed in a duel at the prenuptial feast. The mansion was then closed forever and left to the ravages of nature. A gray solid stone still stands. Only the most adventurous come here on a moonlit night.

At one time, Sephardic Jews who came from Brazil made up a quarter of the island's population, and it's believed that Jews introduced sugar production into the Leewards. Outside the center of Charlestown, at the lower end of Government Road, the **Jewish Cemetery** has been restored and is the resting place of many of the early shopkeepers. Most of the tombstones date from 1690 to 1710.

A U.S. archaeological team believes an old stone building in partial ruin on Nevis is probably the oldest **Jewish synagogue** in the Caribbean, according to historian Dr. Vincent K. Hubbar, a resident of the island and author of *Swords, Ships, and Sugar: A History of Nevis to 1900.* Preliminary findings in 1993 traced the building's history to one of the two oldest Jewish settlements in the West Indies, Hubbard noted, and current work at the site plus historic documents in England establish its existence prior to 1650. The original function of the building site, adjacent to the government administration building in Charlestown, has been long forgotten. However, because of Nevis's relatively large Jewish population in the 17th century and its well-known Jewish cemetery, many scholars and historians believed a synagogue must have existed but didn't know exactly where.

One of the island's newest attractions is the 8-acre **Botanical Garden of Nevis** (© **869/469-3509**), which lies 3 miles south of Charlestown on the Montpelier Estate. Rain-forest plants grow in re-created Mayan ruins in a

---

Value **Cheap Thrills: What to See & Do for Free (Well, Almost) on Nevis**

- **Hike the Rain-Forest Trail.** One of the great nature walks in this part of the Caribbean begins at Stoney Hill at the top of Rawlins Road above Golden Rock Estate at Gingerland in the southeastern corner of the island, and winds its way through a rain-forest setting. The trail is relatively easy to walk, and you pass by rich flora, including nutmeg trees, breadfruit trees, and groves of cocoa. You'll also see rich bird life, including forest thrushes, yellow warblers, hummingbirds, tropical mockingbirds, black-crowned herons, and scaly breasted thrashers. It's possible to see wild monkeys, too, especially between Golden Rock and Stoney Hill. Allow about 3 hours coming and going for this trail.

- **View a Nostalgic Sight.** Regrettably, a hurricane ruined an already ruined sight in Nevis: the decaying Bath Hotel (completed in 1778) in Bath Village, about half a mile from Charlestown. But nothing else conjures up the glory that was Nevis. Still emanating from the hillside, the thermal springs once attracted the elite from North America, with temperatures rising as high as 108°F (locals have reported miraculous cures). Guests drank and gambled in the hotel's casino. There are legends of entire plantation estates changing hands in its casino heyday, as well as a fair share of bloody duels of honor. When the hotel fell on bad days, it was turned into a brothel. It might be best to wander around and take in the sights without romping in the waters. There are plans for restoration, but nothing definite at the moment.

- **Drive Around the Island.** One of the great drives in this part of the Caribbean is around Nevis. Inland roads are rutted and best left to adventurers, but anybody can drive around the coast. The road is relatively good, unless tropical storms have caused highway damage. The most important island landmarks lie along this road,

---

hillside site overlooking the Caribbean. The on-site restaurant serves an English tea with scones and double Devonshire cream. You can also order a ploughman's lunch (French bread, pickled onions, and cheese). If you patronize the restaurant and gift shop, the fee of $9 to the gardens is eliminated. The garden is open Monday to Saturday 9am to 5pm.

A bit incongruous for Nevis, **Caribbean Cove,** Stoney Grove (© **869/ 469-1286**), is an amusement park that's just as popular with locals as visitors. A 2-acre multimillion-dollar facility, it was created by Joseph Murphy, a Philadelphia businessman, who wanted to create a slice of Walt Disney World. Among the attractions is an 18-hole miniature golf course loosely following the history of Nevis, focusing on times when pirates ruled the seas, complete with sculptured caves, waterfalls, a lagoon, blasting cannons, and even a simulated rain forest. A deli offers sandwiches, including Philly cheese steaks, in honor of Murphy's hometown. There's a gift shop, plus live entertainment, including bands, comedians, fashion shows, and a restaurant. Admission is $4, and hours are daily 10am to 10pm.

including Nisbet Plantation (now a hotel), former home of the wife of Lord Nelson. Vistas and panoramic ruins of the sugarcane plantation days greet you at nearly every turn. The trip evokes the days when not only sugarcane but sea island cotton flourished here. Time your trip so you can break up the drive, plus have lunch and lounge at Pinney's Beach.

- **Stroll Around Charlestown.** In colorful decay, the capital of Nevis is like a miniature West Indian port. Some Nevisians, however, hope it'll one day become the capital of their own nation—if Nevis ever breaks its association with St. Kitts. The biggest excitement here is when the ferries come in from St. Kitts. Otherwise, Charlestown is sleepy, and that's part of its charm. In about an hour you can wander around the whole town. After leaving the pier, turn right at the old Cotton House and Ginnery and stroll through the marketplace. This is best enjoyed in the morning. After that, you can make a left onto Prince William Street and follow it to Memorial Square, honoring the Nevisians who died in the two world wars. After that, wander at will and perhaps browse through some handcraft shops.

- **Spend a Day at Pinney's Beach.** Many visitors in Nevis for an entire week spend every day on Pinney's Beach. It's one of the finest beaches in the Caribbean; its reef-protected waters are gin clear and idyllic for snorkeling or swimming. Rainbow-hued fish often can be seen close to the shore. There are miles and miles of powdery sand, ideal for sunbathing or long walks. A sleepy lagoon lies through the palm trees at the sand strip's windward edge. You'll think you've been miraculously delivered to the South Pacific. If you get bored, you can also visit the nearby Museum of Nevis History to learn more about Alexander Hamilton (see "Seeing the Sights," above).

The **Nevis Jockey Club** organizes and sponsors thoroughbred races every month. Local horses as well as some brought over from other islands fill out a typical five-race card. If you want to have a glimpse of what horse racing must have been like a century or more ago, you'll find the Nevis races a memorable experience. For information, contact Richard Lupinacci, a Jockey Club officer and owner and operator of the Hermitage Plantation (© 869/469-3477).

7 Shopping

Normal store hours are Monday to Friday 8am to noon and 1 to 4pm, but on Thursday some places close in the afternoon, and on Saturday some stay open to 8pm. Most are closed Sunday.

For original art, visit **Eva Wilkins's Studio,** Clay Ghaut, Gingerland (© 869/469-2673). The late Eva Wilkins became the island's most famous artist, and Prince Charles even showed up to look at her work. Until her death in 1989, she painted island people, local flowers, and scenes of Nevis life. She worked in both black-and-white and color prints, which her custodians still sell today. Prints are available in some of the local shops, but her originals sell for $100 and more. You can visit her former atelier, which is on the grounds of an old sugar-mill plantation her father owned, near Montpelier.

Hand-painted or tie-dyed cotton and batik clothing are featured at **Island Hopper,** in the T.D.C. Shopping Mall, Main Street, Charlestown (© 869/ 469-0893), which also has locations on St. Kitts and Antigua. From beach wraps to souvenirs, a wide selection of products is available. In a stone building about 200 feet from the wharf, near the marketplace, the **Nevis Handicraft Cooperative Society,** Cotton House, Charlestown (© 869/469-1746), contains locally made gift items, like unusual objects of goatskin, local wines made from a variety of fruits grown on the island, hot-pepper sauce, guava cheese, jams, and jellies.

8 Nevis After Dark

Nightlife isn't the major reason to visit Nevis. Summer nights are quiet, but there's organized entertainment in winter, with steel bands often performing at the major hotels. Most action takes place at the **Four Seasons Resort,** Pinney's Beach (© 869/469-1111), on Friday and Saturday. The **Old Manor Estate,** Gingerland (© 869/469-3445), often brings in a steel band on Friday. On Saturday, the action swings over to the **Golden Rock,** Gingerland (© 869/ 469-3346), where a string band enlivens the scene. Fridays and Saturdays can get raucous at **Eddy's** on Main Street (see "Great Deals on Dining," earlier in this chapter), when West Indian buffets are presented and live bands entertain.

The best place on a Wednesday night is **Pinney's Beach Hotel,** Pinney's Beach (© 869/469-5207), which stages a dinner and dance. The **Oualie Beach Hotel** at Oualie Beach (© 869/469-9735) offers a Saturday buffet, accompanied by a string band.

Disco reigns supreme at **Tequila Sheila's** at Cades Bay (see "Great Deals on Dining," earlier in this chapter) on Saturday night.

One of the best beach bars on island is the **Beachcomber,** Pinney's Beach (© 869/469-1192), known for its happy hour and barbecues. Sometimes live bands appear. Another favorite in winter only is the **Sunset Terrace at Cliff Dwellers** on Tamarind Bay (© 869/469-0262). This is the best place for a sundowner. You must take a not-always-reliable tram ride up the side of a sheer cliff to get here, but there's no more dramatic perch in all Nevis for a tropical punch.

Moments A Killer Bee in the Moonlight

Head for **Sunshine's Bar & Grill,** Pinney's Beach (© 869/469-5817) and order "The Killer Bee." Sunshine, the owner, won't tell you what goes into it. "First there's a little rum, maybe a lot of rum, and then some passion fruit juice. And that's all I'm tellin'." When you arrive in Nevis, check to see if Sunshine is throwing one of his "Full Moon" parties, a raucous island event with a roaring bonfire and a limbo contest. But even without the party, Sunshine's bar is the most fun place to be on Nevis on any night, even a Monday. "Monday, Sunday—it's all the same at Sunshine's," one of the staff told us.

17

Puerto Rico

Puerto Rico boasts a vast array of sights, activities, and entertainment. You'll find hundreds of beaches, countless watersports, acres of golf courses, miles of tennis courts, casinos galore, more discos than any other place in the Caribbean, and shopping bargains to equal those of St. Thomas.

Lush Puerto Rico is some 1,000 miles southeast of the tip of Florida and has 272 miles of Atlantic and Caribbean coastline. Its culture dates back 2,000 years. Old San Juan is its great historic center, with 500 years of recorded history and beautifully restored Spanish colonial architecture. The countryside is dotted with centuries-old coffee plantations, sugar estates, foreboding caves, and enormous boulders with mysterious petroglyphs carved by the Taíno (original settlers of the island). You can travel along colorful but often narrow and steep roads and meandering mountain trails that lead to tropical settings. To see the real Puerto Rico, you need to leave San Juan behind, especially the high-priced Condado Beach area, and explore these back roads.

Of all the Caribbean islands, Puerto Rico is the very best choice for budget travelers, with inexpensive *paradores* (government-sponsored inns), small guesthouses, local inns, and mom-and-pop restaurants, many overlooking the sea. A number of restaurants serve fresh fish and native Puerto Rican dishes. Following in the Spanish tradition, Puerto Rico also has cafes, where you can enjoy a cup of coffee as well as a *comida criolla* (local dinner). Sometimes a dinner costs only $12, or even less, at a roadside kiosk.

You can base yourself at one hotel and still do a lot of exploring elsewhere if you don't mind driving for a couple of hours. It's possible to branch out and see a lot of the island even if you're staying in San Juan.

1 Essentials

VISITOR INFORMATION

Out on the island, it's best to go to the local city hall for tourist information. Ask for a copy of *Qué Pasa,* the official visitors' guide.

For information before you leave home, contact one of the following **Puerto Rico Tourism Company** offices: 666 Fifth Ave., New York, NY 10103 (© **800/ 223-6530** in the U.S., or 212/586-6262); 3575 W. Cahuenga Blvd., Suite 405, Los Angeles, CA 90068 (© **800/874-1230** in the U.S.); or 901 Ponce de León Blvd., Suite 101, Coral Gables, FL 33134 (© **800/815-7391** in the U.S., or 305/445-9112).

In **Canada** you can stop by 41-43 Colbourne St., Suite 301, Toronto, ON M5E 1E3 (© **800/667-0394** or 416/368-2680) for information.

The official website is **www.prtourism.com.**

GETTING THERE

Before you book your own airfare, read the section "Package Deals," in chapter 2—it can save you a bundle!

Puerto Rico is by far the most accessible of the Caribbean islands, and frequent air service can get you there. **American Airlines** (ⓒ 800/433-7300 in the U.S.) has designated San Juan its hub for the entire Caribbean. The major Puerto Rico airport is in San Juan, where most flights from the U.S. mainland arrive. Other major airports serve the two other major cities, Mayagüez and Ponce. American alone offers 39 nonstop daily flights to San Juan from Baltimore, Boston, Chicago, Dallas–Fort Worth, Hartford, Miami, Newark, New York (JFK), Orlando, Philadelphia, Tampa, Fort Lauderdale, and Washington (Dulles), plus flights to San Juan from Montréal and Toronto with changes in Chicago or Miami. There are also at least two daily flights from Los Angeles to San Juan that touch down in Dallas or Miami en route. American also offers many money-saving packages that include your hotel or resort; contact **American Airlines FlyAway Vacations** (ⓒ 800/321-2121 in the U.S.) to find out about the current offerings.

American Eagle (ⓒ 800/433-7300 in the U.S.) is the undisputed leader among the short-haul local commuter flights of the Caribbean. Collectively, American Eagle, along with its larger associate, American Airlines, offers service to dozens of destinations on more than 30 islands of the Caribbean and the Bahamas.

Delta (ⓒ 800/241-4141 in the U.S.) has four daily nonstop flights from its international hub in Atlanta. Delta has nine nonstops on Saturday and seven on Sunday. Ask about its packages by calling **Delta Dream Vacations** at ⓒ 800/872-7786 in the U.S.

United Airlines (ⓒ 800/241-6522 in the U.S.) offers daily nonstop flights from Chicago to San Juan. **Northwest** (ⓒ 800/447-4747 in the U.S.) has one daily nonstop to San Juan from Detroit, as well as at least one (and sometimes more) connecting flights to San Juan from Detroit. Northwest also offers flights to San Juan, some of them nonstop, from both Memphis and Minneapolis, with a schedule that varies according to the season and the day of the week. **TWA** (ⓒ 800/221-2000 in the U.S.) offers three daily nonstop flights between New York and San Juan. There are also daily nonstop flights to San Juan from St. Louis on Saturday and Sunday in winter, but none in summer.

US Airways (ⓒ 800/428-4322 in the U.S.) also competes, with daily flights between Baltimore and San Juan (these flights stop in Charlotte, North Carolina, but don't require a change of planes). The airline also offers three daily nonstop flights from Philadelphia and one from Pittsburgh. You can also ask about packages offered by **US Airways Vacations** (ⓒ 800/455-0123 in the U.S.).

Finally, **Iberia** (ⓒ 800/772-4642 in the U.S.) has two weekly flights from Madrid to San Juan, leaving on Tuesday and Saturday.

GETTING AROUND

BY PLANE **American Eagle** (ⓒ 787/749-1747) flies from Luís Muñoz International Airport to Mayagüez, which can be your gateway to the west of Puerto Rico. Fares vary widely according to the season, the restrictions associated with your ticket, and whatever special promotion might be in effect, but expect to pay $140 to $180 per person round-trip. Try to book your passage as early as possible prior to your flight.

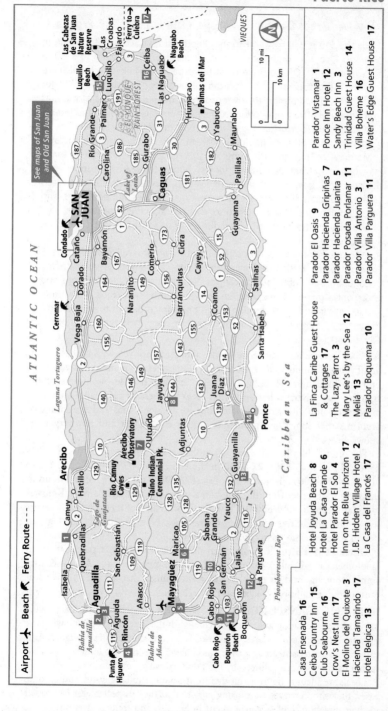

Puerto Rico

Airport ✈ **Beach** ↙ **Ferry Route** - - -

See maps of San Juan and Old San Juan

ATLANTIC OCEAN

Caribbean Sea

VIEQUES

Casa Ensenada **16**
Ceiba Country Inn **15**
Club Seabourne **16**
Crow's Nest Inn **17**
El Molino del Quixote **3**
Hacienda Tamarindo **17**
Hotel Belgica **13**

Hotel Joyuda Beach **8**
Hotel La Casa Grande **6**
Hotel Parador El Sol **4**
Inn on the Blue Horizon **17**
J.B. Hidden Village Hotel **2**
La Casa del Francés **17**

La Finca Caribe Guest House & Cottages **17**
The Lazy Parrot **3**
Mary Lee's by the Sea **12**
Meliá **13**
Parador Boquemar **10**

Parador El Oasis **9**
Parador Hacienda Gripiñas **7**
Parador Hacienda Juanita **5**
Parador Posada Porlamar **11**
Parador Villa Antonio **3**
Parador Villa Parguera **11**

Parador Vistamar **1**
Ponce Inn Hotel **12**
Sandy Beach Inn **3**
Trinidad Guest House **14**
Villa Boheme **16**
Water's Edge Guest House **17**

Value Great Discounts Through the LeLoLai VIP Program

For the $10 it will cost you to join Puerto Rico's **LeLoLai VIP** ("Value in Puerto Rico") program, you can enjoy the equivalent of up to $250 in travel benefits. Of course, most of the experiences linked to LeLoLai are of the rather touristy type, but it can still be a good investment. You'll get discounts on admission to folklore shows, guided tours of historic sites and natural attractions, lodgings, meals, shopping, activities, and more.

Paradores Puertorriqueños, the island's modestly priced network of country inns, gives cardholders 10% to 20% discounts on room rates Monday to Thursday. Discounts of 10% to 20% are offered at many restaurants, from San Juan's toniest hotels to several *mesones gas-tronómicos,* government-sanctioned restaurants that serve Puerto Rican fare. Shopping discounts are offered at many stores and boutiques, and cardholders get 10% to 20% discounts at many island attractions. The card also entitles you to free admission to some of the island's folklore shows.

For more information about the LeLoLai VIP card, call ⓒ **787/723-3135** or go to the El Centro Convention Center at Ashford Avenue on the Condado. Although you can call for details before you leave home, you can only sign up for this program once you reach Puerto Rico. Many hotel packages include participation in this program as part of their offerings.

BY CAR   Some local car-rental agencies might tempt you with slashed prices, but if you're planning to tour the island, you should keep in mind that you won't find any local branches should you run into car trouble. And some of the agencies that advertise low-cost deals don't take credit cards and want cash in advance. You also have to watch out for hidden extras and the insurance problems that sometimes proliferate among the smaller and not very well-known firms.

The old reliables include **Avis** (ⓒ **800/331-1212** in the U.S., or 787/791-2500), **Budget** (ⓒ **800/527-0700** in the U.S., or 787/791-3685), and **Hertz** (ⓒ **800/654-3001** in the U.S., or 787/791-0840). Each offers minivan transport to its office from the San Juan airport. Another alternative is **Kemwel Holiday Auto** (ⓒ **800/678-0678** in the U.S.). None of these companies rents Jeeps, four-wheel-drive vehicles, or convertibles. Note that car theft is high on Puerto Rico, so extra precaution is a good idea.

Distances in Puerto Rico are often posted in kilometers rather than miles (a kilometer is .62 miles), but speed limits are in miles per hour. Added security comes from an antitheft double-locking mechanism that has been installed in most of the rental cars available on Puerto Rico.

BY PUBLIC TRANSPORTATION   *Públicos* are cars or minibuses that provide low-cost transportation and are designated with the letter *P* or *PD* following the number on their license plates. They usually operate only during daylight hours, carry up to six passengers at a time, and charge rates that are loosely governed, with a baffling set of qualifiers, by the Public Service Commission.

Locals are adept at figuring out their routes along rural highways, and in some cases, they simply wave at a moving *público* that they suspect might be headed in their direction. Unless you're fluent in Spanish and feeling adventurous, we suggest that you phone either of the numbers below, describe where and when you want to go, and agree to the prearranged price between specific points. Then, be prepared to wait. Although, at least in theory, a *público* might be arranged between most of the towns and villages of Puerto Rico, by far the most popular routes are between San Juan and Ponce and between San Juan and Mayagüez. Fares vary according to whether a *público* will make a detour to pick up or drop off a passenger at a specific locale. If you want to deviate from the predetermined routes, you'll pay more than if you wait for a *público* at vaguely designated points beside the main highway or at predefined points that include airports and, in some cases, the main plaza (central square) of a town.

Information about *público* routes between San Juan and Mayagüez is available from **Lineas Sultana,** Calle Esteban González 898, Urbanización Santa Rita, Rio Piedras (© 787/765-9377). Information about *público* routes between San Juan and Ponce is available from **Choferes Unidos de Ponce,** Terminal de Carros Públicos, Calle Vive in Ponce (© 787/721-2400). The fare from San Juan to Ponce is $20. Although prices are admittedly low, the routes are slow, with frequent stops, often erratic routing, and lots of inconvenience.

SIGHTSEEING TOURS

If you want to see more of the island but don't want to rent a car or manage the inconveniences of public transportation, perhaps an organized tour is for you.

Castillo Sightseeing Tours & Travel Services, Calle Laurel 2413, Punta La Marias, Santurce (© 787/791-6195), maintains offices at some of San Juan's major hotels. They can also arrange pickup at other accommodations in one of their six air-conditioned buses. One of the most popular half-day tours runs from San Juan to El Yunque Rain Forest; it departs in the morning, lasts 4 to 5 hours, and costs $32 per person. The company also offers a 4-hour city tour of San Juan that costs $32 and includes a stopover at the Bacardi rum factory. Full-day snorkeling tours to the reefs near the coast of a deserted island off Puerto Rico's eastern edge aboard one of two sail- and motor-driven catamarans go for $69, with lunch, snorkeling gear, and piña coladas included.

Fun Fact **Special Events**

Sanjuneros and visitors alike eagerly look forward to the annual **Casals Festival,** the Caribbean's most celebrated cultural event. June 1 to 20, the bill at San Juan's performing arts center includes a glittering array of international guest conductors, orchestras, and soloists come to honor the memory of Pablo Casals, the renowned cellist who was born in Spain to a Puerto Rican mother. When Casals died in Puerto Rico in 1973 at age 97, the festival was 16 years old and attracting the same class of performers who appeared at the festival he founded in France after World War II. Ticket prices range from $18 to $45, with a 50% discount offered to students, seniors over 60, and persons with disabilities. Tickets are available through the performing arts center in San Juan at © 787/ 721-7727.

The island's **Carnival** celebrations feature float parades, dancing, and street parties in the week leading up to Ash Wednesday (which in 2002 is Feb 13). The festivities in Ponce are marked by masqueraders wearing brightly painted horned masks, the crowning of a Carnival queen, and the closing "burial of the sardine." Hotel rates go up (some considerably) at this time of year. For information, call © 787/840-4141.

For a day excursion to the area's best islands, beaches, reefs, and snorkeling, contact **Bill and Donna Henry** at the Puerto Del Rey Marina in Fajardo (© **787/860-4401**). Bill has been sailing for 45 years, and their 50-foot boat *Gulfstar* was featured in Disney's *New Swiss Family Robinson,* where it was called the *Albatross.* They offer snorkeling trips from 10am to 5pm, with two to six passengers paying $75 each. A barbecue chicken meal is cooked onboard (Donna will prepare vegetarian or kosher food if notified). Sunset cruises for $55 per person are also offered, including drinks and hors d'oeuvres from 5 to 7pm. A minimum of four passengers must sign up for this.

 FAST FACTS: Puerto Rico

Banks Most major U.S. banks have branches in San Juan and are open Monday to Friday 8:30am to 2:30pm.

Currency The **U.S. dollar** is the coin of the realm. Canadian currency is accepted by some big hotels in San Juan, although reluctantly.

Documents Because Puerto Rico is part of the United States, American citizens don't need a passport or visa. Canadians, however, should carry some form of identification, such as a birth certificate. Citizens of the United Kingdom should have a passport.

Electricity The electricity is 110-volt AC (60 cycles), as it is in the continental United States and Canada.

Emergencies In an emergency, call © **911.**

Language English is understood at the big resorts and in most of San Juan. Out in the island, Spanish is still *numero uno.*

Safety Use common sense and take precautions. Muggings are commonly reported on the Condado and Isla Verde beaches in San Juan, so you might want to confine your moonlit-beach nights to the fenced-in and guarded areas around some of the major hotels. The countryside of Puerto Rico is safer than San Juan, but caution is always the rule. Avoid narrow little country roads and isolated beaches, night or day.

Taxes There's a government tax of 7% in regular hotels or 9% in hotels with casinos. The airport departure tax is included in the price of your ticket.

Telecommunications Puerto Rico is on the North American telephone system; the area code is **787.** Place a call to or from Puerto Rico just as you would from within the United States or Canada.

Time Puerto Rico is on Atlantic standard time year-round, making it 1 hour ahead of U.S. eastern standard time. In winter when it's noon in Miami, it's 1pm in San Juan. But from April to late October (during daylight saving time on the east coast), Puerto Rico and the U.S. east coast keep the same time.

Tipping Some hotels add a 10% service charge to your bill. If they don't, you're expected to tip for services rendered. Tip as you would in the United States (15%–20%).

Weather Puerto Rico is cooler than most of the other Caribbean islands because of its northeast trade winds. Sea, land, and mountain breezes also help keep the temperatures at a comfortable level. The climate is fairly stable all year, with an average temperature of 76°F. The only variants are found in the mountain regions, where the temperature fluctuates between 66° and 76°F, and on the north coast, where the temperature ranges from 70° to 80°F.

2 San Juan ☆☆☆

San Juan, the capital of Puerto Rico, is a major city—actually an urban sprawl of several municipalities along the island's north coast. Its architecture ranges from classic colonial buildings that recall the Spanish empire to modern beach-front hotels reminiscent of Miami Beach.

San Juan breaks down into several divisions: **San Juan Island,** containing the city center and the old walled city (Old San Juan); **Santurce,** a large peninsula linked to San Juan Island by a causeway; **Condado,** a narrow peninsula stretching between San Juan Island and Santurce; **Puerto de Tierra,** the section east of Old San Juan that contains many government buildings; **Miramar,** a lagoon-front section south of Condado; and **Isla Verde,** detached from the rest of San Juan by an isthmus.

ESSENTIALS

ARRIVING   If you're not traveling on a package deal that includes transfers to your hotel, you'll see lots of options after landing at San Juan's **Luís Muñoz Marín Airport** (© 787/791-1014). A wide variety of vehicles refer to themselves as *limosinas* (their Spanish name).

One company with a sign-up desk in the arrivals hall of the international airport, near the American Airlines arrival facilities, is the **Airport Limousine Service** (© 787/791-4745). It offers minivan transport from the airport to various neighborhoods of San Juan for prices that are lower than for similar routings offered by taxis. Whenever 8 to 10 passengers can be gathered, the fare for transport, with luggage, to any hotel in Isla Verde is $55 to $75 per van to the Condado or to Old San Juan.

The island's **Public Service Commission** (© 787/756-1401) sets flat rates between the Luís Muñoz Marin Airport and major tourist zones as follows: From the airport to any hotel in Isla Verde, $8; to any hotel in the Condado district, $12; and to any hotel in Old San Juan, $16. Tips of between 10% and 15% of that fare are expected.

VISITOR INFORMATION   Tourist information is available at the **Luís Muñoz Marín Airport** (© 787/791-1014). Another office is at **La Casita,** Pier 1, Old San Juan (© 787/722-1709). Open Sunday to Wednesday 9am to 8pm, and Thursday and Friday 9am to 5:30pm.

ORIENTATION   The city center is on **San Juan Island,** connected to the rest of the metropolitan area by causeways. The western half of San Juan Island contains the walled city of **Old San Juan.** The eastern half is known as **Puerto de Tierra,** and contains many government buildings. Across the causeways is the neighborhood of **Miramar,** which fronts the Laguna del Condado. **Condado** is the narrow peninsula that loops around the top of Miramar almost all the way back to San Juan Island. It's where you'll find many of the best beaches. Just east of Condado is the residential neighborhood of **Ocean Park.**

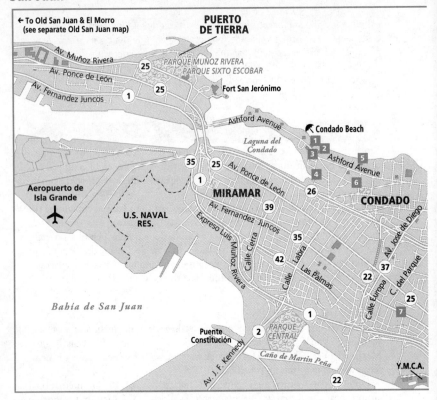

San Juan

← To Old San Juan & El Morro
(see separate Old San Juan map)

PUERTO
DE TIERRA

Av. Muñoz Rivera

PARQUE MUÑOZ RIVERA
PARQUE SIXTO ESCOBAR

Av. Ponce de León

25

25

Av. Fernandez Juncos

1

Fort San Jerónimo

Ashford Avenue

Condado Beach

Laguna del
Condado

1

2

3

Ashford Avenue

5

35

25

Av. Ponce de León

26

4

6

1

MIRAMAR

CONDADO

Aeropuerto de
Isla Grande

39

Av. Fernandez Juncos

Av. José de Diego

U.S. NAVAL
RES.

Expreso Luis Muñoz Rivera

Calle Cerra

35

Calle Labra

Las Palmas

Calle Europa

C. del Parque

42

22

37

Bahía de San Juan

1

25

7

Puente
Constitución

2

PARQUE
CENTRAL

Av. J. F. Kennedy

Caño de Martín Peña

Y.M.C.A.

22

South of Condado and Ocean Park is **Santurce.** To the east is the International Airport, and even farther east is **Isla Verde,** home of some of the Caribbean's most upscale resort hotels, connected to the rest of San Juan by an isthmus.

GETTING AROUND   Walking is the best way to get around Old San Juan. The historic core of the old city is very compact. If your feet tire of the cobblestoned old streets, board one of the free open-air trolleys that slowly make their way through the old city. You can board a trolley at any point along its route (either side of the Calle Fortaleza or Calle San José are good bets), or you can go to the Marina or La Puntilla for departures.

The rest of the city is not so pedestrian-friendly. You'll want to take buses, taxis, or your own car to get around the rest of San Juan, including Condado and Isla Verde. The **Metropolitan Bus Authority** (© 787/767-7979) operates buses in the greater San Juan area. Bus stops are marked by upright metal signs or yellow posts, reading PARADA. Bus terminals in San Juan are in the dock area and at Plaza de Colón. A typical fare is 25¢ to 50¢. The higher fee is for the faster buses that make fewer stops; call for more information about routes and schedules.

Taxis are metered; tips between 10% and 15% of the fare are customary. The initial charge for destinations in the city is $1, plus 10¢ for each $\frac{1}{10}$ mile and 50¢ for every suitcase, with a minimum fare of $3. Taxis are invariably lined up outside the entrance to most of the island's hotels, and if not, a staff member can almost always call one for you. If you want to arrange a taxi on your own,

Alelí by the Sea	**1**
Arcade Inn	**5**
At Wind Chimes Inn	**8**
Atlantic Beach Hotel	**2**
Beach Buoy Inn	**10**
Borinquen Beach Hotel	**11**
Casa de Playa Beach Hotel	**13**
Casa del Caribe	**6**
El Canario by the Lagoon Hotel	**4**
Embassy Condado	**3**
Green Isle Inn	**12**
Hostería del Mar	**9**
Numero Uno Guest House	**7**
Villa Verde Inn	**12**

call the **Mejor Cab Company** (© 787/723-2460). If you want to take a cab to a destination outside the city, you must negotiate a flat fee with the driver. For complaints or questions, contact the **Public Service Commission** (© 787/751-5050), which regulates cabs.

FAST FACTS   One of the most centrally located **pharmacies** is the **Puerto Rico Drug Co.,** Calle San Francisco 157 (© 787/725-2202), in Old San Juan; open Monday to Friday 7am to 9:30pm, Saturday 8am to 9:30pm, and Sunday 8:30am to 7:30pm. **Walgreens,** 1130 Ashford Ave., Condado (© 787/725-1510), is a 24-hour pharmacy.

In a **medical emergency,** call © 787/721-2116. **Ashford Memorial Community Hospital,** 1451 Ashford Ave. (© 787/721-2160), maintains a 24-hour emergency room.

The Travel Network, 1035 Ashford Ave., Condado (© 787/725-0960), handles **American Express** services. The office is open Monday to Friday 9am to 5pm and Saturday 9 to 11am.

ACCOMMODATIONS YOU CAN AFFORD

Most hotels lie in Condado and Isla Verde, areas out by the airport that border the beach. Or you can stay in Old San Juan—but factor in the cost of daily transportation to the beach if that's where you want to go.

All hotel rooms in Puerto Rico are subject to a 7% to 9% tax, which isn't included in the rates listed below. Most hotels also impose a 10% service charge.

IN OLD SAN JUAN

Hotel Milano *(Finds)* This is a good and undiscovered option for those who prefer to lodge directly in the historic heart of Old San Juan. Obviously beach buffs will book elsewhere. The five-story, colonial-style hotel lies near El Morro and is within walking distance of the major historical sights and the best shopping. The interior is tasteful with stucco walls, some wooden floors, paneled windows, and antiques and pictures of Old San Juan. Rooms are small but well maintained, clean, and comfortable, and each has a compact, tiled bathroom with a shower. The top-floor restaurant is an added bonus. Breakfast is served here to guests, who take in the panoramic view of the rooftops of the historic old town.

Calle Fortaleza 307, San Juan, PR 00901. ℂ **787/729-9050.** Fax 787/722-3379. www.hotelmilanopr.com. 21 units. Year-round $80 double, $130 double with view. Rates include continental breakfast. AE, MC, V. Bus: Old Town trolley. **Amenities:** Restaurant. *In room:* A/C, TV.

ON THE CONDADO

Alelí by the Sea *(Value)* This is a lone budget holdout in a sea of expensive hotel options. Right on the Condado, it's a charming little guesthouse that opens onto the beach 1 block off Ashford Avenue. Most of the bedrooms, which are small to midsize, overlook the ocean, and all of them have rattan furnishings and compact, tiled shower-only bathrooms. A pleasant touch is the second-floor terrace overlooking the Atlantic, where guests gather to watch the sunsets.

Calle Seaview 1125, Condado, San Juan, PR 00907. ℂ **787/725-5313.** Fax 787/721-4744. 9 units. Winter $75–$105 double. Off-season $62–$85 double. AE, MC, V. Bus: B-21 or C-10. **Amenities:** Communal kitchen, laundry. *In room:* A/C, TV, no phone.

Arcade Inn This no-frills hotel has attracted families and college students traveling in groups since the 1960s. It's a stucco-covered building with vaguely Spanish colonial detailing on a residential street lined with similar buildings. The small accommodations have slightly battered furniture with well-worn but still comfortable beds. The shower-only bathrooms are cramped. There are very few amenities here, but the beach is only 100 yards away.

8 Taft St., Condado, San Juan, PR 00911. ℂ **787/725-0668.** Fax 787/728-7524. arcadeinn@aol.com. 20 units. Winter $65 single; $70 double. Off-season $60 single; $65 double. DC, MC, V. Bus: B-21. *In room:* A/C, TV, fridge.

Atlantic Beach Hotel On Condado Beach, this place is proud of its status as the best-known gay hotel on Puerto Rico. The five-story hotel, with vaguely Art Deco styling, is a friendly refuge, mostly patronized by men. The rooms are outfitted with tropical fabrics and accessories and rattan furnishings. The mattresses aren't the newest, but, as one repeat visitor told us, "We stay here for the gay ambience, not expecting any grand comfort." Nonetheless, it's a clean and decent place and sometimes takes on the spirit of a house party. Each unit has a small shower-only bathroom. There's a simple snack-style bar and restaurant, with a Sunday-afternoon tea dance that attracts many of the city's gay men.

1 Vendig St., Condado, San Juan, PR 00907. ℂ **787/721-6900.** Fax 787/721-6917. www.atlanticbeachhotel. net. 37 units. Winter $95–$135 single; $120–$150 double. Off-season $80–$115 single; $95–$135 double. AE, DC, DISC, MC, V. Bus: B-21 or C-10. **Amenities:** Restaurant, bar. *In room:* A/C, TV.

At Wind Chimes Inn *(★)* This restored and renovated Spanish manor, 1 short block from the beach and 3½ miles from the airport, is one of the best guest-houses on the Condado. Upon entering a tropical patio, you'll find tile tables surrounded by palm trees and bougainvillea. There's plenty of space on the deck and a covered lounge for relaxing, socializing, and eating breakfast. Dozens of decorative wind chimes add melody to the daily breezes. The good-size rooms offer a choice of size, beds, and kitchens. Beds have firm mattresses, and shower-only bathrooms, although small, are efficiently laid out.

1750 Ashford Ave., Condado, San Juan, PR 00911. © 800/946-3244 or 787/727-4153. Fax 787/728-0671. www.atwindchimesinn.com. 17 units. Winter $80–$129 single or double. Off-season $75–$99 single or double. Rates include continental breakfast. AE, DC, DISC, MC, V. Parking $5. Bus: B-21 or AS. **Amenities:** Pool. In room: A/C, TV, safe, ceiling fans.

Casa del Caribe *(Value* Don't expect the Ritz, but if you're looking for a bargain on the Condado, this is it. This renovated guesthouse was built in the 1940s, later expanded, and then totally refurbished with a tropical decor late in 1995. A very Puerto Rican ambience has been created, with emphasis on Latin hospitality and comfort. On a shady side street just off Ashford Avenue, behind a wall and garden, you'll discover Casa del Caribe's wraparound veranda. The small but cozy guest rooms have ceiling fans and air conditioners, and most feature original Puerto Rican art. The bedrooms are most inviting, with firm mattresses and efficiently organized shower-only bathrooms. The front porch is a social center for guests, and you can also cook out at a barbecue area. The beach is a 2-minute walk away, and the hotel is also within walking distance of some mega-resorts, with their glittering casinos.

Calle Caribe 57, San Juan, PR 00907. © 787/722-7139. Fax 787/725-3995. caribbeanwinds@yunque.net. 13 units. Winter $75–$130 single or double. Off-season $55–$75 single; $65–$95 double. Rates include continental breakfast. AE, DISC, MC, V. Parking $5. Bus: B-21. In room: A/C, TV, ceiling fans.

Embassy Condado This two-story guesthouse sits about a block inland from Condado Beach. On a quiet dead-end street surrounded by a residential neighborhood, it offers a relaxed atmosphere—you could live in a swimsuit or shorts for your entire stay. The medium-size rooms have rattan furniture and tropical accessories, as well as good beds with firm mattresses. Each has a small shower-only bathroom. The hotel features a rooftop sun deck and a restaurant (across the road) that offers a view over the beach.

1126 Seaview, Condado, San Juan, PR 00907. © 787/725-8284. Fax 787/725-2400. http://home.att.net/ ~ embassyguesthouse. 14 units. Winter $85–$115 single or double; $148 suite. Off-season $75–$85 single or double; $115 suite. Extra person $15. AE, DISC, MC, V. Bus: B-21 or C-10. **Amenities:** Restaurant, babysitting. In room: A/C, TV, kitchenette or access to one, no phone.

IN ISLA VERDE

Green Isle Inn Unassuming and somewhat battered by the tropical sun, this hotel stands across the busy avenue from the beach used by the larger and much more expensive Intercontinental Hotel. Each of the simple low-slung rooms has summery furniture that was upgraded in 1996, including replacement of mattresses. Each unit has a compact shower-only bathroom. There's a small pool, but most guests prefer the nearby sea. No meals are served, but dozens of inexpensive hamburger joints are nearby.

Calle Uno 36, Villamar, Isla Verde, San Juan, PR 00979. © 800/677-8860 in the U.S., or 787/726-4330. Fax 787/268-2415. www.greenisleinn.com. 44 units. Winter $79–$84 single or double. Off-season $63–$72 single or double. AE, DC, MC, V. Bus: B-21 or C-10. **Amenities:** Pool. In room: A/C, TV, kitchenette.

Villa Verde Inn True, the living here is rather basic, but it's cheap and clean. This somewhat unremarkable but reasonably priced hotel lies opposite Banco Popular in Isla Verde, about a 5-minute walk to the beach. It's around the corner from the Green Isle Inn, and the aura is that of a 1950s architectural mistake. Behind its plain facade is an interior with rattan furnishings and chrome tables that are duplicated in the small bedrooms, which have worn furnishings and dropped ceilings—yes, a bit tatty, but decent, each with a compact little shower-only bathroom. The better rooms have microwaves, fridges, and balconies. Don't check in if you're seeking a room with a view as the inn faces a freeway.

Urbanización Villamar, Isla Verde, San Juan, PR 00979. ✆ 787/727-9457. Winter $67 double. Off-season $62 double. AE, DISC, MC, V. Bus: A-5. **Amenities:** Babysitting. *In room:* A/C, TV, fridge (some units), microwave (some units), minibar.

IN OCEAN PARK
Beach Buoy Inn About a block from the beach, this affordable B&B deserves to be better known than it is. Its small rooms aren't decorated as nicely as those at the At Wind Chimes Inn (see above), but they're clean and decent; the efficiencies have two double beds each. All have firm mattresses and some have small refrigerators; the bathrooms are small and have shower stalls. Although this place is a comfortable, snug nest, it's short on amenities: no restaurant, no bar, and no pool, but these are available nearby. The staff is especially helpful and friendly.

1853 McLeary, Ocean Park, San Juan, PR 00911. ✆ 800/221-8119 or 787/728-8119. Fax 787/268-0037. 15 units. Winter $80.50 single or double; $76.50–$88.50 efficiency. Off-season $75.05 single or double; $81.90 efficiency. Children 11 and under stay free in parents' room. Rates include continental breakfast. AE, MC, V. Free parking. Bus: B-21. *In room:* A/C, TV, fridge (some units).

WORTH A SPLURGE
On the Condado
El Canario by the Lagoon Hotel One of the area's better B&Bs, the European-style El Canario is in a residential neighborhood a short walk from Condado Beach. It's very much in the Condado styling, evoking Miami Beach in the 1960s. The rooms are generous in size and have balconies. Most units have twin beds with firm mattresses. The bathrooms are sleek and contemporary, each with a tub-and-shower combo and enough room to spread out your stuff. Extras include in-room safes, free coffee in the lobby, a tour desk, and a self-service laundry. The staff can also make arrangements for you to have access to a nearby health club. If the hotel doesn't have room for you, it can book you into its sibling properties, El Canario Inn or El Canario by the Sea.

Calle Clemenceau 4, Condado, San Juan, PR 00907. ✆ 800/533-2649 in the U.S., or 787/722-5058. Fax 787/723-8590. www.canariohotels.com. 40 units. Winter $95 single; $100–$115 double. Off-season $75 single; $90–$105 double. Rates include continental breakfast and morning newspaper. AE, DC, DISC, MC, V. Bus: B-21 or C-10. **Amenities:** Access to health club, tour desk, laundry. *In room:* A/C, TV, safe.

In Isla Verde
Borinquen Beach Hotel Lying just 1 block from the beach and a 5-minute drive from the airport, this is a good deal. This modest one-story guesthouse has been popular with islanders and visitors for more than 2 decades. The unassuming white facade is in keeping with the plain interior decor with its pastel-painted walls, communal lounge and kitchen, and small serving area where guests can order coffee. The rooms are small and plain, but clean and comfortable enough, and each has a small bathroom with shower stall. The overall aura here is very laid-back, but the low prices and convenient location keep the place booked with holiday makers year-round.

Av. Isla Verde 58, Isla Verde, San Juan, PR 00979. ✆ 787/728-8400. Fax 787/268-2411. 12 units. Year-round $92.20 double; $97.65 apt with kitchenette. Extra person $21. AE, MC, V. Free parking. Bus: A-5. *In room:* A/C, TV, no phone.

Casa de Playa Beach Hotel *(Finds)* Jutting out over the sand on the mile-long Isla Verde beach, this bargain oasis is a find. If you're less interested in being in the center of San Juan than you are in spending time on the beach, check out this modest choice. The hotel consists of two two-story buildings, with a porch around the second floor and a small garden in front. Some rooms have small refrigerators. Furnishings are a bit modest and functional but comfortable nonetheless, with much-used, but still firm, mattresses. Rooms include tidily maintained, small, shower-only bathrooms. Standard but inexpensive Italian food is served at a beach bar and restaurant, Fredo's. The hotel doesn't have everything—no pool, no room service—but the price is hard to beat in Isla Verde.

Av. Isla Verde 86, Isla Verde, San Juan, PR 00979. ℭ **800/916-2272** or 787/728-9779. Fax 787/727-1334. 21 units. Winter $92 single; $115 double; $170 suite. Off-season $81 single; $100 double; $140 suite. Children 9 and under stay free in parents' room. Rates include continental breakfast. AE, DC, DISC, MC, V. Bus: B-21 or C-10. **Amenities:** Restaurant, beach bar. *In room:* A/C, TV, fridge (some units).

In Ocean Park

Hostería del Mar ⭐ Lying a few blocks from the Condado casinos are the white walls of this distinctive landmark. It's in a residential seaside community that's popular with locals looking for beach action on weekends. The hotel boasts medium-size oceanview rooms. Those on the second floor have balconies; those on the first floor open onto patios. The guest-room decor is invitingly tropical, with wicker furniture, good beds, pastel prints, and ceiling fans, plus small but efficient shower-only bathrooms. There's no pool, but a full-service restaurant here is known for its vegetarian, macrobiotic, and Puerto Rican plates, all freshly made. The place is simple, yet it has its own elegance, and the hospitality is warm.

1 Tapia St., Ocean Park, Santurce, San Juan, PR 00911. ℭ **787/727-3302.** Fax 787/268-0772. www. prhtasmallhotels.com. 24 units. Winter $115–$155 single or double; $175 apt. Off-season $80–$100 single or double; $125–$185 apt. Children 11 and under stay free in parents' room. AE, DC, DISC, MC, V. **Amenities:** Restaurant. *In room:* A/C, TV.

Número Uno Guest House ⭐ As a translation of its name implies, this is the best of the small-scale, low-rise guesthouses in Ocean Park. It was originally built in the 1950s in a prestigious residential neighborhood adjacent to the wide sands of Ocean Park Beach. There's a garden with palmettos and a pool, easy access to a sandy beach, and all the distractions of several mega-resorts close at hand. The accommodations, ranging from small to medium, have wicker or rattan furnishings and a double, queen, or king-size bed. The bathrooms are also medium in size, and each has a tub-and-shower combination. Budget travelers should be careful when booking as rooms come in three categories, including some economy specials. There are also moderately priced singles and doubles, but some of the singles and doubles with sea views are priced higher than rooms in many first-class hotels. Always specify when booking exactly what type of room you want.

Calle Santa Ana 1, Ocean Park, San Juan, PR 00911. ℭ **787/726-5010.** Fax 787/727-5482. roman@caribe. net. 12 units. Year-round $60–$165 single, $145–$235 single with sea view; $80–$185 double, $165–$255 double with sea view. Rates include continental breakfast. AE, MC, V. Bus: B-21. **Amenities:** Restaurant, bar, pool. *In room:* A/C, safe.

GREAT DEALS ON DINING
IN OLD SAN JUAN

Butterfly People Café CONTINENTAL/AMERICAN This butterfly venture with gossamer wings (see "Shopping," below) is on the second floor of a restored mansion in Old San Juan. Next to the world's largest gallery devoted to butterflies, you can dine in the cafe, which overlooks a patio and has 15 tables inside. The cuisine is tropical and light European fare made with fresh ingredients. You might begin with gazpacho or vichyssoise, follow with quiche or a daily special, and finish with chocolate mousse or the tantalizing raspberry chiffon pie with fresh raspberry sauce. Wherever you look, you see framed butterflies.

Calle Fortaleza 152. ℂ 787/723-2432. Main courses $5.50–$13. MC, V. Mon–Sat 10am–6pm. Bus: Old Town trolley.

Café Berlin INTERNATIONAL/VEGETARIAN This indoor/outdoor cafe-style restaurant overlooking Plaza de Colón is a favorite of locals. No one is quite sure how it got its name, as this cafe isn't German; instead, it's known for its vegetarian dishes, including a specialty, an eggplant tofu sandwich with the works. You can also order chicken and turkey dishes, along with a delectable mahimahi, salmon, shrimp, and quiche. You can make up various combinations of dishes. The cafe specializes in fresh bread, used in its tasty lunch sandwiches. You can also drop in for breakfast to sample homemade pastries.

Calle San Francisco 407. ℂ 787/722-5205. Main courses $9–$17. AE, MC, V. Daily 9am–10pm. Bus: Old Town trolley.

Cafe Puerto Rico CREOLE/PUERTO RICAN On the landmark Plaza de Colón, this restaurant offers balconies overlooking one of the most charming of Old Town squares. The setting is colonial, with beamed ceilings and tile floors, with ceiling fans whirling overhead. The white walls evoke the colonial Caribbean. The menu features the hearty regional fare so beloved by the locals. Tasty options include fried fish filet, paella, and lobster cooked as you like it. Eggplant parmigiana is an excellent vegetarian option, and you might also order eye round stuffed with ham in Creole sauce. On weekends live bands play here, and the sound of romantic boleros or salsa fill the air. The cafe is an especially good value then because you get your food and entertainment for just the price of dinner.

Calle O'Donnell 208. ℂ 787/724-2281. Main courses $9–$17. AE, MC, V. Daily 11:30am–11pm (bar open till 2am Thurs–Sat). Bus: Old Town trolley.

Carli Café Concierto ⍟ INTERNATIONAL This stylish restaurant at the base of the Banco Popular building in Old San Juan is a new arena for the music of owner Carli Muñoz. The gold disc hanging on the walls attests to Carli's success in his previous role as a pianist for the Beach Boys. Nowadays, he entertains his dinner guests with a combination of standards, romantic jazz, and original material on his grand piano. Diners can choose to sit outside on the Plazoleta, where they can enjoy a panoramic view of the bay, or they can eat inside against a backdrop of a tasteful decor of terra-cotta walls, black marble tables, and a black-and-white tiled floor. The chef tempts visitors with an imaginative international menu, including such delights as a quail rockettes stuffed with dried fruit and sage or a classic filet mignon with wild mushrooms. The filet of salmon and a mouth-watering rack of lamb are among the finest main dishes. Carli plays every night. The bar, with its mahogany and brass fittings, is an ideal spot to kick back.

Banco Popular building. ℂ 787/725-4927. Reservations recommended. Main courses $12–$27. AE, MC, V. Mon–Thurs 4pm–midnight; Fri–Sat 4pm–2am (dinner till 11:30pm). Bus: M-2 or M-3.

El Buen Samaritano *(Finds)* PUERTO RICAN   Only the most experimental visitors would venture in here, despite the fact that it provides insights into the subculture of this thriving inner-city neighborhood. In fact, we've included this authentic little eatery to answer the often-posed question, "Where do the locals dine?" It stands adjacent to City Hall's back door, on one of our favorite "backwater" streets in the Old Town. Almost no English is spoken; it's as Creole and ethnic as anything on the island, and it contains no more than four tables in a setting Hemingway would've praised. Everything is predictably filling and starchy, including roast pork with yellow rice and beans and red snapper filet in pungent tomato sauce. The menu, which depends largely on what's available in the market, will be recited lethargically by a member of the family who owns this hole-in-the-wall. Except during the midday crush, no one will mind if you opt for just a cup of thick Puerto Rican coffee, a beer, or a soda.

Calle Luna 255 (near San Justo St.). ℂ **787/721-6184.** Platters and main courses $8–$15; daily specials $5. No credit cards. Daily 7am–9pm. Bus: A-5.

El Patio de Sam AMERICAN/PUERTO RICAN   This is a popular gathering spot for American expats, newspeople, and shopkeepers, and is known for having the best burgers in San Juan. Even though the dining room isn't outdoors, it has been transformed into a patio. You'll swear you're dining alfresco: Every table is placed near a cluster of potted plants, and canvas panels and awnings cover the skylight. For a satisfying lunch, try the black bean soup, followed by the burger platter, and top it off with a Key lime tart. Except for the hamburgers, some other items on the menu haven't met with favor among many visitors, who've written us that the food was overpriced and the service confused. Nevertheless, it remains Old Town's most popular dining room. It now offers live entertainment, Tuesday to Saturday, with Spanish guitar some nights and classical piano others.

Calle San Sebastián 102 (across from the Iglesia de San José). ℂ **787/723-1149.** Sandwiches, burgers, salads $7.50–$10.50; main courses $12–$26. AE, DC, DISC, MC, V. Sun–Thurs 11am–11pm; Fri–Sat 11am–midnight. Bus: A-7, T-1, or T-2.

Hard Rock Cafe AMERICAN   Along with rock 'n' roll memorabilia and loud rock music, you can feed on juicy burgers, well-stuffed sandwiches, fajitas, barbecued chicken, chili, and pork ribs. On days when cruise ships pull into port (usually Tues and Sun), the place is likely to be mobbed.

Calle Recinto Sur 253. ℂ **787/724-7625.** Burgers, sandwiches, and platters $7–$21. AE, DISC, DC, MC, V. Daily 11:30am–1:30am. Bus T-1.

Jibarito *(Finds)* CREOLE/PUERTO RICAN   The name of this restaurant translates as "hillbilly." As you might guess from the name, this place has a rustic aura, both the decor and the regional menu. The popularity of this eatery is due to its owner, Doña Aida, who opened the door of this former colonial house in the old town a quarter century ago. In lieu of air-conditioning, ceiling fans stir the air. The menu consists mostly of dishes your mama would have cooked for you—if your mother were Puerto Rican. You can order mashed plantain served with shrimp and meat dishes, codfish Creole in tomatoes and peppers, lamb chops, or plantain with ground meat.

Calle Sol 280. ℂ **787/725-8375.** Main courses $7–$12. AE, MC, V. Daily 11am–9pm. Bus: Old Town trolley.

La Bombonera *(Value)* PUERTO RICAN   This place has been offering exceptional value in homemade pastries, well-stuffed sandwiches, and endless cups of coffee since 1902. Its atmosphere evokes turn-of-the-century Castile transplanted to the New World. The food is authentically Puerto Rican, home-made, and inexpensive, with regional dishes like rice with squid, roast leg of pork, and seafood *asopao*. For dessert, you might select an apple, pineapple, or prune pie, or one of many types of flan. Service is polite, if a bit rushed, and the place fills up quickly at lunchtime.

Calle San Francisco 259. 🕿 787/722-0658. Reservations recommended. American breakfast $4–$8; main courses $6.50–$15. AE, DISC, MC, V. Daily 7:30am–8pm. Bus: M-2, M-3, or T-1.

La Danza *(Value)* PUERTO RICAN   The friendly, jovial Señora Burgos welcomes guests to this choice dining room and has done so for some 4 decades. Opposite the Chapel of Christ, La Danza is known in Old Town for its all-day special, paella for two with fried plantains, garlic bread, two glasses of wine, and coffee—all for $20. Smoking is permitted at the outside tables, and weekend diners are often treated to live street entertainment. There is also an intimate bar, where locals sometimes pop in for a fast pick-me-up. Begin with one of the choice appetizers, especially the salt cod cakes or the small boiled sweet corn cakes. Main dishes include breaded fish and fish in a traditional Creole sauce. Some diners prefer to fill up on *asopao*, the thick stew of Puerto Rico. Other regional fare includes chicken-and-rice stew accompanied by fried plantains.

Calle Fortaleza 56. 🕿 787/723-1642. Main courses $7–$17. MC, V. Fri–Wed 11:30am–8pm. Bus: Old Town trolley.

La Mallorquina PUERTO RICAN   San Juan's oldest restaurant, founded in 1848, has been run by the Rojos family since 1900. If you look carefully at the floor adjacent to the old-fashioned mahogany bar, you'll see the building's orig-inal gray-and-white marble flooring that the owners are laboriously restoring, square foot by square foot, to its original condition. Lunches here tend to attract a following of local office workers; dinners are more cosmopolitan and more leisurely, with many residents of the Condado and other modern neighborhoods selecting this place specifically because of its old-fashioned, old-world charm.

The food has changed little here over the years, with special emphasis on *asopao* made with rice and chicken, shrimp, or lobster and shrimp. *Arroz con pollo* is almost as popular. Begin with garlic soup or gazpacho, end with a flan, and you'll have a meal that's authentically Puerto Rican.

Calle San Justo 207. 🕿 787/722-3261. Reservations not accepted at lunch, recommended at dinner. Dinner main courses $15–$36 (highest price is for lobster). AE, MC, V. Mon–Sat noon–10pm. Closed Sept. Bus: A-7, T-1, or T-2.

Los Yelos *(Value)* PUERTO RICAN/CREOLE   If you decide to bypass the store next door, "Condom World," you can enter this tiny little joint that has only eight tables. It's a real insider's place, and serves decent food full of flavor under bare fluorescent bulbs. The spartan decor is more than compensated for by the really bargain food served in this working-class neighborhood. The break-fast served here is Old San Juan's most reasonable in price, complete with eggs, potatoes, and ham. For your main course, you could enjoy a generous helping of roast chicken, or something light—codfish salad. Pork is smothered in onions and served with yellow rice, and you can also order *sancocho*, that robust meat and vegetable stew. Many dishes come with *mangú*, a plantain mash. The fixed-price menu is the town's greatest food buy. The place doesn't have a liquor license.

Calle San Francisco 353. 🕿 787/725-9362. Main courses $5–$7; breakfast $1.75–$4; fixed-price menu $5. No credit cards. Mon–Sat 6am–6pm. Bus: Old Town trolley.

Luigi's ★★ GENOVESE   There's a formal and even romantic atmosphere here at night. When chef-owner Luigi Sanguineti came to Puerto Rico from Genoa in the late 1980s, he liked the place so much he decided to bring "a little bit of Genoa" to the old town. After gaining a reputation as one of the island's foremost European chefs, Luigi finally opened his own place in 2000. Since then he's been delighting the palates of locals and visitors with his high-quality Italian cuisine. Try the gnocchi with pesto or the eggplant lasagna, perhaps starting with a savory antipasto prepared by Luigi himself. His lobster ravioli is San Juan's finest, and another dish we like a lot is the shrimp risotto.

104 Diez de Andino. ✆ 787/977-0134. Reservations recommended. Main courses $10–$22. MC, V. Mon–Wed noon–10pm; Thurs–Sat noon–11:30pm; Sun noon–5pm. Bus: Old Town trolley.

IN CONDADO

Café del Angel CREOLE/PUERTO RICAN   Don't come here for the decor. The juice bar up front looks like it was transported from Miami's Flagler Street in 1950, and the plastic green furniture won't compel you to get *Architectural Digest* on the phone. If indeed there is an "angel," as the cafe's name suggests, it is in the kitchen. The chef serves remarkably good food at affordable prices. The place has been in operation for more than a decade. Paintings and figures of its namesake, angels, decorate the dining room. Some 100 hungry diners can be fed here at one time, in a relaxed atmosphere that is welcoming and friendly. The service is also efficient. Prepare for some real island flavor, as in the traditional *mofongo relleno con camarones,* which is sautéed, mashed plantain with shrimp. You can order a generous helping of tender beefsteak sautéed with onions and peppers or a perfectly grilled chicken. The roast pork is subtly seasoned with lemon and fresh garlic. *Pastel,* a kind of creamy polenta of cornmeal, is served with many dishes, and the fresh garlic bread is complimentary.

1106 Ashford Ave. ✆ 787/643-7594. Reservations needed. Main courses $7–$9. MC, V. Wed–Mon 7am–10pm. Bus: B-21.

Cafe Mezzanine INTERNATIONAL   On the mezzanine level of one of the Condado's best hotels, this comfortable and cozy eatery for many years was the most famous Howard Johnson's in the Caribbean. It attracts some of the most prestigious politicians and financiers to its booths and tables (many luminaries live nearby and consider it their neighborhood diner). Depending on the time of day, you can be served pancakes, omelets, muffins, hash browns, and sausages; or you can order lunch and dinner foods like fish fries, teriyaki steaks, clam platters, and an array of sandwiches and burgers, as well as typical Puerto Rican dishes.

In the Radisson Ambassador Plaza Hotel & Casino, 1369 Ashford Ave. ✆ 787/721-7300. Main courses $7–$17; full American breakfast $6.25–$11.50; Mon–Fri daily specials $11. AE, MC, V. Mon–Thurs 6:30am–2pm and 5–11pm; Fri–Sat 6:30am–11pm. Bus: B-21 or C-10.

Cielito Lindo MEXICAN   This serves the Condado's best Mexican cuisine. Sure, it doesn't compare with what you'll find in Mexico or even Arizona and Texas, but it is a refreshing change of pace from a steady diet of Creole cuisine. When you step across the threshold of this little 35-seat eatery, you'll find yourself transported to Old Mexico, with wall tiles, festive death masks, and authentic Mexican posters. The menu would make Emiliano Zapata feel right at home. Along with the inevitable burritos and tacos, you will find yourself tempted by the guacamole and enchiladas, which can be washed down with a selection of imported Mexican beer. Refrijoles and chalupa, along with Tampique steak and enchiladas, are some of the justifiably popular dishes.

Calle Magdalena 1108. ⒸⒸ 787/723-5597. Main courses $3.25–$16. AE, MC, V. Mon–Fri 11am–11pm; Sat 5–11pm. Bus: B-21.

Via Appia ITALIAN   A favorite of Sanjuaneros visiting Condado for the day, Via Appia offers food that's sometimes praiseworthy rather than merely passable. Its pizzas are the best in the neighborhood. Savory pasta dishes, like baked ziti, lasagna, and spaghetti with several of your favorite sauces, are also prepared. All of this can be washed down with sangría. During the day, freshly made salads or sandwiches are available.

1350 Ashford Ave. ⒸⒸ 787/725-8711. Pizza $9–$15; main courses $8–$16; sandwiches $4–$6. AE, MC, V. Daily 11am–midnight. Bus: A-7.

IN ISLA VERDE

Metropol Ⓕ CUBAN/PUERTO RICAN/INTERNATIONAL   Metropol is the happiest blend of Cuban and Puerto Rican food we've ever discovered. The black-bean soup is among the island's finest, served in the classic Havana style with a side dish of rice and chopped onions. Endless garlic bread accompanies most dinners, likely to include Cornish game hen stuffed with Cuban rice and beans or marinated steak topped with a fried egg. Smoked chicken or chicken fried steak are also heartily recommended; the portions are huge. Plantains, yucca, and all that good stuff accompany most dishes. Finish with a choice of thin or firm custard. Most dishes are at the lower end of the price scale.

Av. Isla Verde. ⒸⒸ 787/791-4046. Main courses $8–$27. AE, MC, V. Daily 11am–10:30pm. Bus: A-7.

Panadería España Repostería SANDWICHES   The Panadería España makes San Juan's definitive Cuban sandwich—a cheap meal in itself. Consisting of sliced baked pork packed in crusty bread, it's about the only thing offered except for drinks and coffee dispensed from behind a much-used bar. There's also an assortment of gourmet items from Spain, arranged as punctuation marks on shelves set against an otherwise all-white decor. The place has been serving simple breakfasts, drinks, coffee, and Cuban sandwiches virtually every day since it opened around 1970.

Centro Villamar. ⒸⒸ 787/727-3860. Sandwiches $4.50–$8.50. AE, DISC, MC, V. Daily 6am–10pm. Bus: B-21 or C-10.

Repostería Kassalta Ⓥalue SPANISH/PUERTO RICAN   In a commercial neighborhood 4 miles east of Old San Juan, this is the most famous of San Juan's cafeteria/bakery/delicatessens because of its reasonable prices and eat-in and takeout foods. The cavernous room is flanked with modern sun-flooding windows and glass-fronted display cases filled with meats, sausages, and pastries. At one end of the room, patrons line up to place their orders at a cash register, and then they carry their selections to one of the tables. It helps to know Spanish. Try a steaming bowl of the best *caldo gallego* in Puerto Rico—laden with collard greens, potatoes, and sausage slices and accompanied by hunks of bread, this soup makes a meal in itself. Also popular are Cuban sandwiches (made with sliced pork, cheese, and fried bread), steak sandwiches, octopus salad, and an assortment of omelets.

Calle McLeary 1966. ⒸⒸ 787/727-7340. Full American breakfast $5.50; soups $5; sandwiches $3.80–$8. MC, V. Daily 6am–10pm. Bus: B-21 or C-10.

AT VILLA PALMERAS

La Casita Blanca Ⓕ Ⓕinds CREOLE/PUERTO RICAN   Island politicians are said to have the best nose for good home-cooking. We don't know if that is true

> ### ⌒Moments Picnic Fare & Where to Eat It
>
> Puerto Rico is usually ideal for picnicking year-round. The best place to fill a picnic basket is the **Repostería Kassalta** (see "In Isla Verde," above), a cafeteria/bakery/deli with lots of goodies. Puerto Rican families often come here to order delicacies for their Sunday outings. The best places for a picnic are **Muñoz Marín Park,** along Las Américas Expressway, west of Avenida Piñero, and the **Botanical Gardens** operated by the University of Puerto Rico in the Río Piedras section.

or not, but one of their favorite places is this eatery. Governors or governor wannabes also come here to order excellent regional fare. This is a converted family home that opened its door to diners in the mid-1980s, and it's been a favorite of locals from all walks of Puerto Rican society since. In a popular *barrio,* it is off the tourist trail and best reached by taxi. You'll need to make a reservation for lunch but should have no trouble finding a table at dinner. The traditional Creole menu includes such delights as *guisado y arroz con gandule* (beef stew with rice and small beans) or *bacalao* (salt cod fish with yucca). Guaranteed to put hair on your chest is *patita* (pig's trotters in a Creole sauce). Veal with sautéed onions is popular, as is grilled red snapper or the chicken fricassee. A typical chicken *asopao,* a soupy rice stew, is also served. Fried plantains, rice, and beans come with most dishes.

Calle Tapia 351. ℂ 787/726-5501. Reservations recommended at lunch. Main courses $6.50–$17; Sun buffet $12. No credit cards. Mon–Thurs 11:30am–7pm; Fri–Sat 11:30am–10pm; Sun noon–5pm.

HITTING THE BEACHES

Some public stretches of shoreline around San Juan are overcrowded, especially on Saturday and Sunday; others are practically deserted. If you find that secluded, hidden beach of your dreams, proceed with caution. Muggings have been known to occur on sparsely populated sands. For more information about the island's many beaches, call the **Department of Sports and Recreation** (ℂ 787/728-5668).

All beaches on Puerto Rico, even those fronting the top hotels, are open to the public, although you will be charged for parking and for use of *balneario* facilities, such as lockers and showers. Public beaches shut down on Monday; if Monday is a holiday, the beaches are open for the holiday but closed the next day, Tuesday. Beach hours are 9am to 5pm in winter, to 6pm off-season. Major public beaches in the San Juan area have changing rooms and showers; Luquillo Beach also has picnic tables.

Famous among beach buffs since the 1920s, **Condado Beach** put San Juan on the map as a tourist destination. Backed up by high-rise hotels, it seems more like Miami Beach than any other in the Caribbean. You can book all sorts of watersports at kiosks along the beach or at the activities desk of the various hotels. There are also plenty of outdoor bars and restaurants when you tire of the sands. Condado is especially busy wherever a high-rise resort is located. People-watching is a favorite sport along these golden strands.

At the end of Puente Dos Hermanos, the westernmost corner of the Condado is the most popular strip. This section of the beach is small and shaded by palms, and a natural rock barrier calms the turbulence of the waters rushing in, making for protected, safe swimming in gin-clear waters. The lagoon on the other side of the beach is ideal for windsurfing and kayaking.

A favorite of San Juaneros themselves, golden-sand **Isla Verde Beach** is also ideal for swimming, and it, too, is lined with high-rise resorts and luxury condos. Isla Verde has picnic tables, so you can pick up the makings of a lunch and make it a day at the beach. This strip is also good for snorkeling because of its calm, clear waters; many kiosks will rent you equipment. Isla Verde Beach extends from the end of Ocean Park to the beginning of a section called Boca Cangrejos. The best beach at Isla Verde is in front of the Hotel El San Juan. Most sections of this long strip have separate names, such as El Alambique, which is often the site of beach parties, and Punta El Medio, bordering the new Ritz-Carlton, also a great beach and very popular even with the locals. If you go past the luxury hotels and expensive condos behind the Luís Muñoz Marín International Airport, you arrive at the major public beach at Isla Verde. Here you'll find a *balneario* with parking, showers, fast-food joints, and watersports equipment. The sands here are whiter than the golden sands of the Condado, and are lined with coconut palms, sea-grape trees, and even almond trees, all of which provide shade from the fierce noonday sun.

One of the most attractive beaches in the Greater San Juan area is **Ocean Park Beach,** a mile of fine gold sand in a neighborhood east of Condado. This beach attracts both young people and a big gay crowd. Access to the beach at Ocean Park has been limited recently, but the best place to enter is from a section called El Ultimo Trolley. This area is also ideal for volleyball, paddleball, and other games. The easternmost portion, known as Punta Las Marias, is best for windsurfing. The waters at Ocean Park are fine for swimming, although they can get rough at times.

Rivaling Condado and Isla Verde beaches, **Luquillo Beach** 🏆🏆 is the grandest in Puerto Rico and one of the most popular. It's 30 miles east of San Juan near the town of Luquillo. Here you'll find a mile-long half-moon bay set against a backdrop of coconut palms. Saturday and Sunday are the worst times to go, as hordes of San Juaneros head here for fun in the sun. Watersports kiosks are available, offering everything from windsurfing to sailing. Facilities include lifeguards, an emergency first-aid station, ample parking, showers, and toilets. You can easily have a local lunch here at one of the beach shacks offering cod fritters and tacos.

SPORTS & OTHER OUTDOOR PURSUITS

CRUISES For the best cruises of San Juan Bay, go to **Caribe Aquatic Adventures** (see "Scuba Diving," below). Bay cruises start at $25 per person.

HORSE RACING Great thoroughbreds and outstanding jockeys compete all year at **El Comandante,** Avenida 65 de Infantería, Route 3, km 15.3, at Canovanas (✆ 787/724-6060), Puerto Rico's only racetrack, a 20-minute drive east of the center of San Juan. Post time varies from 2:15 to 2:45pm on Monday, Wednesday, Friday, Saturday, and Sunday.

Tips **Let the Swimmer Beware**

You have to pick your spots carefully if you want to swim along Condado Beach. The waters along the Condado Plaza Hotel are calmer than in other areas because of a coral breakwater. However, the beach near the Marriott is not good for swimming because of rocks and an undertow. Proceed with caution.

SCUBA DIVING   In San Juan, the best outfitter is **Caribe Aquatic Adventures** (© 787/724-1882 or 787/765-7444), which operates a dive shop in the rear lobby of the Radisson Normandie Hotel. The company offers diving certification from both PADI and NAUI as part of 40-hour courses priced at $465 each. A resort course for first-time divers costs $97. They have a variety of full-day diving expeditions to various reefs off the east coast of Puerto Rico. If your time is severely limited, you can take a half-day dive of sites near San Juan. But since the best dive sites are farther away, the serious scuba diver will want to take a full-day tour. They also offer windsurfing excursions (see "Windsurfing," below).

SNORKELING   Snorkeling is better in the outlying portions of the island than in overcrowded San Juan. But if you don't have time to explore greater Puerto Rico, you'll find that most of the popular beaches, such as Luquillo and Isla Verde, have pretty good visibility. One of the best places is the San Juan Bay marina near the Caribe Hilton. Snorkeling equipment generally costs $15 per day and is available from the kiosks on the public beaches. Watersports desks at the big San Juan hotels at Isla Verde and Condado can also make arrangements for equipment rental and point you to the best places for snorkeling. If your hotel doesn't offer such services, you can also contact **Caribe Aquatic Adventures** (see "Scuba Diving," above), which caters to both snorkelers and scuba divers. Other possibilities for equipment rentals are at **Caribbean School of Aquatics,** Taft No. 1, Suite 10F, San Juan (© 787/728-6606), and **Mundo Submarino,** Laguna Gardens Shopping Center, Isla Verde (© 787/791-5764).

TENNIS   Nonguests can use the courts at the **Caribe Hilton & Casino,** Puerta de Tierra (© 787/721-0303), and at the **Condado Plaza Hotel & Casino,** 999 Ashford Ave. (© 787/721-1000), if they make reservations. There are also 17 public courts, lighted at night, at **San Juan Central Municipal Park,** at Calle Cerra (exit on Route 2; © 787/722-1646). Fees are $4 an hour 8am to 6pm, $5 per hour 6 to 10pm.

WINDSURFING   A favorite spot is the sheltered waters of the Condado Lagoon in San Juan. Throughout the island, many of the companies featuring snorkeling and scuba diving also offer windsurfing equipment and instruction, and dozens of hotels offer facilities on their own premises. Another good spot is at the Radisson Normandie Hotel, where **Caribe Aquatic Adventures** has its main branch (© 787/721-1000 or 787/765-7444). Board rentals cost $25 to $30 per hour; lessons cost $45.

STEPPING BACK IN TIME: SEEING OLD SAN JUAN

The Spanish moved to Old San Juan in 1521, and the city played an important role as Spain's bastion of defense in the Caribbean. Today, the streets are narrow and teeming with traffic, but a walk through Old San Juan (El Viejo San Juan) is like a stroll through 5 centuries of history. You can do it in less than a day. In a 7-square-block landmark area in the westernmost part of the city, you can see many of Puerto Rico's chief historical attractions and do some shopping along the way.

CHURCHES

Capilla de Cristo   The chapel was built to commemorate what legend says was a miracle. In 1753, a young rider lost control of his horse in a race down this very street during the fiesta of St. John's Day, plunging over the precipice. Moved by the accident, the secretary of the city, Don Mateo Pratts, invoked

Moments Touring El Yunque Tropical Rain Forest

Some 25 miles east of San Juan lies the **Caribbean National Forest,** known as **El Yunque** ★★★, the only tropical forest in the U.S. National Forest Service system. It was given its status by President Theodore Roosevelt. With 28,000 acres, it contains some 240 tree species (only half a dozen of which are found on the mainland United States). In this world of cedars and satinwood (draped in tangles of vines), you'll hear chirping birds, see wild orchids, and perhaps hear the song of the tree frog, the coquí. The entire forest is a bird sanctuary and may be the last retreat of the rare Puerto Rican parrot.

El Yunque is high above sea level, and the peak of El Toro rises to 3,532 feet. You can be fairly sure you'll be showered on, as more than 100 billion gallons of rain falls here annually, but the showers are brief and there are lots of shelters. El Yunque offers a number of walking and hiking trails. The most scenic is the rugged El Toro, passing through four forest systems en route to the 3,532-foot Pico El Toro, the highest peak in the forest. The signposted El Yunque Trail leads to three of the recreation area's most spectacular lookouts, and the Big Tree Trail is an easy walk to panoramic La Mina Falls. Just off the main road is La Coca Falls, a sheet of water cascading down mossy cliffs.

Nearby, the Sierra Palm Interpretive Service Center offers maps and information and arranges for guided tours of the forest. A 45-minute drive southeast from San Juan (near the intersection of Rtes. 3 and 191), El Yunque is a popular half-day or full-day outing. Major hotels provide guided tours.

El Portal Tropical Forest Center, Route 191, Rio Grande (© **787/888-1810**), an $18-million exhibit and information center, opened its doors in the tropical rain forest, with 10,000 square feet of space. Three pavilions offer exhibits and bilingual displays. Actor Jimmy Smits narrates a documentary called *Understanding the Forest.* The center is open daily 9am to 5pm, charging no admission. Guided tours cost $5 adults, $3 children.

Christ to save the youth, and had the chapel built when his prayers were answered. Today it's a landmark in the old city and one of its best-known monuments. The chapel's gold-and-silver altar can be seen through its glass doors. Since the chapel is open only on Tuesdays, most visitors have to settle for a view of its exterior.

Calle del Cristo (directly west of Paseo de la Princesa). Free admission. Tues 10am–2pm. Bus: Old Town trolley.

Catedral de San Juan   San Juan Cathedral was begun in 1540 and has had a rough life. Looting, a lack of funds, and hurricanes have continually hampered its construction and reconstruction. Over the years, a circular staircase and two adjoining vaulted Gothic chambers have been added. Many beautiful stained-glass windows also escaped pillagers and natural disasters. In 1908, the body of Ponce de León was disinterred from the nearby Iglesia de San José and placed

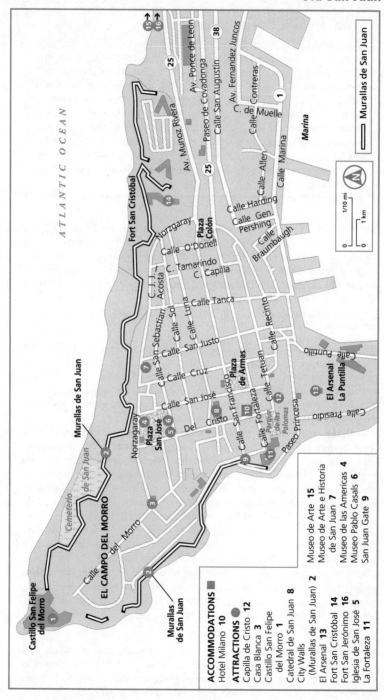

Old San Juan

ATLANTIC OCEAN

Castillo San Felipe del Morro

Murallas de San Juan

EL CAMPO DEL MORRO

Cementerio de San Juan

Calle del Morro

Fort San Cristóbal

Av. Munoz Rivera

Paseo de Covadonga

Av. Ponce de Leon

Calle San Augustin

Av. Fernandez Juncos

C. de Contreras

C. de Muelle

Marina

Calle Marina

Calle Allen

Calle Harding

Calle Gen. Pershing

Calle Braumbaugh

Norzagaray

Plaza Colón

Calle O'Donell

C. Tamarindo

C. Capilla

C. J. Acosta

Calle Tanca

Calle San Sebastian

Calle Sol

Calle Luna

Calle San Justo

Calle Recinto

Calle Cruz

Calle San José

Calle San Francisco

Plaza de Armas

Calle Tetuan

Calle Puntillo

El Arsenal

La Puntilla

Calle Presidio

Calle Fortaleza

Parque de las Palomas

Paseo Princesa

Del Cristo

Norzagaray

Plaza San José

ACCOMMODATIONS
Hotel Milano 10

ATTRACTIONS
Capilla de Cristo 12
Casa Blanca 3
Castillo San Felipe del Morro 1
Catedral de San Juan 8
City Walls (Murallas de San Juan) 2
El Arsenal 13
Fort San Cristóbal 14
Fort San Jerónimo 16
Iglesia de San José 5
La Fortaleza 11

Museo de Arte 15
Museo de Arte e Historia de San Juan 7
Museo de las Americas 4
Museo Pablo Casals 6
San Juan Gate 9

Murallas de San Juan

1/10 mi

1 km

⌒ *Finds* **Jogger's Trail or Romantic Walk**

After hurricane damage, **El Morro Trail,** a jogger's paradise, has been restored. The trail provides Old Town's most scenic views across the harbor. The first part of the trail extends to the **San Juan Gate.** The walk then goes by El Morro, a 16th-century fort, and eventually reaches a scenic area known as Bastion de Santa Barbara. The walk passes El Morro's well-preserved walls until the trail ends at the entrance to the fortress. The walkway is designed to follow the undulating movement of the ocean, and sea grapes and tropical vegetation surround benches for your rest. The trail is more romantic at night when the walls of the fortress are illuminated. Stop in at the tourist office for a map and set off on the adventure.

here in a marble tomb near the transept, where it remains. Since 1862, the cathedral has contained the wax-covered mummy of St. Pio, a Roman martyr persecuted and killed for his Christian faith. To the right of the mummy, you might notice a bizarre wooden statue of Mary with four swords stuck in her bosom. The cathedral faces Plaza de las Monjas (the Nuns' Square), a shady spot where you can rest and cool off.

Calle del Cristo 153 (at Caleta San Juan). ℂ 787/722-0861. Free admission. Daily 8:30am–4pm. Bus: Old Town trolley.

Iglesia de San José   Initial plans for this church were drawn in 1523, and Dominican friars supervised its construction in 1532. (The church is currently closed for extensive renovations; check its status before heading here.) Before entering, look for the statue of Ponce de León in the adjoining plaza—it was made from melted-down British cannons captured during Sir Ralph Abercromby's unsuccessful attack on San Juan in 1797.

Both the church and its monastery were closed by decree in 1838, and the royal treasury confiscated the property. Later, the Crown turned the convent into a military barracks. The Jesuits restored the badly damaged church. This was the place of worship for Ponce de León's descendants, who are buried here under the family's coat-of-arms. The conquistador, killed by a poisoned arrow in Florida, was interred here until his removal to the Catedral de San Juan in 1908.

Although badly looted, the church still has some treasures, including *Christ of the Ponces,* a carved crucifix presented to Ponce de León; four oils by José Campéche, the leading Puerto Rican painter of the 18th century; and two large works by Francisco Oller, the stellar artist of the late 19th and early 20th centuries. Many miracles have been attributed to a painting in the Chapel of Belém, a 15th-century Flemish work called *The Virgin of Bethlehem.*

Plaza de San José, Calle del Cristo. ℂ 787/725-7501. Free admission. Church and Chapel of Belém, Mon–Wed and Fri 7am–3pm; Sat 8am–1pm. Bus: Old Town trolley.

FORTS

Castillo San Felipe del Morro ✹   Called "El Morro," this fort stands on a rocky promontory dominating the entrance to San Juan Bay. Constructed in 1540, the original fort was a round tower, which can still be seen deep inside the lower levels of the castle. More walls and turrets were added, and by 1787, the fortification attained the complex design you see today. The English and the Dutch both attacked this fortress repeatedly.

The National Park Service protects the fortifications of Old San Juan, which have been declared a World Heritage Site by the United Nations. You'll find El Morro an intriguing labyrinth of dungeons, barracks, ramps, and vaults, with lookouts that provide some of the most dramatic views in the Caribbean. Historical information is provided in a video in English and Spanish. The nearest parking is the underground facility beneath the Quincentennial Plaza at the Ballajá barracks (Cuartel de Ballajá) on Calle Norzagaray. Sometimes park rangers lead hour-long tours for free, although you can also visit on your own. Your ticket here entitles you to free admission to Fort San Cristóbal (see below) on the same day.

At the end of Calle Norzagaray. ✆ 787/729-6960. Admission $2 adults, $1 seniors and ages 13–17, free for children 12 and under. Daily 9am–5pm. Bus: A-5, B-21, or B-40.

Fort San Cristóbal ☆   This huge fortress, begun in 1634 and reengineered in the 1770s, is one of the largest the Spanish ever built in the Americas. Its walls rise more than 150 feet above the sea. San Cristóbal protected San Juan against attackers coming by land as a partner to El Morro, to which it is linked by a half-mile of monumental walls and bastions filled with cannon-firing positions. A complex system of tunnels and dry moats connects the center of San Cristóbal to its "outworks," defensive elements arranged layer after layer over a 27-acre site. You'll get the idea if you look at the scale model on display. Like El Morro, the fort is administered and maintained by the National Park Service.

Be sure to see the Garita del Diablo, or the Devil's Sentry Box, one of the oldest parts of San Cristóbal's defenses, and famous in Puerto Rican legend. The devil himself, it is said, would snatch away sentinels at this lonely post at the edge of the sea. In 1898, cannons on top of San Cristóbal fired the first shots of the Spanish-American War in Puerto Rico during an artillery duel with a U.S. Navy fleet. Sometimes park rangers lead hour-long tours for free, although you can visit on your own.

In the northeast corner of Old San Juan (uphill from Plaza de Colón on Calle Norzagaray). ✆ 787/729-6960. Admission $2 adults, $1 ages 13–17, free for children 12 and under. Daily 9am–5pm. Bus: A-5, B-21, or B-40; then the free trolley from Covadonga station to the top of the hill.

Fort San Jerónimo   Completed in 1608, this fort was damaged in the English assault of 1797 before being reconstructed 2 years later. Today it is in the hands of the Institute of Puerto Rican Culture. If you want to see the view from the inside, you must call the Caribe Hilton. Security here will open the gate to let you inside, but you have to make a special request.

Calle Rosales, east of the Caribe Hilton, at the entrance to Condado Bay. ✆ 787/724-0700. Free admission. Wed–Sat 9am–3pm. Bus: T-1.

OTHER HISTORIC SITES

The **city walls** around San Juan (*murallas de San Juan*) were built in 1630 to protect the town against both European invaders and Caribbean pirates, and indeed were part of one of the most impregnable fortresses in the New World. Even today, they're an engineering marvel. At their top, notice the balconied buildings that served for centuries as hospitals and also residences of the island's various governors. The thickness of the walls averages 20 feet at the base and 12 feet at the top, with an average height of 40 feet. Between Fort San Cristóbal and El Morro, bastions were erected at frequent intervals. The walls come into view as you approach from San Cristóbal on your way to El Morro. To get here, take the T-1 bus.

San Juan Gate, Calle San Francisco and Calle Recinto Oeste, built around 1635, just north of La Fortaleza, several blocks downhill from the cathedral, was the main gate and entry point into San Juan—that is, if you arrived by ship in the 18th century. The gate is the only one remaining of the several that once pierced the fortifications of the old walled city. To get here, take the B-21 bus.

El Arsenal The Spaniards used shallow craft to patrol the lagoons and mangroves in and around San Juan. Needing a base for these vessels, they constructed El Arsenal in the 19th century. It was at this base that they staged their last stand, flying the Spanish colors until the final Spaniard was removed in 1898, at the end of the Spanish-American War. Changing art exhibitions are held in the building's three galleries.

La Puntilla. ✆ **787/724-5969**. Free admission. Wed–Sun 8:30am–4:30pm. Bus: B-21.

Casa Blanca Ponce de León never lived here, although construction of the house (built in 1521) is sometimes attributed to him. The house was erected 2 years after the explorer's death; work was ordered by his son-in-law, Juan García Troche. The parcel of land was given to Ponce de León as a reward for services rendered to the Crown. His descendants lived in the house for about 2½ centuries, until the Spanish government took it over in 1779 for use as a residence for military commanders. The U.S. government also used it as a home for army commanders. On the first floor, the Juan Ponce de León Museum is furnished with antiques, paintings, and artifacts from the 16th through the 18th centuries. In back is a garden with spraying fountains, offering an intimate and verdant respite from the monumental buildings of old San Juan.

Calle San Sebastián 1. ✆ **787/724-4102**. Admission $2. Tues–Sat 9am–noon and 1–4:30pm. Bus: B-21.

La Fortaleza The office and residence of the governor of Puerto Rico is the oldest executive mansion in continuous use in the western hemisphere, and has served as the island's seat of government for more than 3 centuries. Yet its history goes back even farther, to 1533, when construction began on a fortress to protect San Juan's Spanish settlers during raids by Carib tribesmen and pirates. The original medieval towers remain, but as the edifice was subsequently enlarged into a palace, other modes of architecture and ornamentation were also incorporated, including baroque, Gothic, neoclassical, and Arabian. La Fortaleza has been designated a national historic site by the U.S. government. Informal but proper attire is required.

Calle Fortaleza, overlooking San Juan Harbor. ✆ **787/721-7000**, ext. 2211. Free admission. 30-min tours of the gardens and building (conducted in English and Spanish) given Mon–Fri, every hour 9am–4pm. Bus: B-21.

MUSEUMS

Museo de Arte 🎯🎯 Puerto Rico's most important gallery, which opened in 2000 and was constructed at the cost of $55 million, is a state-of-the-art showcase for the island nation's rich cultural heritage as reflected mainly through its painters. Housed in a former city hospital in Santurce, the museum features both a permanent collection and temporary exhibitions. Prominent local artists are the star—for example, Francisco Oller (1833–1917), who brought a touch of Cézanne or Camille Pissarro to Puerto Rico (Oller actually studied in France with both of these Impressionists). Another leading star of the permanent collection is Jose Campeche, a late 18th-century classical painter. The museum is like a living textbook of Puerto Rico, beginning with its early development and going on to showcase camp aspects, such as the poster art created here in the mid–20th century. All the important modern island artists are also presented, including the best known, the late Angel Botello, but also such contemporaries as Rafael Tufiño and Arnaldo Roche Rabell.

299 de Diego Avenue, Santurce. (℃) **787/977-6277.** Admission $5 adults, $3 children under 12. Thurs–Tues 10am–5pm; Wed 10am–8pm. Bus: A-5.

Museo de las Americas One of the major new museums of San Juan, Museo de las Americas showcases the artisans of North, South, and Central America, featuring everything from carved figureheads from New England whaling ships to dugout canoes carved by Carib Indians in Dominica. It is unique in Puerto Rico and well worth a visit. Also on display is a changing collection of paintings by artists from throughout the Spanish-speaking world, some of which are for sale, and a permanent collection called "Puerto Rican *Santos*," which includes a collection of carved wooden depictions of saints.

Cuartel de Ballajá. (℃) **787/724-5052.** Free admission, but donations accepted. Tues–Fri 10am–4pm; Sat–Sun 11am–5pm. Bus: Old Town trolley.

Museo Pablo Casals Adjacent to Iglesia de San José, this museum is devoted to the memorabilia left to the people of Puerto Rico by the musician Pablo Casals. The maestro's cello is here, along with a library of videos (played upon request) of some of his festival concerts. This small 18th-century house also contains manuscripts and photographs of Casals. The annual Casals Festival draws worldwide interest and attracts some of the greatest performing artists; it's still held during the first 2 weeks of June.

Plaza de San José, Calle San Sebastián 101. (℃) **787/723-9185.** Admission $1 adults, 50¢ children. Tues–Sat 9:30am–4:45pm. Bus: Old Town trolley.

Museo de Arte e Historia de San Juan Located in a Spanish colonial building at the corner of Calle MacArthur, this cultural center was the city's main marketplace in the mid–19th century. Local art is displayed in several galleries, and audiovisual materials (in English and Spanish) reveal the history of the city (hourly 9am–4pm Mon–Fri). Sometimes major cultural events are staged in the museum's large courtyard.

Calle Norzagaray 150. (℃) **787/724-1875.** Free admission, but donations accepted. Wed–Sun 10am–5pm. Bus: Old Town Trolley, then a short walk.

SHOPPING ✰✰✰

U.S. citizens don't pay duty on items they purchase in Puerto Rico and bring back to the United States. And you can still find great bargains on Puerto Rico, where the competition among shopkeepers is fierce.

The streets of **Old Town,** such as Calle San Francisco and Calle del Cristo, are the major venues for shopping. Note, however, that most stores in Old San Juan are closed on Sunday.

Local handcrafts can be good buys, including needlework, straw work, ceramics, hammocks, papier-mâché fruits and vegetables, and paintings and sculptures by Puerto Rican artists. Collectors seek Puerto Rican *santos* (saints). These carved wooden religious idols vary greatly in shape and size, and devout locals believe they have healing powers—often the ability to perform *milagros,* or miracles.

The biggest and most up-to-date shopping plaza in the Caribbean Basin is **Plaza Las Americas,** in the financial district of Hato Rey, right off the Las Americas Expressway. The complex, with its fountains and advanced architecture, has more than 200 mostly upscale shops. The stores here (and their wares) are about what you'd find in a big mall back home. Prices are comparable to those Stateside.

ART

If you're interested in acquiring Puerto Rican art, there are many possibilities. **Galería Botello,** 314 av. Franklin D. Roosevelt at Hato Rey (© 787/754-7430), is a contemporary Latin American gallery, a living tribute to the late Angel Botello, one of Puerto Rico's most outstanding artists. His paintings and bronze sculptures, evocative of his colorful background, are done in a style uniquely his own. On display are his and other local artists' paintings and sculptures, as well as a large collection of Puerto Rican antique *santos* (saints).

    Galería Fosil Art, Calle del Cristo 200 (© 787/725-4252), is a specialty gallery, displaying unique art pieces from limestone and coral that might have existed at the time of the dinosaurs. The work is the creation of Radamés Rivera. One of the gallery's most noted artists is Yolanda Velasquez, who paints in an abstract style. The gallery also showcases the work of some 40 other artists, ranging from Mexico to Cuba.

    Galería Palomas, Calle del Cristo 207 (© 787/725-2660), is another leading choice. Works range from $300 and include some of the leading painters of the Latin American world, and are rotated every 2 to 3 weeks. The setting is a 17th-century colonial house. Of special note are works by such local artists as Homer, Moya, and Alicea.

    Galería San Juan, at the Gallery Inn, Calle Norzagaray 206 (© 787/722-1808), specializes in the sculpture and paintings of Jan D'Esopo, a Connecticut-born artist who has spent much of her time in Puerto Rico. Many of her fine pieces are in bronze.

BOOKS

For travel guides, maps, and just something to read on the beach, there are two good bookstores. Try **Bell, Book & Candle,** 102 de Diego Ave., Santurce (© 787/728-5000), a large general-interest bookstore that carries fiction and classics in both Spanish and English, plus a huge selection of postcards. **Libreria Cronopios,** Calle San José 255 (© 787/724-1815), is the leading choice in the old town, with the largest selection of titles. It sells a number of books on Puerto Rican culture as well as good maps of the island.

FASHION

Nono Maldonado, 1051 Ashford Ave., midway between the Condado Plaza and the Ramada Hotel (© 787/721-0456), is named after its owner, a Puerto Rican designer who worked for many years as the fashion editor of *Esquire* magazine. This is one of the most fashionable and upscale haberdashers in the Caribbean. Selling both men's and women's clothing, it has everything from socks to dinner jackets as well as ready-to-wear versions of Maldonado's twice-a-year collections. There is also a Maldonado boutique in the El San Juan Hotel in Isla Verde.

    Polo Ralph Lauren Factory Store, Calle del Cristo 201 (© 787/722-2136), has prices that are often 35% to 40% less than what you'd find on the U.S. mainland. One upstairs room is devoted to home furnishings.

    Speedo Authentic Fitness, Calle Fortaleza (© 787/724-3089), sells sportswear for women and men, specializing in shorts, jackets, and swimwear. There's also one of the town's better collections of sandals here.

FURNISHINGS

DMR Gallery, Calle Luna 204 (© 787/722-4181), is a unique specialty store, offering carved and handmade furniture, the work of a well-known local designer, Nick Quijano. Some of his work is displayed in the Museum of Puerto Rico. Quijano turns furniture into art.

GIFTS/UNIQUE ARTS & CRAFTS

Butterfly People, Calle Fortaleza 152 (© 787/723-2432), is a gallery/cafe in a handsomely restored building in Old San Juan. Butterflies, preserved forever in artfully arranged boxes, range from $20 for a single mounting to thousands of dollars for whole-wall murals. Most of these butterflies come from farms around the world, some of the most beautiful from Indonesia, Malaysia, and New Guinea. Tucked away, on the same premises, is **Malula Antiques.** Specializing in tribal art from the Moroccan sub-Sahara and Syria, it contains a sometimes startling collection of primitive and timeless crafts and accessories.

Barrachina's, Calle Fortaleza 104, between Calle del Cristo and Calle San José (© 787/725-7912), is more than a jewelry store. This is also the birthplace, in 1963, of the piña colada. It's a favorite of cruise ship passengers, offering one of the largest selections of jewelry, perfume, cigars, and gifts in San Juan. There's a patio for drinks, plus a Bacardi rum outlet selling bottles cheaper than stateside, but at the same prices as the Bacardi distillery. You'll also find a costume-jewelry department, a gift shop, a restaurant, and a section for authentic silver jewelry.

Xian Imports, Calle de la Cruz 153 (© 787/723-2214), is set within a jumbled, slightly claustrophobic setting where you'll find compactly arranged porcelain, sculptures, paintings, and Chinese furniture, much of it antique. The island's decorators favor it as a source for unusual art objects.

El Artesano, Calle Fortaleza 314 (© 787/721-6483), is a curiosity. You'll find Mexican and Peruvian icons of the Virgin Mary; charming depictions of fish and Latin American birds in terra-cotta and brass; all kinds of woven goods; painted cupboards, chests, and boxes; and mirrors and Latin dolls.

Galería Bóveda, Calle del Cristo 209 (© 787/725-0263), is a long narrow space crammed with exotic jewelry, clothing, greeting cards of images of life in Puerto Rico, some 100 handmade lamps, antiques, Mexican punched tin and glass, and Art-Nouveau reproductions, among other items.

Olé, Calle Fortaleza 105 (© 787/724-2445), deserves an "olé!" Browsing this store is a learning experience. Practically everything comes from Puerto Rico or Latin America. If you want a straw hat from Ecuador, hand-beaten Chilean silver, Christmas ornaments, or Puerto Rican *santos* (saints), this is the place.

Puerto Rican Arts & Crafts, Calle Fortaleza 204 (© 787/725-5596), set in a 200-year-old colonial building, is one of the premier outlets on the island for authentic artifacts. Of particular interest are papier-mâché Carnival masks from Ponce. Taíno designs inspired by ancient petroglyphs are incorporated into most of the sterling silver jewelry sold here. There's an art gallery in back, with silk-screened serigraphs by local artists, and a gourmet Puerto Rican food section with such items as coffee, rum, and hot sauces. The store also exhibits and sells small carved *santos,* representations of the Catholic saints and the infant Jesus laboriously carved by artisans in private studios around the island.

Convento de los Dominicos, Calle Norzagaray (© 787/721-6866), is housed in the offices of the Instituto de Cultura Puertoriqueña. This old

Dominican convent has one of the best displays of crafts in the old town, including *santos* (saints), Indian artifacts, Carnival masks, and baskets. All pieces are made on the island, not in Taiwan.

Haitian Gallery, Calle Fortaleza 367 (© 787/725-0986), carries Haitian paintings, as promised by its namesake, but also lots of souvenirs and handcrafts, including ceramics, from many places in South America, such as Colombia, Venezuela, Peru, and Ecuador.

JEWELRY

Bared & Sons, Calle Fortaleza 65, at the corner of Calle San Justo (© 787/724-4811), now in its fourth decade, is the main outlet of a chain of at least 20 upscale jewelry stores on Puerto Rico. On the ground floor, cruise ship passengers shop for gemstones, gold, diamonds, and watches. One floor up, there's a monumental collection of porcelain and crystal. It's a great source for hard-to-get and discontinued patterns discounted from Christofle, Royal Doulton, Wedgwood, Limoges, Royal Copenhagen, Lalique, Lladró, Herend, Baccarat, and Daum.

The **Gold Ounce,** Plaza los Muchachos, Calle Fortaleza 201 (© 787/724-3102), is the direct factory outlet for the oldest jewelry factory on Puerto Rico, the Kury Company. Don't expect a top-notch jeweler here: Many of the pieces are replicated in endless repetition. But don't overlook the place for 14-karat-gold ornaments. Some of the designs are charming, and prices are about 20% less than at retail stores in the United States. In addition, the outlet has opened an art store, called **Arts and More,** featuring regional works, plus a store called **The Cigar Shop.**

Joyería Riviera, Calle de La Cruz 205 (© 787/725-4000), is an emporium of 18-karat gold and diamonds, and the island's leading jeweler. Adjacent to Plaza de Armas, the shop has an impeccable reputation. This is the major distributor of Rolex watches on Puerto Rico.

Eduardo Barquet, Calle Fortaleza 200, at the corner of Calle La Cruz (© 787/723-1989), is known as a leading value-priced place to buy fine jewelry in Old San Juan.

Yas Mar, Calle Fortaleza 205 (© 787/724-1377), sells convincing, glittering fake diamonds for those who don't want to wear or can't afford the real thing. It also stocks real diamond chips, emeralds, sapphires, and rubies, too.

Leather & Pearls, Calle Tanca 252, at the corner of Calle Tetuán (© 787/724-8185), are two products that don't always go together, but at this outlet form a winning combination. Majorca pearls and fine leather garments (bags, shoes, suitcases, briefcases, and accessories) are sold here from manufacturers that include Gucci and Fendi.

Joseph Manchini, Calle Fortaleza (© 787/722-7698), displays the works of its namesake and the shop's owner. He conceives almost anything you'd want in gold, silver, and bronze. Some of old town's most imaginative rings, bracelets, and chains are displayed here. If you don't like what's on sale, you can design your own jewelry, including pieces made from sapphire, emerald, and rubies.

SAN JUAN AFTER DARK
THE PERFORMING ARTS

Qué Pasa, the official visitor's guide to Puerto Rico, lists cultural events, including music, dance, theater, film, and art exhibits. The tourist office distributes it free.

A major cultural venue in San Juan is **Teatro Tapía,** Avenida Ponce de León (© 787/721-0180), across from Plaza de Colón, one of the oldest theaters in the western hemisphere (built about 1832). Much of Puerto Rican theater history is connected with the Tapía, named after the island's first prominent playwright, Alejandro Tapía y Rivera. Various productions, some musical, are staged here throughout the year and include drama, dance, and cultural events. You'll have to call the box office (open Mon–Fri 10am–6pm) for specific information. Tickets generally range in price from $17 to $40.

THE CLUB & MUSIC SCENE

Modeled after an artist's rendition of the once-notorious city of Mesopotamia, **Babylon,** in El San Juan Hotel & Casino, 6063 Av. Isla Verde, Isla Verde (© 787/791-1000), is circular, with a central dance floor and a wraparound balcony where onlookers can scope out the action below. The crowd is usually in the 25-to-45 age group. This place has one of the best sound systems in the Caribbean. You might want to make a night of it, stopping into the El San Juan's bars and casino en route. The club is open Thursday to Saturday 9:30pm to 3am. Guests of the hotel enter free; otherwise, there's a $10 cover.

Cafe Matisse, Ashford Avenue (© 787/723-7910), is a hot spot for Latin sounds. Although it's also a restaurant, it's best known as a bar where live music, often salsa, is usually part of the ambience. Depending on the night of the week, you can also hear rumba, merengue, blues, jazz, or rock-and-roll. Overall, the site is convivial, has a sense of Big Apple cool, and plays hot music that makes everyone want to dance, dance, dance. It's open Tuesday to Saturday 5pm to around 2am or later, depending on the crowd. The only time a $3 cover is imposed is on a night when an expensive band is brought in.

Laser, Calle del Cruz 251 (© 787/725-7581), is set in the heart of the old town near the corner of Calle Fortaleza. This disco is especially crowded when cruise ships pull into town. Once inside, you can wander over the three floors, listening to whatever music happens to be hot, with lots of additional merengue and salsa thrown in as well. Depending on the night, the age of the crowd varies. It's open Thursday to Saturday 9pm to 4am. Women enter free after midnight on Saturday. The cover is $8.

Café Bohemia, in El Convento Hotel, Calle Cristo 100 (© 787/723-9200), transforms itself from a Spanish restaurant in the early evening to an old town jazz club from 11pm to 2am, when the food service stops. This is becoming an old town hot spot when live music is presented Tuesday, Friday, and Saturday evenings.

The best jazz in old town is heard at **"The Blue,"** 9 Plaza de Mercado (© 787/723-9962), whose walls are decorated with some of the jazz greats (or former greats) of the jazz world. It's a great place to hang out any night except Sunday and Monday when it's closed. Unlike El Patio de Sam, the Continental menu is quite decent too. The chef will even prepare you an individual paella studded with lobster and chunks of red snapper.

Star Gate, Avenida Robert Todd, Santurce (© 787/725-4664), is where the young man of San Juan takes his date. Both often dress up to patronize this disco-bar, where they dance and drink until the late hours. Wednesday night is the most casual, Friday and Saturday the most formal. Cover charge is $10. Open Wednesday, Thursday, and Saturday and Sunday 9:30pm to 4am, Friday 6pm to 4am. Some of the best live music along the Condado is played here.

THE BAR SCENE

Two of the most dramatic bars in San Juan are at **El San Juan Hotel & Casino,** 6063 Av. Isla Verde, Isla Verde (℃ **787/791-1000**). There is no more beautiful bar in the Caribbean than the **Palm Court** ⭑⭑ here, open daily 5pm to 4am. Set in an oval wrapped around a sunken bar area, amid marble and burnished mahogany, it offers a view of one of the world's largest chandeliers. After 9pm Tuesday to Saturday, live music, often salsa and merengue, emanates from an adjoining room (the El Chico Bar). There's also a fine **Cigar Bar,** with a magnificent repository of the finest cigars in the world. Some of the most fashionable women in San Juan—and men, too—can be seen puffing away in this chic rendezvous, while sipping a cognac.

Ireland and its ales meet the tropics at **Shannon's Irish Pub,** Calle Bori 46, Río Piedras (℃ **787/281-8466**). This is definitely a Gallic pub with a Latin beat. A sports bar, it's the regular watering hole of many university students, a constant supplier of high-energy rock and roll and 10 TV monitors. There's live music Wednesday through Sunday—everything from rock to jazz to Latin. There are pool tables, and a simple cafe serves inexpensive food daily 11:30am to 1am. A $3 cover is imposed after 7pm.

HOT NIGHTS IN GAY SAN JUAN

The Beach Bar, on the ground floor of the Atlantic Beach Hotel, 1 Calle Vendig (℃ **787/721-6900**), is crowded and animated. It's the site of a hugely popular Sunday afternoon gathering that gets really crowded beginning around 4pm and stretches into the wee hours. There's an occasional drag show on a dais at one end of the outdoor terrace. There's also an open-air rectangular bar. The Beach Bar is open daily 11am to at least 1am.

Cups, Calle San Mateo 1708, Santurce (℃ **787/268-3570**), is a Latin tavern, the only place in San Juan that caters almost exclusively to lesbians. Men (gay or straight) aren't particularly welcome. Although the club is open Wednesday through Saturday 7pm to 4am, entertainment such as live music or cabaret is presented only on Wednesday at 9pm or Friday at 10pm.

Eros, 1257 Ponce de León, Santurce (℃ **787/722-1131**), is the town's most popular gay disco, with strippers and shows. Most of the crowd is in its late 20s. Rum-based drinks, merengue, and the latest dance tunes are on tap; the place really gets going after around 10:30pm. It's open Wednesday to Sunday 10pm to 5am. The cover is $5.

CASINOS ⭑⭑

Gambling is big in Puerto Rico. Many people come here to do little more than that. As a result, there are plenty of options.

The casino generating all the excitement today is the 18,500-square-foot **Casino at Ritz-Carlton San Juan Spa & Casino,** 6961 State Rd., Isla Verde (℃ **787/253-1700**), the largest in the whole Caribbean. It combines the elegant decor of the 1940s with tropical fabrics and patterns. This is one of the plushest and most exclusive entertainment complexes in the Caribbean. You almost expect to see Joan Crawford arrive, on the arm of Clark Gable. It features traditional games such as blackjack, roulette, baccarat, craps, and slot machines.

One of the splashiest of San Juan's casinos is at the **Wyndham Old San Juan Hotel & Casino,** Calle Brumbaugh 100 (℃ **787/721-5100**). Five-card stud competes with some 240 slot machines and roulette tables.

You can also try your luck at **El San Juan Hotel & Casino** on Avenida Isla Verde (℃ **787/791-1000**) in Isla Verde (one of the most grand), and the

Condado Plaza Hotel & Casino, 999 Ashford Ave. (© **787/721-1000**). There are no passports to flash or admissions to pay, as in European casinos.

The Stellaris Casino at the **San Juan Marriott Resort,** 1309 Ashford Ave. (© **787/722-7000**), is one of the island's newest, as is El Tropical Casino at **Crown Plaza Hotel & Casino,** Route 187, km 1.5, Isla Verde (© **787/253-2929**). El Tropical is open 24 hours a day and is the only theme casino in San Juan, re-creating El Yunque Tropical Rain Forest.

Most casinos are open daily noon to 4pm and again 8pm to 4am. Jackets for men are requested after 6pm.

3 Dorado 𝒜

The name itself evokes a kind of magic. Along the north shore of Puerto Rico, about a 40-minute drive (22 miles) west of the capital, a world of luxury resorts and villa complexes unfolds. The big properties of the Hyatt Dorado Beach Hotel and Hyatt Regency Cerromar Beach Hotel sit on the choice white-sand beaches. These properties cost far more than even our most generous budget allows, but you can still spend a day in the area, enjoying the sands.

GREAT DEALS ON DINING

El Malecón PUERTO RICAN   If you'd like to discover an unpretentious local place serving good Puerto Rican cuisine, then head for El Malecón, a simple concrete structure minutes away from a small shopping center. It has a cozy family ambience and is especially popular on weekends. Some members of the staff speak English, and the chef is best with fresh seafood. The chef might also prepare a variety of items that are not listed on the menu. Most of the dishes are at the lower end of the price scale; only the lobster is expensive.

Rte. 693, km 8.2. © 787/796-1645. Main courses $10–$37. AE, MC, V. Daily 11am–11pm.

SPORTS & OTHER OUTDOOR PURSUITS

GOLF   The Robert Trent Jones, Sr.–designed courses at the **Hyatt Regency Cerromar** and the **Hyatt Dorado Beach** 𝒜𝒜 match the finest anywhere. The two original courses, known as east and west (© **787/796-8961** for tee times), were carved out of a jungle and offer tight fairways bordered by trees and forests, with lots of ocean holes. The somewhat newer and less noted north and south courses (© **787/796-8915** for tee times) feature wide fairways with well-bunkered greens and an assortment of water traps and tricky wind factors. Each course has a 72 par. The longest is the south course, at 7,047 yards. Guests of the Hyatt hotels get preferred tee times and lower fees than nonguests. For the north and south courses, Hyatt guests pay $75; nonguests, $85. At the east and west courses, Hyatt guests are charged $100 for the east or $85 for the west; nonguests, $135 for the east or $115 for the west. Golf carts at any of the courses rent for $20, whether you play 9 or 18 holes. The north and south and the east and west courses each maintain separate pro shops, each with a bar and snack-style restaurant. Both are open daily 7am until dusk.

WINDSURFING & OTHER WATERSPORTS   The best place on the island's north shore is along the well-maintained beachfront of the Hyatt Dorado Beach Hotel near the 10th hole of the east golf course. Here, **Penfield Island Adventures** (© **787/796-1234,** ext. 3200, or 787/796-2188) offers 90-minute **windsurfing lessons** for $60 each; board rentals cost $50 per half day. Well-supplied with a wide array of windsurfers, including some designed

Value Cheap Thrills: What to See & Do for Free (Well, Almost) on Puerto Rico

- **Seek Out the Secrets of Rum-Making.** The Bacardi distillery, the world's largest rum distillery, lies a short hop across San Juan Bay by ferry. It offers daily tours through its 127 acres and its plant, where 100,000 gallons are distilled daily. Complimentary rum drinks are offered at the beginning of the tour, and a well-stocked gift shop sells an assortment of items. The prices of Bacardi rums are better than those at home, and some rums not sold on the mainland also make excellent presents. It's open Monday to Saturday 9am to 4:30pm; tours are given every 30 minutes. For more information, call ℂ 787/788-1500.
- **Stroll Along San Juan's Most Colorful Boulevard.** Streets around the world have become known for observing the passing scene. In Old San Juan, it's the Paseo de La Princesa, a 19th-century esplanade where Spanish colonial gentry once strolled and took the balmy Caribbean air. Its beauty shines again after a 2-year $2.8-million restoration. The *paseo* sweeps from the piers that welcome cruise ships past La Princesa, a restored former 1800s prison, around the old city walls beneath Casa Blanca (the ancestral home of the Ponce de León family), and continues to the entrance of the famed 16th-century El Morro. Outdoor tables with umbrellas are shaded by more than 20 trees, and delicious *criollo* dishes are dispensed from specially designed food carts with gaily colored awnings.
- **Find the Secret Beaches.** Some of Puerto Rico's most beautiful and isolated beaches lie on the southwestern coast. Stretching between Ponce, in the east, and Cabo Rojo, on Puerto Rico's extreme southwestern tip, they flank some of the least densely populated parts of the island. Drive west from Ponce along Highway 2, branching south along Route 116 to Guánica, the self-anointed gateway and capital of this string of secret beaches. Don't expect a lot—you're likely to see only a handful of simple bars, tacky luncheonettes, and gas stations. By far the most accessible and appealing beach is Caña Gorda, about a quarter-mile south of Guánica, at the edge of a legally protected marsh known for its rich bird life and thick reeds. It's a sprawling expanse of pale beige sand dotted with ramshackle-looking *bohios* (huts) crafted from tree branches and

specifically for beginners and children, the school benefits from the almost uninterrupted flow of the north shore's strong, steady winds and an experienced crew of instructors. A **kayaking/snorkeling** trip (ℂ 787/796-4645), departing daily at 9:15am and 11:45am, and lasting 1½ hours, costs $50. Two-tank boat **dives** go for $125 per person. **Waverunners** can be rented for $60 per half hour for a single rider, and $75 for two riders. A **Sunfish** rents for $50 for 1 hour, $68 for 2 hours.

palm fronds. Stray even farther west from Ponce, along coastal highways like 324, 304, and 323, and you'll pass beaches like Tamarindo, Manglillos, Rosado, and Playa Santa. Most westerly is Bahía Sucia, at the end of rutted and badly potholed roads.

• **Hike & Bird-Watch in Guánica State Forest.** Directly west from Ponce is the Guánica State Forest, where you'll find the best-preserved subtropical ecosystem on the planet. The Cordillera Central cuts off the rain coming in, making this a dry region of cacti and bedrock. Some 50% of all the island's terrestrial bird species can be seen here, and some 750 plants and tree species grow in the area. UNESCO has named Guánica a World Biosphere Reserve.

• **Take the Caribbean's Most Spectacular Drive.** The 165-mile Ruta Panorámica runs across the top of the Cordillera Central, a panoramic mountain range with cool temperatures and lush forests. All 40 roads along the route are well marked. The drive links the western city of Mayagüez with Yabucoa in the southeast and can be traversed at either side. The highway stretches the entire length of Puerto Rico. Along this drive you'll see glimpses of rural Puerto Rico that've largely disappeared elsewhere. A detailed highway map will be provided by one of the tourist offices. Allow a solid 8 hours of driving nonstop. There are a number of *paradors* (government-sponsered guesthouses, usually in remote areas) along the route.

• **Wander in the Carite Forest Preserve.** In southeastern Puerto Rico, lying off the Ponce Expressway near Cayey, Carite is a 6,000-acre reserve with a dwarf forest that was produced by the high humidity and moist soil. From several peaks you get panoramic views of Ponce and the Caribbean Sea. On one peak is Nuestra Madre, a Catholic spiritual meditation center that permits visitors to stroll the grounds. Fifty species of birds live in the Carite Forest Preserve, which also has a large natural pool called Charco Azul. A picnic area and campgrounds are shaded by eucalyptus and royal palms. The forest borders a lake of the same name. Entrances to the forest are signposted from the town of Cayey, which is reached after an hour's drive from Ponce or San Juan.

4 Northwestern Puerto Rico

Dubbed an ear to heaven, the **Arecibo Observatory** ✦ (© 787/878-2612) contains the world's largest and most sensitive radar/radiotelescope. The telescope features a 20-acre dish or radio mirror set in an ancient sinkhole. It's 1,000 feet in diameter and 167 feet deep and allows scientists to examine the ionosphere, the planets, and the moon with powerful radar signals and to monitor natural radio emissions from distant galaxies, pulsars, and quasars.

Scientists are using it as part of the Search for Extraterrestrial Intelligence (SETI). This research effort speculates that advanced civilizations elsewhere in the universe might also communicate via radio waves. The 10-year, $100-million search for life in space was launched on October 12, 1992, the 500-year anniversary of the New World's discovery by Columbus.

Unusually lush vegetation flourishes under the giant dish, including ferns, wild orchids, and begonias. Assorted creatures like mongooses, lizards, and dragonflies have also taken refuge there. Suspended in outlandish fashion above the dish is a 600-ton platform that resembles a space station. Tours at $3.50 for adults and $1.50 for children are available Wednesday to Friday noon to 4pm and Saturday and Sunday 9am to 4pm. There's a souvenir shop on the grounds. The observatory lies a 90-minute drive west of San Juan, outside the town of Arecibo. From Arecibo, it's a 35-minute drive via routes 22, 134, 635, and 625 (the site is signposted).

Río Camuy Cave Park ⚐, 1⅓ hours west of San Juan on Route 129, at km 18.9 (© **787/898-3100**), contains the third-largest underground river in the world. It runs through a network of caves, canyons, and sinkholes that have been cut through the island's limestone base over the course of millions of years. Known to the pre-Columbian Taíno peoples, the caves came to the attention of speleologists in the 1950s and were opened to the public in 1986.

You first see a short film about the caves, then descend into the caverns in open-air trolleys. The trip takes you through a 200-foot-deep sinkhole and a chasm where tropical trees, ferns, and flowers flourish, along with birds and butterflies. The trolley then goes to the entrance of Clara Cave of Epalme, one of 16 in the Camuy Caves network, where you begin a 45-minute walk, viewing the majestic series of rooms rich in stalagmites, stalactites, and huge natural sculptures. The park has added the Tres Pueblos Sinkhole and the Spiral Sinkhole to its slate of attractions. The caves are open Tuesday to Sunday 8am to 4pm. Tickets are $10 for adults or $7 for children 2 to 12; seniors pay $5. Parking is $2. For more information, phone the park.

5 Rincón ⬥

At the island's westernmost point, Rincón, 6 miles north of Mayagüez, has one of the most exotic beaches on the island, Punta Higuero, which draws surfers from around the world. In and around this small fishing village are some unique accommodations.

If you rent a car at the San Juan airport, it'll take approximately 2½ hours to drive here via the busy northern Route 2, or 3 hours via the scenic mountain route (no. 52) to the south. We recommend the southern route through Ponce. In addition, there are four flights daily from San Juan to Mayagüez on **American Eagle** (© **800/433-7300**). These flights take 40 minutes, and round-trip fares range from $99 to $189. From the Mayagüez airport, Rincón is a 30-minute drive to the north on Route 2 (go left or west at the intersection with Rte. 115).

ACCOMMODATIONS YOU CAN AFFORD

El Molino del Quixote   This place is known by locals mainly for the cuisine of Doña Carmencita, who welcomes both locals and visitors to her guesthouse 10 minutes from the center of town. But Doña also offers rooms, and has done so since opening this place in 1986. She calls her three apartments cabañas, each coming with two bedrooms, a living room, a fully equipped kitchen, and a terrace overlooking the garden. The decor is basic and the apartments are well maintained, the beds clean and comfortable, each unit coming with a small, tiled bathroom with shower. At night diners flock here to the informal, breezy seaside restaurant, where Doña serves the best paella in Rincón. You also order grilled fresh fish or her special lobster in garlic sauce.

Campo de Playa, Rincón, PR 00677. © 787/823-4010. 3 units. Year-round $92.50–$105.50. No credit cards. **Amenities:** Restaurant, bar. *In room:* A/C, TV, kitchen.

J. B. Hidden Village Hotel   Named after the initials of its owners (Julio Bonilla, his wife, Jinnie, and their son, Julio Jr.), this isolated hotel opened in 1990. Half a mile east of nearby Aguada, on a side street running off Route 4414, it's nestled into a valley between three forested hillsides and offers a quiet refuge to vacationers who enjoy exploring the area's beaches. Each room, with views of the pool, contains furnishings in the basic motel style, and most are a bit small. The mattresses are relatively new, and the bathrooms are basic, each with a shower. The restaurant offers a view over a neighboring ravine.

Rd. 416 (P.O. Box 937), Piedras Blancas, Sector Villarrubia, Aguada, PR 00602. © 787/868-8686. Fax 787/ 868-8701. 38 units. Year-round $55–$68.50 single; $71–$86.65 double; $94.15–$114.50 semi-suite. AE, MC, V. **Amenities:** Restaurant, pool. *In room:* A/C, TV.

The Lazy Parrot *(Kids)*   This extensively remodeled family-run inn is in a residential neighborhood a half-mile walk or drive from at least half a dozen beaches. The pastel-colored accommodations have recently been upgraded and have small refrigerators; one room, with a bunk-bed arrangement, is ideal for families. As befits a former private home, rooms come in a variety of sizes. Some of the mattresses need renewing; others seem fairly new.

Even if you don't stay here, you might want to patronize the Lazy Parrot Restaurant, which offers good views from its main dining room, where your best bet is the catch of the day. It's more romantic at a table in the candlelit floral garden, where the coquí (tree frog), hummingbird, wild parrot, and butterflies can be seen year-round.

413 Punta (P.O. Box 430), Rincón, PR 00677. © 787/823-5654. Fax 787/823-0224. www.lazyparrot.com. 7 units. Year-round $75–$95 single or double. Extra person $10. AE, DISC, MC, V. **Amenities:** Restaurant, pool. *In room:* A/C, TV, minifridge, no phone.

Parador Villa Antonio   Ilia and Hector Ruíz offer apartments by the sea in this privately owned and run parador. The beach outside is nice, but the local authorities don't keep it as clean as they ought to. Surfing and fishing can be enjoyed just outside your front door, and you can bring your catch right into your cottage and prepare a fresh seafood dinner in your own kitchenette (there's no restaurant). Be aware that the air-conditioning doesn't work properly here, and in general better maintenance is needed. Nonetheless, this is a popular destination with families from Puerto Rico who crowd in on the weekends, occupying the motel-like rooms with balconies or terraces. Furnishings are well used but offer reasonable comfort, and bathrooms are small with shower stalls.

Rte. 115, km 12.3 (P.O. Box 68), Rincón, PR 00677. © 800/443-0266 in the U.S., or 787/823-2645. Fax 787/ 823-3380. www.villa-antonio.com. 61 units. Year-round $85.50–$117.75 double. AE, DC, MC, V. **Amenities:** Pool, 2 tennis courts, playground. *In room:* A/C, TV, kitchenette.

Sandy Beach Inn *(Finds)*   At the top of a hill overlooking—you guessed it: Sandy Beach—this little inn opens toward the Mona Passage and the sea beyond, where at certain times of the year you can see whales passing by on their journey to wherever. Many Rincón locals come here to order delectable, fresh seafood on the inn's terrace, but there are rooms to rent as well. The location is a 30-minute drive north from the airport at Mayagüez. The complex consists of an older four-story building and a newer three-story wing with brighter apartments and rooms. The decor is tasteful but rather plain, although the midsize accommodations are comfortable and well appointed, each coming with a small bathroom with shower and tub. Those on the upper floors, of course, have the best views of the sea. The quality of the cuisine comes as a surprise for such a simple place, until you learn that the chef, Julia Avila, was the former chef of the deluxe Horned Dorset Primavera, the most upscale hotel and restaurant in eastern Puerto Rico.

Carretera Vista Linda, Punta Rincón, PR 00677. © 787/823-1146. Fax 787/823-1034. www.sandybeachinn. com. 13 units. Year-round $50–$75 double; $90 apt. Rates include continental breakfast. AE, MC, V. **Amenities:** Restaurant, bar. *In room:* A/C, TV, minibar.

GREAT DEALS ON DINING

Sandy Beach Inn (see above) offers the most delectable seafood platters in the area. You can also visit the guesthouse El Molino del Quixote (see above) for the most delectable paella in the area and its fresh grilled fish.

Bambino's CREOLE/SEAFOOD   Close to the Parador Villa Antonio in the south of town, this is a family dining room where locals go to fill up on delicious Italian specialties served at affordable prices. In operation for more than a decade here, the kitchen enjoys an enviable reputation for its fresh seafood, the menu changing daily based on the catch of the day or what was available at the market. The decor is basic but tasteful, with whitewashed walls and pictures of Italian scenes decorating the dining area. Some tables are nestled between palm trees and tropical plants. The pastas are good—our favorite being the spaghetti marinara, that is, until we ordered the lobster ravioli. Red snapper is prepared to perfection here, as is mahimahi.

Carretera 115, Rincón. © 787/823-3744. Main courses $9–$18. AE, MC, V. Daily 11am–11pm.

The Black Eagle *(Value* STEAKS/SEAFOOD   This restaurant—the best in the neighborhood—serves up enormous portions of fresh seafood at low prices. It's in an isolated black-and-white house adjacent to the beach, about a quarter of a mile north of the center of Rincón, close to the Black Eagle marina (with which it's not associated). In the wood-paneled dining room, you might begin with a house special Black Eagle, a deceptively potent pink cocktail. Menu items include lobster or shrimp cocktail, a 32-ounce porterhouse steak (the restaurant's trademark dish), grilled lobster, pan-fried conch, and *asopao* of lobster or shrimp. All main courses come with salad, bread, and vegetables.

Rte. 413, km 1.0 *interio,* Barrio Ensenada. © 787/823-3510. Main courses $10–$25. AE, MC, V. Daily 5–11pm.

HITTING THE BEACHES

One of Puerto Rico's most outstanding surfing beaches is at **Punta Higuero** ⚓, on Route 413 near Rincón. In the winter months especially, uninterrupted Atlantic swells with perfectly formed waves averaging 5 to 6 feet in height roll shoreward, and rideable swells sometimes reach 15 to 25 feet.

6 Mayagüez

Puerto Ricans have nicknamed their third-largest city the "Sultan of the West." This port city, 98 miles southwest of San Juan and not architecturally remarkable, was once the island's needlework capital. There are still crafts-people here who do fine embroidery.

Mayagüez is the honeymoon capital of Puerto Rico. The tradition dates from the 16th century, when, it's said, local fathers in need of husbands for their daughters (because of the scarcity of eligible young men) kidnapped young Spanish sailors who stopped here for provisions en route to South America.

GETTING THERE

American Eagle (✆ 800/433-7300) flies four times daily throughout the year between San Juan to Mayagüez. Flight time is 40 minutes, but there are often delays on the ground at either end. Depending on restrictions and the season you book your flight, round-trip fares range from $140 to $180 per person.

If you rent a car at the San Juan airport and want to drive to Mayagüez, the more efficient route is the northern one combining sections of the newly widened Route 22 with the older Route 2. Estimated driving time for locals is about 90 minutes but about 30 minutes longer for visitors. The southern route, combining the modern Route 52 with a transit across the outskirts of historic Ponce and a final access into Mayagüez via the southern section of Route 2, requires a total of about 3 hours and affords some worthwhile scenery across the island's mountainous interior.

ACCOMMODATIONS YOU CAN AFFORD

Hotel Parador El Sol   This concrete building from 1970 provides reasonable and hospitable accommodations, although it's geared to business travelers. It's 2 blocks from the landmark Plaza del Mercado in the heart of the city and is central to the shopping district and all western-region transportation and high-ways. Furnishings are no frills in the seven-floor restored hotel, but it offers up-to-date facilities, a restaurant, and a pool. Mattresses are firm and renewed as needed, and rooms range from small to medium; bathrooms contain shower units.

Calle Santiago Riera Palmer, 9 Este, Mayagüez, PR 00680. ✆ 787/834-0303. Fax 787/265-7567. 52 units. Year-round $66.70 single; $74.40 double; $88.10 triple. Rates include continental breakfast. AE, MC, V. **Amenities:** Restaurant, pool. *In room:* A/C, TV.

Parador Hacienda Juanita ✪ *Value*   From an 1836 coffee plantation, this complex is now a *parador* named after one of its long-ago owners, a matriarch named Juanita. It sits in relative isolation, surrounded by only a few neighbor-ing buildings and the jungle, 2 miles west of the village of Maricao, beside Route 105 heading to Mayagüez. The pink-stucco house has a long veranda and a living room decorated with antique tools and artifacts of the coffee industry. The Luís Rivera family welcomes visitors and serves drinks and meals in the restaurant. The small rooms have ceiling fans, rocking chairs, and rustic furniture, although the beds are good, with firm mattresses. The bathrooms are small but tidy, with shower stalls. In-room amenities are scarce, but there's a pool, a billiards table, and a Ping-Pong table.

Rte. 105, km 23.5 (P.O. Box 777), Maricao, PR 00606. ✆ 800/443-0266 in the U.S. for reservations only, or 787/838-2550. Fax 787/838-2551. www.haciendajuanita.com. 21 units. Year-round $95 single; $123 double. Children 11 and under stay free in parents' room. Rates include breakfast and dinner. AE, MC, V. **Amenities:** Restaurant, pool. *In room:* Ceiling fans.

GREAT DEALS ON DINING

El Castillo ✪ INTERNATIONAL/PUERTO RICAN   This is the most pro-fessionally managed and large-scale dining room in western Puerto Rico, the

Finds A Side Trip to Mona Island

Known locally as "the Galápagos of the Caribbean," **Mona Island** enjoys many legends of pirate treasure and is known for its white-sand beaches and marine life. The island is virtually uninhabited, except for two policemen and a director of the Institute of Natural Resources. Although the island is closer to Mayagüez than to San Juan, most boat tours of the island leave from the capital.

The island attracts hunters seeking pigs and wild goats, along with big-game fishers, but mostly it's intriguing to anyone who wants to escape civilization. **Playa Sardinera** on Mona Island was a base for pirates. On one side of the island, at **Playa de Pajaros,** are caves where the Taíno people left their mysterious hieroglyphs. Everything needed, including water, must be brought in, and everything, including garbage, must be taken out. For further information, call the **Puerto Rico Department of Natural Resources** at © 787/723-1616.

Surrounded by some of the most beautiful coral reefs in the Caribbean, Mona Island has the most pristine, extensive, and well-developed **reefs** ⚜⚜ in Puerto Rican waters. The tropical marine ecosystem around Mona includes patch reefs, black coral, spore and groove systems, underwater caverns, deep-water sponges, fringing reefs, and algae reefs. The lush environment attracts octopuses, lobster, queen conch, rays, barracuda, snapper, jack, grunt, angelfish, trunkfish, filefish, butterfly fish, dolphin, parrotfish, tuna, flying fish, and more. The crystal waters afford exceptional horizontal vision for 150 to 200 feet as well as good views down to the shipwrecks that mark the site—including some Hispanic galleons. Five species of whales visit the island's offshore waters. Instead of booking an expensive tour, negotiate with a local fisherman to take you over.

Encantos Ecotours (© 787/272-0005) offers bare-bones but ecologically sensitive camping tours to Mona Island at sporadic intervals that vary according to the demand of clients who are interested. The experience includes ground transport to and from San Juan, sea transport departing from Cabo Rojo (a few miles south of Mayagüez), use of camping and snorkeling gear, all meals (expect the equivalent of K rations cooked over a campfire), and fees. The 4-day, 3-night camping trip costs about $550 to $700.

main gastronomic outlet for the largest hotel and casino on this part of the island. Known as the venue for copious lunch buffets, it serves only a la carte items for dinner. These include such dishes as seafood stew served on linguine with marinara sauce, grilled salmon with mango-flavored Grand Marnier sauce, and sea bass filets with a cilantro, white wine, and butter sauce. Steak and lobster are served on the same platter. The food has real flavor and flair.

In the Best Western Mayagüez Resort & Casino, Rte. 104. © 787/832-3030. Breakfast buffet $11.25; Mon–Fri buffet lunch $14; main courses $17–$25. AE, MC, V. Daily 6:30am–11pm.

La Casona de Juanita ⚜ PUERTO RICAN   You'll find some of the best food and the most reasonable prices in this restaurant, which is in the Parador

Hacienda Juanita. The regional cuisine is prepared with flair and zest. The chef makes at least three regional soups daily (the menu is the same for lunch or dinner); our favorite is the shrimp and rice. Look for the daily special or ask for one of the regular house specialties—corned beef and sweet banana pie, Puerto Rican–style beef stew, or local chicken, which can be breaded, fried, or roasted. Everything is served with rice, beans, and fried plantains. For dessert, make it guava shells with a native white cheese or homemade pumpkin custard pudding.

In the Parador Hacienda Juanita, Rte. 105, km 23.5. ℂ 787/838-2550. Main courses $10–$24. AE, MC, V. Sun–Thurs 8am–8pm; Fri–Sat 8am–10pm.

SEEING THE SIGHTS: SURFING BEACHES & TROPICAL GARDENS

Along the western coastal bends of Route 2, north of Mayagüez, lie the best **surfing beaches** in the Caribbean. Surfers from as far away as New Zealand come to ride the waves. You can also check out panoramic **Punta Higuero** beach, nearby on Route 413, near Rincón.

The chief sight is the **Tropical Agriculture Research Station** ⚘ (ℂ 787/ 831-3435), on Route 65 between Post Street and Route 108, adjacent to the University of Puerto Rico at Mayagüez campus and across from the **Parque de los Próceres (Patriots' Park).** At the administration office, ask for a free map of the tropical gardens, which contain a huge collection of tropical species useful to people, like cacao, fruit trees, spices, timbers, and ornamentals. The grounds are open Monday to Friday 7am to 5pm, and there's no admission charge.

7 Boquerón & Cabo Rojo

Boquerón is Puerto Rico's Cape Cod, lying in the southwestern corner of the island and reached by heading south from Mayagüez along Route 102 (becoming 103) for 45 minutes or so, depending on the traffic. Once a tiny fishing village, Boquerón is now a center of tacky restaurants and low-cost beachside inns. It is, in fact, the cheapest place on Puerto Rico to go for a beachside vacation. It's not an elegant resort like Palmas del Mar, but Puerto Ricans, along with a scattering of foreign visitors, like the funky, often raffish, atmosphere of this laid-back retreat.

The big draw is **Boquerón Beach,** one of the island's best beaches, ideal for swimming or windsurfing. It lies off Route 101 near the fishing village of Boquerón, at the head of a scenic bay stretching for 3 miles. The beaches are lined with coconut palms overlooking the coral-dotted waters (beach umbrellas aren't necessary). In the background stands the lush Boquerón Nature Reserve, one of Puerto Rico's important bird sanctuaries. The best sections along Boquerón Beach go by different names, including Los Pozos, Las Salinas, and Villa Taína. The waters are generally clear and most often calm, and the sands golden. Parking is $2 per car. For information about this beach, call ℂ 787/ 724-2500, ext. 130 or 131. You can ask about renting two-room rustic cabins right on the beach.

Directly south of Boquerón is the fishing and resort community at **El Combate Beach.** Very popular with locals, especially on weekends, El Combate is picture-postcard perfect, set against a row of raffish fishing huts and an overcrowded jetty. There are camping facilities in the area and small kiosks that'll help you arrange watersports like windsurfing, snorkeling, and sailing. This area is the headquarters for the U.S. Fish and Wildlife's Caribbean refuges. A visitor center provides information about regional wildlife refuges and local bird-watching trails.

Sleepy Boquerón is part of the municipality of Cabo Rojo. An additional attraction is the **Boquerón Lagoon,** a refuge for ducks and other birds. You can also shop here for crafts at various kiosks in the area.

A coastal mangrove forest and a salt farm sprawl along the southwest tip of the island. You can drive along a dirt road trenched with potholes to the end of the line, where the 19th-century Spanish colonial **Cabo Rojo Lighthouse** awaits. A former pirate hangout, this section—called Punta Jagüey—is one of the Caribbean's most beautiful spots, if you don't mind the rough ride to it. The lighthouse's squat hexagonal blue tower is now boarded up, but few come here just to view the lighthouse. Once here, you're treated to Puerto Rico's most panoramic view of the rugged coast and an inner lagoon with bays on either side. It's worth the detour.

ACCOMMODATIONS YOU CAN AFFORD
BOQUERÓN

Parador Boquemar   The Boquemar, built in the late 1980s, lies near Boquerón Beach in the southwest corner of the island, between Mayagüez and Ponce. The Boquemar rents small but comfortable rooms with modern furnishings and has a well-known restaurant, La Cascada (see "Great Deals on Dining," below). Units have a festive resort look, thanks to the use of rattan and tropical prints, and the shower-only bathrooms are just big enough to do the job. The pool behind the hotel is popular with Puerto Rican families.

101 Rte. 307, Boquerón, PR 00622. (C) **800/933-2158** or 787/851-2158. Fax 787/851-7600. www.boquemar. com. 75 units. Year-round $70 single; $80–$91 double. AE, MC, V. From either Mayagüez or San Germán, take Rte. 102 into Cabo Rojo and then Rte. 100 south; turn right onto Rte. 101 and the hotel will be 2 blocks from the beach. **Amenities:** Restaurant, pool. *In room:* A/C, TV.

CABO ROJO

Hotel Joyuda Beach   On the beach in scenic Cabo Rojo, this 1989 hotel (a favorite of Puerto Rican honeymooners) offers comfortably furnished rooms with small bathrooms. It suffered massive damage during the 1998 hurricane but is now fully functional. This is a good center for touring such attractions as El Combate Beach and the Cabo Rojo Wildlife Refuge. Tennis and golf are just 5 minutes away, and sport-fishing charters, windsurfing, and canoeing can be arranged. The restaurant is nothing more than a simple cafeteria, serving snacks, drinks, and coffee, open daily during daylight hours or whenever the hotel thinks there's enough business.

Rte. 102, km 11.7, Cabo Rojo, PR 00623. (C) **787/851-5650.** Fax 787/255-3750. www.joyudabeach.com. 41 units. Year-round $80.25 single or double. 2 children 11 and under stay free in parents' room. AE, DISC, MC, V. Follow Rte. 102 south of Mayagüez to Joyuda. **Amenities:** Restaurant, room service. *In room:* A/C, TV.

GREAT DEALS ON DINING

Boquerón has several restaurants known for their fresh fish and seafood (they're not strong on fruit and vegetables, except for plantains, rice, and beans). But you can eat well without going to a restaurant. At various **beach shacks** you can buy fresh oysters, a local delicacy. They're shucked right on the spot, and locals douse them with hot sauce. You can also buy skewers of chicken. For another local delicacy, finish off your meal with the incredibly delicious maize ice cream, made with sweet corn and dusted with paprika (don't knock it until you've tried it).

La Cascada PUERTO RICAN   Known for its fresh seafood, this place is popular with San Juan families who flock to the beaches here on weekends and always schedule a dinner at La Cascada. The staff have their good and bad days and service is among the slowest on the coast, but you can get such great-tasting fresh fish that you'll be willing to suffer the inconvenience. The red snapper can be broiled or fried and often is memorable. Begin with one of the salads, perhaps made of conch or octopus, then proceed to rice stew with lobster, shrimp in chili sauce, the chef's special rice with seafood and vegetables, or mashed green plantain stuffed with seafood, including lobster and shrimp. The meat dishes—made from meat that is shipped in frozen—aren't noteworthy, although the chicken stew isn't bad.

At the Parador Boquemar, 101 Rte. 307. (C) **787/851-2158.** Main courses $10–$20. AE, MC, V. Daily 7:30am–noon; Thurs–Tues 4–10pm.

Tino's *(Finds)* PUERTO RICAN   One of the most appealing restaurants along this section of the coast occupies a simple beachfront building beside the highway and sports a clean tile-sheathed interior. It features fresh seafood and well-prepared roster of *mofongos,* a plantain dish. Seafood is brought in every day. Try the red snapper with Spanish sauce, *zarzuela* of shellfish, three versions of the rice dish *asopao,* and broiled or skewered shrimp. There are also flank steaks and filets from a charcoal brazier. The drink of choice is beer or any of the rum concoctions.

Carretera 102, km 13.6, Joyuda/Cabo Rojo. (C) **787/851-2976.** Main courses $13–$19. AE, DC, MC, V. Daily 11am–9:30pm. Drive 3¹⁄₂ miles south on Rte. 102.

8 Ponce ★★

Puerto Rico's second-largest city, Ponce—called "the Pearl of the South"—was named after Loíza Ponce de León, grandson of Juan Ponce de León. Today it's Puerto Rico's principal shipping port on the Caribbean, lying 75 miles west of San Juan. The city is well kept and attractive, as reflected by its many plazas, parks, and public buildings. There's something in its lingering air that suggests a provincial Mediterranean town. Look for the *rejas* (framed balconies) of the handsome colonial mansions.

Maps and information can be found at the **tourist office,** Fox Delicias Mall, on Plaza de las Delicias ((C) **787/843-0465**).

GETTING THERE
Ponce lies 75 miles southwest of San Juan and is reached via Route 52. Allow at least 1¹⁄₂ hours if you drive.

American Eagle ((C) **800/433-7300**) offers one daily flight between San Juan and Ponce (flight time is about 35 min.) for $99 to $205 round-trip, depending on the ticket. However, prices fluctuate, so call for up-to-the-minute details.

ACCOMMODATIONS YOU CAN AFFORD
Hotel Belgica *(Value)*   One of the best values in town, this boxy-looking hotel is a few steps from Ponce's main square. Built in 1911 and renovated several times since, it contains pale-green rooms that are bare-boned but relatively large—however, some don't have windows. If one of them is assigned to you, don't worry about ventilation, as the air-conditioning system is strong. The bathrooms are small and have shower stalls. No meals are served here, but considering the low prices and the fact that many cafes are nearby, no one seems to mind.

Calle Villa 122, Ponce, PR 00731. (C) **787/844-3255.** Fax 787/844-6149. 20 units. Year-round $60 single; $75 double. MC, V. *In room:* A/C, TV.

Mary Lee's by the Sea *(Finds* Owned and operated by Michigan-born Mary Lee Alvarez, a fiercely independent former resident of Cuba and a self-described compulsive decorator, this is an informal collection of cottages, seafront houses, and apartments beside the coastal highway 4 miles east of Guánica. Two of the buildings are California-style houses; the rest are a confusing medley of other structures built since the 1970s. The entire compound is landscaped with flowering shrubs, trees, and vines.

To the north is the Guánica State Forest, a well-known sanctuary for birds and wildlife (see "Side Trips to Guánica State Forest & Historic San Germán," below). Picnic areas, trails, and campsites are located throughout the reserve. The hotel sits next to sandy beaches and a handful of uninhabited offshore cays. For the benefit of its nature-watching guests, the hotel maintains about half a dozen rental boats with putt-putt motors, two waterside sun decks, and several kayaks. A single visit by a maid each week is included in the price, but for an extra fee guests can arrange to have a maid come in daily. Each medium-size unit includes a modern kitchen, an outdoor barbecue pit, and a sense of privacy. Beds are most comfortable with firm mattresses, and the tidy but small bathrooms have room to spread out your stuff.

Don't come here looking for nighttime activities or enforced conviviality: The place is quiet, secluded, and appropriate only for low-key vacationers seeking privacy and isolation with a companion and/or with nature.

Rte. 333, km 6.7 (P.O. Box 394), Guánica, PR 00653. ℂ 787/821-3600. Fax 787/821-0744. 10 units. Year-round $70–$90 studio for 2; $110–$130 1-bedroom apt; $145–$176 2-bedroom apt; $180–$225 3-bedroom apt. Extra person $10. No credit cards. **Amenities:** Rental boats, kayaks. *In room:* A/C, TV, kitchen (some units), barbecue pits.

Meliá A city hotel with southern hospitality, the Meliá, which has no connection with the international hotel chain, often attracts businesspeople. The location is a few steps away from the Cathedral of Our Lady of Guadalupe and from the Parque de Bombas (the red-and-black firehouse). Although the more expensive Hilton outclassed this old and somewhat tattered hotel long ago, many people who can afford more upscale accommodations still prefer to stay here for its old-time atmosphere. The lobby floor and all stairs are covered with Spanish tiles of Moorish design. The desk clerks speak English. The small rooms are comfortably furnished and pleasant enough, and most have a balcony facing either busy Calle Cristina or the old plaza. In some rooms, the mattresses are a bit tired, but others are new. Bathrooms are tiny, each with a shower stall. Breakfast is served on a rooftop terrace with a good view of Ponce, and Mark's Restaurant, under separate management, thrives. You can park your car in the lot nearby.

Calle Cristina 2, Ponce, PR 00731. ℂ 800/742-4276 in the U.S., or 787/842-0260. Fax 787/841-3602. http:// home.coqui.net/melia. 78 units. Year-round $93–$100 single or double. Rates include continental breakfast. AE, DC, MC, V. Parking $3. **Amenities:** Restaurant, bar. *In room:* A/C, TV.

Ponce Inn Hotel A 15-minute drive east of Ponce on Highway 52, opposite the Interamerican University, this hotel offers modest rooms that are conservative and comfortable. This inn took a direct hit during the 1998 hurricane but is now up and running. The storm forced a massive renewal, so all the mattresses are good. The plumbing has been brought up-to-date in the small but well-maintained bathrooms with shower stalls.

Rte. 1, km 123.5, Mercedita, Ponce, PR 00715. ℂ 866/668-4577 or 787/841-1000. Fax 787/841-2560. www. hidpr.com. 121 units. Year-round $101.50 single; $111.50 double; $121.50 suite. Rates include continental breakfast. AE, DC, MC, V. **Amenities:** Restaurant, pool bar, pool, exercise room, Jacuzzi, room service, dry cleaning. *In room:* A/C, TV, coffeemaker, hair dryer.

GREAT DEALS ON DINING

Café Palermo ITALIAN/PUERTO RICAN   Set on the main square of Ponce, opposite the entrance to the cathedral, this is a small but charming bar and restaurant whose creative force derives from its Argentina-born owner Ricardo Cabral. Its paneled, air-conditioned interior is a welcome relief from the heat of the city's downtown core, and as such, it does a brisk bar business with local shoppers and sightseers throughout the afternoon and evening. Many clients come just for a beer and a *ración* of tapas, but if you're looking for a meal, consider heaping portions of such good-tasting menu items as ravioli, spaghetti, Caesar salad, lasagna, beef Milanese, and breaded chicken cutlets. Every Thursday, Friday and Saturday nights, beginning at 9pm, a live guitarist plays music from Argentina, Italy, and Spain, drawing an animated crowd.

Calle Union 3. ✆ 787/812-3873. Tapas $3.75–$6; main courses $8–$15. MC, V. Tues–Sat 4pm–1am.

El Ancla ✯ PUERTO RICAN/SEAFOOD   This is one of Ponce's best restaurants, with a lovely location 2 miles south of the city center on soaring piers that extend from the rocky coastline out over the surf. As you dine, the sound of the sea rises literally from beneath your feet.

Menu items are prepared with real Puerto Rican zest and flavor. An old favorite here is red snapper stuffed with lobster and shrimp, served with fried plantain or mashed potatoes. Other specialties are filet of salmon in a caper sauce, and a seafood medley of lobster, shrimp, octopus, and conch. Most of the dishes are reasonably priced, especially the chicken and conch. One corner of the menu is reserved for lobster, which tops the price scale. The side orders are also delectable, including crabmeat rice or yucca in garlic.

Av. Hostos Final 805, Playa Ponce. ✆ 787/840-2450. Main courses $13–$36. AE, DC, MC, V. Sun–Thurs 11am–9:30pm; Fri–Sat 11am–11pm.

Lupita's Mexican Restaurant MEXICAN/PUERTO RICAN. In a 19th-century building and its adjoining courtyard, a short walk from Ponce's main square, this is the creative statement of Hector de Castro. The specialties are tortilla soup, taco salads, grilled lobster tail with *tostones,* seafood fajitas, and burritos, tacos, and enchiladas with a wide choice of fillings. Some standard Puerto Rican dishes are offered as well. On Friday and Saturday 8pm to midnight, a mariachi band will probably provide entertainment.

Calle Isabel 60. ✆ 787/848-8808. Reservations required on weekends. Main courses $8–$30. AE, DC, MC, V. Sun–Thurs 11am–11pm; Fri–Sat 11am–2am.

BEACHES & OTHER OUTDOOR PURSUITS

A 10-minute drive west of Ponce will take you to **Playa de Ponce,** a long strip of white sand opening onto the tranquil waters of the Caribbean. This beach is usually better for swimming than the Condado in San Juan. There's little in the way of organized sports here, however.

The city owns two **tennis complexes,** one at Poly Deportivos, with nine hard courts and another at Rambla, with six courts. Both are open 9am to 10pm and are lit for night play. You can play free.

SEEING THE SIGHTS

A $40-million project is restoring more than 1,000 buildings in town to their original charm. Architectural styles that combine neoclassical with "Ponce Creole" and Art Deco give the town a distinctive ambience.

Any Ponceño will direct you to the **Museo de Arte de Ponce** ✯, Avenida de las Americas 25 (✆ 787/848-0505), which has a fine collection of European and Latin American art, the best on the island. Among the nearly 400 paintings, sculptures, and artworks on display are exceptional pre-Raphaelite and Italian baroque paintings. The building was designed by Edward Durell Stone and has been called the "Parthenon of the Caribbean." It's open daily 10am to 5pm. Adults pay $4; children 11 and under are charged $2.

Most visitors head for the **Parque de Bombas,** Plaza de las Delicias (© 787/ 284-4141), the main plaza of Ponce. This fantastic old black-and-red firehouse was built for a fair in 1883. It's open Wednesday through Monday 9:30am to 5:30pm.

Around the corner from the firehouse, a trail will lead you to the **Cathedral of Our Lady of Guadalupe,** Calle Concordia and Calle Union (© 787/842-0134). Designed by architects Francisco Porrata Doría and Francisco Trublard in 1931 and featuring a pipe organ installed in 1934, it remains an important place for prayer. It's open Monday to Friday 6am to 3:30pm and on Saturday and Sunday 6am to 1pm and 3 to 8pm.

El Museo Castillo Serrallés, El Vigía 17 (© 787/259-1774), the largest and most imposing building in Ponce, was built high on a hilltop above town by the Serrallés family (owners of a local rum distillery) in the 1930s. This is one of the architectural gems of Puerto Rico and the best evidence of the wealth produced by the turn-of-the-century sugar boom. Guides will escort you through the Spanish Revival house, where Moorish and Andalusian details include panoramic courtyards, a baronial dining room, and a small cafe and souvenir shop. Hours are Tuesday through Sunday 9:30am to 5pm. Admission is $3 for adults, $2 for seniors over 62, and $1.50 for students and children 15 and under.

If you feel a yen for **shopping,** head for the **Fox Delicias Mall,** at the intersection of Calle Reina Isabel and Plaza de Las Delicias, the city's most innovative shopping center.

The oldest cemetery in the Antilles, excavated in 1975, is near Ponce on Route 503 at km 2.7. The **Tibes Indian Ceremonial Center** (© 787/840-2255) contains some 186 skeletons, dating from A.D. 300, as well as pre-Taíno plazas from A.D. 700. Guided tours in English and Spanish are conducted through the grounds. Shaded by trees are seven rectangular ball courts and two dance areas. The arrangements of stone points on the dance grounds, in line with the solstices and equinoxes, suggest a pre-Columbian Stonehenge. A re-created Taíno village includes not only the museum but also an exhibition hall where you can see a documentary about Tibes; you can also visit the cafeteria and souvenir shop. The museum is open Tuesday to Sunday 9am to 4pm. Admission is $2 for adults and $1 for children.

Hacienda Buena Vista, Route 10, km 16.8 (© 787/284-7020 or 787/722-5882), is a 30-minute drive north of Ponce. Built in 1833, it preserves an old way of life, with its whirring waterwheels and artifacts of 19th-century

---

Finds **For the Hannibal in You**

The best outlet for souvenirs and artisan work is in the very center of town: **El Palacio del Coquí Inc.** (Palace of the Tree Frog), Fox Delicias Mall (© 787/841-0216). This is the place to buy the grotesque masks (collectors' items) that are used at Carnival time. One of these masks will make you more frightening than Hannibal. Ask the owner to explain the importance and significance of these masks.

farm production. Once it was one of the most successful plantations on Puerto Rico, producing coffee, corn, and citrus. It was a working coffee plantation until the 1950s, and 86 of the original 500 acres are still part of the estate. The rooms of the hacienda have been furnished with authentic pieces from the 1850s. **Tours,** lasting 2 hours, are conducted Wednesday to Sunday at 8:30am, 10:30am, 1:30pm, and 3:30pm (in English only at 1:30pm). Reservations are required. Tours cost $5 for adults, $2.50 for seniors, and $2 for children. The hacienda lies in the small town of Barrio Magüeyes, on Route 10 between Ponce and Adjuntas.

SIDE TRIPS TO GUÁNICA STATE FOREST & HISTORIC SAN GERMÁN

GUÁNICA STATE FOREST ★★

Heading directly west from Ponce, you reach **Guánica State Forest** (© 787/ 723-1373), which UNESCO has named a World Biosphere Reserve. Here you'll find the planet's best-preserved subtropical ecosystem. The Cordillera Central cuts off the rain coming in from the heavily showered northeast, making this a dry region of cacti and bedrock. Some 50% of all the island's terrestrial bird species can be seen here—you might even spot the Puerto Rican emerald-breasted hummingbird or the Puerto Rican nightjar, a local bird that was believed to be extinct until one was sighted locally. Some 750 plants and tree species grow in the area. To reach the forest, take Route 334 northeast of Guánica to the heart of the forest. A ranger station here will give you a booklet about hiking trails. The most interesting is the mile-long Cueva Trail, which gives you the most scenic look at the various types of vegetation. You might even encounter the endangered bufo lemur toad, once declared extinct but found to still be jumping in this area.

HISTORIC SAN GERMÁN ★★

Only an hour's drive from Ponce or Mayagüez and the beaches of the southern coast, and just over 2 hours from San Juan, San Germán, Puerto Rico's second-oldest town, has been compared to a small-scale outdoor museum. It was founded in 1512 and destroyed by the French in 1528. Rebuilt in 1570, it was named after Germain de Foix, the second wife of King Ferdinand of Spain. Once the rival of San Juan, but without the benefit of Old San Juan's lavish restoration budgets, San Germán harbored many pirates, who pillaged the ships that sailed off the nearby coastline. Indeed, many of today's residents are descended from the smugglers, poets, priests, and politicians who lived here.

Although the pirates and sugar plantations are long gone, the city retains some colorful reminders of those former days. Today it has settled into a slumber, albeit one that has preserved the feel of the Spanish colonial era. Flowers brighten some of the patios here as they do in Seville. Also as in a small Spanish town, many of the inhabitants stroll through the small but choice historic zone in early evening. Nicknamed "Ciudad de las Lomas," or City of the Hills, San Germán boasts verdant scenery that provides a pleasant backdrop to a variety of architectural styles—Spanish colonial (1850s), *criollo* (1880s), neoclassical (1910s), Art Deco (1930s), and international (1960s)—depicted in the gracious old world–style buildings that line some of its streets. So significant are these buildings that San Germán is only the second Puerto Rican city (the other is San Juan) to be included in the National Register of Historic Places.

The city's 249 noteworthy historical treasures are within easy walking distance of one another, but you'll see most of them only from the outside. If some of them are actually open, count yourself fortunate, as they have no phones, keep no regular hours, and are staffed by volunteers who rarely show up. Also, be aware that most of the city's architectural treasures lie uphill from the impossibly congested main thoroughfare (Calle Luna), that streets in the old town tend to run only one way (usually the way you don't want to go), and that you're likely to be confused by the bad signs and dilapidated condition of many of the historic buildings. We usually try to park on the town's main street (Carretera 102, which changes its name within the border of San Germán to Calle Luna), and then proceed on foot through the city's grimy-looking commercial core before reaching the architectural highlights described below.

One of the most noteworthy churches in Puerto Rico is **Iglesia Porta Coeli** ★ (Gate to Heaven), which sits atop a knoll at the eastern end of a cobble-covered square, the Parque de Santo Domingo. Dating from 1606, in a form inspired by the Romanesque architecture of northern Spain, this is the oldest church in the New World. Restored by the Institute of Puerto Rican Culture, and sheathed in a layer of salmon-colored stucco, it contains a museum of religious art with a collection of ancient *santos,* the carved figures of saints that have long been a major branch of Puerto Rican folk art. Look for the 17th-century portrait of St. Nicholas de Bari, the French Santa Claus. Inside, the original palm-wood ceiling and tough, brown ausobo-wood beams draw the eyes upward. Other treasures include early choral books from Santo Domingo, a primitive carving of Jesus, and 19th-century Señora de Monserrate (Black Madonna and Child) statues. Admission costs $1; free for children 12 and under. It's open Wednesday through Sunday 9am to 4:30pm. Call ✆ **787/264-4258** for more information.

Less than 100 feet downhill from the church, at the bottom of the steps that lead from its front door down to the plaza below, is the **Casa Morales** (it's also known as the **Tomás Vivoni House,** after its architect), San Germán's most popular and widely recognized house. It was built in 1913 (during a period of agrarian prosperity) and named for the local architect who designed it. Edwardian style, with wraparound porches, elaborate gables, and elements that might remind you of a Swiss chalet, it was built in 1913, reflecting the region's turn-of-the-century agrarian prosperity.

The long and narrow, gently sloping plaza that prefaces the Iglesia Porta Coeli is the **Parque de Santo Domingo,** one of San Germán's two main plazas. Street signs also identify the plaza as the Calle Ruiz Belvis. Originally a marketplace, the plaza is paved with red and black cobblestones and bordered with cast-iron benches and portrait busts of some of the prominent figures in the town's history. This plaza merges gracefully with an equivalently shaped, identically sized twin, which street signs and maps identify simultaneously as the **Plaza Francisco Mariano Quiñones,** the Calle José Julian Acosta, or the Plaza Principal. Separating the two plazas is the unused, gray-and-white bulk of San Germán's **Viejo Alcaldia (Old Town Hall).** Built late in the 19th century and awaiting a new vision, perhaps as a museum or public building, it's closed to the public.

San Germán's most impressive church—and the most monumental building in the region—is **San Germánde Auxerre** (✆ **787/892-1027**), which rises majestically above the western end of the Plaza Francisco Mariano Quiñones. Designed in the Spanish baroque style, and painted yellow, it was founded in 1573 in the form of a simple chapel with a low-slung thatch roof. Much of what you'll see today is the result of a rebuilding in 1688 and a restoration in 1737 that followed a disastrous earthquake. Inside, you'll find 3 naves, 10 altars, 3 chapels, and a belfry that was rebuilt in 1939 following the collapse of the original during another earthquake in 1918. The central chandelier, made from rock crystal and imported from Barcelona in 1866, is the largest in the Caribbean. The pride of the church is the trompe-l'oeil ceiling, which was elaborately restored in 1993. The building's restoration was completed in 1999 with the insertion of a series of stained-glass windows with contemporary designs. The church can be visited daily 7am to 7:30pm.

There are a handful of lesser sights within or near the town's two main squares that will distract you as well. They include the **Farmacia Martin,** a modern pharmacy that's incongruously set within the shell of a graceful but battered Art Deco building at the edge of the Parque Santo Domingo (22 Calle Ruiz Belvis; ✆ **787/892-1122**). Open Monday to Friday 9am to 10pm and Saturday 9am to 9pm. A cluster of battered and dilapidated clapboard-sided houses line the southern side of the Calle Dr Ueve. The most important of these is at no. 66, the **Casa Acosta y Fores** house. Also noteworthy is a substantial-looking house at the corner of the Calle Dr. Ueve and the Parque Santo Domingo, the **Casa Juan Perichi.** Both were built around 1917 of traditional wood construction, and are fine examples of Puerto Rican adaptations of Victorian architecture. Both, regrettably, are in seriously dilapidated condition, although that might change as San Germán continues the slow course of its historic renovations.

Accommodations & Dining in San Germán

Parador El Oasis   Although it's not state-of-the-art, this hotel evokes some appealing doses of Spanish colonial charm. If you'd like to anchor into this quaint old town, far removed from the beaches, this is a fine place to stay. A three-story building constructed around a pool and patio area, the hotel originated in the late 1700s as a privately owned mansion. The older rooms, positioned close to the lobby, show the wear and tear of the years. The more modern rooms, located in the back, have little character, but they are cleaner and more spacious than the older units. Three units have private balconies, and each of the accommodations has a tiled, shower-only bathroom. The hotel sits on the town's overcrowded main street, about 2 blocks from the historic churches described above.

The in-house restaurant is not the most imaginative choice in town, but year after year it is the most reliable and consistent of those within the town center.

Calle Luna 72, San Germán, PR 00683. ✆ **877/453-2060** in the U.S., or 787/892-1175. Fax 787/892-1156. 52 units. Year-round $70 single or double. Extra person $10; children 11 and under stay free in parents' room. AE, DC, DISC, MC, V. **Amenities:** Restaurant, pool. *In room:* A/C, TV.

9 Northeastern Puerto Rico

Now that we've covered the western portion of Puerto Rico, we'll begin heading east from San Juan. From the capital, Route 3 leads toward the fishing town of Fajardo, where you'll turn north to Las Croabas, about 31 miles from the capital. You'll be near Luquillo Beach, one of the island's best and most popular public stretches of sand. See "Hitting the Beaches," under San Juan, earlier in this chapter, for more information.

In the Luquillo Mountains east of San Juan is another favorite escape from the capital—**El Yunque** ★★★, a tropical forest teeming with hundreds of species of plant and animal life (see the box earlier in this chapter).

ACCOMMODATIONS YOU CAN AFFORD NEAR EL YUNQUE

Some three dozen camping sites are located in parks ranging from Luquillo Beach to El Yunque National Forest. Tent sites are available at about $4 per person, but it's also possible to rent *casetas* (tiny cottages), lean-tos, huts, and even small trailers. Costs average $25 per night. Don't expect luxury; these are bare-bones and rustic. Sometimes a cold shower might be offered; at other times there's no running water or even a toilet. As such, these are recommended only for the most rugged campers.

For more information about the designated areas for camping, contact the **Department of Natural Resources** at ☎ 787/724-8774 or the **Recreation Department** at ☎ 787/724-3647.

Ceiba Country Inn If you're looking for an escape from the hustle and bustle of everyday life, then this is the place for you. This small B&B, built in 1951, is on the easternmost part of Puerto Rico, 4 miles west of Roosevelt Roads U.S. naval base, and to reach this little haven in the mountains you must rent a car. El Yunque is only 15 miles away. The small to medium rooms are on the bottom floor of a large old family home; two contain refrigerators, and each comes with a small bathroom with shower stalls. They're decorated in a tropical motif with flowered murals on the walls painted by a local artist. For a quiet evening cocktail, you might want to visit the small second-floor lounge.

Rd. no. 977, km 1.2 (P.O. Box 1067), Ceiba, PR 00735. ☎ 787/885-0471. 9 units. Year-round $60 single; $75 double. Extra person $5. Rates include breakfast. AE, DISC, MC, V. Free parking. **Amenities:** Cocktail lounge. *In room:* A/C.

TO THE LIGHTHOUSE: EXPLORING LAS CABEZAS DE SAN JUAN NATURE RESERVE

Better known as **El Faro**, or **The Lighthouse** ⭐, this reserve in the north-eastern corner of the island, north of Fajardo off Route 987, is one of the most beautiful and important areas on Puerto Rico—a number of ecosystems flourish in the vicinity.

Surrounded on three sides by the Atlantic Ocean, the 316-acre site encompasses forestland, mangroves, lagoons, beaches, cliffs, offshore cays, and coral reefs. El Faro serves as a research center for the scientific community. It's home to a vast array of flora and fauna, including sea turtles and other endangered species.

The nature reserve is open Wednesday to Sunday; reservations are required, so check by phone before going. For reservations throughout the week, call ☎ 787/722-5882; for reservations on Saturday and Sunday, call ☎ 787/860-2560 (reservations on weekends can be made only on the day of your intended visit). Admission is $5 for adults, $2 for children 12 and under, and $2.50 for seniors. Guided tours are conducted at 9:30am, 10am, 10:30am, and 2pm (in English at 2pm).

GREAT DEALS ON DINING IN FAJARDO

The sleepy town of Fajardo was established as a supply depot for the many pirates who plied the nearby waters. Today a host of private yachts bob at anchor in its harbor, and the many offshore cays provide naturalists with secluded beaches. From Fajardo, ferries make choppy but frequent runs to the offshore islands of Vieques and Culebra (see later in this chapter). Close by are the coral-bordered offshore islands, the most popular being Icacos, a favorite among snorkelers and divers. To get here, take Route 3 from the eastern outskirts of San Juan all the way to Fajardo.

Lolita's MEXICAN   On the western periphery of Fajardo, 2½ miles from the El Conquistador resort, this is the most popular independent restaurant around. The venue is Mexican and informal, the margaritas are cold, and the roster of fajitas, tacos, tortillas, empanadas, and burritos are among the most flavorful in town. Come here expecting a delay as you wait for an available table—if you do, you won't be alone, as many members of the staff at the deluxe El Conquistador and many locals will be there with you.

Hwy. 3. ✆ 787/889-5770. Main courses $12–$19. AE, DC, MC, V. Wed–Thurs 11am–10pm; Fri–Sat 11am–midnight.

10 Two Island Drives

Puerto Rico is a relatively small island, barely 100 miles long and about 35 miles wide, but it has a wide variety of natural scenery. From your car you can see terrain ranging from the rain forests and lush mountains of El Yunque to the lime deposits of the north and the arid stretches along the south shore, where irrigation is necessary and cacti grow wild. Seasonal changes also transform the landscape: In November the sugarcane fields are in bloom, and in January and February the flowering trees along the roads are covered with red and orange blossoms. Springtime brings delicate pink flowers to the Puerto Rican oak and deep-red blossoms to the African tulip tree, while summer is a flamboyant time when the roadsides seem to be on fire with blooming flowers.

Puerto Rico has colorful but often narrow and steep roads. While driving on mountain roads, blow your horn before every turn; this will help to avoid an accident. Commercial road signs are forbidden, so make sure you take along a map and this guide to keep you abreast of restaurants, hotels, and possible points of interest. There are white roadside markers noting distances in kilometers (1km is equal to 0.62 miles) in black lettering. Speed limits are given in miles per hour.

Two programs that have helped the Puerto Rico Tourism Company successfully promote Puerto Rico as "The Complete Island" are the *paradores puertorriqueños* and the *mesones gastronómicos.*

The *paradores puertorriqueños* are a chain of privately owned/operated country inns under the auspices of the Commonwealth Development Company. These hostelries are easily identified by the Taíno grass hut that appears on their signs and logos. The Puerto Rico Tourism Company started the program in 1973, modeling it after Spain's *parador* system, although it's a poor cousin. Each *parador* is in a historic or particularly beautiful spot. They vary in size, but all share the virtues of affordability, hospitable staffs, and high standards of cleanliness.

The *paradores* are also known for their food—each serves Puerto Rican cuisine of excellent quality, with meals starting at $15. There are now *paradores* at locations throughout the island, many within an easy drive of San Juan. For reservations or further information, contact the **Paradores Puertorriqueños Reservation Office,** P.O. Box 902-3960, Old San Juan Station, San Juan, PR 00902 (✆ **800/443-0266** in the mainland U.S., 800/981-7575 in Puerto Rico, or 787/721-2884 in San Juan).

As you tour the island, you'll find few well-known restaurants, except for those in major hotels. However, there are plenty of roadside places and simple taverns. If you long for authentic island cuisine, you can rely on *mesones gastronómicos* (gastronomic inns). This established dining network, sanctioned by the Puerto Rico Tourism Company, highlights restaurants recognized for excellence in preparing and serving Puerto Rican specialties at modest prices.

Mesón gastronómico status is limited to restaurants outside the San Juan area that are close to major island attractions.

What follows are two driving tours of the Puerto Rican countryside. The first will take you to the lush tropical forests and sandy beaches of eastern Puerto Rico, the second to the subterranean sights of Karst Country and on to the west and south coasts. They're both extended tours—the first takes about 2 days to complete and the second about 6 days—but Puerto Rico's small size and many roads will give you many places to pick up or leave the tour. In fact, there are several points where we give you the opportunity to cut your tour short and head back to San Juan.

DRIVING TOUR 1	THE RAIN FORESTS & BEACHES OF THE EAST

Start:	San Juan.
Finish:	San Juan.
Time:	Allow about 2 days, but you might want to stay longer at places along the way.
Best Times:	Any sunny day Monday to Friday.
Worst Times:	Saturday and Sunday, when the roads are often impossibly crowded.

This tour will take you through some of Puerto Rico's most spectacular natural scenery, including El Yunque Rain Forest and Luquillo Beach. You'll travel through the small towns of Trujillo Alto, Gurabo, Fajardo, Naguabo, Humacao, Yabucoa, San Lorenzo, and Caguas before returning to San Juan.

From Condado, signs point the way southeast to Route 1. Near Rio Piedras on your right, Route 3 is the famous highway most motorists take to visit Luquillo Beach and El Yunque. Route 1 naturally blends into Route 3, which is sometimes called Avenida 65 de Infantera after the Puerto Rican regiment that fought in World War II and the Korean War.

To begin the tour, at the intersection of Route 3 and Route 181, head south toward Trujillo Alto. South of Trujillo Alto, connect with Route 851, which continues until it comes to an intersection with Route 941. At this point get on Route 941, which runs southwest. To your right, you'll soon come to the first worthy stopover, Lake of Loíza.

❶ Lake of Loíza

Near this lake, surrounded by mountains, you might see local farmers (*jíbaros*) riding horses laden with products going to or from the marketplace. (Don't confuse Lake of Loíza with the northern coastal town of Loíza, known for its African heritage and its music.)

Leave the town by heading east along Route 30. Before you approach the town of Juncos, signs point the way to Route 185, which will lead you to the small town of Lomas. Continue north along Route 185, following the signs to the major artery of Route 3. Allow a leisurely hour of driving time for this trek after having left the lake.

Once you've connected with Route 3, take it east toward El Yunque, and then turn right (south) onto Route 191, which climbs into the forest surrounding El Yunque's peak and that of its taller sibling, El Toro. This is part of the Caribbean National Forest, the most panoramic and dramatic part of the eastern drive through Puerto Rico.

After viewing the lake, continue on Route 941, which swings in southeast through Puerto Rico's tobacco country to Gurabo.

❷ Gurabo

You'll know you're nearing this town by the sweet aroma of drying tobacco leaves. Part of the town of Gurabo is set on the side of a mountain, and the streets consist of steps.

Leave Gurabo by heading east on Route 30. Near Juncos, turn left onto Route 185 north, follow it up through Lomas, and then get on Route 186 south. This road offers views of the ocean beyond the mountains and valleys. At this point you'll be driving through the lower section of the Caribbean National Forest; the vegetation is dense, and you'll be surrounded by giant ferns. The brooks descending from the mountains become waterfalls on both sides of the road.

At about 25 miles east of San Juan is El Yunque.

❸ El Yunque Rain Forest

Consisting of about 28,000 acres, this rare natural treasure is the only tropical rain forest in the U.S. National Forest system. Its Spanish name derives from its distinctive anvil shape. It lies in the Luquillo Mountains, a name that harks back to the benign Indian god *Yuquiyú,* who, according to ancient legend, ruled from the forest's mighty peaks and protected the Taíno, the island's original inhabitants. Today, El Yunque offers you close encounters of the natural kind, from picnics amid rare flora and fauna to hikes along the panoramic trails. If the outdoors appeals, give yourself at least a day to explore this natural wonderland.

Backtrack on Route 191 until you reach Route 3. Five miles east from the intersection is Luquillo Beach.

❹ Luquillo Beach

Edged by a vast coconut grove, this crescent-shaped beach is not only the best beach on Puerto Rico but also one of the finest in the Caribbean. You pay $1 to enter with your car, and you can rent a locker, take a shower, and use the changing rooms. Luquillo Beach becomes crowded on weekends, so if possible, go on a weekday, when you'll have more sand to yourself. Picnic tables are available as well.

The beach is open Tuesday to Sunday 9am to 5pm; it's closed Monday (if Mon is a holiday, the beach will be open Mon and closed Tues). Before entering the beach, you might want to stop at one of the roadside thatched huts that sell Puerto Rican snacks and pick up the makings of a picnic.

From Luquillo, return to Route 3 east and drive for about 5 miles, until the first exit, to Fajardo. Make a left onto Route 194, heading toward the eastern shore. Turn left at the traffic light at the corner of the Monte Brisas Shopping Center; stay on this road until the next traffic light, turn right, and continue to the intersection with Route 987. Turn left onto Route 987 and continue north until you reach the entrance to Las Cabezas de San Juan Nature Reserve.

❺ Las Cabezas de San Juan Nature Reserve

Better known as El Faro, or The Lighthouse, Las Cabezas de San Juan Nature Reserve dates from 1882 and is surrounded on three sides by the Atlantic Ocean. This northeast corner of Puerto Rico is one of the most beautiful areas. See "To the Lighthouse: Exploring Las Cabezas de San Juan Nature Reserve," above.

After visiting the reserve, take the same road back, heading south to Route 3. Then follow the highway signs south into Fajardo.

❻ Fajardo

This fishing port was hotly contested during the Spanish–American War. Puerto Ricans are fond of giving nicknames to people and places, and for many years, the residents of Fajardo have been called *cariduros* (the hardfaced ones). Don't let the label mislead you; the locals are very friendly. Sailors and fishers are attracted to the shores of Fajardo and nearby Las Croabas, with several seafood restaurants. If you have time, you can take a very satisfying trip by ferry from Fajardo to Vieques or Culebra, small islands off the Puerto Rican coast that make urban troubles seem far away (see later in this chapter).

Continue south on Route 3, following the Caribbean coastline. At Cayo Lobos, just off the Fajardo port, the Atlantic meets the Caribbean. Here the vivid colors of the Caribbean seem subdued compared to those of the deep blue ocean.

Go through the town of Ceiba, near the Roosevelt Navy Base. After you drive about 8.5 miles, you'll reach Naguabo Beach.

⑦ Naguabo Beach

At Naguabo Beach you can have coffee and *pastelillos de chapin,* pastry turnovers that were used as tax payments during Spanish colonial days. At km 70.9 of Route 3, take a brief detour to the town of Naguabo, but only if you want to enjoy the town plaza's scented, shady laurel trees, imported from India. There isn't much else to see.

Continue south along Route 3, going through Humacao.

⑧ Humacao

When Humacao's sugarcane fields bloom during November and December, the tops of the fields change colors according to the time of day. Humacao itself isn't of much interest, but it has a *balneario*-equipped beach with changing facilities, lockers, and showers.

From here you can detour to Palmas del Mar, which is signposted immediately to the south after you leave Naguabo Beach. To go to Palmas del Mar, continue on 3, going south/southwest, to 53 south to 906 south, to 906R southeast.

⑨ Palmas del Mar

This is a sprawling deluxe vacation resort. You can stop here or continue along Route 3 through Yabucoa, nestled amid some hills. The view along the road opens up at Cerro La Pandura, a mountain from which there's a panoramic outlook over giant boulders onto the Caribbean.

Directly west of Yabucoa you can connect to Route 182, heading west through some of the most dramatic scenery in Puerto Rico along the mountain chain of Cuchilla de Pandura. This road changes its number unexpectedly to Route 181 (but it's still the same road). After a sharp bend, it becomes Route 7740 (again, the same road), and before it reaches the mountain station of Cerro la Santa it becomes Route 184. Stay on Route 184, heading northwest and following the signs to Route 52, the major highway cutting across the heart of Puerto Rico. If you continue southwest on Route 52, you'll come to Ponce. But if you want to return to San Juan, where the driving tour began, go northeast, following the signs back into the heart of Puerto Rico's capital.

ACCOMMODATIONS YOU CAN AFFORD ALONG THE WAY

Trinidad Guest House 💥💥 *Kids*   This is the latest reincarnation of one of the best-known *paradors* in Spain, Parador Martorell, which existed until late in 2000, when new owners took over and renamed the property. This guesthouse stands at the island's most impressive beach. When you arrive, you'll enter an open courtyard, which will have to suffice for your alfresco outings, because there are no grounds. The main reason for staying here is Luquillo Beach, which has shady palm groves, crescent beaches, coral reefs for snorkeling and scuba diving, and a surfing area. For the family who likes to spend the day on the beach, this is a fine and modestly priced choice. Bedrooms are small to midsize, each comfortably furnished, coming with a compact, tiled bathroom with a shower stall. Families share many of the rooms, which come with or without private bathroom. Not all units are air-conditioned. Breakfast always features plenty of freshly picked fruit and homemade breads and compotes.

6A Ocean Dr., Luquillo, PR 00773. (At km 36.2 along Rte. 3, turn toward the shore, then turn left and drive 4 short blocks.) ✆ **787/889-2710.** Fax 787/889-0640. trinidad51@aol.com. 11 units, 7 with bathroom. $70–$75 single or double without bathroom, $86–$107 single or double with bathroom. Rates include continental breakfast. MC, V. **Amenities:** Babysitting. *In room:* A/C (some units), TV.

WESTERN PUERTO RICO & THE SOUTHWEST COAST

Start:	San Juan.
Finish:	San Juan.
Time:	Between 2 and 6 days, depending on how much of the itinerary you want to complete. The tour could run longer if you spend extra time at some of the stops along the way.
Best Times:	Monday to Friday, any sunny day.
Worst Times:	Weekends, when the roads are overcrowded with drivers from San Juan.

This tour begins with a foray into the famous Karst district of Puerto Rico. Along the way, you'll see the Taíno Indian Ceremonial Ball Park, Río Camuy Cave Park, and Arecibo Observatory. You'll then emerge from the island's interior to begin a roundabout tour of the west and south coasts, taking in Guajataca Beach, Mayagüez, San Germán, Phosphorescent Bay, Ponce, Coamo, and numerous other towns and attractions.

A broad highway, Route 22 links San Juan with its western frontiers. The first major stop is the city of Arecibo, directly north of Karst Country. However, there's an interesting detour along the way.

Take Highway 22 west from San Juan until you reach the intersection with Route 140, at which point you head south (signposted to the town of Jayuya). Unless you're in a hurry, you can allow a leisurely hour's drive from San Juan. But traffic is often heavy along Highway 22, since this is a major trucking route for carrying supplies to and from the capital.

Route 140 will take you south through some of the most dramatic mountain scenery in Puerto Rico. At the intersection with Route 141, cut onto this highway and follow it south. It's signposted all the way to Jayuya.

① Jayuya

A village in the middle of the Cordillera Central and home to the **Parador Hacienda Gripiñas,** Jayuya is a former coffee plantation where you can catch a very authentic and unique glimpse of the old days (see "Accommodations You Can Afford Along the Way," at the end of this tour).

If you decide to make this restful side-trip, pick up the trail again by returning on Route 527 to Route 140, then travel west on Route 140 until you pass Lake Caonillas. Here turn onto Route 111 west, and in about 10 miles you'll reach Utuado.

② Utuado

Utuado is a small mountain town boasting the **Hotel La Casa Grande,** with accommodations, a restaurant, and a pool (see "Accommodations You Can Afford Along the Way," at the end of this tour).

From Utuado, continue west for 20 minutes on Route 111 to km 12.3, where you'll find the Taíno Indian Ceremonial Park.

③ Taíno Indian Ceremonial Park

Archaeologists have dated this site to about 2 centuries before Europe's discovery of the New World. It's believed that the Taíno chief Guarionex gathered his subjects on this site to celebrate rituals and practice sports. Set on a 13-acre field surrounded by trees, some 14 vertical monoliths with colorful petroglyphs are arranged around a central sacrificial stone monument. The ball complex also includes a museum, open daily 9am to 5pm; admission is free. There's also a gallery, Herencia Indigena, where you can buy Taíno relics at reasonable prices, including the sought-after *Cemis* (Taíno idols) and figures of the famous little frog, the coquí. The

Taínos have long gone, and much that was here is gone with them. The site is of special interest to those with academic pursuits, but of only passing interest to the lay visitor. However, it makes a good stop along the route. You can walk around and stretch your legs before continuing with the tour.

Continue west on Route 111 for another 20 minutes, to the town of Lares, and then turn onto Route 129 north. Drive about 3½ miles, then turn right onto Route 4456, and you'll soon reach the Río Camuy Caves.

❹ Río Camuy Caves

The world's third-largest underground river, Río Camuy runs through a network of caves, canyons, and sinkholes that have been cut through the island's limestone base over the course of millions of years. The caves, known to both the pre-Columbian Taíno peoples and local Puerto Rican farmers, came to the attention of speleologists in the 1950s. See "Northwestern Puerto Rico," earlier in this chapter, for more details.

After your tour of the caves, follow the signs northeast (it's signposted) to the hamlet of Bayaney along Route 134. This takes only 10 minutes. Pass through the town and continue along Route 134 north until you reach the intersection with Route 635 heading east toward the town of Esperanza. Before reaching the town, take a small road (Rte. 625) south for 10 minutes to the Arecibo Observatory.

❺ Arecibo Observatory

Officially the National Astronomy and Ionosphere Center of Cornell University, this observatory has the world's largest and most sensitive radar/radiotelescope. It features a 20-acre dish, or radio mirror, set in an ancient sinkhole 1,000 feet in diameter and 167 feet deep, allowing scientists to examine the ionosphere, planets, and moon with powerful radar signals and to monitor natural radio emissions from distant galaxies, pulsars, and quasars. See "Northwestern Puerto Rico," earlier in this chapter, for more details.

When you're ready to leave the observatory, follow Route 625 north until reaching the town of Esperanza. From here, continue north on the same road (now called Rte. 635) toward Arecibo. Signs will point the way to Highway 22, the major traffic artery linking San Juan with the west. On the southern outskirts of Arecibo, you can either return east to San Juan if your time is limited or continue with the tour, this time heading west along Highway 22. This express highway from San Juan will come to an end on the western outskirts of Arecibo. At the point where Highway 22 terminates, pick up Route 2 and follow it west for about 8 miles, until you come to Quebradillas.

❻ Quebradillas

Beautiful Guajataca Beach and two *paradores* are only a 15-mile trip from Arecibo along Route 2 in the vicinity of this small town near the sea. Guajataca is fine for sunning and collecting shells, but it's a *playa peligrosa* (dangerous unless you're a strong swimmer). Parador Vistamar is located here (see "Accommodations You Can Afford Along the Way," at the end of this tour).

Instead of continuing west along Route 2 to the dull city of Aguadilla, you can cut south from Quebradillas along Route 113, which in 7 miles will take you to Lago de Guajataca, one of Puerto Rico's most beautiful lakes. After traversing its 2½-mile shoreline, you'll see signposts pointing the way to the town of San Sebastián, a 7-mile drive west along Route 119. As you travel this region, you'll be on the northern border of the richest coffee-growing district.

Once you reach San Sebastián, follow Route 109 southwest to the town of La Parade and continue west along this route until reaching the slightly larger town of Añasco. This is an area of many coffee plantations, but they're private and not open to visitors.

Once at Añasco, you'll be just 6½ miles northeast of Mayagüez. To reach it, continue along Route 109 for about 10 minutes until you get back on the previously traveled Route 2.

❼ Mayagüez

Mayagüez is the Commonwealth's western port city (see "Mayagüez," earlier in this chapter).

When you're ready to leave Mayagüez, continue southeast along Route 2 for 11½ miles, until you reach San Germán.

⑧ San Germán

Puerto Rico's second-oldest town and a little museum piece included in the National Register of Historic Places (see "Ponce," earlier in this chapter).

On a knoll at one end of town stands the chapel of the **Iglesia Porta Coeli** ✿. This is one of the gems of the town's 249 noteworthy sites.

After visiting San Germán, and if you're now ready for some beaches, allow 40 minutes to travel 6 miles on Route 102 west to Cabo Rojo, from which you can make a connection onto Route 307, heading south to Boquerón Beach.

⑨ Boquerón Beach

This is one of Puerto Rico's best beaches for swimming. There's a comfortable *parador* with a good restaurant only 2 blocks away (**Parador Boquemar;** see "Accommodations You Can Afford," above). The beach also has facilities, including lockers and changing places, plus kiosks that rent watersports equipment.

After time at the beach at Boquerón, you can discover more beaches in the east.

From Boquerón, leave along Route 101 heading east and following the signs to the town of Lajas. Once at Lajas, get on Route 116 heading directly south. Once you reach the intersection with 304, get on this road and drive directly south to La Parguera.

⑩ La Parguera

This is a small fishing village with the **Parador Villa Parguera** and the **Parador Posada Porlamar** (see "Accommodations You Can Afford Along the Way," at the end of this tour).

If you have the good fortune to find yourself in La Parguera on a moonless night, go to Phosphorescent Bay. A boat leaves Villa Parguera pier nightly 7:30pm to 12:30am, depending on the demand, and heads for this small bay to the east. Here a pitch-black night will facilitate a marvelous show, since you can see fish leave a luminous streak on the water's surface and watch the boat's wake glimmer in the dark. This phenomenon is produced by a large colony of dinoflagellates, a microscopic form of marine life that produces sparks of chemical light when their nesting is disturbed.

Next, take Route 304 up to Route 116 and drive west through Ensenada. At Guánica, you can turn south and follow Route 333 out to Caña Gorda Beach for lunch or a swim. While here, look for the cacti that flourish in this unusually dry region. Back on Route 116, drive north to Palomas, where you can take Route 2 into Ponce.

⑪ Ponce

This is an old colonial city with many interesting restaurants, inns, and sights (see "Ponce," above).

When you're ready to leave Ponce, take Route 1 east toward Guayama. At the town of San Isabel, you might want to take an interesting detour north along Route 153 to Coamo.

⑫ Coamo

Along the way to this town, you'll see signs pointing to the Baños de Coamo. Legend has it that these hot springs were the Fountain of Youth sought by Ponce de León. It's believed that the Taíno, during pre-Columbian times, held rituals and pilgrimages here as they sought health and well-being. Between 1847 and 1958, the site was a center for rest and relaxation for Puerto Ricans and others, some on their honeymoons, others in search of the curative powers of the geothermal springs. The baths are in poor condition—you can use them, but the experience is hardly special today.

After a look at the baths, you can backtrack. But instead of going all the way back to Route 1, get on Route 52, heading east for a 20-mile drive to Guayama.

⑬ Guayama

This is a green and beautiful small town with steepled churches and the **Casa Cautiño Museum,** on the main plaza of town (✆ 787/864-0600). It's open Wednesday to Sunday 10am to 4pm, and admission is $1 for adults and 50¢ for seniors, students, and children 7 to 12 (free for 6 and under). This museum is in a turn-of-the-century mansion once occupied by the Cañuelo family. It contains all their original belongings and is a showplace for fine furnishings and pictures of the prize horses for which Guayama is famous. Just minutes from town is Arroyo Beach, a tranquil place to spend an afternoon but lacking facilities.

> To begin the final leg back to San Juan, take Route 15 north. If you take this road in spring or summer, you'll be surrounded by the brilliant colors of flowering trees. This route connects with express Highway 52 going north to San Juan, a trip of about an hour, depending on traffic.

ACCOMMODATIONS YOU CAN AFFORD ALONG THE WAY
AT JAYUYA

Parador Hacienda Gripiñas   A former coffee plantation about 2½ hours from San Juan, the Hacienda Gripiñas is reached by a long, narrow, and curvy road. The plantation ambience is everywhere—created by ceiling fans, splendid gardens, hammocks on a porch gallery where you can sit and enjoy a piña colada, and more than 20 acres of coffee-bearing bushes. You'll taste the home-grown product when you order the inn's aromatic brew.

Most of the modest rooms have ceiling fans, and, although the rooms vary in size, they're kept neat as a pin. Badly needed renovations were completed in 1999. Mattresses are now firm, and the shower-only bathrooms, although small, are neatly arranged. For meals, stick to the restaurant's Puerto Rican dishes rather than its international cuisine. You can swim in the two chilly mountain pools (away from the main building), soak up the sun, or enjoy the nearby sights, like the Taíno Indian Ceremonial Ball Park at Utuado. Boating is possible 30 minutes away at Lake Caonillas. The *parador* is also near the Río Camuy Cave Park.

Rte. 527, km 2.5 (P.O. Box 387), Jayuya, PR 00664. ℂ 787/828-1717. Fax 787/828-1719. www. haciendagripinas.com. 20 units. Year-round $95 single; $125 double. Rates include breakfast and dinner. AE, MC, V. From Jayuya, head east via Rte. 144; at the junction with Rte. 527, go south for 1½ miles. **Amenities:** Restaurant, 2 pools. *In room:* A/C, TV.

AT UTUADO

Hotel La Casa Grande 🏕   This hotel lies on 107 acres of a former coffee plantation in the mountainous heartland of the island about 2½ hours from San Juan. It has been vastly improved since its takeover by Steven Weingarten and his wife, Marlene, who's a gourmet cook. Steven is still a practicing attorney in New York City, commuting to Puerto Rico on a regular basis. Each comfortably but simply furnished medium-size room has a ceiling fan, balcony, hammock, and mountain view, plus a good bed with a firm mattress and a compact, tiled bathroom with shower. There's a pool, and nature trails are carved out of the jungle.

Marlene presides over Jungle Jane's Restaurant, which serves an array of delectably prepared international and Puerto Rican dishes. Even if you're not a guest, you can feast here daily. It might make an ideal luncheon stop if you're touring in the area.

P.O. Box 616, Caonillas, Utuado, PR 00761. ℂ 888-343-2272 in the U.S., or 787/894-3939. Fax 787/894-3532. www.hotelcasagrande.com. 20 units. Year-round $85 single or double. AE, MC, V. From Utuado, head south via Rte. 111 until you reach Rte. 140; then head west until you come to the intersection with Rte. 612 and follow 612 south for about ½ mile. **Amenities:** Restaurant, bar, pool, laundry. *In room:* Ceiling fans, no phone.

AT QUEBRADILLAS

Parador Vistamar   High atop a mountain, this 1970s *parador,* one of the largest on Puerto Rico, overlooks greenery and a seascape in the Guajataca area.

The small rooms are comfortably furnished with good beds, but the overall look is a rather bland island-style motel. Each unit comes with a compact, tiled bathroom with shower stall. This is hardly a festive resort, but you get reasonable comfort at a decent price. There are gardens and intricate paths carved into the side of the mountain where you can enjoy the fragrance of the tropical flowers. Or you might choose to search for the calcified fossils that abound on the carved mountainside. For a unique experience, you can try your hand at freshwater fishing in the only river on Puerto Rico with green waters, just down the hill from the hotel. Flocks of rare tropical birds are frequently seen in the nearby mangroves.

A short drive from the hotel will bring you to the Punta Borinquén Golf Course. Tennis courts are just down the hill from the inn itself. Sightseeing trips to the nearby Arecibo are available. Another popular visit is to the plaza in Quebradillas, where you can tour the town in a horse-driven coach. Back at the hotel, prepare yourself for a typical Puerto Rican dinner or choose from the international menu in the dining room with its view of the ocean.

6205 Rte. 113N (P.O. Box T-38), Quebradillas, PR 00678. ✆ **787/895-2065.** Fax 787/895-2294. www. paradorvistamar.com. 55 units. Year-round $76–$112.50 single or double. Extra person over age 12 costs $20; up to 2 children age 12 and under stay free in parents' room. AE, DC, MC, V. At Quebradillas, head northwest on Rte. 2, then go left at the junction with Rte. 113 for ½ mile. **Amenities:** Restaurant. *In room:* A/C, TV.

AT LA PARGUERA

Parador Posada Porlamar   Life in a simple fishing village plus all the modern conveniences you want in a vacation are what you'll find here. The rooms are plain and, although neat, don't invite lingering; some are better than others, as they're larger and contain more recently renewed mattresses and in a few cases a balcony with a minibar, plus a small sitting room. The best are on the third floor. If possible, ask to look at a room before committing yourself; of course, you can do that only when the hotel isn't full. All units come with small, shower-only bathrooms. Paradora Villa Parguera (see below) has more style and flair. The area is famous for its Phosphorescent Bay and good fishing, especially for snapper. If you like to collect seashells, you can beachcomb. Other collectors' items found here are fossilized crustacea and marine plants. If you want to fish, you can rent a boat at the nearby villages, and you can even cook your catch in a communal kitchen. The inn has added a pool and a dive shop and can arrange snorkeling, kayaking, windsurfing, water-skiing, and boat rides.

Rte. 304 (P.O. Box 405), La Parguera, Lajas, PR 00667. ✆ **787/899-4015.** Fax 787/899-5558. www. posadaporlamar.com. 35 units. Year-round Sun–Thurs $75–$95 single or double (rates include continental breakfast); Fri–Sat $145 double (rates include breakfast and dinner). AE, MC, V. Drive west along Rte. 2 until you reach the junction of Rte. 116; then head south along Rte. 116 and Rte. 304. **Amenities:** Restaurant, pool, dive shop. *In room:* A/C, TV, coffeemaker, hair dryer, safe.

Parador Villa Parguera   The water in the nearby bay is too polluted for swimming, but guests here can still enjoy a view of the water and take a dip in the pool. This *parador*—a classic fishermen's inn—is known for its seafood dinners (the fish aren't caught in the bay), its comfortable and colorfully decorated rooms, and its location next to the phosphorescent waters of one of the coast's best-known bays. The rooms have either a balcony or a terrace. Furnishings are in a tropical motif, with firm mattresses resting on good beds. Units range from small to medium, and each has a small, tiled bathroom with a shower stall.

The spacious dining room offers daily specials, as well as chef's favorites, like fish filet stuffed with lobster and shrimp. Both international and Puerto Rican specialties are served. Nonguests are welcome. There's a play area for children.

Because the inn is popular with the residents of San Juan on weekends, there's a special weekend package for a 2-night minimum stay.

304 Main St. (P.O. Box 273), La Parguera, Lajas, PR 00667. ☎ **787/899-7777.** Fax 787/899-6040. www. villaparguera.com. 62 units. Year-round Sun–Thurs $96–$107 single or double; Fri–Sat $350–$375 double-occupancy packages for 2 days (including half board). 2 children 9 and under stay free in parents' room. AE, DC, MC, V. Drive west along Rte. 2 until you reach the junction with Rte. 116; then head south along Rte. 116 and Rte. 304. **Amenities:** Restaurant, pool. *In room:* A/C, TV.

11 Vieques ⓧ

About 6 miles east of the big island of Puerto Rico lies Vieques (Bee-*ay*-kase), an island about twice the size of Manhattan, with some 9,400 inhabitants and scores of palm-lined white-sand beaches. Since World War II, some two thirds of the 21-mile-long island has belonged to the U.S. military. Much of the government-owned land is now leased for cattle grazing, and when there are no military maneuvers the public can visit the beaches, which are sometimes restricted. Being allowed use of the land doesn't, however, totally cover local discontent and protest at the presence of the Navy and Marine Corps personnel on the island.

GETTING THERE

The **Puerto Rico Port Authority** (☎ 787/863-0852) operates two ferries a day from the eastern port of Fajardo to Vieques in about 45 to 60 minutes each way. The round-trip fare is $4 for adults and $2 for children 10 and under. Tickets on the morning ferry leaving on Saturday and Sunday sell out quickly, requiring passengers to be in line at the ticket window in Fajardo before 8am to be certain of a seat on the 9:30am boat. Otherwise, they must wait until the 3pm ferry. In Vieques call ☎ 787/741-8331 for more information.

  Vieques Airlink (☎ 787/722-3736) operates flights from Isla Grande Airport in San Juan. Five flights leave throughout the day, taking 20 minutes and costing $43 one-way or $80 round-trip. Service from San Juan is also provided by **Isla Nena Airlines** (☎ 787/791-5110).

GETTING AROUND

Public cabs or vans called *públicos* transport people around the island. **Island Car Rental,** Route 201 (☎ 787/741-1666), is one of the two largest car-rental companies, with an inventory of stripped-down Suzukis that usually offer dependable, bare-bones transport to many of the island's beautiful but hard-to-reach beaches. Rates begin at $45 per day.

ACCOMMODATIONS YOU CAN AFFORD

Crow's Nest Inn ⓧ   Liz O'Dell, one of the most hospitable innkeepers on Vieques, runs this inviting little lodge on 5 hilltop acres with ocean views, with the nearest beach a 5-minute car ride away. The units are housed in a pair of two-story buildings separated by a large patio and gardens overlooking the ocean. The rooms are decorated in a typical Caribbean motif with sitting areas, kitchenettes, ceiling fans, and reading lights over the good beds; all but two are air-conditioned. The bathrooms are tidily maintained, with tiled shower units. The guesthouse operates a good restaurant, serving Puerto Rican and international dishes at breakfast and dinner. This is an adult retreat, and children under 12 are discouraged. Two locals will take you out fishing, and 2-hour horseback rides through the hills can be arranged.

P.O. Box 1521, Barrio Florida, Vieques, PR 00765. ☎ **787/741-0033.** Fax 787/741-1294. www.crowsnestvieques. com. 12 units. Year-round $65–$85 single or double; $140 suite. AE, MC, V. **Amenities:** Restaurant, pool. *In room:* A/C, kitchenette, ceiling fans, no phone.

La Casa del Francés ⭐⭐   This quirky inn is about a 15-minute drive southeast of Isabel Segunda, just north of the center of Esperanza. Set in a field near the southern coastline, it has columns and an imposing facade. In the 1950s, it was acquired by Irving Greenblatt, who installed a pool and, with his partner, Frank Celeste, transformed 18 of its high-ceilinged rooms into an old-fashioned R&R oasis for his executives. The eclectic rooms are rather plain and the beds old, but there's plenty of space, except in the small, shower-only bathrooms. Many of the units enjoy access to the two-story verandas ringing the white facade.

However, note that readers have had mixed reactions to this inn. Some praise it, while others have complained. If you don't like the personality of Mr. Greenblatt (and many readers don't), you really won't fit in here.

The fixed-price dinners are attended by many island residents who enjoy the Italian, barbecue, or Puerto Rican buffets presented beneath a 200-year-old mahogany tree.

P.O. Box 458, Barrio Esperanza, Vieques, PR 00765. (787/741-3751. Fax 787/741-2330. www.enchanted-isle. com/lacasa. 18 units. Winter $153.50 single or double. Off-season $98 single or double. MAP (available in winter only) $20 per person. AE, MC, V. **Amenities:** Restaurant, pool. *In room:* Ceiling fans, no phone.

La Finca Caribe Guest House & Cottages   This bare-bones place, on a forested hillside 3 miles from Sun Bay in the center of the island north of Esperanza, caters to budget-conscious travelers and youthful adventurers. The present owners, the Merwin family, have renamed it *finca*, which means "a rustic estate" in Spanish. The centerpiece of the property is a plywood-sided house built by a previous owner with student assistants in 1986. Today the guesthouse enjoys a spacious porch with hammocks and swinging chairs. The rooms are rustic and small, with thin mattresses. A series of outbuildings contains a bathhouse and communal kitchen. On a hill, the family-style two-story wooden cottage sleeps three to four comfortably; it comes with a kitchen, a bathroom, decks, and a living area. A *casita*, another cottage nestled in the garden, can accommodate three with its sleeping loft and queen bed. It has a private deck and its own kitchen. A nonchlorinated pool was installed, and bike rentals are available.

Rte. 995, km 2.2, Barrio Pilon (P.O. Box 1332), Vieques, PR 00765. ☎ **787/741-0495.** www.lafinca.com. 6 units, none with bathroom; 2 cottages. Year-round $65 single; $80 double; cottage $525–$800 weekly 2 to 4 occupants. Extra person $15 (in single or double). MC, V. **Amenities:** Pool, bike rental, babysitting. *In room:* No phone.

Water's Edge Guest House *Value*   Just north of town, this is one of the best-appointed guesthouses on the island. Built of adobe cinderblock, stucco, and terra-cotta tile, it's a two-story building in a Mexican hacienda design. There's a second-floor deck for ocean-facing rooms. All the medium-size rooms are tastefully furnished. The mattresses are firm enough for a good night's sleep and the tiny bathrooms with shower units are adequate for the purpose. After new owners took over in 1998, the rooms were completely redone and brightened with Caribbean colors and mosquito netting over the beds. A good beach is only a few steps away, and there's a pool on site. You can have breakfast or dinner here at The Oasis at Water's Edge.

P.O. Box 1374, Isabel Segunda, Vieques, PR 00765. ☎ **787/741-1128.** Fax 787/741-0690. www. watersedgeguesthouse.com. 11 units. Winter $76.30 single; $92.65 double; $136.25 suite. Off-season $65.40 single; $81.75 double; $98.10 suite. Children 11 and under stay free in parents' room. AE, MC, V. **Amenities:** Restaurant, pool, babysitting. *In room:* Minifridge, ceiling fans.

WORTH A SPLURGE

Hacienda Tamarindo ✦   This is the only rival to the Inn on the Blue Horizon, and it's one charming hacienda—the creation of Linda and Burr Vail, who fled cold Vermont. It lies on a hill swept with trade winds, opening onto panoramic views of the Caribbean. An ancient tamarind tree, for which the inn takes its name, stands in the middle of the lobby, rising up three floors. Each of the rooms is individually decorated by Linda, an interior decorator who furnished them with original art, often antiques, and collectibles. They contain first-rate mattresses and good-size bathrooms with tiled showers; some bathrooms offer Jacuzzis and private terraces. About half the rooms are air-conditioned; the others are cooled by trade winds. A full breakfast with tropical fruit is offered on the terrace on the floor above. For dinner all you have to do is stroll down the hill to the Inn on the Blue Horizon, with its well-known Cafe Blu.

Children under 15 aren't permitted, as this is mainly an adult retreat. The inn provides box and poolside picnic lunches, and a well-stocked bar is available, operating on the honor system. A stroll past palms and mahogany trees will bring you to a pool, where the view is panoramic.

Rte. 996 (P.O. Box 1569), Vieques, PR 00765. ☎ 787/741-8525. Fax 787/741-3215. www.enchanted-isle. com/tamarindo. 16 units. Year-round $145–$160 single or double; $200 suite. Rates include breakfast. AE, MC, V. **Amenities:** Bar, pool, massage. *In room:* A/C (some units), no phone.

Inn on the Blue Horizon ✦   Although known mainly for its restaurant, Cafe Blu, the finest on the island (see below), this is also one of the leading inns on Vieques. It was created by two transplanted New Yorkers, Billy Knight and James Weis, who added four more rooms for a total of nine. The rooms are medium in size, opening onto views of the courtyard or the ocean. The beds are double, queen-size, or king-size. Each accommodation is individually decorated, often with antiques. Three of the rooms are in the main house, and the other six are in a trio of *casitas*. Seven of the units contain porches with oversized chairs for taking in that ocean view. Each unit has a neatly arranged, compact, tiled bathroom with a shower. Trade winds are sufficient to keep the rooms cooled, although two rooms in the main house are air-conditioned. Children 13 and under are not accepted.

Rte. 996 (P.O. Box 1556), Vieques, PR 00765. *C* **787/741-3318.** Fax 787/741-0522. www.innonthebluehorizon. com. 9 units. Year-round $204–$290 single or double. AE, MC, V. **Amenities:** Restaurant, bar, pool. *In room:* Ceiling fans, no phone.

GREAT DEALS ON DINING

Cafe Blu *✦* CONTINENTAL/CARIBBEAN   At last Vieques offers a restaurant that can compete in quality with some of the finer dining rooms of San Juan. Transplanted New Yorkers James Weis and Billy Knight have opened this charming eatery and hired creative Michael Glatz as its chef. He's a graduate of the Culinary Institute of America, with 18 years' experience in fine restaurants before coming here. To get you going, try his couscous crab cakes with fresh baby spinach leaves, sprinkled with a sun-dried tomato–lemon oil, or his mushroom papparedelle with shiitake mushrooms, fresh sage, and roasted garlic. Depending on what's available at the market, he's inspired to make a special soup every day. His main courses are equally distinguished, ranging from sweet spice pork tenderloin, pan-seared and oven-roasted with dark rum, to charcoal-grilled boneless chicken breast with curried pineapple-and-ginger chutney.

By all means come here for a drink. *Newsweek* named its Blue Bar as one of the top bars in the world.

In the Inn on the Blue Horizon, Rte. 996. *C* **787/741-3318.** Reservations required. Main courses $15–$25. AE, MC, V. Thurs–Sun 6–10pm.

La Campesina *✦* INTERNATIONAL   Designed to reflect indigenous dwellings, this unusual and excellent restaurant is built a few steps from one of the richest archeological deposits of Taíno artifacts in the Caribbean. It's on the southwestern end of the island (follow the coast road from Esperanza) in the untrammeled fishing village of La Hueca. In a room lined with baskets and weavings amid trailing vines of jasmine and flickering candles, you can enjoy a cuisine of distinctly tropical or uniquely Puerto Rican flair. Fresh herbs like cilantro, tasty varieties of local vegetables, and fruits like papaya, mango, and tamarind served in relishes and pastries, complement the menu. Nightly specials might include avocado rémoulade, conch fritters, lobster ravioli, local fish, and great steak.

La Hueca. *C* **787/741-1239.** Reservations recommended. Main courses $12–$17. MC, V. Tues–Sat 6–10pm. Closed Oct–Nov 15.

Trade Winds STEAK/SEAFOOD   You'll find this restaurant at the ocean esplanade on the south side of the island in the fishing village of Esperanza. It features the Topside Bar for relaxing with drinks with a view of the water, and the Upper Deck for open-air dining. Menu items include several shrimp dishes, Jamaican jerk beef, and fresh fish daily. The chef's specialty is grilled plantain with shrimp and lobster. A pasta of the day is also featured, served with a house or Caesar salad. Included in the price of a main dish are bread and butter, a salad, two fresh vegetables, and a choice of rice or potato.

At the Trade Winds Guest House, Flamboyan 107C, Barrio Esperanza. *C* **787/741-8666.** Reservations recommended. Meals $12–$24. AE, MC, V. Winter Wed–Sun 7:30am–2pm and 6–9:30pm; off-season Thurs–Sat 6–9:30pm.

HITTING THE BEACHES

On the south coast, **Esperanza,** once a center for the island's sugarcane industry and now a pretty little fishing village, lies near **Sun Bay (Sombe) public beach.** Sun Bay is a magnificent government-run crescent of sand. The fenced area has picnic tables, a bathhouse, and a parking lot. Admission is $1 per car.

Few of the island's 40-some beaches have even been named, but most have their loyal supporters—loyal, that is, until too many people learn about them, in which case the devotees can always find another good spot. The U.S. Navy named some of the strands, such as **Green Beach,** a beautiful clean stretch at the island's west end. **Red** and **Blue Beaches,** also with Navy nomenclature, are great jumping-off points for snorkelers. Other popular beaches are **Navia, Half Moon, Orchid,** and **Silver,** but if you continue along the water, you might find your own nameless secluded cove with a fine strip of sand. **Mosquito Bay,** sometimes called Phosphorescent Bay because it glows with phosphorescence on moonless nights, is a short way east of Esperanza (see below).

THE LUMINOUS WATERS OF PHOSPHORESCENT BAY

One of the major attractions on the island is **Mosquito Bay** ⟨⋆⟩, also called **Phosphorescent Bay,** with its glowing waters produced by tiny bioluminescent organisms that live near the surface. These organisms dart away from boats, leaving eerie blue-white trails of phosphorescence. *The Vieques Times* wrote: "By any name the bay can be a magical, psychedelic experience, and few places in the world can even come close to the intensity of concentration of the dinoflagellates called pyrodiniums (whirling fire). They are tiny ($\frac{1}{500}$-in.) swimming creatures that light up like fireflies when disturbed, but nowhere are there so many fireflies. Here a gallon of bay water may contain almost three-quarter of a million." The ideal time to tour is on a cloudy, moonless night, and you should wear a swimsuit since it's possible to swim in these glowing waters.

Shannon Grasso (✆ 787/741-0720) operates trips aboard her *Luminosa I* and *Luminosa II* from La Casa del Francés (see "Accommodations You Can Afford," above). These trips aren't offered around the time of the full moon. The charge for these trips is $20 for adults and $12 for children, and most jaunts last about 90 minutes.

SEEING THE SIGHTS

The Fort Conde de Morasol Museum, Magnolia 471 (✆ 787/741-1717), is the major man-made attraction on the island. In the 1840s, Count Mirasol convinced the Spanish government to build a defensive fortress here. Today the carefully restored fort houses a museum of art and history celebrating the story of Vieques. There are Indian relics, displays of the Spanish conquest, and old flags of the Danes, British, and French. The French sugarcane planters and their African slaves are depicted, and there's even a bust of Simón Bolívar based on a visit to Puerto Rico by the great liberator. A unique collection of maps shows how the world's cartographers envisioned Vieques. Since the U.S. Navy occupies more than two thirds of the island, its presence and controversial role are chronicled. The museum and fort are open Wednesday to Sunday 10am to 4pm, charging $1 for adults and 50¢ for children.

12 Culebra

A tranquil little island, Culebra lies in a mini-archipelago of 24 chunks of land, rocks, and cays in the sea, halfway between Puerto Rico and St. Thomas, U.S. Virgin Islands. Just 7 miles long and 3 miles wide, with nearly 2,000 residents, the inviting island is in U.S. territorial waters belonging to Puerto Rico, 18 miles away. This little-known year-round vacation spot in what was once called the Spanish Virgin Islands was settled as a Spanish colony in 1886, but like Puerto Rico and Vieques, it became part of the United States after the 1898 Spanish–American War. In fact, Culebra's only town, **Dewey,** was named for Adm. George Dewey, American hero of that war, although the locals call the fishing village **Puebla.**

For a long time, beginning in 1909, Culebra was used by the U.S. Navy as a gunnery range, and it even became a practice bomb site in World War II. In 1975, after years of protest over military abuse of the island's environment, the Navy withdrew from Culebra, with the understanding that the island be kept as a nature preserve and habitat for the many rare species of birds, turtles, and fish that abound there.

GETTING THERE

From the port of Fajardo, the **Puerto Rico Port Authority** operates two ferries a day from the Puerto Rican mainland to Culebra, taking about an hour each way. The round-trip fare is $4.50 for adults and $1 for children 3 to 11. For information and reservations, call ℂ **787/742-3161** on Culebra or ℂ **787/863-0705** in Fajardo.

Culebra is served by craft flying in from San Juan International Airport via **Vieques Air Link** (ℂ **787/722-3736**) or **Isla Nena Air Service** (ℂ **787/741-6362**).

ACCOMMODATIONS YOU CAN AFFORD

Casa Ensenada   This is an old but still sturdy guesthouse right on the waterfront at Culebra harbor. The owner, Jackie Pendergast, came here on holiday a decade or so ago and fell in love with the place, making it her home. She welcomes guests to this offbeat island, housing them in one of her three apartments, each capable of accommodating from two to four guests. The units are named Pequeño, Mediano, and Grande, each with its own bedroom, small living room, and kitchen, with ceiling fans whirling overhead. The larger of the units opens onto a view of the bay at Ensenada Honda. Each unit has a small, tiled bathroom with shower. Guests relax in the patio with its hammocks or cook burgers on the gas grill to be served at picnic tables.

142 Calle Escudero, Dewey, Culebra, PR 00775. ℂ 787/742-3559. Fax 787/742-0278. 3 units. Winter $80–$130 apt. Off-season $65–$115 apt. Extra person $10. MC, V. **Amenities:** Kayak and motor boat rental. *In room:* A/C, TV, kitchen, ceiling fans.

Club Seabourne   Across the road from an inlet, about an 8-minute drive from town, is a concrete-and-wooden structure set in a garden of crotons and palms, lying at the mouth of one of the island's best harbors, Ensenada Honda. One of the island's few bonafide hotels, it offers eight villas, two cottages, one crow's nest, and four rooms inside the clubhouse. All units contain small shower-only bathrooms. The villas, set up as duplexes with staggered balconies and private entrances, are spacious and comfortable, opening onto views of Fulladosa Bay. Within each villa is one king-size bed and one twin bed, each with a comfortable mattress. The Crow's Nest is on the second floor of the clubhouse, with a queen-size bed, private entrance, and small balcony. Because of lush tropical landscaping, this nest doesn't offer much of a view. Each of the two rooms inside the clubhouse has a private patio, a queen-size bed, and an entry through the dining room. The two-bedroom cottage is the only unit with kitchen amenities. The cottage has a queen-size bed and two twin beds. Dive packages and watersports can be arranged at the office.

Fulladoza Rd. (P.O. Box 357), Culebra, PR 00775. ℂ 787/742-3169. Fax 787/742-3176. 15 units. Year-round $95–$125 clubhouse double; $110 Crow's Nest; $125 studio villa; $135 cottage. Rates include continental breakfast. AE, MC, V. From Dewey, follow Fulladoza Rd. along the south side of the bay for 1½ miles. **Amenities:** Pool. *In room:* A/C, no phone.

Villa Boheme   Directly on the harbor, opening onto Ensenada Honda Bay, this is the oldest established guesthouse on Culebra. It's not fancy in any way, but most guests are attracted to its laid-back style. Of the 11 rooms, 3 are efficiencies with their own kitchens. Those units on the second and third floors look out onto a deck area, and rooms on the third floor, the most desirable of all, have private balconies overlooking the water. The house is a traditional Caribbean structure with white walls and an open patio surrounded by palm trees and hammocks where guests hang out.

P.O. Box 218, Dewey, Culebra, PR 00775. ℂ/fax 787/742-3508. www.villaboheme.com. 11 units. Winter $87–$125 double. Off-season $70–$109 double. Extra person $15. AE, MC, V. **Amenities:** Communal kitchen, bike rental, kayaks. *In room:* A/C.

GREAT DEALS ON DINING

Club Seabourne PUERTO RICAN/CARIBBEAN   This is the major restaurant on the island. Overlooking Fulladoza Bay, the club's dining room features fresh lobster, shrimp, snapper, grouper, conch, steaks, and the occasional Puerto Rican specialty. Without ever rising to greatness, the cookery is always competent, the specialties tasty, especially if you stick to the seafood dishes. It also has a large patio and a nightly happy hour.

Fulladoza Rd. ℂ 787/742-3169. Reservations recommended. Main courses $8–$21. AE, MC, V. Daily 8am–2pm and 6–10pm. From Puebla, follow Fulladoza Rd. along the south side of the bay for 1½ miles.

El Caobo CREOLE/PUERTO RICAN   Lying on the main drag at the end of town, this is a modest choice but it remains popular with islanders. Doña Tina Ayala opened this pavilion next door to her home in 1990. The decor is simple with plastic-covered tables and some photographs of island scenes. There is a bar as modestly appointed as the restaurant that stays open until 10pm, serving a steady flow of beer, rum, and salsa. Doña personally cooks the dishes, an array of Creole specialties featuring such concoctions as *mofongo relleno* (mashed plantain with chicken or pork).

Barriada Clark H4. ℂ 787/742-3235. Main courses $7–$12. No credit cards. Daily 8am–8pm.

Mamacita's PUERTO RICAN/INTERNATIONAL   In Castelar near the pier, Mamacita's is the place to go for down-home Culebran cookery. The front is very West Indian in aura, with a bar partially exposed to the air, large windows, and huge ceiling fans. Impressive palms surround the saloon with its plain tables. The bar gets especially crowded on weekends. From the menu, there are several tempting options, including grilled sea bass and, on occasion, grilled Caribbean lobster. Of course, you can always ask that a steak be thrown on the grill for you. Other delectable selections are the fish salads, made with octopus, lobster, or mussels.

64 Castelar, Dewey. ℂ 787/742-0090. Reservations recommended on weekends. Main courses $12–$20; lunch platters $7.50. No credit cards. Daily 10:30am–3pm and 6–9pm. Bar daily 5–10:30pm.

BEACHES & A WILDLIFE REFUGE

The four tracts of the **Culebra Wildlife Refuge,** plus 23 other offshore islands, are managed by the U.S. Fish and Wildlife Service. Culebra is one of the most important turtle-nesting sites in the Caribbean. Large seabird colonies, notably terns and boobies, are seen.

Culebra's **white-sand beaches** (especially **Flamenco Beach**), the clear waters, and long coral reefs invite swimmers, snorkelers, and scuba divers. The landscape ranges from scrub and cactus to poincianas, frangipanis, and coconut palms.

Culebrita, which means Little Culebra, is a mile-long coral-isle satellite of Culebra, known for its hilltop lighthouse, the oldest in the West Indies, or so it's said. A favorite goal of boaters and a venue for kayaking, it possesses one of Puerto Rico's better beaches on its north side. The islet is also known for its nature's aquariums, or tide pools.

18

Saba

An extinct volcano, with no beaches or flat land, cone-shaped Saba is 5 square miles of rock—just 2½ miles wide at its widest point—carpeted in lush foliage that includes orchids (which grow in profusion), giant elephant ear, and Eucharist lilies. At its zenith, Mount Scenery, Saba reaches 2,900 feet. Under the sea, the volcanic walls that form Saba continue a sheer drop to great depths, making for some of the most panoramic dives in the Caribbean. Divers and hikers are increasingly attracted to the island, not the party person or gambler—and certainly not the beach buff.

Unless you're a serious hiker or diver, you might confine your look at Saba to a day trip from St. Maarten. If you're a self-sufficient type who demands almost no artificial amusement, then sleepy Saba might be your hideaway. You can find reasonably priced lodgings and cut-rate meals all over the island. In other words, Saba is a bargain for those who appreciate its unique charms.

Saba lies 150 miles east of Puerto Rico and 90 miles east of St. Croix. Most visitors fly over from the Dutch-held section of St. Maarten, 28 miles to the north.

1 Essentials

VISITOR INFORMATION

Before you go, you can get information at the **Saba Tourist Office,** P.O. Box 6322, Boca Raton, FL 33427 (© **800/722-2394** or 561/394-8580).

On the island, the **Saba Tourist Board** is at Lambees Place in the heart of Windwardside (© **599/416-2231**). It's open Monday to Thursday 8am to noon and 1 to 5pm and Friday 8am to noon and 1 to 4:30pm. The Internet address for Saba is **www.sabatourism.com**.

GETTING THERE

BY PLANE You can leave New York's JFK airport or Newark, New Jersey, in the morning and be at Captain's Quarters on Saba for dinner that night by taking a direct flight on either of the two airlines, **American Airlines** (© **800/433-7300** in the U.S.) flying out of JFK and **Continental Airlines** (© **800/231-0856**) flying out of Newark, that currently fly from the United States to **St. Maarten** (see chapters 17 and 22 for complete information and for other airlines with connections through San Juan). From Queen Juliana Airport there, you can take the 12-minute hop to Saba on **Winair (Windward Islands Airways International;** © **599/4-62255**).

Arriving by air from St. Maarten, travelers step from Winair's 20-passenger planes onto the tarmac of the **Juancho E. Yrausquin Airport** (© **599/416-2255**). The airstrip is one of the shortest (if not the shortest) landing strips in the world, stretching only 1,312 feet along the aptly named Flat Point, one of the few level areas on the island.

Many guests at hotels on St. Maarten fly over to Saba on the morning flight, spend the day sightseeing, and then return to St. Maarten on the afternoon flight. Winair connections can also be made on Saba to both St. Kitts and St. Eustatia.

GETTING AROUND

The traditional means of getting around on Saba is on foot, but we suggest that only the sturdy in heart and limb walk from The Bottom up to Windwardside. Many do, but you'd better have shoes that grip the ground, particularly after a recent rain.

BY TAXI   Taxis meet every flight. Up to four persons are allowed to share a cab, and there's no central number to call for service. The fare from the airport to Windwardside is $8 and $12.50 to The Bottom. A taxi from Windwardside to The Bottom is $6.50.

BY RENTAL CAR   None of the major U.S. rental companies maintains a branch on Saba, partly because most visitors opt to get around by taxi. In the unlikely event you should dare to drive a car on Saba, locally operated companies include **Johnson's Rental,** Windwardside (℮ **599/416-2269**), renting about six Mazdas, starting at $40 per day and including a full tank of gas and unlimited mileage. Some insurance is included in the rates, but you might be held partly responsible for any financial costs in the event of an accident. Because of the very narrow roads and dozens of cliffs, it's crucial to exercise caution when driving.

BY HITCHHIKING   Hitchhiking has long been an acceptable means of transport on Saba, where everybody seemingly knows everybody else. And if you hitchhike, you'll probably get to know everybody else, too. On our most recent sightseeing tour, our taxi rushed a sick child to the plane and picked up an old man to take him up the hill because he'd fallen and hurt himself.

 FAST FACTS: **Saba**

Banks The main bank on the island is **Barclays,** Windwardside (℮ **599/ 416-2216**), open Monday to Friday 8:30am to 2pm.

Currency Saba, like the other islands of the Netherlands Antilles, uses the **Netherlands Antilles guilder (NAf),** valued at 1.80NAf to U.S.$1. However, prices given here are in U.S. currency unless otherwise designated, since U.S. money is accepted by almost everybody.

Customs You don't have to go through Customs when you land at Juancho E. Yrausquin Airport, as this is a free port.

Documents The government requires that all U.S. and Canadian citizens show proof of citizenship, such as a passport or a birth certificate with a raised seal along with a government-issued photo ID. A return or ongoing ticket must also be provided. U.K. citizens must have a valid passport.

Drugstore Try **The Pharmacy,** The Bottom (℮ **599/416-3289**), open Monday to Friday 7:30am to 5:30pm.

Electricity Saba uses 110 volts AC (60 cycles), so most U.S.-made appliances don't need transformers or adapters.

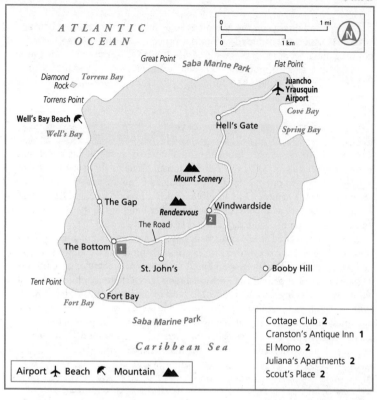

Cottage Club **2**
Cranston's Antique Inn **1**
El Momo **2**
Juliana's Apartments **2**
Scout's Place **2**

Airport ✈ Beach 🏊 Mountain ▲▲

Medical Care Saba's hospital complex is the **A. M. Edwards Medical Centre,** The Bottom (℡ **599/416-3289**).

Police Call ℡ **599/416-3237.**

Safety Crime on this island, where everyone knows everyone else, is practically nonexistent. But who knows? A tourist might rob you. It would be wise to safeguard your valuables.

Taxes The government imposes an 8% tourist tax on hotel rooms. If you're returning to St. Maarten or flying over to St. Eustatius, you must pay a $5 departure tax. If you're going anywhere else, however, a $10 tax is imposed.

Telecommunications Cables and international telephone calls can be placed at **Antelecon,** The Bottom (℡ **599/416-3211**). To call Saba from the United States, dial **011** (the international access code), then **599** (the country code for the Netherlands Antilles), and finally **4** (the area code for all Saba) and the five-digit local number. To make a call within Saba, only the five-digit local number is necessary.

Time Saba is on Atlantic standard time year-round, 1 hour earlier than eastern standard time. When the United States is on daylight saving time, clocks on Saba and the U.S. east coast read the same.

Tipping Restaurants on the island generally add a service charge of 10% to 15%. Ask if it's included before paying your tab. Most of the bigger hotels add a service charge, ranging from 10% to 15%; others include the charge in their tariff quotations. Taxi drivers expect tips of about 10% to 15%; maids should get $1.50 per day.

2 Accommodations You Can Afford

Cottage Club ✪ Small, intimate, and immersed in the architectural and aesthetic traditions of Saba, this hotel complex occupies about a half acre of steeply sloping and carefully landscaped terrain, a 2-minute walk from the center of the island's capital. Only its lobby evokes a historic setting: Designed of local stone, and set at an altitude above the other buildings of the complex, it's full of a collection of island antiques and lace curtains.

Each medium-sized studio apartment has a semiprivate patio, a living-room area, and a queen-size bed with a firm mattress. Bathrooms have showers and are well maintained. These units are housed in clapboard replicas of antique cottages—two studios per cottage—with red roofs, green shutters, white walls, and yellow trim. The interiors are breezy, airy, and comfortable. If you'd like a room with an ocean view, request no. 1 or no. 2. There's no bar or restaurant on the premises, but a nearby supermarket will deliver supplies on request. The owners of the establishment are three Saban brothers (Gary, Mark, and Dean) whose extended families all seem to assist in the maintenance of the place.

Windwardside, Saba, N.A. ℂ **599/412-2486.** Fax 599/416-2476. www.cottage-club.com. 10 units. Winter $145 studio apt for 1 or 2. Off-season $105 studio apt for 1 or 2. 3rd and 4th person $25 each; children 12 and under stay free in parents' room. MC, V. **Amenities:** Pool. *In room:* TV, kitchenette, ceiling fans.

Cranston's Antique Inn ✪ *(Finds)* Everyone congregates for rum drinks and gossip on the front terrace of this inn near the village roadway, north of Fort Bay. It's an old-fashioned house, more than 100 years old, with antique four-poster beds in all the rooms. Mr. Cranston, the owner, will gladly rent you the same bedroom where Queen Juliana spent a holiday in 1955. Aside from the impressive wooden beds, the furnishings are mostly hit or miss, and not much has changed since the Queen checked in oh-so-long-ago. The bedrooms are quite tiny, although the floral spreads jazz them up a bit. Come here for the old-time atmosphere and the cheap prices, not for any grand style. The biggest improvement is that all the rooms now have private—but extremely cramped—shower-only bathrooms.

Mr. Cranston has a good island cook, and she makes use of locally grown spices. Island dishes include goat meat, roast pork from Saba pigs, red snapper, and broiled grouper.

The Bottom, Saba, N.A. ℂ **599/416-3203.** Fax 599/416-3469. 6 units. Winter $125 single or double. Off-season $99 single or double. DISC, MC, V. **Amenities:** Restaurant, bar, pool. *In room:* A/C, TV.

El Momo A steep 10-minute trek up from Windwardside, this is Saba's least expensive accommodation. It's in a tropical garden and puts you close to nature in a fun, funky atmosphere. You'll soon get to know "the crew," including snakes, lizards, and iguanas. Angelica and Oliver, the mom and pop of the place, rent five small gingerbread cottages (really huts) that are merely sleeping rooms with platform beds. You may find the mattresses a bit thin, but tropical fabrics dress them up. *Warning:* The walls are rather thin, too, so you might not want to plan an amorous adventure. The only room with a bathroom is the honeymoon cottage; the rest share a communal area where guests hang a solar shower bag on hooks. One section is for those who like to take their shower out in the open with an audience; another offers a privacy wall. Ecotourists, backpackers, and scuba divers love the place. The small pool has a footbridge, fancifully called "the only bridge on Saba." Simple meals are prepared, with advance notification, for guests, who pay around $9 for wholesome dinners. An honor bar on the premises provides beer and wine but no hard liquor.

Jimmy's Hill (P.O. Box 519), Windwardside, Saba, N.A. ℂ **599/416-2265**. Fax 599/416-2265. www. elmomo.com. 5 units. Year-round $40 single; $50 double. DC, MC, V. **Amenities:** Restaurant, bar, small pool. *In room:* A/C, TV.

Juliana's Apartments   Built in 1985, this hostelry is set on a hillside. Each guest room is modern, immaculate, and simple but comfortably furnished. All have access to a sundeck and balconies opening onto beautiful views of the Caribbean, except nos. 1, 2, and 3, which are in the rear. Opt for one of upper-level rooms (7, 8, or 9), as they offer the best views. The shower-only bathrooms are small but adequate, and housekeeping wins high marks here. Also available are a 2½-room apartment, complete with kitchenette, and a renovated original Saban cottage, with two bedrooms, a spacious living room, a dining room, a TV, and a fully equipped kitchen.

Windwardside, Saba, N.A. ℂ **599/416-2269**. Fax 599/416-2389. www.julianas-hotel.com. 10 units. Winter $100 single; $125 double; $150 apt; $165 cottage. Off-season $70 single; $90 double; $125 apt; $145 cottage. Extra person $20. Dive packages available. AE, DISC, MC, V. **Amenities:** Restaurant, pool, recreation room, car rental. *In room:* Ceiling fans, no phone.

Scout's Place   Right in the center of the village, funky Scout's Place is hidden from the street and set on the ledge of a hill. With only 13 rooms, it's still the second-largest inn on the island. The old house has a large covered open-air dining room, where every table has a view of the sea. It's informal with a decor ranging from Surinam hand-carvings to red-and-black wicker peacock chairs to silver samovars. Guest rooms open onto an interior courtyard filled with flowers, and each has a view of the sea. The rooms are small and rather plain, except for the four-poster beds; many have linoleum floors and tiny TVs. The best units are on the lower floor, as they have French doors opening onto balconies fronting the ocean. Furniture is haphazard, but mattresses, although much used, are still comfortable. Bathrooms are also small, with shower only. The apartment with kitchenette is suitable for up five.

Windwardside, Saba, N.A. ℂ **599/416-2740**. Fax 599/416-2388. www.sabadivers.com. 13 units. Year-round $85 single or double; $100 apt for 2. Extra person $20. Rates include continental breakfast. MC, V. **Amenities:** Restaurant, bar, pool, dive shop. *In room:* TV (some units), fridge, ceiling fans, no phone.

3 Great Deals on Dining

At **Y2K Grill and Bakery,** Windwardside (ℂ **599/416-5390**), you'll find the island's best array of freshly baked bread, rolls, and sweets like pies and cakes. The staff also makes homemade soup, sandwiches, and even pizza daily. You can also pick up coffee and cold sodas. Daily lunch specials are offered 11:30am to 3pm. A deck and gazebo overlook Windwardside at Lambees Place next to the post office.

Guido's Pizzeria AMERICAN/PIZZA   Marcia Guido and her son, Giovanni, own this bustling pizzeria, where you can find basic familiar food. The pizzas come with all the standard toppings, even anchovies, served on crusts that are made fresh daily. There's also spaghetti and meatballs, burgers, and meatball sandwiches. As you wait for your meal, you might want to try your hand at the pool table. On Friday and Saturday nights, it's the hottest spot on the island (see "Saba After Dark," later in this chapter).

Windwardside. ✆ 599/416-2230. Main courses $7.50–$11; pizzas $5.50–$11. MC, V. Mon–Fri 6–10pm.

Lollipop's ☆ CARIBBEAN   Locals who gravitate here like the personality of owner Carmen Caines so much that they've nicknamed her "Lollipop." She's warm and gracious and even has guests picked up at their hotel and delivered to her spot, then taken back. She presents her West Indian fare on an outdoor terrace as well as indoors, cooking whatever was good at the market that day (that usually means fresh grilled fish). She's known for her land crab and also prepares a wicked curried goat. Shrimp and lobster are also regularly featured. Lollipop is so sweet that after dinner you'll want to give her a kiss, too!

St. John's. ✆ 599/416-3330. Reservations recommended for dinner. Dinner (including soup/salad, main course, bread, dessert, coffee, free transport from/to your hotel) $18–$26; lunch $7–$14. MC, V. Daily 8am–11pm.

Mango Royal INTERNATIONAL   Part of this restaurant's allure has to do with its placement beside the largest pool on Saba, its high-altitude views that sweep northward over the sea, and its flaming torches that add a flickering glamour to the site during the dinner hour. You can dine on an indoor/outdoor terrace, or—for more privacy—within a lattice-covered structure inspired by a gazebo. Menu items at lunch include salads, sandwiches, and relatively simple versions of grilled fish. Evening meals are more elaborate, with offerings such as goat meat with mint sauce, lobster bisque, Saba spiced shrimp with Peking dumplings, grilled chicken with tropical herbs, barbecued beef kebabs, and fettuccine with cream sauce.

In the Queens's Garden Resort, Troy Hill, The Bottom. ✆ 599/416-63694. Reservations recommended. Lunch platters $10–$13; dinner main courses $16–$27. AE, DC, MC, V. Daily 7am–2pm and 7–9:30pm.

Saba Chinese Bar & Restaurant (Moo Goo Gai Pan)   Amid a cluster of residential buildings on a hillside above Windwardside, this place is operated by a family from Hong Kong. It offers some 120 dishes, an unpretentious decor of plastic tablecloths and folding chairs, and food so popular that many residents claim this is their most frequented restaurant. Meals include an array of Cantonese and Indonesian specialties—lobster Cantonese, Chinese chicken with mushrooms, sweet-and-sour fish, conch chop suey, several curry dishes, roast duck, and *nasi goreng*. It doesn't rank with the great Chinese restaurants of New York, San Francisco, and Hong Kong, but it's good, change-of-pace fare.

Windwardside. ✆ 599/416-2353. Main courses $8–$20. V. Daily 11am–10pm.

Scout's Place INTERNATIONAL   This is a popular dining spot among day-trippers to the island, so you should have your driver stop by early to make a reservation for you. Lunch at Scout's is simple, good, and filling, and the prices are low, too. Dinner is more elaborate, with tables placed on an open-sided terrace, the ideal spot for a drink at sundown. Fresh seafood is a specialty, as is curried goat. The sandwiches are the island's best, made with fresh-baked bread. Locals come from all over the island to sample them. Each day, a selection of homemade soups is also offered, perhaps pumpkin or pigeon pea. Scout's chef is proud of his ribs as well. Fresh local fruits and vegetables are used whenever possible. Even if you don't like the food, it's the best place on the island to catch up on the latest gossip.

In the Scout's Place hotel, Windwardside. ⓒ **599/416-2740.** Reservations required 2 to 3 hr. in advance. Lunch $10–$15; fixed-price dinner $12–$25. MC, V. Daily 9am–6pm.

Sunset Bar & Restaurant CARIBBEAN   You'll enjoy West Indian special-ties in a homelike atmosphere at this basic restaurant. For your main course, you might want to go for something simple, such as the baked chicken served with rice and peas, potato salad, and your choice of local specialties. Other dishes include spareribs or pork chops with vegetables. The pastries and breads are home-baked.

The Bottom. ⓒ **599/416-3332.** Main courses $6–$14; lunch $4–$10. No credit cards. Daily 8am–2pm and 6pm–midnight.

4 Sports & Outdoor Pursuits

HIKING   The island is as beautiful above the water as it is below. A favorite target for hikers is the top of **Mount Scenery** ✸✸, a volcano that erupted 5,000 years ago. Allow half a day and take your time climbing the 1,064 sometimes-slippery concrete steps up to the cloud-reefed mountain. You'll pass along a nature reserve complete with a lush rain forest with palms, bromeliads, elephant ears, heliconia, mountain raspberries, lianas, and tree ferns. In her pumps, Queen Beatrix of the Netherlands climbed these steps and, on reaching the sum-mit, declared: "This is the smallest and highest place in my kingdom." One of the inns will pack you a picnic lunch. The higher you climb, the cooler it grows, about a drop of 1°F every 328 feet; on a hot day this can be an incentive. The peak is 2,855 feet high.

If you're seeking beaches, forget Saba: It's better to remain on the sands of St. Maarten. Saba's only beach, **Wells Bay Beach,** disappears entirely during the winter. Sports here are limited primarily to diving and hiking.

One of our favorite hikes—with some of Saba's most panoramic views—is the **Crispeen Track,** reached from Windwardside as the main road descends to the hamlet of St. John's. Once at St. John's, the track heads northeast going through a narrow but dramatic gorge covered in thick tropical foliage. The vegetation grows lusher and lusher, taking in banana and citrus fields. As you reach the higher points of a section of the island called Rendezvous, the fields are no longer cultivated and resemble a rain forest, covered with such flora as philo-dendron, anthurium, and the wild mammee. Hiking time to Rendezvous is about an hour.

If you don't want to explore the natural attractions of the island on your own, the **Saba Tourist Office,** P.O. Box 527, Windwardside (ⓒ **599/416-2231**), can arrange tours of the tropical rain forests. Jim Johnson (ⓒ **599/416-3307**), a fit, 40-ish Saban guide, conducts most of these tours, and knows the terrain better than anyone else on the island (he's sometimes difficult to reach, however). Johnson will point out orchids, golden heliconia, and other flora and fauna, as well as the rock formations and bromeliads you're likely to see. Tours can accom-modate one to eight hikers and usually last about half a day; depending on your particular route and number of participants, the cost can be anywhere from $40 to $80. Actual prices, of course, are negotiated.

SCUBA DIVING   Dive sites around Saba, all protected by the Saba Marine Park, have permanent moorings and range from shallow to deep. Divers see pin-nacles, walls, ledges, overhangs, and reefs—all with abundant coral and sponge

Kids Cheap Thrills: What to See & Do for Free (Well, Almost) on Saba

- **Traverse "The Road."** Regardless of what road you travel in the Caribbean, there's nothing to compare with 9-mile-long "The Road." Its hairpin curves climb from the little airport up the steep, steep hillside to the lush interior of Saba. In days of yore, engineer after engineer came to the island and told Sabans they'd have to forget ever having a road on their volcanic mountain. Josephus Lambert Hassell, a local, had high hopes. In the 1930s, he began to take a correspondence course in engineering while he plotted and planned The Road. Under his guidance, his fellow islanders built The Road over the next 2 decades or so. In recent years, it's been necessary to reconstruct The Road, but it's there waiting to thrill you. At the top of The Road stands Windwardside, at 1,804 feet, Saba's second largest settlement and the island's midpoint.

- **Climb Mount Scenery.** There's no more aptly named mountain in the Caribbean, all 2,855 feet of it, reached by 1,064 concrete steps built into the mountainside. Mount Scenery is the island's central volcano and (mercifully) long extinct, and you reach it through a rain forest. Allow at least 3 hours to make this climb and bring along a jug of water. At the top you're rewarded with one of the most panoramic views in all the Caribbean. On a clear day you can view the neighboring islands of St. Kitts, St. Eustatius, St. Maarten, and St. Barthélemy. Along the way to the top of the mountain you'll be enthralled by such vegetation as begonias, orchids, mangoes, palms, red ferns, and especially the golden heliconias that often grow 6 feet tall.

- **Hike Around Saba.** The volcanic island has many hiking trails for both the neophyte and the more experienced hiker. All are reached by paths leading off from The Road. The tourist office can advise you about hiking and which trails are best and most scenic. Our

formations and a wide variety of reef and pelagic marine life. There's also a fully operational decompression chamber/hyperbaric facility located in the Fort Bay harbor.

Sea Saba Dive Center, Windwardside (© 599/416-2246), has nine experienced instructors eager to share their knowledge of Saba Marine Park: famous deep and medium-depth pinnacles, walls, spur-and-groove formations, and giant boulder gardens. Their two 40-foot, uncrowded boats are best suited for a comfortable day on Saba's waters. Daily boat dives are made between 9:30am and 1:30pm, allowing a relaxing interval for snorkeling. Courses range from resort through dive master. Extra day and night dives can be arranged. A one-tank dive costs $50, a two-tank dive, $90.

Saba Deep Dive Center (★★, P.O. Box 22, Fort Bay, Saba, N.A. (© 599/416-63347), is a full-service dive center that offers scuba diving, snorkeling, equipment rental/repair, and tank fills. Mike Myers and his staff of NAUI and PADI instructors and dive masters make an effort to provide personalized

favorite is the Crispeen Track, reached from Windwardside as the main road descends to the hamlet of St. John's. Here you'll encounter some of Saba's most panoramic views. Once at St. John's, the track heads northeast going through a narrow but dramatic gorge covered in thick tropical foliage. As you traverse this trail, the vegetation grows more and more lush, including banana and citrus fields. As you reach the higher points of a section of the island called Rendezvous, the fields are no longer cultivated and resemble a rain forest, covered with such flora as philodendron, anthurium, and wild mammee. Hiking time to Rendezvous takes about an hour.

- **Dive to the Coral Gardens.** Circling the entire island and including four offshore underwater mountains (seamounts), the **Saba Marine Park,** Fort Bay (© **599/416-3295**), preserves the island's coral reefs and marine life. The park is zoned for various pursuits. The all-purpose recreational zone includes Wells Bay Beach, Saba's only beach, but it's seasonal—it disappears with the winter seas, only to reappear in late spring. There are two anchorage zones for visiting yachts and Saba's only harbor. The five dive zones include a coastal area and four seamounts, a mile offshore. In these zones are more than two dozen marked and buoyed dive sites and a snorkeling trail. You plunge into a world of coral and sponges, swimming with parrotfish, doctorfish, and damselfish. The snorkel trail, however, isn't for the neophyte. It can be approached from Wells Bay Beach but only May through October. Depths of more than 1,500 feet are found between the island and the seamounts, which reach a minimum depth of 90 feet. There's a $3 per dive visitor fee. Funds are also raised through souvenir sales and donations. The park office at Fort Bay is open Monday to Friday 8am to 5pm, Saturday 8am to noon, and Sunday 10am to 2pm.

service and great diving, whether you're an old pro or with an entire family of first-timers. A certification course goes for $375. A single-tank dive costs $50; a two-tank dive, $90. Night dives are $65. The center is open daily 8am to 6pm. On the same property, the **In Two Deep Restaurant** and the **Deep Boutique** offer air-conditioned comfort, a view of the harbor area and the Caribbean Sea, good food and drink, and a wide selection of clothes, swimwear, lotions, and sunglasses. The restaurant is open for breakfast and lunch.

5 Seeing the Sights

Tidy white houses cling to the mountainside, and small family cemeteries adjoin each dwelling. Lace-curtained, gingerbread-trimmed cottages give a Disneyland aura.

The first Jeep arrived on Saba in 1947. Before that, Sabans went about on foot, climbing from village to village. Hundreds of steps had been chiseled out of the rock by the early Dutch settlers in 1640. Engineers told them it was impossible, but Sabans built a single cross-island road by hand. Filled with hairpin turns, it zigzags from Fort Bay, where a deep-water pier accommodates large tenders from cruise ships, to a height of 1,600 feet. Along the way it has fortress-like supporting walls.

Past storybook villages, the road goes over the crest to **The Bottom.** Derived from the Dutch word *botte* ("bowl-shaped"), this village is nestled on a plateau and surrounded by rocky volcanic domes. It occupies about the only bit of ground, 800 feet above the sea. It's also the official capital of Saba, a Dutch village of charm, with chimneys, gabled roofs, and gardens.

From The Bottom you can take a taxi up the hill to the mountain village of **Windwardside,** perched on the crest of two ravines at about 1,500 feet above sea level. This village of red-roofed houses, the second most-important on Saba, is the site of the two biggest inns and most of the shops.

From Windwardside you can climb steep steps cut in the rock to yet another village, **Hell's Gate,** teetering on the edge of a mountain. There's also a serpentine road from the airport to Hell's Gate, where you'll find the island's largest church. Only the most athletic climb from here to the lip of the volcanic crater.

6 Shopping

After lunch you can go for a stroll in Windwardside and stop at the boutiques, which often look like someone's living room—and sometimes they are. Most stores are open Monday to Saturday 9am to noon and 2 to around 5:30pm; some are also open shorter hours on Sunday.

The traditional **drawn threadwork** of the island is famous. Sometimes this work, introduced by a local woman named Gertrude Johnson in the 1870s, is called Spanish work, because it was believed to have been perfected by nuns in Caracas. Selected threads are drawn and tied in a piece of linen to produce an ornamental pattern. It can be expensive if a quality linen has been used.

Try to go home with some **"Saba Spice,"** an aromatic blend of 150-proof cask rum, with such spices as fennel seed, cinnamon, cloves, and nutmeg, straight from someone's home brew. It's not for everyone (most find it too sweet), but it'll make an exotic bottle to show off at home.

Most streets in Windwardside have no names, but because it's so small shops are easy to find.

Ex-Manhattanite Jean Macbeth runs **Around the Bend,** at Scout's Place, Windwardside (© **599/416-2519**), a classy little boutique featuring gifts, oddments, and what she calls "pretties," all one-of-a-kind. Charming locally made wooden Saba cottage wall plaques are sold along with magnets, switch plates, bright parrot and toucan pinwheels, Caribbean perfumes, and spices. Naturally, there's a collection of hand-painted silk-screened T-shirts.

In recent years, the **Saba Artisan Foundation,** The Bottom (© **599/416-3260**), has made a name for itself with its hand-screened resort fashions. The clothes are casual and colorful. Among the items sold are men's bush-jacket shirts, numerous styles of dresses and skirts, napkins, and place mats, as well as yard goods. Island motifs are used in many designs. Also popular are the famous Saban drawn-lace patterns. The fashions are designed, printed, sewn, and marketed by Sabans. Mail-order as well as wholesale-distributorship inquiries are invited.

7 Saba After Dark

If you're thinking about going to Saba to do some partying, you might want to think about another island. Saba is known for its tucked-away, relaxed, and calm atmosphere. However, don't be too dismayed; there's something to do at night.

Scout's Place, Windwardside (© **599/416-2740**), is the place to hang out if you want to relax, enjoy a drink, and have a laugh, especially on weeknights. A hotel and restaurant, Scout's Place does moonlight as a local watering hole, entertaining guests, tourists, and locals alike with a distinct Saban/Caribbean atmosphere. You won't do much dancing (well, that depends on how much you've had to drink), but it's much better than the weeknight alternative—nothing. It's open daily, noon to around midnight (actual closing hours depend on business or the lack of it). There's no cover.

Normally a pizzeria, **Guido's,** Windwardside (© **599/416-2230**), serves simple food and drinks weeknights, but it becomes the most happening place on the island on Friday and Saturday nights, as this is really the only place to get a drink *and* boogie down. As a disco, it's known as Mountain High Club. They have a dance floor to shake on and a sound system to shake to—they even have a disco ball. Weeknights are similar to Scout's Place: a simple dining crowd. Hours are Monday to Thursday 6pm to midnight and Friday and Saturday 6pm to 2am. There's no cover.

If you'd like to combine the ambience of a British pub with a saloon that might have been found in the Arizona Badlands, head for **Swinging Doors,** Windwardside (© **599/416-2506**), Saba's good-ol'-boy watering hole where locals start consuming the brew at 9am and keep drinking until late at night (no set closing hour).

19

St. Eustatius

Often called *Statia*, this Dutch-held island is just an 8-square-mile pinpoint in the Netherlands Antilles (just 2 miles wide at its widest point), still basking in its 18th-century heritage as the "Golden Rock." One of the true backwaters of the West Indies, it's just awakening to tourism.

You might want to visit first on a day-trip from St. Maarten to see if you'd like it for an extended stay. As Caribbean islands go, it's rather dull, with no nightlife, and the volcanic black-sand beaches aren't especially alluring. Some pleasant strips of beach exist on the Atlantic side, but the surf is dangerous for swimming.

If you're a hiker or a diver, the outlook improves considerably. You can hike around the base of **The Quill,** an extinct volcano on the southern end of the island. Wandering through a tropical forest, you encounter wild orchids, philodendron, heliconia, anthurium, fruit trees, ferns, wildlife, and birds, with the inevitable oleander, hibiscus, and bougainvillea.

The island's reefs are covered with corals and enveloped by marine life. At one dive site, known as **Crack in the Wall,** or sometimes "the Grand Canyon," pinnacle coral shoots up from the floor of the ocean. Darting among the reefs are barracudas, eagle rays, black-tip sharks, and other large ocean fish.

Statia is 150 miles east of Puerto Rico, 38 miles south of St. Maarten, and 17 miles southeast of Saba. The two extinct volcanoes, The Quill and Little Mountain, are linked by a sloping agricultural plain known as **De Cultuurvlakte,** where yams and sweet potatoes grow. Overlooking the Caribbean on the western edge of the plain, **Oranjestad** (Orange City) is the capital and the only village, consisting of both an Upper and Lower Town, connected by the stone-paved, dogleg Fort Road.

Columbus sighted Statia in 1493, on his second voyage, and Jan Snouck claimed the island for the Netherlands in 1640. The island's history was turbulent before it settled down to peaceful slumber under Dutch protection; from 1650 to 1816, Statia changed flags 22 times! Once the trading hub of the Caribbean, Statia was a thriving market for both goods and slaves. Before the American Revolution, the population of Statia didn't exceed 1,200, most of whom were slaves engaged in raising sugarcane. When war came and Britain blockaded the North American coast, Europe's trade was diverted to the Caribbean. Dutch neutrality lured many traders, which led to the construction of 1½ miles of warehouses in Lower Town. The American revolutionaries obtained gunpowder and ammunition through Statia—perhaps one of the first places anywhere to recognize as a country the newly declared United States of America.

The good news for the budget traveler is that rates here are often described as being "a steal."

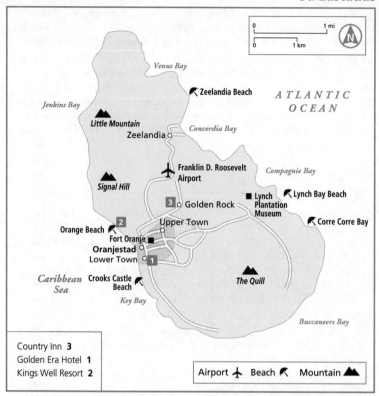

Country Inn **3**
Golden Era Hotel **1**
Kings Well Resort **2**

Airport ✈ Beach 🏝 Mountain ▲▲

1 Essentials

VISITOR INFORMATION

On the island the **Tourist Bureau** is at 3 Fort Oranjestraat (© **599/318-2433**), open Monday through Friday 8am to noon and 1 to 5pm (4:30 on Fri).

The Internet address for Statia is **www.turq.com/statia**.

GETTING THERE

St. Eustatius can be reached from Dutch **St. Maarten's Queen Juliana Airport** via the 20-seat planes of **Windward Islands Airways International (Winair)** (© **599/318-2362** on St. Maarten). The five flights a day take only 20 minutes to hop the waters to Statia's **Franklin Delano Roosevelt Airport** (© **599/ 318-2362**). From here you can also make connections for flights to Saba or St. Kitts; two flights a day to Saba, and two a week to St. Kitts.

The little airline, launched in 1961, has an excellent safety record and has flown such passengers as David Rockefeller. Always reconfirm your return passage once you're on Statia.

GETTING AROUND

BY TAXI Taxis are your best bet. They meet all incoming flights, and on the way to the hotel your driver will offer himself as a guide during your stay on the island. Taxi rates are low, probably no more than $3.50 to $5 to your hotel from the airport. If you book a 2- to 3-hour tour (and in that time you should be able to cover all the sights), the cost is about $40 per vehicle. To summon a taxi, call **Rainbow Taxis** at *©* **599/318-2811,** or **Josser Daniel** at *©* **599/318-2358.**

BY RENTAL CAR   Avis (*©* **800/331-1212** in the U.S., or 599/318-2421), offering unlimited mileage, is your best bet if you want to reserve a car in advance. Drivers must be 21 and present a valid license and credit card. Avis is located at the airport. You can also search for a cheaper deal at one of the local companies, but don't expect cars to be too well maintained. Try **Rainbow Car Rental** at *©* **599/318-2811** or **Walter's** at *©* **599/318-2719.** Walter's rents both cars and jeeps.

 FAST FACTS: St. Eustatius

Banks **Barclay's Bank,** Wilhelminastraat, Oranjestad (*©* **599/318-2392**), the only bank on the island, is open Monday to Thursday 8:30am to 3:30pm and Friday 8:30am to 12:30pm and 2 to 4:30pm. On weekends, most hotels will exchange money.

Currency The official unit of currency is the **Netherlands Antilles guilder (NAf)**, exchanged at a rate of 1.80NAf to each U.S.$1, but nearly all places will quote you prices in U.S. dollars.

Customs There are no Customs duties because the island is a free port.

Documents U.S. and Canadian citizens need proof of citizenship, such as a passport or a birth certificate with a raised seal and a government-authorized photo ID, along with an ongoing ticket. If you're using a birth certificate or voter registration card, you'll also need some photo ID. British subjects need a valid passport.

Electricity It's the same as in the United States, 100-volt AC (60 cycles).

Language Dutch is the official language, but English is commonly spoken as well.

Medical Care A licensed physician is on duty at the **Queen Beatrix Medical Center,** 25 Princessweg in Oranjestad (*©* **599/318-2211**).

Safety Although crime is rare here, it's wise to secure your valuables and take the kind of discreet precautions you would anywhere. Don't leave valuables unguarded on the beach.

Taxes There's a $5 tax if you're returning to the Dutch-held islands of St. Maarten or Saba; if you're going elsewhere, the tax is $10. Hotels on Statia collect a 7% government tax.

Telecommunications Ask for assistance at your hotel if you need to send a cable. St. Eustatius maintains a 24-hour-a-day telephone service—and sometimes it takes about that much time to get a call through!

To call Statia from the States, dial **011** (the international access code), then **599** (the country code for the Netherlands Antilles), and finally **318** (the area code for Statia) and the four-digit local number. To make a call within Statia, only the five-digit local number is necessary.

Time St. Eustatius operates on Atlantic standard time year-round. Thus in winter, when the United States is on standard time, if it's 6pm in Oranjestad, it's 5pm in New York. During daylight saving time in the United States, the island keeps the same time as the U.S. east coast.

Tipping Tipping is at the visitor's discretion, although most hotels, guest-houses, and restaurants include a 10%–15% service charge.

Water The water here is safe to drink.

Weather The average daytime temperature ranges from 78° to 82°F. The annual rainfall is only 45 inches.

2 Accommodations You Can Afford

Don't expect deluxe hotels or high-rises—Statia is strictly for escapists. Sometimes guests are placed in private homes. A 15% service charge and 7% government tax are added to hotel bills.

Country Inn   This is about as basic a hotel as we're willing to recommend. Opened in the early 1990s, about a 5-minute walk from the airport and a reasonable stroll to several well-recommended beaches, it's in a residential neighborhood of weathered concrete buildings. Some of your neighbors might be docile cows and goats belonging to the owners, Wendell and Iris Pompier. Each small room contains a radio, an alarm clock, a small fridge, and a queen-size bed with a mattress that's likely in need of renewal. The bathrooms are cubicles, and each has a shower. In all, it's a decent place to stay and a good value. A launderette and facilities for scuba diving are nearby.

Concordia, St. Eustatius, N.A. ℭ **599/318-2484.** Fax 599/318-2484. 6 units. Year-round $45 single; $55 double. No credit cards. *In room:* A/C, TV, mini-fridge, radio.

Golden Era Hotel ✮   Set directly on the water, this modern hotel is clean, serviceable, and comfortable. Twelve units offer full or partial sea views (the most stunning panorama is from no. 205). All accommodations are tasteful and spacious, with king- or queen-size beds. Regrettably, the shower-only bathrooms are so tiny that it's hard to maneuver. You can, if you wish, sit on the toilet and wash your face at the same time. Lunch and dinner are served daily in the simply decorated bar and dining room.

Lower Town, Oranjestad, St. Eustatius, N.A. ℭ **599/318-2345.** Fax 599/318-2445. goldera@goldenrock.net. 20 units. Winter $70 single; $88 double; $104 triple. Off-season $60 single; $75 double; $90 triple. MAP (breakfast and dinner) $30 per person extra. AE, DISC, MC, V. **Amenities:** Restaurant, bar, pool. *In room:* A/C, fridge, no phone.

Kings Well Resort ✮✮   This is the choice address on Statia. Set on the Caribbean side of the island, about half a mile north of Oranjestad, this secluded choice occupies about ⅔ acre, perched on an oceanfront cliff, 60 feet above the surf. Construction on the hotel started in 1994 and has progressed slowly ever since. If you're looking for a laid-back, escapist vacation, this is your place. (Your nearest neighbors will be in the local cemetery.) Most views look out to the southwest, ensuring colorful sunsets that tend to be enhanced by drinks served from the bar at the Kings Well Restaurant (see "Great Deals on Dining," below).

There are no room keys, so don't expect much security. The accommodations are small and rather sparsely furnished; each is unique. Beds are draped with mosquito netting; rooms 1 and 4 contain waterbeds. The rooms in the rear are larger and face the sea, and those in front open onto a shared sea-view balcony. Bathrooms are small, with showers only. There's no pool, no air-conditioning, and few amenities other than the peace and calm that reign here.

Oranje Bay Rd. 1, Oranjestad, St. Eustatius, N.A. ✆/fax **599/318-2538**. 8 units. Winter $78–$90 single; $84–$102 double; $114–$126 efficiency. Off-season $72–$84 single; $84–$96 double; $108 efficiency. Rates include breakfast. DISC, MC, V. **Amenities:** Restaurant, bar. *In room:* TV, fridge.

3 Great Deals on Dining

Blue Bead Bar & Restaurant ⭐ INTERNATIONAL   Set beside the beach, in a wood-sided Antillean house brightly painted in neon shades of blue and yellow, this restaurant combines West Indian funkiness with a polite staff and well-prepared cuisine. Menu items are whimsical and charming, and rely on culinary inspiration from around the world. The best examples include grilled chicken salads, spicy Thai-style fish, beef skewers in a peanut-based satay, and grilled steaks and fish. The restaurant's name derives from the blue-glazed ceramic beads, originally used as money by Statia's slaves, that sometimes wash up on the island's beaches after severe storms.

Bay Rd., Lower Town, Oranjestad. ✆ **599/318-2453**. Main courses $6.50–$12.50 lunch, $12–$20 dinner. AE. Mon–Sat 11:30am–10pm; Sun 6–10pm. Bar daily 10am–10:30pm.

Chinese Bar and Restaurant CHINESE   This place caters to locals and offers standard Chinese-restaurant fare with a bit of local influence thrown in, including such dishes as curried shrimp. The atmosphere is very laid-back. For instance, even though the terrace isn't set up for dining, you can request to have your table moved there for an alfresco meal. The portions are hearty and range from the typical sweet-and-sour pork and a variety of shrimp dishes to chop suey and chow mein. This is the best place on the island for vegetarian food.

Prinses Weg, Oranjestad. ✆ **599/319-2389**. Main courses $8–$12. No credit cards. Mon–Sat noon–3pm and 7:30–11pm.

Kings Well Restaurant INTERNATIONAL   The restaurant here is more successful and more complete than the simple hotel in which it's housed (see "Accommodations You Can Afford," above). Set about a half-mile north of Oranjestad and perched on a cliff about 60 feet above the surf, it features an open kitchen and great sunset panoramas. Enjoy a fruity drink from the rustic bar before your meal. Lunches feature deli-style sandwiches and a selection of platters from the dinner menu, which is more elaborate. Dishes might include grilled Colorado beefsteaks, fresh lobster, pan-fried grouper or snapper with parsley-butter sauce, plus a few German meat dishes like sauerbraten.

Oranje Bay, Oranjestad. ✆ **599/318-2538**. Lunch platters $5–$12; dinner main courses $10–$19. DISC, MC, V. Daily 11:30am–2pm and 6–8:30pm.

L'Etoile CREOLE   Caren Henríquez's simple second-floor restaurant is well known on Statia for its local cuisine, but you don't run into too many tourists here. Favored main dishes include the ubiquitous "goatwater" (a stew), mountain crab, stewed whelks, tasty spareribs, and Caribbean-style lobster. Caren is also known for her *pastechis*—deep-fried turnovers stuffed with meat. Expect a complete and very filling meal.

6 Van Rheeweg, northeast of Upper Town. ✆ **599/318-2299**. Reservations required. Main courses $10–$20. AE, MC, V. Sun–Fri 9am–1pm and 5–9pm; Sat 9am–1pm and 5–10pm.

Stone Oven CREOLE   A small house with a garden patio and a cozy Caribbean decor, this restaurant serves very simple food. To dine like many islanders do, you can try the bullfoot soup or the goatwater stew. For the less

Value **Cheap Thrills: What to See & Do for Free (Well, Almost) on St. Eustatius**

- **Catch Crabs at Night.** We're perfectly serious. If you're interested, you can join Statians in a crab hunt. The Quill's crater is the breeding ground for these large crustaceans. At night they emerge from their holes to forage, and that's when they're caught. Either with flashlights or relying on moonlight, crab hunters climb The Quill, catch a crab, and take the local delicacy home to prepare stuffed crab-back. Your hotel can usually hook you up with this activity.

- **Stroll Through Upper and Lower Towns.** Upper Town and Lower Town on the west coast facing the leeward side are two parts of Oranjestad, the island's capital. Gradually many of Oranjestad's historic buildings are being restored. The ruins of Fort Orange, dating from 1636, are worth a visit. Presented in 1939 by Franklin Roosevelt to the people of Statia, a plaque in the parade grounds reads: HERE THE SOVEREIGNTY OF THE UNITED STATES OF AMERICA WAS FIRST FORMALLY ACKNOWLEDGED TO A NATIONAL VESSEL BY A FOREIGN OFFICIAL. At the Historical Foundation Museum you can pick up a brochure outlining how you can tour both sections. Lower Town sits below Fort Oranjestraat and some steep cliffs and is reached from Upper Town on foot. Take the cobblestone Fort Road if you're walking between the two. Now these places look like ghost towns, but in the 18th century they were filled with warehouses doing a booming trade. As you walk along the water you'll see the crumbling ruins of this prosperous period. The sea is now reclaiming many of these abandoned warehouses.

- **Hike Up to The Quill.** There's no more dramatic walk in all Statia than The Quill. Having last erupted some 4,000 years ago, The Quill is tranquil today. Lying at the southern end of Statia, it's a 2,000-foot-high extinct volcano with a lush rain forest inside its once-active crater. Five marked trails of varying difficulty lead up to the rim, and each one takes about 2 hours. When you reach the summit, there are additional trails to follow if you have the time and stamina. To reach The Quill, we prefer Quill Track I, the most direct route, even though it is a steep climb. It starts on the south side of Oranjestad on Welfare Road, and it goes up the western side of the rim of the crater, to an elevation of 1,300 feet. Along the way you'll see some interesting vegetation, including pink poui. To look at the lush flora within the volcano is worth the climb.

adventurous, there are fried pork chops and beef stew. Most of the dishes are served with your choice of rice and peas, french fries, fried plantains, and sweet potatoes. Many know this place as a bar where people sometimes dance when the mood and the music are right. Most dishes are at the low end of the price scale.

15 Faeschweg, Upper Town, Oranjestad. © **599/318-2809.** Main courses $6–$12.50. No credit cards. Daily 10am–2pm and 5pm–"until."

4 Hitting the Beaches

Most of the beaches of Statia are small, narrow strips of sand, either volcanic black or a dull mudlike gray. Regrettably, the preferred beaches are not on the tranquil Caribbean side, but on the turbulent Atlantic side, where the waters are often too rough for swimming. Beachcombers delight, however, in their search for the fabled **blue-glass beads,** which were manufactured in the 1600s by a Dutch West Indies Company. These beads were used as money for the trading of such products as tobacco, cotton, and rum. They were even used to purchase slaves. These beads—real collector's items—often are unearthed after a heavy rainfall or tropical storm.

Orange Beach is also called Smoke Alley Beach. On the Caribbean side of the island, it lies off Lower Town. This is one of the small volcanic beaches on the southwest shore, with beige or black sands and waters suitable for a leisurely swim. You virtually have the beach to yourself until late afternoon, when locals start to arrive for a dip.

Also on the leeward or Caribbean side is **Crooks Castle Beach,** south of Oranjestad. The waters, filled with giant yellow sea fans, sea whips, and pillar coral, attract snorkelers, while beachcombers are drawn to the many blue beads that have been unearthed here.

On the southwest Atlantic side of the island, **Corre Corre Bay** has a strip of dark golden sand. It's about half an hour down Mountain Road and is worth the trip to get here, although the waters are often too churned up for comfortable swimming. Two bends north of this beach, the light-brown-sand **Lynch Bay Beach** is more sheltered from the wild swells of the Atlantic. Nonetheless, the surf here is still almost always rough, plus there's a dangerous undertow; this beach is better used for sunbathing than swimming.

Also on the Atlantic side, **Zeelandia Beach** is 2 miles long and filled with dark, dark beige and volcanic-black sand. One tourist promotion speaks of its "exciting Atlantic surf and invigorating trade winds," but fails to warn of the dangerous undertow. Only one small, designated section is safe for swimming. The beach is suitable, however, for wading, hiking, and sunbathing. The place is nearly always deserted.

5 Sports & Other Outdoor Pursuits

HIKING Hiking is the most popular activity on the island. Those with the stamina can climb the slopes of The Quill (see "Cheap Thrills: What to See & Do for Free (Well, Almost) on St. Eustatius," above). The **tourist office** (© 599/ 318-2433) will supply you with a list of a dozen trails with varying degrees of difficulty and can arrange for you to go with a guide whose fee is $20 or more (that has to be negotiated, of course).

WATERSPORTS On the Atlantic side of the island, at Concordia Bay, the **surfing** is best. However, there's no lifeguard protection. **Snorkeling** is available through the Caribbean Sea to explore the remnants of an 18th-century man-of-war and the walls of warehouses, taverns, and ships that sank below the surface of Oranje Bay more than 200 years ago.

Dive Statia is a full PADI diving center on Fishermen's Beach in Lower Town (© 599/318-2435), offering everything from beginning instruction to dive master certification. Its professional staff guides divers of all levels of experience to spectacular walls, untouched coral reefs, and historic shipwrecks. Dive Statia offers one- and two-tank boat dives, costing $45 to $75, including equipment. Night dives and snorkel trips are also available.

Many adventurers come to Statia to enjoy water-skiing, but it's expensive. **Scubagua,** operating out of the Golden Era Hotel, Bay Road, Lower Town (© **599/318-2345**), will hook you up with the sport for $90 per hour.

TENNIS Statia maintains two courts at the **Community Center,** Rosemary Laan in Upper Town (© **599/318-2249**), costing only $2 per hour. You'll have to bring your own rackets and balls, but there is a changing room.

6 Seeing the Sights

Oranjestad stands on a cliff looking out on a beach and the island's calm anchorage, where in the 18th century you might've seen 200 vessels offshore. **Fort Oranje** was built in 1636 and restored in honor of the 1976 U.S. bicentennial celebration. Perched atop the cliffs, its terraced rampart is lined with the old cannons.

The **St. Eustatius Historical Foundation Museum,** Upper Town (© **599/ 318-2288**), is also called the de Graaff House in honor of its former tenant, Johannes de Graaff. After British Admiral Rodney sacked Statia for its tribute to the United States, he installed his own headquarters in this 18th-century house. Today a museum, the house stands in a garden, with a 20th-century wing crafted from 17th-century bricks. There are exhibits on the process of sugar refining as well as shipping and commerce. Archaeological artifacts from the colonial period and a pair of beautiful 18th-century antique furnished rooms are also on view. There's a section devoted to the pre-Columbian period. In the wing annex is a massive piece of needlework by an American, Catherine Mary Williams, showing the flowers of Statia. The museum is open Monday to Friday 9am to 5pm and Saturday and Sunday 9am to noon; admission is $2 for adults and $1 for children.

A few steps away, a cluster of 18th-century buildings surrounding a quiet courtyard is called **Three Widows' Corner.** Nearby are the ruins of the first **Dutch Reformed church** on Kerkweg ("Church Way"). To reach it, turn west from Three Widows' Corner onto Kerkweg. Tilting headstones record the names of the characters in the island's past. The St. Eustatius Historical Foundation recently completed restoration of the church. Visitors may climb to the top level of the tower and see the bay as lookouts did many years before.

Once Statia had a large colony of Jewish traders, and you can explore the ruins of **Honen Dalim,** the second Jewish synagogue in the western hemisphere. Built around 1740 and damaged by a hurricane in 1772, it fell into disuse at the dawn of the 19th century. The synagogue stands beside Synagogpad, a narrow lane whose entrance faces Madam Theatre on the square. The walls of a *mikvah* (ritual bath) rise beside the **Jewish burial ground** on the edge of town. Most poignant is the memorial of David Haim Hezeciah de Lion, who died in 1760 at the age of 2 years, 8 months, 26 days; carved into the baroque surface is an angel releasing a tiny songbird from its cage.

You can also visit the **Lynch Plantation Museum** at Lynch Bay (© **599/ 318-2338**), but you'll have to call to arrange a tour. Donations are accepted; otherwise admission is free. Locals still call this place the Berkel Family Plantation, although today it's a museum depicting life on Statia a century ago. The history of the island is shown in antiques, fishing and farming equipment, even pictures and old Bibles. Usually Ismael Berkel is on hand to show you around.

This is a special sight because it's personal and still very much a place of residence instead of some deadly dull museum.

7 Shopping

At **Mazinga Giftshop,** Fort Oranje Straat, Upper Town (© **599/318-2245**), you'll find an array of souvenirs—T-shirts, liquor, costume jewelry, 14-karat-gold jewelry, cards, drugstore items, beachwear, children's books, handbags, and paperback romances. You may have seen more exciting stores in your life, but this is without parallel for Statia. You can buy books and magazines at the **Paper Corner,** Van Tonningenweg, Upper Town (© **599/318-2208**).

8 St. Eustatius After Dark

Las Vegas it isn't. Nightlife pickings here are among the slimmest in the Caribbean. Even though most visitors are satisfied by drinks and dinner, there are a few spots to wander after hours. Weekends are the best and busiest time to go out on Statia. **Exit Disco** (© **599/318-2543**) at the Stone Oven Restaurant, 16A Faeschweg, Upper Town, Oranjestad, often has dancing and local bands on weekends, and you can also enjoy simple West Indian fare here. For local flavor, try **Cool Corner** (© **599/318-2523**), across from the St. Eustatius Historical Foundation Museum, in the center of town.

20

St. Kitts

A volcanic island of the once-British Leewards, St. Kitts has become a resort mecca in recent years. Its major crop is sugar and has been since the 17th century. But tourism now overwhelms, as its southeastern peninsula, site of the best white-sand beaches, has been set aside for massive hotel and resort development. Most of the island's other beaches are of gray or black volcanic sand.

Although far more active and livelier than its companion island, Nevis (see chapter 16), St. Kitts is still fairly sleepy. But go now, before its inherent Caribbean character changes forever. The island doesn't offer a wide range of accommodations, particularly on the lower end of the price scale, but if you really look, you can find some good deals. As for dining, if you avoid the high-priced resorts and eat at some of the little taverns where the locals go, you'll at least be able to keep food costs within reason.

The Caribs, the early settlers, called St. Kitts *Liamuiga* ("fertile isle"). Its mountain ranges reach up to nearly 4,000 feet, and in its interior are virgin rain forests, alive with hummingbirds and wild green vervet monkeys. The monkeys were brought in as pets by the early French settlers and turned loose in the forests when the island became British in 1783. These native African animals have proliferated and can be seen at the Estridge Estate Behavioral Research Institute. Another import, this one British, is the mongoose, brought in from India as an enemy of rats in the sugarcane fields. However, the mongooses and rats operate on different time cycles—the rats ravage while the mongooses sleep. Wild deer are found in the mountains. Sugarcane climbs right up the slopes, and there are palm-lined beaches around the island. As you travel around St. Kitts, you'll notice ruins of old mills and plantation houses. You'll also see an island rich in trees and other vegetation.

St. Kitts, 23 miles long and 6½ miles wide, rides the crest of that arc of islands known as the northerly Leeward group of the Lesser Antilles. It's separated from the associated state of Nevis by a 2-mile-wide strait, and its administrative capital is Basseterre.

1 Essentials

VISITOR INFORMATION

Tourist information is available from the tourist board's **U.S. offices** at 414 E. 75th St., New York, NY 10021 (© **800/582-6208** or 212/535-1234). In **Canada,** an office is at 365 Bay St., Suite 806, Toronto, ON M5H 2V1 (© **416/376-0881**), and in the **United Kingdom** at 10 Kensington Court, London, W8 5DL (© **020/7376-0881**). **On the island,** the local tourist board operates at Pelican Mall, Bay Road in Basseterre (© **869/465-4040**), open Monday and Tuesday 8am to 4:30pm and Wednesday to Friday 8am to 4pm.

⌒ *Fun Fact* **Party Times in St. Kitts**

Carnival in St. Kitts is celebrated not in the days leading up to Ash Wednesday, but from Christmas Eve until January 2. The festivities include parties, dancing, talent shows, and the crowning of the Carnival Queen. The final day of the celebration is known as "Last Lap," and features a repeat of many of the activities, including a multitude of bands, jamming in the streets of Basseterre.

Another popular party time is the **St. Kitts Music Festival,** held the last weekend in June (Thurs–Sun). The Soca/Calypso night is usually the festival's popular opening event. You can also hear reggae, jazz, rhythm and blues, and gospel performances over the 4 days. For more information about the 2002 festival, call the Department of Tourism at ℰ **869/ 465-4040.**

GETTING THERE

Dozens of daily flights on **American Airlines** (ℰ **800/433-7300**) land in San Juan. From here, **American Eagle** (same phone) makes four daily nonstop flights into St. Kitts.

If you're already on St. Maarten and want to visit St. Kitts (with perhaps a side trip to Nevis), you can do so aboard one of the most remarkable little airlines in the Caribbean. Known by its nickname, **Winair** (ℰ **869/465-8010**), Windward Islands Airways International makes three to four flights a week from St. Maarten to St. Kitts, with easy connections to and from other Dutch islands like Saba and St. Eustatius and about a dozen other destinations throughout the Caribbean.

Another possibility involves transfers into St. Kitts or Nevis through Antigua, St. Maarten, or San Juan on the Antigua-based carrier **LIAT** (ℰ **800/468-0482** in the U.S. and Canada, or 869/465-8613). **Air Canada** (ℰ **800/776-3000**) flies from Toronto to Antigua, and **British Airways** (ℰ **800/247-9297** in the U.S., or 0345/222-111 in England) flies from London to Antigua.

GETTING AROUND

BY TAXI   Since most taxi drivers are also guides, a **taxi** is the best means of getting around. You don't even have to find a driver at the airport—one will find you. They also wait outside the major hotels. Before heading out, however, you must agree on the price since taxis aren't metered. Also ask if the rates quoted to you are in U.S. dollars or Eastern Caribbean dollars. To go from Robert L. Bradshaw International Airport to Basseterre costs about EC$16 ($5.95); to Sandy Point, EC$37 ($13.70) and up. For more information, call the **St. Kitts Taxi Association,** at ℰ **869/465-8487.**

BY RENTAL CAR   A U.S.-based rental firm that maintains a representative on St. Kitts is **Avis,** South Independence Square (ℰ **800/331-1212** in the U.S., or 869/465-6507). It charges from $30 per day, $300 per week, plus $15 per day for collision damage, with a $950 deductible, or $75 per day for collision with no deductible. Tax is 5% extra, and a week's rental allows a seventh day for free. The company offers free delivery service to the airport or to any of the island's hotels, and drivers must be between ages 25 and 75. **Delisle Walwyn & Co.,** Liverpool Row, Basseterre (ℰ **869/465-8449**), is a local company that offers cars and jeeps. This might be your best deal on the island. You can also check two other local companies: **Sunshine,** Cayon Street in Basseterre and a

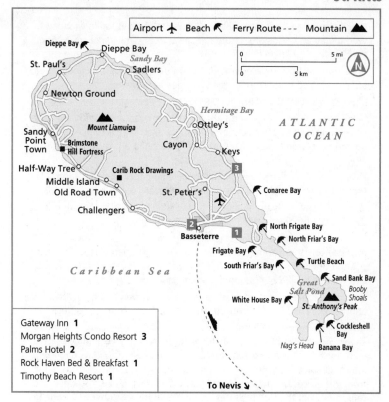

Airport ✈ Beach 🏖 Ferry Route - - - Mountain ▲▲

0 _____ 5 mi
0 _____ 5 km

Dieppe Bay 🏖
Dieppe Bay
St. Paul's
Sandy Bay
Sadlers
Newton Ground
Hermitage Bay
Mount Liamuiga ▲▲
Ottley's
**ATLANTIC
OCEAN**
Sandy
Point
Town
Brimstone
Hill Fortress
Cayon
Keys
Half-Way Tree
Carib Rock Drawings
Middle Island
Old Road Town
St. Peter's
3
Conaree Bay 🏖
Challengers
✈
2
Basseterre
1
North Frigate Bay
North Friar's Bay 🏖
Frigate Bay 🏖
Caribbean Sea
Turtle Beach 🏖
South Friar's Bay 🏖
Sand Bank Bay 🏖
*Great
Salt Pond*
*Booby
Shoals*
White House Bay 🏖
St. Anthony's Peak
▲▲
Cockleshell
Bay 🏖
Nag's Head Banana Bay

Gateway Inn **1**
Morgan Heights Condo Resort **3**
Palms Hotel **2**
Rock Haven Bed & Breakfast **1**
Timothy Beach Resort **1**

To Nevis ↘

kiosk at the Golden Rock Airport (© **869/465-2193**), and **TDC Rentals,** West
Independence Square in Basseterre (© **869/465-2991**).

    Driving is on the left! You'll need a local driver's license, which can be obtained
at the **Traffic Department,** on Cayon Street in Basseterre, for EC$50 ($18.50).
Usually a member of the staff at your car-rental agency will drive you to the Traffic Department to get one.

 ***FAST FACTS*: St. Kitts**

Banking Hours You'll find banks open Monday to Thursday 8am to noon
and Friday 8am to noon and 3 to 5pm.

Currency The local currency is the **Eastern Caribbean dollar (EC$),** valued
at about $2.70 to U.S.$1. Many prices, however, including those of hotels,
are quoted in U.S. dollars. Always determine which "dollar" locals are
talking about.

Customs You're allowed in duty-free with your personal belongings.
Sometimes luggage is subjected to a drug check.

Drugstores Try **Parris Pharmacy,** Central Street at Basseterre (© **869/
465-8569**), open Monday to Wednesday 8am to 5pm, Thursday 8am to
1pm, Friday 8am to 5:30pm, and Saturday 8am to 6pm. You can also try

City Drug, Fort Street in Basseterre (© **869/465-2156**), open Monday to Wednesday and Friday to Saturday 8am to 7pm, Thursday 8am to 5pm, and Sunday 8 to 10am only.

Electricity On St. Kitts, electricity is 230-volt AC (60 cycles), so you'll need an adapter and a transformer for U.S.-made appliances.

Emergencies Dial the **police** at © **911.**

Entry Requirements U.S. and Canadian citizens can enter with proof of citizenship, such as a birth certificate with a raised seal, accompanied by a government-issued photo ID. British subjects need a passport but not a visa.

Hospital In Basseterre, there's a 24-hour emergency room at **Joseph N. France General Hospital,** Cayon Street (© **869/465-2551**).

Language English is the language of the island, and it is spoken with a decided West Indian patois.

Safety This is still a fairly safe place to travel. Most crimes against tourists—and there aren't a lot—are robberies on Conaree Beach, so exercise the usual precautions. It would be wise to safeguard your valuables, and women should not go jogging alone along deserted roads.

Taxes The government imposes a 7% tax on rooms and meals, plus another EC$27 (U.S.$10) airport departure tax (but not to go to Nevis).

Telecommunications Telegrams and telexes can be sent from **Skantel,** Cayon Street, Basseterre (© **869/465-1000**), Monday to Friday 8am to 6pm, Saturday 7:30am to 1pm, and Sunday and public holidays 6 to 8pm. International telephone calls, including collect calls, can also be made from this office. The area code for St. Kitts and Nevis is **869.** You can make calls to or from the United States as you would for any other area code in North America.

Time St. Kitts is on Atlantic standard time all year. This means that in winter, when it's 6am in Basseterre, it's 5am in Miami or New York. When the U.S. goes on daylight saving time, St. Kitts and the U.S. East Coast mainland are on the same time.

Tipping Most hotels and restaurants add a service charge of 10% to cover tipping. If not, tip 10% to 15%.

Water The water on St. Kitts and Nevis is so good that Baron de Rothschild's chemists selected St. Kitts as their only site in the Caribbean to distill and produce CSR (Cane Sugar Rothschild), a pure sugarcane liqueur.

Weather St. Kitts lies in the tropics, and its warm climate is tempered by the trade winds. The average air temperature is 79°F, and the average water temperature is 80°F. Dry, mild weather is usually experienced from November to April; May to October it's hotter and rainier.

2 Accommodations You Can Afford

Gateway Inn   Built by local entrepreneurs in the early 1990s, this self-catering complex offers 10 medium-size apartments, each with a separate bedroom and living/dining area and a fully equipped kitchen. The furnishings include mostly rattan pieces with upholstery and curtains sporting a floral Caribbean motif. The place doesn't offer grand comfort, but it is a good value. The bathrooms are quite small with shower units. The complex is in a secluded position about an 11-minute walk to either the beach or the island's public golf course. There's no restaurant or bar, but maid service is provided in the rooms. Guests can shop at a mini-mart convenience store that is within walking distance.

Frigate Bay (P.O. Box 1253, Basseterre), St. Kitts, W.I. ℭ **869/465-7155.** Fax 869/465-9322. gateway@ caribsurf.com. 10 apts. Winter $80 apt for 2. Off-season $60 apt for 2. Extra person $15. AE, MC, V. **Amenities:** Watersports, maid service, babysitting, laundry. *In room:* A/C, TV, kitchen.

Morgan Heights Condo Resort   Despite the name, Morgan Heights is more of a condo complex than a resort. There's a minimum of assistance from the staff, but each of the small- to medium-size units is well maintained and fairly inviting, with good beds and small, shower-only bathrooms. Each two-bedroom apartment has wicker furniture, a covered patio overlooking the Atlantic Ocean, and a kitchen. The suites are a more recent addition. Although there's a view of the water, the beach is a 10-minute drive away. The whole complex is located on a sandy offshore east coast island known as Canada Estate.

Canada Estate (P.O. Box 735, Basseterre), St. Kitts, W.I. ℭ **869/465-8633.** Fax 869/465-2972. morgan heights@mail.skbee.com. 14 units. Winter $95 1-bedroom condo; $150–$175 suite. Off-season $75 1-bedroom condo; $125 suite. Extra person $20 in winter, $15 off-season. AE, DC, MC, V. **Amenities:** Restaurant, pool. *In room:* A/C, TV, minibar.

Palms Hotel   Occupying the upper floor of a two-story antique building surrounding The Circus, this hotel enjoys a central location. Some of the rooms are accessible only via an outdoor veranda; others open off an enclosed hall inside the 200-year-old site. Although there's lots of hubbub in the square in the morning, after 4pm it quiets down considerably. There are a small bar and cafe on the premises. The accommodations are high-ceilinged, spacious, and simply but comfortably furnished. The mattresses are in need of renewal. The bathrooms are small, each with a tiled shower unit. The main drawback to this place is the slowness of the staff, whose languorous pace can be exasperating. Swimming is an option at Frigate Bay, a 5-minute drive from the hotel.

The Circus (P.O. Box 64), Basseterre, St. Kitts, W.I. ℭ **869/465-0800.** Fax 869/465-5889. www.palmshotel. com. 12 units. Year-round $95 junior suite; $125 1-bedroom suite; $180 2-bedroom suite. AE, MC, V. **Amenities:** Bar, cafe. *In room:* A/C, TV, mini-fridge, coffeemaker.

Rock Haven Bed & Breakfast ✶ *(Finds*   Owners Judith and Keith Blake provide lots of charm at this private home. Both were born on St. Kitts and came back after years in Toronto, Canada, working as a dentist and a dietician, respectively. Although relatively new, the house was built with lots of Caribbean features, including decorative gingerbread, wide verandas, hardwood floors, and a location midway up one of the hills overlooking Frigate Bay Beach—high enough to benefit from the nearly constant ocean breezes. The larger of the two suites has a private patio and a kitchenette; the other doesn't have a kitchen but has reading areas and plenty of space for a cozy family holiday. Mattresses are first rate, and the medium-size bathrooms contain up-to-date plumbing such as excellent showers. The Blakes recommend that guests have a car of their own, making access to the island's attractions a lot easier. Breakfast, the only meal served, is a high point of the day, served with a sense of personalized hospitality.

Frigate Bay (P.O. Box 821, Basseterre), St. Kitts, W.I. ℭ **869/465-5503.** Fax 869/466-6130. blakekj@ caribsurf.com. 2 units. Winter $100 single or double without bathroom, $110 single or double with bathroom.

Off-season $85 single or double without bathroom, $95 single or double with bathroom. Rates include breakfast. No credit cards. **Amenities:** Breakfast room. *In room:* TV.

Timothy Beach Resort *Kids*   Located at the foot of a green mountain, 3 miles east of Basseterre, this condo resort is a family favorite, with swimming, sailing, and watersports at its doorstep. Although short on island atmosphere, it opens onto one of the finest beaches on St. Kitts. Naturally, the most sought-after units in this complex are those opening directly onto the beach,. There's also a pool, and it's just a short drive from an 18-hole golf course. The rooms are furnished in a Caribbean motif, and the larger accommodations have kitchens. Units here are timeshares, so there are no routine amenities. Most have decent mattresses and medium-size bathrooms with tub-and-shower combos.

Frigate Bay (P.O. Box 1198, Basseterre), St. Kitts, W.I. © 800/288-7991 in the U.S. and Canada. Fax 869/466-7085. www.timothybeachresort.com. 60 units. Winter $110–$135 single or double; $160 studio suite; $190 1-bedroom apt for up to 4; $315 2-bedroom apt for up to 6. Off-season $90–$105 single or double; $115 studio suite; $140 1-bedroom apt for up to 4; $225 2-bedroom apt for up to 6. AE, MC, V. **Amenities:** Restaurant, pool. *In room:* A/C, coffeemaker, iron, ceiling fans, no phone.

3 Great Deals on Dining

Most guests eat at their hotels; however, St. Kitts has a scattering of good restaurants, where you're likely to have spiny lobster, crab back, pepperpot, breadfruit, and curried conch. The drink of the island is CSR (Cane Spirit Rothschild), a pure sugarcane liqueur developed by Baron Edmond de Rothschild. Islanders mix it with Ting, a bubbly grapefruit soda.

Chef's Place CARIBBEAN   This small air-conditioned place is in the heart of Basseterre's business district. You can dine on the balcony overlooking the street. The hearty breakfasts include eggs, bacon, and pancakes. One of the specialties is the local version of jerk chicken. Another recommended dish, generally served on Saturday (a St. Kitts tradition), is goatwater stew and souse. Steamed fish, based on the catch of the day, is your best bet, unless you want to drop in on Friday to sample the local beloved specialty: pigtails and snout.

Upper Church St., Basseterre. © 869/465-6176. Reservations recommended for dinner. Lunch or dinner EC$20–EC$25 ($7.40–$9.25). No credit cards. Mon–Sat 8am–10pm.

Glimbara Diner CARIBBEAN   Don't expect grand cuisine from this workaday but honest eatery. Established in 1998 in a simple family-run guesthouse in the heart of town, it is a local favorite, thanks to the hardworking staff and down-to-earth cuisines. Small and cozy, and painted in shades of pink and white, it serves Creole cuisine that varies with the mood and inspiration of the cook, plus conventional U.S.-style platters, including hamburgers and hot dogs, usually served with fries and soda. Examples might include large or small portions of the stew-like goatwater, pumpkin or bean soup, and several kinds of fried or grilled fish, which might be accompanied by coleslaw or green salad. Ask for a local fruit punch known as *fairling* or the grapefruit soda called Ting.

In the Glimbara Guest House, Cayon St., Basseterre. © 869/465-1786. Main courses EC$12–EC$18 ($4.45–$6.65). AE, MC, V. Daily 7am–11pm.

J's Place ✦ *Finds* CARIBBEAN   Some of the best local food—cooked without fuss but filled with flavor—is found at this spot near the Brimstone Hill fortress. Most visitors to the fort stop here for a reasonably priced lunch of burgers, sandwiches, and salads, including the "famous" lobster salad. Although the restaurant closes at 7pm, many habitués stop off here for an early dinner. In the late afternoon, the menu expands, offering such regional favorites as goat and conch water (actually a stew), mutton with rice and peas, fried or steamed kingfish, and grilled Caribbean lobster.

Value **Cheap Thrills: What to See & Do for Free (Well, Almost) on St. Kitts**

- **Explore a Nostalgic Town.** The capital of St. Kitts, Basseterre, may have a French name, but it shows its long control by Britain. On a wide bay in the southwest of the island, it invites the stroller interested in seeing glimpses of its often fading Georgian and Victorian architecture. The best place to begin is Independence Square, a public park with flowering gardens in the historic center. The square is surrounded on three sides by Georgian buildings, many in need of paint. You can view St. George's Anglican Church on Cayon Street, with its crenellated tower. The Circus hardly evokes Piccadilly, but its centerpiece is the Berkeley Memorial Clock, the island's Big Ben, a cast-iron Victorian clock tower with four faces and a fountain at its base. The town is also filled with shops and some art galleries. Finally, you can head down to the pier where the ferry departs for Nevis. It's best to visit on a Saturday morning for market day—the splendid array of tropical fruits and vegetables invites your camera.
- **Tour a Beer Factory.** Devotees claim that Carib Beer is the finest in the West Indies, although Jamaicans, with their Red Stripe, dispute the claim. On the outskirts of town, Carib Breweries St. Kitts Ltd. (© 869/465-2309) offers free tours Monday to Friday 10am to 2pm. This brewery produces 750,000 cases annually of not only Carib Beer but SKOL, Guinness, Royal Extra Stout, Giant Malt, and Vita Malt. At the end of the tour, you're offered a complimentary tasting, the cold beer an ideal drink on a hot day in St. Kitts.
- **Tour a Sugar Factory.** Near the Carib Brewery (see above), the St. Kitts Sugar Manufacturing Corp. provides an insight into how important sugarcane was and is to the island economy. The ideal months to visit are February to July, when the cane is harvested and brought here to begin the sugar-making process whereby raw cane is turned into bulk sugar. A very light liqueur, CSR, is also produced at this factory, and it's enjoyed with a local grapefruit drink, Ting. *Warning:* This drink can be addictive. Free tours are available, but you should call © 869/465-8157 for an appointment.
- **Picnic at Dieppe Bay.** Either at your hotel or at a deli in Basseterre, get the makings of a picnic lunch and head for Dieppe Bay in the far north of St. Kitts. The island has better beaches than this, but none has the drama of the volcanic sand here. In the startling sunlight, the black sand sparkles with gold flecks. The protection of an offshore reef makes for tranquil waters, and a lovely coconut grove provides welcome shade and is the ideal spot for your lunch. The major reason to come here is to take in the coastline of the fabled "Black Rocks," particularly dramatic formations of huge lava boulders.

Romney Grounds. ✆ **869/465-6264**. Main courses EC$20–EC$45 ($7.40–$16.65); lunch from EC$15 ($5.55). No credit cards. Daily 11am–7pm.

Turtle Beach Bar & Grill ✰✰ SEAFOOD   Set directly on the sands above Turtle Beach, this airy, sun-flooded restaurant is one of the most popular lunch stops for those doing a whirlwind tour of St. Kitts. Many guests spend the hour before their meal swimming or snorkeling beside the offshore reef; others simply relax on the verandas or in hammocks under the shade trees, perhaps with a drink in hand. Scuba diving, ocean kayaking, windsurfing, and volleyball are available, and a flotilla of rental sailboats is moored nearby. Menu specialties are familiar stuff, but prepared with an often scrumptious flavor. Typical dishes might be stuffed broiled lobster, conch fritters, barbecued swordfish steak, prawn salad, and barbecued honey-mustard spareribs.

Southeastern Peninsula. ✆ **869/469-9086**. Reservations recommended. Main courses $10–$24. AE, MC, V. Daily 10am–6pm. Follow the Dr. Kennedy Simmonds Hwy. over Basseterre's Southeastern Peninsula; then follow the signs.

WORTH A SPLURGE

Stonewalls CARIBBEAN/INTERNATIONAL   Surrounded by ancient stone walls, this casual, open-air bar in a tropical garden in Basseterre's historical zone is cozy and casual. It's the type of Caribbean bar you think exists but can rarely find. In a garden setting of banana, plantain, lime, and bamboo trees, Wendy and Garry Speckles present an innovative and constantly changing menu. The fare might be Caribbean, with fresh kingfish or tuna and a zesty gumbo, or an authentic, spicy Dhansak-style curry. Hot-off-the-wok stir-fries are served, along with sizzling Jamaican-style jerk chicken. Appetizers might include piquant conch fritters. A small but carefully chosen wine list is available. The bar here is one of the most convivial places on the island for a drink.

Princes St. ✆ **869/465-5248**. Reservations recommended. Main courses EC$40–EC$60 ($14.80–$22.20). AE, MC, V. Mon–Sat 5–11pm.

4 Hitting the Beaches

Beaches are the primary concern of most visitors. The narrow peninsula in the southeast that contains the island's salt ponds also boasts the best white-sand beaches. All beaches, even those that border hotels, are open to the public. However, if you use the beach facilities of a hotel, you must obtain permission first and will probably have to pay a small fee.

For years, it was necessary to take a boat to enjoy the beautiful, unspoiled beaches of the southeast peninsula. But in 1989, the Dr. Kennedy Simmonds Highway (named for the nation's first prime minister), a 6-mile road beginning in the Frigate Bay area, opened to the public. To traverse this road is one of the pleasures of a visit to St. Kitts. Not only will you take in some of the island's most beautiful scenery, but you'll also pass lagoonlike coves and fields of tall guinea grass. If the day is clear (and it usually is), you'll have a panoramic vista of Nevis. The best beaches along the peninsula are **Frigate Bay, Friar's Bay, Sand Bank Bay, White House Bay, Cockleshell Bay,** and **Banana Bay.** Of all these, Sand Bank Bay gets our nod as the finest strip of sand. Both Cockleshell Bay and Banana Bay also have their devotees. These two beaches run a distance of 2 miles, all with powder-white sands. So far, despite several attempts, this area isn't filled with high-rise resorts.

A live steel band plays on Sundays from 12:30 to 3pm at the **Turtle Beach Bar and Grill** (© 869/469-9086), Turtle Beach, making it the place for afternoon cocktails on the beach.

For excellent **snorkeling,** head to the somewhat rocky **White House Bay,** which opens onto reefs. Schools of rainbow-hued fish swim around a sunken tugboat from long ago—a stunning sight.

South Friar's Bay is lovely, although its pristine qualities might be forever disturbed by the construction of a new Hyatt. Friar's has powder-fine sand as well, and many locals consider it their favorite. **Frigate Bay,** with its powder-white sand, is ideal for swimming as well as windsurfing and water-skiing.

As a curiosity, you might want to visit **Great Salt Pond** at the southeastern end of St. Kitts. This is an inland beach of soft white sand, opening onto the Atlantic Ocean in the north and the more tranquil Caribbean Sea in the south.

The beaches in the north of St. Kitts are numerous but are of gray volcanic sand and much less frequented than those of the southeast peninsula. Many beachcombers like to frequent them, and they can be ideal for sunbathing, but swimming is much better in the southeast, as waters in the north, sweeping in from the Atlantic, can be turbulent.

The best beach on the Atlantic side is **Conaree Bay,** with a narrow strip of gray-black sand. Bodysurfing is popular here. **Dieppe Bay,** another black-sand beach on the north coast, is good for snorkeling and windsurfing but not for swimming. This is the site of the island's most famous inn, the Golden Lemon, which you might want to visit for lunch. If you should be on this beach during a tropical shower, do not seek shelter under the dreaded machineel trees, which are poisonous. Rain falling off the leaves will feel like acid on your skin.

5 Sports & Other Outdoor Pursuits

BOATING   Most outfitters are found at Frigate Bay on the southeast peninsula. The best one to go to is provocatively named **Mr. X Watersports,** Frigate Bay (© 869/465-0673). Here you can rent kayaks or arrange windsurfing for $15 an hour. You can also rent a Sunfish at $20 per hour or hook up with a snorkeling tour lasting 2 hours and costing $25 per person.

DIVING, SNORKELING & OTHER WATERSPORTS   Among the best diving spots is **Nagshead,** at the south tip of St. Kitts. This is an excellent shallow-water dive starting at 10 feet and extending to 70 feet. A variety of tropical fish, eagle rays, and lobster are found here. The site is ideal for certified divers. Another good spot is **Booby Shoals,** lying between Cow 'n' Calf Rocks and Booby Island, off the coast of St. Kitts. Booby Shoals has abundant sea life, including nurse sharks, lobster, and stingrays. Dives are up to 30 feet in depth, ideal for both certified and resort divers.

A variety of activities is offered by **Pro-Divers,** at Turtle Beach (© 869/465-3223). You can swim, float, paddle, or go on scuba-diving and snorkeling expeditions from there. A two-tank dive costs $80 with your own equipment or $60 without equipment. Night dives are $60. A PADI certification is available for $350, and a resort course costs $75. Snorkeling trips lasting 3 hours are offered for $35 per person.

HIKING   Kris Tours (© 869/465-4042) takes small groups into the crater of Mount Liamuiga. You can also be led on hiking tours through a rain forest to enjoy the lushness of the island. If a group wants to, this outfitter will also conduct tours to Verchild's Mountain, which isn't a difficult trek. Tours cost $50 per person for a half day.

HORSEBACK RIDING   The best stable is **Trinity Stable** (© **869/ 465-3226**). It charges $45 for a half-day tour through a rain forest. You might also get to see the wild lushness of the North Frigate Bay area and the rather desolate Conaree Beach. You must call for a reservation, and you'll be told where to meet and offered any advice, including what to wear.

6 Seeing the Sights

The British colonial town of **Basseterre** is built around a so-called **Circus,** the town's round square. A tall green Victorian clock stands in the center. After Brimstone Hill Fortress, this **Berkeley Memorial Clock** is the most photographed landmark of St. Kitts. In the old days, wealthy plantation owners and their families used to promenade here.

At some point, try to visit the **marketplace.** Here, country people bring baskets brimming with mangos, guavas, soursop, mammy apples, and wild strawberries and cherries just picked in the fields, and tropical flowers abound. Another major landmark is **Independence Square.** Once an active slave market, it's surrounded by private homes of Georgian architecture.

You can negotiate with a taxi driver to take you on a tour of the island for about $60 for a 3-hour trip, and most drivers are well versed in the lore of the island. Lunch can be arranged at the **Rawlins Plantation Inn** or the **Golden Lemon.** For more information, call the **St. Kitts Taxi Association,** The Circus, Basseterre (© **869/465-8487** during the day or 869/465-7818 at night).

The **Brimstone Hill Fortress** ⊛ (© **869/465-6211**), 9 miles west of Basseterre, is the major stop on any tour of St. Kitts. This historic monument, among the Caribbean's largest and best preserved, is a complex of bastions, barracks, and other structures ingeniously adapted to the top and upper slopes of a steep-sided 800-foot hill. The fortress dates from 1690, when the British attempted to recapture Fort Charles from the French. In 1782, an invading force of 8,000 French troops bombarded it for a month before its small garrison, supplemented by local militia, surrendered. The fortress was returned to the British the following year, and they embarked on an intense program of building and reconstruction that resulted in the imposing military complex that came to be known as the "Gibraltar of the West Indies."

Today the fortress is the centerpiece of a national park of nature trails and a diverse range of plant and animal life, including the **green vervet monkey.** It's also a photographer's paradise, with views of mountains, fields, and the Caribbean Sea. On a clear day, you can see six neighboring islands. Visitors enjoy self-guided tours among the many ruined or restored structures, including the barracks rooms at Fort George, which compose an interesting museum. The gift shop stocks prints of rare maps and paintings of the Caribbean. Admission is $5, half-price for children. The Brimstone Hill Fortress National Park is open daily 9:30am to 5:30pm.

In the old days, a large tamarind tree in the hamlet of **Half-Way Tree** marked the boundary between the British-held sector and the French half, and you can visit the site.

It was near the hamlet of **Old Road Town** that Sir Thomas Warner landed with the first band of settlers and established the first permanent colony to the northwest at Sandy Point. Sir Thomas's grave is in the cemetery of St. Thomas Church. A sign in the middle of Old Road Town points the way to **Carib Rock**

Moments Into the Volcano

Mount Liamuiga was dubbed "Mount Misery" long ago, but it sputtered its last gasp around 1692. This dormant volcano on the northeast coast is one of the major highlights for hikers on St. Kitts today. The peak of the mountain often lies under a cloud cover.

The ascent to the volcano is usually made from the north end of St. Kitts at Belmont Estate. The trail winds through a rain forest and travels along deep ravines up to the rim of the crater at 2,625 feet. The actual peak is at 3,792 feet. Figure on 5 hours of rigorous hiking to complete the round-trip walk, with 10 hours required from hotel pickup to return.

The caldera itself has a depth of some 400 feet from its rim to the crater floor. Many hikers climb or crawl down into the dormant volcano. However, the trail is steep and slippery, so be careful. At the crater floor is a tiny lake along with volcanic rocks and various vegetation.

Greg's Safaris, P.O. Box Basseterre (© **869/465-4121**), offers guided hikes to the crater for $80 per person (a minimum of six participants needed), including breakfast and a picnic at the crater's rim. The same outfit also offers half-day rain-forest explorations for $35 per person.

Drawings, all the evidence that remains of the former inhabitants. The markings are on black boulders, and the pictographs date from prehistoric days.

Most visitors to St. Kitts like to spend at least 1 day on the neighboring island of Nevis. **LIAT** provides twice-daily flights to and from Nevis. Make reservations at the LIAT office on Front Street in Basseterre (© **869/465-8613**) instead of at the airport. In addition, the government passenger ferry *M.V. Caribe Queen* departs from each island between 7 and 7:30am on Monday, Tuesday, Wednesday, Friday, and Saturday, returning at 4 and 6pm (check the time at your hotel or the tourist office). The cost is $4 each way.

7 Shopping

The good buys here are in local handcrafts, including leather items made from goatskin, baskets, and coconut shells. Some good values are also to be found in clothing and fabrics, especially Sea Island cottons. Store hours vary, but are likely to be 8am to noon and 1 to 4pm Monday to Saturday.

If your time on the island is limited, head first for the **Pelican Shopping Mall,** containing some two dozen shops, banking services, a restaurant, and a philatelic bureau. Some major retail outlets in the Caribbean, including Little Switzerland, have branches at this mall. But don't confine all your shopping here. Check out the offerings along the quaintly named **Liverpool Row,** which has some unusual merchandise. **Fort Street** is also worth traversing.

Ashburry's, The Circus/Liverpool Row, Basseterre (© **869/465-8175**), is a local branch of a chain of luxury-goods stores based on St. Maarten. This well-respected emporium sells discounted luxury goods, including fragrances, fine porcelain, crystal by Baccarat, handbags by Fendi, watches, and jewelry. Prices are 25% to 30% below what you might pay in retail stores in North America, but the selection is similar to dozens of equivalent stores throughout the Caribbean.

Cameron Gallery, 10 N. Independence Sq., Basseterre (✆ **869/465-1617**), is the island's leading gallery. Britisher Rosey Cameron-Smith displays her watercolors and limited-edition prints of scenes from St. Kitts and Nevis. In her work, she makes an effort to capture the essence of true West Indian life. Rosey is well known on the island for her paintings of Kittitian Carnival clowns, and she also produces greeting cards, postcards, and calendars, and displays the works of some 10 to 15 other artists.

Island Hopper, The Circus, Basseterre (✆ **869/465-1640**), lies below the popular Ballahoo Restaurant. Island Hopper is one of St. Kitts's most patronized shops, with goods ranging from fashion to handcrafts. There's a lot of merchandise, both West Indian and international, on two floors. Notice the all-silk shift-style dresses from China, the array of batiks made on St. Kitts, and outfits suited for everything from formal to casual sportswear. Some 50% of the merchandise sold is from the islands, most of it from St. Kitts itself.

Kate Design, Mount Pleasant (✆ **869/465-7740**), is set in an impeccably restored West Indian house, on a hillside below the Rawlins Plantation. This is the finest art gallery on St. Kitts. Virtually all the paintings are by English-born Kate Spencer, whose work is well known throughout North America and Europe. Her still lifes, portraits, and paintings of island scenes range from $200 to $3,000 and have received critical acclaim. Also for sale are a series of Ms. Spencer's silk-screened scarves, each crafted from extra-heavy stone-washed silk.

Linen and Gold Shop, in the Pelican Mall, Bay Road, Basseterre (✆ **869/465-9766**), offers a limited selection of gold and silver jewelry, usually in bold modern designs. But the real appeal of this shop are the tablecloths and linens. Laboriously handcrafted in China from cotton and linen, they include everything from doilies to napkins to oversized tablecloths. The workmanship is as intricate as anything you'll find in the Caribbean. **The Palms,** in the Palms Arcade, Basseterre (✆ **869/465-2599**), specializes in island "things," including handcrafts; larimar, sea opal, pottery, and amber jewelry; West Indies spices, teas, and perfumes; tropical clothes by Canadian designer John Warden; and Bali batiks by Kisha.

Romney Manor, Old Road, 10 miles west of Basseterre (✆ **869/465-6253**), is the most unusual factory on St. Kitts. It was built around 1625 as a manor house for sugar baron Lord Romney, during the era when St. Kitts was the premier stronghold of British military might in the Caribbean. For years, it has been used as the headquarters and manufacturing center for a local clothier, Caribelle Batik, whose tropical cottons sell widely to cruise ship passengers and holiday-makers from at least three outlets in the eastern Caribbean. The range of merchandise consists of small items like scarves and separates, going on to caftans and dresses, along with an extensive collection of wall hangings. In 1995, a tragic fire and hurricane completely gutted the building. The manor has now been rebuilt and extended. Consider a stop here if only to admire the 5 acres of lavish gardens, where 30 varieties of hibiscus, rare orchids, huge ferns, and a 250-year-old saman tree still draw horticultural enthusiasts. Entrance to the gardens is free.

8 St. Kitts After Dark

The **Turtle Beach Bar and Grill** (✆ **869/469-9086**), Turtle Bay on the southeast peninsula, has a popular seafood buffet on Sunday with a live steel band 12:30 to 3pm; on Saturday it's beach disco time. There's no cover charge.

St. Kitts's only casino is at the **Allegro Jack Tar Village,** Frigate Bay (© 869/465-8651). It's open to all visitors, who can try their luck at roulette, blackjack, poker, craps, and slot machines. The casino is open daily 10:30am to 2am. There's no cover charge.

Night spots here come and go (mostly go). Currently, **Henry's Night Spot,** Dunn's Cottage, Lower Cayon Street, in Basseterre (© 869/465-3508), is one of the island's most frequented dance clubs. **Bayembi Cultural Entertainment Bar & Café,** just off The Circus in Basseterre (© 869/466-5280), couldn't look junkier, but it's a hot and happening place with a jazz guitarist on Wednesday and the inevitable karaoke on Saturday. Its daily happy hours pack everyone in at sunset. On Friday and Saturday, locals often head for **J's Place,** Romney Grounds across from Brimstone Hill (© 869/465-6264). The place is often jumping until the early hours. Another fun joint is **Doo-Wop Days,** Memory Lane, Frigate Bay (© 869/465-1960), painted in sherbet colors. The place looks like a junkyard, with its old 1940s photographs of such singers as Frank Sinatra and Chuck Berry, its velvet Elvis paintings, and pillows in the shape of guitars. Many nights there's live music, especially from doo-wop groups of yesterday. Saturday is karaoke night.

21

St. Lucia

In recent years, St. Lucia (pronounced "*Loo*-sha")—second largest of the Windward Islands—has become one of the most popular destinations in the Caribbean, with some of its finest resorts. The heaviest tourist development is concentrated in the northwest, between the capital, **Castries,** and the northern end of the island. Here you'll find the string of white-sand beaches that put St. Lucia on world tourist maps.

The rest of the island remains relatively unspoiled, a checkerboard of green-mantled mountains, gentle valleys, banana plantations, a bubbling volcano, giant tree ferns, wild orchids, and fishing villages. There's a hint of the South Pacific about it, and a mixed French and British heritage.

In the 1990s, many luxurious and expensive all-inclusive resorts were developed. Alas, there aren't that many inexpensive or even moderately priced properties anymore, so you have to search for bargains. Finding low-cost dining is also difficult. If you'd really like to see St. Lucia, contemplate an off-season visit, when many hotels slash their prices by 40%.

St. Lucia lies about 20 miles from Martinique. This mountainous island of some 240 square miles has around 120,000 inhabitants. Castries is built on the southern shore of a large, almost landlocked harbor surrounded by hills. The approach to the airport is very impressive.

1 Essentials

VISITOR INFORMATION

In the **United States,** the tourist information office is at 820 Second Ave., New York, NY 10017 (© **800/456-3984** or 212/867-2950). In the **United Kingdom,** information can be obtained at 421A Finchley Rd., London NW3 6HJ (© **020/7431-3675**).

On the island, the **St. Lucia Tourist Board** is located at Pointe Seraphine, Castries Harbour (© **758/452-4094**). In Soufrière the tourist office is on Bay Street (© **758/459-7200**).

The Internet address for St. Lucia is **www.stlucia.org**.

GETTING THERE

Before you book your own airfare, read the section "Package Deals," in chapter 2—it can save you a bundle!

The island maintains two separate airports, whose locations cause endless confusion to most newcomers. Most international long-distance flights land at **Hewanorra International Airport** (© **758/454-6644**) in the south, 45 miles from Castries. If you fly in here and you're booked into a hotel in the north, you'll have to spend about an hour and a half going along the potholed East Coast Highway. The average taxi ride costs $50 for up to four passengers. Flights

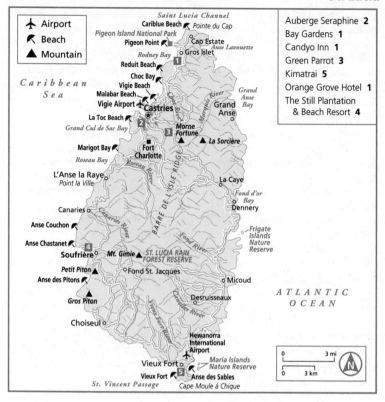

✈ Airport	Auberge Seraphine **2**
🗲 Beach	Bay Gardens **1**
▲ Mountain	Candyo Inn **1**
	Green Parrot **3**
	Kimatrai **5**
	Orange Grove Hotel **1**
	The Still Plantation & Beach Resort **4**

from other parts of the Caribbean usually land at the somewhat antiquated **Vigie Field** (℗ 758/452-2596), in the island's northeast, whose location just outside Castries affords much more convenient access to the capital and most of the island's hotels.

You'll probably have to change planes somewhere else in the Caribbean to get to St. Lucia. **American Eagle** (℗ 800/433-7300 or 758/452-1820) serves both of the island's airports with nonstop flights from the airline's hub in San Juan. Connections from all parts of the North American mainland to the airline's enormous hub in San Juan are frequent and convenient. American also offers some good package deals.

Air Canada (℗ 800/268-7240 in Canada, 800/776-3000 in the U.S., or 758/454-6038) has a nonstop flight to St. Lucia that departs year-round on Saturday from Toronto. **LIAT** (℗ 800/468-0482 in the U.S. and Canada, or 758/452-3015) has small planes flying from many points throughout the Caribbean into Vigie Airport, near Castries. Points of origin include islands like Barbados, Antigua, St. Thomas, St. Maarten, and Martinique. Know in advance that LIAT flights tend to island-hop en route to St. Lucia.

Air Jamaica (℗ 800/523-5585 or 758/454-8869) serves the Hewanorra airport in St. Lucia with nonstop service from either JFK or Newark daily, except Wednesday and Friday. Another option is **BWIA** (℗ 800/292-1183 for North American reservations, or 758/452-3778), which has two flights weekly from

JFK on Thursday and Sunday nonstop to Hewanorra, two weekly flights from Miami on Monday and Thursday, and two weekly flights from London's Gatwick Airport to Hewanorra on Tuesday and Sunday.

British Airways (© **800/247-9297** in the U.S., or 0345/222-111 in England) offers three flights a week from London's Gatwick Airport to St. Lucia's Hewanorra airport. All these touch down briefly on Antigua before continuing to St. Lucia.

GETTING AROUND

BY TAXI   Taxis are ubiquitous on the island, and most drivers are eager to please. The drivers have to be quite experienced to cope with the narrow, hilly, switchback roads outside the capital. Special programs have trained them to serve as guides. Their cars are unmetered, but the government fixes tariffs for all standard trips. Always determine if the driver is quoting a rate in U.S. dollars or Eastern Caribbean dollars (EC$).

Most tours of the island cost EC$350 ($129.50), divided among four people. Some companies specialize in these tours, which can also be cut to a half day if that's your wish. Try **Barnard's Travel,** Micoud Street in Castries (© **758/ 452-2214**).

BY RENTAL CAR   First, *remember to drive on the left* and try to avoid some of the island's more obvious potholes. You'll need a St. Lucia driver's license, which can easily be purchased at either airport when you arrive or at the car-rental kiosks when you pick up your car. Present a valid driver's license from home to the counter attendant or government official and pay a fee of $21.

The big U.S.-based rental companies maintain offices on St. Lucia: **Budget** (© **800/527-0700** or 758/452-0233), **Avis** (© **800/331-1212** or 758/ 452-2700), and **Hertz** (© **800/654-3001** or 758/452-0679). All three companies maintain offices at (or will deliver cars to) both of the island's airports. Each also has an office in Castries and, in some cases, at some of the island's major hotels.

You can sometimes get lower rates by booking through one of the local rental agencies, where rates begin at $60 per day. Try **C.T.L. Rent-a-Car,** Grosislet Highway, Rodney Bay Marina (© **758/452-0732**), which rents Suzuki Muritis and Suzuki Samurais. In addition, **Cool Breeze Car Rental,** New Development, Soufrière (© **758/454-7729**), is also a good bet if you're staying in the south.

Drive carefully and honk your horn while going around the island's blind hairpin turns.

BY LOCAL BUS   Minibuses (with names like "Lucian Love") and jitneys connect Castries with main towns like Soufrière and Vieux Fort. They're generally overcrowded and often filled with produce on the way to market. At least they're cheap, unlike taxis. Buses for Cap Estate, in the northern part of the island, leave from Jeremy Street in Castries, near the market. Buses going to Vieux Fort and Soufrière depart from Bridge Street in front of the department store.

 FAST FACTS: St. Lucia

Banking Hours Banks are open Monday to Thursday 8am to 1pm and Friday 8am to noon and 3 to 5pm.

Currency The official monetary unit is the **Eastern Caribbean dollar (EC$)**. It's about 37¢ in U.S. currency, or EC$2.70 = U.S.$1. Most of the prices quoted in this chapter are in U.S. dollars, as they're accepted by nearly all hotels, restaurants, and shops.

Customs At either airport, Customs might be a hassle if there's the slightest suspicion, regardless of how ill-founded, that you're carrying illegal drugs.

Documents U.S., British, and Canadian citizens need a valid passport, plus an ongoing or return ticket.

Drugstore The best is **William Pharmacy,** Williams Building, Bridge Street, in Castries (© **758/452-2797**), open Monday to Thursday 8am to 4:30am, Friday 8am to 5:30pm, and Saturday 8am to 1pm.

Electricity Visitors from the United States will need to bring an adapter and transformer, as St. Lucia runs on 220- or 230-volt AC (50 cycles).

Emergency Call the police at © **999**.

Hospitals There are 24-hour emergency rooms at **St. Jude's Hospital,** Vieux Fort (© **758/454-6041**), and **Victoria Hospital,** Hospital Road, Castries (© **758/452-2421**).

Language Although English is the official tongue, St. Lucians don't speak it the way you probably do. Islanders also speak a French-Creole patois, similar to that heard on Martinique.

Safety St. Lucia has its share of crime, like every place else these days. Use common sense and protect yourself and your valuables. If you've got it, don't flaunt it! Don't pick up hitchhikers if you're driving around the island. Of course, the use of narcotic drugs is illegal, and their possession or sale could lead to stiff fines or jail.

Taxes The government imposes an 8% occupancy tax on hotel-room rentals, and there's an $11 departure tax.

Telecommuniations The area code for St. Lucia is **758**. You make calls to or from St. Lucia just as you would with any other area code in North America. On the island, dial all seven digits of the local number. Faxes can be handed in at hotel desks or at the offices of **Wireless** in the NAS Building on the waterfront in Castries (© **758/452-3301**).

Time St. Lucia is on Atlantic standard time year-round, placing it 1 hour ahead of New York or Miami. However, when the United States is on daylight saving time, St. Lucia matches the clocks of the U.S. east coast.

Tipping Most hotels and restaurants simply add a 10% service charge.

Weather This little island, lying in the path of the trade winds, has year-round temperatures of 70°F to 90°F.

2 Accommodations You Can Afford

Most of the leading hotels on this island are pretty pricey—you really have to look for the bargains. Once you reach your hotel, chances are you'll feel pretty isolated, but that's what many guests want. Many St. Lucian hostelries have kitchenettes where you can prepare meals. Prices are usually quoted in U.S. dollars. Don't forget the 8% hotel tax and the 10% service charge added to your bill.

Auberge Seraphine   This two-story concrete-sided building painted cerulean blue and white is a 15-minute walk from Vigie Beach, overlooking the marina and the harbor of Castries. Owned and operated by the St. Lucia–born Joseph family, whose hotel skills derived from a long sojourn in England, the hotel offers well-maintained but very simple accommodations. They're generally spacious and decorated with bright colors, often tropical prints. The bathrooms, though small, are clean and have tiled showers. Most activities surround an open terrace whose surface is sheathed with terra-cotta tiles and that rings a small round-sided pool. Don't expect too many amenities, as the place's charm derives partly from its simplicity.

Vigie Cove (Box 390), Castries, St. Lucia, W.I. ℰ 758/453-2073. Fax 758/451-7001. www.sluonestop. com/auberge. 22 units. Year-round $85 single; $100 double; $120 for double occupancy of suite. AE, MC, V. **Amenities:** Pool. In room: A/C, TV.

Bay Gardens (Value (Kids)   This hotel offers one of the best values, as well as some of the best service, on the island. It's not right on the sands, but Reduit Beach, one of St. Lucia's finest, is a 5-minute walk or a complimentary 2-minute shuttle ride away. One of the newest and most up-to-date hotels on the island, Bay Gardens opens onto a large atrium lobby with a designer fountain pool and bamboo furnishings. Joyce and Desmond Destang are among the most hospitable hosts on the island. The medium-size bedrooms are decorated in vivid florals, and each has a terrace or balcony, as well as tropical art and accessories. The tiled bathrooms have tub-and-shower combos. Families might want to consider renting one of the eight apartments, each of which is a self-contained unit with a kitchenette. One child is accommodated without charge. The international restaurant, Spices, serves some of the island's best hotel food. Look for weekly rum punches, barbecues, Caribbean buffets, and live music on occasion.

Rodney Bay (P.O. Box 1892), Castries, St. Lucia, W.I. ℰ 800/223-9815 in the U.S., or 758/452-8060. Fax 758/ 452-8059. baygardens@candw.lc. 71 units, 8 apts. Winter $95 single; $110–$140 double. Off-season $75–$89 single; $95–$120 double. AE, DISC, MC, V. **Amenities:** Restaurant, access to nearby health club, car rental, room service (7–9:30pm), babysitting, laundry. In room: Dataport, fridge, coffeemaker, safe.

Candyo Inn   Amid the congestion of the fast-food restaurants and all-inclusive hotels flanking the edges of Rodney Bay, this is a two-story pink concrete hotel with a hardworking staff. There's a small pool and a simple bar on the premises, but most of the allure derives from the low rates, simple but comfortable rooms, and location a 5-minute walk from the beach. The only meal served in the restaurant is breakfast, with an occasional light snack on special request. Each medium-size room contains white-painted furniture with flowered upholstery, a white-tile floor, a small private balcony, and a cramped shower-only bathroom. The best deal is the suites, as they boast sitting areas, bathrooms with showers and tubs, and kitchenettes. The name of the hotel derives from an amalgam of the names of the owner's daughters, Candice and Yola.

Rodney Bay (P.O. Box 386), Castries, St. Lucia, W.I. ℰ 758/452-0712. Fax 758/452-0774. 12 units. Mid-Dec to mid-Apr $75 single or double; $90 suite. Mid-Apr to mid-Dec $65 single or double; $75 suite. AE, MC, V. **Amenities:** Breakfast room, bar, pool. In room: A/C, TV, kitchenette (in suites).

Green Parrot (★ (Value   About 1½ miles southeast of Castries, this inn operates the most famous restaurant (also called Green Parrot) on St. Lucia. But savvy bargain hunters have known for years that it also offers some of the least expensive lodgings on the island. Built of stone and stucco, the complex overlooks Castries Harbour, and the small rooms are housed in units built up the hillside. The furnishings are more functional than stylish, but everything is clean and comfortable, and the beds have good mattresses. The small bathrooms with shower units evoke U.S. economy motels. Try for a spacious room with a patio or, better yet, a balcony opening onto one of the most famous harbor views in the West Indies. The inn's shuttle takes guests on the 15-minute run between Castries and Vigie Beach.

Red Tape Lane, Morne Fortune, St. Lucia, W.I. © **758/452-3399**. Fax 758/453-2272. 60 units. Winter $65 single; $92 double. Off-season $59 single; $77 double. AE, MC, V. **Amenities:** Pool, beach shuttle. In room: A/C, TV.

Kimatrai   On the island's relatively undeveloped southeastern coast, just north of Vieux Fort, this hotel is about ¼ mile from a beach whose surf is usually rougher than that of beaches on more sheltered regions of the island. But unless you'd planned to spend hours paddling in saltwater, that might not affect your appreciation of this otherwise very acceptable hotel. The small rooms are outfitted with pastels and simple accessories, and the apartments and bungalows contain kitchenettes. Mattresses are a bit used but still comfortable, and the shower-only bathrooms are routine. The staff is helpful. A plain restaurant serves Creole food at very reasonable prices. A car would make your stay at this relatively isolated hotel more appealing.

Vieux Fort (P.O. Box 238), Castries, St. Lucia, W.I. © **758/454-6328**. Fax 758/454-5086 17 units. Year-round EC$143 ($53) single; EC$175 ($65) double; EC$2,300 ($850) 2-week rental of 1-bedroom apt for 2; EC$2,700 ($1,000) 2-week rental of 2-bedroom apt; EC$3,100 ($1,150) 2-week rental of bungalow. DISC, MC, V. **Amenities:** Restaurant. In room: A/C, TV, kitchenette (some units).

Orange Grove Hotel ⊕   This hilltop retreat, off the road leading to the super-expensive Windjammer Landing, is much improved, making it one of the island's most appealing choices. It offers comfort and convenience at a good price. The beach is just 15 minutes away by car, and there's a shuttle bus daily. The suites are spacious and well furnished, but even the standard rooms are well appointed, with West Indian rattan furnishings and tropical prints to enliven the scene. The accommodations also have separate living and sitting areas, along with patios or balconies overlooking the view. Each room has a king-size bed or two twin beds, each with a good mattress. Each unit has a compact, tiled bathroom with shower stall. A simple restaurant serves Creole and international cuisine.

Grosislet Hwy. (P.O. Box GM 702), Castries, St. Lucia, W.I. © **758/452-0021**. Fax 758/452-8094. 62 units. Year-round EC$126 ($47) single; EC$212 ($79) double; EC$220 ($82) suite. Children 11 and under stay free in parents' room. AE, MC, V. **Amenities:** Restaurant, pool, beach shuttle, room service. In room: A/C, TV.

The Still Plantation & Beach Resort   The Still has long been one of the most popular restaurants in the area (see "Great Deals on Dining," below), and in 1995, the owners opened a small inn right on the beach. Less than a mile east of Soufrière, it's on the grounds of a plantation that grows citrus, cocoa, and copra. A pool landscaped into the lush tropical scene adds to the allure, and walks are possible in almost all directions. The cheapest rentals—four studio apartments—have no kitchens, but the others do. The most expensive one-bedroom units open onto a beach, and the site itself opens onto views of the towering Pitons nearby. Furnishings are of the standard motel variety with no special styling. The tub-only bathrooms are tidily maintained, but a bit small and short on shelf space.

P.O. Box 246, Soufrière, St. Lucia, W.I. © **800/223-9815** in the U.S., or 758/459-7224. Fax 758/459-7301. www.thestillresort.com. 19 units. Year-round $50–$65 single or double without kitchen, $75–$85 single or double with kitchen; $110 2-bedroom apt for 5 (with kitchen). AE, MC, V. **Amenities:** Restaurant, bar; pool. In room: A/C, TV, kitchen (most units).

3 Great Deals on Dining

As virtually every hotel on St. Lucia seems to be going all-inclusive, the independent restaurants have had to sail through rough waters. But there are quite a few, nevertheless, of varying quality. Most restaurants are open for lunch and dinner, unless otherwise noted. The big problem about dining out at night, as it is on nearly all Caribbean islands, is getting to that special hideaway and back again with adequate transportation across the dark, potholed roads.

Bread Basket CONTINENTAL   This small bakery offers homemade breads, pastries, and a wide selection of sandwiches. Overlooking the marina, it features alfresco dining on the deck, where patrons can view million-dollar yachts and Pigeon Island. The forte here is the baked goods, from croissants to pies and cakes. This eatery serves full American breakfasts and light lunches, with a few heartier specials, such as stuffed crab backs and fish-and-chips. The sandwiches include roast beef, chicken, and tuna salad served on freshly baked bread. To finish your meal, try the cheesecake—the best on the island. At dinner, you'll find perfectly cooked steaks and succulent pastas.

Rodney Bay. ⓒ 758/452-0647. Breads and pastries EC$3–EC$8 ($1.10–$3); sandwiches EC$5.75–EC$12 ($2.25–$4.50); main courses EC$25–EC$65 ($9.25–$24). No credit cards. Mon–Sat 7am–5pm; Sun 7am–7pm.

Camilla's Restaurant & Bar WEST INDIAN   Set a block inland from the waterfront and one floor above street level, this is a decent Caribbean-style restaurant with simple, unpretentious food. It's operated by a local matriarch, Camilla Alcindor, who'll welcome you for coffee, a soda, or Perrier. The food is straightforward but flavorful. Opt for the fish and shellfish (Caribbean fish Creole, or lobster Thermidor) rather than the beef; the chicken curry is a savory choice as well. Lunches are considerably less elaborate and include an array of sandwiches, cold salads, omelets, and burgers. Our favorite tables are the pair that sit on a balcony overlooking the energetic activities in the street below. Otherwise, the inside tables can get a bit steamy on a hot night, as there's no air-conditioning.

7 Bridge St., Soufrière, St. Lucia, W.I. ⓒ 758/459-5379. Main courses $10–$33. AE, DISC, MC, V. Mon–Sat 8pm–midnight.

Chak Chak Bolomé CARIBBEAN   This simple restaurant, near the Hewanorra Airport, offers a savory West Indian cuisine. Don't expect to be pampered here. The meals are basic, and most of the main courses are served with rice, vegetables, and salad. The menu features an assortment of curried stews and Creole-style fish. You can find sirloin steaks, pork and lamb chops, and baked chicken as well. For a quick bite, the restaurant also serves burgers and sandwiches. Customers can eat outside on a small patio, and on Friday and Saturday nights there's disco dancing from 8pm until closing. Look for the weekend specials, such as fish cakes or fish fingers. Want to go really local? Try the fish-head broth served with local green bananas.

Beanfield, Vieux Fort. ⓒ 758/454-6260. Main courses EC$20–$65 ($7.50–$24). No credit cards. Daily 9am–midnight.

The Hummingbird WEST INDIAN/INTERNATIONAL   The restaurant is the best part of the Hummingbird Beach Resort complex. Tables are set on a stylish veranda adjacent to the sands of Hummingbird Beach. The menu includes Creole-style conch, lobster, burgers, steaks, and fillets of both snapper and grouper, punctuated with such American staples as burgers and BLTs. A tiny gift shop on the premises sells batik items crafted by members of the staff.

At the Hummingbird Beach Resort, on the waterfront just north of the main wharf at Soufrière. © 758/459-7232. Platters EC$40–EC$70 ($15–$26). AE, DISC, MC, V. Daily 8am–11pm.

J.J.'s. ⍟ SEAFOOD On a hill overlooking the bay, about ¼ mile from Marigot Bay Beach, this lively restaurant serves seafood in many guises. The terrace provides outdoor dining with a view of the yachts as they come into the harbor. The starters include stuffed crab backs and fish cakes; the featured platter is a special mix of Creole-style squid and fish along with chicken. Other options include curried chicken and grilled steaks. Prepared in a number of ways here, conch is especially tasty, as are the grilled kingfish and tuna. For a place to dance and mingle with the locals, try J.J.'s on Friday and Saturday nights, when things get cranked up with live entertainment.

Marigot Bay Rd. © 758/451-4076. Main courses EC$35–EC$70 ($13–$26). MC, V. Daily 8am–11:30pm.

Key Largo ITALIAN This local hangout serves only pizzas and salads, in a casual environment. Pizzas are one size (12 in.), with a very thin crust with tomato sauce and mozzarella. The house specialties include the Union Jack (bacon, egg, sausage, and tomato slices) and the signature Key Largo (shrimp and artichokes). Featured on the salad menu are prawn and chicken options. Specialty coffees are served: espresso, cappuccino, and Key Largo coffee (with lime juice, dark rum, brown sugar, Kahlúa, and a frothy head of whipped milk). For a cooler, spirited drink, try the Caribbean punch.

Rodney Heights. © 758/452-0282. Pizzas EC$20–EC$36 ($7.50–$13.25). AE, MC, V. Daily 9am–3pm and 5–11pm.

Razmataz! ⍟ (Finds) INDIAN Across from the Royal St. Lucian Hotel, this welcome entry into the island cuisine features delectable tandoori dishes, among other offerings. It's in an original Caribbean colonial timbered building with lots of gingerbread, decorated in a medley of colors and set in a garden, a 2-minute walk from the beach. A tempting array of starters greets you, from fresh local fish marinated in spicy yogurt and cooked in the tandoor to mulligatawny soup (made with lentils, herbs, and spices). Tandoori delights include shrimp, fresh fish like snapper or mahimahi, chicken, and mixed grill, not to mention the best assortment of vegetarian dishes on the island.

There's live music on weekends, and the owner is often the entertainer.

Rodney Bay Marina. © 758/452-9800. Reservations recommended. Main courses EC$24–EC$55 ($9–$20.25). MC, V. Fri–Wed 5:30–10:30pm.

The Still CREOLE This is the most authentic and atmospheric place for lunch while you're touring the Soufrière area in the south. The first thing you'll see as you drive up the hill from the harbor is a very old rum distillery set on a platform of thick timbers. The site is a working cocoa and citrus plantation that has been in the same St. Lucian family for four generations. The front blossoms with avocado and breadfruit trees, and a mahogany forest is a few steps away. The bar near the front veranda is furnished with tables cut from cross-sections of mahogany tree trunks. In the more formal and spacious dining room, you can feast on excellently prepared St. Lucian specialties, depending on what's fresh at the market that day. Try to avoid the place when it's overrun with cruise ship passengers or tour groups. There are far better restaurants on St. Lucia, but if it's lunchtime and you're near Diamond Falls, you don't have a lot of choices.

The Still Plantation & Beach Resort, Soufrière. © 758/459-7224. Main courses EC$25–EC$55 ($9.25–$20.25). AE, DC, DISC, MC, V. Daily 8am–5pm.

4 Hitting the Beaches

Since most of the island hotels are built right on the beach, you won't have to go far to swim. All beaches are open to the public, even those along hotel properties. However, if you use any of the hotel's beach equipment, you must pay for it. We prefer the beaches along the western coast, as the rough surf on the windward (east) side makes swimming there potentially dangerous. The best hotels are all on the western coast for a reason.

Leading beaches include **Pigeon Island** off the north shore, part of the **Pigeon Island National Park** (see "Seeing the Sights," below). The small beach here has white sand and is an ideal place for a picnic. Pigeon Island is joined to the "mainland" of St. Lucia by a causeway, so it's easy to reach.

The most frequented beach is **Reduit Beach** at Rodney Bay, a mile of soft beige sand fronting very clear waters. Many watersports kiosks can be found along the strip bordering Rex St. Lucian Hotel. With all its restaurants and bars, you'll find plenty of refueling stops.

Choc Bay is a long stretch of sand and palm trees on the northwestern coast, convenient to Castries and the big resorts. Its tranquil waters lure swimmers and especially families (including locals) with small children.

The 2-mile white-sand **Malabar Beach** runs parallel to the Vigie Airport runaway, in Castries, to the Rendezvous resort. **Vigie Beach,** north of Castries Harbour, is also popular. It has fine beige sands, sloping gently into crystalline water. **La Toc Beach,** just south of Castries, opens onto a crescent-shaped bay containing golden sand.

Marigot Bay is the quintessential Caribbean cove, framed on three sides by steep emerald hills and skirted by palm trees. There are some small but secluded beaches here. The bay itself is an anchorage for some of the most expensive yachts in the Caribbean.

One of the most charming and hidden beaches of St. Lucia is the idyllic cove of **Anse Chastanet,** north of Soufrière. This is a beach connoisseur's delight. Towering palms provide shade from the fierce noonday sun, while lush hills are a refreshing contrast to the dark sandy strip. Heading south on the windward side of the island is **Anse des Sables,** opening onto a shallow bay swept by trade winds that make it great for windsurfing.

The dramatic crescent-shaped bay of **Anse des Pitons** is at the foot of and between the twin peaks of the Pitons, south of Soufrière. The Jalousie Hilton transformed the natural black-sand beach by covering it with white sand; walk through the resort to get to it. It's popular with divers and snorkelers. While here, you can ask about a very special beach reached only by boat, the black volcanic sands and tranquil waters of **Anse Couchon.** With its shallow reefs, excellent snorkeling, and picture-postcard charm, this beach has become a hideaway for lovers. It's south of L'Anse la Raye.

Finally, you'll discover miles of white sand at the beach at **Vieux Fort,** at the southern end of the island. Reefs protect the gin-clear waters here, making them tranquil and ideal for swimming.

5 Sports & Other Outdoor Pursuits

BOATING   The most dramatic trip offered is aboard the *Brig Unicorn* (© **758/452-6811**), used in the filming of the famous *Roots* miniseries. Passengers sail to Soufrière and the twin peaks of the Pitons, among other natural attractions of the island. The vessel itself is 140 feet long. The cost of a full-day sail is $80. The ship is moored at Vigie Cove in Castries.

CAMPING   Camping is now possible on St. Lucia, courtesy of the **Environmental Educational Centre,** a division of the St. Lucia National Trust (© 758/452-5005). This reserve, opened in 1998, features 12 campsites (with many more to be added) along a beautiful stretch of beach on historic Anse Liberté in the fishing town of Canaries, 25 miles southwest of Castries and 8 miles north of Soufrière. Beachfront campsites are available for around $20 per night offering a view of the harbor and of Martinique on a clear day. Each campsite features nearby community bathrooms and toilets, and community cooking areas dotted with three to four grills. Some cooking can be done at your campsite in each of the stone stoves provided, a feature designed to contain campfires. The reserve offers 5 miles of hiking trails, and staff members can give tours of the area and the rich emancipation history of the Anse Liberté, which literally translated means "freedom harbor." It was here that much of the Brigand (St. Lucian term for "emancipation" or "freedom fighters") activity was organized, and arms and supplies were stockpiled for the effort in the caves that can be found along a hike. Camping equipment is also available for rent.

HIKING   A tropical rain forest covers a large area in the southern half of St. Lucia, and the St. Lucia Forest & Lands Department has proved to be a wise guardian of this resource. One of the most popular trails is the **Barre De L'Isle Trail,** located almost in the center of St. Lucia, southeast of Marigot Bay; it's a fairly easy trail that's even recommended for children. This forest reserve divides the western and eastern halves of the island. A mile-long trail cuts through the reserve. There are four panoramic lookout points, offering a dramatic view of the sea where the Atlantic Ocean meets the Caribbean. It takes about an hour to walk this trail, which lies about a 30-minute ride from Castries. Guided hikes can usually be arranged through the major hotels or through the **Forest & Lands Department** (© 758/450-2231 or 758/450-2078).

HORSEBACK RIDING   North of Castries, you can rent a horse at **Cas-En-Bas.** To make arrangements, call René Trim (© 758/450-8273). The cost is $40 for 1 hour; a 2-hour ride goes for $50. Ask about a picnic trip to the Atlantic, with a barbecue lunch and drink included, for $70. Departures on horseback are at 8:30am, 10am, 2pm, and 4pm.

PARASAILING   It's said that the most panoramic view of the northwest coast is sailing high over Rodney Bay. Parasailing is the key to this, and it's available at the watersports kiosk at the **Hotel Rex St. Lucian** at Rodney Bay (© 758/452-8351). The cost is $40.

SCUBA DIVING   In Soufrière, **Scuba St. Lucia,** in the Anse Chastanet Hotel (© 758/459-7000), offers one of the world's top dive locations at a five-star PADI dive center. At the southern end of Anse Chastanet's ¼-mile-long, soft, secluded beach, it features premier diving and comprehensive facilities for divers of all levels. Some of the most spectacular coral reefs of St. Lucia, many only 10 to 20 feet below the water surface from the beach, provide shelter for many marine denizens and a backdrop for schools of reef fish.

Many professional PADI instructors offer four dive programs a day. Photographic equipment is available for rent (film can be processed on the premises), and instruction is offered in picture taking, the price depending on the time and equipment involved. Experienced divers can rent the equipment they need on a per-item basis. The packages include tanks, backpacks, and weight belts. PADI certification courses are available. A 2- to 3-hour introductory lesson is $75 and includes a short theory session, equipment familiarization, development of skills in shallow water, a tour of the reef, and all equipment. Single dives cost $35, and hours are 8am to 5:45pm daily.

Another full-service scuba center is available on St. Lucia's southwest coast at the new **Jalousie Hilton** at Soufrière (© 758/459-7666), which offers competition for the longer established program at Anse Chastanet. The PADI center here offers dives in St. Lucia's National Marine Park; there are numerous shallow reefs near the shore. The diver certification program is available to hotel guests and other visitors age 12 or over. Prices range from a single dive for $55 to a certification course for $425. A daily resort course for $70 is offered Monday to Saturday for noncertified divers; it includes a supervised dive from the beach. All these prices include equipment, tax, and service charges.

TENNIS   The best place for tennis is the **St. Lucia Racquet Club,** adjacent to Club St. Lucia (© 758/450-0551). It opened in 1991 and quickly became one of the finest tennis facilities in the Lesser Antilles. Its seven courts are maintained in state-of-the-art condition, and there's also a good pro shop. You must reserve 24 hours in advance. Guests of the hotel play for free; nonguests are charged $20 a day. To rent a tennis racquet costs $7.40 per hour.

If you're in the southern part of the island, the **Jalousie Hilton** at Soufrière (© 758/459-7666) offers a good new program. Vernon Lewis, the top-ranked player on St. Lucia and an 11-time Davis Cup singles winner, is the pro. You'll find four brand-new Laykold tennis courts, three of which are lit for night play. Guests of the hotel play for free (although they pay for lessons). Nonguests are welcomed and can play for $20 per hour.

WATERSPORTS   Unless you're interested in scuba (in which case you should head for the facilities at the Anse Chastanet Hotel), the best all-around watersports center is **St. Lucian Watersports,** at the Rex St. Lucian Hotel (© 758/452-8351). Water-skiing costs $15 for a 10- to 15-minute ride. Windsurfers can be rented for $18 for half an hour or $22 an hour. Snorkeling is free for hotel guests; nonguests pay $10 per hour, including equipment, and water-skiing is arranged for $12 for 15 minutes.

6 Seeing the Sights

Lovely little towns, beautiful beaches and bays, mineral baths, banana plantations—St. Lucia has all this and more. You can even visit a volcano.

Most hotel front desks will make arrangements for guided tours that take in all the major sights. For example, **Sunlink Tours,** Reduit Beach Avenue (© 758/452-8232), offers many island tours, including full-day boat trips along the west coast of Soufrière, the Pitons, and the volcano for $80 per person. Plantation tours go for $56, and Jeep safaris can be arranged for $80. One of the most popular jaunts is a rain-forest ramble for $55, and there's also a daily shopping tour for $20. The company has tour desks or representatives at most of the major hotels.

CASTRIES

The capital city has grown up around its **harbor,** which occupies the crater of an extinct volcano. Charter captains and the yachting set drift in here, and large cruise ship wharves welcome vessels from around the world. Because it has been hit by several devastating fires that destroyed almost all the old buildings (most recently in 1948), the town has a look of newness, with glass-and-concrete (or steel) buildings replacing the French colonial or Victorian look typical of many West Indian capitals.

The **Saturday-morning market** in the old tin-roofed building on Jeremy Street in Castries is our favorite people-watching site on the island. The countrywomen dress up in their traditional garb and cotton headdresses; the number of knotted points on top reveals their marital status (ask one of the locals to explain it). The luscious fresh fruits and vegetables of St. Lucia are sold, as weather-beaten men sit close by, playing *warrie,* a fast game that involves pebbles on a carved board. You can also pick up such St. Lucian handcrafts as baskets and unglazed pottery.

PIGEON ISLAND NATIONAL PARK

St. Lucia's first national park, the **Pigeon Island National Park** ⓐ, was originally an island flanked by the Caribbean on one side and the Atlantic on the other. It's now joined to the mainland island by a causeway. On its west coast are two white-sand beaches. There's also a restaurant, Jambe de Bois, named after a wooden-legged pirate who once used the island as a hideout for his men.

Pigeon Island offers an **Interpretation Centre,** equipped with artifacts and a multimedia display on local history, ranging from the Amerindian occupation of A.D. 1000 to the Battle of the Saints, when Admiral Rodney's fleet set out from Pigeon Island and defeated Admiral De Grasse in 1782. The **Captain's Cellar Olde English Pub** lies under the center and is evocative of an 18th-century English bar.

Pigeon Island, only 44 acres in size, got its name from the red-neck pigeon, or *ramier,* that once made this island home. It's ideal for picnics, weddings, and nature walks. The park is open daily 9am to 5pm, charging an entrance fee of EC$10 ($3.75). For more information, call the **St. Lucia National Trust** at ⓒ **758/452-5005.**

MARIGOT BAY ⭐⭐

Movie crews, including those for Rex Harrison's *Dr. Doolittle* and Sophia Loren's *Fire Power,* have used this bay, one of the most beautiful in the Caribbean. Lying 8 miles south of Castries, it's narrow yet navigable by yachts of any size. Here Admiral Rodney camouflaged his ships with palm leaves while lying in wait for French frigates. The shore, lined with palms, remains relatively unspoiled, but some building sites have been sold. Again, it's a delightful spot for a picnic if you didn't take your food basket to Pigeon Island. A 24-hour ferry connects the bay's two sides.

RODNEY BAY ⭐

Reached after a 15-minute drive north of Castries, one of the most scenic bays in the Caribbean is named after Admiral Rodney. It's an 80-acre site set on a man-made lagoon. This has become a chic center for nightlife, hotels, and restaurants—in fact, it's the most active place on the island at night. Its marina is one of the top watersports centers in the Caribbean and a destination every December for the Atlantic Rally for Cruisers, when yachties who cross the Atlantic meet here and compare stories.

SOUFRIÈRE

This little fishing port, St. Lucia's second-largest settlement, is dominated by two pointed hills called **Petit Piton** and **Gros Piton** ⭐⭐⭐. The Pitons, volcanic

Value Cheap Thrills: What to See & Do for Free (Well, Almost) on St. Lucia

- **Shop at the Public Market.** As Caribbean capitals go, Castries is dull architecturally and has few sights to hold your interest—with one exception. The public market is one of the most fascinating in the West Indies, and it goes full blast every day except Sunday. It's most active on Friday and Saturday mornings. Not that you could miss it, but it lies a block from Columbus Square along Peynier Street, running down toward the water. You'll find rows of stalls under a covered market and out on the street. The array of color alone is astonishing, as are the display of fruits and vegetables, many of which may be unfamiliar. The varieties of bananas alone is daunting. By all means sample one. They're allowed to ripen on the tree, and they taste completely different from those picked green and sold at supermarkets in the U.S. Many of the vendors are from neighboring islands or countries, including the Guianese, who for some reason always seem to be hawking electronics.

- **Spend a Day on Pigeon Island.** Few places in St. Lucia hold the allure of Pigeon Island, which is now linked to St. Lucia by a causeway between Gros Islet and Cap Estate. You can spend a day here, exploring the island, swimming at the beach, and hiking, especially on the grounds of Fort Rodney. You can still explore the grounds of scores of military buildings constructed by the English. The best climb is to the top of Fort Rodney, whose cannon installations evoke the naval conflicts of the English and French that eventually led to British control of the island in 1814. Few small islands in the Caribbean have had such a turbulent history. You'll find caves once used by the cannibalistic Carib Indians. Pigeon Island was also the stamping grounds of some of the sea's most notorious pirates, including Jambe de Bois, or François Leclerc (Peg Leg). He attacked and captured several galleons in the mid–16th century.

- **Take the Waters at Diamond Falls.** The Soufrière Estate in the south of St. Lucia sprawls across 2,000 acres, a land grant made in 1713 by Louis XII. Today it's the Diamond Botanical Gardens, and it is still owned by the descendants of the original Devaux brothers, to whom the French king granted the land. Mrs. Joan Du Bouley Devaux has turned the area into a lush tropical Eden. Deep in the gardens is the Diamond Waterfall, created from water bubbling up from sulfur springs. Close to the falls, curative mineral baths are fed by these underground sulfur springs. You can slip into your swimsuit and bathe for half an hour for $2.50. For $3.75, you're given a private bath. As a young girl, Joséphine Bonaparte enjoyed these mineral baths while visiting her father's nearby plantation.

- **Explore the Scenic Outline at Morne Fortune.** To the south of Castries looms Morne Fortune, the inappropriately named "Hill of Good Luck" (no one ever had much luck here). It forms a stunning backdrop to the capital of Castries. Subjected to fierce battles, devastating hurricanes, and fires that have wiped it out, Morne Fortune today offers what many justifiably view as the most scenic lookout perch in the Caribbean. In the 18th century some of the most savage battles between the French and the British took place here. Today that's but a nostalgic memory as you wander about, looking at the beautifully planted private gardens, aflame with scarlet and purple bougainvillea. Former barracks, stables, and gun replacements are diverted to other purposes today, like Government House on Government House Road, the official residence of the governor-general of St. Lucia. It's one of the few examples of Victorian architecture remaining in St. Lucia (the once-rich heritage of Victorian buildings were destroyed by fires). As you take in the view, you'll see Vigie airport to the north and Pigeon Point beyond that. On a clear day you can see all the way to Martinique. To the south a view of the Pitons is possible.

- **Discover "Forgotten" Grande Anse.** The northeast coast is the least visited part of the island but contains dramatic rockbound shores, interspersed with secret sandy coves. You can reach it via a bad road. The terrain is arid, like parts of Arizona, and it is most unwelcoming, but fascinating nonetheless. Many locals tackle the road in a four-wheel-drive, especially the part from Desbarra to Grande Anse, where the road is the most bumpy. At Grande Anse live some rare bird species, notably the white-breasted thrasher. (While here, be careful to avoid a close encounter with a fer-de-lance, the only poisonous snake on the island. But visitors rarely report seeing them.) Grande Anse with its series of beaches—Grande Anse, Petite Anse, and Anse Louvet—is a nesting ground for sea turtles, including the hawksbill, the green turtle, the leatherback, and loggerhead. Nesting seasons last from February to October. Today the government has set Grande Anse aside as a nature reserve, so it can never be developed.

- **Walk in a Rain Forest.** More than 12% of the forests covering St. Lucia, nearly 20,000 acres, is a government-protected rain forest. In the south of this reserve are the Edmund Forest Reserve and the Quilesse Forest Reserve, site of a 7-mile-long Rain Forest Walk between the villages of Mahaut in the east leading to Fond St. Jacques in the west. This walk is one of the most dramatic in the Caribbean, taking in a quartet of St. Lucia's main bodies of water, the Vieux Fort, Roseau, Canelles, and Troumasse rivers. In a good year, some 150 inches of rain fall on this reserve, and showers are frequent throughout the walk, so dress accordingly. There are various panoramic lookout points, and you pass a number of small hamlets as you go along country roads. You'll note an abundance of rich flora, including wild orchids perfuming the air, bromelaids, and anthuriums. Bird life is evident everywhere, especially hummingbirds and purple-throated caribs. Count yourself lucky if you spot the rare and highly endangered St. Lucia parrot, known locally as a *jacquot*—it was hunted to near extinction for its meat.

cones rising to 2,460 and 2,619 feet, have become the very symbol of St. Lucia. Formed of lava and rock and once actively volcanic, they're now clothed in green vegetation. Their sheer rise from the sea makes them a landmark visible for miles around, and waves crash around their bases. It's recommended that you attempt to climb only Gros Piton, but to do so requires the permission of the **Forest and Lands Department** (© 758/450-2231) and a knowledgeable guide.

Near Soufrière lies the famous "drive-in" volcano, **Mount Soufrière** ☆. It's a rocky lunar landscape of bubbling mud and craters seething with fuming sulfur. You literally drive your car into an old (millions of years) crater and walk between the sulfur springs and pools of hissing steam. Entrance costs EC$3 ($1.10) per person and includes the services of your guide, who will point out the blackened waters, among the few of their kind in the Caribbean. Hours are daily 9am to 5pm; for more information, call © 758/459-5500.

Nearby are the **Diamond Mineral Baths** ☆ (© 758/452-4759), surrounded by a tropical arboretum. Constructed in 1784 on the orders of Louis XVI, whose doctors told him these waters were similar in mineral content to the waters at Aix-les-Bains, they were intended to provide recuperative effects for French soldiers fighting in the West Indies. Later destroyed, they were rebuilt after World War II. They have an average temperature of 106°F and lie near one of the geological attractions of the island, a waterfall that changes colors (from yellow to black to green to gray) several times a day. For EC$7 ($2.50), you can bathe and try out the recuperative effects for yourself.

From Soufrière in the southwest, the road winds toward **Fond St-Jacques**, where you'll have a good view of mountains and villages as you cut through St. Lucia's **Cape Moule-à-Chique** tropical rain forest. You'll also see the **Barre de l'Isle** divide.

7 Nature Reserves

The fertile volcanic soil of St. Lucia sustains a rich diversity of bird and animal life. Some of the richest troves for ornithologists are in protected precincts off the St. Lucian coast, in either of two national parks, Fregate Islands Nature Reserve and the Maria Islands Nature Reserve.

The **Fregate Islands** are a cluster of rocks a short distance offshore from Praslin Bay, midway up St. Lucia's eastern coastline. Barren except for tall grasses that seem to thrive in the salt spray, the islands were named after the scissor-tailed frigate birds (*Fregata magnificens*) that breed here every year between May and July. Large colonies of the graceful birds fly in well-choreographed formations over islands you can visit only under the closely supervised permission of government authorities. Many visitors believe the best way to admire the Fregate Islands (and respect their fragile ecosystems) is to walk along the nature trail the government has hacked along the clifftop of the St. Lucian mainland, about 150 feet inland from the shore. Even without binoculars, you'll be able to see the frigates wheeling overhead. You'll also enjoy eagle's-eye views of the unusual geology of the St. Lucian coast, which includes sea caves, dry ravines, a waterfall (which flows only during rainy season), and a strip of mangrove swamp.

The **Maria Islands** are larger and more arid and almost constantly exposed to salt-laden winds blowing up from the equator. Set to the east of the island's southernmost tip, off the town of Vieux Fort, they contain a strictly protected biodiversity. The approximately 30 acres of cactus-dotted land comprising the two largest islands (Maria Major and Maria Minor) are home to more than

120 species of plants, lizards, butterflies, and snakes that are believed to be extinct in other parts of the world. These include the large ground lizard (*Zandolite*) and the nocturnal, nonvenomous kouwes (*Dromicus ornatus*) snake.

The Marias are also a bird refuge, populated by such species as the sooty tern, the bridled tern, the Caribbean martin, the red-billed tropicbird, and the brown noddy, which usually builds its nest under the protective thorns of prickly pear cactus.

If permission is granted, visitors can set foot in either park as part of a group that arrives by boat under the supervision of a qualified guide. The cost is $30 per person for the Fregates and $114 per person for the Marias, for guided tours that last a full day and include lunch for the Marias jaunt. They must be arranged through the staff of the **St. Lucia National Trust** (© 758/452-5005), which will supply further details.

8 Shopping

CASTRIES

Most of the shopping is in Castries, where the principal streets are **William Peter Boulevard** and **Bridge Street.** Many stores will sell you goods at duty-free prices (providing you don't take the merchandise with you from the store, but have it delivered directly to the airport or cruise dock). There are some good (but not remarkable) buys in bone china, jewelry, perfume, watches, liquor, and crystal.

At **Noah's Arkade,** Jeremie Street (© 758/452-2523), many of the Caribbean handcrafts and gifts are routine tourist items, yet you'll often find something interesting if you browse. They sell local straw place mats, baskets, rugs, wall hangings, maracas, shell necklaces, locally made bowls, dolls dressed in banana leaves, and *warri* boards. Branches are found at Hewanorra International Airport and the Pointe Seraphine duty-free shopping mall.

POINTE SERAPHINE

Built for the cruise ship passenger, Pointe Seraphine, in Castries, has the best collection of shops on the island, together with offices for car rentals, organized taxi service (for sightseeing), a *bureau de change,* a Philatelic Bureau, an Information Centre, and international telephones. Cruise ships berth right at the shopping center. Under red roofs in a Spanish-style setting, the complex requires you to present a cruise pass or an airline ticket to the shopkeeper when buying goods. Visitors can take away their purchases, except liquor and tobacco, which are delivered to the airport. All shops in the complex keep the same hours. In winter, the center is open Monday to Friday 8am to 5pm and Saturday 8am to 2pm; off-season hours are Monday to Saturday 9am to 4pm. It's also open when cruise ships are in port.

Among the stores, you'll find a **Bennetton** (© 758/452-7685). In addition to T-shirts, tennis shirts, and shorts, there's an assortment of women's pants suits, men's business suits, and children's wear. Prices are about 20% lower than stateside. The inventory at **Little Switzerland** (© 758/452-7587) includes a broad-based array of luxury goods. Prices of the porcelain, crystal, wristwatches, and jewelry are usually around 25% less than those of equivalent goods in North American, but wise shoppers are usually alert to the special promotions (with savings of up to 40% below stateside retail prices) that influence the prices.

Although it doesn't even try to stock the porcelain, crystal, perfume, and luggage of Little Switzerland, **Colombian Emeralds** (© 758/453-7233) has a more diverse selection of watches and gemstones. There are two adjoining buildings, one of which sells only gold chains (14- and 18-karat) and watches; the other features a sophisticated array of precious and semiprecious stones. Gemstones are often reasonable in price. Of special value are the watches, which sometimes sell for up to 40% less than in North America. **Studio Images** (© 758/452-6883) offers a collection of designer fragrances, including some exotic locally made concoctions, often at prices representing 20% to 40% off stateside costs. The store also carries the latest brands of Sony electronics, plus leather accessories from Ted Lapidus as well as Samsonite luggage.

A wide collection of souvenirs is also sold. **The Land Shop** (© 758/452-7488) specializes in elegant handbags, garment bags, and briefcases. Prices are at least 25% less than in North America. Also available is a selection of shoes, but the inventory for women is more varied and interesting than the choices for men.

Oasis (© 758/452-1185) sells brand-name resort clothing and beachwear at duty-free prices. Look for Revo sunglasses, Reef and Naot footwear, Kipling bags, Gottex swimwear, and casual clothing by Gear. **Peer** (© 758/453-0815) stocks high-quality creative, colorful prints and embroidery designs on T-shirts, shorts, campshirts, and more. There is a large range for children, as well as bags, caps, women's wear, and bright tropical prints. It's a good place to visit for a wearable souvenir or gift.

GABLEWOODS MALL

On Gros Islet Highway, 2 miles north of Castries, this mall contains three restaurants and one of the island's densest concentrations of shops. The best clothing and sundry shop is **Top Banana** (© 758/451-6389), which sells beachwear, scuba and snorkeling equipment, gifts, inflatable rafts, and casual resort wear. Other branches of this store can be found at both the Rex St. Lucian Hotel and the Windjammer Hotel.

Made in St. Lucia (© 758/453-2788) sells only gifts and souvenirs made by local craftspersons in St. Lucia. The array of merchandise includes woodcarvings, clay cooking pots, sandals, a medley of spices and cooking sauces, a wide assortment of T-shirts, paintings, and such jewelry items as necklaces and "love beads" made from seeds and dried berries.

NEAR CASTRIES

Bagshaws, La Toc (© 758/451-9249), just outside Castries, is the leading island hand-printer of silk-screen designs. The birds (look for the St. Lucia parrot), butterflies, and flowers of St. Lucia are incorporated into their original designs. The highlights are an extensive household line in vibrant prints on linen, as well as clothing and beachwear for both men and women, and the best T-shirt collection on St. Lucia. At La Toc Studios, the printing process can be viewed Monday to Friday. There are three other retail outlets: in the Pointe Seraphine duty-free shopping mall, in Rodney Bay, and at the Best of St. Lucia shop at Hewanorra International Airport, Vieux Fort.

Caribelle Batik, Howelton House, 37 Old Victoria Rd., The Morne (© 758/452-3785), just a 5-minute drive from Castries, is where you can watch St. Lucian artists creating intricate patterns and colors through the ancient art of batik. You can also purchase batik in cotton, rayon, and silk, made up in casual and beach clothing, plus wall hangings and other gift items. Drinks are served in the Dyehouse Bar and Terrace, in the renovated Victorian-era building.

Vincent Joseph Eudovic is a master artist and woodcarver whose sculptures have gained increasing fame. You can view and buy his work at **Eudovic Art Studio,** Goodlands, Morne Fortune (© **758/452-2747;** fax 758/459-0124). He usually carves his imaginative freeform sculptures from local tree roots, such as teak, mahogany, and red cedar. Ask to be taken to his private studio, where you'll see his own remarkable creations.

CHOISEUL

The coastal village of Choiseul, southwest of Castries, was named during St. Lucia's French-speaking regime and has ever since been the home of the descendants of Carib Indians whose bloodlines mingled long ago with African slaves. The village's artistic centerpiece is the **Choiseul Art & Craft Center,** La Fargue (© **758/459-3226**), a government-funded retail outlet and training school that perpetuates the tradition of handmade Amerindian pottery and basketware. Look for place mats, handbags, and even artfully contrived bassinets, priced from EC$270 ($100) each, that might make a worthwhile present for parents-to-be.

9 St. Lucia After Dark

There isn't much night life on St. Lucia, except the entertainment offered by hotels. In winter, at least one hotel offers a steel band or calypso music every night. Otherwise, check to see what's happening at **Capone's** (© **758/ 452-0284**) and **The Green Parrot** (© **758/452-3167**), both in Castries.

Up on Pigeon Island is **Captain's Cellar** (© **758/450-0253**), not very St. Lucian, but draws a lot of expats to its informal English pub site, especially on weekends when live jazz is featured.

Rodney Bay (© **758/450-0022**), near La Creole Restaurant, lies at Rodney Bay marina, luring dancing feet to its wild disco nights. Some of the best zouk and salsa are played here.

Indies, at Rodney Bay (© **758/452-0727**), is a split-floor dance club with a large wooden dancing area and stage. There's also a trio of bars, with smoking and nonsmoking sections. The DJs keep the joint jumping, with both West Indian and international sounds, often American. The action gets going Wednesday, Friday, and Saturday, from 11pm to 4am. The cover ranges from EC$15 to EC$25 ($5.50–$9.25). Indies has opened a bar around the side of the building called the Back Door, featuring alternative music and reggae. A sort of rock and sports bar, it serves snacks until 3am.

Moments Jumping Up and Jumping Down

On Friday night there's only one place to be: The beachfront district that lies about a mile north of the hamlet of Rodney Bay wakes up and becomes one of the best street parties in the Caribbean. From the gigantic sound system the sounds of West Indian music fills the night. "After an uptight week," a local told us, "this is where we go to get lowdown and dirty." Dancing goes on until well after midnight, and no one goes hungry. Fresh local island conch (often marinated in lime juice) and some of the best barbecues on the island are likely to turn up here, but this scene is not for the timid or faint of heart.

The Lime at Rodney Bay is a restaurant that operates **The Late Lime Night Club,** Reduit Beach (© 758/452-0761), offering entertainment Wednesday to Sunday, beginning at 10pm and lasting until the crowd folds. Wednesday, Friday, and Saturday are disco nights. Sunday is country night. Admission is EC$10 ($3.75).

If you'd like to go barhopping, **Banana Split,** on St. George's Street in Castries (© 758/450-8125), is a popular hangout that often offers live entertainment, as does **Shamrocks Pub,** Rodney Bay (© 758/452-8725). This Irish-style pub is especially popular among boaters and gets really lively on weekends.

22

St. Maarten & St. Martin

For an island with a big reputation for its restaurants, hotels, and energetic nightlife, St. Maarten/St. Martin is small—only 37 square miles, about half the area of the District of Columbia. The island is split between the Netherlands and France: **St. Maarten** is the Dutch half and **St. Martin** the French half. Legend has it that a gin-drinking Dutchman and a wine-guzzling Frenchman walked around the island to see how much territory each could earmark for his side in 1 day; the Frenchman outwalked the Dutchman, but the canny Dutchman got the more valuable piece of property.

The divided island is the smallest territory in the world shared by two sovereign states. The only way you know you're crossing an international border is when you see the sign BIEN-VENUE, PARTIE FRANÇAISE—attesting to the peaceful coexistence between the two nations on the island. The island was divided in 1648, and visitors still ascend Mount Concordia, near the border, where the agreement was reached. Even so, St. Maarten changed hands 16 times before it became permanently Dutch.

Returning visitors who have been off the island for a long time are often surprised at the St. Maarten/St. Martin greeting them today. No longer a sleepy Caribbean backwater, it has become a boomtown. The 100% duty-free shopping has turned it into a shoppers' heaven, and the Dutch capital, Philipsburg, bustles with cruise ship passengers who arrive by the hordes. Although Mother Nature has rearranged them a bit, the 36 beaches of white sand remain unspoiled, and the clear turquoise waters are as enticing as ever. Sunshine is virtually guaranteed year-round, making all sorts of watersports and sailing possible. The nightlife is among the best in the Caribbean, but much has been lost to the bulldozer as well.

The Dutch side of the island, for the most part, is cheaper than the French side, especially its restaurants (but of course, they're not as good, either). And you'll find lots of deals, in package tours and villa rentals, so shop around and try not to pay the rack rate. Stay out of the swank places, book a guesthouse or a small inn, and avoid the upmarket French-style restaurants, and you'll probably fare all right in both St. Maarten and St. Martin.

Northernmost of the Netherlands Antilles, St. Maarten/St. Martin lies 144 miles southeast of Puerto Rico. A lush island, rimmed with bays and beaches, it has a year-round temperature of 80°F. The Dutch capital, **Philipsburg,** curves like a toy village along Great Bay. The town lies on a narrow sand isthmus separating Great Bay and Great Salt Pond. Commander John Philips, a Scot in Dutch employ, founded the capital in 1763. To protect Great Bay, Fort Amsterdam was built in 1737. The main thoroughfare is busy Front Street, which stretches for about a mile and is lined with stores that sell international merchandise, such as French designer fashions and Swedish crystal. More shops are dotted along the little lanes, known as

St. Maarten & St. Martin

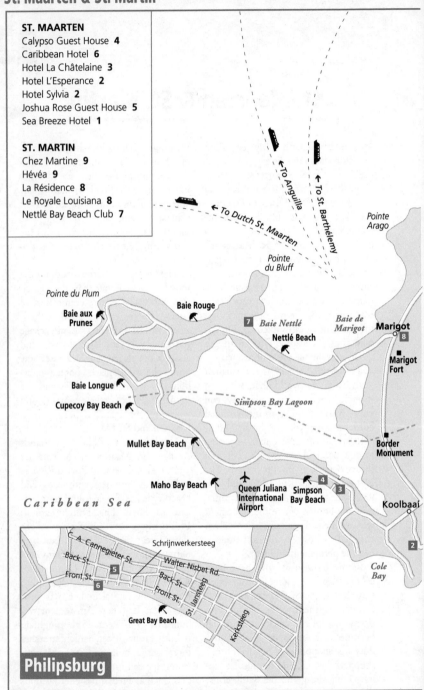

ST. MAARTEN
Calypso Guest House **4**
Caribbean Hotel **6**
Hotel La Châtelaine **3**
Hotel L'Esperance **2**
Hotel Sylvia **2**
Joshua Rose Guest House **5**
Sea Breeze Hotel **1**

ST. MARTIN
Chez Martine **9**
Hévéa **9**
La Résidence **8**
Le Royale Louisiana **8**
Nettlé Bay Beach Club **7**

To Anguilla

To St. Barthélemy

Pointe Arago

To Dutch St. Maarten

Pointe du Bluff

Pointe du Plum

Baie Rouge

7 *Baie Nettlé*

Nettlé Beach

Baie de Marigot

Marigot **8**

Baie aux Prunes

Marigot Fort

Baie Longue

Simpson Bay Lagoon

Cupecoy Bay Beach

Mullet Bay Beach

Border Monument

Maho Bay Beach

Queen Juliana International Airport

Simpson Bay Beach **4**

3

Koolbaai

Caribbean Sea

2

Cole Bay

C. A. Cannegieter St.

Schrijnwerkersteeg

Back St.

Walter Nisbet Rd.

Front St. **5**

Back St.

6

Front St.

St. Jansteeg

Ketksteeg

Great Bay Beach

Philipsburg

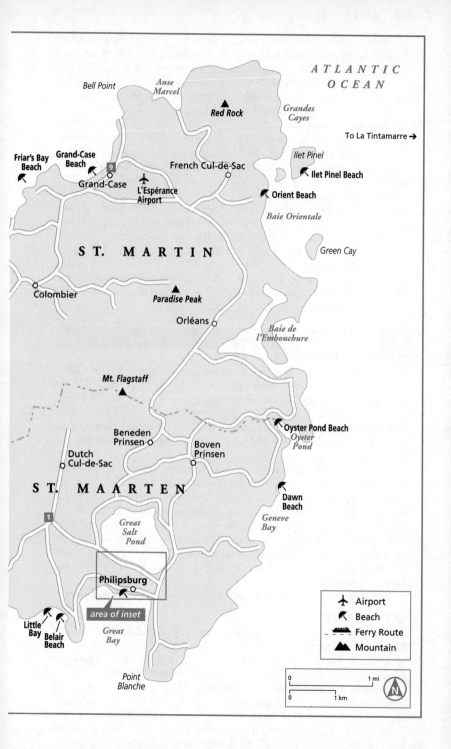

ATLANTIC
OCEAN

Bell Point
Anse
Marcel

Red Rock

Grandes
Cayes

To La Tintamarre →

Friar's Bay
Beach

Grand-Case
Beach

Grand-Case

9

L'Espérance
Airport

French Cul-de-Sac

Ilet Pinel

Ilet Pinel Beach

Orient Beach

Baie Orientale

S T.   M A R T I N

Green Cay

Colombier

Paradise Peak

Orléans

Baie de
l'Embouchure

Mt. Flagstaff

Beneden
Prinsen

Boven
Prinsen

Oyster Pond Beach

Oyster
Pond

Dutch
Cul-de-Sac

S T.   M A A R T E N

1

Great
Salt
Pond

Dawn
Beach

Geneve
Bay

Philipsburg

area of inset

Little
Bay

Belair
Beach

Great
Bay

Point
Blanche

✈	Airport
🏖	Beach
🚋	Ferry Route
▲	Mountain

0   1 mi
0   1 km

N

steegijes, that connect Front Street with Back Street, another shoppers' delight.

The French side of the island has a slightly different character, with no dazzling sights and no spectacular nightlife. Even the sports scene here isn't as well organized as that on many Caribbean islands (although the Dutch side has golf and other diversions). Most people come to St. Martin to relax on its many white-sand beaches and to sample "France in the tropics." St. Martin not only has some of the best cuisine in the Caribbean but is filled with an extraordinary number of bistros and restaurants. It boasts a distinctly French air. Policemen, for example, wear *képis.* The towns have names like Colombier and Orléans, the streets are *rues,* and the French flag flies over the *gendarmerie* in **Marigot,** the capital. Its advocates cite it as distinctly more sophisticated, prosperous, and cosmopolitan than its neighboring *départements d'outre-mer,* Guadeloupe and Martinique.

Marigot isn't quite the same size as Philipsburg. It has none of the frenzied pace of the Dutch city, which is often overrun with cruise ship passengers. In fact, Marigot looks like a French village transplanted to the Caribbean. If you climb the hill over this tiny port, you'll be rewarded with a view from the old fort there. About 20 minutes by car beyond Marigot is Grand-Case, a small fishing village that's an outpost of French civilization with many good restaurants and a few places to stay.

1 Essentials

VISITOR INFORMATION

If you're going to Dutch St. Maarten, contact the **St. Maarten Tourist Office,** 675 Third Ave., Suite 1807, New York, NY 10017 (© **800/786-2278** in the U.S., or 212/953-2084). In Canada, contact the **St. Maarten Tourist Office,** 243 Ellerslie Ave., Willowdale, Toronto, Ontario M2N 1Y5 (© **416/223-3501**). Once on the island, go to the **Tourist Information Bureau,** in the Imperial Building at 23 Walter Nisbeth Rd. (© **599/54-22337**), open Monday to Friday 8am to 5pm.

For French St. Martin, you can obtain information from one of the French Government Tourist Offices: 675 3rd Avenue, Suite 1807, New York, NY 10017 (© **212/475-8970**); 9454 Wilshire Blvd., Suite 715, Beverly Hills, CA 90212 (© **310/271-6665**); and 676 N. Michigan Ave., Suite 3360, Chicago, IL 60611 (© **312/751-7800**). You can also call France-on-Call at (© **900/990-0040** at the rate of 50¢ per minute. The tourist board on French St. Martin, called the **Office du Tourisme,** is at the rue de Sandy Ground (© **0590/87-57-21**), open Monday to Friday 8:30am to 1pm and 2:30 to 5:30pm and Saturday 8am to noon.

The Internet address for both sections of the island is **www.st-martin.org**.

GETTING THERE

There are two airports on the island. St. Maarten's **Queen Juliana International Airport** (© **599/54-54211**) is the second busiest in the Caribbean, topped only by San Juan, Puerto Rico. But you can also fly to the smaller **L'Espérance Airport** in Grand-Case on French St. Martin (© **0590/87-53-03**).

American Airlines (© **800/433-7300** in the U.S.) offers more options and more frequent service into St. Maarten than any other airline—one daily nonstop flight from both New York's JFK and Miami. Additional nonstop daily flights into St. Maarten are offered by American and its local affiliate **American Eagle** (© **800/433-7300** in the U.S.) from San Juan. Ask for one of the airline's tour operators, because you can usually save a lot of money by booking one of American's package tours.

Delta (© **800/221-1212** in the U.S.) now offers a nonstop flight from Atlanta. **US Airways** (© **800/428-4322** in the U.S.) offers nonstop service from Philadelphia on Saturday and Sunday and from Charlotte, North Carolina, on Sunday. **Continental Airlines** (© **800/231-0856** in the U.S.) offers daily flights out of its hub in Newark, New Jersey, and **LIAT** (© **800/468-0482** in the U.S. and Canada), with three flights out of San Juan. These latter flights stop first at Tortola (capital of the British Virgin Islands) before going on to St. Maarten. Even so, the trip usually takes only 90 minutes.

ALM Antillean Airlines (© **800/327-7230** in the U.S.) offers nonstop and once-daily direct service in winter to St. Maarten from the airline's home base on Curaçao. Off-season, there are two flights Sunday to Tuesday and again on Friday. US Airways offers nonstop service from Philadelphia on Saturday and Sunday and from Charlotte, North Carolina, on Sunday.

If you're coming from St. Barts, however, there are at least two airlines available to haul you and your possessions on the short route directly to French-speaking St. Martin: **Air Guadeloupe** (© **0590/87-53-74** on St. Martin) and **Air Caraibes** (© **0590/87-73-46**). Collectively, they maintain between 15 and 20 daily flights, each about 10 minutes long, from St. Barts, about a third of which land at L'Espérance.

GETTING AROUND

BY TAXI   Taxis are unmetered on both sides of the island, so always agree on the rate before getting into an unmetered cab. Rate schedules are slightly different on the two sides. **St. Maarten taxis** have minimum fares for two passengers, and each additional passenger pays $4 extra. One piece of luggage per person is allowed free; each additional piece is $1. Fares are 25% higher between 10pm and midnight and 50% higher between midnight and 6am. **St. Martin fares** are also for two passengers, but allow a supplement of about $1 for each suitcase or valise. These fares are in effect 7am to 10pm; after that, they go up by 25% until midnight and rise by 50% after midnight.

On the **Dutch side,** a typical fare from Queen Juliana Airport to the Maho Beach area is $5; from Philipsburg to Queen Juliana Airport, $10. On the **French side,** taxi fares from Marigot to Grand-Case are $10, from Juliana Airport to Marigot and from Juliana Airport to La Samanna $14.

For late-night cab service on St. Maarten, call © **599/54-54317.** A **Taxi Service & Information Center** operates at the port of Marigot (© **0590/87-56-54**) on the French side of the island.

BY MINIBUS   Minibus is a reasonable means of transport on St. Maarten/St. Martin if you don't mind inconveniences, and at times overcrowding. Buses run daily 7am to midnight and serve most of the major locations on both sides of the island. The most popular run is from Philipsburg to Marigot on the French side. Privately owned and operated, minibuses tend to follow specific routes, with fares ranging from $1.15 to $2, depending on where you're going.

BY RENTAL CAR   Especially if you want to experience both the Dutch and the French sides, you might want to **rent a car.** The taxi drivers' union strictly enforces a law that forbids anyone from picking up a car at the airport. As a result, every rental agency delivers cars directly to your hotel, where an employee will complete the paperwork. If you prefer to rent your car on arrival, head for one of the tiny rental kiosks across the road from the airport, but beware of long lines.

Budget (℡ **800/472-3325** in the U.S., 599/54-54030 on the Dutch side, or 590/87-38-22 on the French side), **Hertz** (℡ **800/654-3131** in the U.S., 599/54-54314 on the Dutch side, or 590/87-40-68 on the French side), and **Avis** (℡ **800/331-1084** in the U.S., 599/54-52847 on the Dutch side, or 590/87-50-60 on the French side) all maintain offices on both sides of the island. **National** (℡ **800/328-4567** in the U.S., 599/54-42168 in Cole Bay, or 599/5-96856 at Queen Juliana Airport) has offices only on the Dutch side. All these companies charge roughly equivalent rates. All the major car-rental agencies require that renters be at least 25 years old. Your credit-card issuer might provide insurance coverage, so check before your trip; otherwise, it may be wise to buy the fairly cheap collision-damage waiver (CDW) when you rent.

Drive on the right-hand side (on both the French and Dutch sides of the island), and expect traffic jams near the major towns. International road signs are observed, and there are no Customs formalities at the border between the two sides of the island.

BY BIKE OR SCOOTER   Of course, it's far cheaper to get around the island by **scooter or bike** than by rented car. The best deal on such rentals is at **Rent Scoot,** Low Lands Road, Nettle Bay (℡ **0590/87-20-59**), just across the border on the French side. It rents scooters for $24 per day, with motorbikes beginning at $39.

 FAST FACTS: **St. Maarten & St. Martin**

Banking Hours   On the Dutch side, most banks are open Monday to Thursday 8:30am to 1pm and Friday 8:30am to 1pm and 4 to 5pm. On the French side, they're also usually open every weekday afternoon 2 to 4 or 5pm, not only on Friday.

Currency   The legal tender on the Dutch side is the **Netherlands Antilles guilder (NAf)**; the official exchange rate is 1.80NAf = U.S.$1. On the French side, the official monetary unit is the **French franc (F)**, which is divided into **100 centimes.** Occasionally, a shop will accept U.S. dollars, converting them into francs at a rate somewhat less favorable than you'd have gotten if you had changed them at a bank or *bureau de change.* The exchange rate used to calculate the dollar values given in the chapter is 6.9F to U.S.$1 (1F= U.S.14½¢). As this is sure to fluctuate a bit, use this rate for general guidance only. Beginning in February 2002, the **euro (€)** will be accepted for general use throughout France, even though authorities expect both the French franc and the euro to coexist for an indeterminate time after the euro's introduction. At press time, the euro converted into French francs at a rate of €1 = 6.58F, and the U.S. dollar converted into euros at a rate of U.S.$1 = €.92.

Documents   U.S., British, and Canadian citizens need a passport, plus an ongoing or a return ticket and a confirmed hotel reservation.

Electricity   Dutch St. Maarten uses the same voltage (110-volt AC, 60 cycles) with the same electrical configurations as the United States, so adapters and transformers are not necessary. However, on French St. Martin transformers and adapters are necessary. To simplify things, many hotels on both sides of the island have installed built-in sockets suitable for both the European and North American forms of electrical currents.

Emergencies On the Dutch side, call the **police** at ℂ **599/54-22222** or an **ambulance** at ℂ **599/54-22111**. On the French side, you can reach the **police** by dialing ℂ **17** or 0590/87-50-06. In case of **fire**, dial ℂ **18**.

Hospitals On the Dutch side, go to the **Medical Center**, Welegen Road, Cay Hill (ℂ **599/54-31111**). On the French side, the local hospital is **Hospital de Marigot**, Rue de l'Hôpital, Marigot (ℂ **0590/29-57-57** or 0590/29-57-48).

Language The language on the St. Maarten side is officially Dutch, but most people speak English. The same is true for St. Martin, with English and French both widely spoken, although this is a French possession. A patois is spoken only by a small segment of the local populace.

Safety Crime is on the rise on the island and, in fact, has become quite serious. If possible, avoid night driving—it's particularly unwise to drive on remote, unlit, back roads at night. Also, let that deserted, isolated beach remain so. You're safer in a crowd, but under no circumstances should you leave anything unguarded on the beach. The crime wave hitting Dutch St. Maarten also plagues French St. Martin.

Taxes & Service There's no departure tax imposed for departures from L'Espérance Airport on the French side. However, for departures from Juliana Airport on the Dutch side, a departure tax of $20 is assessed ($6 if you're leaving the island for St. Eustatius or Saba).

On the Dutch side, an 8% government tax is added to hotel bills, and, in general, hotels also add a 10% or 15% service charge.

Telecommunications To call Dutch St. Maarten from the United States, dial **011** (the international access code), then **599** (the country code for the Netherlands Antilles), followed by **54** and then the five-digit local number.

To make a local call on Dutch St. Maarten, dial **54**, then the five-digit local number. But if you're calling "long distance" from the Dutch side of the island to the French side of the island, dial **00**, followed by **590** (the international access code for French St. Martin) and the six-digit local number. If you're on the French side of the island and want to call anyone on the Dutch side, you treat the call the same way: Dial **00**, followed by **599**, then **54** and the five-digit local number. Know in advance that calls between the French and Dutch sides are considered long-distance calls and are much, much more expensive than you might imagine, considering the relatively short distances involved.

French St. Martin is linked to the Guadeloupe telephone system. To call French St. Martin from the United States, dial **011** (the international access code), then **590** (the country code for Guadeloupe), and then the six-digit local number. To make a call from French St. Martin to any point within French St. Martin, no codes are necessary; just dial the local six-digit French number.

Time St. Maarten and St. Martin operate on Atlantic standard time year-round. Therefore, in winter when the United States is on standard time, if it's 6pm in Philipsburg, it's 5pm in New York. During daylight saving time in the United States, the island and the U.S. east coast are on the same time.

Tipping Most hotels on both sides of the island add a 10% or 15% service charge to your bill; make sure you understand whether it's already included in the price quoted to you. Most restaurants also add a service charge to your bill. If service has not been added (unlikely), it's customary to tip around 15% in restaurants. Taxi drivers also expect a 15% tip.

Water The water on the island is safe to drink. In fact, most hotels serve desalinated water.

Weather The island has a year-round temperature of about 80°F.

2 Accommodations You Can Afford

IN ST. MAARTEN

Remember, a government tax of 8% and a 10% to 15% service charge are added to your hotel bill. Ask about this when you book a room to save yourself a shock when you check out.

Calypso Guest House This is one of the smallest hotels on the island's Dutch side—a welcome contrast to the massive hotels that otherwise dominate the island. A 5-minute drive from both the airport (whose loud noises usually stop around dusk) and Simpson Bay Beach, it has a plain but worthwhile restaurant and rooms that are somewhat bigger (considering the low costs) than you might expect. The rooms have terra-cotta floor tiles, white walls, and simple (mostly wicker) furnishings, including a good bed with a firm mattress and a small but tidy bathroom.

Simpson Bay (P.O. Box 112), Philipsburg, St. Maarten, N.A. ☎ 599/54-54233. Fax 599/54-52881. 8 units. Winter $96 apt for 1; $110 apt for 2; $160 2-bedroom apt for 4. Off-season $65 apt for 1; $80 apt for 2; $110 2-bedroom apt for 4. Extra person $15. AE, MC, V. **Amenities:** Restaurant, bar. *In room:* A/C, TV, kitchenette.

Caribbean Hotel This hotel is popular with business travelers from other Caribbean islands, as well as cost-conscious vacationers looking for inexpensive lodgings in the heart of the Dutch capital, very close to the beach. It's in a three-story building with shops on the ground floor; climb a flight of steps to the second-floor reception area to register. The rooms, like the hotel's exterior, are outfitted in black and white, with occasional touches of red. Each unit has a balcony with a view over the back of the hotel (which is quieter) or Front Street and the beach. Rooms are small and have a sterile look but are clean, with decent but rather thin mattresses. The bathrooms are cramped, and each has a shower stall. At these great rates you don't get a lot of resort-type amenities—it's up to you to make your own fun. No meals are served on the premises, but many bars and cheap eateries are within walking distance.

90 Front St. (P.O. Box 236), Philipsburg, St. Maarten, N.A. ☎ 599/54-22028. 45 units. Year-round $45 single; $65 double. AE, MC, V. *In room:* A/C, TV.

Hotel L'Esperance *(Kids* The management exudes hospitality, as reflected by the bar that operates on the honor system. This two-story white Mediterranean-style building is in a residential area about 10 minutes from Philipsburg; it's a 10- to 15-minute walk from Belaire Beach or about 10 to 15 minutes by car from the area's other good beaches. The lower apartments open onto patios, while the upper units have balconies. Each one-bedroom apartment has a living area, a dining area, a refrigerator, and a two-burner stove. Each unit has a mid-size bathroom, mostly with tub-and-shower combination. The larger apartments have full kitchens, where you can prepare your own meals, and there's also a small restaurant that serves mainly sandwiches and snacks. Because of its low cost and welcoming atmosphere, this is a haven for families.

4 Tiger Rd., Cay Hill, St. Maarten, N.A. ℂ 599/54-25355. Fax 599/54-24088. www.lesperancehotel.com. 23 units. Winter $80 1-bedroom apt; $115 2-bedroom apt. Off-season $60 1-bedroom apt; $90 2-bedroom apt. Children 11 and under stay free in parents' apt. AE, DISC, MC, V. **Amenities:** Restaurant, bar, pool, babysitting. In room: A/C, TV, kitchenette.

Hotel Sylvia   The rooms here are simple but spotless. Near Philipsburg and a 10-minute walk from the nearest beach, this two-story white concrete building is also quite close to some of St. Maarten's best restaurants and shopping. The rooms are decorated with somewhat worn carpeting and have either queen- or king-size beds with mattresses that could stand to be replaced. Second-floor rooms open onto balconies. The rooms have air-conditioning, but the apartments, which have kitchens, are equipped with ceiling fans. The bathrooms are cramped, with shower stalls. The restaurant serves three rather standard but affordable meals a day. Hotel Sylvia is for adults; children aren't encouraged.

1 Leopard Rd., Cay Hill, St. Maarten, N.A. ℂ 599/54-23389. 14 units. Year-round $50–$60 single or double; $60 apt. No credit cards. **Amenities:** Restaurant. In room: A/C in some units, TV.

Joshua Rose Guest House   If you'd like to avoid transportation costs, you can stay in Philipsburg and walk wherever you need to go. This guesthouse on Back Street is perfect for that, only 1 block from the beach and within an easy walk of the entertainment, shopping, and restaurants. This family-owned facility rents small, clean rooms with a vintage 1970s look. Some rooms open onto balconies with attractive mountain views. Don't expect much in the way of bedroom space, but units are suitable for one or two. The mattresses are comfortable, but the shower-only bathrooms are cramped. The hotel has a bar, plus a Chinese restaurant that serves passable fare for lunch and dinner—at very low prices. And if you really want to save money, you can use the communal kitchen.

7 Back St., Philipsburg, St. Maarten, N.A. ℂ 800/223-9815 in the U.S., or 599/54-24317. Fax 599/54-30080. joshuarose49@hotmail.com. 14 units. Winter $50–$55 single; $70–$80 double. Off-season $40–$50 single; $50–$60 double. Children under 12 $10. AE, DISC, MC, V. **Amenities:** Restaurant, bar, communal kitchen. In room: A/C, TV.

Sea Breeze Hotel (Value)   It'll be a Dutch treat—at least for your wallet— if you stay here, far removed from the high prices of the megaresorts. This simple white concrete building is only 5 minutes from Philipsburg and a 5-minute walk from Belaire Beach. The small rooms are clean, comfortable, and plain but decently maintained, each furnished with a firm mattress on the double or twin beds. The bathrooms are a bit cramped and have inadequate shelf space, but they're well cared for and each has a tiled shower. To help you keep costs even lower, some accommodations have small kitchenettes; others have just refrigerators. The lower-floor rooms have porches, and the upper units open onto balconies.

20 Cay Hill, Philipsburg, St. Maarten, N.A. ℂ 599/54-26054. Fax 599/54-26057. reservations@sea-breeze. com. 30 units. Winter $79 single; $92 double. Off-season $55 single; $67 double. Extra person $15. AE, MC, V. **Amenities:** Restaurant, bar, pool, babysitting. In room: A/C, TV.

WORTH A SPLURGE

Hotel La Châtelaine ✦   This pink-sided apartment complex lies on an idyllic strip of white-sand beach. The only drawback is its proximity to the roar of the jets arriving and departing from the airport. (Luckily, air traffic is very light after 7pm.) The resort's focal point is a small but charming octagonal pool with a gazebo. Most visitors forsake the pool in favor of a chaise longue on the sands of nearby Simpson Bay. The hotel offers studio, one-bedroom, or two-bedroom apartments; the studios have kitchenettes and the others have complete kitchens. Some units can accommodate up to four by using living room couches for sleeping, and up to six can stay in a two-bedroom apartment with the addition of a roll-away bed (but that gets really crowded). Mattresses are a bit thin but fairly new, and all the shower-only bathrooms are motel standard.

Simpson Bay Beach (P.O. Box 2065), Philipsburg, St. Maarten, N.A. © 599/54-54269. Fax 599/54-53195. htlchtln@sintmaarten.net. 12 units. Winter $204–$223 1-bedroom apt; $299–$373 2-bedroom apt. Off-season $143 1-bedroom apt; $213–$274 2-bedroom apt. Extra person $30. AE, MC, V. Children 6 and under not accepted. **Amenities:** Pool. *In room:* A/C, TV, kitchenette.

IN ST. MARTIN

Hotels on French St. Martin add a *taxe de séjour*, or government tax, and a 10% service charge. This visitors' tax on hotel rooms differs from hotel to hotel, depending on its classification, but the minimum is $3 a day.

Chez Martine   Chez Martine, one of Grand-Case's best-known restaurants, offers small guest rooms on the upper floor of its white two-story building at the edge of the bay, within easy walking distance of many other restaurants and bars. The furnishings include two single or two double beds, each with a good mattress and wicker headboard, wicker chairs, and a small desk; some rooms have a sea view. The shower-only bathrooms, although small, are adequate and very well kept.

Blvd. de Grand-Case 140 (B.P. 637), Grand-Case, 97150 St. Martin, F.W.I. © 0590/87-51-59. Fax 0590/ 87-87-30. chezmartine@powerantilles.com. 6 units. Winter $110 single or double. Off-season $85 single or double. Extra person $17. Rates include breakfast. AE, DC, MC, V. **Amenities:** Restaurant, bar. *In room:* A/C, fridge.

Hévéa *(Value)*   On sloping land across from the white sands of Grand-Case Beach, this small but charming guesthouse has named its accommodations after local flowers, shrubs, and trees. The setting is an old but much-renovated Creole house, with rooms surrounding a landscaped patio. The accommodations are small, but each contains carefully chosen antique artifacts and a fine twin or double bed with a good French mattress. Although none has a view of the sea, the relatively modest prices make this hotel a worthy and sometimes colorful choice. There's an expensive restaurant on the premises (Hévéa), open only for dinner. The cafes and restaurants of Grand-Case are a short walk away.

Blvd. de Grand-Case 163, Grand-Case, 97150 St. Martin, F.W.I. © 0590/87-56-85. Fax 0590/87-83-88. 5 units. Winter $58–$72 single; $80–$94 double; $122–$136 studio apt with kitchen for 2. Off-season $34–$59 single; $55–$70 double; $71–$103 studio apt with kitchen for 2. AE, MC, V. **Amenities:** Restaurant.

La Résidence *(★)*   La Résidence is in the commercial center of Marigot, which makes it a favorite of business travelers. Its concrete facade is enlivened with neo-Victorian gingerbread fretwork. A bar with a soaring tent serves drinks to guests who relax on wicker and bentwood furniture. The small bedrooms, which have small, shower-only bathrooms, are arranged around a landscaped central courtyard with a fish-shaped fountain. Each room contains minimalist decor, and all but a few have sleeping lofts and a duplex design of mahogany-trimmed stairs and balustrades.

Rue du Général-de-Gaulle (B.P. 679), Marigot, 97150 St. Martin, F.W.I. © 800/423-4433 in the U.S., or 590/87-70-37. Fax 590/87-90-44. laresidence@wanadoo.fr. 22 units. Year-round $92–$98 single or double. Rates include continental breakfast. AE, MC, V. **Amenities:** Restaurant, bar. *In room:* A/C, TV, minibar.

Le Royale Louisiana ☆   Occupying a prominent position in the center of Marigot, 10 miles north of Queen Juliana Airport, this hotel is designed in a hip-roofed French-colonial Louisiana style; its rambling balconies are graced with ornate balustrades. It's about a 10-minute drive to the nearest good beach; you'll want a car if you stay here. Each small- to medium-size guest room has big, sun-filled windows and modern furniture. Standard rooms have king- or queen-size beds. Each duplex, ideal for families, has a sitting room with a sofa bed on the lower floor and a bedroom and bathroom on the upper level. Note that duplex rates are not based on the number of occupants. Bathrooms are well maintained but a bit cramped, with shower stalls.

Rue du Général-de-Gaulle, Marigot, 97150 St. Martin, F.W.I. ✆ 590/87-86-51. Fax 590/87-96-49. louisiana@top-saint-martin.com. 58 units. Winter 513F (€77.95, $74.35) single or double; 720F (€109.40, $104.35) duplex. Off-season 410F (€62.30, $59.40) single or double; 640F (€97.25, $92.75) duplex. Rates include continental breakfast. AE, MC, V. **Amenities:** Restaurant, bar. *In room:* A/C, TV.

Nettlé Bay Beach Club ☆   This is a stylish and appealing colony of villas scattered across a landscaped garden that opens onto four bays, each fronted with its own pool. Each villa is a two-story Creole-style cottage set with some degree of privacy into its own garden. Although each villa can be rented as a complete two-story, two-bedroom house that's suitable for a group of up to six, either the upper floor or the lower floor can be rented as a self-contained studio or one-bedroom apartment, respectively. If your plan is to rent just one floor of any of these cottages, try to book the lower floors, which are larger and more comfortable. Regardless of their size, each unit has terra-cotta floors, wicker furniture, a shower-only bathroom, and a veranda or terrace. All the apartments have kitchens, as do some but not all of the studios. If you go for one of the cheaper units, living here can be quite reasonable.

Baie Nettlé (B.P. 4081), 97064 St. Martin, F.W.I. ✆ 590/87-68-68. Fax 590/87-21-51. dgnbbcsxm@power antilles.com. 169 units. Year-round $120–$205 studio; $150–$250 1-bedroom apt for up to 4; $255–$420 2-bedroom villa for up to 6. AE, MC, V. **Amenities:** Restaurant, bar, snack bar, pool; 3 lit Laykold tennis courts. *In room:* A/C, TV.

3 Great Deals on Dining
IN ST. MAARTEN

A favorite for the partying crowd is **Everyt'ing Cool,** 95 Front St. in Philipsburg (✆ 599/54-31011), although many do go there just to eat. The place is known for its 81 varieties of both alcoholic and nonalcoholic piña coladas. You can come for the everyday party deal, for which you get a locker, a floating mattress, sports on the beach, and lunch and drinks, all for $20. The place closes at 5pm daily.

The Boathouse ☆ AMERICAN/INTERNATIONAL   One of the Dutch side's most enduringly popular bars and restaurants occupies a funky wooden building that's capped with the rickety hull of a battered fishing boat. That seafaring theme continues inside, where a soaring network of heavy timbers are accented with soft pinks, blues, and greens, as well as lots of nautical accessories. Come here for the bar, a wraparound affair that attracts good-natured expatriates and locals alike, and for the generous portions dished up by the hardworking kitchen staff. Lunches consist of sandwiches, pastas, and salads. (Especially worthwhile are the shrimp salad and the grilled chicken Caesar salad.) Main courses at dinner are more substantial, including filet mignon, pepper steak, surf and turf, and red snapper that's either charcoal-grilled or stuffed with shrimp and crabmeat and served with a white-wine cream sauce. Live bands play most Fridays after 11pm, when the already active bar gets even busier.

74 Airport Rd., Simpson Bay. ℂ 599/54-45409. Reservations recommended for dinner. Lunch main courses $7–$16; dinner main courses $13–$20. MC, V. Mon–Sat 11:30am–2:30pm; daily 5:30–10:30pm.

Cheri's Café ⭐⭐ AMERICAN   American expatriate Cheri Baston's island hot spot is the best bar on the island. Touristy but fun and sassy, a great place to meet people, it's outfitted in an irrepressible color scheme of hot pink and white. This open-air cafe, serving some 400 meals a night, is really only a roof without walls, and it's not even on a beach. But people flock to it anyway, devouring 18-ounce steaks, simple burgers, and grilled fresh-fish platters. The clientele covers everybody from rock bands to movie stars, high rollers at the casino to beach bums. Some come for the cheap eats, others for the potent drinks, many to dance and flirt. The bartender's special is the frozen Straw Hat, made with vodka, coconut, tequila, pineapple and orange juices, and strawberry liqueur—maybe even one more ingredient, although nobody's talking. There's live music every night beginning at 8pm.

45 Cinnamon Grove Shopping Centre, Maho Beach. ℂ 599/54-53361. Reservations not accepted. Main courses $9.75–$19.75. MC, V. Wed–Mon 11am–midnight. Closed Sept.

Crocodile Express Café DELI/GRILL/INTERNATIONAL   Start the day overlooking Simpson Bay by enjoying extra-thick French toast made from homemade egg bread with fresh tropical fruits on top, or order eggs any style. There's continuous service throughout the day, beginning with breakfast and followed by lunch, with snacks in the afternoon. Many patrons file in for dinner as early as 5:30pm. Hearty deli fare includes well-stuffed sandwiches, but at night you might prefer grilled local fish or tasty kebabs. A specialty is grilled chicken breast West Indian style, marinated in tropical fruit juices and served with grilled onions. On Thursday, it's all-you-can-eat barbecued chicken and ribs, costing $13. Meals are followed by home-baked pies and other desserts, and drinks include fresh mango and frozen passion fruit. On the beach, Wednesdays 5 to 9pm, there's a beach-party barbecue and a limbo show, with nail-dancing, fire-eating, magic, and steel-band music.

Casino Balcony, at the Pelican Resort Club, Simpson Bay. ℂ 599/54-42503. Dinner main courses $6.50–$15; sandwiches and salads $3.25–$9.50; breakfast $2–$7.25. DISC, MC, V. Daily 8am–10pm.

Don Carlos Restaurant MEXICAN/CARIBBEAN/INTERNATIONAL This down-home restaurant is just 5 minutes east of the airport, with a view of arriving and departing planes from the floor-to-ceiling windows. It serves breakfast, lunch, and dinner, providing consistently decent fare at reasonable prices. Owner Carl Wagner invites you for a drink in his Pancho Villa Bar before your meal in his hacienda-style dining room with a multilingual staff. Quantity, instead of quality, is the rule here, but diners seem to view this place as a fun choice.

Airport Rd., Simpson Bay. ℂ 599/54-53112. Main courses $9.75–$28.50. AE, DC, DISC, MC, V. Daily 7:30am–10pm.

The Greenhouse AMERICAN   Open to a view of the harbor, the Greenhouse is filled with plants. As you dine, breezes filter through the open-air eatery. The menu features the catch of the day as well as burgers, pizza, and salads. Dinner specials might include fresh lobster Thermidor, Jamaican jerk pork, or salmon in light dill sauce. Some of the island's best steaks are served here, each cut certified Angus beef, including a New York strip, a T-bone, a porterhouse, or a filet mignon. The chef specializes in chicken, ranging from mango chicken to chicken parmigiana. Happy Hour is daily 4:30 to 7pm and features half-price appetizers and two-for-one drinks. The DJ not only spins out tunes but also gives prizes to bingo champs and trivia experts. There are also pool tables and video games to keep you entertained.

Bobby's Marina (off Front St.), Philipsburg. ✆ 599/54-22941. Main courses $11–$20. AE, MC, V. Daily 11am–1am.

Indiana Beach INTERNATIONAL   The theme of this place revolves around the exploits and adventures of cinematic hero Indiana Jones, as portrayed by Harrison Ford in the popular films. You'll find a small forest of potted palms and plants; murals showing Temples of Doom and Egyptian hieroglyphs; and in the garden outside, caged birds, snakes, and a crocodile. Inside, you might think you've wandered over to the island's French side by accident, as you'll find a very French staff that isn't the least shy about imposing their language on English-speaking guests. The fare is always reliable and often superb. Menu items include a combination seafood platter; grilled snapper with mango sauce; grilled filet mignon with a choice of mushroom, pepper, or béarnaise sauce; and a selection of fish imported from the French mainland (grilled sea bass with fennel, Dover sole with butter sauce, or fresh tuna with béarnaise sauce). Looking for an appropriately racy cocktail? Consider the Indiana Beach, made with dark rum, Dubonnet, and passion fruit liqueurs.

Simpson Bay. ✆ 0599/54-42797. Reservations recommended. Lunch main courses $8–$15; dinner main courses $15–$25. AE, MC, V. Daily 7am–11am, noon–3pm, and 6–11pm.

Lynette's ★★ (Finds WEST INDIAN   This is the most noteworthy West Indian restaurant on St. Maarten. It's completely unpretentious and rich in local flavors and understated charm. The creative forces here are St. Maarten–born Lynette Felix, along with Clayton Felix, who serve up flavorful ethnic food. The menu reads like a lexicon of tried-and-true Caribbean staples, including *colombos* (ragouts) of goat and chicken, stuffed crab backs, curried seafood, and filet of snapper with green plantains. An ideal lunch might be a brimming bowlful of pumpkin (squash) soup followed by one of the main-course salads. The herbed lobster version, when available, is particularly succulent. The dishes here have true island flavor.

Simpson Bay Blvd., near the airport. ✆ 599/54-52865. Reservations recommended. Main courses $11–$32; Wed all-you-can-eat seafood buffet $35. AE, MC, V. Daily 11:30am–10:30pm.

Shiv Sagar EAST INDIAN   This restaurant serves the island's only Indian cuisine, and because of its large selection of vegetarian dishes, it's the best choice for noncarnivores. The cuisine features mainly Mogul and Kashmiri specialties. Rôtis are prepared before diners in a traditional tandoori oven, and the curries are zesty and spicy. You can also order a number of unusual specialties, such as red snapper cooked in a blend of hot spices. The open-air bar out front is one of the friendliest on the island.

20 Front St., Philipsburg. ✆ 599/54-22299. Reservations recommended. Main courses $14.75–$16.75. AE, MC, V. Mon–Sat 11:30am–3pm and 6:30–10pm; Sun 11:30am–3pm.

Turtle Pier Bar & Restaurant CARIBBEAN/INTERNATIONAL   Less than a quarter mile from the airport, on sunblasted scrubland adjacent to the lagoon, this restaurant offers well-prepared food, stiff drinks, and the added benefit of a 50-member menagerie (zoo) many diners see as an intriguing prelude to their meal. Members of the zoo include a number of birds, such as colorful parrots that talk; turtles; rabbits; iguanas; monkeys; lobsters; and even a shark that swims nervously back and forth in a holding tank. Menu items include Creole-style grouper, roasted duck with ginger or guavaberry sauce, conch fritters, stuffed *christophene,* and several preparations of lobster and burgers. A particularly popular burger is a Turtle Pier—a beef patty atop an English muffin, with lots of spinach, béarnaise sauce, and coleslaw. A particularly popular drink is a frozen colada. Wednesdays feature a live band and a $26 fixed-price dinner that includes a 1-pound lobster.

114 Airport Rd., Simpson Bay. ⓒ 599/54-52562. Lunch main courses $6.50–$17.25; dinner main courses $12–$50. AE, DISC, MC, V. Daily 7:30am–10pm; bar remains open daily to 11 or 11:30pm.

BEST FIXED-PRICE MENU

Pelican Reef Restaurant and Seafood House ⚐ STEAK/SEAFOOD/ INTERNATIONAL   This American steakhouse not only serves what are reputed to be the island's best steaks, but also offers tasty chops and seafood. Hosts Marvin and Jean Rich offer fine, friendly service and good-quality ingredients, artfully served with a view over Simpson Bay. Signature dishes are a hearty slab of prime rib on the bone; whole Caribbean lobster, baked and stuffed; grilled fish filet, perhaps red snapper, from local waters; rack of baby lamb; and a thick veal chop. The El Gaucho steak is a chateaubriand cut from Argentina, a tasty treat that is lean and uniquely rich in flavor because the cattle were grass-fed on the pampas. Served grilled on a wooden plank, it's accompanied by a cognac-and-peppercorn sauce, vegetables, and steak fries. Save room for the conch fritters with two sauces, and follow with a "chocolate island" or the frozen fantasy dessert. A special feature of the wine list is a "tasting" of fine armagnacs, unique because they're from single estates and are made from 100% *ugni blanc,* a rare grape used only in the making of armagnacs and cognacs.

Waterfront Marina, at the Pelican Resort Club, Simpson Bay. ⓒ 599/54-42503, ext. 5950. Reservations recommended. Main courses $13.75–$30; fixed-price menus $21–$32. AE, DISC, MC, V. Daily 5:30–10:30pm.

IN ST. MARTIN

Hévéa ⚐⚐ FRENCH/CREOLE   Normandy-born restaurateurs own this formal place, the most obviously French restaurant in Grand-Case. There's a touch of class here, with Louis XV chairs, Norman artifacts, and candlelight. There are fewer than a dozen tables, so advance reservations are usually crucial. Start with the Caesar salad, which is the best on the island. In honor of their Norman roots, the owners prepare such classic dishes as a cassoulet of scallops with *fumet* of crab and Noilly Prat; *darne* of kingfish; scallops *Dieppoise* (with a cream-flavored mussel sauce); and one of the great dishes of the conservative French repertoire, escalopes of veal *Pays d'Auge,* made with apple brandy (Calvados) and cream. You might also try more experimental dishes, such as mahimahi in puff pastry or lasagna with two kinds of salmon. To remind you that you're in the West Indies, there's a set-price all-Creole menu, a platter of West Indian smoked fish, and American-style lobster with tomato sauce and herbs.

163 blvd. de Grand-Case, Grand-Case. ⓒ 590/87-56-85. Reservations required. Main courses 105F–220F (€15.95–€33.45, $15.20–$31.90); menu Creole (featuring West Indian items) 145F (€22.05, $21). AE, MC, V. Dec–Mar daily noon–2:30pm; Dec–Apr dinner daily 6:30–11pm. Closed May–Nov.

Kakao *(finds)* INTERNATIONAL   This French Polynesian–style open-air pavilion beside the sands of Orient Beach is always hopping, always hip. Amid dark-stained timbers, thatch-covered roofs, and nautical pieces that include the artifacts from several demolished or sunken yachts, you can drink, eat, sun, lie on lounge chairs, or simply gossip with the Euro-Caribbean crowd that hangs out here. Frozen piña coladas go for $6 each, and beer for $2.50, and no one will mind if you just have a liquid lunch. But if you're hungry, check out the menu's pizzas, grilled steaks and fish, burgers, ice cream, and banana splits. This place is a bit more family friendly, and a bit less irreverent and raunchy, than its next-door neighbor, the Kon Tiki.

Orient Beach. ℂ 590/87-43-26. Pizzas 60F–84F (€9.10–€12.75, $8.70–$12.15); main courses 66F–108F (€10.05–€16.40, $9.55–$15.65). AE, MC, V. May–Nov daily 8am–7pm; Dec–Apr daily 8am–10pm.

Kon Tiki FRENCH/INTERNATIONAL   From the parking lot where you'll leave your car, this is the most distant of the several bars that flank the sands of Orient Bay. Inside, you'll find everything you need to amuse yourself for a day at the beach. Facilities include three bars, a watersports facility, volleyball courts, and a bandstand, where there's often live music. Chaises longues with mattresses rent for $6 for a full day's use, and there's a staff member who'll bring such party-colored drinks as a Sex on the Beach ($5). If you opt to spend part of a day here, you won't be alone: Previous clients have included the late John Kennedy, Jr., Diana Ross, Miss France, and French singer and heart-throb Johnny Halliday.

Orient Beach. ℂ 590/87-43-27. Reservations not necessary. Burgers, sandwiches, pizzas, platters $4.50–$15. AE, MC, V. Daily 9am–7pm (till 9:30pm Nov–May).

La Brasserie de Marigot (★ (Value FRENCH   Gruff but friendly, this is a well-managed, fast-paced brasserie right in the heart of town, with sidewalk tables. It's an excellent choice for good food at reasonable prices, and it draws local French-speaking residents, many from the French mainland. This building was originally a bank; it still has a marble-and-brass decor, and its green leather banquettes lend a retro 1950s style. Menu items include a succulent version of garlicky fish soup, frogs' legs in garlic sauce, snails in garlic butter sauce, breast of duckling in orange sauce, Provençal-style shrimp, pot-au-feu, and filet of beef with mushroom sauce—all those good dishes that the French enjoy at blue-collar bistros. You can order interesting terrines here, and wine is sold by the glass, carafe, or bottle. The kitchen also prepares a handful of Caribbean dishes, such as swordfish in garlic sauce. If it's on the menu, check out the tartare of shark, seasoned with onions, chives, and an ample dose of lime juice.

11 rue du Général-de-Gaulle, Marigot. ℂ 590/87-94-43. Main courses 58F–100F (€8.80–€15.20, $8.40–$14.50). AE, MC, V. Mon–Sat 7:30am–9pm.

Le Bar de la Mer INTERNATIONAL   Its walls adorned with primitive Haitian paintings and its tables overlooking the food and handcrafts market of Marigot, this restaurant offers a menu of well-prepared dishes. There's a dish for virtually every budget and taste, including pastas, pizzas, grilled local fish, burgers, lobster, and barbecued ribs. Mornings attract local merchants and office workers who appreciate the croissants, steaming cups of tea and coffee, and a tipple of wine or two as a means of jump-starting their day. Every night there's a barbecue on the beach, and live entertainment is often featured.

Rue Felix-Eboué 2, Marigot. ℂ 590/87-81-79. Pizzas, burgers, pastas, and salads 50F–80F (€7.60–€12.15, $7.25–$11.60); platters 82F–200F (€12.45–€30.40, $11.90–$29); breakfast 35F–49F (€5.30–€7.45, $5.05–$7.10). AE, MC, V. Daily 8am–1am.

Rainbow Café (★ FRENCH/INTERNATIONAL   Set on the northeastern end of the row of restaurants that line either side of the main road of Grand Case, this little bistro thrives under the direction of Dutch-born Fleur Radd and Buffalo, New York–born David Hendricks. The house containing the cafe opens onto views over the sea. Meals are served within an artfully simple dining room

---

Value Going Native: *Accras,* Ragouts, *Boudins* & Curries

For cheap Creole food in Grand-Case, try **Lo-Lo's Food Court** (*Cour des Restaurants Lo-Lo*) on the boulevard de Grand-Case, adjacent to the beachfront in the commercial heart of town. At least a half-dozen local entrepreneurs, some without benefit of running water or refrigeration, serve stews, fish, ragouts, *boudins* Creole, curried rice, macaroni and cheese, and *accras de morue,* which you either carry away in Styrofoam containers or consume at picnic tables on site. These food stands do a thriving business with beachgoers throughout the high season. (Frankly, we're a little nervous about that lack of water and refrigeration problem, so we tend to head for the village's bona-fide restaurants instead.) But if your heart is set on trying the local fare here, you'll be safe heading for one of the most consistently reliable vendors, **The Rib Shack,** Lo-Lo no. 6 (© **590/29-38-15**). Open daily 8am to 10:30pm, it's one of the best enterprises in Lo-Lo's Food Court. The day's menu is marked on a chalkboard with platters priced from $2 to $7, except for lobster, which can go as high as $40 a platter, depending on its size. Sheryll Compper and her family are the proprietors here, offering food that's spicy enough to satisfy your deepest island cravings. Go for lunch, when all the food is freshest, rather than later in the day.

---

outfitted in dark blue and white. Menu items evolve almost every evening—perhaps snapper in a Parmesan-onion crust with tomato-flavored vinaigrette or chicken breast marinated in lemon grass and ginger, with grilled balsamic-glazed vegetables. There's also salmon in puff pastry with spinach and citrus-dill butter sauce, and a fricassee of scallops and shrimp served with Caribbean chutney.

176 blvd. de Grand-Case, Grand-Case. © 590/87-55-80. Reservations recommended. Main courses 130F–210F (€19.75–€31.90, $18.85–$30.45). MC, V. Daily 6–11pm. Closed Sun Apr–Nov.

Yvette's ✸ *Finds* WEST INDIAN   Owner Yvette Hyman-Connor prides herself on the simplicity of her "home cooking." The setting is a part-wood, part-concrete white-sided house just off the main street that runs through the hamlet of Orléans, flanked with a dusty garden. Menu items are partly inspired by the cuisine of Aruba, where Ms. Hyman-Connor spent many years before returning to her native St. Martin. This place draws a lot of locals, many of whom wouldn't ever consider having a meal at any of St. Martin's grander places. The most popular items are curried coconut chicken, stewed fresh conch with onions and fresh tomatoes, conch dumplings boiled in a conch shell in herb- and wine-scented water, and a lobster-and-shrimp combo. Consider prefacing a meal with one of the house special cocktails, a rum-based guavaberry or lime punch. If you'd like to sample really authentic Creole cuisine, you can do no better than Yvette's.

Orléans. © 0590/87-32-03. Main courses $8–$27. No credit cards. Daily noon–2:30pm and 6:30–10:30pm.

4 Hitting the Beaches

The island has 36 beautiful white-sand beaches, and it's fairly easy to find a place to park your beach towel. Most beaches have recovered from the erosion caused by the 1995 hurricane. Regardless of where you stay, you're never far from the water. If you're a beach sampler, you might want to use the changing facilities at some of the bigger resorts for a small fee. Nudists should head for the French side of the island, although the Dutch side is getting more liberal about such things. *Warning:* If it's too secluded, be careful. It's unwise to carry valuables to the beach; there have been reports of robberies on some remote strips.

The popular **Cupecoy Bay Beach** is very close to the Dutch–French border, on the western side of the island. It's a string of three white-sand beaches set against a backdrop of caves, beautiful rock formations, and cliffs that provide morning shade. There are no restaurants, bars, or other facilities here, but locals come around with coolers of cold beer and soda. The beach has two parking lots, one near Cupecoy and Sapphire beach clubs, the other a short distance to the west. Parking costs $2. You must descend stone-carved steps to reach the sands. Cupecoy is also the island's major gay beach.

Also on the west side of the island, west of the airport, **Mullet Bay Beach** has white sand and is shaded by palm trees. Once it was the most crowded beach on the island, but St. Maarten's largest resort, Mullet Bay, remained closed at press time, so the crowds aren't so bad anymore. Weekdays are best, as many locals flock here on weekends. Watersports equipment can be rented at a kiosk here.

Another lovely spot near the airport, **Maho Bay Beach,** at the Maho Beach Hotel and Casino, is shaded by palms and is ideal in many ways, if you don't mind the planes taking off and landing. This is one of the island's busiest beaches, buzzing with windsurfers. Food and drink can be purchased at the hotel.

Stretching the length of Simpson Bay Village are the mile-long white sands of crescent-shaped **Simpson Bay Beach,** west of Philipsburg before you reach the airport. This beach is popular with windsurfers, and it's an ideal place for a stroll or a swim. Watersports equipment rentals are available here, but there are no changing rooms or other facilities.

Great Bay Beach is preferred if you're staying along Front Street in Philipsburg. This mile-long beach is sandy, but since it borders the busy capital, it may not be as clean as some of the more remote choices. On a clear day, you'll have a view of Saba. Immediately to the west, at the foot of Fort Amsterdam, is picturesque **Little Bay Beach,** but it, too, can be overrun with tourists. When you tire of the sands here, you can climb up to the site of Fort Amsterdam itself. Built in 1631, it was the first Dutch military outpost in the Caribbean. The Spanish captured it 2 years later, making it their most important bastion east of Puerto Rico. Only a few of the fort's walls remain, but the view is panoramic.

On the east side of the island, **Dawn Beach** is noted for its underwater life, with some of the island's most beautiful reefs immediately offshore. Visitors talk ecstatically of its incredible sunrises. Dawn is suitable for swimming and offers year-round activities such as sand-castle-building contests and crab races. There's plenty of wave action for both surfers and windsurfers. The road to this beach is bumpy, but worth the effort. Nearby are the pearly white sands of **Oyster Pond Beach,** near the Oyster Bay Beach Resort. Bodysurfers like the rolling waves here.

Top rating on St. Martin goes to **Baie Longue** on the west side of the island, a beautiful beach that's rarely overcrowded. The chic and very expensive La Samanna resort opens onto this beachfront. Its reef-protected waters are ideal for snorkeling, but there is a strong undertow. Baie Longue is to the north of Cupecoy Bay Beach, reached via the Lowlands Road. Don't leave any valuables in your car here, as many break-ins have been reported along this stretch of highway.

If you continue north along the highway, you'll reach another long and popular stretch of sand and jagged coral, **Baie Rouge.** Swimming is excellent here, and snorkelers are drawn to the rock formations at both ends of the beach. This intimate little spot is especially lovely in the morning. There are no changing facilities, but a local kiosk sells cold drinks.

Isolated, but well-known among St. Martin's beach-going crowd, **Friar's Bay Beach** lies at the end of a winding country road; its clearly signposted entrance intersects with the main highway between Grand-Case and Marigot. Although you certainly won't be alone here, this is a less-visited beach with ample parking. There's some topless sunbathing, depending on who happens to show up. You'll not want for food or rum-laced tropical drinks when you get there, as at least three beachfront kiosks ply their trade throughout the day and early evening. None has a phone, and all offer lunch and light fare. Our favorite is the **Friar's Bay Beach Café,** set directly on the sands of Friar's Bay Beach, midway between two of its competitors. This funky open-air pavilion is plastered with the personal motto ("Let Rock Prevail") of its owner, Laurent, known to his visitors as Lo-Lo. Whatever you order here is likely to be served on wooden boards or marble slabs, and usually accompanied with beer or a sunset-colored drink. Expect such dishes as a tartare of tomatoes with fresh mozzarella and tarragon; a "butcher's platter" stocked with chicken wings, ribs, various kabobs, guacamole, and roasted potatoes; and an "FBBC" (Friar's Bay Beach Café) sandwich, stuffed with mozzarella, fresh garlic, tomatoes, and bacon, all of it passed under a grill for the "au gratin" crust. Every afternoon before sunset, the cafe sponsors a free yoga-style meditation class. Open daily 9am to 7:30pm.

White-sand **Grand-Case Beach** is right in the middle of the town of Grand-Case and is likely to be crowded, especially on weekends. The waters are very calm here, making swimming excellent, and making it a good choice for families with kids. A small but select beach, it has its own charm, with none of the carnival-like atmosphere found on other beaches.

On the eastern side of the island, **Orient Beach** is the island's only official nudist beach, so anything (or nothing, as it were) goes in terms of attire. There's steady action here: bouncy Caribbean bands, refreshments of all kinds, watersports, and clothing, crafts, and jewelry vendors. Everyone comes to enjoy this stretch of velvety white sands. The coral reef off the beach here is teeming with marine life, making for great snorkeling. Club Orient, the nude resort, is at the end of the beach; voyeurs from cruise ships can always be spotted here. This is also a haven for windsurfers.

Finally, for the most isolated and secluded beach of all, you have to leave St. Martin. **Ilet Pinel,** off the coast at Cul de Sac, is reached by a boat ride off the northeast coast (you can hire a local boatman to take you from Cul de Sac for about $5 one-way). The island has no residents (except wild goats), phones, or electricity. You will find fine white-sand beaches, idyllic reefs with great snorkeling, and waters great for bodysurfing. There are even two beach bars that rent lounge chairs and serve dishes such as lobster, ribs, and grilled chicken.

5 Sports & Other Outdoor Pursuits

HORSEBACK RIDING   Increasingly popular, horseback riding is possible at **Bayside Riding Club,** Route Galion Beach, Orientale (© **590/87-36-64**). Rides along the beach are a highlight, and prices start at $50 for a 2-hour ride.

SCUBA DIVING   Scuba diving is excellent around St. Martin, with reef, wreck, night, cave, and drift diving; the depth of dives is 20 to 70 feet. Off the

Value Cheap Thrills: What to See & Do for Free (Well, Almost) on St. Maarten & St. Martin

- **Chase Butterflies.** Far from the crowds, you might want to seek a bucolic part of St. Martin—the little village of Orléans (also called the French Quarter), which is the island's oldest French settlement. Its houses (called *cases*) are set in meadows that blossom with hibiscus, bougainvillea, and wisteria. On the road to Bayside and Galion is the charming **Butterfly Farm,** Route de Baie L'Embouchure (© 0590/ 87-31-21), run by two Englishmen who created this Eden-like setting. Visitors are offered a rare insight into the amazing transformations between an egg and a butterfly. You'll learn all about these delicate creatures and meet such beauties as the Brazilian blue morpho and the Cambodian wood nymph. Morning visits are ideal.

- **Spend a Day at a Nudist Beach.** Many cruise ship passengers, in St. Martin only for 2 or 3 hours, head immediately to the wild and wacky beach at Orient Bay, especially if they have a voyeuristic streak. This is one of the best-known clothing-optional beaches in the Caribbean, and most of the bodies on display are at the naturalist resort Club Orient, at the middle of the beach. In the center are several local hangouts, often with bars and restaurants featuring live bands playing great music throughout the day. Our favorite spot is the open-air bar/restaurant **Kontiki** (© 0590/87-43-27), where most patrons are clothed; the nudie area for the less inhibited drinker is a short stroll away. You can stick around for lunch, ordering reasonably good sushi or fresh lobster from saltwater holding tanks. After lunch you can rent a jet ski, go parasailing, join in a hobie cat race, or try some snorkeling.

- **People-Watch in Philipsburg.** At Wathey Square (pronounced "watty") in the center of the Dutch capital of St. Maarten, you can sit and watch the world go by. This is the heartbeat of this thriving little town, with its duty-free shops. It's filled with tourists and cruise ship passengers, trinket peddlers, vendors, and all sorts of shops. That building across the street from the square, with its white cupola, dates from 1793 and has been everything from a jail to a fire station, but today it's the town hall and courthouse. Directly off the square is the town's largest collection of shops, restaurants, and cafes. Take any narrow alley leading to an arcade for an adventure. Once you reach these arcades you'll find flower-filled courtyards, more shops, and plenty of eateries. The town is filled with West Indian cottages decorated with a gingerbread trim.

- **Visit Remote Ilet Pinel.** At the north end of Orient Bay on the Atlantic coast, Etang de la Parrière is the island's most beautiful cove, its sand banks filled with hundreds of ancient shells. Offshore here to the north is the remote Ilet Pinel, with fine white-sand beaches and reefs idyllic for snorkeling. Sometimes schools of rainbow-hued fish surround this island. The only inhabitants, other than visitors for the day, are wild goats feeding on the cacti and scrub brush. In an hour you can traverse the entire island. At Cul de Sac, the settlement on the French side, for $5 you can take a shuttle boat to this little bit of Eden.

northeastern coast on the French side, dive sites include Ilet Pinel, for shallow diving; Green Key, a barrier reef; and Tintamarre, for sheltered coves and geologic faults. To the north, Anse Marcel and neighboring Anguilla are good choices. Most hotels will arrange for scuba excursions on request.

The island's premier dive operation is **Marine Time,** whose offices are based in the same building as L'Aventure, Chemin du Port, 97150 Marigot (© **0590/ 87-20-28**). Operated from in front of the Market Dock in downtown Marigot by British-born Philip Baumann and his Mauritius-born colleague, Corine Mazurier, it offers morning and afternoon dives in deep and shallow water, wreck dives, and reef dives at $45 per dive. A resort course for first-timers with reasonable swimming skills is $80 and includes 60 to 90 minutes of instruction in a pool, then a one-tank dive above a coral reef. Full PADI certification costs $400, requires 5 days, and includes classroom training, sessions with a SCUBA tank in the safety of a pool, and three open-water dives. You can also arrange snorkeling trips with this outfitter, costing $25 for half a day or $75 for a full day, plus $10 for equipment rental.

You can also try **Blue Ocean Watersport & Dive Center,** B.P. 4079, Baie Nettlé, St. Martin (© **0590/87-89-73**). A certified one-tank dive costs $45, including equipment. A PADI certification course is available for $350 and takes 4 to 5 days. Three one-tank dives are offered for $120 or five dives for $175. Snorkeling trips are more modestly priced at $35 and are conducted daily 10am to 1pm and 2 to 5pm.

Dutch St. Maarten's crystal-clear bays and countless coves make for good **snorkeling** and **scuba diving.** Underwater visibility reportedly runs from 75 to 125 feet. The biggest attraction for scuba divers is the 1801 British man-of-war, HMS *Proselyte,* which came to a watery grave on a reef a mile off the coast. Most of the big resort hotels have facilities for scuba diving, and their staff can provide information about underwater tours, for photography as well as night diving.

The best watersports, and the best value, are found at **Pelican Watersports,** Pelican Resort and Casino, Simpson Bay (© **599/54-42640**). Its PADI-instructed program features the most knowledgeable guides on the island, each one familiar with St. Maarten dive sites. Divers are taken out in custom-built 28- and 35-foot boats, and many return to claim they've been led to some of the best reef diving in the Caribbean. A single-tank dive costs $45 and a double-tank dive $90. Snorkeling trips can also be arranged, as can trips to nearby islands, including Saba, Anguilla, and St. Barts.

SNORKELING   The calm waters ringing the shallow reefs and tiny coves found throughout the island make it a snorkeler's heaven. But the waters off the northeastern shores of French St. Martin have been classified as a regional underwater nature reserve, **Réserve Sous-Marine Régionale.** The area, comprising Flat Island (also known as La Tintamarre), Ilet Pinel, Green Key, Proselyte, and Petite Clef, is thus protected by official government decree. The use of harpoons is strictly forbidden. Snorkeling can be enjoyed individually or on sailing trips. Equipment can be rented at almost any hotel.

One of St. Martin's best-recommended sites for snorkeling, sunning, and generalized beach diversions is **Carib Watersports** (© **0590/87-51-87**), an independently operated clothing store, art gallery, and watersports kiosk occupying a building on the beachfront of the Grand-Case Beach Club. Its French and American staff, supervised by Michigan-born Marla Welch, functions as a source of info on island activities and can confirm travel plans or schedules for leisure activities. It also rents paddleboats with parasols for $20 an hour, low-velocity motorized boats for $25 an hour, and chaises longues with beach umbrellas. Their main allure, however, is its guided hour-long snorkeling trips to St. Martin's offshore reefs. The most visible of them are the waters surrounding Creole Rock, an offshore clump of reef-ringed boulders that are rich in underwater fauna. The cost of the experience, which departs every day at 2:30pm, with a return 2 hours later during high season (or whenever demand warrants it), costs $30 per person, all equipment included. Reservations are recommended.

TENNIS   You can try the courts at most of the large resorts, but you must call first to make reservations, and, of course, preference is given to guests. On the Dutch side are three lit courts at the **Pelican Resort Club** at Simpson Bay (✆ **0599/54-25-03**); another three lit courts are at the **Divi Little Bay Beach Resort,** Little Bay Road (✆ **0599/52-54-10**); and yet another three courts are at the **Maho Beach Hotel,** Maho Bay (✆ **0599/55-21-15**). On the French side, the **Privilège Resort & Spa,** Anse Marcel (✆ **0590/87-38-38**), offers six lit courts; the **Hotel Mont Vernon,** Baie Orientale (✆ **0590/87-62-00**), has two lit courts; and the **Nettlé Beach Club,** Sandy Ground Road (✆ **0590/87-6-68**), has three lit courts.

WATER-SKIING & PARASAILING   Most of French St. Martin's large beachfront hotels maintain facilities for water-skiing and parasailing, often from makeshift kiosks that operate from the sands of the hotel's beaches. Water-skiing averages $40 per 20-minute ride. Two independent operators are situated side-by-side on Orient Bay, close to the cluster of hotels near the Esmeralda Hotel: **Kon Tiki Watersports** (✆ **0590/87-46-89**) and **Bikini Beach Watersports** (✆ **0590/87-43-25**). Jet skis rent for $40 to $45 per half-hour session, and parasailing costs $50 for a vertiginous 10-minute experience aloft or $80 if two go together.

Jet skiing and water-skiing are also especially popular in Dutch St. Maarten. The unruffled waters of Simpson Bay, the largest in the West Indies, are ideal for these sports.

WINDSURFING   Because of prevailing winds and waters that are protected from violent waves by offshore reefs, most windsurfers gravitate to the strips of sand on the island's easternmost edge, most notably **Coconut Grove Beach, Orient Beach,** and to a lesser extent, **Dawn Beach,** all of which are in St. Martin. The best of the several outfits that specialize in the sport is **Tropical Wave,** Coconut Grove, Le Galion Beach, Baie de l'Embouchure (✆ **0590/87-37-25**). Midway between Orient Beach and Oyster Pond, amid a sunblasted, scrub-covered landscape that's isolated from the island's big hotels, its combination of wind and calm waters is considered by windsurfing aficionados as almost ideal. Operated by American-born Patrick Turner, Tropical Wave is the island's leading sales agent for Mistral Windsurfers. They rent for $20 an hour, with instruction priced at $30 an hour.

In St. Maarten, visitors usually head to **Simpson Bay** for windsurfing.

6 Cruises & Sightseeing Tours

DAY CRUISES

A popular pastime is a day of picnicking, sailing, snorkeling, and sightseeing aboard one of several boats that provide such services. The sleek sailboats usually pack large wicker hampers full of victuals and stretch tarpaulins over sections of the deck to protect sun-shy sailors.

Experienced skippers also make 1-day voyages to St. Barts in the French West Indies and to Saba, another of the Dutch Windwards in the Leewards; they stop long enough for passengers to familiarize themselves with the island ports, shop, and have lunch. To arrange a trip, ask at your hotel or at the **St. Maarten Tourist Bureau,** 23 Walter Nisbeth Rd. in Philipsburg (© **599/54-22337**).

If you'd like to see some of the other islands nearby, *Voyager I* and *Voyager II* offer the best deal. There are daily sails to St. Bart's costing $57 round-trip or to Saba, going for $57 round-trip. Children under 12 ride for half-price. These trips are a good value and are well worth the time and money. For more details, call **Dockside Management** in Philipsburg (© **599/54-24096**).

SIGHTSEEING TOURS

The only companies offering bus tours of the island are **Dutch Tours,** Cougar Road, 8 Unit One (© **599/54-23316**), and **St. Maarten Sightseeing Tours** (© **599/54-53921**), whose buses can accommodate between 22 and 52 people. They're configured only for large groups and are very difficult to prearrange.

In Dutch St. Maarten, you can also hire a taxi driver as your guide; a 2½-hour tour of the entire island costs $35 to $40 for up to two passengers and $7.50 to $10 for each additional passenger.

In French St. Martin, you can book 2-hour sightseeing trips around the island, either through **St. Martin's Taxi Service & Information Center** in Marigot (© **0590/87-56-54**) or at any hotel desk. The cost is $50 for one or two passengers, plus $10 for each additional person.

7 Shopping ★★

IN ST. MAARTEN

Not only is St. Maarten a free port, but also it also has no local sales taxes. Prices are sometimes lower here than anywhere else in the Caribbean except St. Thomas, with which it's locked in a head-to-head race. However, you must be familiar with the prices of what you're looking for to know what actually is a bargain. On some items we've priced (fine liqueurs, cigarettes, Irish linen, German cameras, French perfumes) we've found prices 30% to 50% lower than in the United States or Canada. Many well-known shops on Curaçao have branches here.

Besides the boutiques at resort hotels, the main shopping area is in the center of **Philipsburg.** Most of the shops are on two leading streets, **Front Street** (called Voorstraat in Dutch), which is closer to the bay, and **Back Street** (Achter-straat), which runs parallel to Front Street.

In general, at major retail outlets such as H. Stern, the jewelers, or Little Switzerland, the price marked on the merchandise is what you're supposed to pay. At small, very personally run shops, where the owner is on site, some bargaining might be in order. Most shopkeepers will remind you that their merchandise is already discounted, sometimes considerably, and they might add, "We've got to make some profit, now, don't we?"

Antillean Liquors, Queen Juliana Airport (© **599/54-54267**), has a complete assortment of liquor and liqueurs, cigarettes, and cigars. Prices are generally lower here than in other stores on the island, and the selection is larger. The only local product sold is the Guavaberry island liqueur.

Del Sol (Sun Powered Products), 11 Old St. (© **599/54-28784**), sells men's and women's sportswear. Embedded into the mostly black-and-white designs are organic crystals that react to sunlight (specifically, ultraviolet light), which transforms the fabric into a rainbow of colors. Step back into the shadows, and your T-shirt will revert to its original black-and-white design. The same technology is applied to yo-yos, which shimmer psychedelically when you bob them up and down.

Colombian Emeralds International, Old Street Shopping Center (© 599/54-23933), sells unmounted emeralds from Colombia, as well as emerald, gold, diamond, ruby, and sapphire jewelry. Prices are approximately the same as in other outlets of this famous Caribbean chain, and if you're seriously shopping for emeralds, this is the place. There are some huckster vendors around the island pawning fakes off on unsuspecting tourists; Colombian Emeralds offers the genuine item.

Belgian Chocolate Shop, 109 Old St. (© 599/54-28863), is the best of its kind on the island. Contrary to popular rumor, only *some* of the velvety chocolates sold in this upscale shop are pornographic, portraying parts of the human anatomy. Chocolates seem to fly out of this shop, especially on days when cruise ships are berthed at the nearby piers.

Guavaberry Company, 8–10 Front St. (© 599/54-22965), sells the rare "island folk liqueur" of St. Maarten, which for centuries was made only in private homes. Sold in square bottles, the product is made from rum that's given a unique flavor with rare guavaberries usually grown in the hills in the center of the island. (Don't confuse guavaberries with guavas—they're very different.) The liqueur has a fruity, woody, almost bittersweet flavor. You can blend it with coconut for a unique guavaberry colada or pour a splash into a glass of icy champagne.

Greenwich Galleries, 20 Front St. (© 599/54-23842), is the most interesting and sophisticated art gallery on either side of the island, with Bajan pottery in tones of sea greens and blues, replicas of Taéno artifacts, enameled metal cutouts that are both quirky and perplexing, and a wide range of paintings and lithographs by artists from as far away as Holland and Britain.

Little Switzerland, 52 Front St. (© 599/54-22523), is part of a chain of stores spread throughout the Caribbean. These fine-quality European imports are made even more attractive by the prices, often 25% or more lower than stateside prices. Elegant famous-name watches, china, crystal, and jewelry are for sale, plus perfume and accessories. Little Switzerland has the best overall selection of these items of any shop on the Dutch side.

New Amsterdam Store, 66 Front St. (© 559/54-22787), has been a tradition in the islands since 1925. This general store sells a little bit of everything—from fine linen to fashion, footwear to swimwear, and even porcelain. If your time is limited, you might want to visit this place first. Prices here are competitive with other stores in town touting similar merchandise.

The **Caribbean Camera Centre,** 79 Front St. (© 599/54-25259), has a wide range of merchandise, but it's always wise to know the prices charged back home before making a major purchase. Cameras here might be among the cheapest on St. Maarten; however, we've discovered better deals on St. Thomas.

Little Europe, 80 Front St. (© 599/54-24371), is an upscale purveyor of all the "finer things" in life—Hummels, jewelry, and watches by Concorde, Piaget, Corum, and Movado. Cruise ship passengers favor it because its prices are inexpensive compared to North American boutiques.

At the **Shipwreck Shop,** Front Street (© 599/54-22962), you'll find West Indian hammocks, beach towels, salad bowls, baskets, jewelry, T-shirts, postcards, books, woodcarvings, native art, sea salt, cane sugar, and spices—in all, a treasure trove of Caribbean handcrafts. If you're looking for affordable gifts or handcrafts in general, this might be your best bet.

IN ST. MARTIN

Many day-trippers come over to Marigot from the Dutch side just to visit the French-inspired boutiques and shopping arcades. Because it's also a duty-free port, you'll find some of the best shopping in the Caribbean. There's a wide selection of European merchandise, much of it luxury items such as crystal, fashions, fine liqueurs, and cigars, sometimes at 25% to 50% less than in the United States and Canada. Whether you're seeking jewelry, perfume, or St-Tropez bikinis, you'll find it in one of the boutiques along **rue de la République** and **rue de la Liberté** in Marigot. Look especially for French luxury items, such as Lalique crystal, Vuitton bags, and Chanel perfume.

Prices are often quoted in U.S. dollars, and salespeople frequently speak English. Credit cards and traveler's checks are generally accepted. When cruise ships are in port on Sundays and holidays, some of the larger shops stay open.

At harborside in Marigot, there's a lively **morning market** with vendors selling spices, fruit, shells, and handcrafts. Shops here tend to be rather upscale, catering to passengers of the small but choice cruise ships that dock offshore.

At **Port La Royale,** the bustling center of everything, mornings are even more active: Schooners unload produce from the neighboring islands, boats board guests for picnics on deserted beaches, a brigantine sets out on a sightseeing sail, and a dozen different little restaurants are readying for the lunch crowd. The largest shopping arcade on St. Martin, it has lots of boutiques.

Havane Boutique, 50 Marina Port La Royale (© **590/87-70-39**), is a hyperstylish menswear store, more couture than ready-to-wear. **Serge Blanco "15" Boutique,** Marina Port La Royale (© **590/29-65-49**), is a relatively unknown name in North America, but in France, Blanco is revered as one of the most successful rugby players of all time. His menswear is sporty, fun, and elegant. Everything is manufactured in or near Blanco's home town of Biarritz in southwestern France. Clothes include polo shirts, shorts, and wonderful latex jackets.

Gingerbread & Mahogany Gallery, 4–14 Marina Royale (© **590/ 87-73-21**), is among the finest galleries. Owner Simone Seitre is one of the most knowledgeable purveyors of Haitian art in the Caribbean. Even if you're not in the market for an expensive piece, you'll find dozens of charming and inexpensive handcrafts. The little gallery is a bit hard to find (on a narrow alleyway at the marina), but it's worth the search.

Another complex, the **Galerie Périgourdine,** facing the post office, also has a cluster of boutiques. Here you might pick up designer wear for both men and women, including items from the collection of Ted Lapidus.

Act III, 3 rue du Général-de-Gaulle (© **590/29-28-43**), is perhaps the most glamorous women's boutique in St. Martin. It prides itself on its evening gowns and chic cocktail dresses. If you've been invited to a reception aboard a private yacht, this is the place to find the right outfit. Designers include Alaïa, Thierry Mugler, Gianni Versace, Christian Lacroix, Cerruti, and Gaultier. The bilingual staff is accommodating, tactful, and charming.

Comptoir des Iles du Nord, rue de la Liberté (© **590/29-19-68**), offers unusual art objects from Bali and around the world—stuff to catch the eye of any aspiring interior decorator. There's even an inventory of dolls, dolls' clothing, dollhouses, and dolls' accessories, as well as vintage men's and women's clothing.

J'Aime ça by Bettina, Passage Louisiane (℗ **590/87-29-76**), sells lace garments, the kind that are demure with undergarments and more than a bit naughty without. Lace, lace, and more lace—in colors that include white, ecru, and black—is fashioned into skirts, tops, jumpsuits, shirts and blouses, and even "summer coats" that have lots of style but virtually no warmth, thanks to the peek-a-boo holes artfully crafted into each square yard.

La Romana, 12 rue de la République (℗ **590/87-88-16**), specializes in chic women's clothing that's a bit less pretentious and more fun and lighthearted than the selection at Act III. Italian rather than French designers are emphasized, including lines such as Anna Club and Ritmo de la Perloa, plus La Perla swimwear, Moschino handbags, and perfumes. A small collection of menswear is also available. The popular chain **Little Switzerland** has a branch here, on rue de la République (℗ **590/87-50-03**). This outlet is different from the one on the Dutch side, with a concentration on French products. The widest array of duty-free luxury items in St. Martin is available here, including French perfume and leather goods. **Maneks,** 24 rue de la République (℗ **590/87-54-91**), has a little bit of everything: video cameras, electronics, household appliances, liquors, gifts, souvenirs, beach accessories, film, watches, T-shirts, sunglasses, and Majorca pearls. The staff even sells Cuban cigars, but remember that they can't be brought back into the United States. **Roland Richardson,** 6 rue de la République (℗ **590/87-84-08**), has a beautiful gallery. A native of St. Martin, Richardson is one of the Caribbean's premier artists, working in oil, watercolors, pastels, and charcoal. Called a "modern-day Gauguin," he is known for his landscapes, portraits, and colorful still lifes. His work has been exhibited in more than 70 one-man and group exhibitions in museums and galleries around the world.

A charming roadside Creole cottage is home to **Gloria Lynn Studio,** 83 blvd. de Grand-Case (℗ **590/87-77-24**), which offers some of the most interesting paintings in Grand-Case. Inside, you'll find artworks produced by four members of the Lynn family (Gloria, Marty, Peter, and Robert). Their shared theme is island life and island sociology.

8 St. Maarten & St. Martin After Dark

IN ST. MAARTEN

After-dark activities begin early here, as guests start off with a sundowner, perhaps on the garden patio of **Pasanggrahan,** 15 Front St., Philipsburg (℗ **599/54-23588**). The most popular bar on the island is **Cheri's Café** ★★ (see "Great Deals on Dining," earlier in this chapter).

Many hotels sponsor **beachside barbecues** (particularly in winter) with steel bands, native music, and folk dancing. Outsiders are welcomed at most of these events, but call ahead to see if it's a private affair.

The **Casino Royale,** at the Maho Beach Hotel on Maho Bay (℗ **599/54-52115**), has 16 blackjack tables, 6 roulette wheels, and 3 craps and 3 Caribbean stud-poker tables. The casino offers baccarat, minibaccarat, and more than 250 slot machines. It's open daily 1pm to 4am. The **Casino Royale Piano Bar** is open nightly from 9:30pm, featuring the best of jazz, pop, and Caribbean music. There's no cover, and there's a complimentary buffet of snacks.

One of the island's newest casinos, the **Dolphin,** is at The Caravanserai on Beacon Hill Road (℗ **599/54-54000**). Gamblers start pouring in here at 1pm daily, some staying until 3 the next morning.

Sunset Beach Bar, 2 Beacon Hill Rd. (© **599/54-53998**), is set directly on the sands of Airport Beach and resembles an oversized gazebo. This place is mobbed most afternoons and evenings with office workers, off-duty airline pilots, beach people, and occasional celebs like Sandra Bullock. No one seems to mind the whine of airplane engines overhead or the fumes that filter down from aircraft that seem to fly at precarious altitudes just a few dozen feet overhead. Drinks are cheap, and you can order burgers, sandwiches, steaks, fish, chicken, and hot dogs from an outdoor charcoal grill.

The **Pelican Resort Club,** Simpson Bay (© **599/54-42503**), has a popular Vegas-style casino with a panoramic view of the bay. It offers 2 craps tables, 3 roulette tables, 9 blackjack tables, 2 stud-poker tables, and 120 slot machines. The Pelican also features horse racing, bingo, and sports nights with events broadcast via satellite, plus nightly dancing on the Pelican Reef Terrace and island shows featuring Caribbean bands. It's open daily 1pm to 3am.

Indiana Beach Restaurant & Bar and Indy's Bar, Kimshore (© **599/54-42797**), are immediately adjacent to one another and set beside the sands of Simpson Bay. They jointly reign as queen (or king) of the night every Thursday after 8:30pm, when they're mobbed with singles, who enjoy the two-for-one frozen margaritas after 10pm. (See "Great Deals on Dining," above.)

Sports fans gravitate to the **Lightning Casino,** Cole Bay (© **599/54-43290**), where wide-screen TVs show baseball, soccer, boxing, hockey, basketball, and football, along with horse racing. This casino is near the airport and will send a shuttle to pick you up, regardless of where you are on island.

The Roman-themed **Coliseum Casino,** on Front Street in Philipsburg (© **599/54-32102**), tries to attract high rollers, and has the highest table limits ($1,000 maximum) on St. Maarten. The Coliseum features more than 200 slot machines, 4 blackjack tables, 3 poker tables, and 2 roulette wheels. The Coliseum is open daily 11am to 3am.

Right in the heart of Philipsburg's shopping-crazed Front Street, **Rouge et Noir** (© **599/54-22952**) has a futuristic design. It offers slot machines, a Sigma Derby horse machine, video Keno, and video poker. It opens Monday to Saturday at 9am and Sunday at 11am to snag cruise ship passengers.

Also in the heart of Philipsburg, **Portofino,** Back Street (© **590/29-08-28**), is a lot of fun. A few nights a week, live rock and roll and country-western music is presented, with a French accent, between 10pm and 1am. There's no cover charge, and the cross-cultural pollination is charming. A menu lists all kinds of pizzas and pastas to stave off starvation.

IN ST. MARTIN

Some St. Martin hotels have dinner-dancing, piano-lounge music, and even discos, but the most popular after-dark pastime is leisurely dining. In Grand-Case, **Calmos Café,** blvd. de Grand-Case no. 4 (© **590/29-01-85**), is funky and low-key. This beachfront shack draws a young, hip crowd, with an occasional pop icon like Linda Evangelista dropping in. Management has posted a sign that says NO SNOBS near the entrance. In winter, there's sometimes live music after 9:30pm. Most people come just to flirt, gossip, and drink, but there's also good, affordable food, such as a Greek salad, a tuna salad, and "New Wave burgers" that are slathered with goat cheese. The house special drink is a Ti Punch that's a local variation on an old-fashioned rum punch.

The island attracts a lot of gay visitors, especially to its nude beaches, but there's little gay nightlife, except at the **Pink Mango,** Residence Laguna Beach at Nettlé Bay (© **0590/87-59-99**). To reach this charming and rather small club, go to the far right section of the former hotel's parking lot, walk along the building, and keep to the left. When you see a rainbow flag, press a buzzer. Gay men of all ages flock here, and a few women do, too. The club opens nightly at 10pm but doesn't really get crowded until midnight. It keeps going until 3am or later.

23

St. Vincent & the Grenadines

One of the major Windward Islands, sleepy **St. Vincent** is just beginning to awake to tourism, which hasn't yet reached massive dimensions the way it has on nearby St. Lucia. Sailors and the yachting set have long known of St. Vincent and its satellite bays and beaches in the **Grenadines.**

You visit St. Vincent for its botanical beauty and the Grenadines for the best sailing waters in the Caribbean. Don't come for the nightlife, grand cuisine, or beaches. There are some white-sand beaches near Kingstown on St. Vincent, but most of the others ringing the island are of black sand. The yachting crowd seems to view St. Vincent merely as a launching pad for the 40-plus-mile string of the Grenadines, but the island still has a few attractions that make it worth exploring on its own.

St. Vincent rewards you with a number of inexpensive inns and small West Indian taverns once you've paid the rather high airfare to reach it. The Grenadines, stamping ground of yachties, royalty, and high society (often British), are hardly what one thinks of first in contemplating a budget holiday in the sun. However, even here there are a few places to stay where you can keep costs affordable. The island in the Grenadines that offers the widest range of affordable food and lodging is Bequia.

An emerald island 18 miles long and 11 miles wide, St. Vincent has fertile valleys, rich forests, lush jungles, rugged peaks, waterfalls, foam-whitened beaches, outstanding coral reefs (with what experts say is some of the world's clearest water), a volcano nestled in the sky and usually capped by its own private cloud, and 4,000 feet up, Crater Lake. Unspoiled by the worst fallout that mass tourism sometimes brings, the islanders actually treat visitors like people: Met with courtesy, they respond with courtesy. British customs predominate, along with traces of Gallic cultural influences, but all with a distinct West Indian flair.

South of St. Vincent, the small chain of islands called the Grenadines extends for more than 40 miles and offers the finest yachting area in the eastern Caribbean. The islands are strung like a necklace of precious stones and have romantic-sounding names like Bequia, Mustique, Canouan, and Petit St. Vincent. A few of the islands have accommodations, but many of the islands are so small and so completely undeveloped they attract only beachcombers and stray boaters. We'll explore Bequia, Union Island, and Mayreau. Populated by the descendants of African slaves and administered by St. Vincent, the Grenadines collectively add up to a landmass of 30 square miles. These bits of land, often dots on nautical charts, may lack natural resources, yet they're blessed with white-sand beaches, coral reefs, and their own kind of sleepy beauty. If you don't spend the night in the Grenadines, you should at least go over for the day to visit one of the islands and enjoy a picnic lunch (which your hotel will pack for you) on one of the long stretches of beach.

St. Vincent

✈ Airport	
↖ Beach	
▲ Mountain	

Beachcombers Hotel **3**
Casa de Columbus **2**
Cobblestone Inn **1**
Coconut Beach Hotel **2**
Heron Hotel **1**

Fancy
■ Falls of Baleine
Kearton's Bay
▲ La Soufrière
Crater Lake
Wallibou Beach ↖
▲ Morne Garu Mountains
Richmond Beach ↖
Wallibou River
○ Richmond
Chateaubelair Islet
▲ Richmond Peak
Troumaka ○ Chateaubelair
▲ Mt. Brisbane
○ Georgetown
Leeward Hwy.
Windward Hwy.
Wallilabou Bay
Barrouallie ○
○ Colonarie
Peter's ↖ Hope
Sans Souci
Jackson's Point
○ Layou
Greiggs
○ Biabou
ATLANTIC OCEAN
Buccament ↖ Bay Beach
▲ Mt. St. Andrew
Mesopotamia
Questelle's Bay ↖ Beach
MARRIQUA VALLEY
1 ○ E. T. Joshua Airport
↖ Argyle Beach
Kingstown ✈
Vigie Hwy.
○ Stubbs
2
Caribbean Sea
Indian Bay Beach ↖
Villa Beach
Young Island ↖ **3**
Bequia Channel

0 — 5 mi
0 — 5 km
Ⓝ

1 Essentials

VISITOR INFORMATION

In the United States, you can get information at the **St. Vincent and Grenadines Tourist Office,** 801 Second Ave., 21st Floor, New York, NY 10017 (℃ **800/729-1726** or 212/687-4981). In **Canada,** you can go to 32 Park Rd., Toronto, Ontario N4W 2N4 (℃ **416/924-5796**).

On St. Vincent, the local **Department of Tourism** is on Upper Bay Street, Government Administrative Centre, Kingstown (℃ **784/457-1502**).

The Internet address for St. Vincent and the Grenadines is **www. svgtourism.com**.

GETTING THERE

In the eastern Caribbean, St. Vincent—the gateway to the Grenadines (the individual islands are discussed later in this chapter)—lies 100 miles west of Barbados, where most visitors from North America fly first and then make connections to get to St. Vincent's **E. T. Joshua Airport** and on to the Grenadines. For details on getting to Barbados from North America, see chapter 5. However, the transfer through Barbados is no longer necessary, as **American Eagle** (℃ **800/433-7300** or 784/456-5000) has one direct flight to St. Vincent daily from San Juan, so getting here is more convenient than ever before.

Air Martinique (© 784/458-4528) runs once-daily service between Martinique, St. Lucia, St. Vincent, and Union Island.

Increasing numbers of visitors to St. Vincent prefer the dependable service of one of the best charter airlines in the Caribbean, **Mustique Airways** (© 784/458-4380). The airline makes frequent runs from St. Vincent to the major airports of the Grenadines. With advance warning, it will arrange specially chartered (and reasonably priced) transport for you and your party to and from many of the surrounding islands (such as Grenada, Aruba, St. Lucia, Antigua, Barbados, and Trinidad). The price of these chartered flights is less than you might expect and often matches the fares on conventional Caribbean airlines. Currently the airline owns seven small aircraft, none of which carry more than nine passengers.

GETTING AROUND

BY TAXI The government sets the rates for fares, but **taxis** are unmetered; always ask the fare and agree on the charge before getting in. Figure on spending EC$15 to EC$20 ($5.50–$7.50)—or maybe more—to go from the E. T. Joshua Airport to your hotel.

If you don't want to drive yourself, you can also hire taxis to take you to the island's major attractions. Most drivers seem to be well-informed guides (it won't take you long to learn everything you need to know about St. Vincent). You'll spend EC$40 to EC$50 ($14.75–$18.50) per hour for a car carrying two to four passengers.

BY RENTAL CAR Driving on St. Vincent is a bit of an adventure because of the narrow twisting roads. *Drive on the left.* To drive like a Vincentian, you'll soon learn to sound your horn a lot, as you make the sharp curves and turns. If you present your valid U.S. or Canadian driver's license at the police department on Bay Street in Kingstown and pay a fee of EC$75 ($27.75), you'll obtain a temporary permit to drive.

Avis (© 800/331-1084 in the U.S., or 784/456-2929 locally) has a branch at the airport. Local rental firms include **Kim's Rentals,** on Grenville Street in Kingstown (© 784/456-1884), or **Star Garage,** also on Grenville Street in Kingstown (© 784/456-1743). Make sure your car has a spare tire because the roads are full of potholes.

BY BUS Flamboyantly painted open **buses** travel the principal roads of St. Vincent, linking the major towns and villages. The price is low, depending on where you're going, and the experience will connect you with the people of the island. The central departure point is the bus terminal at the New Kingstown Fish Market. Fares range from EC$1.50 to EC$6 (55¢–$2.20).

 FAST FACTS: **St. Vincent & the Grenadines**

Banking Hours Most banks are open Monday to Thursday 8am to either 1 or 3pm and Friday either 8am to 5pm or 8am to 1pm and 3 to 5pm, depending on the bank.

Currency The official currency of St. Vincent is the **Eastern Caribbean dollar (EC$)**, worth about U.S.37¢, or EC$2.70 = U.S.$1. Most of the quotations in this chapter appear in U.S. dollars, unless otherwise noted. Most restaurants, shops, and hotels accept payment in U.S. dollars or traveler's checks.

Documents British, Canadian, or U.S. citizens should have proof of identity and a return or ongoing airplane ticket. Passports or birth certificates with a photo ID are sufficient.

Electricity Electricity is 220-volt AC (50 cycles), so you'll need an adapter and a transformer. Some hotels have transformers, but it's best to bring your own.

Language English is the official language.

Medical Care There are two hospitals on St. Vincent, **Kingstown General Hospital,** Kingstown (© **784/456-1185**), and **Medical Associates Clinic,** Kingstown (© **784/457-2598**).

Pharmacies On St. Vincent try **Deane's Pharmacy,** Halifax Street, Kingstown (© **784/457-2056**), open Monday to Friday 8:30am to 4:30pm and Saturday 8:30am to 12:30pm.

Post Office The **General Post Office,** on Halifax Street in Kingstown (© **784/456-1111**), is open Monday to Friday 8:30am to 3pm and Saturday 8:30 to 11:30am. There are smaller post offices in 56 districts throughout the country, including offices on the Grenadine islands of Bequia, Mustique, Canouan, Mayreau, and Union Island.

Safety St. Vincent and its neighboring islands of the Grenadines are still safe islands to visit. In Kingstown, the capital of St. Vincent, chances are you'll encounter little serious crime. However, take the usual precautions and never leave valuables unguarded.

Taxes The government imposes an airport departure tax of EC$30 ($11) per person. A 7% government occupancy tax is charged for all hotel accommodations.

Telecommunications To call St. Vincert from the United States, dial 1 then 784 (the area code for St. Vincent) and the local seven-digit number.

Time Both St. Vincent and the Grenadines operate on Atlantic standard time year-round: When it's 6am on St. Vincent, it's 5am in Miami. During daylight saving time in the United States, St. Vincent keeps the same time as the U.S. east coast.

Tipping Hotels and restaurants add a 10% to 15% service charge, and it is customary to tip the same percentage when the service charge isn't automatically added to the bill. Tip taxi drivers 12% of the fare.

Weather The climate of St. Vincent and the Grenadines is pleasantly cooled by the trade winds all year. The tropical temperature is in the 78° to 82°F range. The rainy season is May to November.

2 Accommodations You Can Afford

Don't expect high-rise resorts here, as everything is rather small. The places are comfortable, not fancy, and you usually get a lot of personal attention from the staff. Most hotels and restaurants add a 7% government tax and a 10% to 15% service charge to your bill; ask whether these taxes are included in the prices quoted.

Beachcombers Hotel ⚘ (*Value*   This relative newcomer, opened by Richard and Flora Gunn in a tropical garden right on the beach, immediately became a far more inviting choice than the traditional budget favorites, the Heron and the Cobblestone. A pair of chalet-like buildings house the tastefully decorated accommodations, all cooled by ceiling fans, although a few rooms have air-conditioning. The standard of cleanliness and maintenance is the finest on the island. Try for room 1, 2, or 3, as they are the best rooms, and they also open onto the water. Two rooms have small kitchenettes. The shower-only bathrooms are a bit cramped. The hotel has a spa (Mrs. Gunn is a massage and beauty therapist). And, astonishingly for a B&B, the Beachcombers offers a steam room and sauna. The Beachbar & Restaurant, a favorite gathering place for locals, fronts an open terrace and serves excellent cuisine. The Gunns' daughter Cheryl, who mastered her cookery skills in England, is the chef.

Villa Beach (P.O. Box 126), Kingstown, St. Vincent, W.I. ℂ **784/458-4283**. Fax 784/458-4385. www.beach combershotel.com. 12 units. Year-round $65 single; $90 double. AE, MC, V. **Amenities:** Restaurant, bar, spa, steam room, Turkish bath, sauna, room service, library, babysitting, laundry. *In room:* Fridge, ceiling fans.

Casa de Columbus   Built in 1972 a few feet from the sea, in a residential neighborhood that's one of the most sought-after on St. Vincent, this is a modestly priced hotel that has been renovated several times. Don't expect personalized intimacy; the setting is anonymous but serviceable, and it provides easy access to many neighboring resorts whose bars, restaurants, and sports facilities can sometimes be made available to you. You can swim on a narrow beach near the hotel's foundation, but a more desirable site might be Indian Bay Beach, whose sands are a 5-minute walk away. If you don't feel inspired to cook, you can go to the lattice-ringed Caribbean bistro, Sam's, on the premises, which serves lunch and dinner. The accommodations aren't frilly or fancy, but contain white walls, carpets, patterned draperies, wood furnishings, touches of rattan, and sometimes views over the offshore upscale resort of Young Island. The rooms are small and rather motel-like but offer good beds and rather tiny but tidily maintained bathrooms with showers. This is the place to be on Saturday night, when the owners invite you to "Come and Drink Us Dry," to the sounds of a live band.

Indian Bay (P.O. Box 538), Kingstown, St. Vincent, W.I. ℂ **800/742-4276** or 784/458-4001. Fax 784/ 457-4777. indianbay@casadecolumbus.com. 14 units, some with kitchenette. Year-round $95 per person. Extra person $45. Rates are all-inclusive. AE, MC, V. **Amenities:** Restaurant, bar. *In room:* A/C, TV.

Cobblestone Inn   Built as a warehouse for sugar and arrowroot in 1814, the core of this historic hotel is made of stone and brick. Today it's one of St. Vincent's most famous hotels, known for its labyrinth of passages, arches, and upper halls. To reach the high-ceilinged reception area, you pass from the waterfront through a stone tunnel into a chiseled courtyard. At the top of a massive sloping stone staircase, you're shown to one of the simple old-fashioned rooms. Most units contain TVs, and some have windows opening over the rooftops of town. Most of the rooms are small, although some are medium in size; the most spacious is no. 5, but it opens onto a noisy street. Mattresses are well worn but still comfortable, and the bathrooms are very tiny, with thin towels. Meals are served on a third-floor aerie high above the hotel's central courtyard. Rows of windows and rattan furnishings in the adjacent bar create one of the most frequented hideaways in town. You'll have to drive about 3 miles to the nearest beach.

Bax St. (P.O. Box 867), Kingstown, St. Vincent, W.I. ℂ **784/456-1937**. Fax 784/456-1938. 20 units. Year-round $65 single or double; $70 triple. AE, DISC, MC, V. **Amenities:** Restaurant, bar, babysitting, laundry. *In room:* A/C.

Coconut Beach Hotel   This owner-occupied inn/restaurant/bar is 5 minutes south of the airport and a 5-minute drive from Kingstown. The hotel, which grew out of a villa built in the 1930s by one of the region's noted eccentrics, lies across the channel from the much more expensive Young Island. Its seaside setting makes it a good choice for swimming and sunbathing. Island tours, such as sailing the Grenadines, can be arranged, as can diving, snorkeling, and mountain climbing. Each small room is furnished in a modern style but contains a fairly good bed, although the mattresses look well used; the tiny bathrooms have rather thin towels. A beach bar at water's edge serves tropical drinks, and an open-air restaurant opens onto a view of Indian Bay and features West Indian and Vincentian dishes, prepared from local foods. Steaks, Cornish game hens, and hamburgers round out the fare.

Indian Bay (P.O. Box 355), Kingstown, St. Vincent, W.I. ✆/fax **784/457-4900**. inforequest@ cobblestoneinnsvg.com. 11 units. Year-round $55–$70 single or double. Rates include breakfast. AE, MC, V. **Amenities:** Restaurant, beach bar. *In room:* Ceiling fan, no phone.

Heron Hotel   This respectable but slightly run-down hotel is among the most historic buildings on St. Vincent. It was built of local stone and tropical hardwoods late in the 18th century as a warehouse, and it later provided lodging for colonial planters doing business along the then-teeming wharves of Kingstown. Operating in its present format since 1960, it occupies the second story of a building whose ground floor is devoted to shops. Some of the simple and rather small rooms overlook an inner courtyard; others face the streets. Room 15 is the largest. Accommodations have time-worn furnishings, including mattresses that are ready for retirement, rather garish floral draperies, single beds, and extremely cramped bathrooms with thin towels. Although you don't get grand comfort here, the price is extremely reasonable and the staff most hospitable. There's a restaurant, whose busiest time of day is lunch. (The restaurant might close after dusk, so dinner reservations are important.)

Upper Bay St. (P.O. Box 226), Kingstown, St. Vincent, W.I. ✆ **784/457-1631**. Fax 784/457-1189. 13 units. Year-round $54 single; $70 double. Extra person $45. Rates include full breakfast. AE, MC, V. **Amenities:** Restaurant. *In room:* A/C.

3 Great Deals on Dining

Unlike on many Caribbean islands, many Vincentian hotels serve authentic West Indian cuisine. There are also a few independent eateries.

Aggie's ✿ *Finds* WEST INDIAN/SEAFOOD   On the island's southern end in Kingstown, this eatery provides a lively environment with warm hospitality. The matriarch who runs the place is Agatha Richards, affectionately called Aggie by her well-satisfied customers. This local hangout specializes in West Indian seafood at reasonable prices. What's in season determines which soups are offered (perhaps green pea, *callaloo*, or pumpkin), or try the fish or conch chowder. House specialties might include lobster, souse, conch, shrimp, fish, and whelk, or try the chicken, served baked or fried, or one of the curried beef and mutton dishes. A Creole buffet is featured at lunch noon to 3pm on Friday with your choice of three meats such as pork, chicken, and fish. It's Creole day on Saturday, with specialties like souse, Creole-style fish, and pilau.

Egmont St., Kingstown. ✆ **784/456-2110**. Reservations recommended. Main courses EC$25–EC$55 ($9.25–$20.35). AE, MC, V. Daily 9am–4pm.

Basil's Bar & Restaurant ✿ SEAFOOD/INTERNATIONAL   This brick-lined enclave is a less famous annex of the legendary Basil's Beach Bar on

Mustique. It occupies an early 19th-century sugar warehouse, on the waterfront in Kingstown beneath the previously recommended Cobblestone Inn (see "Accommodations You Can Afford," above). The air-conditioned interior is accented with exposed stone and brick, soaring arches, and a rambling mahogany bar that remains open throughout the day. The food is quite creditable, but nowhere near as good as that enjoyed by Princess Margaret or Mick Jagger at Basil's other bar on Mustique. The menu could include lobster salad, shrimp in garlic butter, sandwiches, hamburgers, and barbecued chicken. Dinners feature grilled lobster, escargots, shrimp cocktail, grilled red snapper, and grilled filet mignon. You can order meals here throughout the day and late into the evening (until the last satisfied customer leaves).

Bay St., Kingstown. ✆ **784/457-2713.** Reservations recommended. Main courses EC$37–EC$65 ($13.75–$24). AE, MC, V. Mon–Sat 8am–10pm.

Bounty (Value) AMERICAN/WEST INDIAN In the redbrick Troutman Building, in the center of Kingstown, you'll find the extremely affordable Bounty serving the local workers (the true power-lunch venue is Basil's, above). A friendly staff greets you. Fill up on pastries of all kinds, rôtis (Caribbean burritos), hot dogs, hamburgers, and sandwiches, along with homemade soups. Fish-and-chips are also served, along with quiche and pizza. The cookery is just as simple as the surroundings, and the interesting collection of drinks includes passion fruit and golden apple. On site is a gallery selling works by local artists.

Egmont St., Kingstown. ✆ **784/456-1776.** Snacks and sandwiches $1.50–$4.50; main courses $7.50–$16. No credit cards. Mon–Fri 8am–5pm; Sat 8am–1:30pm.

Lime N' Pub Restaurant ★ (Value) WEST CARIBBEAN/INDIAN This is one of the island's most popular restaurants, and it sits opposite the super-expensive Young Island Hotel, right on Young Island Channel. It's the most congenial pub on St. Vincent, with a wide selection of pub grub, including pizza. There's even a live lobster pond. A local band livens things up a few times a week in winter. In the more formal section of this indoor and alfresco restaurant, you can partake of some good West Indian food, along with dishes from India or the international kitchen. The rôtis win high praise, but we always order the fresh fish and lobster dishes instead. Coconut shrimp is generally excellent. Service is among the most hospitable on the island.

Opposite Young Island at Villa. ✆ **784/458-4227.** Main courses EC$55–EC$95 ($20.25–$35.25). AE, DC, MC, V. Daily noon–midnight.

Rooftop Restaurant & Bar WEST INDIAN/INTERNATIONAL This restaurant does a thriving business because of its well-prepared food and its location three stories above the center of Kingstown. After you climb some flights of stairs, you'll see a bar near the entrance, an indoor area decorated in earth tones, and a patio open to the breezes. Lunch stresses traditional Creole recipes using fresh fish, chicken, mutton, beef, and goat. Dinners are more international and include lobster, excellent snapper with lemon butter–and–garlic sauce, steak with onions and mushrooms, and several savory preparations of pork. Every Wednesday and Friday a karaoke sing-along is featured, and Saturday is family night, with a barbecue along with a steel band in attendance after 6pm. In addition, 60 drinks are featured at the bar.

Bay St., Kingstown. ✆ **784/457-2845.** Reservations recommended for dinner. Main courses EC$30–EC$65 ($11–$24); lunch platters EC$30 ($11). AE, DISC, MC, V. Mon–Wed 9am–10pm; Thurs–Fri 9am–midnight; Sat 10am–4pm.

4 Hitting the Beaches

All beaches on St. Vincent are public, and many of the best ones border hotel properties, which you can patronize for drinks or lunch. Most of the resorts are in the south, where the beaches have golden-yellow sand. Young Island has the only beach of truly white sand on St. Vincent, but it's reserved for patrons of the expensive resort property. Many of the beaches in the north have sands of a lava-ash color. The safest swimming is on the leeward beaches; the surf on the windward (that is, eastern) beaches is often rough and can be quite dangerous.

Villa Beach, only a 10-minute drive from Kingstown, is the island's most frequented beach, although its sands are hardly large enough to accommodate the crowds that flock there. Weekends can be particularly bad. The narrow strip of sand fronts the better beach of Young Island. The tranquil Caribbean waters make swimming safe here. Dive shops and simple cafes dot the shoreline. Nearby **Indian Bay Beach** is similar to Villa Beach and also attracts lots of Vincentians on weekends. Monday to Thursday, however, you'll probably have plenty of room on the narrow strip. The sand here is slightly golden in color but tends to be rocky. The reef-protected tranquil waters are ideal for both swimming and snorkeling. You'll find both bars and restaurants here.

Heading north from Kingstown, you'll reach **Buccament Bay,** where the waters are clean, clear, and tranquil enough for swimming. This beach is very tiny, however, and its sand is of the black volcanic variety. In the same area, **Questelle's Bay Beach** (pronounced Keet-*eels*) is also on the leeward, tranquil Caribbean side of the island. The black-sand beach, next to Camden Park, is very similar to Buccament Bay.

The best beaches, all with black volcanic sand, are found at **Kearton's Bay,** near the hamlet of Barrouallie, and at **Peter's Hope** and **Richmond Beach,** all reached along the leeward highway running up the east coast of St. Vincent.

Only the most die-hard frequent the beaches on the east coast, or windward side. This is where the big breakers roll in from the Atlantic. Don't plan to go swimming in these rough waters—a beach picnic might be more appropriate.

5 Sports & Other Outdoor Pursuits

FISHING It's best to go to a local fisherman (or woman) for advice if you're interested in this sport, which your hotel can also arrange for you. The government of St. Vincent doesn't require visitors to take out a fishing license. If you arrange things in time, it's sometimes possible to accompany the fishermen on a trip, perhaps 4 or 5 miles from shore. A modest fee should suffice. The fishing fleet leaves from the leeward coast at Barrouallie. They've been known to return to shore with everything from a 6-inch redfish to a 20-foot pilot whale.

HIKING Exploring St. Vincent's hot volcano, **La Soufrière,** is an intriguing adventure. As you travel the island, you can't miss its cloud-capped splendor. This volcano has occasionally captured the attention of the world. The most recent eruption was in 1979, when it spewed ashes, lava, and hot mud that covered the vegetation on its slopes and forced thousands of Vincentians to flee its fury. Belching rocks and black curling smoke filled the blue Caribbean sky. Jets of steam spouted 20,000 feet into the air. About 17,000 people were evacuated from a 10-mile ring around the volcano.

Fortunately, the volcano is in the sparsely settled northern part of the island. It lies away from most of the tourism and commercial centers, and even if it

---

Finds **A Journey into a Rain Forest**

If you don't want to face Soufrière, try the other best hikes on the island, the **Vermont Nature Trails.** These marked trails (get a map at the tourist office) take you through a rain forest. You'll pass long-ago plantations that nature has reclaimed and enter a world of tropical fruit trees. If it's your lucky day, you might even see the rare St. Vincent parrot with its flamboyant plumage. Wear good hiking shoes and mosquito repellent. Call **Sailor's Wilderness Tours** in Kingstown at ℂ **784/457-1274** to get directions.

---

should erupt again, volcanologists don't consider it a danger to visitors lodged at beachside hotels along the leeward coast. At the rim of the crater you'll be rewarded with one of the most panoramic views in the Caribbean—that is, if the wind doesn't blow too hard and make you topple over into the crater itself!

Take extreme caution. Looking inside, you can see the steam rising from the crater. Even if you're an experienced hiker, don't attempt to explore the volcano without a guide. And wear suitable hiking clothes and be sure you're in the best of health before making the arduous journey. The easiest route is the 3-mile-long eastern route leaving from Rabacca. Some people attempt this on their own. The more arduous trail, longer by half a mile, is the western trail from Chateaubelair, which definitely requires a guide. The round-trip to the crater takes about 5 hours. (The trail back down is much easier, we assure you.)

St. Vincent Forestry Headquarters, in the village of Campden Park, about 3 miles from Kingstown along the west coast (ℂ **784/457-8594**), offers a pamphlet giving hiking data to La Soufrière. It's open Monday to Friday 8am to noon and 1 to 4pm. **HazEco Tours** (ℂ **784/457-8634**) offers guided hikes up to La Soufrière, costing $120 per couple, including lunch.

SNORKELING & SCUBA DIVING   The best area for snorkeling and scuba diving is the Villa/Young Island section on the southern end of the island.

Dive St. Vincent, on the Young Island Cut (ℂ **784/457-4928**), has been owned and operated by a transplanted Texan, Bill Tewes, for more than a decade. The best dive company in the country, Dive St. Vincent now has two additional dive shops: **Dive Canouan,** at the Tamarind Beach Hotel on Canouan Island (ℂ **784/458-8044**), and **Grenadines Dive,** at the Sunny Grenadines Hotel on Union Island (ℂ **784/458-8138**). The shops have a total of six instructors and three dive masters, as well as seven dive boats. The chain of dive shops allows visitors to dive or be certified with a consistency of quality while sailing throughout St. Vincent and the Grenadines. All shops offer dive/snorkel trips as well as sightseeing day trips and dive instruction. Single-tank dives are $50 and two-tank dives $90, including all equipment and instructors and/or dive master guides. Dive packages are also available.

TENNIS   **Young Island Resort** on Young Island (ℂ **784/458-4826**) and the **Grand View Beach Hotel** at Villa Point (ℂ **784/458-4811**) have tennis courts.

6 Seeing the Sights

Special events include the weeklong **Carnival** in early July, one of the largest in the eastern Caribbean, with steel band and calypso competitions, along with the crowning of the king and queen of the carnival.

KINGSTOWN

Lush and tropical, the capital isn't as architecturally fascinating as St. George's on Grenada. Some English-style houses do exist, many looking as if they belonged in Penzance, Cornwall, instead of the Caribbean. However, you can still meet old-timers if you stroll on Upper Bay Street. White-haired and bearded, they load their boats with produce grown on the mountain before heading to some secluded beach in the Grenadines. This is a chief port and gateway to the Grenadines, and you can also view the small boats and yachts that have dropped anchor here. The place is a magnet for charter sailors.

At the top of a winding road on the north side of Kingstown is **Fort Charlotte** (© **784/456-1165**), built on Johnson Point around the time of the American Revolution, enclosing one side of the bay. The ruins aren't much to inspect; the reason to come here is the view. The fort sits atop a steep promontory some 640 feet above the sea. From its citadel, you'll have a commanding sweep of the leeward shores to the north, Kingstown to the south, and the Grenadines beyond. On a clear day you can even see Grenada. Three cannons used to fight off French troops are still in place. You'll see a series of oil murals depicting the history of black Caribs. Admission is free, and the fort is open daily 6am to 6pm.

The second major sight is the **Botanic Gardens** ⚘, on the north side of Kingstown at Montrose (© **784/457-1003**). Founded in 1765 by Gov. George Melville, these are the oldest botanical gardens in the West Indies. In this Windward Eden, you'll see 20 acres of such tropical exotics as teak, almond, cinnamon, nutmeg, cannonball, and mahogany; some trees are more than 2 centuries old. One of the breadfruit trees was reputedly among those original seedlings brought to this island by Captain Bligh in 1793. There's also a large *Spachea perforata* (Soufrière tree), a species believed to be unique to St. Vincent and not found in the wild since 1812. The gardens are open daily 6am to 6pm; admission is free.

THE LEEWARD HIGHWAY ⚘⚘

The leeward, or west, side of the island has the most dramatic scenery. North of Kingstown, you rise into lofty terrain before descending to the water again. There are views in all directions. Here you can see the massive **Carib Rock,** with a human face carving dating back to A.D. 600. This is one of the finest petroglyphs in the Caribbean.

Continuing north you reach **Barrouallie,** where there's a Carib stone altar. Even if you're not into fishing, you might want to spend some time in this whaling village, where some people still occasionally set out in brightly painted boats armed with harpoons, Moby Dick style, to seek the elusive whale. But environmentalists should note that while Barrouallie may be one of the last few outposts in the world where whaling is carried on, Vincentians point out that it doesn't endanger an already endangered species since so few are caught each year. If one is caught, it's an occasion for festivities.

The leeward highway continues to **Chateaubelair,** the end of the line. Here you can swim at the attractive **Richmond Beach** before heading back to Kingstown. In the distance, the volcano, La Soufrière, looms menacingly in the mountains.

The adventurous set out from here to see the **Falls of Baleine,** 7½ miles north of Richmond Beach on the northern tip of the island, accessible only by boat. Baleine is a freshwater falls that comes from a stream in the volcanic hills. If you're interested in making the trip, check with the tourist office in Kingstown for tour information.

> ⌒*Value* **Cheap Thrills: What to See & Do for Free**
> **(Well, Almost) on St. Vincent & the Grenadines**
> ────────────────────────────────────
>
> - **Hike Through a Lush Eden.** St. Vincent might not be much on
>   beaches, but it's a hiker's paradise, filled with lush tropical forests
>   and the volcano La Soufrière. You can book the services of a guide
>   through the tourist office or go it alone if you're skilled in handling
>   yourself in the outdoors. The tourist office will provide you with a
>   map. The Vermont Nature Trails are a network of well-marked
>   paths winding through a beautiful tropical rain forest. The ground
>   beneath you will often be carpeted by huge ferns that look as if
>   they're from the dawn of time, and you'll be shaded by a vast
>   canopy of hardwood trees. Caribbean pine, 75-foot bamboo stands,
>   and deep ravines are part of the landscape. Count yourself lucky if
>   you see the endangered St. Vincent parrot.
> - **Spend a Day on Bequia.** A scenic ride on an inexpensive government-
>   owned mailboat will deliver you to the enchanting Grenadine island
>   of Bequia, where time has seemingly stood still. Its capital is Port Eliz-
>   abeth, one of the Caribbean's best sheltered harbors, 9 miles south of
>   the parent island of St. Vincent. Part of the fun of going here is to
>   meet and talk to some of the Bequinians, with their long tradition of
>   seafaring and shipbuilding. There's not a lot to do here, and that's
>   part of the fun. You can wander the port, soak up local color, enjoy a
>   Creole lunch, and spend the rest of the day on the sandy beach.
> - **Drive Through the Marriaqua Valley.** Also known as the
>   Mesopotamia Valley, this rugged valley is one of the most dramatic
>   drives in the Caribbean. It begins at the Vigie Highway, just east of
>   the airport, and climbs northeast before heading north to the

THE WINDWARD HIGHWAY

The Windward Highway runs along the eastern Atlantic coast from Kingstown.
Waves pound the surf, and panoramic seascapes are all along the rocky shores.
If you want to go swimming along this often-dangerous coast, stick to the sandy
spots, as they offer safer shores. Along this road you'll pass coconut and banana
plantations and fields of arrowroot.

North of Georgetown is the **Rabacca Dry River,** which shows the flow of lava
from the volcano when it erupted at the beginning of the 20th century. The
journey from Kingstown to here is only 24 miles, but it will seem like much
longer. If you want to go the final 11 miles along a rugged road to **Fancy,** the
northern tip of the island, you'll need a really rugged four-wheel-drive vehicle.

MARRIQUA VALLEY 🐦

Sometimes known as the Mesopotamia Valley, the Marriqua Valley is one of the
lushest cultivated valleys in the eastern Caribbean. Surrounded by mountain
ridges, the drive takes you through a landscape planted with nutmeg, cocoa,
coconut, breadfruit, and bananas. The road begins at the Vigie Highway, east of
the airport; surrounded by mountain ridges, it opens onto a panoramic view of
Grand Bonhomme Mountain, rising 3,180 feet. At Montréal, you'll come upon

village of Mesopotamia. Along the way you'll pass rustic scenes like boys riding overburdened donkeys and farmers putting blue plastic on their crops to protect them from insects and birds. As you pass the fields of coconut, sweet corn, arrowroot, peanuts, and coconut palms, you'll know why this valley is called the breadbasket of St. Vincent. Surrounded by mountain ridges, the road opens onto a panoramic view of 3,180-foot Grand Bonhomme Mountain. Passing through deep tropical forests, you arrive at Montreal Gardens, 12 miles north of Kingstown. Here you can have lunch and go for a swim in the natural mineral springs.

• **Wander Kingstown.** Although often confused with the more famous Kingston, capital of Jamaica, this tiny town of some 25,000 Vincentians has its own unique personality. On the southwestern coast, it wraps itself around Kingstown Bay and is set against a backdrop of hills and ridges. A bustling port, it invites wandering and people-watching. Most interest centers on the waterfront, where schooners from many other islands, including South America, unload their cargo. The best time to visit is Saturday morning, when the marketplace at the south end of town is at its most active. If you need a sightseeing goal, make it Fort Charlotte on the north side of the capital, lying at the end of a winding road on a promontory rising 650 feet above sea level. Originally used by the British to defend St. Vincent from the French, it was named for George III. At the fort you'll be rewarded with the most panoramic view of St. Vincent and the Grenadines.

natural mineral springs where you can have lunch and take a dip. Only rugged vehicles should make this trip.

Around Kingstown, you can also enjoy the **Queen's Drive,** a scenic loop into the high hills to the east of the capital. From here, the view is panoramic over Kingstown and its yacht-clogged harbor to the Grenadines in the distance.

7 Shopping

You don't come to St. Vincent to shop, but once you're here, you might pick up some of the Sea Island cotton fabrics and clothing that are specialties. In addition, Vincentian artisans make pottery, jewelry, and baskets that have souvenir value at least.

Since Kingstown consists of about 12 small blocks, you can walk and browse and see just about everything in a morning's shopping jaunt. Try to be in town for the colorful, noisy **Friday-morning market.** You might not purchase anything, but you'll surely enjoy the riot of color.

Juliette's Fashions, Back Street (© **784/456-1143**), owned and operated by the same entrepreneur who runs Juliette's Restaurant, is the best-stocked and most glamorous women's clothing store on St. Vincent, but that's not saying a lot. Beneficiary of its owner's frequent buying trips to Miami and New York, it's one of the few outlets on the island to sell semiformal eveningwear. At **Sprott Brothers, Homeworks,** Bay Street (© **784/457-1121**), you can buy clothing designed by Vincentians, along with an array of fabrics, linens, and silk-screened T-shirts—even Caribbean-made furniture.

Noah's Arkade, Bay Street (© **784/457-1513**), sells gifts from the West Indies, like woodcarvings, T-shirts, and a wide range of books and souvenirs. Noah's has shops at the Frangipani Hotel in Bequia. **St. Vincent Philatelic Services,** Bonadie's Building, Bay Street (© **784/457-1911**), is the Caribbean's largest operating bureau, and its issues are highly acclaimed by stamp collectors around the world. Stamp enthusiasts can visit or order by mail. The familiar **Y. de Lima,** Bay and Egmont streets (© **784/457-1681**), is full of cameras, stereo equipment, toys, clocks, binoculars, and jewelry, the best selection on the island. Caribbean gold and silver jewelry are also featured.

Time for more shopping? The typical Caribbean duty-free goods are found at **Voyager,** Halifax Street (© **784/456-1686**), including quality jewelry, French perfumes, leather goods, and Swiss watches. As you're leaving you can drop into **Carsyl Duty-Free Liquors** at the airport (© **784/457-2706**), where you'll find liquor at prices often 40% off stateside prices. To add to your music collection, you can visit **Music World** at Egmont Street (© **784/547-1884**), where you can listen to and buy the latest soca, reggae, and calypso music.

8 St. Vincent After Dark

Most nightlife here revolves around the hotels, where activities are likely to include barbecues and dancing to steel bands. In season, at least one hotel seems to have something planned every night during the week. Beer is extremely cheap at all the places noted below.

During party nights, when it rocks and rolls (usually Fri, Sat, and Sun), the **Aquatic Club,** adjacent to the departure point of the ferry from St. Vincent to Young Island (© **784/458-4205**), is the loudest, most raucous nightspot on St. Vincent. On weekend nights, things heat up by 11pm and continue until as late as 3am. The other nights of the week the place functions just as a bar, with a spate of recorded music but without the high-volume live bands. Centered on an open-sided veranda and an outdoor deck, the place is open daily 8pm to 2 or 3am. There's no cover.

The Attic, in the Kentucky Building, at 1 Melville and Back sts. (© **784/457-2558**), features jazz and easy-listening music. Music is live only on Friday and Saturday; Tuesday and Thursday it's recorded, and Wednesday is karaoke night. Fish and burgers are available. There's usually a cover of EC$10 to EC$15 ($3.75–$5.50).

Emerald Valley Casino, Penniston Valley (© **784/456-7824**), is not one of the Caribbean's glamorous casinos. This down-home nightspot offers a trio of roulette tables, three blackjack, and one Caribbean stud poker. You can also play craps here. There's a bar, and you can also order food. If you've got nothing else to do, you might consider a visit. Open Wednesday to Monday 9pm to 3am.

Touch Entertainment Centre (TEC), Grenville Street (© **784/457-1825**), opposite KFC on the top floor of the Cambridge Building, is the best-known nightspot around. With advanced lighting, it's a soundproof air-conditioned environment, popular with tourists. Every Wednesday in summer is disco night, especially for the young and restless. Friday and Sunday nights the club has a house party with a DJ. Surprisingly, it isn't open on Saturday. Cover charge ranges from EC$10 to EC$15 ($3.75–$5.50).

9 The Grenadines: Bequia ⟨⭑⟩, Union Island & Mayreau ⟨⭑⟩

GETTING THERE

BY PLANE Four of the Grenadines—Bequia, Mustique, Union Island, and Canouan—have small airports, the landing spots for flights on **Mustique Airways** (© 784/458-4380 on St. Vincent). Its planes are technically charters, but flights depart St. Vincent for Bequia daily at 8am. The cost is $70 round-trip.

BY BOAT The ideal way to go, of course, is to rent your own yacht, as many wealthy visitors do. But a far less expensive method of transport is to go on a mail, cargo, or passenger boat as the locals do, but you'll need time and patience. However, boats do run on schedules. The **government mailboat,** the *M/V Baracuda* (© 784/456-5180), leaves St. Vincent on Monday and Thursday at 10:30am, stops at Bequia, Canouan, and Mayreau, and arrives at Union Island at about 3:45pm. On Tuesday and Friday, the boat leaves Union Island at about 6:30am, stops at Mayreau and Canouan, reaches Bequia at about 10:45am, and makes port at St. Vincent at noon. One-way fares from St. Vincent are: to Bequia, EC$15 ($5.50); to Canouan, EC$30 ($11); to Mayreau, EC$20 ($7.50); and to Union Island, EC$25 ($9.25).

You can also reach Bequia Monday to Saturday on the *Admiral I* and *II.* For information on these sea trips, inquire at the **Tourist Board,** Bay Street in Kingstown (© 784/457-1502).

BEQUIA

Only 7 square miles of land, Bequia (pronounced *Beck*-wee) is the largest and northernmost island of the Grenadines (only 9 miles south of St. Vincent). It offers quiet lagoons, reefs, and long stretches of nearly deserted beaches. Descended from seafarers and other early adventurers, its population of some 6,000 will give you a friendly greeting if you pass them along the road. Of the inhabitants, 10% are of Scottish ancestry, who live mostly in the Mount Pleasant region. A feeling of relaxation and informality prevails.

GETTING AROUND

Rental cars, owned by local people, are available at the port, and you can hire a **taxi** at the dock to take you around or to your hotel if you're spending the night. Taxis are reasonably priced, but an even better bet are the so-called **dollar cabs,** which take you anywhere on the island for a small fee. They don't seem to have a regular schedule—you just flag one down.

Before going to your hotel, drop in at the circular **Tourist Information Centre,** Port Elizabeth (© 809/458-3286). Here you can ask for a driver who's familiar with the attractions of the island (all of them are). You should negotiate the fare in advance.

ACCOMMODATIONS YOU CAN AFFORD

Frangipani Hotel ⟨⭑⭑⟩ The core of this pleasant guesthouse originated as the private home of a 19th-century sea captain. Since it became a hotel it has added accommodations that border a sloping tropical garden in back. The complex overlooks the island's most historic harbor, Admiralty Bay. The five rooms in the original house are smaller and much less glamorous (and less expensive) than the ones in the garden, which are handcrafted from local stone and hardwoods and have tile floors, carpets of woven hemp, wooden furniture (some made on St. Vincent), firm mattresses, and balconies. Most of the rooms have a small bathroom with a shower; the hall bathrooms are adequate and tidy. The in-house restaurant is open-sided and overlooks the yacht harbor. Guests can play tennis or arrange for scuba, sailboat rides, or other watersports nearby. (The nearest scuba outfitter, Sunsports, is fully accredited by PADI.) The hotel presents live music every Monday in winter and an outdoor barbecue every Thursday at 7:30pm, with a steel band.

P.O. Box 1, Bequia, the Grenadines, St. Vincent, W.I. ✆ 784/458-3255. Fax 784/458-3824. 15 units. Winter $35 single without bathroom, $120–$130 single with bathroom; $55 double without bathroom, $150–$170 double with bathroom. Off-season $30 single without bathroom, $80–$100 single with bathroom; $45 double without bathroom, $90–$120 double with bathroom. Extra person $40; children 12 and under $15. AE, DISC, MC, V. **Amenities:** Restaurant, bar, tennis courts, boating, dive shop, babysitting, laundry. *In room:* Ceiling fans, no phone.

Gingerbread   About a minute's walk from the edge of Port Elizabeth, this is the gingerbread-accented architectural statement of a British entrepreneur who firmly believes in self-reliant holidays (each unit has a kitchen). The approach is formal, even a bit chilly. But if you're able to entertain yourself in a laissez-faire environment with a stiff dose of British reserve, you might find the place appealing. The units are simply but tastefully furnished with a reinterpretation of British living in the Caribbean tropics. Upstairs units have four-poster queen-size beds, usually with draped mosquito netting; downstairs units have twin beds and lower ceilings but the same amenities. Mattresses are new and comfortable, and the bathrooms, though small, are neatly arranged, each with a shower stall. Throughout are terra-cotta floor tiles from Italy, country-comfortable color schemes of blue and white, and a distinct sense that a sophisticated decorator performed some magic here. The Gingerbread restaurant is described below, in "Great Deals on Dining."

Belmont Walkway, Admiralty Bay, Bequia, the Grenadines, St. Vincent, W.I. ✆ 784/458-3800. Fax 784/458-3907. ginger@caribsurf.com. 9 units. Winter $150–$175 single or double. Off-season $120–$140 single or double. AE, MC, V. **Amenities:** Restaurant, tennis courts. *In room:* A/C, TV, kitchen.

Julie's and Isola's Guest Houses   These twin places are owned by two of the most kindhearted hoteliers on the island, Julie and Isola McIntosh. Julie, a mason, laid many of the bricks for both hotels, which lie across the street from each other about a block from the water in the center of Port Elizabeth. Isola's Guest House is the more modern; Julie's is slightly older. The rooms in both tend to be hot, small, and noisy at times, but these inns are an enduring favorite nonetheless. Mattresses have entertained many guests before you checked in, but there's still comfort in them. The shower-only bathrooms are very cramped. Good West Indian food is served in the dining room. The bill of fare is likely to include pumpkin fritters, very fresh fish, and curried dishes.

P.O. Box 12, Port Elizabeth, Bequia, the Grenadines, St. Vincent, W.I. ✆ 784/458-3304. Fax 784/458-3812. 20 units. Year-round $39 single; $65 double. Rates include half-board. MC, V. **Amenities:** Restaurant. *In room:* Fans.

Keegan's Guest House   Ringed with white-painted picket fences that separate its sandy garden from the unpaved road outside, this is a simple but clean and respectable guesthouse adjacent to Lower Bay Beach. Built in the early 1980s, it presents an angular white-fronted facade, an uncomplicated interior, and well-swept verandas. All rooms have ceiling fans, tile-covered floors, good mattresses, tiny bathrooms with shower stalls, off-white walls, maid service, and (on the upper floors) narrow balconies; the apartment has a kitchenette. There's

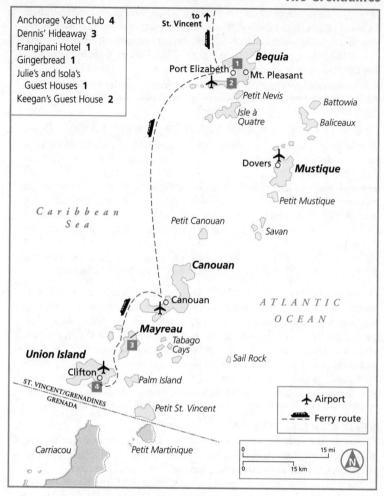

Anchorage Yacht Club **4**
Dennis' Hideaway **3**
Frangipani Hotel **1**
Gingerbread **1**
Julie's and Isola's
    Guest Houses **1**
Keegan's Guest House **2**

to ↑
St. Vincent

Bequia
Port Elizabeth **1**
 ○ Mt. Pleasant
2
Petit Nevis
Battowia
Isle à
Quatre
Baliceaux

*Caribbean
Sea*

Dovers ○ *Mustique*
Petit Mustique

Petit Canouan
Savan

Canouan
○ Canouan

*ATLANTIC
OCEAN*

Mayreau
3 Tabago
Cays
Sail Rock

Union Island
Clifton ○
4 Palm Island

ST. VINCENT/GRENADINES
GRENADA
Petit St. Vincent

Carriacou
Petit Martinique

0 ____ 15 mi
0 ____ 15 km

✈ Airport
- - - Ferry route

a kiosk-style beach bar. The simple food is based on West Indian traditions, with ample use of chicken, vegetables, conch, and local fish.

Lower Bay, Bequia, the Grenadines, St. Vincent, W.I. ☎ 784/458-3530. Fax 784/457-3313. 11 units. Year-round $75–$90 single or double; $400–$510 per week apt for 1–4. Extra person $90. Room (but not apt) rates include breakfast and dinner. MC, V. **Amenities:** Restaurant, bar. *In room:* TV, ceiling fans.

GREAT DEALS ON DINING

The food is good and healthful here—lobster, chicken, and steaks from such fish as dolphin, kingfish, and grouper, plus tropical fruits, fried plantain, and coconut and guava puddings made fresh daily. Even the beach bars are kept spotless.

Frangipani ⋆⋆ CARIBBEAN   This waterside dining room is one of the best restaurants on the island. The yachting crowd often comes ashore to dine here. With the exception of the juicy steaks imported for barbecues, only local food is used in the succulent specialties. Lunches, served throughout the day, include sandwiches, salads, and seafood platters. Dinner specialties include conch chowder, baked chicken with rice-and-coconut stuffing, lobster, and an array of fresh fish. A fixed-price menu is available at night. The Thursday-night barbecue with live entertainment is an island event.

In the Frangipani Hotel, Port Elizabeth. (*©* 809/458-3255. Reservations required for dinner. Breakfast $5–$8; lunch $12–$30; dinner main courses $12–$30; fixed-price dinner $14–$35. AE, MC, V. Daily 7:30am–5pm and 7–9pm. Closed Sept.

Friendship Bay Resort ✿ INTERNATIONAL/WEST INDIAN   Guests dine in a candlelit room high above a sweeping expanse of seafront on a hillside rich with the scent of frangipani and hibiscus. Lunch is served at the beach bar Spicy 'n Herby, but dinner is more elaborate. Meals are based on fresh ingredients and might include grilled lobster in season, curried beef, grilled or broiled fish (served Creole style with spicy sauce), shrimp curry, and charcoal-grilled steak flambé. Dishes are flavorsome and well prepared. An island highlight is the Friday- and Saturday-night jump-up (a Caribbean version of a hoedown) and barbecue.

Port Elizabeth. (*©* 784/458-3222. Reservations required for dinner. Main courses EC$30–EC$48 ($11–$17.75); lunch EC$40–EC$90 ($14.75–$33.25). AE, MC, V. Daily 7:30am–10pm. Closed Sept–Oct 15.

Gingerbread INTERNATIONAL   This restaurant is cozy, calm, and more closely tuned to European models than many of its counterparts on Bequia. In a second-floor dining room overlooking a boardwalk, a garden, and the sea, you'll be served meals that include an array of grilled and baked fish, shellfish, and a broad selection of curries that include versions made with pork, fish, beef, and shrimp. The specialty drink of the place is a *passionata,* made with passionfruit juice, rum, and selected island spices.

In the Gingerbread hotel, Belmont Walkway, Admiralty Bay. (*©* 784/458-3800. Reservations recommended for dinner. Lunch main courses $6–$12; dinner main courses $14–$18. AE, MC, V. Daily 8am–9:30pm.

SEEING THE SIGHTS

Obviously, the **secluded beaches** are tops on everyone's list of Bequia's attractions. As you walk along the beaches, especially near Port Elizabeth, you'll see craftspeople building boats by hand, a method they learned from their ancestors. Whalers sometimes still set out from here in wooden boats with hand harpoons, just as they do from a port village on St. Vincent.

Dive Bequia, Gingerbread House, Admiralty Bay (P.O. Box 16), Bequia, St. Vincent, W.I. (*©* **784/458-3504**), specializes in diving and snorkeling. Scuba dives cost $55 for one dive, $90 for two dives in the same day, and $420 for a 10-dive package. Introductory lessons go for $20 per person; a four-dive open-water certification course is $400. A snorkeling trip is $20 per person. These prices include all the necessary equipment.

The main harbor village, **Port Elizabeth,** is known for its safe anchorage, **Admiralty Bay.** The bay was a haven in the 17th century for the British, French, and Spanish navies, as well as for pirates. Descendants of Captain Kydd (a.k.a. Kidd) still live on the island. Today the yachting set anchors here, often bringing a kind of excitement to the locals.

Frankly, after you leave Port Elizabeth there aren't many sights, and you'll probably have your driver, booked for the day, drop you off for a long, leisurely lunch and some time on a beach. However, you'll pass a fort with a harbor view and drive on to Industry Estates, which has a Beach House restaurant serving a fair lunch. At **Paget Farm,** you can wander into an old whaling village and maybe inspect a few jawbones left over from the catches of yesterday.

At **Moonhole,** a vacation and retirement community is built into the cliffs practically as a freeform sculpture. These are private homes, of course, and you're not to enter without permission. For a final look at Bequia, head up an 800-foot hill that the local people call **The Mountain.** From that perch, you'll have a 360-degree view of St. Vincent and the Grenadines to the south.

SHOPPING

Shopping isn't a particularly good reason to come to Bequia, but there are some interesting stores. The best of the shops scattered along the water is **The Crab Hole,** next to the Plantation House, Admiralty Bay (✆ **784/458-3290**), where they invite guests to visit their silk-screen factory in back. Later you can make purchases at their shop in front, including sterling silver and 14-karat gold jewelry.

At **Noah's Arkade,** in the Frangipani Hotel, Port Elizabeth (✆ **784/ 458-3424**), island entrepreneur Lavinia Gunn sells Vincentian and Bequian batiks, scarves, hats, T-shirts, and a scattering of pottery. There are also dolls, place mats, baskets, and homemade jellies concocted from grapefruit, mango, and guava, plus West Indian cookbooks and books on tropical flowers and reef fish. This place stands a few steps from the terrace bar of the Frangipani Hotel.

Anyone on the island can show you the way to the workshops of **Sargeant's Model Boatshop Bequia,** Front Street, Port Elizabeth (✆ **784/458-3344**), which lies west of the pier past the oil-storage facility. Sought out by yacht owners looking for a scale-model reproduction of their favorite vessel, Lawson Sargeant is the self-taught woodcarver who established this business. The models are carved from a soft local wood called gumwood, then painted in brilliant colors of red, green, gray, or blue; whatever your fancy dictates. When a scale model of the royal family's yacht, *Britannia,* was commissioned in 1985, it required 5 weeks of work and meticulous blueprints and cost $10,000. You can pick up a model of a Bequia whaling boat for much less. The Sargeant family usually keeps 100 model boats in many shapes and sizes in inventory.

UNION ISLAND

Midway between Grenada and St. Vincent, Union Island is one of the southernmost of the Grenadines. It's known for its dramatic 900-foot peak, Mount Parnassus, which yachting people can often see from miles away. For those cruising in the area, Union is the port of entry for St. Vincent. Yachters are required to check with Customs upon entry.

Perhaps you'll sail into Union on a night when the locals are having a big drum dance, in which costumed islanders dance and chant to the beat of drums made of goatskin.

GETTING THERE

The island is reached by chartered or scheduled aircraft, by cargo boat, by private yacht, or by mailboat (see "Getting There" at the beginning of this section). **Air Martinique** (✆ **784/458-4528**) flies to Union Island from both Martinique and St. Vincent. **Mustique Airways** (✆ **784/458-4380** on St. Vincent) makes one flight per day to Union Island Monday to Thursday at a cost of $64 round-trip. Children under 12 fly half-price.

ACCOMMODATIONS YOU CAN AFFORD

Anchorage Yacht Club ✯   This club occupies a prominent position a few steps from the bumpy airplane landing strip that services at least two nearby resorts and about a half dozen small islands nearby. As such, something of an airline hub aura permeates the place as passengers shuttle between their airplanes and boats and the bar and restaurant here. Although at least two other hotels are nearby, this is the most important. It functions as a hotel, restaurant, and bar, with a busy marine-service facility (under different management) in the same compound. The yachting set meets in the wood-and-stone bar, which serves breakfast, lunch, and dinner daily.

Each of the small rooms is set between a pair of airy verandas and has white-tile floors and simple, somewhat sun-bleached modern furniture, including good beds with firm mattresses. The bathrooms are very small and towels a bit thin. The most popular units are the bungalows and cabañas beside the beach.

Clifton, Union Island, the Grenadines, St. Vincent, W.I. (✆ 784/458-8221. Fax 784/458-8365. 12 units. Winter $110 single; $135 double; $175 bungalow or apt. Off-season $70 double; $80 bungalow or apt. Extra person $35. Rates include continental breakfast. MC, V. **Amenities:** Restaurant, bar, dock, marina, fishing, snorkeling. *In room:* A/C, no phone.

GREAT DEALS ON DINING

Lambi's Guest House & Restaurant ✯ *Value* CREOLE/SEAFOOD   Built partially on stilts into the sea on the waterfront in Clifton, this is the best place to sample the local cuisine. *Lambi* means "conch" in Creole patois, and naturally this is the specialty. You can order various other fresh fish platters as well, depending on the catch of the day. Lobster and crab are frequently available. You can also order the usual, like chicken, steaks, and lamb or pork chops, but all this is shipped in frozen. Fresh vegetables are used whenever possible. In winter, a steel band entertains nightly in the bar, and limbo dancers or fire dancing will enthrall you.

Upstairs has been turned into a hotel of 41 rooms, Lambi's Guest House. Rooms are dorm-simple but come with two double beds and a tiny bathroom. There are ceiling fans, but no air-conditioning. Year-round prices are EC$50 ($18.50) single, EC$75 ($27.75) double, and EC$90 ($33.25) triple.

Clifton Harbour, Union Island. (✆ 784/458-8549. Fax 784/458-8395. Main courses EC$35–EC$50 ($13–$18.50); 50-dish buffet EC$50 ($18.50). MC, V. Daily 7am–midnight.

MAYREAU

A tiny cay, 1½ square miles of land in the Grenadines, Mayreau is a privately owned island shared by a hotel and a little hilltop village of about 170 inhabitants. It's on the route of the mailboat that plies the seas to and from St. Vincent, also visiting Canouan and Union Island. It's completely sleepy unless a cruise ship anchors offshore and hustles its passengers over for a lobster barbecue on the beach.

ACCOMMODATIONS YOU CAN AFFORD

Dennis' Hideaway *Finds*   Most of the energy here goes into the restaurant and supermarket, although rooms are available to overnight guests. All electricity is produced by the complex's own generator. The isolation contributes to a neighborly sense of raffish fun. The tiny rooms have ceiling fans and simple but solid furniture, including well-worn mattresses. You're given some rather thin towels for the communal bathroom. Dennis will charm and entertain you while you enjoy lunch or dinner here; on some nights he even plays the guitar. The view alone would justify coming here, but the West Indian food is another good reason. Since there's water in all directions, seafood is naturally the choice on the bill of fare. The selection might include lobster, shrimp, or conch. For those who want meat, Dennis usually has lamb or pork chops. A steel band plays on Wednesday and Saturday, when bountiful buffets are featured.

Saline Bay, Mayreau Island, The Grenadines, St. Vincent, W.I. ©/fax **784/458-8594.** www.dennis-hideaway.com. 2 units, neither with bathroom. Winter $70 single or double. Off-season $55 single or double. Rates include breakfast. AE, MC, V. **Amenities:** Restaurant. *In room:* Ceiling fans.

24

Trinidad & Tobago

Trinidad, birthplace of calypso and the steel pan, used to be visited only by business travelers in Port-of-Spain. The islanders were more interested in its oil, natural gas, and steel industries than in tourism. But all that has changed. Trinidad is a serious tourist destination, with a spruced-up capital and a renovated airport. The island's sophistication and cultural mélange, which is far greater than that of any other island in the southern Caribbean, is also a factor in increased tourist interest in Trinidad. Conversely, **Tobago,** its sibling island, is just as drowsy as ever—and that's its charm.

Charted by Columbus on his third voyage in 1498, Trinidad is named after the Holy Trinity he saw represented in three massive peaks on the southern coast. Through the years, the country has been peopled by immigrants from almost every corner of the world— Africa, the Middle East, Europe, India, China, and the Americas. It's against such a background that the island has become the fascinating mix of cultures, races, and creeds that it is today.

Trinidad, which is about the size of Delaware, and its neighbor island, tiny Tobago, 20 miles northeast, together form a nation popularly known as "T&T." The islands of the new country are the southernmost outposts of the West Indies. Trinidad lies only 7 miles from the Paria Peninsula in Venezuela, to which it was connected in prehistoric times.

The Spanish settled the island, which the Native Amerindians had called Iere, or "Land of the Hummingbird." The Spaniards made their first permanent settlement in 1592, and they held on to Trinidad longer than they did any of their other real estate in the Caribbean. The English captured Trinidad in 1797, and it remained British until the two-island nation declared its independence in 1962. The Republic of Trinidad and Tobago is a parliamentary democracy, with a president and a prime minister. The British influence is still clearly visible, from the strong presence of the British dialect to the islanders' fondness for cricket.

1 Essentials

VISITOR INFORMATION

In the United States, information about Trinidad and Tobago is available by calling the **Trinidad & Tobago Tourism Office** at 350 Fifth Ave., Suite 6316, New York, NY 10118 (© **800/748-4224**). Canadians are supplied information at **Taurus House,** 512 Duplex Ave., Toronto, Ontario M4R 2E3 (© **800/ 267-7600** or 416/485-7827). There's also an office in England at **International House,** 47 Chase Side, Enfield, Middlesex EN2 6NB2 (© **0181/367-3752**).

Once you're in Trinidad, you can get information from **TIDCO,** 10–14 Phillips St., Port-of-Spain (© **868/623-1932**). There's also an information desk at **Piarco Airport** (© **868/669-5196**). On Tobago, you can go to the **Tobago**

Division of Tourism, N.I.B. Mall, Level 3, Scarborough (© **868/639-2125**). Tobago also maintains an information desk at **Crown Point Airport** (© **868/ 639-0509**).

The Internet address for the islands is **www.tidco.co.tt**.

 FAST FACTS: **Trinidad & Tobago**

Banking Hours Most banks are open Monday to Thursday 8am to 2pm and Friday 9am to noon and 3 to 5pm.

Currency The **Trinidad and Tobago dollar (TT$)** is loosely pegged to the U.S. dollar at an exchange rate of about U.S.$1 = TT$6.28 (TT$1 = U.S.16¢). Ask what currency is being referred to when rates are quoted. We've used a combination of both in this chapter, depending on the establishment. U.S. and Canadian dollars are accepted for payment, particularly in Port-of-Spain. However, you'll usually do better by converting Canadian or U.S. dollars into local currency. British pounds should be converted into the local currency. Unless otherwise specified, dollar quotations appearing in this chapter are in U.S. currency.

Customs Readers have reported long delays in clearing Customs on Trinidad. Personal effects are duty-free, and visitors may bring in 200 cigarettes or 50 cigars plus 1 quart of "spirits."

Documents Visitors arriving in Trinidad and Tobago should have an ongoing or return ticket from their point of embarkation. A visa isn't required for tourist/business stays of less than 6 weeks. You'll be asked to fill out an immigration card on your arrival, and you should save the carbon copy of this, as it must be returned to immigration officials when you depart. Citizens of the United States, Britain, and Canada need passports to enter Trinidad and Tobago.

Electricity The electricity is either 110- or 230-volt AC (60 cycles), so ask when making your hotel reservations if you'll need transformers and/or adapters.

Embassies & High Commissions In Port-of-Spain on Trinidad, the **U.S. Embassy** is located at 7–9 Marli St., 15 Queen's Park West (© **868/ 622-6371**); the **Canadian High Commission** is located at Maple House, 3 Sweet Briar Rd., St. Clair (© **868/622-6232**); and the **British High Commission** is located at 19 St. Clair Ave., St. Clair (© **868/622-2748**).

Emergencies Call the **police** at © **999**. To report a **fire** or summon an **ambulance**, dial © **990**.

Language English is the official language, although you'll hear it spoken with many accents, including British. Hindi, Chinese, French, and Spanish are also spoken.

Safety As a general rule, Tobago is safer than its larger neighbor, Trinidad. Crime does exist on Trinidad, but it's not of raging dimensions. If you can, avoid the downtown streets of Port-of-Spain at night, especially those around Independence Square, where muggings have been reported. Evening jaunts down Wilson Street and the Market of Scarborough are also discouraged. Visitors are open prey for pickpockets during

Carnival time, so be alert during large street parties. It would also be wise to safeguard your valuables and never leave them unattended at the beach or even in a locked car.

Taxes The government imposes a 15% value-added tax (VAT) on room rates. It also imposes a departure tax of TT$85 ($13.50) on every passenger older than 5 years.

Telecommunications The area code for Trinidad and Tobago is **868**. Make calls to or from the islands as you would to any other area code in North America. On either island, just dial the local seven-digit number.

Time Trinidad and Tobago are on the same time as the U.S. east coast in winter. But when the United States goes on daylight saving time, Trinidad and Tobago do not; then, when it's 6am in Miami, it's 7am in Trinidad and Tobago.

Tipping The big hotels and restaurants add a 10% to 15% service charge to your final tab.

Weather Trinidad has a tropical climate all year, with constant trade winds maintaining mean temperatures of 84°F during the day, 74° at night, with a range of 70° to 90°F. The rainy season runs May to November, but it shouldn't deter you from visiting; the rain usually lasts no more than 2 hours before the sun comes out again. However, carry along plenty of insect repellent if you come then.

2 Trinidad ★★

Trinidad is completely different from the other islands of the Caribbean, and that forms part of its charm and appeal. The island itself is 50 miles long and 40 miles wide. The limbo was born here, as were calypso and steel drum music. Visitors in increasing numbers are drawn to this island of many rhythms.

Trinidad isn't for everyone, though. Because Port-of-Spain is one of the most bustling commercial centers in the Caribbean, more business travelers than tourists are drawn here. The island has beaches, but the best of them are far away from the capital. The city itself is hot, humid, and slightly on the dirty side, while the hilly suburbs are as charming as a southern city set in a tropical paradise.

Although Port-of-Spain, with its shopping centers, fast-food joints, modern hotels, and active nightlife, draws mixed reviews from readers, the countryside is calmer. Far removed from the traffic jams of the capital, you can explore the fauna and flora of the island. There are an estimated 700 varieties of orchids alone, plus 400 species of birds.

Prices on Trinidad are often lower than those on many other islands in the West Indies, such as Barbados. Port-of-Spain abounds in inexpensive inns and guesthouses. Most of the dining places cater to locals, so dining prices reflect the low wages.

The people are part of the attraction on this island, the most cosmopolitan in the Caribbean. Trinidad's polyglot population includes Syrians, Chinese, Americans, Europeans, East Indians, Parsees, Madrasis, Venezuelans, and the last of the original Amerindians. You'll also find Hindustanis, Javanese, Lebanese, African descendants, and Creole mixtures. The main religions are Christianity, Hinduism, and Islam. In all, there are about 1.2 million inhabitants whose language is English, although you might hear speech in a strange argot, Trinibagianese.

Trinidad

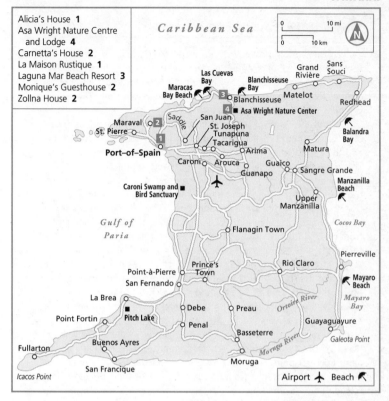

Alicia's House **1**
Asa Wright Nature Centre and Lodge **4**
Carnetta's House **2**
La Maison Rustique **1**
Laguna Mar Beach Resort **3**
Monique's Guesthouse **2**
Zollna House **2**

Caribbean Sea

0 — 10 mi
0 — 10 km

Grand Rivière   Sans Souci
Las Cuevas Bay   Blanchisseuse Bay
Maracas Bay Beach   **3** Blanchisseuse   Matelot
Redhead
San Juan   **4** ■ Asa Wright Nature Center
Maraval   **2**   St. Joseph
St. Pierre   Tunapuna   Balandra Bay
1   Tacarigua
Port–of–Spain   Arima   Matura
Caroni   Arouca   Guaico
Guanapo   Sangre Grande
Manzanilla Beach
Caroni Swamp and ■ Bird Sanctuary
Upper Manzanilla
Gulf of Paria   *Cocos Bay*
Flanagin Town
Pierreville
Point-à-Pierre   Prince's Town   Rio Claro
San Fernando   Mayaro Beach
La Brea   *Mayaro Bay*
Debe   Preau   *Ortoire River*
Point Fortin   ■ **Pitch Lake**   Guayaguayure
Penal   *Galeota Point*
Fullarton   Buenos Ayres   Basseterre
Moruga River
San Francique   Moruga
Icacos Point   Airport ✈   Beach 🅡

Port-of-Spain ✈, in the northwestern corner of the island, is the capital, with the largest concentration of the population, about 120,000 people. With the opening of its $2-million cruise ship complex in Port-of-Spain, Trinidad now has become a major port of call for Caribbean cruise lines.

One of the most industrialized nations in the Caribbean and the third-largest exporter of oil in the Western Hemisphere, Trinidad is also blessed with the huge 114-acre Pitch Lake, from which comes most of the world's asphalt. It's also the home of Angostura bitters, the recipe for which is a closely guarded secret.

GETTING THERE

From North America, Trinidad is one of the most distant islands in the Caribbean. Because of the legendary toughness of Trinidadian Customs, it's preferable to arrive at **Piarco Airport** during the day (presumably when your stamina might be at its peak) if you can schedule it.

Most passengers from eastern North America fly **American Airlines** (② **800/ 433-7300** or 868/664-4661), which has connections through San Juan. American also offers a daily nonstop flight to Trinidad from Miami, which is especially useful for transfers from the midwest and the west coast.

From New York, **BWIA** (② **800/292-1183**) offers one daily flight into Port-of-Spain, depending on the day of the week and the season. Several of these are nonstop; most touch down en route, usually on Barbados or Antigua, before continuing without a change of planes to Trinidad, the airline's home base. From

Fun Fact **The Carnival of Trinidad**

Called "the world's most colorful festival," the **Carnival of Trinidad** is a spectacle of dazzling costumes and gaiety. Hundreds of bands of masqueraders parade through the cities on the Monday and Tuesday preceding Ash Wednesday, bringing traffic to a standstill. The island explodes with music, fun, and dancing.

Some of the Carnival costumes cost hundreds of dollars. For example, "bands" might depict the birds of Trinidad, such as the scarlet ibis and the keskidee; or a bevy of women might come out in the streets dressed as cats. Costumes are also satirical and comical.

Trinidad is the land of calypso, which grew out of the folk songs of the African–West Indian immigrants. The lyrics command great attention, as they're rich in satire and innuendo. The calypsonian is a poet-musician, and lyrics have often been capable of toppling politicians from office. In banter and bravado, the calypsonian gives voice to the sufferings and aspirations of his people. At Carnival time the artist sings his compositions to spectators in tents. There's one show a night at each of the calypso tents around town, from 8pm to midnight. Tickets for these are sold in the afternoon at most record shops.

Carnival parties, or fêtes, with three or four orchestras at each one, are public and advertised in the newspaper. For a really wild time, attend a party on Sunday night before Carnival Monday. To reserve tickets, contact the **National Carnival Committee,** Queen's Park Savannah, Port-of-Spain, Trinidad, W.I. (✆ **868/627-1358**). Hotels are booked months in advance, and most inns raise their prices—often considerably—at the time.

You can attend rehearsals of steel bands at their headquarters, called panyards, beginning about 7pm. Preliminary band competitions are held at the grandstand of Queen's Park Savannah in Port-of-Spain and at Skinner Park in San Fernando, beginning 2 weeks before Carnival.

Miami, BWIA usually offers a daily nonstop to Port-of-Spain, departing every afternoon and arriving on Trinidad in the early evening. Port-of-Spain is also serviced by as many as two additional flights per day, touching down on Barbados, Antigua, Grenada, and St. Lucia.

Air Canada (✆ **888/247-2262** in the U.S.) offers one nonstop flight from Toronto to Port-of-Spain.

GETTING AROUND

BY TAXI   There are only unmetered taxis on Trinidad, and they're identified by their license plates, beginning with the letter *H*. There are also "pirate taxis"—private cars that cruise around and pick up passengers like a regular taxi. Maxi Taxis or vans can also be hailed on the street. A taxi ride from Piarco Airport into Port-of-Spain generally costs $20 ($30 after 10pm).

To avoid the anxiety of driving, you can rent taxis with local drivers for your sightseeing jaunts. Although it can be costly, it alleviates the hassles of badly marked (or unmarked) roads and contact with the sometimes-bizarre local driving patterns; if a rented taxi and driver is too expensive for you, you can take an organized tour. Most drivers will serve as guides. Their rates, however, are based on route distances, so get an overall quotation and agree on the actual fare before setting off.

BY RENTAL CAR   Because the island is one of the world's largest exporters of asphalt, Trinidad's some 4,500 miles of roads are well paved. However, outback roads should be avoided during the rainy season as they're often narrow, twisting, and prone to washouts. Inquire about conditions, particularly if you're headed for the north coast.

The fierce traffic jams of Port-of-Spain are legendary, and night driving anywhere on the island is rather hazardous. If you're brave enough to set out on a venture via rental car, arm yourself with a good map and beware: The car will probably have a right-hand–mounted steering wheel; hence, *you'll drive on the left.* Visitors with a valid International Driver's License or a license from the United States, Canada, France, or the United Kingdom may drive without extra documentation for up to 3 months.

The major U.S.-based car-rental firms currently have no franchises on the island, so you have to make arrangements with a local firm (go over the terms and insurance agreements carefully). Count on spending about $40 to $60 per day or more, with unlimited mileage included.

Your best bet is one of the local car-rental firms that maintain offices at Piarco Airport. They include **Econo-Car Rentals** (© **868/669-2342**), **Thrifty** (© **868/669-0602**), and **Auto Rentals** (© **868/669-2277**). *A word of warning:* Although these local rental firms technically accept reservations, a car might not be waiting for you even if you reserve. Sometimes if a prospective renter shows up for an off-the-street booking, he or she gets the car you might have already reserved for a later pickup. The rule seems to be that a customer in hand is better than one that might—or might not—wing in on a plane later.

BY BUS   All the cities of Trinidad are linked by regular bus service from Port-of-Spain. Fares are low (about 50¢ for runs within the capital). However, the old buses are likely to be overcrowded. Always try to avoid them at rush hours, and beware of pickpockets.

ACCOMMODATIONS YOU CAN AFFORD

The number of hotels is limited, and don't expect your Port-of-Spain room to open directly on a white-sand beach—the nearest beach is a long, costly taxi ride away. Don't forget that a 15% government tax and a 10% service charge will be added to your hotel and restaurant bills. All hotels raise their rates during Carnival (the week before Ash Wednesday).

Alicia's House ✮   This is a genteel guesthouse inspired by British models. It's in an upscale residential neighborhood, a short walk north of Queen's Park Savannah, the Botanical Gardens, and the dining and entertainment facilities of the Hilton Hotel. Locals claim Alicia's House sits on what used to be a sprawling plantation. During a slave uprising, the leaders of the revolt slaughtered 200 of their compatriots, which led to the closing of the property. Ghosts of those who were murdered are reputed to wander the streets of St. Ann's but shouldn't disturb your sleep.

The setting is a flat-roofed two- and three-story white-painted concrete building whose yard was neatly fenced in for privacy, with a ring-around garden and a pool in back. Ivan and Barbara Dara are your hosts (they named the place after their daughter, Alicia). The rooms contain wooden or rattan furniture, including good beds, small refrigerators, ceiling fans, white walls, wooden floors, and touches of homey bric-a-brac. They vary greatly in size. The biggest one is named Admiral Rooney (not a naval commander but an island flower), with mahogany furniture and a giant tub. Alicia's Room is like a small apartment, with twin cherry-red sofas and large closets. The Back Room is tiny but airy and bright and offers a private spiral staircase going down to the pool. The bathrooms are fitted in wherever possible and are immaculately maintained; each has a shower. Because of local zoning laws, no liquor is served on the premises, but guests are welcome to bring their own.

7 Coblentz Gardens, St. Ann's, Port-of-Spain, Trinidad, W.I. © 868/623-2802. Fax 868/623-8560. 19 units. Year-round $36–$48 single; $46–$60 double; $70 triple; $94 quad. AE, MC, V. **Amenities:** Pool. *In room:* A/C, TV, mini-fridge, ceiling fans.

Carnetta's House   This home is in the suburb Andalusia in cool and scenic Maraval, about a 15-minute ride from the central business district of Port-of-Spain and a 45-minute ride from Maracas Bay. It's owned by Winston and Carnetta Borrell, both keen naturalists (he was a former director of tourism) and both a wealth of information about touring the island. Winston is a grand gardener, filling the property with orchids, ginger lilies, and anthuriums, among other plant life. Carnetta grows her own herbs and uses them to produce some of the finest meals around. The rooms have floral themes and are furnished in a tropical style. For the most privacy, request a guest room on the upper floor. Our preferred nest is "Le Flamboyant," opening onto the little inn's patio. Most of the rooms are medium in size, and each has a small and immaculately maintained bathroom. Mountain bikes can be rented for $7.50 per day and cars for $50 per day.

28 Scotland Terrace, Andalusia, Maraval, Trinidad, W.I. © 868/628-2732. Fax 868/628-7717. www. carnettas.com. 6 units. Year-round $50–$55 single or double. Dinner $12 extra. AE, DC, MC, V. **Amenities:** Restaurant. *In room:* A/C, TV.

Laguna Mar Beach Resort ★★ *finds*   On the north coast, this beachfront property, owned by Fred and Barbara Zollna, who also operate Zollna House (see below), is set on 28 acres of rain forest at the Marianne River and its swimming lagoon. A place for those who seek solitude, it lures nature lovers with a free-flowing freshwater spring and natural pools, along with tropical plants and flowers. Coconut palms, coffee, and cocoa are cultivated throughout the estate, and birds, butterflies, and other forest creatures are abundant. In nesting season, leatherback turtles lay their eggs in the soft sand of the beach. The Blanchisseuse area is well known for its fishing, and you can fish off the beach or in the river. This place is recommended for its scenic setting in lush surroundings, not for its grand comforts. Nonetheless, the small rooms are neat and tidy, with comfortable beds and equally small bathrooms with shower. The Cocos Hut Restaurant, with its sliding roof, was formerly used for drying coffee and coconut. Today it serves local and international food, and there are also barbecue pits and rafts. A campsite is also available.

Blanchisseuse, Trinidad, W.I. © 868/628-3731. Fax 868/628-3737. www.lagunamar.com. 15 units. Winter $65 single; $75 double. Off-season $45 single; $55 double. Extra person $15. MC, V. **Amenities:** Restaurant. *In room:* Ceiling fans.

La Maison Rustique   A great little Victorian B&B trimmed in gingerbread, this recommendation enjoys an in-the-heart location near Queen's Park Savannah. La Maison Rustique (which is far from rustic) allows you to sit on the veranda for a daily high tea. The delightful owner, Maureen Chin-Asiong, serves breakfast in a teahouse and will cater to special diets if asked. She's a baker supreme—just taste her croissants and popovers—and a graduate of the Wilton School of Cake Decorating in Chicago. She'll even pack you a picnic basket if you're going touring for the day. The rooms are neat and homey, very comfortably furnished and immaculately maintained, with firm mattresses. Each small bathroom has a shower stall. Guests in the rooms without bathrooms will find the public bathrooms adequate (there's rarely a line). The nearest beach is a 45-minute drive away, but guests may be admitted to a nearby country club.

16 Rust St., St. Clair, Port-of-Spain, Trinidad, W.I. ℂ 868/622-1512. 6 units, 3 with bathroom; 1 studio cottage. Year-round $44 single without bathroom, $55 single with bathroom; $75 double with bathroom; $105 cottage. Children 9 and under stay free in parents' room. Rates include full breakfast. MC, V. *In room:* Ceiling fans, no phone.

Monique's Guesthouse   In the lush Maraval Valley just an 8-minute (3-mile) drive north of the center of Port-of-Spain, Monique's offers 20 newly rebuilt bungalow-style rooms. Some are large enough to accommodate up to four people, and 10 rooms offer kitchenettes with their own porches and cable TV. The biggest are units 25 and 26, which could possibly sleep up to six, but that would be a bit crowded. One room is designed for elderly travelers or those with disabilities. Accommodations have open balconies so you can enjoy the tropical breezes and scenic hills. The bathrooms are well organized and spotless; each has a shower. The air-conditioned dining room and bar offers a medley of local and international dishes, and Maracas Bay is only a 25-minute drive away. Mike and Monica Charbonné will be here to welcome you.

114–116 Saddle Rd., Maraval, Trinidad, W.I. ℂ 868/628-3334. Fax 809/622-3232. www.best-caribbean. com/moniques. 20 units. Year-round $55–$65 single or double. AE, DC, MC, V. **Amenities:** Restaurant, bar. *In room:* A/C, TV, kitchenette (some units).

Zollna House   On a hillside in the Maraval Valley with a view of Port-of-Spain and the Gulf of Paria, Zollna House is 2 miles from the capital. The two-story building has comfortably furnished rooms, two large porches, two indoor lounges, a beverage bar and games room, and dining areas on two floors, as well as a patio/barbecue setup outdoors. The mattresses are well used but still comfortable, and the two units with bathrooms have small private showers. The lush garden features flowering shrubs and fruit trees, home to a variety of birds. The house, white with black trim, is almost obscured by trees, but you can find it by going along Saddle Road, turning onto La Seiva Road, and going uphill for about a quarter mile. It's operated by Gottfried (Fred) Zollna, a German-American resident on Trinidad since 1965, and his Trinidadian wife, Barbara. They have a reputation for their easygoing hospitality and can advise on what to see and do. They also own a 35-foot yacht and often take their guests sailing in the Gulf of Paria. The Laguna Mar Beach Resort on the north coast of Trinidad is also owned by the Zollnas.

12 Ramlogan Terrace, La Seiva, Maraval, Trinidad, W.I. ℂ 868/628-3731. Fax 868/628-3737. 3 units, 2 with bathroom. Year-round $30 single without bathroom, $45 single with bathroom; $50 double without bathroom, $65 double with bathroom. Rates include American breakfast. MC, V. **Amenities:** 2 dining rooms, 2 lounges, sailing, game room. *In room:* Ceiling fans.

WORTH A SPLURGE

Asa Wright Nature Centre and Lodge (Finds)   There really isn't anything else like this in the Caribbean. Known to bird-watchers throughout the world, this center sits on 196 acres of protected land at an elevation of 1,200 feet in the rain-forested northern mountain range of Trinidad, north of Arima, beside Blanchisseuse Road. Hummingbirds, toucans, bellbirds, manakins, several varieties of tanagers, and the rare oilbird are all found on the property. Back-to-basics accommodations are available in the lodge's self-contained rooms, in guest rooms in the 1908 Edwardian main house, or in one of the cottages built on elevated ground above the main house. Even though they offer less privacy, we prefer the two guest rooms in the main house, as they have more atmosphere and are decorated with dark wood antiques and two king-size beds. Furnishings in the cottages are rather plain but comfortable. Mattresses are a bit thin, but the bird-watchers who "flock" here don't complain, as they're a hearty lot. Guided tours are available on the nature center's grounds, which contain several well-maintained trails, including a natural pool with a waterfall in which guests can swim in lieu of a beach that involves a 90-minute drive to the coast. Summer seminars are conducted with expert instructors in natural history, ornithology, and nature photography. The minimum age is 14 years if accompanied by an adult and 17 if unaccompanied.

Spring Hill Estate, Arima, Trinidad, W.I. (For more information or to make reservations, call the toll-free number or write **Caligo Ventures**, 156 Bedford Rd., Armonk, NY 10504.) ✆ **800/426-7781** in the U.S., or 868/ 667-4655. Fax 868/667-4540. www.asawright.org. 25 units. Winter $155 single; $240 double. Off-season $120 single; $180 double. Rates include all meals, afternoon tea, and a welcoming rum punch. MC, V. **Amenities:** Dining room, pond. *In room:* Ceiling fans, no phone.

GREAT DEALS ON DINING

The food on Trinidad should be better than it is, considering all the culinary backgrounds that have shaped the island, including West Indian, Chinese, French, and Indian. Stick to local specials like stuffed crabs or *chip-chip* (tiny clam-like shellfish), but skip the armadillo and opossum stewpots. Spicy Indian rôtis (Caribbean burritos) filled with vegetables or ground meat seem to be everyone's favorite lunch, and everyone's favorite drink is a fresh rum punch, flavored with the home-produced Angostura bitters. Except for a few fancy places, dress tends to be very casual.

For the fastest, cheapest lunch in town, try a rôti. In Port-of-Spain you'll find them for sale at stalls on the street. Our favorite is **Nanny's Rôti Limited,** a funky little spot at the corner of Richmond and Sackville streets. One visitor called these rôtis a kind of "Indo-Caribbean tortilla stuffed with shrimp, beef, or chicken." For less than $5 you can order a rôti—a meal unto itself—along with a beer.

Rafters ✦ *Value* SEAFOOD   Rafters is a good-value dining choice housed in a century-old grocery shop in the central business district of a suburb of Port-of-Spain, a short walk off the Savannah. Wednesday to Saturday there are buffets, and you can also order from an a la carte menu devoted mainly to local seafood. The food is more plentiful than refined, but is a very good value. Buffets begin at 7pm. On Wednesday to Saturday there are carvery buffets. On the regular menu, house specialties include seafood Creole. You can also order U.S. choice beefsteaks. In the lounge, a snack-and-sandwich menu is offered daily in a relaxed atmosphere, attracting folks of all ages and occupations.

6A Warner St., Newtown. ✆ 868/628-9258. Reservations recommended. Main courses TT$40–TT$125 ($6.50–$20); buffets from TT$100 ($16). AE, DC, MC, V. Mon–Fri 11:30am–10:30pm; Sat 6:30pm–11pm.

Restaurant Singho CHINESE   This restaurant contains an almost mystically illuminated bar and aquarium. It's on the second floor of one of the capital's largest shopping malls, midway between the commercial center of Port-of-Spain and the Queen's Park Savannah. Many of its dishes are quite tasty and spicy. A la carte dishes include shrimp with oyster sauce, shark-fin soup, stewed or curried beef, almond pork, and spareribs with black-bean sauce. The takeout service is one of the best known in town. The Wednesday-night buffet has an enormous selection of main dishes, along with heaps of rice and fresh vegetables. Even dessert is included in the set price.

Long Circular Mall, Level 3, Port-of-Spain. ℂ **868/628-2077.** Main courses TT$85–TT$100 ($13.50–$16); Wed night buffet TT$100 ($16). AE, MC, V. Daily 11am–11pm.

Veni Mangé ℛ CREOLE/INTERNATIONAL   Built in the 1930s about a mile west of Port-of-Spain's center, Veni Mangé (whose name translates as "come and eat") is painted in coral tones and has louvered windows on hinges that ventilate the masses of potted plants. It was opened by two of the best-known women in Trinidad, Allyson Hennessy and her sister, Rosemary Hezekiah. Allyson, the Julia Child of Trinidad, hosts a daily TV talk show that's broadcast throughout Trinidad. Best described as a new generation of Creole women, both Allyson and Rosemary (whose parents were English/Venezuelan and African-Caribbean/Chinese) entertain with their humor and charm.

Start with the bartender's special, a coral-colored fruit punch that's a luscious mix of papaya, guava, orange, and passion fruit juices. On some days they do an authentic *callaloo* soup, which, according to Trinidadian legend, can make a man propose marriage. Save room for one of the main courses, such as curried crab or West Indian hotpot (a variety of meat cooked Creole style), or perhaps a vegetable-lentil loaf. The helpings are large, and if you still have room, order the pineapple upside-down cake, homemade soursop ice cream, or coconut mousse. Dinner is served only on Wednesday and is something of a social event among regulars. On Friday, the bar buzzes but no formal food is served, only snacks and finger foods.

67A Ariapata Ave. ℂ **868/624-4597.** Reservations recommended. Main courses $5–$15. AE, MC, V. Daily 11:30am–3pm; Wed 7:30–10pm; Fri 7–10pm.

Woodford Café ℛ TRINIDADIAN/WEST INDIAN   In a conservative-looking West Indian house with jalousied windows overlooking a residential neighborhood, about a 5-minute walk southwest of the Savannah, this is a well-respected place where most of the food is richly steeped in local culinary traditions. Inside, you'll find a color scheme of peach and white, a hardworking staff, and at least 25 paintings, mostly by Trinidadian and Bajan artists. The most visible of them is an oversized triptych of a Trinidadian landscape by a local rising star on the arts scene, Peter Sheppherd. Menu items include at least a dozen vegetarian side dishes, any of which can be combined into an all-vegetarian meal. (Examples are red beans, lentils, black-eyed peas, stewed *christophene*, yams, macaroni pie, corn, salad, and several preparations of potatoes.) There's also an array of slow-stewed meats and fish, such as curried conch or fish and stewed chicken, beef, pork, oxtail, and shrimp.

62 Tragarete Rd., Newtown. ℂ **868/622-2233.** Main courses $3.50–$8.50. AE, MC, V. Mon–Tues 11am–3:30pm; Wed–Sat 1–10pm.

HITTING THE BEACHES

Trinidad isn't thought of as beach country, yet it has more beach frontage than any other island in the West Indies. The only problem is that most of its beaches are undeveloped and in distant places, far removed from Port-of-Spain. The closest of the better beaches, **Maracas Bay** (on the N. Coast Rd.), is 18 miles from Port-of-Spain and a delight to visitors, with its protected cove and quaint fishing village at one end. Enclosed by mountains, it has the expected charm of a Caribbean fantasy: white sands, swaying coconut palms, and crystal-clear water. It's likely to be crowded because many beach buffs, often locals, flock here for fun in the sun. There's another major drawback—a strong current—so be extremely careful. You'll find an array of snack bars and toilets. Chances are you'll be here for lunch. In addition to rôtis, one of the local seafood treats is a fish sandwich called "shark and bake." Sample it at **Patsy's Shack** or one of the other fast-food joints. At Patsy's you can also order one of the most refreshing fruit drinks on the island. It's called *grenadillo* and tastes very much like passion fruit.

Farther up the north coast is **Las Cuevas Bay,** which is far less crowded than Maracas Bay. Lying directly off the North Coast Road is a narrow strip of sand set against a backdrop of palm trees. There are changing rooms, and vendors come around selling the luscious tropical fruit juices of Trinidad. Las Cuevas is named after the underwater caves nearby.

To reach the other beaches, you'll have to range much farther afield, perhaps to **Blanchisseuse Bay** on the North Coast Road. This is a narrow strip of sand set against a palm-fringed backdrop, excellent for a picnic on the beach, but there are no facilities unless you're staying at the Laguna Mar Beach Resort. This is one of the best places in Trinidad for a beach picnic. You can also negotiate with one of the local fishers at anchor about taking you on an inexpensive boat ride along the coast, and maybe doing a little fishing as well. Also on the northeast coast is **Balandra Bay.** This area is frequented by bodysurfers and sheltered by rocky outcroppings, but the waters generally aren't good for swimming.

Another beach worth a look is **Manzanilla Beach,** which lies along the east coast of Trinidad, between Cocos Bay and Matura Bay. Because its waters open onto the often turbulent Atlantic on the windward side, it is not ideal for swimming. But it has some picnic facilities, and the view of the water is dramatic. The water here, however, is often muddied by the Orinoco River flowing in from South America. Many rich Trinidadians have vacation homes here.

SEEING THE SIGHTS

The Travel Centre, Uptown Mall, Edward Street, Port-of-Spain (© **868/ 623-5096**), offers sightseeing tours in late-model sedans, with a trained driver-guide. Prices are quoted on a seat-in-car basis. Private arrangements will cost more. Several tours are offered regularly.

The daily **City Tour,** which lasts 2 hours and costs $22 per person for two or $16 per person for three or more, will take you past (but not inside) the main points of interest of Port-of-Spain. You'll see tropical splendor at its best on a Port-of-Spain/Maracas Bay/Saddle Road jaunt, which leaves at 1pm daily and lasts 3½ hours. The tour begins with a drive around Port-of-Spain, passing the main points of interest in town and then going on through the mountain scenery over the "Saddle" of the northern range to the popular beach Maracas Bay. The cost is $35 per person for two or $25 per person for three or more.

An **Island Circle Tour** is a 7- to 8-hour journey that includes a lunch stop (the tour price doesn't include lunch) and a welcome drink. Leaving at 9am daily, your car goes south along the west coast with a view of the Gulf of Paria, across the central plains, through Pointe-à-Pierre and San Fernando, and on eastward into rolling country overlooking sugarcane fields. Then you go down into the coconut plantations along the 14-mile-long Mayaro Beach for a swim and lunch before returning along Manzanilla Beach and back to the city. The cost is $75 per person for two or $55 per person for three or more.

An especially interesting trip is to the **Caroni Swamp and Bird Sanctuary** (© **868/623-1932**), a 4-hour trek by car and flat-bottomed boat into the sanctuary where you'll see rich Trinidad bird life. The tour guides recommend long pants and long-sleeved, casual attire along with lots of insect repellent. The cost is $75 per person for two or $55 per person for three or more.

PORT-OF-SPAIN   One of the busiest harbors in the Caribbean, Trinidad's capital, Port-of-Spain, can be explored on foot. Start out at **Queen's Park Savannah** ✈, on the northern edge of the city. Called the Savannah, it consists of 199 acres, complete with soccer, cricket, and rugby fields and vendors hawking coconut water. What's now the park was once a sugar plantation until it was swept by a fire in 1808 that destroyed hundreds of homes.

Among the Savannah's outstanding buildings is the pink-and-blue **Queen's Royal College** ✈, containing a clock tower with Westminster chimes. Today a school for boys, it stands on Maraval Road at the corner of St. Clair Avenue. On the same road, Trinidadians affectionately call the family home of the Roodal clan **"the gingerbread house."** It was built in the baroque style of the French Second Empire. In contrast, the family residence of the Strollmeyers was built in 1905 and is a copy of a German Rhenish castle. Nearby stands **Whitehall,** which was once a private mansion but today has been turned into the office of the prime minister of Trinidad and Tobago. In the Moorish style, it was erected in 1905 and served as the U.S. Army headquarters in World War II. These houses, including Hayes Court, the residence of the Anglican bishop of Trinidad, and others form what's known as **"the Magnificent Seven"** ✈ big mansions standing in a row.

On the south side of Memorial Park, a short distance from the Savannah and within walking distance of the major hotels, stands the **National Museum and Art Gallery,** 117 Frederick St. (© **868/623-5941**), open Tuesday to Saturday 10am to 6pm and Sunday 2 to 6pm. The free museum contains a representative exhibit of Trinidad artists, including an entire gallery devoted to Jean Michel Cazabon (1813–88), permanent collections of artifacts giving a general overview of the island's history and culture, Amerindian archaeology, British historical documents, and a small natural-history exhibit including geology, corals, and insect collections. There's also a large display filled with costumes dedicated to the colorful culture of Carnival.

At the southern end of Frederick Street, the main artery of Port-of-Spain's shopping district, stands **Woodford Square.** The gaudy **Red House,** a large neo-Renaissance structure built in 1906, is the seat of the government of Trinidad and Tobago. Nearby stands **Holy Trinity Cathedral,** whose Gothic look might remind you of the churches of England. Inside, search out the marble monument to Sir Ralph Woodford made by the sculptor of Chantry.

Another of the town's important landmarks is **Independence Square,** dating from Spanish days. Now mainly a parking lot, it stretches across the southern part of the capital from the **Cathedral of the Immaculate Conception** to Wrightson Road. The neo-Gothic Roman Catholic church was built in 1815 and consecrated in 1832. The cathedral has an outlet that leads to the **Central Market,** on Beetham Highway on the outskirts of Port-of-Spain. Here you can see all the spices and fruits for which Trinidad is known. It's one of the island's most colorful sights, made all the more so by the wide diversity of people who sell their wares here.

At the north of the Savannah, the **Royal Botanical Gardens** (© **868/ 622-4221**) cover 70 acres and are open daily 9:30am to 6pm; admission is free. Once part of a sugar plantation, the park is filled with flowering plants, shrubs, and rare and beautiful trees, including an orchid house. Seek out the raw beef tree: An incision made in its bark is said to resemble rare, bleeding roast beef. Licensed guides will take you through and explain the luxuriant foliage to you. In the gardens is the **President's House,** official residence of the president of Trinidad and Tobago. Victorian in style, it was built in 1875.

Part of the gardens is the **Emperor Valley Zoo** (② **868/622-3530**), in St. Clair, which shows a good selection of the fauna of Trinidad as well as some of the usual exotic animals from around the world. The star attractions are a family of mandrills, a reptile house, and open bird parks. You can take shady jungle walks through tropical vegetation. Adults pay TT$4 (65¢), children 3 to 12 are charged TT$2 (30¢), and children under 3 are admitted free. It's open daily 9:30am to 6pm.

AROUND THE ISLAND   For one of the most popular attractions in the area, the **Asa Wright Nature Centre,** see "Accommodations You Can Afford," earlier in this chapter.

On a peak 1,100 feet above Port-of-Spain, **Fort George** was built by Governor Sir Thomas Hislop in 1804 as a signal station in the days of the sailing ships. Once only hikers could reach it, but today it's accessible by an asphalt road. From its citadel, you can see the mountains of Venezuela. Locals refer to the climb up the winding road as "traveling up to heaven," since nature's bounty is at its greatest along this route. The drive is only 10 miles, but to play it safe, allow about 2 hours.

Pointe-a-Pierre Wild Fowl Trust, 42 Sandown Rd., Point Cumana (② **868/ 658-4230,** ext. 2512), is a bird sanctuary a 2-hour drive south of Port-of-Spain. The setting is unlikely, near an industrial area of the state-owned Petrotrin oil refinery, with flames spouting from flare stacks in the sky. However, in this seemingly inhospitable clime, wildfowl flourish in a setting rich with luxuriant vegetation like crape myrtle, flamboyant soursop and mango trees, and even black sage bushes, said to be good for high blood pressure. In this setting live a number of birds, including endangered species like the toucan and purple gallinule. You can spot the yellow-billed jacana and plenty of Muscovies. The sanctuary sprawls across 26 acres. Adults pay $5 to enter, and those aged 12 and under pay $2. Hours are Monday to Friday 8am to 5pm, Saturday and Sunday by appointment only 11am to 4pm.

Enhanced by the blue and purple hues of the sky at sunset, clouds of scarlet ibis—the national bird of Trinidad and Tobago—fly in from their feeding grounds to roost at the **Caroni Bird Sanctuary** ⊕⊕ (② **868/645-1305**). The 40-square-mile sanctuary is a big mangrove swamp interlaced with waterways and framed by mangrove trees. The setting couldn't be more idyllic, with blue, mauve, and white lilies; oysters growing on mangrove roots; and caimans resting on mudbanks. The sanctuary lies abut a half-hour drive (7 miles) south of Port-of-Spain. Reservations are required. Admission is $10 for adults and $5 for children. Visitors are taken on a launch through these swamps to see the birds (bring along some insect repellent). For your exploration of this wonderland, the most reliable tour operator is **James Meddoo,** Bamboo Grove Settlement, 1 Butler Highway (② **868/662-7356**). Meddoo has toured the swamps for some 25 years. His tour leaves daily at 4pm; it lasts 2½ hours and costs $10 per person, $5 for children ages 5 to 14, and free for children 4 and under.

Pitch Lake ⊕ is on the west coast of Trinidad, with the village of Le Brea on its north shore. To reach it from Port-of-Spain, take the Solomon Hocoy Highway. It's about a 2-hour drive, depending on traffic. One of the wonders of the world, with a surface like elephant skin, the lake is 300 feet deep at its center.

It's possible to walk on its rough side, but we don't recommend that you proceed far. Legend has it that the lake devoured a tribe of Chayma Amerindians, punishing them for eating hummingbirds in which the souls of their ancestors reposed. The lake was formed millions of years ago, and it's believed that at one time it was a huge mud volcano into which muddy asphaltic oil seeped. Churned up and down by underground gases, the oil and mud eventually formed asphalt. According to legend, Sir Walter Raleigh discovered the lake in 1595 and used the asphalt to caulk his ships. Today, the bitumen mined here is used to pave highways throughout the world. A 120-mile tour around the lake takes 5 hours. You can tour Pitch Lake on your own, or you can request a guided tour by calling © **868/648-7426.** Cost is approximately $5 per person. **Trinidad & Tobago Tours** (© **868/628-1051**) also runs tours of Pitch Lake. You'll find some bars and restaurants at Le Brea.

The **Saddle** ℛ is a humped pass on a ridge that divides the Maraval Valley and the Santa Cruz Valley. Along this circular run you'll see the luxuriant growth of the island, including grapefruit, papaya, cassava, and cocoa. Leaving Port-of-Spain by Saddle Road, going past the Trinidad Country Club, you pass through Maraval Village, with its St. Andrew's Golf Course. The road rises to cross the ridge at the spot from which the Saddle gets its name. After going over the hump, you descend through Santa Cruz Valley, rich with giant bamboo, into San Juan, and back to the capital along Eastern Main Road or via Beetham Highway. You'll see panoramic views in every direction; this tour takes about 2 hours and covers 18 miles.

Nearly all cruise ship passengers are hauled along Trinidad's "Skyline Highway," the **North Coast Road.** Starting at the Saddle, the road winds for 7 miles across the Northern Range and down to Maracas Bay. At one point, 100 feet above the Caribbean, you can, on a clear day, see as far away as Venezuela in the west or Tobago in the east, a sweep of some 100 miles. Most visitors take this route to **Maracas Beach,** the most splendid beach on Trinidad.

SHOPPING

One of the large **bazaars** of the Caribbean, Port-of-Spain has luxury items from all over the globe, including Irish linens, English china, Scandinavian crystal, French perfumes, Swiss watches, and Japanese cameras. Even more interesting are the **Asian bazaars,** where you can pick up items in brass. Reflecting the island's culture are calypso shirts or dresses, sisal goods, woodwork, cascadura bracelets, silver jewelry in local motifs, and saris. For souvenir items, visitors often like to bring back figurines of limbo dancers, carnival masqueraders, or calypso singers.

Art Creators and Suppliers, Apt. 402, Aldegonda Park, 7 St. Ann's Rd., St. Ann's (© **868/624-4369**), lies in a banal apartment complex, but the paintings and sculptures sold are among the finest in the Caribbean. Karen De Lima, Rosa Foster, and Stella Beaubrun, the creative forces behind the gallery, are recognized for their knowledge of Trinidadian art. The works sold here are fairly priced samples of the best on Trinidad. Among the artistic giants are Glasgow, Robert Mackie, Boscoe Holder, Sundiata, Keith Ward, and Jackie Hinkson.

Gallery 1-2-3-4, in the Normandie Hotel, 10 Nook Ave., St. Anne's Village (© **868/625-5502**), is more iconoclastic than any other gallery on the island. This art center displays its paintings in a space of minimalist walls and careful lighting. The gallery opened in 1985 and has attracted the attention of the art world because of its wide selection of Caribbean artists.

Value Cheap Thrills: What to See & Do for Free (Well, Almost) on Trinidad & Tobago

- **Have a Close Encounter with Nature.** For getting close to nature, there's nothing in the Caribbean quite like the Asa Wright Nature Center and Lodge in Trinidad. Refer to "Accommodations You Can Afford," above, if you'd like to stay here, but you can also visit just for the day. This 200-acre wildlife sanctuary lies in the island's rain-forested northern range, where it's not unusual to spot 20 to 30 species of birds before you've had your morning coffee. Commonly spotted are such species as the turquoise-billed toucan, chestnut woodpecker, white-bearded manakin, bearded bellbird, and rufous-browned pepperstrike. The center offers guided walks, and birding from the veranda of the center's main lodge is one of the world's most pleasant ornithological experiences.

- **Take Afternoon Tea at a Monastery Estate.** Evoking Trinidad's long British heritage, the quaint custom of afternoon tea in the Caribbean is still practiced at the Pax Guest House, on the Mount St. Benedict Monastery Estate (© **868/662-4084** for information and directions). Tea is served daily in the garden 3 to 6pm. Pax offers an assortment of international teas, homemade pastries, cakes, and breads. The guesthouse is situated on 600 acres of land that includes a rain forest, nature trails, tennis courts, and much more.

- **Limin' at a Funky Little Bar.** On the sleepy island of Tobago, a local told us that limin' (just doing nothing) is a favorite pastime. There's no better place to pursue this activity than the First Historical Cafe/Bar at Mile Marker 8 on the Windward Main Road in the Studley Park district en route to Charlotteville. The place doesn't even have a phone, but the roadside eatery lies in a typically Creole building with a backporch dining area. Painted in flamboyant colors, it rises above a cliff that's some 25 feet high. The walls are covered with boards inscribed with a specific piece of data about Tobago's history. Owner Kenneth Washington, who for decades was a public servant, is the bar's guiding light and main attraction. This is the best

---

The Market, 10 Nook Ave., St. Ann's (© **868/624-1181**), is one of the most fashionable shopping complexes in Trinidad. It contains about 20 boutiques, which carry some of the island's best jewelers, designers, and art dealers. You'll find a wide assortment of merchandise, including clothing, cosmetics, bags, shoes, china, decorative tableware, handcrafts, and designer jewelry and accessories. The complex forms an interconnected bridge among the Normandie Hotel and Restaurant, the restaurant La Fantasie, and Gallery 1-2-3-4.

Stecher's, in Excellent City Mall (© **868/623-5912**), is the best bet for those luxury items. Stecher's sells crystal, watches, jewelry, perfumes, Georg Jensen silver, Lladró, Wedgwood, Royal Doulton, Royal Albert, Aynsley, Hutschenreuther china, and other in-bond items that can be delivered to Piarco

place to go to meet people on the island. By all means, opt for one of those fruit punches, the fruit plate, or a fish sandwich.

- **Take a Nostalgic Look at a Great House.** The ghost of Comte Charles Joseph de Lopinot, a French aristocrat, is said to still prowl the grounds of his former Great House, especially on a stormy night or when the moon is full. This historic complex is a restored cocoa-estate Great House, where the count used to live. He came to Trinidad at the dawn of the 19th century and selected this panoramic site to build his magnificent home. The restored estate has been turned into a museum, and a guide will show you through daily 10am to 6pm for free. You'll see displays of antiques, pottery, and other artifacts of the era. Sometimes small groups of musicians playing *parang* (traditional Christmas music with Spanish origins) roam through the property, entertaining visitors. To reach the estate, take the Eastern Main from Port-of-Spain to Arouca. It's sign-posted from here, but there's no number to call for information.

- **Visit Remote "Little Tobago."** This islet lies a mile offshore from the little town on Speyside on the island of Tobago. The boat ride takes only about 20 minutes and can easily be arranged with one of the fishers. The crossing by boat is likely to be rough, as is the wet landing, with its swells and whitecaps. But once you're on Little Tobago you'll see that the effort is worth it. It's best to go in the early morning or late afternoon, when you'll see the biggest collection of wild birds, a total of 52 species. They include the magnificent frigatebird and even the sooty tern. Laughing gulls breed here from April to September. The islet is arid and hilly, but there's a network of marked trails, the longest of which is only half a mile. Our favorite is Sea View Trail, a short walk east along the lower tiers of the islet. Another interesting hike, taking about an hour, is along George Ride Trail, going through interior forests to a viewing platform facing across Alexander Bay. Along the way here you can say hi to the crested oropendola or the blue-crowned motmot.

International Airport on your departure. You don't have to go downtown to shop here, as you'll find branches at Long Circular Mall and West Mall, in residential areas of Port-of-Spain. You can also pay a last-minute call at the three tax-free airport branches—one outlet for famous perfumes, another for sunglasses, Cartier watches, lighters and pens, leather goods, Swarovski crystal, and local ceramics. Another branch sells tobacco and liquor. There's also a branch at the Cruise Ship Complex at the Port-of-Spain docks.

Y. De Lima, 23 Queen St. (© **868/623-1364**), is another good store for duty-free cameras and watches, but its main focus is local jewelry. The third-floor workroom will make whatever you want in jewelry or bronze work. You could emerge with anything from steel-drum earrings to a hibiscus-blossom broach.

With any extra time remaining for shopping, check out some handcraft outlets, notably **The Boutique,** 43 Syndeham Ave., St. Ann's (© **868/624-3274**). Among other wares, this is a showcase for batik silks created by Althea Bastien, one of Trinidad's finest artisans. Her fabric art is highly prized but reasonable in price. If you'd like to go home with some music of Trinidad, head for **Rhyner's Record Shop,** 54 Prince St. (© **868/623-5673**), which has the best selection of soca and calypso recordings. There's another branch at the airport.

TRINIDAD AFTER DARK

Trinidad Hilton, Lady Young Road, Port-of-Spain (© **868/624-3211**), stages a Poolside Fiesta show every Monday night, with a folkloric performance beginning at 7pm and continuing live until midnight. It features lots of live music, calypso, a steel band, and limbo. It's the most spectacular on Trinidad. The cover (including a buffet dinner with grills) is $20.

Other fun joints worth checking out include **Smokey & Bunty,** Western Main Road at Dengue Street in St. James (no phone). Self-billed as a sports bar, it's more a local hangout. If you have a rumor to spread in Port-of-Spain, get it going here. It's the local gossip center. The **Blue Iguana,** Main Street, Chaguanas (no phone), is the best place to go late at night when the clubs close and you're still in a party mood. It lies about half an hour west of Port-of-Spain, and it opens at 10pm Wednesday to Sunday, seemingly closing when the last customer staggers out.

3 Tobago ⊛⊛⊛

Dubbed "the land of the hummingbird," Tobago lies 20 miles northeast of Trinidad, to which it's connected by frequent flights. It has long been known as a honeymooner's paradise. The physical beauty of Tobago is stunning, with its forests of breadfruit, mango, cocoa, and citrus, through which chartreuse-colored iguanas dart.

Unlike bustling Trinidad, Tobago is sleepy, and Trinidadians come here, especially on weekends, to enjoy the wide sandy beaches. The legendary home of Daniel Defoe's *Robinson Crusoe,* Tobago is only 27 miles long and 7½ miles wide. The people are hospitable, and their villages are so tiny that they seem to blend with the landscape. Tobago's idyllic natural beauty makes it one of the greatest escapes in the Caribbean. It's for those who like a generous dose of sand, sun, and solitude, in a mellow atmosphere.

Columbus probably sighted fish-shaped Tobago in 1498, when he charted Trinidad, but the island was so tiny he paid no attention to it in his log. For the next 100 years it lay almost unexplored. In 1628, when Charles I of England gave it to one of his nobles, the earl of Pembroke, the maritime countries of Europe suddenly showed a belated interest. From then on, Tobago was fought over no fewer than 31 times by the Spanish, French, Dutch, and English, as well as marauding pirates and privateers.

After 1803, the island settled down to enjoy a sugar monopoly unbroken for decades. Great Houses were built, and in London it used to be said of a wealthy man that he was "as rich as a Tobago planter." The island's economy collapsed in 1884, and Tobago entered an acute depression. The ruling monopoly, Gillespie Brothers, declared itself bankrupt and went out of business. The British government made Tobago a ward of Trinidad in 1889, and the sugar industry was never revived.

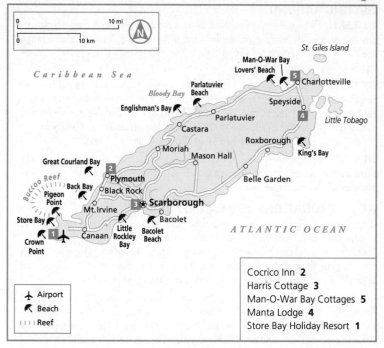

Cocrico Inn **2**
Harris Cottage **3**
Man-O-War Bay Cottages **5**
Manta Lodge **4**
Store Bay Holiday Resort **1**

The island's village-like capital lies on the southern coast and provides a scenic setting, with its bay surrounded by a mountainside. **Scarborough,** which is also the main port, is a rather plain town, however. The local market, the Gun Bridge, the Powder Magazine, and Fort King George, provide a good day's worth of entertainment. Most of the shops are clustered in the streets around the market.

GETTING THERE

BY PLANE Tobago's small **airport** lies at Crown Point (© **868/639-0509**), near the island's southwestern tip. Trinidad is the transfer point for many passengers heading on to the beaches of Tobago. **LIAT** (© **800/468-0482** in the U.S. and Canada, or 868/639-0276) maintains one daily flight from Trinidad to Tobago. If you'd like to skip Trinidad completely, you can book a LIAT flight with direct service to Tobago from Barbados or Grenada. **American Airlines** (© **800/433-7300**), operates one daily round-trip flight between San Juan and Tobago. American Airlines also operates a daily nonstop flight between Miami and Trinidad; once on Trinidad, you can make a connecting flight into Tobago, via BWIA (© **800/292-1183**), which offers several flights daily.

BY BOAT It's possible to travel between Trinidad and Tobago by ferry service managed/operated by the **Port Authority of Trinidad and Tobago** (© **868/623-2901** in Port-of-Spain, 868/639-2417, or 868/639-2416 in Scarborough, Tobago). Call for departure times and more details. Ferries leave once a day (trip time is 5½–6 hr.). The round-trip fare is TT$50 ($8) in economy or TT$60 ($9.50) in tourist.

GETTING AROUND

BY TAXI   From the airport to your hotel, take an unmetered taxi, which will cost $8 to $36, depending on the location of your hotel. You can also arrange (or have your hotel do it for you) a sightseeing tour by taxi. Rates must be negotiated on an individual basis.

BY RENTAL CAR   To rent a car you have to rely on local companies—no international car-rental agencies are here as of yet. Options include **Rattan's Car rentals** at Crown Point Airport (© **868/639-8271**) and **Singh's Auto Rentals,** Grafton Beach Resort (© **868/639-0191**). Another possibility is **Thrifty** at Rex Turtle Beach Hotel, Courland Bay, Black Rock (© **868/639-8507**).

BY BUS   Inexpensive public buses travel from one end of the island to the other several times a day. Expect an unscheduled stop at any passenger's doorstep, and never, never be in a hurry.

ACCOMMODATIONS YOU CAN AFFORD

The hotels of Tobago attract those who seek hideaways instead of high-rise resorts packed with activity. Sometimes to save money, it's best to take the MAP (breakfast and dinner) plan when reserving a room. There's a 15% value-added tax added to all hotel bills, and often a service charge of about 10%. Always ask if the VAT and service charge are included in the prices quoted to you.

Cocrico Inn   Built around 1978, this unpretentious L-shaped building is best known for its popular bar and restaurant. There's a pool, a paved-over sun terrace, and simple landscaping. In the center of Tobago's largest settlement, it's close to grocery stores and bars; Great Courland Beach lies half a mile away, Turtle Beach is 1 mile away, and golf and tennis can be arranged within a reasonable distance. The rooms aren't very large but have white walls, wall-to-wall carpeting, wooden furnishings, and standing fans or ceiling fans; the more expensive doubles have kitchenettes. The furnishings are a bit drab, but there's general comfort here. The staff is most hospitable and keeps the small, shower-only bathrooms decently maintained, each equipped with a shower unit. The restaurant is a respectable diner-style place; its home-style cooking features lots of local seafood and fresh produce.

North St. at Commissioner St. (P.O. Box 287), Plymouth Village, Tobago, W.I. © **800/223-9815** in the U.S., or 868/639-2961. Fax 868/639-6565. www.hews-tours.com/cocricoinn.html. 16 units. Winter $50–$65 single; $60–$85 double; $105–$135 triple. Off-season $40–$55 single; $50–$70 double; $85–$120 triple. MAP $22 per person. AE, MC, V. **Amenities:** Restaurant, bar, pool. *In room:* TV, kitchenette (some rooms), ceiling fans.

Harris Cottage   Its brick-sided construction marks this place distinctly from its many rather ramshackle guesthouse competitors. It lies about a mile from the center of Scarborough, in a fashionable residential neighborhood, a 4-minute walk from the white sands of Bacolet Beach. Built in the late 1980s and owned by Roger Harris, it offers cozy and family-oriented accommodations, with carpeted floors, separate dressing areas, and morning breakfasts on the veranda. The rooms are genuinely comfortable, albeit small, as are the tidily maintained bathrooms with shower stalls. A garden surrounds the house, adding welcome touches of greenery. A rental car is available for $35 per day.

Bacolet, Scarborough, Tobago, W.I. © **868/639-2111.** Fax 868/639-2285. 3 units. Year-round $35 single; $70 double. Rates include breakfast. MAP $15 per person. MC, V. *In room:* A/C, TV.

Man-O-War Bay Cottages *Finds*   If you're seeking a Caribbean cottage hideaway, then the Man-O-War might be for you. The cottages are a part of Charlotteville Estate, a 1,000-acre cocoa plantation open to visitors, who may wander through at will. Pat and Charles Turpin rent several cottages on a sandy beach. Each unit is complete with a kitchen, a good bed, a spacious living and dining room, a tiny private bathroom with shower, and a porch opening onto the sea. The place is simplicity itself, so don't expect room phones or air-conditioning. (But for $12 a maid will clean the unit and prepare a meal.) Near the colony is a coral reef that's ideal for snorkelers. The Turpins will also arrange a boat rental if you want to explore Lovers' Beach. Bird-watchers often book these cottages, and scuba diving and guided nature tours are available.

Charlotteville Estate, Charlotteville, Tobago, W.I. © 868/660-4327. Fax 868/660-4328. www.man-o-warbay cottages.com. 9 cottages. Year-round $65 1-bedroom cottage; $85 2-bedroom cottage; $105 3-bedroom cottage; $135 4-bedroom cottage. MC, V. *In room:* Kitchen.

Store Bay Holiday Resort This is an L-shaped motel-style building painted off-white with a green stripe. The rooms have recently been painted and redecorated, the mattresses have been much used but still have life and comfort in them, and the shower-only bathrooms are tiny but tidy. For the most part, furnishings are a bit time-weary and a few carpets are well worn. Because there's a much-used kitchenette with a new refrigerator in each room, you might be tempted to cook your own meals. The rooms flank a pool, although you'll probably walk about 350 yards to reach the Store Bay Beach. No meals are served, but there are cafes and restaurants nearby.

Store Bay Rd., Crown Point, Tobago, W.I. © 868/639-8810. Fax 868/639-7507. sbaymair@cablenet.net. 15 units. Year-round $45–$85 single or double; $95–$140 suite for up to 8. V. **Amenities:** Pool. *In room:* A/C, kitchenette, fridge.

WORTH A SPLURGE

Manta Lodge ★★ *Finds* One of the newer properties on the island, this complex caters to serious bird-watchers and even more serious divers. It overlooks a beach named for the monster manta rays islanders call "Tobago taxis." The mantas frequent the nearby dive sites. The lodge, built by Trinidad-born Sean Robinson, is a colonial-style concrete building across the road from the beach, with a garden in front. The loft rooms are especially popular with divers; each has airconditioning and a sundeck. The superior and more expensive rooms have verandas and air-conditioning, while ceiling fans cool the cheaper rooms, but they have verandas as well. Surprisingly, the beds are the most sumptuous in Tobago, with the best linen and the finest mattresses. Amenities in the rooms include roomy closets, along with medium-size tiled bathrooms. Service and amenities are at a minimum, but ice can be obtained on request. There's a pool as well as a restaurant and bar, which serves island food and drink.

Speyside (P.O. Box 433), Tobago, W.I. © 868/660-5268. Fax 868/660-5030. www.mantalodge.com. 22 units. Winter $95–$135 single; $115–$170 double. Off-season $75–$110 single; $95–$145 double. Extra person $15. MAP $35 per person. AE, DC, MC, V. **Amenities:** Restaurant, bar, pool, room service, babysitting. *In room:* A/C (some units), ceiling fan.

GREAT DEALS ON DINING

Jemma's Seaview Kitchen ★ *Finds* TOBAGONIAN A short walk north of the hamlet of Speyside, on Tobago's northeastern coast, this is one of the very few restaurants in the Caribbean designed as a treehouse. Although the simple kitchen is firmly anchored to the shoreline, the dining area is set on a platform nailed to the massive branches of a 200-year-old almond tree that leans out over the water. Some 50 tables are available on a wooden deck that provides a rooflike structure for shelter from the rain. The charming staff serves up main courses that come with soup or salad. Lunch platters include shrimp, fish, and chicken, while dinners feature more elaborate portions of each, as well as steaks, curried lamb, grilled or curried kingfish, lamb chops, and lobster served grilled or Thermidor style. Most dishes are at the lower end of the price scale. No liquor is served.

Speyside. © 868/660-4467. Reservations recommended. Main courses TT$50–TT$190 ($8–$30.50). MC, V. Sun–Fri 8am–9pm.

Kiskadee Restaurant CREOLE/CARIBBEAN Five miles from Scarborough, the Kiskadee is casual. Its tables overlook a tropical garden and the sea. Specialties include the catch of the day, steamed or grilled or in a curry. Other courses include baked chicken, sirloin steak, and Chinese-style stir-fry. The cooks pay special attention to the homemade soups, including kettles of pumpkin, *callaloo*, potato, and cucumber. The kitchen doesn't exactly extend itself in preparing these dishes, but the flavors are zesty and spicy.

In the Turtle Beach Hotel, Courland Bay. © 868/639-2851. Reservations recommended for those not staying in the hotel. Fixed-price menu TT$185 ($29.50). AE, DISC, MC, V. Daily 7:30–10am, 12:30–2:30pm, and 7–10pm.

Papillon ✿ SEAFOOD/INTERNATIONAL Near the Tobago Golf Club on the corner of Buccoo Bay Road and Mount Irvine, this restaurant offers international specialties with an emphasis on seafood, including kingfish steak, stuffed flying fish, and lobster Buccoo Bay (marinated in sherry and broiled with garlic, herbs, and butter sauce). The interior is adorned with pictures referring to the novel and film *Papillon,* a story about a convict who settles in the Caribbean. For a change of pace, try curried goat, beef Stroganoff, or grilled lamb and beef. There's a patio for alfresco dining.

Buccoo Bay Rd., Buccoo Bay. © 868/639-0275. Reservations recommended. Main courses TT$40–TT$60 ($6.50–$9.50) lunch, TT$70–TT$125 ($11.25–$20) dinner. AE, MC, V. Daily 7:30am–2:30pm and 7–11pm.

WORTH A SPLURGE

The Cocoa House ✿✿ WEST INDIAN/TOBAGONIAN Proud of its eco-sensitivity (waste water and paper trash are recycled here), this eating house is a worthy choice because of its allegiance to tried-and-true Tobagan food. It derives its name from its unusual design for a roof made of the fronds of the Timit palm. During balmy evenings, the roof retracts, allowing views of the setting sun and—a bit later—of the moon and stars. Old-fashioned drying rooms for cocoa pods were designed with retractable roofs, allowing direct access to the sun as a means of drying the raw product. Menu items include a well-flavored roster of dishes like crabmeat or pork and dumplings; jerk versions of shrimp, chicken, pork, and beef; duck with orange or pineapple sauce; and *pilau,* a French-inspired dish that combines rice, chicken, and beef.

In Footprints Eco Resort, Golden Lane, Colloden Bay Rd. © 868/660-0118. Reservations recommended for lunch, required for dinner before 1pm on day of your intended arrival. Main courses $6–$10 lunch; $20–$34 dinner. AE, MC, V. Daily 7am–9pm.

Kariwak Village Restaurant ✿✿ CARIBBEAN Even if you're not a guest at the Kariwak Village resort, consider visiting at dinnertime. The chefs here prepare one of the choicest menus on the island, a four-course repast that changes nightly based on what's best and freshest at the market. On our latest rounds, we began with a creamy breadfruit soup, followed by freshly grilled fish, rice, stuffed butternut pumpkin, and *christophene* (a squashlike vegetable). The price even includes dessert and coffee, a very good value. In an open-air setting, you can enjoy recorded music from Trinidadian steel bands. The owner, Cynthia Clovis, grows herbs and vegetables in an on-site organic garden. The Friday or

Saturday evening buffet is one of the best spreads on the island, with live music to boot. Shrimp and steak are favorites, but save room for the specialty: green banana salad seasoned with fresh herbs.

In the Kariwak Village resort, Local Rd., Store Bay. ℂ **868/639-8442**. Reservations recommended. Breakfast $10; lunch $8–$12; 4-course dinner $22–$27. AE, MC, V. Daily 7am–11pm.

HITTING THE BEACHES

On Tobago sands you can still feel like Robinson Crusoe in a solitary cove—at least for most of the week before the Trinidadians fly over to sample the sands on a Saturday.

A good beach, **Back Bay,** is within an 8-minute walk of the Mount Irvine Bay Hotel on Mount Irvine Bay. Along the way you'll pass a coconut plantation and an old cannon emplacement. Sometimes there can be dangerous currents here, but you can always enjoy exploring Rocky Point with its brilliantly colored parrotfish. In July and August, the surfing is the finest in Tobago, and it's also likely to be good in January and April. Snorkeling is generally excellent, even in winter. There are picnic tables, so get the makings for your picnic in Scarborough before coming here, but you can buy cold beer and drinks at an on-site snack bar.

Also try **Man-O-War Bay,** one of the finest natural harbors in the West Indies, at the opposite end of the island, near the fishing village of Charlotteville. Once here, you'll come to a long sandy beach, and you can also enjoy a picnic at a government-run rest house. Sometimes the local fishers will come around hawking the day's catch, even cleaning the fish for you. Many guests who have a kitchen or kitchenette in their living quarters buy fish and prepare it themselves for dinner.

Pigeon Point, on the island's northwestern coast, is the best-known bathing area with a long coral beach. Thatched shelters provide changing rooms, as well as tables and benches for picnics. This beach is public but adjoins a former great coconut estate for which you pay TT$10 ($1.60) to enter the grounds, including the use of its facilities. Pigeon Point is a Caribbean cliché in that it's set against a backdrop of royal palms. This beach is becoming increasingly commercial, with food kiosks and some crafts shops, plus a diving concession. You can rent paddleboats from one of the local outfitters here to sail in the tranquil waters.

The true beach buff will want to head for **King's Bay Beach,** south of the town of Speyside in the northeast, near the hamlet of Delaford (a sign between Roxborough and Speyside will direct you here). Against a backdrop of towering green hills, it's one of the island's best places for swimming. The grayish crescent-shaped beach is well protected here. Perhaps you'll resist the young men who offer themselves as guides to a local waterfall, but the climb and sight are worth the trip. Also approached from Roxborough on the north side of the island, **Parlatuvier Beach** is a classic half-moon crescent. The scene of villagers and fishing boats is like a picture postcard advertising Tobago. The setting is more bucolic than the swimming, however.

Lover's Beach in the northeast of the island is aptly named. The remote beach lies near **Man-O-War Bay** to the east of Charlotteville. This beach is accessible only by boat and is famous locally for its pink sand, formed by dozens of crushed seashells ages ago. If you want to visit it, local boatmen are willing to take you out for a fee to be negotiated. If you'd like to spend several hours here with a loved one, you can make arrangements to be picked up at an agreed-on time.

Great Courland Bay is known for its long expanse of tranquil, gin-clear waters, and is flanked by Turtle Beach, named for the sea creatures who nest here. Near Fort Bennett, Great Courland Bay and Turtle Beach lie south of Plymouth, off the coast near the hamlet of Black Rock. This is one of the longest sandy beaches on the island and the site of several hotels, including a marina that attracts visiting yachties. Beach lovers will also seek out **Bacelot Beach,** west of Scarborough and opening onto Bacelot Bay. It's a dark sandy beach with waters tranquil for swimming. This beach has seen its share of film crews, as it was used as a setting for the movies *Heaven Knows, Mr. Allison,* and *Swiss Family Robinson.*

If you can't stand crowds and want the sands all to yourself, head for **Englishman's Bay,** on the north coast, east of Plymouth and past the hamlets of Moriah and Castara. Here, this lovely beach is virtually deserted. We don't know why: It's charming, secluded, and good for swimming. **Little Rockley Bay** is good for escapists but not worth seeking out unless you're going to be on Tobago for several days. It lies west of the capital of Scarborough and is reached by taking the sign-posted Milford Road off the main highway. The beach here is rather craggy and not suited for either sunbathing or swimming. But beachcombers can be seen wandering its shoreline, and you can enjoy a panoramic view of Scarborough from here.

SPORTS & OTHER OUTDOOR PURSUITS
SNORKELING, DIVING & MORE   The unspoiled reefs off Tobago teem with a great variety of marine life. Divers can swim through rocky canyons 60 to 130 feet deep, and underwater photographers can shoot pictures they won't find anywhere else. Snorkeling over the celebrated Buccoo Reef is one of the specialties of Tobago. Hotels routinely arrange for their guests to visit this underwater wonderland.

Wreck divers have a new adventure to enjoy, with the sinking of the *Maverick,* a former ferry between Trinidad and Tobago. In 1997, the *Maverick* was sunk in 100 feet of water near Mount Irvine Bay Hotel on Tobago's southwest coast, making it accessible to divers. The ship lays the foundation for a new reef to support sea life, including resident and migrating fish as well as coral and sponges.

Dive Tobago, Pigeon Point (P.O. Box 53), Scarborough, Tobago, W.I. (© **868/639-0202**), is the oldest and most established dive operation, run by Jay Young. It offers easy resort courses, single dives, and dive packages. Equipment is available to rent. It caters to the beginner as well as to the experienced diver. A basic resort course, taking half a day and ending in a 30-foot dive, costs $55, but for certification you must pay $350. Young is a certified PADI instructor. A one-tank dive goes for $40.

Tobago Dive Experience, at the Turtle Beach Hotel, Black Rock (© **868/639-7034**), offers scuba dives, snorkeling, and boat trips. All dives are guided, with a boat following. Exciting drift dives are available for experienced divers. Manta rays are frequently seen 10 minutes from the shore, and there's rich marine life with zonal compaction. A one-tank dive costs $39 with no equipment or $46 with equipment; a two-tank dive costs from $70. A resort course costs $65.

Man Friday Diving, Charlotteville (© **868/660-4676**), is a Danish-owned dive center with certified PADI instructors along with PADI dive masters. The location is right on the beach of Man-O-War Bay at the northernmost tip of Tobago. With more than 40 dive sites, Man Friday is always able to find suitable locations for diving, no matter what the water conditions are. Guided boat trips for certified divers go out twice a day except Sundays, at 9:30am and 1pm.

A resort course costs $75; a PADI open-water certification is $375. A one-tank dive costs $35, and a night dive goes for $50.

TENNIS   The best courts are at the **Mount Irvine Bay Hotel** (© 868/ 639-8871), where two good courts are available for TT$11.50 ($1.85) per half hour or TT$23 ($3.70) per hour.

SEEING THE SIGHTS

Tobago's capital, **Scarborough,** need claim your attention only briefly before you climb up the hill to **Fort King George,** about 430 feet above the town. Built by the English in 1779, it was later captured by the French. After that it jockeyed back and forth among various conquerors until nature decided to end it all in 1847, blowing off the roofs of its buildings. The cannons still mounted had a 3-mile range, and one is believed to have come from one of the ships of Sir Francis Drake (you can still see a replica of the *Tudor Rose*). One building used to house a powder magazine, and you can see the ruins of a military hospital. Artifacts are displayed in a gallery on the grounds.

If you'd like to get a close-up view of Tobago's exotic and often rare tropical birds, as well as a range of other island wildlife and lush tropical flora, **naturalist-led field trips** are the answer. The trips lead you to forest trails and coconut plantations, along rivers and past waterfalls. Each trip lasts about 2 to 3 hours, so you can take at least two per day if you like. One excursion goes to two nearby islands. The price per trip is $45 to $54 per person. For details, contact **Pat Turpin,** Man-O-War Bay Cottages, Charlotteville (© **868/660-4327** or 868/660-4328). From Scarborough, you can drive northwest to **Plymouth,** Tobago's other town. Perched on a point at Plymouth is **Fort James,** which dates from 1768, when the British built it as a barracks. Now it's mainly in ruins.

From Speyside, you can make arrangements with a local fisher to go to **Little Tobago,** a 450-acre offshore island where a bird sanctuary attracts ornithologists. Threatened with extinction in New Guinea, many birds, perhaps 50 species in all, were brought over to this little island in the early part of this century.

Off Pigeon Point lies **Buccoo Reef** 𝒦𝒦, where sea gardens of coral and hundreds of fish can be seen in waist-deep water. This is the natural aquarium of Tobago. Nearly all the major hotels arrange boat trips to these acres of submarine gardens, which offer the best scuba diving and snorkeling. Even nonswimmers can wade knee-deep in the waters. Remember to protect your head and body from the tropical heat and to guard your feet against the sharp coral. After about half an hour at the reef, passengers reboard their boats and go over to **Nylon Pool,** with its crystal-clear waters. In this white-sand bottom, about a mile offshore, you can enjoy water only 3 or 4 feet deep. After a swim, you'll be returned to the Buccoo Village jetty in time for a goat and crab race.

Eco-consciousness on the island was enhanced by the opening of the **Franklyn Water Wheel and Nature Park** at Arnos Vale, Arnos Vale Estate, Franklyn Road (© **868/660-0815**). This is the site of Tobago's best-preserved water wheel, which once helped provide power to a sugar estate. It has been refurbished, and the site offers walking trails and a restaurant. There's also an outdoor theater, and the old machinery itself is still in place for the most part. Walkways allow you to see the sights without upsetting Mother Nature. Many hiking trails are possible on the 12-acre estate, where you can see butterflies and iguanas, plus mango and citrus orchards—you can even pick your own fresh fruit. Admission is TT$10 ($1.60) for adults or TT$5 (80¢) for children. You can visit any time during the day and can gain entrance to the site as long as the restaurant is open (until 10pm).

SHOPPING

In Tobago's capital, **Scarborough,** you can visit the local market Monday to Saturday morning and listen to the sounds of a Creole patois. Scarborough's stores have a limited range of merchandise, more to tempt the browser than the serious shopper.

But if you're in town, you'll find **Farro's,** Wilson Road (no phone), lying across from the marketplace. Here you can pick up the tastiest condiments on the island, which are packed into little straw baskets for you to carry back home. Sample the delectable lime marmalade, any of the hot sauces, the guava jelly, and most definitely the homemade and -canned chutney from the tamarind fruit. If you're seeking handcrafts, especially straw baskets, head for the **Souvenir & Gift Shop,** Port Mall (© 868/639-5632), also in Scarborough.

Cotton House Fashion Studio, Old Windward Road, in Bacolet (© 868/639-2727), is the island's best choices for "hands-on" appreciation of the fine art of batik. Batik is an Indonesian tradition in which melted wax, brushed onto fabric, resists dyes on certain parts of the cloth, thereby creating unusual colors and designs. This outlet contains the largest collections of batik clothing and wall hangings on Tobago. Dying techniques are demonstrated to clients, who can try their skills at the art form for free.

TOBAGO AFTER DARK

Your best bet for entertainment is at the **Mount Irvine Bay Hotel** at Mount Irvine Bay (© 868/639-8871), where you might find some disco action or a steel band performing by the beach or poolside. The **Rex Turtle Beach Hotel,** Great Courland Bay (© 868/639-2851), is the place to be on Wednesday night, when it stages a Caribbean buffet dinner with cultural entertainment and dancing. You get real West Indian flavor here. Every Saturday a steel band entertains at a barbecue dinner from 7 to 10pm.

The Grafton Beach Resort at Black Road owns one of the island's most charming bars, **Buccaneer's Beach Bar** (© 868/639-0191), across from the resort. Here you'll find a wide wood terrace sheltered by a grove of almond trees. It evokes the feeling of a treehouse, but the sea is right at your feet. Not only can you drink here, but you can enjoy daily specials written on a surfboard—burgers, fried fish, and the like (don't expect the elegant beachside Creole cooking of Martinique). If your order gets too fancy, it's referred to the kitchens at Grafton Beach Resort itself. Even after the beach bar closes, you can stick around to see what's happening at the resort itself. Every night some cabaret-like entertainment is organized. If you can, catch the local troupe, Les Couteaux Cultural Group, which performs a version of Tobagonian history set to dance. The group frequently appears here.

Still want some local action? Drop in at **Bonkers,** Store Bay Road at Crown Point (© 868/639-7173), which is an active bar that often has disco action. Here you'll hear the best on-island sounds of soca, reggae, or jazz. If you've been "bad," the DJ might order you to walk the gangplank into the pool. Disco parties are occasionally held at **The Lush,** Shirvan Road in Mount Irvine (© 868/639-0225). Otherwise, this is one of the island's friendliest alfresco pubs. Drop in to see what's happening.

25

The U.S. Virgin Islands

The U.S. Virgin Islands are known for their sugar-white beaches, which are among the world's finest. The most developed island in the chain is **St. Thomas,** which has the Caribbean's largest concentration of shopping in its capital, Charlotte Amalie. With a population of some 50,000, St. Thomas isn't exactly a secluded tropical retreat; you'll hardly have its beaches to yourself. The place abounds in bars and restaurants, even fast-food joints, and has a vast selection of hotels in all price ranges, making it great for the budget traveler.

St. Croix is bigger, but more tranquil, than St. Thomas. A favorite with cruise ship passengers (as is St. Thomas), St. Croix touts its shopping and has more stores than most islands in the Caribbean, especially in and around Christiansted, although it's not as dense with stores as Charlotte Amalie. Its major attraction is Buck Island, a U.S. National Park that lies offshore. St. Croix is peppered with inns and hotels and is condo heaven.

St. John, the smallest of the three islands, is also the most beautiful and the least developed. It has only two big hotels. Some two-thirds of this island is set aside as a U.S. National Park. Even if you visit only for the day while based on St. Thomas, you'll want to sample the island's dreamy beach, Trunk Bay.

The U.S. Virgin Islands lie in two bodies of water: St. John is entirely in the Atlantic Ocean, St. Croix is entirely in the Caribbean Sea, and St. Thomas separates the Atlantic and the Caribbean. These islands, directly in the belt of the subtropical easterly trade winds, enjoy one of the world's most perfect year-round climates. At the eastern end of the Greater Antilles and the northern tip of the Lesser Antilles, the U.S. Virgins are some 60 miles east of Puerto Rico and 1,100 miles southeast of Miami.

1 Essentials

VISITOR INFORMATION

Before you go, contact the **U.S. Virgin Islands Division of Tourism,** 1270 Ave. of the Americas, Suite 2801, New York, NY 10020 (© **212/332-2222**). Branch offices are at 225 Peachtree St. NE, Suite 260, Atlanta, GA 30303 (© **404/688-0906**); 500 N. Michigan Ave., Suite 2030, Chicago, IL 60611 (© **312/670-8784**); 2655 Le Jeune Rd., Suite 907, Coral Gables, FL 33134 (© **305/442-7200**); 3460 Wilshire Blvd., Suite 412, Los Angeles, CA 90010 (© **213/739-0138**); and 900 17th St. NW, Suite 500, Washington, DC 20006 (© **202/293-3707**).

Offices outside the United States are found in **Canada** at 3300 Bloor St. W., Suite 3120, Centre Tower, Toronto, ON M8X 2X3 (© **416/233-1414**), and in **Britain** at 2 Cinnamon Row, Plantation Wharf, York Place, London SW11 3TW (© **020/7978-5262**).

The Internet address for the U.S. Virgin Islands is **www.usvi.net**.

GETTING THERE

It's possible to fly directly to St. Croix from the mainland United States and even possible to fly from St. Thomas to St. Croix, but you can't fly to St. John. The only way to get to St. John is by a ferry from St. Thomas or Jost Van Dyke or Tortola in the British Virgin Islands.

TO ST. THOMAS OR ST. CROIX FROM THE U.S.   Nonstop flights to the U.S. Virgin Islands from either New York or Atlanta usually take 3¾ and 3½ hours, respectively. The flight time between St. Thomas and St. Croix is only 20 minutes. Flying to San Juan from mainland cities and changing planes may save you money over the APEX nonstop fare.

American Airlines (© 800/433-7300 in the U.S.) offers frequent service into St. Thomas and St. Croix from the U.S. mainland, with five daily flights from JFK to St. Thomas. Summer flights can vary; call for more information. Passengers originating in other parts of the world are usually routed to St. Thomas through American's hubs in Miami or San Juan, both of which offer nonstop service (often several times a day) to St. Thomas. Connections from Los Angeles or San Francisco to St. Thomas or St. Croix are usually made through New York, San Juan, or Miami. One especially convenient nonstop flight from Miami, available only June to August, departs Miami at 5pm and continues to St. Croix, where the plane stays overnight. This late afternoon departure from Miami allows for connections to the U.S.V.I. from many other destinations within the United States, including same-day connections from such remote places as Los Angeles. American can also arrange lots of great discount packages that include both airfare and hotel. Flights from Puerto Rico to the U.S. Virgin Islands are on American's partner, **American Eagle** (© 800/433-7300 in the U.S.), which has 13 nonstop flights daily.

Delta (© 800/221-1212 in the U.S.), in winter, offers two daily nonstop flights between Atlanta and St. Thomas, the first departing in the morning and the second in the afternoon. The latter flight also provides an air link to St. Croix. In off-season, only one flight might be available. **TWA** (© 800/ 221-2000 in the U.S.) doesn't fly nonstop to any of the Virgin Islands but offers connections to other carriers through San Juan. TWA flies into San Juan five times daily from New York's JFK and twice daily from St. Louis with a touchdown in Miami. **Cape Air Airlines** (© 800/352-0714 in the U.S.) began service between St. Thomas and Puerto Rico in autumn 1998. The Massachusetts-based airline provides seven flights daily between 7am and 5pm. If needed, more frequent departures may be added.

TO ST. CROIX FROM ST. THOMAS   It's now easier than ever before to travel between St. Thomas and St. Croix. **American Eagle** (© 800/433-7300 in the U.S.) has three flights a day, costing $80 to $110 per person one-way. In addition, **Seaborne Seaplane** (© 340/773-6442), offers 10 or 11 round-trip flights daily, going for $130 to $150 per person one-way. Flight time is only 30 minutes.

Those who want to make the 40-mile crossing from St. Thomas to St. Croix by **hydrofoil** should call the new service at © 340/776-7417. A hydrofoil, *Katrun II,* departs twice daily from the harbor at Charlotte Amalie going to the harbor of Christiansted. The trip takes about an hour and costs $90 round-trip.

A **ferry service** from St. Thomas to Puerto Rico, with a stop in St. John, is available once every 2 weeks, maybe more if demand merits it. The trip from Puerto Rico to Charlotte Amalie takes about 2 hours, costing $80 one-way or

$100 round-trip, including ground transportation to the San Juan airport or Condado. For more information, call © **340/776-6282.**

TO ST. JOHN   The easiest and most common way to get to St. John is by **ferry** (© **340/776-6282**), which leaves from the Red Hook landing pier on St. Thomas's eastern tip; the trip takes about 20 minutes each way. Beginning at 6:30am, boats depart more or less every hour, with minor exceptions throughout the day. The last ferry back to Red Hook departs from St. John's Cruz Bay at 11pm. Because of such frequent departures, even cruise ship passengers temporarily anchored in Charlotte Amalie for only a short stay can visit St. John for a quickie island tour. The one-way fare is $3 for adults or $1 for children 10 and under. Schedules can change without notice, so call in advance before your intended departure.

To reach the ferry, take the **Vitran** bus from a point near Market Square (in Charlotte Amalie) directly to Red Hook. The cost is $1 per person each way. In addition, privately owned taxis will be willing to negotiate a price to carry you from virtually anywhere to the docks at Red Hook.

It's also possible to board a **boat** for St. John directly at the Charlotte Amalie waterfront for a cost of $7 each way. The ride takes 45 minutes. The boats depart from Charlotte Amalie at 9am and continue at intervals of between 1 and 2 hours, until the last boat departs around 5:30pm. (The last boat to leave St. John's Cruz Bay for Charlotte Amalie departs at 3:45pm.) Call © **340/776-6282** for more information.

 FAST FACTS: **The U.S. Virgin Islands**

Banks Banks are generally open Monday to Thursday 9am to 2:30pm and Friday 9am to 2pm and 3:30 to 5pm. It's not hard to find a bank with an ATM on St. Thomas or St. Croix. Chase Manhattan Bank has branches, with ATMs, on all three islands.

Currency The **U.S. dollar** is the unit of currency in the Virgin Islands.

Customs Every U.S. resident can bring home $1,200 worth of duty-free purchases, including 5 liters of liquor per adult. If you go over the $1,200 limit, you pay a flat 5% duty, up to $1,000. You can also mail home gifts valued at up to $100 per day, which you don't have to declare. (At other spots in the Caribbean, U.S. citizens are limited to $400 or $600 worth of merchandise and a single bottle of liquor.)

Documents U.S. and Canadian citizens are required to present some proof of citizenship to enter the Virgin Islands, such as a birth certificate with a raised seal along with a government-issued photo ID. A passport isn't strictly required, but carrying one is a good idea. Residents from other countries, including Britain, are required to carry a valid passport, and in some cases a visa. In other words, requirements are the same as for a foreigner entering mainland U.S. gateways.

Driving Remember to *drive on the left.* This comes as a surprise to many visitors, who expect that U.S. driving practices will hold here. Of course, you should also obey speed limits, which are 20 mph in towns, 35 mph outside.

Electricity It's the same as on the mainland: 120-volt AC (60 cycles). No transformer, adapter, or converter is needed for U.S. appliances.

Emergencies In an emergency, dial ✆ **911**.

Mail The Virgin Islands are part of the U.S. Postal Service, so postage rates are the same as on the mainland.

Safety The U.S. Virgin Islands have more than their share of crime. St. John is safer than St. Thomas or St. Croix, but even on St. John there is crime—possessions that are left unattended are likely to be stolen. Travelers should exercise extreme caution both day and night when wandering the back streets of Charlotte Amalie on St. Thomas and both Christiansted and Frederiksted on St. Croix. Muggings are commonplace. Avoid, if possible, night strolls or drives along quiet roads, and never go walking on the beaches at night.

Taxes There is no departure tax for the U.S. Virgin Islands. Hotels add on an 8% tax (always ask if it's included in the original price you're quoted).

Telecommunications The phone system for the U.S. Virgin Islands is the same as on the U.S. mainland. The area code is **340**.

Time The U.S. Virgins are on Atlantic standard time year-round, which places the islands an hour ahead of U.S. eastern standard time. When the U.S. east coast goes on daylight saving time, the Virgin Islands have the same time.

Tipping Tip as you would on the U.S. mainland: 15% in restaurants, 10% to 15% to taxi drivers, $1 or $2 per round to bartenders, at least $1 or $2 per day for chambermaids. Some hotels add a 10% to 15% surcharge to cover service, so check before you wind up paying twice.

Water There's ample water for showers and bathing in the Virgin Islands, but you are asked to conserve. Hotels will supply you with all your drinking water. Many visitors drink the local tap water with no harmful aftereffects. Others, more careful or with more delicate stomachs, should stick to bottled water.

Weather From November to February, temperatures average about 77°F. The average temperature divergence is 5° to 7°F. Sometimes in August the temperature peaks in the high 80s, but the subtropical breezes keep it comfortably cool in the shade. The temperature in winter might drop into the low 60s, but this happens rarely. If you're visiting in August, make sure you carry along mosquito repellent.

2 St. Thomas ★★★

St. Thomas, the busiest cruise-ship harbor destination in the West Indies, is not the largest of the U.S. Virgins (St. Croix, 40 miles south, holds that distinction). But bustling **Charlotte Amalie** is the capital of the U.S. Virgin Islands, and the shopping hub of the Caribbean. The beaches on this island are renowned for their white sand and calm, turquoise waters, including the very best of them all, **Magens Bay.** Despite all the overdevelopment, *National Geographic* rated St. Thomas as one of the top destinations in the world for sailing, scuba diving, and fishing. Hotels on the north side of St. Thomas face the Atlantic and those on the south side front the calmer Caribbean.

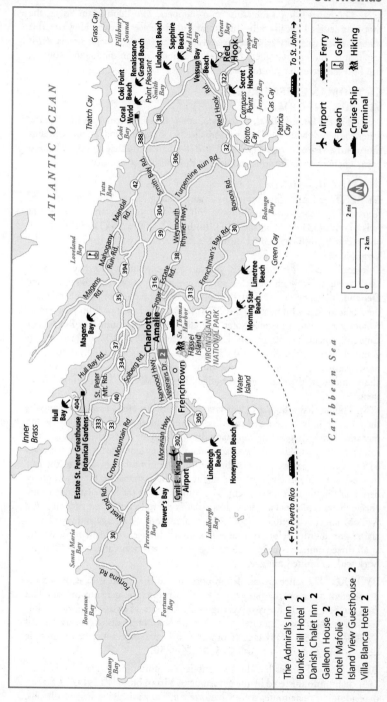

St. Thomas

Legend:
- ✈ Airport
- ↙ Beach
- ⛴ Cruise Ship Terminal
- ⛴ Ferry
- ⛳ Golf
- 🥾 Hiking

To St. John →

← To Puerto Rico

ATLANTIC OCEAN

Caribbean Sea

Grass Cay
Pillsbury Sound
Thatch Cay
Great Bay
Red Hook
Coquet Bay

Lindquist Beach
Sapphire Beach
Grand Beach
Renaissance
Point Pleasant
Vessup Bay Beach
Coki Point Beach
Coral World
Coki Bay
Smith Bay
Red Hook
Secret Harbour
Compass Point
Jersey Bay
Gas Cay
Rotto Cay
Patricia Cay

Loveland Bay
Tutu Bay
Mandal Rd.
Mahogany Run Rd.
Smith Bay Rd.
Turpentine Run Rd.
Weymouth Rhymer Hwy.
Frenchman's Bay Rd.
Bovoni Rd.
Bolongo Bay
Green Cay

Magens Rd.
Magens Bay
Hull Bay
Inner Brass
Santa Maria Bay

Estate St. Peter Greathouse Botanical Gardens
St. Peter Mt. Rd.
Hull Bay Rd.
Solberg Rd.
Harwood Hwy.
Veterans Dr.
Charlotte Amalie
Frenchtown
St. Thomas Harbor
Hassel Island
VIRGIN ISLANDS NATIONAL PARK
Water Island

Crown Mountain Rd.
Moravian Hwy.
Brewer's Bay
Cyril E. King Airport
Lindbergh Beach
Honeymoon Beach
Morning Star Beach
Limetree Beach

West End Rd.
Perseverance Bay
Fortuna Rd.
Bordeaux Bay
Botany Bay
Fortuna Bay
Lindbergh Bay

Sugar Estate Rd.

0   2 mi
0   2 km

The Admiral's Inn 1
Bunker Hill Hotel 2
Danish Chalet Inn 2
Galleon House 2
Hotel Mafolie 2
Island View Guesthouse 2
Villa Blanca Hotel 2

St. Thomas is a boon for cruise ship shoppers, who flood Main Street, the shopping center, basically 3 to 4 blocks long in the center of town. However, this center, which gets very crowded, is away from all beaches, major hotels, most restaurants, and entertainment facilities. At a hotel "out on the island," you can still find the seclusion you may be seeking.

ST. THOMAS ESSENTIALS
VISITOR INFORMATION
Stop off in the **Grand Hotel,** at Tolbod Gade 1, near Emancipation Park, on the waterfront in downtown Charlotte Amalie. No longer a hotel, it now contains shops and a **visitor center** (© **340/774-8784**), open Monday to Friday 8am to 5pm. There's also an information desk at the cruise ship terminal.

GETTING AROUND
BY RENTAL CAR   St. Thomas has many leading North American car-rental firms at the airport and competition is stiff. Before you go, compare the rates of **Avis** (© **800/331-1084** in the U.S.), **Budget** (© **800/626-4316** in the U.S.), and **Hertz** (© **800/654-3001** in the U.S.). There's no tax on car rentals in the Virgin Islands.

Instead of calling Hertz or Avis, you can often save money by renting from a local agency, although vehicles sometimes aren't as well maintained. Try **Dependable Car Rental,** 3901 B Altona, behind the Bank of Nova Scotia and the Medical Arts Complex (© **340/774-2253**), which will pick up prospective renters at the airport or their hotel. A final choice is **Discount Car Rental,** 14 Content, outside the airport on the main highway (© **340/776-4858**), which grants drivers a 12% discount on rivals' rates. Its rates are usually among the most reasonable on the island, beginning at $47 per day in winter. The firm closely monitors prices charged at Budget, Hertz, and Avis, and then undercuts them.

St. Thomas has a high accident rate. Many visitors aren't used to driving on the left, the hilly terrain shelters blind curves and entrance ramps, and some motorists drive after having too many drinks. In many cases, the roads are narrow and the lighting is poor; we recommend collision-damage insurance. It costs $15 to $20 per day extra, depending on the fine print, but be alert to the fact that even if you purchase it, you might still be responsible for a whopping deductible if you have an accident. The company with the least-attractive insurance policies is Hertz. The Hertz deductible is the full value of the car, while the Avis or Budget deductible is $500. Ask about insurance coverage and your financial responsibilities before you rent. The minimum age requirement for drivers at all three companies is 25. The cheapest car rentals begin at around $250 per week with unlimited mileage.

BY TAXI   The chief means of transport around the island is taxis, which are unmetered; agree on the fare with the driver before you get into the car. Taxi fares are $30 to $34 for two passengers for 2 hours of sightseeing; each additional passenger pays another $12. For 24-hour radio-dispatch service, call © **340/774-7457.** Many taxis transport 8 to 12 passengers in vans to multiple destinations. For taxi tours, call © **340/774-4550.**

BY BUS   St. Thomas has the best public transportation of any island in the U.S. chain. Administered by the government, **Vitran** buses (© **340/774-5678**), depending on their route, serve Charlotte Amalie, its outlying neighborhoods, and the countryside as far away as Red Hook. Vitran stops are found at intervals

---

Fun Fact **Carnival**

The annual **Carnival** celebration, held after Easter, is a spectacular event, with echoes of the islanders' African heritage. "Mocko Jumbies," people dressed as spirits, parade through the streets on stilts nearly 20 feet high. Steel and *fungi* bands, "jump-ups," (Caribbean hoedowns), and parades bring the event to life. Events take place islandwide, but most of the action is on the streets of Charlotte Amalie. Contact the visitors' center in St. Thomas for a schedule of events.

---

beside each of the most important traffic arteries on St. Thomas, including the edges of Veterans Drive in the capital. You rarely have to wait more than 30 minutes during the day, and the Vitran buses run from 5:30am to 10:30pm. A one-way ride costs 75¢ within Charlotte Amalie and $1 for rides from Charlotte Amalie to outer neighborhoods. Although you might still have to walk some distance to your final destination, the Vitran buses are a comfortable and usually air-conditioned form of transport. Call for more information about Vitran buses, their stops, and schedules.

BY VAN OR MINIBUS   Less structured and more erratic than Vitran buses are the **taxi vans,** a mini-flotilla of privately owned vans or minibuses that make unscheduled stops along major traffic arteries of the island. Charging the same rates as the Vitran buses, and operated by a frequently changing cast of local entrepreneurs, they may or may not have their end destination written on a cardboard sign displayed on the windshield. They tend to be less comfortable than Vitran buses and not as well maintained, but some residents opt for a ride if one happens to arrive near a Vitran stop at a convenient moment and if it's headed in the right direction. If you're in doubt, it's much better to stick to the Vitran buses.

FAST FACTS

Royal Roy Lester Schneider Hospital, the largest on the island with the best-equipped emergency room, is at 48 Sugar Estate, Charlotte Amalie (© **340/776-8311**), a 5-minute drive east of the town's commercial center.

ACCOMMODATIONS YOU CAN AFFORD

Nearly every beach on St. Thomas has its own hotel, and the island also has more quaint inns than anyplace else in the Caribbean. If you want to stay here on the cheap, consider one of the guesthouses in the Charlotte Amalie area. All the glittering, expensive properties lie in the East End.

Remember that hotels in the Virgin Islands slash their prices in summer by 20% to 60%. Unless otherwise noted, the rates listed below do *not* include the 8% government tax.

Sometimes you can make a deal on an inexpensive condo or apartment rental that might not be as expensive as it sounds. We've found that **Calypso Realty,** P.O. Box 12178, St. Thomas, U.S.V.I. (© **800/747-4858** in the U.S., or 340/774-1620), has the best deals. This agency is especially noted for its offerings at discount prices from April to mid-December. It features apartments, condos, houses, and villas, the apartments or small condos being cheaper, of course. A studio overlooking Pillsbury Sound often goes for $100 per night off-season or $145 per night in winter.

The Admiral's Inn On a peninsula in Frenchtown, near the western entrance to Charlotte Amalie's harbor, this famous inn was battered by recent hurricanes but is now up and running again. It often attracts divers and other travelers who aren't too particular about where they spend the night. Although the Admiral's Inn has had its share of admirers, it disappoints many readers, who complain about lack of security and a sometimes unhelpful staff. Luckily, units that were in bad need of refurbishment before the hurricane received much-needed facelifts. They contain one or two queen-size beds with new mattresses, plus dressing areas flanking well-maintained tiled bathrooms with shower stalls. A saltwater beach and sea pool lie a few paces from the lanai-style ocean-view units. There's a pool with a large sundeck, plus a poolside bar that is open for guests in the morning and afternoon. You can have dinner at the Chart House Restaurant, which is on the premises but not affiliated with the inn.

Villa Olga (P.O. Box 306162), Frenchtown, Charlotte Amalie, St. Thomas, U.S.V.I. 00802. © 800/423-0320 in the U.S., or 340/774-1376. Fax 340/774-8010. 16 units. Winter $129–$169 single or double. Off-season $95–$115 single or double. Extra person $20; children 11 and under stay free in parents' room. Rates include continental breakfast. AE, DISC, MC, V. **Amenities:** Restaurant, bar, pool. *In room:* A/C, TV, fridge (some units).

Bunker Hill Hotel We recommend this place only if the other hotels are booked up (as is often the case). This district is a bit questionable, so caution is advised—especially at night. This clean and centrally located guest lodge is suitable for anyone who'll sacrifice some comfort—like putting up with street noises—for economy's sake. Four rooms have balconies, and some offer a view of the lights of Charlotte Amalie and the sea. Despite some minor improvements, the furnishings in the small rooms are simple and the mattresses are well worn. The shower-only bathrooms are also exceedingly small. Guests share a communal kitchen, and on the premises is a deli that serves soups, sandwiches, and drinks. The closest beach is Lindbergh Bay, a 15-minute drive away.

7 Commandant Gade, Charlotte Amalie, St. Thomas, U.S.V.I. 00802. © 340/774-8056. Fax 340/774-3172. www.bunkerhillhotel.com. 18 units. Winter $80 single; $90 double; $115 suite. Off-season $60 single; $70 double; $95 suite. Rates include continental breakfast. AE, MC, V. **Amenities:** Deli, communal kitchen. *In room:* A/C, TV, fridge.

Danish Chalet Inn Above Charlotte Amalie on the western edge of the cruise ship harbor, a 5-minute walk from the harbor front, this trio of buildings sits on a steeply inclined acre of land dotted with tropical shrubs and bougainvillea. The heart and soul of the place is the panoramic terrace, with a 180-degree view over the cruise ships and an honor bar. The small rooms are neat, clean, and colorful. All but the cheapest rooms have refrigerators and air-conditioning; the others have ceiling fans. The mattresses are well worn but with some comfort still in them. The shared bathrooms are generally adequate and well maintained; you rarely have to wait in line. The hotel has no pool, but it does have a semisecluded Jacuzzi spa. The nearest beaches are Morningstar and Beachcomber, about a 4-minute drive away. Breakfast is the only meal served.

9E9J Nordsidevej (Solberg Rd.) (P.O. Box 4319), Charlotte Amalie, St. Thomas, U.S.V.I. 00803. © 800/635-1531 in the U.S., or 340/774-5764. Fax 340/777-4886. www.danishchaletinn.com. 11 units, 6 with bathroom. Winter $79 single or double without bathroom, $89–$99 single or double with bathroom. Off-season $64 single or double without bathroom, $78–$88 single or double with bathroom. Extra person $15. Rates include continental breakfast. MC, V. **Amenities:** Bar, Jacuzzi, concierge, tour desk, car rental, laundry. *In room:* A/C in most, fridge, ceiling fans.

Galleon House The rates at Galleon House are among the most competitive around, so if you don't mind a place operated without state-of-art maintenance and a staff attitude many readers have complained about, this is a good place to stay. You walk up a long flight of stairs to reach a concrete terrace that doubles as the reception area. The small rooms are in scattered hillside buildings, each with a firm mattress, so-so air-conditioning, and a cramped shower-only bathroom. Breakfast is served on a veranda overlooking the harbor, and Magens Beach is 15 minutes by car or taxi from the hotel.

Government Hill (P.O. Box 6577), Charlotte Amalie, St. Thomas, U.S.V.I. 00804. ☎ 800/524-2052 in the U.S., or 340/774-6952. Fax 340/774-6952. www.st-thomas.com/galleonhouse. 14 units, 12 with bathroom. Winter $69 single; $79 double without bathroom, $99 double with bathroom. Off-season $49 single; $59 double without bathroom, $89 double with bathroom. Rates include continental breakfast. AE, DISC, MC, V. **Amenities:** Pool. In room: A/C, TV, ceiling fan.

Hotel Mafolie

An old favorite, with lots of fans and only a few detractors, the sprawling Mafolie is about 850 feet above Charlotte Amalie and offers a panoramic harbor view. It has bounced back after hurricane damage with major renovations that make it better than ever. Although the hotel attracts honeymooners, the ambience isn't the stuff of dreamy postcards, but the rooms are comfortable, with a rather uninspired decor. Rooms are small but not necessarily cramped, and the mattresses are fairly new and comfortable. The shower-only bathrooms are like a cheap stateside motel's. Breakfast is served at the pool bar. The restaurant, Lindy's, is home to a celebrated view of Charlotte Amalie harbor, a perfect backdrop for enjoying a drink and a Caribbean sunset. It offers alfresco dining Monday to Saturday, with an extensive menu specializing in shrimp, crab, and lobster dishes. The chefs seem to do crab the best—steamed, split, and served with tangy mustard or cooked in herbs, spices, and garlic. Desserts might be Mary Russ's award-winning fruit tart, Key lime pie, or chocolate chip–macadamia nut tart. A shuttle transports visitors to Magens Bay, about a 5-minute ride.

7091 Estate Mafolie, Mafolie Hill, Charlotte Amalie, St. Thomas, U.S.V.I. 00802. ☎ 800/225-7035 or 340/774-2790. Fax 340/774-4091. www.mafolie.com. 22 units. Winter $97 single; $105–$115 double; $145 mini-suite for up to 4. Off-season $78 single; $85–$95 double; $115 mini-suite for up to 4. Children 11 and under stay free in parents' room; children 12 and over $15 each. AE, MC, V. **Amenities:** Restaurant, bar, pool, beach shuttle. In room: A/C, TV, safe.

Island View Guesthouse ★ Value

The casual Island View is located in a hilly neighborhood of private homes and villas about a 7-minute drive west of Charlotte Amalie and a 20-minute drive from the nearest beach at Magens Bay. Set 545 feet up Crown Mountain, it has sweeping views over Charlotte Amalie and the harbor. It contains main-floor rooms (two without private bathroom) and some poolside rooms, plus six units in a recent addition (three with kitchens and all with balconies). The bedrooms are cooled by breezes and fans, and the newer ones have air-conditioning. Each has a shower-only bathroom. Furnishings are very basic, but the price is right. A self-service, open-air bar on the gallery operates on the honor system. A terrace, with gorgeous views, is the site for breakfast each morning, and cocktails in the evening. The staff will help you arrange all kinds of outings and excursions.

11-C Contant (P.O. Box 1903), Charlotte Amalie, St. Thomas, U.S.V.I. 00803. ☎ 800/524-2023 for reservations only, or 340/774-4270. Fax 340/774-6167. www.st-thomas.com/islandviewguesthouse. 15 units, 13 with private bathroom. Winter $72 single without bathroom, $77–$105 single with bathroom; $77 double without bathroom, $110 double with bathroom; $115 suite. Off-season $50 single without bathroom, $55.75 single with bathroom; $55 double without bathroom, $80 double with bathroom; $90 suite. Rates include continental breakfast. AE, MC, V. From the airport, turn right onto Rte. 30; then cut left and continue to the unmarked Scott Free Rd., where you turn left; look for the sign. No children under 15. **Amenities:** Bar, pool. In room: A/C (some units), TV, ceiling fans.

WORTH A SPLURGE

Villa Blanca Hotel *★★* *Value*   Small, intimate, and charming, this hotel lies east of Charlotte Amalie on 3 secluded acres of hilltop land, among the most panoramic on the island, with views over the harbor and the green rolling hills. The hotel's main building served as the private home of its present owner, Blanca Terrasa Smith, between 1973 and 1985. After the death of her husband, Mrs. Smith added a 12-room annex in the garden and opened her grounds to paying guests. Today, a homey and caring ambience prevails. Each room has tile floors, a ceiling fan and/or air-conditioning, a tiled shower-only bathroom, a well-equipped kitchenette, a good bed with a firm mattress, and a private balcony or terrace with sweeping views either eastward to St. John or westward to Puerto Rico and the harbor of Charlotte Amalie. No meals are served. On the premises are a freshwater pool and a large covered patio where you can enjoy the sunset. The closest beach is Morningstar Bay, about a 4-mile drive away.

Villa Blanca is the honeymoon bargain of the island. The "Honeymoon Hideaway" package, for 8 days and 7 nights, costs $875 per couple in winter and only $575 per couple from May 1 to mid-December, including welcome drinks, a bottle of champagne, and flowers.

4 Raphune Hill, Rte. 38, Charlotte Amalie, St. Thomas, U.S.V.I. 00801. ✆ **800/231-0034** in the U.S., or 340/776-0749. Fax 340/779-2661. www.st-thomas.com/villablanca. 14 units. Winter $125–$145 single or double; off-season $75–$120 single or double. AE, DC, MC, V. **Amenities:** Pool. *In room:* A/C (some units), TV, kitchenette, ceiling fans, no phone.

GREAT DEALS ON DINING

The cuisine on St. Thomas is among the top in the entire West Indies. But prices are high, and many of the best spots can be reached only by taxi. With a few exceptions, the finest and most charming restaurants aren't in Charlotte Amalie but elsewhere on the island. However, the town does offer the best options for budget travelers.

If you're in a villa, an apartment, or a condo rental, patronize the **Pueblo supermarkets.** You'll find them across from the Havensight Mall (where the cruise ships dock), at the Sub Base, and also at the Lockhart Gardens and Four Winds shopping centers.

IN CHARLOTTE AMALIE

Bumpa's AMERICAN   This open-air deli joint is on the second level of a little old West Indian house with a canvas-roof porch that offers a panoramic harbor view. It isn't that special, but it is an ideal choice for a filling, low-priced breakfast or lunch. The shopping hordes find this a favorite refueling stop. The cook prepares a fresh soup for lunch, and you can also get sandwiches and freshly made salads. Many patrons stop in just to order Ben & Jerry's ice cream, one of the homemade pies, or a refreshing lemonade on a hot day.

38-A Waterfront. ✆ **340/776-5674.** Main courses $5.50–$7.50. No credit cards. Daily 7am–5pm. Closed Sept.

Diamond Barrel AMERICAN/WEST INDIAN   This popular local eatery and hangout is active throughout the day. The decor (what there is of it) is appropriately nautical, with rattan pieces and murals of sealife. Breakfast is fairly standard, but at lunch you can sample good regional fare like the catch of the day and various chicken dishes. You might begin with the oxtail soup or whatever's in the kettle that day. If you want to go really local, opt for the stewed mutton or pickled pigs' feet, although you might settle more happily for the salmon patties. On site is a bakery providing fresh pastries and other baked goods. Expect cafeteria-style service with simple tables where you can eat your meal.

18 Norre Gade. (C) 340/774-5071. Main courses $7–$13; lunch $6–$12; breakfast $3–$8. No credit cards. Daily 6am–5pm.

Gladys's Café ✦ WEST INDIAN/AMERICAN

Antigua-born Gladys Isles is a warm and gracious host. She worked at the Palm Passage for years as a waitress, but when she developed a following that demanded so much of her time, she decided to open her own place. Her cafe is housed in a 1700 pump house with a stonework courtyard that has a well (one of only three on the island) in the middle. Considering the portions, quality, and price, her breakfast is the best value in town. The lunch offerings are various sandwiches, salads, and fresh seafood, like excellent swordfish and dumplings. The house specialty is hot chicken salad made with pieces of sautéed white meat with red-wine vinegar, pine nuts, and dill weed, all nestled on a bed of lettuce. Dinner is served only on Friday, when a popular jazz band plays. Try a local lobster, pasta, fresh fish, or perfect steaks.

Royal Dane Mall. (C) 340/774-6604. Reservations required for parties of 4 or more. Main courses $7–$15; breakfast $3.50–$7. AE, MC, V. Mon–Thurs and Sat 6:30am–4pm; Fri 7am–11pm; Sun 7am–5pm.

The Green House AMERICAN/CARIBBEAN

Fronted with big sunny windows, this waterfront restaurant attracts cruise ship passengers who've shopped and need a place to drop. The food isn't the island's best but is satisfying if you're not too demanding. Many diners drop in during the afternoon to sample one of the tasty omelets, especially the Caribbean Creole three-egg concoction. The house specializes in chicken, often with exotic fruit flavors like mango-banana chicken and coconut chicken. Appetizers are often good enough to make a meal by themselves, ranging from conch fritters to stuffed jalapeño peppers. A kettle of soup is always on the stove. You can also make a meal of the fresh salads, perhaps Jamaican jerk chicken or pasta salad primavera. What's most popular on the menu? The big, juicy burgers made with Angus beef. There's also a wide selection of seafood and chef's specialties like slow-roasted and wood-smoked baby-back ribs. On Wednesday and Friday you can hear live reggae music; on other nights, it's the sounds selected by a DJ.

Veterans Dr. (C) 340/774-7998. Main courses $12–$25; omelets $6–$8. AE, DISC, MC, V. Daily 11am–10am.

Hard Rock Cafe AMERICAN

Occupying the second floor of a pink-sided mall whose big windows overlook the ships moored in the harbor, this restaurant is a member of the international chain that defines itself as the Smithsonian of Rock 'n' Roll. Entire walls are devoted to the memorabilia of John Lennon, Eric Clapton, Bob Marley, and others. Throughout most of the day the place functions as a restaurant, serving barbecued meats, salads, sandwiches, burgers (including a well-flavored veggie burger), fresh fish, steaks, and the best fajitas in the Virgin Islands. On Friday and Saturday a live band performs, at which time a small dance floor gets busy and the bar trade picks up considerably.

In International Plaza, the Waterfront. (C) 340/777-5555. Main courses $9–$20. AE, DC, DISC, MC, V. Mon–Sat 11am–11pm; Sun 11am–9pm.

Little Bopeep CARIBBEAN

This little tavern serves some of the best West Indian food on the island. The menu changes daily, and no one puts on any airs. Lunch is the only meal served, and it's likely to be intriguing and spicy. Try the jerk chicken (a secret recipe), curried chicken, or curried conch. Fried plantains accompany most dishes.

Barberl Plaza. ℂ **340/774-1959.** Main courses $5–$13. No credit cards. Mon–Sat 7:30–11am (takeout only) and 11:30am–4pm.

Tickles Dockside Pub AMERICAN   Tickles is dedicated to the concept of comfort and reasonably priced food in a friendly atmosphere. Diners at this open-air restaurant can relax while watching the sailboats and cruise ships on the water. The menu offers a simple American fare of burgers (like a chicken burger) and sandwiches (like a Reuben made with your choice of ham, turkey, or corned beef, grilled with Tickles's special Russian dressing, Swiss cheese, and sauerkraut). Start with a plate of "gator eggs" (lightly breaded jalapeño peppers stuffed with cheese) or the "sweet lips" (strips of sweet fried chicken in the shape of lips with honey-mustard sauce). If you're in the mood for seafood, you might want to try the fish-and-chips, beer-battered white fish fried and served with Swiss-fried potatoes. Vegetarians delight in the burger made just for them, and the cooks also turn out an array of American classics like chicken Alfredo, prime ribs, baby-back ribs, and fried catfish.

Crown Bay Marina. ℂ **340/776-1595.** Main courses $9–$23; lunch $7–$12. AE, DC, MC, V. Daily 7am–10:30pm.

WORTH A SPLURGE

Randy's Wine Bar & Bistro ✯ CONTINENTAL   This is an oddity, catering to deli devotees (usually from New York), cigar aficionados, and bistro fans. As one local customer, who goes here every day, said to us, "It's anything you want it to be." The store sells a good selection of wines, along with the standard liquors and cigars. If you don't like the bistro wine list, you can buy a bottle of wine from the store and bring it into the bistro, but you'll pay a $5 corkage fee. The deli serves the usual sandwiches and salads, while the bistro dishes up a delectable cuisine, especially if you stick to the fresh fish, steak, and lobster. Look for the daily specials, like pork tenderloin in Dijon mustard sauce. At lunch you might want to try the portobello mushroom sandwich marinated in balsamic vinegar with basil mayonnaise, or the Carnegie Reuben with half a pound of meat. For dinner, shrimp scampi is always a favorite. Tuesday night brings out locals eager to sample the prime rib.

In Al Cohen's Plaza, 4002 Raphune Hill. ℂ **340/775-5001.** Main courses $14–$35; lunch $7–$14. AE, MC, V. Bistro, daily 10am–1am; deli, daily 9am–5pm.

Zorba's Cafe GREEK   If you're in the mood for Greek food, head here. Jimmy Boukas is the owner of this casual place in a 19th-century building at the heart of town. Guests can sit in the courtyard surrounded by banana and palm trees. We highly recommend the *spanikopita* (spinach-and-feta pie), the *moussaka* (eggplant casserole), and the gyros, but be sure to save room for the homemade baklava. On our recent rounds, we found the tastiest treats to be the Greek lemon chicken and the perfectly seasoned tender Greek-style lamb shanks.

1854 Hus, Government Hill. ℂ **340/776-0444.** Main courses $15–$25; lunch $8–$15. AE, MC, V. Mon–Sat 11am–3:30pm and 6–10pm; Sun 6–10pm.

AT FRENCHTOWN

Between the harbor and the airport on the outskirts of Charlotte Amalie, you'll find the **Frenchtown Deli,** in the Frenchtown Mall (ℂ **340/776-7211**). Home-baked breads, fresh salads, and beer, soda, and wine are sold. Some of the island's best and thickest sandwiches are served here, and their Green Mountain coffee is the best. Full-service breakfasts begin at $3.50, with lunches starting at $4.

Most dinners are $15, and that's for two, making this *the* bargain of St. Thomas. You can eat your dinner on the premises or take it out. Hours are Monday to Friday 6am to 8pm, Saturday 7am to 6pm, and Sunday 8am to 4pm. It's a good place to stock up on supplies if you've rented a place with a kitchenette or would like the makings of a picnic.

Hook, Line & Sinker AMERICAN   Both locals and visitors flock to this rendezvous, where they get friendly service, good food at reasonable prices, and a panoramic harbor view. The setting evokes a New England seaport village, and the restaurant has a pitched roof and skylights, along with wraparound French doors and windows. A "Cheers"-like crowd frequents the bar. Breakfast, except for Sunday brunch, is the standard old menu, but at lunch you can try everything from Caesar salad to various grilled chicken dishes. The dinner menu is usually a delight. The new chef devotes more time to preparing seafood than previous cooks did here—wait until you sample his mango-rum tuna, Jamaica-inspired jerk swordfish, or yellowtail in banana curry sauce or stuffed with mushrooms and red peppers and covered in garlic sauce. Locals call his soups outrageous: They're more like hearty stews, as exemplified by the sausage-and-potato combo.

2 Honduras, Frenchtown. ℭ **340/776-9708.** Main courses $9–$25; lunch $6–$10; Sun brunch $8–$14. AE, MC, V. Mon–Fri 11:30am–4pm and 6–10pm; Sat 8–10:30am, 11:30am–4pm, and 6–10pm; Sun 10am–2:30pm.

IN RED HOOK

Duffy's Love Shack ☆ *Finds* AMERICAN/CARIBBEAN   This is a fun and happening place where you can mingle with the locals. As the evening wears on, the customers become the entertainment, often dancing on tables and forming conga lines. Yes, Duffy's also serves food, standard American cuisine with Caribbean flair and flavor. The restaurant is open-air, with lots of bamboo and a thatched roof over the bar. Even the menu appears on a bamboo stick, like an old-fashioned fan. Start with a Caribbean egg roll or black-bean cakes, then move on to cowboy steak or voodoo pineapple chicken (in a hot garlic-and-pineapple sauce). Surf-and-turf here means jerk tenderloin and mahimahi (dolphin). After 10pm, a late-night menu appears, mostly sandwiches. The bar business is huge, and the bartender is known for his lethal rum drinks.

6500 Red Hook Plaza, Rte. 38. ℭ **340/779-2080.** Main courses $9–$16. No credit cards. Daily 11:30am–2am.

Fungi's on the Beach CARIBBEAN   Opening onto Pineapple Beach, this is a funky native bar. It's a lot of fun, and the food is good, too. Come here for some of the juiciest burgers on the island and the most delectable tasting pizza. You can also order Caribbean specialties, such as conch in butter sauce and roast suckling pig, along with such island favorites as johnnycakes, plantains, rice and beans, and *callaloo* soup. Stewed chicken is a local favorite. The place has an outdoorsy atmosphere with a reggae theme. Nightly entertainment—reggae and more reggae—is also a feature.

Point Pleasant. ℭ **340/775-4145.** Main courses $7–$20. AE, MC, V. Daily 11:30am–10pm.

Polli's Tillet Gardens TEX-MEX   The setting for this likable restaurant is an open garden-style pavilion near a splashing fountain and adjacent to a collection of arts and crafts boutiques. Named and modeled after a similar restaurant in Hawaii, it features a roster of frozen margaritas and especially a golden margarita (with Cuervo Gold and Galliano liqueur; $5 each) that seems tailor-made to precede a Tex-Mex meal. Menu items are among the most savory and flavorful Mexican food on St. Thomas. Examples are fajitas (made with your choice of beef, chicken, seafood, or tofu), burritos supreme, seafood enchilada platters, fajita quesadillas, and some of the best-priced and juiciest steaks on the island. Children's plates, including tacos and cheese quesadillas or enchiladas, are also dished up.

4125 Anna's Retreat, Rte. 38, midway between Red Hook and Charlotte Amalie. (C) **340/775-4550.** Lunch main courses $6–$14; dinner main courses $8–$17. AE, DC, MC, V. Mon–Thurs 11:30am–9:30pm; Fri–Sat 11:30am–10:30pm.

Wok & Roll CHINESE   Across from the dock for the St. John ferry, this small Chinese restaurant (below the Warehouse Bar) is housed in a cinder-block building with a blue roof. A patio seats about 25 people, but the majority of the business is takeout. The restaurant serves typical Asian dishes like chow mein and sweet-and-sour pork, along with specials like Shanghai spring rolls, shrimp in lobster sauce, and Hong Kong lo mein. The famous dish here is the crab rangoon. Newly added to the menu is calamari in black bean sauce.

6200 Smith Bay. (C) **340/775-6246.** Main courses $5.50–$12. No credit cards. Mon–Thurs 11am–10pm; Fri–Sat 11am–10:30pm; Sun 5–10pm.

AT BOLONGO & COWPET BAYS

Iggie's Restaurant AMERICAN/CONTINENTAL   Sports fans and others patronize this action-packed seaside place—with giant TVs broadcasting the latest games—it's the island's best sports bar and grill. To make things even livelier, karaoke singalongs are staged. The place has indestructible furniture, lots of electronic action, and an aggressively informal crowd. Bring the kids along; no one will mind if they make a ruckus. The menu is geared to such kid favorites as burgers, oversized sandwiches, and pastas. It changes nightly, and often there's a theme name, such as "lobster night" or "Italian night." Most popular is "carnival night," when a West Indian all-you-can-eat buffet is served along with a limbo show. You can call to find out what the special theme nights are. Try one of the sudsy tropical drinks, like Iggie's Queen (coconut cream, crème de Noya, and rum), or the Ultimate Kamikazi, the ingredients of which are a secret.

At the Bolongo Bay Beach Club, Bolongo Bay, 50 Estate Bolongo (Rte. 30). (C) **340/775-1800.** Burgers and sandwiches $8–$10; main courses $11–$25. AE, MC, V. Daily 11:30am–11pm.

Jerry's Beachfront Bar & Restaurant ITALIAN/SEAFOOD   This is a refreshing waterside spot for a meal near the East End. The decor includes lots of exposed, much-weathered wood, a color scheme of blue and white, and a large bar where nobody seems to mind dallying a bit before a table becomes available. The owners—veterans and survivors of several other popular waterfront eateries around the island—are proud of such lunch specialties as seafood bisque, soup of the day, Parmesan sandwiches, hoagies, meatball heros, and Caesar salads. Evening meals are more elaborate and, in most cases, more leisurely. Look for well-prepared dishes like shrimp Sambuca, pasta bayou (with andouille sausages, shrimp, and smoked Gouda in creamy pink sauce), barbecued babyback ribs, shrimp scampi, and both red and white versions of conch and scampi. Naturally, the drinks are potent enough to encourage you to linger.

In the Anchorage Condos (next to the St. Thomas Yacht Club), Cowpet Bay. (C) **340/779-2462.** Reservations recommended in winter. Main courses $8–$15; set-price menu $22. AE, MC, V. Daily 10am–10pm; Sun brunch 11am–3pm.

ON THE NORTH COAST

Texas Pit BBQ BARBECUE The owners hail from Texas, where they know not only how to barbecue but how to make a fiery sauce to wake up your palate . . . and everything else. This is just a takeaway stand, with no place to sit and eat, but locals flock here. It's been around for nearly 2 decades, and in spite of hurricanes is still going strong. Chicken, tender ribs, and Texas-style beef are dished up in cowboy-size portions, along with the usual accompaniments of rice, coleslaw, and potato salad. One local pronounced the ribs here the island's best, but we're still sampling other places before giving a final verdict.

Sub Base. ℭ 340/776-9579. Main courses $7–$12; combination platters $13–$17. No credit cards. Mon–Sat 5–11pm.

NEAR MAFOLIE HILL

Sibs Mountain Bar & Restaurant AMERICAN Older residents of St. Thomas remember this place as a social fixture that was called Sibilly's Bar when it was first built of concrete and wood in 1927. In recent times, it received an update from new owners who added another dining area in back, hooked up some of the biggest TV screens on the island, and shortened its name to Sibs. Today, it combines an ongoing presentation of sports events with pool tables and electronic bar games. No one will mind if you stay in the front bar, soaking up the sweaty athleticism of the place, but if you're hungry, head for the rear dining room, which offers a terrace and views that sweep out over Charlotte Amalie. Menu items are generously proportioned and well seasoned and include burgers, some of the best ribs in St. Thomas, pastas, pizzas, and fresh fish.

Mafolie Hill. ℭ 340/774-8967. Main courses $8–$25. AE, MC, V. Daily 5–10pm; bar daily 4pm–4am.

PICNIC FARE & WHERE TO EAT IT

You can create a successful picnic with the culinary expertise of the **Cream and Crumb Shop,** Building 6, Havensight Mall (ℭ **340/774-2499**), open daily 6:30am to 5pm. Located at the point where most cruise ships dock for day excursions onto St. Thomas, this cheerful modern shop is easy to miss amid the crush of tax-free jewelers and perfume shops. The thick deli sandwiches ($4.50 to $7.50), fresh salads (shrimp, chicken, potato, or crabmeat), and homemade pastries are all excellent. The shop also specializes in pizza and serves frozen yogurt and ice cream—these might not be the most practical picnic items, but they're still awfully good. With these ingredients, you can head for your favorite beach. We recommend **Magens Bay,** not just for its beauty, but for its picnic tables, too. Other ideal spots are **Drake's Seat** or any of the secluded **high-altitude panoramas** along the island's western end.

HITTING THE BEACHES

Chances are, your hotel will be right on the beach, or very close to one. All the beaches in the Virgin Islands are public, and most lie anywhere from 2 to 5 miles from Charlotte Amalie.

THE NORTH SIDE The gorgeous white sands of **Magens Bay** lie between two mountains 3 miles north of the capital. *Condé Nast Traveler* named this beach one of the world's 10 most beautiful. The turquoise waters here are calm and ideal for swimming, although the snorkeling isn't as good. The beach is no secret, and it's usually terribly overcrowded, but it gets better in the midafternoon. Changing facilities, snorkeling gear, lounge chairs, paddleboats, and kayaks are available. There is no public transportation to get here (although some hotels provide shuttle buses); from Charlotte Amalie, take Route 35 north all the way. The gates to the beach are open daily 6am to 6pm (after 4pm, you'll need insect repellent). Admission is $1 per person and $1 per car. Don't bring valuables and certainly don't leave anything of value in your parked car.

A marked trail leads to **Little Magens Bay,** a separate clothing-optional beach (especially popular with gay and lesbian visitors). This is also former president Clinton's preferred beach on St. Thomas (no, he doesn't go nude).

Coki Point Beach, in the northeast near Coral World, is good but often very crowded. It's noted for its warm, crystal-clear water, ideal for swimming and snorkeling (you'll see thousands of rainbow-hued fish swimming among the beautiful corals). Locals even sell small bags of fish food, so you can feed the sea creatures while you're snorkeling. From the beach, there's a panoramic view of offshore Thatch Cay. Concessions can arrange everything from water-skiing to parasailing. An East End bus runs to Smith Bay and lets you off at the gate to Coral World and Coki. Watch out for pickpockets.

Also on the north side is luscious **Renaissance Grand Beach,** one of the island's most beautiful. It opens onto Smith Bay and is near Coral World. Many watersports are available here. The beach is right off Route 38.

THE EAST END   Small and special, **Secret Harbour** is near a collection of condos. With its white sand and coconut palms, it's the epitome of Caribbean charm. The snorkeling near the rocks is some of the best on the island. No public transportation stops here, but it's an easy taxi ride east of Charlotte Amalie heading toward Red Hook.

Sapphire Beach is set against the backdrop of the Sapphire Beach Resort and Marina, where you can have lunch or order drinks. There are good views of offshore cays and St. John, a large reef is close to the shore, and windsurfers like this beach a lot. Snorkeling gear and lounge chairs can be rented. Take the East End bus from Charlotte Amalie, going via Red Hook. Ask to be let off at the entrance to Sapphire Bay; it's not too far to walk from here to the water.

White-sand **Lindquist Beach** isn't a long strip, but it's one of the island's prettiest. It's between Wyndham Sugar Bay Beach Club and the Sapphire Beach Resort. Many films and TV commercials have used this photogenic beach as a backdrop. It's not likely to be crowded, as it's not very well known.

THE SOUTH SIDE   **Morning Star** (also known as Frenchman's Bay Beach) is near the Marriott Frenchman's Reef Beach Resort, about 2 miles east of Charlotte Amalie. Here, among the often young crowds (many of whom are gay), you can don your skimpiest bikini. Sailboats, snorkeling equipment, and lounge chairs are available for rent. The beach is easily reached by a cliff-front elevator at Frenchman's Reef.

Limetree Beach, set against a backdrop of sea-grape trees and shady palms, lures those who want a serene spread of sand where they can bask in the sun and even feed hibiscus blossoms to iguanas. Snorkeling gear, lounge and beach chairs, towels, and drinks are available. There's no public transportation, but the beach can easily be reached by taxi from Charlotte Amalie.

WEST OF CHARLOTTE AMALIE   Near the University of the Virgin Islands in the southwest, **Brewer's Bay** is one of the island's most popular beaches. The strip of white coral sand is almost as long as the beach at Magens Bay. Unfortunately, this isn't the place for snorkeling. Vendors sell light meals and drinks. From Charlotte Amalie, take the Fortuna bus heading west; get off at the edge of Brewers Bay, across from the Reichhold Center.

> **_Finds_ Secret Beaches**
>
> At this point you'd think all the beaches of overrun St. Thomas had been destroyed, but there are two less-trampled strands of sand we recently came upon. A sparkling beach of white sand, **Vessup Bay Beach,** is found at the end of Bluebeard's Road (Route 322) as it branches off Route 30 near the hamlet of Red Hook. Against a rocky backdrop, the beach curves around a pristine bay studded with vegetation, including cacti, agave plants, and sea grape. One end of the beach is less populated than the other. A watersports concessionaire operates here. Another find is **Hull Bay,** on the north shore, just west of Magens Bay, which is overpopulated these days with cruise ship passengers. Surfers are attracted to the waves along the western tip of Hull Bay, and in the more tranquil strands, local St. Thomas fishermen anchor. Part of the beach is in shade. Don't expect much in watersports, but there is a combined restaurant and open-air bar.

Lindbergh Beach, with a lifeguard, restrooms, and a bathhouse, lies at the Island Beachcomber Hotel and is used extensively by locals, who sometimes stage political rallies here as well as Carnival parties. It's not good for snorkeling. Drinks are served on the beach. Take the Fortuna bus route west from Charlotte Amalie.

SPORTS & OTHER OUTDOOR PURSUITS

DEEP-SEA FISHING   The U.S. Virgins have excellent deep-sea fishing; some 19 world records (8 for blue marlin) have been set in these waters in recent years. Outfitters abound at the major marinas like Red Hook. We recommend angling off the *Fish Hawk* (© 340/775-9058), which Captin Al Petrosky sails out of Fish Hawk Marina Lagoon on the East End. The 43-foot diesel-powered craft is fully equipped with rods and reels. All equipment (but not meals) is included in the price: $500 per half day for up to six passengers. Full-day excursions start at $950.

FITNESS CENTERS   The most reasonably priced club on the island is the **Bayside Fitness Center,** 7140 Bolongo (© 340/693-2600), part of the Bolongo Beach complex. The club offers weights, cardio machines, treadmills, and a sauna. The cost of a day pass is $12 for nonresidents; it's free to guests of the Bolongo complex. Hours are Monday to Friday 6am to 9pm and Saturday and Sunday 8am to 5pm.

HORSE & PONY TOURS   Half Moon Stables (© 340/777-6088) offers horse and pony tours of the East End. A secluded trail winds through lush, green hills to a pebble-covered beach. These hour-long guided tours are a great way to explore areas of the island rarely seen from tour buses or rental cars. The cost is $55 per person per hour. Western and English saddles are available.

KAYAK TOURS   Virgin Island Ecotours (© 340/779-2155 for information) offers 2½-hour kayak trips through a mangrove lagoon on the southern coastline. The cost is $50 per person. The tour is led by professional naturalists who allow enough time for 30 minutes of snorkeling.

SAILING   On St. Thomas, most of the boat business centers on the Red Hook and Yacht Haven marinas.

The 50-foot *Yacht Nightwind,* Sapphire Marina (© **340/775-4110,** 24 hours a day), offers full-day sails to St. John and the outer islands. The $100 price includes continental breakfast, champagne buffet lunch, and an open bar aboard. You're also given free snorkeling equipment and instruction.

New Horizons, 6501 Red Hook Plaza, Suite 16, Red Hook (© **340/775-1171**), offers wind-borne excursions amid the cays and reefs of the Virgin Islands. The two-masted, 63-foot ketch has circumnavigated the globe and has been used as a design prototype for other boats. Owned and operated by Canadian Tim Krygsveld, it contains a hot-water shower, serves a specialty drink called a New Horizons Nooner (with a melon-liqueur base), and carries a complete line of snorkeling equipment for adults and children. A full-day excursion, with an Italian buffet lunch and an open bar, costs $100 per person. Children 2 to 12, when accompanied by an adult, pay $55. Excursions depart daily, weather permitting, from the Sapphire Beach Resort & Marina. Call for reservations and information.

New Horizons has another vessel, **New Horizons II,** a 44-foot custom-made speedboat that takes you on a full-day trip to some of the most scenic highlights of the British Virgin Islands, costing $115 for adults or $95 for children 2 to 12.

You can avoid the crowds by sailing aboard the **Fantasy,** 6700 Sapphire Village, no. 253 (© **340/775-5652;** fax 340/775-6256), which departs from the American Yacht Harbor at Red Hook at 9:30am daily. It takes a maximum of six passengers to St. John and nearby islands for swimming, snorkeling, beachcombing, and trolling. Snorkel gear with expert instruction is provided, as is a champagne lunch; an underwater camera is available. The full-day trip costs $100 per person. A half-day sail, morning or afternoon, lasts 3 hours and costs $65. Sunset tours are also popular, with an open bar and hors d'oeuvres, costing $50 per person.

American Yacht Harbor ★★, Red Hook (© **800/736-7294** in the U.S., or 340/775-6454), offers both bare-boat and fully crewed charters. It leaves from a colorful yacht-filled harbor set against a backdrop of heritage Gade, a reproduction of a Caribbean village. The harbor is home to sailing charters. There are also four restaurants on the property, serving everything from continental to Caribbean cuisine.

Finds Into the Deep

If you really want to get to the bottom of it all, board the air-conditioned *Atlantis* submarine, which takes you on a 1-hour voyage (the whole experience is really 2 hours, when you include transportation to and from the sub) to depths of 90 feet, where an amazing world of exotic marine life unfolds. You'll have up-close views of coral reefs and sponge gardens through the sub's 2-foot windows. *Atlantis* divers swim with the fish and bring them close to the windows for photos.

Passengers take a surface boat from the West Indies Dock, right outside Charlotte Amalie, to the submarine, which is near Buck Island (the St. Thomas version, not the more famous Buck Island near St. Croix). The fare is $72 for adults, $36 for ages 4 to 17; children 3 and under are not allowed. The *Atlantis* operates daily November through April, Tuesday through Saturday May through October. Reservations are a must (the sub carries only 30 passengers). For tickets, go to the Havensight shopping mall, building 6, or call © **340/776-5650.**

Another reliable outfitter is **Charteryacht League** 🦈🦈, at Flagship (© **800/ 524-2061** in the U.S., or 340/774-3944).

Sailors might want to check out the *Yachtsman's Guide to the Virgin Islands,* available at major marine outlets, at bookstores, through catalog merchandisers, or directly from **Tropic Isle Publishers,** P.O. Box 610938, North Miami, FL 33261-0938 (© **305/893-4277**). This annual guide, which costs $16, is supplemented by sketch charts, photographs, and landfall sketches and charts showing harbors and harbor entrances, anchorages, channels, and landmarks, plus information on preparations necessary for cruising the islands.

SCUBA DIVING & SNORKELING 🦈🦈   With 30 spectacular reefs just off St. Thomas, the U.S. Virgin Islands have been rated one of the most beautiful areas in the world for scuba diving snorkeling by *Skin Diver* magazine. For **snorkeling,** we like the waters off **Coki Point,** on the northeast shore of St. Thomas; especially enticing are the coral ledges near Coral World's underwater tower. **Magens Bay** 🦈🦈 also has great snorkeling year-round. For information on snorkeling cruises, see "Sailing," above.

The best dive site off St. Thomas, especially for novices, has to be **Cow and Calf Rocks,** off the southeast end (45 minutes from Charlotte Amalie by boat); here you'll discover a network of coral tunnels riddled with caves, reefs, and ancient boulders encrusted with coral. The *Cartanser Sr.,* a sunken World War II cargo ship that lies in about 35 feet of water, is beautifully encrusted with coral and now home to a myriad of colorful resident fish. Another popular wreck dive is the *Maj. General Rogers,* the stripped-down hull of a former Coast Guard cutter.

Experienced divers might want to dive at exposed sheer rock pinnacles like **Sail Rock** and **French Cap Pinnacle,** which are encrusted with hard and soft corals and frequented by lobsters and green and hawksbill turtles. They are also exposed to open-ocean currents that can make these very challenging dives.

St. Thomas Diving Club, 7147 Bolongo Bay (© **877/LETSDIVE** or 340/ 776-2381), is a full-service, PADI five-star IDC center, the best on the island. An open-water certification course, including four scuba dives, costs $385. An advanced open-water certification course, including five dives that can be accomplished in 2 days, goes for $275. Every Thursday, participants are taken on an all-day scuba excursion that includes a two-tank dive to the wreck of the **HMS *Rhone*** in the British Virgin Islands; the trip costs $125. A scuba tour of the 350-foot wreck of the *Witshoal* is offered every Saturday for experienced divers only; the cost is $95. You can also enjoy local snorkeling for $35.

DIVE IN!, in the Sapphire Beach Resort & Marina, Smith Bay Road, Route 36 (© **800/524-2090** or 340/775-6100), is a well-recommended, complete diving center that offers some of the finest services in the U.S. Virgin Islands, including professional instruction (beginner to advanced), daily beach and boat dives, custom dive packages, underwater photography and videotapes, snorkeling trips, and a full-service PADI dive center. An introductory course costs $65, with a one-tank dive going for $62, two-tank dives for $75. A six-dive pass costs $203.

TENNIS   The best tennis on the island is at the **Wyndham Sugar Bay Beach Club** 🦈🦈, 6500 Estate Smith Bay (© **340/777-7100**), which has the first stadium tennis court in the Virgin Islands, seating 220. Six additional Laykold courts are lit at night, and there's also a pro shop. The cost is $8 an hour for nonguests.

Another good resort for tennis is the **Bolongo Bay Beach Resort,** Bolongo Bay (ⓒ **340/775-1800**), which has two courts lit until 10pm. They're free to members and hotel guests, but cost $10 for nonguests.

Marriott Frenchman's Reef Tennis Courts, Flamboyant Point (ⓒ **340/ 776-8500,** ext. 444), has four courts. Again, nonguests are charged $8 per hour per court. Lights stay on until 10pm.

WINDSURFING   Windsurfing is available through the major resorts and at some public beaches, including Brewer's Bay, Morning Star Beach, and Limetree Beach. The **Renaissance Grand Beach Resort,** Smith Bay Road, Route 38 (ⓒ **340/775-1510**), is the major hotel offering windsurfing. It's available only to guests with no charge. You might want to stay here if you plan to do a lot of windsurfing.

SEEING THE SIGHTS
CHARLOTTE AMALIE ✦
The capital of St. Thomas, Charlotte Amalie, where most visitors begin their sightseeing on this small island, has all the color and charm of an authentic Caribbean waterfront town. In days of yore, seafarers from all over the globe flocked to this old-world Danish town, as did pirates and members of the Confederacy, who used the port during the American Civil War. (Sadly, St. Thomas was the biggest slave market in the world.)

The old warehouses once used for storing pirate goods still stand and, for the most part, house today's shops. In fact, the main streets (called *Gade,* because of the islands' Danish heritage) have virtually become a shopping mall and usually packed. (See "Shopping," below, for our specific recommendations.) Sandwiched among these shops are a few historic buildings, most of which can be covered on foot in about 2 hours.

Before starting your tour, stop off in the so-called **Grand Hotel,** near Emancipation Park. No longer a hotel, it contains, along with shops, a **visitor center,** Tolbod Gade 1 (ⓒ **340/774-8784**), that's open Monday to Friday 8am to 5pm and Saturday 8am to noon.

Fort Christian   This imposing structure, which dates from 1672, dominates the center of town. It was named after the Danish king, Christian V, and has been everything from a fort to a governor's residence to a jail. It became a national historic landmark in 1977, but still functioned as a police station, court, and jail until 1983. Now a museum, the fort houses displays on the island's history and culture. Cultural workshops and turn-of-the-century furnishings are just some of the exhibits. A museum shop features local crafts, maps, and prints.

In the town center. ⓒ 340/776-4566. Free admission. Mon–Fri 9:30am–4:30pm.

Seven Arches Museum   Browsers love checking out the private home of longtime residents Philibert Fluck and Barbara Demaras. This is an 18th-century Danish house, completely restored to its original condition and furnished with West Indian antiques. You can walk through the yellow ballast arches and visit the great room, with its wonderful view of the busiest harbor in the Caribbean. Night-blooming cacti and iguanas are on the roof of the slave quarters. The admission includes a cold tropical drink served in a walled garden filled with flowers.

Government Hill. ⓒ 340/774-9295. Admission $5. Daily 10am–4pm or by appointment.

Synagogue of Beracha Veshalom Vegmiluth Hasidim ✦   This is the oldest synagogue in continuous use under the American flag and the second oldest in the western hemisphere. It was erected in 1833 by Sephardic Jews, and still maintains the tradition of having sand on the floor, commemorating the exodus from Egypt. The structure was built of local stone, along with ballast brick from Denmark and mortar made of molasses and sand.

Next door, the **Weibel Museum** showcases 300 years of Jewish history. It keeps the same hours as the synagogue.

15 Crystal Gade. ✆ **340/774-4312.** Free admission. Mon–Fri 9am–4pm.

ELSEWHERE ON THE ISLAND

Route 30 (Veterans Drive) will take you west of Charlotte Amalie to **Frenchtown.** (Turn left at the sign to the Admiral's Inn.) Early French-speaking settlers arrived on St. Thomas from St. Bart's after they were uprooted by the Swedes. Many island residents today are the direct descendants of those long-ago immigrants, who were known for speaking a distinctive French patois. This colorful village contains a number of restaurants and taverns. Because Charlotte Amalie has become somewhat dangerous at night, Frenchtown has picked up its after-dark business and is the best spot for dancing, drinking, and other local entertainment.

Coral World Marine Park & Underwater Observatory ✦
This marine complex features a three-story underwater observation tower 100 feet offshore. Inside, you'll see sponges, fish, coral, and other aquatic creatures in their natural state. An 80,000-gallon reef tank features exotic marine life of the Caribbean; another tank is devoted to sea predators, with circling sharks and giant moray eels. Activities include daily fish and shark feedings and exotic bird shows. The latest addition to the park is a semisubmarine that lets you enjoy the panoramic view and the "down under" feeling of a submarine without truly submerging.

Coral World's guests can take advantage of adjacent **Coki Beach** for snorkel rentals, scuba lessons, or simply swimming and relaxing. Lockers and showers are available. Also included in the marine park are the Tropical Terrace Restaurant, duty-free shops, and a nature trail.

6450 Coki Point, a 20-min. drive from Charlotte Amalie off Rte. 38. ✆ **340/775-1555.** Admission $18 adults, $9 children 3–12. Daily 9am–5pm.

Estate St. Peter Greathouse Botanical Gardens ✦
This estate consists of 11 acres set at the foot of volcanic peaks on the northern rim of the island. The grounds are laced with self-guided nature walks that will acquaint you with some 200 varieties of West Indian plants and trees, including an umbrella plant from Madagascar. From a panoramic deck in the gardens, you can see some 20 of the Virgin Islands, including Hans Lollick, an uninhabited island between Thatched Cay and Madahl Point. The house itself, filled with local art, is worth a visit.

At the corner of Rte. 40 (6A St. Peter Mountain Rd.) and Barrett Hill Rd. ✆ **340/774-4999.** Admission $8 adults, $2 children 4–12 years. Daily 9am–4pm.

Paradise Point Tramway
This contraption affords visitors a dramatic view of Charlotte Amalie harbor, with a ride to a 697-foot peak. The tramway, similar to those used at ski resorts, operates four cars, each with a 10-person capacity, for the 15-minute round-trip ride. It transports customers from the Havensight area to Paradise Point, where they can disembark to visit shops and the popular restaurant and bar.

Departure Point Route 30 at Havensight. ✆ **340/774-9809.** Round-trip $12 adults, $6 children 6–12 years. Daily 9am–5pm.

Fun Fact **Into the Deep for Nondivers**

Nondivers can get some of the thrill long known to scuba aficionados by participating in **Sea Trek at the Coral World Marine Park & Underwater Observatory.** For $68 you can get a full immersion undersea with no experience needed. Participants are given a helmet and a tube to breathe through. The tube is attached to an air source at the observatory tower. You then enjoy a 200-yard, 20-minute stroll in water 18 feet deep. You're on the sea floor taking in the rainbow-hued tropical fish and the coral reefs as you go along. It's a marvelous way to get to experience the world as seen from the eyes of a fish.

SHOPPING ★★★

The discounted, duty-free shopping in the Virgin Islands makes St. Thomas a shopping mecca. It's possible to find well-known brand names here at savings of up to 60% off mainland U.S. prices. *But be warned:* Savings are not always so good. Before you leave home, check prices in your local stores if you think you might want to make a major purchase, so you can be sure that you are in fact getting a good deal. Having sounded that warning, we'll mention some St. Thomas shops where we have found really good buys.

The best buys here include china, crystal, perfume, jewelry (especially emeralds), Haitian art, fashion, watches, and items made of wood. Cameras and electronic items, based on our experience, are not the good buys they're reputed to be. St. Thomas is also the best place in the Caribbean for discounts on porcelain, but remember that U.S. brands can often be purchased for 25% off the retail price on the U.S. mainland. Look for the imported patterns for the biggest savings.

Most shops, some of which occupy former pirate warehouses, are open Monday to Saturday 9am to 5pm. Some stores open Sunday and holidays if a cruise ship is in port. *Note:* Friday is the biggest cruise ship day at Charlotte Amalie (we once counted eight ships in port at once), so try to avoid shopping then—it's a zoo.

Nearly all the major shopping on St. Thomas is along the harbor of Charlotte Amalie. Cruise ship passengers mainly shop at the **Havensight Mall,** where they disembark at the eastern edge of Charlotte Amalie. The principal shopping street is **Main Street** or **Dronningens Gade** (its old Danish name). North of this street is another merchandise-loaded street called **Back Street** or **Vimmelskaft.**

Many shops are also spread along the **Waterfront Highway** (also called **Kyst Vejen**). Between these major streets or boulevards are a series of side streets, walkways, and alleys, all filled with shops. Major shopping streets are **Tolbod Gade, Raadets Gade, Royal Dane Mall, Palm Passage, Storervaer Gade,** and **Strand Gade.**

All the major stores on St. Thomas are located by number on an excellent map in the publication *St. Thomas This Week,* distributed free to all arriving plane and boat passengers.

It's illegal for most street vendors to ply their trades outside a designated area called **Vendors Plaza,** at the corner of Veterans Drive and Tolbod Gade. Hundreds converge at 7:30am, remaining here usually no later than 5:30pm, Monday to Saturday. (Very few remain in place on Sunday, unless a cruise ship is scheduled to arrive.)

When you completely tire of French perfumes and Swiss watches, head for **Market Square** as it's called locally, or more formally, **Rothschild Francis Square.** Here, under a Victorian tin roof, locals with machetes will slice open fresh coconuts for you so you can drink the milk, and women wearing bandanas will sell ackee, cassava, or breadfruit they harvested themselves.

ART The **Gallery Camille Pissarro,** Caribbean Cultural Centre, 14 Dronningens Gade (℗ **340/774-4621**), lies in the house where Pissarro, dean of Impressionism, was born on July 10, 1830. This art gallery—reached by climbing a flight of stairs—honors the illustrious painter. In three high-ceilinged rooms you'll discover all the available Pissarro paintings relating to the islands, which were created from 1852 to 1856. Many prints and note cards of local artists are also available, and the gallery also sells original batiks, alive in vibrant colors.

The **Jim Tillett Art Gallery & Silk Screen Print Studio,** Tillett Gardens, 4126 Anna's Retreat, Tutu (℗ **340/775-1929**), is reached by following Route 38 east from Charlotte Amalie. Since 1959 Tillett Gardens, once an old Danish farm, has been the island's arts-and-crafts center. Including an art gallery and a screen-printing studio, this tropical compound is a series of buildings housing studios, galleries, and an outdoor garden restaurant and bar. Prints in the galleries start as low as $10. The best work of local artists is displayed here—originals in oils, watercolors, and acrylics. The Tillett prints on fine canvas are all one of a kind, and the famous Tillett maps on fine canvas are priced from $30. If you're not interested in buying any art, perhaps you'd prefer watching the daily iguana feedings in the garden.

Mango Tango Art Gallery, Al Cohen's Plaza, Raphune Hill, Route 38 (℗ **340/777-3060**), is one of the largest art galleries in St. Thomas, with close contacts with about half a dozen internationally recognized artists. Except for prints and posters, which are cheaper, original artworks begin at $200. Represented are internationally reputed artists who spend at least part of their year in the Virgin Islands, many of them sailing during breaks from their studio time. Well-known examples are Don Dahlke, Max Johnson, Anne Miller, David Millard, Dana Wylder, and Shari Erickson.

Native Arts and Crafts Cooperative, Tarbor 1 (℗ **340/777-1153**), is the largest arts-and-crafts emporium in the U.S. Virgin Islands, combining the output of 90 artisans into one sprawling shop. Contained in the former headquarters of the U.S. District Court, a 19th-century brick building adjacent to Charlotte Amalie's tourist information office, it specializes in items small enough to be packed in a suitcase or trunk that almost never need to be shipped. Examples are spice racks, paper towel racks, lamps crafted from conch shells, salad utensils and bowls, crocheted goods, and straw goods.

BOOKSTORES The **Dockside Bookshop,** Havensight Mall (℗ **340/774-4937**), is the place to go if you need a beach read. Head for this well-stocked store near the cruise ship dock, east of Charlotte Amalie. The shop has the best selection of books on island lore, as well as a variety of general reading selections.

BRIC-A-BRAC **Carson Company Antiques,** Royal Dane Mall, off Main Street (℗ **340/774-6175**), invites browsers. Its clutter and eclecticism might appeal to you, especially if you appreciate small spaces loaded with merchandise, tasteless and otherwise, from virtually everywhere. Much of it is calibrated to appeal to the tastes of cruise ship passengers looking for bric-a-brac that usually accumulates on shelves back on the U.S. mainland. Bakelite jewelry is cheap and cheerful, and the African artifacts are often interesting.

ELECTRONICS   Royal Caribbean, 33 Main St. (© **340/776-4110**), is the largest camera and electronics store in the Caribbean. This store and its outlets carry Nikon, Minolta, Pentax, Canon, and Panasonic products. It's a good source for watches, including brand names like Seiko, Movado, Corum, Fendi, and Zodiac. They also have a complete collection of Philippe Charriol watches, jewelry, and leather bags, and a wide selection of Mikimoto pearls, 14- and 18-karat jewelry, and Lladró figurines. There's another branch at Havensight Mall (© **340/776-8890**).

EROTIC ACCESSORIES   Lover's Lane, Raadets Gade 33 (© **340/ 777-9616**), is for erotic tastes. Despite the fact that this store expends a lot of effort to present its merchandise as items to be enjoyed within marital respectability, some of it is pretty raunchy. That doesn't prevent a visit here from being amusing and even a lot of fun. Day visitors from cruise ships sometimes make a visit here a required stop, usually to perk up the sometime tame roster of shipboard activities. One floor above street level of a building beside Veteran's Drive, the shop sells provocative lingerie; edible panties; inflatable men, women, and sheep; massage aids of every conceivable type; the largest inventory of electric or battery-operated vibrators in the Virgin Islands; and all the lace, leather, or latex you'll ever need.

FASHION   Cosmopolitan, Drakes Passage and the waterfront (© **340/ 776-2040**), has been in business since 1973. Its shoe salon features Bally of Switzerland, and Bally handbags are a popular addition. In swimwear, it offers one of the best selections of Gottex of Israel for women and Gottex, Hom, Lahco of Switzerland, and Fila for men. A menswear section offers Paul & Shark from Italy and Burma Bibas sports shirts. The shop also features ties by Versace and Pancaldi of Italy (priced at least 30% less than on the U.S. mainland) and Nautica sportswear for men discounted at 10%.

FRAGRANCES   Tropicana Perfume Shoppe, 2 Main St. (© **800/233-7948** or 340/774-0010), at the beginning of Main Street, is billed as the largest perfumery in the world. It offers all the famous names in perfumes, skin care, and cosmetics. They carry Lancôme and La Prairie among other products, and men will also find Europe's best colognes and aftershave lotions.

GIFTS & LIQUORS   Al Cohen's Discount Liquors, Long Bay Road (© **340/774-3690**), occupies a big warehouse at Havensight, across from the West Indian Company docks where cruise ship passengers disembark. You can make purchases from one of the island's biggest storehouses of liquor and wine. The wine department is especially impressive. The quarters have been recently expanded and remodeled, and there are now more brands and items on sale than ever before. You can also purchase fragrances, T-shirts, and souvenirs.

    A. H. Riise Gift & Liquor Stores, 37 Main St. at A. H. Riise Gift & Liquor Mall (perfume and liquor branch stores at the Havensight Mall; © **800/ 524-2037** or 304/776-2303), is St. Thomas's oldest outlet for luxury items like jewelry, crystal, china, and perfumes. It also offers the widest sampling of liquors and liqueurs on the island. Everything is displayed in a 19th-century Danish warehouse, extending from Main Street to the waterfront. The store boasts a collection of fine jewelry and watches from Europe's leading craftspeople, like Vacheron Constantin, Bulgari, Omega, and Gucci, as well as a wide selection of Greek gold, platinum, and precious gemstone jewelry.

Imported cigars are stored in a climate-controlled walk-in humidor. Delivery to cruise ships and the airport is free. A. H. Riise offers a vast selection of fragrances for both men and women, along with the world's best-known names in cosmetics and treatment products. Waterford, Lalique, Baccarat, and Rosenthal, among others, are featured in the china and crystal department. Specialty shops in the complex sell Caribbean gifts, books, clothing, food, art prints, note cards, and designer sunglasses.

Caribbean Marketplace, Havensight Mall, Building III (© **340/776-5400**), offers the best selections of island handcrafts, in addition to some distinctively Caribbean food items, including Sunny Caribbee products, a vast array of condiments (ranging from spicy peppercorns to nutmeg mustard). There's also a wide selection of Sunny Caribbee's botanical products. Other items range from steel-pan drums from Trinidad to wooden Jamaican jigsaw puzzles, from Indonesian batiks to bikinis from the Cayman Islands. Do not expect very attentive service.

Down Island Traders, Veterans Drive (© **340/776-4641**), offers a taste of the Caribbean. The aroma of spices will lead you to these markets, which have Charlotte Amalie's most attractive array of spices, teas, seasoning, candies, jellies, jams, and condiments, most of which are packaged from natural Caribbean products. The owner carries a line of local cookbooks, as well as silk-screened T-shirts and bags, Haitian metal sculpture, handmade jewelry, Caribbean folk art, and children's gifts. Be sure to ask for the collection of tropical coconut-mango bath and body products and the Calypso Spa Sun Care line.

It had to happen. **The Virgin Islands Brewing Company,** across from the Havensight Mall (© **340/777-8888**), was originally founded on St. Croix but has invaded St. Thomas with two local beers, Blackbeard Ale and Foxy's Lager. At the company store, you're given free samples and can purchase six-packs of the home-brewed suds along with T-shirts, caps, and polo shirts.

JEWELRY   Blue Carib Gems and Rocks, 2 Back St., behind Little Switzerland (© **340/774-8525**), has unique items. For a decade, the owners of this shop scoured the Caribbean for gemstones, and these stones have been brought directly from the mines to you. The raw stones are cut, polished, and then fashioned into jewelry by the lost-wax process. On one side of the premises you can see the craftspeople at work, and on the other view their finished products. A lifetime guarantee is given on all handcrafted jewelry. Since the items are locally made, they're duty-free and not included in the $1,200 Customs exemption.

Cardow Jewelers, 39 Main St. (© **340/776-1140**), is often called the Tiffany's of the Caribbean. This outlet boasts the world's largest selection of fine jewelry. This fabulous shop, where more than 20,000 rings are displayed, offers savings because of its worldwide direct buying, large turnover, and duty-free prices. Unusual and traditional designs are offered in diamonds, emeralds, rubies, sapphires, Brazilian stones, and pearls. Cardow has a whole wall of Italian gold chains and also features antique-coin jewelry. The Treasure Cove, a discount area in the store, has cases of fine gold jewelry all priced under $200.

LINENS   Mr. Tablecloth, 6 Main St. (© **340/774-4343**), receives a constant supply of new shipments of top-quality linen from the Republic of China, including Hong Kong. Now it has the best selection of tablecloths and accessories, plus doilies, in Charlotte Amalie. Also check out their display of place mats, aprons, and runners.

MUSIC   Modern Music (at the Nisky Center, © **340/777-7877,** and at Four Winds Mall, © **340/775-3310**) features nearly every genre of music, from rock

⌒ **Value**   **Cheap Thrills: What to See & Do for Free (Well, Almost) on the U.S. Virgin Islands**

- **Spend a Day on Honeymoon Beach.** The fourth largest of the U.S. Virgins, with 500 acres of land, Water Island off the coast of St. Thomas is only half a mile long. Visitors head out here to spend the day on **Honeymoon Beach,** where they swim, snorkel, sail, waterski, or just sunbathe on the palm-shaded beach and order lunch or a drink from the beach bar. The U.S. government, previous owner of Water Isle, has transferred it to the U.S.V.I. government and has spent some $3 million cleaning and sprucing it up. The island lies about ¼ mile out in the harbor of Charlotte Amalie. It was once a part of the peninsula of St. Thomas but a channel was cut through it, allowing U.S. submarines to reach their base in a bay to the west.

- **Escape to Hassel Island.** Despite the maritime mob scene at Charlotte Amalie in St. Thomas, the harbor's nearest and most visible island, **Hassel Island,** is almost completely deserted—its membership in the National Parks network prohibits most forms of development. There are no hotels or services of any kind, and swimming is limited to narrow rocky beaches. Even so, many visitors hire a boat to drop them off for an hour or two of relief from the cruise ship congestion.

- **Snorkel on St. John.** The coastline of St. John measures nearly 50 miles, including an equal number of bays, a few odd cays, and many secluded coves. Many of its bays and beaches aren't reachable by land because of the rugged terrain. But some of the best spots are accessible, including the north-shore bays at Hawksnest, Trunk, Maho, Leinster, and Cinnamon. All of St. John is in the Atlantic, which means its waters are more turbulent than those of the other islands, which open onto the Caribbean Sea. On St. John's east coast or windward side, the winds are stronger and the waves bigger, but the leeward or western side is calmer and more suited for snorkelers. If you have time to snorkel on only one bay, make it Leinster Bay, home to Watermelon Cay. Surrounded by gin-clear, tranquil waters, it invites you to explore its world of sponges in tropical hues, giant

to jazz to classical, and especially Caribbean. You'll find new releases from Caribbean stars such as Jamaica's Byron Lee and the Virgin Islands's The Violators, as well as U.S. artists.

ST. THOMAS AFTER DARK

St. Thomas has more nightlife than any other of the Virgin Islands, but it's not as extensive as you might think. The big resort hotels offer the most varied programs.

St. Thomas might be the most cosmopolitan of the Virgin Islands, but it's no longer the gay paradise it was in the 1960s and 1970s—the action has shifted mainly to San Juan. The major gay scene in the U.S. Virgins is in Frederiksted on St. Croix. That doesn't mean gays and lesbians aren't attracted to St. Thomas—they are—but many of the clubs that used to cater exclusively to

sea stars, and perhaps the odd turtle swimming by along with an occasional nurse shark or schools of blue tangs and fields of sea fans.

- **Have a Close Encounter of the Wildlife Kind.** One of the most rarely visited parts of St. Croix, the island's southwestern tip is composed of salt marshes, tidal pools, and low vegetation inhabited by birds, turtles, and other wildlife. More than 3 miles of ecologically protected coast lie between Sandy Point (the island's westerly tip) and the shallow waters of the Westend Saltpond. Home to colonies of green and hawksbill turtles, the site is also a resting ground for leatherback turtles. It's one of only two such places in U.S. waters. The site is also home to thousands of birds, including herons, brown pelicans, Caribbean martins, black-necked stilts, and white-crowned pigeons. Sandy Point gave its name to a rare form of orchids, a brown and/or purple variety. Part of the continued viability of the site as a wildlife refuge depends on its inaccessibility, except on Saturday and Sunday 6am to 6pm. The site is most easily reached by driving to the end of Route 66 (Melvin Evans Highway) and continuing down a gravel road. Earthwatch, a nonprofit organization staffed mostly by volunteers working cooperatively with advisors from universities around the world, maintains a monitoring program here. For inquiries about guided weekend visits to the site, call the **St. Croix Environmental Association** at © **340/773-1989.**

- **Visit the Easternmost Point of the United States.** Diehards get up before sunrise to see the sun come up over Point Udall, a rocky promontory that's the easternmost point of the United States, jutting into the Caribbean Sea. But considering the climb via a rutted dirt road, you might want to wait until the sun comes up before heading here. Once at the top, you'll be rewarded with one of the most panoramic views in the U.S. Virgin Islands. On the way to the lookout point, you'll see the Castle, a local architectural oddity. It looks like the St. Croix version of the Taj Mahal. Its occupant is mysterious, known locally only as the Contessa. Point Udall is reached along Route 82 (it's signposted).

them are gone. Today there are pockets of gays who attend predominantly straight places.

THE PERFORMING ARTS   The **Reichhold Center for the Arts,** University of the Virgin Islands, 2 John Brewer's Bay (© **340/693-1550**), the premier venue in the Caribbean, lies west of Charlotte Amalie. Call the theater or check with the tourist office to see what's on at the time of your visit. The lobby displays a frequently changing free exhibit of paintings and sculptures by Caribbean artists. A Japanese-inspired amphitheater is set into a natural valley, with seating space for 1,196. The smell of gardenias adds to the beauty of the performances. Several repertory companies of music, dance, and drama perform here. Performances begin at 8pm (call the theater to check), and tickets run $10 to $45.

THE BAR, CLUB & MUSIC SCENE The **Bar at Paradise Point**★★, Paradise Point (✆ **340/777-4540**), is best for a sundowner. Any savvy insider will tell you to head here for your sunset watching. It's 740 feet above sea level, across from the cruise ship dock, providing excellent photo ops and sunset views. There's a tram you can ride up the hill. Get the bartender to serve you a Bushwacker (his specialty)—you'll have to guess what's in it. Sometimes a one-man steel band is on hand to serenade the sunset watchers, who after a few of those painkillers don't know if the sun has set or not. You can also order inexpensive food here, such as barbecued ribs, hot dogs, and hamburgers, beginning at $4. It opens at 11am daily; closing time varies, depending on business. Happy hour with discounted drinks begins at 5pm, with no set cut-off time.

If you must be in Charlotte Amalie at night (there are safer places to be), head to **The Green House** ★★, Veterans Drive (✆ **340/774-7998**), for drinking, dining, and perhaps listening to some of the best music on the island, either live or recorded. What's even better are the two-for-one happy hours including a generous free buffet Monday through Saturday. There's only a modest cover charge when live bands play.

Baywinds, at the Renaissance Grand Beach Resort, Smith Bay Road (✆ **340/775-1510**), is one of the most romantic places to be in the evening. This is a posh trade wind–cooled poolside club where loving couples dance at the side of the luxurious pool as moonlight glitters like diamonds off the ocean in the background. Music ranges from jazz to pop. The club is open nightly with live music and dinner 6pm to midnight.

Dungeon Bar, Bluebeard's Hill (✆ **340/774-1600**), overlooks the yacht harbor and offers piano-bar entertainment nightly. It's a popular gathering spot for both guests and visitors. You can dance 8pm to midnight on Thursday and 8pm to 1am on Saturday. Entertainment varies from month to month, but a steel band comes in on some nights and other nights are devoted to karaoke (Mon) or jazz (Wed). Drink specialties are named after Bluebeard himself—Bluebeard's Wench, Cooler, and Ghost. There's no cover, and it's open Tuesday to Friday 4pm to midnight and Saturday to Monday 4pm to 1am.

Epernay, rue de St-Barthélemy, Frenchtown (✆ **340/774-5348**), is adjacent to Alexander's Restaurant. This stylish watering hole with a view of the ocean adds a touch of Europe to the neighborhood. You can order glasses of at least six brands of champagne and vintage wines by the glass. Appetizers cost $6 to $10 and include sushi and caviar. You can also order main courses, plus tempting desserts, such as chocolate-dipped strawberries. It's open Monday to Wednesday 11:30am to 11pm and Thursday to Saturday 11:30am to midnight.

Fat Tuesday, 26A Royal Dane Mall (✆ **340/777-8676**), is on the waterfront in downtown Charlotte Amalie. This spot serves up frozen concoctions: In the party-like atmosphere, patrons enjoy specialties like the Tropical Itch (a frozen punch made with bourbon and 151-proof rum) or the Moko Jumbi Juice (made with vodka, bourbon, 151-proof rum, and banana and cocoa liqueurs). There's also a variety of beers, highballs, and shooters (like the Head Butt, containing Jagermeister, Bailey's, and amaretto). Each night the bar has special events, like Monday-night football or T.G.I.F. night. There's no cover, and hours are daily 10am to midnight or even 1am (perhaps later on Friday and Saturday).

The Greenhouse, Veterans Drive (✆ **340/774-7998**), is directly on the waterfront. This is one of the few nightspots we recommend in the heart of Charlotte Amalie. You can park nearby and walk to the entrance. Each night a different entertainment is featured, ranging from reggae to disco. There's no cover except on Wednesday and Friday, when a $5 to $7 charge is imposed to cover the cost of live reggae music.

Larry's Hideaway, 10 Hull Bay (© **340/777-1898**), has a laid-back atmosphere. Many local fans like to hide away here on lazy Sunday afternoons especially. The atmosphere is still funky, and it's a cheap place to eat if you devour the hot dogs and hamburgers served until 3:45pm. After 5pm, you can order affordable main courses in the restaurant, including the catch of the day and the chef's pork stew.

Latitude 18, Red Hook Marina (© **340/779-2495**), is the hot spot on the east coast where the ferries depart for St. John. Its interior ceiling is adorned with boat sails. It's both a restaurant and bar, opening nightly at 6pm. Live entertainment is regularly featured, especially on Tuesday and Saturday. This spot is especially popular with locals.

Turtle Rock Bar, in the Mangrove Restaurant at the Wyndham Sugar Bay Beach Club, 6500 Estate Smith Bay (© **340/777-7100**), is a few minutes' drive west of Red Hook. This popular bar presents live music, steel bands, and karaoke. There's space to dance, but most patrons just sway and listen to the steel-pan bands that play from 2pm to closing every night or the more elaborate bands that play on Tuesday, Sunday, and some other nights. Thursday night is karaoke night. If you're hungry, burgers, salads, steaks, and grilled fish are available at the Mangrove Restaurant a few steps away. There's no cover, and happy hour (when most drinks are half price) is 4 to 6pm every night.

The major venue for nightlife in St. Thomas is **The Old Mill,** 193 Contant (© **340/776-3004**), the largest and newest entertainment complex to open on the island, with three separate venues. The courtyard sports bar offers a variety of games, including four pool tables. The more elegant wine and champagne bar is in a restored 18th-century historic sugar mill, where guest can relax to the sound of jazz and blues. More than 100 different types of wines and champagnes from all over the world are served here. There's also a dance club, the largest of its kind in the U.S. Virgins, featuring a sunken dance floor combined with a state-of-the-art lighting and sound system. Open Thursday to Sunday. Go after 9am (no set closing times).

Walter's Livingroom, 3 Trompeter Gade (© **340/774-5025**), is dimly and rather flatteringly lit. This two-level watering hole attracts locals, often gay men, in season, drawing more off-island visitors in winter. Located about 100 yards from the island's famous synagogue, in a clapboard townhouse built around 1935, Walter's cellar bar features an intimate atmosphere with music from the 1950s, 1960s, and 1970s.

3 St. John ★★★

The smallest and least populated of the U.S. Virgin Islands, St. John is known for its lush, unspoiled beauty. More than half its land, as well as its shoreline, was set aside and protected in 1956 as the Virgin Islands National Park.

Ringed by a rocky coastline, crescent-shaped bays, and white-sand beaches, the island contains an array of bird and wildlife that's the envy of ornithologists and zoologists around the world. Miles of serpentine hiking trails lead to spectacular views and the ruins of 18th-century Danish plantations. Mysterious geometric petroglyphs incised into boulders and cliffs can be pointed out by island guides; of unknown age and origin, the figures have never been deciphered.

The boating set seeks out its dozens of sheltered coves for anchorages and swimming. The hundreds of coral gardens surrounding St. John's perimeter are protected as rigorously as the land surface by the National Park Service. Any attempt to damage or remove coral from these waters is punishable by large and strictly enforced fines.

About 3 to 5 miles east of St. Thomas, St. John lies just across Pillsbury Sound. The island is about 7 miles long and 3 miles wide, with a total land area of some 20 square miles.

ST. JOHN ESSENTIALS

VISITOR INFORMATION

St. John Tourist Office (© 340/776-6450) is located near the Battery, a 1735 fort that's a short walk from where the ferry from St. Thomas docks. It's open Monday to Friday 8am to 1pm and 2 to 5pm. If you have Internet access, head to **www.stjohnusvi.com**.

GETTING AROUND

BY PUBLIC TRANSPORTATION The most popular way to get around is by local **Vitran bus** service, the same company that runs bus service on St. Thomas. Buses run between Cruz Bay and Coral Bay and cost $1 for adults and 75¢ for children (4 and under free). A **surrey-style taxi** is more fun, however (© **340/693-7530**). Typical fares are $5 to Trunk Bay, $8 to Cinnamon Bay, or $10 to Maho Bay. Between midnight and 6am, fares are increased by 40%. Call for more information.

BY CAR OR JEEP The roads are undeveloped and uncluttered, and offer panoramic vistas. Because of these views, many visitors opt to rent a car (sometimes with four-wheel drive) to tour the island. You might consider one of the open-sided Jeep-like vehicles. Most people need a car for only a day or two. During the busiest periods of midwinter, there's sometimes a shortage of cars, so try to reserve early.

The island has only two gas stations. (A third gas station on the island dispenses gas only to government vehicles.) Because of the distance between gas stations, it's never a good idea to drive around St. John with less than half a tank.

The two largest car-rental agencies on St. John are **Hertz** (© **800/654-3001** in the U.S., or 340/693-7580) and **Avis** (© **800/331-1212** in the U.S., or 340/776-6374); Budget isn't represented. If you're a Budget fan, you can rent a car from its fleet on St. Thomas, then take the vehicle over to St. John by car ferry. If you want a local firm, try **St. John Car Rental,** across from the post office in Cruz Bay (© **340/776-6103**). Its stock is limited to Jeep Wranglers, Jeep Cherokees, and Suzuki Sidekicks.

FAST FACTS

In a medical emergency, dial © **911.** Otherwise, go to **St. John Myrah Keating Smith Community Health Clinic,** 28 Sussanaberg (© **340/693-8900**), reached along Route 10, 7 miles east of Cruz Bay. A leading drugstore is **St. John Drugcenter,** in the Boulon Shopping Center, Cruz Bay (© **340/776-6353**), which also sells film, cameras, magazines, and books; it's open Monday to Saturday 9am to 6pm and Sunday 10am to 2pm.

ACCOMMODATIONS YOU CAN AFFORD

The choice of accommodations on St. John is limited, and that's how most people would like to keep it. And except for the campgrounds recommended below, the tabs at most of the establishments here are far beyond the pocketbook of the average traveler. However, the following places will provide you a low-cost holiday on St. John.

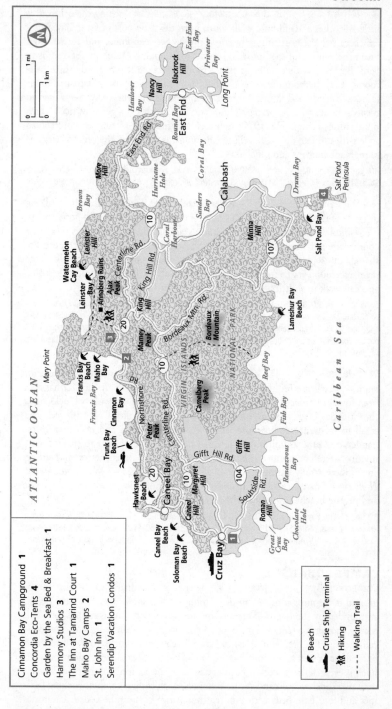

Garden by the Sea Bed & Breakfast ⭐ *Finds* Overlooking the ocean, this little B&B lies a 10-minute walk south from the little port of Cruz Bay. It has easy access to the north-shore beaches and lies between Frank and Turner Bays. From the gardens of the house, a 1-minute path along Audubon Pond leads to Fank Bay Beach. Be sure to reserve a room ahead, as it offers only three bedrooms. Each bedroom features elephant bamboo canopy beds, Japanese fountains, and hardwood floors. Artifacts from around the world have been used to furnish the units. Don't expect phones or TVs, as this is a getaway, not a communications center. The 1970s house is designed in a Caribbean gingerbread style with cathedral beamed ceilings. Breakfast is served on the veranda (try the homemade muffins and quiche).

P.O. Box 1469 Cruz Bay, St. John, U.S.V.I. ℂ **340/779-4731.** www.gardenbythesea.com. 3 units. Winter $170–$190 double. Off-season $115–$130 double. No credit cards. *In room:* Ceiling fans, no phone.

The Inn at Tamarind Court Right outside Cruz Bay but still within walking distance of the ferryboat dock, this modest place consists of a small hotel and an even simpler West Indian inn. Bedrooms are small, evoking those in a little country motel. Most have twin beds. Shower-only bathrooms in the inn are shared; units in the hotel have small private bathrooms. The social life here revolves around its courtyard bar and restaurant, Pa Pa Bulls. From the hotel, you can walk to shuttles that take you to the beaches.

South Shore Rd. (P.O. Box 350), Cruz Bay, St. John, U.S.V.I. 00831. ℂ **800/221-1637** or 340/776-6378. Fax 340/776-6722. www.tamarindcourt.com. 23 units, 13 with bathroom. Winter $89 single or double without bathroom, $108 single or double with bathroom; $145 apt; $165 suite. Off-season $59 single or double without bathroom, $78 single or double with bathroom; $98 apt; $128 suite. Rates include continental breakfast. AE, DISC, MC, V. *In room:* Ceiling fans, no phone.

St. John Inn *Value* The old Cruz Inn, once the budget staple of the island, enjoys a new lease on life. Although its rates have gone up, its quality has also been much improved. The inn overlooks Enighed Pond, only a few blocks from the Cruz Bay Dock area. Accommodations have a light, airy, California feel. The small to medium-size bedrooms have wrought-iron beds and new mattresses, handcrafted pine armoires, and a touch of Ralph Lauren flair to make for an inviting nest. The junior suites contain full sofa beds, kitchenettes, and sitting areas. Shower-only bathrooms are small. The inn offers a 43-foot motor yacht, *Hollywood Waltz,* for daily excursions to private snorkeling spots along the coast and private beaches on uninhabited islands.

P.O. Box 37, Cruz Bay, St. John, U.S.V.I. 00831. ℂ **800/666-7688** in the U.S., or 340/693-8688. www.stjohn inn.com. 12 units. Winter $120–$195 single or double. Off-season $60–$120 single or double. Extra person $15. AE, DISC, MC, V. **Amenities:** Bar, pool. *In room:* A/C, TV, kitchenette in some, fridge, coffeemaker, hair dryer on request.

CAMPGROUNDS

Cinnamon Bay Campground ⭐ This U.S. National Park Service campground is the most complete in the Caribbean. The site is directly on the beach, surrounded by thousands of acres of tropical vegetation. Life is simple here: You have a choice of a tent, a cottage, or a bare site. At the bare campsites, you basically get just the site, with no fancy extras. Each canvas tent is 10 by 14 feet and has a floor as well as a number of extras, including all cooking equipment; your linen is even changed weekly. Each cottage is 15 by 15 feet, consisting of a room with two concrete walls and two screen walls. Each cottage contains cooking facilities and four twin beds with thin mattresses; two cots can be added. Lavatories and cool-water showers are in separate buildings nearby. Camping is limited to a 2-week period in any given year.

P.O. Box 720, Cruz Bay, St. John, U.S.V.I. 00831. ✆ **340/776-6330.** Fax 340/776-6458. www.cinnamonbay. com. 126 units, none with bathroom. Winter $105 cottage for 2; $80 tent site; $25 bare site. Off-season $70 cottage for 2; $62 tent site; $20 bare site (5-day minimum). Extra person $15. AE, MC, V. **Amenities:** Restaurant, grocery store, snorkeling, windsurfing. *In room:* No phone.

Maho Bay Camps 🦅   Right on Maho Bay, this is an interesting concept in ecology vacationing, where you camp close to nature, but with considerable comfort. It's set on a hillside above the beach surrounded by the Virgin Islands National Park. To preserve the existing ground cover, all 114 tent-cottages are on platforms, above a thickly wooded slope. Utility lines and pipes are hidden under wooden boardwalks and stairs. Each tent-cottage, covered with canvas and screens, has two twin beds with thin mattresses, a couch, electric lamps and outlets, a dining table, chairs, a propane stove, an ice chest (cooler), linen, thin towels, and cooking and eating utensils. Guests share communal bathhouses. Maho Bay Camps is more intimate and slightly more luxurious than its nearest competitor, Cinnamon Bay.

P.O. Box 310, Cruz Bay, St. John, U.S.V.I. 00831. ✆ **800/392-9004,** 212/472-9453 in New York City, or 340/776-6226. Fax 340/776-6504, or 212/861-6210 in New York City. www.maho.org. 114 tent-cottages, none with bathroom. Winter $110–$125 tent-cottage for 2 (minimum stay of 7 nights). Off-season $75 tent-cottage for 2. Extra person $15. AE, DISC, MC, V. **Amenities:** Restaurant; snorkeling, windsurfing. *In room:* No phone.

VILLA & CONDO RENTALS

Villa vacations are on the rise on St. John. These private homes and condos deliver spaciousness and comfort, as well as privacy, and come with fully equipped kitchens, dining areas, bedrooms, and such amenities as VCRs and patio grills. Rentals go from large multiroom resort homes to simply decorated one-bedroom condos. Villa rentals year-round typically run from about $1,295 to $2,375 per week, an affordable option for multiple couples or families looking for a large house. Condos generally range from $225 to $375 per night per unit. However, in the off-season you can get substantial reductions, perhaps $135 to $210 per night or $770 to $1,225 per week.

For information on privately owned villas and condos on St. John, call ✆ **800/372-8784.** You can also try **Caribbean Villas & Resort Management** (✆ **800/338-0987** in the U.S., or 340/776-6152) or **Villa Portfolio Management** (✆ **800/858-7989** or 340/693-9100).

Serendip Vacation Condos   Set on sloping land on a hillside above Cruz Bay, these condos with angular lines and concrete verandas are shielded by masses of shrubbery. Each unit has slightly dated furniture, concrete latticework, a ceiling fan, a radio, and a terrace or balcony, plus a double or twin beds, each with a good mattress. The shower-only bathrooms are in good order. Maid service is usually not included as part of a rental here. Tennis courts and watersports are available nearby. A gas-heated barbecue grill on the grounds is available. Costs here are especially attractive for vacationers who include extra guests in their plans.

P.O. Box 293, Cruz Bay, St. John, U.S.V.I. 00831. ✆/fax **340/776-6646.** www.st-john.com/serendip. 10 units. Winter $135 studio apt for 1 or 2; $165 1-bedroom apt for 2. Off-season $70 studio apt for 1 or 2; $125 1-bedroom apt for 2. Extra person $25; children 3–10 $15 each; children 2 and under stay free in their parents' apt. AE, MC, V. **Amenities:** Concierge, car rental, massage, babysitting. *In room:* A/C, kitchenette, fridge, coffeemaker, hair dryer, radio.

WORTH A SPLURGE

Concordia Eco-Tents ⚛ (Finds)   This is the newest addition to Stanley Selengut's celebrated Concordia development project on the southern tip of St. John, overlooking Salt Pond Bay and Ram Head Point. These solar- and wind-powered tent-cottages combine sustainable technology with some of the most spectacular views on the island. The light framing, fabric walls, and large screened-in windows lend a treehouse atmosphere to guests' experience. Set on the windward side of the island, the tent-cottages enjoy natural ventilation from the cooling trade winds. Inside, each has two twin beds with rather thin mattresses in each bedroom, one or two twin mattresses on a loft platform, and a queen-size futon in the living-room area (each can sleep up to six people comfortably). Each kitchen comes equipped with a running-water sink, propane stove, and cooler. In addition, each Eco-Tent has a small private shower, rather meager towels, and a composting toilet.

The secluded hillside location, surrounded by hundreds of acres of pristine national park land, requires guests to arrange for a rental vehicle. Beaches, hikes, and the shops and restaurants of Coral Bay are only a 10-minute drive from the property.

20–27 Estate Concordia, Coral Bay, St. John, U.S.V.I. 00830. (℃) **800/392-9004** in the U.S. or 212/472-9453 for reservations. Fax 212/861-6210. www.maho.org/ecotents.html. 11 tent-cottages. Winter $120 tent for 1 or 2. Off-season $75–$85 tent for 1 or 2. Extra person $25 in winter, $15 in off-season. AE, DISC, MC, V. **Amenities:** Pool. *In room:* No phone.

Harmony Studios ⚛   Built on a hillside above Maho Bay Camps, this is a small-scale cluster of 12 luxury studios in six two-story houses with views sweeping down to the sea. The complex is designed to combine both ecological technology and comfort; it's one of the few resorts in the Caribbean to operate exclusively on sun and wind power. Most of the building materials are derived from recycled materials, including reconstituted plastic and glass containers, newsprint, old tires, and scrap lumber. The managers and staff are committed to offering educational experiences, as well as the services of a small-scale resort. The studios have tiled shower-only bathrooms, kitchenettes, dining areas, and outdoor terraces. Guests can walk a short distance downhill to use the restaurant, grocery store, and watersports facilities at the Maho Bay Camps.

P.O. Box 310, Cruz Bay, St. John, U.S.V.I. 00831. (℃) **800/392-9004** in the U.S. and Canada, 212/472-9453 in New York City, or 340/776-6226. Fax 340/776-6504, or 212/861-6210 in New York City. www.maho.org/harmony.html. 12 units. Winter $175–$210 studio. Off-season $105–$135 studio. Extra person $25. 7-night minimum stay in winter. MC, V. **Amenities:** Restaurant, windsurfing, snorkeling. *In room:* Ceiling fans, no phone.

GREAT DEALS ON DINING

Joseph's INTERNATIONAL   Cruz Bay's newest hangout is a hip and happy-go-lucky place that can be a lot of fun, thanks to the humor of the men from Boston and New Jersey who opened it in 1997. It promotes itself as a "Bar/Lounge and porch," and a "place for fine lounging with good food." Within 200 yards of the public docks, it's a pavilion open on two sides, with lots of comfortable chairs, touches of wrought iron, and a bar that dispenses the largest and most potent martinis in St. John. Lobster ravioli is the house specialty.

Cruz Bay. (℃) **340/693-9200.** Main courses $15–$24; lunch from $8. AE, MC, V. Mon–Sat 5–10pm; bar daily 4pm–2am.

La Tapa ⚛ INTERNATIONAL   This is one of our favorite restaurants in Cruz Bay, where you can sample the tapas, Spanish-inspired bite-size morsels of fish, meat, or marinated vegetables, accompanied by pitchers of sangria. There's a tiny bar with no more than five stools, a two-tiered dining room, and lots of original paintings (the establishment doubles as an art gallery for emerging local artists). Menu items are thoughtful and well conceived, and include fast-seared tuna with a Basque-inspired relish of onions, peppers, garlic, and herbs; filet mignon with Gorgonzola, caramelized onions, and port; and linguine with shrimp, red peppers, and leeks in a peanut sauce.

Centerline Rd., across from Scotia Bank, Cruz Bay. ℂ **340/693-7755**. Reservations recommended. Tapas from $4; main courses $18–$36. AE, MC, V. Fri–Wed 5:30–10pm.

The Lime Inn SEAFOOD   This lively open-air restaurant is located at the Lemon Tree Mall in the heart of Cruz Bay. It's known for its fresh-grilled Caribbean-style lobster as well as its grilled seafood, ranging from shrimp to the fresh catch of the day. If you're not in the mood for seafood, try one of the daily chicken and pasta specials or a grilled steak. For a combination of both land and sea, the Lime Inn offers a tender grilled filet mignon stuffed with crabmeat. The most popular night of the week here is Wednesday, when you can enjoy an all-you-can-eat, peel-and-eat shrimp feast for $18.

In the Lemon Tree Mall, Konges Gade, Cruz Bay. ℂ **340/776-6425**. Reservations recommended. Main courses $6.25–$20; lunch $4–$10. AE, MC, V. Mon–Fri 11:30am–3pm and 5:30–10pm; Sat 5:30–10pm. Closed 3 weeks in July.

Luscious Licks VEGETARIAN/VEGAN   On the eastern side of the island at Cruz Bay, next to Mongoose Junction, this eatery offers open-air dining with a view of the water. The walls are appointed with small chalkboards, which have various quotations and pithy everyday sayings written on them. The menu offers a varied selection of vegetarian dishes—from soups, such as split pea, to the house specialty, the stroller (a flour tortilla filled with hummus, bean sprouts, carrots, avocado, broccoli, tahini, and yogurt). Diners can enjoy the pita sandwiches with fillings ranging from Swiss cheese to hummus, tabouleh, or marinated tofu. Your drink comes from the vegetable and fruit juice bar. For a finish, try a selection from the ice-cream bar located off the patio, which features Ben & Jerry's.

Cruz Bay. ℂ **340/693-8400**. Main courses $5–$8. No credit cards. Mon–Sat 10am–4pm.

Margaritas MEXICAN/VEGETARIAN   The name Margaritas tells you what to expect. On the western side of the island at Cruz Bay, next to Mongoose Junction, this eatery offers open-air dining with a view of the water. Tables are placed both outside and inside the building, whose decor evokes fantasy version of Santa Fe, with religious icons competing for wall space with decorated tiles and Mexican sombreros. It's a bit corny, but the food is tasty. The menu offers a wide choice of standard Mexican fare and a decent selection of vegetarian dishes. The cooking isn't fantastic, but it is quite acceptable, especially if you down one or even two of those *margaritas gigante.*

Cruz Bay. ℂ **340/693-8400**. Main courses $7–$18l lunch $7–$12. Mon–Sat 11am–9pm.

Miss Lucy's ★ *Finds* WEST INDIAN   Before becoming the island's most famous woman chef, Miss Lucy was a big hit with tourists as St. John's first female taxi driver. For the broadest array of island cookery, nobody does it better than Miss Lucy. Her food is prepared the way it used to taste in the Caribbean, long before anyone had ever heard of high-rise resorts. Her paella is the most scrumptious on the island, a kettle brimming with hot Italian sausage, deep-fried chicken, shrimp, and mussels over perfectly cooked saffron rice. Traditional conch fritters appear with picante sauce, and you can gobble them down with Miss Lucy's *callaloo* soup. Her fish is pulled fresh from Caribbean waters, and does she ever know how to cook it. When a local fisherman catches a wahoo, he is often likely to bring it here for Miss Lucy to cook. Main dishes come with *fungi*, a cornmeal and okra side dish. At one of her "full moon parties," she'll cook a roast suckling pig. For dessert, try her banana pancakes.

Salt Pond Rd., near Estate Concordia, Coral Bay. ✆ **340/693-5244.** Reservations recommended. Main courses $15.50–$22.50. AE, MC, V. Tues–Sat 11am–3pm and 6–9pm; Sun 10am–2pm.

Mongoose Restaurant/North Shore Deli ⭐ AMERICAN   There's a hint of New Age California at this popular deli and outdoor restaurant, which occupies a setting that's soothing, woodsy, and very, very tropical. The to-go service at the deli provides one of the best options on St. John for an overstuffed sandwich. There's a cluster of wooden tables near the deli if you prefer to eat here. Breads are baked fresh every day.

More substantial, and more esoteric, fare is served in the restaurant, where the vegetation of a tropical forest extends up to the deck, and where a high roof and a lack of walls give the impression of eating outdoors. You can always precede or end a meal at the center-stage bar. Perennially popular drinks include rum-and-fruit-based painkillers and a dessert-inspired "chocolate chiquita" (rum, bananas, and chocolate ice cream). Menu items at lunch include quesadillas, burgers, grilled chicken, and blackened tuna sandwiches. At dinner, they include fresh grilled or sautéed fish, often served with a salsa made from local fruits; margarita-marinated shrimp; mahimahi with cashew crust; and lots of vegetarian options as well.

Mongoose Junction. ✆ **340/693-8677.** Sandwiches in deli $5–$9; main courses in restaurant $7–$12 at lunch, $14–$28 at dinner. AE, DISC, MC, V. Deli daily 7am–7pm; restaurant Mon–Sat 8:30am–pm; Sun 10am–9pm.

Morgan's Mango ⭐⭐ CARIBBEAN   The chefs here roam the Caribbean looking for tantalizing flavors, which they adapt for their ever-changing menu. The restaurant is easy to spot, with its big canopy, the only protection from the elements. The bar wraps around the main dining room and offers some 30 frozen drinks. Thursday is Margarita Night, when soft music plays. Some think the kitchen tries to do too much with the nightly menu, but it does produce some zesty fare—everything from Anegada lobster cakes to a spicy Jamaican pickapepper steak. Try flying fish served as an appetizer, followed by Haitian voodoo snapper pressed in Cajun spices, then grilled and served with fresh fruit salsa. Equally delectable is mahimahi in a Cruzan rum and mango sauce. The knockout dessert is the mango-banana pie.

Cruz Bay (across from the National Park dock). ✆ **340/693-8141.** Reservations recommended. Main courses $8–$25. AE, MC, V. Daily 5:30–10pm. Bar opens at 5pm.

Shipwreck Landing SEAFOOD/CONTINENTAL   Eight miles east of Cruz Bay on the road to Salt Pond Beach, Shipwreck Landing offers palms and tropical plants on a veranda overlooking the sea. The intimate bar specializes in tropical frozen drinks. Lunch isn't ignored here, and there's a lot more than sandwiches, salads, and burgers—try pan-seared blackened snapper in Cajun spices or conch fritters. The chef shines brighter at night, though, offering a pasta of the day along with such specialties as a rather tantalizing Caribbean blackened shrimp. A lot of the fare is routine, including New York strip steak and fish-and-chips, but the grilled mahimahi in lime butter is worth the trip. Entertainment, including jazz and rock, is featured Wednesday night, with no cover.

34 Freeman's Ground, Rte. 107, Coral Bay. (C) 340/693-5640. Reservations requested. Main courses $10–$22; lunch from $6–$12. AE, DISC, MC, V. Daily 11am–10pm. Bar daily 11am–11pm.

Vie's Snack Shack ★ *Finds* WEST INDIAN Vie's looks like little more than a plywood-sided hut, but its charming and gregarious owner is known as one of the best local chefs on St. John. Her garlic chicken is famous. She also serves conch fritters, johnnycakes, island-style beef patés, and coconut and pineapple tarts. Don't leave without a glass of homemade limeade. The place is open most days, but as Vie says, "Some days, we might not be here at all"—so you'd better call before you head out.

East End Rd. (12½ miles east of Cruz Bay). (C) 340/693-5033. Main courses $7–$12. No credit cards. Tues–Sat 10am–5pm (but call first!).

Woody's Seafood Saloon SEAFOOD/AMERICAN Just 50 yards from the ferry dock, this local dive and hangout at Cruz Bay is more famous for its beers on tap than for its cuisine. A mix of local fishers, taxi drivers, tour guides, aimless on-island drifters, and an occasional husband and wife show up here to sample the spicy conch fritters and mingle with the islanders. Shrimp appears in various styles, and you can usually order fresh fish and other dishes, including blackened shark, drunken shellfish, and mussels and clams steamed in beer. But fancy cookery is just not the style of this place. You can always get a burger here, reggae on Wednesday, and, as a patron said, "a little bit of everything and anything" on a Saturday night.

Cruz Bay. (C) 340/779-4625. Main courses dinner, $8–$20; lunch, $6–$11. AE, DC, MC, V. Mon–Thurs 11am–1am; Fri–Sun 11am–2am.

HITTING THE BEACHES

The best beach, hands down, is **Trunk Bay** ★★★, the biggest attraction on St. John. To miss its picture-perfect shoreline of white sand would be like touring Paris and skipping the Eiffel Tower. One of the loveliest beaches in the Caribbean, it offers ideal conditions for diving, snorkeling, swimming, and sailing. The only drawback is the crowds (watch for pickpockets). Beginning snorkelers in particular are attracted to the underwater trail near the shore (see "Sports & Other Outdoor Pursuits," below); you can rent snorkeling gear here. Lifeguards are on duty. Admission is $4 per person for those over age 16. If you're coming from St. Thomas, both taxis and "safari buses" to Trunk Bay meet the ferry from Red Hook when it docks at Cruz Bay.

Caneel Bay, the stamping ground of the rich and famous, has seven beautiful beaches on its 170 acres, and all are open to the public. **Caneel Bay Beach** is open to everyone and easy to reach from the main entrance of the Caneel Bay resort. A staff member at the gatehouse will provide directions. **Hawksnest Beach** is one of the most beautiful beaches near the Caneel Bay properties. It's not a wide beach, but it is choice. Since it lies near Cruz Bay, where the ferry docks, it is the most overpopulated, especially when cruise ship passengers come over from St. Thomas. Safari buses and taxis from Cruz Bay will take you along Northshore Road.

The campgrounds of **Cinnamon Bay** have their own beach, where forest rangers sometimes have to remind visitors to put their swim trunks back on. This is our particular favorite, a beautiful strip of white sand with hiking trails, great windsurfing, ruins, and wild donkeys (don't feed or pet them!). Changing rooms and showers are available, and you can rent watersports equipment. Snorkeling is especially popular; you'll often see big schools of purple triggerfish. This beach is best in the morning and at midday, as afternoons are likely to be windy.

A marked **nature trail,** with signs identifying the flora, loops through a tropical forest on even turf before leading straight up to Centerline Road.

Maho Bay Beach is immediately to the east of Cinnamon Bay, and it also borders campgrounds. As you lie on the sand here, you can take in a hillside of pitched tents. This is also a popular beach, often with the campers themselves.

Francis Bay Beach and **Watermelon Cay Beach** are just a few more of the beaches you'll encounter traveling eastward along St. John's gently curving coastline. The beach at **Leinster Bay** is another haven for those seeking the solace of a private sunny retreat. You can swim in the bay's shallow water or snorkel over the spectacular and colorful coral reef, perhaps in the company of an occasional turtle or stingray.

The remote **Salt Pond Bay** is known to locals but often missed by visitors. It's on the beautiful coast in the southeast, adjacent to **Coral Bay.** The bay is tranquil, but the beach is somewhat rocky. It's a short walk down the hill from a parking lot (*beware:* a few cars have recently been broken into). The snorkeling is good, and the bay has some fascinating tidal pools. The Ram Head Trail begins here and, winding for a mile, leads to a belvedere overlooking the bay. Facilities are meager but include an outhouse and a few tattered picnic tables.

If you want to escape the crowds, head for **Lameshur Bay Beach,** along the rugged south coast, west of Salt Pond Bay and accessible only via a bumpy dirt road. The sands are beautiful and the snorkeling is excellent. You can also take a 5-minute stroll down the road past the beach to explore the nearby ruins of an old plantation estate that was destroyed in a slave revolt.

Does St. John have a nude beach? Not officially, but lovely **Solomon Bay Beach** is a contender, although park rangers of late have sometimes asked people to put their swimwear back on. Leave Cruz Bay on Route 20 and turn left at the park service sign, about a quarter mile past the visitor center. Park at the end of a cul-de-sac, then walk along the trail for about 15 minutes. Go early, and you'll practically have the beach to yourself.

SPORTS & OTHER OUTDOOR PURSUITS ☆☆

Come to St. John for some of the best snorkeling, scuba diving, swimming, fishing, hiking, sailing, and underwater photography in the Caribbean, the centerpiece of the island being Virgin Islands National Park. The island is known for its coral-sand beaches, winding mountain roads, hidden coves, and trails that lead past old, bush-covered sugarcane plantations.

HIKING   St. John's **Virgin Islands National Park** is laced with a wide choice of clearly marked **walking paths.** At least 20 of these originate from Northshore Road (Rte. 20) or from the island's main east–west artery, Centerline Road (Rte. 10). Each is marked at its starting point with a preplanned itinerary; the walks can last anywhere from 10 minutes to 2 hours.

Another series of hikes traversing the more arid eastern section of St. John originate at clearly marked points along the island's southeastern tip, off Route 107. Many of the trails wind through the grounds of 18th-century plantations, often past ruined schoolhouses, rum distilleries, molasses factories, and Great Houses, many of which are covered with lush, encroaching vines and trees.

Because of the island's semi-wild state, with terrain ranging from arid and dry (in the east) to moist and semitropical (in the northwest), many hikers and trekkers consider a visit here among the most rewarding in the Virgin Islands. The island boasts more than 800 species of plants, 160 species of birds, and more than 20 hiking trails maintained in fine form by the island's crew of park rangers.

Maps of the island's hiking trails are available from the national park headquarters at Cruz Bay, but one of our favorite tours requires only about a half-mile stroll (about 30 minutes, round-trip, not including stops to admire the views) and departs from clearly marked points along the island's north coast, near the junction of Routes 10 and 20. Identified by the National Park Service as Trail no. 10, the **Annaberg Historic Trail** is a self-guided tour that includes the partially restored ruins of a manor house built during the 1700s and overlooking the island's north coast. Signs along the way give historical and botanical data. To visit the ruins costs $4 per person for those over 16.

If you want to prolong your hiking experience, the **Leinster Bay Trail** (Trail no. 11) begins near the point where Trail no. 10 ends, leading past mangrove swamps and coral inlets rich with plant and marine life, often with markers identifying some of the plants and animals.

National Park Service (© **340/776-6330** or 340/776-6201) provides a number of ranger-led activities in the park. One of the most popular is the 2½-mile **Reef Bay Hike.** A park ranger leads the hike down the Reef Bay Trail interpreting the natural and cultural history along the way. Included is a stop at the only known petroglyphs on the island and a tour of the sugar mill ruins. Reservations are required for this hike and can be made by phone. Tours are conducted at 10am on Monday and Thursday, costing $15 per person. Visitors are encouraged to stop by the **Cruz Bay Visitor Center** where you can pick up the park brochure, which includes a map of the park, and the *Virgin Islands National Park News,* which has the latest information on activities in the park.

WATERSPORTS   The most complete line of watersports available on St. John is offered at the **Cinnamon Bay Watersports Center** on Cinnamon Bay Beach (© **340/776-6330**). For the adventurous, there's windsurfing, kayaking, and sailing.

The **windsurfing** here is some of the best anywhere, for the beginner or the expert. High-quality equipment is available for all levels, even for kids. You can rent a board for $15 an hour; a 2-hour introductory lesson costs $45. Want to paddle to a secluded beach, explore a nearby island with an old Danish ruin, or jump overboard anytime you like for snorkeling or splashing? Then try a sit-on-top **kayak;** one- and two-person kayaks are available for rent for $10 to $17 per hour. You can also sail away in a 12- or 14-foot Hobie monohull **sailboat,** which can be rented for $20 to $30 per hour.

Snorkeling equipment can be rented from the Watersports Beach Shop for $4, plus a $25 deposit. Two of the best snorkeling spots around St. John are **Leinster Bay** ✦✦ and **Haulover Bay** ✦✦. Leinster Bay offers some of the best snorkeling in the U.S. Virgins. With calm, clear, and usually uncrowded waters, the bay is filled with an abundance of sea life, especially brilliantly hued tropical fish in rainbow colors. Visibility is usually excellent. Haulover Bay is a favorite among the locals. It is often deserted, and the waters are often clearer than in other spots around St. John. The ledges, walls, and nooks here are set very close together, making the bay a lot of fun for anyone with a little bit of experience.

Divers can ask about scuba packages at **Low Key Watersports,** Wharfside Village (© **800/835-7718** in the U.S., or 340/693-8999). All wreck dives are two-tank/two-location dives. A one-tank dive costs $55 per person, with night dives going for $75. Snorkel tours are also available at $55 to $75 per person, and parasailing is possible at $55. The center uses its own custom-built dive boats and also offers and specializes in watersports gear, including masks, fins, snorkels, and "dive skins." It also arranges day sailing charters, kayaking tours, and deep-sea sport-fishing.

Cruz Bay Watersports, P.O. Box 252, Palm Plaza, St. John, U.S.V.I. 00831 (© **800/835-7730** in the U.S., or 340/776-6234), is a PADI and NAUI five-star diving center on St. John. Certifications can be arranged through a dive master, for $350. Certification classes start daily, as well as two-tank reef dives with all the dive gear for $85. Beginner scuba lessons start at $95, and wreck dives (Wednesday and Friday), night dives, and dive packages are available at accommodations that range from budget to first class. Snorkel tours are available daily as well as trips to the British Virgin Islands (bring your passport), the latter costing $85, including food and beverages.

At **Trunk Bay** 🐾🐾, you can take the **National Park Underwater Trail** (© **340/776-6201**), stretching for 650 feet, allowing you to identify what you see, everything from false coral to colonial anemones. You'll pass lavender sea fans and schools of silversides. Equipment rental costs $4, with a $25 refundable deposit, and rangers are on hand to provide information. If time is limited, try to visit the **Annaberg Ruins** on Leinster Bay Road, where the Danes maintained a thriving plantation and sugar mill after 1718. It's located off North Shore Road east of Trunk Bay on the north shore. Admission is $4 for those over 16. On certain days of the week (dates vary) park rangers give guided walks of the area.

Trunk Bay, one of the world's most beautiful beaches, is also the site of one of the world's first marked underwater trails (bring your mask, snorkel, and fins). It lies to the east of Cruz Bay along North Shore Road. **Fort Berg** (also called Fortsberg), at Coral Bay, dating from 1717, played a disastrous role during the 1733 slave revolt—it served as the base for soldiers who brutally crushed the rebellion.

SHOPPING 🐾

Compared to shopping on St. Thomas, St. John's shopping isn't much, but what's here is intriguing. The boutiques and shops of Cruz Bay are individualized and quite special. Most of the shops are clustered at **Mongoose Junction,** in a woodsy area beside the roadway, about a 5-minute walk from the ferry dock. We've already recommended restaurants in this complex (see "Great Deals on Dining," earlier in this chapter), and it also contains shops of merit.

The most fun shopping on the island takes place on **St. John Saturday** 🐾, a colorful, drum-beating, spice-filled feast for the senses, held on the last Saturday of every month. This daylong event begins early in the morning in the center of town and spills across the park. Vendors hawk handmade items, ranging from jewelry to handcrafts and clothing, and especially food made from local ingredients. One vendor concocts soothing salves from recipes passed on by her ancestors; another designs and makes porcelain earrings; another flavors chicken and burgers with her own wonderful secret hickory barbecue sauce; yet another hollows out and carves gourds from local calabash trees.

Before you set sail for St. Thomas, you'll want to visit the recently expanded **Wharfside Village,** just a few steps from the ferry-departure point on the waterfront, opening onto Cruz Bay. Here in this complex of courtyards, alleys, and shady patios is a mishmash of all sorts of boutiques, along with some restaurants, fast-food joints, and bars.

Bamboula, Mongoose Junction (© **340/693-8699**), has an unusual and very appealing collection of gifts from the Caribbean, Haiti, India, Indonesia, and

Central Africa. Its exoticism is unexpected and very pleasant. The store has added clothing for both men and women under its own label—hand-batiked soft cottons and rayons made for comfort in a hot climate. Many locally crafted items, ideal as gifts, are also sold. **The Canvas Factory,** Mongoose Junction (© **340/776-6196**), produces its own handmade, rugged, and colorful canvas bags in the factory at Mongoose Junction. Their products range from sailing hats to soft-sided luggage. **The Clothing Studio,** Mongoose Junction (© **340/776-6585**), is the Caribbean's oldest hand-painted clothing studio, in operation since 1978. You can watch talented artists create original designs on fine tropical clothing, including swimwear and daytime and evening clothing, mainly for babies and women.

Coconut Coast Studios, Frank Bay (© **340/776-6944**), lies a 5-minute stroll from the heart of Cruz Bay (follow along the waterfront bypassing Gallows Point). This will lead you to the studio of Elaine Estern and Lucinda Schutt, two of the best watercolorists on the island. Especially known for her Caribbean landscapes, Elaine is the official artist for Westin Resorts, St. John; Lucinda is the artist for Caneel Bay. **Donald Schnell Studio,** Mongoose Junction (© **340/776-6420**), is a studio and gallery where Mr. Schnell and his assistants have created one of the Caribbean's finest collections of handmade pottery, sculpture, and blown glass. The staff can be seen working daily and are especially noted for their rough-textured coral work. Water fountains are a specialty item, as are house signs and coral-pottery dinnerware. The studio will mail works all over the world; go in and discuss any particular design you may have in mind.

Fabric Mill, Mongoose Junction (© **340/776-6194**), features silk-screened and batik fabrics from around the world. Vibrant rugs and bed, bathroom, and table linens add the perfect touch to your home if you like a Caribbean flair. Whimsical soft sculpture, sarongs, and handbags are also made in this studio shop.

R and I Patton Goldsmithing, Mongoose Junction (© **340/776-6548**), on the island since 1973, is one of the oldest businesses here, and three quarters of the merchandise is made on St. John. It has a large selection of island-designed jewelry in sterling silver, gold, and precious stones. Also featured are the works of goldsmiths from outstanding American studios, plus Spanish coins.

ST. JOHN AFTER DARK

Bring a good book. After dark, St. John is no St. Thomas when it comes to nightlife, and everybody here seems to want to keep it that way. Most people are content to have a long, leisurely dinner and then head for bed.

The **Caneel Bay Bar,** at the Caneel Bay Resort (© **340/776-6111**), presents live music nightly 8:30 to 11pm. The most popular drinks are a Cool Caneel (local rum with sugar, lime, and anisette) and the trademark of the house, a Plantation Freeze (lime and orange juice with three kinds of rum, bitters, and nutmeg). This place is very touristy. If you'd like to go where the locals go for drinking and gossiping, try **JJ's Texas Coast Café,** Cruz Bay (© **340/776-6908**), across the park from the ferry dock. Your Texan host, J.J. Gewels, makes everybody feel welcome—at least if he likes you. The Tex-Mex food is the island's best, and the margaritas are deservedly called lethal. Also at Cruz Bay, check out the action at **Fred's** (© **340/776-6363**), across from The Lime Inn. The most laid-back bar on the island, it brings in island bands on Wednesday, Friday, and Sunday, and is also the best place to go to dance, at least on those nights. It's just a little hole-in-the-wall and can get crowded fast.

The best sports bar on the island is **Skinny Legs,** Emmaus, Coral Bay, beyond the fire station (© **340/779-4982**). It's only a shack made out of tin and wood, but it serves the best hamburgers on St. John. The chili dogs aren't bad either. The yachting crowd likes to hang out here, and it often seems like the richer they are, the poorer they dress—many of them look as if they're refugees, though in fact they've disembarked from $1.5-million yachts. The bar has a satellite dish to televise major sporting events. Live music is presented at least once a week; otherwise it's the dartboard or horseshoe pits for you.

Morgan's Mango, although primarily a restaurant, is also one of the hottest watering holes along the island, lying in Cruz Bay across from the national park dock (© **340/693-8141**). Thursday is margarita night, when a soft rock duo plays. Count yourself lucky if you get in on a crowded night in winter. The place became famous locally when it turned away actor Harrison Ford, who was vacationing at Caneel Bay.

4 St. Croix ★★★

At 84 square miles, St. Croix is the largest of the U.S. Virgin Islands. At the east end (which actually is the easternmost point of the United States), the terrain is rocky and arid. The west end is lusher, and even includes a small "rain forest" of mango, mahogany, tree ferns, and dangling lianas. Between the two extremes are beautiful beaches, rolling hills, pastures, and, increasingly, miles of condos.

Columbus named the island *Santa Cruz* (Holy Cross) when he landed here on November 14, 1493. He anchored his ship off the north shore, but was quickly driven away by the spears, arrows, and axes of the Carib Indians. The French laid claim to the island in 1650, and the Danes purchased it from them in 1773. Under Danish rule, slave labor and sugarcane fields proliferated during a golden era for both planters and pirates, which came to an end in the latter half of the 19th century. Danish influence still permeates the island today.

ST. CROIX ESSENTIALS
VISITOR INFORMATION
You can begin your explorations at the **visitors' bureau,** Queen Cross Street, in Christiansted (© **340/773-0495**), a yellow-sided building with a cedar-capped roof near the harbor. It was originally built as the Old Scalehouse in 1856. In its heyday, all taxable goods leaving and entering the harbor were weighed here. Open Monday to Friday 8am to 5pm.

GETTING AROUND
BY TAXI   At Alexander Hamilton Airport you'll find official **taxi** rates posted. Per person rates require a minimum of two passengers; a single person pays double the posted fares. Expect to pay about $12 to $15 for one or two riders from the airport to Christiansted and about $10 for one or two from the airport to Frederiksted. The cabs are unmetered, so agree on the rate before you get in.

The **St. Croix Taxicab Association** (© **340/778-1088**) offers door-to-door service.

BY BUS   Air-conditioned **buses** run between Christiansted and Frederiksted about every 30 minutes daily, from 5:30am to 9pm. Beginning at Tide Village, to the east of Christiansted, buses go along Route 75 to the Golden Rock Shopping Center. Then they make their way to Route 70, with stopovers at the Sunny Isle Shopping Center, La Reine Shopping Center, St. George Village Botanical Garden, and Whim Plantation Museum, before reaching

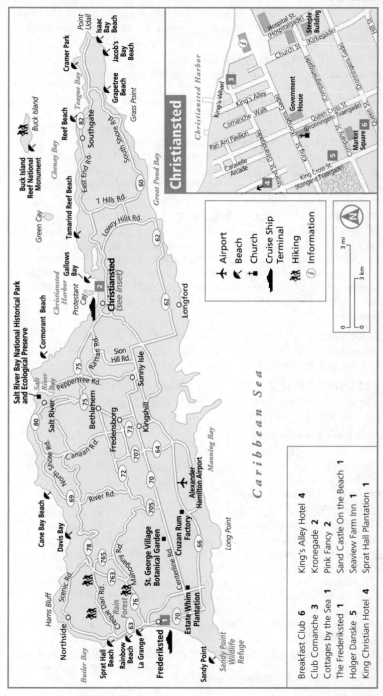

St. Croix

Christiansted

Hospital St. (Hospitalgade)
Steeple Building
Church St. (Kirkegade)
Christiansted Harbor
King's Wharf
3
Government House
King's Alley
Comanche Walk
Pan Am Pavilion
Queen Cross St. (Dronningens Tvaergade)
Company St. (Compagniegade)
Caravelle Arcade
5
Market Square
6
4
Strand St. (Strandgade)
King Cross St. (Kongens Tvaergade)
King St. (Kongens Gade)
Queen St. (Dronningens Gade)
Hill St.

Point Udall
Isaac Bay Beach
Jacob's Bay Beach
Cramer Park
Grapetree Beach
Reef Beach
82
Southgate
Teague Bay
Grass Point
Chenay Bay
Buck Island
Buck Island Reef National Monument
Reef Beach
Tamarind Reef Beach
East End Rd.
South Shore Rd.
Great Pond Bay
60
1 Hills Rd.
Lowry Hills Rd.
Green Cay
62
Longford
62
Gallows Bay
Christiansted Harbor
Christiansted (see inset)
Protestant Cay
2
Cormorant Beach
Salt River Bay National Historical Park and Ecological Preserve
Salt River Bay
Raftan Rd.
Sion Hill Rd.
Sunny Isle
Peppertree Rd.
75
75
Salt River
80
Bethlehem
North Shore Rd.
69
Canaan Rd.
Fredensborg
Kingshill
73
707
64
Manning Bay
Alexander Hamilton Airport
72
70
River Rd.
705
66
Long Point
Cane Bay Beach
Davis Bay
78
765
Mahogany Rd.
763
Centerline Rd.
Cruzan Rum Factory
St. George Village Botanical Garden
Hams Bluff
Scenic Rd.
Blue Dan Rd.
Rain Forest
76
63
70
Estate Whim Plantation
Northside
Sprat Hall Beach
Rainbow Beach
La Grange
1
Frederiksted
Butler Bay
Sandy Point
Sandy Point Wildlife Refuge

Caribbean Sea

N

Airport
Beach
Church
Cruise Ship Terminal
Hiking
i Information

0   3 mi
0   3 km

Breakfast Club **6**
Club Comanche **3**
Cottages by the Sea **1**
The Frederiksted **1**
Holger Danske **5**
King Christian Hotel **4**

King's Alley Hotel **4**
Kronegade **2**
Pink Fancy **2**
Sand Castle On the Beach **1**
Seaview Farm Inn **1**
Sprat Hall Plantation **1**

Frederiksted. Bus service is also available from the airport to each of the two towns. Fares are $1 or 50¢ for senior citizens. For more information, call ℭ **340/778-0898.**

BY RENTAL CAR   Okay, we've warned you: The roads are often disastrous. Sometimes the government smoothes them out before the big season begins, but don't count on it. Car-rental rates on St. Croix are reasonable. However, because of the island's higher than usual accident rate (which is partly because many visitors aren't used to *driving on the left*), insurance costs are higher than on the mainland.

Avis (ℭ **800/331-2112**), **Budget** (ℭ **888/227-3359** in the U.S., or 340/778-9636), and **Hertz** (ℭ **800/654-3001** in the U.S., or 340/778-1402) all maintain their headquarters at the island's airport; look for their kiosks near the baggage claim areas. Not to beat a dead horse, but do remember: *Driving is on the left.*

BY BIKE   **St. Croix Bike and Tours,** 5035 Cotton Valley, Christiansted (ℭ **340/773-5004**), offers bike rentals and guided bicycle tours. The outfitter rents 21-speed mountain bikes, which are suitable for the rugged terrain of St. Croix. They also feature a 12-mile historical-ecotour of moderate exertion level along the rolling western coast and a 14-mile ridgeline tropical mountain bike tour for the experienced biker or fitness buff. Guides are knowledge-able about the social, political, and natural history of the island. Call for more information.

FAST FACTS

For medical care on St. Croix, go to the **St. Croix Hospital,** 6 Diamond Bay, Christiansted (ℭ **340/778-6311**).

ACCOMMODATIONS YOU CAN AFFORD

All rooms are subject to an 8% hotel room tax, which is *not* included in the rates given below.

IN CHRISTIANSTED

The trick is to reserve one of the cheaper rooms at Club Comanche instead of the most expensive. If you do, you'll be nailing down one of the bargain rooms of Christiansted. But even this traditional budget leader doesn't match the deal offered by the Breakfast Club.

Breakfast Club 𝒦 *Value*   Here you'll get the best value of any bed-and-breakfast on St. Croix. This comfortable place combines a 1950s compound of efficiency apartments with a traditional-looking stone house that was rebuilt from a ruin in the 1930s. Each of the units has a cypress-sheathed ceiling, a tile floor, and simple, summery furniture. Shower-only bathrooms are small and adequately maintained. The centerpiece of the place is the hot tub on a raised deck, where impromptu parties are likely to develop at random hours of the day or night, and where views stretch as far off as St. John. Toby Chapin, the Ohio-born owner, cooks one of the most generous and appealing breakfasts on the island; try the banana pancakes or the chile rellenos.

18 Queen Cross St., Christiansted, St. Croix, U.S.V.I. 00820. ℭ 340/773-7383. Fax 340/773-8642. http://nav. to/thebreakfastclub. 9 units. Year-round $60 single; $75 double. Rates include breakfast. AE, V. Free parking. **Amenities:** Jacuzzi. *In room:* Kitchenette, no phone.

Club Comanche   Right on the Christiansted waterfront, this is a famous old West Indian inn, based around a 250-year-old Danish-inspired main house, once the home of Alexander Hamilton. Extensively remodeled over the years, some of its small to medium-size rooms have slanted ceilings with carved four-poster beds, old chests, and mahogany mirrors. Reached by a covered bridge, a more modern addition passes over a shopping street to the waterside. Some rooms are at poolside or harborfront buildings. Since accommodations come in such a wide range of styles and sizes, your opinion of this place is likely to be influenced entirely by your room assignment. Since the hurricanes, all the mattresses have been replaced, and beds are most comfortable, often king-size. The bathrooms remain small but have been renewed, each with a shower. The club also offers the most popular restaurant in Christiansted. Four minutes by ferry will take you to the beach at Hotel on the Cay.

1 Strand St., Christiansted, St. Croix, U.S.V.I. 00820. © **800/524-2066** or 340/773-0210. Fax 340/713-9145. www.usvi.net/hotel/comanche. 45 units. Winter $75–$125 single or double; $175 suite. Off-season $60–$110 single or double; $120 suite. AE, DC, V. **Amenities:** Restaurant, bar, pool. *In room:* A/C, TV.

Holger Danske ⟨★⟩ ⟨*Value*⟩   This is one of the best bets in town for the budget traveler. Freshly remodeled and refurbished, right in the heart of Christiansted, it's a Best Western. The inn provides pleasantly furnished but small accommodations, each with a private furnished balcony. Following hurricane damage, the rooms have been renewed, with fresh mattresses and rejuvenated plumbing in the shower-only bathrooms. Some units also offer efficiency kitchens. It has a pool patio and a garden path walkway, but only the superior rooms open onto the harbor and its offshore cay. Watersports and other activities are close at hand, as are a bevy of shops and restaurants. The nearest beach is a 4-minute ferry ride away.

1200 King Cross St., Christiansted, St. Croix, U.S.V.I. 00821. © **800/528-1234** or 340/773-3600. Fax 340/773-8828. www.bestwestern.com/reservations/carib/vi/main.html. 44 units. Winter $104–$155 single or double. Off-season $90–$135 single or double. AE, DC, DISC, MC, V. **Amenities:** Pool, access to nearby watersports. *In room:* A/C, TV, fridge.

King Christian Hotel   This hotel is directly on the waterfront. Each of its front rooms has two double beds, a refrigerator, and private balcony overlooking the harbor. No-frills economy-wing rooms have two single beds or one double but no view or balcony. Rooms are either small or medium, and under new management. All units have been redone, with fresh mattresses on the comfortable beds, new rugs and draperies, and renewed bath fixtures in the shower-only bathrooms. You can relax on the sundeck or shaded patio or in the freshwater pool. The staff will make arrangements for golf, tennis, horseback riding, and sightseeing tours, and there's a beach just a few hundred yards across the harbor, reached by ferry. Mile Mark Charters watersports center offers daily trips to Buck Island's famous snorkeling trail as well as a complete line of watersports.

59 King St. (P.O. Box 24467.CBS), Christiansted, St. Croix, U.S.V.I. 00824. © **800/524-2012** in the U.S., or 340/773-6330. Fax 809/773-9411. www.kingchristian.com. 39 units. Winter $112 economy single, $118 superior single; $147 economy double, $159 superior double. Off-season $89 economy single, $110 superior single; $125 economy double, $120 superior double. AE, DC, DISC, MC, V. **Amenities:** 2 restaurants, bar, exercise room, tour desk, bike rental, car rental, business center. *In room:* A/C, TV, dataport, fridge, coffeemaker, iron, safe.

King's Alley Hotel ⟨★⟩   The King's Alley Hotel stands at water's edge, near Christiansted Harbor's yacht basin, a 4-minute ferry ride to the nearest beach at Hotel on the Cay. The inn is furnished with a distinct Mediterranean flair, and many of its small to medium-size rooms overlook its pool terrace surrounded by tropical plants. The galleries opening off the rooms are almost spacious enough for entertaining. All rooms have twin or king-size beds with good mattresses, and the newly added deluxe units contain four-poster mahogany beds. The medium-size bathrooms are very comfortable, with showers and good lighting. Right outside your door are boutiques and restaurants. Breakfast can be ordered if you walk over to one of the nearby cafes.

57 King St., Christiansted, St. Croix, U.S.V.I. 00820. © **800/843-3574** or 340/773-0103. Fax 340/773-4431. 35 units. Winter $105 single; $119–$165 double. Off-season $99 single; $108–$148 double. AE, DC, MC, V. **Amenities:** Pool. *In room:* A/C, TV.

Kronegade Inn 🌴 *Finds* Opened in 1994, this small inn in Christiansted offers a certain down-home charm at reasonable rates. Some guests call it the best-kept secret in Christiansted. The inn offers 12 suites or apartments, each with full kitchen, radio, and ceiling fan. The beds are most comfortable with firm mattresses, and bathrooms, though small, are tidily maintained, each with a shower. The nearest beach is at the offshore Hotel on the Cay, a 4-minute ferry ride away, where Kronegade guests are allowed to use the beach and facilities. The decor is in a tropical motif with white rattan furnishings. The inn doesn't offer food service, but a number of restaurants and cafes are nearby.

1112 Western Suburb, Christiansted, St. Croix, U.S.V.I. 00820. © **340/692-9590**. Fax 340/692-9591. www. kronegadeinn.com. 16 units. Winter $87 suite for 1 or 2; $107 2-bedroom suite. Off-season $75 suite for 1 or 2; $95 2-bedroom suite. AE, MC, V. *In room:* A/C, TV, kitchen ceiling fans, radio.

Pink Fancy 🌴🌴 This small, unique hotel is a block from the Annapolis Sailing School. You get more atmosphere here than anywhere else in town. The oldest part of the four-building complex is a historic 1780 Danish town house. In the 1950s, the hotel became a mecca for writers and artists, including, among others, Noël Coward. New owners have made major renovations, installing more antiques and fine furnishings. Guest rooms have a bright, tropical feel, with ceiling fans, floral prints, and rattan furnishings. The deluxe rooms are furnished with canopy or iron beds, as well as antiques and artwork. The medium-size bathrooms have combination shower/tubs. A 3-minute launch ride takes guests to The Beach on the Cay, a sandy islet in Christiansted's harbor.

27 Prince St., Christiansted, St. Croix, U.S.V.I. 00820. © **800/524-2045** in the U.S., or 340/773-8460. Fax 340/ 773-6448. www.pinkfancy.com. 13 units. Winter $95–$125 single or double. Off-season $75–$105 single or double. Extra person $20. Rates include continental breakfast. Ask about packages and weekly rates. AE, DC, DISC, MC, V. **Amenities:** Pool. *In room:* A/C, TV, kitchenette, fridge.

AT FREDERIKSTED

Cottages by the Sea *Value* These isolated cottages are on the water right outside Frederiksted, about 6 miles from the airport. In 1998, *Caribbean Travel & Life* voted this the best bargain of the U.S. Virgins. The enterprise was launched with 4 cottages back in the late 1970s and has increased to 20. The managers, Vicki McFee and Richard Mercure, like to keep it quiet, so no children under age 8 are allowed. Some cottages are made of cinder blocks and others of wood. The timeworn interiors include paneling, and all cottages have air-conditioning, TVs, and private patios. The look is a bit spartan but reasonably comfortable. Most rooms have king-size or twin beds, with freshly renewed mattresses, along with tight, compact bathrooms with shower. Maintenance is excellent, however. There are big patios out front where guests can grill their dinners. Watersports have to be arranged elsewhere, but guests are welcome to go snorkeling in the waters just outside the grounds.

127A Smithfield, Frederiksted, St. Croix, U.S.V.I. 00840. © **800/323-7252** or 340/772-1753. Fax 340/ 772-1753. maccottage@worldnet.att.net. 22 units. Winter $95–$119 cottage for 1 or 2; $175 villa for 4. Off-season $70–$99 cottage for 1 or 2; $140 villa for 4. Extra person $20 in winter, $15 off-season. AE, DISC, MC, V. In room: A/C, TV, fridge, coffeemaker.

The Frederiksted ⚡   This contemporary four-story inn is a good choice if you want to stay in the heart of historic Frederiksted. It's located in the center of town, about a 10-minute ride from the airport. Much of the activity takes place in the outdoor tiled courtyard, where guests enjoy drinks and listen to live music on Friday and Saturday nights. The cheery rooms are like those of a U.S. motel, perhaps showing a bit of wear, and with good ventilation but bad lighting. They're done in a tropical motif of pastels. The best (and most expensive) rooms are those with an ocean view; they're subject to street noise, but they have the best light. Each accommodation has a small, tiled shower-only bathroom. The nearest beach is Dorch Beach, a 1-mile walk or a 5-minute drive from the hotel, along the water.

20 Strand St., Frederiksted, St. Croix, U.S.V.I. 00840. © **800/595-9519** in the U.S., or 340/772-0500. Fax 340/ 772-0500. www.frederikstedhotel.com. 40 units. Winter $100–$110 single or double. Off-season $90–$100 single or double. Extra person $10. AE, DISC, MC, V. **Amenities:** Pool. In room: A/C, TV, kitchenette, fridge.

Sand Castle On the Beach   This small place is the best-known gay hotel in Frederiksted. It lies half a mile from the town's shopping and dining facilities. Rooms are comfortably furnished but small; all have good mattresses, tiny private bathrooms, and extras such as VCR, computer hookups, and coolers. There are two pools, a hot tub, and a beachfront patio, where you'll often encounter middle-aged men in G-strings. The on-site restaurant is excellent.

Frederiksted Beach (P.O. Box 1908), Frederiksted, St. Croix, U.S.V.I. 00841. © **800/524-2018** or 340/772-1205. Fax 340/772-1757. onthebeach@virginislands.net. 23 units. Winter $115–$159 single or double. Off-season $65–$145 single or double. Rates include continental breakfast. AE, DISC, MC, V. **Amenities:** Restaurant, 2 pools, Jacuzzi. In room: A/C, TV/VCR, dataport, kitchenette, fridge, coffeemaker, hair dryer, iron/ironing board.

Seaview Farm Inn   This is one of the most artfully unstructured small-scale inns on St. Croix, with views that extend out over Frederiksted's cruise ship piers. There's no pool and not many formal amenities, but the inn has a great location near the northern tip of the Great Salt Pond, with Dorsch Beach within a 5-minute walk, allowing guests to appreciate the sense of living in a backwater hideaway. Set on 3 acres of rolling land, the four-building complex originally has a stylized West Indian decor. Each of the unexpectedly large units contains a private porch, a living room with a kitchenette, a separate bedroom, a shower-only bathroom, a supply of paperback books for low-key reading, and beach towels and beach chairs. Most have iron four-poster beds and comfortable wicker and rattan furnishings. The ingredients for the day's continental breakfast are stocked in the refrigerators.

180 Estate Two Brothers (about a mile south of central Frederiksted), Frederiksted, St. Croix, U.S.V.I. 00840. © **800/792-5060** in the U.S., or 340/772-5367. Fax 340/772-5060. www.seaviewfarm.net. 8 suites. Winter $100 single or double. Off-season $65 single or double. Rates include continental breakfast. DC, MC, V. **Amenities:** Restaurant, bar. In room: Kitchenette, ceiling fans.

WORTH A SPLURGE
Sprat Hall Plantation ⚡ (Finds)   This resort, 1 mile north of Frederiksted, is the oldest plantation Great House (and the only French-built plantation house left intact) in the Virgin Islands. Dating from St. Croix's French occupation of

1650 to 1690, it's set on 20 acres and has private white-sand beaches. The plantation has room for about 40 people, depending on how many guests use the cottage units, which all have radios.

The units in the Great House have been designated for nonsmokers because of the value of the antiques. An annex was built in the 1940s, and each of its units has simple furnishings and a view of the sea. If you prefer your Caribbean living old-fashioned and homey, ask for a room in the Great House. The cottages aren't very romantic but have been remodeled and refurnished with queen-size beds with good mattresses; you'll find greater comfort elsewhere on the island, although nothing that even comes close to matching the history and legacy of this place. You can be assured of good food at the Beach Restaurant or in the Sprat Hall Restaurant. Guests are requested to dress with decorum—no jeans or T-shirts, please. Only guests of the hotel and/or their invited guests can attend dinners. On the grounds is a worthwhile equestrian stable. The Hurd and Young families run the operation and offer hiking and bird-watching, as well as snorkeling, swimming, and shore fishing. Jetskiing and water-skiing can be arranged.

Rte. 63 (P.O. Box 695), Frederiksted, St. Croix, U.S.V.I. 00841. © **800/843-3584** or 340/772-0305. Fax 340/772-2880. www.st-croix.com/sprat. 17 units. Winter $110–$120 single; $120–$130 double; $150 suite; $200 cottage; $150 Great House room. Off-season $90–$100 single; $100–$110 double; $130 suite; $200 cottage; $130 Great House room. No credit cards. **Amenities:** 2 restaurants, 2 bars, stable, hiking, bird-watching. *In room:* A/C, TV, radio.

GREAT DEALS ON DINING
IN & AROUND CHRISTIANSTED

The Bombay Club INTERNATIONAL   This is one of the most enduring restaurants in Christiansted. It's concealed from the street by the brick foundations of an 18th-century planter's town house. You enter through a low stone tunnel and eventually find yourself near its bar and the courtyard that contains many of its tables. The food, while not overly fancy, is plentiful, flavorful, and reasonably priced. Menu items include the catch of the day, regional dishes like conch, veal dishes, beef filet, and pasta. The island's best fresh lobster pasta is served here. The catch of the day is likely to be wahoo, tuna, or mahimahi.

5A King St. © **340/773-1838.** Reservations recommended. Main courses $10–$18. MC, V. Mon–Fri 11am–4pm and 5–10pm; Sat–Sun 6–10pm.

Cheeseburgers in Paradise AMERICAN   Three miles outside Christiansted, this restaurant isn't owned by Jimmy Buffett, but does make the best burgers on the island. You get almost a half pound of meat with all the fixin's. A margarita accompanies many a burger plate. Cheeseburgers aren't all: You can choose from an array of burritos, freshly made salads, a tasty grilled chicken sandwich, and daily specials. The pizza oven is heated up on Thursday. Dinners run the gamut from barbecued ribs to stir-fry. The fresh fish dishes are excellent, and the chef has a winning way with chicken and cooks a big prime rib on Saturday. Live music is presented Thursday to Sunday.

67 Southgate. © **340/773-1119.** Main courses $8–$10. MC, V. Daily 11am–11pm (bar open later).

Comanche Club ★ CARIBBEAN/CONTINENTAL   Relaxed yet elegant, Comanche is one of the island's most popular restaurants. It's not the best, but the specialties are eclectic—everything from fish and conch chowder to shark cakes. Each night, a different special and a different local dish is featured. Other choices include salads, a cold buffet, curries, fish sautéed with lemon butter and capers, and typical West Indian dishes such as conch Creole with *fungi* (cornmeal mash). There's also standard international dishes such as filet mignon in a béarnaise sauce.

1 Strand St. © **340/773-9145.** Reservations recommended. Main courses $13–$25; lunch from $12. AE, MC, V. Mon–Sat 11:30am–2:30pm and 5:30–9:30pm.

Fort Christian Brew Pub *(Finds* CAJUN   This fish house and brewery boasts one of the best harbor views in Christiansted. It's the only licensed microbrewery in the U.S. Virgins Islands. Beer choices include a pale ale ("Frigate"), a red beer ("Blackbeard's"), and a dark stout ("Jump-Up"), all of which have already earned a formidable reputation on the island. Many patrons here come just to drink, staying until the pub's closing at around 1am. But if you're hungry, check out the roster of burgers and sandwiches that is served on street level at lunch and dinner. In the evening, the upstairs dining room offers a two-fisted menu that includes a 16-ounce ribeye with caramelized onions. A favorite of ours is Bourbon Street Jambalaya. Maybe it's better in New Orleans, but this version tastes very much of Louisiana, as does the shrimp étouffée, slow-cooked in a blend of Creole spices and stock. The blackened or pan-seared catfish takes you way down south. For something West Indian, order the red snapper with *fungi* (okra and cornmeal).

King's Alley Walk. © **340/713-9820.** Reservations recommended for upstairs dining room, not for meals in the Brew Pub. Platters in Brew Pub $8–$12; main courses in upstairs restaurant $12–$24. MC, V. Mon–Sat 11am–11pm (bar open until 1am).

Harbormaster Restaurant AMERICAN   A 4-minute ferry ride across the harbor from Christiansted, this is where guests at the local town inns head for a day at the beach (it's the nearest, best beach). While here, you don't want to go back into Christiansted for lunch, so the hotel has decided to accommodate its many day visitors by offering this quite acceptable restaurant. The cookery isn't the island's best, but it's good. You get the usual array of salad platters, sandwiches, omelets, and burgers. Many main dishes are more elaborate and appealing, especially the grilled filet of dolphin (or swordfish); the conch in lemon, garlic, and butter sauce; and the barbecued ribs. The chef also prepares a good dinner, but only 1 night a week: the Tuesday evening West Indian barbecue. You pay $23 for all you can eat and are entertained by steel band music.

At the Hotel on the Cay, Protestant Cay. © **340/773-2035.** Main courses $6.50–$17.50; breakfast from $3.50. AE, DISC, MC, V. Daily 7:30am–5pm; Tues 7–9:30pm.

Harvey's CARIBBEAN/CONTINENTAL   Ignore the plastic and the flowery tablecloths that give this place the aura of a 1950s time warp, and try to grab one of its dozen or so tables. If you do, you can enjoy the thoroughly zesty cooking of island matriarch Sarah Harvey, who takes joy in her work and definitely aims to fill your stomach with her basic but hearty fare. Try one of her homemade soups, especially the *callaloo* or chicken. She'll even serve you conch in butter sauce as an appetizer. For a main dish you might choose from barbecue chicken, barbecue spareribs, boiled filet of snapper, and even lobster when they can get it. *Fungi* comes with just about everything. For dessert, try one of the delectable tarts, made from guava, pineapple, or coconut.

11B Company St. © **340/773-3433.** Main courses $5–$10. No credit cards. Mon–Sat 11:30am–5pm.

The Hideaway AMERICAN   Three miles west of Christiansted, this open-air restaurant fronts one of the island's best beaches. Even if you don't go here for dinner, you might want to patronize it at lunch. It's a true hideaway, known for serving one of the island's best breakfasts, including good stuff like eggs Benedict and salmon with sour cream. The chef also makes some of the island's best omelets. At lunch, you get the usual burgers and sandwiches, as well as hot main-dish specialties. At night, the menu is considerably upgraded, based on the market that day. You can usually get fresh fish prepared as you like it, along with lobster (sometimes available). The baby-back ribs are a winner, and chicken and beef are prepared in interesting ways. On Wednesday, it's beach barbecue time, all you can eat for $18.

At the Hibiscus Beach Hotel, La Grande Princesse. ℂ **340/773-4042.** Reservations recommended. Main courses $11–$25; lunch $7–$12. AE, DISC, MC, V. Daily 7am–10pm.

Junie's Bar and Restaurant WEST INDIAN/SEAFOOD   A favorite of locals and particularly the island's taxi drivers, this restaurant occupies a white-painted cement building about a half-mile south of Christiansted's main core. The wooden tables, metal chairs, bowls of cut flowers, and well-scrubbed kind of simplicity add to the appeal. Your hosts, Junie Allen and her daughter Denise, prepare a flavor-filled but basic medley of West Indian staples, including a roster of drinks you might not have tasted before. Examples are sea moss, a kind of eggnog flavored with pulverized seaweed; mauby, fermented from rainwater and tree bark; and ginger beer. Good-tasting menu items include boiled fish, conch, or lobster in butter sauce; stewed goat; Creole-style lobster; and pork chops with greens and yams. Desserts feature carrot cake, cheesecake, and Key lime pie.

132 Peter's Rest. ℂ **340/773-2801.** Lunch main courses $8–$12; dinner main courses $8–$22. AE, DC, DISC, MC, V. Mon–Sat 11:30am–11pm; Sun 11am–8pm.

Luncheria Mexican Food _Value_ MEXICAN/CUBAN/PUERTO RICAN This Mexican restaurant offers great value. You get the usual tacos, tostadas, burritos, nachos, and enchiladas, as well as chicken fajitas, enchiladas verde, and _arroz con pollo_ (spiced chicken with brown rice). Daily specials feature both low-calorie and vegetarian choices (the chef's refried beans are lard-free), and whole-wheat tortillas are offered. The complimentary salsa bar has mild to hot sauces, plus jalapeños. More recently, some Cuban and Puerto Rican dishes have appeared on the menu, including a zesty chicken curry, black-bean soup, and roast pork. The bartender makes the island's best margaritas.

In the historic Apothecary Hall Courtyard, 2111 Company St. ℂ **340/773-4247.** Main courses $7–$12. No credit cards. Mon–Sat 11am–9pm.

Marina Bar & Grill CARIBBEAN/CONTINENTAL   Some in-the-know boaters head here for their morning pick-me-up, a spicy Bloody Mary to get their blood circulating. You can join them for breakfast, which is rather standard fare, with bagels, muffins, and eggs as you like them. Lunch is also a bit standard; many opt for one of the burgers, even a veggie burger. The best bet is one of the daily specials. In the evening the menu perks up, and fresh fish is the best item to order. Dinner is often accompanied by steel drum music. If you show up Monday night, you can get in on the crab races. Locals are fond of dining here, sitting on the waterfront watching the seaplane land.

At the Kings Landing Yacht Club. ℂ **340/773-0103.** Main courses $5.50–$12. AE, MC, V. Daily 24 hours.

Nolan's Tavern ★★ INTERNATIONAL/WEST INDIAN   Nolan's is a warm, cozy tavern with no pretensions. It's across from the capital's most promi-nent elementary school, the Pearl B. Larsen School. Your host is Nolan Joseph, a Trinidad-born chef who makes a point of welcoming guests and offering "tasty food and good service." No one will mind if you stop in just for a drink. Mr. Joseph, referred to by some diners as "King Conch," prepares that mollusk in at least half a dozen ways, including versions with curry, Creole sauce, and garlic-pineapple sauce. He reportedly experimented for 3 months to perfect a means of tenderizing the conch without artificial chemicals. His ribs are also excellent.

5A Estate St. Peter (2 miles east of Christiansted's harbor), Christiansted East. ✆ 340/773-6660. Reservations recommended only for groups of 6 or more. Burgers $7–$9; main courses $12.75–$20. AE, DISC, MC, V. Kitchen daily 5–9pm; bar from 3pm.

Paradise Café DELI/AMERICAN   This neighborhood favorite draws locals seeking good food and great value. Its brick walls and beamed ceiling were originally part of an 18th-century Great House. New York–style deli fare is served during the day. Enjoy the savory homemade soups or freshly made salads, to which you can add grilled chicken or fish. At breakfast, you can select from an assortment of omelets, or try the steak and eggs. Dinners are more elaborate. The 12-ounce New York strip steak and the freshly made pasta specialties are good choices. Appetizers include stuffed mushrooms and crab cakes.

53B Company St. (at Queen Cross St., across from Government House). ✆ 340/773-2985. Breakfast $4.50–$9.50; lunch $4–$9.50; dinner $14–$22. No credit cards. Mon–Sat 7:30am–10pm.

Stixx on the Waterfront INTERNATIONAL/AMERICAN   This rustic eatery is on the waterfront in downtown Christiansted. This two-story place at the Pan Am Pavilion has a deck extending out over the harbor, and it has been said that this restaurant sells more lobster than anywhere else on the island, thus making it the house specialty. The good-tasting menu is varied from chicken to seafood. Stixx is also known for its stuffed mushrooms, the swordfish served with a mango salsa, and grilled vegetables over angel-hair pasta, with surf-and-turf specials once or twice a week.

39 Strand St. ✆ 340/773-5157. Reservations recommended. Main courses $10–$30; lunches from $5.50; all-you-can-eat Sun brunch $10. AE, MC, V. Daily 7am–10pm.

WORTH A SPLURGE
South Shore Café ✪ AMERICAN   Set in a breezy building on an isolated inland region ("in the middle of nowhere") 2 miles southeast of Christiansted, this is a charming and intensely personalized restaurant, whose family-style dining has helped make the place a success since its debut. Diane Scheuber is the owner. Her decorating quirks (including a collection of umbrellas—her trademark—hanging from the ceiling of the lattice-trimmed dining room) add a funky note to what are usually well-turned-out meals with a rural North American twist. Excellent examples are ravioli stuffed with sweet potatoes and spring onions, tomato-based Sicilian clam chowder, baked brie with Cruzan rum sauce, local grilled fish with herb-flavored butter sauce, and homemade grilled chicken lasagna with sun-dried tomatoes and sherry-flavored cream sauce.

Junction of Rtes. 62 and 624. ✆ 340/773-9311. Reservations required. Main courses $12–$25. MC, V. Mid-Dec to Apr Wed–Sun 6–9pm; May to mid-Dec Thurs–Sun 6–9pm.

THE NORTH SHORE
Cormorant Beach Club Restaurant ✪ INTERNATIONAL   This is the premier gay restaurant on St. Croix. Both the restaurant and its bar are a mecca for gay and gay-friendly people who appreciate its relaxed atmosphere,

Finds Buck Island: Unspoiled Nature & World-Class Snorkeling

The crystal-clear waters and the white coral sand of **Buck Island** 🌟🌟, a satellite of St. Croix, are legendary. Some visitors, including Arthur Frommer, have called it the single most important attraction of the Caribbean. In years past, the island was frequented by the swashbuckling likes of Morgan, LaFitte, Blackbeard, and even Captain Kidd. Now the U.S. National Park Service has marked an underwater snorkeling trail in the waters offshore, attracting a new generation of seafarers. The park covers about 850 acres, including the land area, which has a sandy beach with picnic tables and barbecue pits, as well as restrooms and a small changing room. There are two major underwater trails for snorkeling on the reef, plus many other labyrinths and grottoes for more serious divers.

You can also take a **hiking trail** through the tropical vegetation covering the island. Despite the fact that access to Buck Island is only via chartered tours and boat trips, this is one of the most-visited rock spits in the Caribbean.

Only ⅓-mile wide and a mile long, Buck Island lies 1½ miles off the northeastern coast of St. Croix. A barrier reef shelters many reef fish, including queen angelfish and smooth trunkfish. The attempt to return the presently uninhabited Buck Island to nature has been successful—even endangered brown pelicans are producing young here. Small boats run between St. Croix and Buck Island, and snorkeling equipment is supplied. You head out in the morning, and nearly all charters allow for 1½ hours of snorkeling and swimming. You can have a memorable ramble through sun-flooded and shallow waters off the rocky coast. Circumnavigating the island on foot will take about 2 hours. Buck Island's trails meander from several points along its coast to its sun-flooded summit, affording views over nearby St. Croix.

A couple of warnings: Bring protection from the sun's sometimes merciless rays, and even more important, don't rush to touch every

well-prepared food, and gracefully arched premises overlooking the sea. The menu isn't particularly ambitious, but food items are full of flavor and generous. Lunch specialties include meal-size salads, club sandwiches, burgers, and fresh fish. Dinner might begin with carrot-ginger soup or Caribbean spring rolls with chutney; main courses include steak au poivre, chicken breast stuffed with spinach and feta, grilled New Zealand lamb chops, and grilled filets of salmon with roasted poblano orange sauce. Desserts feature tropical fruits baked into tempting pastries.

4126 La Grande Princesse. ℂ **340/778-8920.** Reservations recommended. Lunch main courses $7–$12; dinner main courses $12–$25. AE, DC, DISC, MC, V. Daily 11:30am–3pm and 6–9pm.

Crucian Grill INTERNATIONAL   Many guests at this luxury resort come to this informal restaurant because of its authentic island dishes, zesty flavors, and reasonable prices. It offers a wide array of lunch fare, ranging from sandwiches

plant you see. The island's western edge has groves of poisonous manchineel trees, whose leaves, bark, and fruit cause extreme irritation if they come into contact with human skin.

Buck Island's greatest attraction is its **underwater snorkeling trail,** which rings part of the island. Equipped with a face mask, swim fins, and a snorkel, you'll be treated to some of the Caribbean's most beautiful underwater views. Plan on spending at least two thirds of a day at this extremely famous ecological site.

Mile Mark Watersports, in the King Christian Hotel, 59 King's Wharf, Christiansted (© **800/523-DIVE** in the U.S., or 340/773-2628), conducts twice-daily tours of Buck Island. It offers two ways to reach the reefs. One is a half-day tour aboard a glass-bottomed boat departing from the King Christian Hotel. Tours are daily 9:30am to 1pm and 1:30 to 5pm, costing $35 per person, all snorkeling equipment included. A more romantic half-day journey is aboard one of the company's sailboats, which, for $35 per person, offers the sea breezes and the thrill of harnessing the wind's power to reach the reef. A full-day tour, offered daily 10am to 4pm on the company's 40-foot catamaran, can take up to 20 participants to Buck Island's reefs. Included in the tour are a West Indian barbecue picnic on the isolated sands of Buck Island's beaches and plenty of opportunities for snorkeling. The full-day tour costs $75.

Captain Heinz (© **340/773-3161** or 340/773-4041) is an Austrian-born skipper with more than 25 years of sailing experience. His trimaran, *Teroro II,* leaves Green Cay Marina H Dock at 9am and 2pm, never filled with more than 24 passengers. The snorkeling trip costs $50, with all gear and safety equipment provided. The captain is not only a skilled sailor but also a considerate host. He'll even take you around the outer reef, which the other guides don't, for an unforgettable underwater experience.

to coconut shrimp and conch fritters (both tasty specialties). Freshly made salads run the gamut from chicken Caesar to hearts of palm. You can also order hamburgers; try the Jamaican jerk burger. A full selection of main courses for dinner is offered as well, including a Caribbean spiced seafood brochette. You might also try the excellent Mangrove Mama's mahimahi, which is grilled and served on a bed of sesame seaweed with green mango salsa, or the jerk-spiced pork tenderloin in gingered guava glaze.

In Sunterra Resorts Carambola Beach. © **340/778-3800.** Main courses $10–$18; sandwiches $7.50–$9.50. AE, DC, DISC, MC, V. Daily 7am–6pm.

IN & AROUND FREDERIKSTED

Blue Moon INTERNATIONAL/CAJUN   The best little bistro in Frederik-sted becomes a hot, hip spot during Sunday brunch and on Friday nights, when it offers entertainment. The 200-year-old stone house on the waterfront is a favorite of visiting jazz musicians, and tourists have now discovered (but not ruined) it. It's decorated with funky, homemade art from the States, including a trashcan-lid restaurant sign. The atmosphere is casual and cafelike. Begin with the "lunar pie," with feta cheese, cream cheese, onions, mushrooms, and celery in phyllo pastry, or else the artichoke-and-spinach dip. Main courses include the catch of the day and, on occasion, Maine lobster. The clams served in garlic sauce are also from Maine. Vegetarians opt for the spinach fettuccine. There's also the usual array of steak and chicken dishes. Save room for the yummy guava pie.

17 Strand St. ⓒ 340/772-2222. Reservations recommended. Main courses $16.50–$25. AE, DISC, MC, V. Tues–Fri 11:30am–2pm; Tues–Sat 6–9:30pm; Sun 11am–2pm and 6–9pm. Closed Aug.

Dowies CARIBBEAN/AMERICAN   Regulars appreciate this place for its complete lack of pretense, its hearty portions, and its West Indian format. Sheltered from the sun and rain with a corrugated tin roof, with tables set on a bed of gravel in the open air, this local diner occupies a prominent position in the heart of Frederiksted. Actually, it's a bit more elegant then the Formica-sheathed countertops you might've expected: Madras-patterned tablecloths cover most surfaces, and diners can choose from a cosmopolitan choice of American and West Indian food. Breakfast includes omelets (meat, vegetarian, and seafood); as well as French toast and any imaginable kind of eggs. On Friday and Saturday, an additional option is a Cruzan breakfast with saltfish, johnnycakes, and banana fritters. Lunches include platters of grilled fish, served with beans, rice, and stewed greens; a prize-winning version of fish pudding; bullfoot soup; stewed conch in butter sauce; grilled or jerk chicken meatloaf plates; and sandwiches. After around 2:30pm, everyone goes home and the place is shut up tight.

111 Market St. ⓒ 340/772-0845. Breakfasts $3.75–$5.50; lunch platters $4–$10. MC, V. Tues–Sat 7:30am–2:30pm.

Sprat Hall Beach Restaurant ★ *Finds* CARIBBEAN   This informal spot is on the west coast, near Sprat Hall Plantation. It's the best place on the island to combine lunch and a swim. The restaurant has been in business since 1948, feeding both locals and visitors. Try such local dishes as conch chowder, pumpkin fritters, *tannia* soup, and the fried fish of the day. These dishes have authentic island flavor, perhaps more so than any other place on St. Croix. You can also get salads and burgers. The bread is baked fresh daily. The owners charge $2 for use of the showers and changing rooms.

1 mile north of Frederiksted on Rte. 63. ⓒ 340/772-5855. Lunch $8–$15. Daily 11:30am–3pm and 5:30–10pm.

Villa Morales PUERTO RICAN   This inland spot is one of the premier Puerto Rican restaurants on St. Croix. You can choose between indoor and outdoor seating areas. No one will mind if you come here just to drink; a cozy bar is lined with the memorabilia collected by several generations of the family who maintain the place. Look for a broad cross-section of Hispanic dishes here, including many that Puerto Ricans remember from their childhood. Savory examples include fried snapper with white rice and beans, stewed conch, roasted or stewed goat, and stewed beef. Meal platters are garnished with beans and rice. Most of the dishes are at the lower end of the price scale. About once a month, the owners transform the place into a dance hall, bringing in live salsa and merengue bands (the cover ranges from $5 to $12).

Plot 82C, off Route 70 (about 2 miles from Frederiksted), Estate Whim. © **340/772-0556.** Reservations recommended. Breakfast $4–$8; lunch main courses $7–$14; dinner main courses $6–$28. MC, V. Thurs–Sat 10am–10pm.

HITTING THE BEACHES

Beaches are St. Croix's big attraction. The problem is that getting to them from Christiansted, which is home to most of the hotels, isn't always easy. It can also be expensive, especially if you want to go back and forth each day on your stay. Of course, you can always rent a condo right on the water.

The most celebrated beach is offshore **Buck Island,** part of the U.S. National Park network. Buck Island is actually a volcanic islet surrounded by some of the most stunning underwater coral gardens in the Caribbean. The white-sand beaches on the southwest and west coasts are beautiful, but the snorkeling is even better. The islet's interior is filled with such plants as cactus, wild frangipani, and pigeonwood. There are picnic areas for those who want to make a day of it. Boat departures are from Kings Wharf in Christiansted; the ride takes half an hour. For more information, see the box "Buck Island: Unspoiled Nature & World-Class Snorkeling," above.

Your best choice for a beach in Christiansted is the one at the **Hotel on the Cay.** This white-sand strip is on a palm-shaded island. To get here, take the ferry from the fort at Christiansted; it runs daily 7am to midnight. The 4-minute trip costs $3, free for guests of the Hotel on the Cay.

Five miles west of Christiansted is the **Cormorant Beach Club,** where some 1,200 feet of white sand shaded by palm trees attracts a gay crowd. Since a reef lies just off the shore, snorkeling conditions are ideal.

We highly recommend both **Davis Bay** and **Cane Bay,** with swaying palms, white sand, and good swimming and snorkeling. Because they're on the north shore, these beaches are often windy, and their waters are not always tranquil. The snorkeling at Cane Bay is truly spectacular; you'll see elkhorn and brain corals, all lying some 250 yards off the "Cane Bay Wall." Cane Bay adjoins Route 80 on the north shore. Davis Beach doesn't have a reef; it's more popular among bodysurfers than snorkelers. There are no changing facilities. It's near Carambola Beach Resort.

On Route 63, a short ride north of Frederiksted, lies **Rainbow Beach,** which offers white sand and ideal snorkeling conditions. Nearby, also on Route 63, about 5 minutes north of Frederiksted, is another good beach, called **La Grange.** Lounge chairs can be rented here, and there's a bar nearby.

Sandy Point, directly south of Frederiksted, is the largest beach in all the U.S. Virgin Islands. Its waters are shallow and calm, perfect for swimming. Try to concentrate on the sands and not the unattractive zigzagging fences that line the beach. Take the Melvin Evans Highway (Route 66) west from the Alexander Hamilton Airport.

There's an array of beaches at the East End of the island; they're somewhat difficult to get to, but much less crowded than beaches in other parts of the island. The best choice here is **Isaac Bay Beach,** ideal for snorkeling, swimming, and sunbathing. Windsurfers like **Reef Beach,** which opens onto Teague Bay along Route 82 (East End Road), a half-hour ride from Christiansted. You can get food at Duggan's Reef. **Cramer Park** is a special public park operated by the Department of Agriculture. It's lined with sea-grape trees and has a picnic area, a restaurant, and a bar. **Grapetree Beach** is off Route 60 (the South Shore Road). Watersports are popular here.

⟨Moments Into the Deep Without Getting Wet

St. Croix Water Sports Center (✆ **340/773-7060**), located at the Hotel on the Cay, features the Oceanique, a semi-submersible vessel that's part submarine and part cruiser. It takes visitors on 1-hour excursions through Christiansted harbor and along Protestant Cay. The inch-thick windows lining the vessel's underwater observation room provide views of St. Croix's colorful marine life in a cool and dry environment. This trip is especially popular with children and nonswimmers. Day and night excursions are available for $35 for adults and $25 for children. Call for reservations.

WATERSPORTS & OTHER OUTDOOR PURSUITS

FISHING The fishing grounds at **Lang Bank** are about 10 miles from St. Croix. Here you'll find kingfish, dolphin fish, and wahoo. Using light-tackle boats to glide along the reef, you'll probably turn up jack or bonefish. At **Clover Crest,** in Frederiksted, local anglers fish right from the rocks.

Serious sport-fishers can board the *Fantasy,* a 38-foot Bertram special available for 4-, 6-, or 8-hour charters, with bait and tackle included. It's anchored at St. Croix Marina, Gallows Bay. Reservations can be made by calling ✆ **340/ 773-7165** during the day or 340/773-0917 at night. The cost for six passengers is $350 to $400 for 4 hours, $550 to $590 for 6 hours, and $600 for 8 hours.

HIKING Scrub-covered hills make up much of St. Croix's landscape. The island's western district, however, includes a dense, 15-acre forest known as the **"Rain Forest"** (although it's not a real one). The network of footpaths here offers some of the best nature walks in the Caribbean. For more details on hiking in this area, see "The Rain Forest," below. **Buck Island** (see the box "Buck Island: Unspoiled Nature & World-Class Snorkeling," above), just off St. Croix, also offers some wonderful nature trails.

The **St. Croix Environmental Association,** 6 Company St., Christiansted (✆ **340/773-1989**), has regularly scheduled hikes from December to March. A minimum of four people are required, costing $25 per person.

HORSEBACK RIDING **Paul and Jill's Equestrian Stables,** Sprat Hall Plantation, Route 58 (✆ **340/772-2880**), the largest equestrian stable in the Virgin Islands, is known throughout the Caribbean for the quality of its horses. It's set on the sprawling grounds of the island's oldest plantation great house. The operators lead scenic trail rides through the forests, past ruins of abandoned 18th-century plantations and sugar mills, to the tops of the hills of St. Croix's western end. Beginners and experienced riders alike are welcome. A 2-hour trail ride costs $50. Tours usually depart daily in winter at 10am and 4pm, and in the off-season at 5pm, with slight variations according to demand. Reserve at least a day in advance.

KAYAKING Many people say that the beauty of St. Croix is best seen on a kayak tour offered by **Caribbean Adventure Tours** (✆ **340/773-4599**). Using stable sit-on-top ocean kayaks, you traverse the tranquil waters of Salt River of Columbus landfall fame and enjoy the park's ecology and wildlife, including going into secluded estuaries and mangrove groves. Some of the landscape was used as ancient Indian burial grounds. The highlights of the trip are snorkeling on a pristine beach and paddling to where Columbus and his crew came ashore some 500 years ago. The tour, which lasts 3 hours, costs $45 per person.

SAFARI TOURS   The best are offered by **St. Croix Safari Tours (℃ 340/ 773-6700**) in a 25-passenter open-air bus tour run by a hip tour guide who knows all about the botanical, culinary, and history of the island. Tours crisscross the island with stops at plantation houses, historic Frederiksted, the Salt River landfall of Columbus, and a drive through the rain forest, with a stop for lunch. There are lots of photo ops.

SNORKELING & SCUBA DIVING 🤿🤿   Sponge life, black coral (the finest in the West Indies), and steep drop-offs into water near the shoreline make St. Croix a snorkeling and diving paradise. The island is home to the largest living reef in the Caribbean, including the fabled north-shore wall that begins in 25 to 30 feet of water and drops to 13,200 feet, sometimes straight down. See "Hitting the Beaches," above, for information on good snorkeling beaches. The **St. Croix Water Sports Center** (see "Windsurfing," below) rents snorkeling equipment for $20 per day if your hotel doesn't supply it.

Buck Island 🤿🤿 is a major scuba-diving site, with a visibility of some 100 feet. It also has an underwater snorkeling trail. All the outfitters offer scuba and snorkeling tours to Buck Island. See the box "Buck Island: Unspoiled Nature & World-Class Snorkeling," above.

Other favorite dive sites include the historic **Salt River Canyon** (northwest of Christiansted at Salt River Bay), which is for advanced divers. Submerged canyons walls are covered with purple tube sponges, deep-water gorgonians, and black coral saplings. You'll see schools of yellowtail snapper, turtles, and spotted eagle rays. We also like the gorgeous coral gardens of **Scotch Banks** (north of Christiansted), and **Eagle Ray** (also north of Christiansted), the latter so named because of the rays that cruise along the wall there. **Cane Bay** 🤿🤿 is known for its coral canyons.

Davis Bay is the site of the 12,000-foot-deep Puerto Rico Trench. **Northstar Reef,** at the east end of Davis Bay, is a spectacular wall dive, recommended for intermediate or experienced divers only. The wall here is covered with stunning brain corals and staghorn thickets. At some 50 feet down, a sandy shelf leads to a cave where giant green moray eels hang out.

The ultimate night dive is at the **Frederiksted Pier.** The old pier was damaged by Hurricane Hugo and torn down to make way for a new one. The heavily encrusted rubble from the old pier remains beneath the new one, carpeted with rainbow-hued sponges and both hard and soft coral, preserving a fantastic night dive where you're virtually guaranteed to see seahorses and moray eels.

At **Butler Bay,** to the north of the pier on the west shore, three ships were wrecked: the *Suffolk Maid,* the *Northwind,* and the *Rosaomaira,* the latter sitting in 100 feet of water. These wrecks form the major part of an artificial reef system made up mostly of abandoned trucks and cars. This site is recommended for intermediate or experienced divers.

Dive St. Croix, 59 King's Wharf (℃ **800/523-DIVE** in the U.S., or 340/ 778-1522; fax 340/773-7400), operates the 38-foot dive boat *Reliance.* The staff offers complete instruction, from resort courses through full certification, as well as night dives. A resort course is $80, with a two-tank dive going for $80. Scuba trips to Buck Island cost $70, and dive packages begin at $350 for five dives.

V.I. Divers Ltd., in the Pan Am Pavilion on Christiansted's waterfront (℃ **340/773-6045**), is the oldest and one of the best dive operations on the island. *Rodale's Scuba Diving* magazine rated its staff as among the top 10 world-wide. This full-service PADI five-star facility offers two-tank boat dives, guided snorkeling trips to Green Cay, night dives, and a full range of scuba-training programs. Introductory two-tank dives, which require no experience, cost $95, including all instruction and equipment. A six-dive package goes for $210, and a 10-dive package for $330. A two-tank boat or beach dive is $75. Night dives go for $60. A 2-hour guided snorkel tour costs $35, the boat snorkeling trip to Green Cay, $35.

Other recommended outfitters include **Anchor Dive** (℡ **800/532-DIVE** in the U.S.), **The Buccaneer** (℡ **800/255-3881** in the U.S.), the **Cane Bay Dive Shop** (℡ **340/773-9913**), **St. Croix Ocean Recreational Experience** (S.C.O.R.E.; ℡ **340/778-8907**), and **St. Croix Ultimate Bluewater Adventure** (℡ **877/789-72822** in the U.S.).

TENNIS   Some authorities rate the tennis at the **Buccaneer** ★★, Gallows Bay (℡ **340/773-3136,** ext. 736), as the best in the Caribbean. This resort offers a choice of eight courts, two lit for night play, all open to the public. Nonguests pay $10 per person per hour; you must call to reserve a court. A tennis pro is available for lessons, and there's also a pro shop.

WINDSURFING   Head for the **St. Croix Water Sports Center** (℡ **340/773-7060**), located on a small offshore island in Christiansted Harbor and part of the Hotel on the Cay. It's open daily 10am to 5pm. Windsurfing rentals are $30 per hour. Lessons are available. Sea Doos, which seat two, can be rented for $45 to $55 per half hour. The center also offers parasailing for $65 per person and rents snorkeling equipment for $25 per day.

SEEING THE SIGHTS

Taxi tours are a great way to explore the island. For one or two passengers, the cost is often $40 for 2 hours or $60 for 3 hours. All prices should be negotiated and agreed on in advance. For more information, call the **St. Croix Taxi Association** at ℡ **340/778-1088.**

THE RAIN FOREST ★

Unlike the rest of St. Croix, a verdant parcel in the island's western district is covered with dense forest, a botanical landscape very different from the scrub-covered hills on other parts of the island. Set amid the sparsely populated terrain of the island's northwestern corner, north of Frederiksted, the area grows thick with mahogany trees, kapok (silk-cotton) trees, turpentine (red birch) trees, samaan (rain) trees, and all kinds of ferns and vines. Sweet limes, mangos, hog plums, and breadfruit trees, which have sown themselves in the wild since the plantation era, are woven among the forest's larger trees. Bird life includes crested hummingbirds, pearly-eyed thrashers, green-throated caribs, yellow warblers, and perky banana quits.

Although the district isn't technically a tropical rain forest, it's known by virtually everyone as the Rain Forest. How best to experience its botanical charms? Some visitors opt to drive along Route 76 (also known as Mahogany Road), stopping the car beside any of the footpaths meandering off the highway into dry riverbeds and glens on either side. (It's advisable to stick to the best worn of the footpaths to avoid losing your way and to retrace your steps after a few moments of admiring the local botany.)

Equally feasible is a hike beside those highways of the island's western sector where few cars ever venture. Three of the most viable are the **Creque Dam Road**

(Routes 58/78), the **Scenic Road** (Route 78), and the **Western Scenic Road** (Routes 63/78). Consider beginning your trek near the junction of Creque Dam Road and Scenic Road. (Although passable by cars, it's likely you'll see only a few along these roads during your entire walking tour.)

Your trek will cover a broad triangular swath, beginning at the abovementioned junction, heading north and then west along Scenic Road. The road will first rise and then descend toward the coastal lighthouse of the island's extreme northwestern tip, **Hamm's Bluff.** Most trekkers decide to retrace their steps after about 45 minutes of northwesterly walking, returning to their parked cars after admiring the land and seascapes. Real diehards, however, can continue trekking all the way to the coastline, head south along the coastal road (Butler Bay Road), then head east along Creque Dam Road to their parked car at the junction of Creque Dam Road and Scenic Road. Embark on this longer expedition only if you're really prepared for a prolonged trek (about 5 hours) and some serious nature-watching.

CHRISTIANSTED ★★

The picture-book harbor town of the Caribbean, **Christiansted** is a handsomely restored (or at least in the process of being restored) Danish port. On the northeastern shore of the island, on a coral-bound bay, the town is filled with Danish buildings erected by prosperous merchants in the booming 18th century. These red-roofed structures are often washed in pink, ocher, or yellow. Arcades over the sidewalks make ideal shaded colonnades for shoppers. The whole area around the harbor front has been designated a historic site, including **Government House,** which is looked after by the National Park Service.

You can begin at the **visitors' bureau,** Queen Cross Street (© **340/773-0495**), a yellow-sided building with a cedar-capped roof near the harbor front. It was built as the Old Scalehouse in 1856 to replace a similar structure that burned down. In its heyday, all taxable goods leaving and entering the harbor were weighed here. The scales that once stood here could accurately weigh barrels of sugar and molasses weighing up to 1,600 pounds each.

Steeple Building   This building's full name is the Church of Lord God of Sabaoth. It was built in 1753 as St. Croix's first Lutheran church, until it was deconsecrated in 1831; the building subsequently served at various times as a bakery, a hospital, and a school. Today, it houses exhibits relating to island history and culture.

On the waterfront off Hospital St. © 340/773-1460. Admission $2 (also includes admission to Fort Christiansvaern). Daily 8:30am–4:30pm.

Fort Christiansvaern   This fortress overlooking the harbor is the best-preserved colonial fortification in the Virgin Islands. The National Park Service maintains it as a historic monument. Its original four-pronged, star-shaped design was in accordance with the most advanced military planning of its era. The fort is now the site of the St. Croix Police Museum, which has exhibits on police work on the island from the late 1800s to the present.

© 340/773-1460. Admission $2. Mon–Fri 8am–4:45pm; Sat 9am–4:45pm.

St. Croix Aquarium   This aquarium has expanded with many exhibits, including one devoted to "night creatures." In all, it houses some 40 species of marine animals and more than 100 species of invertebrates. A touch pond contains starfish, sea cucumbers, brittle stars, and pencil urchins. The aquarium allows you to become familiar with the marine life you'll see while scuba diving or snorkeling.

Caravelle Arcade. © 340/773-8995. Admission $5 adults, $2 children. Tues–Sat 11am–4pm.

FREDERIKSTED ⟨★⟩

This former Danish settlement at the western end of the island, about 17 miles from Christiansted, is a sleepy port town that comes to life only when a cruise ship docks at its shoreline. In 1994, a 1,500-foot pier opened to accommodate the largest cruise ships. The pier facility is designed to accommodate two large cruise vessels and two mini–cruise ships simultaneously.

Frederiksted was destroyed by a fire in 1879, and the citizens rebuilt it with wood frames and clapboards on top of the old Danish stone and yellow-brick foundations.

Most visitors begin their tour at russet-colored **Fort Frederik,** next to the cruise ship pier (© **340/772-2021**). Some historians claim this was the first fort to sound a foreign salute to the U.S. flag, in 1776. It was here on July 3, 1848, that Gov.-Gen. Peter von Scholten emancipated the slaves in the Danish West Indies. The fort, at the northern end of Frederiksted, has been restored to its 1840 appearance and is today a national historic landmark. In 1998, a bust was unveiled here of General Buddhoe, the young black man who led the insurrection of slaves into town to demand their freedom on July 3, 1848. You can explore the courtyard and stables, and a local history museum has been installed in what was once the Garrison Room. Admission is free, and it's open Monday to Saturday 8:30am to 4:30pm.

Just south of the fort, the Customs House is an 18th-century building with a 19th-century two-story gallery. Here you can go into the **visitors' bureau** at Strand Street (© **340/772-0357**) and pick up a free map of the town.

ELSEWHERE AROUND THE ISLAND

North of Frederiksted you can drop in at **Sprat Hall,** the island's oldest plantation, or continue along to the rain forest, which covers about 15 acres, including the 150-foot-high **Creque Dam.** The terrain is private property, but the owner lets visitors go inside to explore. Most visitors come here to see the jagged estuary of the northern coastline's **Salt River.** The Salt River is where Columbus landed on November 14, 1493, the only known site where the explorer ever landed on what's now U.S. territory. Marking the 500th anniversary of Columbus's arrival, then-President George Bush signed a bill creating the 912-acre **Salt River Bay National Historical Park and Ecological Preserve.** The landmass encompasses the site of the original Carib village explored by Columbus and his men, including the only ceremonial ball court ever discovered in the Lesser Antilles. The park contains the largest mangrove forest in the Virgin Islands, sheltering many endangered animals and plants, plus an underwater canyon attracting scuba divers from around the world. The **St. Croix Environmental Association,** 3 Arawak Building, Gallows Bay (© **340/773-1989**), conducts tours of the area and can provide details. Tours cost $20 for adults and $12 for children under 10.

Estate Mount Washington Plantation is the island's best preserved sugar plantation and a highlight along the St. Croix Heritage Trail. It flourished from 1780 to 1820, when St. Croix was the second largest producer of sugar in the West Indies. The on-site private residence is closed to the public, but you can go on a self-guided tour of the 13 acres at any time of the day you wish (there is no admission charge, although donations are appreciated). You'll see what is the best antique store on St. Croix, but can visit only if you call ✆ **340/772-1026** and ask for an appointment. The plantation site lies at the very southwestern tip of the island, off Route 63, a mile inland from the highway that runs along the Frederiksted coast.

Cruzan Rum Factory This factory distills the famous Virgin Islands rum, which some consider the finest in the world. Guided tours depart from the visitors' pavilion; call for reservations and information. There's also a gift shop.

W. Airport Rd., Rte. 64. ✆ **340/692-2280**. Admission $4. Tours given Mon–Fri 9–11:30am and 1–4:15pm.

Estate Whim Plantation Museum This restored great house is unique among those of the many sugar plantations whose ruins dot the island. It's composed of only three rooms. With 3-foot-thick walls made of stone, coral, and molasses, the house resembles a luxurious European château. A division of Baker Furniture Company used the Whim Plantation's collection of models for one of its most successful reproductions, the Whim Museum–West Indies Collection. A showroom here sells the reproductions, plus others from the Caribbean, including pineapple-motif four-poster beds, cane-bottomed planters' chairs with built-in leg rests, and Caribbean adaptations of Empire-era chairs with cane-bottomed seats.

Also on the premises is a woodworking shop that features tools and exhibits on techniques from the 18th century, the estate's original kitchen, a museum store, and a servant's quarters. The ruins of the plantation's sugar-processing plant, complete with a restored windmill, also remain.

Centerline Rd. (2 miles east of Frederiksted). ✆ **340/772-0598**. Admission $6 adults, $2 children. June–Oct Tues–Sat 10am–3pm; Nov–May Mon–Sat 10am–4pm.

St. George Village Botanical Garden of St. Croix This is a 16-acre Eden of tropical trees, shrubs, vines, and flowers. The garden is a feast for the eye and the camera, from the entrance drive bordered by royal palms and bougainvillea to the towering kapok and tamarind trees. It was built around the ruins of a 19th-century sugarcane workers' village. Self-guided walking-tour maps are available at the entrance to the garden's great hall. Facilities include rest rooms and a gift shop.

127 Estate St. (just north of Centerline Rd., 4 miles east of Frederiksted), Kingshill. ✆ **340/692-2874**. Admission $6 adults, $1 children 12 and under; donations welcome. Nov–May daily 9am–5pm; June–Oct Tues–Sat 9am–4pm.

ORGANIZED TOURS

BUS TOURS Organized tours operate according to demand. Many are conducted at least three times a week during the winter, with fewer departures in summer. A typical 4-hour tour costs $25 per person. Tours usually go through Christiansted and include visits to the botanical gardens, Whim Estate House, the rum distillery, the rain forest, the St. Croix Leap mahogany workshop, and the site of Columbus's landing at Salt River. Check with your hotel desk, or call **Travellers' Tours,** Alexander Hamilton Airport (✆ **340/778-1636**), for more information.

TAXI TOURS Many visitors explore St. Croix on a taxi tour (✆ **340/778-1088**), which for a party of two costs $40 for 2 hours or $60 for 3 hours. The fare should be negotiated in advance. Extra fees are charged for the following sights: $10 for the botanical gardens, $10 for Whim Estate House, and $8 for the rum distillery.

The Heritage Trail

St.Croix Heritage Trail, launched at the millennium, helps visitors relive the Danish colonial past of the island. All you need is a brochure and map, available at the visitors' bureau, Queen Cross Street, in Christiansted (© **340/773-0495**), and you can set out on this 72-mile road, which is teeming with historical and cultural sights. The St. Croix Heritage Trail is one of the 50 nationwide Millennium Legacy Trails launched in 2000.

The route, among other of the trail's historic sites, connects the two major towns of Christiansted and Frederiksted, going past the sites of former sugar plantations.

The trail traverses the entire 28-mile length of St. Croix, passing cattle farms, suburban communities, even industrial complexes and resorts. So it's not all manicured and pretty. But much of it is scenic and worth the drive. Allow at least a day for this trail, with stops along the way.

Nearly everyone gets out of the car at Point Udall, the easternmost point under the American flag. You'll pass an eclectic mix of churches and even a prison. The route consists mainly of existing roadways, and that pamphlet you picked up will identify everything you've seeing.

The highlight of the trail is the Estate Mount Washington (see p. 666), a strikingly well-preserved sugar plantation. Another highlight is Estate Whim Plantation (see p. 667), one of the best of the restored Great Houses with a museum and gift shop. Another stop along the way is along Salt River Bay, which cuts into the northern shoreline. This is the site of Columbus Landfall in 1493.

Of course, you'll want to stop and get to know the locals. We recommend a refreshing stop at Smithens Market along the trail. Lying off Queen Mary Highway, vendors here offer freshly squeezed sugar-cane juice and sell locally grown fruits and homemade chutneys.

WALKING TOURS For a guided walking tour of either Christiansted or Frederiksted, contact **St. Croix Heritage Tours** (© 340/778-6997). The tour of Christiansted departs Tuesday at 9:30am, and costs $12 per person or $6 for children. The Frederiksted tour leaves on Wednesday at 10:15am, and costs $8 per person or $4 for children. Call for details and to arrange meeting places.

SHOPPING ✸✸✸

In **Christiansted,** where the core of our shopping recommendations are found, the emphasis is on hole-in-the-wall boutiques selling one-of-a-kind merchandise; the selection of handmade items is especially strong. Knowing it can't compete with Charlotte Amalie, Christiansted has forged its own creative statement and has now become *the* chic spot for merchandise in the Caribbean. All the shops are within half a mile or so of one another.

Following the hurricanes of 1995, a major redevelopment of the waterfront at Christiansted was launched. The **King's Alley Complex** (© 340/778-8135) opened as a pink-sided compound, filled with the densest concentration of shopping options on St. Croix. The $1.2-million project was built on a 50-foot strip of land from Strand Street to King Street, the town's main thoroughfare. It bustles with merchants, vendors, and restaurants.

The Coconut Vine, Pan Am Pavilion, Strand Street (© **340/773-1991**), is a little boutique, one of the most colorful and popular on the island. A storefront on the Pan Am Pavilion opens to a world of color and style. Hand-painted batiks for both men and women are the specialty for this tropical shop. **Crucian Gold,** 59 King's Wharf (© **340/773-5241**), offers unique gold creations of island-born Brian Bishop. He designs all the gold jewelry himself, and less expensive versions of his work come in sterling silver. The most popular item is the Crucian bracelet, which contains a True Lovers' Knot in its design. The outlet also sells hand-tied knots (bound in gold wire), rings, pendants, and earrings.

Elegant Illusions Copy Jewelry, 55 King St. (© **340/773-2727**), a branch of a hugely successful chain based in California, sells convincing copy jewelry. The lookalikes range from $9 to $1,000 and include credible copies of the baroque and antique jewelry your great-grandmother might have worn. If you want the real thing, you can go next door to **King Alley Jewelry** (© **340/773-4746**), owned by the same company and specializing in fine designer jewelry, including Tiffany and Cartier.

Folk Art Traders, Strand Street (© **340/773-1900**), is a gem. Since 1985, the operators of this store have traveled throughout the Caribbean (in the bush) to acquire a unique collection of local art and folk-art treasures, not only Carnival masks, pottery, ceramics, and original paintings, but also hand-wrought jewelry. The assortment is wide-ranging, including batiks from Barbados and high-quality iron sculpture from Haiti. There's nothing else like it in the Virgin Islands. **From the Gecko,** 1233 Queen Cross St. (© **340/778-9433**), is a hip and eclectic clothier/gift shop. You can find anything from hand-painted U.S.V.I. cottons and silks to the old West Indian staple, batiks. Items will give you gift ideas. We found the Indonesian collection among the most imaginative in the U.S.V.I.—everything from ornate candleholders to banana-leaf knapsacks.

About 60% of the merchandise in **Gone Tropical,** 5 Company St. (© **340/773-4696**), is made in Indonesia (usually Bali). The prices of new, semi-antique, or antique sofas, beds, chests, tables, mirrors, and decorative carvings are the same as or less than those of similar pieces you might've bought new at more conventional furniture stores. The store also sells worthy art objects (which can be shipped wherever you want), as well as jewelry, batiks, candles, and baskets. **Little Switzerland,** 1 Strand St. (© **340/773-1976**), has branches throughout the Caribbean and is the island's best source for crystal, figurines, watches, china, perfume, flatware, leather, and lots of fine jewelry. It specializes in all the big names, such as Paloma Picasso leather goods. For luxuries like a Rolex watch, an Omega, or heirloom crystal like Lalique, Swarovski, and Baccarat, this is the place. At least a few items are said to sell for up to 30% less than on the U.S. mainland, but don't take anyone's word for that unless you've checked prices carefully.

Many Hands, 21 Pan Am Pavilion, Strand Street (© **340/773-1990**), sells Virgin Islands handcrafts exclusively. The merchandise includes West Indian spices and teas, shellwork, stained glass, hand-painted china, pottery, and hand-made jewelry. Their collection of local paintings is intriguing, as is their year-round Christmas tree. **The Royal Poinciana,** 1111 Strand St. (© **340/773-9892**), is the most interesting gift shop on St. Croix. In what looks like an antique apothecary, you'll find such Caribbean-inspired items as hot sauces (fire water), seasoning blends for gumbos, island herbal teas, Antillean coffees, and a scented array of soaps, toiletries, lotions, and shampoos. There's also a selection of museum-reproduction greeting cards and calendars as well as fun and educational gifts for children.

Purple Papaya, 39 Strand St., Pan Am Pavilion (© **340/713-9412**), is the best place to go for inexpensive island gifts. It has the biggest array of embroidered T-shirts and sweatshirts on island. Although you're in the Caribbean and not Hawaii—there is a large selection of Hawaiian shirts and dresses, along with beachwear for the whole family, plus island souvenirs.

Sonya Ltd., 1 Company St. (© **340/778-8605**), is the domain of Sonya Hough, the matriarch of a cult following of locals who wouldn't leave home without wearing one of her bracelets. She's most famous for her sterling silver or gold (from 14- to 24-karat) interpretations of the C-clasp bracelet. Locals communicate discreet messages by how it's worn: If the cup of the C is turned toward your heart, it means you're emotionally committed. If the cup of the C is turned outward, it means you're available to whoever strikes your fancy. She also sells rings, earrings, and necklaces. **Urban Threadz/Urban Kidz,** 52C Company St. (© **340/773-2883**), is the most comprehensive clothing store in Christiansted's historic core, with a big-city scale and appeal that's different from the tropical-boutique aura of nearby T-shirt shops. It's the store where islanders prefer to shop, because of the clothing's hip urban styles. Men's garments are on the street level and women's upstairs, and the inventory includes everything from Bermuda shorts to lightweight summer blazers and men's suits. They carry Calvin Klein, Nautica, and Oakley, among others.

Waterfront Larimar Mines, The Boardwalk/King's Walk (© **340/692-9000**), sells the largest selection of the Caribbean's own gemstone, **larimar.** Everything sold in this shop is produced by the largest manufacturer of gold settings for larimar in the world. Discovered in the 1970s, larimar is a pale-blue pectolyte prized for its sky-blue color. It's extracted from mines in only one mountain in the world, on the southwestern edge of the Dominican Republic, near the Haitian border. **The White House,** King's Alley Walk (© **340/773-9222**), takes a stand against those who appear only in black. Going against a trend, this outlet lives up to its name. Everything is white or off-white—nothing darker than beige is allowed on the premises. The style of clothing for women ranges from dressy to casual and breezy.

ST. CROIX AFTER DARK

St. Croix doesn't have the nightlife of St. Thomas, so to find the action, you might have to hotel- or bar-hop or consult *St. Croix This Week,* which is distributed free to cruise ship and air passengers and is also available at the tourist office.

Try to catch a performance of the **Quadrille Dancers,** the cultural treat of St. Croix. Their dances have changed little since plantation days; the women wear long dresses, white gloves, and turbans, and the men are attired in flamboyant shirts, sashes, and tight black trousers. When you've learned their steps, you're invited to join the dancers on the floor. Ask at your hotel if and where they're performing.

THE PERFORMING ARTS The 1,100-seat **Island Center** (© **340/778-5272**), half a mile north of Sunny Isle, continues to attract big-name entertainers to St. Croix. Its program is widely varied, ranging from jazz, nostalgia, and musical revues to Broadway plays. Consult *St. Croix This Week* or call the center to see what's being presented. The Caribbean Community Theatre and Court-yard Players perform regularly. Call for performance times. Tickets run $8 to $30.

BARS & CLUBS   Blue Moon ★★, 17 Strand St. (© **340/772-2222**), is a little dive that's also a good bistro, the hottest and hippest spot in Frederiksted on Friday nights, when a five-piece ensemble provides the entertainment. The good news is that there's no cover, so you'll have to spend money only on drinks. Stick around to try some of the food from an eclectic menu that samples flavors from the Bayou Country to Asia. Closed in August.

The **Marina Bar,** in the King's Alley Hotel, King's Alley/The Waterfront (© **340/773-0103**), occupies a panoramic position on the waterfront, on a shaded terrace overlooking the sea and Protestant Cay. Although the place remains open throughout the day, the real festivities begin right after the last seaplane departs for St. Thomas (around 5:30pm) and continue energetically to 8:30pm. Sunset-colored cocktails made with rum, mangos, bananas, papaya, and grenadine are the libations of choice. You can stave off hunger pangs with burgers, sandwiches, and West Indian–style platters. The bar has live entertain-ment most nights, usually steel bands. On Monday you can bet on crab races.

Mt. Pellier Hut Domino Club, Montpellier (© **340/772-9914**), is a one-of-a-kind club. It came into being as a battered snack shack established to serve players of a never-ending domino game. Gradually it grew into a drinking and entertainment center, although the game is still going strong. Today, the bar charges $1 to view a beer-drinking pig (Miss Piggy) and has a one-man band, Piro, who plays on Sunday. The bartender will also serve you a lethal rum-based Mamma Wanna. The **Terrace Lounge,** in the Buccaneer, Route 82, Estate Shoys (© **340/773-2100**), is for a grand night on the town. Every night this lounge off the main dining room of one of St. Croix's most upscale resorts welcomes some of the Caribbean's finest entertainers, often including a full band. Call to see what's happening.

The **Cormorant Beach Club Bar,** 4126 La Grande Princesse (© **340/778-8920**), has gone gay. One of the island's most romantic bars is along La Grande Princesse northwest of Christiansted, opening onto one of the island's best beaches. It's a Caribbean cliché, but that's why people often come to the islands in the first place, to enjoy tropical drinks in a moonlit setting with palm trees swaying in the night winds. Guests—usually gay men—sit at tables overlooking the ocean or around an open-centered mahogany bar, surrounded by an enlarged gazebo, wicker love seats, comfortable chairs, and soft lighting. Excellent tropical drinks are mixed, including the house specialty, a Cormorant cooler made with champagne, pineapple juice, and Triple Sec.

2 Plus 2 Disco, along the La Grande Princesse (© **340/773-3710**), is a real Caribbean disco. This joint features the regional sounds of the islands, not only calypso and reggae, but also salsa, rhythm and blues, and soca (a hybrid of calypso and reggae). Usually you get a sweaty DJ selecting the music, except on weekends, when local bands are brought in. Not fancy or large, the disco has a black-tile dance floor with a simple lighting system. Come here for Saturday Night Fever. Hours are Tuesday to Sunday 8:30pm to 2am and Friday and Saturday 8pm to either 5 or 6am. A cover of $5 to $10 is imposed when there's live entertainment.

GAMBLING   Divi Casino, in the Divi Carina Bay Resort, 25 Estate Turner Hole (© **340/773-9700**), has brought gambling to St. Croix for the first name.

After much protest and controversy, gambling was finally introduced in the spring of 2000. Many visitors who heretofore went to such islands as Aruba for gambling now stay within the realm of U.S. possessions. The 10,000-square-foot casino boasts 12 gaming tables and 275 slot machines. No passport in needed to enter, but you do need some form of ID. There is no cover charge either. In lieu of a nightclub, the casino offers nightly live music on an open stage on the casino floor. There are two bars, a main bar plus a smaller cafe-style bar where you can order light meals. Open Monday to Thursday noon to 4am and Friday to Sunday noon to 6am.

Index

Accommodations. *See also* Rental properties; *and specific destinations*
all-inclusive, 51–52, 241–242, 248–249, 253–254, 317, 516
best bets, 14–15
general information on, 50–53
money-saving tips, 38–39
package tours, 40–42
Admiralty Bay (Bequia), 578
Aguasol Theme Park (Jamaica), 2, 333
Airfares, 38, 42–44, 56–59
Ajoupa-Bouillon (Martinique), 399–400
Alcázar de Colón (Dominican Republic), 236
Alice in Wonderland (Tortola), 154
Altos de Chavón (Dominican Republic), 242–247
Amber, in Dominican Republic, 238, 239, 251
Andromeda Botanic Gardens (Barbados), 118
Anegada, 156–157, 166–167
Annaberg Historic Trail (St. John), 645
Annandale Falls (Grenada), 273
Anse-à-l'Ane (Martinique), 390, 393
Anse-Bertrand (Guadeloupe), 295
Anse Chastanet (St. Lucia), 524
Anse Couchon (St. Lucia), 524
Anse de la Gourde (Guadeloupe), 306
Anse des Pitons (St. Lucia), 524
Anse des Sables (St. Lucia), 524

Anse du Souffleur (Guadeloupe), 294, 306–307
Anse Mitan (Martinique), 388, 389–390
Anses d'Arlets (Martinique), 393–394
Antigua, 20, 60–77
accommodations, 14, 64–66
cheap thrills, 74–75
information sources, 61
nightlife, 18, 77
restaurants, 66–68
shopping, 73–77
sights and activities, 68–73
special events, 62
transportation, 62–63
traveling to, 61–62
weddings, 54
Antigua & Barbuda, Museum of (Antigua), 71
Antigua Rum Distillery, 73
Antilla (Aruba), 88, 89
Apple Bay (Tortola), 155
Aquariums, 198, 206, 288, 665–666
Arawak Beach (Guadeloupe), 306
Arawak Indians, 71, 93, 138, 203, 294, 303, 325, 356, 363, 373, 385
Arecibo Observatory (Puerto Rico), 451–452, 472
Arikok National Park (Aruba), 93
Arnos Vale (Tobago), 605
Aruba, 1, 20, 78–95
accommodations, 83–86
cheap thrills, 92–93
information sources, 78, 80
nightlife, 94–95
restaurants, 86–87
shopping, 13, 91–94
sights and activities, 87–91
special events, 81

transportation, 80–81
traveling to, 80
weddings, 54
Asa Wright Nature Centre (Trinidad), 589–590, 594, 596
Asta Reef (Barbados), 113
Athenry Gardens (Jamaica), 363
Atlantis submarine
Aruba, 90
Barbados, 114–115
Grand Cayman, 180
St. Thomas, 624
Ayo (Aruba), 90

Baby Beach (Aruba), 88, 91
Bacardi Distillery (Puerto Rico), 450
Bacelot Beach (Tobago), 604
Back Bay (Tobago), 603
Baie Longue (St. Martin), 551
Baie Mahault (Guadeloupe), 296, 316
Baie Mahault (La Désirade), 316
Baie Rouge (St. Martin), 552
Balandra Bay (Trinidad), 592
Balata Cathedral (Martinique), 385
Baleine Falls (St. Vincent), 571
Ballets Guadeloupeans, 309
Ballets Martiniquais, 387, 388
Banana Bay (St. Kitts), 510
Baoruco (Dominican Republic), 241
Barahona Peninsula (Dominican Republic), 241–242
Barbados, 1, 20, 96–124
accommodations, 102–107
cheap thrills, 120–121

Barbados *(cont.)*
information sources, 96, 98
nightlife, 18, 122–124
restaurants, 16, 107–110
shopping, 13, 119–122
sights and activities, 111–119
special events, 99
transportation, 98–100
traveling to, 98
weddings, 54
Barbados Gallery of Art, 116
Barbados Museum, 116, 123–124
Barbados National Trust, 112, 117, 121
Barbados Synagogue, 115
Barbados Wildlife Reserve, 118
Barbuda, Museum of Antigua & (Antigua), 71
Barnett Estates (Jamaica), 333
Barrouallie (St. Vincent), 569, 571
Bas du Fort (Guadeloupe), 288, 306
Baseball, in Dominican Republic, 235
Basse-Pointe (Martinique), 401
Basse-Terre (Guadeloupe), 282–286, 295–305, 307
Basseterre (St. Eustatius), 503–513
Baths, the (Virgin Gorda), 157, 164
Bathsheba (Barbados), 103, 108, 111, 112, 118
Bayahibe (Dominican Republic), 243
Beaches, 5, 8. *See also specific beaches*
Anegada, 167
Antigua, 68–70, 70, 74
Aruba, 87–88
Barbados, 111
Bequia, 578
Bonaire, 133, 134, 136
Culebra, 482
Curaçao, 198–199, 206
Dominica, 217
Dominican Republic, 5, 242, 250
Cabarete, 256–257
Samaná, 259
Santo Domingo, 234–235
Sosúa, 252–253

Grand Cayman, 5, 178–179
Grenada, 5, 270–271, 273
Guadeloupe, 293, 294, 306–307
Iles des Saintes, 310, 313
Jamaica, 5, 375
Kingston, 367
Montego Bay, 331
Negril, 344–345
Ocho Rios, 354
Port Antonio, 362
Runaway Bay, 349
Jost Van Dyke, 167
La Désirade, 316
Martinique, 5, 384, 389–390, 393–397, 403
Nevis, 5, 8, 410–411, 415
nudist, 293, 298, 306, 310, 313, 331, 338, 344, 345, 354, 396, 551, 552, 553, 561, 622, 644
Puerto Rico, 8, 449–451, 454, 456, 457, 461, 479–480
San Juan, 435–436
Saba, 489
St. Croix, 661
St. Eustatius, 500
St. John, 8, 643–644
St. Kitts, 509, 510–511
St. Lucia, 524
St. Maarten, 550–551
St. Martin, 551–552
St. Thomas, 621–623
St. Vincent, 569
Tobago, 603–604
Tortola, 5, 154–155
Trinidad, 591–592
Virgin Gorda, 164
Beef Island (Tortola), 141, 144, 146, 157, 159
Bellfield Great House (Jamaica), 333
Bequia, 18, 26, 572, 575–579
Beracha Veshalom Vegmiluth Hasidim Synagogue (St. Thomas), 626–627
Bermúdez National Park (Dominican Republic), 246
Berwyn **(Barbados),** 113
Beth Haim Cemetery (Curaçao), 204–205
Betty's Hope (Antigua), 73
Bianca **(Grenada),** 271
Bibliothèque Schoelcher (Martinique), 385

Bicycling
Anegada, 166
Antigua, 81
Bonaire, 127, 135–136, 137
Dominican Republic, 258
Iles des Saintes, 311
Jamaica, 322, 365
La Désirade, 316
Martinique, 380
St. Croix, 650
St. Maarten/Martin, 540
Bird-watching
Anegada, 166
Antigua, 73, 74
Aruba, 92
Barbados, 118
Bonaire, 20, 125, 133, 137, 138, 139
Culebra, 482
Curaçao, 203
Dominica, 218, 220
Dominican Republic, 242, 246
Grand Cayman, 183
Grenada, 267, 274, 275, 276
Guadeloupe, 298, 300
Jamaica, 324, 364, 373, 375
Little Cayman, 187, 189
Martinique, 376–377
Nevis, 414
Puerto Rico, 438, 450, 451, 452, 457, 458, 460, 463
St. Croix, 633, 664
St. John, 635, 644, 654
St. Kitts, 503
St. Lucia, 529, 530–531, 594
Tobago, 598, 601, 605, 627
Trinidad, 11, 584, 589–590, 592–593, 594, 596, 597
Blackbeard (Edward Teach), 141, 156, 185, 369
Black River (Jamaica), 373–375
Blanchisseuse Bay (Trinidad), 592
Blauwbaai (Curaçao), 198
Bloody Bay Wall (Little Cayman), 189
Blossom Village (Little Cayman), 187
Blue Beach (Puerto Rico), 480
Blue Lagoon (Jamaica), 345, 362

Blue Mountain-John Crow Mountain National Park (Jamaica), 364–365

Boat charters. *See also* Sailing
Nevis, 411
St. Kitts, 511
St. Thomas, 623–625

Boating. *See* Kayaking; Rafting, in Jamaica; Sailing

Boat travel and cruises
Antigua, 70
Aruba, 88
Barbados, 114
to the Caribbean, 44–50
Carriacou, 281
Curaçao, 199
Grand Cayman, 180
Grenada, 272
Jamaica, 334
Martinique, 384
Puerto Rico, 422, 436, 480
St. Lucia, 524–525, 526
St. Maarten/Martin, 555–556
Tortola, 156–157

Boca Chica (Dominican Republic), 234–235, 237

Boca Cocolishi (Bonaire), 133, 138

Boca Grandi (Aruba), 91

Boca Onima (Bonaire), 138

Boca Slagbaai (Bonaire), 133, 136

Boca Tabla (Curaçao), 203

Bodden Town (Grand Cayman), 182

Boiling Lake (Dominica), 10–11, 218, 220

Bolongo Bay (St. Thomas), 620, 625, 626

Bonaire, 1, 11, 20–21, 125–140
accommodations, 129–131
cheap thrills, 137
information sources, 125
nightlife, 18, 140
restaurants, 131–132
shopping, 139–140
sights and activities, 133–139
transportation, 126–127
traveling to, 125–126
weddings, 54–55

Bonaire Marine Park, 134–135

Bonney, Ann, 339

Booby Island, 5, 338

Booby Shoals (St. Kitts), 511

Boquerón (Puerto Rico), 457–459

Boquerón Beach (Puerto Rico), 457, 473

Boston Beach (Jamaica), 362

Botabano (Grand Cayman), 181

Bottom, the (Saba), 484, 485, 486, 488, 489, 492

Bottom Bay (Barbados), 111

Bouillante (Guadeloupe), 300–301

Bout Sable Bay (Dominica), 217

Brandon's Beach (Barbados), 111

Brewer's Bay (St. Thomas), 622, 626

Brewers Bay (Tortola), 15, 149, 155

Bridgetown (Barbados), 96, 98–103, 115–116, 120–121
nightlife, 123
restaurants, 109–110
shopping, 119–122

Brighton Beach (Barbados), 111

Brimmer Hall Estate (Jamaica), 355

Brimstone Hill Fortress (St. Kitts), 512

British Virgin Islands, 21, 141–169
information sources, 141
traveling to, 141–142
weddings, 55

Bubali Pond (Aruba), 92

Buccament Bay (St. Vincent), 569

Buccoo Reef (Tobago), 8, 604, 605

Buck Island Reef National Park (St. Croix), 8, 11, 607, 658–659, 661, 662, 663

Butler Bay (St. Croix), 663

Butterfly Farm (St. Martin), 553

Cabarete (Dominican Republic), 256–259

Cabarete Beach (Dominican Republic), 256

Cabo Rojo (Puerto Rico), 457–459

Cabrits National Park (Dominica), 221

Callinago Beach (Guadeloupe), 306

Camping, 15–16
Jamaica, 324
Jost Van Dyke, 15–16, 168
Martinique, 382
Puerto Rico, 460, 466
St. John, 16, 638–639
St. Lucia, 525
Tortola, 15, 149

Canashito Caves (Aruba), 90, 93

Cane Bay (St. Croix), 8, 661, 663–664

Cane Bay Wall (St. Croix), 8, 661

Caneel Bay (St. John), 643

Cane Garden Bay (Tortola), 5, 154–155
accommodations, 147, 148, 149
restaurants, 152, 153

Canouan, 570, 575

Capilla de Cristo (Puerto Rico), 437–438

Cardiff Hall Public Beach (Jamaica), 349

Careenage, the (Barbados), 110, 115, 120

Carenage, the (Grenada), 263, 264, 266, 270, 273, 275, 277

Caribbean Cove (Nevis), 414

Carib Breweries (St. Kitts), 509

Carib Indian Reservation (Dominica), 12, 219, 221

Carib Indians, 12, 21, 209, 219, 221, 294, 295, 376, 385, 443, 503, 512–513, 528, 533, 648

Carib Rock Drawings (St. Kitts), 512–513

Carite Forest Preserve (Puerto Rico), 451

Carlisle Bay (Antigua), 69

Carnival
Antigua, 62
Aruba, 81
Grenada, 264
Guadeloupe, 284
Martinique, 379
Puerto Rico, 421
St. Kitts, 504
St. Thomas, 613
St. Vincent, 570
Trinidad, 586

Caroni Bird Sanctuary (Trinidad), 11, 592–593, 594

Carriacou, 262, 274, 278–281

Carriacou Museum, 281

Carriacou Parang Festival, 281

Cartanser Sr. (St. Thomas), 625

Casa Blanca (Puerto Rico), 442

Casa Cautiño Museum (Puerto Rico), 473–474

Casa del Cordón (Dominican Republic), 236

Casals, Pablo, Museum (Puerto Rico), 443

Casals Festival (Puerto Rico), 421, 443

Casibari (Aruba), 90

Casinos
  Antigua, 77
  Aruba, 94
  Bonaire, 140
  Curaçao, 208
  Dominican Republic, 252
  Guadeloupe, 309–310
  Martinique, 388, 393
  Puerto Rico, 448–449
  St. Croix, 671–672
  St. Kitts, 515
  St. Maarten/Martin, 559
  St. Vincent, 574
  U.S. Virgin Islands, 2–3, 672

Castillo San Felipe del Morro (Puerto Rico), 2, 440–441, 450

Castries (St. Lucia), 516–519, 526–527, 528, 531–532

Casuarina Beach (Barbados), 111

Catalina Beach (Dominican Republic), 243–244

Cattlewash (Barbados), 111

Caya G. F. Betico Croes (Aruba), 89, 91

Cayman Brac, 170, 185–187

Cayman Brac Museum, 187

Cayman Islands, 21, 170–189. *See also* Cayman Brac; Grand Cayman; Little Cayman
  information sources, 170, 172
  special events, 172
  traveling to, 172
  weddings, 55

Cayman Islands National Museum (Grand Cayman), 181

Cayman Islands Pirates' Week, 172

Cayman Turtle Farm (Grand Cayman), 181

Centre d'Art Musée Paul-Gauguin (Martinique), 398

Centre St-Jean-Perse (Guadeloupe), 286–287

Champagne Garden (Nevis), 412

Charlestown (Nevis), 22–23, 404–407, 413, 415–416

Charlotte Amalie (St. Thomas), 3, 14, 15, 19, 607, 608, 610, 612–613, 626–627
  nightlife, 632–635
  restaurants, 616–618
  shopping, 628–632

Charters. *See* Boat charters; Fishing

Chateaubelair (St. Vincent), 571

Chikuzen (Tortola), 154

Children, best resorts for, 15

Choc Bay (St. Lucia), 524

Choiseul (St. Lucia), 533

Christiansted (St. Croix), 607, 648, 650, 661, 663–664, 665–666, 668
  accommodations, 650–652
  nightlife, 670–672
  restaurants, 654–657
  shopping, 14, 668–670

Christoffel National Park (Curaçao), 200, 203–204, 205

Chute de l'Ecrevisse (Guadeloupe), 300

Chutes du Carbet (Guadeloupe), 304

Cinnamon Bay (St. John), 16, 638–639, 643–644, 645

Clarence House (Antigua), 73

Climate, 32–33, 59

Club Med, 37, 42, 51, 52, 306

Clugny Beach (Guadeloupe), 296, 307

Coamo (Puerto Rico), 473

Cockleshell Bay (St. Kitts), 510

Coki Point Beach (St. Thomas), 9, 622, 625, 627

Columbus, Christopher, 22, 156, 160, 212, 215, 224, 236–237, 245, 299, 310, 313, 315, 355, 373, 376, 398, 403, 404, 494, 582, 598, 648, 662–663, 666, 668

Columbus Lighthouse (Dominican Republic), 236–237

Columbus Park Museum (Jamaica), 349

Conaree Bay (St. Kitts), 511

Concord Falls (Grenada), 274

Condado (Puerto Rico), 423, 426–427, 428, 433–434

Condado Beach (Puerto Rico), 435, 436

Condo rentals. *See* Rental properties

Coppermine Point (Virgin Gorda), 165

Coral Bay (St. John), 644

Coral World Marine Park & Underwater Observatory (St. Thomas), 627, 628

Cornwall Beach (Jamaica), 331

Corre Corre Bay (St. Eustatius), 500

Cousteau, Jacques, 187, 301, 307, 308, 313

Coward, Noël, 350, 355, 356, 357, 652

Cowpet Bay (St. Thomas), 620

Coyaba River Garden and Museum (Jamaica), 356

Crack in the Wall (St. Eustatius), 494

Cramer Park (St. Croix), 661

Crane Beach (Barbados), 111, 118

Creole Beach (Guadeloupe), 306

Creque Dam (St. Croix), 664–665, 666

Cricket, 96, 116, 593

Crooks Castle Beach (St. Eustatius), 500

Crop Over Festival (Barbados), 99

Croydon Plantation (Jamaica), 334

Cruises. *See* Boat travel and cruises

Cruzan Rum Factory (St. Croix), 667

Cuba, 317
  air travel to, 320

Culebra (Puerto Rico), 480–482

Culebra Wildlife Refuge (Puerto Rico), 482

Culebrita (Puerto Rico), 482

Cupecoy Bay Beach (St. Maarten), 551

Curaçao, 21, 190–208
accommodations, 193–195
cheap thrills, 204–205
information sources, 190
nightlife, 208
restaurants, 17, 195–198
shopping, 13, 206–208
sights and activities, 198–206
transportation, 192
traveling to, 190–192
weddings, 55
Curaçao Country House Museum, 203
Curaçao Liqueur Distillery, 204
Curaçao Maritime Museum, 203
Curaçao Museum, 202–203
Curaçao Seaquarium, 206
Curaçao Underwater Marine Park, 8, 200, 203
Currency and exchange, 30, 31
Antigua, 63
Aruba, 82
Barbados, 100
Bonaire, 128
British Virgin Islands, 142
Cayman Islands, 172–173
Curaçao, 192
Dominica, 212
Dominican Republic, 227
Grenada, 265
Guadeloupe, 284, 285
Jamaica, 322
Martinique, 380, 381
Nevis, 406
Puerto Rico, 422
Saba, 484
St. Eustatius, 496
St. Kitts, 505
St. Lucia, 518–519
St. Maarten/Martin, 540
St. Vincent, 564
Tortola, 146
Trinidad and Tobago, 583
U.S. Virgin Islands, 609
Currency converter, 59
Customs regulations, 28–30

Daaibooi (Curaçao), 198
Darkwood Beach (Antigua), 69
Davis Bay (St. Croix), 661, 663
Dawn Beach (St. Martin), 551, 555

Dead Chest Island, 156
Deshaies (Guadeloupe), 296–300
Devil's Bay National Park (Virgin Gorda), 164
Devon House (Jamaica), 368, 370–371
Dewey (Culebra), 480, 481–482
Diamond Beach (Martinique), 5, 394
Diamond Botanical Gardens (St. Lucia), 528
Diamond Mineral Baths (St. Lucia), 530
Diamond Rock (Martinique), 5, 394
Dickenson Bay (Antigua), 68–69, 70
Dieppe Bay (St. Kitts), 509, 511
Disabled travelers, 35–36
Diving. See Scuba diving
Doctor's Cave Beach (Jamaica), 331
Dolphin watching, on Dominica, 219, 222
Dominica, 4, 21, 209–223
accommodations, 213–215
cheap thrills, 220–221
information sources, 209–210
nightlife, 222–223
restaurants, 215–217
shopping, 221–222
sights and activities, 217–221
special events, 212–213
transportation, 210–211
traveling to, 210
Dominica National Park, 10–11, 217–218
Dominican Republic, 1, 4, 21, 224–261
cheap thrills, 246–247
information sources, 224–225
transportation, 226–227
traveling to, 225–226
Dorado (Puerto Rico), 449–450
Dos Pos (Bonaire), 137
Dottins (Barbados), 113
Dow's Hill Interpretation Center (Antigua), 72–73
Driftwood Beach (Antigua), 69
Dunn's River Falls (Jamaica), 354, 356

Dutchman's Bay (Antigua), 71
Dutch World Radio (Bonaire), 136–137

Eagle Beach (Aruba), 88, 92
Eden Brown Estate (Nevis), 413
Edgar Clerc Archaeological Museum La Rosette (Guadeloupe), 294
Edinburgh Castle (Jamaica), 355
Edmund Forest Reserve (St. Lucia), 529
El Arsenal (Puerto Rico), 442
El Combate Beach (Puerto Rico), 457
El Faro (Puerto Rico), 466, 469
El Faro a Colón (Dominican Republic), 236–237
El Morro (Puerto Rico), 2, 440–441, 450
El Yunque Rain Forest (Puerto Rico), 438, 465, 466, 469
Emperor Valley Zoo (Trinidad), 594
Englishman's Bay (Tobago), 604
Entertainment Village (Jamaica), 2, 358–359
Entry requirements, 27–28
Estate Mount Washington Plantation (St. Croix), 666–667, 668
Estate St. Peter Greathouse Botanical Gardens (St. Thomas), 627
Estate Whim Plantation Museum (St. Croix), 667

Fairy Hill Beach (Jamaica), 362
Fajardo (Puerto Rico), 466–467, 469
Falmouth (Jamaica), 344, 346–347
Falmouth Harbour (Antigua), 65, 68, 76–77
Farley Hill National Park (Barbados), 119
Fern Gully (Jamaica), 355

Ferries (and mail boats)
  British Virgin Islands, 142,
    144, 167–168
  Carriacou, 279
  Dominica, 210
  Grenadines, 575
  Iles des Saintes, 311
  La Désirade, 316
  Marie-Galante, 314
  Martinique, 379, 380, 388
  Nevis, 406, 513
  Puerto Rico, 608–609
  St. John, 609
  St. Kitts, 513
  St. Thomas, 608–609
  Tobago, 599
  Trinidad, 599
Festivals. *See* Carnival; *and
  specific festivals*
Fig Tree Drive (Antigua),
  73, 74
Firefly (Jamaica), 356
Fishing
  Aruba, 88
  Barbados, 112
  Bonaire, 135
  Cayman Brac, 186
  Dominican Republic,
    258, 260
  Guadeloupe, 296
  Little Cayman, 187,
    188, 189
  Puerto Rico, 456, 457
  St. Croix, 662
  St. Thomas, 623
  St. Vincent, 569
Flamenco Beach (Puerto
  Rico), 482
Fleming, Ian, 350, 354–355
Floating Market (Curaçao),
  202
Flower Forest (Barbados),
  116–117
Flynn, Errol, 12–13, 344,
  356, 359–363
Folkestone Underwater
  Park (Barbados), 113
Folly Great House
  (Jamaica), 363
Fontein Cave (Aruba), 91
Fort Amsterdam (Curaçao),
  201
Fort Charles (Jamaica), 369
Fort Charlotte (St. Vincent),
  571
Fort Christian (St. Thomas),
  626
Fort Christiansvaern
  (St. Croix), 665
Fort Clarence (Jamaica), 367

Fort Conde de Morasol
  Museum (Puerto Rico),
  480
Fort-de-France
  (Martinique), 378–388
Fort Fleur-d'Epée
  (Guadeloupe), 288
Fort Frederick (Grenada),
  273
Fort Frederik (St. Croix),
  666
Fort George (Grenada), 272
Fort George (Trinidad), 594
Fort King George (Tobago),
  599, 605
Fort Napoléon (Iles des
  Saintes), 313
Fort Nassau (Curaçao), 204
Fort Oranje (Bonaire), 136
Fort San Cristóbal (Puerto
  Rico), 441
Fort San Felipe (Dominican
  Republic), 251
Fort San Jerónimo (Puerto
  Rico), 441
Foursquare Plantation
  (Barbados), 118
Francia Plantation
  (Barbados), 117
Francis Bay Beach
  (St. John), 644
Franklyn Water Wheel and
  Nature Park (Tobago), 605
Frederiksted (St. Croix), 14,
  648, 650, 663, 666, 668
  accommodations,
    652–654
  nightlife, 19, 670–672
  restaurants, 659–661
French Cap Pinnacle
  (St. Thomas), 625
Frenchman's Cove Beach
  (Jamaica), 362
Frenchtown (St. Thomas),
  618–619, 627, 634
Friar's Bay (St. Kitts), 510,
  511
Friar's Bay Beach
  (St. Martin), 552
Frigate Bay (St. Kitts), 510,
  511
Frigate Islands Nature
  Reserve (St. Lucia), 530
Funchi Beach (Bonaire),
  133, 136

Gambling. *See* Casinos
Gauguin, Paul, Museum
  (Martinique), 398

Gay and lesbian travelers,
  36–37, 51
  Antigua, 77
  Cayman Islands, 170
  Dominican Republic, 240
  Martinique, 388, 396–397
  Puerto Rico, 426, 436, 448
  St. Croix, 653, 657–658,
    661, 671
  St. John, 635
  St. Maarten/Martin, 551,
    561
  St. Thomas, 622, 632–633
George Town (Grand
  Cayman), 170, 172,
  173–174, 176–178, 181,
  182, 184–185
Giddy House (Jamaica), 369
Ginger Island, 154
Gingerland (Nevis), 404,
  415–416
Glovers Island, 272
"Goat Island" (Dominican
  Republic), 242, 246
Goldeneye (Jamaica),
  354–355
Golden Rock (Nevis), 413,
  414, 416
Golf
  Antigua, 70
  Aruba, 88
  Curaçao, 200
  Dominican Republic, 250
  Grenada, 271
  Martinique, 384
  Nevis, 411
  Puerto Rico, 449
Gorda Peak (Virgin Gorda),
  165
Gosier (Guadeloupe),
  288–290, 306, 309–310
Gotomeer (Bonaire), 137
Gouyave (Grenada), 273,
  275
Governor Gore Bird
  Sanctuary (Little Cayman),
  189
Grand Anse Beach
  (Grenada), 5, 262, 266,
  268–271, 276
Grand Ballets Martiniquais,
  387, 388
Grand-Bourg (Marie-
  Galante), 314–315
Grand-Case Beach
  (St. Martin), 552
Grand Cayman, 170,
  172–185
  accommodations, 15,
    174–176
  cheap thrills, 182–183

information sources, 170, 172, 173
nightlife, 185
restaurants, 176–178
shopping, 184–185
sights and activities, 178–184
transportation, 173–174
traveling to, 172
weddings, 55
Grande Anse (Grenada), 268
Grande Anse (Martinique), 393
Grande Anse (St. Lucia), 529
Grand Etang National Park (Grenada), 262, 271, 275, 276
Grande-Terre (Guadeloupe), 282–295, 306–309
Grand' Rivière (Martinique), 401
Grapetree Beach (St. Croix), 661
Great Bay Beach (St. Maarten), 551
Great Bird Island, 71
Great Courland Bay (Tobago), 603–604
Great Harbour (Jost Van Dyke), 167, 168–169
Great houses
    Barbados, 116, 117, 118
    Curaçao, 203
    Grand Cayman, 181–182
    Jamaica, 333–334, 350, 355, 356–357, 363, 371, 372, 373
    St. Croix, 666–667
    St. Thomas, 627
    Tobago, 597, 598
Great River (Jamaica), 332
Green Beach (Puerto Rico), 480
Greenwood Great House (Jamaica), 333
Grenada, 1, 12, 21–22, 262–278
    accommodations, 266–268
    cheap thrills, 274–275
    information sources, 262–263
    nightlife, 278
    restaurants, 17, 268–270
    shopping, 276–277
    sights and activities, 270–276
    transportation, 264–265
    traveling to, 263–264
Grenada Cooperative Nutmeg Association, 273, 275

Grenada National Museum, 273
Grenadines, the, 12, 26, 562, 575–581
    cheap thrills, 572–573
    information sources, 563
    transportation, 564
    traveling to, 563–564, 575
Grenville (Grenada), 275, 276
Guadarikiri Cave (Aruba), 91
Guadeloupe, 1–2, 11, 22, 282–310
    activities, 307–309
    cheap thrills, 298–299
    information sources, 282
    nightlife, 309–310
    transportation, 282, 284
    traveling to, 282
Guadeloupe, Aquarium de la, 288
Guadeloupe, Parc Naturel de, 11, 298, 300, 303–304, 307
Guadirikiri Cave (Aruba), 93
Guajataca Beach (Puerto Rico), 472
Guánica State Forest (Puerto Rico), 451, 460, 463
Guayama (Puerto Rico), 473–474
Gun Hill Signal Station (Barbados), 117
Gurabo (Puerto Rico), 468–469

Hacienda Buena Vista (Puerto Rico), 462–463
Hadikurari (Aruba), 87–88
Half Moon Bay (Antigua), 69
Hamilton, Alexander, 404, 413, 415, 650–651
Hamm's Bluff (St. Croix), 665
Hampstead Beach (Dominica), 217
Hard Rock Cafes, 431, 617
Harmony Hall (Jamaica), 356–357
Harrison's Cave (Barbados), 10, 117
Hassel Island (St. Thomas), 632
Hastings (Barbados), 102–103, 108, 109
Hato Caves (Curaçao), 205
Haulover Bay (St. John), 9, 645

Havensight Mall (St. Thomas), 621, 628–631
Hawksbill Beaches (Antigua), 69
Hawksnest Beach (St. John), 643
Health concerns, 33–34
Hell! (Grand Cayman), 181, 183
Hell's Gate (Saba), 492
Hellshire Beach (Jamaica), 367
Hellshire Hills (Jamaica), 345
Heritage Quay (Antigua), 75, 76, 77
Hiking
    Antigua, 70, 72
    Barbados, 112, 121
    Curaçao, 205
    Dominica, 217–218, 219–220
    Dominican Republic, 258
    Grand Cayman, 183–184
    Grenada, 271, 274
    Guadeloupe, 304, 307
    Iles des Saintes, 313
    Jamaica, 364–365
    Martinique, 384, 391, 395, 399, 403
    Nevis, 411, 412, 414
    Puerto Rico, 451, 460, 463
    Saba, 489, 490–491
    St. Croix, 3, 658–659, 662, 664–665, 666, 668
    St. Eustatius, 499, 500
    St. John, 644–645
    St. Kitts, 511–512, 513
    St. Lucia, 525, 529
    St. Vincent, 569–570, 572
    Tortola, 155, 156
    Virgin Gorda, 165
Hillsborough (Carriacou), 274, 278, 280, 281
Hilma Hooker (Bonaire), 135
Hodges Beach (Dominica), 217
Holetown (Barbados), 99, 107, 113, 123
Holy Trinity Cathedral (Trinidad), 593
Honen Dalim (St. Eustatius), 501
Honeymoon Beach (Water Island), 632
Honeymooners
    best resorts for, 14–15
    weddings, in the Caribbean, 54–56

Hooiberg (Aruba), 90
Hooker (Bonaire), 135
Horseback riding
  Aruba, 89
  Barbados, 112
  Curaçao, 200, 205
  Dominican Republic, 244,
    258
  Jamaica, 332, 348, 357
  Martinique, 390–391
  Nevis, 411
  St. Croix, 662
  St. Kitts, 512
  St. Lucia, 525
  St. Maarten/Martin, 552
  St. Thomas, 623
  Tortola, 156
Horse racing, 235, 415, 436
Horseshoe Reef (Anegada),
  166
Hull Bay (St. Thomas), 623
Humacao (Puerto Rico), 470
Hurricane season, 32–33

Icacos (Puerto Rico), 466
Iglesia Porta Coeli (Puerto
  Rico), 464, 473
Iles des Saintes, 12, 307,
  310–313
Ilet à Goyave, 301
Ilet Pinel (St. Martin),
  552, 553
Indian Bay Beach
  (St. Vincent), 569
Indian Castle Beach (Nevis),
  410–411
Indian Town National Park
  (Antigua), 73–74
Information sources, 27.
  See also Websites; *and
  specific destinations*
Insurance, 34–35
Isaac Bay Beach (St. Croix),
  661
Isabel de Torres (Dominican
  Republic), 251
Isla Verde (Puerto Rico),
  423, 424, 427–428,
  428–429, 434
Isla Verde Beach (Puerto
  Rico), 436

Jabrun du Nord
  (Guadeloupe), 294
Jabrun du Sud
  (Guadeloupe), 294
Jack Tar Village (Dominican
  Republic), 252
Jack Tar Village (St. Kitts),
  515

Jamaica, 4, 22, 317–375.
  *See also specific
  destinations*
  accommodations tips, 324
  cheap thrills, 344–345
  information sources, 318
  transportation, 320–322
  traveling to, 319–320
  weddings, 55–56
  what's new, 2
Jamaica Grande's Beach
  (Jamaica), 354
Jamaica National Library,
  368
Jamaica People's Museum
  of Craft & Technology,
  370
James Bond Beach
  (Jamaica), 354
Jardín Botánico (Dominican
  Republic), 237
Jardin de Balata
  (Martinique), 385
Jayuya (Puerto Rico), 471,
  474
Jewish Cultural Historical
  Museum (Curaçao), 202
John Crow Mountain
  National Park (Jamaica),
  364–365
Johnson's Point (Antigua),
  69
Jolly Harbour (Nevis),
  68, 69
Jolly Roger (Antigua), 70
Jost Van Dyke, 141–142,
  167–169

Karpata Ecological
  Center (Klein Bonaire),
  134
Kayaking
  Bonaire, 136
  Carriacou, 274
  Culebra, 482
  Dominica, 218
  Dominican Republic, 250,
    256
  Puerto Rico, 435, 450
  St. Croix, 662–663
  St. John, 645
  St. Thomas, 623
Kearton's Bay (St. Vincent),
  569
King's Bay Beach (Tobago),
  603
King's House (Jamaica), 368
Kingston (Jamaica), 318,
  319–322, 365–371

Kingstown (St. Vincent),
  562–565, 567–568, 571,
  573–574
Klein Bonaire, 8, 134, 136
Knip Bay (Curaçao), 198
Kralendijk (Bonaire),
  125–129, 136, 139–140

Lac Bay Beach (Bonaire),
  133, 136, 139
La Désirade (Guadeloupe),
  315–316
La Fortaleza (Puerto Rico),
  442
Lago Enriquillo (Dominican
  Republic), 242
La Grand-Anse
  (Guadeloupe), 296–300,
  307
Lamentin (Guadeloupe), 296
Lameshur Bay Beach
  (St. John), 644
La Minitas (Dominican
  Republic), 243
Landhuis Brievengat
  (Curaçao), 205, 208
Lang Bank (St. Croix), 662
L'Anse Noire (Dominica),
  217
La Parguera (Puerto Rico),
  473, 475–476
La Réserve Cousteau
  (Guadeloupe), 307
La Romana (Dominican
  Republic), 242–244
La Sagesse Nature Center
  (Grenada), 16, 267, 271
Las Cabezas de San Juan
  Nature Reserve (Puerto
  Rico), 466, 469
Las Cuevas Bay (Trinidad),
  592
La Soufrière (Guadeloupe),
  11, 282, 302–303,
  304–305
La Soufrière (St. Vincent),
  569–570, 572
Las Terrenas (Dominican
  Republic), 259, 260
La Toc Beach (St. Lucia), 524
Laudat (Dominica), 217, 219
Layou River (Dominica), 219
Le Bas du Fort
  (Guadeloupe), 288, 306
Le Carbet (Martinique), 398
Le Diamant (Martinique),
  394–395
Le François (Martinique),
  403

Leinster Bay (St. John), 9, 632–633, 644, 645
LeLoLai VIP Program (Puerto Rico), 420
Le Marin (Martinique), 395–396
Le Moule (Guadeloupe), 294, 306
Le Prêcheur (Martinique), 399
Le Rocher du Diamant (Martinique), 5, 394
Les Deux Mamelles (Guadeloupe), 300
Les Grand Ballets Martiniquais, 387, 388
Les Heures Saines (Guadeloupe), 308
Les Saintes, 12, 307, 310–313
Les Salines (Martinique), 396
Les Trois-Ilets (Martinique), 388–393
Levera Beach (Grenada), 271, 273
Levera National Park (Grenada), 271, 274
Leyritz (Martinique), 398, 400–401
Lime Cay (Jamaica), 367
Limetree Beach (St. Thomas), 622, 626
Lindbergh Beach (St. Thomas), 623
Lindquist Beach (St. Thomas), 622
Little Bay Beach (St. Maarten), 551
Little Cayman, 170, 187–189
Little Magens Bay (St. Thomas), 622
Little Rockley Bay (Tobago), 604
Little Tobago, 597, 605
Loblolly Bay (Anegada), 167
Loíza Lake (Puerto Rico), 468
Long Bay (Antigua), 70
Long Bay (Tortola), 155
Los Haitisses (Dominican Republic), 260
Los Tres Ojos (Dominican Republic), 237
Lover's Beach (Tobago), 603
Lovers' Leap (Jamaica), 375
Luperón Beach (Dominican Republic), 250
Luquillo Beach (Puerto Rico), 8, 435, 436, 465, 469

Lyford (Jamaica), 355
Lynch Bay Beach (St. Eustatius), 500
Lynch Plantation Museum (St. Eustatius), 501–502

Machoucherie River (Dominica), 219, 220
Macouba (Martinique), 391
Mafolie Hill (St. Thomas), 615, 621
Magens Bay (St. Thomas), 9, 610, 621–622, 625
Mahaut (Guadeloupe), 300
Maho Bay Beach (St. John), 16, 639, 644
Maho Bay Beach (St. Maarten), 551
Mahoe Bay (Virgin Gorda), 164
Mail boats. See Ferries
Maison de la Canne (Martinique), 393
Maj. General Rogers (St. Thomas), 625
Malabar Beach (St. Lucia), 524
Mallards Bay Beach (Jamaica), 354
Manchebo Beach (Aruba), 88
Mandeville (Jamaica), 371–373
Man-O-War Bay (Tobago), 603
Manzanilla Beach (Trinidad), 592
Maracas Bay (Trinidad), 591–592, 595
Maria Islands Nature Reserve (St. Lucia), 530–531
Marie-Galante, 12, 307, 313–315
Marigot (St. Martin), 538–542, 549–550, 558–559
Marigot Bay (St. Lucia), 524, 527
Marijuana (ganja), 135, 322, 325, 338
Markets
   Antigua, 75
   Aruba, 89, 93
   Barbados, 108, 120
   Bonaire, 136
   Curaçao, 202, 204–205
   Dominica, 221
   Dominican Republic, 238
   Grenada, 272, 275, 276
   Guadeloupe, 286, 288

   Jamaica, 335, 344, 358, 359, 370, 371
   Martinique, 386
   St. John, 646
   St. Kitts, 509, 512
   St. Lucia, 527, 528
   St. Martin, 558
   St. Thomas, 628, 629
   St. Vincent, 573
   Tobago, 599, 606
   Trinidad, 593
Marley, Bob, 617
   Museum (Jamaica), 368–369
Marriages, in the Caribbean, 54–56
Marriqua Valley (St. Vincent), 572–573
Marshall's Pen (Jamaica), 371, 373
Martha Brae River (Jamaica), 347
Martinique, 22, 376–403
   cheap thrills, 390–391
   information sources, 378
   money-saving tips, 382
   transportation, 379–380
   traveling to, 378–379
Martinique, Parc Naturel Régional de la, 384, 391, 398
Mastic Trail (Grand Cayman), 183–184
Matouba (Guadeloupe), 303
Maverick (Tobago), 604
Mayagüez (Puerto Rico), 418, 451, 454–457, 472–473
Mayreau, 580–581
Megaliths (Antigua), 73
Mesopotamia Valley (St. Vincent), 572–573
Middle Quarters (Jamaica), 375
Mikve Israel-Emanuel Synagogue (Curaçao), 202
Mona Island (Puerto Rico), 10, 456
Money, 30–32. See also Currency and exchange
Money-saving tips, 38–40, 50
Mongoose Junction (St. John), 642, 646–647
Monkey Shoals (Nevis), 411
Montego Bay (Jamaica), 324–336
   accommodations, 325, 328–329
   beaches, 331
   nightlife, 336
   restaurants, 329–331

Montego Bay (Jamaica)
(cont.)
    shopping, 334–336
    sights and activities,
        331–334
    special events, 321
    traveling to, 319–320
Montserrat, 69, 72
Moonhole (Bequia), 579
Morgan Lewis Sugar Mill
    (Barbados), 117
Morne des Esses
    (Martinique), 402
Morne Fortune (St. Lucia),
    528–529
Morne Rouge (Martinique),
    399
Morne Rouge Bay
    (Grenada), 270–271
Morne Trois Pitons National
    Park (Dominica), 217,
    219–220
Morning Star Beach
    (St. Thomas), 622, 626
Mosquito Bay (Puerto Rico),
    480
Mount Brandaris (Bonaire),
    138
Mount Liamuiga (St. Kitts),
    23, 511, 513
Mount Nevis (Nevis), 411
Mount Pelée (Martinique),
    398, 399–400
Mount Sage (Tortola),
    155–156
Mount Scenery (Saba), 483,
    489, 490
Mount Soufrière (St. Lucia),
    530
Mount Washington
    Plantation (St. Croix),
    666–667, 668
Mullet Bay Beach
    (St. Maarten), 551
Mullins Beach (Barbados),
    111
Musée de la Pagerie
    (Martinique), 392
Musée Départemental de la
    Martinique, 385
Musée du Rhum St-James
    (Martinique), 401–402
Musée Rhum Clement
    (Martinique), 403
Musée Volcanologique
    (Martinique), 399
Museo Castillo Serrallés
    (Puerto Rico), 462
Museo de Arte (Puerto
    Rico), 442–443
Museo de Arte de Ponce
    (Puerto Rico), 461–462

Museo de Arte e Historia
    de San Juan (Puerto
    Rico), 443
Museo de Arte Moderno
    (Dominican Republic),
    237
Museo de las Americas
    (Puerto Rico), 443
Museo de las Casas Reales
    (Dominican Republic),
    237
Museo Pablo Casals (Puerto
    Rico), 443
Museum of Antigua &
    Barbuda (Antigua), 71
Museum of Dominican
    Amber (Dominican
    Republic), 251
Museum of Nevis History,
    413, 415
Mustique, 26, 575

Naggo Head (Jamaica),
    367
Nagshead (St. Kitts), 511
Naguabo Beach (Puerto
    Rico), 470
National Library (Dominican
    Republic), 237
National Library of Jamaica,
    368
National Museum and Art
    Gallery (Trinidad), 593
National Theater
    (Dominican Republic),
    237
Natural Bridge (Aruba),
    90–91
Nature trails. See Hiking
Navy Island, 344, 359–362
Negril (Jamaica), 336–346
    accommodations,
        338–341
    beaches, 344–345
    nightlife, 346
    restaurants, 17, 341–343
    sights and activities,
        344–346
    traveling to, 338
Nelson's Dockyard National
    Park (Antigua), 60, 64,
    71–72
Nevis, 12, 22–23, 404–416,
    513
    accommodations,
        407–408
    cheap thrills, 414–415
    information sources, 405
    nightlife, 416
    restaurants, 408–410
    shopping, 415–416

    sights and activities,
        410–415
    transportation, 406
    traveling to, 405–406
Nevis Botanical Garden,
    413–414
Nevis History, Museum of,
    413, 415
Nevis Jockey Club, 415
Nevis synagogue, 413
Newcastle Beach (Nevis),
    411
Nightlife. See also Casinos;
    and specific destinations
    best bets, 18–19
    money-saving tips, 39–40
No Name Beach (Klein
    Bonaire), 134
Nonsuch Cave (Jamaica),
    363
Norman Island, 12, 141, 157
North Shore Shell Museum
    (Tortola), 17, 151, 156
Northstar Reef (St. Croix),
    663
Nukove Beach (Bonaire),
    133
Nylon Pool (Tobago), 605

Ocean Park (Puerto Rico),
    423, 428, 429
Ocean Park Beach (Puerto
    Rico), 436
Ocho Rios (Jamaica), 22,
    318, 350–359
    accommodations, 350,
        352
    beaches, 354
    nightlife, 358–359
    restaurants, 352–354
    shopping, 357–358
    sights and activities,
        354–357
    transportation, 320–322
    traveling to, 319–320, 350
Oistins Fish Festival
    (Barbados), 99
Oistins Fish Market
    (Barbados), 108, 120
Old Man Bay (Grand
    Cayman), 182
Old San Juan (Puerto Rico),
    2, 417, 423, 424,
    429–433, 437–444, 450
O'Neal Botanic Gardens
    (Tortola), 157
1,000 Steps Beach
    (Bonaire), 133, 136
Orange Beach
    (St. Eustatius), 500

Oranjestad (Aruba), 80–83, 89–90, 92–93
  nightlife, 94–95
  restaurants, 86–87
  shopping, 91–94
Oranjestad (St. Eustatius), 494–497, 498–499, 501–502
Orient Beach (St. Martin), 552, 553, 555
Orléans (St. Martin), 550, 553
Oualie Beach (Nevis), 410, 412
Our Lady of Guadalupe Cathedral (Puerto Rico), 462
Owen Island (Little Cayman), 187
Oyster Pond Beach (St. Martin), 551

Package tours, 40–42
Paget Farm (Bequia), 579
Palmas del Mar (Puerto Rico), 470
Palm Beach (Aruba), 87, 89, 92, 94
Papillote Forest (Dominica), 16, 214, 216
Paradise Beach (Barbados), 111
Paradise Beach (Jamaica), 349
Paradise Point Tramway (St. Thomas), 627
Paradise Reef (Antigua), 69, 71
Parasailing, 70, 525, 555
Parc des Floralies (Martinique), 392
Parc Naturel de Guadeloupe, 11, 298, 300, 303–304, 307
Parc Naturel Régional de la Martinique, 384, 391, 398
Parlatuvier Beach (Tobago), 603
Parque de Bombas (Puerto Rico), 462
Parque Independencia (Dominican Republic), 235
Parque Nacional Bahoruco (Dominican Republic), 242
Parque Nacional Isla Cabritos (Dominican Republic), 242, 246
Parque Nacional Jaragua (Dominican Republic), 242
Paynes Bay (Barbados), 108, 110, 111

Pearl's Beach (Grenada), 271
Pedro St. James National Historic Site (Grand Cayman), 181–182
Peter Island, 156, 157
Petit-Bourg (Guadeloupe), 305
Petit Canal (Guadeloupe), 294
Philipsburg (St. Maarten), 535, 538–542, 545–548, 551, 553, 556–558
Phosphorescent Bay (Puerto Rico), 480
Picard Beach (Dominica), 217
Picard River (Dominica), 219, 220
Pigeon Island National Park (St. Lucia), 524, 527, 528, 533
Pigeon Point (Antigua), 68
Pigeon Point (Tobago), 603
Pineapple Beach (Antigua), 70
Pink Beach (Bonaire), 133
Pink Gin Beach (Grenada), 271
Pinney's Beach (Nevis), 5, 8, 404, 410, 411, 415
Pirates Week (Cayman Islands), 172
Pitch Lake (Trinidad), 594–595
Plage Anse Crawen (Iles des Saintes), 313
Plage Caravelle (Guadeloupe), 306
Plage de Clugny (Guadeloupe), 296, 307
Plage de La Caraïbe (Guadeloupe), 307
Plage de la Malendure (Guadeloupe), 307
Plage de la Perle (Guadeloupe), 307
Plage de la Tillette (Guadeloupe), 307
Plage de Pompierre (Iles des Saintes), 313
Plage Figuier (Iles des Saintes), 313
Playa Abao (Curaçao), 198
Playa de Pajaros (Puerto Rico), 456
Playa de Ponce (Puerto Rico), 461
Playa Dorada (Dominican Republic), 246, 250
Playa Esmeralda (Dominican Republic), 235

Playa Forti (Curaçao), 203
Playa Funchi (Bonaire), 133, 136
Playa Grande (Dominican Republic), 5, 252
Playa Juan Dolio (Dominican Republic), 235
Playa Kenepa (Curaçao), 198
Playa Lagun (Curaçao), 198
Playa Sardinera (Puerto Rico), 456
Plymouth (Tobago), 600, 605
Pointe-a-Pierre Wild Fowl Trust (Trinidad), 594
Pointe-à-Pitre (Guadeloupe), 282–288
Pointe de la Grande Vigie (Guadeloupe), 295
Pointe des Châteaux (Guadeloupe), 293–294, 298
Pointe des Colibris (Guadeloupe), 293
Pointe du Bout (Martinique), 384, 388–393
Pointe Noire (Guadeloupe), 297, 298, 299–300
Pointe Seraphine (St. Lucia), 531–532
Point Salines (Grenada), 276
Point Udall (St. Croix), 633, 668
Ponce (Puerto Rico), 459–463, 473
Port Antonio (Jamaica), 322, 323, 359–365
Porte d'Enfer (Guadeloupe), 295, 306
Port Elizabeth (Bequia), 578
Port Louis (Guadeloupe), 294–295
Port-of-Spain (Trinidad), 582–587, 590–598
Port Royal (Jamaica), 335, 369
Portsmouth (Dominica), 214–215, 221, 222
President's House (Trinidad), 594
Presqu'ile de la Carabelle Nature Preserve (Martinique), 403
Prickly Pear Island (Antigua), 69
Prospect Plantation (Jamaica), 357
Puebla (Culebra), 480, 482
Puerto Plata (Dominican Republic), 245–252

Puerto Rico, 4–5, 23, 417–480. *See also* *specific destinations*
cheap thrills, 450–451
information sources, 417
special events, 421
tours, 421–422
transportation, 418, 420–422
traveling to, 418
weddings, 56
what's new, 2
Puerto Rico Trench, 10, 663
Punta Brabo (Aruba), 88
Punta Higuero (Puerto Rico), 454, 457

Quadrille Dancers (St.Croix), 670
Quebradillas (Puerto Rico), 472, 474–475
Queen Elizabeth II Botanic Park (Grand Cayman), 182–183
Queen Emma Pontoon Bridge (Curaçao), 201, 204
Queen Juliana Bridge (Curaçao), 201
Queen's Park Savannah (Trinidad), 593
Queen's Royal College (Trinidad), 593
Questelle's Bay Beach (St. Vincent), 569
Quilesse Forest Reserve (St. Lucia), 529
Quill, the (St. Eustatius), 494, 499, 500

Rabacca Dry River (St. Vincent), 572
Rafting, in Jamaica, 332, 347
Río Grande, 12–13, 362–363
Rainbow Beach (St. Croix), 661
Red Beach (Puerto Rico), 480
Redcliffe Quay (Antigua), 66, 67–68, 70, 75–76
Red Hook (St. Thomas), 609, 619–620, 623–624, 635, 643
Reduit Beach (St. Lucia), 524, 526
Reef Beach (St. Croix), 661

Reggae music, in Jamaica, 321, 332, 333, 336, 346, 358, 367, 368
Reggae Sunfest (Jamaica), 321
Reggae Sunsplash (Jamaica), 321
Regional Museum of Archaeology (Dominican Republic), 244
Renaissance Grand Beach (St. Thomas), 622, 626
Rental properties, 52–53
Barbados, 102
Carriacou, 280
Grand Cayman, 176
Jamaica, 324
Martinique, 382
St. John, 639–640
St. Thomas, 613
Tortola, 149
Virgin Gorda, 160, 162–163
Réserve Sous-Marine Régionale (St. Martin), 554
Resorts, 50–51. *See also* *specific destinations*
all-inclusive, 51–52, 241–242, 248–249, 253–254, 317, 516
best bets, 14–15
Restaurants. *See also* *specific destinations*
best bets, 16–17
money-saving tips, 39
Rhone, HMS (Tortola), 9, 154, 165, 625
Rhone National Marine Park, 154, 156
Richmond Beach (St. Vincent), 569, 571
Rincón (Bonaire), 138, 139
Rincón (Puerto Rico), 452–454
Río Camuy Caves (Puerto Rico), 452, 472
Río Grande (Jamaica), rafting, 12–13, 362–363
River rafting. *See* Rafting, in Jamaica
Road Town (Tortola), 141, 142, 144, 146, 147–148, 155, 156, 157
restaurants, 150, 151, 152–153
shopping, 157–158
Rocher du Diamant (Martinique), 5, 394
Roches Gravées (Guadeloupe), 303

Rodger's Beach (Aruba), 88, 91
Rodney Bay (St. Lucia), 524, 527
Roseau (Dominica), 209, 210–213, 215–217, 221–222, 222–223
Rose Hall Great House (Jamaica), 334
Route de la Trace (Martinique), 390, 398
Route de la Traversée (Guadeloupe), 300
Royal Botanical Gardens (Trinidad), 593–594
Rum Point (Grand Cayman), 182, 183
Runaway Bay (Jamaica), 348–350
Ruta Panorámica (Puerto Rico), 451

Saba, 5, 10, 12, 23, 483–493
accommodations, 486–487
cheap thrills, 490–491
information sources, 483
nightlife, 493
restaurants, 487–489
shopping, 492
sights and activities, 489–492
transportation, 484
traveling to, 483–484
Saba Marine Park, 489–491
Saba Spice, 492
Sage Mountain National Park (Tortola), 155–156
Sailing. *See also* Boat charters
Anegada, 166
Antigua, 60
Sailing Week, 62
Aruba, 87, 89
Bonaire, 133
October Sailing Regatta, 126
Carriacou, 281
Culebra, 482
Curaçao, 199
Grand Cayman, 180
Grenada, 272
Guadeloupe, 307
Jamaica, 332
Martinique, 384
Nevis, 411
St. John, 645
St. Kitts, 511
St. Thomas, 623–625
Tortola, 156

St. Ann's Bay (Jamaica), 355
St. Ann's Fort (Barbados), 116
St. Bernard's Roman Catholic Church (Bonaire), 136
St. Christoffelberg (Curaçao), 203
St. Croix, 3, 26–27, 607, 633, 648–672
    accommodations, 650–654
    information sources, 607, 648
    nightlife, 19, 670–672
    restaurants, 17, 654–661
    shopping, 14, 668–670
    sights and activities, 661–668
    transportation, 648, 650
    traveling to, 608–609
    weddings, 56
St. Croix Aquarium, 665–666
St. Croix Heritage Trail, 3, 666, 668
St. Croix Rain Forest, 662, 664–665
Ste-Anne (Guadeloupe), 291–292, 306
Ste-Anne (Martinique), 396–397
Ste-Marie (Guadeloupe), 299
Ste-Marie (Martinique), 401–402
Ste-Rose (Guadeloupe), 296
St. Eustatius, 5, 23, 494–502
    accommodations, 497–498
    cheap thrills, 499
    information sources, 495
    nightlife, 502
    restaurants, 498–499
    shopping, 502
    sights and activities, 500–502
    transportation, 495–496
    traveling to, 495
St. Eustatius Historical Foundation Museum, 501
St-François (Guadeloupe), 292–293, 308, 309, 310
St. George's (Grenada), 263–266, 272–273, 275
    nightlife, 278
    restaurants, 268–270
    shopping, 276–277
St. George Village Botanical Garden (St. Croix), 667

St. Jago de la Vega (Jamaica), 369–370
Saint James Distillery (Martinique), 401–402
St. John, 12, 26–27, 607, 635–648
    accommodations, 636–640
    information sources, 607, 636
    nightlife, 647–648
    shopping, 646–647
    sights and activities, 643–646
    transportation, 636
    traveling to, 608–609
    weddings, 56
St. John's (Antigua), 60, 61–64, 66–68, 71, 73–77
St. John's Cathedral (Antigua), 71
St. Kitts, 23, 503–515
    accommodations, 506–508
    cheap thrills, 509
    information sources, 503
    nightlife, 514–515
    restaurants, 508–510
    shopping, 513–514
    sights and activities, 510–513
    transportation, 504–505
    traveling to, 504
St. Kitts Music Festival, 504
St. Louis Roman Catholic Cathedral (Martinique), 385
St. Lucia, 23, 26, 516–534
    accommodations, 519–521
    cheap thrills, 528–529
    information sources, 516
    nightlife, 533–534
    restaurants, 522–523
    shopping, 531–533
    sights and activities, 524–531
    transportation, 518
    traveling to, 516–518
    weddings, 56
St. Maarten, 26, 535–561
    accommodations, 542–544
    cheap thrills, 553
    information sources, 538
    nightlife, 19, 559–560
    restaurants, 545–548
    shopping, 556–558
    sights and activities, 550–556

    transportation, 539–540
    traveling to, 538–539
St. Martin, 26, 535–561
    accommodations, 544–545
    cheap thrills, 553
    information sources, 538
    nightlife, 560–561
    restaurants, 548–550
    shopping, 558–559
    sights and activities, 550–556
    transportation, 539–540
    traveling to, 538–539
St. Michael's Cathedral (Barbados), 115
St. Nicholas Abbey (Barbados), 119
St. Peter Greathouse Botanical Gardens (St. Thomas), 627
St-Pierre (Martinique), 398–399
St. Stanislaus Church (Dominican Republic), 244
St. Thomas, 3, 26–27, 607, 610–635
    accommodations, 14, 15, 613–616
    cheap thrills, 632–633
    information sources, 607, 612
    nightlife, 18, 19, 632–635
    restaurants, 616–621
    shopping, 628–632
    sights and activities, 621–628
    transportation, 612–613
    traveling to, 608–609
    weddings, 56
St. Vincent, 12, 26, 562–574
    accommodations, 565–567
    cheap thrills, 572–573
    information sources, 563
    nightlife, 574
    restaurants, 567–568
    shopping, 573–574
    sights and activities, 569–573
    transportation, 564
    traveling to, 563–564
St. Vincent Botanic Gardens, 571
Salako Beach (Guadeloupe), 306
Salt flats, of Bonaire, 137, 138, 139
Salt Island, 9, 154
Salt Pond Bay (St. John), 644

Salt River (St. Croix), 662, 666
Salt River Bay National Historical Park and Ecological Preserve (St. Croix), 666
Salt River Canyon (St. Croix), 663
Samaná (Dominican Republic), 247, 259–261
Sam Lord's Castle Resorts (Barbados), 121
Sand Bank Bay (St. Kitts), 510
Sandy Beach (Barbados), 111, 113
Sandy Point (St. Croix), 661
San Felipe del Morro Castillo (Puerto Rico), 2, 440–441, 450
San Germán (Puerto Rico), 463–465, 473
San Germánde Auxerre (Puerto Rico), 464–465
San José (Puerto Rico), 440
San Juan (Puerto Rico) , 2, 23, 422–449
    accommodations, 14, 425–429
    beaches, 435–436
    information sources, 417, 423
    layout of, 423–424
    nightlife, 18, 446–449
    restaurants, 429–435
    shopping, 443–446
    sights and activities, 435–443
    transportation, 418, 420–422, 424–425
    traveling to, 418, 423
San Juan Cathedral (Puerto Rico), 438, 440
San Juan city walls (Puerto Rico), 441
San Juan Gate (Puerto Rico), 440, 442
San Nicolas (Aruba), 86, 91, 93
San San Beach (Jamaica), 362
Santa Barbara Beach (Curaçao), 196, 199
Santa María la Menor Cathedral (Dominican Republic), 236
Santo Domingo (Dominican Republic), 1, 21, 227–240, 247
    accommodations, 229–232
    beaches, 234–235

nightlife, 239–240
restaurants, 232–234
shopping, 13–14, 238–239
sights and activities, 234–237
traveling to, 225–226
Sapphire Beach (St. Thomas), 622, 625
Sauteurs (Grenada), 273
Savane-à-Mulets (Guadeloupe), 305
Savane des Pétrifications (Martinique), 397
Savaneta (Aruba), 91
Savannah Bay (Virgin Gorda), 164
Scarborough (Tobago), 26, 583, 599–600, 605, 606
Schooner Harbor (Aruba), 89
Scotts Head Beach (Dominica), 217
Scuba diving, 9–10
    Anegada, 166
    Antigua, 70–71
    Aruba, 89
    Barbados, 112–113
    Bequia, 578
    Bonaire, 9, 134–135, 137
    Cayman Brac, 186–187
    Curaçao, 200, 206
    Dominica, 217, 218–219
    Dominican Republic, 250, 258
    Grand Cayman, 9–10, 179–180
    Grenada, 271–272
    Grenadines, 570
    Guadeloupe, 307–308
    Iles des Saintes, 310, 313
    Jamaica, 332, 346, 349, 354, 363
    Little Cayman, 9–10, 189
    Martinique, 391–392, 393
    Nevis, 411–412
    Puerto Rico, 437, 450, 456
    Saba, 10, 489–491
    St. Croix, 10, 659, 663–664
    St. Eustatius, 500–501
    St. John, 645–646
    St. Kitts, 511
    St. Lucia, 525–526
    St. Maarten/Martin, 552, 554
    St. Thomas, 625
    St. Vincent, 570
    Tobago, 604–605
    Tortola, 154
    Virgin Gorda, 9, 164–165
    websites, 23

Sea kayaking. See Kayaking
Seaquarium Beach (Curaçao), 198
Seasons, 33
Secret Harbour (St. Thomas), 622
Senior citizen travelers, 37–38
Seroe Colorado (Aruba), 91
Seven Arches Museum (St. Thomas), 626
Seven Mile Beach (Grand Cayman), 5, 178, 182–183
Seven Mile Beach (Jamaica), 5, 338, 344–345
Seville Great House (Jamaica), 350
Shete Boka National Park (Curaçao), 204, 205
Shirley Heights (Antigua), 72, 74–75
Shopping. See also Markets; and specific destinations
    best destinations for, 13–14
    money-saving tips, 40
Silver Sands Beach (Barbados), 107, 111, 114
Simpson Bay Beach (St. Maarten), 551, 555
Single travelers, 38
1627 and All That (Barbados), 123–124
Smith's Cove (Grand Cayman), 179
Smugglers Cove (Tortola), 155
Snorkeling, 8–9
    Antigua, 69, 70–71
    Aruba, 89, 91
    Barbados, 112–113
    Bonaire, 8, 136, 137
    Cayman Brac, 186
    Curaçao, 8, 200, 206
    Dominica, 217, 220–221
    Dominican Republic, 250
    Grand Cayman, 8, 179–180, 182
    Grenada, 271–272
    Guadeloupe, 296
    Jamaica, 332, 346, 349, 354, 363
    Martinique, 391–392
    Nevis, 411
    Puerto Rico, 437, 450
    St. Croix, 8, 659, 661, 663–664
    St. Eustatius, 500
    St. John, 9, 632–633, 645
    St. Kitts, 511
    St. Lucia, 526

St. Maarten/Martin, 554–555
St. Thomas, 9, 623, 625
St. Vincent, 570
Tobago, 8, 604–605
Virgin Gorda, 164
Solomon Bay Beach (St. John), 644
Somerset Falls (Jamaica), 364
Sorobon Beach (Bonaire), 139
Sosúa (Dominican Republic), 252–256
Souffleur (La Désirade), 316
Soufrière (Guadeloupe), 11, 282, 302–303, 304–305
Soufrière (St. Lucia), 516, 521, 522, 523, 527, 530
Soufrière (St. Vincent), 569–570, 572
Soufrière Bay Beach (Dominica), 217
Spaans Lagoen (Aruba), 91
Spanish Town (Jamaica), 369–370
Spanish Town (Virgin Gorda), 160, 162, 163
Spring Bay (Virgin Gorda), 164
Statia. See St. Eustatius
Steeple Building (St. Croix), 665
Stevenson, Robert Louis, 12, 141, 157
Stingray City (Grand Cayman), 8, 9, 179, 180
Sulphur Springs (Dominica), 220
Sun Bay (Puerto Rico), 479
Sunbury Plantation House (Barbados), 118
Surfing. See also Windsurfing
    Puerto Rico, 457
    St. Eustatius, 500
    Tobago, 603
    Tortola, 155

Taíno Indian Ceremonial Park (Puerto Rico), 471–472
Tarare Point (Guadeloupe), 306
Tennis
    Antigua, 71
    Aruba, 89
    Barbados, 113
    Bonaire, 136
    Curaçao, 200
    Dominican Republic, 244
    Grenada, 272
    Guadeloupe, 308
    Jamaica, 332–333, 354
    Martinique, 392
    Nevis, 412–413
    Puerto Rico, 437, 461
    St. Croix, 664
    St. Eustatius, 501
    St. Lucia, 526
    St. Maarten/Martin, 555
    St. Thomas, 625–626
    St. Vincent, 570
    Tobago, 605
Terre-de-Haut, 310–313
Tibbetts (Cayman Brac), 186–187
Tibes Indian Ceremonial Center (Puerto Rico), 462
Titou Gorge (Dominica), 10, 218, 220
Tobago, 26, 582–584, 598–606
    accommodations, 600–601
    cheap thrills, 596–597
    information sources, 582–583
    nightlife, 606
    restaurants, 17, 601–603
    shopping, 606
    sights and activities, 603–605
    transportation, 600
    traveling to, 599
Tombeau des Caraïbes (Martinique), 399
Tortola, 21, 141, 144–160
    accommodations, 146–149
    cheap thrills, 156–157
    information sources, 141, 144
    nightlife, 18, 158–160
    restaurants, 17, 150–153
    shopping, 157–158
    sights and activities, 154–157
    transportation, 146
    traveling to, 141–142
Tortuga Rum Company (Grand Cayman), 184
Tours. See also Boat travel and cruises; and specific destinations
    package, 40–42
Trafalgar Falls (Dominica), 220
Trafalgar Square (Barbados), 115, 120
Transportation, 40. See also Bicycling; Ferries
Travel agents, 27

Traveler's checks, 30
Travel websites, 27, 43–44, 56–59
Treasure Beach (Jamaica), 375
"Treasure Island," 12, 141, 157
Trinidad, 26, 582–598
    accommodations, 587–590
    cheap thrills, 596–597
    information sources, 582–583
    nightlife, 598
    restaurants, 590–591
    shopping, 595–598
    sights and activities, 591–595
    special events, 586
    transportation, 586–587
    traveling to, 585–586
Trinidad National Museum and Art Gallery, 593
Trinidad Royal Botanical Gardens, 593–594
Trinité (Martinique), 403
Trois-Ilets (Martinique), 392–393
Trois-Rivières (Guadeloupe), 303
Trunk Bay (Virgin Gorda), 164
Trunk Bay National Park (St. John), 8, 9, 607, 643, 646
Turner's Beach (Antigua), 69
Turtle Beach (Jamaica), 354
Turtle Beach (Tobago), 603–604
Tyrol Cot Heritage Village (Barbados), 116

Union Island, 575, 579–580
University of the West Indies (Jamaica), 365, 368
U.S. Virgin Islands, 26–27, 607–672
    cheap thrills, 632–633
    information sources, 607
    traveling to, 608–609
    weddings, 56
    what's new, 2–3
Utuado (Puerto Rico), 471, 474

Valley of Desolation (Dominica), 11, 217, 220
Vauclin (Martinique), 395

Versailles (Guadeloupe), 300
Vessup Bay Beach (St. Thomas), 623
Vieques (Puerto Rico), 476–480
Vigie Beach (St. Lucia), 524
Villa Beach (St. Vincent), 569
Villa rentals. *See* Rental properties
Virgin Gorda, 11–12, 21, 141, 160–166
  accommodations, 15, 160, 162–163
  information sources, 141
  nightlife, 165–166
  restaurants, 163–164
  shopping, 165
  sights and activities, 164–165
  transportation, 160
  traveling to, 141–142, 160
Virgin Gorda Peak National Park, 165
Virgin Islands. *See* British Virgin Islands; U.S. Virgin Islands
Virgin Islands Brewing Company, 3, 631
Virgin Islands National Park (St. John), 644–645

Walter Fletcher Beach (Jamaica), 331, 333
Washington-Slagbaai National Park (Bonaire), 133, 136, 137, 138
Waterfort Arches (Curaçao), 201–202

Water Island, 632
Watermelon Cay Beach (St. John), 644
Weather, 32–33, 59. *See also specific destinations*
Websites, 27. *See also specific destinations*
  travel, 27, 43–44, 56–59
Weddings, in the Caribbean, 54–56
Welchman Hall Gully (Barbados), 117
Westend Saltpond (St. Croix), 633
Westpunt (Curaçao), 199
Whale-watching
  Dominica, 219, 222
  Dominican Republic, 259, 260
  Puerto Rico, 453, 456
Whim Plantation Museum (St. Croix), 667
White Bay (Jost Van Dyke), 15–16, 167, 168
White Bay Beach (Nevis), 411
Whitehall (Trinidad), 593
White House Bay (St. Kitts), 510, 511
White River (Dominica), 219, 220
Wickhams Cay (Tortola), 144, 151, 159
Wilhelmina Park (Aruba), 89
Willemstad (Curaçao), 190–193, 195–198, 201–202, 206–208, 208
Windsurfing
  Antigua, 71
  Aruba, 87–88, 91

  Barbados, 113–114
  Bonaire, 133, 136
  Dominican Republic, 250, 257, 258
  Guadeloupe, 308
  Jamaica, 332
  Martinique, 392
  Nevis, 413
  Puerto Rico, 435, 436, 437, 449–450
  St. Croix, 661, 664
  St. John, 645
  St. Kitts, 511
  St. Lucia, 526
  St. Maarten/Martin, 555
  St. Thomas, 626
  Tortola, 154–155
Windwardside (Saba), 483–493
Witshoal **(St. Thomas),** 625
Woburn (Grenada), 272, 276
Woodford Hill Bay (Dominica), 217
Woodlands (Grenada), 271, 276
Worthing (Barbados), 102, 106–109, 124

Young Island (St. Vincent), 569, 570
Y. S. Falls (Jamaica), 375

Zeelandia Beach (St. Eustatius), 500
Zombie Pool (Guadeloupe), 304

FROMMER'S® COMPLETE TRAVEL GUIDES

Alaska
Amsterdam
Argentina & Chile
Arizona
Atlanta
Australia
Austria
Bahamas
Barcelona, Madrid & Seville
Beijing
Belgium, Holland & Luxembourg
Bermuda
Boston
British Columbia & the Canadian
  Rockies
Budapest & the Best of Hungary
California
Canada
Cancún, Cozumel & the Yucatán
Cape Cod, Nantucket &
  Martha's Vineyard
Caribbean
Caribbean Cruises & Ports of Call
Caribbean Ports of Call
Carolinas & Georgia
Chicago
China
Colorado
Costa Rica
Denmark
Denver, Boulder & Colorado Springs
England
Europe
European Cruises & Ports of Call
Florida
France

Germany
Great Britain
Greece
Greek Islands
Hawaii
Hong Kong
Honolulu, Waikiki & Oahu
Ireland
Israel
Italy
Jamaica
Japan
Las Vegas
London
Los Angeles
Maryland & Delaware
Maui
Mexico
Montana & Wyoming
Montréal & Québec City
Munich & the Bavarian Alps
Nashville & Memphis
Nepal
New England
New Mexico
New Orleans
New York City
New Zealand
Nova Scotia, New Brunswick &
  Prince Edward Island
Oregon
Paris
Philadelphia & the Amish Country
Portugal
Prague & the Best of the Czech
  Republic

Provence & the Riviera
Puerto Rico
Rome
San Antonio & Austin
San Diego
San Francisco
Santa Fe, Taos & Albuquerque
Scandinavia
Scotland
Seattle & Portland
Shanghai
Singapore & Malaysia
South Africa
South America
Southeast Asia
South Florida
South Pacific
Spain
Sweden
Switzerland
Texas
Thailand
Tokyo
Toronto
Tuscany & Umbria
USA
Utah
Vancouver & Victoria
Vermont, New Hampshire
  & Maine
Vienna & the Danube Valley
Virgin Islands
Virginia
Walt Disney World & Orlando
Washington, D.C.
Washington State

FROMMER'S® DOLLAR-A-DAY GUIDES

Australia from $50 a Day
California from $70 a Day
Caribbean from $70 a Day
England from $70 a Day
Europe from $70 a Day

Florida from $70 a Day
Hawaii from $80 a Day
Ireland from $60 a Day
Italy from $70 a Day
London from $85 a Day

New York from $90 a Day
Paris from $80 a Day
San Francisco from $70 a Day
Washington, D.C., from $70
  a Day

FROMMER'S® PORTABLE GUIDES

Acapulco, Ixtapa & Zihuatanejo
Alaska Cruises & Ports of Call
Amsterdam
Aruba
Australia's Great Barrier Reef
Bahamas
Baja & Los Cabos
Berlin
Big Island of Hawaii
Boston
California Wine Country
Cancún
Charleston & Savannah
Chicago
Disneyland

Dublin
Florence
Frankfurt
Hong Kong
Houston
Las Vegas
London
Los Angeles
Maine Coast
Maui
Miami
New Orleans
New York City
Paris

Phoenix & Scottsdale
Portland
Puerto Rico
Puerto Vallarta, Manzanillo &
  Guadalajara
San Diego
San Francisco
Seattle
Sydney
Tampa & St. Petersburg
Vancouver
Venice
Virgin Islands
Washington, D.C.

FROMMER'S® NATIONAL PARK GUIDES

Family Vacations in the National
  Parks
Grand Canyon

National Parks of the American
  West
Rocky Mountain
Yellowstone & Grand Teton

Yosemite & Sequoia/
  Kings Canyon
Zion & Bryce Canyon

Frommer's® Memorable Walks

Chicago
London

New York
Paris

San Francisco

Frommer's® Great Outdoor Guides

Arizona & New Mexico
New England

Northern California
Southern New England

Vermont & New Hampshire

Suzy Gershman's Born to Shop Guides

Born to Shop: France
Born to Shop: Hong Kong,
  Shanghai & Beijing

Born to Shop: Italy
Born to Shop: London

Born to Shop: New York
Born to Shop: Paris

Frommer's® Irreverent Guides

Amsterdam
Boston
Chicago
Las Vegas
London

Los Angeles
Manhattan
New Orleans
Paris
Rome

San Francisco
Seattle & Portland
Vancouver
Walt Disney World
Washington, D.C.

Frommer's® Best-Loved Driving Tours

Britain
California
Florida
France

Germany
Ireland
Italy

New England
Scotland
Spain

Hanging Out™ Guides

Hanging Out in England
Hanging Out in Europe

Hanging Out in France
Hanging Out in Ireland

Hanging Out in Italy
Hanging Out in Spain

The Unofficial Guides®

Bed & Breakfasts and Country
  Inns in:
    California
    New England
    Northwest
    Rockies
    Southeast
Beyond Disney
Branson, Missouri
California with Kids
Chicago
Cruises
Disneyland

Florida with Kids
Golf Vacations in the
  Eastern U.S.
The Great Smokey &
  Blue Ridge Mountains
Inside Disney
Hawaii
Las Vegas
London
Mid-Atlantic with Kids
Mini Las Vegas
Mini-Mickey
New England & New York
  with Kids

New Orleans
New York City
Paris
San Francisco
Skiing in the West
Southeast with Kids
Walt Disney World
Walt Disney World for
  Grown-ups
Walt Disney World for Kids
Washington, D.C.
World's Best Diving Vacations

Special-Interest Titles

Frommer's Adventure Guide to Australia & New
  Zealand
Frommer's Adventure Guide to Central America
Frommer's Adventure Guide to India & Pakistan
Frommer's Adventure Guide to South America
Frommer's Adventure Guide to Southeast Asia
Frommer's Adventure Guide to Southern Africa
Frommer's Britain's Best Bed & Breakfasts and
  Country Inns
Frommer's France's Best Bed & Breakfasts and
  Country Inns
Frommer's Italy's Best Bed & Breakfasts and Country
  Inns
Frommer's Caribbean Hideaways

Frommer's Exploring America by RV
Frommer's Gay & Lesbian Europe
Frommer's The Moon
Frommer's New York City with Kids
Frommer's Road Atlas Britain
Frommer's Road Atlas Europe
Frommer's Washington, D.C., with Kids
Frommer's What the Airlines Never Tell You
Israel Past & Present
The New York Times' Guide to Unforgettable
  Weekends
Places Rated Almanac
Retirement Places Rated